ENCYCLOPEDIA OF AMERICAN LIVES

The SCRIBNER ENCYCLOPEDIA *of*
AMERICAN LIVES

The SCRIBNER ENCYCLOPEDIA *of*

AMERICAN LIVES

VOLUME THREE

1991–1993

KENNETH T. JACKSON
EDITOR IN CHIEF

KAREN MARKOE
GENERAL EDITOR

ARNOLD MARKOE
EXECUTIVE EDITOR

CHARLES SCRIBNER'S SONS
AN IMPRINT OF THE GALE GROUP
NEW YORK   DETROIT   SAN FRANCISCO   LONDON   BOSTON   WOODBRIDGE, CT

Charles Scribner's Sons
An imprint of The Gale Group
1633 Broadway
New York, NY 10019

Library of Congress Cataloging-in-Publication Data

The Scribner encyclopedia of American lives / Kenneth T. Jackson,
    editor in chief ; Karen Markoe, general editor ; Arnold Markoe,
    executive editor.
      p.   cm.
    Includes bibliographical references and index.
    Contents: v. 1. 1981–1985
    ISBN 0-684-80492-1 (v. 1 : alk. paper)
    1. United States—Biography—Dictionaries. I. Jackson, Kenneth
  T. II. Markoe, Karen. III. Markoe, Arnie.
CT213.S37   1998
920.073—dc21   98-33793
                                       CIP

ISBN 0-684-80620-7 (v. 3 : alk. paper)

1 3 5 7 9 11 13 15 17 19 20 18 16 14 12 10 8 6 4 2
PRINTED IN THE UNITED STATES OF AMERICA

The paper in this publication meets the minimum requirements of the American National Standard for Information Services—Permanence of Paper for Printed Library Materials, ANSI Z39.48-1992.

EDITORIAL *and* PRODUCTION STAFF

Managing Editor
TIMOTHY J. DeWERFF

Project Editor
TARA M. STRICKLAND

Editorial Assistants
MICHELLE BECKER   SARA FEEHAN
LEE ANN FULLINGTON   KASY MOON   CHARLES SCRIBNER IV

Editors
CAROL J. CIASTON   JOHN FITZPATRICK   KATHY MOREAU   CARYN RADICK

Copy Editors, Researchers
HELEN A. CASTRO   GRETCHEN GORDON   ELEANOR R. HERO   JEAN F. KAPLAN
MICHAEL LEVINE   LINDA SANDERS   CINDI SHERMAN
MELISSA A. DOBSON   JESSICA HORNIK EVANS   JANE HEECKT   LOUISE B. KETZ
ANNA LOVE LEHRE   MARCIA MERRYMAN MEANS   CHERYL MacKENZIE   MARTHA SCHÜTZ

Proofreaders
MARCEL CHOUTEAU   MARGIE DUNCAN   MARK GOLDMAN
ERICH J. KAISER   KIM A. NIR

Picture Researchers
KATHLEEN DROSTE
MARGARET CHAMBERLAIN   DEAN DAUPHINAIS   DOUGLAS PUCHOWSKI

Designer
BRADY McNAMARA

Compositor
IMPRESSIONS BOOK AND JOURNAL SERVICES, INC.

Publisher
KAREN DAY

PREFACE

This third volume in the *Scribner Encyclopedia of American Lives* (*SEAL*) series contains the biographies of 306 persons who died in the three-year period between 1 January 1991 and 31 December 1993. This marks a change from the five-year intervals of previous volumes to three-year intervals. The shift was made in order to keep the volumes at a manageable heft as the cumulative name and occupations indexes of all the biographees in the series, numbering 1,306 through this volume, continue to expand. Henceforth, each succeeding volume will likewise contain indexes of all previous entries.

The format of this book is alphabetical. Each essay in it appraises the circumstances and influences that shaped the life of an individual subject. Each entry also includes the full dates of birth and death, the full names and occupations of parents, the number of siblings, the educational institutions attended and degrees granted, the names of spouses and the dates of marriages and divorces, and the number of children. Wherever possible, the book also includes information on residences, cause of death, and place of burial. The length of an article was determined both by the relative significance of the subject and by the completeness of biographical material available.

In selecting a few hundred subjects from the millions of Americans who died in 1991, 1992, and 1993, the editors followed a rigorous process. First, they compiled a list of several thousand candidates from a variety of sources. Second, they classified the names according to profession or occupation. Third, they submitted the lists to specialists or groups of specialists who helped to rank the potential biographees. The final list, however, is solely the responsibility of the editors, who weighed the relative significance of particular politicians and poets, chemists and criminals, business leaders and baseball players.

The 306 individuals who are profiled in this book obviously lived extraordinary lives and in conspicuous ways set themselves apart from the rest of us. Some won fame on the battlefield or in the halls of government. Others distinguished themselves by their books, their research efforts, or their creative genius. Still others became household names because of their achievements as performing artists or sports heroes. But taken together, these unusual individuals reflect the diversity of the nation they called home. They came from every race, ethnic group, socioeconomic class, and region of the United States. Many were born to privilege; others were born to poor parents. All took advantage of their natural gifts to leave a permanent mark on a continental nation. In general, the editors have included individuals, such as Marlene Dietrich, who made major professional or artistic contributions while living in the United States, whether or not they ever actually became American citizens.

Some of the choices of subjects were easy, and many of the names in this book, such as Miles Davis in music, Martha Graham in dance, Thurgood Marshall in law and civil rights, Albert Sabin in science, Frank Capra in motion pictures, Thomas Watson in business machines, César Chávez in farmworker organizing, and Sam Walton in merchandising, will be familiar to almost everyone. But this volume also includes persons who were not much in the news during their lifetimes and who are only now receiving the recognition they deserve.

As is the case in any large-scale research effort, *SEAL* depended on the hard work and cooperation of hundreds of contributors, many new to this venture. We acknowledge again the diligent research efforts undertaken by our 244 writers. Resourceful photo editors located photographs for almost every subject. Happily, the editors of this volume all had worked together on similar ventures and chose to do so again. The result of this collaboration is a book that we trust will be useful, reliable, and enjoyable.

In particular, we wish to thank Tara M. Strickland of the Visual Education Corporation in Princeton, New Jersey, who as project editor oversaw the copyediting and proofreading of this volume. Her cooperative spirit, cheerfulness under pressure, and high standards were essential in moving this book to publication. We also wish to thank our longtime collaborator Timothy J. DeWerff, who managed the entire effort from his office at Scribners with his unique combination of wide intelligence, superb judgment, meticulous organization, and reliable good humor. Similarly, Richard H. Gentile has provided valuable insight and advice throughout our many years of collaboration as he has demonstrated time and again his encyclopedic knowledge of American history. Finally, we wish to record our continuing gratitude to Karen Day, the publisher of Charles Scribner's Sons. Her personal commitment to this project has always been the essential ingredient in its success, and everyone who uses this volume will be in her debt.

Kenneth T. Jackson, Editor in Chief
Karen E. Markoe, General Editor
Arnold Markoe, Executive Editor

CONTENTS

The SCRIBNER ENCYCLOPEDIA *of*

AMERICAN LIVES

A

ABBOTT, Berenice (*b*. 17 July 1898 in Springfield, Ohio; *d*. 11 December 1991 in Monson, Maine), major American photographer noted for her documentary record of New York City.

Abbott was the daughter of Charles E. Abbott and Alice Bunn. Her parents divorced soon after her birth and she was raised alone by her mother, separated from her three siblings until the age of six. After the divorce, her mother moved with her to Columbus, Ohio, where Abbott attended public schools, rarely seeing her father. She attended Ohio State University for one term in the fall of 1917, then dropped out. Moving to New York City, she supported herself as a waitress, artist's model, and actress in the Provincetown Playhouse in Greenwich Village. In Manhattan, she met the surrealist photographer and artist Man Ray, who became an important influence on her. When he offered her employment as a darkroom assistant, Abbott relocated to Paris, France, to work with him in 1923. There she met the photographer Eugène Atget. Realizing the immense value of his work and influenced by his formal portraits of everyday life, Abbott purchased Atget's negative files and images after his death in 1927. She also set up a portrait studio at which she created psychological images of major artists, such as James Joyce and Jean Cocteau, and of the collector Peggy Guggenheim. She held her first solo show at the Galerie au Sacre du Printemps in 1926.

Abbott forged her own artistic philosophy and increased her stature among modernists by attacking soft-focus pictorialism in favor of documentary photography drawn from the examples of the French pioneers Gaspard-Félix Tournachon ("Nadar") and Atget. From Atget, she learned the importance of refusing commissions and picking one's own subjects, and she was inspired by his epic chronicling of Parisian life, lessons she would apply in New York City.

In 1929 Abbott returned to the United States for a brief visit but was stunned by the changes occurring in New York City. She determined to photograph them as Atget had recorded Parisian cityscapes. She then arranged to have her massive collection of Atget's work shipped to New York. Thirty-five years later she published the monograph *The World of Atget* (1964), considered one of the finest commentaries by one photographer on another. In 1968 she sold the collection to the Museum of Modern Art.

Living again in Greenwich Village, Abbott supported herself by magazine commissions. Abbott revealed Atget's influence and her own creativity in an eight-year study of New York's buildings and residents. Working first with a handheld camera, she then purchased an 8-by-10-inch view camera with which she sacrificed the speed and flexibility of the small camera for added detail and control. A historian of photography, she studied the work of Mathew Brady, David Octavius Hill, Nadar, and Atget to comprehend, in her words, "the sources of an authentic photographic tradition," taking important lessons from each artist. As did her forebears, Abbott experienced financial

Berenice Abbott. © TODD WATTS

difficulty. She proved too temperamental for a job at *Fortune* magazine and had to abandon a stylish apartment she had rented at the luxurious Hotel des Artistes off Central Park West. She enjoyed the patronage of Lincoln Kirstein and Julien Levy, who showed some of her work at the newly established Museum of Modern Art. Levy then opened a gallery where he presented Abbott's first one-person show in 1932.

Abbott spent the first years of the Great Depression vainly seeking grant support from museums, foundations, and private donors for her New York City project. In the fall of 1933, she began teaching photography at the New School for Social Research, a post that she held until 1958. The following year she collaborated with the architectural historian Henry Russell Hitchcock on two projects. The first recorded the Victorian architecture of H. H. Richardson for the Museum of Modern Art, while the second involved preparing an exhibition of pre–Civil War architecture for Wesleyan University. These projects provided needed funds and sharpened Abbott's style as direct, selfless, and functional.

In 1934 Abbott gained exposure in another one-person show in New York City and in *This Is New York,* a guide-book edited by Gilbert Seldes that featured twelve Abbott photographs, including the iconic *Midtown Night View*. Her first major break occurred in 1934, when the Museum of the City of New York mounted a major exhibition of her work. That same year, Abbott met Elizabeth McCausland, an art critic, who became her lifelong companion. The pair traveled around the eastern United States together and applied unsuccessfully for a joint Guggenheim Foundation Grant to photograph and write about the rest of the country.

Sponsored by the Museum of the City of New York, Abbott secured a post in the Works Progress Administration (WPA), which allowed her to photograph New York City full time. Influenced by Lewis Mumford's *Sticks and Stones: A Study of American Architecture and Civilization* (1924), which espoused a sociological analysis of city life, Abbott constructed a three-part organization of her study, including "material aspect," "means of life," and "people and how they live." Abbott then accumulated ideas for subjects, sought permission for restricted sites and cajoled residents to use their homes for better street angles, and considered the best times of day for shooting. Teaching, commissions, and freelance jobs also altered her routine. The type of cameras she used limited her progress: her lack of a miniature camera, for example, curtailed her ability to photograph crowd scenes. She constantly played with the organization of the project, which left some parts unfinished and added an air of chaos; a key conceptual omission in her work was a section on middle-class housing. She also waged and overcame several bureaucratic battles with the Federal Art Project (FAP), the division of the WPA that administered her project.

Despite these problems, Abbott's work drew significant notice, including stories in *Life* magazine, special exhibits by the WPA, and a second exhibit at the Museum of the City of New York, titled "Changing New York," in 1937. At the end of the 1930s, the WPA lost its political battle for survival, and Abbott grew anxious about an income. Wrangling with the government was easy compared to the battles that she and McCausland encountered with E. P. Dutton, the publisher selected for the exhibition book. McCausland was more explicitly left-wing than Abbott, and the editors at Dutton rejected all of the former's plans for book layout, editorial composition, and focus. In the final run, Abbott had little control over the book's design. Moreover, the FAP paid her little for required prints and then issued more images without her permission. The great personal costs and limited financial reward did not detract from the enormous achievement of the project, published as *Changing New York* in 1939.

Abbott made no further studies of New York except for a collection published as *Greenwich Village: Today and Yesterday* in 1949, with text written by Henry W. Lanier. Another project, intended to compare her earlier urban studies with 1950s landscapes, lapsed when she could not find a publisher. As her mastery of technique became more complete, Abbott published *A Guide to Better Photography* (1941) and *The View Camera Made Simple* (1948). Her artistic interests then turned to scientific photography of physics and biology. She worked from 1944 to 1949 as picture editor of *Science Illustrated*. Abbott created new techniques and equipment to shoot images of magnetic fields, soap bubbles, and penicillin developing in a petri dish. She patented several methods, including the Supersight Process, which made direct photographs on 16-by-20-inch negatives that created virtually grainless images when transformed into contact sheets. Her sociological photography lapsed. A new project documenting the American panorama down U.S. Route 1 from Maine to Florida, accompanied by poems by Muriel Ruykeser, was largely completed but remains unpublished.

Abbott became famous in the 1950s for her scientific images. In 1958 she joined the Physical Science Study Committee at the Massachusetts Institute of Technology to help develop a textbook that would teach basic principles of physics to high school students. The text, *Physics,* appeared in 1960, and Abbott's explanatory photographs were widely exhibited in schools and museums for the next thirty years. In 1965 McCausland died, and Abbott left New York City to live in Monson. In 1968 she published a book, *A Portrait of Maine,* with text written by Chenoweth Hall. With the arrival of photography as a collectible art form in the 1970s, Abbott received new appreciation, and she published a limited portfolio of her earlier works. Dover Books produced an inexpensive reprint of *Changing New York,* retitled *New York in the 1930s* (1973), which further popularized her work. In 1989 the New York Public Library mounted the initial retrospective of her work, accompanied by a catalog edited by Julia Van Haaften.

Abbott died of congestive heart failure in Monson. She left no survivors. In 1997 the Museum of the City of New York published a complete edition of *Changing New York.*

Abbott's influence on twentieth-century American photography is immense. Compatible with the visions of Walker Evans and the WPA photographers, her clear, concise, yet populist approach to urban scenes and people influenced the later work of William Klein, Robert Frank, and Garry Winograd. Her sharply defined images are by far the best available record of New York life at mid-century. The critic Hank O'Neal has contended that the reputation of Abbott's scientific photography may someday outstrip her cityscapes. As a female photographer, her recording of urban humanity anticipated the work of Diane Arbus and Nan Goldin.

★

There is no full biography of Abbott. The standard accounts are in editions of her photography, including Hank O'Neal, *Berenice Abbott, American Photographer* (1982); and Julia Van Haaften, ed., *Berenice Abbott, Photographer: A Modern Vision* (1989). *Berenice Abbott: Changing New York* appeared in a full version edited by Bonnie Yochelson in 1997. Articles include Elizabeth McCausland, "Camera Eye Records Ever 'Changing New York,'" *Springfield Sunday Union and Republican* (24 Oct. 1938); Julia Newman, "Berenice Abbott—Pioneer, Past and Present," *U.S. Camera* (Feb. 1960); and Erwin Leiser, "Berenice Abbott," *Du* (Jan. 1981): 35–38. An obituary is in the *New York Times* (12 Dec. 1991). Her photographs are in public and private collections all over the world.

GRAHAM RUSSELL HODGES

ABRAVANEL, Maurice (*b.* 6 January 1903 in Salonika, Greece; *d.* 22 September 1993 in Salt Lake City, Utah), conductor and teacher best known as the longtime music director of the Utah Symphony Orchestra.

Abravanel was the youngest of four children of Edouard de Abravanel, a pharmacist, and Rachel Bitty, a homemaker. Edouard descended from an old Sephardic Jewish family, originally of Spain but resident in Salonika since 1517. Maurice moved with his family to Lausanne, Switzerland, when he was five years old. He began studying piano at age nine and by his late teens was performing at a local theater and writing music criticism for a local newspaper. His father wished him to become a physician and he accordingly studied at the Lausanne Gymnasium (secondary school) from 1917 to 1919, the University of Lausanne from 1919 to 1921, and the University of Zurich from 1921 to 1922. However, by 1922 he had decided that he wanted to be a musician and moved to Berlin, Germany. There he studied harmony and counterpoint with the composer Kurt Weill in 1922 and 1923, beginning a friendship of great importance to his professional life.

In 1924 Abravanel became a singers' coach at the Neustrelitz Opera. He became choral director of the Zwickau Opera in 1925. In 1927 he became a regular conductor at the Altenburg Opera and married a singer, Friedel Schacko. He had his first major engagement on 17 January 1931 when he guest-conducted Verdi's *La forza del destino* (*The Force of Destiny*) at the Berlin State Opera. His success led to numerous other guest performances at the State Opera. He left Germany for Paris when the Nazis came to power in 1933.

Abravanel served as assistant to the renowned German-born conductor Bruno Walter at the Paris Opéra and also guest-conducted the Paris Symphony Orchestra. He became the music director of George Balanchine's Les Ballets 1933 and in that capacity commissioned and conducted the

Maurice Abranavel, 1974. © JAMES L. AMOS

premiere performance of Kurt Weill's ballet *Die sieben Tod-sünden* (*The Seven Deadly Sins,* 1933). He spent most of the years between 1934 and 1936 in Australia, conducting operas in Melbourne and Sydney and originating regular series of symphony orchestra concerts in both cities.

In late 1936 Abravanel came to the United States under a three-year contract to conduct at the Metropolitan Opera in New York City. He was the youngest conductor in the history of the Met. He made his American debut with Camille Saint-Saëns's *Samson et Dalila* on 6 December 1936. For the next two years he conducted numerous performances of French and German operas at the Met. He resigned at the end of his second year, however, when the opportunity came to conduct Kurt Weill's musical play *Knickerbocker Holiday* on Broadway in 1938. (Broadway was still doing well during the Great Depression, while the Met was experiencing a severe retrenchment.) That same year, Abravanel and his wife separated; they were divorced in 1940. He continued as a conductor of Broadway shows until 1947, leading premiere performances of Weill's *Lady in the Dark* (1940), *One Touch of Venus* (1943), and *Street Scene* (1947). He became an American citizen in 1943.

In June 1947 Abravanel signed a contract to conduct the Utah Symphony Orchestra, based in Salt Lake City, because he wanted to build a superior musical organization as a full-time music director—an opportunity he did not have in Berlin, New York, or Paris. On 20 September of that year he married Lucy Menasse Carasso, a widow with two young sons.

The Utah Symphony, founded in 1940, had become an orchestra composed entirely of professional musicians only during the 1946–1947 season. Due to the symphony's inability to provide full-time work for its musicians in those early years, most of the players held daytime jobs outside the orchestra for the first two decades of its operation. The organization suffered a severe financial crisis, almost resulting in bankruptcy, during the 1948–1949 season. Abravanel, with the support of civic leaders of Salt Lake City, officials of the Mormon Church, and the ensemble's board of directors, became the driving force in creating financial stability, vastly expanding the orchestra's activities. He also worked toward achieving a full fifty-two weeks of employment per year for the musicians (finally accomplished in 1980). As conductor, he both attracted and recruited new musicians to the orchestra.

Abravanel, in his lengthy tenure with the Utah Symphony, drilled the orchestra into a precise and flexible ensemble capable of performing the entire classical repertoire. He continually increased the number of concerts in Salt Lake City, in other cities and towns in Utah, and in surrounding states. Over considerable opposition he insisted on including twentieth-century music in the orchestra's programs. He forged strong alliances between the orchestra and both the University of Utah and the Mormon Church (the ensemble played all of its Salt Lake City concerts in the Mormon Tabernacle). The orchestra and Abravanel became widely known both in the United States and abroad through a total of 111 recordings, made between 1952 and

1978. Among them were a widely acclaimed series of the symphonies of Gustav Mahler, as well as the complete symphonies of Brahms, Sibelius, and Tchaikovsky. Under Abravanel's direction the orchestra made tours to Europe in 1966, 1975, and 1977, and to South America in 1971, receiving largely favorable reviews. The ensemble also toured widely in the western United States. In addition to his work with the Utah Symphony, Abravanel spent his summers from 1955 to 1979 in Santa Barbara, California, where he was music director of the Music Academy of the West, a school for advanced vocal and instrumental students.

Abravanel underwent open-heart surgery on 29 November 1976. By mid-February 1977 he had returned to the podium and conducted the remainder of the Utah Symphony's season. He then led the orchestra on a lengthy European tour in the fall of 1977, followed by another strenuous winter season in 1977–1978. Worn down by ill health and strain, he conducted fewer concerts in 1978–1979 and submitted his resignation on 6 April 1979. He conducted his last concert in Salt Lake City on 21 April of that year. In 1982 he taught conducting at the Berkshire Music Center at Tanglewood in Massachusetts, the summer home of the Boston Symphony Orchestra. He returned to Tanglewood every summer until his death, holding the title "artist in residence" and serving as an informal mentor to the students there. Lucy Abravanel died in 1985; on 2 July 1986 he married Carolyn Chaney Firmage at Tanglewood. He died of natural causes in 1993 in Salt Lake City.

Abravanel conducted the Utah Symphony Orchestra for thirty-two years, a tenure exceeded only by Eugene Ormandy's forty-four years with the Philadelphia Orchestra. His great achievement was to build a fine symphonic ensemble almost from scratch in an area far removed from the major urban centers of the United States.

★

The papers of Maurice Abravanel are in the Special Collections Department of the University of Utah Marriott Library in Salt Lake City, Utah. Karin Hardy, *Register of the Papers of Maurice Abravanel (1903–)* (1988), is an excellent, well-indexed guide to this collection. The only biography, written by a longtime friend and professional associate, is Lowell M. Durham, *Abravanel!* (1989). Ronald Sanders, *The Days Grow Short: The Life and Music of Kurt Weill* (1980), discusses Weill's lengthy friendship and professional collaboration with Abravanel. Andrew L. Pincus, *Tanglewood: The Clash Between Tradition and Change* (1998), briefly describes Abravanel's special relationship with that institution. Robert R. Craven, ed., *Symphony Orchestras of the United States: Selected Profiles* (1986), includes a useful sketch of the history of the Utah Symphony Orchestra. An obituary is in the *New York Times* (23 Sept. 1993).

JOHN E. LITTLE

ACCARDO, Tony ("Big Tuna") (*b.* 28 April 1906 in Chicago, Illinois; *d.* 27 May 1992 in Chicago, Illinois), gangster and mob boss of organized crime in Chicago, who was hailed as the "Genuine Godfather."

Accardo was born in Chicago's "Little Sicily" to Francesco Accardo, a shoemaker, and his wife, Maria Tillota, a homemaker. Baptized Antonino Leonardo Accardo, he was the second of six children.

Accardo attended James Otis Elementary School in Chicago from 1911 to 1916, and then went on to Washington Grade School. Not impressed with the education that he was receiving, his parents filed a delayed birth certificate, claiming that he was born on 28 April 1904 so that, officially sixteen, he would be of legal age to leave school in 1920 at the actual age of fourteen. He never returned to school.

Living in the knock-around world of Chicago's "Little Sicily," Accardo was just another punk doing his share of muggings and stealing. With Prohibition came a new cottage industry—bootleg whiskey. Young Accardo was arrested eight times for bootlegging before he was old enough to vote, although he bragged that he never spent a night in jail (although he was indicted no fewer than four times between 1948 and 1982) because the mob "owned" the police and the judges.

Early in 1926 Accardo met Chicago's mob boss, Al Capone, and was initiated into the Capone mob at the age of twenty. He served as Capone's chauffeur and guarded the boss by sitting for hours in the lobby of Capone's suite in the Lexington Hotel in Chicago, screening visitors. Before Accardo's twenty-third birthday, he had solidified his reputation as a Capone mobster.

On the morning of 14 February 1929, the Capone gang massacred seven members of the North Side Gang, a rival Chicago gang. Many suspected Accardo of complicity in the 1929 Saint Valentine's Day Massacre. Four Capone mobsters did the shooting; Accardo may have been one of them. Accardo was also known to have great prowess with a baseball bat, though not in baseball. His prowess lay in smashing the skulls of rival gang members, various Capone foes, and loan-shark debtors. For this Capone nicknamed him "Joe Batters." (Many said Accardo had "more brains at breakfast than Capone had all day.") Later in his life the media nicknamed him "Big Tuna," for Accardo's love of sportfishing.

In 1934 Accardo married Clarice Evelyn Porter, the daughter of Polish immigrants. Within twelve years, they had two daughters and adopted two sons. One of their sons, Anthony Ross Accardo, won millions of dollars in the Illinois state lottery later in life.

The 1930s were profitable years for the Chicago mob. Accardo was involved in everything connected with the mob. By 1930 his official position was that of "capo"—

Anthony "Big Tuna" Accardo *(left)* and his attorney George Callahan read a subpoena from the Senate Crime Investigating Committee, 1950. © BETTMANN/CORBIS

captain of the street crew. When the Chicago Crime Commission released the first list of public enemies on 31 July 1931, Accardo ranked seventh. Gradually, he assumed more important leadership positions, especially after Frank Nitti, the mob boss, shot and killed himself in 1943. Paul ("The Waiter") Ricca, a close confidant of Accardo, succeeded as head of the mob but was sent to prison later that year. Only in his mid-thirties, Accardo was now the boss. In 1946, with Ricca in the penitentiary, Accardo brought in the disciplined glory days for the mob. He took over bookmaking by controlling the wire services that carried racing information so that bookmakers could set the odds, pay off the winners, and collect on bets.

By 1957 the mob was fully under Accardo's control. Even its public image was acceptable to most people in Chicago because the organization seemed to kill only its own members, it didn't deal in narcotics, and it kept many areas of Chicago under control. Federal Bureau of Investigation (FBI) director J. Edgar Hoover believed that the FBI should have little interest in the mob because its operations were usually limited and local and did not involve interstate commerce. There was little national interest in disciplining the mob.

This changed in November 1957, when mob families in New York and other states were once again warring with each other. The national leaders of organized crime decided to have a meeting of members of all the major families so that they could settle their differences and end internecine warfare. They met on 14 November 1957 in Apalachin, New York. A New York State trooper alerted the Bureau of Alcohol, Tobacco, and Firearms (ATF) to investigate whether any laws were being broken. Soon the media got hold of the story and broadcast the fact that the country's leading mob figures had met in Apalachin. This caught the attention of Hoover. Crossing state lines to conspire to commit a crime was a matter for the FBI. With the exposure of the mob menace and an aroused American public, Hoover took action.

From that time on, Accardo and company were subjects of investigation. Accardo had withstood the Kefauver investigations into organized crime and racketeering in 1950 by pleading the Fifth Amendment. In the spring of 1958 Accardo was investigated for income tax fraud. The McClellan Committee investigation of organized crime later subpoenaed Accardo. Appearing before the committee, he gave only his name and address and invoked his Fifth Amendment right to remain silent 172 times.

By the late 1950s the mob, under Accardo's leadership, had accomplished all of its goals. Although he enjoyed unbridled prosperity, Accardo had become bored with the job. In his early fifties, in good physical, financial, and mental health, Accardo was urged by his wife, Clarice, to step aside.

It was time. Knowing that he could never quit—"mobsters only get out of the mob feet first" was an old expression—he decided to become the "consigliere," the wise counselor. Thus, he didn't step down; he stepped aside.

The new boss was Sam Giancana. A flamboyant, natty dresser and publicity seeker who loved the limelight and ignored Accardo's advice to "keep your head down," Giancana didn't last long. As a result, the mob did not prosper under Giancana's leadership. Giancana went to jail in 1965, was released in 1966, and fled to Mexico. He returned to Chicago and was murdered on 18 June 1975. After his death came a series of successors, but none with Accardo's skills, leadership ability, or staying power.

Accardo finally retired. On the evening of 27 May 1992, he died of heart and respiratory failure in a Chicago hospital at the age of eighty-six. He is buried in Queen of Heaven Cemetery in Hillside, Illinois, in the family crypt. To the right of his burial site is the crypt of Paul Ricca, Accardo's closest friend.

Although Accardo killed and broke many laws, even law enforcement agents respected him. He preferred to settle disputes without bloodshed. Accardo was the most important leader in organized crime and the last link to the Capone era.

★

There are several sources of information on the life and times of Tony Accardo. Foremost is *Accardo: The Genuine Godfather* (1995), by former FBI agent William F. Roemer. Bill Brashler, *The Don* (1977); William F. Roemer's autobiography, *Roemer: Man Against the Mob* (1989); William F. Roemer, *War of the Godfathers* (1991); and Robert J. Schoenberg, *Mr. Capone* (1993), all reference Accardo. Also helpful is Sandy Smith, "The Charmed Life of Gangster Tony Accardo," *Saturday Evening Post* (24 Nov. 1962). An obituary is in the *Chicago Tribune* (30 May 1992).

JOHN KARES SMITH

ACUFF, Roy Claxton (*b.* 15 September 1903 in Maynardville, Tennessee; *d.* 23 November 1992 in Nashville, Tennessee), country musician, singer, and music business executive, nicknamed the "King of Country Music."

Acuff was born in rural Tennessee, the third of five children of Neill Acuff, a small-town lawyer, part-time Baptist preacher, and amateur fiddler, and Ida Carr, a homemaker who played piano and guitar. Acuff played harmonica and Jew's harp as a child and sang with his brothers, sisters, and parents in church and at home. In 1919 the family relocated to Fountain City, near Knoxville, Tennessee. Acuff attended Central High School there, playing baseball and appearing in amateur dramatic productions. He appears to have graduated in 1924, though he was still playing baseball with the school's team the following year. Acuff

Roy Acuff, 1940. © BETTMANN/CORBIS

continued to play ball on a semiprofessional level through the 1920s; he was also involved in a few minor run-ins with the law. In 1929 he was invited to join the New York Yankees, but he suffered a severe case of sunstroke while playing baseball that summer. Acuff spent most of 1930 bedridden, and his baseball career was over.

While recuperating, Acuff began playing the fiddle, picking up the rudiments from his father and listening to recordings of such fiddlers as Gid Tanner and Fiddlin' John Carson. He decided to pursue a musical career. During 1931 he played on the streets of Knoxville, fiddling and performing yo-yo tricks for spare change. In the spring of 1932 he joined Doc Hower's Medicine Show, a local traveling troupe, as a musician and a comedian/actor. Hower sold a patent medicine with the colorful name Moc-a-Tan (sometimes spelled Mocoton), promising relief from most major ailments. After the tour ended that fall, Acuff played around Knoxville with his brother Claude (known as "Spot") and Red Jones in a group called the Three Rolling Stones. In 1934 he formed his first band, originally known as the Tennessee Crackerjacks. The band worked locally over the next few years, performing on radio in Knoxville and for local events. In mid-1936 a scout for the American Recording Company (ARC) label, a recording company that specialized in blues and country music, approached the band. That October, the band, now calling themselves the Crazy Tennesseans, recorded its first songs in Chicago. A second session followed in 1937.

Acuff's relaxed singing style and the modern sound of his band made the group immediately popular. In 1938 the group was invited to join the prestigious Grand Ole Opry radio program in Nashville, Tennessee. The Opry was recognized as the most important place a country musician could perform. Acuff was tapped as a master of ceremonies as well as a performer and made the Opry his home until his death. That same year the group's recording of "Wabash Cannonball" became a major country hit. In 1939, perhaps sensitive to the "down-home" image of the group's name, Acuff decided to rename his backup band the Smoky Mountain Boys; some say that the Opry manager Harry Stone insisted on the name change, fearing to offend his rural listeners with the name the Crazy Tennesseans. Also that year the National Broadcasting Company (NBC) began broadcasting a portion of the Opry show nationally, featuring Acuff. A year later he went to Hollywood with other Opry cast members to star in a film, *The Grand Ole Opry* (1940), based on the popular radio show. The low-budget mixture of comedy and romance was not much of an artistic or box-office success. Nonetheless, Acuff appeared in seven similar, B-grade motion pictures during the 1940s.

Acuff was a shrewd businessman who recognized that country music was a popular, moneymaking form of entertainment. Rather than sell his songs to other music publishers—some of whom reportedly offered him $1,000 to $1,200 per song, a large sum for that time—Acuff decided to form his own music-publishing company. In 1942 he put up the money to start Acuff-Rose Publishing, along with the pianist and songwriter Fred Rose. Acuff's wife—Mildred Louise Douglas, whom he had married in 1936—became an active figure in Acuff-Rose and in the record company, Hickory Records, which Acuff-Rose started in 1952. Their only son, Roy Neill Acuff, also became involved with Acuff-Rose after a brief career as a country singer during the 1960s. The true genius behind the company was Rose's son, Wesley, who in 1948 signed the singer/songwriter Hank Williams, who became one of the most popular country performers of all time.

During World War II Acuff enjoyed his greatest success as a performer. His recordings were so well known that, according to the legendary war correspondent Ernie Pyle, Japanese pilots would yell, "To hell with Roosevelt! To hell with Babe Ruth! To hell with Roy Acuff!" as they flew kamikaze missions over Okinawa. Acuff recorded several patriotic songs during this period, including the hit "Cowards over Pearl Harbor" (1942), which undoubtedly contributed to the Japanese animosity toward him. He also

scored several top-ten country hits, including 1944's "The Prodigal Son" and the two-sided hit "I'll Forgive You But I Can't Forget"/"Write Me Sweetheart." Acuff also flirted with politics in the mid-1940s. A popular figure in Tennessee, he ran for governor in 1948. He won the Republican nomination, but he failed to win the general election. Nonetheless, he pulled more votes than any other Republican had ever won in the largely Democratic state. Acuff remained active in Republican politics throughout his life.

After the war Acuff continued to record and perform with various backup musicians, all called the Smoky Mountain Boys. Unlike other country groups, Acuff's band did not feature banjo or mandolin and barely featured the fiddle; instead, its sound was characterized by the slide guitar work of a series of Dobro players. The Dobro, a wooden-bodied guitar that has a round, metal resonator plate inserted into the faceplate, was in some ways the predecessor of the modern pedal steel guitar. Dobroist Pete Kirby (known as "Bashful Brother Oswald") was the most famous musician associated with Acuff and helped establish the instrument as a key to the modern country sound.

In 1949 Acuff saw his last major hit for nearly a decade, the bathetic ballad "Wreck on the Highway." Throughout the 1950s Acuff remained a popular attraction on the Opry and on tour, often including country comedy and skits as part of his act. As an emcee at the Opry he would often perform yo-yo tricks between acts as a way of amusing the audience. Acuff scored his last major country hits in 1958 and 1959, including his last top-ten country hit, "Once More" (1958), though he would remain on the country charts throughout the 1970s.

In 1962 Acuff became the first living person to be inducted into the Country Music Hall of Fame. Three years later an automobile accident left him severely injured, and he decided to retire from active touring and focus on his work at the Opry. His wife stepped forward to handle his business affairs while he recuperated. In 1974, the Grand Ole Opry show left downtown Nashville and moved to an elaborate theme park, called Opryland U.S.A. Shortly before the Opry made its move, Acuff's wife died. Giving up his home, Acuff moved into a cabin on the Opryland grounds, where he lived for the rest of his life. Further cementing his relationship with Opryland, the Acuff-Rose music-publishing business was sold to Opryland's owners in 1985 for $22 million.

Toward the end of his life, Acuff received several honors, including a Grammy Lifetime Achievement Award in 1987 (conferred by the National Association of Recorded Arts and Sciences) and the National Medal of Art and Kennedy Center Lifetime Achievement awards in 1991. He continued to emcee and work at the Opry throughout the early 1990s, though his appearances became less frequent toward the end of his life. Acuff appeared at a show honoring the career of the country comedian Minnie Pearl—with whom he had often performed—just a month before he died of congestive heart failure. Following his wishes for little pomp or ceremony, Acuff was buried on the day of his death at a small, private service at Spring Hill Cemetery in Nashville.

As both a performer and a music publisher, Acuff was a driving force in modernizing country music. His simple vocal style, tasteful and low-key accompaniments, and heart-throbbing repertoire of material were hallmarks of the postwar country sound. Tall and gangly, Acuff disliked the "hillbilly" image, despite the fact that his act often featured the kind of backwoods comedy that was long associated with hillbillies. He did much to modernize country music's image and also helped make Nashville the center of the country music business. Thanks to his recognition of the value of his own songs, he was able to build a music-publishing empire that still dominates the country scene.

★

In the early 1980s Acuff donated his collection of memorabilia and musical instruments to Opryland in Nashville, where it remains on display. The collection is described in Douglas B. Green and George Gruhn, *Roy Acuff's Musical Collection at Opryland* (1982). Acuff coauthored his autobiography, *Roy Acuff's Nashville: The Life and Good Times of Country Music,* with William Neely (1983); it is somewhat weak on insights into his life and career. Elizabeth Schlappi compiled a complete discography of Roy Acuff and his groups, *Roy Acuff and His Smoky Mountain Boys,* in 1966 and published a serviceable biography under the same name in 1978, which was issued in a second edition in 1993, following Acuff's death. A. C. Dunkleberger wrote a short biography, *King of Country Music: The Life Story of Roy Acuff* (1971). An obituary is in the *Los Angeles Times* (24 Nov. 1992).

RICHARD CARLIN

ADLER, Stella (*b.* 10 February 1902 in New York City; *d.* 21 December 1992 in Los Angeles, California), flamboyantly theatrical actress, director, and producer, considered by many professionals to have been the best American teacher of acting and the Stanislavsky Method.

Adler was the youngest daughter of Jacob Pavlovich Adler, the legendary actor and manager, and Sara Lewis Levitska, the famed tragedienne. Their Independent Yiddish Art Company's translations of Shakespeare and other classic and modern dramas attracted Yiddish-speaking intellectuals to New York's Lower East Side theaters.

Onstage at the age of four in her father's 1906 production of *Broken Hearts,* Stella soon acted regularly with her parents and five siblings, the core of the repertory company. Stella's "first true consciousness, was . . . in a dressing room" amidst her father's costumes and makeup, watching

Stella Adler. ARCHIVE PHOTOS/MUSEUM OF THE CITY OF NEW YORK

him become "another man." These experiences and Jacob's personal attention to his favorite child's training permanently affected her views about theater and life.

Formal education was embarrassingly fragmentary for the busy child actress, but she later saw her early exposure to classic dramas and the contextual research demanded by her father as excellent preparation for her later career. In her teens she attended New York University, pursuing the cultural and historical knowledge—the lack of which she later deplored in young American actors—required to perform classics.

Adler made her London debut as Naumi in her father's 1919 revival of *Elisha Ben Avuya,* written for him a decade earlier. In 1922 she married Horace Eliasheff; the marriage ended shortly after the birth of Ellen, Adler's only child. As "Lola" Adler, she first acted on Broadway on 31 October 1922, playing the butterfly Apatura Clythia in *The World We Live In* (*The Insect Comedy*).

In 1925 Adler found herself dissatisfied with commercial theater and seeking a "theatre with a signature" like the Moscow Art Theatre, whose 1923 American tour astonished professionals. She made a life-altering decision to attend classes at the American Laboratory Theatre, led by Richard

Boleslavsky and Maria Ouspenskaya, former members of the Moscow troupe. In classes and productions there from 1925 through 1927, she encountered Lee Strasberg and Harold Clurman, who were already discussing a new theater based on European and Russian models.

Clurman's passion for theater had ignited at age six, when he saw Jacob Adler as *Uriel Acosta*. In 1930 he found in Stella Adler the "the very flesh of my secret yearning" and rushed her into a volatile, combative love affair that lasted thirteen years before they married in 1943 and seventeen more years until they divorced. In 1992, in her last interview, she called Clurman a "savior," responsible for "the opening of my talent, of my mind."

In 1931 Clurman, Strasberg, and Cheryl Crawford formed the Group Theatre; Adler joined the soon-to-be-famous ensemble for a summer in Connecticut, using Konstantin Stanislavsky–inspired techniques (such as affective memory) to rehearse its first New York season. Adler played Geraldine Connelly in the Group's first production, *The House of Connelly* (1931), and Doña Josefa in *Night over Taos* (1932). Lovers' quarrels with Clurman were often over Group issues as she sought to define her place within the collective.

Adler later remarked that her best role was the cast-aside secretary, Sarah Glassman, in *Success Story* (1932). Adler's acting and Strasberg's direction created a performance so real that many experienced actors came repeatedly to study Adler in her last scene, keening over the lover she had just killed. It was an "acting feat," Robert Lewis recalled, that made one "wonder when he would see the like again."

But as Gwyn Ballantyne in *Gentlewoman* (1934), Adler so hated her performance and Strasberg's emphasis on "affective memory"—actors dredging their personal lives for emotions to relive on stage—that she took a leave from the Group to go abroad with Clurman. In Paris they met Stanislavsky. Dismayed at her complaint that his system made her hate acting, he worked with Stella for five weeks in private sessions that she had stenographically recorded.

Adler returned, inspired, to report and offer Group members classes based on her Stanislavsky sessions, emphasizing the actor's use of imagination to find "truth within the play's given circumstances" instead of Strasberg's affective memory exercises. Robert Lewis, Sanford Meisner, and Elia Kazan attended her "liberating" classes. Strasberg's jealous resentment, barely hidden then, emerged years later as bitter denigrations of Adler's teaching.

Adler's greatest critical success came in a role she shrank from until Clurman, directing his first production, slyly implied that she might not be able to do it. As the unglamorous, fifty-year-old Bessie Berger in *Awake and Sing!* (1935), she contributed a lighter side to Clifford Odets's angry characterization and, Robert Lewis claimed, set a standard for Jewish-mother parts never approached since.

When money troubles shortened the Group's next season in spring 1937, Adler and Clurman went to Hollywood. "Too Jewish-looking" for filmdom's Jewish moguls, she had her nose shortened, changed her name to Stella Ardler, and starred in Paramount's 1937 comedy *Love on Toast*. She directed the Group's successful international tour of Odets's *Golden Boy* (1938–1939) but returned to Hollywood to play a femme fatale in *Shadow of the Thin Man* (1941); later she assisted Arthur Freed in producing the 1942 Metro-Goldwyn-Mayer (MGM) musicals *DuBarry Was a Lady* and *For Me and My Gal*. Her last film role was in *My Girl Tisa* (1948).

From 1939 to 1942 Stella taught at Erwin Piscator's Dramatic Workshop at the New School; her classes evolved into the Stella Adler Acting Studio, which she opened in New York in 1949. She continued to act onstage for some years, but her desire to teach gradually replaced her need to perform. "Critically pummeled" as Madame Rosepettle in the 1961 London premiere of *Oh, Dad, Poor Dad, Mama's Hung You in the Closet and I'm Feeling So Sad*, she abandoned the stage. Meanwhile, her studio grew into a conservatory with a two-year program in play analysis and characterization taught by Adler and a faculty of twelve. Later she headed the Yale Drama School's acting department (1966–1967), again taught at the New School (1970–1972), and gave classes for New York University drama students at her own conservatory thereafter.

Adler divorced Clurman in 1960 and married the novelist Mitchell Wilson. He died on 26 February 1973. In 1986 she added a Los Angeles Conservatory and divided her teaching time between the two coasts. American acting had already been changed by such alumni of Adler's teaching as Marlon Brando, Warren Beatty, Robert De Niro, Ellen Burstyn, and Harvey Keitel.

Adler recorded her approach and exercises in *The Technique of Acting* (1988), the only book she published during her life. Her inspiring script analyses for performance are preserved in her posthumously published lectures, *Stella Adler on Ibsen, Strindberg, and Chekhov* (1999). Its informative biographical preface is based on the editor Barry Paris's final Los Angeles interview with her, shortly before her death from heart failure at age ninety.

Adler's lecture on Ibsen began: "Jacob Adler said . . . unless you give the audience something that makes them bigger—better, do not act." Stella Adler's life embodied that rule.

★

Memories of childhood are in Stella Adler's introduction to Lulla Rosenfeld's translation of Jacob Adler's autobiography *A Life On the Stage* (1999); all the Adlers appear in Rosenfeld's *Bright Star of Exile: Jacob Adler and the Yiddish Theatre* (1977). Harold Clurman vividly renders their romance and Group Theatre years in *The Fervent Years* (1945). The December 1976 issue of *Educational Theatre Journal,* entirely devoted to the Group Theatre, contains interviews and previously unpublished memorabilia; additional material appears in Wendy Smith, *Real Life Drama: The Group Theatre and America* (1990). Memoirs of Group members and works like Jay Williams's *Stage Left* (1974) and Foster Hirsch's *A Method to Their Madness* (1984) portray Adler from other viewpoints. Robert Brustein offers a valuable and affectionate tribute in "Stella for Star," *New Republic* (1 Feb. 1993). An obituary is in the *New York Times* (22 Dec. 1992). Her rambling 1981 videotaped interview in the Theatre on Film and Tape Archive at New York's Library of the Performing Arts does not do justice to Adler's charismatic personality and flamboyant classroom performance, both vividly apparent in "Awake and Dream!," the 1989 PBS *American Masters* video by Merrill Brockway and Catherine Tatge.

DANIEL S. KREMPEL

AMECHE, Don (*b.* 31 May 1908 in Kenosha, Wisconsin; *d.* 6 December 1993 in Scottsdale, Arizona), actor of radio, stage, screen, and television remembered especially for the film *The Story of Alexander Graham Bell* (1939) and later in life for his Academy Award for *Cocoon* (1985).

Ameche was born Dominic Felix Amici, the second of eight children of Felix Amici, an Italian-born saloon proprietor, and Barbara Etta Hertle, of German and Scotch-Irish de-

Don Ameche. © BETTMANN/CORBIS

scent. Sometime after arriving in the United States, his father changed the family name to "Ameche"; since classmates called Dominic "Don," he became known as "Don Ameche." After attending St. Berchman's Seminary in Marion, Iowa, from 1921 to 1922, Ameche attended another Catholic boys' school, Columbia Academy in Dubuque, Iowa, where he graduated with honors in 1925. He entered the academy's collegiate counterpart, Columbia College (now called Loras College) in Dubuque, where he studied for a year. His father wanted him to study law, however, so Ameche enrolled as a pre-law student at Marquette University in Milwaukee, Wisconsin, from 1926 to 1927. He was then accepted into the Bachelor of Laws program at Georgetown University Law School in Washington, D.C., where he remained for less than one term in 1927. Finally, he registered for introduction to law at the University of Wisconsin at Madison from September 1928 to February 1929. He never received a college or law degree.

While at the University of Wisconsin, a friend urged him to try out for a campus play, and Ameche won a lead role in George Bernard Shaw's *The Devil's Disciple.* He then successfully auditioned for an Al Jackson Stock Company production in Madison and enjoyed several more productions with that company. He then headed to New York City, where he made his Broadway debut in the small role of Perkins in *Jerry-for-Short,* which played through most of the 1929–1930 season. In 1930 Ameche acted in *Excess Baggage* (Greenwich, Connecticut) and the short-lived *Illegal Practice* (Chicago). He also worked with Texas Guinan in her traveling vaudeville show for a few weeks.

Ameche won parts on the Chicago radio programs *Empire Builders* (appearing from 1930 to 1931) and *The First Nighter* (appearing from 1930 to 1936) and later *Grand Hotel* (appearing from 1933 to 1936). Other radio commitments during the 1930s were *Foreign Legion* (1933) and host of *The Chase and Sanborn Hour* (1937–1939), starring Edgar Bergen and his dummy, Charlie McCarthy. On 26 November 1932, Ameche married Honore Prendergast, his childhood sweetheart whom he had met at a Catholic church choir in Dubuque; they raised a family of six children.

An NBC radio publicist, aware of Ameche's popularity as a radio persona and light baritone singing voice, urged Ameche to make his first screen test in New York City for Metro-Goldwyn-Mayer (MGM) in 1935. Another friend used his influence with Twentieth Century–Fox to have Ameche make another screen test two months later. Ameche had already made a film short, *Beauty at the World's Fair* (1933), though Paramount refused to release this mediocre piece. The filmmakers brought a suit against the Paramount producers, but the suit was dropped when the filmmakers realized that their case would be weakened because Ameche, who agreed with the negative assessment of the short, was prepared to testify in court to that same assessment. Upon MGM's rejection of Ameche's screen tests, Darryl F. Zanuck at Twentieth Century–Fox reviewed the tests and offered a contract to Ameche, who remained with that studio until 1945. Ameche eventually joined Alice Faye and Tyrone Power in becoming the three new hot box-office favorites whom Zanuck brought into the studio and often costarred together. Ameche played a promising dual role in his first feature motion picture, *Sins of Man* (1936). He acquired confidence and on-screen relaxation from Henry King, the director of *Ramona* (1936), from the novel by Helen Hunt Jackson; Ameche played Alessandro, a Native American in love with the title character, played by Loretta Young. He and Young were soon together again in *Ladies in Love* (1936) and *Love Under Fire* (1937). He joined the famed Olympic ice-skater Sonja Henie in her screen debut in *One in a Million* (1936) and appeared with her again in *Happy Landing* (1938). For his fourth film with Young, *Love Is News* (1937), the six-foot-tall, brown-eyed Ameche wore a thin moustache, which became his trademark.

Some of Ameche's best-known films were released in 1938 and 1939: *In Old Chicago* (1938); *Alexander's Ragtime Band* (1938); the tongue-in-cheek musical interpretation of *The Three Musketeers* (1939); an outstanding screwball comedy, *Midnight* (1939), with Claudette Colbert and John Barrymore; and the film with which moviegoers for several decades would most identify Ameche, *The Story of Alexander Graham Bell* (1939). For years thereafter, the American public called the telephone "the Don Ameche." Ameche played the American songwriter Stephen Foster in *Swanee River* (1939) and Edward Soloman, the first husband of Lillian Russell, in *Lillian Russell* (1940).

In another court case, a $170,000 suit was filed against Ameche in 1940 because of his refusal to be loaned out to Paramount for *The Night of January 16*, a mystery script that he found very poor; the case was dropped the same year. In 1940 he gave testimony before the House of Representatives Interstate Commerce Committee—in the presence of numerous fans—to oppose the Neely Anti-Block Booking Bill, which would free movie theaters from "blind" purchasing contracts with studios. (Blind purchasing contracts were arrangements in which theaters purchased films from studios before production began.) Ameche objected to these contracts because no synopses could be given to the theaters before production began, since films often changed extensively during production. Throughout the early 1940s Ameche acted in many more comedies and dramas, period dress stories, several melodramas and mysteries, and a few wartime stories, such as *Four Sons* (1940), *Confirm or Deny* (1941), *Wing and a Prayer* (1944), and *Guest Wife* (1945). Among his last films at Twentieth Century–Fox before his contract ended was his favorite,

Ernst Lubitsch's *Heaven Can Wait* (1943). Ameche felt that Lubitsch evoked from him one of his best performances in this period comedy/fantasy. In it he played Henry Van Cleve, a deceased man who regrets his mistakes as he describes his life story to the devil.

Ameche decided against renewing his studio contract so that he could freelance, a career choice that he later regretted. By the conclusion of his contract in 1945, he had made thirty-three films; for four of them he was loaned out to Paramount, MGM, and Columbia. From 1945 through the 1970s he made close to a dozen more films—sometimes in small character roles—with a variety of studios. Over the airwaves, Ameche had great success, especially whenever he teamed up with Frances Langford in their sketches on the Bickersons—a married couple who first appeared on the *Chase and Sanborn Hour* and reappeared on the *Drene Show* (1946–1957) and the *Morgan-Ameche-Langford Show* (1947–1948). In the early 1940s Ameche attempted to establish a Buffalo, New York, franchise within the National Football League. He was among the millionaires who established the All-America Football Conference, which played four seasons (1946–1949). His ownership group, including the film producer Louis B. Mayer and the actors Bing Crosby and Bob Hope, established the Los Angeles Dons, based at the Los Angeles Memorial Coliseum, as one of the western division teams. Ameche also owned, raced, and bred thoroughbreds, stabled at Lexington, Kentucky.

In 1950 he returned to Broadway and started working for the television studios. He acted in the plays *Silk Stockings* (1955), *Holiday for Lovers* (1957), *Goldilocks* (1958), *13 Daughters* (1961), and *Henry, Sweet Henry* (1967). He joined nationwide tours and gave dinner theater presentations of *I Married an Angel* (1964), *The Odd Couple* (1968), and *No, No Nanette* (1972–1974). Ameche first appeared on television in "The Door" episode of the *Chevrolet Tele-Theater* (1949), and then in a religious film, *The Triumphant Hour* (1950). His first regular contract was to replace Edward Everett Horton in the fall of 1950 in the musical variety show *Holiday Hotel;* this program evolved into *Don Ameche's Musical Playhouse* (September 1950 to October 1951). The Bickersons soon found themselves regularly before the television cameras in *Star Time* (1950–1951), and then on the *Frances Langford–Don Ameche Show* (1951–1952). Ameche was the original host for *Coke Time with Eddie Fisher* (1953).

Ameche served as emcee for several game shows, such as *Take a Chance* (1950) and, in the early 1960s, as a panelist on *To Tell the Truth*. He appeared in the television musical *High Button Shoes* (1956) with Nanette Fabray; starred with Joan Bennett in *Junior Miss* on CBS's *DuPont Show of the Month* (1957); played the Mafia leader Albert Anastasia in *Climax* (1958); and started a short-lived comedy series (also with Bennett), *Too Young to Go Steady* (1959). He even had a five-day-a-week radio program, *Don Ameche's Real Life Stories,* in 1958. He traveled overseas with a crew to tape live performances of circuses and ice shows from more than twenty countries for *International Showtime* (1961–1965). A film of some of those episodes, *Rings Around the World,* was released to movie theaters by Columbia (1966).

After decades away from motion picture studios, Ameche recharged his acting career with *Won Ton Ton, the Dog Who Saved Hollywood* (1976). He appeared in the popular comedy hit *Trading Places* (1983) with Eddie Murphy and Ralph Bellamy. His final Broadway work came as the stage manager during the closing weeks of Lincoln Center Theater's award-winning revival of Thornton Wilder's *Our Town* (1989). On 24 March 1986, Ameche won his only Academy Award (best supporting actor) for his exhilarating, comic, and athletic performance in *Cocoon* (1985). Among his last films was David Mamet's *Things Change* (1988) with Joe Mantegna, with whom he shared the Venice Film Festival's best actor award. Ameche died of prostate cancer. Despite his separation from his wife, Ameche's ashes are buried near her in the Prendergast plot at Resurrection Catholic Cemetery in Dubuque.

For more than half a century Ameche performed as one of the most charming, debonair personalities in various forums of the entertainment world. He was a prime mover during radio's golden days and an important actor on television as well. In Hollywood, Ameche never won recognition as a "great" actor but ranked among the top twenty-five box-office attractions during the 1930s and 1940s. His spectacular screen and television revival starting in the 1970s made him a popular actor to a new generation. His elegant charm, beautiful and soothing voice, affable and energetic masculinity, and handsome looks, when combined with his flawless professionalism and personal integrity, worked together to make him a beloved, reassuring, and comforting "friend," whose company radio listeners, theatergoers, and film attendees eagerly sought time and time again.

★

An interview with Dr. Ronald D. Davis (March 1977) is available at the Ronald Davis Oral History Collection, DeGolyer Library, Southern Methodist University, Dallas. This interview is also accessible on microform as "The Reminiscences of Don Ameche" through the Library of Congress. The Billy Rose Theatre Collection at the New York Public Library for the Performing Arts at Lincoln Center holds clippings, scrapbooks, and photographs. For informative biographical material see James Robert Parish and Michael R. Pitts, *Hollywood Songsters* (1991), which includes a sample but unique "Album Discography," and James C. Madden, "Don Ameche: Parlayed a Pleasing Voice into a Successful Film Career," *Films in Review* 23 (Jan. 1972): 8–22, in-

cluding filmography. There are extensive articles, often with interviews, in the *New York Times,* including Chris Chase, "At the Movies: Don Ameche Explains His Absence from Films" (17 June 1983). See also listings in *Current Biography* (1965 and the obituary in the 1994 yearbook). For extensive bibliographies primarily in the Hollywood journals see Mel Schuster, *Motion Picture Performers: A Bibliography of Magazine and Periodical Articles, 1900–1969* (1972) and *Supplement No. 1, 1970–1974* (1976). To focus on Ameche's association with football, see Phil Barber, "The All-America Football Conference," in Bob Carroll et al., eds., *Total Football: The Official Encyclopedia of the National Football League* (1997). Obituaries are in the *New York Times* (8 Dec. 1993), the *Los Angeles Times* (8 Dec. 1993), and *Variety* (20 Dec. 1993).

MADELINE SAPIENZA

ANDERSON, Carl David, Jr. (*b.* 3 September 1905 in New York City; *d.* 11 January 1991 in San Marino, California), experimental physicist who, while conducting cosmic ray investigations in 1932, discovered the positron—the fundamental atomic particle having the same mass but opposite in electric charge to the negatively charged electron. For his discovery he won the Nobel Prize for physics in 1936.

Anderson was the only child of immigrants from Sweden who had arrived in the United States in 1895. His father, also named Carl David, and his mother, Emma Adolfina

Carl David Anderson, Jr., upon arrival in New York City aboard the SS *Aquitania,* 1937. © BETTMANN/CORBIS

Ajaxson, were both from farming families in Sweden. When he was twelve years old, the family moved to Los Angeles, where his father managed small restaurants. Anderson attended Los Angeles Polytechnic High School where, supplementing his ambition in high jumping, he evinced his initial interest in science by joining the science club. He graduated in 1924. Because the limited financial resources of the family precluded attending a college out of town, Anderson commuted as an undergraduate to the California Institute of Technology (Caltech) in nearby Pasadena, from which he graduated with a B.S. degree in 1927. Anderson's enrollment in Caltech, though initially dictated by fiscal restraints, turned out to be fortunate. The physics department became, under the stewardship of Robert A. Millikan, one of the leading institutions of physical scientific research in the United States, indeed in the world.

Anderson spent his entire career at Caltech. Beginning as a research fellow in 1930, he joined Caltech's faculty as assistant professor of physics in 1933. In 1937 he was promoted to associate professor and in 1939 to full professor. Upon his retirement from active research and teaching, he was named professor emeritus in 1977, completing an uninterrupted association with Caltech of fifty-three years.

Under Millikan's direction, Anderson's graduate work emphasized experimental rather than theoretical physics. The eminent theoretician J. Robert Oppenheimer, who in late 1942 became the principal scientific director of the Manhattan Project (the American atomic bomb project), taught Anderson's first course in quantum mechanics. Oppenheimer persuaded Anderson to complete successfully the course after other students had found it too formidable and dropped out.

Anderson's doctoral thesis addressed the scattering of electrons from gaseous atoms bombarded by X rays. His Ph.D. degree was awarded in 1930 with the magna cum laude citation. After securing his doctorate, Anderson was asked by Millikan to remain and assist him in his study of the extraterrestrial ionizing radiation discovered and measured in 1911 and 1912 by the Austrian (later U.S.-naturalized) physicist Victor F. Hess. This radiation was given the now universally employed designation "cosmic rays" by Millikan, and was a subject of intensive investigation by Millikan and his colleagues at Caltech, as well as scientific groups around the world. Anderson's assignment was to build a cloud chamber especially suited for the detection of electrons in cosmic-ray measurements. The first cloud chamber had been built and developed by the Scottish physicist Charles Thomson Rees Wilson at Cambridge University from 1895 to 1900. Wilson received the Nobel Prize for his invention in 1927.

Essentially, the cloud chamber depends upon the formation of vapor trails similar to those seen behind aircraft flying at high altitudes with corresponding low atmospheric pressure. The essential apparatus consists of an artificial mist of water vapor in an evacuated chamber. A piston connected to the chamber is moved quickly outward, lowering the pressure and suddenly causing a mist cloud to form. When an ionizing particle traverses the cloud, droplets condense along electrically charged particles (or ions), forming a path that can be photographed.

Anderson and Millikan designed a cloud chamber positioned between the poles of a powerful electromagnet capable of deflecting the parts of the high-energy, electrically charged particles found in cosmic rays. Anderson ultimately made and studied more than 1,000 cosmic ray photographs. As the result of the action produced by the electromagnet, he observed deflections of cloud chamber paths in opposite directions, indicating that some were negative and some positive. It was evident that the negative paths were attributable to electrons. Because the only positively charged particle known in the early 1930s was the proton, which was more than 1,800 times heavier, Anderson initially assumed that this was what he had encountered. However, further experiments led him to the possibility that the positively charged particle had the same mass as the negative electron. For months this inference was strenuously resisted by Millikan, and it took courage for Anderson to challenge the judgment of his prestigious mentor in what he later characterized as "frequent and at times somewhat heated discussions."

Finally, after inserting a lead plate across the center of the cloud chamber to reduce the charged particle's high energy, on 2 August 1932 Anderson obtained an unmistakable photograph exhibiting both the positive charge and a mass equivalent to the negatively charged electron. This and subsequent photographs finally persuaded Millikan that Anderson had discovered a "positive electron." Anderson wrote a letter announcing the discovery that appeared in *Science* on 9 September 1932. General skepticism initially confronted Anderson's discovery. The great Danish physicist Niels Bohr (Nobel Prize, 1922) dismissed the possibility of a positive electron. In 1934, however, two physicists at Cambridge University, Patrick M. S. Blackett (Nobel Prize, 1948) and Giuseppe P. S. Occhialini, reported cloud chamber investigations of their own in which positron tracks were observed.

Interestingly, Anderson was totally unaware that the leading theoretician of quantum mechanics, Paul A. M. Dirac (Nobel Prize, 1933), had predicted the existence of a positive analog of the electron in 1928. As Anderson himself stated in a retrospective article in the December 1961 issue of the *American Journal of Physics:* "The discovery of the positron was wholly accidental . . . if a researcher had taken the Dirac theory at face value he could have discovered the positron in a single afternoon."

In 1936 Anderson shared the Nobel Prize in physics for

his discovery of the positron with Victor F. Hess, whose balloon flights of 1911 and 1912 had identified cosmic rays. Recognizing that Anderson was only thirty-one years old at the time of the award, the presenter made the following observation: "We congratulate you on this great success attained in your young years and we wish to express the hope that your further investigations will bring to science many near and equally important results."

Anderson continued his cosmic ray studies at Caltech beyond his discovery of the positron. In 1937, while performing cloud chamber measurements at Pike's Peak in Colorado, he and his former student and colleague Seth Neddemeyer made known the discovery of a "hereto unknown particle" with an average life of two-millionths of a second. In 1938 he announced the existence of the aforementioned—which he called the mesotron, later shortened to meson—a fundamental nuclear particle having either positive, negative, or no electric charge and intermediate in mass between the electron (or positron) and the heavier proton. The discovery of mesons and their role in fundamental nuclear particle interactions became another vital landmark in contemporary nuclear physics. With his meson discovery and other research achievements, Anderson certainly fulfilled the hope expressed by the Nobel Prize presenter just a year earlier.

In addition to his impressive research career, Anderson was an exceptional scientific administrator. Between 1962 and 1970 he was chairman of Caltech's division of physics, mathematics, and astronomy. Anderson was one of those considered prior to Oppenheimer for the position of scientific director of the Manhattan Project. For reasons not known, he declined, though he did do military rocket research for the government during World War II.

Anderson married Lorraine Elvira Bergman on 30 June 1946. She died in 1984. They had two children. Anderson died at the age of eighty-six in San Marino. The cause of death was undisclosed.

With reference to his working-class beginnings, his mother was quoted at the time of his Nobel Prize win: "If he has special ability, I don't know where he got it." One journalistic appraisal characterized him as "shy and retiring" and another saw him as having "a very approachable manner [that] brands him as one of the more human scientists." His discoveries of the positron and meson in cosmic rays certainly place Anderson in the pioneering forefront of modern physics, with its focus on nuclear structure, on the existence of antimatter, and on striving for the resolution of undecided cosmological questions.

★

Carl David Anderson, Jr., "Apparent Existence of Easily Deflectable Positives," *Science* (9 Sept. 1932), published the month after Anderson's discovery of 2 August 1932, is a letter written at the behest of Anderson's mentor Richard A. Millikan after Millikan finally agreed that the observed track was indeed the positive light particle and not the heavier proton Millikan had conjectured. Anderson's paper "The Positive Electron," *Physical Review* vol. 43, (1933): 491, exhibited the historic photograph of the cloud chamber positron track mentioned above. *Physics: Nobel Lectures, Including Presentation Speeches and Laureates' Biographies 1922-1941* (1967) gives a transcript of the presentation speech by Professor H. Pleijel, which gives a coherent picture of the important connection between the scientific work of Anderson and the earlier cosmic ray research of Victor F. Hess. Robert A. Millikan, *Autobiography of Robert A. Millikan* (1950), gives a thorough account of the California Institute of Technology's activities in physics research and thus the environment in which Anderson spent his entire scientific career. In Emilio Segrè, *From X-Rays to Quarks: Modern Physicists and Their Discoveries* (1980), "The Wonder Year 1932: Neutron, Positron, Deuterium and Other Discoveries," is of special interest. Abraham Pais, *Inward Bound: Of Matter and Forces in the Physical World* (1986), treats Anderson's positron and meson work in detail. Frank Close, Michael Marten, and Christie Sutton, *The Particle Explosion* (1987), has two of the earliest photographs of positron tracks as well as discussion of the contributions by other researchers in the field. Frank N. Magill, ed., *The Nobel Prize Winners: Physics,* vol. 1 (1989), has a good summary of Anderson's life and scientific accomplishments. Yuval Ne'eman and Yoram Kirsh, *The Particle Hunters* (2d ed., 1989), is an excellent popular presentation of the impact of Anderson's discovery on the development of modern physics; the 2 August 1932 cloud chamber photograph that appeared in the first positron paper by Anderson is presented here. Obituaries are in the *New York Times* and *Los Angeles Times* (both 12 Jan. 1991).

LEONARD R. SOLON

ANDERSON, George Whelan, Jr. (*b.* 15 December 1906 in Brooklyn, New York; *d.* 20 March 1992 in McLean, Virginia), admiral and chief of naval operations during the Cuban missile crisis of 1962.

Anderson was the son of George W. Anderson, the owner of a real estate agency, and Clara Green, a homemaker. Raised and educated in Brooklyn as a devout Roman Catholic, he graduated from Brooklyn Preparatory School in 1923. He then excelled at the U.S. Naval Academy, from which he graduated in 1927, twenty-eighth in a class of 579 midshipmen. After three years aboard the light cruiser *Cincinnati* in the Pacific, he qualified as a naval aviator at Pensacola, Florida, in 1930. He flew catapult scout planes attached to two successive light cruisers in the Atlantic until 1933, when he became a test pilot at the Norfolk, Virginia, naval air station. Anderson's flying skills earned him an assignment to the crack Fighting Squadron Two, aboard the aircraft carrier *Lexington* in 1935, and two years later to

George Whelan Anderson, Jr., U.S. Sixth Fleet Commander, 1959. AP/
WIDE WORLD PHOTOS

ship's company of the carrier *Yorktown,* which he helped
place in commission. From 1939 to 1940, in the rank of
lieutenant, he briefly flew patrol planes in Seattle.

Because of his exceptional intelligence and knowledge
of airplanes, and in spite of his relatively junior rank, Anderson was transferred early in 1940 to the U.S. Navy's
Bureau of Aeronautics at the behest of its chief, Rear Admiral John H. Towers. He was placed in charge of long-
range programs and allocations of the navy's aircraft during
the mobilization of 1940–1941. Promoted to lieutenant
commander in 1941, he designed the navy's wartime aircraft program in the three weeks following the Japanese
attack on Pearl Harbor that December. Anderson worked
closely with counterparts in the U.S. Army, industry, and
in Britain. He accompanied Towers and General Dwight
D. Eisenhower to London in May 1942 for an important
aircraft allocation conference with British prime minister
Winston Churchill. His reward for these wartime accomplishments was promotion to commander and assignment
as prospective navigator and tactical officer of the second
carrier to be named *Yorktown* in March 1943. Following
her commissioning, Anderson participated in raids on
Japanese-occupied Marcus and Wake Islands in the Pacific.

Anderson's organizational and administrative talents
and experience led Towers, now a vice admiral, to utilize

him as head of the plans division of Pacific Fleet air forces
during the offensive of November 1943 to March 1944. He
remained as one of two key assistants when Towers was
deputy fleet commander in chief during the rest of the offensive. Recalled to Washington, D.C., in the rank of captain in June 1945, Anderson served on the navy's Strategic
Planning Division, interservice Joint Planning Staff, and
related agencies during the final months of World War II
and through the early cold war period.

With his wife, Muriel Buttling, to whom he was married
from 3 October 1933 until her death in 1947, he had one
daughter and two sons. His youngest son, Thomas Patrick
Anderson, became a decorated carrier pilot during the
Vietnam War and died in 1978 when he crashed while
trying to land his plane aboard his carrier. Anderson
married Mary Lee Lamar, widow of Rear Admiral William
D. Sample, on 15 May 1948, by whom he gained a stepdaughter.

After service as captain of the Atlantic antisubmarine
aircraft carrier *Mindoro* from 1948 to 1949, Anderson was
a student at the National War College and then fleet operations officer of the Sixth Fleet in the Mediterranean. In
1950 Eisenhower, then Supreme Allied Commander in Europe, specifically requested that Anderson be his senior U.S.
officer in Plans and Operations, a major post that Anderson
occupied from December 1950 to July 1952. He then commanded the attack carrier *Franklin D. Roosevelt* in the Mediterranean until becoming special assistant to Admiral Arthur W. Radford, chairman of the Joint Chiefs of Staff, in
July 1953, being promoted to rear admiral one year later.
During tensions with Communist China from 1955 to
1956, Anderson commanded the Taiwan Patrol Force, then
served as chief of staff on the Pacific Fleet's Joint Staff.
Advanced to vice admiral, he was chief of staff to Admiral
Felix B. Stump, the Commander in Chief Pacific from 1957
to 1958. Following a navy tradition of earning flag rank
(all ranks above captain) at sea instead of ashore, he was
permitted reversion in rank to rear admiral to command a
carrier division that supported Marine Corps landings in
Lebanon in 1958. Again promoted to vice admiral, Anderson commanded the Sixth Fleet and concurrently the
North Atlantic Treaty Organization's (NATO) striking
and support forces in southern Europe between 1959 and
1961.

In June 1961 President John F. Kennedy appointed Anderson chief of naval operations (CNO). He was chosen
from a pool of 109 candidates, ten of whom were senior to
him. Anderson assumed leadership of the navy and four-
star rank on 1 August. He soon ran afoul of the new
secretary of defense, Robert S. McNamara, who asserted
increased civilian authority over the military by microman-
aging decisions without much experience in or knowledge
of military matters. This became apparent when McNa-

mara forced the navy and air force to adopt the same experimental tactical fighter plane, the TFX, in spite of Anderson's opposition to it based on his belief that it would be unsuitable for carrier-based operations. When the plane entered naval service as the F-111, Anderson was proved correct. Similarly, McNamara overrode navy plans, championed by Anderson, to replace its oil-driven aircraft carriers entirely with nuclear-powered ones, a policy that was adopted in the 1980s. Anderson also criticized McNamara for authorizing an inadequate pay raise for military personnel.

Anderson brilliantly directed President Kennedy's "quarantine" (naval blockade) of Soviet Russian vessels carrying potentially nuclear-tipped missiles into communist Cuba during the Cuban crisis of October 1962. McNamara's inexperience in conducting naval blockades, however, resulted in at least three heated confrontations with Anderson in the Pentagon command center during the course of the operation. Although Anderson attempted to confer privately with McNamara about the issues of U.S. warships tracking Soviet submarines in the Caribbean and U.S. naval vessels firing warning shots to stop Soviet tankers, McNamara became openly distraught for fear of losing control of this delicate international confrontation. As a result, despite the navy's complete success in the blockade, Anderson did not receive reappointment to an expected second two-year term as CNO. He retired in August 1963 and then served from 1963 to 1966 as U.S. ambassador to Portugal, advising that nation on an orderly transition of its African colonies to independence. From 1973 to 1977 he was a member of, and eventually chaired, the U.S. president's Foreign Intelligence Advisory Board.

Anderson was an imposing individual at 6 feet, 2 inches, and 190 pounds—and, with deep blue eyes and later silvery hair, sufficiently handsome to draw the nickname "Gorgeous George" from other navy personnel. He inspired immense loyalty from naval personnel, to whom he preached cleanliness in behavior and language (in spite of his own penchant for off-color humor). A perfectionist, he was appreciated for his keen intellect, technical knowledge, and diplomatic, managerial, and command abilities. He died in McLean of congestive heart failure and was buried at Arlington National Cemetery in Arlington, Virginia.

★

An oral history transcript of Anderson (1980) is deposited at the U.S. Naval Institute, Annapolis, Maryland. His World War II service is treated in Clark G. Reynolds, *Admiral John H. Towers: The Struggle for Naval Air Supremacy* (1991), and his role in the Cuban crisis is covered in Dino A. Brugioni, *Eyeball to Eyeball: The Inside Story of the Cuban Missile Crisis* (1991). An obituary is in the *New York Times* (22 Mar. 1992).

CLARK G. REYNOLDS

ANDERSON, Judith (*b.* 10 February 1898 in Adelaide, Australia; *d.* 3 January 1992 in Montecito, California), actress known for outstanding stage interpretations of Medea and Lady Macbeth and Academy Award nominee for Alfred Hitchcock's film *Rebecca* (1940).

Anderson was born Frances Margaret Anderson-Anderson, the youngest of four children of James Anderson-Anderson and Jessie Margaret Saltmarsh Anderson-Anderson. Anderson attended Rose Park (1908–1912) and Norwood (1913–1915) private schools in Adelaide. Her father, a silver mine owner, gambled away much of his wealth; after he deserted his family in 1903, Anderson's mother supported her children by operating a grocery store. At age seven, Anderson saw the great opera singer Dame Nellie Melba perform and resolved to move audiences as she did. Taking voice and piano lessons, Anderson at first aspired to an operatic career as a contralto but soon decided to become an actress. Elocution lessons helped her win national recitation awards.

After her family relocated to Sydney, Australia, in 1915, "Francee Anderson" made her professional stage debut there later that year at the Theatre Royal with the Julius Knight Company as Stephanie in *A Royal Divorce*. She worked with this company through 1916. She also toured New Zealand in *Turn to the Right,* performed by a pre-

Judith Anderson, 1944. © BETTMANN/CORBIS

dominantly American cast, who urged her to act in the United States. In January 1918, accompanied by her mother (her strongest moral support until her death in 1950), Anderson left for Hollywood. She failed to impress the film producer Cecil B. DeMille and, after four months, moved to New York City. Anderson worked for $40 a week with the Emma's Bunting Stock Company at the Fourteenth Street Theatre, where she progressed through the ranks (1918–1919). She toured with William Gillette in *Dear Brutus* (1920) and played with stock companies in Albany, New York, and Boston (1921).

Under the stage name "Frances Anderson," she made her Broadway debut as Mrs. Bellmore in *On the Stairs* on 25 September 1922. In 1923 she adopted the stage name "Judith Anderson." When she opened as Elise Van Zile in *Cobra* (1924), she propelled herself into higher spheres of professional acting and won sensational praise from critics and theatergoers alike. The playwright and producer David Belasco cast her in *The Dove* (1925). She even opened in vaudeville at the Palace in a "playlet" entitled *Thieves* (1926). In January 1927 she returned to Australia in *Cobra* and other plays until stricken with pneumonia. She returned to the United States, and by the end of the year, she had opened in New York as Antoinette Lyle in *Behold the Bridegroom.* She played the lead in *Anna* (1928) and, in the summer of 1928, replaced the vacationing Lynn Fontanne as Nina Leeds in Eugene O'Neill's Pulitzer Prize–winning nine-hour play, *Strange Interlude.* In 1930 she made her film debut in a small role in a short, *Madame of the Jury.*

On tour, Anderson appeared in Luigi Pirandello's *As You Desire Me* (1930–1931). For the Theatre Guild, she appeared as Lavinia in O'Neill's *Mourning Becomes Electra* (1932), which subsequently went on tour. From 1934 to 1936 she was busy with other plays, including her favorite role, the Woman, in the not-too-successful play *Come of Age* (1934). She starred as Delia Lovell in another Pulitzer Prize–winning play, Zoë Akins's *The Old Maid* (1935).

In 1936 Anderson took on her first Shakespeare role when she played Queen Gertrude in the Guthrie McClintic production of *Hamlet,* with the famed Shakespearean actor John Gielgud in the title role and Lillian Gish as Ophelia. Anderson gave her first performance as Lady Macbeth in an Old Vic production in London opposite Laurence Olivier in 1937. Her first American Lady Macbeth opened in New York in 1941, opposite Maurice Evans. Anderson married Benjamin Harrison Lehman, a professor of English at the University of California at Berkeley, in 1937; they divorced two years later.

Anderson made her film debut in Twentieth Century–Fox's *Blood Money* (1933). She appeared in fifteen films released during the 1940s alone, followed by ten more over the decades through 1985. The only role for which Anderson was nominated for an Academy Award (as best sup-

porting actress) was as the sinister Mrs. Danvers in Alfred Hitchcock's *Rebecca* (1940), costarring Laurence Olivier and Joan Fontaine.

During World War II, Anderson entertained Allied troops in live theatrical presentations on the home front and on bases close to the battle lines, especially in the South Pacific. Anderson said that the troops craved serious presentations just as much as the more popular musical and comedy routines. Her group of entertainers included a few instrumentalists, a singer, and a pianist. On film, Anderson was one of the many stars in *Stage Door Canteen* (1943) and acted in two wartime stories for Warner Brothers: *All Through the Night* (1942) and *Edge of Darkness* (1943). After the war, in 1946, she married Luther Greene, a theatrical producer; they divorced in 1951. Anderson never had children.

During the postwar period, Anderson erupted into the pages of theatrical history with her monumental interpretation of Euripides' *Medea* (1947), a "free adaptation" written by the poet Robinson Jeffers. In 1948 Anderson was given a Tony Award and a Donaldson Award for her interpretation of Medea, was designated "first lady of the theatre" by the General Federation of Women's Clubs, and was recognized with the award for diction by the American Academy of Arts and Sciences.

From 1950 to 1953 she was busy on Broadway, including a role in *The Tower Beyond Tragedy* (1950) and a dramatic reading of *John Brown's Body* (1953). The 1950s also included tours of *Medea* to theaters in Berlin, Paris, and throughout Australia. Her varied film activities of the late 1940s and 1950s included the roles of Herodias in *Salome* (1953); Memnet, the nurse in service to Pharaoh's daughter in DeMille's memorable remake of *The Ten Commandments* (1956); and Big Mama in Tennessee Williams's *Cat on a Hot Tin Roof* (1958).

In the 1950s Anderson ventured into television, when she starred in "The Silver Cord" (*Pulitzer Prize Playhouse,* 1951) and other dramatic works, including *Macbeth* (*Hallmark Hall of Fame,* 1954), for which she received an Emmy for best actress. She received a second Emmy when *Macbeth* was reproduced in 1960. The American Shakespeare Festival Theatre and Academy, in its opening season at Stratford, Connecticut, cited her Lady Macbeth for one of seven awards presented at New York's Waldorf-Astoria (1955). Other honors throughout her career included an honorary degree from Northwestern University (1953), investiture at Buckingham Palace (12 July 1960) by Queen Elizabeth II with the insignia of a Dame Commander of the Most Excellent Order of the British Empire, and an honorary degree from Fairfield University (1964) upon the 400th anniversary of Shakespeare's birth.

Anderson's live performance scheduling did not slacken in the later decades of her life. In the 1960s there were tours in the United States and Canada as well as new productions, including Anton Chekhov's *The Seagull* at the Edinburgh Festival in 1960 and at the Old Vic. She followed in the tradition of Sarah Bernhardt and other tragediennes by playing the lead in a condensed version of *Hamlet* (1970–1971) and then performed again in *Medea,* this time as the Nurse.

Anderson's television ventures during her final decades included a new production of *Elizabeth the Queen* with Charlton Heston (*Showcase Theatre,* 1968). As an octogenarian she played the role of the wealthy matriarch Minx Lockridge for *Santa Barbara,* a television soap opera; she appeared regularly on the show from 1984 through 1987. On 11 June 1984, New York's Lion Theater was renamed the Judith Anderson Theater; the honored actress presented Lady Macbeth's letter scene and expressed grateful words of tribute to her audiences, who had so motivated her throughout the decades. Suffering from cancer, she died of pneumonia at her home in Montecito, near Santa Barbara, California.

Though she was famed in the world of screen and television for her award-winning performances in *Rebecca* and *Macbeth,* Dame Judith Anderson shines forth most brilliantly on the pages of theatrical history for her classical style of acting in an almost eight-decade stage career. Her acting life offered a wide variety of stage roles not only in the development of female leads but also in an expansive range of theatrical genres, from plays of antiquity to contemporary works—in sharp contrast to Hollywood's more restricted typecasting of her as suspicious or sinister characters, usually in secondary or supporting roles. She favored roles that allowed her to achieve the most "musical" interpretation of the language as she developed her characterizations, and she preferred works that engaged audiences in elevated contemplation or joyful appreciation of life. During the final decades of her life, she regretted the "ugliness and tawdriness" on stage and screen that deprived audiences of a meaningful theatrical or film experience.

★

The Dame Judith Anderson Collection, from 1915 through the 1980s, is held at the Department of Special Collections, University of California, Santa Barbara. The Billy Rose Theatre Collection at the New York Public Library for the performing Arts at Lincoln Center has clippings, scrapbooks, photographs, and programs. For biographical information see Alice M. Robinson, Vera Mowry Roberts, and Milly S. Barranger, eds., *Notable Women in the American Theatre: A Biographical Dictionary* (1989), which includes a bibliography, and William C. Young, *Famous Actors and Actresses on the American Stage* vol. 1 of *Documents of American Theater History* (1975). There is a short filmography in Christopher Young, "Judith Anderson: Her Grade-A Acting Ability Wasn't Enough for Success on the Screen," in *Films in Review*

21 (Apr. 1970): 193–196. *Current Biography* has entries in 1941 and 1961 as well as an obituary in the 1992 yearbook. See references to Anderson in Daniel Blum, *A Pictorial History of the American Theatre 1860–1985* (6th ed., 1986); Brooks Atkinson, *Broadway* (1970); and Ronald Hayman, *John Gielgud* (1971). For extensive bibliographies, primarily citing Hollywood journals, see Mel Schuster, *Motion Picture Performers: A Bibliography of Magazine and Periodical Articles, 1900–1969* (1971), and *Supplement No. 1, 1970–1974* (1976). Obituaries are in the *New York Times* (4 Jan. 1992), *Los Angeles Times* (4 Jan. 1992), London *Times* (6 Dec. 1992), and *Variety* (13 Jan. 1992). Some of Anderson's films are available on commercial videocassettes, and there are numerous recordings of her dramatic readings. For example, there are tapes of *Medea* at the Kennedy Center for the Performing Arts and a conversation (taped in 1976), including a monologue from *Hamlet,* with Clifton Fadiman for the Center for the Study of Democratic Institutions, Santa Barbara, California, available at the Library of Congress and elsewhere.

MADELINE SAPIENZA

ANDERSON, Marian (*b.* 27 February 1897 in Philadelphia, Pennsylvania; *d.* 8 April 1993 in Portland, Oregon), concert singer who was one of the great contraltos of the twentieth century.

Anderson was the eldest of three daughters of John Berkley Anderson, a dealer in coal and ice who died when she was twelve years old, and Annie Delilah Rucker, a homemaker who took in laundry and worked in the Wanamaker Department Store. John Berkley had come with his family to Philadelphia from the Tidewater of eastern Virginia during the 1890s. Annie Delilah, who was born in Lynchburg, Virginia, came to Philadelphia shortly before her marriage.

Anderson's father died in 1910 after a brief illness. Graduating from Stanton Grammar School in 1912, Anderson did not continue her schooling for three years because her family could not make do without the money she was able to earn from singing. In 1915, with the help of funds raised by the Philadelphia black community, eighteen-year-old Anderson entered the business-oriented William Penn High School. Her progress was slow because of her lack of interest in the curriculum and because her singing took her away from school more and more frequently. Three years later she transferred to the more progressive South Philadelphia High School for Girls, where she graduated in 1921. Although poverty and racial discrimination prevented her from realizing her ambition to attend a music conservatory, she was given a scholarship to enroll in the summer course in opera performance taught by Oscar Saenger at the Chicago Conservatory of Music in the summer of 1919.

Anderson's precocious musical talent was discovered in Union Baptist Church, where she sang in the junior choir

Marian Anderson. © BETTMANN/CORBIS

from the age of six, known throughout her neighborhood in South Philadelphia by the age of ten as "the baby contralto." At thirteen she joined the senior choir. Her formal vocal studies did not begin until she was eighteen. Her first teachers were Mary Saunders Patterson and Agnes Reifsnyder, but it was Giuseppe Boghetti, her longtime teacher and coach, who saw the vast potential Anderson had for a major career as a singer.

After high school Anderson began to tour with Billy King, a young black pianist and choir director. She performed in a Town Hall recital in 1924 and earned a first place finish among 300 vocal contestants in a 1925 concert sponsored by Lewisohn Stadium, in conjunction with the National Music League, both in New York City. These, however, did little to broaden opportunities for concerts much beyond black colleges and churches in the south. By the end of the 1920s, tired of the routine of touring and dissatisfied with the slow pace of her artistic progress, especially in the German art song, a repertory she had longed to master since the days she had heard Roland Hayes perform, she decided she could advance her career artistically only by studying abroad. Anderson studied in London in 1928, making her debut at the Wigmore Hall, 15 June 1928, and, on a Rosenwald Fellowship, spent parts of 1930 and 1931 studying in Berlin with Kurt Johnen.

Anderson's fame in Europe began in the 1933–1934 season with a historic tour throughout the cities and provinces of Scandinavia, accompanied by the Finnish pianist Kosti Vehanen, during which she gave 116 concerts in seven months. In May 1934 she made her Paris debut. During the next eighteen months Anderson sang to great acclaim in every musical center from Spain to the Soviet Union, revealing herself to be a mature and accomplished interpreter of a wide range of the recitalist's repertoire. Only in Salzburg, Austria, in August 1935, did she meet resistance, when the authorities of the Salzburg Festival refused on racial grounds to allow her to sing at the festival. Eventually, submitting to public pressure, the authorities allowed Anderson the use of the Mozarteum, with the understanding that the concert would not be officially recognized as part of the Salzburg Festival. It was at a second concert in Salzburg a few days later, attended by many musicians and celebrities, that Arturo Toscanini uttered the famous encomium: "What I have heard today one is privileged to hear only once in a hundred years."

In 1929 Anderson had come briefly under the management of the powerful American concert manager Arthur Judson, but because of the Great Depression and Judson's overly cautious and unimaginative handling of a black artist, the first under his management, Anderson's American career had not progressed the way she had hoped. In 1935 Anderson was offered a contract by the famed American impresario Sol Hurok, under whose management Anderson returned to America for a triumphant concert in Manhattan's Town Hall in December 1935. In little more than a few years, Anderson's great artistic maturity and Hurok's inventive and persistent management made her one of the most popular American concert artists. During the 1938 season Anderson gave sixty concerts in the United States, and during the 1939 season, eighty concerts. In January 1939 Hurok was able to boast to the press that Anderson had earned $238,000 during 1938, an astonishing record for a concert singer in those years.

In 1939 the Daughters of the American Revolution denied Anderson the use of Constitution Hall on racial grounds for an Easter Sunday concert. First Lady Eleanor Roosevelt's highly publicized resignation from the DAR in protest catapulted Anderson into national prominence as a potent symbol in the struggle for racial equality. Through the work and imagination of a cadre of determined black Washington leaders, including Walter White, secretary of the National Association for the Advancement of Colored People (NAACP), and Charles Houston, an NAACP attorney, as well as Howard University officials, who led a well-organized protest movement against the DAR and later the Washington School Board, Anderson gave an outdoor concert to a throng of 75,000 people on Easter Sunday on the steps of the Lincoln Memorial.

Franz Rupp, the eminent German émigré pianist and chamber musician, became Anderson's accompanist in 1941, a partnership that lasted a quarter of a century. The two made yearly tours of the United States and frequent tours of South America and, beginning in 1949, many visits to Europe, where Anderson had not sung for more than a decade. Anderson had made some recordings of Negro spirituals for the Victor Talking Machine Company in 1924, and of operatic arias and *Lieder,* including a celebrated series of songs by Jean Sibelius, for the HMV label, at the end of the 1920s and early 1930s. Her recording career began in earnest with Rupp in 1941, the beginning of a collaboration with RCA that produced many recordings of German *Lieder,* especially Franz Schubert, Robert Schumann, and Johannes Brahms, as well as spirituals. With orchestra Anderson recorded the Brahms "Alto Rhapsody," Gustav Mahler's *Kindertotenlieder,* and Bach and Handel arias.

In 1943 Anderson married Orpheus Fischer, an architect, whom she had known since high school. They settled in Danbury, Connecticut, on a 105-acre farm.

During the 1950s, as a African American woman of extraordinary artistic accomplishment, gracious and soft-spoken publicly, never openly critical of government policy on racial or social issues, Anderson was embraced by the public and in government circles alike as a woman capable of building bridges between peoples of different races and backgrounds. In 1953 Anderson was invited by the Japanese Broadcasting Corporation to give a series of concerts in Japan, making her among the first Western artists to appear in Japan in the postwar period. On 7 January 1955 she made her operatic debut at the Metropolitan Opera in New York City in the role of Ulrica in Giuseppe Verdi's *Un ballo in maschera,* the first black singer to be engaged by the Met in its seventy-one-year history. In 1957 Anderson was invited by the State Department to undertake a tour of Southeast Asia, both as a distinguished artist and goodwill ambassador, in which she gave twenty-six concerts in twelve countries. The following year President Dwight Eisenhower appointed her as a member of the thirteenth United Nations delegation. In view of the success of her Asian tour, she was assigned to the Trusteeship Council as alternate delegate.

Although Anderson retired from the concert stage in 1965, after a farewell American tour that took her to more than fifty cities, she gave lectures and narrated Aaron Copland's "Lincoln Portrait" and, on occasion, other works with narrator, until she was nearly eighty. In 1986 her husband died of heart failure. Anderson was living with her nephew, the Oregon Symphony music director James De Preist, when she died of heart failure at the age of ninety-six after suffering a series of strokes. Anderson was cre-

mated and her ashes interred in her mother's grave in Eden Cemetery in Philadelphia.

Anderson received numerous prizes and awards and nearly thirty honorary degrees during her career. In 1941 she was given the Bok award and used the $10,000 prize money to establish the Marian Anderson Scholarship Fund for young singers. In 1939 she was awarded the Spingarn Medal by the NAACP. President Lyndon B. Johnson presented her with the Medal of Freedom in 1963, and in 1978 she was awarded the Congressional Medal.

Anderson was one of the supremely great concert singers of the twentieth century. Her voice, instantly recognizable in timbre, extended nearly three octaves from low D to high C and was capable of an extraordinary range of shadings and color. She had a remarkable linguistic gift, which enabled her to sing in eight languages with clarity, vividness, and a natural feeling for the phonetic characteristics of each language. Particularly impressive was the range of her stylistic understanding, her ability to negotiate the differing demands of composer and period, idiom and genre, mood and feeling. Many consider her interpretation of Negro spirituals incomparable in their emotional range, in the way she reached inward to express her own beliefs without ever appearing to interpret. Anderson was particularly impressive in songs that are melodically direct and strongly characterized, or songs that have a realistic narrative with individually drawn characters, such as Schubert's "Der Erlkönig" and "Der Tod und das Mädchen." But her repertoire was enormous, taking in not only the whole of nineteenth-century German *Lieder* but seventeenth- and eighteenth-century *arie antiche,* arias of Johann Sebastian Bach and George Frideric Handel, French songs of Claude Debussy, Gabriel Fauré, and others as well as songs of the Russian composers Sergei Rachmaninoff and Pyotr Ilyich Tchaikovsky. Anderson was particularly noted for her interpretation of the songs of Sibelius and of other Scandinavian composers.

★

The Marian Anderson Papers are housed in the Annenberg Rare Book and Manuscript Library of the University of Pennsylvania and consist of diaries, scrapbooks, newspaper clippings, autobiographical material, promotional material, awards, memorabilia, personal and general correspondence, music, books, phonograph recordings, and tapes. The only biography of Marian Anderson, comprehensive and written with the full cooperation of the Anderson family, is Allan Keiler's *Marian Anderson: A Singer's Journey* (2000), which contains a complete repertory and discography. An autobiography, *My Lord, What a Morning: An Autobiography* (1956), ghostwritten by Howard Taubman from taped sessions with Anderson, reveals her gracious and modest personality but is guarded and understated about controversial or personal matters. Kosti Vehanen's *Marian Anderson: A Portrait*

(1941) is a colorful and highly appreciative memoir of their decade-long artistic relationship. There are many published interviews of Anderson, but only in Emily Kimbrough's "My Life in a White World," *Ladies' Home Journal* (Sept. 1960), is Anderson really open about racial and personal experiences. An obituary is in the *New York Times* (9 Apr. 1993).

ALLAN KEILER

ANDREWS, (Carver) Dana (*b.* 1 January 1909 in Collins, Mississippi; *d.* 17 December 1992 in Los Angeles, California), actor and star of some of the most memorable Hollywood films of the 1940s.

Andrews was born Carver Dana, but as an actor he was known by his middle name. He was the third of nine children born to the Reverend Charles Forrest Andrews, a Baptist minister, and Annis Speed, a homemaker. When Andrews was a young child, the family moved from Collins to Louisville, Kentucky, and later to Huntsville, Texas, where he attended Huntsville High School, graduating in 1926.

At Sam Houston State Teachers College in Huntsville, Andrews studied business administration. Andrews quit

Dana Andrews. THE KOBAL COLLECTION

college in 1929 to work as an accounts clerk for Gulf Oil in Austin, Texas. Two years later, he left his job and hitchhiked to Los Angeles to try to break into the movies. He was followed years later by a younger brother, the actor Steve Forrest. While working odd jobs, he studied acting and performed in repertory at the Pasadena Playhouse, making his stage debut in 1935. At the Pasadena Playhouse he met an aspiring actress, Janet Murray, whom he married in 1932; they had one child before she died in 1935. That year, he was spotted by a scout for the independent movie producer Samuel Goldwyn, who signed Andrews to a contract for $150 per week. The contract allowed him to continue his Pasadena studies, and the salary financed his marriage in 1939 to the actress Mary Todd, with whom he had three children. They were divorced in 1968.

For several years, Andrews shared the fate of Goldwyn contract players, who waited for roles and were often loaned out to other studios. He debuted as a supporting actor in *The Westerner* (1940), directed by William Wyler, and was cast in minor roles in several B movies. After Goldwyn split Andrews's contract with Twentieth Century–Fox, the producer Darryl F. Zanuck cast him as Captain Tim in John Ford's *Tobacco Road* (1941). When the war depleted the ranks of male stars at Fox and Goldwyn, Andrews, who was over draft age and had four children, received choice roles. He was the personification of despair as the innocent victim of a lynch mob in William Wellman's powerful film *The Ox-Bow Incident* (1943). He also won the lead in *The Purple Heart* (1944), playing a pilot shot down during the 1942 Doolittle air raid on Tokyo and facing torture and death at the hands of the Japanese.

For a brief time in the mid-1940s, Andrews dominated the high-gloss Hollywood film. He played the intense, cynical police detective in *Laura* (1944), Otto Preminger's stylish murder mystery costarring Gene Tierney, Clifton Webb, and Andrews's offscreen friend Vincent Price. In Lewis Milestone's *A Walk in the Sun* (1945), among the best of American war movies, he portrayed Sergeant Tyne, who was suddenly put in charge of an infantry company that had to storm German machine gunners in an Italian farmhouse. In the decade's most emblematic movie, William Wyler's *The Best Years of Our Lives* (1946), he played the "fallen angel" Captain Fred Derry, the decorated B-17 bombardier who went back to his job as a soda jerk after the war, who asked, "Have you had any trouble getting readjusted?" *The Best Years of Our Lives* was a box-office smash, and Andrews spent early 1947 on Goldwyn publicity tours and giving radio interviews. In *Boomerang* (1947), which the director Elia Kazan shot in the style of a documentary in a Connecticut town, Andrews starred as a district attorney defying public opinion to exonerate an accused murderer.

Andrews's career then waned, as Samuel Goldwyn grew

exasperated by his star's excessive drinking. Andrews appeared in the syrupy movie *My Foolish Heart* (1949) opposite Susan Hayward and with Farley Granger in *Edge of Doom* (1950), a cheap melodrama. *I Want You* (1952) was his last picture under the Goldwyn contract. Andrews then freelanced and formed his own production company, but aside from a supporting role with Elizabeth Taylor in *Elephant Walk* (1954), his stardom was over. "They want top box office names for blockbusters," Andrews remarked. "And I'm not in that category." In 1957 he pleaded guilty to a drunk driving charge and was later sued by a producer for delays on the set caused by his alcoholism. Andrews did summer stock with his wife and took over Henry Fonda's part in *Two for the Seasaw* on Broadway in 1958. He helped lead the Screen Actors Guild, serving as vice president from 1957 to 1963 and as president from 1964 to 1965, using his position to attack a system that forced actresses to do nude scenes.

Turning to real estate in Orange County in the early 1960s, he built apartment houses and hotels and made, he claimed, more money than he ever did with Goldwyn. He had a couple of walk-on roles, unveiling his Southern drawl to play military officers in Otto Preminger's *In Harm's Way* (1965) and *The Battle of the Bulge* (1965). Television audiences saw him as the president of Bancroft College in the daytime soap opera *Bright Promise,* which ran from 1969 until 1972. He talked about his drinking problem on public service spots for the U.S. Department of Transportation, in cooperation with the National Council on Alcoholism, in 1972. Andrews lived in an Alzheimer's disease treatment center for several years before his death from congestive heart failure and pneumonia at Los Alamitos Medical Center in Los Angeles in 1992.

Andrews was never nominated for a major acting award. He was tied to Samuel Goldwyn. As he later acknowledged, "Mr. Goldwyn made a lotta bad pictures. I was in a couple of 'em." But for a while he made decent money and, in fact, remained with Goldwyn for twelve years, a record at the studio. His courageous, slightly broken demeanor carried some of the most riveting Hollywood films of the 1940s, and he vied with Henry Fonda in providing audiences with examples of quiet integrity in an embattled decade. At the end of *The Best Years of Our Lives,* Andrews embraced his costar Teresa Wright, telling her: "You know what it'll be, don't you, Peggy? It may take us years to get anywhere. We'll have no money, no decent place to live. We'll have to work, get kicked around." The words were those of screenwriter Robert Sherwood, but Dana Andrews gave them an unforgettable conviction.

★

Andrews was never the subject of a Hollywood biography. Carol Easton included a brief interview with Andrews in her

Search for Sam Goldwyn: A Biography (1976), and there is anecdotal material in A. Scott Berg, *Goldwyn: A Biography* (1989), and Elia Kazan, *A Life* (1988). Cynthia Brown wrote a fine biographical appreciation in Amy L. Unterburger, ed., *Actors and Actresses,* vol. 3 of *International Dictionary of Films and Filmmakers,* (3d ed., 1997). Obituaries are in the *Los Angeles Times* (18 Dec. 1992) and the *New York Times* (19 Dec. 1992).

JOEL SCHWARTZ

APPLING, Lucius Benjamin, Jr. ("Luke") (*b.* 2 April 1907 in High Point, North Carolina; *d.* 3 January 1991 in Cumming, Georgia), Hall of Fame shortstop with the Chicago White Sox from 1930 through 1950.

Appling was one of six children born to Lucius Benjamin Appling, a woodcarver, and Dola Sappenfield, a homemaker. He began his athletic career at Fulton High School in Atlanta, from which he graduated in 1928, before playing baseball and football at Atlanta's Oglethorpe College for two years. He played minor-league baseball for part of the 1930 season for the Atlanta Crackers. Atlanta sold Appling to the Chicago Cubs, which traded him to the White Sox before he arrived in Chicago. At the end of the 1930 season he made a few appearances with the White Sox, then became the club's regular shortstop in 1931. He played there

Luke Appling. TRANSCENDENTALGRAPHICS

until 1950, setting a major-league record for durability at shortstop at that time.

Appling was an outstanding hitter. His trademark was a slashing line-drive single to center or right-center field. He set the all-time White Sox records for hits, doubles, runs scored, and runs batted in. His most outstanding season was 1936, when he hit .388 and drove in 128 runs. He won batting championships in 1936 and again in 1943 when he hit .328. In 1940 he hit .348 but lost the batting championship to Joe DiMaggio's .352. In all but four of his years as a player he hit over .300. He retired with a .310 career batting average. Although not a smooth fielder in his first years in Chicago, he became an accomplished shortstop under the tutelage of Jimmy Dykes, the White Sox manager and third baseman in the mid-1930s. Only 587 of Appling's 2,749 hits went for extra bases. He hit only forty-five home runs throughout his entire major-league career, half of which was played in spacious Comiskey Park.

Appling, who rarely struck out, fouled off an average of fifteen pitches per game. This skill caused great frustration for both opponents and owners: White Sox owners once figured that Appling cost them about $2,300 a year in balls fouled into the stands. On one occasion the Senators owner Clark Griffith refused Appling's request for free seats in Washington, D.C., so Appling stood at home plate and fouled sixteen consecutive pitches into the stands. On a hot afternoon at Comiskey Park, with Charles ("Red") Ruffing of the Yankees pitching, Appling fouled off fourteen pitches in a row before Ruffing finally walked him. The next White Sox batter promptly hit a home run.

Appling was the outstanding player on mediocre teams in the 1930s and 1940s, and he was selected as the White Sox player of the century in a 1949 poll of 5,000 White Sox fans and in a 1969 poll of the Chicago Chapter of Baseball Writers of America. He was selected as the outstanding White Sox shortstop in a poll taken by the Chicago *Tribune* in 2000. He was a member of the American League All-Star team four times and elected to the Baseball Hall of Fame in 1964.

Appling, at five feet, ten inches, and 185 pounds, was initially described as a gangly youth, but filled out into a solidly built player. His nickname, "Old Aches and Pains," came from the maladies and injuries, real or imagined, he complained of on a regular basis. He was baseball's favorite hypochondriac. He said that he always played the best when he felt the worst. But he had only two major injuries in his twenty-year career. He broke a finger in 1930 shortly after arriving in Chicago, causing him to miss the end of his initial season; and in 1938 he had a broken ankle, which limited him to eighty-one games. Yet Appling complained about fallen arches, indigestion, dizzy spells, torn leg tendons, insomnia, gout, astigmatism, stiff neck, mysterious pains in his kneecap, and, at least once, vertigo. In his worst season, 1942, when he hit only .262, he blamed his perfor-

mance on the fact that he felt good all year. Teammates, the press, and ownership took Luke's complaints in stride as long as he kept hitting and showing his tremendous zeal for the game. He missed two seasons, 1944 and 1945, when he was drafted into the army in 1943. He reported to Fort Sheridan, north of Chicago, and was honorably discharged in 1945.

Following his retirement in 1951, Appling began a forty-year career as manager and coach. In the 1950s he managed the Memphis Chicks of the Southern Association and subsequently the Indianapolis club of the American Association. He managed for a brief period of time at the major-league level with Kansas City in 1967. He coached in Baltimore, Detroit, Oakland, Cleveland, Chicago (White Sox), and Kansas City. He ended his career in baseball with a seventeen-year relationship with the Atlanta Braves beginning in 1974 as coach, minor-league instructor, and minor-league batting coach. He retired from the Braves just two days prior to his death and was scheduled to appear at a baseball-card show two days later.

Appling died at age eighty-three while undergoing surgery on an abdominal aneurysm at Lakeside Community Hospital in Cumming, Georgia. He and his wife, Fay Dodd, to whom he remained married until his death, had two daughters and one son. He is buried in Sawnee View Gardens Mausoleum in Cumming.

Appling was the most dynamic player on a mediocre team at midcentury. He was a quality, all-around player whose magnetic, outgoing personality made him the most famous player on the White Sox as well as a perennial member of White Sox all-century teams. His entire life was committed to playing, coaching, and managing the game that he loved.

★

There are no full-length biographies of Appling. The best information is from the clippings files of the *Sporting News;* Warren Brown, *The Chicago White Sox* (1952), and Richard C. Lindberg, *The White Sox Encyclopedia (1997)*. Obituaries are in the *New York Times* (4 Jan. 1991) and *Annual Obituary* (1991).

HARRY JEBSEN, JR.

ARNALL, Ellis Gibbs (*b.* 20 March 1907 in Newnan, Georgia; *d.* 13 December 1992 in Atlanta, Georgia), progressive governor of Georgia from 1943 to 1947.

Arnall was born into a comfortable middle-class northern Georgia family. His father, Joe Gibbs Arnall, owned a small chain of supermarkets, with one store in each of three northern Georgia towns. The future governor's mother, Bessie Lena Ellis, was the daughter of an Alabama legislator and had been a teacher at a women's college.

Arnall was president of his high school student body and quarterback of the football team. In 1924 he left

Ellis Arnall holds a "snooping" device during testimony against the Food and Drug Administration, 1965.
© BETTMANN/CORBIS

Newnan High School without earning his diploma and entered Mercer University in Macon, Georgia, transferring after three months to the University of the South in Sewanee, Tennessee. Following his graduation from college with an A.B. degree in 1928, he entered law school at the University of Georgia in Athens, Georgia, where he earned his LL.B. and graduated first in his class in 1931.

After practicing law in his hometown of Newnan for a year, Arnall ran for and won a seat in the Georgia House of Representatives. Within two years he was elected speaker of the house and soon afterward became floor leader for Governor Eugene Talmadge.

On 6 April 1935 Arnall married Mildred DeLaney Slemons; they had two children. In 1939 he was made attorney general of Georgia by Talmadge's successor, E. D. Rivers, an appointment that was endorsed by popular election in 1940. By 1941 Talmadge was once again the governor of the state. Maintaining that some members of the faculty in the state's public colleges supported racial integration, Talmadge bullied the Board of Regents into terminating the appointments of ten professors. As a result, the Southern Association of Colleges and Secondary Schools revoked the accreditation of most of Georgia's state colleges. This gave Arnall the issue on which he ran for governor against Talmadge in 1942. He defeated Talmadge in the Democratic primary and went on to win the governorship in the general election.

A popular and energetic reformer, Governor Arnall presided over the modernization of the state's antiquated constitution. Perhaps the most dramatic of the many other reforms that he instituted was the abolition of Georgia's notorious chain gang system in which convicts were regularly chained, shackled, and whipped. So infamous was the system that, in 1932, it had been the subject of the celebrated motion picture *I Am a Fugitive from a Chain Gang,* based on a book written by Robert E. Burns, a convict who had escaped from one of Georgia's chain gangs. Additionally, Arnall established a Board of Pardons and Paroles and successfully demanded that juveniles and adults, and first and subsequent offenders, no longer be housed together, and that prisoners receive vocational training. He was also responsible for Georgia being the first state to give eighteen-year-olds the right to vote (which he accomplished by packing the legislature gallery with crippled war veterans under the age of twenty-one). He did away with the poll tax, one of the ways by which the state's impoverished black citizens were effectively disenfranchised. Under Arnall's administration, a civil service system replaced cronyism in the hiring of state employees, a teachers' retirement system was created, and a cap was imposed on the amount of money that could be spent in statewide political campaigns. Many Georgians called him "Benedict Arnall" because of his devotion to reforming and his failure to "uphold the Southern way of life."

Arnall's by now national reputation was enhanced by virtue of one of the most bizarre episodes in the history of state politics in the United States. In 1946 Talmadge was once again elected governor, defeating Lieutenant Governor M. E. Thompson and succeeding Arnall, who was barred from seeking a second consecutive term by a provision then in the state's constitution. However, Talmadge died before the scheduled mid-January inauguration date. Simultaneous claims of the right to succeed to the governorship for the remainder of Arnall's term were then made by Thompson, who invoked a recently enacted constitutional provision; by Herman Talmadge, Eugene's son, whose claim rested on his appointment by the legislature under a provision of the constitution that Thompson claimed had been superseded; and by Arnall himself, whose elected term had not yet expired. The Georgia courts decided in Arnall's favor and he retained his governorship throughout the sixty-seven-day interregnum leading up to the 18 January 1947 inauguration of the new governor, M. E. Thompson.

For the next five years Arnall held a number of important positions both in private industry and in the federal government. His most significant achievement during this period was a series of legal decisions that resulted from a lawsuit he had brought when he was governor and had personally tried before the United States Supreme Court. Known collectively as the "railroad rate cases," this litigation involved Arnall's charge that the railroad industry had illegally set freight rates at a higher level in the South and the West than in the North and the East. In a series of precedent-setting decisions that helped expand the powers of the federal government, the Supreme Court held that the government had the constitutional authority to equalize freight rates in interstate commerce.

In 1952 Arnall moved to Atlanta, where his legal practice and the pursuit of various business interests absorbed his attention for the next decade and a half. In 1966 he re-emerged on the Georgia political stage in order to oppose Lester Maddox—an arch segregationist whose views were anathema to Arnall—in the Democratic primary for governor. His other opponent in that primary race was a little-known state senator by the name of Jimmy Carter. Arnall led in the primary, Maddox finished second, and Carter was third. Because none of the candidates had attained a majority, a runoff was required. Arnall, confident of victory, barely campaigned during the runoff, and in a stunning upset, Maddox won handily. The general election ended in an impasse. Howard ("Bo") Callaway, the Republican candidate, received 3,000 more votes than Maddox, but because Arnall received a substantial number of write-in votes, once again no candidate received a majority. It then fell to the legislature to choose between Callaway and Maddox. The overwhelmingly Democratic legislature chose Maddox.

The 1966 election represented Arnall's last foray into electoral politics. He returned to his legal practice and his business interests. His wife Mildred died in 1980. On 15 July 1981 he married Ruby Hamilton McCord. In 1990

Arnall suffered a massive stroke and was largely confined to a nursing facility in Atlanta, where he died of pneumonia at the age of eighty-five. He is buried in Oak Hill Cemetery in his hometown of Newnan.

★

Arnall's personal papers are in the possession of his family. Several oral interviews with Arnall are archived in the William Russell Pullen Library of Georgia State University, in Atlanta. His book *The Shore Dimly Seen* (1946) presents his views on many social and political issues. For a political biography, see Harold P. Henderson, *The Politics of Change in Georgia: A Political Biography of Ellis Arnall* (1991). Arnall in the context of the "new South" is discussed in Harold P. Henderson, *Georgia Governors in an Age of Change: From Ellis Arnall to George Busbee* (1998), edited by Gary L. Roberts. An obituary is in the *Atlanta Journal and Constitution* (14 Dec. 1992).

JACK HANDLER

ARNESON, Robert Carston (*b.* 4 September 1930 in Benicia, California; *d.* 2 November 1992 in Benicia, California), ceramic sculptor and leader of the 1960s San Francisco Bay Area "funk art" movement.

Arneson was born to Arthur and Helena Arneson in Benicia, a small town approximately twenty-five miles northeast of San Francisco. Encouraged by his father, who was a draftsman, Arneson began drawing at an early age. As a teenager, he sketched comics that often featured superheroes or football players in heroic roles. At age seventeen Arneson's cartoons, which depicted highlights from local sports events, were published in the local weekly newspaper, the *Benicia Herald*.

Robert Arneson, 1974. ARCHIVE PHOTOS

After graduating from Benicia High School, Arneson attended the College of Marin in Kentfield, California. He studied art and, ironically, received a grade of "D" in his ceramics class. By the spring of 1951 Arneson had transferred to California College of Arts and Crafts in nearby Oakland, where he received a partial scholarship to study commercial art. Although he took a brief hiatus from his art studies for a semester, Arneson returned and graduated in 1953 with a bachelor's degree in art education.

Arneson soon began teaching high school art just outside of San Francisco. In 1955 he married Jeanette Jensen; they had four sons. Because ceramics was required for the high school class curriculum, Arneson enrolled in a local pottery class and started reading ceramics magazines. By the spring of 1956, his skills in clay had improved and Arneson was confident enough to take ceramics classes at San Jose State College and at California College of Arts and Crafts.

As his abilities developed, Arneson began to think of ceramic art as "sculpture" rather than just pottery. Excited by the nonutilitarian potential for the craft, in 1957 Arneson enrolled in the Master of Fine Arts program at Mills College in Oakland. Arneson received his M.F.A. degree one year later and in 1959 began teaching high school students again while also devoting time to his art. Influenced by the ceramic sculptor Peter Voulkos, who also rejected the traditional notion of making craft objects from clay, Arneson produced works with no functional design. He was invited in 1960 to show his work at the Oakland Museum.

By the early 1960s many American artists were using elements from popular culture as inspiration for their art. Artists like Jasper Johns, Roy Lichtenstein, and Andy Warhol incorporated commercial images and techniques to reflect the rise of mass media's dominance in American culture. In 1961 Arneson sculpted the work *No Deposit, No Return*, a clay bottle topped with an actual bottle cap, relating his work to this contemporary movement.

In 1962 Arneson had a one-man show at the M. H. DeYoung Museum in San Francisco and began teaching at the University of California, Davis, as assistant professor of art and design. At the university Arneson taught with other important contemporary artists such as William T. Wiley and Wayne Thiebaud. For his next significant exhibition in 1963, "California Sculpture," at the Kaiser Center in Oakland, he contributed a ceramic sculpture in the form of a toilet, entitled *Funk John*. The sculpture was rejected by the museum's administration. This piece was emblematic of the fledgling San Francisco Bay Area "funk art" movement, which rebelled against traditional good taste with wit and satire. By the mid-1960s "funk" functioned as a reaction to the predominant abstract expressionist and pop art movements by incorporating lively colors and imagery with humor and narrative content. Arneson also introduced technical innovations, such as new glazing methods, into the vocabulary of his work.

Upon receiving a grant from the Institute of Creative Arts at the University of California, Arneson spent 1967 in New York working on paintings. One year later his sculpture *Typewriter* was included in the Museum of Modern Art's show "Dada, Surrealism, and Their Heritage." In 1968 he received a teaching promotion at the University of California, Davis, and his work was included in the prestigious Whitney Biennial exhibition in New York in 1970. While Arneson's professional career was thriving, his personal life was experiencing major changes. In 1969 a fire nearly burned down his house, and in 1970 Arneson and his wife divorced, with Arneson receiving custody of their four sons. Hence, Arneson decided to take a sabbatical leave from teaching in 1970. He then switched his focus to ceramic portraits and employed different mold-making techniques. In 1971 he received a grant from the National Endowment for the Arts and in 1973 he wed Sandra Shannonhouse, a sculptor; they had one daughter. In 1974 Arneson received artistic recognition when his career was highlighted in a retrospective exhibition at the Chicago Museum of Contemporary Art.

After being diagnosed with cancer in 1975, Arneson moved back to his hometown of Benicia, where he continued to develop self-portrait sculptures and portrait busts of artists. He received another grant from the National Endowment for the Arts in 1978, which allowed him to travel to France, Belgium, Holland, and Switzerland.

In 1981 Arneson was selected to create a portrait bust of the assassinated San Francisco mayor George Moscone. The resulting commission featured a colorful ceramic bust on top of a pedestal inscribed with text and images that referred to the deceased politician's life. Because some of this mentioned specifics of the mayor's murder (including a Twinkie that referred to the murderer's "Twinkie defense," mock bullet holes, and drips of red paint that implied blood), the sculpture was rejected and Arneson was criticized for his artistic choices. After this incident Arneson began to explore the social and political potential of his art.

In the 1980s Arneson became concerned with the threat of nuclear holocaust and produced sculptures that addressed the horrors of such a war. These pieces led to other works that dealt with Americans' fears regarding military power. At the same time, he also fabricated drawings that appropriated colorful stylistic elements from Vincent van Gogh and Jackson Pollock. Arneson received an honorary doctorate of fine arts from the Rhode Island School of Design in 1985, and another from the San Francisco Art Institute in 1987. In 1986 Arneson's career was again recognized in a retrospective exhibition compiled by the Des Moines Art Museum in Iowa. This show traveled to Washington, D.C., and Portland, Oregon.

Throughout the 1980s Arneson intermittently battled cancer, a struggle that was examined in several of his last series. Working in bronze, the artist fashioned images of spiritual waste and bodily decay. Although these works caustically depict the trials of chemotherapy, the sculptures maintain Arneson's signature element of humor and retain a witty, rebellious quality. Arneson succumbed to liver cancer at his home in Benicia on 2 November 1992.

From early in his career, Arneson overturned traditional methods of working in clay. His ceramic sculptures proved to the art establishment that clay was a medium worthy of fine art discussion. A major figure in the San Francisco–based funk art movement, Arneson remained somewhat of an iconoclast in later years, never following current art world trends. Through his many creative investigations, he always asserted the importance of subject matter in art. His sculptures proved to be some of the most significant contributions to the field of ceramics in the twentieth century.

★

Many catalogs of Arneson's work have been published in conjunction with museum exhibitions of his art. Neal Benezra, *Robert Arneson: A Retrospective* (1986), features an in-depth review of Arneson's life and career. *Robert Arneson* (1986), which accompanied an exhibit at the Hirshhorn Museum and Sculpture Garden in Washington, D.C., also features examples of his work. Tom E. Hinson, *Robert Arneson: Portrait Sculptures* (1987), and Steven A. Nash, *Arneson and Politics: A Commemorative Exhibition* (1993), focus on important aspects of his work. Nancy Moore, *California Art: 450 Years of Painting and Other Media* (1998), devotes a section to the San Francisco funk art movement and Arneson's role in the history of California art. Many articles highlight Arneson's career and discuss his artistic choices, including Donald Kuspit, "Arneson's Outrage," *Art in America* (May 1985): 134–139. An account of Arneson's work with emphasis on his last series of sculptures is Robert C. Hobbs, "Robert Arneson: Critical Clay," *Sculpture Magazine* (Nov.–Dec. 1993): 20. Obituaries are in the *Los Angeles Times* (4 Nov. 1992) and London *Guardian* (10 Nov. 1992).

RENEE COPPOLA

ARRAU, Claudio (*b.* 6 February 1903 in Chillán, Chile; *d.* 9 June 1991 in Mürzzuschlag, Austria), concert pianist who enjoyed an eight-decade career and who is widely regarded as one of the great musicians of the twentieth century.

One of three children, Arrau was the son of Carlos Arrau, an eye doctor, and Lucretia Leon. Arrau was one year old when his father died, and his mother began teaching piano in order to support the family. She kept her young son with her during lessons, and he quickly showed prodigious talents on the keyboard. Arrau made his public concert debut at age five in his hometown and a year later was performing

Claudio Arrau. © BETTMANN/CORBIS

in Chile's capital, Santiago. He so impressed Chilean authorities that, when he was seven, his entire family was sent to Berlin so he could study with the greatest piano teachers. He did not receive formal academic schooling. In 1913 he began studying with Martin Krause, who became a father figure to the young pianist. A pupil of Franz Liszt and a well-known music critic, Krause was greatly impressed by Arrau, proclaiming him his favorite student and declaring he would be his "masterwork."

In 1918 Krause died in the great flu epidemic, and Arrau was once again left fatherless. However, he continued working at the piano, winning the prestigious Liszt in 1919 and 1920. At age seventeen Arrau made his debut at London's Royal Albert Hall as well as in Berlin with the Berlin Philharmonic, both great successes. On 20 October 1923, when he was twenty years old, he made his U.S. debut at Carnegie Hall as part of his first tour of America. The tour, however, was a failure; only five of the thirty planned dates actually materialized, and his Carnegie Hall debut was to a nearly empty house. Arrau returned to Berlin somewhat crestfallen and for a time stopped playing, suffering from depression. After several years of therapy, he returned to performing in the late 1920s. His career was greatly boosted in 1927 when he won the prestigious International Geneva Prize; among the judges was the renowned pianist Artur Rubinstein.

No longer a child prodigy, Arrau found it hard to compete with the many other virtuosos touring Europe in the 1920s and 1930s. In order to draw attention to himself, in 1935 he played the complete keyboard works of Johann Sebastian Bach in a series of twelve concerts in Berlin. The resulting publicity led him to tackle Mozart's keyboard works the following year, and in 1938 he performed the first of many series in which he played all thirty-two of Beethoven's piano sonatas. From 1924 to 1940 he was also a teacher at Berlin's Stern Conservatory of Music. On 8 July 1937 he wed Ruth Schneider, with whom he had three children.

Leaving Berlin on the eve of World War II, Arrau returned to Chile, opening a piano school in its capital. However, he soon left the country because of his disillusionment with the Chilean government. He made his second Carnegie Hall appearance in February 1941, and this time his fame was such that he filled the hall. The concert was favorably reviewed and covered in the popular media. In 1942 Arrau played more than 100 concerts throughout the country. He decided to settle in the United States, although he did not become a naturalized citizen until 1979.

From the 1950s Arrau became an international superstar of the piano, traveling extensively and performing with major orchestras around the world. He was particularly beloved in his native Chile, where he was always warmly received. However, he refused to perform there once the Socialists took control of the government. In 1978, as a protest against the repressive Chilean regime then in power, he renounced his Chilean citizenship. As part of his eightieth birthday celebration, in 1984 he made a sentimental and hugely successful return to his homeland after more than a decade away. His concerts in Santiago, televised and covered widely in the press, became an event of intense national pride.

In his later years Arrau was much celebrated. Each notable birthday, beginning when he was in his seventies, was an occasion for awards, special recitals, new recordings, and gala events. He continued to perform into his eighties, maintaining a rigorous concert schedule. He died of a massive stroke while preparing for a recital that was to be held at the recently established Brahms museum in Austria. He is buried in Municipal Cemetery in Chillán.

Arrau was an influential interpreter of the great classical and Romantic repertoire. His many recordings include landmark renditions of Beethoven's and Brahms's piano concertos, Liszt's twelve Transcendental Etudes, and Chopin's complete works for piano and orchestra, many of which have continued to be available on CD. He was also a scholar of Beethoven's works, producing an urtext edition of the piano sonatas that was published in 1978. The music critic Nicolas Slonimsky noted that his playing "combined a Classical purity and precision of style with a rhapsodic éclat."

★

Ingo Harden, *Claudio Arrau: Ein Interpretenportrait* (1983), is a German-language interpretative biography. Two major Spanish-language biographies of Arrau, published in Chile, are Inés María Cardone, *Claudio Arrau: Lo que nunca se dijo de su viaje a Chile* (1984), and Sergio Dorantes Guzmán, *Arrau: El gran artista latinoamericano* (1991). Joseph Horowitz, *Conversations with Arrau* (1982), is a book-length interview. The revised version is *Arrau on Music and Performance* (1999). An extended interview with Arrau is in David Dubal, *Reflections from the Keyboard: The World of the Concert Pianist* (1984; 2d ed. 1997). An extended critical work by Herbert Kupferberg appeared in *Musical America* (Mar. 1988). Obituaries are in the *New York Times* (10 June 1991) and London *Times* (11 June 1991).

RICHARD CARLIN

ARTHUR, Jean (*b.* 17 October 1900 in Plattsburgh, New York; *d.* 19 June 1991 in Carmel, California), movie star best known for her roles in romantic comedies, notably *Mr. Deeds Goes to Town* (1936), *Easy Living* (1937), and *The More the Merrier* (1943).

Arthur was born Gladys Georgianna Greene, the fourth and last child of Hubert Greene and Hannah Nelson, five to eight years earlier than she would later admit to after becoming a star. Her mother was a homemaker until Hubert left her when Arthur was about nine years old; she then ran a boarding house in Portland, Maine, where they had moved in 1910. Arthur's father, a photographer, returned to and left the family repeatedly. His professional connections may have helped Arthur get modeling jobs after the family moved to New York City in 1915.

Arthur dropped out of high school during her junior year. Noticed by Twentieth Century–Fox talent scouts, she signed a contract with that studio in 1923; in Hollywood, she took a name redolent of heroism—a blend of Jeanne d'Arc and King Arthur. Among her early appearances was a brief turn as a secretary in Buster Keaton's *Seven Chances* (1925). During most of the silent era she specialized in Westerns.

Paramount signed her to a contract and cast her with William Powell and Louise Brooks in an early talkie, *The Canary Murder Case* (1929). But the studio dropped her in 1931, a setback that Arthur dealt with in boldly unorthodox style. She returned to New York and went on the Broadway stage at a time when the Great Depression was cutting sharply into box-office receipts. The plays she appeared in are deservedly forgotten, but she got good notices, learned her craft, and came to the attention of Harry Cohn, the boss of Columbia Pictures, who signed her to a long-term contract.

Jean Arthur, 1959. © BETTMANN/CORBIS

Back in Hollywood, Arthur took an offbeat role in John Ford's *The Whole Town's Talking* (1935); it made her a star. As Wilhelmina ("Bill") Clark, she swaggered and lounged about the office in which she worked—a liberating sight for women at the time. For the rest of the 1930s she played much the same type: the working girl who of necessity developed a tough skin, beneath which beat a tender heart that her male counterpart could win by figuring out a sufficiently deft approach. Two things kept this strong female persona from alienating audiences. Arthur was wholesomely pretty but not inaccessibly beautiful; unlike, say, her resplendent Columbia Pictures colleague Rita Hayworth, she seemed a plausible catch for an average-looking man. And then there was Arthur's voice: a smoothly cracked instrument that captivated the ear, a trademark as distinctive as Mae West's bosom or Betty Grable's legs.

Arthur gave what was arguably her finest performance during this period as Mary Smith, who toiled at a magazine called *The Boy's Constant Companion,* in *Easy Living* (1937), a romantic comedy written by Preston Sturges and directed by Mitchell Leisen. In its memorably screwball opening, Arthur's character, while riding on a double-decker bus, is engulfed by a sable coat thrown from a penthouse by a millionaire in a snit over his wife's extravagance.

Arthur had caught the eye of the director Frank Capra, who cast her in three of his biggest hits—opposite Gary Cooper in *Mr. Deeds Goes to Town* (1936), and with James Stewart in *You Can't Take It With You* (1938) and *Mr. Smith Goes to Washington* (1939). By then her longstanding shyness and anxiety had evolved into an almost paralyzing fear of acting. "Never have I seen a performer plagued with such a chronic case of stage 'jitters'," Capra wrote in his autobiography. "I'm sure she vomited before and after every scene." But he learned to be firm with her, and "in front of a camera . . . that whining mop would magically blossom into a warm, lovely, poised, and confident actress." Howard Hawks had trouble directing Arthur in the exhilarating adventure movie *Only Angels Have Wings* (1939). Afterward he told her, "Jean, I think you're the only person I've ever worked with that I don't think I helped a bit." Even so, Hawks admitted that she was "good" in the role.

Arthur came to loathe her boss, Harry Cohn, who kept sending her scripts she felt obliged to turn down. The back-and-forth became almost a game, according to the writer-director Garson Kanin: "It seemed clear from the quality of the submissions that Cohn was simply going through the motions, that he would be horrified if by any chance Jean were to accept one of these scripts." Kanin broke one stalemate by cowriting a screenplay about comically unorthodox rooming arrangements in wartime Washington, D.C., selling it to Arthur, tempting Cohn with the bait of a free script, then reading part of it aloud to him. The result was *The More the Merrier* (1943), which produced Arthur's only Academy Award nomination (she lost to Jennifer Jones in *The Song of Bernadette*).

Whether because of or in spite of her grousing, few actresses got better roles than Arthur did in her heyday. But she saw it differently. When her contract with Columbia lapsed in 1944, she ran through the lot shouting, "I'm free! I'm free!" By then she had been in eighty-seven movies; there were to be only two more.

The rest of Arthur's career was largely a shambles of false starts, withdrawals, and psychosomatic illnesses that led to the cancellation of plays mounted specially for her (such as "Born Yesterday" in Philadelphia and a national tour and revival of "St. Joan"). She had only an occasional success, such as her 1950 "Peter Pan" on Broadway and her last screen appearance, as an all-American mother in George Stevens's Western classic *Shane* (1953). She attended Stephens College in Columbia, Missouri, to get the education she had missed out on (although she never received a degree), underwent psychoanalysis, taught acting at Vassar College and other colleges. Her first marriage, a one-day union in 1928 with photographer Julian Anker, was annulled; her second, in 1932, to Frank J. Ross, Jr., who produced some of her films, ended in divorce seventeen years later, in 1949. Arthur had no children. Late in life, she acknowledged an affinity with one of the characters she had played: Peter Pan, the child who never grew up. Both Hawks and Billy Wilder, who directed her in *A Foreign Affair* (1948), reported that she eventually apologized for having resisted their coaching.

In 1965 Arthur guest-starred in an episode of the television series *Gunsmoke* and enjoyed herself so much that she agreed to do a series of her own the following year. The *Jean Arthur Show* featured her in a blonde wig (to hide her now-white hair) as defense attorney Patricia Marshall. But the scripts proved to be fatuous, and the show died after thirteen episodes. She turned down other offers, holding out for parts that would be more "fun." They failed to materialize.

Arthur's consolations in later years included Driftwood, her house at Carmel, where, she said, "I have a very good life" with close friends "and the sea on three sides of me." She died of a heart ailment at the age of ninety, in the Carmel Convalescent Hospital. Her ashes were scattered at sea.

None of Jean Arthur's insecurity or prickliness showed up on film—in itself a tribute to her acting skills. She embodied a sociological phenomenon—the early-twentieth-century influx of single young women to big cities in search of work—and demonstrated that a tough woman need not be intimidating to men. She beguiled both sexes with a voice that remains one of the joys of cinema.

★

A complete biography is John Oller, *Jean Arthur: The Actress Nobody Knew* (1997). There is a chapter on Arthur in each of two books about the genre she virtually made her own: James Harvey, *Romantic Comedy in Hollywood: From Lubitsch to Sturges* (1987); and Elizabeth Kendall, *The Runaway Bride: Hollywood Romantic Comedy of the 1930s* (1990). Frank Capra's recollections of Arthur can be found in his *The Name Above the Title* (1971); Garson Kanin's in his *Hollywood* (1974); Howard Hawks's in Joseph McBride, *Hawks on Hawks* (1982); and Billy Wilder's in Cameron Crowe, *Conversations with Wilder* (1999). See also Dennis Drabelle, "Jean Arthur," *Film Comment* (Mar./Apr. 1996). An obituary is in the *New York Times* (20 June 1991).

DENNIS DRABELLE

ASHE, Arthur Robert (*b.* 10 July 1943 in Richmond, Virginia; *d.* 6 February 1993 in New York City), tennis player who was the first black male to win major championships; he used his athletic celebrity to serve his international political beliefs.

Ashe could trace his American ancestry back to 1735, when his slave forebear was brought to Yorktown, Virginia—nearly a half-century before, as Ashe would wryly point out, the colonies would gain their freedom from England

Arthur Ashe, c. 1989. © NEAL PRESTON/CORBIS

in that same place. The family members were enslaved in the North Carolina and Virginia Piedmont, with Ashe's grandfather moving to Richmond sometime early in the twentieth century.

His father, Arthur Ashe, Sr., was a sturdy, inscrutable disciplinarian who kept a tight rein on his two sons—and on life in general. Ashe remembered little of his mother, the former Mattie Cunningham, a homemaker who died when he was six years old. His father remarried five years later to Lorraine Kimbrough, and Ashe grew up in a home full of love and security, even amid a city of racial segregation.

The Ashe home was located in Brook Field, a playground for the black youth of Richmond. Arthur Sr., a man of many talents, served as a watchman and a maintenance man for Brook Field. The facilities included a tennis court, so young Ashe took up the game and soon began to develop a reputation within the small African-American tennis community.

The summer when he turned ten years old, Ashe was sent to Lynchburg, in western Virginia, where a black physician, R. Walter Johnson, had built a clay court next to his house. It was a rare opportunity for a black player to learn the game, facing good competition. Ashe, skinny but eminently coachable, thrived. Although Ashe was a person of charm and humor, under Johnson's tutelage he developed a cool athletic disposition, wearing a placid mask on court. Johnson told Ashe that when the chance came to play white boys, he must show neither displeasure in defeat nor delight in victory.

Although Ashe's promise was obvious, his future was circumscribed by segregation, and so for his senior year he moved to St. Louis, where he boarded with a white tennis family and attended Sumner High School. Ashe then moved on to the University of California at Los Angeles (UCLA) on a tennis scholarship in 1961, prospering there as an athlete as well as a student, and as a member of the ROTC also. Even more, he patiently endured the discomfort of being a curiosity. Althea Gibson, an African-American woman, had won Grand Slam tennis titles in the late 1950s, but Ashe was the first black male player of consequence anywhere in the world. As he moved up into the rankings, entering the U.S. top ten at number six in 1963, an apposition was invariably attached to every first mention of his name: "Arthur Ashe, the first Negro tennis player to . . ."

Ashe graduated from UCLA in 1966 as the intercollegiate champion, ranked second in the United States, and shortly thereafter entered the army as a second lieutenant, reaching the rank of first lieutenant before his discharge in 1968. He had delicately walked a tightrope between the black world that idolized its tennis pioneer and the white country club society where most tournaments were still played by amateur men and women. But now, in 1968, the roiling, rebellious times began to press onto him. Black leaders urged Ashe to support other prominent African-American athletes in a boycott of the Mexico City Olympics. When Ashe refused, maintaining his independence, he began, for the first time, to hear whispers that he was an Uncle Tom, afraid to unsettle the white tennis establishment.

Incredibly, in the midst of anguish and controversy, Ashe's game suddenly blossomed. As the lead singles player on the U.S. Davis Cup team, he won eleven straight matches. In August 1968 Ashe took the U.S. Amateur championship in Boston. Later in the year came the U.S. Open, which had at last joined all the other major sports in allowing professionals as well as amateurs to compete in the major championships. Ashe himself remained an amateur, seeded fifth, but his hot streak continued, and in the finals, where he faced Tom Okker of the Netherlands, he won 14–12, 5–7, 6–3, 3–6, 6–3, his first Grand Slam. The victory made front-page news, and at a time when athletes were growing impertinent, Ashe—demonstrably bright,

polite, and engaging—became a popular hero for blacks and whites alike.

Ashe, who lived in New York City for most of his adult life, closed out 1968 by leading the U.S. team to its first Davis Cup victory in five years, and then headed successful Cup defenses over Romania and West Germany in the next two years. In 1970 he also won his second Grand Slam title, taking the Australian Open. He had by now turned professional and was instrumental in organizing the players' union, the Association of Tennis Professionals (ATP). He was also growing more critical in his public comments about South Africa's system of apartheid, or racial separation, and on domestic racial issues as well. For the rest of his playing career, in fact, Ashe would be as well known for his opinions as for his strokes.

In 1973 he led the ATP in its boycott of Wimbledon, and that same year, he personally negotiated an invitation to enter South Africa, where he broke the athletic color line, playing in that nation's Open. Ashe lost to Jimmy Connors in the singles, but he won the doubles. Notwithstanding how well he played, his appearance in South Africa was an event of significance and controversy. In fact, some prominent black figures pleaded with him not to go, arguing that Ashe's deal with the government served only to validate apartheid. Ashe replied: "Of course, I know they're using me, but I'm using them too." He also contended that if change were ever to come, then sports was a logical, symbolic starting place.

Blacks in South Africa thronged to see him—especially on the tennis court, where Ashe's demands had been met so that all races were allowed seating in all parts of the stadium. He also traveled throughout South Africa, and most memorably, publicly debated a professor of anthropology at Stellenbosch, the country's leading university. The trip was, altogether, a success and served to establish Ashe as the rare athlete who was a serious international figure.

On the tennis side, however, Ashe allowed his outside interests to divert him from his game, and while he would make the world top ten for eleven years running (and twelve years overall), he began to drift down the ladder. So when Ashe reached the Wimbledon final against Jimmy Connors in 1975, just before his thirty-second birthday, it was viewed as a pleasant consolation for the popular veteran. Connors, rampant upon the court, was a heavy favorite to win. Ashe's style had always been suited to fast courts, especially grass. The keystone of his game was his powerful serve, which he managed to unleash more with coordination than with strength. He remained rail-thin all his life, rarely carrying more than 155 pounds on his six-foot, one-inch frame. He did possess a classic backhand, but Ashe could not win with ground strokes; he needed to attack the net. Thus, no one was prepared, least of all Connors, when Ashe completely adjusted his game for the Wimbledon final. He served off-speed, hitting slices and chops, forcing Connors to come to the net, taking him out of his usual game. Ashe won 6–1, 6–1, 5–7, 6–4. It was not only the cap to his career but the most brilliantly orchestrated match ever played in the sport.

Ashe married Jeanne-Marie Moutoussamy, a photographer, on 20 February 1977; they had one child. His tennis career came to an abrupt end in July 1979 when, although only thirty-six years old, he suffered a serious heart attack. Then, in 1983, after heart-bypass surgery, he was given a blood transfusion. The blood was tainted with the HIV virus, and he was diagnosed with AIDS in 1988.

Ashe did serve, however, as the captain of the Davis Cup team from 1981 to 1985, winning the Cup twice. Most of his time, though, was devoted to charity and to writing. His most comprehensive project was *A Hard Road To Glory* (1993), a three-volume history of the African-American athlete. He won an Emmy for writing the television adaptation and also worked as a network sports commentator. He contributed columns and essays, most often to the *Washington Post,* and spoke out forcefully on the issues that engaged him. Only months before he died, in fact, frail and failing, he was arrested and imprisoned in Washington, D.C., in a protest on behalf of Haitian democracy. Ashe also concentrated his efforts on bringing more minority urban youth into tennis. As far back as 1968, he had co-founded the National Junior Tennis League, and he was elected chairman of the Black Tennis and Sports Foundation. When Ashe was first diagnosed with AIDS, he chose to keep the illness a secret, knowing that once his condition was revealed, he would be forced to constantly deal publicly with the disease—becoming, as he described it, "a professional patient." It was a tribute to the esteem in which he was held in that, even as the word began to leak out, many journalists kept his secret. Finally, *USA Today* forced his hand in April 1992, and he revealed his condition. Immediately, Ashe began to assist the cause of combating AIDS, most prominently working to set up the Arthur Ashe Institute for Urban Health in Brooklyn, New York. He found himself showered with the most extraordinary affection. In a way, Ashe was able to read his eulogies while he was still alive. *Sports Illustrated,* for example, named him Sportsman of the Year for 1982. It was the only time that the award had been given to a former athlete. In 1985 he was inducted into the International Tennis Hall of Fame.

Ashe died on 6 February 1993 at age forty-nine. He is buried in Woodland Cemetery in Richmond. He was praised for his humanity, nobility, and principles more than for his tennis championships. In 1997 the center court at the U.S. Open site in New York City was named the Arthur Ashe Stadium. After sustained public debate, in 1997 a statue of Ashe—holding a tennis racket and a book—was erected on Monument Avenue in Richmond, only blocks from statues of three Confederate generals—Robert E. Lee, Stonewall Jackson, and J. E. B. Stuart—and the Confederate president, Jefferson Davis.

Ashe was, in fact, that rare athlete whose goodness transcended his greatness, and he stands—with the likes of Jackie Robinson, Billie Jean King, and Muhammed Ali—as a sports figure of cultural significance.

★

Ashe wrote *Portrait in Motion* (1975), a diary of one tennis year. It is especially valuable inasmuch as it covers in detail the period of his first trip to South Africa. He was also the author of an autobiography, *Off the Court* (1981). Ashe's memoir, *Days Of Grace* (1993), written in collaboration with Arnold Rampersad, was published posthumously. It is conspicuous for its candor and lack of self-pity. For tennis facts and a summary of his career, the best source is *Bud Collins' Tennis Encyclopedia* (3d ed., 1997). "The Sportsman of the Year: The Eternal Example," by Kenny Moore in *Sports Illustrated* (21 Dec. 1992), is the most complete post-AIDS tribute. Some Ashe memorabilia may be found at the International Tennis Hall of Fame in Newport, Rhode Island. There is an obituary in the *New York Times* (7 Feb. 1993). An HBO documentary, *Arthur Ashe: Citizen of the World* (1995), concentrates, as the title suggests, more on the man than on the player.

FRANK DEFORD

ASHMAN, Howard Elliot (*b.* 17 May 1950 in Baltimore, Maryland; *d.* 14 March 1991 in New York City), lyricist and playwright best known for his Academy Award–winning songs, written in collaboration with the composer Alan Menken, for Walt Disney Pictures' films *The Little Mermaid* (1989) and *Beauty and the Beast* (1991).

Ashman was one of two children of Raymond Albert Ashman, an ice-cream cone manufacturer, and Shirley Thelma Glass, a homemaker. He attended Boston University and received a B.A. from Goddard College in Plainfield, Vermont, in 1971. He earned an M.F.A. from Indiana University in Bloomington in 1974.

Ashman then moved to New York City, becoming a book editor at Grosset and Dunlap, where he found time to indulge his love of playwriting. His works included *'Cause Maggie's Afraid of the Dark* and *Dreamstuff,* a musical version of *The Tempest*—both produced in 1976. *The Confirmation* was produced in 1978. *Dreamstuff* was his first work in association with the off-off-Broadway WPA Theatre, for which Ashman accepted the post of artistic director in 1977. He remained the organization's guiding force until 1982.

In 1979 Ashman drew attention as lyricist, co-librettist (with Dennis Green), and director of *God Bless You, Mr.*

Howard Ashman (*left*) and Alan Menken, in a portrait for *The Little Mermaid.* AP/WIDE WORLD PHOTOS

Rosewater. Ashman had given the fledgling composer Alan Menken his big break, choosing him over a number of competitors to write the music for the stage adaptation of the author Kurt Vonnegut's tale of an eccentric multimillionaire bent on giving away his fortune. Menken told *People* magazine in 1991, "With Howard, I realized I was dealing with somebody monumentally talented. I knew great things were going to come."

Ashman worked brief stints as guest director of Westchester Regional Theatre in Harrison, New York, from 1979 to 1980 and as stage director of Arena Stage in Washington, D.C., from 1980 to 1981. He continued his association with Menken, and the pair soon found success with the 1982 off-Broadway hit *Little Shop of Horrors.* The musical about a shy flower-store clerk whose fate becomes entangled with a man-eating plant won the New York Drama Critics Circle Award for best musical of 1982 to 1983. It also won the 1982 Drama Desk Award for outstanding lyrics, the 1982 Outer Critics Circle Awards for best lyrics and best off-Broadway musical, the 1983 London Evening Standard Award, and a 1983 Grammy nomination for best cast show album. The pair composed two additional songs for the musical's 1986 film adaptation, which earned Ashman his first Academy Award nomination for the rhythm-and-blues-tinged "Mean Green Mother from Outer Space." The musical became the highest-grossing and third-longest-running musical in off-Broadway history. With *Our*

Town, it remains the most-produced play in American high schools.

In 1986 Ashman wrote the Broadway production of *Smile* with Marvin Hamlisch and received a 1987 Tony Award nomination for best book. Soon after, Walt Disney Pictures decided to venture into the realm of animated musicals for the first time in more than ten years. The film producer David Geffen, who had worked on *Little Shop of Horrors,* recommended Ashman to Disney, and Ashman brought in Menken.

Ashman and Menken collaborated on the 1989 feature *The Little Mermaid,* which was deemed an instant classic because of its unforgettable music. Ashman, who also served as the film's producer, decided that an animated crab character should have a Jamaican accent. Thus was born the calypso song "Under the Sea," which won Ashman the 1989 Academy Award for best original song. The song also won a Golden Globe Award, and the soundtrack won a Grammy for best album for children. Reflecting in the *Chicago Tribune* in 1989, Ashman said, "Writing about crabs singing to mermaids involves the same craft as writing about man-eating plants from outer space. In both cases, the songs have to mesh with the story and push it forward."

Three days after the 1989 Academy Awards ceremony, while at the Beacon, New York, cottage that Ashman shared with his partner, the architect William Lauch, Ashman told Menken that he had tested positive for HIV. The pair persevered in their collaboration, next penning *Beauty and the Beast* (1991), which Ashman also executive-produced. The film won 1992 Academy Awards for best original score and for its title song, which was deemed best original song. The song also won a Golden Globe Award, and the soundtrack again won the Grammy for best album for children.

Ashman also finished work on three songs for *Aladdin* (1992), the score of which Menken completed with lyricist Tim Rice. "Friend Like Me" received 1993 Academy Award and Golden Globe Award nominations for best original song; "Prince Ali" also received a Golden Globe Award nomination for best original song.

Ashman's death at age forty from complications of AIDS preceded the release of the final two films. In 1995, four years after his death, the WPA Theatre saluted its former artistic director with *Hundreds of Hats,* a revue of Ashman's songs.

In 1997 Menken told the *New York Times* that "the intensity of a life close to the end" came through in the songs from *Beauty and the Beast.* "It's tragic what didn't get written," he continued. "We had a great career ahead of us." A Walt Disney official commented, "In animation, we have two guardian angels. One is Walt Disney, who continues to touch every frame of our movies. The other is Howard Ashman, who continues to touch every note of our movies."

Ashman can be credited in large part with the renaissance of the animated Disney musical, which continued throughout the 1990s. The wave of films introduced numerous songs and images into popular culture and the indelible memories of a generation of children. The final credits of *Beauty and the Beast* contained this dedication to Ashman: "To our friend Howard, who gave a mermaid her voice and a beast his soul."

★

Ashman's Disney songwriting is featured in *The Illustrated Treasury of Disney Songs* (1998). He was interviewed in *Starlog* magazine (Mar. 1990). Interviews with his collaborator Alan Menken appeared in *People* (16 Dec. 1991) and the *New York Times* (13 July 1997). A brief biography is in *Contemporary Theatre, Film, and Television,* vol. 12 (1994). Obituaries are in the *New York Times* and the *Los Angeles Times* (both 15 Mar. 1991).

LEIGH DYER

ASIMOV, Isaac (*b.* 2 January 1920, or as early as 4 October 1919 in Petrovichi, Russia; *d.* 6 April 1992 in New York City), writer of science fiction and science popularizations, including the *Foundation Trilogy* (1951, 1952, 1953), and one of the most prolific authors of the twentieth century.

Asimov and his younger sister arrived in the United States with their parents, Judah Asimov and Anna Rachel Berman, in 1923, at the invitation of their mother's half brother, Joseph Berman. They settled in Brooklyn, New York, where Asimov's mother was a homemaker and in 1926 Asimov's father bought the first of a series of candy stores. The stores, with living quarters above, became a major part of Asimov's childhood which, he felt, deprived him of his father's attention at an early age. In 1927 Asimov's mother gave birth to his brother, Stanley, who would make a journalism career at *Newsday* and retire as the newspaper's vice president in charge of editorial administration. Asimov became a naturalized U.S. citizen in 1928.

Asimov was a precocious child who learned to read on his own before starting school. Later he would skip grades, graduate from Boys High School in Brooklyn in 1935, enter Seth Low Junior College at the age of fifteen, and earn a bachelor's degree from Columbia University in 1939 at the age of nineteen. He worked as civilian researcher at the U.S. Navy Yard in Philadelphia, upon the recommendation of the science fiction author Robert A. Heinlein, who was also working there (as an honorable way to avoid the draft). Asimov was then reclassified by the draft board, inducted into the army on 1 November 1945, and discharged a year later. He returned to Columbia to earn his Ph.D., which he received in 1948. Asimov married Gertrude Blugerman in 1942; they were separated in 1970 and divorced in 1973.

They had two children. Asimov married psychoanalyst Janet Jeppson as soon as his divorce was final.

Asimov discovered science fiction magazines in his father's store at the age of nine and began writing stories at the age of eleven. In 1938 he took his first story to the editor John W. Campbell, Jr., at Asimov's favorite magazine, *Astounding Science Fiction*. His first published story, "Marooned Off Vesta," was published in *Amazing Stories* in March 1939, and his second, "Trends," appeared in the July 1939 issue of *Astounding Science Fiction*. One of his most famous stories, "Nightfall," which earned him his first cover, was published in September 1941.

By that time Asimov had developed a close relationship with Campbell that would last until Campbell's death in 1971. For the first dozen years it consisted of Asimov traveling by subway to Campbell's office with a story idea, discussing it, and then bringing back the story for Campbell's comments and, usually, acceptance. In this way Asimov developed the robot stories that made up the collection *I, Robot* (1950), the first of which, "Robbie," was published in September 1940 in *Super Science* and the second, "Reason," in April 1941 in *Astounding Science Fiction;* and the stories that made up *The Foundation Trilogy* (1951, 1952, 1953), the first of which, "Foundation," was published in May 1942 in *Astounding Science Fiction*.

In 1950 Asimov, fearing the loss of his major market if

Isaac Asimov. AP/WIDE WORLD PHOTOS

Astounding Science Fiction stopped publication or Campbell retired, began contributing stories and serials to *Galaxy Science Fiction* and in 1953, to *Fantasy and Science Fiction*. For the latter he also wrote a regular science column beginning in 1958. His columns won a "Special Hugo" in 1963. Most of his articles were collected into books of essays. Meanwhile he had branched out into novel publication with Gnome Press and then, starting in 1950, with Doubleday, which would remain the publisher for his science fiction until his death.

Meanwhile Asimov's academic career had begun in 1949 with an appointment at the Boston University School of Medicine, where he was a popular lecturer in biochemistry. His lack of interest in research led to his dismissal in 1958 (although he insisted that he had tenure and fought to keep his title of associate professor). He then lectured at the university about once a year and in 1979 was promoted to full professor. By that time his writing of science fiction and his newfound ability to write academic texts and books about science were bringing in more income than his regular salary.

Asimov's dismissal coincided with the launching of the first Russian satellite, *Sputnik*. Asimov recognized the need for more and better science education, and for some twenty years he wrote nonfiction rather than fiction. His first nonfiction book was *Biochemistry and Human Metabolism* (1952). In addition to his books on chemistry and biochemistry, he published books on mathematics, astronomy, earth sciences, physics, biology, history, the Bible (*Asimov's Guide to the Bible*, 2 vols. 1968, 1969), literature (*Asimov's Guide to Shakespeare*, 2 vols. 1970), humor and satire (*The Sensuous Dirty Old Man*, 1971; *Lecherous Limericks*, 1975), and general science (*The Intelligent Man's Guide to Science*, 1960; *Asimov's Biographical Encyclopedia of Science and Technology*, 1964, 1972, 1982).

Asimov also wrote mystery novels (*Murder at the A.B.A.*, 1976) and mystery stories collected in nine volumes (*Tales of the Black Widowers*, 1974). He edited dozens of anthologies beginning with *The Hugo Winners* (1962) and continuing with other Hugo volumes until his death, as well as such anthologies as *Where Do We Go From Here?* (1971) and *Before the Golden Age* (1974). He wrote five science fiction juveniles as Paul French, beginning with *Lucky Starr and the Pirates of the Asteroids* (1953), and a series of children's books (with his wife Janet) about a robot named Norby, beginning with *Norby, the Mixed-up Robot* (1983).

His abstinence from the writing of science fiction (except for occasional short stories) was briefly interrupted in 1966 by the publication of the novelization of the film *Fantastic Voyage* and then, in 1972, with his Nebula- and Hugo-award-winning *The Gods Themselves*. But it was not until the early 1980s that his Doubleday editors insisted that he write another science fiction novel. His science fic-

tion editor added, " . . . when we say 'a science-fiction novel' we mean 'a Foundation novel.'" Asimov produced *Foundation's Edge* (1982), which became his first best-seller and won a Hugo Award. He spent the last decade of his life writing science fiction novels, several of which also became best-sellers, and weaving together his robot novels, which began with *The Caves of Steel* in 1954, and his *Foundation* novels (which originally included no robots).

Asimov was guest of honor at the World Science Fiction Convention in 1966, where his *Foundation* trilogy won a Hugo for best all-time series, and frequently served as toastmaster at other conventions. He was an accomplished public speaker and gave many commencement addresses at places he could reach by train (he was agoraphobic and afraid of flying). A special issue of *Fantasy and Science Fiction* (October 1966) was dedicated to him, and a magazine, *Isaac Asimov's Science Fiction Magazine,* was created in his honor in 1976. He wrote an editorial column for that magazine until his death. He was named "Humanist of the Year" in 1984 by the American Humanist Society and later became president. He was presented the Science Fiction Writers of America Grand Master Award in 1987.

Hollywood often talked about filming Asimov's fiction, and one major project, *I, Robot,* even reached the stage of a completed screenplay by the science fiction writer Harlan Ellison. It was not until eight years after Asimov's death, however, that the actor Robin Williams starred as a robot in an adaptation of Asimov's Hugo- and Nebula-award-winning novelette *The Bicentennial Man* (1976).

Writing was Asimov's life and brought him his greatest moments of pleasure. He had expressed the desire to die with his nose caught between two typewriter keys, but at the end, suffering with heart and kidney failure, he was too weak to write. His last novel, *Forward the Foundation,* published posthumously in 1993, depicted the psychohistorian Hari Seldon, who had developed equations by which he could predict the general outline of the future, still working as he died, "the future he created unfolding all around him. . . ." It could have been Asimov's own epitaph.

Asimov celebrated the milestones in his life not by anniversaries but by books published: *Opus 100* in 1969; *Opus 200* in 1979; his autobiography, *In Memory Yet Green* and *In Joy Still Felt* in 1979 and 1980; and his memoirs, *I. Asimov,* in 1994. In *Opus 100* he recalled mentioning to his first wife his ambition to write 100 books, and she replied, "What good will it be if you then regret having spent your life writing books while all the essence of life passes you by?" And Asimov replied, "But for me the essence of life is writing. In fact, if I do manage to publish a hundred books, and if I then die, my last words are likely to be 'Only a hundred!'"

By his death Asimov had published 470 books, including hundreds of nonfiction books on a vast array of subjects.

Harvard professor George G. Simpson called him "one of our natural wonders and national resources." Asimov preferred to be thought of as a science fiction writer and, in fact, became best known for his *Foundation Trilogy* and later best-selling *Foundation* novels, and his robot stories and novels. He died of heart and kidney failure in New York City. He was cremated and his ashes are in the possession of his daughter Robyn.

★

Asimov's manuscripts and personal papers are in Mugar Memorial Library, Boston University. His autobiographical works are *In Memory Yet Green* (1979), which covers the years 1920–1954; *In Joy Still Felt* (1980), which covers the years 1954–1978; and *I. Asimov: A Memoir* (1994), classified by subject and started in the hospital in 1990. James Gunn, *Isaac Asimov: The Foundations of Science Fiction* (1982, 1996), provides biographical information. See also Joseph F. Patrouch, Jr., *The Science Fiction of Isaac Asimov* (1974); Joseph D. Olander and Martin H. Greenberg, eds., *Isaac Asimov* (1977); Jean Fielder and Jim Mele, *Isaac Asimov* (1982). An obituary is in the *New York Times* (7 Apr. 1992).

JAMES GUNN

ATWATER, Harvey Leroy ("Lee") (*b.* 27 February 1951 in Atlanta, Georgia; *d.* 29 March 1991 in Washington, D.C.), political consultant who developed the strategy known as "negative campaigning" and who became chairman of the Republican National Committee after engineering George Bush's victory in the 1988 presidential election.

Lee Atwater, 1988. © WALLY MCNAMEE/CORBIS

Atwater was the eldest of three children born to Harvey Dillard Atwater, an insurance claims adjuster, and Alma Page, a high school teacher. His parents moved several times during his childhood before settling in Columbia, South Carolina, when he was nine years old. His grades at A. C. Flora High School were poor because he spent much of his time playing guitar with a rhythm and blues band. Upon graduation in June 1969 he wanted to play music professionally but bowed to his parents' wishes and went to college. His poor academic record closed the door to most colleges, but his mother got him into Newberry College, a small school forty miles from Columbia.

During the summer of 1971 Atwater interned in the Washington, D.C., office of South Carolina senator J. Strom Thurmond, a Democrat who had bolted his party in 1948 to campaign for the presidency on the States' Rights (Dixiecrat) party ticket. Thurmond was now a Republican in a state still dominated by the Democratic party. In Atwater's view, Democrats represented the establishment and Republicans were the outsiders, and he dreamed of reestablishing the Republican party as the majority party in the United States.

When Atwater returned to Newberry in the fall of 1971, he joined the College Republicans, plunged into a fight for control of the organization's South Carolina chapter, and won election as the state chairman. While still in college, he managed his first political campaign, getting his candidate, a Republican running against an incumbent Democrat, elected the mayor of Forest Acres, a suburb of Columbia. He also became a delegate to the Republican National Convention in Miami in 1972.

After graduation in 1973 Atwater served as executive director of the College Republicans' national office in Washington, D.C., but returned to Columbia in 1974 to establish a political consulting firm. He managed the campaigns of many South Carolina Republicans and began to perfect the tactics known as negative campaigning. During Senator Thurmond's 1978 reelection campaign, Atwater ran advertisements emphasizing remarks critical of South Carolina allegedly made by Thurmond's Democratic opponent to a New York City audience. The Democrat appeared disloyal to his state and hence unfit to be its senator. Thurmond won in a landslide.

In the same year, Atwater played a role in the successful congressional campaign of the Republican Carroll Campbell, whose Democratic opponent, Max Heller, was Jewish.

Though Atwater denied having anything to do with it, a third party candidate in the race attacked Heller for refusing to believe in Jesus Christ, thus raising the issue of Heller's faith.

Meanwhile, Atwater earned an M.A. degree in journalism from the University of South Carolina in 1977. On 24 June 1978 he married Sally Dunbar, a special education teacher. The couple had three children. In 1981 he moved to a small townhouse in Washington, D.C.; his wife joined him fully in 1982.

In 1980 a reporter asked Tom Turnipseed, the Democratic candidate for a South Carolina congressional seat, if it was true that he had undergone psychiatric treatment and electroshock therapy. Turnipseed accused Atwater of planting the question, but Atwater refused comment on an accusation made by a man who, he said, had been "hooked up to jumper cables." Atwater eventually apologized for the remark, but the damage was done.

Republicans were not immune to Atwater's negative tactics. During the 1980 campaign for the Republican presidential nomination, Atwater helped deliver South Carolina for Ronald Reagan by creating the impression that Reagan's chief opponent, George Bush, was a staunch supporter of gun control. Reagan easily won the crucial contest and gained his party's nomination. After Bush accepted the vice presidential nomination, Atwater served as the regional director of the Reagan-Bush campaign in a four-state area that included South Carolina.

Atwater's reward was a job in the Reagan White House in the Office for Political Affairs, which he left in 1984 to serve as deputy director of the successful Reagan-Bush reelection campaign. He then joined a prestigious Washington political consulting firm. From 1986 to 1988 he spearheaded Bush's successful effort to gain his party's presidential nomination.

As Bush's campaign manager in 1988, Atwater achieved notoriety because of a television advertisement that suggested that the Democratic nominee, Michael Dukakis, was "soft on crime." In 1986, while Dukakis was governor of Massachusetts, Willie Horton, Jr., who had served ten years of a sentence for first-degree murder, received a weekend pass from a state prison and did not return. In April 1987 the fugitive Horton raped a woman in Maryland. The furlough program was enacted before Dukakis became governor, but he had vetoed a bill denying furloughs to people, such as Horton, convicted of first-degree murder. Atwater maintained that the issue raised by the advertisement—which was aired by a political action committee, and not by the official Bush campaign—was the issue of crime and not of race. But the fact that Horton was black and his victim white was seen by critics as an effort to interject race into the campaign.

To celebrate Bush's inauguration Atwater, an accomplished guitarist, organized and participated in an event featuring rhythm and blues artists. Although he became chairman of the Republican National Committee in January 1989, Atwater began playing guitar in nightclubs and recorded an album, *Red Hot & Blue* (1990), with B. B. King, which received a Grammy nomination in January 1991 for best contemporary blues recording.

As chairman of the Republican National Committee, Atwater began an aggressive effort to attract black voters to the Republican party. Some black leaders apparently were willing to forget Willie Horton, for Atwater was named a trustee of historically black Howard University in Washington, D.C. He was forced to resign in March 1989, however, after student demonstrators took over the school's administration building to protest his appointment.

On 5 March 1990 Atwater collapsed during a speech, and doctors discovered an inoperable brain tumor. Despite aggressive treatment with both radiation and chemotherapy, Atwater, who clung to the chairmanship of the Republican National Committee until January 1991, lost his battle with cancer a year after it was diagnosed. He died at George Washington University Hospital in Washington, D.C. He is buried in Columbia.

Although he apologized to many targets of his attacks during the final months of his life, Atwater may forever be linked to the concept of negative campaigning. Personal attacks on opponents were hardly new to American electoral politics, but Atwater, a professed student of Sun Tzu and Machiavelli, elevated such attacks to a coherent strategy designed to bring victory by seeking an opponent's weaknesses—real or apparent—and ruthlessly emphasizing or exaggerating them to destroy the opponent's image in the eyes of the voters.

★

John Joseph Brady, *Bad Boy: The Life and Politics of Lee Atwater* (1997), is a popular account of Atwater's career based on extensive interviews with people who knew him. A brief biographical sketch may be found in *Current Biography 1989*. David Remnick, "Why Is Lee Atwater So Hungry?" *Esquire* (Dec. 1986), emphasizes Atwater's unconventional, "down-home" style and his determination to win at any cost. Eric Alterman, "Playing Hardball," *New York Times Magazine* (30 Apr. 1989), is good on Atwater's use of negative campaigning. In "Lee Atwater's Last Campaign," written for *Life* (Feb. 1991) with Todd Brewster, Atwater discussed his fight against cancer and took the opportunity to express regret for some of his "nakedly cruel" political attacks. Obituaries are in the *Atlanta Constitution* and the *New York Times* (both 30 Mar. 1991).

ROMAN ROME

B

BALDWIN, Hanson Weightman (*b.* 22 March 1903 in Baltimore, Maryland; *d.* 13 November 1991 in Roxbury, Connecticut), military editor at the *New York Times,* prolific author, and winner of a Pulitzer Prize.

Baldwin was the only son of four children born to Oliver Perry Baldwin, Jr., the managing editor of the *Baltimore Sun,* and Caroline Sutton, a homemaker. Baldwin attended high school at the Boys Latin School in Baltimore and the United States Naval Academy in Annapolis, from which he graduated with a B.S. degree in 1924. He served aboard battleships and a destroyer for three years, but resigned from the navy in 1927 to pursue a career in journalism. In 1928, as a cub reporter for the *Baltimore Sun,* he covered one of the first naval tests of the "lung" or escape device from submarines, as well as the arrival of the Graf Zeppelin.

In 1928 and 1929 Baldwin quit journalism for a year, shipping out to South America as a quartermaster. He also went to Labrador, Canada, as the director of a volunteer group of college students in Sir William Grenfell's work, helping establish hospitals, orphanages, nursing stations, schools, and cooperative stores near the Arctic Circle. In 1929 he became a general assignment reporter for the *New York Times* in New York City. In June 1931 Baldwin married Helen Bruce. They had two children.

Baldwin was appointed the military editor of the *Times* in 1937, from which time he contributed a column as well as news articles. While at the *Times* he covered fleet maneuvers in the Caribbean Sea and the Pacific and Atlantic oceans. He studied the military preparedness of Germany, France, Great Britain, and Poland and analyzed the events leading up to World War II. During the war he predicted possible Axis strategy. He also summed up trends of how the war was progressing.

With Wayne Francis Palmer, Baldwin coedited *Men and Ships of Steel* (1935), a history of the U.S. Navy with 275 pictures. Baldwin then wrote *The Caissons Roll: A Military Survey of Europe* (1938). Based on a survey that he conducted in 1937 and containing much material already published in the *Times,* the volume provided an overview of the military situation in Europe. Baldwin recounted the tremendous military build-up taking place there. He provided estimates and statistics pertaining to tank equipment and naval operations, and also predicted the probable centers of future European wars. In *The Caissons Roll,* Baldwin additionally expressed the view that the two sides in the Spanish civil war were equally "evil" and advocated the localization of the conflict; argued that France was safe behind the Maginot Line; and asserted that the Spanish civil war showed that war could not be won in the air. Baldwin predicted a second world war but did not foresee it happening as early as 1939. He also stated that Germany and Italy would base their strategy on a fast action, attacking their enemies from land and air simultaneously.

Hanson Baldwin, 1952. AP/WIDE WORLD PHOTOS

D day, 6 June 1944. Baldwin watched the invasion from the cruiser *Augusta,* and landed with General Omar Bradley. In the postwar years, Baldwin wrote about the formation of the North Atlantic Treaty Organization (NATO), the new roles for sea and air power, atomic weapons development, newly introduced missiles and jets, and the arms race. He was often aligned with the Pentagon officials in his views on military strategy and tactics. In 1959 he got an exclusive in breaking the news of high altitude atomic bomb tests, known as Project Argus, by the United States. He had to wait seven months before getting permission to release the story because of what the government contended were national security concerns.

In 1965, during the Vietnam War, Baldwin wrote an article in the *New York Times Magazine* titled "We Must Choose: (1) Bug Out; (2) Negotiate; (3) Fight." In it, he suggested that the United States send one million troops, if required, to secure a victory in Southeast Asia. Baldwin's influence was such that his views were read by the president of the United States, members of Congress, and military chiefs. In a 1966 conference, Defense Secretary Robert S. McNamara disputed Baldwin's contention that the Vietnam War had overextended the armed forces.

Baldwin retired from the *Times* in 1968. Subsequently, he contributed occasional articles to the newspaper. A tall, slender, and courtly man, with a quiet manner that contrasted with his forceful opinions, Baldwin enjoyed swimming, tennis, skiing, and reading for relaxation.

During his career Baldwin was presented with numerous awards and prizes, including the Syracuse University Distinguished Service Medal in 1944 and honorary degrees from Drake University and the Clarkson Institute of Technology. Baldwin wrote for a wide variety of magazines, including *Harper's,* the *North American Review, Aviation, Foreign Affairs*, and the *Reader's Digest*. He also lectured extensively. Baldwin died in his home of heart failure at age eighty-eight and was buried at sea.

Baldwin was the leading military journalist of his day, and he espoused thoughtful discussion of military matters and strategies. His Pulitzer Prize for his writing from Guadalcanal and the Western Pacific in World War II serves to recognize his significance and impact on the world of journalism.

With Shepard Stone, Baldwin edited *We Saw It Happen* (1938), comprising articles by thirteen *Times* correspondents on the news behind the news. His *Admiral Death* (1939) consisted of twelve true stories of adventures at sea. He next wrote *What the Citizen Should Know About the Navy* (1941, with illustrations by André Jandot). The book contained information on the use of the fleet, naval bases, various types of fighting ships and planes, equipment, and communications, and descriptions of various careers in the navy.

Baldwin's work *United We Stand! Defense of the Western Hemisphere* (1941) created a stir. Giving a comprehensive survey of the military strengths and weaknesses of the United States, Baldwin said that within a year the United States would have to choose between peace and entry into World War II. In his *Times* articles during 1941, Baldwin pointed out that Great Britain and the United States were reacting to the Germans rather than taking the initiative. It was only in June 1941 that he concluded the Germans could be defeated, but only with speed of decision, rapidity of action, and a total war effort.

Baldwin won the Pulitzer Prize in 1943 for his distinguished writing from Guadalcanal and the Western Pacific during World War II. He also covered the Allied invasion of North Africa, as well as the landings at Normandy on

★

Baldwin's papers are in the Yale University Library, in New Haven, Connecticut. A biographical article on Baldwin can be found in *Current Biography 1942* (1943). Information about Baldwin can be found in Meyer Berger, *The Story of the New York Times, 1851–1951* (1951) An obituary is in the *New York Times* (14 Nov. 1991).

MARTIN JAY STAHL

BARBER, Walter Lanier ("Red") (*b.* 17 February 1908 in Columbus, Mississippi; *d.* 22 October 1992 in Tallahassee, Florida), sportscaster and author, best known for his folksy southern accent and colorful language as a broadcaster for the Brooklyn Dodgers and New York Yankees on radio and television.

Barber was one of three children born to William L. Barber, a locomotive engineer for the Atlantic Coast Line Railroad, and Selena Martin, an English teacher. He was nicknamed "Red" because of his hair color. Sidney Lanier, the southern poet, was a distant relative. Barber's family moved to Sanford, Florida, when he was ten years old. He graduated from Sanford High School in 1926 and picked celery, drove trucks, and worked as both a roustabout and a road builder. Barber attended the University of Florida at Gainesville from 1928 through 1930, hoping to become an English teacher, and worked as a janitor to help pay tuition costs. His career ambitions changed, however, after he was selected to read the paper of a professor who forgot to appear for his scheduled airtime on the campus radio station, WRUF. Barber dropped out of school in 1930 to become chief announcer and director for WRUF.

The short, wiry Barber met Lylah Scarborough, a nurse, while recuperating from an automobile accident at the Uni-

Red Barber as host of "Red Barber's Star Review," 1945. AP PHOTO/ WEAF

versity of Florida hospital. They married on 28 March 1931 and had one child.

Cincinnati Reds owner Powel Crosley, Jr., hired Barber in 1934 to broadcast Reds baseball games over his radio stations, WSAI and WLW, in Cincinnati. Barber's first such broadcast was the first major league game he had ever seen. He remained with the Reds through 1938, impressing listeners with his voice, style, and sensibility.

In 1939 New York removed a ban on the radio broadcast of baseball games (imposed after a 1934 agreement between the Brooklyn Dodgers, New York Yankees, and New York Giants), and Barber began announcing Brooklyn Dodgers baseball games with Al Helfer on WOR radio and television. On 29 August 1939 Barber broadcast the first major league baseball game ever televised, between the Cincinnati Reds and the Brooklyn Dodgers at Ebbets Field. Barber covered Dodgers games through 1953, building a reputation as a fair, accurate announcer known for his colorful, dramatic reporting. Without pretentiousness, he spoke conversationally and with soft-voiced authority in a chatty, easygoing style and introduced listeners to colorful southern terms. Barber called the broadcast booth "a catbird seat" and described players arguing with umpires as going to "the rhubarb patch." He labeled batters enjoying a hitting streak as "tearing up the pea patch." No announcer better captured the sequence of events that makes baseball unique: the fidgety tension of batter against pitcher; the blind destiny of the ball; and the bang-bang climax. In 1954 Barber started broadcasting New York Yankee baseball games on WOR radio and television. His impartial style contrasted with legendary announcer Mel Allen, who openly rooted for the home team. The Yankees fired Barber in 1966, two years after Allen's dismissal, when he honestly reported the smallest crowd ever to attend a game at Yankee Stadium. Barber revealed that the crowd numbered just 413 and asked the television cameras to show the stands. The producer, however, had ordered television camera operators not to show the empty seats.

While announcing in New York, Barber lived on Lynwood Drive in Scarsdale, New York, and then on River Road in Scarborough, New York. He served as sports director for CBS in New York from 1946 to 1951 and provided sports coverage for newsreels from 1940 through 1948. Besides broadcasting thirteen World Series and four All-Star Games, he covered eight Orange Bowls, two Rose Bowls, one Sugar Bowl, five Army-Navy football contests, and four National Football League (NFL) title games for CBS radio and television from 1946 to 1955.

Barber's most dramatic broadcasts were game four of the 1947 World Series, when Cookie Lavagetto of the Brooklyn Dodgers broke up a no-hit bid by Bill Bevens of the New York Yankees; game three of the 1951 National League playoffs, when Bobby Thomson of the New York

Giants clouted a game-ending home run off Ralph Branca of the Brooklyn Dodgers; the 1935 football game in which Notre Dame scored two touchdowns in the final minutes to defeat Ohio State, 18–13; and the 1940 NFL championship game when the Chicago Bears humiliated the Washington Redskins, 73–0. He also covered the consecutive no-hitters by Johnny Vander Meer of the Cincinnati Reds in June 1938 and Jackie Robinson's historic first game and season with the Brooklyn Dodgers in 1947.

In his 1968 autobiography, *Rhubarb in the Catbird Seat,* Barber reviewed his announcing career. Barber mentioned dedication, loyalty, professionalism, and skill as the essential qualities of an effective baseball broadcaster. The deeply religious, Mississippi-born Barber also described how he nearly quit as announcer when Branch Rickey signed Jackie Robinson as the first modern major league black player. Additionally, he discussed his difficulties with the New York Yankees management and with the new breed of sportscaster.

Barber's moving *Walk in the Spirit* (1969) told the inspirational stories of Lou Gehrig, Ben Hogan, Roy Campanella, and other athletes who had overcome adversity and used them to illustrate various biblical verses. His next work, *The Broadcasters* (1970), provided anecdotes about Dizzy Dean, Graham McNamee, Ted Husing, and other baseball announcers. Sportscasters were among the first celebrities of mass communication, demonstrating cantankerous, eccentric behavior, verbal flamboyance, irascibility, and egotism. Barber disliked the trend toward hiring former athletes as broadcasters. He also authored *Show Me the Way to Go Home* (1971) and *1947: When All Hell Broke Loose in Baseball* (1982), the latter chronicling Jackie Robinson's major league debut and manager Leo Durocher's suspension.

Barber, a licensed Episcopal lay reader and preacher for the Diocese of New York, broadcast sports commentaries on Fridays from 1981 to 1992 on National Public Radio's *Morning Edition* and wrote a monthly column for the *Christian Science Monitor.* Barber chaired the Board of the Youth Consultation Service helping troubled teenagers and unwed mothers, led fund-raising for the Saint Barnabas Home, a temporary shelter for children in New York City, and helped the American Red Cross blood donor campaign. After moving to Tallahassee during his retirement, he wrote a weekly column for the *Tallahassee Democrat* and tended his flower garden. He continued as a licensed Episcopal lay reader and preacher until the age of seventy.

Barber was elected to the National Sportscasters and Sportswriters Hall of Fame in 1973, the Florida Sports Hall of Fame in 1979, the American Sportscasters Hall of Fame in 1984, and the National Association of Broadcasters' Broadcasting Hall of Fame in 1989. He won the Ford C. Frick Award from the National Baseball Hall of Fame in

1978, the George Polk Award from Long Island University's Department of Journalism in 1985, and the George Foster Peabody Award in 1990 and served on the Veterans Committee of the National Baseball Hall of Fame. Barber died of pneumonia and kidney complications in Tallahassee.

★

Barber's autobiography, *Rhubarb in the Catbird Seat* (1968), with Robert Creamer, describes his distinguished broadcasting career. His *1947: When All Hell Broke Loose in Baseball* (1982), recounts his personal struggles as a religious southerner in accepting Jackie Robinson as the first black player in modern major league baseball. His other books include *The Rhubarb Patch: The Story of the Modern Brooklyn Dodgers* (1954), *Walk in the Spirit* (1969), *The Broadcasters* (1970), and *Show Me the Way to Go Home* (1971). Lylah Barber, *Lylah: a Memoir* (1985), contains his wife's reminiscences. Curt Smith, *Voices of the Game* (1992), assesses Barber's impact on baseball's broadcasting history. Bob Edwards, *Fridays with Red: A Radio Friendship* (1995), discusses Barber's National Public Radio commentaries. Quentin Reynolds, "The Two Lives of Red Barber," *Reader's Digest* (Aug. 1954), sheds light on Barber's role as an Episcopal lay reader. Articles that illuminate Barber's early career include Richard G. Hubler, "The Barber of Brooklyn," *Saturday Evening Post* (21 Mar. 1942); *Current Biography 1943*; and John K. Hutchens, "Red Barber in a New Role," *New York Times Magazine* (31 Dec. 1944). Vin Scully, "Unforgettable Red Barber," *Reader's Digest* (Apr. 1993), contains reminiscences by another distinguished sportscaster. His entry in *Contemporary Authors,* vol. 141 (1994) summarizes his literary impact. Obituaries are in the *New York Times* (23 Oct. 1992), *Newsweek* (2 Nov. 1992), *Sports Illustrated* (2 Nov. 1992), and *Time* (2 Nov. 1992).

DAVID L. PORTER

BARDEEN, John (*b.* 23 May 1908 in Madison, Wisconsin; *d.* 30 January 1991 in Boston, Massachusetts), theoretical physicist, educator, and two-time Nobel Prize winner who co-invented the transistor.

Bardeen was one of four children of Charles Russell Bardeen, a professor of anatomy and dean of the medical school at the University of Wisconsin, and Althea Harmer, an interior designer. His mother died in 1920 and his father married Ruth Hames later that year; the couple had a daughter, Bardeen's half sister.

Bardeen attended elementary school in Madison, skipping three grades before entering University High School. He later transferred to Madison Central High School, from which he graduated in 1923. Bardeen enrolled at the University of Wisconsin, where in 1928 he earned a B.S. degree, and in 1929 an M.S. degree, both in electrical engineering. From 1930 to 1933 he worked as a geophysicist at the Gulf Research and Development Corporation in Pittsburgh.

John Bardeen. AP/WIDE WORLD PHOTOS

In 1933 Bardeen began doctoral studies in mathematical physics at Princeton University. Working with the renowned Eugene Wigner, he focused on quantum theory as applied to solids and wrote his thesis on the attractive forces of electrons within metals. He received his Ph.D. from Princeton in 1936, a year after having accepted a postdoctoral research fellowship from Harvard University. There he worked with Professors John Van Vleck and Percy Bridgman on the problems in electrical conduction and cohesion in metals. The fellowship ended in 1938, and Bardeen taught physics as an assistant professor at the University of Minnesota from 1938 to 1941. During World War II, from 1941 to 1945, he served as a civilian physicist for the Naval Ordnance Laboratory in Washington, D.C.

In 1945 Bardeen took a job with Bell Telephone Laboratories in Murray Hill, New Jersey. Working with Walter H. Brattain and William Bradford Shockley in research on semiconductors, the three attempted to create a solid-state amplifier that would replace vacuum tubes in electronic devices. They concentrated on silicon and germanium, two of the better-understood semiconductors of that time. Shockley's idea was to control electron flow within the semiconductor by applying an electric field from outside, expecting that the field would produce amplification. When Shockley's experiments failed, Bardeen hypothesized that atoms on the surface of the semiconductor might be preventing electrical signals from getting to the interior and producing the desired effect. The group shifted its focus temporarily in order to study and better understand surface phenomena in semiconductors.

By December 1947 Bardeen and Brattain had made the first successful semiconductor amplifier. It consisted of a piece of germanium with two closely spaced pieces of gold on one side (point contacts) and a broad tungsten contact on the other side. When an electrical current was fed to one of the gold contacts, it appeared in greatly amplified form on the other side. The device had transferred current from a low resistance input to a high-resistance output. The invention was named "transistor" because it exhibited the property of *trans*fer re*sist*ance. The transistor could perform the functions of a vacuum tube in one-fiftieth of the space and with one-millionth of the power. It created virtually limitless possibilities in the field of electronics. The public used transistors in hearing aids in 1953 and in transistor radios in 1954. By the late 1950s the first transistorized computers were available. In 1956 Bardeen, Brattain, and Shockley shared the Nobel Prize in physics for their research on semiconductors and the discovery of the transistor effect.

Bardeen left Bell Labs in 1951 to become professor of physics and electrical engineering at the University of Illinois at Urbana-Champaign. There he began earnest research on the phenomenon of superconductivity, which had interested him since graduate school. In 1955 Bardeen teamed with Leon Cooper and John Robert Schrieffer to investigate how certain metals, at very low temperatures, suddenly lose all electrical resistance. By 1957 the trio had been successful in demonstrating their theory that electrons within the metals, when subjected to the necessary low temperatures, were aligned and moving in such a way as to create a coherent, rather than random, state, resulting in the superconductive effect. The theory, which became known as the BCS theory (for Bardeen Cooper Schrieffer), is widely considered to be one of the most important developments of modern theoretical physics. In 1972 the three men shared the Nobel Prize in physics for their jointly developed theory on superconductivity. Bardeen became only the third Nobel laureate to win the prize twice and the only person in history up until that point to have received two Nobel prizes in the same field.

Bardeen retired in 1975 but remained professor emeritus at the University of Illinois until his death. His professional memberships included the National Academy of Sciences, the American Academy of Arts and Sciences, the American Physical Society, of which he was president in 1968–1969, and the Royal Society of Great Britain. He was a member of the Center for Advanced Study at the University of Illinois from 1951 to 1975. Bardeen was on the President's Science Advisory Committee from 1959 to 1962 and on the White House Science Council in the 1980s. He served as consultant to the Xerox Corporation in Rochester, New York, from 1952 to 1982 and was a member of its board of directors from 1961 to 1974. He was an associate editor of *Physical Review* from 1949 to 1952 and then again in 1956 for several years. Bardeen's many awards and honors included the Stuart Ballantine Medal of the Franklin Institute (1952), the Oliver E. Buckley Solid State Physics Prize of the American Physical Society (1954), the John Scott Medal of the City of Philadelphia (1955), the Fritz London Award (1962), the National Medal of Science of the National Science Foundation (1965), the Presidential Medal of Freedom (1977), the Lomonosov Prize of the USSR Academy of Sciences (1988), and sixteen honorary degrees.

In July 1938 Bardeen married Jane Maxwell, a biologist and teacher. They had three children. Friends described Bardeen, an avid golfer, as a family man and as remarkably intelligent, soft-spoken, and modest. He died of a heart attack following surgery in Boston and is buried in Forest Hill Cemetery in Madison.

Bardeen once told a reporter, "I knew the transistor was important, but I never foresaw the revolution in electronics it would bring." In 1990 *Life* magazine named Bardeen one of the 100 most influential Americans of the twentieth century. On Bardeen's death, Dr. Robert M. Berdahl, then vice chancellor of the University of Illinois, said of him, "There are few people who had a greater impact on the whole of the twentieth century."

★

A Collection of Professor John Bardeen's Publications on Semiconductors and Superconductivity was published in 1989. The text of Bardeen's 1956 Nobel lecture and a short biography appear in *Nobel Lectures in Physics, 1942–1962* (1964). Bardeen is profiled twice in *The Nobel Prize Winners: Physics* (1989). A special issue of *Physics Today* (Apr. 1992) details Bardeen's life and work. Obituaries are in the *New York Times*, *Boston Globe*, and *Los Angeles Times* (all 31 Jan. 1991). An oral history transcript, "Reminiscences of John Bardeen" (1963), is at the Oral History Collection at Columbia University.

VICTORIA TAMBORRINO

BARNETT, Marguerite Ross (*b.* 22 May 1942 in Charlottesville, Virginia; *d.* 26 February 1992 in Wailuku, Hawaii), political scientist and educator; the first African-American woman to become the president of a major university.

Barnett, the only child of Dewey Ross Barnett and Mary Douglass, grew up in Buffalo, New York, and graduated

Marguerite Ross Barnett. AP/WIDE WORLD PHOTOS

from Bennett High School in 1959. She earned a B.A. degree in political science from Antioch College in 1964 and subsequently pursued graduate studies at the University of Chicago, where she was awarded M.A. and Ph.D. degrees in political science in 1966 and 1972, respectively.

As a graduate student, Barnett's academic interests centered on Indian politics. With financial support from two University of Chicago sponsors (the Committee on Southern Asian Studies and the Committee on Comparative Politics), as well as the Princeton University Fund for Research in the Humanities and Social Sciences, she conducted research in India between 1967 and 1969 for her doctoral dissertation. This study of ethnic and cultural pluralism in the modern Indian state of Tamil Nadu later became the foundation for Barnett's highly acclaimed book, *The Politics of Cultural Nationalism in South India* (1976), which received the American Political Science Association's top book prize in 1981.

After graduate school Barnett became an educator and held many teaching positions throughout her distinguished career. She began as a lecturer at the University of Chicago in 1969 and joined the Princeton University faculty as an assistant professor in 1970. Barnett was the James Madison Bicentennial Preceptor at Princeton from 1974 to 1976 and then taught at Howard University, where she chaired the Department of Political Science between 1977 and 1980. In 1980, while still at Howard, Barnett became codirector of the Ethnic Heritage Project: Study of an Historic Black Community, Gum Springs, Virginia, funded by the U.S. Department of Education.

From August 1980 to August 1983 Barnett was a member of the faculty at Columbia University in New York City, serving as professor of politics and education, professor of political science, and director of the Institute for Urban and Minority Education. In 1982 she became the coprincipal investigator on the Constitution and American Culture and the Training Program for Special Project Directors, sponsored by the National Endowment for the Humanities.

After years in the classroom, Barnett's interests turned to university administration, the area in which she would establish her place in American history. In 1983 she was appointed vice chancellor for academic affairs at City University of New York (CUNY), a twenty-one college system of 180,000 students. During her tenure at CUNY, she established a program to assist disadvantaged high school students in their transition from high school to college. In 1986 she was named chancellor and professor of political science at the University of Missouri at St. Louis. There she established numerous new degree programs, oversaw an 18-percent increase in enrollment, and made a significant contribution to the fiscal well-being of the university by doubling federal grant monies and raising more than $9 million in new donations. Additionally, she implemented the transition program for disadvantaged students that she had so successfully developed at CUNY.

Barnett left the University of Missouri at St. Louis in 1990 to become the president of the University of Houston, a post she held for one and one-half years until her death in 1992. Her appointment at that institution was groundbreaking, as she became the first African American woman to head a major American research university. Barnett arrived at the University of Houston, which she considered to be on the "cusp of greatness," with innovative changes in mind. Her agenda focused on the leading role she believed public urban universities should play in addressing a wide range of economic and social issues, from homelessness to environmental quality to space exploration.

Shortly after Barnett's arrival at the university, she established the Texas Center for University-School Partnership, a cooperative venture among business, education, and community leaders to study and promote school reform. Barnett also instituted her outreach program for underprivileged students, to become known at the University of Houston as the Bridge Program. This endeavor was

awarded the Anderson Medal from the American Council on Education as the outstanding public school initiative in the United States in 1991. Barnett's other accomplishments at the University of Houston during her brief tenure included the creation of the Texas Center for Environmental Studies, the recruitment of nationally prominent faculty members, and a fund-raising campaign that generated more than $150 million for the university.

Recognized as a scholar in the field of political science and a leader in the field of education, Barnett pursued research and writing throughout her career. She is the author or editor of six books on contemporary black politics, education policy, and Indian politics, as well as dozens of articles.

Barnett served on numerous boards and commissions, including the President's Commission on Environmental Quality, Educational Testing Service, Council on Foreign Relations, Overseas Development Council, Student Loan Marketing Association, American Council on Education, Committee on Economic Development, Monsanto Company, Houston Grand Opera, and Houston Symphony.

Barnett had one child by a marriage (18 December 1962) to Stephen A. Barnett. That marriage ended in divorce. On 30 June 1980 Barnett married Walter Eugene King, a former member of the parliament of Bermuda and a former professional golfer. In November 1991 Barnett took a medical leave of absence from the University of Houston to seek treatment for a neuroendocrinological disorder. She died on 26 February 1992 in Wailuku, Hawaii, of a blood disorder involving hypoglycemia with metastatic cancer.

Described as an "animated woman whose pace exhausted even her most energetic colleagues," Marguerite Ross Barnett, political scientist, educator, and administrator, was a woman of many "firsts." She was the first female and the first African American to head the University of Houston and the first black woman to lead a major research university. These accomplishments, however, were not as significant to her as was her agenda at the University of Houston and the role she believed research universities must play as they move into the twenty-first century—that of "helping society solve its key conundrums . . . in the same way land-grant institutions helped solve the problems of the 19th century."

★

The collection of Barnett's personal papers is housed in the M. D. Anderson Library, Department of Special Collections and Archives, University of Houston. While no full-scale biography of Barnett exists, her life is detailed in several biographical encyclopedia essays. The most notable are Jessie Carney Smith, ed., *Notable Black American Women* (1992); Darlene Clark Hine, ed., *Black Women in America: An Historical Encyclopedia* (vol. 1, 1993); and Jessie Carney Smith, ed., *Epic Lives: One Hundred Black*

Women Who Made a Difference (1993). Katherine S. Mangan, "President Sees University of Houston on 'the Cusp of Greatness,'" *Chronicle of Higher Education* 37, issue 25 (6 Mar. 1991): A3, focuses on Barnett's position at the University of Houston. An obituary is in the *New York Times* (27 Feb. 1992).

PAMELA W. BELLOWS

BARRETT, William Christopher (*b.* 30 December 1913 in New York City; *d.* 8 September 1992 in Tarrytown, New York), philosopher, cultural historian, and educator who brought existentialism into the main current of American intellectual life in the late 1940s and later, through his books and teaching, instructed two generations in modern philosophy, political thought, and twentieth-century literary and artistic experiment.

Son of John Patrick Barrett, a grocer, and Delia Connolly, a cook, Barrett was the youngest of four children raised in the Catholic faith. He grew up in the borough of Queens, attended public high school in Long Island City, and showed an early interest in the classics, particularly Aristotle. At the City College of New York he caught the Marxist wave of the early Great Depression years and that influence made him at home with the New York intellectuals later in the decade. After receiving his bachelor's degree in 1933 he continued his education at Columbia University

William Barrett, 1964. AP/WIDE WORLD PHOTOS

in New York, spent 1936 on a fellowship at the University of Chicago, and then earned his Ph.D. at Columbia with a dissertation on Greek philosophy in 1938.

In 1937 he met the legendary poet and critic Delmore Schwartz, who soon drew him into the circle of *Partisan Review* writers that included Phillip Rahv, Lionel Trilling, and Mary McCarthy. A Gentile in the predominantly Jewish world of Marxist intellectuals, Barrett enjoyed the curious position of an insider who was outside. Yet he was never quite committed to the rough-and-tumble of politics and personalities in New York literary journalism and pursued a career in teaching, first at the University of Illinois at Urbana from 1938 to 1940 and then at Brown University in Providence, Rhode Island, from 1940 to 1942. At Brown he met and married Juliet Bigney, a secretary working at Pembroke College; their marriage lasted from 1941 until her death in 1979 and produced two children. Barrett spent the early World War II years with the Office of Strategic Services, and in 1944–1945 served with the State Department as vice consul in Rome. Once back in the United States, he resumed his friendships in New York, wrote on postwar Italy for *Partisan Review* under the pseudonym of Moses Brown, was named an editor of the magazine in 1946, and held a Rockefeller Foundation fellowship during 1946–1947.

Barrett's *Partisan Review* years, 1946–1953, saw the emergence of two strong themes in his thought: the focus on existentialism, including its roots and permanent importance in world philosophy, and the battle with totalitarianism, especially in its postwar Communist form. Barrett's famous exposition of the "new" movement called existentialism came out in the magazine in 1947; during the same period his anti-Stalinist editorials argued the democratic leftist point of view. In 1952 Barrett led the International Seminar at Harvard, an enterprise geared to demonstrating the vigor of the anticommunist American intellectual. Vaguely disaffected with *Partisan*'s turn against anticommunism after Stalin's death, Barrett incorporated a teaching position into his workaday life before leaving *Partisan Review* for good in 1953. He took a position at New York University that lasted from 1950 to 1979, then taught at the United States Military Academy in upstate New York for two years, and then at Pace University in New York City as Distinguished Professor of Philosophy from 1982 to 1992.

Irrational Man, published in 1958, was Barrett's first major work. An exploration of thinkers and writers who revolted against abstraction and scientific positivism, the book is a close reflection on the meaning of being as expounded by Søren Kierkegaard, Martin Heidegger, and Friedrich Nietzsche. Boldly at odds with reductive analytic philosophy, Barrett championed the often poetic exploration of man's nature; in so doing he also provided concise and exceptionally lucid accounts of whole bodies of protoexistentialist thought. During the 1960s Barrett pursued his literary career as reviewer for the *Atlantic* and later as the magazine's columnist in "Reader's Choice."

His next major book, *Time of Need* (1972), surveyed the artistic and fictional dimensions of the existentialist phenomenon, studying figures such as Alberto Giacometti and Pablo Picasso, Samuel Beckett and William Faulkner. The analysis of novels, he argued, allowed him access to the elemental and primal world that, as Georg Wilhelm Friedrich Hegel had argued, was taking place behind the backs of mere reporters. Fiction for Barrett was a form of existential history, not the vague realm of fancifulness dismissed by analytic philosophers.

The Illusion of Technique: A Search for Meaning in a Technological Civilization, published in 1978, was a different kind of book—more polemical and explicitly opposed to the direction of modern civilization. Much of the material first appeared in the neoconservative magazine *Commentary,* a fact that registered Barrett's abandonment of his youthful leftism and his return to the Catholic Church. Barrett's purpose was to trace the development of three philosophers—Ludwig Wittgenstein, Heidegger, and William James—who moved beyond the truths of logic and science and explored being. Metaphysical when others were pragmatic or ideological, Barrett was a philosopher out of his time. He attacked the instrumentalism of the late twentieth century and its emphasis on method at the expense of value.

Barrett's 1982 memoir, *The Truants: Adventures Among the Intellectuals,* was his own mental history as well as the story of a generation of writers and thinkers. Without any private revelation of the confessional sort, he manages to show the temperament and soul of a thinker grappling with intense conflicts between human feeling and principle. Central to the book is Barrett's early devotion to Schwartz—a philosopher's devotion to a mostly demented poet. Other attractions, and eventual recoils, involve the nihilistic Rahv and the all-too-rational Trilling. The characters are "truants," escapees from essential truths who take refuge in their abstract formulations—Marxism, Freudianism—and neglect the sources of life and spiritual discovery. Barrett describes the great critic Edmund Wilson as unable to see anything in Rome other than his own ideas. Along with the truancy there was also the aggression and destructiveness of this class of intellectuals: their infighting, battling over leftist politics, and brilliance wasted on polemics. In an elegiac mood—recalling his illusions about politics, especially—Barrett creates a very spiritual account of a group of secular thinkers and critics.

The 1970s and early 1980s were a time of honors, including a Guggenheim Fellowship in 1975, a National Endowment for the Humanities senior fellowship in 1976, and a Mellon Fellowship in 1981. Barrett's last book, *The Death of the Soul: From Descartes to the Computer* (1986), takes the spiritual measure of thinkers from the seventeenth to the twentieth century, finds much of empiricism dangerous to the soul of man, evaluates Immanuel Kant's awareness of moral states beyond our "finite station," and analyzes the soul-denying elements in Jean-Paul Sartre and postmodern deconstruction. The book is an accessible and elegant study of the challenges to metaphysics in the modern world. Barrett died in suburban Tarrytown, his home since 1962, of esophageal cancer. He is buried in Sleepy Hollow Cemetery in Tarrytown.

Barrett was a lifelong existentialist, even when that philosophy was crowded off the stage by the politics of the New Left, deconstruction, feminism, and new versions of pragmatism and positivism. Believing that philosophy was coextensive with literature and art and that religious impulses were a vital component of the self, he had little appeal for academic specialists. Yet his combination of clear reasoning and recognition of the mysteries of being make him an important guide to modern philosophy.

★

Barrett's miscellaneous papers are held at the time of this writing by his daughter, Susan Barrett, but are eventually to be archived at the Library of Congress. Hilton Kramer's review of the book *The Truants* shows how it is "a permanent part of our literature," *New York Times Book Review* (7 Feb. 1982). Mark Shechner's review of the book in *Nation* (27 Feb. 1982) gives useful opinions about Barrett's place among the New York intellectuals. James Atlas gives a sharply focused short analysis of *The Illusion of Technique* in *Time* (4 Sept. 1978). An obituary is in the *New York Times* (10 Sept. 1992).

DAVID CASTRONOVO

BARTHOLOMEW, Frederick Llewellyn ("Freddie")
(*b.* 12 February 1924 in London, England; *d.* 22 January 1992 in Sarasota, Florida), famed motion picture child actor of the 1930s, especially remembered for *David Copperfield* (1935), *Little Lord Fauntleroy* (1936), and *Captains Courageous* (1937).

Bartholomew was one of three children born to Cecil Llewellyn Bartholomew, a wounded veteran of World War I and minor civil servant, and Lillian May Bartholomew, a homemaker. At the age of three, Bartholomew was sent to live with his paternal grandparents in Warminster, England, and was placed under the immediate care of his father's sister, Myllicent Mary Bartholomew, or "Aunt Cissie." Speaking with impressive diction at about the age of three, Bartholomew reputedly made "stage" appearances and gave recitations at church-related gatherings and received early dramatic training with Italia Conti (an actress in England who from 1911 developed expertise in training young

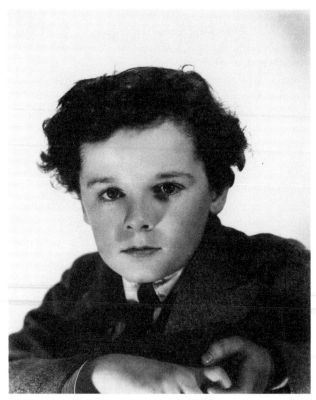

Freddie Bartholomew. THE KOBAL COLLECTION

children as actors). He went on to appear in several British films, including *Fascination* (1931) and *Lily Christine* (1932). His aunt, looking ahead to a film career for him, took him to New York City in 1934 and arranged for a Hollywood representative to present them to the movie executive David O. Selznick at the Metro-Goldwyn-Mayer (MGM) studios in Culver City, California. At that time Selznick was searching among ten thousand applicants for the perfect boy to play young David Copperfield for his film production of Charles Dickens's great novel. (Another version of this story says that Bartholomew was discovered by Selznick and the MGM director George Cukor in England.)

Selznick immediately signed Bartholomew for *David Copperfield* (1935) and gave him a seven-year contract with MGM at a starting salary of $175 dollars a week, soon to reach $500. The studio was forced to slow down its original shooting schedule to comply with laws that limited child actors to four hours of studio work a day. On the set of *David Copperfield,* Bartholomew was only allowed to associate with his guardian (Aunt Myllicent), a state-appointed welfare worker, and a tutor because it was feared that a child of his young age would quickly lose his accent if he came in contact with non-English children. In the successful motion picture, which had a cast that included Basil Rathbone, W. C. Fields, Lionel Barrymore, and Edna May Oliver, Bartholomew became a "child star." Barthol-

omew's weekly salary increased to $1,000 after his appearance as Sergei, the only child in a loveless marriage between Greta Garbo and Rathbone in MGM's stunning rendering of the Russian novelist Leo Tolstoy's *Anna Karenina* (1935). The role of the loving, curly-haired Sergei, whose first appearance in the film showed him tiptoeing near his mother with a pledge to protect her always, intensified the tragic love story.

Bartholomew played the lead in Sir James Barrie's *Peter Pan* in his only performance on Cecil B. DeMille's *Lux Radio Theatre* (23 February 1936). His next film was *Professional Soldier* (1936), in which he played a young king who befriends the soldier of fortune sent to kidnap him. He then appeared as Ceddie in *Little Lord Fauntleroy* (1936) as the epitome of the noble-minded young boy, devoted to his mother, docile, and obedient—in sharp contrast to Mickey Rooney's athletic, street-smart character. This Selznick International Pictures production cost $600,000 to make but grossed $1.7 million. Another film, *The Devil Is a Sissy* (1936) focused on the three young male child stars best known at that time—Bartholomew, Rooney, and Jackie Cooper—who together in one film tried to rival the box-office potency of Hollywood's top child actress, Shirley Temple. Bartholomew soon was loaned to Twentieth Century–Fox to play the youthful Jonathan Blake (played as an adult by Tyrone Power) in *Lloyd's of London* (1936). Bartholomew's next motion picture was *Captains Courageous* (1937), from the novel by the British writer Rudyard Kipling. Bartholomew's role of Harvey is often considered his best performance. The film starred Spencer Tracy, who won an Academy Award for best actor for his performance in it as Manuel, a Portuguese fisherman.

Perhaps because of Batholomew's fame and his salary ($2,500 a week after *Captains Courageous*), his personal life underwent a period of emotional stress as his parents took legal action to become, along with Bartholomew's two teenage sisters, beneficiaries of his Hollywood success and to challenge his aunt's guardianship rights. In late October 1935, a California court had approved Aunt Myllicent as Bartholomew's guardian. In April of 1936, Bartholomew's mother appeared in court in California to file a petition to nullify the aunt's guardianship, but a superior court judge denied that petition. Attorneys for both sides met to offer compromise measures, which were approved by the judge in June. According to their agreement, some of Bartholomew's money would be reserved for him in a trust fund; a 10 percent portion would be paid out to his father and 5 percent portions to each of his two sisters; and the rest was directed toward supporting Aunt Myllicent and Bartholomew.

In 1937 Aunt Myllicent filed suit to challenge the validity of her nephew's contract with MGM. In a settlement agreement, MGM offered a new contract at $2,000 a week for forty weeks of film work in addition to $300 a week for six weeks of personal appearances. But Bartholomew's family troubles persisted. In late 1937, his parents presented another unsuccessful court challenge to Aunt Myllicent's authority as guardian. The court gave Aunt Myllicent complete control over Bartholomew's finances and investments. Without counsel, on 19 June 1939 his parents filed a $1 million suit against Aunt Myllicent and their own former attorney for compensation for Bartholomew's earnings and lost companionship. His sisters also initiated their own lawsuit in September 1939. In late September 1939 Bartholomew sought recourse through the courts, requesting that his parents, sisters, and other relatives stop suing him; by that time he had already paid $83,000 in legal fees.

Three films released in 1938 highlighted Bartholomew in his last starring roles: *Kidnapped,* a well-received rendering of Robert Louis Stevenson's adventure; *Lord Jeff,* in which Bartholomew swindles jewels until sent to a mariners' academy and is reformed by Mickey Rooney and others; and the musical *Listen, Darling,* where his teenage interest in Judy Garland helps her find a suitable prospect. In his two 1939 releases, Bartholomew played secondary roles to Jackie Cooper: in *Spirit of Culver,* filmed in part at Culver Military Academy in Indiana, Bartholomew still retains a rather elitist, helping role; but in *Two Bright Boys,* the opportunism of his on-screen father slowly evolves into humanitarian concerns. He did make his Broadway debut as a vaudeville headliner (13 October 1938) at the Loew's State Theatre for one week. Having grown to six feet tall, Bartholomew finished his teens with two films released in 1940, *The Swiss Family Robinson* and *Tom Brown's School Days,* and one film each in 1941 and 1942, *Naval Academy* and *Cadets on Parade,* respectively. His final MGM contract film was *A Yank at Eton* (1942). *Junior Army* (1943) and *The Town Went Wild* (1945) were his final films during the war years. Bartholomew became a U.S. citizen in 1943. He enlisted in the Army Air Forces on 13 January 1943 and was assigned to maintenance work on B-17 bombers in the United States. While he was at the Amarillo Army Air Field in Amarillo, Texas, an old back injury became so aggravating that extensive hospitalization was required. He received a medical discharge from the military in January 1944 as a private first class. After his discharge, Bartholomew returned to acting; he started with summer stock and acted with and directed small theater groups in California. He returned to Hollywood to appear as himself in *Sepia Cinderella* in 1947.

On 25 April 1946 Bartholomew married Maely Daniele, the publicity director of his theater group; they had no children and divorced in 1953. Later that year he married Aileen Paul, star of Manhattan television's *New York Cook* show; they had two children. He later divorced Aileen and

married Elizabeth Grabill. In 1949 Bartholomew hosted an afternoon film presentation on New York City television and soon became the associate station director. He also began working as a director and producer of videos and commercial advertisements. In 1951 he appeared as a priest in a final comedy film, *St. Benny the Dip.* In 1954, now known in the business world as "Frederick C. Bartholomew," he joined Benton & Bowles, a leading advertising agency; on 16 November he became the vice president of its radio and television staff. Among the various Hollywood and network television accounts handled under his immediate attention was the *Andy Griffith Show*; he served as one of the executive producers of *As the World Turns* and *Search for Tomorrow,* and as one of the directors of *Edge of Night.* He rarely granted interviews, though he did appear as a commentator in the documentary *MGM: When the Lion Roars* (1992). In 1989, on the recommendation of his doctor, Bartholomew moved from Long Beach Island, New Jersey, to Bradenton, Florida. He died of emphysema at Sarasota Memorial Hospital and was cremated.

Bartholomew will be remembered as one of the handful of outstanding child actors from the 1930s who projected such unique personalities in film classics that their names and faces will never be forgotten. For years and even decades after his initial and most popular film work, Bartholomew epitomized the kind-hearted little gentleman who was stylishly neat in his dress and well versed in the best of manners and who spoke in the most beautifully precise English. Generally, the hardships of the young characters that he played were overcome in uplifting, redemptive endings. Yet his own life, particularly the legal clashes over his fortune and affections, resolved itself in a heartrending manner. People who met him later in life immediately commented upon his kindness and joviality, as captured in photographs of those later years. Still, the adult "Frederick C. Bartholomew" distanced himself from the fame and pain of his childhood.

★

The D'Arcy Masius Benton & Bowles Archives, 1929–1989, Rare Book, Manuscript, and Special Collections Library at Duke University in Durham, North Carolina, contain archives of the advertising agency where Bartholomew worked. For an excellent biographical summary, see David Shipman, *The Great Men Stars: The Golden Years* (1979). There is a good article in James Robert Parish and Ronald L. Bowers, *The MGM Stock Company: The Golden Era* (1973). See also the entry in David Thomson, *A Biographical Dictionary of Film* (3d ed., 1994). For information about articles in the Hollywood journals, see Mel Schuster, *Motion Picture Performers: A Bibliography of Magazine and Periodical Articles, 1900–1969* (1971), and *Supplement No. 1, 1970–1974* (1976). Most of the available information about Bartholomew, especially his legal difficulties, can be found in the *New York Times* (27 Oct.

1935; 9, 19, 23 Apr. 1936; 26 May 1936; 5, 9, 26 June 1936; 4 Apr. 1937; 2 Nov. 1937; 10 Dec. 1937; 12 Feb. 1938; 22 Nov. 1938; 17 Jan. 1939; 20 June 1939; 6, 28 Sept. 1939). Articles in the *New York Times* that include discussion of Bartholomew in relation to the cluster of other child actors of the time are Eunice Fuller Barnard, "Children of Hollywood's Gold Rush: A New Get-Rich-Quick Scheme Dazzles Their Parents, But Prizes Are Won by the Few" (4 Oct. 1936), and "What Price Glory for Screen Starlets? Their Hollywood Work-Routine Is Exacting and There Are Long School Hours Also" (11 Oct. 1936); and Douglas W. Churchill, "Life of the Child Star: A Hollywood Fairy Tale" (29 May 1938). An appreciation is in the London *Times* (1 Feb. 1992). Obituaries are in the *New York Times* (24 Jan. 1992), London *Times* (25 Jan. 1992), and *Variety* (27 Jan. 1992).

MADELINE SAPIENZA

BAUZÁ, Mario   (*b.* 28 April 1911 in Havana, Cuba; *d.* 11 July 1993 in New York City), musician who was essential to the incorporation of Caribbean African and Caribbean Hispanic rhythms and melodies into jazz.

Mario Bauzá was one of six children born to Hilario and Dolores Bauzá, but Mario was raised through nearly all of his childhood by his godparents, Arturo Andrade and Sofia Dominguez Andrade. The Andrades were members of an influential Havana family, Vieta-Placencia, and were materially quite secure. Arturo Andrade was a music teacher and realized that young Mario had an innate gift for melody and rhythm. As part of Andrade's disciplined parenting style, four-year-old Mario received weekly music lessons in solfege (melody and rhythm skills) with Modesto Fraga, conductor of the Havana Municipal Band. During that time, Mario began to play the oboe, which he did not much enjoy, saying that it "sounded Chinese" to him.

After quitting the oboe, Mario's godfather provided the boy with a specially sized clarinet for Mario's seven-year-old hands in order to study the clarinet with Gabriel Siam. For the next eight years, Mario studied at the Havana Conservatory of Music, winning a scholarship to La Scala in Italy in his final year. Mario declined the scholarship, refusing to go to Europe. He felt that European orchestral studies were not appropriate to Afro-Cuban musicians. Instead, at the age of fifteen, he became one of three clarinetists in the Havana Symphony Orchestra.

Mario also performed with many popular dance bands in Cuba. He performed in New York City for one month in 1926, with the Orquesta Antonio Maria Romeu. During that trip he heard the dynamic jazz ensembles of Fletcher Henderson and Charles Johnson as well as the Paul Whiteman Orchestra. He became fascinated by the saxophone sections in these early swing bands and bought an alto sax in New York and taught himself to play it. Back in Cuba, Bauzá began incorporating some of the jazz he had heard

Mario Bauzá, 1993. AP/WIDE WORLD PHOTOS

in New York into the music of Cuban bands. He dreamed of synthesizing Afro-American jazz and Afro-Cuban dance music, envisioning a new music that had the rich harmonies and spontaneities of jazz and the architectural rhythmic syncopations (*claves, cáscaras,* and *bombos*) and complex orchestral call-and-response patterns of his beloved Cuban dance music.

In 1930 Bauzá traveled again to New York, this time with the Orquesta Don Azpiazú, and began to introduce Cuban music to the New York jazz scene. He played with Noble Sissle's society orchestra. When Antonio Machin, a fellow Cuban musician, needed a replacement trumpet player for a recording session, Bauzá bought a $15 trumpet from a Fifty-ninth Street pawnshop and taught himself to play it in just two weeks. He modeled his trumpet playing after Louis Armstrong. His strong tone and rhythmic accuracy earned him a chair on many 1930s Cuban recordings in the United States. The jazz drummer and bandleader Chick Webb hired Bauzá as a section trumpeter in 1933 and within a year named him musical director of that historic group. A year later, Bauzá persuaded Webb to hire a then-unknown young singer named Ella Fitzgerald. After six years collaborating with Webb and Fitzgerald, he left to perform with the Don Redman and Fletcher Henderson jazz orchestras, helping with musical arrangements and unerringly hiring the best young players.

Bauzá returned to Cuba briefly in 1936 to marry his childhood sweetheart, Stella (Estela) Grillo. They returned to the United States and a year later sent for Stella's brother and fellow musician, Frank Raúl Grillo, known to all as "Machito." The visionary collaborations of Bauzá and Machito would soon change the American musical scene.

By 1938 Bauzá was performing with the Cab Calloway Orchestra at the Cotton Club in New York City. At a jam session, he heard a young trumpet player named John Birks Gillespie (though everybody called him "Dizzy") and saw to it that Calloway hired this future giant of jazz. Bauzá resigned from Calloway's band in 1940 and formed the Afro-Cubans with Machito. After several months of rehearsal, the band, a group of Latin and black musicians who played authentic Cuban rhythms in the big-band style, debuted at the Park Plaza, though many New York booking agents objected to the directness of the term "Afro-Cuban."

Apparently, the crowds did not mind so much. For the next seven years, the band played at Harlem clubs and the Concord Hotel in the Catskills, recorded nearly fifty singles (the first in 1941 for Decca Records), and eventually helped open the Palladium Ballroom, "the home of the mambo." The band flourished through Bauzá's skills at orchestration, collaboration, band management, and spectacle. Cuban and Puerto Rican legends like Noro Morales. Marcellino Guerra, Chano Pozo, Tito Puente, and Bobby Rodriguez often teamed up with the jazz greats Charlie Parker, Dizzy Gillespie, Buddy Rich, Herbie Mann, and Cannonball Adderley.

For thirty-five years, the Afro-Cubans worked constantly and served as a proving ground for all the talented players Bauzá hired. His arrangements were most instrumental to the group's success, as were Machito's singing and conducting. The Afro-Cubans opened for Thelonious Monk at the Hollywood Bowl and performed on the recording executive Norman Granz's album *Jazz at the Philharmonic*. As the years passed, Bauzá put aside the trumpet and concentrated on writing and orchestrating.

By 1975 Bauzá and Machito had gone their separate musical ways. Bauzá launched the Afro-Cuban Jazz Orchestra with the singer Graciela, another of Machito's sisters. The band took ten long years to find perfection. During this time, Stella Bauzá, his wife for forty-seven years, died. Though Mario and Stella never had children, Mario remained the proud uncle and godfather to an ever-expanding family.

Bauzá received the New York City Mayor's Award for Art and Culture in 1984. Two years later, he recorded, along with Graciela, the critically acclaimed album *Afro-Cuban Jazz*. Five more years of world tours ensued. In 1990 he married Lourdes Noboa. The following year, at the age of 80, Bauzá recorded the very first album on which he did not share credit or top billing, *Tanga*. Within two years, two more historic albums emerged, *My Time Is Now* and *944 Columbus*. Each was recognized as the work of a master craftsman. Six months after his last album's completion, Bauzá died at home, at the pinnacle of his writing success.

Without the pioneering artistry of Mario Bauzá, the history of Afro-Cuban music in the twentieth century would have been very different. Bauzá was essential to the early incorporation of Caribbean African and Caribbean Hispanic rhythms and melodies into jazz. He was equally essential to the incorporation of jazz harmonies and improvisation techniques into the mid-century Cuban society orchestra. Bauzá was the principal interlocutor between two previously isolated musical communities—New York jazz and Cuban dance music. The synthesis of these two styles in the 1940s was critical to the further expansion of bebop into what is called Afro-Cubop. This synthesis also paved the way for the later infusions of mambo, cha cha, samba, bossa nova, rock steady, reggae, and ska into North American dance music.

★

There is as yet no full-length study of Bauzá, but see John Tumpak, "Historical Impact of Webb and Bauzá," *Dancing USA* 15, no. 1 (Feb./Mar. 1997), and Michael Erlewine, ed., *All Music Guide to Jazz,* 2d ed. (1996). An obituary by Peter Watrous is in the *New York Times* (12 July 1993). Bauzá is interviewed in *Musica* (1984), a documentary film directed by John D. Wise tracing the history of Latin jazz in the United States from the 1940s to the 1970s.

JAMES McELWAINE

BECK, David (*b.* 16 June 1894 in Stockton, California; *d.* 26 December 1993 in Seattle, Washington), labor leader who served as president of the International Brotherhood of Teamsters from 1952 to 1957.

Beck was one of two children of Lemuel Beck, a carpet cleaner and part-time auctioneer, and Mary Tierney, a laundress. At the age of four Beck moved with his family to Seattle, which was to be his permanent home. Beck attended public schools only until the ninth grade, when grinding financial poverty forced him to seek full-time employment. Beck always valued education and remained a voracious reader throughout his life. He first worked a series of odd jobs and then found steady employment driving a laundry truck.

Employment as a driver led Beck to the unions, and in 1914 he began a forty-three-year career in the labor movement. He joined the International Brotherhood of Team-

Dave Beck, *c.* 1950s. © CORBIS

held its 1925 convention in Seattle. The Teamsters' president, Dan Tobin, was especially impressed by Beck. Tobin's chance to support Beck came quickly. Two Seattle businessmen who worked with Beck to rationalize competition in the laundry industry invited him to be a partner in their business. Rather than lose a promising leader, Tobin named Beck the West Coast organizer for the IBT.

With a broader official capacity, Beck used the Seattle Joint Council to establish statewide control in Washington State. He always defined Teamster jurisdiction broadly and used a top-down organizing strategy to unionize not only drivers but also freight handlers and warehouse workers. Once control was established in Washington, Beck led successful major organizing drives in British Columbia, Canada, and Oregon. Beck next turned his attention to California, where only the San Francisco Bay Area was well organized. Beck determined that the key to organizing California was to establish a strong Teamsters presence in the most notorious open shop city in the nation, Los Angeles. Throughout 1937 Beck used two innovative strategies to organize Los Angeles: he first organized over-the-road (long distance) drivers for the first time and then used this foundation to establish a withering secondary boycott that shut down almost all handling and transportation of freight in and out of Los Angeles. Capitulation by major businesses came quickly.

The California victory made Beck the unquestioned leader of organized labor on the West Coast. He solidified his power by setting up the West Coast Conference of Teamsters with himself as president. Through his Seattle offices, Beck now controlled Teamster locals in eleven western states. At first, IBT officers resisted this development, but they later warmed to the innovation because it provided much greater control over the locals and helped rationalize competition and regulate wages. Beck used his power in the 1940s to become a major community figure in Seattle, well known in business and civic organizations. In 1938 he was named to the University of Washington Board of Regents and served one term as president.

Beck's continued success on the West Coast led to his appointment as international vice president in 1940 and as executive vice president in 1947. The West Coast Conference became the model for the geographic IBT structure. His greater role within the IBT prepared him to be Tobin's successor. In 1952, when Tobin finally stepped down, Beck was elected president and remained in office until 1957. He was arguably the most powerful labor leader in America. Teamster membership had grown from 420,000 in 1939 to 1,100,000 in 1952 and to 1,600,000 when Beck left office. It was the largest and most successful union in the American Federation of Labor-Congress of Industrial Organization (AFL-CIO). Beck was also named to the executive council of the AFL and vice president in 1953; in 1955 he became vice president of the AFL-CIO.

sters (IBT) and quickly became active in union affairs. Beck volunteered for service in World War I in April 1918 and served as a machinist in the navy in Killingholme, England. While on leave in 1918, Beck married Dorothy Leschander; they had one child.

After being discharged from the navy in August 1919, Beck returned to Seattle and to his laundry route, but his primary focus soon became union activity. Throughout his career he remained consistent to a set of principles that emphasized business unionism. He was fond of saying that running a union was like running Boeing or Safeway. He was dedicated to the capitalist economic system and believed that unions should work with businessmen to rationalize competition. He wanted business to earn the highest possible profit, because he believed that workers would then earn higher wages. Beck thought that unions had no place in politics, and he was consistently and thoroughly antiradical. He used strikes only as a last resort and was a lifelong critic of unions that put politics or radical ideas ahead of bread-and-butter gains for the rank and file.

During the 1920s Beck was a fast-rising leader within the Seattle Teamsters Local 566. He served as secretary-treasurer and then president of his local and of the Seattle Teamsters Joint Council in 1925. As the decade closed, Beck was a major force within the Pacific Northwest labor movement. He was an indefatigable organizer and a powerful orator, and his successes began to attract the attention of IBT leadership. This interest culminated when the IBT

Teamster success, however, brought problems. Beck's ascension to the presidency coincided with the beginnings of labor union investigations conducted by Senator John McClellan's Select Committee on Improper Activities. Senator Robert F. Kennedy, who investigated Beck and other Teamster officers doggedly, staffed the committee. Kennedy learned that throughout his career Beck had become very wealthy through personal real estate investments, sometimes made with union funds. To procure property, Beck frequently borrowed large sums from the union and from companies with whom Beck negotiated contracts. Refusing to testify, Beck claimed Fifth Amendment privileges 117 times in three days. One outcome of this strategy was that Beck was removed from the AFL-CIO executive board. He was indicted on federal charges of income tax evasion and on state charges of grand larceny. These allegations, combined with the failing health of his wife, persuaded Beck to resign from the IBT presidency in 1957. Jimmy Hoffa replaced him.

Beck was convicted on both counts of the indictment and sentenced to five years in prison for each of the convictions. His wife died in 1961, and in June 1962 he began his prison term, which ended two and a half years later. In 1965 the governor of Washington pardoned him, and in 1975 President Gerald Ford did the same. Beck never returned to union activities, choosing instead to manage his finances very successfully and to address civic organizations. In 1967 he married his second wife, Helen, who died in 1977. Beck died in a Seattle hospital at the age of ninety-nine. He is buried in Seattle.

Beck dedicated his life to building a powerful union based on business principles. His strategies and organizational concepts redefined the IBT and played a major role in helping establish the Teamsters as the most powerful union in the United States. Partnership with business and a tight focus on wages and benefits guided his actions.

★

Beck has attracted little scholarly attention, principally because there is no central repository of his papers. John Dennis McCallum, *Dave Beck* (1978), is essentially a long interview. Donald Garnel, *The Rise of Teamster Power in the West* (1972), measures Beck's influence in the Pacific Northwest, and Charles Waite's published dissertation, *The Business of Unionism: Race, Politics, Capitalism and the West Coast Teamster, 1940–1952* (1996), explores the shortcomings of Beck's business union strategy. There is an obituary in the *New York Times* (28 Dec. 1993).

R. DAVID MYERS

BELL, James Thomas ("Cool Papa") (*b.* 17 May 1901 in Starkville, Mississippi; *d.* 7 March 1991 in St. Louis, Missouri), fabled Negro League outfielder widely considered the fastest man ever to play professional baseball.

Bell and his seven siblings were raised on a farm about two miles from Starkville, a farming community of 2,700 on the outskirts of the Mississippi blues country. (It was around the time of Bell's birth that white anthropologists "discovered" the Delta Blues in rural Mississippi.) Bell's father, Jonas Bell, sharecropped cotton and corn. His mother, Mary Nichols (who was three-eighths Native American), did odd jobs, including taking in laundry. Bell attended Starkville's one-room elementary school for blacks but left school in the seventh grade.

In 1920 Bell joined the many African Americans escaping the impoverished South for urban centers of the Midwest, bringing their music and their baseball with them. Bell moved to St. Louis because, he later said, "you could just live better and make more money." Four of his older brothers already lived in St. Louis, where they played for a black semiprofessional team, the Compton Hill Cubs, on Sundays and holidays. Soon the wiry Bell (who was five feet, eleven inches tall and weighed 145 pounds) was playing for the team too as a knuckleball pitcher while also earning a respectable $21.20 per week laboring at the Independent Packing Company and attending Sumner Evening School (from which he probably did not graduate) at night. The team disbanded in August 1921, and in 1922 Bell joined another semiprofessional team, the East St. Louis Cubs, making $20 per week for pitching on Sundays. On 3 May 1922 he signed with the St. Louis Stars, a major

James "Cool Papa" Bell, 1990. AP/WIDE WORLD PHOTOS

power in the Negro National League, for $90 a month. He reportedly earned his famous nickname as a rookie with the Stars when he calmly struck out the feared slugger Oscar Charleston in a high-pressure situation. The players began calling him "Cool," which manager Bill Gatewood later modified to "Cool Papa." Bell pitched and played the outfield occasionally until 1924, when, at Gatewood's urging, he made two changes that would be crucial to his later success: he began playing center field exclusively, and he learned to switch hit. (Although a left-handed thrower, Bell had always batted right-handed.) Bell eventually became a defensive star in center field, known for playing unusually shallow because his speed enabled him to reach most balls hit over his head.

Soon after switching positions, Bell's base running brought him renown as the fastest player in baseball. Because Negro League teams neither played traditional schedules nor kept accurate statistics, the exploits of their players survive mostly in anecdotal tales of dubious veracity. The stories about Bell's blazing speed are among the most colorful. He was said to have once been hit by his own batted ball as he slid into second base. Another tale, the legendary pitcher Satchel Paige's favorite, said Bell was so fast he could shut out the lights and get into bed before the room got dark. Bell himself claimed to have stolen 175 bases in 200 games during the 1933 season. Such exaggerations notwithstanding, there is ample evidence to document Bell's disruptiveness on the base paths. In the 1934 East-West all-star game, he drew a leadoff walk in the eighth inning, then stole second and scored on a weak hit for the only run in a 1–0 victory. Many years later, on 24 October 1948, the forty-seven-year-old Bell scored from first base on a sacrifice bunt in an exhibition game against a major league all-star team.

Bell played ten seasons with the Stars, which by the late 1920s had become the premier franchise in the Negro National League. Led by the trio of Bell, shortstop Willie Wells (Bell's closest friend), and first baseman Mule Suttles, St. Louis won championships in 1929 and 1930. The Stars disbanded in 1931 along with the Negro National League, however, and Bell spent the rest of his career moving from team to team in the often financially unstable Negro Leagues. From 1933 to 1938 he played for the Pittsburgh Crawfords, a conglomeration of superstars often considered to be the greatest black team ever. In addition to Bell, the team's lineup included Josh Gibson at catcher, playing manager Oscar Charleston at first base, Judy Johnson at third base, and pitcher Satchel Paige. In 1943 Bell joined the Homestead Grays and helped them to three consecutive championships.

On 8 September 1928, Bell married Clara Belle Thompson. They honeymooned in Cuba, where Bell had signed a contract to play winter ball. On 3 January 1929 he became the first player in Cuban League history to hit three *jonrones* (home runs) in one game. He led the league in both homers and stolen bases that season, the first of four winters he spent in Cuba. Latin America was a popular destination for many African American players, who were drawn to the Caribbean leagues by warm weather, high salaries, and a relative lack of racism. Bell played so often in Latin America that he eventually became fluent in Spanish. In 1937 Bell and other Negro League stars were lured to the Dominican Republic by exorbitant salary offers from the dictator Rafael Trujillo, who used his personal baseball team as a publicity tool to preserve his political power. From 1938 to 1941 Bell also played in the Mexican League, where he earned his highest salary of $450 a month.

In 1948 Bell became playing manager of a Kansas City Monarchs farm team, where his charges included the young shortstop Ernie Banks. In 1951, when Bell was fifty years old, the St. Louis Browns offered him a major league contract, but Bell declined, saying he was too old to play his best. He retired from baseball later that year, after playing for twenty-nine summers and twenty-one winters.

Talented as he was, baseball did not make Bell rich. Left without a pension, he immediately found work as a custodian at City Hall in St. Louis. He was eventually promoted to night watchman there, a job he held until his retirement in April 1973. On 12 August 1974 Bell received baseball's highest honor when he was inducted into the National Baseball Hall of Fame in Cooperstown, New York. He was the fifth Negro League star to be elected to the Hall, where his Stars uniform, and his sunglasses, remain on permanent display. In the ensuing years Bell lived on Social Security, his small pension from the city of St. Louis, and a stipend from the baseball commissioner's office. He and Clara continued to reside in a modest home on St. Louis's Dickson Avenue, which was renamed James "Cool Papa" Bell Avenue in 1987.

On 20 January 1991, after sixty-two years of marriage, Clara Bell died. A month later Bell was hospitalized after a heart attack, and he died in St. Louis on 7 March 1991. He was survived by their only child, Connie Bell Brooks, and was buried at St. Peter's Cemetery in St. Louis. His will specified that he have twelve pallbearers at his funeral, six black and six white.

Bell impressed most who met him as a gentle, dignified, and soft-spoken man, and he left behind a legacy of unparalleled achievement on the baseball diamond. Given the lack of statistics, the degree of Bell's greatness will likely always be debated. But he was clearly one of the most important figures to emerge from baseball's Negro Leagues. The anecdotal stories that contributed so much to Bell's legend are an essential part of African American oral tradition and a grim reminder that segregation caused a talent so great to be appreciated by so few. "So many people say

I was born too early," Bell said shortly before his death. "But that's not true. They opened the doors too late."

★

No full-length biography of Bell exists, and factual information about him is hard to come by. The best source is the collection of research files maintained by the National Baseball Hall of Fame Library, which contain newspaper articles, correspondence, interviews, and the scrapbook Bell kept of his playing career. Two other essential works of oral history contain chapters on him: John Holway, *Voices from the Great Black Baseball Leagues* (1975), and Donald Honig, *Baseball When the Grass Was Real: Baseball from the Twenties to the Forties Told by the Men Who Played It* (1975). The *Negro Leagues Book* (1994), edited by Dick Clark and Larry Lester, is the definitive source for information on the black teams' rosters and statistics. An obituary is in the *New York Times* (9 Mar. 1991). An extensive interview with Bell was done by the Oral History Program of the University of Missouri-St. Louis in 1971.

ERIC E. ENDERS

BELLAMY, Ralph Rexford (*b.* 17 June 1904 in Chicago, Illinois; *d.* 29 November 1991 in Santa Monica, California), versatile leading man of stage, screen, radio, and television famed for his realistic portrayal of President Franklin D. Roosevelt in the Dore Schary play *Sunrise at Campobello* (1958) and the 1960 film of the same name.

Ralph Bellamy, 1971. THE KOBAL COLLECTION

Bellamy was one of two children born to advertising executive Charles Rexford Bellamy and homemaker Lilla Smith. Bellamy graduated from New Trier High School in the Chicago suburb of Winnetka, Illinois, in 1922. He chose not to follow in his father's footsteps and at the age of eighteen set out on a career as an actor that would last for more than six decades. For two years Bellamy toured in the Chautauqua circuit and in repertory and stock companies in the Midwest, working backstage as well as onstage in a wide variety of roles. In 1924 at the age of twenty, he tried his luck on Broadway but failed to find a job, instead returning to his Midwest theatrical adventures. With 400 roles in his background, he invaded New York again in 1930 to join his friend and fellow actor Melvyn Douglas, landing a part in Lynn Riggs's *Roadside,* a play that lasted only eleven performances.

Nevertheless, this was long enough for him to be spotted by a talent scout for the Hollywood producer Nicholas Schenck, who signed him to a United Artists contract. Schenck, however, was not impressed by the tall, husky, twenty-six-year-old actor and lent him to MGM for his Hollywood debut in *The Secret Six* (1931), featuring superstars Jean Harlow, Clark Gable, and Wallace Beery. This was followed by a part in *West of Broadway* (1931), starring John Gilbert.

The slow-starter from Illinois was now off to the races.

In 1931 he left Schenck to freelance and worked at Fox Studios for a year, then at Columbia Pictures for five years. Most of his films during this period were quickly shot and run-of-the-mill. However, in 1937 Bellamy was cast by the director Leo McCarey to play a likeable Oklahoma millionaire in the sophisticated comedy *The Awful Truth,* in which he loses his love interest, Irene Dunne, to the handsome, dashing Cary Grant.

Bellamy won an Academy Award nomination for best supporting actor, but even here he lost out—this time to Joseph Schildkraut, who took home the Oscar for his work in the Warner Brothers classic film *The Life of Emile Zola.* Despite the prestige of the nomination, Bellamy continued to face the pattern of losing leading ladies to better-looking and more charming men in subsequent pictures. He lost Carole Lombard to Fred MacMurray in *Fools for Scandal* (1938), Ginger Rogers to Fred Astaire in *Carefree* (1938), and Rosalind Russell to Cary Grant, again, in *His Girl Friday* (1940).

In 1942 Bellamy realized that his career as the other man, the perennial loser, would only lead to disaster. He reversed course and returned to the Broadway stage in 1943 to play a truly heroic role as a liberal, anti-Nazi college professor in *Tomorrow the World* by James Gow and Arnaud D'Usseau. In 1945 he essayed another strong character as a presidential candidate in *State of the Union,* the

Howard Lindsay–Russel Crouse comedy that won the Pulitzer Prize and the New York Drama Critics Circle Award. In 1949 he played a tough detective in Sidney Kingsley's realistic, hard-hitting drama *Detective Story*.

With his "other man" image in the past, Bellamy could now plunge ahead with a variety of roles in the newly emerging television field. He appeared as private eye Mike Barrett in *Man Against Crime* (1949–1954), the first live half-hour weekly series drama on television. The show ran for two years live and then three more years on film. His new reputation as a tough guy won him an important part as a defense attorney in the 1955 film *The Court-Martial of Billy Mitchell*.

Once again a popular star, Bellamy made numerous guest appearances in the golden days of live television. In 1955 he won an Emmy Award nomination for his acting in "Fearful Decision," an episode on the United States Steel Hour. The following year he received critical acclaim in the controversial drama *The Filmmaker* on the Goodyear Playhouse. Bellamy portrayed a traditional Hollywood mogul fighting the challenge of television films being made by the studios. Other shows that utilized his talents were *Climax!* (1954–1958) and *Playhouse 90* (1956–1961). In a 1957 "Studio One" two-parter, he teamed up with William Shatner to play father-and-son attorneys in Reginald Rose's *The Defenders,* which became one of history's outstanding dramatic television series.

Bellamy was lured back to Broadway for the memorable role of President Franklin D. Roosevelt in *Sunrise at Campobello* (1958). Bellamy researched the life of a paralyzed person by visiting hospitals, working with physiotherapists, and consulting Eleanor Roosevelt and her children. His brilliant performance won him a Tony and the Drama Critics Best Actor Award.

Returning to Hollywood to do the film version in 1960, Bellamy was once again in demand as a character actor. Roman Polanski cast him as a demonic doctor in the cult film *Rosemary's Baby* (1968). In 1983 he was once again called upon to play Roosevelt in the Herman Wouk television miniseries *The Winds of War.* That same year he and another veteran actor, Don Ameche, were cast in support of the rising young comedian Eddie Murphy in *Trading Places*. Ultimately, Bellamy made more than 100 films. In 1987 the quality of his work was officially recognized by the Motion Picture Academy, which awarded him an honorary Oscar for lifetime achievement.

His final film was in support of two popular Hollywood stars, Richard Gere and Julia Roberts, in Garry Marshall's box office hit *Pretty Woman*. This took place in 1990, one year before his death. Ralph Bellamy died on 29 November 1991 of a respiratory infection. He is buried at Forest Lawn Cemetery in Los Angeles.

The acting community also remembers Bellamy for his

fight on behalf of labor. He was one of the founders of the Screen Actors Guild and served as president of Actor's Equity for four three-year terms (1952–1964). He led the union in its struggle against the vicious blacklisting of actors by Senator Joseph McCarthy and the House Un-American Activities Committee. His fellow actors rewarded his stewardship by naming him president emeritus for life.

Bellamy's personal life was as varied as his professional career. His first three marriages, to Alice Delbridge from 1922 to 1931, to Catherine Willard from 6 July 1931 to 6 August 1945, and to Ethel Smith from 1945 to 1947, all ended in divorce. His fourth wife, Alice Murphy, whom he married in 1949, survived him. He had two children with his second wife, Catherine.

Bellamy's long and distinguished career established him as an actor of amazing skill in comedy, drama, and melodrama. He won immortality in the role of President Franklin D. Roosevelt on stage, screen, and television and will be remembered fondly by his fellow actors and many generations of fans.

★

Bellamy's autobiography, *When the Smoke Hit the Fan* (1979), is purely anecdotal and fails to mention any of his first three wives or his children. His early Hollywood years are carefully recalled in a chapter in James Robert Parish and William T. Leonard, *Hollywood Players, the Thirties* (1976). Obituaries are in the *New York Times* and *Los Angeles Times* (both 30 Nov. 1991), London *Times* and *Daily Variety* (both 2 Dec. 1991), and *People* (12 Dec. 1991).

MALVIN WALD

BERBEROVA, Nina Nikolaevna (*b.* 8 August 1901 in Saint Petersburg, Russia; *d.* 26 September 1993 in Philadelphia, Pennsylvania), Russian émigré writer whose autobiography, *The Italics Are Mine* (1969), chronicled nearly a century of intellectual life in tsarist Russia, the early Soviet Union, and exile in Paris.

Berberova was the only child of Nikolai Ivanovich Berberov, an Armenian civil servant in Russia's Ministry of Finance whose family had acquired land and moved into the gentry class under Catherine the Great, and Natalia Ivanovna Karaulova. Berberova's maternal great-grandfather, Karaulov, a landowner in the province of Tver, was the model for Ivan Goncharov's fictional hero Oblomov—the prototypical "superfluous man" of the nineteenth century, a recurrent literary type in many Russian novels including Aleksandr Pushkin's *Eugene Onegin* and Mikhail Lermontov's *Hero of Our Time*.

Berberova had a privileged childhood in tsarist Russia that came to an end with World War I. She briefly enrolled in the department of philology at Rostov University, but

Nina Berberova. © NABOKOV/GAMMA LIAISON

the Bolshevik Revolution interrupted her education. She was one of the last of her class to attend a university in Russia. Returning to Saint Petersburg, now called Petrograd, she joined the Poets' Guild and became part of the vibrant but increasingly imperiled literary life of that city. In 1922 she and the symbolist poet Vladislav Khodasevich (1886–1939), with whom she had fallen in love, left Russia together and traveled throughout Europe. They spent part of the time as members of Maksim Gorky's peripatetic household, before Gorky returned to Russia. About Gorky she observed, perhaps harshly, "It was always more important for him to be heard than to speak out."

In 1925 Berberova and Khodasevich finally settled into the Russian intellectual community in Paris, which she called a "unique generation of deprived, broken, silenced, stripped, homeless, destitute, disenfranchised and therefore half-educated poets." Among the writers she describes in her autobiography are Andrey Bely, Vladimir Nabokov, Ivan Bunin (winner of the 1933 Nobel Prize for Literature), Marina Tsvetayeva, and Boris Pasternak, and scores of others. She singles out Nabokov as a genius who was "able to bring in a renewal of style."

Berberova remained in Paris for twenty-five years, and for most of that time she wrote short fiction, cultural criticism, and news articles for Russian-language publications including *Poslednie Novosti* (The Latest News) and later *Russkaya Mysl'* (Russian Thought). She describes the Russian community of these years, struggling to maintain itself even as Stalinist Russia conspired to destroy it, hating the Soviet regime yet "entangled in a common web."

In 1932 Berberova left Khodasevich, although she remained on good terms with him and Olga, the woman he subsequently married. In 1937 she married Nikolai Makeyev, a Russian émigré painter, and moved to Longchene, a rural suburb of Paris, where they lived in extreme poverty throughout World War II. They divorced nine years later in 1946, and in 1950, Berberova emigrated once again, this time to the United States, where in 1954 she married the musician George Kochevitsky in order to become a U.S. citizen. They divorced in 1983.

During her early years in the United States, Berberova edited books for the Chekhov Publishing House in New York City and served on the editorial board of the Russian literary journal *Mosty* (Bridges). She began a new career in 1958 when she joined the Slavic department at Yale University, in New Haven, Connecticut. In 1963 she moved to Princeton University, in New Jersey, where she taught Russian literature until she retired in 1971, following which she continued to teach and lecture at various institutions in the United States, including Cornell, Columbia, Bryn Mawr College, Middlebury College, and the University of Pennsylvania. She received honorary doctorates from Middlebury and Yale.

When Berberova was in her eighties, she enjoyed unexpected good fortune. In 1985 the French publishing house Actes Sud began issuing her fiction in French translation. Her books sold so well that she remained on the French best-seller lists for nearly a decade, which brought her financial independence and great personal satisfaction. Her fiction in French translation attracted the notice of Jacqueline Kennedy Onassis, who brought Berberova to the attention of American publishers and readers. Actes Sud translated and published her fiction in more than twenty-two languages, including English.

In 1989 she paid a visit to her homeland, sixty-seven years after leaving, courtesy of an invitation from the Union of Writers. Two years later she watched the collapse of the Soviet Union. She had outlived the Revolution. Berberova died in a nursing home in Philadelphia of complications from a fall at the age of ninety-two.

Most of Berberova's fiction was written during her years in Paris, and her disaffected heroines reflect Berberova's life on the edge of desperation, lonely yet claustrophobically confined to a narrow existence. *The Book of Happiness* (1999; originally published in Russian as *Kniga schast'e*) is her most autobiographical novel. The protagonist, Vera, grows up in a comfortable household in tsarist Saint Petersburg but after the Revolution marries an invalid and emigrates to Paris, where she leads a life of drudgery. Only at the end of the novel is there a glimpse of redemption, when she falls in love for the first time: "She felt like saying that despite the fact that it was going to be an uphill road, the round-the-world journey was over."

The French director Claude Miller adapted Berberova's 1934 novella *The Accompanist* for his film, *L'Accompagnatrice* (1992), about an impoverished young pianist hired to accompany a beautiful but selfish opera singer; the accompanist becomes so obsessed with her employer's life that she ruins her own. The film was a commercial success in France and in the United States.

In addition to her autobiography and fiction, Berberova wrote a biography of Tchaikovsky, in which she openly discusses his homosexuality, and a life of Aleksandr Blok, the finest symbolist poet of Russia's "Silver Age." Berberova was an important part of the modernist movement in twentieth-century Russian literature, and because of her personal descriptions of so many Russian writers, she provides an invaluable record of an entire era.

★

Berberova's papers are in the Beinecke Rare Book and Manuscript Library at Yale University and in the Boris I. Nicolaevsky Collection in the Hoover Institution of War, Revolution, and Peace at Stanford University. The Beinecke collection contains correspondence, manuscripts, photographs, personal papers, and memorabilia chiefly from the years 1950 to 1993. The papers are written in Russian, English, French, and German. The bulk of her early papers (1922–1950) are at the Hoover Institution. Berberova's autobiography, *The Italics Are Mine* (1969; originally published in Russian as *Kursiv moi: avtobiografiia*), is the best source of her life. Berberova's English translator, Marian Schwartz, has written an eloquent introduction to *The Ladies from St. Petersburg,* (1995; originally published in Russian as *Baryni*), and Ken Kalfus reviewed it for the *New York Times Book Review* (1 Nov. 1998). Claire Messud reviewed *Cape of Storms* (1999; originally published in Russian as *Mys bur*) for the *New York Times Book Review* (9 Jan. 2000). An obituary is in the *New York Times* (29 Sept. 1993).

LESLEY S. HERRMANN

BIGART, Homer William (*b.* 27 October 1907 in Hawley, Pennsylvania; *d.* 16 April 1991 in Portsmouth, New Hampshire), one of the most admired and honored reporters in American journalism, considered by his peers to be the outstanding war correspondent of his generation. His precise, understated, and often witty prose twice won him the Pulitzer Prize.

Bigart was the son of Anna Schardt, a homemaker, and Homer S. Bigart, a sweater manufacturer in the Pocono Mountains of eastern Pennsylvania. Like his two sisters, he attended the local public schools and, following his graduation from Hawley High School in 1925, entered the Carnegie Institute of Technology in Pittsburgh to become an architect. The faculty soon learned that he could not draw,

Homer Bigart, war correspondent for the *New York Herald,* 1944. © BETTMANN/CORBIS

he said, "and invited me to find another school." In the autumn of 1927, he enrolled at New York University, taking courses during the day and working as a copy boy on the *Herald Tribune* at night. He left school without a degree during the Great Depression in 1929 to pursue his newspaper career.

For a time it appeared as if that career would never materialize. A painfully slow writer, Bigart agonized over every word. Even as a seasoned prizewinner with a reputation for crisp, elegant prose, he pecked out his articles one word at a time, taking long pauses between pecks as he struggled to find the precise language he wanted. He also had a pronounced stammer that worsened under stress, so he found it virtually impossible to phone in stories to the rewrite desk. Over time he transformed this weakness into an art form—"the Bigart Big Dummy Act," his colleagues called it—that misled officials into believing he was not too bright, and in an attempt to help him, they responded to his persistent questioning with details and insights they initially intended to keep hidden. His editors believed one secret of his success was his willingness to dig more deeply for facts than anyone else.

His early editors allowed him to write an occasional obituary and report on Sunday sermons, but after five years at the *Tribune* he had risen only to the lowly rank of head copy boy. He later said that the only thing that kept him from being the oldest copy boy in the history of journalism was his 1934 appointment to a general reporting job which, over the next several years, took him through a series of out-of-town assignments in St. Louis, New Orleans, and the coal fields of Pennsylvania to the *Tribune*'s metropolitan desk. In 1942 he departed for the war in Europe.

This was the beginning of Bigart's storied career. He initially reported from London on the Allies' massive air assault on Nazi Germany as one of the first correspondents to fly on a nighttime raid in February 1943. Sent to Italy, he reported on the Seventh Army in Sicily in July 1943 and in Salerno in September. He landed with the Fifth Army at Anzio on the first day of fighting, 22 January 1944, and covered the Eighth Army's mountain campaign north of Naples in the spring. He was one of three journalists to enter Cassino on the afternoon it finally fell to the British on 19 May 1944. By then he had become notorious among the press corps for his insistence on being close to the fighting and taking any risk to be first with a story. In a semiserious warning, his *Tribune* colleague Tex O'Reilly told a newcomer to the front, "Keep away from Homer. He's always trying to build his reputation at the cannon's mouth."

After covering the U.S. invasion of southern France and the liberation of Marseilles in August and September, Bigart was sent to the Pacific for the final months of the war, beginning with General Douglas A. MacArthur's triumphant return to Leyte in the Philippines in October 1944 and Corregidor, Philippines, early in the new year. He landed with the Marines on Iwo Jima in February 1945 and again with the Tenth Army on Okinawa from April to June. He returned from a B-29 run over Kumagaya, Japan, on 15 August 1945 to file what is believed to be World War II's last eyewitness combat report. ("The radio tells us that the war is over," Bigart wrote, "but from where I sit it looks suspiciously like a rumor.") On 2 September 1945, he reported the Japanese capitulation on board the *Missouri*. ("Japan," he wrote, "paying for her desperate throw of the dice at Pearl Harbor, passed from the ranks of the major powers at 9:05 A.M. today when Foreign Minister Mamoru Shigemitsu signed the document of unconditional surrender.") Among the first correspondents to enter Hiroshima to survey the damage from the first atomic bomb, Bigart received his first Pulitzer Prize in 1946 for his Pacific reporting.

In the postwar period the *Tribune* sent him on a roving assignment through Europe, first in Germany; then in Prague, Czechoslovakia; and finally in Warsaw, Poland, where he was branded a "reactionary" because of his reporting on communist terrorism. He spent much of 1946 and 1947 in Palestine, getting "in the hair of the British" while reporting sympathetically on the Jewish independence movement.

Bigart covered the 1948 Greek civil war, where his criticism of American officials disbursing aid and his dispatches on the Greek government's mass executions led to accusations that his reporting was distorted and untrue. The controversy opened the way to Bigart's most spectacular scoop: an exclusive interview with the Greek partisan leader General Markos (Markos Vafiades), the result of a dangerous mission that was accomplished in secret and at great personal risk. George Polk, a CBS correspondent, had been murdered just a few weeks earlier in attempting to contact Markos; whether he was killed by the partisans or by the Greek army remains one of journalism's unsolved mysteries. After an arduous, 200-mile, overland journey on foot from Belgrade, Yugoslavia, to a small village in the Pindus range of Greece, Bigart got his story, which earned him the first George Polk Memorial Prize and, at the direction of the American secretary of state, protection by a twenty-four hour security guard until he left Athens.

Bigart won his rare second Pulitzer Prize in 1951—an award shared with other combat correspondents that year—for his dispatches from the Korean War, where MacArthur publicly reproached him for "biased reporting" after he criticized the general for miscalculating the readiness of China to enter the war once American forces approached the Yalu River. Bigart was perhaps as famous among his fellow correspondents for his months-long slanging match with his *Tribune* colleague in Korea, Marguerite Higgins, whom he actively disliked, in part because he believed the war zone was no place for a woman.

In 1955, as the financial health of the *Herald Tribune* worsened, Bigart jumped to the *New York Times,* which sent him to the Middle East to cover events in Iran and Israel, most notably the trial of the Nazi war criminal Adolph Eichmann in 1961. The next year he went to Vietnam. Within weeks of his posting, he came to hate the assignment, and early on—some say he was the first reporter to do so—he wrote that the burgeoning war, in spite of the Pentagon's contrary assertions, was a tragedy and a mistake. Saying that he had had enough of battlefield death, he returned home in June 1962 for a decade of domestic reporting, covering such stories as the civil rights movement in the South, poverty and hunger in the United States, and the 1971 trial of William Calley, an army lieutenant charged with ordering a massacre at Mai Lai in Vietnam. Bigart retired from the *New York Times* in 1972 to West Nottingham, New Hampshire.

A tall, portly man, Bigart was a notable and witty raconteur in reporters' bars wherever he went, but he was also shy and intensely private, revealing little or nothing about himself. He married Alice Kirkwood Veit, a *Herald Tribune* staffer, on 15 March 1951; they divorced before her death in 1959. His second wife, Alice Weel, whom he married on 6 July 1963, died in 1969. On 3 October 1970, he married Else Holmelund Minarik, a writer of children's books, who brought a daughter to the marriage. He had no children of his own.

Bigart's life revolved around the two papers for which he worked, and of the two his greater love was the *Herald Tribune,* which, he told the managing editor of the *New York Times,* always sent him first class; the *Times,* he added, was run by bureaucrats. Having been barred or expelled from eight countries for alleged "biased reporting" and frequently at odds with American officials wherever he was posted, he professed a profound dislike for authority in general and editors in particular, once referring to them as "pallid clerks who are in charge of my destiny." In a celebrated story, a young *Times* reporter was talking with Bigart from a phone booth in Harlem during the 1966 riots when angry protestors began shaking the booth. Bigart, who was in the *Times*'s midtown building and apparently at that moment locked in some office struggle with an editor, listened to the young man express his fears and told him not to worry. "At least," he said, "you're dealing with sane people."

In 1991 Bigart died of cancer at the Edgewood Center in Portsmouth where he had been hospitalized for two months. In keeping with his wishes, there was no funeral.

Bigart wrote no books, composed no memoirs, and produced fewer than ten magazine articles or book reviews in his long career. He said that because writing came so hard for him, he needed the daily deadlines that only newspapers provided. When the writing was done, a fellow war correspondent once said, "Nine times out of ten you could count on his being the best." He won nearly every major prize or award the profession offered.

★

Bigart's papers (1932–1972) are in the State Historical Society of Wisconsin, Madison. They include his press clippings, his World War II correspondence (1943–1945), and letters to his family from Belgrade, Madrid, Paris, and Saigon (1946–1962). His reporting is available in the microfilm editions of the *New York Herald Tribune* and *New York Times.* The *Times*'s edition is indexed; the *Tribune*'s is not. A selection of his wartime dispatches is in *Forward Positions: The War Correspondence of Homer Bigart,* compiled and edited by Betsy Wade (1992). Some of his dispatches are included in Library of America, *Reporting World War II: American Journalism 1938–1946,* 2 vols. (1995) and *Reporting Vietnam: American Journalism 1959–1975,* 2 vols. (1998). There is no biography, but see Harrison E. Salisbury's "Foreword," Betsy Wade's "Introduction," and the "Appendix" in *Forward Positions.* Salisbury's profile of Bigart is also in *Heroes of My Time* (1993). Other useful sources are *Editor and Publisher,* 12 March 1949; *Newsweek,* 2 October 1944, and 22 January 1951; Keyes Beech, *Tokyo and Points East* (1954); Antionette May, *Witness to War: A Biography of Marguerite Higgins* (1983); Richard Kluger, *The Paper: The Life and Death of the New York Herald Tribune* (1986); and William Prochnau, *Once Upon a Distant War: Young War Correspondents and the Early Vietnam Battles* (1995). An obituary is in the *New York Times* (17 Apr. 1991).

ALLAN L. DAMON

BLACK, Eugene Robert (*b.* 1 May 1898 in Atlanta, Georgia; *d.* 20 February 1992 in Southampton, New York), financier who as third president of the World Bank (International Bank for Reconstruction and Development), from 1949 to 1962, made the newly established institution into a major global force, powering the economic development of emerging nations.

Black was the eldest of three children born to Eugene Robert Black, Sr., a prominent Atlanta banker and lawyer who was president of the Atlanta Trust Company, governor of Atlanta's Federal Reserve Bank, and a governor of the Federal Reserve Board, and Gussie King Grady, a homemaker and daughter of the Southern editor Henry Woodfin Grady. After graduating from the Peacock School, a private academy for young men in Atlanta, Black attended the University of Georgia, graduating with a B.A. cum laude in 1918. During the First World War he served briefly as an ensign in the U.S. Navy. In 1918 he married Dolly Blalock, with whom he had two children before her death in 1928. Black's second marriage in 1930, to Suzette Heath, with whom he had one child, lasted until his death.

In late 1918 Black returned to Atlanta, joining the local office of the New York investment bank Harris, Forbes and Company, reorganized the following year as the Chase-Harris-Forbes Corporation. Black became assistant vice president by 1933, acquiring a reputation as a bond market expert. In 1933 he joined the Chase National Bank of New York as a vice president, becoming senior vice president in 1937. Offered a position as undersecretary of the U.S. Treasury in 1936, Black initially accepted, but financial considerations led him to withdraw. As World War II ended he became more involved with Chase's international activities, making several trips to Europe between 1945 and 1947.

Black's bond market expertise and his international exposure led John J. McCloy, the second president of the new International Bank for Reconstruction and Development, to make him the infant organization's American executive director, which he became in February 1947. Founded in 1944, the bank was intended to finance postwar economic reconstruction, but its capital was limited. Operations on the scale envisaged necessitated tapping the American capital market, and McCloy hoped Black's connections would enhance the bank's credibility. His strategy succeeded a few months later, when the bank floated a $250 million bond issue on Wall Street.

In July 1949 Black succeeded McCloy as the World Bank's third president. The bank's early loans went primarily to European countries to finance their recovery from wartime ravages. These countries included France, whose Credit National in 1947 received the first loan of $250 million, the Netherlands, Denmark, and Luxembourg. The adoption in 1948 of the Marshall Plan European Recovery Program led the bank to switch its emphasis to building

Eugene Black (*right*), president of the World Bank, with Japanese prime minister Shigeru Yoshida, 1954. © BETTMANN/CORBIS

the economies of developing nations. In April 1948, while still executive director, Black organized its first such loan to Chile. Throughout Black's presidency, which lasted until ill health caused his resignation in 1962, providing funding and advice to promote economic development in emerging nations remained the bank's major preoccupation. In that period, the bank suffered no defaults when lending $6 billion of its own funds and substantially more money raised on the open market.

During Black's tenure the bank's number of subscribing member nations rose from forty-eight to eighty; its capital grew from $8.3 billion to $20.5 billion; its lending portfolio quintupled, and its staff expanded commensurately. Black reorganized its operations into three geographic departments (Asia and the Middle East; Europe, Africa, and Australia; and the Western Hemisphere) and a technical operations department. In 1955, 1956, and 1960 respectively he introduced three additional subagencies: the Economic Development Institute, to train potential borrowers; the International Finance Corporation, which provided loans to the private sector in developing countries; and the International Development Association, which offered the poorest countries longer-term loans at lower interest rates.

Tall, rangy, impeccably tailored, and usually sporting a homburg hat, the genial Black combined great charm with a reputation for subjecting projects submitted to him to hard-nosed evaluation. An economic conservative with a social conscience, Black insisted that loans should only finance projects that would generate income for repayment. With few exceptions, the bank's lending financed indus-

trial, agricultural, and power projects that would stimulate the private sector. Black jealously guarded the bank's independence from political control, causing him to deprecate bilateral aid programs that might subject bank projects to international political interference. He was annoyed when in 1955–1956 American suspicion that Egyptian president Gamal Abdel Nasser was pro-Soviet brought the collapse of projected joint Anglo-American-Bank financing he had arranged for Egypt's Aswan High Dam.

As president Black spent about two-thirds of his time traveling and established warm personal relationships with many international politicians and financiers. He emphasized the importance of "mutual trust" between the bank and its clients. On occasion he helped to mediate international disputes, resolving the assorted financial claims of Britain, France, and the Suez Canal Company after the Suez crisis of 1956 and in 1960 settling an Indo-Pakistani dispute over the Indus waters.

On retirement Black returned to the Chase Manhattan Bank as a consultant and director. In April 1965 President Lyndon B. Johnson chose Black to create a United Nations–sponsored multinational Asian Development Bank to provide investment funds and research staff to Southeast Asian nations, an attempt to deflect criticism of American involvement in Vietnam. Black also helped to organize other, generally more short-lived, American assistance projects in Southeast Asia. In January 1969 Johnson awarded Black the Medal of Freedom for these efforts.

As special financial consultant to the United Nations from 1963 to 1970, Black attempted to collect overdue obligations from member states that had defaulted on their dues. A passionate baseball fan, he was often mentioned as a potential baseball commissioner. Until 1970, when he retired from most active positions, he held numerous prestigious directorships and trusteeships. He and his wife gradually gave up homes in Washington, Brooklyn, and Florida, keeping only a place in Southampton, Long Island. Black died from heart and kidney failure in Southampton, where he was privately buried.

Black's major achievement was to place the nascent World Bank on a solid footing. A fundamentally conservative banker, he devised an efficient institutional structure whose operational standards won the international financial community's confidence, an essential precondition to raising funds on the open market. Despite Black's emphasis on working with recipient countries and funding only financially viable enterprises, subsequent critics have suggested the bank often effectively encouraged high-profile and environmentally detrimental projects of limited value to the host countries.

★

Black's papers are in the archives of the University of Georgia at Athens. He summarized his socioeconomic philosophy in *The Diplomacy of Economic Development and Other Papers* (1963). There is no biography of Black, though he figures largely in Catherine Caufield, *Masters of Illusion: The World Bank and the Poverty of Nations* (1996); Catherine Gwin, *U.S. Relations with the World Bank, 1945–1992* (1994); Devesh Kapur et al., *The World Bank: Its First Half Century* (1997); and Edward S. Mason and Robert E. Asher, *The World Bank Since Bretton Woods* (1973). Material on his association with Chase Manhattan is included in John Donald Wilson, *The Chase: The Chase Manhattan Bank, N.A., 1945–1985* (1986). Black's role during successive presidential administrations is covered in useful short essays in Eleanora W. Schoenebaum, ed., *Political Profiles: The Truman Years* (1978); Eleanora W. Schoenebaum, ed., *Political Profiles: The Eisenhower Years* (1980); Nelson Lichtenstein, ed., *Political Profiles: The Kennedy Years* (1976); and Nelson Lichtenstein, ed., *Political Profiles: The Johnson Years* (1976). Obituaries are in the *New York Times,* (21 Feb. 1992); *Washington Post* (21 Feb. 1992); and London *Times* (22 Feb. 1992). Transcripts of various oral history interviews by Black are held by the Chase Manhattan Archives and the Dwight D. Eisenhower and Lyndon B. Johnson presidential libraries.

PRISCILLA ROBERTS

BLOCK, Joseph Leopold (*b.* 6 October 1902 in Chicago, Illinois; *d.* 17 November 1992 in Chicago, Illinois), industrialist and civic leader who presided over the postwar expansion of Chicago's Inland Steel Company.

Block was the oldest of four children born to Leopold E. Block and Cora Bloom. His grandfather and namesake, a

Joseph Block as new chairman of the board of Inland Steel Corporation, 1959. AP/WIDE WORLD PHOTOS

prosperous Cincinnati scrap-iron dealer, had founded Inland Steel in Chicago in 1893 and ran it as a family business, and Block's father, uncles, and cousins were part of its growth and prosperity. Block's father moved to Chicago in 1897 when the family acquired the East Chicago Iron and Forge Company. Renamed Inland Iron and Forge and managed by Block's father, the company introduced the use of angles rolled from a web of rails, which produced a lighter, tougher material. The manufacture of fashionable iron beds increased Inland's sales over 75 percent. In 1900 the Blocks sold Inland Iron and Forge and contracted a million-dollar package to establish an open-hearth steelmaking plant, the Indiana Harbor Works in East Chicago, Indiana. With profits from Inland Steel and the Indiana Harbor Works, the Blocks purchased coal and iron mines, barges, and Chicago real estate.

Block grew up in Chicago and like his brother and cousins, attended the Harvard School for Boys. He left Chicago for Cornell University in 1920, intending to pursue a career in journalism. He wrote for the Cornell *Daily Sun* and earned an editorial position as an underclassman. When he announced to his father that he planned to marry, Leopold Block insisted that young Joe leave Cornell at the end of his second year and join the family business. Block began as a trainee at the Indiana Harbor Works in the summer of 1922. On 19 January 1924 Block married Lucille Eichengreen; they had two children.

Inland grew dramatically due to the demand for rolled

steel during World War I. In the early 1920s, Americans directed much of their consumer budgets toward automobiles and appliances. Agriculture and transportation created even larger markets for steel. Block started at Inland Steel Company in 1922, moved to sales in 1923, became assistant vice president in 1927, and vice president of sales and director in 1929, effective in 1930. A lively, wiry, highly principled salesman, Block believed in and instructed his salesmen in "face-to-face" selling. Inland's customers were well known to management, and Block built customer loyalty by selling Inland's innovations in steel manufacture through district offices that could respond quickly to customers' demands. In 1930 Block had become a member of Inland Steel Company's board of directors, and in 1936 he was named vice president in charge of sales. Because the company had anticipated the growth of industry and agriculture in the Midwest, had provided a high level of service as well as generous employee benefits and promotion opportunities, and had made sound investments, it weathered the Great Depression.

In 1941 Block took a leave of absence from Inland and left Chicago for Washington, D.C., to serve as a "dollar-a-year" consultant to the War Production Board. Responding to President Franklin Roosevelt's call for a massive buildup of military supplies, Block coordinated the increase of national steel plate production from 700,000 to 1.3 million tons per month and organized its efficient distribution. Proud of his work in the war effort, Block kept his annual dollar paychecks framed in his Chicago office.

In 1945 Block returned to Chicago. He used his position as head of sales at Inland Steel to maneuver the company into a position of major importance in national industry. Responding to postwar consumer, industrial, and agricultural demands, Block supported renewed research and development. At the same time that he moved the company toward superior customer satisfaction, he made explicit that an Inland employee had the "opportunity . . . to earn his living and rise from the bottom to the top rung of the ladder on merit, irrespective of race, creed, or class." For Chicago's varied ethnic communities, Block's promise meant jobs that offered security, respect, and a realistic potential for promotion. Block guaranteed Inland's AA bond rating by continually improving the company's existing mills, production technology, transportation, and resources.

In 1952 Block became executive vice president and chair of Inland's finance committee, and in 1953 he became Inland's eighth president. Block led two major expansion programs. He approved Skidmore, Owings, and Merrill's design for a nineteen-story steel and glass office building in downtown Chicago. Always a Chicago booster, Block resisted the corporate exodus to the suburbs. In 1956 he assumed the position of chief executive officer at Inland. In 1957 he headed the Chicago Association of Commerce and Industry and for two years, 1957–1959, he led the Chicago Community Fund, which supported local charities. Block had been a director of the Jewish Federation since 1931, and through Inland, he supported local community building projects, including donating land for the Joseph L. Block Junior High School and an adjacent housing development. He headed the Crusade for Mercy from 1965 to 1967. As president, Block expanded the Inland fleet to seven ships, including the two largest ore carriers on the Great Lakes. He opened additional iron mines in Ontario, Canada, built automated slabbing and cold rolling steel mills, and upgraded the production of high-quality, flat-rolled steel. With an investment of $360 million, Block authorized the construction of an enormous facility at Indiana Harbor on a 436-acre landfill. Production at Inland increased from 5.2 million tons in 1952 to 6.5 million in 1959.

In 1959 Block, promoted to chairman of the board, represented steel industry producers during a major strike. His position—that labor, management, and government would benefit mutually and resist foreign competition if they would balance their interests and responsibility to their constituents with mutual fair dealing—was a reflection of his personal code of ethics. The early 1960s saw a period of instability, foreign competition, and intense labor demands. The steel industry decided to institute price increases. Block, called a renegade, refused to participate. Subpoenaed by Senator Estes Kefauver, Block refused to provide production cost data unless every other industry was called to the same task.

Under Block's leadership, Inland invested more than $1.3 billion in growth. Block was committed to promoting from within and supporting policies that moved women and minorities into significant positions within the company. The "Ten Goals" he wrote in 1953, emphasizing social responsibility and integrity, governed all of Block's dealings both within and outside the company. In 1962 Block led a second expansion and modernization program, building a hot strip mill that could take nine-inch slabs of steel and roll them into strips of metal one-quarter-inch thick and one-quarter-mile long, a computer-controlled facility that covered nearly a half mile. The nation's first basic oxygen steelmaking complex opened in 1965. Through the 1960s and early 1970s, Block served Presidents John F. Kennedy, Lyndon B. Johnson, and Richard Nixon on the President's Advisory Committee on Labor-Management Policy. In November 1967 Block retired as CEO of Inland Steel but remained active on the board as a director and as chair of the executive committee until 1971. Early in 1992 he agreed to serve as the honorary chair of Inland's 100th anniversary celebration. At the age of ninety he died of congestive heart failure at Northwestern University Hospital. He is entombed at Rosehill Cemetery and Mausoleum in Chicago.

Block, a third-generation principal of his family's steel business, led Inland Steel during periods of unprecedented growth and prosperity. A lifelong admirer of Abraham Lincoln, he attempted to imbue a powerful industry with ethical principles that reflected his family and personal integrity.

★

Information on Block's career is in the Inland Steel collection (CPA #12) of the Calumet Regional Archives at Indiana University, North Library. Corporate publications, Jack Morris's *Inland Steel at 100* (1993), and *The Story of Inland Steel Company* (1989), outline Block's contributions to Inland's growth and provide a history of the family's early years in the steel industry in Illinois and Indiana. Overviews of Block's personal and corporate life are available in Bruce Seely, ed., *Encyclopedia of American Business History and Biography: The Iron and Steel Industries in the 20th Century* (1994), and in Charles Moritz, ed., *Current Biography Yearbook* (1961). An interview with Block, "Labor Prices Go up Faster than Steel Prices," supplements an article on the steel industry, "How Steel Will Change America," *U.S. News and World Report* (7 June 1957). Block's speeches on a number of topics are published in *Vital Speeches of the Day* (15 Sept. 1962 and 1 Feb. 1963). *Time* (3 Nov. 1967) and *Newsweek* (6 Nov. 1967) cover his contributions at the time of his retirement. A discussion of Block's influence on industry ethics is in "High Ethical Standards and an Operating Background" in *Iron Age New Steel* (August 1995). Obituaries are in the *New York Times* and *Chicago Tribune* (both 18 Nov. 1992).

WENDY HALL MALONEY

Allan Bloom, 1987. AP/WIDE WORLD PHOTOS

BLOOM, Allan David (*b.* 14 September 1930 in Indianapolis, Indiana; *d.* 7 October 1992 in Chicago, Illinois), teacher, philosopher, and author who gained wide attention with his best-selling book *The Closing of the American Mind* (1987), an erudite and passionate meditation on the state of higher education in the United States.

Bloom was one of the two children of Allan Bloom and Malvina Glasner, both of whom were social workers. His father served as executive secretary of the Jewish Community Center Association of Indianapolis, Midwest regional director of the American Jewish Community Association in Chicago, and executive secretary of the Rockford (Illinois) Jewish Community Board.

Bloom's future as a scholar was set when he first saw the University of Chicago at the age of fifteen. "I had discovered my life," he disclosed in *The Closing of the American Mind: How Higher Education Has Failed Democracy and Impoverished the Souls of Today's Students* (1987). He entered that institution after the family had moved to Chicago, and he subsequently received bachelor of arts (1949) and master of arts (1953) degrees there. He capped off his

studies at the University of Chicago with a Ph.D. in social thought in 1955. His doctoral dissertation, "The Political Philosophy of Isocrates," illuminated his lifelong veneration of that philosopher.

Bloom then embarked upon an academic career that led him from lecturer at the University of Paris (1954–1955) to lecturer at the University of Chicago (1955–1960). This was followed by teaching posts at Yale (1962–1963) and Cornell (1963–1970), where he was critical of administrators for giving in to the demands of African-American students for curriculum changes after major turmoil on that campus, which included threats to faculty members. After Cornell he was a visiting professor for one semester each at the University of Tel Aviv and the University of Paris before settling in as a professor in the department of political science at the University of Toronto (1970–1979). He returned to his first love, the University of Chicago, in 1979, and remained there until his death. His teaching and writing led him to the role of codirector of the John M. Olin Center for Inquiry into the Theory and Practice of Democracy (1983–1992). He was given the title of John U. Nef Distinguished Service Professor in the Committee on Social

Thought, an elite interdisciplinary graduate department, at the University of Chicago in 1992.

Living the life of a devoted academic, Bloom's major focus was political philosophy. He was a disciple of Leo Strauss, a conservative, German-born philosopher who, like Bloom, spent most of his career at Chicago. Bloom mastered both French and classical Greek, using these skills to read classics in the original languages, a practice he advocated for serious students. He wrote numerous articles and several books, acquiring a reputation as a serious critic of education and as a translator. Among his best-known translations are *Politics and the Arts* (1960) and *Emile; or, On Education* (1979), both by Jean-Jacques Rousseau, and *The Republic* (1968), by Plato.

Bloom was little known outside academic circles until the publication of *The Closing of the American Mind: How Higher Education Has Failed Democracy and Impoverished the Souls of Today's Students* (1987). With a foreword by Saul Bellow, a Nobel laureate and close friend, the book made Bloom an instant celebrity and sold more than one million copies. It held the number-one spot on the *New York Times* best-seller list for ten weeks and made Bloom wealthy.

The major theme of the work was that the study of the classics, with emphasis on theory, is the hallmark of a good education. Bloom argued that undergraduate students should concentrate on major questions of life and being. He maintained that the concept of relativism, including cultural relativism, that had emerged on college campuses in the 1960s—that is, giving equal weight to a wide variety of subjects and cultures—and the emphasis on the practical application of information were ultimately leading to the downfall of democracy. He postulated that opening up curricula to include every current fad topic was, paradoxically, leading to the closing of the American mind.

In his review of the book in the *New York Times* (23 March 1987), Christopher Lehmann-Haupt wrote, "By turns passionate and witty, sweetly reasoned and outraged, it commands one's attention and concentrates one's mind more effectively than any other book I can think of in the past five years. Even its most devout enemies will learn from it." Roger Kimball, also reviewing the book for the *New York Times* (5 April 1987) wrote, "*The Closing of the American Mind* is that rarest of documents, a genuinely profound book, born of a long and patient meditation on questions that may be said to determine who we are, both as individuals and as a society." In 1999 the *National Review* placed the book at number forty-eight on its list of the one hundred most significant nonfiction works of the twentieth century.

Bloom's celebrity in the years following the publication of the book was double-edged. Fame and wealth were accompanied by countless verbal attacks by academicians who labeled his views of education ultraconservative and elitist. In doing so they overlooked contrary evidence. For example, although he appeared antifeminist, he wrote, "I am not arguing here that the old family arrangements were good or that we should or could go back to them. I am only insisting that we not cloud our vision to such an extent that we believe that there are viable substitutes for them just because we want or need them." In 1996, with Bloom's thoughts still goading academicians, *The Opening of the American Mind*, by Lawrence W. Levine, was published as a counterpoint to Bloom's book.

Bloom went on to publish *Giants and Dwarfs* (1990), a collection of essays written from 1960 to 1990, but it did not add luster to his reputation. *Love and Friendship*, his final book, was published posthumously in 1993.

During his career, Bloom accumulated many honors and awards, including the Clark Distinguished Teaching Award at Cornell University (1968), a Guggenheim Fellowship (1978–1979), and the Prix Jean-Jacques Rousseau (1987), granted by the City of Geneva. In 1992 he was named the University of Chicago's first John U. Nef Distinguished Service Professor.

Bloom dedicated his life to his teaching and writing. A tall, balding man, he tended to stutter when he was excited. He was a bachelor and lived a very private life. He was almost constantly engaged in conversation with his friends and students, both in person and on the telephone. He had a passionate interest in classical music and had an enormous collection of classical compact discs. The publication in 2000 of the novel *Ravelstein*, by Saul Bellow, created a stir as the title character is undeniably a thinly veiled portrait of Bloom. Bellow received negative press for betraying his friend by revealing deeply personal traits.

Bloom's death at the University of Chicago's Bernard Mitchell Hospital was attributed by university officials to peptic ulcer bleeding complicated by liver failure (although statements were made about the cause of death being AIDS-related complications). He was survived by his mother, his stepfather, and his sister. He is buried in his family's plot in Philadelphia, Pennsylvania.

By writing *The Closing of the American Mind*, Allan Bloom provoked educators to examine seriously the state of higher education in the United States. Although his detractors were vociferous, Bloom also garnered many accolades for his unpopular stance, and some colleges reestablished core curricula. More than a decade after its publication the book continued to serve as a reference point for serious debate.

★

There is no biography of Bloom. His curriculum vitae is available at the John M. Olin Center at the University of Chicago. Bloom makes several personal comments in *The Closing of the*

American Mind. Numerous reviews of the book have appeared, and scholars have made many references to it, but none reveal anything about Bloom's personal life. On the significance of Bloom's work see (in addition to the *New York Times* reviews cited above) a review by Frank Kermode in the *New York Times* (27 Oct. 1996) of *The Opening of the American Mind: Canons, Culture and History* (1996), by Lawrence W. Levine; "The University Is Not the U.S. Army: A Conversation with Lawrence W. Levine," in *Humanities 18, no. 1* (Jan.–Feb. 1997): 4–9; and "The Closing of the American Mind, Revisited," by S. J. D. Green, in the *Antioch Review* 56, no. 1 (winter 1998): 26–36. D. T. Max, "With Friends Like Bellow," in the *New York Times Magazine* (16 Apr. 2000), offers a glimpse into Bloom's friendship with Saul Bellow. An obituary is in the *New York Times* (8 Oct. 1992). For the present essay Nathan Tarcov, director of the John M. Olin Center, provided family information through personal correspondence.

MYRNA W. MERRON

BLUME, Peter (*b.* 27 October 1906 in Smorgon, Russia; *d.* 30 November 1992 in New Milford, Connecticut), artist whose meticulously crafted, brilliantly colored paintings are commentaries on the political and social realities of his day or serve as allegories of the regeneration of life.

Blume was born in a small town in Russia. He was one of three children of Harry Blume, a garment worker, and Rose Gopin, a homemaker. The family emigrated to the United States in 1911, settling in Brooklyn where Blume attended public school. Blume became a naturalized U.S. citizen in either 1917 or 1921. Blume left high school in his early teens to work at a newsstand, then in a jewelry factory, and finally in a lithography plant. At about age fifteen he enrolled full-time in art classes given at the Educational Alliance in Manhattan, attending from 1919 to 1924. Occasionally he sat in on sketch classes offered at the Beaux-Arts Institute of Design and also studied briefly at the Art Students League. When he was eighteen—now self-supported, doing commercial lithography and engraving—Blume rented his own studio in Manhattan.

In 1926 the artist acquired his first dealer, Charles Daniel, through whose gallery he made his first sale: the semi-abstract still life *Cyclamen* (1925). With the money earned from the sale of this work, he took off to New England and painted several canvases in the austere precisionist style, incorporating local settings. *Maine Coast* (1926), with figures posed ambiguously within and outside an old house, prefigures the dreamlike narratives with hidden meanings characteristic of his later painting. *Winter, New Hampshire* (1927); *The White Factory* (1928); and *The Bridge* (1928)—inspired by the Queensboro Bridge in New York—with their immaculately defined architectural forms, have been

Peter Blume, 1960. © BETTMANN/CORBIS

compared to the work of his contemporaries Charles Sheeler and Charles Demuth.

Back in New York City, where Blume frequently sketched along the Hudson River piers, he began work on *Parade* (1930), his first large canvas. The composition is an unlikely combination of allusions to riverside industrial sites and to the armored figures that fascinated him in the Metropolitan Museum of Art's medieval galleries. The face of the man with a lifted visor is that of the editor and critic Malcolm Cowley, Blume's longtime friend. The painting was the featured work in his first solo exhibition, held at the Daniel Gallery in 1930.

After a visit to Cowley in Sherman, Connecticut, in 1929, Blume established a studio there; he lived in Sherman the rest of his life. In the spring of 1930 he went on an automobile trip to Charleston, South Carolina, stopping along the way in Scranton, Pennsylvania. Setting up a temporary studio in Charleston, he began *South of Scranton,* the painting that established his name. The work is a composite of the images that caught his eye on his trip: slag heaps above a Scranton street, a locomotive, and in the background a view of Charleston Harbor and a battleship at anchor, with young men doing calisthenics on its deck. As in *Parade,* the artist contrasted the vulnerability of human beings with the harshness of their machine-age environment. Always a slow, painstaking worker (in the manner of early Netherlandish masters), Blume finished *South of Scranton* in 1931, the year he married Grace Douglas Gibbs Craton on 9 March. It was shown at the Carnegie International Exhibition in Pittsburgh three years later and was awarded first prize. Many viewers, puzzled and antagonized by its jumble of images, its arbitrary scale, and strange lighting, proclaimed that it revealed the sinister influence of modern European art.

A Guggenheim fellowship, awarded in 1932–1933 and renewed in 1936, enabled Blume to travel to Europe. Repelled by Mussolini's Fascist government, he began *The Eternal City,* on which he worked from 1934 to 1937. It was exhibited at the Julian Levy Galleries in Manhattan in 1937. Perhaps his best-known painting, it is another surreal assemblage of finely wrought details, in a setting that is unmistakably the Roman Forum. From the midst of the ruins springs—like a jack-in-the-box—the head of Mussolini painted a startling acid green. In 1947 Blume was elected an associate member of the National Academy of Design.

With *The Rock* (1948), a new theme entered Blume's art. Developed from some 500 preliminary drawings, it took seven years to complete. Images of a blasted rock, a burned-out building, and figures working on a new construction (a visual allusion to Fallingwater, the Frank Lloyd Wright house Blume had once visited) combine to symbolize—in his own words—"the continual process of man's rebuilding out of a devastated world." He addressed this theme of regeneration in varying ways from then on. Thus, *Passage to Etna* (1956) is a metaphor for continuity, expressed in the contrast between ancient ruins and daily life in a Sicilian town. The painter had visited Sicily in 1952; four years later he was back in Italy as an artist-in-residence at the American Academy in Rome. From sketches done there he completed *Tasso's Oak* (1958): a dead tree on the Janiculum hill, under which old women sit knitting. Opposed to these symbols of aging and decay are the one tree branch still in leaf and the young lovers who run hand-in-hand up the hill.

Blume's *Winter* (1964), finished in Rome where Blume had returned to the American Academy, is another narrative of death and resurrection. In a forbidding rocky landscape, sprigs of foliage are visible amid the granite outcroppings, and birds of many colors flock in the snow: life and sound in contrast to frozen silence. Still later he worked out the continuity of life theme in the *Seasons* series of the 1960s—regeneration in nature; in *Recollections of the Flood* (1969)—the restoration of a work of art after the Florence flood of 1966; and in *The Metamorphoses* (1979)—mythological transformations.

In addition to easel paintings, Blume did murals under the auspices of the U.S. Treasury Department for post offices in Canonsburg, Pennsylvania; Rome, Georgia; and Geneva, New York. Completed between 1937 and 1940, all three were based on local landscapes. He also worked in watercolor and produced a large body of pencil drawings, generally as preparatory studies for his canvases. In the 1970s he turned to sculpture and did a series of elegantly finished, mannerist-inspired figures, *Bronzes About Venus.*

Blume, who was elected to the National Institute of Arts and Letters in 1951, died in a nursing home in New Milford after a stroke. He had had no children.

Blume has mistakenly been classified as an American surrealist. Unlike the surrealists, however, he did not set out to shock or to reveal the unconscious, and by the 1930s his own eclectic style had been formed. A true original, he remained unaffected by succeeding trends in American art.

★

An article on Blume appeared in *Current Biography 1956.* There is a brief entry on the artist in the *Grove Dictionary of Art,* vol. 4 (1996). Additional information on his career and analyses of his work are found in *Paintings and Drawings in Retrospect, 1925 to 1964* (1964), a catalog of an exhibition held jointly at the Currier Gallery of Art, Manchester, New Hampshire, and the Wadsworth Atheneum, Hartford, Connecticut; *Peter Blume* (1968), a catalog from the Kennedy Galleries, New York, with text by Frank Getlein; and *Peter Blume* (1976), the catalog of a retrospective at the Museum of Contemporary Art, Chicago. An obituary by the critic Roberta Smith is in the *New York Times* (1 Dec. 1992).

ELEANOR F. WEDGE

BOOTH, Shirley (*b.* 30 August 1898 in New York City; *d.* 16 October 1992 in Chatham, Massachusetts), stage, film, and television actress known for her character parts, whose work won a number of awards, including Tonys, Emmys, and an Academy Award.

Booth was born Thelma Booth Ford, one of two daughters to Albert James Ford, an executive with International Business Machines Corporation, and Virginia Wright, a homemaker. Shortly after her birth, the family moved from Manhattan to the Flatbush section of Brooklyn, New York. Her first public appearance was at age three when she sang "In the Good Old Summertime" in a Sunday school show. In Public School 152 in Brooklyn she amused her classmates with her imitations of the teacher. When her composition "Autobiography of a Thanksgiving Turkey" was chosen for her to read aloud to the student body, the shy child rose to the occasion.

When Booth was seven, the family moved to Philadelphia, Pennsylvania, where they lived at a residential hotel. Another resident, J. Hammond Daly, an actor employed by a local stock company, befriended the family. Some years

Shirley Booth, with an Oscar for her performance in *Come Back, Little Sheba*, 1953. AP/WIDE WORLD PHOTOS

later after the family had moved to Hartford, Connecticut, they met again. Daly was still playing in stock and Booth asked him if there were any parts for her. Although Mr. Ford disapproved of acting and his daughter's interest in the stage, he agreed that Daly would introduce his daughter to the company manager. Booth suffered no stage fright, only, as expressed in her *Life* magazine interview with Robert Coughlan, "delight and a sense of freedom."

After a summer of playing stock, she returned home but the following summer rejoined the stock company. Finally, against her father's wishes she moved to New York City, seeking a stage career. She was not fourteen, as she claimed, but twenty-three when she got a job as an ingenue, for $35 a week, with the Poli stock company and was assigned to a unit playing in New Haven, Connecticut. Her father forbade her to use his name, so she changed her name from Thelma, which she had never liked, to Shirley, and dropped the Ford. For the next ten years she traveled with Poli and other stock companies, alternating stock with occasional New York runs, most of them brief. Stock was her "bread and butter." She worked in more than 600 different plays, ranging from *The Wild Duck* to *Little Old New York*,

in a variety of roles. Her favorite part was Sadie Thompson in *Rain*. Booth learned to memorize quickly because there was a new play every week, a new musical every fourth week, and four to five matinees and six evening performances each week. Booth also became a close observer of people, learning a variety of gestures, expressions, and mannerisms to flesh out the characters she was playing.

In 1925 she debuted on Broadway as the ingenue in *Hell's Bells,* playing opposite another future star, Humphrey Bogart. The play ran for four months. Other short runs on Broadway followed, including *Buy, Buy Baby* (1926), *High Gear* (1927), and *The War Song* (1928).

On 23 November 1929 Booth married Eddie Poggenburg, who changed his name to Gardner. Gardner produced a show, starring Booth, of skits based on the short stories of Dorothy Parker. In 1934 the director George Abbott saw Booth in a performance and when he was casting for *Three Men on a Horse* (1935), he remembered her as being perfect for the part of Mabel, a gangster's "moll" with a horribly "refined" Brooklyn accent. This substantial part served as Booth's big break and established her as an up-and-coming actress.

The play ran two years and Booth got excellent reviews. She left stock and devoted herself to Broadway. Her next role was in *Excursion* (1937). A string of long-playing hits followed, including *Too Many Heroes* (1937) and *The Philadelphia Story* (1939). Booth's portrayal of Liz Imbrie, the photographer in *The Philadelphia Story,* earned praise from the critics and the star, Katharine Hepburn. The following year she played a writer in *My Sister Eileen* (1940). Reluctant to be typecast as a comedian, Booth turned down a comedy part to try out for the serious anti-Nazi drama *Tomorrow the World* (1943). The producer, Theron Bamberger, was concerned that the public would associate her with comedy and laugh. Booth said, as recalled in a 1953 *Time* magazine article, "Don't worry. Getting laughs isn't quite that easy." In the play, costarring Ralph Bellamy, Booth portrayed a teacher combating fascism. It ran for two years with 499 performances and was a notable financial success.

Booth was not only starring on Broadway, she was also on radio, playing the part of Miss Duffy on *Duffy's Tavern.* The show was created by her husband, who played Archie, the manager. Gardner wrote the part of Miss Duffy, a sharp-tongued woman with a classic Brooklyn accent, for Booth who played it from 1941 to 1943. When she and Gardner divorced in 1942, she finished the season. Her departure was a serious loss to the show, and Gardner mounted a nationwide search for her replacement. In a number of guest appearances on other radio shows, Booth used her "Miss Duffy" voice, playing different characters.

Booth married William H. Baker, Jr., formerly an investment broker, on 24 September 1943. Following World

War II, they moved to a dairy farm in Bucks County, Pennsylvania, and Booth temporarily retired from the theater. Baker died in 1951. There were no children from either marriage.

Booth's first musical was *Hollywood Pinafore* (1945), playing the part of a gossip columnist named Louhedda Hopsons (a sly reference to Hedda Hopper and Louella Parsons). One of her songs was "Little Miss Butter-up," George Kaufman's version of the Gilbert and Sullivan "Buttercup" classic. In 1949 Booth received her first Antoinette Perry (Tony) Award for best feminine supporting role in *Goodbye, My Fancy*. Living on her farm in Pennsylvania, she commuted to Broadway to play the acid-tongued congresswoman's secretary. She invariably got more laughs than the star, played by Madeleine Carroll.

However, the role that most people associate with Shirley Booth is that of Lola Delaney, the frumpy housewife of an alcoholic husband in William Inge's domestic tragedy *Come Back, Little Sheba* (1950). Initially, Booth did not want the part. When Lawrence Langner of the Theatre Guild showed her a draft of the play, she read it and liked it, but said it wasn't for her. She wanted something "lighter." Langner persisted, and persuaded her to try the part. The play opened 15 February 1950 on Broadway. From this moment, after 3,500 performances in twenty-two different Broadway plays, Booth was finally a major star. After the final curtain went down opening night, Booth made the traditional visit to Sardi's restaurant to await the reviews. When she walked in the crowd gave her a standing ovation, and the unsuspecting Booth looked behind her, curious to see who was being applauded. Her performance, opposite Sidney Blackmer as Doc, resulted in a Tony for best actress and the New York Drama Critics Circle Award.

Following her favorite dictum—"An actress should make you forget everything she has done before"—Booth took a secondary role in her next play, the musical *A Tree Grows in Brooklyn* (1951). Her husband died suddenly while the show was in production, but Booth only missed two rehearsals and went back to work in the best tradition of the theater: the show must go on. When *A Tree Grows in Brooklyn* opened, Booth, playing the free-spirited Aunt Sissy, stopped the show with her rowdy number "Love Is the Reason." Critic John Mason Brown in the *Saturday Review of Literature* (1951) said Booth woke up the show and "her Sissy is among the best things she has done." She won *Billboard*'s award for the best female performance in a musical.

After much speculation as to who would play Lola in the film version of *Come Back, Little Sheba* (1952), the assignment was given to Booth. She did not expect the role, since she had previously been passed over for the film versions of *Three Men on a Horse, My Sister Eileen,* and *The Philadelphia Story,* and filmmakers were reportedly suggesting Bette Davis, Joan Crawford, or Judy Holliday. Playing Lola on film required some changes of Booth, to keep her in tune with the younger Doc of Burt Lancaster. The film was shot in one month, and her performance earned a number of awards, including an Academy Award and the best actress honors from the National Board of Review, the New York Film Critics Circle, and the Cannes International Film Festival.

Booth returned to Broadway, starring as Leona Samish, the lonely spinster in Arthur Laurents's *The Time of the Cuckoo* (1952). For the first time her name stood alone on the marquee of the theatre. The title of the play was not there; the marquee of the Empire Theatre simply said Shirley Booth. She won another Tony for this role, although she was never happy with the part of a woman who felt sorry for herself. In an interview in *Cosmopolitan* she remarked, "I had to fight myself to play her." Self-pity was never her style. When Hollywood offered her the role for the film, which became *Summertime* (1955), Booth turned down the part, and Katharine Hepburn took it. From 1953 to 1961 Booth played a number of roles to high critical praise, although the plays themselves were not so well regarded. Although Booth never saw herself as a Hollywood star, she did other films, including *About Mrs. Leslie* (1954) with Robert Ryan, *Hot Spell* (1958), and *The Matchmaker* (1958), playing Dolly Levi. In 1961 she disappointed many of her peers by "defecting" to television, signing a five year contract to play a housemaid, Hazel Burke, on a weekly show of the same name. *Hazel* was based on the *Saturday Evening Post* cartoon character created by Ted Key. The character was outspoken and sassy. Booth added the elements of warmth and lightheartedness to the character. Almost from the start it topped the Nielsen ratings. For this show (1961–1966), she received a number of awards, including Emmys in 1962 and 1963.

When the series ended, Booth starred in a television adaptation of *The Glass Menagerie* (1966), winning another Emmy for her portrayal of Amanda Wingfield. By 1970 she was back on Broadway in the musical *Look to the Lilies* and a revival of Noël Coward's *Hay Fever*. Neither play was a financial or a critical success. In the spring of 1973 Booth shot a half season of episodes for a television comedy *A Touch of Grace,* playing a perky widow who had moved in with her daughter and son-in-law, but the show was cancelled. She retired after the series folded to her 1810 home on Cape Cod, Massachusetts, living the rest of her life in relative seclusion. Always a private person, Booth once said, "I save my exuberance for the stage." Booth died in her home from a stroke.

Although Booth acted in film and on television, most of her professional life was devoted to the stage. She appeared in more than forty Broadway plays, equally at home in drama and comedy. Critics continually remarked on her versatility. During the 1950s she was described as the "Queen of the American Theatre," and in 1953 she appeared on the cover of *Time* magazine. Booth brought to her roles enormous talent, great technique, warmth, and honesty.

★

Booth's scrapbooks and photographs are in the Museum of the City of New York. A lengthy article by Katherine Laris is in *Notable Women in the American Theatre: A Biographical Dictionary* (1989). Periodical articles include John Mason Brown, "Shirley Booth in the Rescue," *Saturday Review of Literature* (5 May 1951): 23–24; "Actress," *The New Yorker* (19 May 1951); Harry Gilroy, "Hollywood Can't Change Shirley Booth," *New York Times Magazine* (27 Apr. 1952); Robert Coughlan, "New Queen of the Drama," *Life* (1 Dec. 1952); Jay Kaye, "Shirley Booth: Broadway's Choice," *Coronet* (Dec. 1953): 48–51; "The Trooper," *Time* (10 Aug. 1953); Jon Whitcomb, "Shirley Booth," *Cosmopolitan* (Sept. 1958); and Thomas Congdon, "At Home with 'Hazel'," *Saturday Evening Post* (22 Sept. 1962). Obituaries are in the *Los Angeles Times* and *New York Times* (both 21 Oct. 1992), and London *Independent* (22 Oct. 1992). A tribute, "Maid to Order," is in *People Weekly* (2 Nov. 1992).

MARCIA B. DINNEEN

BOYLE, Katherine ("Kay") (*b.* 19 February 1902 in Saint Paul, Minnesota; *d.* 27 December 1992 in Mill Valley, California), writer of fiction, nonfiction, and poetry best known for her novellas and short stories, for which she twice won the O. Henry Memorial Award, and for her social and political activism.

Boyle and her older sister, Joan, were born into a family marked by conflicts between its suffragette women and the authoritarian, patriarchal figure of the author's grandfather Jesse Peyton Boyle, who founded the West Publishing Company. The three generations of the family lived and traveled together, with vacations in the Poconos in Pennsylvania and summer voyages to Europe. Katherine Evans, Kay's mother, supported the socialist Eugene Debs, read to her daughters from Gertrude Stein's *Tender Buttons,* and encouraged their artistic aspirations. Boyle's father, Howard Peterson Boyle, lost most of the family fortune through mismanagement.

Throughout her life Boyle carried the lessons of her family situation: women had a right to careers independent of marriage; dominant and especially heroic men were to be admired, unless they threatened a woman's independence; and social and political activism were the individual's obligation. Boyle attended schools briefly and irregularly in Washington, D.C.; Philadelphia; Atlantic City, New Jersey; and Cincinnati, but never earned a degree, seeing it as irrelevant to her writer's calling.

Kay Boyle. LIBRARY OF CONGRESS

Early in 1922 Boyle moved to New York City, where her sister Joan was a fashion designer for *Vogue.* On 24 June, Boyle married Richard Brault, a French veteran of World War I. Two of her reviews appeared in *The Dial,* and Harriet Monroe published Boyle's first poem in *Poetry.* In November 1922 Boyle joined the staff of Harold Loeb's *Broom* under Lola Ridge, who was a friend of the anarchist Emma Goldman and who inoculated Boyle with progressive ideas. *Broom* printed a few of Boyle's poems. She met many writers through Ridge, including William Carlos Williams, who became a lifelong friend.

In the spring of 1923 Boyle and her husband went to France, where they stayed with the Brault family in Saint-Malo. The stultifying atmosphere of provincial Brittany furnished material for Boyle's first novel, *Plagued by the Nightingale* (1931), in which a young American woman struggles against French bourgeois culture and attempts to avoid pregnancy. A pattern was established: Boyle would convert the stuff of her life into fiction, using the story line to analyze and provide the moral justification for her actions. Contemporary reviews ranged from Katherine Anne Porter's favorable *New Republic* summation to the *New York Times,* which complained of a lack of substance beneath a polished surface. *Plagued by the Nightingale* marked Boyle's invention of an inexperienced young American woman as the point-of-view character. Later many critics and Boyle herself would come to see the prevalence of this figure as a weakness in her novels.

Residence in Harfleur, where Brault was employed, provided the material for *Gentlemen, I Address You Privately* (1933), a sympathetic novel about homosexuality. After Boyle became ill in the damp northern coastal climate, she accepted the invitation of the Detroit-born tubercular poet Ernest Walsh and joined him in March 1926 at sun-drenched Grasse. Soon Boyle and Walsh became lovers; he died on 16 October, and Boyle later gave birth to their daughter. She claimed that Walsh was her one great love, and in rapid succession she wrote poems, short stories, and the novel *Year Before Last* (1932) based on her life with the dying poet.

Following Walsh's death, Boyle lived with Brault in Stoke-on-Trent, until 1928 when she joined, for six months, the Paris commune run by Raymond Duncan; this led to the novel *My Next Bride* (1934). She quickly garnered a wide acquaintanceship that included Harry and Caresse Crosby, who published Boyle's 1929 volume *Short Stories*; Eugene Jolas, editor of *transition* magazine, who printed many of her poems and stories; and Sylvia Beach, Constantin Brancusi, Hart Crane, Marcel Duchamp, James Joyce, Robert McAlmon, Francis Picabia, and Gertrude Stein. To these were soon added Archibald MacLeish, Ezra Pound, Nancy Cunard, Samuel Beckett, and William L. Shirer. Tall, thin, and beautiful, Boyle was photographed by Man Ray.

Jonathan Cape brought out Boyle's first commercially produced volume, *Wedding Day and Other Stories,* in 1930; the reviews were mixed, as they always would be, but she was praised in the *Nation* and the *New York Times*. In July 1931 the *New Yorker* published "Kroy Wen," a clever piece about overwork and linguistic dysfunction, the first of her many stories to appear in the magazine. She has been credited with inventing a type of *New Yorker* story: the narrative line begins in the middle of an action, usually at a critical point and without a formal exposition, then reaches a conclusion without any hint of moral judgment. No such judgment was needed, Boyle implied: "All human misery," she said, stemmed from a "failure of love." Meanwhile, she and Brault were divorced on 9 January 1931.

After leaving the commune, Boyle lived with Laurence Vail, an American writer and artist whom she married in April 1932. He introduced Boyle to cross-country skiing and mountain climbing, sports that would feature in her fiction. Boyle received a Guggenheim fellowship in 1934. Residence in Austria resulted in her novel *Death of a Man* (1936), in which Boyle attempted to show how, under oppressive economic conditions, even decent folk could embrace fascism. The title story of her 1936 collection *The White Horses of Vienna* won an O. Henry Award. Two of her novellas published in 1938, *The Crazy Hunter* and *The Bridegroom's Body,* rank among the best of the century, and the same year her first volume of poetry, *A Glad Day,* appeared, remarkable for the intensity of its love lyrics.

Boyle and Vail had three daughters and escaped to New York from a Europe at war in 1941, the same year in which her short story "Defeat" garnered her second O. Henry Award. By this time Boyle had met Joseph Franckenstein, an antifascist Austrian baron who followed her to the United States. They were married in February 1943 (soon after her divorce from Vail) and had a daughter and a son. Franckenstein's experiences in the U.S. Army ski corps provided Boyle with episodes for her novel *His Human Majesty* (1949), and their life together in postwar Germany, where she reported on the Nazi war-crimes trials and he edited the *Frankfurter Neue Zeitung,* led to *The Smoking Mountain: Stories of Postwar Germany* (1951). During the U.S. congressional inquiry into subversive activity led by Senator Joseph McCarthy in the early 1950s, Franckenstein and Boyle were accused of harboring Communist sympathies, and he lost his position in 1953; their names were cleared only after a long struggle.

Boyle's novel *Generation Without Farewell* (1960) marked a successful return to long fiction, and in 1961 Boyle received another Guggenheim grant. Before Franckenstein's death in 1963, Boyle had become an antiwar activist and started teaching English and creative writing at San Francisco State University, where she remained until 1979. Her revision of McAlmon's *Being Geniuses Together, 1920–1930* (1968), to which she added supplementary chapters, is an important sourcebook on the expatriate generation.

Boyle purchased a four-story Victorian house in the Haight-Ashbury section of San Francisco, and she was sentenced to thirty days in prison for picketing the Oakland Induction Center in protest against the Vietnam War. *Testament for My Students and Other Poems* (1970), *The Long Walk at San Francisco State and Other Essays* (1970), and *The Underground Woman* (1975) reflect her antiwar activities. She also founded the San Francisco chapter of Amnesty International. *Fifty Stories,* a collection representing her lifetime production, appeared in 1980. *Words That Must Somehow Be Said,* a selection of essays, appeared in 1985, and *Collected Poems* in 1991. Her total output came to nearly forty volumes. For the last several years of her life Boyle lived in a retirement community called the Redwoods, where she died of natural causes. She is buried in San Francisco.

Perhaps more than any other American writer, Kay Boyle epitomized and often anticipated the pulse of the twentieth century.

★

The major archive of Boyle's extant manuscripts and papers is at the Morris Library, Southern Illinois University, Carbondale.

There is also important Boyle material at the Beinecke Library, Yale University; the Berg Collection, New York Public Library; the James Laughlin archive, Harvard University; the Harold Loeb archive, Firestone Library, Princeton University; the Harry Ransom Humanities Research Center, University of Texas, Austin. The only full-scale biography is Joan Mellen, *Kay Boyle: Author of Herself* (1994), but Sandra Whipple Spanier, *Kay Boyle: Artist and Activist* (1986), is especially valuable for its appraisal of Boyle's writing. For interviews and analyses see Elizabeth S. Bell, *Kay Boyle: A Study of the Short Fiction* (1992), and Marilyn Elkins, *Metamorphosing the Novel: Kay Boyle's Narrative Innovations* (1994). Two collections of essays are Marilyn Elkins, ed., *Critical Essays on Kay Boyle* (1997), and Sandra Whipple Spanier, ed., *Kay Boyle: A Special Issue of Twentieth Century Literature* 34, no. 3 (1988). The most complete bibliography is that included in David V. Koch, "Kay Boyle," *Dictionary of Literary Biography, American Writers in Paris, 1920–1939*, 4 (1980). An obituary is in the *New York Times* (29 Dec. 1992).

IAN S. MACNIVEN

BRANNAN, Charles Franklin (*b.* 23 August 1903 in Denver, Colorado; *d.* 2 July 1992 in Denver, Colorado), government official and advocate for farmers' rights, best known for the Brannan Plan, developed during his tenure as secretary of agriculture under President Harry S. Truman.

Brannan was the son of John Brannan, an electrical engineer, and Ella Louise Street. He graduated from West Denver High School in 1921 and spent some time at Regis College before transferring to the University of Denver, where he went to law school, earning an LL.B. in 1929. Upon being admitted to the bar in 1929, he practiced law in Denver. He married Eda Seltzer on 29 June 1932; they had no children.

Brannan started his career in government service in 1935, when he was appointed assistant regional attorney of the U.S. Department of Agriculture's Resettlement Administration in Denver. In 1937 he became the regional attorney at the Office of the Solicitor, Department of Agriculture, in that city, and in 1941 advanced to regional director of the Farm Security Administration for Colorado, Wyoming, and Montana. In 1944 President Franklin D. Roosevelt appointed Brannan assistant secretary of agriculture under Claude R. Wickard; Brannan continued under the next secretary of agriculture, Clinton P. Anderson. During that posting he was agricultural adviser to the American delegation to the United Nations Conference for International Organization in San Francisco, and vice chairman of the board of directors of Commodity Credit Corporation.

Brannan was a champion for the family farm and an early and enthusiastic New Dealer. He became an aggressive apostle of the Roosevelt-Truman farm program. When

Charles Brannan, 1956. AP/WIDE WORLD PHOTOS

Republicans attacked the Democrats' agricultural policies during the 1948 election, Brannan took to the stump, making about eighty speeches in thirty farm states. He was a decisive force in earning Truman the farm vote and helping make the upset election victory over Thomas Dewey a reality. Some of the largest Truman upsets were in the farm states—including Ohio, Wisconsin, and Iowa—that Dewey had carried against Franklin D. Roosevelt in 1944.

On 2 June 1948 Brannan was inducted as secretary of agriculture, following his appointment by President Truman. He held the post until January 1953. As secretary, Brannan is best remembered as the author, in 1949, of a set of controversial legislative proposals that became known as the Brannan Plan. This was the first post–World War II initiative to attain steady prices for farmers while ensuring that the cost of commodities was determined by market forces. Brannan described the plan in the May 1949 *Democratic Digest* as "a farm income and price support program which is dedicated to the interests of all the people." Its aim, Brannan stated, was to "build bigger industrial markets and employment, maintain high-level production of farm commodities, conserve natural resources, maintain reserves for national security and strengthen the rural community." The plan was supported by the National Farmers Union but fiercely contested by the American Farm Bureau Federation and a coalition of Republicans and conservative Democrats in Congress, who defeated the legislation in July 1949. In an interview in 1981 Brannan reiterated that the Brannan Plan "was the first real, direct and open attempt to give consumers the benefit of our abundance."

Upon his retirement from government service in 1953, Brannan resumed private law practice. His primary client was the National Farmers Union and its subsidiary insurance and related business enterprises. Within a year, he had become the union's general counsel; he served in this capacity until 1990. This work allowed him to continue to support the ideas expressed in the Brannan Plan as well as his emphasis on conservation of soil and water. He continued to push farmers to be "rightfully" preoccupied with conservation of soil and related water problems. He pointed out that farmers, their organizations, and the government were ignoring the "enormous amounts" of water being used to increase production and that a water crisis was imminent. He stressed that the most important hazard was water pollution and that it was time to start "cleaning up our rivers," in order to "safeguard permanent abundance and prosperity" in the United States.

Brannan was active in numerous community and national organizations. He served as president of the University of Denver Alumni Association and vice president of the Harry S. Truman Library Institute for National and International Affairs from 1981 until his death. He died in 1992, while he was in a Denver hospital undergoing tests for a heart ailment, and is buried in the Denver area.

Brannan emphasized that the government and farm organizations must work together in shaping farm policy, and that no one person or organization should be the sole representative of the farmers of America. His contributions include the introduction of agriculture price-support recommendations, a successful grain storage program, and the ratification of the International Wheat Agreement (1949). He was also effective as the adviser to the Economic and Social Council of the United Nations and as chairman of the U.S. delegation to the Inter-American Conference on Agriculture. Parts of the Brannan Plan eventually became law as late as 1973.

★

Brannan's papers, covering the years 1933–1991, are housed at the Harry S. Truman Presidential Library in Independence, Missouri. Information on Brannan is also in the records of the National Farmers Union at the University of Colorado. Brannan's role in shaping agriculture policy in the Truman administration is discussed in David McCullough, *Truman* (1992). See also John Kerr Rose, *The Brannan Plan: A Proposed Farm Program* (1950),

and Reo M. Christenson, *The Brannan Plan: Farm Politics and Policy* (1959). An obituary is in the *Washington Post* (5 July 1992).

JOAN GOODBODY

BROOKS, Richard (*b.* 18 May 1912 in Philadelphia, Pennsylvania; *d.* 11 March 1992 in Beverly Hills, California), novelist, screenwriter, and director of the motion pictures *Blackboard Jungle* (1955), *Elmer Gantry* (1960), and *In Cold Blood* (1967).

Brooks was born Reuben Sax, the son of Crimean Jewish immigrant laborers. After graduating from Overbrook High School in Philadelphia in 1929, he studied communications and theater at Temple University. Financial hardship and a dispute with his parents caused him to drop out in 1932, one semester short of graduation. He spent the next several years riding the rails and finding his own way. During this period he reinvented himself as Richard Brooks, an aspiring writer. He was also married for two weeks, ending the hasty union when he threw a Christmas tree out the window. Little is known of these early years; Brooks revealed few details even to intimates, establishing a passion for privacy that would characterize his entire career.

After holding journalistic and other jobs in New Orleans, Nebraska, Oklahoma, and Texas, Brooks returned to Philadelphia, where he worked for the *Philadelphia Record* beginning in 1934 and then the *Atlantic City Press Union* in 1936. He was in New York City by 1937, writing radio scripts for WNEW and the NBC Blue Network and serving as announcer and commentator as well. In 1940 he helped

Richard Brooks at the 1962 premiere of *Lawrence of Arabia*. © BETTMANN/CORBIS

organize the Mill Pond Theatre of suburban Roslyn, New York, with a program of introducing new plays. After an argument with a colleague, Brooks moved to Hollywood in 1941, where he continued to write dramatic scripts for radio—one a day for over a year. He broke into the movies as a scriptwriter for Universal Pictures, where he advanced from doctoring B pictures to writing exotic adventures like *White Savage* (1943) and *Cobra Woman* (1944).

Brooks enlisted in the Marine Corps in 1943, serving in a filmmaking unit at Quantico, Virginia. He wrote and narrated a documentary about the invasion of the Mariana Islands. Out of this military experience came his first novel, *The Brick Foxhole* (1945), a study of the boredom and pressures of barracks life. This book, which concerns the murder of a homosexual, was later filmed as *Crossfire* (1947), with the theme somewhat diluted. Brooks was nearly court-martialed because he failed to clear his novel with Marine Corps authorities in advance. Among the writers who rallied to his defense was Sinclair Lewis, a contact that had important consequences for Brooks's later career.

Returning to Hollywood, Brooks became associated with more important pictures. For the producer Mark Hellinger he collaborated on the screenplays of such hard-hitting crime dramas as *The Killers* (from Ernest Hemingway's short story, 1946), and *Brute Force* (1947). With the director John Huston he cowrote *Key Largo* (1948). Huston became a lifelong friend; Hellinger, who died suddenly in 1948, became a major influence. Brooks's third and final novel, *The Producer* (1951), is a rough portrait of Hellinger. It contains the telling line, "I can't take risks; I'm an independent producer."

Always seeking his own independence, Brooks signed with Metro-Goldwyn-Mayer (MGM) in 1949. There he sought to direct his own scripts, beginning with *Crisis* (1950), a dark film about a doctor's moral dilemma: whether to heal a brutal Latin American dictator whom he personally detests. Brooks was obliged to direct other people's stories in the early 1950s (*The Light Touch, Take the High Ground,* and *Battle Circus*). *Deadline U.S.A.* (1952) is the most personal of his early films; it featured Humphrey Bogart as a tough newspaper editor who investigates a scandal. The picture that vaulted Brooks to the top rank of Hollywood directors was *Blackboard Jungle* (1955), an explosive portrait of juvenile violence in an urban school. The theme was considered risky at the time, and MGM actually withdrew the film from the Cannes Festival for fear of seeming unpatriotic. But Brooks's violent staging captured public attention, initiating a whole cycle of juvenile delinquency films. *Blackboard Jungle* also helped launch the careers of two young stars, Sidney Poitier and Vic Morrow, and Brooks's savvy introduction of "Rock Around the Clock" into the background score helped drive the urban pulse of rock and roll into the public consciousness.

Brooks's concerns for violent subjects were now expressed in major efforts like *The Last Hunt* (1956), about the slaughter of the buffalo, and *Something of Value* (1957), a vivid picture about the Mau Mau rebellion in Kenya. He overreached with his melodramatic adaptation of *The Brothers Karamazov* (1958) but had greater success adapting Tennessee Williams to the screen in *Cat on a Hot Tin Roof* (1958) and *Sweet Bird of Youth* (1962), both with Paul Newman. The absurd studio-imposed happy ending for the latter was the last straw for Brooks's strained relationship with MGM. Thereafter he became an independent producer (Pax Enterprises) as well as writer-director.

His first independent production had come two years earlier for United Artists: *Elmer Gantry* (1960) is a burly, bustling masterpiece that is often said to improve on Sinclair Lewis's satiric novel about traveling evangelists. Brooks had received the novelist's encouragement to make a free adaptation of the book years earlier. He found the perfect incarnation of Gantry in his old friend Burt Lancaster, who humanizes the con-man-turned-preacher while romancing the deluded, yet passionately sincere, evangelist played by Jean Simmons. The film was widely praised for its vivid Americana, its imaginative use of color, and its lively performances. It was nominated for multiple Academy Awards and received three Oscars, including one for Brooks's screenplay. Brooks also fell in love with Jean Simmons on this project. They were married in 1961 and had one daughter. (Brooks's second marriage, to Harriet Levin in 1945, had ended in divorce.)

Brooks's next project was the colossal failure *Lord Jim* (1965), filmed under difficult conditions in prewar Malaysia and Cambodia. He rebounded with a taut Western, *The Professionals* (1966), and the beautifully photographed crime drama *In Cold Blood* (1967), one of Hollywood's last major black-and-white productions. *The Happy Ending* (1969) is an odd mixture of satire, melodrama, and feminism that was designed to showcase the talents of Jean Simmons, who was widely praised and earned an Oscar nomination for her work. After an uncharacteristic comedy, *$* [*Dollars*] (1971), and another Western, *Bite the Bullet* (1975), Brooks invested much effort in *Looking for Mr. Goodbar* (1977), a story about a young woman's troubled sexuality and eventual murder. Fighting to finance the film and make it his own way, Brooks went so far as to mortgage his home against the project. (The strain seems to have ended his marriage with Simmons; they divorced in 1976.) The resulting movie was praised for its vivid performances but criticized for overly explicit moralizing. Nevertheless, it became the greatest financial success of Brooks's career. However, Brooks's next two pictures failed miserably at the box office: the incoherent satires of nuclear terrorism (*Wrong Is Right,* 1982) and Las Vegas gambling (*Fever Pitch,* 1985). Brooks's health declined thereafter.

A highly uneven artist whose passionate idealism could be undercut by strident moralizing, Brooks nevertheless traced an extraordinary career path from straitjacketed studio writer to independent filmmaker. A rumpled, pipe-smoking, crew-cut figure in a baggy shirt, he got his own way by passion, guile, and fearless independence. A tough guy of the old school, he could boast of bringing in a picture a month ahead of schedule and a million dollars under budget. His ruthlessness could terrorize. Some called him "bonecrusher Brooks" and "God's angry man." But friends recalled a warm spirit under the gruff exterior. He received a total of eight Academy Award nominations—four for writing and four for directing. The Directors Guild and Writers Guild recognized his unusual combined talent with their joint presentation of the Preston Sturges Award for lifetime achievement in 1990.

Brooks died of heart failure in 1992. He is buried at Hillside Memorial Park in Culver City, California, where his epitaph reads, "First Comes the Word."

★

Brooks's papers are not yet available for study. Some materials are at the Margaret Herrick Library of the Academy of Motion Picture Arts and Sciences, Los Angeles. Patrick McGilligan, *Backstory 2: Interviews with Screenwriters of the 1930s and 1940s* (1991), pp. 27–72, contains a lengthy interview. Other interviews are in *American Film* (Oct. 1977 and June 1991). Richard Schickel offers a personal memoir in *Matinee Idylls* (1999), pp. 211–226. A valuable survey with filmography and bibliography is in *Dictionary of Literary Biography,* vol. 44: *American Screenwriters,* 2d series (1986). The English journal *Movie* 12 (1965) contains extensive interviews and appreciations. A doctoral dissertation by Francis Frost offers "A Historical-Critical Study of the Films of Richard Brooks, with Special Attention to His Problems of Achieving and Maintaining Final Decision-Control" (University of Southern California, 1976). Obituaries are in the *New York Times* (13 Mar. 1992) and *Variety* (16 Mar. 1992).

Brooks has received more critical attention in France than America. Patrick Brion, *Richard Brooks* (1986), is a lavish, large-format tribute that reproduces many French and English interviews and essays. See also *Cahiers du Cinéma* (Feb. 1959 and May/June 1965) and *Positif* (May 1968 and Nov. 1975).

JOHN FITZPATRICK

BROWN, John R. (*b.* 10 December 1909 in Funk, Nebraska; *d.* 22 January 1993 in Houston, Texas), Texas judge who practiced admiralty, maritime, and transportation law.

Brown, the son of E. E. and Elvira Brown, received an A.B. from the University of Nebraska in 1930 and a J.D. from the University of Michigan in 1932. In law school, he "studied like hell and got drunk once a month" while earning the highest grades in the school's history. Upon grad-

uation Brown went to Texas, settling in Houston where, despite not knowing "port from starboard or keel from truck," he was an associate of the Royston and Rayzor law firm in 1932, becoming a junior partner in 1936 and a partner in 1939. When he left in September 1955 he was a senior active partner specializing in admiralty, maritime, and transportation law. His most important case arose from the Texas City disaster in 1947. Two ships filled with ammonium nitrate fertilizer exploded while docked, leveling much of the city and killing over 600 people. Brown was one of the lawyers who brought suit against the federal government. They won at trial but lost on an appeal that the Supreme Court eventually upheld. Congress then appropriated $16 million in claims, significantly less than the original verdict. Three years later, in 1955, the Supreme Court reversed its position on the key issue.

Brown helped build the Republican party in Texas after World War II. He was a member of the challenged delegation that supported Dwight D. Eisenhower at the 1952 convention and became Harris County (Houston) party chairman the next year. In 1955 he was nominated to the Court of Appeals for the Fifth Circuit, which spanned the South from Georgia to Texas. After a bumpy confirmation struggle, in which his role in the Texas City litigation was reexamined and he came close to asking President Eisenhower to withdraw his nomination, Brown took his seat that July.

"We are our brother's keeper because God meant it that way," Brown said during his first year as a judge. He considered himself a Lincoln Republican, and he joined with Judges Richard T. Rives, Elbert P. Tuttle, and John Minor Wisdom to enforce the Supreme Court's 1954 decision in *Brown* v. *Board of Education* and to translate it into a broad mandate for racial justice and equality under law. They "made as much of an imprint on American society and American law as any four judges below the Supreme Court have ever done on any court," observed Burke Marshall, assistant attorney general in the administration of John F. Kennedy. "If it hadn't been for judges like that on the Fifth Circuit, I think *Brown* would have failed in the end."

From his first days as a judge, Brown demonstrated a talent for administration. He assisted successive chief judges in docketing, assigning judges to, and monitoring cases. "If Judge Brown is going to be the acting clerk," a colleague acidly observed, "we need another judge." Shortly after becoming chief judge on 17 July 1967, Brown designed and implemented summary procedures allowing judges to dispense of certain cases on the basis of the briefs alone, without oral argument. By the time of his death, sixty percent of the Fifth Circuit's cases were decided in this way. In 1970 Brown introduced a rule authorizing the court to decide a limited number of cases without issuing an opinion. He also persuaded the United States Judicial

Council, and hence Congress, to create an office of staff lawyers to screen briefs and records in most appellate cases, an innovation many other courts emulated. Brown's predecessor as chief judge, Elbert Tuttle, called him "the premier judicial administrator of this century."

These procedures were indispensable in the late 1960s as the Fifth Circuit had to meet the new demands of the Supreme Court in school desegregation. Thousands of school board cases were clogging the docket, and the judges had "to get the job done," Brown said. "All that can be said about school cases has been said," he told his colleagues. "There is no point in writing further words." Cases were decided by opinion orders. The court had "to 'ride roughshod' to complete the job of school integration in the Deep South," he noted. The "result is in [the] figures."

Brown considered *Gomillon* v. *Lightfoot* (1959), in which the Alabama legislature redrew city boundaries to exclude the largely black area around Tuskegee Institute, to be his most important opinion. "I had never concerned myself much with constitutional problems or issues," he later admitted. Implicitly criticizing his colleagues as "blind" for upholding the redistricting, Brown wrote, "I make no apologies for the view that the business of judging in constitutional fields is one of searching for the spirit of the Constitution in terms of the present as well as the past, not the past alone.... When legislation oversteps its bounds . . . the Courts are the only haven for citizens in the minority." The Supreme Court followed his approach.

An opinion in Brown's view "ought not necessarily to put the reader to sleep." A 1973 concurring opinion on the marketing of detergents certainly did not. Parodying the court's opinion and naming twenty-three brands, Brown noted, "Clearly, the decision represents a *Gamble* since we risk a *Cascade* of criticism from an increasing *Tide* of ecology-minded citizens." The writing style reflected the man: direct and decisive, but with an undeniable flair. Brown included soda pop slogans, puns, biblical references, mythology, and movie titles in opinions, and he wrote one decision as a poem. He was also a pioneer in the area of computers and the law, writing about their interface as early as 1961.

Brown's gregariousness, perpetual quips, and vibrant, usually plaid sport coats ensured that he would not be anonymous. His colleagues called him "peppery, warm, sarcastic, charming, forceful, even pushy." All conceded his enthusiasm and humor. Brown engaged in impromptu sing-alongs and appeared in costumes at judicial conferences, once wearing a Lone Ranger outfit complete with mask. It was a fitting disguise, for as one observer noted, Brown "was essentially a loner who masked his inner self with flamboyant style." His first wife, Mary Lou Murray, whom he married on 30 May 1936 and with whom he had one child, disliked both his becoming a judge and the Su-

preme Court's desegregation decision. After her death in 1977, Brown married Vera Smith Riley on 14 September 1979. He served as a major in the transportation corps during World War II in which he worked in the judge advocate's department and acted as a port commander in the Philippines. He was an active Presbyterian, serving as deacon and then as elder of his church. Brown died of cancer in Houston.

★

Brown's papers are at the O'Quinn Law Library of Houston University in Texas. Other sources include Frank T. Read and Lucy S. McGough, *Let Them Be Judged: The Judicial Integration of the Deep South* (1978); Jack Bass, *Unlikely Heroes: The Dramatic Story of the Southern Judges of the Fifth Circuit Who Translated the Supreme Court's Brown Decision into A Revolution of Equality* (1981); and Harvey Couch, *A History of the Fifth Circuit, 1891–1981* (1984), which discuss the Court of Appeals on the Fifth Circuit on which he served. Articles are found in *Houston Law Review* 34 (spring 1998); "Bench Conference" (interview with Brown), in *Trial* (Jan. 1984); Blake A. Bailey, "Profile: The Colorful Judge John Robert Brown," *Fifth Circ. Reporter* (Sept. 1990); "Salute to the Honorable John R. Brown," 767 F.2d lxvii (1984); "Proceedings," 743 F.2d lxvi (1985); "In Recognition," *Tulane Law Review* 54 (1980); Brown, "Electronic Brains and the Legal Mind: Computing the Data Computer's Collision with Law," *Yale Law Journal* 71 (1961). An obituary is in the *New York Times* (27 Jan. 1993).

ROGER K. NEWMAN

BROWN, Paul Eugene ("P. B.") (*b.* 7 September 1908 in Norwalk, Ohio; *d.* 5 August 1991 in Cincinnati, Ohio), football coach who led the Cleveland Browns to three National Football League championships and was part owner of the Browns and later the Cincinnati Bengals.

Brown was the son of Lester Brown, a dispatcher for the Wheeling and Lake Erie Railroad, and Ida Sherwood, a homemaker. He moved with his parents and sister to Massillon, Ohio, a community renowned for football, when he was nine years old. He first played organized football as a 120-pound sophomore at Massillon's Washington High School. His family had misgivings because of his small size, but his determination overcame their doubts. In the sixth game of the season, with the Massillon Tigers enjoying a safe lead, Brown was sent in at quarterback, and on his first play, he threw a touchdown pass.

Brown played three years of football, basketball, and baseball at Washington High, and was a pole-vaulter and broad jumper on the track team. He graduated from high school in 1926 and enrolled at Ohio State University (OSU) that fall when he was not quite seventeen years old. OSU's coaches would not let him try out for the football team

Coach P. B. Brown (*right*) and Cleveland Browns star quarterback Otto Graham, 1950. ASSOCIATED PRESS AP

because he weighed only 145 pounds. Also, he found the huge student body overwhelming, and after his freshman year, he transferred to Miami University in Ohio, which proved more to his liking.

In his first year at Miami, Brown worked with the freshman football team. By his junior year he was the starting quarterback on the varsity team and the baseball team's center fielder. He graduated in 1930 with a B.A. degree and immediately took a job coaching football and teaching English and history at Severn Middle Preparatory School in Annapolis, Maryland. His wife, Kathryn ("Katy") Kester, whom he married in 1929, was a registered nurse, and she took over the school's infirmary. They had three sons. In his two years at Severn, Brown's football team won sixteen games, lost one, and tied one.

In 1932 Brown went back home to Massillon as head football coach and teacher at Washington High School. Over the next nine seasons the Massillon Tigers won eighty games, including the last thirty-three in a row, lost eight, and tied two. In his final year, Tiger games attracted an average of 18,200 spectators in a city with a population of 26,000. Brown coached basketball for several years and became director of athletics for Washington High and the city's recreation director.

In 1941 Brown was named head coach at Ohio State University, "the only job I ever wanted," he said later. At

the age of thirty-three, he was the youngest head coach in the history of the Big Ten, a conference of ten Midwestern athletic powers. In his first season the Buckeyes won six games, lost one, and tied one. Their only loss was to Northwestern University, whose quarterback, Otto Graham, would star with Paul Brown's Cleveland team after World War II. In 1942 the Buckeyes were Big Ten champions and acclaimed as the best in the country. Ohio State's record slipped to 3–6 in 1943 because Brown had to rely on seventeen-year-old freshmen and students who had been refused military duty. During World War II Ohio State had affiliated with the U.S. Army's ROTC program, which did not permit enrollees to play college football, while some of their Big Ten rivals had joined the navy's V-12 program, which did.

Brown was commissioned as a lieutenant, junior grade, in the U.S. Navy in January 1944 and was assigned to organize and coach a football team at the Great Lakes Naval Training Center near Chicago. In two seasons at Great Lakes, Brown's teams posted records of 9–2–1 and 6–3–1 against colleges and other service teams. Brown was still in the navy in 1945 when he agreed to coach the Cleveland entry in the All-America Football Conference (AAFC), a professional league that planned to start play in the 1946 season. In a contest for fans, the name Browns was chosen for the team with strong support from Paul Brown partisans in the Massillon-Canton area south of Cleveland.

The Cleveland Browns quickly established a standard of excellence that brought them the championship in each of the AAFC's four years. Leaders of the National Football League derided the AAFC as "bush," but when Cleveland and two other AAFC teams were absorbed by the NFL in 1950, the Browns soon proved more than equal to the challenge of competing in the older circuit by winning the championship. In Brown's thirteen years of coaching the Browns in the NFL, the team won three league championships and seven conference titles.

After the 1962 season Brown was ousted by Art Modell, who became a part owner of the Browns in early 1961. Brown did not return to football until he helped organize the Cincinnati Bengals in 1968. He then coached the team until his retirement in 1975, after which he continued to run the Bengals' business operations as general manager and vice president until his death. Brown's first wife died of a heart attack during surgery in April 1969. He married Mary, a widow with four children, in June 1973.

Paul Brown was strait-laced and authoritarian in his dealings with players. His teams had a strict dress code calling for jackets and ties in public. In his later years he deplored the players' union and players' agents. He hated showboating and end zone antics after a touchdown. "Act like you've been there before," he urged his players. As a coach, he stressed the fundamentals of blocking, tackling, and precise execution of offensive plays and defensive positioning. Brown died in 1991 in Cincinnati from complications caused by pneumonia.

An early innovator in professional football, Brown was the first head coach to hire full-time, year-round assistant coaches and was the first to give players intelligence and psychological tests to judge their ability to learn and improve. He introduced play books and classroom instruction to pro football. He stressed speed and was the first to test foot speed in the forty-yard dash. He was the first to use messenger guards to send in plays to the quarterback (a practice he could not engage in during his first three years of coaching professional football because unlimited substitution was not permitted until 1949). Brown was also the first coach to use game films to judge players and was among the first coaches to station assistants high up in the stadium for a bird's-eye view of the action. The spotters used a telephone to the bench to suggest plays and defensive alignments.

★

With assistance from sportswriter Jack Clary, Paul Brown published his autobiography, *PB: The Paul Brown Story*, in 1979, four years after his last year as a coach. Clary also published an appreciation of Brown's many contributions to professional football, "Paul Brown," in the winter 1992 issue of *The Coffin Corner*, a bimonthly publication of the Professional Football Researchers Association. Bill Walsh, a former assistant coach for Brown and later head coach of the San Francisco 49ers, and the *New York Times* sportswriter Ira Berkow assessed Brown's place in professional football history in the *Times* in the days following his death (7 Aug. 1991 and 11 Aug. 1991). An obituary is in the *New York Times* (6 Aug. 1991).

ROBERT W. PETERSON

BUELL, Marjorie Lyman Henderson ("Marge") (*b.* 11 December 1904 in Philadelphia, Pennsylvania; *d.* 30 May 1993 in Elyria, Ohio), self-taught artist and cartoonist noted for her creation of Little Lulu.

Buell, or "Marge" as she came to be known worldwide, was the oldest of three daughters of Horace Lyman Henderson, a Princeton University graduate who practiced law in Philadelphia and the Chester County seat, and Bertha Brown, a homemaker. Buell and her two younger sisters were raised in an idyllic country setting where they were given ample opportunities to develop their natural talents. The girls all demonstrated an early flair for art, and they often staged amateur theatricals for family members and friends. Buell herself was an eager reader of wide range, especially of fiction classics and current biographies. The three sisters were also serious horsewomen in their younger years, and one of Buell's sisters owned an equestrian academy as an adult.

Buell's early precociousness in art led to a brief stay at a formal art school (possibly the Philadelphia Art Institute), but she apparently was not happy in this environment. After Buell graduated from Villa Maria Academy in Malvern, Pennsylvania, in 1921, she began experimenting with cartoon drawings in her "studio," a converted chicken coop on her father's gentleman's farm in Malvern. Through her father's contact with the *Philadelphia Ledger*, Buell published her first cartoon panel in 1921 when she was only sixteen. Ruth Plumley Thompson, who wrote most of the *Oz* books after L. Frank Baum died in 1912, was an early mentor and Buell later illustrated *King Kojo*, one of Thompson's books. This relationship and Buell's growing body of published work in the *Ledger* led to further sales of her cartoons to *Life*, *Judge*, *Collier's*, and the *Saturday Evening Post*. "Dashing Dot," a curled and bobbed "sweet young thing" whose boyfriend Dick wears oversized raccoon coats and zoot suits, was one of Buell's early characters. In addition to being a wry and compassionate observer of human nature, Buell also possessed a terrific sense of humor.

In 1935 Buell created "Little Lulu Moppet" at the behest of the *Post* when it lost its popular "Henry" cartoon to the King Features syndication. Although Little Lulu sported corkscrew curls and displayed a more spirited mien, she nonetheless possessed the same air of childhood innocence as Henry. Like "Dashing Dot," Lulu also had a boyfriend, who went by the alliterative name of "Tubby Tom Tompkins." By 1938 the Rand McNally Company had published the first Little Lulu book, an anthology of *Post* cartoons. Five additional anthologies were published by the David McKay Company from 1939 to 1944. In 1943 Lulu talked for the first time when Paramount Pictures released the first of eight animated cartoons, all of which were produced under Buell's supervision. Paramount eventually produced a total of twenty-six Little Lulu films from 1943 to 1947 and two more were released in 1961 and 1962.

Marge married Clarence Addison Buell on 30 January 1936, and the young couple moved to the old family place, Hershey Mill Road, in Malvern. Their union produced two sons. Buell always possessed an affinity for nature, and her sons were the beneficiaries of her love of natural history; indeed, she always encouraged them to study and collect shells, butterflies, and minerals. When the boys were nearly grown, an aunt, Alice Thomas, and her husband, both the epitome of amateur Victorian scholars, bequeathed the Buell family an extensive mineral collection, which the family later expanded together and donated to a local museum. Yearly vacations were usually spent at various resorts in southern New Jersey because Buell was very fond of the seashore.

By 1944 Buell had moved Little Lulu and her friends into the comic book format as well as into advertisements for Kleenex tissues; indeed, this early commercial venture contributed to Buell's "amicable" separation from the *Post*. During the next three decades Buell's venue became so varied that she became more a manager of the Little Lulu empire than its actual creator, although she did retain final say over all newspaper cartoons and comic book stories. Little Lulu collectibles consist of coloring, painting, and activity books; dolls in different dress styles and sizes; animated cartoons and films; phonograph records; games and puzzles; sewing cards, bean bags, balloons, and other toys; greeting cards; children's apparel and accessories; candy and confections; cosmetics and toiletries; towels and drapery fabrics featuring Little Lulu and her friends; and outdoor toys such as swimming rings, beach balls, and wading pools. A number of these items were manufactured in Canada and Brazil; thus, her simple little cartoon characters had a worldwide reach. The Lulu comic books were distributed internationally and in many foreign languages, from Japanese to Turkish. In 1971, Western Publishing Company, which continued to publish Little Lulu material as of the beginning of the twenty-first century, purchased Buell's rights to the Little Lulu trademark, and she retired.

The truth of Buell's life narrative was that she never set out to be an entrepreneur; however, she found herself overtaken by the rapid rate of her success. Her response was to limit the scope of the characters she invented. She made a deliberate decision to channel her creative energy into the design of games for children and into encouraging the development of her own children as well as several nieces. After her husband's retirement, the couple moved from Pennsylvania to Ohio, where they could be closer to their elder son and his family. Even in retirement, however, Buell remained active, joining Sorosis, for example, one of the oldest women's book clubs in the United States.

Throughout the Malvern years, Buell was a pillar of the Good Samaritan Episcopal Church in Paoli, Pennsylvania, serving not only as a Sunday school leader but also as a founding member of a boutique that crystallized out of the crafts fairs that the church periodically held to raise money for local charities. Buell was always a very private person, and she frequently refused to grant interviews to journalists and scholars alike. Despite the fact that she was the first successful female cartoonist in the United States, perhaps in the world, she remained uncomfortable with hearing her work interpreted as socially laden with issues. Buell died of lymphoma at the age of eighty-eight on 30 May 1993; she is interred at Westwood Cemetery in Oberlin, Ohio.

★

Trina Robbins mentions Buell several times in her retrospective, *A Century of Women Cartoonists* (1993); a "Dashing Dot" cartoon as well as two Little Lulu samples (a 1946 Kleenex advertisement and a puzzle page from Dell's *Little Lulu and Tubby in Alaska* [1959]), are included. Obituaries are in the *Washington Post* (2 June 1993), *New York Times* and *St. Louis Post-Dispatch* (both 3 June 1993), *Los Angeles Times* (4 June 1993), *Daily Telegraph* (12 June 1993), *Newsweek* (14 June 1993), *Guardian* (18 June 1993), and *People* (21 June 1993).

EVA M. MADDOX

BURCH, (Roy) Dean (*b*. 20 December 1927 in Enid, Oklahoma; *d*. 4 August 1991 in Potomac, Maryland), telecommunications lawyer, political adviser, and chairman of the Federal Communications Commission and the Republican National Committee.

Burch was born to Bert Alexander Burch and Leola Atkisson in Enid on the eve of the Great Depression. He served in the U.S. Army in Japan after World War II and later attended the University of Arizona, receiving a bachelor of laws degree in 1953.

From 1953 to 1954 Burch served as an assistant attorney general in Arizona before joining the Washington, D.C., staff of Senator Barry M. Goldwater in 1955 as a legislative and administrative assistant. In 1959 Burch returned to Arizona as a partner in the Tucson firm of Dunseath, Stubbs, and Burch. He married Patricia Meeks on 7 July 1961; they had three children.

Burch was an anonymous Arizona lawyer until he was thrust into the national spotlight in 1964. Senator Gold-

Dean Burch, 1969. AP/WIDE WORLD PHOTOS

water, ascending through the Republican leadership, chose Burch to become the Republican National Committee (RNC) chairman. Although he had no previous national political experience, Burch was a tremendous manager who overhauled the RNC headquarters, turning it into a marvel of modern communications and campaign organization.

The race for the Republican presidential nomination in 1964 was a struggle between the party's liberal and conservative wings, embodied personally by Governor Nelson Rockefeller of New York on the left and Senator Goldwater on the right. Under Burch's guidance, the RNC was committed to Goldwater, although Burch himself was seen by many as a moderate influence in the conservative senator's brain trust. When Goldwater appeared to be foundering entering the crucial California primary, Burch went to the state and took over. Many observers credit Burch with bridging the gap between Goldwater and the party's liberal wing, helping to deliver the state and the nomination.

While Burch was a moderate, he was decidedly a Goldwater loyalist, and he rejected attacks on Goldwater for being too conservative. In response to the senator's acceptance speech, in which he said "extremism in defense of liberty is no vice," Burch put the controversy in perspective. "If Goldwater had recited the Lord's Prayer there were certain people at the convention who were going to object to it."

Few observers gave Goldwater a chance to win the general election against the incumbent president, Lyndon B. Johnson, the popular former Texas senator and vice president who had entered the Oval Office after the assassination of President John F. Kennedy in 1963. The Democrats were the majority party, and they were united behind Johnson. Goldwater had many negatives, including a small-state, western political base and an image as a right wing extremist willing to split his own party in a quixotic quest for the presidency.

Nevertheless, when the expected Democratic landslide materialized, the party establishment wanted blood. In addition to the lost presidency, many Republican congressional candidates had been buried in the landslide alongside Senator Goldwater. Burch's own moderate Republicanism was lost in his association with Goldwater and the stridency of the conservative movement. Cries for Burch's scalp came from far and wide, and Burch agreed to play sacrificial lamb in the interest of the party. Indeed, some observers believe that Burch's willingness to step aside amicably helped pave the way for party unity in 1968, when Richard M. Nixon was able to retake the White House for the Republicans. In 1965 Burch returned to his law practice in Tucson. He maintained his close ties to Goldwater, managing the senator's reelection campaign in 1968.

A year later Burch was once again summoned to Washington. In 1969 President Nixon named Burch chairman of the Federal Communications Commission (FCC). During his tenure Burch made tough speeches focusing on children's television programming, denouncing much of the content as "just chewing gum for the eyes." The networks took notice, and Burch's campaign was influential in improving children's television. Burch was less successful in pressuring the networks to cover Nixon favorably.

Burch served as FCC chairman until 1974, when he was appointed counselor to the president, a post with cabinet rank. He retained that post under President Gerald Ford, leaving at the end of 1975 to join the Washington law firm of Pierson, Ball, and Dowd as a partner. Burch specialized in communication law but kept his hand in presidential politics. He helped guide President Ford's successful run for the 1976 Republican presidential nomination.

Burch was also a friend and political ally of the former congressman and Central Intelligence Agency director George Bush, serving as the vice presidential campaign's chief of staff after Bush was named Ronald Reagan's running mate in 1980. Burch also served as liaison between the Reagan and Bush organizations during the transition to the White House. During Bush's 1988 campaign for the White House, Burch was an adviser on the general election and in dealing with conservative forces within the Republican party.

Chronicling the connection between Bush and Goldwater, *Washington Post* columnist David Broder wrote that Burch "took the issues seriously, but was wonderfully irreverent about himself."

Burch stepped down from Pierson, Ball, and Dowd in 1987 to become director general of INTELSAT, the International Telecommunications Satellite Organization, a cooperative representing more than 100 countries that operates the satellite network transmitting most of the world's international telephone calls and television broadcasts. Burch was nominated by the U.S. government and confirmed by INTELSAT's assembly, made up of representatives of all member countries.

Burch was director general of INTELSAT until he died at the age of sixty-three, of bladder cancer. He was survived by his wife, Patricia; two daughters, Shelly Burch Bennett and Dianne Ruth Burch Butterfield; a son, Dean A. Burch; and a grandson. Burch was an important figure in Republican party politics for a quarter-century and, at his death, one of the most respected and influential communications officials in the world.

★

A number of books chronicle the controversial 1964 presidential campaign of the archconservative Arizona Republican Barry Goldwater, including Theodore H. White, *The Making of the President 1964* (1965), and Stephen Shadegg, *What Happened to Gold-*

water? The Inside Story of the 1964 Republican Campaign (1965). There are also several Goldwater biographies, including Lee Edwards, *Goldwater: The Man Who Made a Revolution* (1995), Robert Alan Goldberg, *Barry Goldwater* (1995), and the senator's own memoirs, *Goldwater,* with Jack Casserly (1988). While details of Burch's role in Goldwater's senate office and presidential campaigns are sprinkled throughout these volumes, unfortunately, a truly satisfying portrait of Dean Burch, the man, fails to emerge. Obituaries appear in the *New York Times* and *Washington Post* (both 5 Aug. 1991) and *Time* (19 Aug. 1991).

TIMOTHY KRINGEN

BURDICK, Quentin Northrop (*b.* 19 June 1908 in Munich, North Dakota; *d.* 8 September 1992 in Fargo, North Dakota), lawyer, congressman, and U.S. senator best known for his defense of federal farm subsidies and for securing federal developmental projects for his home state.

Burdick was one of three children of Usher Lloyd Burdick and Emma Robertson, whose families had been among North Dakota's earliest settlers. In 1910 the family moved to Williston, North Dakota, where Emma was a homemaker and Usher practiced law, farmed, and pursued a political career linked to William Langer and the Nonpartisan League (NPL) that eventually led to ten terms in the U.S. House of Representatives. Burdick attended public schools, where he excelled in debate, dramatics, and sports. He was the president of his Williston High School class for three consecutive years and in 1926 captained Williston's undefeated football team. Later that year he entered the University of Minnesota at Minneapolis, where he also played football, won fame as a blocker for Bronko Nagurski, and suffered a knee injury that kept him out of military service during World War II. After graduating with a bachelor's degree in 1931, he entered the University of Minnesota Law School, earning an LL.B. degree in 1932. He then joined his father's law firm in Fargo. On 13 March 1933 he married Marietta Janecky, with whom he had four children. Marietta died in 1958, and on 7 July 1960 Burdick married Jocelyn Birch Peterson, with whom he had one child.

As a young lawyer Burdick worked principally on foreclosure cases, acquiring, he said, a "social conscience." He also joined a reinvigorated NPL, embracing its brand of agrarian radicalism. With NPL backing, he ran for a series of offices, initially as a Republican because of League ties to that party, but from 1946 on as a Democrat. Unlike his father, however, he was long unsuccessful in winning. Between 1934 and 1956 his bids to become state attorney, state senator, lieutenant governor, governor, and U.S. senator all ended in defeat. Not until 1958, following the NPL's switch of affiliation to the Democratic party and his father's de-

cision to retire, did he become North Dakota's first Democratic congressman. He was elected to the seat long held by his father and was known, despite his age, as "young Burdick."

In Congress, Burdick secured membership on the House Interior Committee and set about making himself an authority on water resource development. He was also cosponsor of the unsuccessful Poage-McGovern-Burdick bill, aimed at subsidizing small farmer income. Breaking away from his father's isolationism, he became a supporter of the United Nations, reciprocal trade, and foreign aid. In addition, he voted with the liberal wing of his party on such issues as public works appropriations, minimum wages, and civil rights. His House tenure, however, was short. The death of Senator William Langer led, in June 1960, to a special election to fill his remaining term. In this election Burdick narrowly defeated the Republican nominee, Governor John E. Davis. The contest received national publicity as a referendum on efforts of Secretary of Agriculture Ezra Taft Benson to scrap rigid farm price supports in favor of lower, more flexible ones supported by export aids and land withdrawals. Burdick was a strong critic of the policy, and the election's outcome was hailed as a realization of his slogan, "Beat Benson with Burdick."

In the Senate, Burdick supported the domestic reforms of the John F. Kennedy and Lyndon B. Johnson administrations, was an early critic of the Vietnam War, and remained a persistent champion of farm subsidies and rural development, taking particular pride in a program to train rural health workers that would be renamed in his honor in 1998. His outstanding constituency service, folksy political style, and success in securing federal funds for North Dakota also helped him to build a strong political base, evident in his repeated reelection by large majorities. Before 1987, however, committee reforms and frequent changes in committee assignments prevented him from chairing a committee. While his varied committee service widened his interests to encompass such matters as prison and judicial reform, bankruptcy law, aging, and Indian affairs, he failed to become a senatorial leader on national issues. In his own view, his greatest accomplishment was his success in 1965 in securing authorization for the Garrison Water Diversion Project, a huge public works program altering North Dakota's landscape but later denounced by critics as environmentally unsound and wasteful of public resources.

In 1987 Burdick's clout increased. He became the chair of both the Environment and Public Works Committee and the Appropriations Subcommittee on Agriculture and Rural Development. In these positions he pushed for stronger clean air and farm programs but in general became a less reliable vote for the liberal wing of his party, rejecting in particular the environmentalist positions on waterway and mineral development. His determination to "get everything

Senator Quentin Burdick, 1981. ARCHIVE PHOTOS

that North Dakota is entitled to" also grew, leading critics to dub him the "King of Pork." In 1990, in a move that subsequently backfired, he secured a $500,000 grant to build a museum in Strasburg, the birthplace of bandleader Lawrence Welk. Criticism and ridicule finally led Congress to withdraw the grant.

As a personality, Burdick combined an athletic bearing and vigor, rugged good looks, and an easygoing accessibility with a generally rumpled appearance, a folksy unpretentiousness, and a reassuring sense of stern sincerity and moral rectitude. In a long political career made possible in part by such traits, he left his mark on North Dakota politics and to a lesser extent on the politics of farm subsidization, rural development, and congressional appropriations. His historical significance, however, lay less in his shaping of history than in a career that reflected both the extension of a tradition and its loss of relevance and vitality. Occupying the seats once held by his father and William Langer, he brought a tamer version of the NPL's agrarian radicalism into a world that was being shaped by an urban liberalism, seeking, as other inheritors of the tradition did, to find ways of ensuring its survival through incorporation into the new liberal creed. These remained elusive, and at the time of his death from heart disease, the tradition was being dismissed as a cloak for "pork barrel" deliveries and self-serving protectionism.

★

A large collection of Burdick's papers, primarily documenting his career as a congressman and senator, is located in the Chester Fritz Library at the University of North Dakota in Grand Forks.

There is no biography, but useful biographical sketches can be found in George Douth, *Leaders in Profile: The United States Senate* (1975), and Alan Ehrenhalt, ed., *Politics in America: Members of Congress in Washington and at Home* (1982). Numerous details about Burdick's political career can also be gleaned from the "North Dakota" sections of the *Almanac of American Politics* (1978–1992). The most useful articles in periodicals and yearbooks are "New Faces," *New Republic* (13 Oct. 1958); "Republican Burdick Cheers for Democratic Son," *U.S. News & World Report* (14 Nov. 1958); and "Quentin N. Burdick," *Current Biography 1963*. A variety of tributes are in *Memorial Services Held in the Senate and House of Representatives of the United States Together with Tributes Presented in Eulogy of Quentin N. Burdick, Late a Senator from North Dakota* (1992). An obituary is in the *New York Times* (9 Sept. 1992).

ELLIS W. HAWLEY

BURKE, Kenneth Duva (*b.* 5 May 1897 in Pittsburgh, Pennsylvania; *d.* 19 November 1993 in Andover, New Jersey), writer best known for his literary and social criticism and for his many studies of the rhetorical properties of language, who also wrote poems, short stories, and a novel.

Burke was the only child of James Leslie Burke, a clerk for Westinghouse Electric Company, and Lillyan May Duva, a homemaker. He grew up in Pittsburgh, where he graduated from Peabody High School in 1915. Malcolm Cowley, his lifelong friend and correspondent, was one of his classmates. He moved to Weehawken, New Jersey, with his family in 1915. In 1916 he enrolled for a semester at Ohio

State University in Columbus, and then returned to Weehawken in June. He enrolled at Columbia University in New York City that fall but withdrew in January 1918 because, as he wrote Cowley, he was afraid his formal education was doing him more harm than good and was interfering with his plan to become a "genius." Burke never did receive a degree and, from 1918 on, was entirely self-educated. For the next few years, he lived, worked, wrote, and studied in New York City, where he met many of the leading literary figures of his time and played an active role in the vibrant literary life of the city.

On 19 May 1919 Burke married Lily Mary Batterham, with whom he had three daughters. In 1921 Burke bought the first of his two farmhouses in rural Andover, the town he would live in for the rest of his life. While working in New York City during most of the 1920s, he commuted two hours by train to and from work. He lived in Andover for many years without electricity, running water, or indoor plumbing, until late in the 1960s when his second wife became ill, and he had to modernize his house. He chose a spartan existence because he did not want to clutter up his life any more than necessary with modern technology.

Burke's first ambition as a writer was to become, like Gustave Flaubert, a writer of poetry and prose fiction and an advocate of art for art's sake. His first published book was a collection of surrealistic short stories titled *The White Oxen* (1924). But as Burke was to discover while working as an editor for the literary magazine *Dial* (1924–1929), criticism and not fiction was to be his real calling, his true voice as a writer. Burke began writing critical essays in the mid-1920s even as he was working on his only novel, and it was as a literary critic that he first became well known with the publication of *Counter-Statement* in 1931. His first and only novel, *Towards a Better Life,* was finally published in 1932, and as Burke pointed out, was received with as much fanfare as a feather falling into the Grand Canyon. Burke's determination to become a genius was to be fulfilled through his criticism.

By the end of the 1920s, Burke was well established personally and professionally. He worked for the *Dial* until it ceased publication in 1929 and there met James Sibley Watson, who was to become his patron, and to whom he would dedicate three of his books in gratitude. The Wall Street crash of 1929 brought this period to a calamitous end and ushered in the economic miseries of the Great Depression. These two events had a profound effect on Burke's career and development and coincided with upheavals in his personal life.

In response to the crash and the depression, which seemed to signal the collapse of democracy and capitalism, Burke attempted to work out a more inclusive conception of what it meant to be a critic in the two books he wrote in the mid-1930s: *Permanence and Change* (1935) and *Attitudes Toward History* (2 vols., 1937). These were the kind of books, Burke said, that critics in the 1930s often put together to keep themselves from falling apart. In these books Burke sought a more significant and functional role for both art (literature) and the critic. He developed an approach he called "comic criticism," which was heavily dependent on an ironic perspective and treated literature as necessary equipment for living. It was also in the 1930s that Burke developed his important functional approach to literature as symbolic action, most thoroughly worked out in *The Philosophy of Literary Form* (1941), a collection of Burke's essays and reviews from this period.

Burke quite literally wrote his way through the 1930s, supporting himself and his family with writing and occasional teaching at the New School for Social Research at the University of Chicago and at Syracuse University. He also revamped his personal life. In 1933 he divorced his first wife, Lily Batterham, and married her sister, Elizabeth ("Libbie") Batterham, with whom he had two sons. He bought another farmhouse down the road from the first and lived there with Libbie and the boys until her death in 1969 and his own in 1993. The family, who remained on good terms, still occupies the house.

In 1943 Burke began a permanent part-time teaching

Kenneth Burke. LIBRARY OF CONGRESS

job at Bennington College in Vermont, which lasted until 1961. It was the only regular teaching job he ever had. In the 1940s, Burke also began work on his magnum opus, the three "Motives" books. If ever there was a flowering of his "genius," it was in *A Grammar of Motives* (1945), *A Rhetoric of Motives* (1950), and *A Symbolic of Motives* (modeled on Aristotle's *Poetics*), which was finished by 1956 but never published as a book. Burke called the approach to language and the drama of human relations in these three works "dramatism" because of its emphasis on language as action. Like all of Burke's prose, the Motives books were partly written in response to the major events of Burke's time—in this case, the carnage of World War II, including the Holocaust, and the anxiety of the seemingly interminable cold war with its threat of a nuclear war. Burke was to continue writing and publishing for thirty more years; after dramatism, he developed an approach to the study of language he called "logology," which he applied in *The Rhetoric of Religion* (1961), and in the omnibus collection of his essays titled *Language as Symbolic Action* (1966), and in many still uncollected late (1966–1984) essays.

Burke was a prolific writer of reviews, producing more than 150, and a voluminous and extraordinary letter writer, authoring thousands upon thousands of letters, sometimes over periods of many years, as with the Burke/Cowley letters. He was also an accomplished poet whose *Collected Poems* was published in 1968.

Burke was a small man of prodigious energy and enormous intellect; he was a fabulous talker, a serious drinker, and a lifelong insomniac. He taught, lectured, and gave readings at colleges and universities all over the United States, especially in his later years, after his wife Libbie died in 1969. He died in Andover at the age of ninety-six of natural causes.

In spite of his achievements and reputation, Burke was always paranoid about his own work and its reception and treatment by other critics. He worried about his social status and lack of "Ivy League" credentials. But he could never be described as an unacknowledged or underappreciated or misunderstood genius, having received enormous recognition in his lifetime, including eleven honorary degrees; a score of books and hundreds of essays published about his work; and the formation of a Kenneth Burke Society in 1984 that meets every three years to reappraise and continue the work he started.

★

The main Kenneth Burke archives, in the Special Collections Department at Pennsylvania State University Library, includes many letters from Burke's voluminous correspondence with many of the best-known literary figures of his time. See also *Selected Correspondence of Kenneth Burke and Malcolm Cowley, 1915–1981,* ed. Paul Jay (1988); Jack Selzer, *Kenneth Burke in Greenwich Vil-*lage: Conversing with the Moderns, 1915–1931* (1996); and *The Legacy of Kenneth Burke,* ed. Herbert W. Simons and Trevor Melia (1989). Useful works for the study of Burke include William H. Rueckert, ed., *Critical Responses to Kenneth Burke* (1969); William H. Rueckert, *Kenneth Burke and the Drama of Human Relations* (2d ed., 1982); *Extensions of the Burkeian System,* ed. James W. Chesebro (1993); and Robert Wess, *Kenneth Burke: Rhetoric, Subjectivity, Postmodernism* (1996). An obituary is in the *New York Times* (21 Nov. 1993).

WILLIAM H. RUECKERT

BURR, Raymond William Stacy (*b.* 21 May 1917 in New Westminster, British Columbia, Canada; *d.* 12 September 1993 in Dry Creek Valley, California), television and film actor most noted for his performance in the title role of the TV series *Perry Mason* (1967–1975).

Burr was the oldest of three children born to William Johnston Burr, a hardware dealer, and Minerva Smith, a pianist and music teacher and daughter of a U.S. naval officer. Shortly after he was born, the family moved to China, where they spent five years. His parents divorced when Burr was six, and his mother moved the family to Vallejo, California. His family was hit hard during the Great Depression, and at age thirteen Burr quit the San Rafael Mili-

Raymond Burr. THE KOBAL COLLECTION

tary Academy to find work on a cattle and sheep ranch. He returned to school a year later, but never completed junior high. Working in a variety of jobs after leaving school, he taught, traveled as a salesman, sang in a nightclub, and ran a weather station, all while taking extension courses from Stanford, Columbia, and the University of Chongqing. He had an interest in entertainment, including singing as a young adult, which led to his Broadway debut in the 1941 musical *Crazy with the Heat.*

Later in his life Burr stated that he had been married three times, a surprise to some of his close friends. His sister claimed that only the second marriage was official, prompting some to question the validity of the other unions. In 1939 he married Annette Sutherland. They had one child, a son. Sutherland died in June 1943, allegedly when her plane was shot down by the Germans. In 1946 Burr married Isabella Ward. The marriage lasted only a few months and was annulled in 1947. In 1950 Burr wed Laura Andrina Morgan. She died of cancer in 1955. In 1953 Burr's son died of leukemia. Burr then spent more than thirty years with his friend Robert Benevides.

Burr served in the U.S. Navy from 1944 to 1946 and was discharged with a shrapnel injury. He returned to acting, where his large size (in 1946 he weighed 340 pounds and stood six feet tall) led him to be cast as a villain in many films. His 1946 onscreen debut was in *Without Reservations* with John Wayne and Claudette Colbert. His career eventually encompassed ninety film appearances, including his notable performance as Lars Thorwald in Alfred Hitchcock's *Rear Window* (1954), his well received role as a district attorney in *A Place in the Sun* (1951)—an adaptation of Theodore Dreiser's *An American Tragedy*—and his role in the original *Godzilla, King of the Monsters!* (1954). Between 1951 and 1955 Burr made seven tours with the United Service Organizations (USO) to honor troops fighting in the Korean War, while continuing to make movies.

In 1957 Burr assumed the starring role in CBS's new television drama *Perry Mason,* for which he won two best actor Emmy Awards, in 1959 and 1961. By the end of the show, in 1966, Burr was the highest paid actor in television, earning $18,500 per episode. Although the series was extremely popular with viewers, Burr told *TV Guide* in a 1993 interview that the show "dominated [his] life" and that he regretted taking the role. It was a formulaic program that received little praise from critics. Perry Mason, a defense attorney, won almost every case on more than 290 shows, often upsetting the prosecuting attorney's case by springing new evidence or causing the breakdown of a witness in the middle of a trial. When Mason did lose a case, which happened only three times over the course of nine years, fans protested by sending the studio angry letters.

When *Perry Mason* was canceled, Burr retired with Be-

nevides to Naitaumba, the 1,830-acre island in Fiji that he had bought with Benevides in 1963, intending to raise cattle. In 1967 he returned to Hollywood to shoot the movie *Ironside.* The film's protagonist, Chief Robert Ironside, proved to be such a well-liked character that a television series was developed and Burr took the lead role. The program, about a wheelchair-bound private detective, ran from 1967 to 1975. His portrayal was so convincing that Burr insisted on appearing in variety shows "just to show people [he] could still walk."

Burr maintained an active schedule of TV, miniseries, and movie roles after the end of *Ironside.* In 1985 he reprised the role of Perry Mason in a series of made-for-TV movies, all of which proved to be popular. He had put the final touches on his last Perry Mason movie just before his death. He was planning to donate the proceeds of the movie to cancer research and pushed to complete the movie before personally undergoing treatment.

Burr was an avid orchid grower, and in 1961 he opened a Malibu nursery with Benevides. He donated part of his collection to the California Polytechnic Institute in 1982. He also loved art and established the Swarthe-Burr gallery in Beverly Hills, California, in 1960. His own gallery was launched in Beverly Hills in October 1961. Later in his life, Burr opened the Raymond Burr Vineyards in Dry Creek Valley, California.

Burr died at his ranch in Dry Creek Valley of cancer of the liver. Some sources give the cause of death as cancer of the kidney. He was buried in Fraserview Cemetery, in New Westminster.

Burr felt constrained by his roles as Perry Mason and as Chief Robert Ironside, but he was proud of his convincing work in those roles. He felt that *Perry Mason* in particular informed viewers about the inner workings of the legal system. Speculation frequently circulated about his personal life, but Burr preferred that the public see him only through his roles as an actor. He told *TV Guide,* "Everything else is none of their business."

★

Ona Hill documented Raymond Burr's professional career in *Raymond Burr: A Film Radio, and Television Biography* (1994). Valuable professional and personal information can be found in *Newsmakers 1994* 4 (1994), as well as *Current Biography Yearbook* (1961). An interview with Burr ran in *TV Guide* (25 Sept. 1993). Obituaries are in the *New York Times* (14 Sept. 1993) and *Los Angeles Times* (13 Sept. 1993).

LESLIE JANOS

BUTTS, Alfred Mosher (*b.* 13 April 1899 in Poughkeepsie, New York; *d.* 4 April 1993 in Rhinebeck, New York), architect and inventor of the board game Scrabble.

Alfred Butts, creator of Scrabble, at the Milton Bradley plant that manufactures the game's wooden letters, 1985. ASSOCIATED PRESS AP

Butts was the youngest of five boys born to Allison Butts, a lawyer, and Arrie Elizabeth Mosher, a high school teacher. Both parents were descended from Dutchess County, New York, farm families. Games, especially chess and anagrams, dominated family life. Alfred was said to have added a wild-card letter square to an anagram game that the Butts played, an idea he would later use in Scrabble.

After graduation from Poughkeepsie High School in 1917, Butts studied architecture at the Pratt Institute in Brooklyn and received his degree in architecture in 1924 from the University of Pennsylvania. He practiced for most of his career with the New York firm Holden, McLaughlin and Associates. Butts designed several buildings, most notably the $6.5 million Charles W. Berry Housing project on Staten Island, New York, and the Stanford Free Library, which he cofounded, in Stanfordville, New York.

Butts married Nina Ostrander, a high school teacher, on 3 October 1925. They had no children. They lived for many years in the Jackson Heights neighborhood in the borough of Queens, New York City. Work was scarce after 1929, but Butts did publish an article in *American Architect* (March 1933) outlining a formula for determining the rent of low-cost housing units based on the construction costs. The article's text and charts reveal his attention to detail and analytical skill. When he was unemployed from 1931 to 1935 during the Great Depression, Butts invented what he hoped would be a marketable adult game based on skill, strategy, and chance.

Using 100 anagram letter tiles, four wooden mah-jongg racks, and a cribbage board to keep score, he tinkered with combining anagram and crossword puzzle concepts, naming it at various times, "Lexico," "It," and "Criss-Cross Words." By analyzing the number of times that letters of the alphabet appeared on the front page of the *New York Times,* Butts determined the proportion of individual letters for the game: one Z but twelve E's, and so forth. He weighted the worth of each letter according to its frequency: vowels received one point, Q's and X's, ten. In a 1984 radio interview with Bob Edwards on National Public Radio's *Morning Edition,* Butts recalled, "I made up some sets. Nothing very much happened, though. Then suddenly, I got the idea, how about playing on a board. And that's what developed into what I call criss-cross words." He glued architectural graph paper on a chessboard to create 225 squares. Sixty-one premium squares could double or triple the value of either letters or whole words. Although the game looked like a crossword puzzle, players did not need to know word meanings. The game could be played by two to four players, and each played with seven letter tiles, which were replenished after each play until the tiles were gone. Butts forbade proper names or abbreviations but allowed Greek letters and names from the musical scale. By 1938 the game was essentially in its final form, and Butts had made and sold a number of sets but found no manufacturer. By then he was back at work as an architect.

In 1948 his old friend James Brunot, the former executive director of the War Relief Control Board, approached Butts about manufacturing and distributing the game. Butts would receive three cents for each game sold. They redesigned the game, named it Scrabble, and registered the trademark. Brunot and his wife set up a home manufacturing enterprise, which they moved to an abandoned school building in Dodgington, Connecticut. Over the next four years they made a few thousand sets but lost money. The game caught on in a modest way in the New York summer resorts, and then in 1952 a Macy's executive discovered Scrabble and stocked it at the department store. Thereafter, sales of the game boomed, to the extent that sets had to be rationed to stores nationally. *Life* magazine reported in 1953 that "there are perhaps 10 million players," and by 1954 a million games had sold. The standard set cost $3, and deluxe sets with white plastic tiles sold for $10.

In 1954 the Brunots licensed Selchow and Righter Company to produce, distribute, and market Scrabble in the United States and Canada. Selchow and Righter bought the trademark in 1972. COLECO Industries bought Selchow and Righter in 1986, and Hasbro, owner of Milton Bradley Company, purchased Scrabble in 1989. Outside the United States and Canada, J. W. Spear and Sons, a Mattel subsidiary, owns the trademark.

Butts confessed that he was not a good speller and that his wife often beat him at the game: "You may have seen some of the advertisements of Scrabble where the word 'quixotic' is made. My wife actually made that game. Two hundred and eighty-four points for one word because it went from one triple-the-word score down to the other triple-the-score word which had nine times the score for the word." In 1954 he bought the family homestead of Daniel Butts, his great-great-grandfather, in Standfordville. He and his wife lived there full-time after 1978.

Butts eventually received about five cents per game: "One-third went to taxes, I gave one-third away and the other third enabled me to have an enjoyable life." Butts patented several architectural structural systems. He also painted New York City scenes, and the Metropolitan Museum of Art bought six of them.

Butts was five foot seven, with bespectacled, bright-blue eyes. Professorial in manner and wryly humorous, Butts involved himself in the Standfordville community, voted Republican, collected stamps, and continued to invent board games, including one called Alfred's Other Game, into the last decade of his life, though none of these achieved commercial success. He lived his last years in the Baptist Home of Brooklyn in Rhinebeck, and died at the Northern Duchess County Hospital. He is buried in the Standfordville family plot.

One-third of American households own a Scrabble game and roughly 100 million Scrabble sets have been sold worldwide. Britain's Queen Mother, President Richard Nixon, and India's premier Jawaharlal Nehru were all avid players. Scrabble has been produced in many languages including Russian, Arabic, French, Dutch, Spanish, and Italian, and also in magnetic, Braille, and computerized versions. Deluxe editions in 1998 incorporated three improvements that players in 1954 requested: a bag for letters, a turntable, and a timer. At the 1999 International Scrabble Championship in Melbourne, Australia, Canadian Joel Wapnick spelled *grit* to win by one point, 403–402.

★

There is no biography of Butts, and after the Scrabble craze peaked in the early 1950s he all but disappeared from the public eye until his death in 1993. Butts's article "Pre-Planning Low Cost Housing Projects to Meet Economic Requirements," *American Architect* (Mar. 1933), indicates his meticulous attention to detail and his analytical skills. Robert Wallace, "A Man Makes a Best-Selling Game—Scrabble—And Achieves His Ambition (Spelled Out Above)," *Life* (14 Dec. 1953), and "Word Rage," *Look* (29 Dec. 1953), cover the development of the game and its rise to stardom. Bob Edwards spoke with Butts sometime in 1984 and replayed the brief interview as a tribute after his death. The transcript is available from National Public Radio. Obituaries are in the *New York Times* and *Newsday* (both 7 Apr. 1993), and *U.S. News & World Report* and *Time* (both 19 Apr. 1993). A telephone interview with Eleanor Butts, widow of Alfred Butts's nephew, Charles A. Butts (30 July 2000), provided personal information about Alfred Butts's last forty years.

CATHERINE RIFE SMALL

C

CAGE, John Milton, Jr. (*b.* 5 September 1912 in Los Angeles, California; *d.* 12 August 1992 in New York City), prolific avant-garde composer, teacher, visual artist, and writer of critical pieces and poetry, diaries, and fiction.

Cage was the son of John Milton Cage, Sr., an amateur scientist and inventor, and Lucretia Harvey, a homemaker and occasional newspaper columnist. He first studied piano as a child, taking lessons initially with his aunt. Following two years at Pomona College, in Claremont, California. Cage went to Europe, traveling between 1930 and 1931, studying piano, architecture, and painting with various people. On his return home, he gave occasional lectures on the modern arts to local women's groups. In 1932 he studied briefly with the pianist Richard Buhlig, who recommended that he send some of his compositions to the composer Henry Cowell. In 1934 Cage traveled to New York City to work as Cowell's assistant at the New School and also took lessons from the composer Adolph Weiss (a student of the composer Arnold Schoenberg). A year later, Cage returned to California to study with Schoenberg, who was dismissive of Cage's music. This opposition only made Cage more determined to compose. On 7 June 1934, he married Xenia Andreyevna Kashevaroff, who became a partner in his artistic endeavors.

During the mid-1930s Cage worked as a dance accompanist, first in Los Angeles, then at Mills College in Oakland, California (summer 1937), and finally at the Cornish School in Seattle (1938), where he met the dancer and choreographer Merce Cunningham. The two would become lifelong collaborators and partners. That same year, Cage "invented" the prepared piano by placing small screws, nuts, pieces of rubber, and other items into the piano's mechanism in order to change it from primarily a melodic to a percussive instrument; the side benefit of this invention was that the player could never be sure what sound would occur when he hit each key. Cage composed almost exclusively for the instrument over the next few years, including his celebrated *Sonatas and Interludes for Prepared Piano* (1946–1948), which led to both a Guggenheim Foundation grant and an award from the National Academy of Arts and Letters after it was premiered in New York City in 1949.

From 1941 to 1942, Cage was in Chicago, where he taught at Laszló Moholy-Nagy's short-lived experimental art school. In 1942 he moved to New York City, where he was reunited with Cunningham; Cage composed music for many of Cunningham's first solo recitals and, in 1953 when Cunningham officially formed a dance company, Cage became its music director, a position he held almost until his death. When he first came to New York City, Cage also met the artist Marcel Duchamp, a founder of the Dada movement, whose theories of art, and sense of humor, had an enormous impact on the composer. In 1945 Cage divorced his wife; that same year, he became interested in Eastern philosophy, attending classes by D. T. Suzuki on

John Cage. CORBIS CORPORATION (NEW YORK)

Zen Buddhism. In summer 1948 he taught at Black Mountain College in North Carolina—a center for avant-garde artists—along with Cunningham; they returned for another summer four years later. During 1949 Cage toured Europe for three months with Cunningham. There, he befriended the avant-garde composer and conductor Pierre Boulez and heard early examples of musique concrète (compositions made directly on audiotape, usually by creating audio collages through cutting and pasting short, unrelated recordings together).

The year 1952 was a banner one for Cage for performances and compositions. His *Music of Changes* was premiered on 1 January by the pianist David Tudor in New York City. It was one of his first pieces composed using, in Cage's words, "chance operations." By tossing dice or drawing cards, Cage would randomly select certain elements of a composition, such as pitch, tempo, duration, or loudness. He soon turned to using the Chinese work of divination, the *I Ching*, as an aid in this work, and eventually developed the *IC* computer program, with Andrew Culver, as a means of speeding the process. Also in 1952 Cage created his first work for audiotape, *Imaginary Land-*

scape, No. 5. Most famous of all, *4'33"*, the notorious "silent" piano piece (which Cage felt highlighted the music that is occurring around us at all times), premiered in Woodstock, New York, on 29 August of that year, also by Tudor. Cage's point—that there is music occurring all around us, at all times—reverberated through all of his later works. The piece is considered an early example of conceptual art.

In 1953 Cage created his most ambitious work for tape, *Williams Mix*, a tape collage composed of thousands of bits of tape, intricately fused onto six audiotapes meant to be played simultaneously, so that the result is an abundance of sounds within only several minutes. A year later, Cage left New York City to settle in an artists' community in Stony Point, New York. During this period, he befriended two New York painters, Jasper Johns and Robert Rauschenberg; both would participate in early "Happenings" (unscripted events featuring contributions by musicians, artists, actors, and others, designed to encourage audience participation) staged by Cage, and each later served as artistic director for Cunningham's dance company. In the second half of the 1950s, Cage taught on occasion at New York City's New School, where his students included many people who later became active in the 1960s Fluxus and Happening movements. (The Fluxus movement was an early 1960s art movement in New York that worked in a variety of media and also encouraged audience participation.) In 1957 he recorded *Indeterminacy*, a two-record set that features Cage reading minute-long stories while Tudor played randomly selected, and unrelated, piano pieces. A year later, Cage was celebrated with a "25th anniversary concert" of his works at New York City's Town Hall, which was released on record. This helped introduce Cage's art to a larger audience.

Cage's reputation was secured in the 1960s. From 1960 to 1961, he was a fellow at Wesleyan University's Center for Advanced Studies (he held this position again in 1970), in Middletown, Connecticut. While there, he assembled a collection of his writings, which was published by the university's press as *Silence* (1961); it has since become a classic of twentieth-century aesthetic philosophy. A year later, Cage founded the New York Mycological Society, reflecting a lifelong interest in mushrooms. (Cage sometimes augmented his income by supplying wild morels to New York's finer restaurants.) In 1962 he toured Japan with Tudor, and, a year later, undertook a world tour with Cunningham's dance company. From 1967 to 1969 he was an associate at the Center for Advanced Study at the University of Illinois in Champaign/Urbana; *HPSCHD* for one to seven amplified harpsichords and one to fifty-one tapes was the outcome of his residency there, which was performed only once, in the university's gymnasium. Cage created his first visual work in 1969. *Not Wanting to Say Anything*

About Marcel consists of a sequence of Plexiglas plates that recalled Duchamp's famous *Bride Stripped Bare by Her Bachelors Even,* which was executed on a large piece of broken glass.

During the 1970s and 1980s Cage worked as a writer, graphic artist, watercolor painter, and composer. In the early 1970s Cage became interested in the writings of Henry David Thoreau, culminating in the work *Lecture on the Weather* for 12 Amplified Voices, optionally with instruments, tape, and film (premiered in Toronto, 26 February 1976). During the second half of the 1970s Cage's long-running fascination with James Joyce began. In 1978 he published *Writings Through* Finnegans Wake, a collection of mesostics (in a mesostic, a word runs down the center of the page; Cage would then randomly select text from a source work, such as Joyce's novel, to place on either side of the central letters); follow-up volumes appeared in the early 1980s. In 1979 Cage completed *Roaratorio, an Irish Circus on* Finnegans Wake, which premiered in Paris.

In 1982 the first exhibit of Cage's scores and prints was given in a major museum retrospective that appeared at New York City's Whitney Museum of Art and the Philadelphia Museum of Art. Cage spent the mid-1980s creating his series of *Europeras.* Eventually the work was produced in five versions, each featuring randomly selected arias, costumes, set pieces, and even librettos. From 1988 to 1989, Cage held the Charles Eliot Norton Chair at Harvard University; as part of his responsibilities, he gave six randomly composed lectures that were subsequently published as *I-VI* (1990). In 1991 he created his last score for Cunningham, *Beach Birds.*

The year 1992 was a gala year for Cage, with many celebrations scheduled for his eightieth birthday. He composed special works for both large orchestras and smaller ensembles, and created his first film, *One*[11], a ninety-minute film whose only visible content was changing gray shadows against a white background. Cage was about to depart for a birthday celebration for him in Germany when he collapsed from heart failure in his New York City loft on 11 August. He died the following day.

Cage was a tall man with a long, distinctive face; he often wore a grin, in keeping with the Buddhist notion of maintaining a happy countenance. Early in his career, he wore his hair in a high brush cut; in the 1970s, he adopted long hair and a beard in the then-fashionable style; later in life, he returned to a less hirsute look. Cage won numerous awards and honors, particularly in the last decade of his life. Following his death, an ever-changing exhibit of his works in all media, called *Rolywholyover,* which Cage had been planning since 1990, toured the world.

Although he was commonly regarded as an apostle of "artistic freedom" and "chance," Cage was an extremely productive inventor who, once he transcended traditional conventions, was able to realize a wealth of indubitably original constraints. The notorious "prepared piano," which prevented the emergence of familiar pianistic sounds, was merely the beginning of a career that included scrupulously alternative kinds of musical scoring, idiosyncratically structured theatrical events, unique literary forms, and much else that was aesthetically new. Cage also revolutionized musical scoring (even collecting an anthology of *Notations,* 1969, that mostly reflects his influence), introducing graphic notations and even prose instructions. He was also a pithy speaker, who produced instantly quotable and memorable sayings, such as "I have nothing to say and I'm saying it—and that's poetry."

★

Cage's music manuscripts are at the New York Public Library; a portion of his manuscripts relating to poetry and writing and the humanities in general are at Wesleyan University (the balance is at the John Cage Trust in New York City); all correspondence is at Northwestern University in Chicago; his materials relating to nature, mycology, marine biology, and horticulture are at the University of California, at Santa Cruz; all other holdings are at the John Cage Trust. A famous early biographical/critical sketch of Cage is included in Calvin Tomkin's *The Bride and the Bachelor* (1965); another early profile was written by Richard Kostelanetz: "The American Avant-Garde: John Cage," *Stereo Review* 22, no. 5 (May 1969); the piece was subsequently included in his book *Masterminds* (1969). An "authorized" biography written by David Revill, *The Roaring Silence,* was published in 1992. Richard Kostelanetz assembled a book of interviews to create *Conversing with Cage* (1988) and edited two collections of articles on Cage, *John Cage* (1971) and *Writings about John Cage* (1993). The composer William Duckworth and Richard Flemming coedited *John Cage at Seventy-five* (1989). Marjorie Perloff and Charles Junkerman edited a collection of articles and interviews from the early 1990s titled *John Cage: Composed in America* (1994). William Duckworth included a long interview with Cage in his book *Talking Music* (1995). A complete annotated bibliography on Cage is due to be published in 2001 by Paul van Emmerick.

RICHARD CARLIN
RICHARD KOSTELANETZ

CAHN, Sammy (*b.* 18 June 1913 in New York City; *d.* 15 January 1993 in Los Angeles, California), lyricist whose songs, used primarily in motion pictures, included numerous popular hits.

Cahn was born Samuel Cohen, the only son and the second of five children of Abraham Cohen and Elka Riss, who had immigrated to the United States from Poland. His father was a restaurateur. His mother, a homemaker, persuaded him to take violin lessons in his childhood. He attended Seward Park High School on Manhattan's Lower East Side

Sammy Cahn. AP/WIDE WORLD PHOTOS

but dropped out before graduating. In his teens he joined a group, Frankie Miggs and His Pals of Harmony, which also featured pianist Saul Kaplan. As Sammy Cahn and Saul Chaplin, they formed a writing partnership, initially penning special material for vaudeville acts. In 1935 they had their first hit with "Rhythm Is Our Business," recorded by Jimmie Lunceford and His Orchestra; Lunceford was credited as a cowriter. Tommy Dorsey's Clambake Seven recorded their follow-up, "(If I Had) Rhythm in My Nursery Rhymes" (co-credited to Lunceford and Don Raye), and it reached the hit parade (the popular song ranking on the weekly *Your Hit Parade* radio show) in January 1936. They had two more songs in the hit parade before the end of the year: "Until the Real Thing Comes Along" (a revision of L. E. Freeman and Mann Holiner's song "Till the Real Thing Comes Along"), recorded by Andy Kirk and His Twelve Clouds of Joy, and "If It's the Last Thing I Do," recorded by Tommy Dorsey and His Orchestra.

The biggest hit of Cahn's early career was "Bei Mir Bist du Schön," for which he and Chaplin provided an English lyric to the original Yiddish song written by Sholom Secunda and Jacob Jacobs. The Andrews Sisters scored their first success with the song, which topped the hit parade in January 1938. The songwriters had begun working for Vitaphone Studios, writing songs for film shorts; from these efforts "Please Be Kind," recorded by Red Norvo and His

Orchestra, with Mildred Bailey on vocals, became another number-one hit in May. They returned to the hit parade eleven months later with "I Want My Share of Love," recorded by Larry Clinton and His Orchestra.

At the end of the 1930s, Warner Brothers, Vitaphone's parent company, transferred Cahn and Chaplin to Hollywood. There they provided songs for the film *Ladies Must Live* (1940), including the minor hit "I Could Make You Care," recorded by Tommy Dorsey, with Frank Sinatra on vocals, thus beginning an association between Cahn and Sinatra. Over his long career, Sinatra recorded more songs by Cahn than by any other songwriter.

Cahn and Chaplin moved from Warner Brothers to Republic Studios and then Columbia Pictures without scoring any more hits, and they ended their partnership in 1942. Shortly after, Cahn did his first writing with composer Jule Styne back at Republic, for the film *Youth on Parade* (1942). Among their compositions was "I've Heard That Song Before," which was recorded by Harry James and His Orchestra for a million-selling record that became the biggest hit of 1943 and was Cahn's first to be nominated for an Academy Award. (He would ultimately receive a total of twenty-six nominations, the most for any songwriter.) With that, he and Styne made their partnership permanent. In 1944 they scored major hits with "Vict'ry Polka," recorded by Bing Crosby and the Andrews Sisters, and "I'll Walk Alone," recorded by Dinah Shore.

Cahn and Styne's first attempt at a Broadway musical, *Glad to See You,* closed out of town in 1944, but "Guess I'll Hang My Tears Out to Dry" from the score later became a standard. Renewing his association with Sinatra, who had become a successful solo singer, Cahn wrote "Saturday Night (Is the Loneliest Night of the Week)" with Styne for the singer, who scored a hit with it in 1945. Sinatra also had a hit with "I Should Care," which Cahn wrote with Axel Stordahl and Paul Weston for the film *Thrill of a Romance* (1945), and insisted that Cahn and Styne be engaged to write songs for his film *Anchors Aweigh* (1945), among them "I Fall in Love Too Easily." The songwriters' most successful song of 1945 was "It's Been a Long, Long Time," with a lyric perfectly timed to appeal to returning GIs and their loved ones; three different recordings of the song each hit number one toward the end of the year. Meanwhile, Cahn married actress Gloria Delson on 5 September 1945. They had two children and were divorced in April 1964.

Cahn and Styne had two number-one hits in 1946, "Let It Snow! Let It Snow! Let It Snow!," recorded by Vaughn Monroe, in January, and "Five Minutes More," recorded by Sinatra, in September. In 1947 they finally succeeded on Broadway, writing the songs for the musical *High Button Shoes,* which opened on 9 October and ran for 727 performances, the longest-running musical of the 1947–1948 season. Returning to Hollywood, they went to work at Warner Brothers, writing songs for Doris Day's film debut, *Romance on the High Seas* (1948), among them the hit "It's Magic." Styne, however, wished to continue writing for the theater, while Cahn preferred the movies, and after writing songs for another Doris Day vehicle, *It's a Great Feeling,* in 1949, the two parted amicably.

Over the next six years, Cahn had no permanent songwriting partner. The composer he worked with most frequently during this period was Nicholas Brodszky, with whom he wrote "Be My Love" for Mario Lanza to sing in the film *The Toast Of New Orleans* (1950); it hit number one, sold a million copies, and earned an Academy Award nomination. Cahn and Brodszky's title song for the Lanza film *Because You're Mine* (1952) was another major hit and Academy Award nominee. The early 1950s marked a decline in original movie musicals, but Cahn kept busy writing title songs for nonmusical films; in 1954 he teamed with Jule Styne again to write "Three Coins in the Fountain," a chart-topping, million-selling hit that finally won him the Academy Award for best song, on his tenth nomination. The same year, he was surprised by the belated top-ten success of "Teach Me Tonight," a song he had written years earlier with Gene de Paul.

In 1955 Cahn formed his third long-term songwriting partnership, with James Van Heusen at the instigation of Sinatra. Their first work together came with the television production of Thornton Wilder's play *Our Town*. For it, they wrote "Love and Marriage," a hit for Sinatra and an Emmy Award winner. Within months, Sinatra was back on the charts with another Cahn–Van Heusen song, "(Love Is) the Tender Trap," from his film *The Tender Trap* (1955). Although the songwriters worked together for the next fourteen years, for Cahn it was not an exclusive partnership. He worked extensively with other composers on film projects and independent songs. His next top-ten hit, in December 1956, came with Sinatra's recording of "Hey! Jealous Lover," which he wrote with Kay Twomey and Bee Walker. The following year, he and Van Heusen wrote "All the Way," which Sinatra sang in *The Joker Is Wild* (1957) and recorded for a top-ten hit; it won the lyricist his second Academy Award.

By the late 1950s, Cahn was working more frequently with Van Heusen and less frequently with others. As the pop singles market turned toward rock and roll, while pop singers remained dominant in the LP format, Cahn and Van Heusen contributed title songs to classic Sinatra albums such as *Come Fly with Me, Only the Lonely, Come Dance with Me!,* and *No One Cares,* released in 1958 and 1959. They also wrote the light-hearted "High Hopes" for Sinatra to sing in the film *A Hole in the Head* (1959), resulting in another Academy Award and a Grammy nomination for song of the year. "The Second Time Around,"

their most successful song of 1960, was written for the Bing Crosby film *High Time,* although Sinatra scored the top of the chart with it; Academy Award and Grammy nominations followed.

Even title song assignments for the movies began to dry up in the early 1960s, though Cahn and Van Heusen wrote "Pocketful Of Miracles" for the film of the same name in 1961. In 1963, their "Call Me Irresponsible" was used in *Papa's Delicate Condition* and won Cahn his fourth Academy Award while also earning another Grammy nomination for song of the year. The songwriters' work in 1964 on the movie musical *Robin and the Seven Hoods,* starring Sinatra, Dean Martin, Sammy Davis, Jr., and Bing Crosby, included "My Kind Of Town," an Oscar nominee that became a Sinatra signature song. The following year, they wrote the title song for the acclaimed Sinatra album *September of My Years,* yet another Grammy song of the year nominee.

By the mid-1960s, there was little demand for their style of writing in Hollywood, and Cahn and Van Heusen wrote the songs for a Broadway musical, *Skyscraper,* which opened in November 1965 and ran for 248 performances. A second show, *Walking Happy,* opened a year later and ran for 161 performances. After this, Cahn's work was only occasional, although it included the title songs for the Julie Andrews vehicles *Thoroughly Modern Millie* (1967) and *Star!* (1968), with Van Heusen, and the unsuccessful 1970 stage musical *Look to the Lilies* with Styne. He married on 2 August 1970, to Virginia "Tita" Basile Curtis, a fashion consultant. They had no children.

Cahn always claimed to be the most highly paid performer in show business, figuring that his song demonstrations to potential singers of his works ended up earning him vast sums when the songs were taken up and used. In 1974 he branched out into performing in public, staging an autobiographical Broadway revue, *Words and Music,* in which he sang his songs and told stories about his life. (The same year, he published his autobiography, *I Should Care.*) The show ran for 127 performances on Broadway, and then Cahn toured it around the United States and in England. He continued to place occasional songs in films until 1987. In 1993 he died of congestive heart failure in Los Angeles, where he is buried in Westwood Memorial Park.

Sammy Cahn was known for his speed and professionalism. In addition to the many well-remembered songs he wrote, he continued throughout his career to turn out special material and parody lyrics, without charge, for his favorite performers. His facility as a lyricist and his earthy manner, along with his long career in Hollywood, caused him to be underestimated both for the quality of his work and its emotional content. He himself downplayed his abilities. In fact, he was a consummate craftsman whose lyrics hold up well against those of the classic songwriters who preceded him by a decade or so on Broadway, and for all his disclaimers, his words revealed him to be an unashamed romantic who reveled in detailing the wonders of love through verse.

★

Cahn's autobiography, *I Should Care* (1974), is the best source for biographical information. Also useful is the recording *An Evening with Sammy Cahn* (1978), an early version of his Broadway show *Words and Music,* which was performed as part of the "Lyrics and Lyricists" series at the Ninety-second Street YMHA in New York. There is no biography. Max Wilk, *They're Playing Our Song* (1973), has a chapter featuring an interview, and David Ewen, *American Songwriters* (1987), contains a good entry. Didier C. Deutsch's annotations to the Columbia House Music Collection's album *The Great American Songwriters: Sammy Cahn* (1992), provides another good, brief biographical essay. An obituary is in the *New York Times* (16 Jan. 1993).

WILLIAM J. RUHLMANN

CAMPANELLA, Roy (*b.* 19 November 1921 in Philadelphia, Pennsylvania; *d.* 26 June 1993 in Woodland Hills, California), Brooklyn Dodgers baseball player who was the premier catcher in the National League during the 1950s and was instrumental in the eradication of baseball's color line.

Campanella was the youngest of four children born to John Campanella, an Italian American owner of a fruit and vegetable market, and Ida Mercer, an African American homemaker. In 1928 the Campanella family moved from the Philadelphia neighborhood of Germantown, to the suburb of Nicetown, where Roy attended Asa Parker Grade School, Gillespie Junior High School, and Simon Gratz High School. At school, students (both black and white) called him "half breed" because of his mixed parentage.

As a youngster Campanella played stickball in the streets and developed a love for baseball. In 1935 he began playing semipro ball on weekends with the Bacharach Giants, a Philadelphia-based team. In 1937, at the age of fifteen, he was discovered by Baltimore Elite Giants catcher-manager Biz Mackey, and Roy left high school, joining the Elites as a third-string catcher to give Mackey some relief behind the plate. In 1939 Mackey was traded and Campanella became a regular. That season the Elites won a four-team postseason Negro National League playoff.

Campanella appeared in three East-West games, which were the Negro Leagues' All-Star game, and was voted the Most Valuable Player (MVP) in the 1941 game. The young catcher remained with the franchise through the 1945 season, except for 1943 and the latter part of 1942 when he played with Monterrey in the Mexican League after a dispute with Elites owner Tom Wilson. During these years Campanella also played several winter seasons in Latin

Roy Campanella. AP/WIDE WORLD PHOTOS

America, primarily in Puerto Rico but also in Cuba and Venezuela.

When Branch Rickey, owner of the Brooklyn Dodgers, began implementing his plan to integrate organized baseball, which had excluded black players since the onset of the twentieth century, Campanella was the second black player he approached. Chuck Dressen, who had seen Campanella play in a series of exhibition games against a white team, recommended him to Rickey and arranged the meeting. Campanella, however, mistakenly thought that Rickey wanted him to play for a new Negro team that he was forming and declined the initial offer. Both Jackie Robinson, who was the first African American player signed by Rickey, and Campanella had been selected for a black all-star team to tour Venezuela following the 1945 season. When Robinson informed Campanella that Rickey had signed him for the Brooklyn Dodgers organization, Campanella realized his mistake and was determined not to repeat his error.

Campanella was ready for the major leagues when he signed with the Dodgers, but Rickey had another role for the young catcher. He wanted Campanella to help integrate the minor leagues before moving him up to the parent Dodgers. Campanella was assigned to play with the Nashua, New Hampshire, team in the New England

League in 1946, with the Montreal Royals in the International League in 1947, and (despite winning the MVP Award in each of these seasons and being declared the best catcher in organized baseball, including the major leagues, by Buffalo manager Paul Richards) with the Saint Paul Saints in the American Association briefly in 1948.

Campanella's performance at Saint Paul earned him a quick promotion to the parent ball club, and he joined the Brooklyn Dodgers in 1948. Beginning in 1949, he was the starting catcher for the Dodger teams that won five National League pennants in a span of eight seasons and barely missed two other flags, losing on the last day of the season (1950) and in a postseason playoff (1951). During this eight year span, Campanella was a fixture behind the plate in the All-Star game, appearing in every game. The Dodger teams of this era later became known as the "Boys of Summer" after the title of Roger Kahn's 1971 book on those great teams.

In each of their pennant-winning seasons with Campanella behind the plate, the Dodgers battled the lordly American League champion New York Yankees in the World Series and seemed jinxed as they lost each time except 1955. That year Campanella was honored for the third time as the National League's Most Valuable Player; his other awards came in 1951 and 1953 (when he was also the *Sporting News* outstanding National League player). The *Sporting News* also selected Campanella to its major league all-star team in 1949, 1951, 1953, and 1955.

The 1957 season was to be Campanella's last, as his career was ended by a near-fatal accident. On 28 January 1958, while driving home from his liquor store at 7th Avenue and 134th Street in Harlem (which he had bought with a loan from Branch Rickey), his station wagon skidded on a patch of ice, and he lost control of his car, which crashed into a telephone pole and turned over. Campanella was left hanging upside down in the station wagon with a broken neck and injured spinal cord that left him paralyzed. The tragic accident left him a quadriplegic confined to his wheelchair for the rest of his life.

Campanella was determined to lead a productive life and persevered through his rehabilitation to inspire others with handicaps. He became a baseball ambassador, conducting his own radio show and speaking to youth groups. He wrote a book, *It's Good to Be Alive,* which was later made into a television movie.

The Dodgers owner Walter O'Malley staged an exhibition game at the Los Angeles Coliseum for Campanella on 7 May 1959. A capacity crowd of over 93,000 fans were on hand for the tribute, while thousands more were turned away. At the time, this was the largest crowd ever assembled for any game of baseball—and this was only an exhibition game. The crowd gave Campanella a thunderous ovation as the Dodgers captain Pee Wee Reese wheeled him onto the field after the completion of the fifth inning. All the lights were turned off in the ballpark, and each person lit a match. The 93,000 points of light illuminating the stadium were awe-inspiring. Campanella's recollection of this spectacle is moving. He wrote later, "I cried without shame as this tremendous throng—all 93,103 of them—stood up in tribute. . . . The Coliseum suddenly burst into a mass of blinking stars."

Had it not been for the accident, Campanella might well have become the first African American manager in the major leagues. He managed for one game at Nashua, when the manager Walt Alston was ejected from the game, and he managed the Vargas ball club during the 1946 winter season in Venezuela.

Campanella was married three times and had eight children, three of whom were adopted. His first marriage was to Bernice Ray in 1939; they had two daughters. The young couple was frequently separated due to Campanella's playing baseball year-round, and eventually the marriage ended in divorce. His second marriage was to Ruthe Willis on 30 April 1941, and the couple had three children. Campanella had also adopted Ruthe's son from a previous marriage. The family established residence in Saint Albans in the borough of Queens in New York City. Later they moved to Glen Cove on Long Island, where Campanella enjoyed his favorite hobbies. Their basement was filled with an extensive system of railroad tracks and model trains. The house contained elaborate tanks of tropical fish, and he had a yacht (the *Princess*) that he loved to take on fishing expeditions.

After the tragic accident, Ruthe's affection waned. Unable to reverse the changing relationship, Campanella filed for legal separation on 2 August 1960. By the spring of 1962, he had moved into an apartment at Lenox Terrace, near his liquor store. On 27 November 1962, he sold his home (named Salt Spray) on Long Island. Two months later, on 26 January 1963, Ruthe died of a cerebral hemorrhage.

On 5 May 1964 he married a neighbor, Roxie Doles. He adopted her two children. Following the wedding, they lived in Hartsdale, New York, until 1978, when they moved to Los Angeles after Roy accepted a job in the Dodgers Community Relations Department. Campanella credited Roxie with helping him get his life back together. The beloved Dodger received baseball's highest honor in 1969, when he was inducted into the National Baseball Hall of Fame at Cooperstown, New York. Campanella died of a heart attack in a Los Angeles suburb at the age of seventy-one, over thirty-five years after his crippling accident He was eulogized by his friends as a "gentle giant" in a private memorial ceremony at Forest Lawn Hollywood Hills.

In his pioneering role to help eliminate the color line, Campanella was a visible sign of racial compatibility. His presence wearing a Brooklyn Dodgers uniform uplifted the spirits of black Americans and enhanced white Americans' awareness of racial equality. During his active baseball career, he personified leadership and excellence on the diamond and served as a role model for young Americans of all racial and ethnic backgrounds. After his tragic accident, the faith, courage, and indomitable strength of character that Campanella demonstrated continue to be an inspiration to handicapped people worldwide.

★

Campanella's autobiography *It's Good to Be Alive* (1959) is an excellent source of information. Another good source is Dick Young's biography, *Roy Campanella* (1952), written after Campanella's first MVP season. See also Milton Shapiro, *The Roy Campanella Story* (1958), and Gene Schoor, *Roy Campanella: Man of Courage* (1959). Among many incidental profiles the best known is Roger Kahn's "Manchild at Fifty" in *The Boys of Summer* (1972). An obituary is in the *Los Angeles Times* (1 July 1993).

JAMES A. RILEY

CAPRA, Frank (*b.* 18 May 1896 in Bisacquino, Sicily; *d.* 3 September 1991 in La Quinta, California), film director most identified with populist New Deal–theme films of the 1930s and the "Why We Fight" armed forces documentaries of the 1940s.

Francesco Capra was the son of Salvatore Capra, a peasant farmer, and Rosaria Nicolosi, a craftsman's daughter. The family immigrated to the United States in 1903. The family settled in Los Angeles, where both parents toiled at menial jobs. Frank attended public schools while working as a newsboy. Industrious and determined, he overcame his mother's opposition to his further education. But the only book he owned for years was *The Three Musketeers,* which he read from age twelve onward, according to his own account, about "two thousand times." Capra performed in school plays while attending Manual Arts High School in modern-day Hollywood. He also heard socialist ideas from teachers and grew fascinated with movies. Some of his classmates were already film extras, but his first job in entertainment was playing guitar in brothels in downtown Los Angeles.

He attended Throop College of Technology (later the California Institute of Technology) in Pasadena and majored in chemical engineering as a reliable means of upward mobility. He also wrote short stories and won a fellowship for a six-week travel expedition around the United States, during which he took numerous photographs for a school presentation. He entered the army in 1917 and became an engineering instructor. He was discharged in December 1918 after contracting influenza. Capra returned to school but lost interest in science before graduation and, seeing his grades drop sharply, turned to the burgeoning movie industry.

Frank Capra. LIBRARY OF CONGRESS

Capra took work picking hops in the Sacramento Valley, where he heard about a call for extras on a western being shot nearby by the director John Ford. He signed on and soon obtained fulltime work as a jack-of-all-trades at the Christie Film Company, which made slapstick comedies on Sunset Boulevard. Released after two months, he sought repeatedly to make a living in movies as a writer, scripting several early unsuccessful silent films.

His first venture at directing was *Fulta Fisher's Boarding House* (1921), shot for $1,700 in a small studio across from San Francisco's Golden Gate Park. Based in part on a Rudyard Kipling poem set in a Calcutta grog shop with assorted rough characters, it featured a Mary Magdalene–style heroine redeemed at the end. *Fulta Fisher's Boarding House* received a few glowing notices and earned a profit, but plans to make a series of films from famous poems quickly fell apart. Capra also directed a short documentary (title unknown) in 1921 celebrating the two-week visit of an Italian naval cruiser to San Francisco, a prototype for Capra's later wartime documentaries; it starred Dorothy Revier, who soon became famous as the model for Columbia Pictures's trademark "torch lady." Capra's first important break came thanks to his romance in the early 1920s with the actress Helen Howell, whose connections helped him rise to near-director status. She reputedly sought him out after viewing *Fulta Fisher's Boarding House* and he began working for a small company whose financial backer was Helen's father. Cheaply produced comedies, sometimes starring Revier or Howell, at first found Capra working as a prop man, then gag writer, and finally assistant director. In 1923 Capra and Howell married; the next year they left San Francisco for Hollywood.

Capra later observed that writing gags had been the "shortcut" to screen success because a skilled comedy writer could advance quickly if studios noticed his talent. By 1924 he was working with the Hal Roach Studios, writing gags for the *Our Gang* comedies and some twenty-five Mack Sennett films, including several starring comic Harry Langdon. Like many other "caption" writers or "titlists" of the silents, his work grew more sophisticated, approaching themes and treatments later used in his major films. Sennett gave Capra his first chance to direct for a major studio in 1925 with *Soldier Boy,* but fired him as an incompetent after the third day of shooting.

Luckily for Capra, Langdon broke with Sennett and moved over to First National Pictures, taking Capra with him as gag writer. Langdon soon sponsored him as a director, first of several scenes in *Tramp, Tramp, Tramp* (1926), a Langdon box-office hit. Capra's direction of the comedian in *The Strong Man* (1926) established his own style—hailed at the time and ranked by subsequent critics as one of the foremost of the silent comedy standards—mixing satire and sentimentalism in social themes, in this case a naïf (played by Langdon) who manages somehow to clean up a corrupt town.

Beginning with *That Certain Thing* (1927), Capra struck up a useful relationship with producer Harry Cohn and cameraman Joe Walker at Columbia Pictures that would last through the best of Capra's career. Known for his exacting approach, he soon turned out feature after feature for the studio, first gaining the credit "A Frank Capra Production" with *Say It with Sables* (1928)—the year he divorced Helen Howell. Paid handsomely and owning Columbia stock, he rapidly became wealthy as the studio prospered. Capra bought a small house in what would become the exclusive Malibu Colony, where (along with the Roosevelt Hotel and the Hollywood Athletic Club) he would frequently spend his time between pictures. He had arrived, but not entirely.

Loaned out by Cohn to Louis B. Mayer and Metro-Goldwyn-Mayer (MGM), Capra went to work in 1928 on *Brotherly Love,* about a prison guard and an inmate who both fall in love with the warden's daughter. Although offering higher production values than Columbia, MGM controlled its directors tightly. Frequently using substitute directors for retakes, the larger MGM produced more im-

personal films. Perhaps because of Capra's rejection of that method, but likely because of a series of continued smaller conflicts over creative control, Capra was fired during the last weeks of shooting. It was a blow to the rising director but also a reminder that whatever its limitations, Columbia offered him the best artistic climate for his work.

Meanwhile, Harry Cohn was gambling Columbia's profits on a near-spectacular that cost eight times more than any of Capra's earlier films. The sound feature *Submarine* (1929), made with full cooperation of the navy, fell into difficulties during production. Cohn replaced his big-name action director Irvin Willet with Capra, who reshot nearly every scene. A critical success, *Submarine* became the largest moneymaker in the studio's short history, catapulting Capra into sound movies.

Capra had developed a feeling for films about the "little guy" and the Hollywood-style redemption of the downcast and even the degraded. The Wall Street crash of 1929 and resulting Great Depression also had a dramatic effect on the instinctively conservative, Republican Capra. He grasped the value of the socially conscious narrative, both for the integrity of the story and for the film's potential box-office success. Undertaking *Ladies of Leisure* (1930), based upon a Broadway play about a prostitute, he wrote a draft of a script and then turned to the leftist writer Jo Swerling, initiating an era of his intimate collaboration with writers sympathetic to unionism, antifascist causes, and even to the Soviet Union. Not only did the social and economic climate of the time affect the way Capra made his films, it also impacted the audiences, who hungered to see their senses of betrayal and estrangement from the American dream reflected on the screen.

Ladies of Leisure had another important influence upon Capra. Stage actress Barbara Stanwyck had only three failed films to show for her Hollywood career thus far and had decided upon a return to Broadway when Capra asked her to test for the lead. She reluctantly agreed, and he discovered in the former chorus girl the female complexity and toughness that he had been seeking. Thanks in no small part to his filming of Stanwyck—with whom Capra subsequently had a romance of several years—Capra learned to direct in ways maximizing his actors' capacities, female and male alike. *Platinum Blonde* (1931), the first of his sound films about the little guy (and written in part by Swerling), received good notices and made a healthy profit. Jean Harlow's role as an heiress and sweetheart won her star status with the film. The comedy also prepared Capra for later films through the narrative of a male lead (played by Robert Williams) who suddenly finds himself surrounded by luxury, only gradually grasping the emptiness of his worldly success.

Capra married Lucille Warner Rayburn in 1932, when he began working with rising screenwriter Robert Riskin.

He and Riskin turned out a series of hits: the screwball comedy *It Happened One Night* (1934), for which Capra received his first Best Director Academy Award; *Lost Horizon* (1937); and *You Can't Take It with You* (1938), for which he received another Academy Award. The social shockers *Mr. Deeds Goes to Town* (1936), written by Riskin about a native fascist movement and for which Capra won his third Best Director Academy Award and starring Gary Cooper, and *Mr. Smith Goes to Washington* (1939), about corruption in Congress and written by the communist Sidney Buchman, stand among the foremost "message" films of 1930s Hollywood. Not surprisingly, contemporary reports from the Federal Bureau of Investigation's Hollywood agents and informers describe Capra's working relationships as highly suspicious at best, potentially subversive at worst.

At the leftward apex of his trajectory, Capra urged studio negotiations with the screenwriters and actors unions, spoke at public events of the Hollywood Anti-Nazi League, walked a local newspaper strike picket line, and bought the rights to Clifford Odets's radical play *Golden Boy*—then traded them away. Although politically mild, *You Can't Take It with You* pokes fun at the fanatical anticommunist "red hunters," who in real life set into motion the congressional investigations resulting a decade later in the Hollywood blacklist. Capra also served simultaneously as president of the Screen Directors Guild and of the Academy of Motion Picture Arts and Sciences (1935–1941).

Capra had become an American icon by the late 1930s but also a tragic private figure. A cover story on Capra in *Time* magazine (8 August 1938) described him as master of the "peculiarly American, peculiarly kinetic humor" and the "top director of the industry." As *You Can't Take It with You* was being previewed grandly for the press, one of his three children died suddenly following a tonsillectomy. According to friends, the director soon after returned to the Catholic church he had abandoned and assumed a melancholy that pursued him the rest of his life.

During World War II Capra became the most important Hollywood director of propaganda-edged documentaries. The seven "Why We Fight" documentaries (including *The Negro Soldier,* written by the communist writer Carlton Moss without credit), won Capra a Distinguished Service Medal in 1945. As Winston Churchill wrote, "I have never seen or read any more powerful statement of our cause or of our rightful case against the Nazi tyranny [than in Capra's war series]."

Emotionally burned out by the war effort and no longer in heavy demand by the studios, Capra formed Liberty Films, with William Wyler, George Stevens, and Sam Briskin, to make *It's a Wonderful Life* (1946), scripted by Capra, Riskin, Swerling, and the communists Albert Maltz and Michael Wilson. Melancholy despite its happy ending, *Wonderful Life* marked a loss of optimism for Capra and also for its star, James Stewart. As Capra biographer Joseph McBride explained, Capra drew upon his own gnawing uncertainties to show his lead's "equation of lack of money with desperation and shame,"—to say nothing of self-doubt and temptation to suicide.

In Hollywood of the blacklist era, Capra made the satirical *State of the Union* (1948) about American politics. Bitterly attacked for the film's mildly critical stance, he retreated, avowing his loyalty to "Americanism" against the rival communist system. But in the new conservative climate, his best talents were wasted. Capra's style deteriorated severely in his next several pictures, and he left Hollywood with great bitterness in 1951. Working intermittently in television and a few further undistinguished films, Capra drifted into a retirement that was marked by participation in numerous film retrospectives and college appearances, where he spoke about his work and his involvement in Hollywood's Golden Age. In a memoir and in public statements, he insisted repeatedly that he had never truly grasped the radical New Dealism that made him both famous and beloved. Perhaps he had understood the sentiments best intuitively, or perhaps, returning to the political conservatism of his youth, he had become ashamed of the social implications of his own cinematic accomplishments. The American Film Institute's Lifetime Achievement Award in 1982 may have reminded Capra, as it did the wider public, that his best work, done in response to social crisis, had been remarkably radical after all.

Capra succumbed to heart failure in La Quinta and is buried in the Coachella Valley Cemetery. His legacy endures decades after his heyday ended, as evidenced by features such as Oliver Stone's *Wall Street* (1987), which offered the little guy hope against the powerful and corrupt, and by use of the term "Capraesque," which denotes the kind of populist sensibility that his work embodied.

★

The Frank Capra Archive is at Wesleyan University, including scripts, correspondence, and other materials. His autobiography is *Frank Capra: The Name Above the Title* (1980), and the outstanding biography is Joseph McBride, *Frank Capra: The Catastrophe of Success* (1992). Other critical works include Bruce Henstell, ed., *Frank Capra: One Man—One Film* (1971); Richard Glatzer and John Raeburn, eds., *Frank Capra: The Man and His Films* (1975); Victor Scherle and William Turner Levy, *The Films of Frank Capra* (1977); and Raymond Carney, *American Vision: The Films of Frank Capra* (1986). Capra's letters that are not in the Wesleyan archive are scattered in many locations, as are production documents of his films.

PAUL BUHLE

CARNOVSKY, Morris (*b.* 5 September 1897 in St. Louis, Missouri; *d.* 1 September 1992 in Easton, Connecticut), character actor, director, and teacher who survived the Hollywood blacklist of the 1950s to thrill audiences with his Shakespearean portrayals.

Carnovsky was the son of Isaac Carnovsky, a grocer, and Jennie Carnovsky, a homemaker. As a child, his father took him to the Yiddish theater. "There was such richness in their portrayals of Jewish life," he recalled in a 1975 interview. "I could savor it. Once I smelled greasepaint, I was committed." In his first acting role, he played the title role of *Disraeli* in a 1916 production at Yeatman High School in St. Louis. In 1920, after graduating Phi Beta Kappa from Washington University in St. Louis, he moved to Boston. There, he made his professional debut with the Henry Jewett Players, an established company at the city's historic Copley Theater.

Carnovsky made his New York stage debut at the famed Provincetown Playhouse in Greenwich Village in December 1922. He played Reb Aaron in Sholem Asch's *The God of Vengeance*. Although the play itself was denounced by critics, the young Carnovsky received favorable reviews. He joined the most celebrated acting group in New York, the Theatre Guild, in 1923. Although he concentrated on supporting roles, in the next seven years Carnovsky became an increasingly visible member of the company. He appeared in such varied parts as Brother Martin in the world premiere of George Bernard Shaw's *Saint Joan* (1924), Alyosha, the youngest of *The Brothers Karamazov* (1927), and the judge in *Volpone* (1928). Finally, in 1929, he achieved stardom in the title role of *Uncle Vanya* in which he was described as "an actor to be reckoned with."

Carnovsky gravitated to one of several splinter groups that formed within the Guild in 1930 and 1931. The new group was led by directors Lee Strasberg and Harold Clurman, who held radically different views about acting and theater. It was a soul-searching experience for Carnovsky, who recalled in 1980, "I'd always had a nagging sense that I wasn't altogether the craftsman I wanted to be." He realized that acting was more than just inspiration: "Listening to Lee, I was eager to reduce this all to a science of acting of the highest degree. This new thing was exciting." Eventually, the informal groups evolved into an ensemble known as the Group Theatre. Carnovsky appeared in the Group's inaugural production of *The House of Connally* (1931) and in many subsequent naturalistic dramas, particularly the works of Clifford Odets. He was hailed as "one

Morris Carnovsky before the House Un-American Activities Committee, refusing to disclose whether he has ever had any Communist affiliations, 1951. © BETTMANN/CORBIS

of the most knowing actors in this or any other theatrical group." In 1937, when the company was on hiatus, he was enticed to Hollywood to play Anatole France in *The Life of Émile Zola* and a supporting role in *Tovarich*. He soon returned to New York to play the father of the young prize-fighter in Clifford Odets's *Golden Boy* (1937), the Group Theatre's greatest box-office hit. One critic commented: "Morris Carnovsky beautifully conveys the silent grief of the affectionate father." Other roles included that of the eccentric landlord in the smash comedy *My Sister Eileen* (1940).

Later that year, he moved to Los Angeles, where he became a leading member of the Actors' Lab, an ensemble made up of former Group Theatre members. In addition to acting, he directed several Actors' Lab productions. In 1941 he married Phoebe Brand, an actress, teacher, and director he met in the Group Theatre. They had one son. Although Carnovsky claimed that he did not like filmmaking, because it did not provide enough time to develop a character, he did appear in a number of films in the mid-1940s. These included roles in the anti-Nazi *Edge of Darkness* (1943), the war dramas *Address Unknown* and *The Master Race* (1944), the part of George Gershwin's father in *Rhapsody in Blue* (1945), the malicious gangster adversary of Humphrey Bogart in *Dead Reckoning* (1946), and, finally, *Cyrano de Bergerac* (1950).

By that time, the cold war anti-Communist frenzy had taken hold of Hollywood. Alumni of the left-leaning Group Theatre came under attack. Called before the House Un-American Activities Committee as a member of "Communist-front" groups, Carnovsky refused to provide the committee with the names of others. As a result, he was blacklisted by Hollywood. "As an experience," he recalled later, "it was revolting, injurious, hurtful. But . . . in an odd way it nurtured me, strengthened me, made me hard, objective. . . . And to that degree I think it fed me as an actor." With some fellow Hollywood outcasts, he returned to New York and launched a successful two-year off-Broadway run of *The World of Sholem Aleichem* (1953).

In his long, distinguished career, Carnovsky had never played Shakespeare. John Houseman of the American Shakespeare Festival in Stratford, Connecticut, a director who "did not give a damn about the blacklist" or Carnovsky's age (almost sixty), recruited him in 1956. By 1957 he had moved from supporting roles to Shylock in a production of *The Merchant of Venice,* which featured Katharine Hepburn as Portia. Critics praised the "dignity" he brought to the part. Carnovsky later admitted that he was able to use the bitterness he experienced during the McCarthy era "and poured into that portrayal." He continued to appear in a variety of Shakespearean productions, culminating in *King Lear* (1963), a role he reprised in Chicago and Los Angeles. Throughout the 1960s and 1970s, Carnovsky con-

tinued to tour the United States in Shakespearean roles and as Galileo in *Lamp at Midnight* (1975).

In 1966 he accepted an appointment in the Theater Arts Department of Brandeis University, enabling him to direct two professional productions a year. As late as 1989, at the age of ninety-two, Carnovsky directed a production of *Ivanov* in Wisconsin. He was elected to the Theater Hall of Fame in 1979. Carnovsky died of natural causes at his home, at the age of ninety-four.

Morris Carnovsky's wide range of professional experiences could be equaled by very few actors of his time. In his book, *The Actor's Eye,* Carnovsky noted: "The very examination of our capabilities as actors in the Group Theatre was an act of love. And fundamentally, that's how I think about everything that an actor does with all his truth and depth. An act of love."

★

Carnovsky's views about acting and his approach to various roles can be found in his *The Actor's Eye* (1984), written with Peter Sander. References can be found in Cindy Adams, *Lee Strasberg: The Imperfect Genius of the Actors Studio* (1980), and *Contemporary Theatre, Film, and Television* (1986). An obituary is in the *New York Times* (2 Sept. 1992).

LOUISE A. MAYO

CASTRO, Bernard (*b.* 11 August 1904 near Palermo, Sicily, Italy; *d.* 24 August 1991 in Ocala, Florida), inventor of the Castro convertible sofa and founder of the Castro Convertible Corporation who was touted as "the man who 'conquered space—living space, that is'" for inventing a sofa that could be turned into a bed.

Castro was fifteen years old in 1919 when he came to the United States from Sicily with his father, Carmello. After they were settled, they sent for Castro's mother, a home-maker, and his only other sibling. Working for a short time in a New York City bank making $8 a week, Castro realized that he really wanted to be a craftsperson and work more with his hands, so he began working as an apprentice with a decorator-upholsterer in a Manhattan furniture shop. Although Castro had attended school in Italy, he never completed high school. In the United States he attended night school to learn English and later earned a diploma from the New York School of Interior Design.

While working as an apprentice, Castro repaired davenport sofas. Frustrated with trying to fix their complicated mechanisms, he became determined to build a beautiful sofa "a child could operate." In 1931, after saving $400, Castro opened his own furniture shop in Manhattan and began working on his concept of a convertible sofa with a mechanism that could turn it into a bed. The timing was right for such an invention. The Great Depression had

Bernard Castro. COURTESY OF BERNADETTE CASTRO

forced many families to remain in or move to apartment housing, so Castro's invention, which turned the davenport into a full-size bed that folded into a sofa, allowed families more room.

While his fortunes in the furniture business were beginning to look bright, Castro met Theresa Barabas. After a three-year courtship, they married in 1941. The Castros had two children.

At the end of World War II the return of soldiers to civilian life led to an acute housing shortage. As families crowded into small, cramped apartments, every bit of space was critical. Castro's invention, known popularly by that time as the Castro convertible, gave them the space they needed. However, were it not for Castro's keen marketing sense, people might have dismissed his invention as a novelty. He made sure that the people who would benefit the most from his sofa design were aware of the product. In 1948 he became one of the first businesspeople to capitalize on the potential of television by buying local airtime on a New York City station to promote his sofa beds. To sell his invention, he enlisted the help of his daughter, who demonstrated that at the age of four she could open the sofa bed. Bernadette became nationally famous as the little girl who could open the sofa bed with the "feather lift mechanism."

Castro insisted that his furniture should be functional, but not at the expense of beauty. He made sure that the sofas his company produced were of quality craftsmanship and were able to blend into any home. His success with furniture allowed him to move his business, which had grown to 500 employees, to suburban New Hyde Park, Long Island. In time his company added two factories to produce his patented sofa beds. By 1963 the company added four more factories to keep up with the demand for his product.

Castro's first patent for his design was granted in 1956 for a spring cover for his sofa bed. Over the next several years, both by himself and with the help of coworkers, he patented several versions of his sofa beds, including one with an integrated television set in 1971. Castro's pragmatism, marketing efforts, and determination stimulated growth within the Castro Convertible Corporation to forty-eight showrooms in twelve states, making him a millionaire. In 1963 the Horatio Alger Association of Distinguished Americans awarded him membership in its organization. He owned residences in Manhattan and on Long Island in New York and in Fort Lauderdale and Ocala in Florida.

In addition to running the Castro Convertible Corporation, Castro and his wife devoted themselves to nonprofit organizations and civic duties. The chair and a founder of a nonsectarian private school, the Golden Hills Academy in Ocala, Castro's wife discussed this endeavor and others in an interview with the *New York Times* on 6 August 1969. Castro liked to open his home for charitable events. For example, in 1972 he held an auction in his thirty-room estate at Lloyd Harbor, Long Island, to benefit the Patients' Service Program of the American Cancer Society. Castro received an honorary doctorate from Mercy College in Westchester, New York, the Knight of Malta in the Roman Catholic Church, and an honorary Green Beret for allowing paratroopers to use 1,000 acres of his ranch in Ocala for practice maneuvers.

Castro never really retired, but he moved to his ranch estate in Ocala. His daughter took over some of the administrative duties involved in running the company, but Castro regularly held business meetings with his company officers and inspected new designs at his ranch until his death. When he was not working on company business, Castro, who was athletic and distinguished-looking, focused on photography, one of his hobbies. He suffered a fatal heart attack at the age of eighty-seven. He is buried next to his son in the family mausoleum on the Ocala ranch. At the time of Castro's death, Castro Convertible Corporation had sold over 5 million of its innovative sofa beds.

★

U.S. Patents 2,752,613; 2,818,584; 2,928,106; 2,960,648; 3,191,198; and 3,608,101, in the College Station Patent and Trademark Depository Library at Texas A & M University, contain information related to Castro's ideas regarding the sofa bed. Additional biographical material is in the *New York Times* (22 Feb. 1964), (6 Aug. 1969), (18 June 1972), and (30 Oct. 1974). An obituary is in the *New York Times* (26 Aug. 1991) and *Time* (9 Sept. 1991).

BRIAN B. CARPENTER

CHAIKIN, Sol (Chick) (*b.* 9 January 1918 in New York City; *d.* 1 April 1991 in New York City), apparel industry labor leader.

Chaikin, who adopted and preferred the name Chick (spelled, at his insistence, without quotation marks) after the summers spent on his uncle's chicken farm, was the son of Sam Chaikin and Beckie Schechtman. He was the only one of three siblings to live beyond childhood. His parents were Russian Jewish immigrants who came to the United States in 1910 to escape the anti-Semitism of turn-of-the-century Russia. They settled in New York City, both finding work in Manhattan's then-thriving garment indus-

Chick Chaikin, 1980. AP/WIDE WORLD PHOTOS

try, Sam as a cloak maker, Beckie as a dressmaker. His parents soon became members of the fledgling International Ladies' Garment Workers Union (ILGWU), an allegiance they maintained for the rest of their lives.

In the 1930s and 1940s organized labor was a way of life for many garment workers, Chaikin's parents included, and their influence directed his life and his choice of career. Graduating from high school in 1934 at the age of sixteen, he received a B.A. degree from the City College of New York in 1938 and a law degree from Brooklyn Law School in 1940.

Choosing the life of a union organizer over the practice of law, Chaikin went to work with the ILGWU in Fall River, Massachusetts, in 1940. On 31 August 1940 he married a schoolteacher named Rosalind Bryon. They had four children. His rapid rise within the union, which began with his appointment as business agent for the union's Boston local, was interrupted by his enlistment in 1943 in the Army Air Forces. He earned several battle stars in combat in the South Pacific and the China-Burma-India theater. Discharged in 1946, he returned to the ILGWU as the manager of the Springfield, Massachusetts, local and in 1948 was elevated to manager of the union's Western Massachusetts District. In 1955 he became director of its Lower Southwest Region and in 1959 was appointed deputy director of the Union's Northeast Department, which covered all of New England and Pennsylvania. Elected a vice president of the union in 1965, he became secretary-treasurer in 1973. In 1975, when incumbent president Louis Stulberg resigned for reasons of poor health, the union's executive board elected Chaikin president of the ILGWU. The election was ratified by the full membership in 1977. Chaikin served for nine years, winning three successive terms, and retired from the presidency in 1986.

Chaikin's ascendance to the presidency occurred at a time of great difficulty for the union. Garment manufacturers in vast numbers were relocating their plants from New York and Pennsylvania to the low-wage states of the South and Southwest, where local right-to-work laws discouraged union membership. In addition, many manufacturers were opening factories in South America and as far away as Southeast Asia, where labor costs were a mere fraction of the cost of labor in the United States. As jobs disappeared, first from the relatively union-friendly northern states and then from the country as a whole, the union's membership declined dramatically. Chaikin's herculean efforts to organize in the South and the Southwest failed to stanch the hemorrhaging of the union's membership.

The approach Chaikin took to minimizing the effects of the industry's flight to developing countries was unabashedly protectionist in nature. He argued that the government should impose high tariffs on garments imported into the country in order to force their retail price upward to a level that would make them competitive with American-made garments, thus preserving union jobs. Although he assiduously lobbied the government to this end, he was never able to convince the president or Congress that the remedy he sought was tenable. As a consequence, the union's membership at the time he relinquished the presidency in 1986 stood at 220,000—approximately half its number when he was first elected in 1975.

After retiring from the union's presidency, Chaikin, an acknowledged expert on international trade, represented the ILGWU at labor and economic conferences around the world. He was also extensively involved, nationally and internationally, in a wide range of educational, social, and political organizations and coalitions. Chick Chaikin died of heart failure in New York City on 1 April 1991 at the age of seventy-three.

Chaikin's greatest and most important contribution to the union was his successful effort to revamp the system by which it was administered. At first the ILGWU's membership was largely composed of Jewish and Italian women, reflecting the ethnicity of the workers employed in the garment industry, which was then largely located in New York City. As many of these jobs moved into Pennsylvania, women of other ethnicities flocked to work in the garment plants. The membership was still largely white, but as manufacturers increasingly moved their work south, the workforce became heavily black and Hispanic. The union's leadership, however, remained in the hands of now aging officers who had first been elected in the organization's infancy, when the ethnicity of its membership was considerably different. Further, although the union's membership was almost exclusively female, virtually all of its officials were male. The result was that the rank and file of the union had become increasingly and perilously disaffected from its leadership. Reversing this circumstance by successfully supporting the election of women and minorities to key positions, Chaikin paved the way for the historic merger of the ILGWU with the country's other major apparel workers union, the Amalgamated Clothing and Textile Workers' Union (ACTWU), in February of 1995. Although UNITE (Union of Needletrades, Industrial, and Textile Workers), with its combined membership, did not solve the economic problems endemic in the industry, it gave organized garment workers considerably more power than they had enjoyed for many years.

★

Chaikin's personal papers are archived with the Union of Needletrades, Industrial, and Textile Workers (UNITE) in New York City. He is the author of *A Labor Viewpoint: Another Opinion* (1980). His widow, Rosalind Bryon Chaikin, is the author of *To My Memory Sing: A Memoir Based on Letters and Poems from Sol Chick Chaikin, an American Soldier in China-Burma-India During World War II* (1997). *Current Biography Yearbook 1979* contains a short biography of Chaikin to that date. An obituary is in the *New York Times* (3 Apr. 1991).

JACK HANDLER

CHANDLER, Albert Benjamin ("Happy") (*b.* 14 July 1898 in Corydon, Kentucky; *d.* 15 June 1991 in Versailles, Kentucky), baseball commissioner, lawyer, governor, and U.S. senator, was best known for defying team owners and helping to end racial segregation in major league baseball.

Chandler, the son of Joseph Chandler, a handyman, rural letter carrier, and telephone operator; and Callie Sanders, a homemaker who left the family when Chandler was only four, grew up in a broken home plagued by poverty. His only brother died at the age of fourteen in a fall from a tree. Chandler attended Corydon High School in Henderson County, Kentucky. After serving as a private in the U.S. Army in 1918 and 1919, he enrolled at Transylvania College in Lexington, Kentucky. His constant smile earned him the nickname "Happy." He earned tuition by working in a laundry and waiting on tables and starred in baseball, football, and basketball. He graduated from Transylvania with a B.A. degree in 1921 and attended Harvard University Law School for one year, leaving for financial reasons. He earned a bachelor of laws degree from the University of Kentucky in 1924.

Happy Chandler, 1946. ASSOCIATED PRESS AP

Chandler married Mildred Watkins on 12 November 1925. They had four children. Chandler commenced law practice in Versailles, Kentucky, in 1924 and played professional baseball. After being selected master commissioner of the Woodford County circuit court in 1928, he served as a Democrat in the state senate in 1930 and 1931 and as lieutenant governor from 1931 to 1935. During the absence of Governor Ruby Laffoon in 1935 he called a special session of the General Assembly to enact a state primary law. Chandler defeated the Laffoon-backed candidate for governor in the Democratic primary and was elected chief executive that November.

Chandler served as governor of Kentucky from December 1935 until October 1939. His administration replaced sales taxes with liquor and income taxes, eliminated 130 state agencies, eradicated a $20 million deficit, reformed prisons, built many hospitals, and secured ratification of a child labor amendment. In 1939 he activated 1,000 National Guardsmen to restore order in Harlan County, where the United Mine Workers had struck to win recognition for a union shop.

Because governors were limited to one term, Chandler opposed incumbent U.S. senator Alben Barkley in the 1938 Democratic primary. President Franklin D. Roosevelt's support helped Barkley win by over 50,000 votes.

When Kentucky's junior U.S. senator, Marvel Logan, died in 1939, Chandler resigned as governor and was appointed to fill the vacant Senate seat. He was elected to fill the remainder of Logan's term in November 1940 and defeated the Republican John Young Brown in November 1942 for a full six-year Senate term.

Chandler chaired a subcommittee of the Senate Military Affairs Committee that visited Alaska and the Aleutian Islands in 1942. He favored defeating Japan before Germany, fearing that Great Britain and the USSR would otherwise not help the United States win the Pacific war. Chandler supported Lend-Lease, reciprocal trade extension, the Bretton Woods Agreement, the United Nations Charter, the extension of Farm Security Administration loans, and the spending of $100 million for soil conservation. At the 1944 Democratic National Convention he unsuccessfully sought the vice presidential nomination.

In November 1945 Chandler resigned from the Senate and replaced the authoritarian Kenesaw Mountain Landis as the commissioner of baseball. He became the goodwill ambassador that baseball needed, acting fairly, honestly, and ethically. Chandler persuaded owners not to sign high school baseball players until they graduated and favored playing more night games. He imposed a five-year ban on the eighteen major league stars who in 1946 jumped to the outlaw Mexican League. Several players filed a suit against major league baseball in 1948; the case was settled out of court, with the players being reinstated when Chandler gave them blanket amnesty in 1949. Many of them returned to the major league that year.

Chandler approved the transfer of Jackie Robinson's contract to the Brooklyn Dodgers in 1947 despite a 15–1 negative vote by team owners. His action and Robinson's excellence on the field paved the way for Willie Mays, Roy Campanella, Hank Aaron, and other black stars. In April 1947 he suspended the Brooklyn Dodgers manager Leo Durocher for the 1947 season for associating with gamblers. Chandler instituted the pension fund for players, signed baseball's first television contract, and ordered that the revenue be used to support the players pension fund. He knew every player by name and face and supported a $5,000 minimum salary for major leaguers.

The owners resented the strong commissioner, preferring a vassal instead. Several owners revolted against Chandler for approving the racial integration of major league baseball, arbitrarily jeopardizing the reserve clause, and investigating the alleged gambling activities of some owners. During the All-Star break in July 1951 they fired him. Chandler secured only nine of the twelve votes necessary for reelection and was forced to resign as commissioner that month. He returned to Versailles to practice law, raise tobacco, and operate a weekly newspaper, the *Woodford Sun*.

Chandler bucked the Democratic party machine by running for governor of Kentucky in 1955. He challenged Governor Lawrence Wetherby and Senators Earle Clements and Alben Barkley, who supported Bertram Combs. Chandler campaigned for ten months, making 900 speeches. His slogan was "Be like your pappy and vote for Happy." After each campaign speech, he sang, "There's a Gold Mine in the Sky." He won the August primary by 18,000 out of 500,000 votes and then defeated Republican Edward Denny by a record 129,000 votes.

Chandler served as governor for a second term from 1955 to 1959. The Adair County Consolidated High School in Columbia was integrated in January 1956 and other schools followed the next September. Most communities accepted the change peacefully. Chandler appointed Robert Humphreys to fill the unexpired Senate term of Alben Barkley in 1956, but the Democratic State Central Committee rejected Humphreys in favor of former governor Lawrence Wetherby to run in the November 1956 election. In 1959 the University of Kentucky Medical Center was named in Chandler's honor.

Chandler unsuccessfully sought the Democratic party nomination for governor in 1963. He then became vice president and director of First Flight Golf Company of Chattanooga, director of Coastal States Life Insurance Company of Georgia, receiver for the Inter-South Life Insurance Company of Louisville, and organizer of the Kentucky Home Life Insurance Company. Chandler chaired the Woodford County Democratic Executive Committee and was Democratic national committeeman for Kentucky.

He was elected to the Kentucky Sports Hall of Fame in 1957 and the National Baseball Hall of Fame in 1982. Chandler served as president of the International Baseball Congress in Wichita, Kansas, as commissioner of the Continental Football League in 1965, and as a trustee of the Ty Cobb Foundation and at the University of Kentucky. He chaired the board of trustees at Transylvania College. Chandler received the bishops' medal of the Episcopal Church in 1959 and the Jefferson Davis medal in 1975. He died of a heart attack at the age of ninety-two. He is buried in Pisgah Church Cemetery in Versailles.

The independent-minded Chandler often defied both the political and baseball establishments. He bucked the Kentucky State Democratic Party and clashed with the team owners who did not want a strong, dominant commissioner. Chandler boldly supported the racial integration of major league baseball, paving the way for black athletes.

★

Chandler's papers and oral history are located at the Margaret I. King Library, University of Kentucky, Lexington, Kentucky, and the National Baseball Library, Cooperstown, New York. His autobiography, *Heroes, Plain Folks, and Skunks* (1989), coauthored with Vance Trimble, describes his political and baseball careers. J. B. Shannon, "'Happy' Chandler: A Kentucky Epic," in *The American Politician* (1938), edited by J. T. Salter, reviews his early political career. Fred J. Hood, ed., *Kentucky: Its History and Heritage* (1978), and Lowell H. Harrison, ed., *Kentucky's Governors, 1792–1985* (1985), recount Chandler's two terms as governor. Jules Tygiel, *Baseball's Great Experiment: Jackie Robinson and His Legacy* (1983), details Chandler's support for the integration of major league baseball. Jerome Holtzman, *The Commissioners* (1998), assesses Chandler's role as baseball commissioner. Articles in *Current Biography 1943* (1943) and *Current Biography 1956* (1956) summarize Chandler's career. Harold H. Martin, "Happy's Last Hurrah!" *Saturday Evening Post* (10 Aug. 1963), provides further information about Chandler as governor. Chandler discusses his role as commissioner in John Underwood, "How I Jumped from Clean Politics to Dirty Baseball," *Sports Illustrated* (26 Apr. 1971 and 3 May 3, 1971). Milton Gross, "The Truth About Happy Chandler," *Sport* (Apr. 1949) and John Drebinger, "A Commissioner's Reign Ends," *Baseball Digest* (Aug. 1951), discuss Chandler's role in the integration of baseball. Other useful articles include "Chandler Casts a Happy Shadow," *Southern Living* (June 1981), and Frank Deford, "Happy Days," *Sports Illustrated* (20 July 1987). Obituaries of Chandler are in the *New York Times* (16 June 1991) and *Time* (24 June 1991).

DAVID L. PORTER

CHÁVEZ, César Estrada (*b.* 31 March 1927 in Yuma, Arizona; *d.* 23 April 1993 in Yuma, Arizona), founder and first president of the United Farm Workers of America (UFW) and one of America's most influential labor leaders of the late twentieth century.

Chávez was one of five children born to Librado Chávez and Juana Estrada, both farmers. He grew up nourished by the values of his family and his rural Mexican-American community in Arizona. From his mother he learned the importance of nonviolence and self-sacrifice; his grandmother impressed upon him the values of the Catholic faith. As a youth he experienced racial discrimination in school and absorbed from the Mexican-American community the folklore of their struggle against oppression during the Mexican revolution. In 1939 the Chávez family lost their farm because of the Great Depression, and they joined the migrant stream flowing west into California. For the next ten years the Chávez family worked as farm laborers, moving from farm to farm in California, taking odd jobs to supplement their income when there was no farm work. Chávez did not graduate from high school.

Chávez joined the navy in 1944 and served as a coxswain apprentice. Two years later he returned to the family home in Delano, California, a small town in the San Joaquin Valley, and resumed work in the fields. On 22 October 1948 Chávez married Helen Fabela, whom he had first met when his family had passed through Delano following the crops. She became an important partner with Chávez as he began to fulfill his dream of doing something to improve the lot of farm workers. The couple eventually settled in San Jose, California, and began a family of eight children while Chávez worked for a lumber company.

In San Jose, Chávez met Father Donald McDonnell, a Catholic priest who, along with Father Thomas McCullough, was trying to work with farm laborers and Mexican *bracero* workers to improve their lot. The Chávez family regularly attended mass in the barrio church, where Chávez learned about the Papal Encyclicals on labor, the teaching of Saint Francis of Assisi, and Mahatma Gandhi.

César Chávez. AP/WIDE WORLD PHOTOS

He read Louis Fisher's *Life of Gandhi* (1950), a book that made a deep impression on him. Gandhi's philosophy of nonviolence would later become the hallmark of Chávez's leadership of the farm worker movement.

In 1952 Fred Ross, an organizer for the Community Service Organization (CSO) in San Jose, met Chávez and was impressed by his sincerity and willingness to work. Soon Chávez was working full time for the CSO, where he quickly rose to the position of executive director of the CSO in California.

In 1962 Chávez resigned from the CSO to devote himself to building an independent farm workers union. He and his family moved back to Delano, where for the next three years Chávez slowly built up membership in the National Farm Worker's Association (NFWA). Using his CSO training, Chávez emphasized the service aspect of his organization. He traveled extensively, talking to the workers to see what they thought about a union and the services it should provide. In 1962, at their first convention, they adopted the distinctive union flag, the black eagle on a red field. By August 1965 they had 1,700 dues-paying members and more than fifty locals.

From the beginning Chávez did not think of "La Causa" as a movement that would be motivated by appeals to race or nationality. When he had worked for the CSO, Chávez had confronted the issue of Mexican chauvinism and had been uncompromising in fighting for the inclusion of blacks within the organization. While the "core" leadership of the NFWA was Mexican American, the staff and hundreds of volunteer workers were predominantly Anglo-American.

On 15 September 1965, Mexican Independence Day, NFWA members voted to support the Filipino grape pickers who were on strike, spontaneously joining a struggle that they had long considered their own. The Delano table and wine grape strike, which was sponsored by the AFL-CIO affiliated Agricultural Workers Organizing Committee (AWOC), was the largest such strike in the history of California. The region covered a 400-square-mile area and involved thousands of workers. Chávez's main activity during the early months of the strike was traveling around the state to various college campuses to galvanize support for the striking farm workers. His emphasis on the workers' civil rights and economic justice fit in with a growing national concern about civil rights.

Dramatic events gave momentum to the strike. On 17 March 1966 Chávez organized a march from Delano to Sacramento, California, to dramatize the struggle and get the support of Governor Pat Brown. The march helped recruit more members and spread the spirit of the strike. As they passed through each small farming town, hundreds of workers greeted them. Some joined the march to carry the union flags to the next town.

Just prior to the end of the pilgrimage, the first grower,

Schenley Corporation, announced that it was willing to sign a contract with the AWOC. On 7 April the agreement was made public. In a triumphant mood, the pilgrimage ended a few days later on the steps of the state capitol. The union had won its first victory. On 22 August 1966, the AWOC and NFWA merged to become the United Farm Workers Organizing Committee (UFWOC), a united union within the AFL-CIO, later to become the United Farm Workers of America (UFW).

During the next four years, the UFW grew in strength, nourished by the support of millions of sympathetic Americans. Hundreds of student volunteers lived on poverty wages in the big cities to organize an international boycott of table grapes. Scores of priests, nuns, ministers, and church members donated time, money, facilities and energies to the cause. Organized labor donated millions of dollars to the UFW strike fund. Millions of Americans gave up eating table grapes. All this was inspired by the example of Chávez, the soft-spoken, humble leader who quietly worked to revolutionize grower-worker relations.

In 1968, at the height of the strike, Chávez began a fast to protest the mounting talk of violence. Soon hundreds of farm worker families began appearing at Forty Acres, the union headquarters near Delano, to show their support for Chávez and to attend the daily mass that he also attended. Martin Luther King, Jr., sent a telegram supporting Chávez. When Chávez finally decided to end his fast on the twenty-fifth day, he asked Senator Robert F. Kennedy to attend. On March 11 they held a mass at a county park with more than 4,000 farm workers in attendance, along with national reporters from the major papers and television cameras. The mass was said on the back of a flatbed truck. In a short speech after the mass Chávez declared to the assembled group: "I am convinced that the truest act of courage, the strongest act of manliness is to sacrifice ourselves for others in a totally nonviolent struggle for justice. To be a man is to suffer for others. God help us to be men!"

By 1969 Chávez had organized a boycott of all California table grapes, and shipments of such produce had practically stopped to the cities of Boston; New York; Philadelphia, Pennsylvania; Chicago; Detroit; Montreal, Canada; and Toronto, Canada. Grape sales fell, while millions of pounds of the fruit rotted in cold storage sheds. Finally, on 29 July 1970, twenty-six Delano growers filed into Reuther Hall on Forty Acres to sign contracts. This victory was without precedent in the history of American agriculture. Never before had an agricultural workers union achieved such sweeping success.

There were immediate indications that the farm workers were facing another formidable challenge from the Teamsters and table grape and iceberg lettuce growers in the Salinas Valley in California, who were conspiring to undercut the UFW's newly won recognition. The Teamsters had signed sweetheart contracts giving the vegetable growers almost all that they wanted while sacrificing workers' benefits. To challenge this, Chávez moved the staff headquarters of the union to Salinas and began organizing workers. Finally he called for a general strike.

In late 1972 California voters considered Proposition 22, an initiative that would outlaw boycotting and limit secret ballot elections to full-time nonseasonal employees. Throughout the fall, the union's "No on 22" campaign gathered momentum through the use of human billboards. On 7 November 1972, Proposition 22 was defeated by a margin of fifty-eight percent. The UFW had used the boycott organization to mobilize support and had proven itself a serious political force.

Meanwhile the lettuce boycott and struggle with the Teamsters continued. Soon violence exploded and two union members were killed. On 1 September, Chávez decided to call off the strike and resume the boycott. The decision to abandon the strike was motivated in part by his desire to avoid future violence but also by his deeply-held feeling that a boycott would be more effective than a strike. The Teamsters finally gave up their campaign to organize field workers and take over UFW contracts late in 1974.

During the Teamster struggle, Chávez decided to organize another march. On 22 February 1975 he began a 110-mile march from San Francisco to Modesto, California, home of the Gallo Wineries. More than 15,000 supporters participated.

The newly elected governor of California, Jerry Brown, supported the cause and helped pass a California Agricultural Labor Relations Act in May 1975, the first law in the continental United States governing farm labor organizing (farm workers in Hawaii had a similar law). The law gave the UFW secret ballot elections, the right to boycott, voting rights for migrant seasonal workers, and control over the timing of elections.

In terms of union building, the period following the passage of the California Farm Labor Act was one of growth in membership and contracts. The UFW had won almost two-thirds of the elections after 1975, and the Teamsters admitted in March 1977 that they were beaten and would not contest future elections. The dues-paying membership of the UFW soared to over 100,000 by 1978.

In the 1980s, as a result of the stalemate promoted by the California's Agricultural Labor Relations Board, Chávez came to the conclusion that the best tactic was to boycott in order to force the growers to sign contracts. He announced on 12 June 1984 that the union would embark on a new grape boycott. He also decided to protest against pesticides usage by beginning a fast on 16 July 1988. The fast went largely unnoticed by the public until the children of Robert Kennedy visited him at La Paz, his home and the UFW headquarters, in Keene, California, to lend their

support. Finally on 22 August, Chávez gave up his water-only fast.

Chávez was confident about the ultimate success of the UFW struggle and remained so until his unexpected death from natural causes in Yuma, Arizona, on 23 April 1993. The tremendous outpouring of condolences and support that followed his death was a testimony to his importance as a leader who touched the conscience of the nation. More than 40,000 people followed his casket for three miles from downtown Delano to the union's old headquarters at Forty Acres. Expressions of regret for his passing came from around the world, from international political, labor, and spiritual leaders as well as from thousands of poor migrant farm workers, to whom he had dedicated his life. He was buried at La Paz, in a rose garden at the foot of the hill he often climbed to watch the sun rise.

Chávez's inspiring leadership of *El Movimiento* changed the way Americans thought about farm workers. Under his direction, the UFW brought the social and economic problems of Mexican Americans into the nation's consciousness. For his accomplishments Chávez was awarded the Aguila Azteca ("Aztec Eagle"), Mexico's highest award presented to people of Mexican heritage who have made major contributions outside of Mexico. In 1994 he was posthumously awarded the Presidential Medal of Freedom, the United States' highest civilian honor, by President Bill Clinton. In August 2000, the state of California declared his birthday an official holiday, recognizing his greatest achievements of moral leadership and a commitment to social justice.

★

The UFW archives at La Paz, in Keene, California, contain materials relating to Chávez and the union. Biographical treatments include Richard Griswold del Castillo and Richard Garcia, *César Chávez: Triumph of the Spirit* (1995). Jacques Levy, *César Chávez: Autobiography of La Causa* (1975), is the most comprehensive source produced by insiders in the union. Also in this category are Eugene Nelson, *Huelga: The First Hundred Days of the Great Delano Grape Strike* (1966), and Mark Day, *Forty Acres: César Chávez and the Farm Workers* (1971). See also Peter Matthiessen, *Sal Si Puedes: César Chávez and the New American Revolution* (1969); Sam Kushner, *The Long Road to Delano* (1975); Ronald Taylor, *Chávez and the Farm Workers* (1975); and Susan Ferriss et al., eds., *The Fight in the Fields: César Chávez and the Farmworkers Movement* (1998). An obituary is in the *New York Times* (24 Apr. 1993).

RICHARD GRISWOLD DEL CASTILLO

COLEMAN, J(ames) P(lemon) (*b.* 9 January 1914 near Ackerman, Mississippi; *d.* 28 September 1991 in Ackerman, Mississippi), politician, Mississippi governor, and federal appeals court judge best known for his efforts to prevent violence while defending segregation during the struggle over civil rights in the South.

The oldest of six children born to Thomas Allen Coleman, a farmer, and Jennie Essie Worrell, a homemaker, Coleman grew up on his parents' small farm where he engaged in the hard physical labor required in agriculture before mechanization. He graduated from high school in 1931. Without funds to attend college Coleman took a truckload of sweet potatoes to the University of Mississippi in 1931 or 1932, hoping to sell them to the cafeteria for tuition money. Although the university refused the vegetables, he was offered a campus job and attended "Ole Miss" from 1932 to 1935 but did not finish his degree.

In 1935 Coleman moved to Washington, D.C., as secretary to newly elected congressman Aaron L. Ford. There he studied law in the evenings at George Washington University and received his LL.B. in 1939. He married Margaret Janet Dennis on 2 May 1937. They had one child.

In 1939 Coleman returned to Ackerman, established a law practice, and won election as district attorney. He served until 1946, when he was elected circuit court judge. In 1950 he was appointed to the state Supreme Court, but he served less than two months before the governor appointed him attorney general to complete an unexpired term. In 1951 Coleman was elected to a full term as Mississippi attorney general.

In 1955 Coleman, the skillful lawyer, demonstrated his political acumen by adopting the persona of country plowboy and winning election as governor over better-known opponents. The U.S. Supreme Court had declared racial segregation in public schools unconstitutional the previous year, and racial issues dominated Coleman's term as gov-

ernor. In the volatile political atmosphere, Coleman feared violent outbreaks by whites and counseled quiet resistance to integration. He launched a public relations campaign to convince Northern voters that race relations were satisfactory in the South and made several national television appearances himself, used the newly established Mississippi Sovereignty Commission and law enforcement agencies to identify and intimidate black residents who might challenge the status quo, and frequently reassured whites that their leaders could prevent change in the white-dominated society. Coleman implemented a major school building program, primarily to improve segregated black schools; won substantial increases in teacher pay; initiated state regulation of utility rates; and vigorously, but unsuccessfully, promoted the writing of a new state constitution to facilitate economic development. Reflecting on his term years later, the former governor declared that "four years of peace and quiet" was his principal accomplishment.

A Democrat, Coleman believed that the South could influence national politics most effectively from within the Democratic party. Consequently, he consistently supported Democratic candidates for national office, even as the national party moved toward support for civil rights.

Prohibited by the state constitution from serving consecutive terms as governor, Coleman won a seat in the state legislature in 1959. He turned down appointments as secretary of the army and ambassador to Australia proffered by President John F. Kennedy after the 1960 election and prepared for another race for governor in 1963. This time Coleman was defeated because of his comparative moder-

J. P. Coleman, 1959. AP/WIDE WORLD PHOTOS

ation on racial issues and his 1960 electoral support of Kennedy, who had subsequently used federal troops to integrate the University of Mississippi. He returned to his private law practice.

In 1965 President Lyndon B. Johnson nominated Coleman to fill a vacancy on the U.S. Court of Appeals for the Fifth Circuit. With jurisdiction over six southern states from Texas to Florida, the Fifth Circuit had taken the judicial lead in advancing civil rights. Fearing that Coleman, whom Congressman John Conyers labeled "the thinking man's segregationist," would stand in the way of continued progress, a coalition of civil rights groups mounted a challenge to his Senate confirmation. After a brief but bruising battle, Coleman was confirmed.

As a federal judge Coleman had responsibility for implementing school desegregation decisions that he had opposed as governor. An analysis of his voting record on the court indicates that he supported the claims of racial minorities most of the time, but less consistently than most of his judicial colleagues. A strong believer in states' rights, Coleman rarely overruled actions by state officials.

In 1979 Coleman was elevated to chief judge of the Fifth Circuit, which had been expanded that year from fifteen judges to twenty-five. Population growth, economic development, and civil rights litigation had combined to make the Fifth Circuit the nation's busiest federal appeals court, and for several years Coleman and Senator James O. Eastland of Mississippi, chairman of the Senate Judiciary Committee, had vigorously advocated division of the Fifth Circuit into two courts. Civil rights supporters on the court and in Congress had blocked the plan, however, because it would have separated Mississippi from the more liberal influences of judges from Texas and Louisiana and joined it with Alabama, Georgia, and Florida in a new circuit certain to be more conservative. Soon after assuming the leadership of a court made unwieldy by its large size and immense workload, Coleman agreed to a compromise that he had previously rejected: keeping Mississippi in the Fifth Circuit with Texas and Louisiana and creating a new Eleventh Circuit for the other three states. Congress quickly enacted the necessary legislation.

Coleman gave up his position as chief judge in February 1981 to permit the senior members of the new Fifth and Eleventh Circuits to preside over the division of the old court into two. In May 1981 he assumed senior status, entitling him to hear cases on a part-time basis, but freeing him from full-time judicial service. He retired from the court fully in February 1984, and reentered private law practice.

Throughout his adult life, Coleman exuberantly pursued an interest in Mississippi history and genealogy. He served as president of the Mississippi Historical Society and published a history of his home county as well as two family histories. Coleman suffered a stroke in December 1990 and died from complications nine months later. He is buried in Enon Cemetery in Ackerman.

Termed a Southern "moderate" in derision by his enemies and respect by his friends, Coleman rejected the label. He called himself a "successful segregationist." He always respected the law, but he mistakenly believed that the South could use the instruments of the law to maintain white domination. As a federal judge he won praise from his colleagues for his fairness and his devotion to the law.

★

Coleman's papers are in the Mississippi Department of Archives and History in Jackson. The Department of Archives and History also has a subject file consisting primarily of newspaper articles. Coleman's judicial performance is analyzed in Elkin Terry Jack, "Racial Policy and Judge J. P. Coleman: A Study in Political-Judicial Linkage" (Ph.D. diss., University of Southern Mississippi, 1979). His political career is the subject of Robbie Sue Lee, "James P. Coleman and the Politics of Race" (M.A. thesis, Mississippi College, 1972), and Connie L. Cartledge, "James P. Coleman: Moderate Politician in an Age of Racial Strife, 1950–1965" (M.A. thesis, Mississippi State University, 1984). Earl Black, *Southern Governors and Civil Rights: Racial Segregation As a Campaign Issue in the Second Reconstruction* (1976), examines Coleman's gubernatorial campaigns, and Deborah J. Barrow and Thomas G. Walker elaborate on Coleman's role in the division of the Fifth Circuit in *A Court Divided: The Fifth Circuit Court of Appeals and the Politics of Judicial Reform* (1988). An obituary is in the *New York Times* (29 Sept. 1991). Coleman gave a number of oral history interviews. They are in the Southern Historical Collection of the University of North Carolina at Chapel Hill, the University of Southern Mississippi in Hattiesburg, and Mississippi College in Clinton.

Vagn K. Hansen

COLES, Charles ("Honi") (*b.* 2 April 1911 in Philadelphia, Pennsylvania; *d.* 11 November 1992 in New York City), only tap dancer to be honored with both Tony and Drama Desk Awards.

Coles was one of three children born to George and Isabel Coles. His father was a jack-of-all-trades who owned a pool hall and a barbershop at various times. His mother was a domestic servant. His older sister gave Coles the nickname "Honey Boy" when he was a child and it stuck. He was teased about it and later changed the spelling to "Honi." He grew up when fast dancing was a ticket to fame and fortune for young blacks, and he learned to tap-dance on the streets of Philadelphia, first watching and then joining in the time step "cutting" contests, in which one youth competed to beat another's time for doing a particular set of steps. By his late teens, Coles had determined to make

Charles "Honi" Coles. AP/WIDE WORLD PHOTOS

a career in show business, practicing alone for a year to enhance his speed, his number of taps per beat, and his complicated patterns. Although he was taller and lankier than the average tap dancer, he made his physical characteristics work for him. His fellow tapper Pete Nugent said that he did "centipede steps," in which his legs and feet seemed to pull in opposite directions.

In 1931 at the age of twenty, Coles joined two brothers, Danny and George Miller, to form the Three Millers and traveled with them to New York City. They appeared at Schiffman's Lafayette Theater in Harlem, performing on narrow planks five feet above the stage. The group was unable to get further bookings, and Coles returned to Philadelphia while the Miller brothers continued as a duo. Coles returned to New York the following year and worked with a variety of acts, including a comedy routine with Bert Howell at the Apollo Theatre in Harlem. At the Hoofer's Club, Coles further developed his own unique style. He considered John Bubbles his mentor, not Bill "Bojangles" Robinson. From 1936 to 1939, Coles was a member of the Lucky Seven Trio, who performed on large cubes painted to look like dice. The group changed their name to the Three Giants of Rhythm while Coles was a member. The

group went through ten costume changes in the course of its act and was much in demand to appear on variety bills with big bands. As Coles once explained to a reporter for the New York *Amsterdam News,* the tap dancer "was the best dressed, the most conditioned, the most conscientious performer on any bill, and in spite of being the least paid, he was the act to 'stop the show.'"

In 1940 Coles finally landed a steady gig as a solo dancer with Cab Calloway's big band, which played Harlem's famed Cotton Club frequently. There Coles met Charles "Cholly" Atkins, who was a member of the Cotton Club Boys. A native of Buffalo, New York, Atkins was an expert wing dancer (a dancer who specializes in a step described as a hop with one foot flung out to the side) who had already appeared in eleven major films. As was the custom of the day, however, his dancing spots in those films were easily excised by vigilant southern censors charged with sparing southern white audiences from film portrayals of blacks as other than servants.

Both Coles and Atkins served in the military during World War II. Coles served in the U.S. Air Force Special Services in China, Burma, and India, achieving the rank of sergeant before being discharged in 1946. On being discharged, Coles and Atkins returned to New York and decided to form a dance team. Frank Schiffman, owner of the Apollo Theatre, gave them their first booking. This was where Coles had met Marion Evelyn Edwards, a dancer in the Apollo's Number One chorus. They had met in 1936, when she was just beginning her career as a ballroom dancer. They were married in 1944, settled in East Elmhurst in the borough of Queens in New York City and had a son and a daughter. Their son died of spinal meningitis at the age of two. Coles already had a son by a previous relationship with a woman named Celeste.

Coles and Atkins developed a highly successful seven-minute act that began with a fast number, continued with a precision "swing dance," and then moved on to a soft-shoe number for which they became famous. The act ended with a challenge dance featuring each man performing his own specialty. They appeared with nearly all the major big bands between 1945 and 1949 and made a triumphant tour of England in 1948. In 1949 they joined the cast of the Broadway show *Gentlemen Prefer Blondes,* regularly stopping the show with the Jule Styne number "Mamie is Mimi." By the time the show closed after two years, tap dancing had fallen from favor, and jobs for tap dancers were scarce. Coles and Atkins, who were known as the last "class act," traditionally reopened the Apollo Theater at the beginning of every fall season with the vocalist Billy Eckstine throughout the 1950s. In the meantime, Coles partnered with his fellow tap dancer Pete Nugent to open the Dancecraft studio on West Fifty-second Street in New York, which they operated from 1954 to 1955.

The team of Coles and Atkins finally broke up in 1960. While Atkins went on to choreograph for the record producer Berry Gordy's young singing acts at Motown Records in Detroit, Coles worked as production manager at the Apollo Theatre. He also served as president of the Negro Actors Guild and was associated with the Copasetics, a tapping fraternity he helped establish in honor of Bill Robinson after his death in 1949. When the tap revival of the 1970s occurred, Coles was at the forefront. He joined the touring company of Broadway's *Bubbling Brown Sugar* in 1976 and subsequently performed as a soloist at New York's Carnegie Hall and Town Hall and with Chicago's Joffrey Ballet. He was featured in the films *The Cotton Club* (1984) and *Dirty Dancing* (1987) as well as in numerous documentaries. In 1983, at the age of seventy-two, Coles won both the Tony and Drama Desk awards for best featured actor and dancer in a musical for the Broadway hit *My One and Only*. Other accolades followed: the *Dance Magazine* Award in 1985, the Capezio Award for lifetime achievement in dance in 1988, and the National Medal of Arts in 1991. Coles died from cancer at home in 1992. He is buried in Pinelawn Cemetery in Farmingdale, New York.

Coles believed that tap dancing was the only dance form America could claim as its own. Through its time out of fashion and during its renaissance, he kept the form alive with his work with the Copasetics, master classes, and artistic consultancies, adjusting his style as he aged. In an interview in 1983, he explained, "Things happen with me now from the knees down, nice and easy."

★

For information on tap dance, Marshall and Jean Stearns, *Jazz Dance: The Story of American Vernacular Dance* (1994), is an invaluable reference. Ted Fox, *Showtime at the Apollo: 50 Years of Great Entertainment from Harlem's World-Famous Theatre* (1983), gives the flavor of the New York entertainment world for African Americans in Coles's time. James Haskins, *Black Dance in America: A History Through Its People* (1990) approaches the subject of black dance through biographies of its most noted practitioners. An obituary is in the *New York Times* (12 Nov. 1992).

JIM HASKINS

COLLINS, (Thomas) LeRoy   (*b.* 10 March 1909 in Tallahassee, Florida; *d.* 12 March 1991 in Tallahassee, Florida), governor of Florida who is best remembered for his moderate leadership with regard to civil rights and his commitment to good government.

Collins was the fourth child of Marvin Herring Collins and Mattie Albritton Brandon. He grew up on the outskirts of Tallahassee, Florida, where his father owned a grocery. Marvin Collins descended from a long line of Methodist preachers, and Collins's mother hoped that her son might

LeRoy Collins, 1960. AP/WIDE WORLD PHOTOS

follow the same calling. Roy, as his family and friends called him, held little interest in the clergy. Although he later became an Episcopalian, he remained a faithful churchgoer, and his religious convictions influenced his later political career. Upon graduating from high school in 1927, Collins moved to Poughkeepsie, New York, to attend Eastman's Business School in 1928. He finished the one-year program in a single semester and quickly moved back to Tallahassee, where he took a job as a bank teller. In 1930 Collins enrolled at Cumberland University in Lebanon, Tennessee, to study in the university's one-year law program. The next year Collins returned to Florida with his LL.B., passed the Florida bar examination with the highest score up to that time, and set up his own law practice. Unfortunately, his practice, like that of many other Florida lawyers in the Great Depression, did not grow quickly.

Collins entered politics largely because of the difficulty in earning a living as a lawyer. In 1932 he sought to marry the former Mary Call Darby but recognized that his practice was not generating the income necessary to support a family and decided to run for the position of Leon County prosecutor. While he ran well, he lost to the incumbent candidate. Despite the defeat, he and Mary Call married on 29 June 1932. They remained married until his death, raising four children.

Collins, a lifelong Democrat, again ran for office in 1934 and was elected state representative for Leon County, a position he held for three two-year terms. In 1940 Collins ran successfully for state senator, holding that position until 1953, interrupted only by World War II. During the war, Collins volunteered for the U.S. Navy, serving as a military prosecutor. Collins's career in the Florida legislature was marked by his commitment to a progressive philosophy that sought to better the condition of the state's citizens. He introduced and supported legislation that improved public schools, promoted automotive safety, and mandated fiscal responsibility. While he often met resistance from powerful rural legislators, he gained prestige in the eyes of many Floridians.

In 1954 Collins ran for the governorship against the very rural interests he had battled in the legislature. The election, which was held to fill the term of the recently deceased incumbent, pitted Collins against the conservative president of the Florida State Senate. Collins won the election on a platform promising government reforms, carrying the more populous counties of south Florida with a message of progress and economic development. As governor, Collins distinguished his tenure by expanding the number of state-supported universities and community colleges, by promoting tourism and economic development, and by striving to remedy the abuses of cronyism. In 1956 voters elected Collins to a full term.

As with most other governors of southern states in the 1950s, the Supreme Court's 1954 ruling in *Brown* v. *Board of Education,* which declared school segregation unconstitutional, shaped Collins's term in office. Collins responded with moderation, defending segregation while calling for adherence to the Court's decision. In 1955 it seemed that most Floridians agreed with this approach. By 1956, however, staunch segregationists were branding Collins an integrationist and attacking his moderate positions. The tactics of his critics, as well as his personal religious convictions, convinced Collins of the immorality of segregation and racism, distancing him from most southern politicians. In 1960 Collins presided as chairman of the 1960 Democratic National Convention, which nominated John F. Kennedy for president of the United States; this further separated Collins from the mainstream of southern politics.

At the end of his governorship, Collins took a break from politics. From 1961 to 1964 he served as the president of the National Association of Broadcasters (NAB). While with the NAB, Collins pushed broadcasters to serve the public interest by reducing violent programming and elim-

inating television cigarette advertising. Although successful in the private sphere, Collins soon returned to government. In 1964 President Lyndon B. Johnson appointed him to head the Community Relations Service (CRS), which was created by the 1964 Civil Rights Act to foster peaceful implementation of civil rights policies. As head of the CRS, Collins was most prominent in orchestrating the successful second voting rights march across the Edmund Pettus Bridge in Selma, Alabama, on 9 March 1965. Later that year, Collins was appointed undersecretary of commerce. In this capacity, he helped negotiate an end to the rioting and unrest in the Los Angeles neighborhood of Watts.

In 1966 Collins left the Commerce Department in order to run for the United States Senate in 1968. As former governor, Collins enjoyed a great deal of popularity in Florida, but his stance against segregation and his role in CRS angered many Floridians. His Republican rival in the 1968 race, Edward John Gurney, drew on this well of opposition. Labeling Collins "Liberal LeRoy," his opponent appealed to conservative discontent and defeated Collins in the general election.

Collins retired from government following his 1968 defeat, but he did not retire from public life. He remained a champion for progressive political values, especially in his opposition to capital punishment. In 1990 Collins was named a finalist for the John F. Kennedy Profile in Courage Award, which is given by the Kennedy Library Foundation to recognize courage in championing political causes. Lung cancer claimed Collins's life in 1991. He was buried in Tallahassee.

In the minds of many Floridians, Collins was the model governor, dedicated to the betterment of his state for all of its citizens. Upon hearing of his death, the Florida Legislature immediately passed a resolution naming Collins the "Floridian of the Century." Not always loved for his politics, Collins earned the respect of all Floridians for his principled stands for a better society.

★

There are two major collections of Collins's personal papers. The Special Collections Department of the University of South Florida Library in Tampa holds a major collection with emphasis on Collins's tenure as governor and his 1968 senatorial campaign. In addition, the Special Collections Department of the Florida State University Library in Tallahassee maintains an important collection of papers related to his tenure in the state legislature as well as his postpolitical life. Tom Wagy has written the only full-length biography of Collins, *Governor LeRoy Collins of Florida: Spokesman of the New South* (1985), a very sympathetic interpretation of his career. His obituary is in the *New York Times* (13 Mar. 1991).

EVAN P. BENNETT

CONN, William David, Jr. ("Billy")   (*b.* 8 October 1917 in East Liberty, Pennsylvania; *d.* 29 May 1993 in Pittsburgh, Pennsylvania), light-heavyweight champion and Hall of Fame boxer.

The oldest of five children of William David Conn, a steamfitter who worked for Westinghouse Electric Company, and Margaret McFarland, an Irish immigrant, Conn grew up in an Irish-American neighborhood. By the time he was thirteen, Conn was an accomplished street fighter. "It was a long time before I got to the street from the alley," Conn said years later. He attended Sacred Heart Grammar School through the eighth grade and did not go on to high school. Conn began working in an East Pittsburgh gym owned by Johnny Ray, a former professional boxer. "I worked there three years and got lots of practice against some real good talent who worked out there," Conn told the *Pittsburgh Post-Gazette* in 1988. He never fought as an amateur and learned his craft sparring with professionals. "Ray worked with Billy, told him how to hold his hands, block punches, and, most of all, explained the principle of the left jab, the punch that was to make Billy famous," the fight trainer Freddie Fierro recalled in 1956.

At the age of seventeen, Conn launched his professional

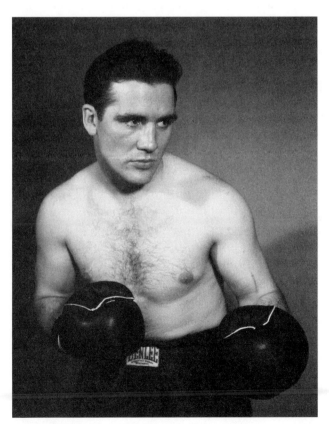

Billy Conn, 1949. © Bettmann/Corbis

career as a welterweight. After winning twelve out of eighteen fights in 1935, he was undefeated in nineteen bouts during 1936, including a hard-fought decision over the welterweight contender Fitzie Zivic. Following this victory, Conn moved up to the middleweight division and defeated four ex-champions in 1937: Babe Risko, Vince Dundee, Teddy Yarosz, and Young Corbett III. After twice defeating the middleweight champion Fred Apostoli in nontitle fights in 1938, he decisioned Melio Bettino on 13 July 1939 for the world's light-heavyweight championship. Conn successfully defended his title twice against Gus Lesnevich in November 1939 and June 1940.

With lightning quickness, the "Pittsburgh Kid" was among the more exciting fighters of his era. Conn, who enjoyed a national following among Irish Americans, wore green trunks adorned with a shamrock. Tall, dark-haired, and ruggedly handsome, Conn looked like a movie star. "The Irishman is indeed a beauteous boxer," the *New York Daily News* noted after Conn won the title, "who could probably collect coinage by joining the ballet league if he chose to flee the egg-eared and flattened nose fraternity."

Conn went on to knock out the heavyweight contender Bob Pastor in the thirteenth round in September 1940, then decisioned Al McCoy in ten rounds and Lee Savold in twelve rounds. In May 1941, he relinquished the light-heavyweight crown to become a full-time heavyweight.

On 18 June 1941, Conn nearly won the heavyweight championship from the legendary Joe Louis. It was supposed to have been a mismatch. Louis, unbeaten in sixteen title fights, was the four-to-one favorite, eleven-to-five to win by knockout. Conn liked his chances. "Louis is a big, slow-moving Negro. Nobody knows this better than Joe himself. He's a dangerous fighter, because he can punch and because he's been taught well," Conn said before the fight. "But he's a mechanical fighter, doing only what he's been told. He can't think under pressure in the ring, and he knows it." Louis replied, "I never heard of him getting no college degrees. He talks too much and I'm going to push some of his gab down his throat."

Louis had no problems with Conn in the early rounds. But in the seventh round, Conn went on the attack and took command of the fight. "Billy was just too fast. I couldn't catch him," Louis said later. "By the time the eighth round came up, I was tired as hell, and I stayed that way until the twelfth. I was completely exhausted and he was really hurting me with left hooks."

Going into the thirteenth round, Conn led on all scorecards. After staggering Louis with a left hook in the twelfth, Conn went for a knockout in the next round. For the first two minutes of the thirteenth, Louis seemed vulnerable. But as Conn tried to end the fight, Louis struck his jaw with a powerful right, then hurt him with a left, and dropped him for the count with a jolting right. "He gave me my toughest fight of all my fights," Louis said years later.

Conn's epic fight made him an instant celebrity. He starred in the title role in a semiautobiographical movie, *The Pittsburgh Kid*, produced in 1941 by Republic Pictures. Shortly after the Louis fight, on 1 July 1941, he was married to Mary Louise Smith. Their marriage produced three sons and a daughter.

After the first Louis fight, Conn won a bruising slugfest with middleweight champion Tony Zale on 14 February 1942. Also in that year Conn enlisted in the U.S. Army and fought exhibition fights with division champions in the European theater. He was discharged as a corporal.

A Louis-Conn rematch was in the works for the summer of 1942. However, when Conn broke his hand in a scuffle with his father-in-law, the Louis fight was delayed. Secretary of War Henry L. Stimson announced that Louis, who was still in the army, would not be making any more title defenses for the duration of the war. The boxing promoter Mike Jacobs finally signed both fighters for a rematch in June 1946. When Louis was asked by reporters if Conn might win by decision, the champion replied, "He can run, but he can't hide." Conn was heavier and slower than he had been in the first fight. Louis knocked him out in the eighth round. Conn won his final two fights in 1948 with ninth-round knockouts. In his final appearance as a professional, Conn boxed with Louis in a six-round 10 December 1948 exhibition.

In his thirteen-year career, Conn won sixty-three fights, lost eleven, and fought one draw. A third of his professional fights were against world champions, and Conn defeated all but Louis. He was elected to the Boxing Hall of Fame in 1965. In 1981 the editors of *Ring* magazine rated his first bout with Louis as boxing's greatest fight.

Following his retirement in 1948, Conn lived off investments from his fight earnings. In the last two years of his life, Conn suffered from a condition known as pugilistic dementia. He died of pneumonia at a Veterans Affairs hospital in Pittsburgh and is buried in Calvary Cemetery.

★

Conn's trainer Freddie Fierro recalls his association with Conn in "The Champion Who Was Born for Laughs," *Boxing and Wrestling* magazine (Feb. 1956). The first Louis-Conn fight is chronicled by Leonard Koppett in *The Way It Was: Great Sports Events from the Past* (1974), edited by George Vecsey, and in *The Great Fights* (1981), by Bert Randolph Sugar and the editors of *Ring* magazine. There is also a profile of Conn in Bert Randolph Sugar's *The 100 Greatest Boxers of All Time* (1984). Frank Deford's profile of Conn, "The Boxer and the Blonde," which appeared in *Sports Illustrated* in 1985, is reprinted in *The World's Tallest Midget: The Best of Frank Deford* (1987). An obituary is in the *New York Times* (31 May 1993).

STEVE NEAL

CONNALLY, John Bowden, Jr. (*b.* 27 February 1917 in Floresville, Texas; *d.* 15 June 1993 in Houston, Texas), governor of Texas, secretary of the U.S. Navy, secretary of the U.S. Treasury, and adviser to three U.S. presidents.

Connally was one of eight children born to John B. Connally, Sr., and Lela Wright, tenant farmers. Connally attended public schools in San Antonio and Floresville, graduating from the high school in Floresville in 1933. That same year he enrolled at the University of Texas, earning his B.A. degree in 1935 and LL.B. in 1941. Tall, lantern-jawed, and possessing a shock of jet-black hair, Connally proved a captivating leading man at the university theater. He won election as student body president in 1938, and between 1939 and 1941 served as an aide to Congressman Lyndon B. Johnson, Democrat of Texas. Connally's restless ambition, love of politics, and close association with Johnson remained important threads throughout his public life. His private life centered around Idanell ("Nellie") Brill, whom he married on 21 December 1940. They had four children.

Connally's early career paralleled that of Johnson. He enlisted in the naval reserves in 1941 and during World War II briefly served as an aide to General Dwight D. Eisenhower. Connally was reassigned to the Pacific theater

John Connally, 1973. ASSOCIATED PRESS AP

and stationed on the aircraft carrier USS *Essex,* on which he experienced some of the fiercest fighting of the war. He attained the rank of lieutenant commander and earned two Bronze Stars for valor. In 1945 Connally returned to Texas to practice law and run an Austin radio station. He managed Lyndon Johnson's 1946 congressional race and successful bid for the U.S. Senate in 1948. Connally's role in fishing up the requisite ballots to ensure Johnson's triumph, by eighty-seven votes, remains in dispute. But the younger man clearly understood the essentials of Texas politics: controlling the machine vote in the Rio Grande Valley and securing large amounts of cash from contributors.

During the 1950s Connally struck a conservative pose, becoming an attorney and lobbyist for the Texas oil magnate Sid W. Richardson. He acquired holdings in real estate and ranching, apparently determined, like Johnson, to escape forever the poverty of his youth. Devoted to politics, Connally bolted his party in 1952 and supported Eisenhower for president. Four years later he returned to the fold, joining with liberal Texans to wrest the state Democratic party from conservative governor Allan Shivers and deliver it to Johnson. Connally's ruthlessness stunned Johnson, who privately remarked that his protégé lacked "even the tiniest trace of compassion." While managing Johnson's unsuccessful bid for the 1960 Democratic presidential nomination, Connally circulated rumors of John F. Kennedy's poor health. Nevertheless, because of his relationship with Johnson, who became Kennedy's running mate, and Texas's pivotal role in the election, the president-elect named Connally secretary of the navy in December 1960.

The subcabinet position did not satisfy Connally's ambition. He maintained cordial relations with Secretary of Defense Robert S. McNamara, even though McNamara usurped authority from the service secretaries. Connally resigned from his navy post late in 1961 to seek the Texas governorship. Financial and organizational support allowed Connally to become visible, and he led the Democratic primary after the initial balloting. Outspending Don Yarborough, his liberal challenger in the runoff, Connally appeared daily on television and crossed ideological lines, promising business growth and improvements in education. He took 51.2 percent of the vote against Yarborough in the Democratic primary and 54.2 percent against Republican Jack Cox in the fall general election. Connally closed his campaign in flashy style, with a nonstop, forty-eight-hour tour of the state.

A year later tragedy transformed Connally into a national figure. On 22 November 1963 he was riding through Dallas in Kennedy's open-topped limousine when an assassin shot the president. Connally survived after sustaining wounds to his back, chest, wrist, and thigh. The governor thought that the rifle might have been aimed at him rather than at the president, since the accused assailant, Lee Har-

vey Oswald, had unsuccessfully petitioned the Navy Department to upgrade his undesirable discharge from the Marine Corps. The Warren Commission's conclusion that a single bullet had passed through Kennedy's neck and Connally's torso and wrist before penetrating the governor's thigh seemed incredible to many Americans, including Connally. His wounding and slow, but highly public, recovery insulated Connally from criticism, easing his reelection in 1964 and 1966.

As governor Connally charted a more conservative course than either Kennedy or Johnson. While investing greater funds in higher education and mental health care, he showed less interest in primary and secondary schooling. Connally was no cheerleader for Johnson's Great Society legislation, except when the states attained control over its programs. His conservatism extended to race, where Connally criticized both the Civil Rights Act of 1964 and federal efforts to protect voting rights, affirming that Texas could advance in these areas without outside prompting. Although Connally appointed African Americans and Hispanics to state offices and distanced himself from the crudest forms of white resistance, he opposed sweeping changes for minorities. In 1966, when Mexican-American workers marched 400 miles on behalf of a minimum farm wage law, Connally traveled thirty miles to meet them and explain his opposition. He then drove away and did not greet the marchers when they arrived in Austin.

Connally's "swagger" became central to his political style. "John Connally epitomized the big man of Texas," wrote James Reston, Jr., his biographer. "Connally personifies confidence," the *Houston Chronicle* purred in 1964. "Defeat is not in his make-up. Retreat is not in his vocabulary." Occupying a weak office, the governor placed loyal associates on state boards and wielded power with relish. One-time Democratic National Committee Chair Robert S. Strauss called Connally "one of the ablest men I ever knew." His elegant attire, good looks, and suave manners fostered a "wheeler-dealer" persona. The governor enhanced his macho image in 1967, when he traveled alongside several well-known sportsmen on a six-week-long safari in Africa. Whatever their differences were over domestic issues, Connally strongly backed Johnson's military intervention in Vietnam.

Connally seemed out of place in a Democratic party moving toward the left, and he declined to run for reelection in 1968. Connally's conservative record and stand on Vietnam hindered his chances for gaining a spot on the Democratic ticket that year. At the party's convention, he led the fight for the administration's Vietnam plank and helped dissuade Vice President Hubert Humphrey, the presidential nominee, from modifying his support of Johnson's war policies. Connally backed Humphrey without zeal, partly because the vice president had not considered him as a running mate. In 1969 Connally joined the Houston law firm of Vinson and Elkins.

Connally gradually found a home among the Republicans. In 1969 President Richard Nixon named him to an advisory commission to reorganize the executive branch. Impressed with the results, he appointed Connally secretary of the treasury in 1971. An air of skepticism greeted the Texan; when asked about his economic credentials, Connally said: "I can add." He secured $250 million in loans to Lockheed Aircraft Corporation and persuaded Nixon to impose wage and price controls to arrest inflation. Under Connally the United States went off the gold standard, which led to a devalued dollar and floating currencies. Bargaining with European and Japanese representatives, Connally won an increase in the price of gold and exchange rates favorable for selling U.S. goods abroad. In the short run, these programs, known as the "New Economic Policy," curtailed inflation and unemployment and facilitated Nixon's reelection. In the long run, the lifting of controls helped prompt the "Great Inflation" of 1973, setting up the "Great Recession" of 1974. But throughout his brief tenure, Connally brought color to a drab cabinet. In 1971, the *New York Times* columnist James Reston tagged him "the spunkiest character in Washington" for telling business and labor leaders "to get off their duffs" if they wanted more jobs, profits, and trade.

In May 1972 Connally left the government to head "Democrats for Nixon." The president thought highly of Connally and weighed making the Texan his running mate in 1972. According to Nixon's national security adviser, Henry A. Kissinger, "Connally's swaggering self-assurance was Nixon's Walter Mitty image of himself." Nixon said that along with himself and Governor Nelson A. Rockefeller of New York, only Connally fully understood the uses of power. In 1973 the Texan registered as a Republican and became, for two months, a presidential adviser during the Watergate affair. Nixon wanted to appoint him vice president after Spiro T. Agnew's resignation, but the idea offended Democrats, whom Connally had spurned, and Republicans remained wary of the convert. Connally soon faced charges of corruption himself. In 1975 a federal court acquitted him of accepting a $10,000 bribe in exchange for backing a raise in price supports for milk producers. After serving on President Gerald R. Ford's Foreign Intelligence Advisory Board, Connally returned to his Houston law firm and sat on several corporate boards.

The Texan never fulfilled the political promise that others saw in him. Although Connally's ties to Nixon hurt his electoral prospects, he showed interest in the Republican vice presidential nomination in 1976 and sought the GOP's presidential nod in 1980. Connally lost the latter contest to Ronald Reagan, after spending $11 million in the primaries and collecting just one convention delegate. He abandoned politics in favor of financial pursuits, but a series of bad investments forced him to declare bankruptcy in 1988. With his once spacious ranch reduced to two hundred acres, Connally admitted, "I know what it is to be poor," but he emerged from bankruptcy within a year. Connally died in Houston of a pulmonary fibrosis in 1993. He is buried at Texas State Cemetery in Austin.

Connally symbolized the movement of white southerners, a historically conservative group, from Democratic to Republican allegiance. But for all his ability and guile, the Texan failed to inspire trust, and he proved unable to secure a place on the national ticket of either party. Connally's notoriety also came from serving powerful presidents whose actions alienated voters and tarnished their brightest protégés.

★

Connally's papers are housed at the Lyndon Baines Johnson Library in Austin, Texas. Connally's memoir (with Mickey Herskowitz) is *In History's Shadow: An American Odyssey* (1993). An early biography is Charles Ashman, *Connally: The Adventures of Big Bad John* (1974). The standard biography is James Reston, Jr., *The Lone Star: The Life of John Connally* (1989). Connally's service in the Nixon administration is covered in Henry Kissinger, *White House Years* (1979); Joan Hoff, *Nixon Reconsidered* (1994); and Allen J. Matusow, *Nixon's Economy: Booms, Busts, Dollars, and Votes* (1998). An obituary is in the *New York Times* (16 June 1993).

DEAN J. KOTLOWSKI

CONNORS, Kevin Joseph Aloysius ("Chuck") (*b.* 10 April 1921 in Brooklyn, New York; *d.* 10 November 1992 in Los Angeles, California), professional baseball and basketball player and actor best known for his title role in the television series *The Rifleman* (1958–1963).

Connors was the older of two children born to Irish immigrants Allen Francis Connors, a watchman, and Marcella Connors, a domestic servant and custodian. His childhood hobbies included hunting, reciting, and baseball. As a teenager, Connors acquired his nickname because while playing baseball he frequently told the pitcher to "Chuck it to me!" During the Great Depression the family moved from a humble home to an unheated apartment at 455 Sixty-first Street in Brooklyn. In 1934 they moved to 358 Senator Street, also in Brooklyn, where they resided for many years.

Connors attributed his ambition to his family's financial hardships. He attended a Catholic grammar school and, from ages thirteen to seventeen, he played baseball for John Flynn, a childless bank teller who formed a youth baseball team named the Bay Ridge Celtics. Flynn helped Connors develop integrity. On athletic scholarships, he attended Adelphi Academy in Brooklyn, from which he graduated

Chuck Connors, 1983. AP/WIDE WORLD PHOTOS

in 1939, and Seton Hall University in South Orange, New Jersey. Connors stood six and a half feet tall and weighed slightly over 200 pounds. Although he did not graduate from Seton Hall, he majored in English and, when he won a recitation contest, discovered that he enjoyed entertaining an audience. He was a voracious reader and loved Shakespeare, often writing his own poetry. But baseball remained his lifelong passion, and he dreamed of playing first base for the Brooklyn Dodgers.

In 1940 Connors persuaded the Dodgers to give him a tryout. This resulted in a contract and a $200 bonus check—the first check he had ever seen in his life—to play for their Newport News minor league team. Over the next thirteen years, Connors played mainly on minor league teams for the Dodgers, the New York Yankees, and the Chicago Cubs. The Newport News team won the 1946 Piedmont League championship, and Connors was the league's home run champion. He played on the Dodgers' Mobile, Alabama, minor league team that won the 1947 Southern Association championship. Connors also played on the Dodgers' Montreal Royals minor league team. While playing for Montreal in 1949, he batted .319, hit twenty home runs, and had 108 runs batted in. His only at-bat for the major league Dodgers was on 1 May 1949, when he hit into a double play, ending the game in a Dodgers loss. A primary obstacle to his becoming the Dodgers' first base-

man was the fact that the legendary Gil Hodges already held that position.

On 20 October 1942 Connors joined the army and was inducted at Fort Dix, New Jersey; he trained in tank warfare. In November he went to Camp Campbell, Kentucky, and then in 1944 to the U.S. Military Academy in West Point as a tank-warfare instructor. He was fortunate to spend his entire tour of duty stateside, and he remained an instructor for the rest of the war. The army discharged Connors on 19 February 1946. While he was in the military, Connors played semiprofessional basketball with the Wilmington (Delaware) Bombers. In 1946 he played for the Rochester (New York) Royals, champions of the National Basketball League. For the next several years, he played both baseball and basketball, the latter during the baseball off-season. From 1946 to 1947 Connors played basketball with the Boston Celtics as their starting center. His strengths were defense and rebounding; he averaged 4.5 points per game. Although he started the 1947–1948 season with Boston and appeared in four games, the 1946–1947 season was his only full season with the team; Connors quit basketball to concentrate on baseball in 1947.

In 1948 Connors met the model Elizabeth Jane Riddell on a blind date. They married on 1 October 1948 and had four sons. On 10 October 1950, the Dodgers traded Connors to the Chicago Cubs, who sent him to play the 1951 season with their Los Angeles Angels minor league team. In so doing, the Cubs also sent Connors to eventual show-business stardom. Connors moved from Brooklyn to Los Angeles in the summer of 1951. In the early 1950s, he and his wife lived at 5813 Penfield Avenue in Woodland Hills. During his first season with the Angels, he batted .321, hit twenty-one home runs, and had seventy-seven runs batted in.

In 1951 Connors got a call from Metro-Goldwyn-Mayer's casting director—a passionate baseball fan—that led to a role in the 1952 movie *Pat and Mike*. His 1952 season with the Angels was his last in baseball, and he retired from the game in February 1953. While in baseball, he played with such greats as Duke Snider, Don Newcombe, Jackie Robinson, Roy Campanella, and Carl Furillo. After baseball and before real success in show business, Connors sold insurance and worked other odd jobs. As he succeeded in show business, he appeared in several movies and popular television shows. From 1953 to 1956, Connors played roles in such movies as *Code Two* (1953) and *The Hired Gun* (1957) and made guest appearances on several television shows, among them, *Wagon Train, Topper, Superman, The Millionaire,* and *Gunsmoke*.

In 1957 Connors played Burn Sanderson, owner of the dog in the title role of Walt Disney's *Old Yeller*. Two scenes in which he befriended two young brothers, which showed how well he could interact with young boys, helped him land the role of Lucas McCain in *The Rifleman,* a television Western set in the late 1870s. *The Rifleman*—created by Sam Peckinpah—ran from 1958 to 1963. McCain lived on a ranch near North Fork, New Mexico, and raised his son, Mark (played by Johnny Crawford), with moral lessons, not spankings. The show's title referred to McCain's wizardry with his modified Winchester rifle, with which he protected himself and others from the dangers of the Wild West. Connors described the show as a "love story between a father and his son," and his role served as a positive parenting model. After its first season, *The Rifleman* was nominated for an Emmy, and Connors won a TV Champion Award and a Golden Globe Award.

In 1961 Connors divorced his first wife. He married Kamala Devi on 10 April 1963. They had no children and were divorced in 1972. In June 1973 he gave a cowboy hat and two Colt .45 revolvers to Soviet leader Leonid Brezhnev, an ardent fan. On 5 September 1977 Connors married Faith Quabius; they did not have children and divorced in 1979. In 1977 he played the slave owner Tom Moore in *Roots,* a television miniseries. On 18 July 1984 Connors received his star on Hollywood Boulevard's Walk of Fame. He worked with some of Hollywood's greatest celebrities, including Katharine Hepburn, Spencer Tracy, John Wayne, and Burt Lancaster. He was inducted into the National Cowboy Hall of Fame in March 1991. Connors died at the age of seventy-one of lung cancer at Cedars-Sinai Medical Center in Los Angeles and was buried at San Fernando Mission Cemetery in Mission Hills, California.

Connors was an unconventional, friendly extrovert with a strong physical presence. Via golf tournaments, he raised millions of dollars for charity. Politically, he supported the Vietnam War and campaigned for President Ronald Reagan. In baseball, his shenanigans entertained fans: He was known to cartwheel from base to base after hitting a home run. He also taunted umpires and other players with Shakespearean quotes. Although he is best remembered for *The Rifleman,* Connors's first love was baseball. He would have preferred to swing a bat than to twirl a rifle.

★

David Fury reveals Connors's life in *Chuck Connors: "The Man Behind the Rifle"* (1997), which contains many black-and-white photos of Connors. It also includes many quotes by Connors, some of his poetry and speeches, and lists of his baseball and basketball statistics, movies, television appearances, and stage plays. Connors is also covered in "Now Batting for Furillo, the 'Rifleman,'" in Tony Salin, *Baseball's Forgotten Heroes: One Fan's Search for the Game's Most Interesting Overlooked Players* (1999). Articles about Connors include "The Rifleman Was a Ham," *TV Guide* (22 Aug. 1959); G. Eells, "Chuck Connors: Man of Dimension," *Look* (21 June 1960); and "Boys Have a Ball at Dad's Work," *Life* (3 Oct. 1960). Obituaries are in Louise Mooney, ed.,

The Annual Obituary 1992 (1993); the *New York Times Biographical Service* (Nov. 1992); and Emily J. McMurray, ed., *Contemporary Theatre, Film, and Television* 11 (1994): 113.

GARY MASON CHURCH

COOPER, John Sherman (*b.* 23 August 1901 in Somerset, Kentucky; *d.* 21 February 1991 in Washington, D.C.), U.S. senator, ambassador to India and East Germany, and member of the Warren commission.

The second of seven children of John Sherman Cooper, Sr., and Helen Gertrude Tartar, Cooper grew to maturity in a politically oriented family. His mother's father and brother had long been active in Republican politics; his father followed both farming and the law but also served as a bank president and county judge, the chief executive position in the county. His mother was a schoolteacher before her birth and again later on, but was a homemaker when her children were born. Cooper received his early education at home but graduated in 1918 from Somerset High School, where he was named class president and class poet. In the fall of that year he entered Centre College in Danville, Kentucky, but transferred to Yale University a year later. Cooper became a member of the exclusive Skull and Bones secret society, captained the basketball team, and was named "best liked" by his class of 1923. He then entered Harvard Law School, but his father's illness caused him to leave before graduation.

John Sherman Cooper as a member of the Warren commission, 1964. ASSOCIATED PRESS AP

Back in Somerset, Cooper soon entered the political arena himself. In 1928 he passed his bar exam (even though he had not graduated), opened a law office, and won election to the Kentucky House of Representatives, where he served one term. With the support of his powerful uncle, Roscoe Tartar, Cooper won election in 1929 as county judge. When he took office in 1930, at age twenty-eight, he was said to be the youngest county judge in the state. Unfortunately, the two terms he served, from 1930 to 1938, coincided with the depths of the Great Depression. Burdened by debt, he nevertheless served without pay several times due to budget issues. Yet he received accolades for his work and cooperated closely with New Deal agencies. Still, the pressure of the office took its toll, and in 1938, suffering from deep depression, Cooper had a nervous breakdown and spent time in several hospitals. That would never be an issue, however, in any of his subsequent races.

Fully recovered by 1939, Cooper sought the Republican nomination for governor, running against a former gubernatorial candidate, King Swope of Lexington. Not well known outside his region despite service on the University of Kentucky board of trustees from 1935 to 1946, Cooper had little chance against the experienced Swope and lost with only 36 percent of the vote. With the coming of World War II the forty-one-year-old Cooper left his law practice and on 14 September 1942 volunteered for the army as a private. Commissioned an officer the next year, he served with General George Patton's Third Army in France, Luxembourg, and Germany. In 1944, Cooper wed Evelyn Pfaff, a young widowed nurse with a daughter; the marriage would barely survive the war, however, ending in divorce in 1947. They had no children.

Awarded a Bronze Star for his wartime work, Cooper was discharged as a captain. In Europe after the conflict ended, he helped reorganize Bavaria's judicial system and worked with displaced refugees. While engaged in those activities, he was elected a circuit judge back home, and he returned to Kentucky to begin that term in January 1946.

Cooper's judicial duties did not last long, however. In 1946, A. B. "Happy" Chandler left his senate seat to become commissioner of baseball. Democrats nominated former congressman John Y. Brown, Sr., and Republicans chose Cooper, who won the election by some 41,000 votes. Serving the rest of Chandler's term from November 1946 until January 1949, Cooper voted with his party only 51 percent of the time, demonstrating an independence that would mark his voting record for the rest of his career. In a state that usually voted Democratic, such actions did not injure him. Still, in 1948 he faced a difficult reelection race, for the vice presidential candidate on the national ticket that year was Kentucky Democrat Alben Barkley. Cooper's Democratic opponent for senator, Virgil Chapman, rode those coattails to victory, although Cooper won many Democratic votes. In 1949 he joined the Washington, D.C., law firm of Gardner, Morison, and Rogers. Later that year he was appointed by President Harry Truman as a delegate to the United Nations General Assembly. He served as an alternate delegate in 1950–1951, and again in 1968 and 1981.

The death of Senator Chapman in 1952 created another senate vacancy. Republicans again put forth Cooper, who defeated the short-term Democratic appointee Tom Underwood by some 28,000 votes. Cooper's service as senator ran from November 1952 until a virtually unbeatable Barkley defeated Cooper in the 1954 race. On 17 March 1955 Cooper married a well-known Washington socialite, Lorraine Rowan Shevlin, and their union would continue until her death on 3 February 1985. They had no children.

In 1955 President Dwight D. Eisenhower rewarded Cooper with an appointment as ambassador to India. Very popular there at a time when America generally was not, Cooper served until 1956, when politics beckoned again. At the personal request of Eisenhower, Cooper returned for yet another senatorial race to fill an unexpired term, this time that of Alben Barkley, who had died. Although a loyal Republican, Cooper usually attracted support from the Democratic faction led by Happy Chandler, who had returned from baseball to become governor. With that support as well as Eisenhower's in a presidential election year, Cooper won easily over former Democratic governor Lawrence Wetherby. Four years later, for the first time in the state's history, a Republican won reelection to the Senate when Cooper defeated another former governor, Keen Johnson, by almost 200,000 votes. In 1966 the incumbent Cooper handily won over John Y. Brown, Sr., but he decided not to seek reelection in 1972.

During his years in the Senate, Cooper was a respected man who often served behind the scenes. In 1960 a *Newsweek* poll of correspondents named him the ablest Republican senator. He supported civil rights legislation, environmental bills, and the Tennessee Valley Authority (TVA), and opposed the antiballistic-missile program and attempts to restrict tobacco supports. Cooper cosponsored the Appalachian Regional Development Act and very early became a critic of U.S. involvement in Vietnam, as chiefly demonstrated by the 1970 Cooper-Church amendment, which prohibited funding for the use of U.S. ground forces in Cambodia. One of his most distressing duties came when he accepted appointment to the Warren commission to investigate the death of his friend John F. Kennedy.

After leaving the Senate in January 1973 Cooper joined the Washington, D.C., firm of Covington and Burling. He interrupted that work to serve as the first U.S. ambassador to the German Democratic Republic (East Germany) from 1974 to late 1976, then returned to the law firm, where he remained until his retirement in 1989. He died quietly, at age eighty-nine, and is buried in Arlington National Cemetery.

Tall, handsome, and distinguished-looking, Cooper looked the political part he played. Yet his success came through an unusual route, for he was a poor campaigner. He mumbled his speeches, displayed a poor memory, seemed always tardy, and stated matters bluntly. Yet, in a Democratic state, he won election after election, revitalizing the Republican Party. People voted for his integrity, sincerity, and conscience; they trusted him to do right. In the Senate, his lack of partisanship won him respect in both parties. Cooper led quietly, but he led.

★

The John Sherman Cooper Collection and the John Sherman Cooper Oral History Project, both at the University of Kentucky Library, provide a wealth of primary materials. The best introduction to the spirit of Cooper is Bill Cooper, "John Sherman Cooper: A Senator and His Constituents," *Register of the Kentucky Historical Society* (1986) (hereinafter *Register*). Richard C. Smoot has written numerous studies: "John Sherman Cooper: The Paradox of a Liberal Republican in Kentucky Politics" (Ph.D. diss., University of Kentucky, 1988); "John Sherman Cooper: The Early Years, 1901–1927," *Register* (1995); and "The Gavel and the Sword: Experiences Shaping the Life of John Sherman Cooper," in John David Smith and Thomas H. Appleton, Jr., eds., *A Mythic Land Apart: Reassessing Southerners and their History* (1997). A detailed look at one facet of Cooper's career is Douglas A. Franklin, "The Politician as Diplomat: Kentucky's John Sherman Cooper in India, 1955–1956," *Register* (1984). Books include Robert Schulman, *John Sherman Cooper: The Global Kentuckian* (1976), and Clarice James Mitchiner, *Senator John Sherman Cooper: Consummate Statesman* (1982). An obituary is in the *New York Times* (23 Feb. 1991).

JAMES C. KLOTTER

D

DALY, John Charles, Jr. (*b*. 20 February 1914 in Johannesburg, South Africa; *d*. 25 February 1991 in Chevy Chase, Maryland), broadcast journalist, host of one of the longest-running television game shows, *What's My Line?,* and head of the Voice of America radio network.

Daly was one of the two children of John Charles Daly, an American geologist and mining engineer working in South Africa, and Helene Grant Tennant, a homemaker. After the death of his father, who succumbed to a tropical fever, Daly's mother took him and his older brother to Boston in the United States. Daly was enrolled in the Tilton School in Tilton, New Hampshire, and went on to junior college there. From 1930 to 1933 he completed his education at Boston College. He maintained his connection with the Tilton School throughout his life, later serving as chairman of its board. A portrait by Charles Andres of Daly in front of Tilton's campus includes some of the buildings he helped fund.

On 7 January 1937, Daly married Margaret Criswell Neal, with whom he had three children. After they were divorced, he married Virginia Warren, a daughter of the U.S. Supreme Court Chief Justice Earl Warren, on 22 December 1960. With her, Daly again had three children. From 1935 to 1937 Daly worked for a transit company in the nation's capital. He then joined NBC as a radio reporter in Washington, soon moving on to CBS. From 1937 to 1949, Daly worked at CBS, first as radio correspondent and

news analyst, then as White House correspondent and special events reporter. It was his voice that interrupted a music program on 7 December 1941 to announce that the Japanese had bombed Pearl Harbor, which triggered the entry of the United States into World War II.

Daly's wartime assignments included reporting from London, the Middle East, and Italy from 1943 to 1944. In August 1943, while covering the U.S. invasion of Sicily, Daly learned that the American general George Patton had slapped two soldiers who Patton believed were malingering in an army hospital. Daly and other correspondents went to Patton's superior, General Dwight D. Eisenhower, to suggest he be removed. Eisenhower, replying that he needed Patton for the war effort, asked the journalists not to report the incident. They kept their promise of silence. But three months later the radio commentator Drew Pearson broke the story, with a resulting uproar against Patton in Congress and the press.

In 1949 Daly moved to ABC as a correspondent. In 1953 he was promoted to vice president in charge of news, special events, sports, and public affairs. In addition to serving as anchor for ABC's nightly news program, Daly helped evolve policies relating to television news coverage. One issue concerned the responsibility for the production of documentary programs. The matter became controversial when David Wolper, an independent producer, filmed a documentary on space. Wolper had an advertiser who sought to place the program on one of the major networks.

However, all three networks turned it down, arguing that because they were responsible for content, they would carry only documentaries created by staff personnel.

Critics contended that this policy gave the networks a virtual monopoly in that influential area. However, the sponsor was able to purchase time, city by city, on a patchwork of individual stations. Meanwhile, the Writers Guild of America (WGA) protested the networks' action. Daly replied to the WGA: "The standards of production and presentation which apply to a professional network news department would not necessarily apply to, for instance, an independent Hollywood producer." NBC and CBS took similar stands.

Daly faced another controversy when Leonard Goldenson, president of American Broadcasting–Paramount Theaters, saw the work of a Time, Inc., film unit headed by Robert Drew. Goldenson entered into an arrangement with Time for Drew and his staff to produce programs for ABC as an ABC documentary unit. Daly felt his policy had been subverted and he resigned from ABC in 1960. He did not, however, give up his long-held post hosting CBS-TV's celebrity game show *What's My Line?* Daly is most remembered for that role, which went back to February 1950 when it premiered. Although *What's My Line?* followed a score

John Daly as the mystery guest on *What's My Line?* in 1967. AP/WIDE WORLD PHOTOS

of other game-panel programs, it proved to have a winning mixture of puzzle, intriguing guests, a witty panel, and an affably erudite host in Daly. It outlasted all its rivals and later imitators to become the longest-running show in its category. Its premise called for the panel to guess the occupation of mystery guests by asking yes-or-no questions. When the guests were notables—such as Eleanor Roosevelt, playwright Noël Coward, and U.S. Supreme Court Justice William O. Douglas—the panelists were blindfolded. Daly presided over the banter with urbane charm and erudition. After seventeen years, in 1967 CBS canceled *What's My Line?* as audience interest waned. Later, reruns and updated versions were aired in syndication. Daly did not appear in any of the updated versions of the show.

Although it was later seen as inappropriate for a network newsperson to star in a purely entertainment program, this was not so in television's early days. Mike Wallace was on *Majority Rules* in 1949 and 1950, and Walter Cronkite was on *It's News to Me* in 1954.

In 1954 Daly was master of ceremonies at the first broadcast of the Miss America beauty pageant, which became an annual presentation. Daly also appeared on an innovative CBS-TV series, *You Are There,* in which historic events were covered as though they were taking place in the television era. For example, the program on the French Revolution showed Daly interviewing an actor playing King Louis XVI. Among his many other credits over the years were serving as narrator on ABC's serious music program *The Voice of Firestone,* and moderator of the *National Town Meeting* (1974).

Daly received the Emmy Award as best reporter or commentator from the National Academy of Television Arts and Sciences (1954). He also received Emmy nominations for best reporter or commentator in 1955, best news commentator in 1956 and 1957, and best news commentator or analyst in 1958.

In 1969 Daly succeeded John Chancellor, a former NBC journalist, as director of the Voice of America radio network, a broadcast service of the United States Information Agency. Daly resigned after one year because personnel changes had been made without his involvement. Daly, who had a long-standing interest in public health and the environment, served on the Water Pollution Control Advisory Board (1960–1962), the National Digestive Diseases Advisory Board of the National Institutes of Health (1962–1987), and the board of trustees of Norwich University. Daly died of cardiac arrest. He is buried in Washington, D.C.

For seventeen years on *What's My Line?* Daly was watched on Sunday evenings by millions of American families who enjoyed his affable personality. Many of them also remembered his reporting, news analysis, and dedication to journalistic professionalism.

Gil Fates, the producer of the program, is the author of *What's My Line?* (1978), which recounts the show's history, including references to John Daly's participation. Fates suggests that the program might have lasted longer had Daly accepted some format revisions. Obituaries are in the *New York Times* (27 Feb. 1991) and *Time* (11 Mar. 1991).

BERT R. BRILLER

DAVIS, Miles Dewey, III (*b.* 26 May 1926 in Alton, Illinois; *d.* 28 March 1991 in Santa Monica, California), jazz trumpeter, composer, bandleader, and painter who helped introduce the neo-bop and modal styles of music.

Davis was one of three children born to Miles Dewey Davis, II, a dental surgeon, and Cleota Henry, a homemaker. Davis's father established his practice in East St. Louis, Illinois, and from the age of one Davis was raised and educated there. Davis's youth was spent in relatively affluent circumstances. He spent vacation times on his father's 200-acre hog farm near Millstadt, Illinois. From early adolescence Davis came to know big-city nightlife in St. Louis, Missouri, across the Mississippi River from East St. Louis.

Miles Davis had the favor of his father to the point of

Miles Davis. LIBRARY OF CONGRESS

indulgence, and from him he inherited a strong sense of family pride predicated on three generations of African American success against oppressive odds. Davis's mother had social pretensions that often rankled her husband and, through him, her son.

Davis began studying trumpet at fourteen, under the tutelage of a dance-band musician named Elwood Buchanan who was indebted to Dr. Davis for dental work. Davis's parents separated at this time. Davis's father took the boy's side in favoring the trumpet over the violin, which his mother preferred. The rancor between Davis's parents and his close identification with his father may have been the source of the deep-seated misogyny in Davis's relations with women. In any event, the choice of Buchanan as his teacher, arbitrary as it might have seemed, proved fateful. Buchanan had played with touring orchestras, including Andy Kirk's Clouds of Joy, and he knew about the new musical currents that would crystallize into the bebop revolution. Buchanan made Davis aware of harmonic departures from conventional scales and encouraged him to play with a crisp, vibratoless tone. Both traits would eventually inspire admiration for and emulation of Davis's mature style.

Davis played professional gigs in St. Louis starting at age sixteen. He was nicknamed "Little" because of his stature; he was only five-foot seven and weighed about 135 pounds. He had a penchant for sharp, conservative attire that led him to favor Brooks Brothers suits and spit-polished oxfords with elevated soles from adolescence until 1967, when he began wearing dashikis, jumpsuits, thick-soled clogs, and other bohemian attire.

At the age of eighteen Davis's high-school romance with Irene Birth resulted in the birth of his first child in 1944. The relationship continued after he moved to New York City, where his second child was born in 1946. Davis and Birth had a third child in 1950, but Davis later denied paternity.

After graduating from Lincoln High School in East St. Louis, Davis moved to New York City in 1944, ostensibly to study at the Juilliard School of Music. Instead, he gravitated toward the jazz clubs playing bebop. He dropped out of Juilliard in his second term to devote himself to jazz, and he developed a close musical association with the saxophonist and bebop genius Charlie ("Bird") Parker. Davis recorded with Parker frequently between 1945 and 1948 and played as the second horn in the front line of Parker's quintets in both Hollywood and New York City during the same period.

Davis's natural proclivities as a trumpeter ran contrary to the bebop style. He favored ballad tempos and he excelled at middle-register melodic variations that used understatement eloquently. In 1948 he led a nine-piece band tailored to that style, with fastidious arrangements by Gil

Evans, Gerry Mulligan, and John Lewis. Although the band, known as the Miles Davis Nonet, played only two weeks (in September 1948 at the Royal Roost in New York City) and recorded only twelve three-minute sides (in 1949 and 1950, collected as *The Birth of the Cool*), it founded the style known as cool jazz. Hallmarks of the style were legato voicings with orderly, thoughtful solos in arranged contexts. Davis's nonet recordings profoundly influenced jazz in the 1950s, contributing to its international dissemination as concert music accessible to a broad audience in college auditoriums, symphony halls, and festival tents.

Even as Davis's early achievements as a leader were establishing him as an influential figure during the period from 1949 to 1954, his own musical talents suffered a sharp decline while he struggled with a debilitating heroin addiction. He finally brought his addiction under control by locking himself in a room at his father's farmhouse and putting himself through cold turkey withdrawal. He emerged to become the most influential stylist and the most admired instrumentalist in jazz in the postwar era.

Davis quickly attained his apogee, leading quintets and sextets from 1955 to 1960 that featured John Coltrane on tenor saxophone. Davis displayed a wistful, introverted, expressive lyricism especially on ballads such as "Round Midnight" (1955), "Jazz Track" (1956), and "Someday My Prince Will Come" (1961). He also introduced modal structures, in which improvised choruses were based on scales rather than chord sequences ("Milestones" 1958; "Kind of Blue" 1959), and he soloed in elegant concerti grossi orchestrated by Gil Evans, such as "Miles Ahead" (1956), "Porgy and Bess" (1958), and "Sketches of Spain" (1960). All of these recordings rank among the most abiding accomplishments of modern jazz.

During the late 1950s, Davis was also enjoying a period of relative calm in his personal life. In 1955 he signed a lucrative contract with Columbia Records that provided him with worldwide distribution for his music and a measure of financial security; the relationship lasted for thirty years, ending when he signed with Warner Brothers in 1985. He married the dancer Frances Taylor on 21 December 1960. They renovated a five-story brownstone on West Seventy-seventh Street on the Upper West Side of Manhattan, and Davis's children came from St. Louis to live with them.

In the early 1960s jazz went through a period of audacious experimentation, but at first Davis held to the musical course he had set. Then, in 1963, he formed a quintet of brilliant young musicians—with Wayne Shorter on saxophone, Herbie Hancock on piano, Ron Carter on bass, and Tony Williams on drums—that led him into radical modal experiments ("Miles Smiles" 1965; "Nefertiti" 1967). He played with the quintet for five years. With Davis's imprimatur, the music of this quintet found a steadfast audience, even as jazz, like opera, ballet, symphony, and other forms of serious music, struggled against the burgeoning rock and folk waves of a surprisingly vital pop music. The adventurous style of Davis's quintet, combining neo-bop elements with harmonic exploration, established what has become the main current of contemporary jazz.

Davis, as characteristically restless in his artistic life as in his personal life, moved his music in yet another direction. In 1968, he began fusing jazz harmonies with rock instrumentation and rhythms to become the most influential exemplar of the style known as jazz-rock fusion ("In a Silent Way" 1969; "Live-Evil" 1970). In recording studios and on stages, he led bands featuring electric guitars, electric keyboards, synthesizers (which he himself began playing during this period), electric bass, drums, and assorted percussion instruments, setting up a wall of percussive sound against which he unloosed declamatory wails on his amplified trumpet, often with electronic "wah-wah" effects. This music found initial commercial success; the double LP recording *Bitches Brew* (1970) was Davis's best-selling record for over twenty years, until it was overtaken posthumously by *Kind of Blue* (1959), his bona fide masterpiece from an earlier period.

Other changes accompanied Davis's adoption of fusion music. Davis began dressing in colorful robes and batik tunics. His performances became continuous, unbroken recitals, segueing between tunes with intervals of dense funk rhythms. In both his musical direction and his personal tastes he was influenced by the soul singer Betty Mabry, whom he married on 30 September 1968 and divorced the next year. (His marriage to Frances Taylor ended in divorce in 1968 but it had effectively ended some four years earlier.) In 1970 his four-year off-and-on relationship with Marguerite Eskridge resulted in the birth of a son, Erin Davis. In 1978 Davis was imprisoned for failing to support the child, but ten years later Erin was living with Davis in Malibu, California, and he was named the main beneficiary in Davis's will.

Davis suffered from sickle-cell anemia, which gave him acute arthritic symptoms and led to hip-replacement operations, brittle bones (he broke both ankles in a car accident in 1972), and other ailments. By the 1970s, he was consuming large quantities of analgesics and other drugs, especially cocaine. In 1975 he retired for six years and became reclusive, devoting himself by his own description to a cocaine habit that cost $500 a day and (in his own words) to "kinky sex and other weird sick shit."

Davis resumed his performance career with a concert at Avery Fisher Hall in New York City as part of the 1981 Kool Jazz Festival. His health appeared to improve under the influence of his third wife, the actress Cicely Tyson, whom he married on Thanksgiving Day in 1981 at the home of the actor and comedian Bill Cosby. Tyson urged him into therapy with acupuncturists and other specialists. For the remaining ten years of his life he led bands of young, often rock-trained, musicians on commercially successful international tours. His music became simplistic, based on melodic riffs that he played repetitively over lush synthesized chords. On stage he wore baggy jumpsuits, outsized sunglasses, and berets. His custom-made Martin trumpets were black enameled or red enameled, with a portable microphone attached to the bell that allowed him to stump around the stage in a restless trek. His performances became exhibitions of shadow, noise, and antics. He teased ovations from his young audiences by raising his pant-legs to show his bright-red cowboy boots or chugging liter bottles of mineral water.

As his music grew ever more trite in his waning years, Davis discovered a remarkable passion for painting. He had begun sketching with felt pens and charcoal as part of Tyson's therapy regime, and his interest quickly extended to oils and acrylics. He pursued his art long after his and Tyson's acrimonious divorce in 1989. His considerable artistic talent, abetted by his musical fame, resulted in gallery shows in the United States, Spain, Germany, and Japan, as well as a handsome folio entitled *The Art of Miles Davis* (1991).

Davis was often hospitalized in the 1980s and early 1990s for various ailments—arthritis, diabetes, gallstones, heart palpitations, liver infection, bleeding ulcer—most of which resulted from his decades of drug addiction. Tabloids and other sources reported that he was suffering from AIDS but the reports were never corroborated. He died in Santa Monica on 28 September 1991. The official causes were pneumonia, stroke, and respiratory failure.

Despite a turbulent, quixotic personal life, Davis managed to harness his creative impulses in ways that helped fulfill the potential of jazz as concert music and expanded its grammar in often unexpected directions. During the years of the bebop revolution, Davis apprenticed under the greatest innovators, and after that he led jazz through no fewer than four stylistic changes. Cool jazz in the early 1950s restored order and textural richness that had been sacrificed by the pyrotechnical excesses of bebop. Neo-bop (or hard bop), beginning around 1954, restored the blues as the primary jazz form and toughened the rhythmic base. The modal experiments of the 1960s freed improvisers from predictable harmonic resolutions based on chord sequences and challenged them, as Davis said it would, to develop their melodic imaginations in freer contexts. The fusion of jazz with electronic instruments and rock (or funk) rhythms proved more ephemeral, initially raising hopes for a productive amalgam but stalling largely because of its predictability. The mainstream of contemporary jazz diffuses from Davis's music in his peak years, the neo-bop and modal styles that he helped to introduce and influen-

tially developed. The best of his recorded legacy, which began in 1945 and was sustained for forty-six years, with consummations abounding in the long period from 1954 to 1971, sounds so fresh that it remains among the best-selling jazz music years after his death. Davis's musical influence remains audible in both the sounds and the styles of the best young musicians.

★

Miles's autobiography, written with Quincey Troupe, *Miles: The Autobiography* (1989), is highly personal and often shocking in Davis's casual references to beating his wives, tangling with managers, and pursuing drugs; this is self-inflicted tabloid journalism with little indication of the author's stature as a musician. Miles Davis and Scott Gutterman, *The Art of Miles Davis* (1991), is a beautiful coffee table book with full-color plates of about seventy of Davis's paintings. Bill Cole, *Miles Davis: A Musical Biography* (1974), is a spotty biography, notable because of the author's affection for Davis's music. The British jazz trumpeter Ian Carr highlights his narrative of the main events of Davis's life with his knowledge of trumpet technique in *Miles Davis: A Biography* (1982). Eric Nisenson, *'Round About Midnight: A Portrait of Miles Davis* (1996), is concerned more with Davis's style than with his music and more with his image than his life, but is succinct and highly readable. Ken Vail, ed., *Miles' Diary: The Life of Miles Davis 1947–61* (1996), is a chronology of Davis's early career with reproductions of clippings and photographs. Jack Chambers, *Milestones: The Music and Times of Miles Davis* (1998), was originally published as two volumes in 1986, but the meticulously-detailed revised edition is compiled in one volume with an additional chapter on the last decade of Davis's life. Gary Carner, ed., *The Miles Davis Companion* (1996), is a collection of articles and documents about Davis, and a useful complement to Bill Kirchner, ed., *A Miles Davis Reader* (1997), another collection of articles and documents. Quincey Troupe, *Miles and Me* (2000), is a personal account of the author's experiences with the irascible trumpeter when he was supposed to be helping Davis assemble his autobiography. Ashley Kahn, *Kind of Blue: The Making of the Miles Davis Masterpiece* (2000), is a detailed account of the recording of the 1959 *Kind of Blue* album by Davis, with his sextet that included John Coltrane, Julian ("Cannonball") Adderley, and Bill Evans.

JACK CHAMBERS

DELACORTE, George Thomas, Jr. (*b.* 20 June 1893 in Brooklyn, New York; *d.* 4 May 1991 in New York City), founder of the Dell Publishing Company and Delacorte Press, and philanthropist whose gifts to New York City became Central Park landmarks.

Delacorte was one of ten children of attorneys George Thomas, Sr., and Cecilia Koenig, and a product of Brooklyn's primary and secondary schools, graduating from Boys High in 1910. Even before he went away to Harvard he

125

George Delacorte in front of the *Alice in Wonderland* sculpture in Central Park, which he donated. New York City, 1982. NANCY R. SCHIFF/ ARCHIVE PHOTOS

dent of New Fiction, but this success was short-lived. Economic hard times hit and Delacorte was fired in 1921. With his severance pay (alternately reported as $10,000 or $15,000) he launched Dell (a diminutive of "Delacorte"), publishing in a one-room office in New York's Masonic Temple Building on West Twenty-third Street. He reveled in the challenge to stay on top of what a mass audience wanted to read. Early publications were ten-cent horoscope and character analysis pamphlets printed on wood pulp paper, and formula fiction publications like *Sweetheart Stories* and *I Confess*, which capitalized on the popularity of romance and confession magazines. After the death of his partner, William A. Johnston, a former *New York World* editor, Delacorte took on every aspect of the business, from editing to distribution to management. Operating on a shoestring, he bought manuscripts in England by the barrel-full, changed the characters and plots to reflect American situations, and repackaged them in the pulp magazines *My Story, Modern Romances, Cupid's Diary, War Stories, Inside Detective*, and *Modern Screen*. By 1931 he had originated three dozen magazines and abandoned more than half of them.

With the onset of the 1930s Delacorte cashed in on the rising popularity of talking movies, issuing movie fan magazines. Ever the promotional-minded innovator, he launched *Ballyhoo*, a biweekly that lampooned advertising; it was wrapped in cellophane with the label "Read a fresh magazine." Soon *Ballyhoo* was selling more than 2 million copies. Despite its success, Delacorte, who practiced rigid economy, never put stock in a single title. Instead he tested the market with one-shots—if it caught on, it lived; if not, he buried it. Joining the pulps in the 1930s were ten-cent comic books—featuring Flash Gordon, Woody Woodpecker, Bugs Bunny, and the entire Walt Disney stable of characters, which Delacorte had brought under license. By the end of the decade he had amassed a comic book line of staggering proportions and Dell, the first to introduce four-color comics, was the world's leading comic book publisher, selling 300 million a year and sometimes 3 million copies in one month alone.

Perhaps because of his fondness for children (Delacorte and Margarita, who died in 1956, had six children), Delacorte avoided the sleaze that came to be associated with the "pulps" and was known as the "Mr. Clean" of the comic book industry, abjuring crime and sex scenes. In the 1940s, with the United States at war, he satisfied mass reading appetites with war romances, comic books, and crossword puzzle books—all cheaply priced. He concentrated on newsstand sales and relied on circulation, not advertising, for revenue. As late as 1949 he continued to reject the idea of putting ads on comic book covers because he felt that he could sell more copies using full-color cover illustrations.

Delacorte developed innovative strategies to ensure

had decided against becoming an attorney like his parents, perhaps because he regarded the profession as "too sedate," a complaint he registered in later years about Harvard itself. He transferred to Columbia College in the fall of 1911, married Margarita von Doerhoff on 30 August 1912, and the following year brought his wife and baby son to his graduation. Upon receipt of his B.A. degree and $100 from his father, he set out to learn the magazine publishing business. He was nineteen years old.

His first job was in advertising and circulation at New Fiction Publishing Company in Manhattan. Here he learned the mass-market magazine publishing business from the ground up, initiating distribution techniques such as handing out cigars to newsstand dealers to ensure prominent display space for New Fiction magazines. He developed a keen sense of the tastes of his readers, and he was to spend the remainder of his publishing career correctly guessing and satisfying those tastes.

Within two years he was business manager and presi-

sales. For example, rather than date magazine issues, he numbered them. Unsold copies distributed in the East were redistributed in the West. To build demand for his titles, he handed out free copies. As an outgrowth of this vast publishing empire, Delacorte launched a line of paperbound books in 1943, initially reprints of classic novels and genre fiction by Ellery Queen, Dashiell Hammett, Dorothy Hughes, and Rex Stout. In 1953 he started Dell First Editions ("Not a Reprint," the cover announced), leading off with *The Body Snatchers* by Jack Finney. By 1957, when he acquired the reprint rights to *Peyton Place,* he had become the leading publisher of twenty-five-cent paperbound books, and by 1962 Dell accounted for 20 percent of all paperbacks published. To ensure a constant supply of material for Dell paperbacks, he formed the hardcover Delacorte Press in 1963, with J. P. Donleavy, Kurt Vonnegut, and Irwin Shaw among his earliest writers.

In 1976, when Dell was sold to Doubleday for a reported $35 million in cash, Delacorte retired. Although he had homes in Sharon, Connecticut; North Palm Beach, Florida; and Manhattan, his generous philanthropy was dedicated to the city in which he made his fortune. When in town he walked daily to his midtown office, often through Central Park, where he visited his gifts—the Delacorte Theater, the animated Delacorte Clock with its dancing bear, goat, monkeys, and elephant, and the Alice in Wonderland statue. Delacorte fountains graced Columbus Circle, Bowling Green, and City Hall Park, as did Delacorte's Folly, an ill-fated geyser that once gushed 400 feet in the air from the foot of Roosevelt Island. Helen Meyer, Dell chairman and Delacorte's right hand for six decades, said that he always liked to see his name on fountains and memorials. When Meyer's daughter was born, Delacorte wired: "If you can't name her after me, you can't have your job back." Meyer named the child Adele. Later, when her son was born, Delacorte wanted him named Cort. Delacorte also contributed more than $6 million to Columbia University, which awarded him an honorary Doctor of Laws degree in 1982.

Tanned and fit, he was an avid tennis player until the age of ninety-one and played golf up to the time of his death. Delacorte died in his sleep in the home that he shared with his second wife, the former Valerie Hoecker, a widow he had married on 15 May 1959. He is buried in the family plot at Woodlawn Cemetery in the Bronx, New York. In his philanthropy as in his publishing, Delacorte was an iconoclastic loner. He did not serve on boards. He gave money to projects he liked and that struck his fancy. A founder of Make New York Beautiful, he encouraged "guys who are going to kick off" to give the city $500,000. In his business, he was an innovator and risk taker with no interest in improving the intellectual atmosphere of America's heartland. Rather, he made money, as a 1962 *New York Herald Tribune* article noted, by "guessing what the lowbrows wanted."

★

Some of the literary and editorial papers and correspondence of Delacorte are in Columbia University's Butler Library Rare Book and Manuscript Division in New York City. A complete set of Dell paperbacks is held in the Library of Congress Special Collections in Washington, D.C., and includes documentation on major changes in cover design. "The Story of Dell Publishing Company, Inc.," *Book Production Magazine* (Nov. 1964), offers background on the company's early days. Several books contain detailed information on the forces that influenced the evolution and development of the American publishing industry, including Theodore Peterson, *Magazines in the Twentieth Century* (1956), J. P. Wood, *Magazines in the United States* (1971), Allen B. Crider, *Mass Market Publishing in America* (1982), and Kenneth C. Davis, *Two-Bit Culture: The Paperbacking of America* (1984). An obituary is in the *New York Times* (5 May 1991).

MARTHA MONAGHAN CORPUS

DE MILLE, Agnes George (*b.* 18 September 1905 in New York City; *d.* 7 October 1993 in New York City), dancer, choreographer of ballets and musicals, stage director, author, labor union leader, and a major influence on the arts in twentieth-century America.

De Mille's father, William de Mille, was a playwright and the brother of the movie director Cecil B. DeMille; her mother, Anna George, was the daughter of the political economist Henry George. The family moved to Hollywood, California, when de Mille was very young. Growing up in the company of the leading literary, theatrical, and political figures of the day, she watched her father and uncle shape a new art form: the movies. The art form that most fascinated her, however, was dance.

As a teenager de Mille saw the legendary ballerina Anna Pavlova dance; from then on, although already too old for serious training, she was obsessed with becoming a dancer. Her father, however, considered dancers not quite respectable and allowed only perfunctory dance instruction for Agnes and her younger sister, Margaret.

De Mille graduated in 1925 from the University of California at Los Angeles (with a cum laude degree in English) and promptly moved to New York City, where she devised and performed unconventional solo recital pieces that emphasized character over traditional ballet movement. As a choreographer, de Mille cleverly exploited her own limitations as a dancer, as in "Ballet Class," in which a little dancer—a hapless pupil with more dedication than talent—performs endless repetitive exercises to the beat of her offstage teacher's stick and dreams of the dancer she hopes to become.

Agnes de Mille. ARCHIVE PHOTOS

From 1932 to 1939 de Mille studied and worked in London with Antony Tudor, Marie Rambert, and other ballet revolutionaries. When World War II threatened Europe, she returned to the United States and formed a touring company that performed her own work. Within a few months, it folded. Undaunted, she danced in nightclubs, taught "acting for dancers," and struggled to find the right outlet for her unconventional blend of theater and dance.

In 1941 the newly formed Ballet Theatre commissioned her to create works for its first two seasons but rejected her third offering. The following year her break finally came: the Ballet Russe de Monte Carlo asked her to choreograph an "American" ballet. She expanded a recital piece she had created in London and the result, with music (at de Mille's insistence) by Aaron Copland, was the landmark *Rodeo*—an intimate, gentle, and funny romance about an awkward cowgirl with a crush on the unattainable champion wrangler. As in all de Mille's work, her choreography synthesized classical ballet, modern dance movement, folk dancing (Americana was a specialty), and natural, everyday gestures to tell a story based on timeless emotions.

The composer Richard Rodgers and the lyricist Oscar Hammerstein saw *Rodeo* and signed de Mille to choreograph their upcoming musical, *Oklahoma!*—a turning point for de Mille and for the Broadway musical. In place of the traditional interchangeable members of the chorus, de Mille used trained dancers and gave each a specific character, revealed in their individual movements.

A lot of the movement was balletic, but instead of the tutus and tights that most theatergoers had equated with "serious" dancing, the dancers wore jeans and gingham dresses. The choreography was not only entertaining, it propelled the story—notably in the dream sequence in which Laurey, the heroine, expresses her sexual conflicts. When *Oklahoma!* opened on Broadway in April 1943, theatrical history and de Mille's reputation were made. From then on it would be taken for granted that show dancing would include ballet and modern dance. Singers would dance and act, dancers would act and sing, and actors would be capable of performing at least a rudimentary song and dance.

With *Oklahoma!* a record-breaking hit, de Mille, who fervently believed that no woman was complete without a husband and child, took a brief break on 14 June 1943 to marry Walter Prude, a concert artists' manager to whom she had been introduced by their mutual friend Martha Graham.

For the rest of the decade Agnes de Mille was the most powerful woman on Broadway. Always torn between the demands of a husband, a chronically ill child (Jonathan, born in 1946), and a career, she nevertheless choreographed eleven more musicals, including *One Touch of Venus* (1943), *Bloomer Girl* (1944), *Carousel* (1945), *Brigadoon* (1947), *Gentlemen Prefer Blondes* (1949), and, less successfully, *Allegro* (1947), which she also directed. Alan Lerner and Frederick Loewe's *Paint Your Wagon*, choreographed by de Mille in 1951, was her last Broadway success.

As her subsequent Broadway projects floundered, de Mille continued to create ballets. Her characters had always represented parts of herself—from *Rodeo's* cowgirl, who wears her heart on her riding breeches and is "always trying something a little beyond her, and whether she succeeds or fails, she is cocky as hell," to the jubilant pioneers in *Oklahoma!* and the audacious whores in *Paint Your Wagon*. Years of psychoanalysis had left her feeling a kinship with the infamous Lizzie Borden, who had been accused of hacking her parents to death with an ax. Out of her empathy with Lizzie's alienation, repressed sexuality, and longing for approval from a weak and rejecting father, Agnes created *Fall River Legend*—a chilling, memorable version of the tragedy first presented by Ballet Theatre in 1948.

Shows failed; ballets failed; a repertory dance company of her own failed—but in de Mille's life, there were no intermissions. In 1952, *Dance to the Piper*, a memoir of her early years, was published and became an instant classic. The ten books that followed are witty, opinionated, enlightening, and generally acknowledged to be among the best books ever written about dance.

In 1956 de Mille presented two award-winning hour-long television shows—"The Art of Ballet" and "The Art of Choreography"—that introduced millions of people to ballet. In 1965 President Lyndon Johnson appointed her to the advisory panel of the first National Council on the Arts and Humanities, which would become the National Endowment for the Arts. For the rest of her life she was a passionate and eloquent spokesperson for public support of the arts.

In 1975, at age sixty-nine, de Mille suffered a massive stroke that left the right side of her body useless. Undaunted, she learned to write with her left hand, and to dictate. The four books she completed in the next eighteen years include some of her best: *Where the Wings Grow*, about her childhood; *Reprieve*, about the stroke and its effect on her; and *Martha,* an insightful and comprehensively researched biography of her longtime friend Martha Graham.

De Mille continued to write, to lecture, even to choreograph from her wheelchair. Unable to demonstrate movement, she had to depend entirely on her formidable command of language, and on assistants who at times seemed able to read her mind. *The Informer* (1988), a reworking of choreography originally devised for the failed 1959 Broadway show *Juno*, dealt with a subject unusual for a ballet—the Irish "troubles" in 1916. It was first presented by American Ballet Theater in 1988. Her final work, *The Other*, premiered in 1992; it was her fifth revision of dances created twenty years earlier for another Broadway failure, *Come Summer*. Set to Schubert songs, its subject was, fittingly, the cycles of life and the inevitability of death—to which Agnes succumbed, after another stroke, shortly after her eighty-eighth birthday.

By popularizing what had been elitist, Agnes de Mille became the first American-born choreographer to reach a mass audience and achieve international acclaim. She choreographed twenty-one ballets and fourteen Broadway shows over a career that spanned fifty years. She brought fresh air into ballet, permanently changed the look of the American musical, and influenced generations of choreographers who followed her. In a male-dominated business, she was the first woman to choreograph and direct a major Broadway musical and the first female president of a national labor union (Society of Stage Directors and Choreographers), which she helped found in 1959. A reviewer called her the best dancer ever to write, and the best writer ever to dance. De Mille said "One cannot be more than a dancer," but no other dancer approached the breadth of her achievements.

★

A voluminous collection of Agnes de Mille's manuscripts, papers, tapes, and filmed dances is archived at the New York Public Library; some of her letters are in the Smith College Archives. All of her books are to some extent autobiographical, but those technically in that category are: *Dance to the Piper* (1952), *And Promenade Home* (1958), *Lizzie Borden: A Dance of Death* (1968), *Speak to Me, Dance with Me* (1973), *Where the Wings Grow* (1978), and *Reprieve* (1981). She also wrote *The Book of the Dance* (1963), *America Dances* (1980), *Portrait Gallery* (1990), and *Martha* (1991). A biography, *No Intermissions: The Life of Agnes De Mille,* by Carol Easton, was published in 1996. An obituary is in the *New York Times* (8 Oct. 1993).

CAROL EASTON

DEMING, W(illiam) Edwards (*b.* 14 October 1900 in Sioux City, Iowa; *d.* 20 December 1993 in Washington, D.C.), statistician and management theorist who used innovative methods to monitor and improve manufacturing quality, first in postwar Japan and later in Britain and the United States.

Deming was the first of three children born to William Albert Deming and Pluma Irene Edwards. The family lived in Iowa, in modest circumstances, until 1906, when they moved to Wyoming. The Demings lived first in Cody, and later in Powell, which was named after John Wesley Powell, the explorer and geologist who became known as the

W. Edwards Deming, 1987. AP/WIDE WORLD PHOTOS

"father of reclamation." Powell had advocated the development of irrigation systems that attracted homesteaders like the Demings to the region's barren lands. William Deming received a forty-acre plot near what later became the town.

The Demings spent approximately their first five years in Powell in a tar paper shack, where Deming's sister, Elizabeth, was born in 1909. Their farm was never a success. To make ends meet, William Deming did freelance work as a law clerk and Pluma Deming gave piano lessons. When Deming grew old enough, he also contributed to the family finances by hauling kindling and coal after school and lighting Powell's gasoline street lamps. Deming's abhorrence of waste, his diligence, and his frugality took root during his childhood and lasted for the rest of his life. These characteristics also influenced his pioneering work in quality management.

In 1917 Deming went to Laramie where he attended the University of Wyoming and earned a B.S. degree in engineering. Deming supported himself by doing odd jobs such as janitorial work and shoveling snow. In the 1920s Deming attended the Colorado School of Mines in Golden, and the University of Colorado, from which he received an M.S. degree in mathematics and physics in 1924. In 1923 he married Agnes Bell, a teacher. She died in 1930, and in 1932 he married Lola Shupe, a mathematician. His second wife died in 1986.

Between his studies in Colorado and getting his doctorate in physics from Yale University in 1928, Deming landed two summer jobs at Western Electric's Hawthorne plant in Chicago that contributed formative experiences to his early career. Working at Hawthorne marked the only time that Deming was employed full-time by a corporation. What he saw at the plant, which employed 46,000 people assembling telephone equipment, left a lasting impression on him.

Although Western Electric, a division of AT&T, was paternalistic and, for the times, progressive, the work at the plant was monotonous. Workers regularly complained about smoke, fumes, and extreme temperatures. Coincidentally, it was here that the legendary Hawthorne experiments—also known as "fatigue studies"—were conducted by Harvard University researchers led by Elton Mayo and Fritz Roethlisberger.

Deming's frontier upbringing had accustomed him to hardship, but he was appalled by the demeaning drudgery of factory life. He also despised what he saw as the manipulative nature of the piece-rate system. Years later he would become an ardent opponent of incentive pay schemes.

AT&T left one other important mark on Deming. In the 1930s, he befriended Walter Shewhart, a physicist at Bell Laboratories who had developed a groundbreaking approach to improving manufacturing systems by studying the variation produced by each process. Shewhart used probability theory and statistics to monitor and identify process problems *before* they produced large numbers of defects. He also used a simple diagram, known as a control chart, to show whether a system was stable and to measure the capabilities of the process over time. Shewhart's system, which was first tested at Hawthorne, could eliminate end-of-the-line inspections, which were costly and did little to improve the system itself. It was also essential for the development and commercialization of complex, high-tech products, such as telephones.

Deming, who had gone to work at the U.S. Department of Agriculture in the 1930s, invited Shewhart to give a series of lectures in Washington, D.C. Deming also helped compile the lectures into a book, *Statistical Method from the Viewpoint of Quality Control* (1939). The ideas he learned from Shewhart and Ronald A. Fisher, a geneticist and pioneer of modern statistical analysis whom he sought out during the same period, were soon put to use at the U.S. Census Bureau, where Deming helped plan the first large-scale use of statistical sampling—the modeling of a carefully selected portion to represent the whole.

After World War II, Deming's work on the census and his statistical expertise caught the attention of General Douglas MacArthur. In 1947 Deming was summoned to Japan to develop its national census of 1951, which was intended to help assess the level of devastation in the country after the war, including the amount of new housing that was needed to accommodate countless Japanese who had been left homeless. That journey proved to be the second seminal influence of his career.

While most of his colleagues kept to their American enclaves, Deming toured the cities and the countryside, seeing firsthand the poverty of postwar life. He also became enamored of Japanese culture, including Kabuki theater, which at the time was off-limits to Allied personnel.

When the Japanese Union of Scientists and Engineers (JUSE) invited Deming to give a series of lectures on statistical process control (SPC)—essentially Shewhart's system for monitoring and improving manufacturing quality—Deming jumped at the chance. The lectures, held in more than a dozen locations from Tokyo to Kyushu, attracted thousands of listeners from both industry and government. One presentation attracted top managers from a number of companies, including Kawasaki Steel and Hitachi. Unlike other U.S. advisers, who kept aloof from the Japanese, Deming's self-deprecating charm (which was little in evidence in the United States in later years) and his mastery of Japanese customs and manners won him a special place in the hearts of the locals.

Deming's lectures in Japan stressed the importance of viewing quality concepts as part of a holistic new management philosophy. Top management would have to take a leading role in quality improvement, Deming insisted, but every member of the organization must play a part. The ultimate goal was to identify and anticipate the needs of customers.

To link consumer research and product manufacturing, Deming introduced what came to be known as the "Deming cycle" (adapted from Shewhart's original concept). This cycle of continuous testing and improvement—"plan, do, check, act," or PDCA—inevitably leads to the redesign of the product. This system was adopted by the Japanese as the basis of the Japanese Total Quality Control (TQC) movement and, eventually, as a way to monitor almost every corporate process. Thus it became the foundation of the Japanese strategic planning system known as policy deployment.

With the possible exception of General MacArthur, Deming was soon hailed as "the most famous and revered American" in Japan. In 1951 the JUSE created the Deming Prize competition in his honor and parlayed the competition into a national event for which virtually every leading Japanese corporation would come to compete. The Deming Prize institutionalized Japan's TQC movement. In 1960, in a final recognition of the enormous impact of both Deming and the prize, Deming became one of the first Americans to receive the Second Class Sacred Treasure, a medal bestowed by Emperor Hirohito.

In the United States, however, Deming continued to labor in relative obscurity. Not until the early 1980s, when American manufacturers found themselves unable to compete against a surge of high-quality foreign imports, did companies seeking the secret of Japan's success discover Deming and the quality movement.

Deming was already an octogenarian when he responded to an urgent appeal from Donald E. Petersen, the new president of Ford Motor Company. (During a three-year period beginning in 1980, Ford's losses totaled $3.26 billion.) Over the next few years Deming worked with a number of major U.S. companies, including Ford and General Motors. To ensure that top management took responsibility for quality, he insisted on meeting with the CEOs of client companies. He insisted that companies follow his fourteen points of management, which he delineated in his landmark work *Out of the Crisis* (1989). He also taught grueling four-day seminars that were attended by hundreds of participants.

Deming's most sweeping policy change addressed the use of multiple suppliers selected on the basis of cost rather than quality. Beginning in 1981 Deming began working with Ford to develop training programs for suppliers aimed both at improving the quality of parts and at breaking down the wall that traditionally had blocked collaboration between Ford and its vendors. The success of the seminars prompted Ford to spin off its training activities into a separate organization, the American Supplier Institute (ASI). As an independent association, the ASI became the center of quality training for all three major automakers and their suppliers. Under Deming's influence, Ford and other manufacturers slashed suppliers and developed stronger links with those who could meet new quality standards.

Deming also had limited success with his ardent opposition to incentive pay. Drawing at least partly on the writings of Abraham Maslow and Douglas McGregor, Deming believed that people have an innate desire to "take pride in their work." If management does a good job of hiring and training employees and creating a well-designed work environment, good performance will follow. Deming argued that tying performance targets to dollar rewards actually *harms* overall performance because it focuses on short-term results, nourishes rivalry, and destroys teamwork. Moreover, Deming argued that pay-for-performance was intrinsically unfair because it ascribes to the people in a group differences that may be caused by the system within which they work.

Although Deming's views on performance appraisal were an exceedingly hard sell, a few companies began to experiment with so-called 180-degree performance appraisals, which included peer and subordinate reviews and tied pay to seniority, skills, and group rewards.

Deming's influence was linked to a number of automotive successes, including the revival of Cadillac in the late 1980s. But his style antagonized many executives, who chafed at his insistence that "85 percent of manufacturing problems" were caused by management.

Deming continued consulting and conducting four-day seminars until his death. His daughters then established the Deming Institute, which holds periodic conferences on quality. Although the quality movement has survived, most recently as part of the Six Sigma movement, which draws many—though not all—of its principles from Deming's teachings, Deming's name was largely forgotten after his death.

★

Frank Voehl, ed., *Deming: The Way We Knew Him* (1994), includes fourteen chapters written by quality-control experts, each on one of Deming's "points for management." Andrea Gabor, *The Man Who Discovered Quality: How W. Edwards Deming Brought the Quality Revolution to America* (1990), features case studies on Ford, Xerox, and General Motors. See also Kaoru Ishikawa, *What Is Total Quality Control?: The Japanese Way* (1985), translated by David J. Lu; and Cecilia S. Kilian, *The World of W. Edwards Deming* (1988). An obituary is in the *New York Times* (21 Dec. 1993), and a memorial tribute by John A. Byrne is in *Business Week* (10 Jan. 1994).

ANDREA GABOR

DE NAGY, Tibor (*b.* 25 April 1908 in Debrecen, Hungary; *d.* 24 December 1993 in New York City), economist, banker, and art dealer whose Manhattan art gallery represented some of the most important American artists of the 1950s.

De Nagy was born in the city of Debrecen, approximately 120 miles west of Budapest. At the time of de Nagy's birth, Debrecen was undergoing tremendous economic growth and it ranked as one of the top business centers in Hungary, after Nagyvárad and Budapest. Well educated and known for his "old world" courtly manner, de Nagy studied economics at University of Frankfurt in Germany and at Kings College, at Cambridge University in England during the 1920s. In 1930 he began his career when he joined the National Bank of Hungary in Budapest.

De Nagy's stepfather, a prominent judge and an avid collector of modern art and rare books, began taking de Nagy to art galleries in Budapest at the age of five. De Nagy started building his own collection in the 1930s, concentrating on seventeenth- and eighteenth-century Flemish and Italian paintings. De Nagy reflected on those years, saying, "I was a spoiled brat; I loved to own things, to surround myself with luxury."

Hungary, split apart after World War I, suffered severely during the Great Depression. Tragically, Hungary was occupied by the Nazis during World War II and it became a battleground between the Red Army and Hitler's armed forces. By the end of the war, nearly half of Debrecen was in ruins due to extensive Allied bombing, and de Nagy's entire art collection had been destroyed by a British airplane that crashed into his villa. After Germany's defeat, de Nagy, who had sought refuge in Poland, returned to Hungary and began to help rebuild its banking system, but he was imprisoned by the Soviet Secret Police in 1946. Allegedly, he escaped in 1948, with a little money raised from the sale

Tibor de Nagy in his gallery, 1960. Copyright © by Fred W. Mc-Darrah

of family jewelry. He stayed briefly in London and then joined his daughter and ex-wife, Agnes Axcel (whom he had divorced in 1946), in New York City.

In 1949, while looking for a banking position, de Nagy befriended John Bernard Meyers, an art editor for *View* magazine and a puppeteer. Meyers convinced him to invest in a marionette company. The Tibor de Nagy Marionette Company was short-lived and unsuccessful, but through the business de Nagy met the abstract expressionist artists Jackson Pollack, William de Kooning, and Franz Kline, all of whom were enthusiastic supporters of the company. These artists encouraged de Nagy and Meyers to start an art gallery. Located on East Fifty-third Street in Manhattan, the new gallery opened in 1950. Finances were difficult during the first year, but the future was secured when the English collector, poet, and artist Dwight Ripley agreed to pay the rent for the next six years.

In de Nagy's words, the gallery was "designed for the special tangibility that is the love of looking." With John Meyers assuming directorship, the gallery began operating just as American abstract expressionism was beginning to make an international impact. The Tibor de Nagy Gallery earned a strong reputation for its willingness to represent a diverse group of artists, both figurative and abstract. Indeed, a number of second-generation abstract expressionist artists had their first shows at the gallery. Among them was the action painter Grace Hartigan, who had her first one-person show at the gallery in 1951. For the show, Hartigan chose to call herself "George Hartigan" with the hope that as a man she would attract more notice. It worked, and the first painting the gallery sold was a Hartigan that went for $75. Hartigan continued to exhibit her work at the gallery throughout the 1950s. Other important abstract artists who had their first shows at the gallery in the 1950s were Alfred Leslie, Kenneth Noland, and Helen Frankenthaler.

Among the representational painters who began their careers at the Tibor de Nagy Gallery were the impressionistic painter Fairfield Porter, who was a mainstay at the gallery for over twenty years, and the pop artists Red Grooms and Larry Rivers. Rivers, whose first show was in 1951, was the first artist who made a profit for the gallery. In a 1953 show, Rivers exhibited what would become one of his most important works, *Washington Crossing the Delaware,* which was later destroyed in a museum fire.

In the 1950s Tibor de Nagy Editions was formed and it was the first publishing house to distribute the works of the New York School poets Frank O'Hara, James Schuyler, and John Ashbery. The publications were in pamphlet form, and the poetry was often accompanied by drawings and prints made by some of the gallery artists. Among those to collaborate were Frank O'Hara and Larry Rivers, who worked on a series of lithographs called *Stones,* and the landscape painter Jane Freilicher, who worked with John Ashbery.

De Nagy became an American citizen in 1953. That same year he went to work for Manufacturers Hanover Trust Banking Company. Following his retirement from the bank in 1970 de Nagy devoted his energies to the gallery. Between 1973 and 1983 he was also a co-owner of the Watson/de Nagy Gallery in Houston. In his later years de Nagy, who continued to speak English with a strong Hungarian accent, returned to Hungary for several visits.

The 1950s were the most vital years for the Tibor de Nagy Gallery; among the collectors who bought from de Nagy were Joseph Hirshhorn, Peggy Guggenheim, and David Rockefeller. By the end of the 1960s, New York City had become the center of the art world, and established galleries, such as the famous Leo Castelli Gallery, were focusing more on investments and public relations. De Nagy's gallery, which moved to 41 West Fifty-seventh Street in the late 1960s, flourished in this new atmosphere but de Nagy geared his sales more towards private rather than corporate collections. De Nagy's reputation and the success of his gallery came to depend on his well-trained eye, his belief in the artists he represented, and his strong business sense. In 1991, two years before his death from stomach cancer, the Tibor de Nagy Gallery mounted a fortieth anniversary exhibition. Twenty-five well-established artists who had exhibited with the gallery over the years were represented, affirming de Nagy's ability to identify art works that could stand the test of time, and provide, in his words, "solid aesthetic values."

★

Laura de Coppet, ed., *The Art Dealers* (1983), contains an autobiographical essay written by de Nagy. Lee Caplin, *The Business of Art* (1989), contains a chapter written by de Nagy entitled "The Integrity of the Artist, Dealer, and Gallery." Tibor de Nagy, *Arts Magazine* (1971), contains a short essay by de Nagy on the philosophy of his art gallery. An obituary is in the *New York Times* (28 Dec. 1993).

PETER SUCHECKI

DENNIS, Sandra Dale ("Sandy") (*b.* 27 April 1937 in Hastings, Nebraska; *d.* 2 March 1992 in Westport, Connecticut), stage and film actress who earned a string of honors, including an Academy Award for best supporting actress for her role in *Who's Afraid of Virginia Woolf?* (1966).

Dennis was one of two children of Jack Dennis, a salesman and railway clerk, and Yvonne Dennis, a secretary. Her family moved to Lincoln, Nebraska, when she was about seven. There she attended public schools, read voraciously, wrote poetry, and both directed and acted in plays. After watching Kim Stanley and Joanne Woodward perform on

Sandy Dennis, 1968. © BETTMANN/CORBIS

television in *A Young Lady of Property,* the fourteen-year-old Dennis decided to become an actress. She appeared in the Lincoln Community Theater's productions of *The Crucible* and, later, *The Rainmaker,* for which she received the best actress award. After graduating from Lincoln High School, Dennis attended Nebraska Wesleyan University and the University of Nebraska, although she never earned a college degree. At age nineteen, Dennis moved to New York City to study acting at the Herbert Berghof Studio.

Waiflike, possessing an elfin face, and exuding girl-next-door innocence, Dennis initially portrayed younger characters on the New York stage. She first appeared as a thirteen-year-old in a revival of Henrik Ibsen's *Lady from the Sea* around 1956. Dennis next played a high school waitress in William Inge's *Bus Stop* before landing a role in 1959 in an off-Broadway production of John Steinbeck's *Burning Bright.* Although that play closed after thirteen performances, in 1961 she accepted a small part in the Broadway production of Graham Greene's *The Complaisant Lover.* One year later, Dennis's portrayal of a young social worker in the comedy *A Thousand Clowns* earned her the Antoinette Perry (Tony) Award for best performance in a supporting role. In 1964 she won a second Tony, this time for best nonmusical female performance, playing the jaunty mistress of a married tycoon in *Any Wednesday.*

By 1964 Dennis was a star on Broadway. She had played

opposite such leading men as Sir Michael Redgrave (*The Complaisant Lover*), Jason Robards, Jr. (*A Thousand Clowns*), and Gene Hackman (*Any Wednesday*). The critics sang her praises. A "charmer (with a face like fresh mint)," glowed Walter Kerr of the *New York Herald Tribune,* following Dennis's performance in *The Complaisant Lover.* "Let me tell you about Sandy Dennis," Kerr quipped, after seeing *Any Wednesday.* "There should be one in every home." Emory Lewis of *Cue* applauded her timing as "far too brilliant in one so young." In the spring of 1965 Dennis left the cast of *Any Wednesday* to film Edward Albee's play *Who's Afraid of Virginia Woolf?*

Dennis's performance in *Who's Afraid of Virginia Woolf?* earned her additional honors and a place in Hollywood history. She costarred alongside Elizabeth Taylor, Richard Burton, and George Segal and worked under the first-time director Mike Nichols in a film that explored, through a late-night party, the troubled marriages of two small-town college professors. Dennis portrayed Honey, Segal's mousy, whimpering wife who becomes intoxicated and at one point performs a jig while chanting, "I dance like the wind." Although the film's adult content and racy dialogue offended censors, the studio president Jack L. Warner stood by the work, which became a box-office hit. The performance of Taylor, who received the Academy Award for best actress, eclipsed that of Dennis. Although the *New York Times* lamented that Nichols was unable to "get more" from both Segal and Dennis, the Academy of Motion Picture Arts and Sciences awarded Dennis the Oscar for best supporting actress of 1966.

Who's Afraid of Virginia Woolf? was neither Dennis's first nor last film. She had played a minor part in Elia Kazan's *Splendor in the Grass* (1961) and followed up her Oscar-winning performance with a starring role in *Up the Down Staircase* (1967). The latter film, based on the novel by Bel Kaufman, told the story of an idealistic young teacher wrestling with student problems in an inner-city school. The *New York Times* film critic Bosley Crowther applauded Dennis's "vivid performance of emotional range and depth," and the International Film Festival held in Moscow awarded her its best actress prize. Dennis's next roles were offbeat. In *The Fox* (1968), based on a novella by the British writer D. H. Lawrence, she portrayed a lesbian, and in *Sweet November* (1968), she played a terminally ill woman who changes lovers monthly. The *New York Times* critic Renata Adler found Dennis's performance in *The Fox* "halting" but graded her "very good" in the wistful *Sweet November.* Dennis won few accolades for her portrayal of a spinster involved with a younger man in *That Cold Day in the Park* (1969). But her leading role in *Thank You All Very Much* (1969), a British film about an unwed mother determined to raise her child alone, drew praise.

Dennis was unable to continue her triumphs. *The Out-of-Towners* (1970), a Neil Simon comedy in which she co-starred with Jack Lemmon, flopped with moviegoers and critics alike. Qualities that had made Dennis seem fresh a decade earlier—sweetness, sincerity, naïveté, and feminine fragility—had become stale. *The Fox* and *Thank You All Very Much,* in which she departed from her character types, failed to find large audiences. Dennis's trademark features—protruding teeth, a muttering speech pattern, and a nasal voice—suggested an annoying nervousness. In 1967 a critic for *Time* worried that "Sandy Dennis is in danger of losing her momentum in mannerisms." The *New Yorker* film critic Pauline Kael griped that she "has made an acting style of postnasal drip," an assessment with which Dennis agreed and worked to correct. Dennis landed supporting roles in such films as *Nasty Habits* (1977), a parody of Watergate set in a convent, Alan Alda's comedy *The Four Seasons* (1981), and Sean Penn's *The Indian Runner* (1991).

By her own admission, Dennis was a "solitary person." She married the jazz musician Gerry Mulligan in 1965; they separated in 1976 but never divorced. They had no children. Once described by Richard Burton as "one of the most genuine eccentrics I know," Dennis enjoyed the outdoors, old movies, books, photography, and, above all, animals. She sought homes for strays and, at one point, kept six dogs and twenty-six cats herself. "You have to keep going," Dennis said of acting, her life's passion, "giving the best you've got to get something intangible." She died in 1992 after a long battle with ovarian cancer. She is buried in Lincoln Memorial Park in Nebraska.

Dennis's outstanding performances will be remembered by film and theater buffs. Her wholesome exterior belied a willingness to portray marginal or out-of-place figures: a mistress, a lesbian, a spinster, a dying woman, an untested teacher, and an unwed mother. Dennis's career also shows how success gained at a young age can prove difficult to sustain.

★

Dennis's autobiography, *Sandy Dennis: A Personal Memoir* (1997), edited by Louise Ladd and Doug Taylor, is charming, episodic, and brief. An insightful profile of the actress is given by Joanne Stang in "Sweet Success," *New York Times* (1 Mar. 1964). For background on Dennis's role in *Who's Afraid of Virginia Woolf?* consult H. Wayne Schuth, *Mike Nichols* (1978), and Mel Gussow, *Edward Albee: A Singular Journey* (1999). An obituary is in the *New York Times* (4 and 5 March 1992).

DEAN J. KOTLOWSKI

DESSAUER, John Hans (*b.* 13 May 1905 in Aschaffenburg, Germany; *d.* 12 August 1993 in Rochester, New York), chemical engineer and research director of the Xerox Corporation who first recognized the potential importance of the electrostatic photocopying process that came to be known as xerography.

Dessauer, one of three sons of Hans and Bertha Dessauer, was educated in Aschaffenburg and Munich, Germany. In Munich he attended the Technical Institute, from which he received a baccalaureate degree in chemistry in 1924. He then attended the Technical Institute of Aachen, earning a master of science degree in 1927 and a doctorate in 1929, in both chemistry and chemical engineering. Shortly after receiving his doctorate he emigrated to the United States.

In his professional autobiography, *My Years with Xerox: The Billions Nobody Wanted* (1971), Dessauer recalled his early years in the United States. From 1929 to 1935 he worked for Ansco, which made photography film and paper, but was fired. As Dessauer wrote, "The man who fired me . . . wrote to suggest he had done me a favor; if he had not pushed me out of Ansco I might never have become associated with the Xerox saga. He may be right." Dessauer then applied for a chemical engineer position with the Rectigraph Company in Rochester, New York, which made and marketed a photocopying camera. He was hired to perfect a new type of photocopy paper to compete with a product made by the Haloid Company in Rochester. Haloid, however, soon acquired Rectigraph. After meeting Joseph R. Wilson, Haloid's president, and his son Joseph C. Wilson, a vice president and later president, Dessauer was persuaded to stay with Haloid. He became an American citizen in 1935, and in 1936 he married Margaret Lee, with whom he had three children.

John Dessauer. ARCHIVE PHOTOS

In 1945 Dessauer, then in charge of Haloid's research and development, read an article in *Radio-Electronic Engineering* about a discovery just patented by the physicist Chester F. Carlson. The discovery was a photographic process that depended on electrostatic attraction of pigment particles to a coated metal plate. "It was as if lightning had struck when I read that article," he recalled some years later. He promptly reported it to "Young Joe" Wilson, who, after consulting experts in New York City, went with Dessauer to the Battelle Memorial Institute in Columbus, Ohio, with which Carlson was affiliated. There they talked at length with Dr. R. M. Schaffert and the other researchers experimenting with Carlson's electrostatic copying process. The next two years were spent in contractual and technological negotiations with Battelle. By 1947 Carlson's photocopying process was showing so much promise that Haloid acquired a license for it and to begin marketing the copiers.

For effective marketing, the copying process needed a name that was shorter than the phrase "electrostatic photocopy," and, after consulting a classics scholar at Ohio State University, the company chose "xerography," a combination of the Greek words *xeros* ("dry") and *graphein* ("to draw" or "to write"). The trade name Xerox was adopted unanimously at Haloid's next board meeting: it was short and symmetrical, and the question of how to pronounce the initial X attracted people's curiosity.

The first Xerox copier did not reach the market for eleven years after the crucial decisions of 1947. Carlson's original patents from 1940, which he had sold to Battelle, expired at the end of seventeen years, in 1957, but Battelle and Haloid had received a number of subordinate patents. In 1956, Haloid bought Carlson's patents from Battelle for 50,000 shares of Haloid stock. During the years of development, the Haloid Company continued to produce photosensitive paper and offset masters called Xerox LithMasters, its principal products. The company also produced two office copying machines named the Photographic Foto-Flo Recorder and the Foto-Flo Model C, used mainly to produce paper offset masters; these machines became a major source of income for Haloid. The principal research effort during the late 1950s led to the release in 1960 of the Xerox 914, which proved to be a tremendous success.

During this period Young Joe Wilson was exploring the possibility of developing the European market through an English affiliate. Xerography attracted the attention of the J. Arthur Rank Organisation in London. Wilson and John Davis, the chairman of the Rank board, exchanged visits and eventually formed Rank-Xerox, which became a major subsidiary. The Xerox 914 was sufficiently successful to prompt construction of large new production facilities in Webster, on the east side of Rochester. Dessauer estimated, conservatively, that during his years at Xerox (1936–1970) sales increased from $7 million to $1 billion per year. After thirty years with Xerox, Dessauer retired in 1970, having left his active vice presidency in 1968. At that time the Xerox research staff numbered almost 1,300, of which 400 were engaged in developing the Xerox 2400, the successor to the 914. After his retirement Dessauer retained his board membership and planned to set up an office aimed at helping people. A devout Catholic, Dessauer told the *New York Times* in June 1970, "I want to devote myself mainly to education, religions, and charitable work."

John Dessauer was a trustee of the New York State Science and Technology Foundation. He held honorary degrees from Fordham University, LeMoyne College, and Clarkson College and was a recipient of the Philipps Award from the Institute of Electrical and Electronics Engineers and the Gold Medal of the Industrial Research Institute. He was a member of the National Academy of Engineering, American Chemical Society, American Institute of Chemists, American Optical Society, American Physical Society, and New York Academy of Sciences.

★

In addition to his autobiography *My Years with Xerox: The Billions Nobody Wanted* (1971), Dessauer was joint editor, with Harold E. Clark, of *Xerography and Related Processes* (1965) and a contributor to *Research Management.* There is a significant review by John Brooks of *My Years with Xerox,* critical of the ghostwriting of Oscar Schisgall, in the *New York Times Book Review* (17 Oct. 1971). Obituaries are in the *New York Times* (14 Aug. 1993) and *Contemporary Authors,* vol. 142 (1994).

DAVID W. HERON

DE VRIES, Peter (*b.* 27 February 1910 in Chicago, Illinois; *d.* 28 September 1993 in Norwalk, Connecticut), American comic novelist known for his extravagant wordplay and sparkling satire of suburban mores.

De Vries was the second of three children of Joost De Vries, a warehouse owner, and Henrietta Eldersveld, a homemaker. His parents, immigrants from the Netherlands, subscribed to Dutch Reformed Calvinism, an austere sect that forbade dancing, card playing, and moviegoing, among other activities. Peter graduated from Chicago Christian School in 1927 and then attended Calvin College in Grand Rapids, Michigan, where he edited the student newspaper, played varsity basketball, and was chosen during his senior year as the state intercollegiate extemporaneous-speaking champion. He graduated with a B.A. degree in English in 1931.

De Vries returned to Chicago and began submitting and publishing poems and humorous sketches in magazines. To support himself he held various jobs, including community-newspaper editor, vending-machine route operator, taffy-apple salesman, radio actor, and furniture mover. In 1938

he was hired as associate editor of the prestigious *Poetry* magazine and four years later he was named coeditor. On 16 October 1943 he married Katinka Loeser, whom he had met when she won *Poetry*'s Young Poets Prize. She would later be known as a short-story writer. They had four children.

In 1944 James Thurber, well known for his comic sketches and cartoons for the *New Yorker,* came to Chicago at De Vries's invitation to give a benefit lecture for *Poetry.* The two hit it off and, when De Vries brought out some of his own comic pieces, Thurber was so taken with them that he promised to show the work to Harold Ross, the editor of the *New Yorker,* and lobby him to give De Vries a job on the magazine. Ross was duly impressed. He offered—and De Vries accepted—a position working two days a week as a poetry editor and two days screening newly submitted cartoons. He left the job in the poetry department in 1947 but continued helping with the cartoons two days a week until his retirement in 1987.

Before leaving Chicago De Vries had written three novels, but he later disowned these, and his reputation rests on the books he published beginning in 1952, with *No, But I Saw the Movie,* a collection of short pieces. This was followed by: *The Tunnel of Love* (1954); *Comfort Me with Apples* (1956); *The Mackerel Plaza* (1958); *The Tents of Wickedness* (1959); *Through the Fields of Clover* (1961); *The Blood of the Lamb* (1961); *Reuben, Reuben* (1964); *Let Me Count the Ways* (1965); *The Vale of Laughter* (1967); *The Cat's Pajamas and Witch's Milk* (1968); *Mrs. Wallop* (1970); *Into Your Tent I'll Creep* (1971); *Without a Stitch in Time* (1972); *Forever Panting* (1973); *The Glory of the Hummingbird* (1974); *I Hear America Swinging* (1976); *Madder Music* (1977); *Consenting Adults; or, The Duchess Will Be Furious* (1980); *Sauce for the Goose* (1981); *Slouching Towards Kalamazoo* (1983); *The Prick of Noon* (1985); and *Peckham's Marbles* (1986).

Despite the high number and varied titles of De Vries's novels, they almost all fall into one of two categories. In the first, the protagonist finds his Midwestern home culturally stifling and makes his way east, taking part in varied comic adventures along the way. In the second group of novels, the hero, already ensconced in New York City or its suburbs (De Vries himself moved from Manhattan to Westport, Connecticut, in 1948), finds himself in an assortment of professional, personal, amorous, and moral fixes, and has to try to find a way out.

In both cases, plot is secondary to humor. De Vries is a specialist in high-class puns ("We're all like the cleaning woman. We come to dust"); droll epigrams ("The murals in restaurants are on a par with the food in museums"); quaint similes (the man with "hair like the grass on a putting green, except for the color of course"); and an original comic figure of speech, merging the literal and the para-

Peter De Vries. © Jerry Bauer

doxical, that has been identified as the De Vriesism (Husband: "Come to bed." Wife: "I'm too tired").

De Vries's one serious novel, *The Blood of the Lamb,* grew out of a personal tragedy: the death of his ten-year-old daughter of leukemia in 1960. In the book the narrator's daughter suffers the same fate and his wife commits suicide. His only slight consolation, he feels, is his capacity to offer compassion to his fellow sufferers.

De Vries, whose sober, sometimes melancholy personal demeanor belied his madcap prose, stopped writing in 1986. His daughter Jan told the *New York Times,* "I asked him why he wasn't working, and he simply said, 'When you know you're done, you're done.' " De Vries's health subsequently deteriorated, and he ultimately died of pneumonia in Norwalk. He is buried in Westport.

Throughout his career De Vries's books sold modestly. But he gradually garnered more admirers over the years—many of them from the other side of the Atlantic. Anthony Burgess called him "surely one of the great virtuosos of modern America" and Auberon Waugh "one of the great comic geniuses of our time." In 1983, in recognition of the virtuosity, humanity, and sheer invention of his humor, he was inducted into the American Academy of Arts and Letters, the nation's most prestigious cultural fraternity. Only three other humorists had preceded him: Mark Twain, Joel Chandler Harris, and E. B. White.

★

De Vries's papers are collected at the Boston University Library in Massachusetts and several of his letters to James Thurber can be found at Ohio State University in Columbus, Ohio. Book-length studies of his work are J. H. Bowden, *Peter De Vries* (1983), and Dan Campion, *Peter De Vries and Surrealism* (1995). For articles and reviews before 1978, see Edwin T. Bowden, *Peter De Vries: A Bibliography 1934–1977* (1978). A thinly-disguised version of De Vries appears as the main character's husband, Gladstone, in Katinka Loeser's collection of short stories *A Thousand Pardons* (1982). Obituaries are in the *New York Times* (29 Sept. 1993) and *London Times* (4 Oct. 1993).

Ben Yagoda

DEWHURST, Colleen (*b.* 3 June 1924 in Montreal, Canada; *d.* 22 August 1991 in South Salem, New York), one of America's foremost actresses, best remembered for her roles in the plays of Eugene O'Neill, which highlighted a career on stage, screen, and television that spanned forty years and earned her two Tony Awards and four Emmys.

Dewhurst was the only child of Fred Dewhurst, a professional football and hockey player, and Frances, his petite and beautiful wife who, descended from a line of Ulster Irish, was devoted to her daughter and to her Christian Science religion. Dewhurst recalled her childhood as particularly happy, although the family moved to Boston, New York, Milwaukee, and several other cities and states when she was young. Her father brought her up as an athlete, and she described herself as the definitive tomboy. A series

Colleen Dewhurst in character for an ABC Sunday Night Movie, 1987. THE KOBAL COLLECTION

of surgeries for tuberculin glands of the neck left her with visible scars and the throaty voice quality for which she is remembered. Her parents divorced when she was twelve years old.

In 1943 Dewhurst graduated from Milwaukee's Riverside High School, the fifteenth school she had attended since the family's move from Montreal. She played Olivia in Shakespeare's *As You Like It* in her senior year. While attending Milwaukee Downer College for Women in 1944, she wrote, cast, and acted in a dramatic skit that won first prize for the freshman class. That same year her mother surprised her with tickets to two plays in Chicago. One was Tennessee Williams's *The Glass Menagerie,* with Laurette Taylor. Thoroughly impressed by the theatrical experience, she dropped out of school in 1945, abandoning plans to be an aviator, and worked as a dental receptionist in Gary, Indiana, before enrolling in the American Academy of Dramatic Arts in New York City in 1946.

After graduating from the academy in 1948, Dewhurst continued her studies with Joseph Kramm and Joseph Anthony of the American Theatre Wing, playing summer stock for the first ten years of her career. While studying with Harold Clurman in 1952, she made her Broadway debut in a small role in a revival of Eugene O'Neill's *Desire Under the Elms.* Two years later Joseph Papp invited her

to join his newly organized Shakespeare Workshop. After participating in a reading, *An Evening with Shakespeare and Marlowe* (1954), she became a New York Shakespeare Festival regular. Her first Obie was awarded to her for her role as Kate in *The Taming of the Shrew* (1956). Later in 1956 she played Tamora in *Titus Andronicus;* in 1957, again under Papp's aegis, she played Lady Macbeth in *Macbeth.* In 1959 she performed opposite George C. Scott in *Antony and Cleopatra.*

Dewhurst's first appearance with Scott was in Edwin Justus Mayer's *Children of Darkness* at the Circle in the Square (1958) in Greenwich Village. The production was directed by José Quintero, who was to become her director in many O'Neill roles, including Josie in *A Moon for the Misbegotten* (1958) at the Spoleto Festival in Italy; Abbie Putnam in *Desire Under the Elms* (1963) at the Circle in the Square, which brought a second Obie; Sara in *More Stately Mansions* (1967) on Broadway; Josie in *A Moon for the Misbegotten* (1973) on Broadway, for which she received her second Tony Award (she received her first Tony Award in 1960 for her portrayal of Mary Follet in Tad Mosel's *All the Way Home*), and, in two 1988 Broadway revivals, Mary Tyrone in *Long Day's Journey into Night* and Essie Miller in *Ah, Wilderness!* Theodore Mann directed her performance as Christine Mannon in the revival of *Mourning Becomes Electra* (1972) at the Circle in the Square. In 1987 she played Carlotta Monterey O'Neill, the playwright's wife, in *My Gene,* a one-woman show at the New York Shakespeare Public Theatre.

Dewhurst is best remembered for the earthy quality and the absolute truth and passion that she brought to the roles of O'Neill's women. She also, however, brought an equal understanding and intuitive response to those of Edward Albee in her interpretation of Amelia in *Ballad of the Sad Cafe* (1964), the Mistress in *All Over* (1971), and Martha in a revival of *Who's Afraid of Virginia Woolf?* (1976).

Dewhurst was also a prolific presence in television and film. She appeared with Candice Bergen on the *Murphy Brown* CBS comedy series for three seasons as Murphy's mother, winning an Emmy Award in 1989 and another in 1991, three days after her death. She also won Emmys for her portrayal of Barbara Petherton in the miniseries *Between Two Women* (1986) and for her performance as Margaret Page in the made-for-television movie *Those She Left Behind* (1989). Of her many films, she played the Archangel in *The Nun's Story* (1959); a psychiatrist in *A Fine Madness* (1966); a madam in *The Cowboys* (1972); a bar waitress in *McQ* (1974), with John Wayne; Mom Hall in Woody Allen's *Annie Hall* (1977); the owner-coach-adviser of an ice-skating rink in *Ice Castles* (1978); a physician in *Tribute* (1980), with Jack Lemmon; and a wise old widow in *Dying Young* (1991), with Julia Roberts and Dewhurst's son, the actor Campbell Scott. While she performed in television and film for the money, her heart belonged to the theater. She was the president of Actors' Equity for two terms from 1985 to 1991 and worked in conjunction with Equity Fights AIDS and Broadway Cares.

Her first marriage in 1947 to James Vickery, a fellow American Academy student actor, ended in divorce after twelve years. Her second marriage was in 1960 to the actor George C. Scott, with whom she had two children. The couple divorced, remarried in 1967, and then divorced a second time in 1972.

An imposing figure both on and off stage, Dewhurst has been described as a striking woman whose face and figure exuded power and femininity. She is remembered for her regal stature (she was five feet, eight inches tall and big-boned), her mature sexuality, her folksy earthiness, and her quick wit. With her companion, the Broadway producer Ken Marsolais, Dewhurst lived on a farm in suburban South Salem in Westchester County, New York, for her last sixteen years. She loved her thirty-five-room farmhouse in South Salem, which was home to eight cats, two dogs, a goat, a parrot, a housekeeper, and a multitude of guests. She summered at her home on Prince Edward Island, Canada. When diagnosed with cervical cancer in 1989, she refused medical intervention due to her Christian Science upbringing. She died at home on her farm at the age of sixty-seven.

★

The Billy Rose Theatre Collection at the New York Public Library for the Performing Arts, Lincoln Center, New York City, contains uncatalogued newspaper clippings and magazine articles about Dewhurst and her productions. *Colleen Dewhurst: Her Autobiography* (1997), written with and completed by Tom Viola, fills in the narrative with interviews of those who knew her best: Edward Albee, Jason Robards, José Quintero, Zoe Caldwell, Maureen Stapleton, and her children, to name a few. Barbara Lee Horn, *Colleen Dewhurst: A Bio-Bibliography* (1993), compiles journalistic literature and includes an extensive section with data on her major roles in all media, including credits, runs, synopses, and review citations. Obituaries are in the *New York Times* (24 Aug. 1991) and *Variety* (26 Aug. 1991).

BARBARA LEE HORN

DICHTER, Ernest (*b.* 14 Aug. 1907 in Vienna, Austria; *d.* 21 Nov. 1991 in Cortlandt Manor, New York), psychologist, marketing research executive, and originator and leading exponent of motivational research in advertising, communications, management, and politics.

Dichter was the eldest of three sons born to a poor family headed by William Dichter, an itinerant salesman, and Mathilda Schneider, a homemaker. While his father was serving in the Austrian army during World War I, his

Ernest Dichter, 1960. ARCHIVE PHOTOS

mother taught the children to use the black market, bartering possessions for food, to keep them from starving. Eventually Ernest was sent with other poor Viennese children to Holland, where he became seriously ill before returning home at the end of the war. At age fourteen he left school to help support his family for several years, but he later earned an undergraduate degree from the University of Vienna. He then went to the Sorbonne, receiving a *licencié ès lettres* in 1930, and returned to the University of Vienna for a Ph.D. in psychology, which he received in 1934. Dichter married Hedy Langfelder, a concert pianist and piano teacher, in 1935. Their marriage produced a son and daughter and lasted until Dichter died in 1991.

Dichter's early interests were in psychoanalysis and other forms of depth psychology, but he wanted to apply them in a practical manner. He began doing psychoanalysis and vocational guidance, but as the Nazis rose to power, the Dichters, who were Jewish, decided to flee Vienna. In 1937 Dichter went to Paris and tried without success to get visas to the United States. In desperation, he went to the American consulate and met with Vice Consul Llewelyn Thompson. He persuaded Thompson to intervene in Washington to allow the Dichters passage to the United States, telling Thompson that he had ideas for motivational research that could improve American business and solve social problems by uncovering the real reasons for people's actions—which were not necessarily the reasons people told themselves and others—and motivating them to change. In 1938 the Dichters emigrated to America.

Shortly after settling in Manhattan, Dichter began his first motivational research project, analyzing the public's interest in Procter & Gamble's Ivory soap. Rejecting questionnaires with yes-or-no answers, Dichter talked with people in depth about their bathing habits. He learned that children liked baths best on their birthday or Christmas and that young women bathed very thoroughly before going out on weekends. He concluded that ritualistic meanings of bathing as a way to wash away sins continued to influence people and advised Procter & Gamble to tell consumers, "Be smart and get a fresh start with Ivory soap." The campaign became a classic.

His next studies, for *Esquire* magazine and the Chrysler Corporation's Plymouth automobile, were also huge successes. In 1940 for Chrysler, Dichter found that men believed they acted alone when buying cars, but in reality their wives and girlfriends wielded considerable influence. He also found that men viewed sedans as "wives" and convertibles as "mistresses." After Chrysler followed Dichter's advice to market itself more to women and use convertibles as "bait" to draw men into showrooms, Plymouth sales increased internationally and Dichter became famous.

For the next three years, Dichter worked full-time for the advertising agency J. Sterling Getchall, analyzing scores of products and consumer motivations for buying or not buying them. In 1943 he joined the Columbia Broadcasting System as a research psychologist and became an American citizen, helping in World War II by analyzing Hitler's speeches and developing counterpropaganda. In 1946, he went out on his own, establishing an independent research organization in Manhattan and widening his reputation through lectures and books (*The Psychology of Everyday Living,* 1947; *Successful Living: A Practical Guide to Help You Influence People,* 1947). In 1953 he moved his Institute for Motivational Research to a twenty-six-room mansion in Croton-on-Hudson, New York. Within a few years he had a staff of sixty-five and nine other offices in the United States and abroad that offered a wide range of services to commercial, political, and civic organizations.

Dichter's successes drew other practitioners to motivational research, and it became a standard service of advertising consultants. But its methods, which relied heavily on interviewing skills and were not easily replicable, and Dichter's overpowering personality and influence, also made it controversial. In 1957, Vance Packard's best-selling *The Hidden Persuaders* focused negative attention on Dichter and motivational research, comparing it to "the chilling world of George Orwell and his Big Brother." Four years later, Betty Friedan in *The Feminine Mystique* charged Dichter and others with confining American women to the role of housewife and reliable consumer by glorifying that role through advertising and then making women feel guilty for not living up to it. Dichter always denied manipulating people and claimed what he practiced was persuasion. "No one forces anyone to purchase a product or believe anything," he said in a 1977 interview (quoted in the *New York Times,* 23 Nov. 1991).

Interest in motivational research declined in the 1960s, but Dichter remained successful. He continued doing corporate work, but over the next two decades he turned more toward management, political and government consulting, and social concerns. He also wrote many books, including *The Strategy of Desire* (1960), *The Disease of Nationalism* (1967), *The Naked Manager* (1974), *Total Self-Knowledge* (1976), and *How Hot a Manager Are You?* (1987). He also taught marketing at Nova University, Mercy College, and Long Island University.

Dichter's many honors included election to the Market Research Council's Hall of Fame and the American Marketing Association's (AMA) fifty-year membership award. His awards from foreign countries included the Golden Medal of Merit from Vienna. His professional memberships included the AMA, American Psychological Association, American Sociological Association, and World Association of Public Opinion.

Dichter was a consultant for several corporations when he died of heart failure at age eighty-three in Cortlandt Manor. He is buried nearby in Putnam Valley.

During his career, Dichter conducted more than 6,500 studies and wrote hundreds of articles and seventeen books for professional and popular audiences. He consulted for some of the world's most influential businesses, including General Motors, AT&T, Johnson & Johnson, Philip Morris, and the *New York Times*; governments and political candidates both domestic and foreign; advertising agencies; and nonprofit organizations. His insights into sexuality and other motivations helped Exxon put a tiger in its tank and Mattel sell its Barbie doll; they also convinced men it could be sexy to give blood and brought more people into public libraries. Although motivational research mostly went out of fashion, Dichter's influence has continued into the twenty-first century through related techniques like psychographics and archetype research, and many of his published works have become standards of the marketing literature.

★

Identical collections of Dichter's books, articles, studies, and correspondence are at the Institute for Publicity and Communications Science, University of Vienna, and in the library of the Institute for Motivational Research, which existed in dormant form under Hedy Dichter in 2000. Dichter wrote his autobiography, *Getting Motivated: The Secret Behind Individual Motivations by the Man Who Was Not Afraid to Ask "Why?"* in 1979. Books that extensively review Dichter's work include Rebecca Piirto, *Beyond Mind Games: The Marketing Power of Psychographics* (1991), and M. G. Lord, *Forever Barbie: The Unauthorized Biography of a Real Doll* (1994). Critical coverage is in Vance Packard, *The Hidden Persuaders* (1957), and Betty Friedan, *The Feminine Mystique* (1963). A two-page biographical essay is in *Current Biography* (1961). Dichter discussed his research methodology and personal history in a 1986 interview with Rena Bartos, "Ernest Dichter: Motive Interpreter," in *Journal of Advertising Research* 26, no. 1 (Feb.–Mar. 1986): 15–20. Lynne Ames interviewed Dichter's widow, Hedy Dichter, in "The View from Peekskill: Tending the Flame of a Motivator," *New York Times* (2 Aug. 1998). Posthumous tributes to Dichter included "A Remembrance of Ernest Dichter," by Emmanuel H. Demby, *Marketing News* 26, no. 6 (Jan. 1992): 21; and an editorial in *Advertising Age* (2 Dec. 1991). An obituary is in the *New York Times* (23 Nov. 1991).

MADELEINE R. NASH

DICKEY, John Sloan (*b.* 4 November 1907 in Lock Haven, Pennsylvania; *d.* 9 February 1991 in Hanover, New Hampshire), lawyer, professor, and foreign affairs specialist best known for his leadership as president of Dartmouth College from 1945 to 1970.

John Sloan Dickey, 1957. AP/WIDE WORLD PHOTOS

Dickey was the son of John W. Dickey, secretary-treasurer of a woven-wire factory, and Gretchen Sloan, a homemaker. One of five children, John graduated from Lock Haven High School in 1925 and was the first member of his family to attend college. He graduated from Dartmouth College in 1929 with a B.A. degree in history, magna cum laude, and was a member of Phi Beta Kappa. He graduated from Harvard Law School in 1932; on 26 November of that year he married Christina Gillespie, with whom he had three children. He was also admitted to the Massachusetts bar and practiced law for thirteen years, six of those (1934–1940) as a partner in the Boston firm Gaston, Snow, Saltonstall, and Hunt.

In addition to his legal practice Dickey undertook a variety of assignments in the U.S. State Department on inter-American issues, economics, and trade. He served as an assistant to the assistant secretary of state for economic affairs, Francis B. Sayre, and as an assistant to the State Department's legal adviser (1934). He then became a special assistant to Secretary of State Cordell Hull and liaison between the State Department and the coordinator of inter-American affairs, Nelson A. Rockefeller, in 1940. During World War II he was chief of the State Department's Division of World Trade Intelligence and special assistant to Secretary Hull on renewal of the Trade Agreements Act (1943). In 1945 Dickey became the first director the State Department's Office of Public Affairs. In this capacity he served as public liaison officer for the U.S. delegation to the forty-six-nation San Francisco conference that drafted the charter on the United Nations (1945), coordinating communication between the delegation and foreign-policy consulting groups.

In 1945 the board of trustees of Dartmouth College appointed Dickey the school's twelfth president, to succeed Ernest Martin Hopkins. He took office less than ninety days following the end of World War II. Among his first initiatives as president, Dickey undertook to raise Dartmouth's stature among the Ivy League colleges by rebuilding its faculty. Through increases in faculty compensation and benefits, he recruited and hired "teacher-scholars" with Ph.D. training, strong publication records, and an interest in teaching. Dickey also increased competition for undergraduate admission, giving the sons of alumni less advantage than before the war, and he set Dartmouth on a course toward more diversity by instructing the admissions office that, henceforth, the freshman class would be selected without racial or religious discrimination.

Dickey was directly involved in academic policy and educational innovation during his tenure. Highlights of his leadership in this area include the Great Issues Course (1947–1966), a somewhat controversial model course for seniors that included convocations and lectures by eminent politicians and intellectuals in philosophy, the arts, government, and economics, to ensure that Dartmouth undergraduates would be prepared as citizens to understand local, national, and international problems. In 1951 Dickey, believing that a Dartmouth education should encourage "conscience as the necessary companion to competence," created the William Jewett Tucker Foundation. The foundation initially promoted the spiritual growth of undergraduates through religious programs, counseling, and workshops; it later expanded its initiatives to include voluntary services and the opportunity to earn academic credit for social activism. He oversaw the reorganization of the 1958–1959 undergraduate academic year into the "Three-three" program (three terms with three courses each term), which permitted students to study each subject in greater depth and provided more time for self-study. In 1962 the college established the Hopkins Center to link the instructional, creative, cultural, and community activities in the humanities and the arts.

From 1957 to 1962 Dickey worked with the trustees and faculty to rejuvenate and expand Dartmouth's antiquated two-year medical school, augmenting the faculty, introducing research, and reviving the M.D. degree, which had not been awarded since 1914. He inaugurated a new department of engineering in 1958 and, with the support of the Sloan Foundation in 1960, set the Thayer School of Engineering on a new course that included graduate education. In 1962, under Dickey, Dartmouth revived doctoral programs in the natural sciences.

Over the course of his tenure Dickey oversaw the construction of twenty new campus buildings, including eight new dormitories and five major complexes, among them the Gilman Biomedical Center and the Kiewit Computation Center. Between 1946 and 1963 Dickey increased Dartmouth's endowment fivefold, from $22 million to $114 million. Effective with alumni, he raised annual contributions from $337,000 to $2 million. Indeed, Dartmouth's 66 percent alumni contribution rate was typically the highest of any major school. However, his chief innovation in fundraising at Dartmouth was to move from a reliance on the annual alumni fund and bequests to a comprehensive development effort that included major foundation support and, beginning in 1957, capital campaigns.

Dickey resigned from the presidency in 1970, Dartmouth's bicentennial year, at the age of sixty-three. By this time student dissent and protest against military recruiting on campus during the Vietnam War had sharpened, culminating in the occupation by the Students for a Democratic Society (SDS) of the main administration building, Parkhurst Hall, on 6 May 1968. Although Dickey handled this incident without the disruption that had occurred on other campuses and later moved to give undergraduates a greater role in college governance, he was disappointed and discouraged by what he viewed as a mounting worldwide rebellion against authority and by the failure of his faculty to maintain an atmosphere of free speech on campus during this period.

Over the course of his presidency Dickey received many honorary degrees, including the Doctor of Laws from Amherst, Brown, Bucknell, Columbia, Harvard, Middlebury, Tufts, Oberlin, Notre Dame, Princeton, and Wesleyan. He served on President Harry S. Truman's 1947 Committee on Civil Rights, the United Nations Collective Measures Committee in 1951, and as consultant to the Secretary of State Acheson on disarmament in 1952. He was recognized nationally for his publications on government and foreign affairs and taught Canadian-American relations as the Bicentennial Professor of Public Affairs at Dartmouth until 1978.

Dickey suffered a stroke in 1982 and remained severely ill, living at the medical center on the Dartmouth campus until his death. He is buried in Pine Knoll Cemetery in Hanover.

As president of Dartmouth for a quarter of a century, Dickey had a pervasive and enduring influence on the school's character and prestige. In his initiatives to revitalize and redesign the college, he is probably unmatched by any of his predecessors. Dickey was above all a champion of the liberal arts. At the heart of his initiatives was his strong belief in the value of the "liberating arts" as the best foundation for undergraduate, graduate, and professional education. His leadership flowed from a philosophy that it was bad education in the twentieth century to advance the power of intellectual competency in undergraduates without "creating a corresponding sense of moral direction to guide the use of that power." Education was a lifelong endeavor, and the mission of institutions such as Dartmouth should be to encourage in its students a sense of personal responsibility or conscience, a sense of commitment and discipline, and a comprehensive "awareness for those later experiences which over the course of a lifetime can add up to an education."

★

Charles E. Widmayer provides the most comprehensive coverage of Dickey's presidency at Dartmouth in *John Sloan Dickey: A Chronicle of his Presidency of Dartmouth College* (1991). In "Dartmouth on Purpose: A Forward" in Ralph Nading Hill, ed., *The College on the Hill, a Dartmouth Chronicle* (1965), Dickey outlines his vision of undergraduate education at Dartmouth. His view on college governance during the period of 1960s student radicalism is laid out in excerpts taken from his 1969 interview with *Yankee* magazine in Edward Connery Lathem and David M. Shribman, eds., *Miraculously Builded in Our Hearts: A Dartmouth Reader* (1999). Obituaries are in the *New York Times* and *Boston Globe* (both 11 Feb. 1991). Close to fifty hours of a taped oral history interview conducted by Jere R. Daniell after Dickey's retirement are located in Special Collections at the Dartmouth Library.

MILDRED G. CARSTENSEN

DIEBENKORN, Richard Clifford (*b.* 22 April 1922 in Portland, Oregon; *d.* 30 March 1993 in Berkeley, California), major mid-century modernist artist. After working for more than twenty years in loose, figurative, and abstract styles, he developed in his *Ocean Park* series one of the most luminous and fully realized groups of nonobjective paintings produced by an American.

The only child of Richard Clifford Diebenkorn, a sales executive, and Dorothy Stephens, Diebenkorn moved to San Francisco when he was two. His grandmother, Florence Stephens, who became a lawyer later in life and was a short story writer and a cultural affairs organizer on the radio, spent summers with the artist when he was a boy and introduced him to Arthurian legends and English history through the illustrated books of Howard Pyle and N. C. Wyeth.

Richard Diebenkorn. ARCHIVE PHOTOS

After graduating from Lowell High School in San Francisco in 1940, Diebenkorn entered Stanford University, majoring in art. He was attracted to the paintings of Arthur Dove, Charles Sheeler, and Edward Hopper. As an undergraduate he painted landscapes and urban scenes of local areas. On 16 June 1943 he married Phyllis Gilman, a fellow student. That year he was called up by the Marine Corps (having enlisted in 1942). During his two-year stint his assignments brought him to Parris Island, South Carolina; Camp Lejeune, North Carolina; Quantico, Virginia; Camp Pendleton, California; as well as Hawaii. While in Virginia he often visited the Phillips Collection in Washington, D.C., and in California he came to know the work of the abstract expressionists William Baziotes and Robert Motherwell. His daughter was born in May 1945 and his son in the spring of 1947.

In late 1946 and early 1947, Diebenkorn stayed at the art colony at Woodstock, New York. He also met the abstract expressionists Baziotes, Mark Rothko, and Bradley Walker Tomlin in New York City. In 1947 he moved to Sausalito (north of San Francisco) and began teaching at the California School of Fine Arts in San Francisco. He met the California modernist artists David Park and Elmer Bischoff, who were instructors at the school, and with whom he would be closely associated during his figurative period beginning in 1956. After receiving an M.F.A. degree from the University of New Mexico at Albuquerque in 1951, he taught for a year at the University of Illinois at Urbana. In 1953 he met the abstract expressionist Franz Kline. From January 1955 until June 1960 he taught at the California College of Arts and Crafts and from the fall of 1961 until 1966 at the San Francisco Art Institute. He was also a guest of the Soviet Artists Congress and was able to see the Henri Matisse collection at the Hermitage Museum in Leningrad. In the summer of 1966 he traveled to southern France and Germany and in the fall was appointed professor of art at the University of California at Los Angeles. For this position Diebenkorn moved from Berkeley, where he had lived since 1953, to the Ocean Park district of Santa Monica, taking over the studio of the color-field painter Sam Francis. He remained in Ocean Park until 1988, when he moved to Healdsburg in northern California.

Diebenkorn, a lean, well-proportioned man who wore a mustache, received his first one-man show in November 1952 at the Paul Kantor Gallery in Los Angeles. By the 1970s, although working far from the center of the art world in New York City, Diebenkorn was recognized as an artist of national, and even international, importance. From February to March 1974 a retrospective exhibition of his drawings was held at the University of California at Santa Cruz. Another major retrospective exhibition, which traveled widely through the country, originated in November 1976 at the Albright-Knox Art Gallery in Buffalo, New York.

Diebenkorn was awarded honorary doctorates from the San Francisco Art Institute in 1975 and from Occidental College in Los Angeles in 1982. In May 1985 he was elected to the American Academy of Arts and Letters.

Diebenkorn's work falls neatly into three periods. After a brief representational phase while at Stanford, as seen in *Palo Alto Circle* (1943), in which the rows of buildings are rendered in the manner of Edward Hopper, he worked in an abstract expressionist format until 1955. His turn to modernism was brought on partly by his exposure to the A. E. Gallatin Collection, on loan from the Philadelphia Museum of Art, and he studied the catalog with its reproductions of works by Matisse, Paul Cézanne, Joan Miró, and Hans Arp for many years. His work from this period was completely nonobjective, with some canvases heavily painted in a gestural manner, containing looping lines or ovular shapes reminiscent of Miró. Other works, which were more planar, suggested the influence of Matisse. A late work of the period, *Berkeley No. 8* (1954), contains strong diagonal lines breaking up the continuity of the surface. At this time Diebenkorn was strongly impressed with Chaim Soutine's turbulent landscapes, which he saw reproduced in a book on the artist.

The summer of 1955 marked a turning point, a catharsis, as the artist felt, "I came to mistrust my desire to explode the picture. . . . Something was missing in the process. I sensed an emptiness as though I were a performer." He produced some paintings of still lifes in interiors showing knives, scissors, books, or other objects on tabletops (*Interior with Book,* 1959), but mostly Diebenkorn painted interiors containing one or two seated or standing figures quietly regarding one another. In these large paintings, forms were grandly displayed while precise detailing was avoided, and although there was an indication of perspective, the strength of the two-dimensional design was forcefully maintained as seen in *Man and Woman in Large Room* (1957).

The third period of the extensive (150 paintings in total) *Ocean Park* series was marked by a return to nonobjectivity that coincided with Diebenkorn's twenty-one-year stay in Santa Monica. These majestic paintings with their broad, flat, carefully ruled-off rectangles of color owe a good deal to the earlier work of Matisse and Piet Mondrian. But the artist synthesized these influences into a formulation all his own. The soft colors, the sense of expansiveness of the rectangles, and the sense of atmosphere and wetness suggest his own environment of brightly lit skies over oceans, beachfront areas, and highways as seen in *Ocean Park No. 66* (1973). Diebenkorn received the National Medal of Art in 1991. Having no part in the abstract expressionism centered in New York City, Diebenkorn produced a West Coast variant of modernism that rivaled it in quality. A national tour of the Richard Diebenkorn Exhibit, spon-

sored by J. P. Morgan and Company, began at the Whitney Museum of American Art in New York City in 1997.

★

There is a catalog of Diebenkorn's works, produced by the Albright-Knox Art Gallery, *Richard Diebenkorn, Paintings and Drawings, 1943–1976* (1976), with essays by Robert T. Buck, Jr., Linda L. Cathcart, Gerald Nordland, and Maurice Tuchman. Another authoritative essay is John Elderfield, *The Drawings of Richard Diebenkorn* (1988). An extensive chronology of the artist's life may be found in Gerald Nordland, *Richard Diebenkorn* (1987). Another source is Jane Livingston, *The Art of Richard Diebenkorn* (1997), with essays by John Elderfield, Ruth E. Fine, and Jane Livingston.

ABRAHAM A. DAVIDSON

DIETRICH, Marlene (*b.* 27 December 1901 in Schöneberg, Germany; *d.* 6 May 1992 in Paris, France), actress whose alluring beauty and unique aura of mystery and sophistication established her as a film icon for many years.

From the very beginning of her career and throughout her life, Marlene Dietrich persisted in creating her own legend, often blurring the facts about her origins and her work. Born Maria (some sources say Marie) Magdalene Dietrich in Schöneberg, Germany, an outlying district of Berlin, the actress was the daughter of Louis Erich Otto Dietrich and Wilhelmina Elisabeth Josephine Felsing (known as "Josephine"). Their first daughter, Elisabeth, whom Dietrich

Marlene Dietrich. AP/WIDE WORLD PHOTOS

never acknowledged, was born a year earlier, in 1900. Dietrich's father, a police lieutenant who had spent years in military service, died suddenly in the summer of 1907, shortly before Dietrich was enrolled in the August Victoria Academy for Girls. Not long afterward, her mother married Eduard von Losch, a colonel in the Royal Grenadiers, who died in battle during World War I.

After the war, Josephine and her two daughters moved to Weimar, a major cultural center in Germany, 140 miles from central Berlin. Dietrich studied music, with the promise of a major career as a violinist, but she gave it up after an injury to her hand. Lured by the hedonistic lifestyle of postwar Berlin, she was soon caught up in the city's frenzied gaiety, seeking to become part of its culturally thriving, sometimes decadent world of cabaret, movies, and innovative theater. For a while she was one of the so-called Thielscher Girls, chorus girls who performed intermittently in cabarets and music halls. Rejected at first by Max Reinhardt's prestigious drama school, she was later permitted to enroll in classes and eventually appeared in many of the school's productions. During this period, there were changes in her personal life. In 1922 she changed her name to "Marlene," and on 17 May 1923 she married Rudolf Sieber, who was then working as an assistant to the film director Joe May. They had one daughter.

Attracting attention with her lustrous blonde hair, long shapely legs, and a gaze that could be either insolent or seductive, Dietrich won increasingly larger roles in the theater and in films. She was noticeable even in her first movie, *The Little Napoleon* (1923), and both critics and audiences were soon aware of her striking presence in such films as *The Joyless Street* (1926, with Greta Garbo*)*, *Manon Lescaut* (1926), *A Modern Du Barry* (1926), and *Café Electric* (1927). By the end of the decade she had prominent roles in *Princess Olala* (1928), *The Woman One Longs For* (1929), *The Ship of Lost Souls* (1929), and other films. She also performed onstage in musical revues such as *It's in the Air* and *Two Neckties,* and in the hit American play *Broadway.* Throughout this period it became increasingly clear that Dietrich regarded Rudolf Sieber as more of a confidante, adviser, and friend than a husband, and her romantic affairs with other men as well as with women were well known at the time.

In 1929, Dietrich began her association with the director Josef von Sternberg, one of the most productive and significant alliances in the history of cinema. A highly eccentric, domineering director whose innovative films were more concerned with imagery and atmosphere than with plot or dialogue, Sternberg found in Dietrich the embodiment of his ideas on filmmaking. In *The Blue Angel* (1930), based on Heinrich Mann's 1905 novel *Professor Unrat,* he cast her as Lola-Lola, the sluttish, heartless café singer who degrades and destroys a respected professor (German film star Emil Jannings in his sound debut), who cannot control his lust for her. Brazenly straddling a chair and singing—or rather croaking—"Falling in Love Again" in her inimitable voice, Dietrich was a worldwide sensation, and when the German studio UFA failed to renew her contract, she signed with Paramount Pictures in Hollywood, arriving in America in April 1930. Her contract specified that she could only be directed by Sternberg.

Their six films together represent a unique collaboration of two artists. Although their stories are vastly different, Sternberg succeeded in creating an indelible image of his star as a bewitchingly beautiful, enigmatic woman whose air of icy aloofness hid a vulnerability, especially in matters of the heart. *Morocco* (1930), their first American film, cast her as Amy Jolly, a jaded cabaret singer who, at the end, follows her legionnaire lover (Gary Cooper) into the desert. In subsequent films, replete with Sternberg's complex, ornate imagery, Dietrich portrayed women whose wicked, even decadent ways were caused by the lust and treachery of men. From the wronged wife and mother who is forced to become a raunchy nightclub performer in *Blonde Venus* (1932), to the notorious Shanghai Lily in *Shanghai Express* (1932), to the simple country girl who evolves into Russia's promiscuous Catherine the Great in *The Scarlet Empress* (1934), Sternberg's Dietrich created the unique image of an elusive, world-weary, and endlessly fascinating woman. Of these films, *Shanghai Express* was probably the most accessible. A flamboyant melodrama set aboard a speeding train in a China torn by civil war, it received an Academy Award nomination for best picture. Lee Garmes's shimmering images of Dietrich—her almost translucent face, her praying hands—helped win him an Oscar for the year's best cinematography.

Too esoteric for the public taste, Dietrich's films with Sternberg did not fare well at the box office. After playing the dangerously seductive Concha Perez in *The Devil is a Woman* (1935), her last film with Sternberg and her personal favorite, the actress's box office appeal began to fade. Her cryptic, languorous personality was going out of fashion. Films such as *Desire* (1936), *The Garden of Allah* (1936), and *Angel* (1937) emphasized her exquisite beauty, but there was a chilly remoteness to her characters that alienated audiences. Moviegoers preferred the earthy vitality of Ginger Rogers and Carole Lombard. Dissatisfied and unhappy at being labeled "box-office poison" by exhibitors, she walked out on her Paramount contract. In 1937, Nazi agents approached Dietrich with an offer to return to German films, but she refused, resulting in the banning of her films in Germany. She became an American citizen on 9 June 1939.

An important change in her career occurred in 1939 when she was cast as Frenchy, the rowdy, raucous saloon singer in the comedic Western *Destry Rides Again.* Reluctant at first to change her image so drastically, Dietrich finally agreed to take the role, and her Frenchy, whether engaging in a hair-pulling free-for-all with Una Merkel or singing "The Boys in the Back Room" in her husky voice, won enthusiastic reviews. Inevitably, Dietrich was now cast in roles far removed from her earlier sophisticated image. In *Seven Sinners* (1940), she played a tawdry café singer in love with naval officer John Wayne; in *The Flame of New Orleans* (1941), she was a brazen adventuress out to snare wealthy Roland Young. Other roles in the early 1940s were not as felicitous—in such movies as *Manpower* (1941), *The Spoilers* (1942), and *Pittsburgh* (1942), Dietrich was cast as an explosive catalyst to the relationship of two friends.

Throughout World War II, she spent most of her time entertaining American troops in battle zones from the South Pacific to North Africa to Italy and Germany. She participated frequently in war bond drives and made anti-Nazi broadcasts in German, for which she was deeply reviled within Germany. Her film roles were few and not very rewarding, with the outstanding exception of Billy Wilder's acerbic comedy *A Foreign Affair* (1948), in which she excelled as Erika von Schlutow, a selfish, opportunistic cabaret singer—and former consort to Nazis—in postwar Berlin. Her renditions of such songs as "Black Market," "Illusions," and "The Ruins of Berlin" were memorable expressions of the prevailing attitude of cynicism. In 1947 General Maxwell Taylor presented her with the Medal of Freedom, the highest civilian honor the United States government bestows, and France named her a Chevalier of the Legion of Honor.

During the 1950s, Dietrich appeared in such movies as *Stage Fright* (1950), *No Highway in the Sky* (1951), and *Rancho Notorious* (1952). She had a small but memorable role in Orson Welles's *Touch of Evil* (1958) as a gypsy-like madam who urges obese sheriff Orson Welles to "lay off the candy bars." She gave one of her best performances as Christine, the enigmatic wife of accused murderer Tyrone Power in Billy Wilder's adaptation of the Agatha Christie stage play *Witness for the Prosecution* (1958). More of her time, however, was devoted to making records and to performing in cabarets. Her cabaret act, which took her from Las Vegas to London, was carefully honed to take full advantage of her film image as a glamorous, worldly woman and actress. She also starred in two radio series called *Café Istanbul* and *Time for Love*. In 1960 she returned apprehensively to Berlin, where, to her relief, she was received with great enthusiasm. By the late 1960s she had perfected her act to the extent that she could risk performing on Broadway, where she made two triumphant appearances in 1967 and 1968. Audiences were delighted by the renditions of her signature songs, including "Falling in Love Again," "Lili Marlene," and "Where Have All the Flowers Gone?" In 1968 she was presented with a Special Tony Award.

Dietrich took a few film roles in the 1960s, most notably as Madame Bertholt, widow of an executed Nazi general, in Stanley Kramer's drama *Judgment at Nuremberg* (1961). She narrated Louis Clyde Stoumen's *The Black Fox* (1962), a documentary that parallels Hitler's rise to power with Goethe's adaptation of the twelfth-century folktale "Reynard the Fox," and she can be spotted briefly in *Paris When It Sizzles* (1964). Her last appearance in films was as a baroness in a forgettable melodrama entitled *Just a Gigolo* (1979). In 1984, the actor Maximilian Schell created *Marlene,* a documentary film about the actress that combined documentary footage, film clips, still photographs, and other material to create a curious but fascinating portrait. Although Dietrich's voice is heard throughout the film, she refused to be photographed. Some months after the death of her husband in 1976, she withdrew to her Paris apartment where she remained a recluse, determined to maintain the illusion of "Marlene Dietrich" until the end. She died of kidney and liver failure in May 1992 at the age of ninety and was buried in Berlin, survived by her daughter and four grandsons.

Early in her career Marlene Dietrich decided to create a unique image of glamour, mystery, and sophistication, and she succeeded beyond all her expectations to become a legendary actress. The true Dietrich remains a puzzle; director Billy Wilder called her "a strange combination of femme fatale, German hausfrau, and Florence Nightingale."

But whether we see her as the gauzy heroine of Josef von Sternberg's exotic romances or the rowdy saloon queen urging us to "see what the boys in the back room will have," Marlene Dietrich is not easy to forget.

★

The Marlene Dietrich Collection in Berlin contains extensive materials on the actress, including photographs, costumes, films, documents, and recordings. Dietrich's unreliable autobiography was published in German in 1979 as *Nehmt nur mein Leben* (Take Only My Life) and in English in 1989 as both *Marlene* and *My Life. Marlene Dietrich's ABC,* her reflections on life, love, and food, was published in 1962 and revised in 1984. Books on her life and career include Homer Dickens, *The Films of Marlene Dietrich* (1968, revised and updated by Jerry Vermilye, 1992); Leslie Frewin, *Dietrich: The Story of a Star* (1967); Charles Silver, *Marlene Dietrich* (1974); Charles Higham, *Marlene: The Life of Marlene Dietrich* (1977); Alexander Walker, *Dietrich* (1984); Steven Bach, *Marlene Dietrich: Life and Legend* (1992), and Donald Spoto, *Blue Angel: The Life of Marlene Dietrich* (1992). *Marlene Dietrich,* by her daughter, Maria Riva, was published in 1993. Josef von Sternberg's autobiography, *Fun in a Chinese Laundry* (1965), includes much information on Dietrich. Obituaries are in the *New York Times* (7 May 1992) and *Variety* (11 May 1992).

TED SENNETT

DIXON, Willie James (*b.* 1 July 1915 in Vicksburg, Mississippi; *d.* 29 January 1992 in Burbank, California), musician, songwriter, record producer, and arranger who was the driving creative force behind the influential Chicago-blues sound of the 1940s and 1950s.

Dixon was the seventh of fourteen children born to Daisy McKenzie, a devoutly Christian restaurant owner, and Charles Dixon, who worked in a sawmill. Seven of the Dixon children died at birth; Willie's six surviving siblings included three older sisters and three younger brothers. His father filed for divorce in 1912 on grounds of adultery; the divorce became final in 1913. Anderson ("A. D.") Bell, who became Dixon's stepfather, and who some have speculated may have been Dixon's biological father, played an important role in Dixon's early development.

Dixon's childhood was spent in a poor integrated neighborhood on the northern edge of Vicksburg, where he attended the Cherry Street elementary school. His mother would regularly make rhymes for her children, a skill that Dixon acquired at a very early age. Dixon's mother also required that he sing in church at the age of five where he received his first formal exposure to music. He was greatly influenced by the country-blues, Dixieland, and ragtime

Willie Dixon. ARCHIVE PHOTOS

musicians who played in the barrelhouse around the corner from his mother's restaurant in Vicksburg during the early 1920s, particularly Little Brother Montgomery and Charley Patton. Dixon and his friends often skipped school to hear them play. In 1926, when he was eleven years old, Dixon, who by this time had stopped going to school altogether, ran away from home. This began years of wanderings that took him on the hobo trails to Chicago, New York City, and all over the South. When Dixon was in his early teens he served two sentences—one for theft and the other for hoboing—on prison-farm camps in Mississippi. It was at these camps that he first became acquainted with various blues styles practiced by inmates.

In the early 1930s Dixon began to sing bass with a gospel quartet called the Union Jubilee Singers. The group toured the towns of Mississippi and broadcast a fifteen-minute radio show from Vicksburg every Friday night. But during the Depression, Dixon's music took a backseat to working at any job he could find. He shoveled coal, worked a short stint with the Civilian Conservation Corps, and traveled by boat to Hawaii working as a ship's laborer.

Dixon had been an overweight child, but by his late teens he had become trim, strong, and interested in boxing. In 1936 he moved to Chicago to pursue a career as a boxer. He won the Illinois State Golden Gloves heavyweight championship and sparred with such nationally known champions as Joe Louis. But Leonard ("Baby Doo") Caston, an aspiring musician who met Dixon at a gym where he was working out, convinced Dixon to drop boxing in favor of music. Caston gave Dixon his first instrument, a one-string washtub bass. The pair made the rounds of the bustling Chicago music scene, often playing in the streets or passing the hat in the clubs. Dixon made his first recording while serving as a vocal coach for the Bumpin' Boys in 1938. In late 1939, Dixon and Caston formed the Five Breezes and recorded eight tracks on RCA's subsidiary Bluebird label.

During the late 1930s, the economic conditions of the Great Depression and the lack of opportunities available for black musicians made Dixon's music career difficult. In the early 1940s his life and career were made even more difficult when he was jailed for refusing to be inducted into the Army during World War II, on the grounds that African Americans shouldn't serve in the military when they were still being denied civil freedoms. After several months of trials and imprisonment, Dixon was released in 1944 but was prohibited from working in the lucrative war industries.

In 1945 Dixon formed the Four Jumps of Jive and cut four tracks for Mercury Records. In 1946 he again joined forces with Leonard Caston to form the Big Three Trio. The band, with Dixon on bass, played regularly from 1946 to 1952 and earned an enthusiastic following of fans. The group released its first record, "Signifying Monkey," which became a chart hit on the Bullet label in 1946. They also had a hit on the Columbia label in 1946 with "Wee Wee Baby, You Sure Look Good to Me." Around this time Dixon met the Chess brothers, two Polish immigrants who created the soon-to-be famous Chess record label in 1950. In years to come Dixon would work on and off as one of the Chess brothers' busiest session musicians and producers.

By the end of the 1940s Dixon had firmly established his musical career in Chicago as a composer, producer, and musician. He became a family man when Elenora Franklin, whom he had met at a Big Three Trio gig in the late 1940s, became his common-law wife. He and Elenora had seven children but were divorced in 1955. In 1957 Dixon married Marie Booker. They had five children and remained together until Dixon's death.

In the 1950s Dixon worked steadily as a composer, producer, backup musician, and arranger on some of the most popular blues and rock-and-roll records of the day, by artists such as the bluesman Muddy Waters and rock-and-roll innovator Chuck Berry. Dixon's "Hoochie Coochie Man," recorded in 1954 by Muddy Waters, sold more than 75,000 copies, and "My Babe," performed by the harmonica player Little Walter Jacobs, became Dixon's first number-one hit on the rhythm-and-blues charts. Dixon also had hits with Chess Records in 1960 when he produced Howlin Wolf's recordings of his own compositions "Spoonful" and "Back Door Man."

The growing popularity of Chicago-style blues and blues-influenced rock-and-roll in the 1950s brought Dixon's music to the attention of a white audience. In the 1960s rock-and-roll bands such as the Rolling Stones, the Doors, Cream, and Led Zeppelin recorded versions of Dixon's songs, sometimes without proper credit to Dixon, which resulted in more than one lawsuit. Dixon regularly toured America and Europe in the late 1950s and 1960s with Memphis Slim, and in 1957 and 1958 he appeared at the prestigious Newport Folk Festival in Rhode Island. In 1968 he formed the Chicago Blues All-Stars and released his first studio album, entitled *I Am the Blues,* which became the title of his 1989 autobiography.

Despite medical ailments that plagued him in later life—particularly diabetes, which led to the amputation of his right leg in 1977—Dixon continued to tour internationally and to appear at blues festivals in the 1970s and 1980s. He received Grammy nominations for *What Happened to My Blues* (1978) and *Backstage Access—Live at Montreux* (1986) and performed live on the 1987 Grammy Awards broadcast. In 1989, his *Hidden Charms* won the Grammy for best blues album.

In 1982 Dixon created the Blues Heaven Foundation, a nonprofit organization devoted to increasing awareness of the blues through educational and legal assistance to blues artists in addition to instrument donations to schools. In 1982, after more than fifty years in Chicago, Dixon and his wife moved to Glendale, California, for the warmer climate. At the age of seventy-six he died of cardiac arrest in Burbank; he is buried in Burr Oak Cemetery in Alsip, Illinois.

Dixon's catalog of over 500 songs—made famous by artists from Bo Diddley and Otis Rush to Elvis Presley—continues to be performed by musicians all over the world. He is generally regarded as the most influential and important bluesman of his day.

★

Dixon's autobiography, written with Don Snowden, is *I Am the Blues: The Willie Dixon Story* (1989). Shorter treatments of his life and career are in *Current Biography Yearbook* (1989) and *The Annual Obituary* (1992). See also Roger Wolmuth, "Willie Dixon," *People Weekly* (11 Sept. 1989); and Thomas Duffy, "Blues Master Willie Dixon Dead at 76," *Billboard* (8 Feb. 1992). Obituaries are in the *New York Times* and *Chicago Sun-Times* (both 30 Jan. 1992).

RICHARD STRINGER-HYE

DOOLITTLE, James Harold (*b.* 14 December 1896 in Alameda, California; *d.* 27 September 1993 in Pebble Beach, California), aviator, engineer, air force commander, and war hero whose career spanned aviation's first century.

The only child of Frank H. Doolittle and Rosa C. Shepherd, James Harold Doolittle spent his early childhood in Nome, Alaska, while his father, a carpenter by trade, prospected for gold. As a teenager, he returned with his mother to California and became interested in boxing. After achieving success as an amateur, he occasionally fought for money at various boxing clubs under the name Jimmy Pierce. He even held his own in an exposition bout against World Bantamweight Champion Kid Williams. Following graduation from Manual Arts High School in 1914, he spent several months in Alaska trying his luck at prospecting before returning to California. In 1915 Doolittle registered at Los Angeles Junior College and two years later entered the University of California School of Mines. To earn money, he worked summers in the mines and continued to fight professionally. His quickness and toughness in the ring might well have earned him notoriety had it not been for the entreaties of both his mother and his girlfriend.

With the entry of the United States into World War I, Doolittle enlisted as a flying cadet in the Army Signal Corps Reserve. He attended the School of Military Aeronautics at the University of California, and then Rockwell Field in San Diego, California, for flight training. He soloed after seven hours and four minutes of flight training instruction. Despite witnessing numerous accidents, many of them fatal, he retained his love of flying. After becoming a second lieutenant in the Signal Corps Reserve, Aviation Section, on 11 March 1918, he was assigned to a series of places,

Major General James Doolittle with the bomb he and his crew dropped on Tokyo, 1942. ASSOCIATED PRESS AP

including Camp Dick, Texas; Wright Field, Ohio; Gerstner Field, Louisiana; and as a flight and gunnery instructor at Rockwell Field. His commander refused his frequent requests for an overseas assignment, and his hope for a war zone tour was shattered by the armistice of November 1918. One positive aspect of his California assignment was that it stationed him near his wife, Josephine ("Joe") Daniels, his high school sweetheart, whom he had married on 24 December 1917. She would remain his wife for seventy-one years in a union that produced two sons.

Doolittle's love of flying prompted him to stay in the air service after the war. A series of assignments in the Southwest followed. After a tour at Kelly Field, Texas, he flew border patrol for the Ninetieth Aero Squadron, stationed at Eagle Pass, Texas. In July 1920 he transferred back to Kelly Field to the Air Service Mechanics School. His promotion to first lieutenant in the air service, regular army, decreased his chances of being cut from the service when only reserve officers were being mustered out. At Kelly he received firsthand instruction from top-notch teachers, and he worked directly on the airplanes and the engines. After assignment to McCook Field in Ohio, he was able to convince the chief of the air service, General Mason M. Patrick, to let him attempt a cross-country flight in less than a day. On 4 September 1922 Doolittle took off from Pablo Beach, Florida. After enduring bad weather, weariness, a paucity of cockpit instrumentation, and a single thirty-minute fuel stop in San Antonio, Texas, he landed at Rockwell Field in San Diego, in an elapsed time of twenty-two hours and thirty minutes (a total flying time of twenty-one hours and nineteen minutes). Doolittle gained instant celebrity for his record flight.

In 1922 Doolittle earned a B.A. degree from the University of California, and in October 1923 he entered the Massachusetts Institute of Technology (MIT) for special engineering courses, earning an M.S. degree the following year. After Doolittle was admitted to a doctoral program at MIT, the army recalled him to McCook to pursue hazardous structural flight testing of a new experimental Fokker fighter. Doolittle flew the aircraft in a series of difficult maneuvers at various speeds to the very limit of its structure and survived a near in-flight failure. For his efforts he received the Distinguished Flying Cross. In addition, his work and resulting test data helped him earn a doctorate in aeronautics from MIT in 1925. That same year, he won the Schneider Cup race in a Curtiss R3C-2 float biplane, bettering both domestic and international competitors at an average speed of 232.573 miles per hour over a straightaway course. At the age of twenty-eight, Doolittle was considered by other aviators to be the most experienced and best educated test pilot in the United States.

During the second half of the decade, Doolittle pursued his interest in aeronautical science and engineering. He took several leaves of absence from the army and headed for Latin America, where he flew many dangerous demonstration flights for various U.S. aviation companies. In addition, he worked on flight instrumentation and blind flying at Mitchel Field's Full Flight Laboratory in New York. At that time, accidents often occurred because pilots could not fly by instruments or did not trust them. Doolittle believed that flying in inclement weather could be mastered if the improvements in aircraft design, flight and navigation instruments, and radio communication could be coordinated. On 24 September 1929 he made the first such "blind flight," using just these tools—the Kollsman precision altimeter, the Sperry gyrocompass, the Sperry artificial horizon, and rudimentary radio navigation aids. The flight encompassed ten months of planning and was perhaps the most important demonstration since the Wright brothers' flight at Kitty Hawk, North Carolina, in 1903. It did much to ensure the rapid expansion of U.S. commercial aviation, which depended upon the integration of advanced aircraft designs, airway developments, and the emergence of innovative avionics and instrumentation systems.

In February 1930 Doolittle decided for financial reasons to resign from the Army Air Corps to work for Shell Oil Company. He successfully applied for a commission as a major in the Air Corps Reserve. At Shell he coordinated the company's aviation departments in San Francisco, St. Louis, and New York City. He also kept the company in the public's eye by continuing to participate in air shows and races. Doolittle's work as aviation manager for Shell Oil Company in supporting the development of high-octane fuels resulted in the Army Air Corps standardizing 100-octane fuel by mid-1936. As a result, when war began in Europe in 1939, the United States was the only nation capable of producing large quantities of 100-octane (or higher) fuel—up to 650,000 gallons per day by mid-1940. Meanwhile Doolittle kept his hand in flying. In 1932 the Granville brothers of Springfield, Massachusetts, invited Doolittle to fly the Gee Bee R-1 racer in the Thompson Trophy Race in Cleveland, which he won with a record speed for the race of 252.287 miles per hour.

In January 1940 Doolittle was appointed president of the Institute of Aeronautical Sciences. In that post, he emphasized to college students the importance of applying the best minds to solving the problems of aeronautics. But he wanted to do more, so as World War II began, he requested recall to active duty. His old friend, and now commanding general of the Army Air Corps, General Henry ("Hap") Arnold, granted his request. On 1 July 1940 Doolittle returned to active duty and went on an inspection and study trip to Great Britain in 1941. On his return, he tested new aircraft like the B-26 Marauder and recommended that the aircraft remain in production.

In early 1942 the United States, still tormented by the shock of Pearl Harbor and the continuing succession of Japanese victories, needed some type of victory to raise morale. To effect this, a scheme was concocted to have army B-25 bombers take off from the navy aircraft carrier *Hornet* and attack the Japanese mainland. Arnold, now commanding general of the Army Air Forces, chose Doolittle to lead the air strike. Colonel Doolittle set about to supervise the training of his volunteer crews and the modification of their B-25s to obtain maximum range. His crews, who had never taken off from a carrier deck, knew nothing about the mission until they were far out to sea. On the morning of 18 April 1942, the Japanese observed the carriers *Hornet* and *Enterprise,* compelling Doolittle to schedule the raid a day earlier and at a greater range from their targets. All sixteen B-25s dropped their bombs, but as a consequence of the 150-mile extended flight path all but one aircraft, which landed in the Soviet Union, ran out of fuel and went down in Japanese-occupied China. Of the eighty crewmen, seventy-one survived, one died, and eight were captured. The Japanese executed four of the captured American airmen as war criminals; the others survived cruel treatment and were freed at the war's end. Most of the pilots, including Doolittle, maneuvered their way to friendly lines. Unfortunately, the Japanese subsequently executed many of the Chinese peasants who had assisted Doolittle's raiders. While the actual damage of the Doolittle raid was slight, the psychological effect on the Japanese was significant: their army and navy had failed to protect their homeland. In June, Japanese strategists decided to attack Midway Island, where they lost four large carriers and one cruiser. One of the decisive battles in human history had taken place because of Doolittle's action. Doolittle was made a brigadier general following the raid and received the Congressional Medal of Honor. Promotion to major general soon followed.

After briefly commanding the Fourth Bombardment Wing (Medium) of the Eighth Air Force stationed in England in July 1942, General Doolittle took over the Twelfth Air Force for the invasion of North Africa. By D-Day, 8 November 1942, Doolittle, who had never commanded a unit larger than a squadron, controlled a force of over 1,244 aircraft and twelve groups, with seventy-five percent of the personnel either untrained or partially trained. Doolittle was transferred again on 18 February 1943, to command the Northwest African Strategic Air Forces (NASAF). This heavy bomber force concentrated on bombing Axis shipping. Within two months, the NASAF had succeeded in cutting off the Nazis in Tunisia. Doolittle flew at least six combat missions during this period.

After Tunisia, Doolittle directed the NASAF through Pantelleria, Sicily, and Italy. His forces bombed Rome and participated in the Regensberg and Schweinfurt raids. When the Fifteenth (Strategic) Air Force was established at Foggia, Italy, in October 1943, its mission was to bomb

Germany. Doolittle and his heavy bombardment wings transferred from NASAF and formed the core of this new air force. As the first commander of the Fifteenth Air Force, Doolittle commanded eleven groups of fighters and bombers with 930 combat aircraft and over 20,000 men. But before he could begin serious operations, he received orders to go to England.

During his thirteen months in the Mediterranean theater, Doolittle had to quickly absorb the fundamentals of managing huge units. In so doing he refined some of the new tactics employed by his units. He encouraged his fighters to employ loose escort, instead of close escort, of bomber formations and encouraged escorts to be more aggressive. His performance impressed the supreme Allied commander in Europe, General Dwight D. Eisenhower, who in January 1944 gave Doolittle command of the "mighty" Eighth Air Force, the largest and most prestigious numbered air force with no fewer than twenty-six heavy bomber groups, twelve fighter groups, 42,000 combat aircraft, and 150,000 personnel. Doolittle changed the role of his fighters from one of escort to one of killer, allowing his fighters to go after the German fighters instead of waiting for the enemy to come to them. This change in policy soon gave the Allies air superiority over Europe. After V-E Day and a brief respite in the United States, Doolittle moved out with his Eighth Air Force to the Pacific and was present for the unconditional Japanese surrender on the battleship *Missouri* on 2 September 1945.

After World War II, Doolittle worked hard to promote a separate air force, making speeches and testifying before Congress. In 1947 he helped found the Air Force Association and became its first president. After resigning from the army air forces, he retained his reserve status and went back to his job at Shell as a vice president and, in April 1946, director, holding the latter position until 1967. He retired from the air force reserve as a lieutenant general in 1959, the only reserve officer to retire at that rank. In 1985 President Ronald Reagan and Senator Barry Goldwater pinned Doolittle with his fourth star, promoting him to full general.

In the postwar period, Doolittle served as a member of the Joint Congressional Aviation Policy Board, as an adviser to the Committee on National Security Organization, and as a member and chairman of the National Advisory Committee for Aeronautics. He made several trips to Korea during the Korean War as a consultant for Chief of Staff of the Air Force General Hoyt S. Vandenberg. From his various advisory roles to the air force and to other agencies of the government while representing Shell, Doolittle knew the organization and functioning of the air force's ballistic missile program. It was for this reason that he agreed to become the chairman of the board as well as the director of Space Technologies Laboratories.

Doolittle became the proverbial "wise man" of every phase of aviation and aerospace science, whose counsel was consistently sought. Prior to his retirement from Shell, he and his wife, Joe, suffered a severe personal tragedy in 1958 with the baffling suicide of their eldest son, thirty-seven-year old Jim Jr., then a major in the air force. Despite this painful loss, they recovered and rebounded. Doolittle became a director of the Mutual of Omaha Insurance Company. His beloved Joe died on 24 December 1988, their seventy first wedding anniversary. Honors would continue to follow him, culminating with the Presidential Medal of Freedom presented to him by President George Bush in 1988. This pioneer of aviation and man of many talents and accomplishments died peacefully in his sleep in Pebble Beach at the age of ninety-six. He was buried with full honors at Arlington National Cemetery in Washington, D.C., in an elaborate ceremony reserved for dignitaries and top officers that included a twenty-one-gun salute and a flyover by eleven aircraft.

★

The private papers of Doolittle, including his personal correspondence, film and photographs, and copies of his published scientific research, as well as his famous desk and chair, are held at the James H. Doolittle Library, University of Texas at Dallas History of Aviation Collection. Doolittle's autobiography is *I Could Never Be So Lucky Again*, written with Carroll V. Glines (1991). Biographies include Thomas Lowell and Edward Jablonski, *Doolittle: A Biography* (1976), and Carroll V. Glines, *Jimmy Doolittle: Master of the Calculated Risk* (1980). Finally, a superb appraisal of his aeronautical and engineering exploits can be found in the winter 1993 issue of *Air Power History*, which, on the occasion of Doolittle's death, dedicated the entire issue of seven articles to the pioneer aviator. An obituary is in the *New York Times* (29 Sept. 1993).

GEORGE M. WATSON, JR.

DORSEY, Thomas Andrew (*b.* 1 July 1899 in Villa Rica, Georgia; *d.* 23 January 1993 in Chicago, Illinois), called "The Father of Gospel Music" for the contributions he made as songwriter, arranger, choir director, and publisher in the development of gospel hymnody. Dorsey helped usher in the Golden Age of Gospel (1930–1960).

Dorsey was the first of three children born to the Reverend Thomas Madison Dorsey and Etta Plant. His father was a farmer and a Baptist preacher who ministered to two rural churches and ran a school during the winter months and his mother was a property owner as a result of an insurance settlement following her first husband's death. Thomas often accompanied his father and thus came to know the characteristic forms of worship and singing in a rural southern black congregation. He learned to play the piano from

Thomas Dorsey, c. 1929. FRANK DRIGGS COLLECTION/ARCHIVE

his mother and shape-note hymnody from his uncle, Corrie M. Hindsman, who was also a pastor. His mother also taught him the significance of "moaning," a deeply felt emotional reading of a hymn, which was the source of the style of embellishment in the gospel blues that Dorsey came to write. In addition, he got some formal instruction from Mrs. Graves in Atlanta, who taught Morehouse College students (although Dorsey himself did not attend Morehouse), and from the Chicago College of Composition. His principal teachers were the people he sought to emulate, Ed Butler and Eddie Heywood, the respective pianists at "81" and "92" (film and vaudeville houses serving Atlanta's African American community), and the African American entertainers—singers, bands, and vaudevillians—who performed in Atlanta theaters.

Dorsey worked at the "81" after his family moved to Atlanta in 1908. He found the move a distasteful experience for a number of reasons, such as encountering color status within the African American community for the first time (Dorsey was very dark-skinned and "African" in his features), and having to begin school over again at a lower grade than he had finished at Villa Rica. Those factors forced him to think about ways of making a living, a step that would begin to define his lifetime work. At this point in his life religious music was not his first order of business, although he did learn the popular hymns featured in the evangelist Billy Sunday's revivals as arranged by his musician, Homer Rodeheaver. He also studied C. A. Tindley's work, which embedded hymn and revival tunes in the id-

ioms and tonalities of the southern black Baptist and Methodist churches. What mattered during his Atlanta years was developing his piano skills— playing at house parties and in bordellos—and gaining a reputation as someone with talent. He would continue in this same path when he relocated to Chicago by way of Gary, Indiana, in 1916. Although he returned to Atlanta between 1917 and 1918, he was back in Chicago to stay by 1919. He did not attend high school.

Dorsey had a significant career as a blues musician during the 1920s before devoting himself completely to religious music in 1932. This change was the result of a conversion experience that marked the end of a two-year period of depression. The death of his wife, Nettie Harper (whom he had married in 1925), in August 1932 after having given birth to a baby boy who died one day later made the change final. He eventually remarried in 1941 and had two children, a son and a daughter, by his second wife, Kathryn Mosely.

Although one of his gospel songs, "If You See My Savior," was a hit at the 1930 National Baptist Convention and, moreover, he worked very briefly as the director of music at the New Hope Baptist Church on Chicago's South Side, his principal work during this period was in blues. The money was better. He played with Will Walker's Whispering Syncopators for four months and began composing and arranging as southern-style blues began to catch on in Chicago. Dorsey was the pianist and the head of the Wild Cats Jazz Band, a group that toured with Ma Rainey. It was during this period that he took the nickname "Georgia Tom" and teamed up with Horace ("Tampa Red") Whittaker. They called themselves "The Hokum Boys" and introduced "hokum music" with the song "It's Tight like That." Hokum music, with its sexual innuendoes and overtones, was one of the reasons why blues became synonymous with vulgarity and worldliness. Between 1928 and 1932 Dorsey made over sixty hokum recordings, either solo or with Tampa Red.

Dorsey's bout with depression and the death of his first wife brought all of this activity to an end. It resulted in his writing one of his greatest songs, "Take My Hand, Precious Lord," a work which has become one of the United States' most beloved hymns. It has been translated into over fifty languages and become, because of the poignancy of Dorsey's lyrics, an Everyman's prayer. The turn from blues to religious music did not signal a change in the kind of writing and arranging that Dorsey did and would do. Instead, he carried what he had learned into writing gospel music. The blues style suited Dorsey's feel for improvisation and embellishment, and the immediacy and power of his lyrics encouraged powerful performances by individuals (Mahalia Jackson would be a Dorsey presenter from 1935 to

1946) and choirs. Dorsey became the director of the Pilgrim Baptist Church Choir in 1931.

Dorsey's music did not catch on immediately. He and others who joined him (such as Sallie Martin, the first singer to work with Dorsey in demonstrating and popularizing his music) had to work very hard to spread the word of gospel music and have it accepted and used in the larger black Baptist churches of Chicago and to be featured at the National Baptist Convention meetings. In addition to trying to sell his music, he formed a publishing house and he and Sallie Martin formed the National Convention of Gospel Choirs and Choruses in 1932, thus effectively giving gospel music an institutional base. There, Dorsey remained active until the 1970s, when failing health forced him into semi-retirement. In 1983 he was featured in the documentary "Say Amen, Somebody." He died of Alzheimer's disease in 1993 after spending the last year of his life in a coma.

Gospel music did not start with Dorsey. He drew on traditions and forms that were part of his training and experience, but he gave them shape and power and thereby contributed enormously to the development of a singular musical form, a fact others acknowledged by making the name "Dorsey" synonymous with gospel music.

★

The major work on Dorsey is Michael Harris, *The Rise of Gospel Blues: The Music of Thomas Andrew Dorsey in the Urban Church* (1992). This is likely to remain the definitive reading of Dorsey's life and work for some time. Other texts that discuss Dorsey in the development of gospel and gospel performers are Anthony Heilbut, *The Gospel Sound: Good News and Bad Times* (1997); Alan Young, *Woke Me Up This Morning: Black Gospel Singers and the Gospel Life* (1997); and Horace Clarence Boyer, *The Golden Age of Gospel* (2000). An obituary is in the *New York Times* (25 Jan. 1993).

ROBERT B. CAREY

DR. SEUSS. *See* Geisel, Theodor A.

DRAKE, Alfred (*b.* 7 October 1914 in New York City; *d.* 25 July 1992 in New York City), actor, singer, writer, and director whose award-winning starring role in the musical *Oklahoma!* revitalized American musical theater.

Alfred Drake, born Alfred Capurro, was the second son of John Capurro and Elena Teresa Maggiolo. The family attended Our Lady of Good Counsel Church in Brooklyn, New York, where Alfred made his first singing appearance. He continued his interest in music by joining the glee club while attending Brooklyn College. In 1935 while still a student at Brooklyn, Drake and his older brother, Arthur, passed the Adelphi Theatre in New York City where au-

Alfred Drake, 1962. © BETTMANN/CORBIS

ditions were being conducted for a summer production of Gilbert and Sullivan's *The Mikado*. Drake auditioned and was hired as an understudy and member of the chorus. When that nine-week engagement ended, he and his brother spent the rest of the summer of 1935 singing with an opera company on the Steel Pier in Atlantic City, New Jersey. (Arthur Capurro had his own career as a singer using the name Arthur Kent.)

Drake returned to Brooklyn College, majoring in English and education, and received his B.A. degree in 1936, but he was no longer interested in a teaching career. He made his Broadway debut as a chorus member in the musical review *White Horse Inn* in 1936. In December of that year the star of the show became ill and Drake was hired as his replacement with hardly any rehearsal. As a result of his performance—he only played the lead for eight performances—Drake was cast in the Rogers and Hart musical *Babes in Arms* in 1937. That show ran for forty weeks and earned Drake good reviews from the New York critics. Over the next four years Drake appeared in musicals, plays, and reviews of various kinds. A versatile performer, he appeared as Orlando in Shakespeare's *As You Like It* in 1941. After that short-lived production he was given the male ingenue role in Emlyn Williams's *Yesterday's Magic,* which starred Paul Muni. Drake's notices were positive, although the play as a whole was not well received. Often, Drake was singled out for praise even if the production was not.

In 1943 Drake was given the role of Curly McLain in *Oklahoma!,* the first of nine musicals created by Richard Rogers and Oscar Hammerstein. *Oklahoma!* was immediately called a landmark of American musical theatre. Daring and imaginative, the musical opens with Curly singing "Oh, What a Beautiful Morning," one of the most celebrated melodies in American music. Laura Wagner, in her article "The Versatile Rogue," quotes critic Elliot Norton of the *Boston Post* who wrote that, in that opening, "American musical comedy took a new turn away from the stilted nonsense towards something like truth and beauty. And Alfred Drake, because he got all that into his manner, his bearing, and his exuberant natural singing voice, became in effect the herald of a new era." It made Drake a star. He was awarded the New York Drama Critics Award for his performance.

Not content with Broadway stardom, Drake left *Oklahoma!* in 1944 to appear in the musical review *Sing Out, Sweet Land* with Burl Ives. The production was successful and critics again praised Drake as an actor and singer. In 1945 Drake was signed to appear in the Columbia Pictures musical *Tar and Spars.* The film was released in 1946. Sammy Cahn and Jule Styne wrote the songs and music. Drake sang two of them: "I'm Glad I Waited for You" and "Love Is a Merry-Go-Round." But Drake was fated never to have a successful film career. Whenever one of his Broadway successes was filmed—*Oklahoma!; Kismet; Gigi; Kiss Me, Kate*—another actor was always chosen to play his role. Years later, Drake explained why. In the winter 1998–1999 issue of *Show Music,* James Klosty excerpts an interview in which he asked Drake why he did not do the film version of *Kiss Me, Kate.* Drake responded that he was under contract with Metro-Goldwyn-Mayer (MGM) to do the film. "Then I was told MGM was worried I was too much of a liberal. The American Legion had decided that I sounded like a commie." MGM cancelled his contract. Besides, Drake explained, MGM already had Howard Keel, who MGM believed could play the role.

Drake returned to Broadway in 1946, starring in *Beggar's Holiday* and then *The Cradle Will Rock* (1947). In 1948 he starred in Cole Porter's *Kiss Me, Kate,* a retelling of Shakespeare's *Taming of the Shrew.* It was immensely popular, earning Drake the Donaldson Award. In 1951 Rodgers and Hammerstein offered Drake the role of the King of Siam in their new musical, *The King and I.* Drake turned them down because the role did not require much singing.

In 1953 the composers Chet Forrest and Robert Wright hired Drake to star in *Kismet,* which became one of his signature roles. His performance earned him another Drama Critics Award and a Tony for best actor. In 1955 Drake made his London debut in *Kismet.* Ten years later he reprised the role at Lincoln Center in New York.

Drake's choice of roles was often unconventional. As Wagner points out, he "didn't accept roles because of any success it might bring him; instead he did them for their artistic merits. All this proved that he was a versatile actor, capable of any role handed him, and he couldn't be typed."

Drake was also highly regarded as a serious actor, director, and writer. In 1957 he played Iago in Shakespeare's *Othello* at the American Shakespeare Festival. He played Benedict to Katherine Hepburn's Beatrice in John Houseman's 1957 production of *Much Ado About Nothing* and appeared in the production of *Hamlet* that starred Richard Burton (1964). Drake also directed the original Broadway cast of *Courtin' Life,* choreographed by George Balanchine. Drake wrote adaptations of plays by Molière, Ugo Betti, and Carlo Goldoni. His last major role was in the 1975 revival of Thornton Wilder's *The Skin of Our Teeth.*

Although a very private man, Drake was well regarded in the theater community. He served as president of the Players' Club, as a member of the Tony Nominating Committee, and as artistic director of the National Lyric Arts Theatre Foundation. In 1964 he was given the Brooklyn College Alumni Association Alumnus of the Year award. He was inducted into the Theatre Hall of Fame in 1981. In 1990 he was awarded a Tony for lifetime achievement.

Drake married Alma Rowena Tollefsen on 29 September 1940. Following their divorce in March 1944, he married Esther Harvey Brown, a member of the cast of *Oklahoma!* He died of heart failure following a long battle with cancer. He is survived by his wife and two daughters.

Drake was one of the most acclaimed and versatile performers of the mid-twentieth century. Actor, singer, writer, and director, he will be long remembered for revitalizing the American musical with his immortal performance as Curly in *Oklahoma!*

★

While there is no full-scale biography of Alfred Drake, he is referenced in all of the standard theatre histories. Drake himself was an engaging writer. In "Actor's Holiday," *Theatre Arts* (Dec. 1950), he gives a delightful account of the British theatre. He is featured in Max Wilks, *OK! The Story of Oklahoma!* (1993). Laura Wagner recounts and interprets his career in "The Versatile Rogue," *Classic Images* (May 1999). Jim Klosty published interviews with Alfred Drake in "Alfred Drake on the Life that Late He Led," *Show Music* (winter, 1998–1999) and "Alfred Drake Revisits the *Oklahoma!* Territory," *Show Music* (spring 1993). He is cited in *Who's Who in the Theatre* in 1983 and in *Current Biography 1944.* Obituaries are in the *New York Times* (26 July 1992) and *Variety* (3 Aug. 1992). He is featured in the five-volume videocassette *Broadway! A History Of The Musical.*

JOHN KARES SMITH

DRYSDALE, Don(ald) Scott (*b.* 23 July 1936 in Van Nuys, California; *d.* 3 July 1993 in Montreal, Canada), baseball pitcher for the Brooklyn and Los Angeles Dodgers during the 1950s and 1960s, baseball broadcaster, and Baseball Hall of Fame inductee.

Drysdale was one of two children born to Scott Sumner Drysdale, a onetime minor league baseball pitcher and repair supervisor for the Pacific Telephone and Telegraph Company, and Verna Ruth Ley, a homemaker. He began to play organized baseball as a nine-year-old in the Valley Junior Baseball League, followed by play at Van Nuys High School and American Legion baseball on a team managed by his father. Drysdale played mainly infield positions, but he was asked by his father to pitch when the scheduled pitcher failed to show up for an American Legion game. Drysdale, a right-handed thrower, pitched a complete game and won. A scout for the Brooklyn Dodgers watched the game and later asked Drysdale to join the Dodger Juniors, a team of high school prospects. During his senior year

Don Drysdale, 1957. © BETTMANN/CORBIS

Drysdale drew interest from baseball scouts when he pitched a no-hitter, striking out twelve batters. After his graduation in 1954, he received scholarship offers from Stanford University and the University of Southern California, while the White Sox, Yankees, Braves, Pirates, and Dodgers wanted to sign him immediately to a professional contract. Instead of attending college, Drysdale signed with the Dodgers in June 1954. Drysdale was sent to the class C Bakersfield club in the California League. In 1955 he moved up to Montreal, the Dodgers top farm club.

In 1956 Drysdale spent his rookie year with the Brooklyn Dodgers. In wins versus losses, his record was 5–5 for the season. In 1957, the Dodgers' last year in Brooklyn, he led the team's pitchers with a record of 17–9. Drysdale started the Dodgers' first home game in Los Angeles, losing to the San Francisco Giants 7–0 in the Los Angeles Coliseum. On 27 September 1958 Drysdale married Eula Eugenia ("Ginger") Dubberly, the 1958 Miss Tournament of Roses. They had one child and divorced in 1970. Drysdale contributed to the Los Angeles Dodgers' capturing the National League pennant in 1959, compiling a record of 17–13 and leading the major leagues with 242 strikeouts. The Dodgers then defeated the Chicago White Sox to win the World Series that year. Drysdale won game four. In 1960 he went 15–14 and again led the major leagues with 246 strikeouts. In 1961 he signed a contract with the Dodgers for $32,500, making him the highest-salaried pitcher in baseball at the age of twenty-four.

Known as "Big D," Drysdale stood six and a half feet tall and weighed about 190 pounds (215 pounds later in his career). As a pitcher, he threw three-quarter sidearm, a range of motion between overhand (throwing over the top) and sidearm (throwing when the arm is parallel to the ground). On the mound he was intimidating not only for his size and pitching motion but also for his tendency to pitch inside to hitters. In 1961 he hit twenty batters, the most in the National League since 1909. He led the league in this category five times and holds the National League career mark with 154 batters hit. Often accused of altering baseballs, Drysdale admitted in his 1990 autobiography that he used spit mixed with slippery elm.

Between 1962 and 1965 Drysdale was one of baseball's dominant hurlers, posting a record of 85–54. In all four of these years he started the most games of any pitcher in the National League, logging more than 300 innings in each of these seasons and leading the league in innings pitched in 1962 and 1964. Drysdale's career season was 1962, when he led the major leagues with a record of 25–9. He led the National League with forty-one games started and topped both leagues with 314⅓ innings pitched and 232 strikeouts, receiving the National League's Cy Young Award in recognition of his achievements. He and his southpaw Hall-of-Fame teammate, Sandy Koufax, dominated baseball's hitters and took the Dodgers to the World Series in 1963, 1965, and 1966.

Drysdale went 23–12 and Koufax notched a 26–8 record as the Dodgers won the National League pennant in 1965. The Dodgers then defeated the Minnesota Twins in the World Series, Drysdale going 1–1 and Koufax going 2–0. After the World Series, Drysdale and Koufax held out in an effort to become the first pitchers to make more than $100,000. After the pair missed most of spring training, the Dodgers signed them to one-year contracts. Koufax agreed to $125,000 and Drysdale signed for $110,000. During 1966, Drysdale's record declined to 13–16. This included two of the Dodgers' four losses during which they dropped the World Series to the Baltimore Orioles. In 1967 Drysdale again posted a discouraging 13–16 record. In 1968 he went 14–12, but, more important, from the period of 14 May through 8 June he threw 58⅔ consecutive scoreless innings, eclipsing Walter Johnson's major league record of fifty-six scoreless innings. This led to 1968 being called the "year of the pitcher." As a result, the pitching mound was lowered in 1969 in an effort to lessen pitchers' domination of hitters. (Drysdale was a broadcaster for the Dodgers in 1988 when the Dodger pitcher Orel Hershiser broke his record.) Drysdale was selected to the National League All-Star team, pitching three scoreless innings to pick up the victory. After his twelfth start of the 1969 season, he retired.

In 1969 Drysdale joined the Montreal Expos as a part-time television announcer and minor league pitching instructor. In 1971–1972, he was an announcer for the Texas Rangers, and he worked as a broadcaster with the Anaheim (then California) Angels from 1973 to 1981. From 1978 to 1986, he worked as an analyst for the American Broadcasting Company's weekly baseball games. Drysdale was inducted into the Baseball Hall of Fame in 1984. On 1 November 1986, he married Ann Elizabeth Meyers, a former All-American basketball star at the University of California at Los Angeles and a member of the Basketball Hall of Fame. They had three children. From 1988 until his death Drysdale worked as a broadcaster for the Dodgers. In 1989 Drysdale became a part owner of the Visalia Oaks, a class A minor league team in the California State League. He died of a heart attack and is buried at Forest Lawn Cemetery in Glendale, California.

Spending his entire career with the Dodgers, Drysdale compiled 209 wins and 166 losses, posting a 2.95 earned run average. Also known as an excellent hitter for a pitcher, Drysdale hit twenty-nine career home runs, including two seasons with seven, and had a respectable batting average of .186. Only twice did he win more than twenty games in a season, but he was a dominant pitcher from 1962 to 1965. He played in five World Series, pitching in seven games, winning three, and losing three (one game was a no decision). Drysdale was selected to eight All-Star teams, posting a 2–1 record. In a time when aggressive pitching dominated the game, "Big D" set the standard.

★

The National Baseball Hall of Fame Library in Cooperstown, New York, has a clippings file on Drysdale. His autobiography is *Once a Bum, Always a Dodger: My Life in Baseball from Brooklyn to Los Angeles,* written with Bob Verdi (1990). Drysdale's records can be found in *Total Baseball: The Official Encyclopedia of Major League Baseball,* 4th ed., edited by John Thorn and Peter Palmer with Michael Gershman (1995). A chapter on Drysdale can be found in Bill Libby's *Star Pitchers of the Major Leagues* (1971). The 1966 holdout by Drysdale and Koufax is covered in William B. Mead, *World of Baseball: The Explosive Sixties* (1989). *Current Biography* (1965) provides background on Drysdale's life before major league baseball. From the many magazine articles written about Drysdale, three in particular give insights into the man and the baseball issues of his time. Don Drysdale, "You've Got to Be Mean to Pitch," *Sport* (30 June 1960), suggests the role of intimidation in baseball. Huston Horn, "Ex-Bad Boy's Big Year," *Sports Illustrated* (20 Aug. 1962), provides background on Drysdale as he neared completion of his best season. Jack Mann, "The $1,000,000 Holdout," *Sports Illustrated* (4 Apr. 1966), offers a balanced appraisal of the situation faced by Drysdale and Koufax as they tried to improve their salaries dramatically during a time when the "reserve clause" precluded negotiation and mediation. (The reserve clause was a traditional provision in a player's contract that reserved the player's services for the following season, even if new terms had not been reached.) Obituaries are in the *New York Times* (5 July 1993) and the *Los Angeles Times* (4 July 1993).

PAUL A. FRISCH

DUKE, Doris (*b.* 22 November 1912 in New York City; *d.* 28 October 1993 in Beverly Hills, California), tobacco heiress whose notoriety stemmed from both her flamboyant lifestyle and, after her death, a sensational battle over her will.

Duke was the only child of James Buchanan Duke, president of American Tobacco Company, and his second wife, Nanaline Holt Inman, a socialite who had an adolescent son from her previous marriage. She grew up in an imposing Fifth Avenue mansion in New York City that felt more like a museum than a home and spent weekends on Duke Farms, her father's estate in Somerville, New Jersey, which later became her primary residence. Her father adored her; her mother largely ignored her.

From the day she was born, Duke was frequently referred to as "the richest girl in the world." She was educated mostly by tutors, although she did attend the Brearley School in New York City from 1922 to 1928. Her mother then enrolled her in Fermata, a finishing school in Aiken, South Carolina. Unhappy there, Duke expressed interest

Doris Duke, 1981. ASSOCIATED PRESS AP

in attending college. Her mother vetoed the idea. In later years Duke was defensive about her relative lack of education and resentful of Duke University, possibly because it represented something that had been denied her. Her father died on 10 October 1925, shortly before her thirteenth birthday, and she inherited an estimated $100 million. Before his death, he is supposed to have warned her: "Do not trust anyone." Her inheritance did not come to her outright but was set up in two trusts. She received only income from the larger trust; Duke University, already a primary beneficiary of a large charitable trust set up by her father, would become a primary beneficiary of this trust as well if she died without children. But the smaller one was turned over to her completely in increments: one-third when she was twenty-one years old, one-third when she was twenty-five, and one-third when she was thirty.

Duke made her debut on 23 August 1930 in Newport, Rhode Island, but she was not happy in society. She was exceedingly tall—six feet, one inch—and very insecure about her appearance. Many considered her self-centered and eccentric. And for one so wealthy, she could be astonishingly cheap, refusing, for example, to tip cab drivers.

On 13 February 1935 she married James H. R. Cromwell, the stepson of the Philadelphia multimillionaire E. T. Stotesbury. The marriage got off to a bad start when the check Cromwell had written to cover the initial expenses of their yearlong honeymoon bounced, and Duke had to pay for their trip around the world herself. The highlight of the trip for her was Hawaii, where she eventually built an ornate Near Eastern palace she called Shangri-La.

During her marriage to Cromwell, Duke had at least two significant extramarital affairs. Her open liaison with Duke Kahanamoku, the 1912 and 1920 Olympic 100-meter freestyle swimming champion, scandalized Honolulu. But Hawaii was still very isolated, so news of it did not reach the mainland. Her dalliance with Alec Cunningham-Reid, a member of the British Parliament with whom she was spotted in several New York City nightclubs in early 1940, created more of a stir. In the summer of 1940 Cunningham-Reid was reviled in his home country when he took off shortly before the Battle of Britain for a Hawaiian vacation with Duke. On 11 July, he arrived in Hawaii where Duke gave birth to a premature daughter, whom she named Arden. The baby, whose father might have been either Reid or Kahanamoku, died twenty-four hours later, and Duke was told that she would not be able to have any more children.

In late 1940, Duke and Cromwell separated. In 1942 she obtained a divorce in Reno, Nevada. But it was of questionable legality since Cromwell had obtained a restraining order barring her from seeking a divorce anywhere but in New Jersey. In 1944 Duke enlisted with the United Seaman Service, and left for Egypt, where she worked at the Egyptian Club in Alexandria. That November her Nevada divorce was upheld. In 1945 and 1946, she worked in Europe as a correspondent for the International News Service.

Her foray into the working world ended when she met Porfirio Rubirosa, a Dominican polo player and diplomat who was renowned for his sexual prowess. They married on 1 September 1947 in the Dominican consulate in Paris, but the marriage was shaky from the start. He was incapable of remaining faithful, she was jealous, and they fought constantly. They got along better after she divorced him on 27 October 1948. Their romantic involvement continued for two more years.

During the 1950s, Duke, herself an accomplished pianist, began to use the celebrity value of her name to gain entrée into the worlds of music and dance. There were late-night jam sessions in her homes, and she frequently worked out with dance troupes. Her most significant romantic liaison was with Joey Castro, a jazz pianist fifteen years her junior, whom she met in 1950. Another significant involvement was with Louis Bromfield, a Pulitzer Prize–winning novelist and conservationist. There was some talk of marriage, but his health was precarious (he died in 1956), and he was wary about the impact her wealth might have on his life.

Meanwhile, her relationship with Castro, which was marked by fierce fights and tearful reconciliations, continued. They broke up in 1964 after she attacked him with a butcher knife, reconciled, then broke up for good in 1966 after he broke her jaw. She turned her attention to restoring her mansion in Newport, assisted by Eduardo Tirella, the landscape architect who had helped design Duke Gardens for her Somerville estate. She made headlines when, on 7 October 1966, a car she was driving slammed Tirella against the gates of her Newport mansion, killing him instantly. His death was ruled an accident. His family filed a wrongful death suit against Duke, and in 1971 she was found guilty of negligence. But the damages she had to pay were minimal.

In 1968, Duke formed the Newport Restoration Foundation and embarked on her most ambitious project: restoring Newport's rundown eighteenth-century buildings. Over the next fifteen years the foundation bought and restored eighty-three houses. Her work helped spur a revival of Newport, which is considered one of the most successful restoration projects anywhere.

In 1985 in Hawaii, she met and developed a bond with Chandi Heffner, a former follower of Hare Krishna. During some channeling sessions, Duke became convinced that Heffner was the reincarnation of her daughter Arden. On 10 November 1988, Duke officially adopted Heffner, who was then thirty-five. But shortly afterward their relationship began to deteriorate. Duke eventually became convinced that she had been taken in by a con artist, and in 1991 she had her lawyer order Heffner off her property. But her lawyers could not undo the adoption. And she knew that it would be extremely difficult to keep Heffner from getting some kind of share in the proceeds of her father's trust after her death.

Duke attracted a good deal of attention in 1988 when Imelda Marcos, wife of the deposed Philippine dictator Ferdinand Marcos, was indicted for racketeering in New York and Duke lent her $5 million for her bail. Duke was quite put out, however, when Marcos failed to return the bail money after she was acquitted.

Until the late 1980s, Duke swam daily and, thanks to extensive plastic surgery, looked decades younger than her actual age. But her experience with Heffner seriously shook her confidence, and she began to rely on her butler, Bernard Lafferty, who some of Duke's other servants began to feel was deliberately keeping Duke's friends, relatives, and acquaintances away from her. The final decline in her health began when she had a face-lift in April 1992 and two days later, disoriented by painkillers, fell and broke her hip. Knee-replacement surgery followed in January 1993, and the painkillers, sleeping pills, antidepressants, wine, and laxatives she took while she was convalescing left her so malnourished and dehydrated that she had to be hospitalized. During her hospital stay, Duke, who had rewritten her will frequently, changed it one last time, making Lafferty the executor (a position that paid $5 million, plus $500,000 a year for life). After she was released from the hospital she had another knee operation, and two days after the operation she had a stroke and was hospitalized for two months. She returned to her home in Beverly Hills, but from that point on she was heavily sedated. The official cause of her death was fluid in the lungs and infection. A few hours after she died, her body was cremated so her ashes could be scattered in the ocean.

Duke left an estate of $1.2 billion and earmarked the vast majority of it for charity, via the Doris Duke Charitable Foundation. The will was not particularly specific, however, simply directing that the money be used for "the improvement of humanity" and mentioning a few special areas of interest: the arts, the environment, animals, and medicine. It was left to the will's executor to set up the foundation and the board. This will was challenged by Heffner, by Dr. Harry B. Demopoulos, who had been named executor in a 1991 will, and by three servants suing for breach of contract. The estate was tied up for the next thirty months in Surrogate's Court in Manhattan in one of the ugliest estate battles ever. Eventually, six law firms were billing the estate. One of her private nurses filed an affidavit contending that Lafferty and one of Duke's doctors had hastened Duke's death with a morphine overdose. Lawyers for Demopoulos presented evidence that during the period when her last will was written, Duke was frequently disoriented. Lawyers for the estate countered with evidence that there were also periods during that time when she was lucid. While Duke was dying, it was revealed, Lafferty ran up her credit-card accounts and made large gifts to the two doctors who were primarily responsible for her care. After her death, Lafferty spent estate money lavishly on himself. In December 1995 Heffner agreed to drop several claims against the estate in return for $65 million. And on 15 May 1996 Lafferty agreed to relinquish his role as the will's executor, the foundation was agreed upon, and the will finally was accepted for probate.

Because of the sensational battle over her will, Duke is likely to be remembered primarily as a victim of her enormous wealth. Ironically, up until her final year she had coped far better than most with the unique pressures that seem to beset those who inherit an inordinate amount of money.

★

Biographies include Tom Valentine and Patrick Mahn, *Daddy's Duchess: An Unauthorized Biography of Doris Duke* (1987); Stephanie Mansfield, *The Richest Girl in the World: The Extrav-*

agant Life and Fast Times of Doris Duke (1992); Pony Duke and Jason Thomas, *Too Rich: The Family Secrets of Doris Duke* (1996); and Ted Schwarz with Tom Rybak, *Trust No One: The Glamorous Life and Bizarre Death of Doris Duke* (1997). It should be noted, however, that some of the more sensational information in *Too Rich* and *Trust No One* is not documented. The *New York Times* also covered the fight over her will, including a particularly detailed account headlined "Court Revisits the Last Days of Doris Duke" (21 May 1995). An obituary is in the *New York Times* (29 Oct. 1993).

LYNN HOOGENBOOM

DUROCHER, Leo Ernest (*b.* 25 July 1905 in West Springfield, Massachusetts; *d.* 7 October 1991 in Palm Springs, California), scrappy baseball player and combative Hall of Fame manager whose battling personality led to success on the field for more than fifty years.

Durocher was one of four children of George Durocher, a railroad engineer, and Clarinda Provost, a homemaker who took in boarders and stitched Spalding baseballs at home, both of French Canadian descent. Only five feet, ten inches in height, but the tallest male in his family, Durocher took after his tough-talking mother and not his more mild-mannered father early on to lead a hardscrabble life.

Leo Durocher. © UNDERWOOD & UNDERWOOD/CORBIS

Growing up in West Springfield, Durocher enjoyed sports like most children but eventually focused his attention on billiards and baseball. Not one for schooling, he would often find himself refining his game in pool halls and became known as somewhat of a hustler because of his young age. While the information is not definitive, it is unlikely that Durocher attended high school. Eventually, it was on the baseball diamond where the smooth-fielding shortstop with the soft hands impressed the locals. Although he was not much of a hitter, a trait that would follow him throughout his professional career, his glove work had local semiprofessional and company teams bidding for his services.

In the spring of 1925 Durocher took a two-week leave from the Wico Electric Company, where he was assembling battery parts while also playing for the company team, to try out for the Hartford Senators of the Eastern League. He started at shortstop all year. His batting average was a woeful .220, but his fielding caught the eye of the New York Yankees scout Paul Krichell. The Yankees, suffering through a losing season, purchased Durocher from Hartford for $7,000. He made one pinch-hitting appearance for the Yankees in October, which proved to be his last big league at bat for two seasons.

The only way for Durocher to prove he belonged in the major league was to show it in the minors. His first stop was in Atlanta of the Southern Association, where he spent the entire 1926 campaign, and in 1927 he was with Saint Paul of the American Association. So while the Yankees were winning the 1927 World Series with Murderers' Row, the heart of the 1927 Yankees batting order and arguably the greatest team of all time, Durocher was toiling in the bushes, where he committed fifty-six errors as the everyday shortstop.

When he returned to the Yankees in 1928, he was picked on incessantly by the stalwarts of the famed Murderer's Row, but the team's manager, Miller Huggins, also a man of small stature, saw something in the smart and aggressive Durocher. It was during Durocher's first full season in the big leagues that his cocky talk led members of the team to call him "Lippy," from which sportswriters Will Wedge and Ford Frick began calling the rookie "The Lip." Huggins kept his pupil around for two seasons, with Durocher, often seen with a notebook marking down managerial moves, playing shortstop and second base for the Bronx Bombers and helping them sweep the St. Louis Cardinals in four games to win the 1928 World Series.

Although Durocher was the starting shortstop for most of the 1929 season, his poor batting (.246), the team's second-place finish to the Philadelphia Athletics (eighteen games back), Huggins's unexpected death near the end of the season, and his own financial woes eventually led to him being sold to the Cincinnati Reds in February 1930.

Durocher's reputation began to be cemented in Cincinnati. Although his offensive production remained weak, his defensive prowess at shortstop and his leadership skills began to shine through despite the team consistently finishing in the second division.

Durocher's private life was somewhat rocky. He was married four times, the first on 5 November 1930 to Ruby Marie Hartley. This union ended in divorce in 1934, but in 1931 they produced a daughter, the only child Durocher is known to have fathered. Each of his other three wives had children when he married them. Durocher married his second wife, Grace Dozier, on 26 September 1934. They divorced in 1943.

With the Reds struggling to another last place finish in the National League early in the 1933 season, the St. Louis Cardinals made a trade for Durocher with the hope that he would be the final link to winning the pennant. The St. Louis general manager Branch Rickey, who formed a love-hate relationship with the shortstop during the almost twenty years they stayed together, acquired Durocher with the pitchers Jack Ogden and Dutch Henry for the pitchers Paul Derringer and Allyn Stout and the infielder Sparky Adams on May 7. The Reds went on to finish in last place in 1933 and 1934, with Derringer eventually becoming a six-time all-star in later years, while the Cardinals were on their way to becoming the notorious "Gashouse Gang."

Despite Durocher's presence, the Cardinals still finished in fifth place in the National League in 1933. Everything came together the following season, with Dizzy Dean winning thirty games and his brother Paul winning nineteen, as St. Louis took the pennant by two games over the New York Giants. The twenty-nine-year-old Durocher, the team's starting shortstop, came through with his best offensive season as he produced career highs in games played (146), at bats (500), runs (62), hits (130), doubles (26), runs batted in (70), and batting average (.260). The Cardinals won the World Championship in seven games over the Detroit Tigers.

Although he was named to all-star teams in 1936, 1938, and 1940, the 1934 season proved to be the highlight of Durocher's playing career. The "Gashouse Gang" finished second in 1935 and 1936. On 5 October 1937 Durocher was sent to the Brooklyn Dodgers, where his infamy grew.

The Dodgers were perennial losers at the time, finishing in fifth place or lower every year since 1932, and Durocher's arrival in 1938 didn't pay immediate dividends. But when Burleigh Grimes was let go as the manager after the season, Durocher replaced him as the player-manager. The team's fortunes soon reversed. An 84–69 record, good enough for third place, helped Durocher become National League Manager of the Year in 1939.

Durocher went on to a twenty-four-year career in the dugout as one of his era's most successful and controversial managers. He favored scrappy players and the running game, played hunches, harassed umpires, and fought with owners and fans. His seventeen years as a player produced a .247 lifetime batting average in 1,637 games with 1,320 hits, 210 doubles, 56 triples, 24 home runs, 575 runs scored, 567 runs batted in, and 31 stolen bases.

A second-place finish in 1940 was followed the next year by Brooklyn's first pennant in twenty-one years. The Dodgers then fell to the powerful New York Yankees in the World Series in five games.

When Rickey, then the Dodgers general manager, decided to bring Jackie Robinson to the majors as their first African-American player in 1947, Durocher was supportive. However, he did not get to manage in the player's rookie year because Commissioner Albert ("Happy") Chandler suspended Durocher for a year for associating with gamblers and other activities.

On 21 January 1947 Durocher married his third wife—the actress Laraine Day. Although Durocher adopted Day's children, this union eventually ended in divorce in 1960.

Durocher returned in 1948 to replace Burt Shotton as the Dodgers manager, but near the All-Star break, Horace Stoneham hired Durocher to manage the Giants. Ironically, it was late in Durocher's tenure as the manager of the Dodgers that he is believed to have said his famous "nice guys finish last" quote. He was talking with some sportswriters before a game at the Polo Grounds when the topic switched to Eddie Stanky, and Durocher was explaining how the "Brat" overcame his physical limitations with a ferocious will to win. Just then the Giants came out for batting practice, led by player-manager Mel Ott. "Nicer guy never drew a breath," Durocher said. "Walker Cooper, Mize, Marshall, Kerr, Gordon, Thomson. Take a look at them. All nice guys. They'll finish last. Nice guys. Finish last."

With Durocher at the helm the Giants moved up to third place in 1950, and then came the "Miracle of Coogan's Bluff." In the middle of August the Dodgers were thirteen and a half games in front, but when the regular season ended they were tied for first place. A three-game playoff followed, with the Giants winning the first game and the Dodgers winning the second game. In game three, the Dodgers scored three runs off the starting pitcher Sal Maglie in the top of the eighth to take a 4–1 lead. But after Dodger starter Don Newcombe was relieved by Ralph Branca in the ninth, Bobby Thomson hit the "shot heard 'round the world," a three-run, game-winning homer, and the Giants were the National League champs. The Giants then lost the 1951 World Series to the Yankees in six games.

The Giants won the pennant by five games in 1954 and played the Cleveland Indians, the team that had won a record 111 games, in the World Series. In a surprising sweep, the Giants became world champions as Willie Mays made his famous catch off Vic Wertz about 425 feet from home plate to save the first game. The Giants were a distant third to the Dodgers in 1955 when Stoneham fired his manager. Durocher then became a broadcaster for NBC, where he stayed for five years (1956–1960).

Durocher became a coach for the Dodgers under Walter Alston in 1961, a job that lasted until 1965. The Cubs made him their manager in 1966. The Cubs finished tenth in his first year at the helm, but finished third the next two seasons and second in 1969 behind the surprising New York Mets.

The sixty-four-year-old Durocher married his fourth wife on 19 June 1969, Chicago media personality Lynne Walker Goldblatt, who was twenty-four years his junior. She eventually tired of his constant gambling, and they divorced in 1981.

Midway through the 1972 season, Durocher left the Cubs and replaced Harry Walker as the Houston Astros manager. The Astros finished 1973 with an 82–80 record, Durocher's last year as a manager before retiring. In his twenty-four years of managing, Durocher had a 2,008–1,709 record and won three National League pennants (1941, 1951, 1954) and one World Series (1954). After retiring, he coauthored *Nice Guys Finish Last* with Ed Linn, which was published in 1975.

Durocher died of natural causes at the age of eighty-six and is buried at Forest Lawn Hollywood Hills Cemetery in Los Angeles.

Combative on the field and gregarious off it, Durocher always seemed to get his team out of trouble, but he always seemed to be able to find it himself. Whether leading a ragtag team to a World Series title as a player, shifting the fortunes of franchises as a manager, or getting suspended by the powers that be in the game, things were never dull when Durocher was around. He retired with more than 2,000 victories as a manager with four different teams, still one of the highest figures of all time, and in 1994 was posthumously inducted into the National Baseball Hall of Fame.

★

The National Baseball Hall of Fame Library in Cooperstown, New York, has a number of clippings files on Durocher that include newspaper and magazine stories from throughout his lengthy baseball career. Durocher's autobiography, *Nice Guys Finish Last* (1975), gives the author's account of life in baseball with some perspective. A book of lesser note that Durocher contributed to is *The Dodgers and Me* (1948). A number of biographies have been written about Durocher over the years. Gene Schoor wrote *The Leo Durocher Story* (1955), but it suffers from being too well meaning and possibly was written for a younger audience. The most informative and well researched biography is Gerald Eskenazi, *The Lip: A Biography of Leo Durocher* (1993). Books that touch on specific parts of Durocher's life include Arthur William Mann, *Baseball Confidential: The Secret History of the War Among Chandler, Durocher, MacPhail, and Rickey* (1951); *Day with the Giants* (1952) by Durocher's former wife Laraine Day; and David Claerbaut, *Durocher's Cubs: The Greatest Team That Didn't Win* (2000). An obituary is in the *New York Times* (8 Oct. 1991).

WILLIAM FRANCIS

E

ECKSTINE, William Clarence ("Billy") (*b*. 8 July 1914 in Pittsburgh, Pennsylvania; *d.* 8 March 1993 in Pittsburgh, Pennsylvania), popular baritone singer whose smooth delivery on love ballads made him a sex symbol in the African American community; he led an influential jazz band in the mid-1940s that served as an important breeding ground for musicians of the emerging bebop style.

Eckstine was born William Clarence Eckstein, the youngest of three children of Clarence William and Charlotte Eckstein. His father held various jobs including chauffeur; his mother was a homemaker. He began singing at age seven, probably in the family's Episcopal church in the East Liberty neighborhood of Pittsburgh.

Although he pursued singing throughout his early life, Eckstine at this stage was more interested in sports than in music. On his own, he went to Armstrong High School in Washington, D.C., and St. Paul Normal and Industrial School in Lawrenceville, Virginia, to play high school football, earning an athletic scholarship to Howard University in 1932. Enrolled as a physical education major, he was injured and withdrew less than a year later.

While in Washington, Eckstine gained a reputation as a singer of ballads and blues through his work with Tommy Myle's band. Imitating the entertainer and orchestra leader Cab Calloway, he won an amateur contest at the Howard Theater in 1933. Returning to Pittsburgh in 1934, Eckstine encountered the tenor saxophonist Budd Johnson—a childhood acquaintance and member of the pianist Earl Hines's orchestra—who advised him to move to Chicago. Eckstine left Pittsburgh in 1936, lived in Buffalo, New York, for most of 1937, and then lived in Detroit before arriving in Chicago in early 1938.

He entertained at Ralph Capone's Club De Lisa until 1939, when Hines heard him and offered him a job with his orchestra, then nearing the end of its long and storied residence at the Grand Terrace Hotel. Together with Johnson, Eckstine helped to revive Hines's sagging fortunes by attracting the best and most innovative young musicians to play in his band.

In 1940 a blues song, "Jelly, Jelly," hastily conceived by Eckstine and Johnson to use up excess studio time, became the singer's first hit with Hines. A classic ballad performance, "Skylark," followed in 1942, and Eckstine's career was launched. In late 1942, "Stormy Monday Blues" by Hines, featuring Eckstine, was the number one rhythm-and-blues (or as it was known then, "race music") song in the country, staying on the chart for fourteen weeks.

Among the young modernists who Eckstine helped attract to the Hines band were the trumpeters "Dizzy" Gillespie and "Little Benny" Harris, the alto saxophonist Charlie Parker (who played tenor while with Hines), the tenor saxophonists Gene Ammons and Wardell Gray, and the vocalist Sarah Vaughan. Unfortunately this seminal band made few recordings. Because of a ban on recordings by the American Federation of Musicians—which in 1942

Billy Eckstine. ARCHIVE PHOTOS

demanded better contract terms with the recording industry—as well as wartime shortages of the materials used to make recording discs, only a few documents of this brief era of jazz survive.

Eckstine, who did not serve in World War II because of a sports injury, left Hines in September 1943 to embark on a solo career in New York City. Following a brief period in which he was billed on Fifty-second Street as "Billy X-Tine," he decided to form a big band of his own. Although the Billy Eckstine Orchestra, launched in June 1944, was an economic failure, it was an important harbinger of things to come in jazz. The band toured the southern United States and had a few hit records for the De Luxe and National labels—mostly ballads, including such staples of Eckstine's later repertoire as "A Cottage for Sale" (1945) and the old Russ Columbo warhorses "Prisoner of Love" and "You Call It Madness" (1946). In 1944 he recorded a Tadd Dameron arrangement of his own composition, "I Want to Talk About You," a sublime statement of love subsequently recorded by the tenor saxophonist John Coltrane and others. Sometime around 1944, Eckstine changed his surname's spelling to "Eckstine."

Eckstine sidemen, the trumpeter Miles Davis and the drummer Art Blakey, went on to become famous bandleaders themselves. The band also boasted, at various times, the trumpeters Gillespie, Fats Navarro, and Kenny Dorham, and the saxophonists Dexter Gordon, Lucky Thompson,

Gene Ammons, Parker, and Sonny Stitt. Some critics and listeners recognized the progressiveness of the music, while others found the juxtaposition of smooth vocal ballads and avant-garde bop instrumentals unsettling. In later interviews Eckstine scoffed at the critics who had faulted his band's sound in the early days, only to reverse their opinion once the group's significance to jazz history was known.

Eckstine had blue eyes and pretty-boy looks, and as a young man he would not hesitate to fight if provoked. In the film short *Rhythm in a Riff* (1946), he is shown singing and conducting the big band, and he solos competently on valve trombone. He began playing trumpet while with Hines, partly as a way of teaching himself to read music, but switched to valve trombone in his own band, he said, to counterbalance the trumpet and saxophone soloists. When he gave up the big band along with the trombone in 1947, he continued to play trumpet in his nightclub act. Dizzy Gillespie absorbed the remnants of the Eckstine band into his own group and added some irreverent clowning, finally achieving wide success with big band bop in 1949.

Turning to Hollywood, Eckstine found doors partly closed because of racial prejudice. Signing with Metro-Goldwyn-Mayer's nascent MGM Records, he had a string of hits working with various arrangers including Russ Case and Pete Rugolo, and rose quickly to become the most popular American male vocalist of 1949–1950. Like Nat King Cole, he presented an image of the contemporary African American male that was strong, sophisticated, romantic, sensitive, and intelligent. His appeal transcended boundaries of race, and he set box office records in New York while being mobbed by the "Billy soxers" who came to hear him sing love songs like "Everything I Have Is Yours" (1947), "Somehow" (1948), "My Foolish Heart" (1949), and his theme, "I Apologize" (1950).

He toured lucratively with the pianist George Shearing in 1950 and 1951, and ignited a fashion craze in the United States and England with his trademark "Mr. B." cotton shirts, which had a rolled, floppy collar. An avid golfer, he was the subject of feature articles in *Life* (1950) and *Look* (1951) magazines. Yet MGM mostly denied Eckstine the opportunity to expand his talent into movies—with the exception of a cameo appearance in the 1952 Esther Williams vehicle, *Skirts Ahoy!* Years later his friend the producer Quincy Jones commented, "They never let him become the sex symbol he could have been. If he'd been white, the sky would have been the limit. As it was he didn't even have his own radio or TV show, much less a movie career. He had to fight the system, so things never quite fell into place."

Eckstine's popularity waned with the arrival of rock music in the early 1950s. He turned again to the jazz scene, helping Count Basie to reestablish his orchestra after its collapse in 1951. He and his wife, June, divorced in 1953 (they had married in 1942, and had no children). Later that year he married Carolle Drake. They had seven children before the marriage ended in divorce in 1977. Eckstine also had an eighth child by another woman during his second marriage. Eckstine made the charts one last time for MGM with "Passing Strangers," a duet with Sarah Vaughan, in 1957. By then he had settled into a comfortable career as a nightclub singer, a position that he was able to maintain for the rest of his life in Las Vegas and Reno, Nevada, and Atlantic City, New Jersey.

After briefly signing with RCA, Eckstine signed with Morris Levy's Roulette label in 1960, recording both *Basie-Eckstine, Inc.* with Count Basie, and *No Cover, No Minimum* with his regular accompanist since 1949, Bobby Tucker. In 1961 he signed a five-album deal with Mercury Records and recorded *Live at Basin Street East* with Quincy Jones's orchestra.

He toured Europe and Asia and maintained homes in Las Vegas and Encino, California, as well as an apartment on 125th Street in the Harlem neighborhood of New York City. Typically he would work thirteen-week engagements at the Las Vegas casinos. The performances and subsequent partying would be followed by a round of golf in the morning, with Eckstine getting to bed in the early afternoon, waking up in time for the evening's performance.

Eckstine signed with Motown Records in 1965, but the resultant two albums did not sell well. The same was true of three albums he made for Stax in the late 1960s and early 1970s. In 1966 he performed with Duke Ellington. By the 1970s he had matured into a beloved celebrity, making guest appearances in television and films—a debonair, living symbol of a more romantic time in history.

In 1979 Eckstine toured with his daughter Gina, a singer. He recorded with saxophonist Benny Carter in 1986 for Mercury, where his son Ed was an executive. That year, he made his final album, *I Am a Singer,* for Kimbo Records. He continued to tour and carry out his nightclub engagements until his death from a stroke. He was cremated and his ashes were distributed among the surviving family members.

Eckstine's name is synonymous with the smooth style of baritone ballad singing that he perfected. Subsequent singers who have shown the Eckstine influence include Joe Williams, Arthur Prysock, Luther Vandross, Kevin Mahogany, and Brian McKnight. While essentially a popular singer, he maintained strong ties to jazz throughout his career, and was highly regarded in both the world of entertainment and the African American community.

★

Eckstine wrote a three-part series about leading his band for the British music magazine *Melody Maker* in 1954; he also granted interviews to *Metronome* (Feb. 1949, July 1950, and Jan. 1951), *Soul* (14 Oct. 1974), and *Jazz Times* (June 1984). Information about Eckstine's bop band may be found in Ira Gitler, *Jazz Masters of the '40s* (1966), Ira Gitler, *Swing to Bop: An Oral History of the Transition in Jazz in the 1940s* (1985), as well as in Scott DeVeaux, *Birth of Bebop: A Social and Musical History* (1997). Further information about the bop era may be found in Dizzy Gillespie, *To Be, or Not . . . to Bop, Memoirs* (1979; rev. ed. 1999). Information about the Earl Hines Orchestra is found in Stanley Dance, *The World of Earl Hines* (1977). An obituary is in the *New York Times* (9 Mar. 1993).

GREGORY K. ROBINSON

ELLIS, John Tracy (*b.* 30 July 1905 in Seneca, Illinois; *d.* 16 October 1992 in Washington, D.C.), educator and historian of the Roman Catholic Church in the United States, best known for his biography of James Cardinal Gibbons and his critiques of American Catholic higher education.

Ellis was the elder of two sons born to Elmer L. Ellis, a Methodist hardware business owner, and Cecilia Murphy, an Irish Catholic homemaker. He was raised in the Roman Catholic faith and educated at Saint Patrick's School and Seneca High School before finishing his secondary schooling at Saint Viator Academy in Bourbonnais, Illinois, from which he graduated in 1923. That fall Ellis enrolled at Saint Viator College, where he was influenced by Father Thomas J. Lynch, a professor of English and history, who instilled in him a love of the past and under whose direction he completed his bachelor's thesis.

After graduation from Saint Viator in June 1927 Ellis accepted a Knights of Columbus Fellowship to Catholic University of America, where he studied under the ecclesiastical historian Peter Guilday. Ellis earned a master's degree in 1928, expanding his thesis, "Anti-Papal Legislation in Medieval England, 1066–1377," into a Ph.D. dissertation (June 1930) and eventually his first book. At the same time, Ellis helped to support himself by serving as a secretary to the famed preacher Fulton J. Sheen.

Ellis began his teaching career immediately after earning his Ph.D., spending the summer of 1930 at Saint Benedict's College in Atchison, Kansas, and the following two academic years at his alma mater, Saint Viator. In the autumn of 1932 he began a two-year stint at the College of Saint Teresa in Winona, Minnesota, teaching the summer terms of 1933 and 1934 at Dominican College and the summers between 1935 and 1937 as director of the Southern Branch of Catholic University in San Antonio. Following a long period of consideration, Ellis requested—but was denied—seminary sponsorship from George Cardinal Mundelein of Chicago. He ultimately found a sponsor in Bishop Francis M. Kelly of Winona, on the conditions that

John Tracy Ellis, 1962. AP/WIDE WORLD PHOTOS

he pay his own way through seminary and that he teach after ordination. Ellis turned down an opportunity to attend the North American College in Rome, opting instead for the Sulpician Seminary in Washington, D.C., so that he could simultaneously teach at Catholic University to earn money for his brother's college expenses. He completed his seminary studies in four years and was ordained at the College of Saint Teresa in Winona in June 1938. Ellis then spent the summer in parochial ministry at Saint John the Baptist Parish in Chicago.

Ellis's career as an historian and educator began in earnest in September 1938 when he accepted an instructorship at Catholic University and began work on his second book. The following winter he was appointed to the editorial board of the *Catholic Historical Review,* initially editing book reviews. Within two years he succeeded his mentor Peter Guilday as managing editor of the *Review* and as secretary of the Catholic Historical Association. Ellis's ca-

reer reached a turning point in July 1941 when the rector of Catholic University, Bishop Joseph Corrigan, asked him to assume responsibility for Guilday's courses in American Catholic history. Having only previously taught classes in European history and feeling unready for such an assignment, Ellis requested and received a year of leave to prepare. He spent the spring 1942 semester at Harvard, studying American social history with Arthur Schlesinger, Sr. and the history of the American West with Frederick Merk. He returned to Catholic University as an assistant professor of history but quickly gained promotion to associate professor after the publication of his second book, *Cardinal Consalvi and Anglo-Papal Relations, 1814–1824* (1942).

The following decade was arguably Ellis's most productive. At the prompting of his close friend John K. Cartwright, Ellis in July 1945 began work on what would become his magnum opus, a biography of James Cardinal Gibbons of Baltimore (1834–1921). The project, to which he devoted seven years of his life, took him to dozens of archives in the United States and Europe. The biography appeared in two volumes to wide acclaim in November 1952. During the same time period Ellis was elevated to full professor (1947), produced two more books, published more than a dozen articles, traveled with the Archdiocese of Washington delegation to Europe for Holy Year celebrations (1950), and served as a U.S. State Department envoy to South America (1952). Largely as a result of the success of his work on Cardinal Gibbons, Ellis was invited to give the 1955 Walgreen Lectures at the University of Chicago, which were published as *American Catholicism* the following year. In the next ten years, he published five more notable books, including *Documents of American Catholic History* (1956), *John Lancaster Spalding, First Bishop of Peoria, American Educator* (1961), *Perspectives in American Catholicism* (1963), and *Catholics in Colonial America* (1965).

During the late 1950s and 1960s Ellis earned a reputation as something of a controversialist. In the autumn of 1956, in the Fordham University quarterly *Thought,* he issued a stinging critique of Catholic anti-intellectualism, raising the ire of prelates across the country. In the following few years, differences with Catholic University administration became more pronounced, due in large measure to Ellis's defense of four banned theologians and his criticism of the university's association with the *New Catholic Encyclopedia,* the policies of whose editor in chief Ellis called "benighted." In 1963 he applied for and received approval for a leave of absence without salary in order to move to San Francisco and begin work on a general history of Catholicism in America. The full multivolume work was never written, according to Ellis, "because the San Franciscans were too sociable and I was too weak," but on the suggestion of Professor John B. McGloin, the University of San Francisco president Charles W. Dullea extended Ellis an invitation to join the faculty in 1964, which he accepted.

Ellis thrived in relative freedom, accepting a lectureship at the North American College in Rome during Vatican II (1965) and visiting professorships at Brown University (1967), Saint Patrick's Seminary of California (1967–1968), Notre Dame (1970), the Graduate Theological Union, Berkeley (1970–1971), Gregorian University (1974–1975), and Angelicum University (1976).

Despite his difficult past with the university's administration and his continued attacks on the church's past transgressions, Ellis accepted in 1976 an invitation to be the first occupant of the Catholic Daughters of the Americas Chair at Catholic University. There he continued to be immensely productive, authoring more than two dozen scholarly articles, pamphlets and books before his retirement from the university in 1989 at the age of eighty-three. Though he suffered from diabetes for the last two decades of his life, Ellis remained in generally good health until undergoing hip surgery at Providence Hospital in Washington, D.C. There he suffered from complications related to his heart and died at age eighty-seven. He is buried in Seneca.

Though known for his remarkable work ethic and precise, fair scholarship, Ellis has exerted lasting influence through his calls for higher standards in Catholic seminaries and colleges and his demand that the church own up to its sometimes dark past. Moreover, he has profoundly shaped the study of American Catholic history through his dozens of graduate students, his long-term leadership in the American Catholic Historical Association, and his almost fifty-year editorship of the *Catholic Historical Review*.

★

Ellis recounted his career in *Faith and Learning: A Church Historian's Story* (1989) and a number of articles, including "Right Reverend Monsignor John Tracy Ellis" in *The Book of Catholic Authors,* vol. 5 (1957), and "Fragments from My Autobiography, 1905–1942," *Review of Politics* 36 (1974): 565–591. Ellis's books include *The Formative Years of the Catholic University of America* (1946), *A Select Bibliography of the History of the Catholic Church in the United States* (1947), *A Commitment to Truth* (1966), *Essays in Seminary Education* (1967), and *Catholic Bishops: A Memoir* (1983). Ellis's detailed curriculum vitae and a complete bibliography of his works appear in a Festschrift, *Studies in Catholic History: In Honor of John Tracy Ellis,* edited by Nelson H. Minnich, Robert B. Eno, and Robert F. Trisco (1985). Obituaries are in the *New York Times* and the *Washington Post* (both 17 Oct. 1992).

RAYMOND D. IRWIN

ENGLE, Paul Hamilton (*b.* 12 October 1908 in Cedar Rapids, Iowa; *d.* 22 March 1991 in Chicago, Illinois), writer and educator who garnered prizes and prestige for his poetry and who brought acclaim to the creative writing program at the University of Iowa during his tenure as director there.

Engle was one of four children of Hamilton Allen Engle, a farmer, and Evelyn Reinheimer, a homemaker. Although Paul helped his father, because of limited resources he also worked at a drugstore, delivered newspapers, and took odd jobs. He paid his own way through Coe College in Cedar Rapids, graduating magna cum laude in 1931.

Engle entered the English graduate program at the University of Iowa in 1931. He completed his master of arts degree in 1932 with the submission of his thesis, "One Slim Feather," a collection of poems, which according to Engle may have been the first creative writing ever accepted for the completion of an advanced degree in the United States. It was published in the Yale Series of Younger Poets as *Worn Earth* (1932).

In 1932 Engle received a fellowship to Columbia University. The next year he not only won the Chicago World's Fair Prize for Poetry sponsored by *Poetry* magazine for his poem "America Remembers," but he also was selected to be a Rhodes scholar at Oxford University in England.

At Merton College in Oxford, Engle studied under the poet Edmund Blunden and completed two volumes of poetry. With *American Song* (1934), he was proclaimed "a new voice in American poetry" in the *New York Times Book Review.* However, *Break the Heart's Anger* (1936) garnered less appreciation from critics who believed that Engle had

Paul Engle. ARCHIVE PHOTOS

lost some of his earlier focus. Oxford awarded Engle a B.A. degree in 1936. On 3 July 1936 in the registry at Oxford, Engle married his hometown girlfriend Mary Nomine Nissen. They would eventually have two daughters.

Engle and his wife returned to Iowa, where in 1937 he began to teach poetry at the University of Iowa. In 1939 he published a book of poems, *Corn,* and again exhibited his Whitmanesque approach to poetry with critically approved style. That same year he received an M.A. degree from Oxford. In 1941 he completed *West of Midnight,* which won the Friends of American Writers Award, and published a novel, *Always the Land,* which dealt with farmers, like his father, in the horse business.

In 1942 Engle became the acting director of the Iowa Writers' Workshop, and in 1943 he assumed the permanent directorship, a position he held until 1965. As head of the workshop, Engle had to administrate and promote as well as teach and write. He undertook raising funds from foundations and businesses as well as competing for university funds. The workshop needed money for faculty, classrooms, and scholarships for developing writers. Engle succeeded in his efforts and gained a national reputation for helping young writers. He recruited Donald Justice, Wallace Stegner, W. D. Snodgrass, Flannery O'Connor, William Stafford, all of whom would become highly regarded authors, as well as many others as students. He brought prestigious professional writers to the workshop as faculty. In all, he made the University of Iowa a widely known literary center.

Engle also experienced professional success from 1943 to 1965. He authored six books of poetry, a children's book, two reminiscences, and one work of fiction; he also edited nine anthologies and a highly regarded textbook, *On Creative Writing* (1964). He wrote the lyrics for an opera, *Golden Child* (1960), which was performed on television. Later the story was published as a novel of the same title (1962). He won Guggenheim scholarships for poetry (1953, 1957, and 1959) and was a Ford Foundation fellow (1952).

In 1965 Engle stepped down as director of the Iowa Writers' Workshop. In 1967, with the Chinese novelist Hualing Nieh, Engle oversaw the creation of the University of Iowa's International Writing Program, which brought together established writers from around the world to experience cross-cultural exchange of literary endeavors. His marriage to Mary ended in divorce in 1970, and on 14 May 1971 he married Hualing Nieh; she brought with her two children from her first marriage. Together they garnered funds and promoted the International Workshop; the success of the program led the diplomat Averell Harriman to nominate them for the Nobel Peace Prize in 1976. That same year Engle turned full directorship of the workshop over to his wife but remained a consultant to and a fundraiser for the program.

From 1965 to 1976 Engle continued to write. He put together another book of poems and with Hualing Nieh translated the poems of Mao Tse-tung. He also published a work of nonpoetry, *Women in the American Revolution* (1976).

In the 1980s Engle published a collection of poems written during a trip to China and helped edit an anthology derived from the International Workshop. He also spent time on reminiscences of his life. (*A Lucky American Childhood* was published posthumously in 1996.) Both Engle and his wife fully retired from the International Workshop in 1987, and in 1990 the American Academy and Institute of Arts presented Engle with its award for distinguished service. In 1991 Poland awarded Engle its government's Order of Merit. On his way to accept the honor, Engle died of a heart attack in Chicago's O'Hare International Airport. He was buried in a private ceremony, with a public memorial service at the University of Iowa.

Paul Engle was one of the leading literary figures in the United States. While public popularity of his poetry peaked in the 1940s, he produced numerous works of criticism, academic, and creative writing during his career. However, his greatest impact on the world of letters was his leadership of the creative writing programs at the University of Iowa, where he possibly nurtured more poets than anyone ever and facilitated the artistic development of a multitude of other aspiring writers.

★

The Special Collections Department, University of Iowa Libraries, is still processing Engle's copious personal papers. His childhood memoirs were published posthumously as *A Lucky American Childhood* (1996). Books that discuss Engle and the Iowa Writers' Workshop are Stephen Wilbers, *The Iowa Writers' Workshop: Origins, Emergence, and Growth* (1980), and Robert Dana, ed., *A Community of Writers: Paul Engle and the Iowa Writers' Workshop* (1999). An extensive biographical sketch of Engle is in Joseph Wilson, *Dictionary of Literary Biography,* vol. 48 (1978): 159–166. Also helpful are *Current Biography 1942*: 248–250, and *Contemporary Authors New Revision Series,* vol. 82 (1981): 114–116. An obituary is in the *Des Moines Register* (24 Mar. 1991).

THOMAS BURNELL COLBERT

EXLEY, Frederick Earl (*b.* 28 March 1929 in Watertown, New York; *d.* 17 June 1992 in Alexandria Bay, New York), autobiographical writer best known for his first novel, *A Fan's Notes* (1968).

Exley and his twin sister, Frances, were two of four children born to Earl Exley, a telephone lineman, and his wife, Charlotte Merkley, a homemaker. A local hero basking in his high school athletic triumphs, the elder Exley raised his family at 393 Moffett Street in Watertown. Frederick attended public school and was confirmed in the Episcopal Church. Like his father, he enjoyed football and basketball, but he always seemed to play in the shadow of Earl's fame.

Shortly after Exley entered Watertown High School in 1943, his father was diagnosed with lung cancer. The death of this seemingly indestructible athlete at the age of forty marked Exley for life, causing him to brood on his own mortality. A serious car accident in May 1946 exacerbated his fears. Hospitalized for six weeks, Exley failed to finish the school year and, as a result, did not receive his diploma until January 1947. After graduation Exley attended a post-graduate course at John Jay High School in suburban Katonah, New York, where he attempted to raise his grades for college while playing on the interscholastic all-star basketball team. His grades at John Jay earned him admission to the pre-dental program at Hobart College in Geneva, New York, in the fall of 1949. A year later, however, he transferred to the University of Southern California after a soured love affair with a high school sweetheart. There Exley changed his major to English, developed a taste for liquor, and had a chance meeting with the All-American football great Frank Gifford, whose success Exley contrasted with his own sense of failure in *A Fan's Notes* (1968).

After completing his B.A. degree in 1953, Exley worked in public relations first with the New York Central Railroad and then with the Rock Island Railroad in Chicago. Fired for drinking and poor work habits, he traveled around the country supporting himself at odd jobs, including brief stints as a bartender in Baltimore and a dishwasher in Miami, before returning to Watertown in the fall of 1957. He spent the next six months in his mother's house lying on the davenport, drinking, and losing touch with reality. Recognizing that Exley was having a breakdown, his family persuaded him to commit himself to Stony Lodge, a private mental hospital in Westchester County, New York.

At Stony Lodge, Exley met Francena Fritz, an attractive social worker and Skidmore College graduate, who continued to visit him after he was hospitalized for a second time at the Harlem Valley Hospital in Wingdale, New York. After Exley's release, the couple married on 31 October 1959 in a civil ceremony at the Hotel Woodruff in Watertown. They settled in suburban Greenwich, Connecticut, where Exley found a teaching position in nearby Port Chester. Temperamentally unsuited for teaching, he soon gave it up, though he later taught for several years in upstate New York, driven by the need to support himself and his family (in 1960 he and his wife had a daughter). He drank heavily and was sometimes abusive to Francena, who, at her father's urging, filed for a Mexican divorce in 1962.

Over the next five years Exley was at loose ends, dividing his time between upstate New York and Florida and returning for a final time to the Harlem Valley Hospital, where he found much of the material for *A Fan's Notes*.

While he was in Florida, he met Nancy Glenn, who helped type the manuscript for his first book. They married on 13 September 1967 and had a daughter before divorcing on 8 January 1971.

Fourteen publishers rejected *A Fan's Notes* before Harper and Row issued the book in 1968 to generally favorable reviews. Hailed as the best novel written in English since F. Scott Fitzgerald's *The Great Gatsby,* it was praised for its humor, its fierce honesty, and its unflinching criticism of the American Dream. Nominated for the National Book Award, it won the William Faulkner Award for best novel of the year as well as the National Institute of Arts and Letters Rosenthal Award for a book "which, though not a commercial success, is a considerable literary achievement." While Exley's first year's royalties were modest, his related earnings were sizable. He sold the film rights to Warner Brothers for $35,000, received a Rockefeller Foundation Award for $10,000, and obtained a $50,000 advance on his next book.

In June 1969 Exley moved into a borrowed apartment on Nineteenth Street in Manhattan, and he spent most of his time at the Lion's Head, a literary bar at 59 Christopher Street. In the fall he fled to the Seaview Hotel on Singer Island, Florida, where he began work on *Pages from a Cold Island* (1975). Despite good intentions, he was more inclined to drink than to write, and he became so depressed he came close to suicide. Through the 1970s, Exley earned money lecturing on college campuses, including the University of Iowa, where he was invited to teach in the Writer's Workshop in 1972. In 1974 *Playboy* paid $4,600 for "St. Gloria and the Troll," an article based on a disastrous interview with Gloria Steinem, which won the magazine's silver medal. In 1975 Random House published *Pages from a Cold Island,* which included the Steinem material as well as an extensive tribute to the late literary critic and writer Edmund Wilson. The reviews were mixed and decidedly less laudatory than those for *A Fan's Notes.* Exley was stung by the critical response, particularly Alfred Kazin's attack in the *New York Times Book Review* (20 April 1975). The book sold poorly and did little to enhance Exley's reputation.

The 1980s were a difficult period for Exley as his drinking began to take its toll. Suffering from high blood pressure, angina, and liver disease, he retreated to Alexandria Bay. His social life, he complained to *Esquire* (March 1986), was "circumscribed within the length of a football field." Nevertheless, there were some bright spots. Exley improved his relationship with his daughter Alexandra, and Frank Gifford invited him to the January 1987 Super Bowl, where his beloved New York Giants defeated the Denver Broncos, 39–20. In 1988 Random House published *Last Notes from Home,* the final volume of Exley's trilogy, which centered on the death of his brother, William, a retired army colonel, in 1972. In 1989, Exley's mother, who had always been his anchor and refuge, died. In October 1990 he was hospitalized for congestive heart failure and remained in poor health until, at age sixty-three, he died of a massive stroke at the Edward John Noble Hospital in Alexandria Bay. An Episcopal memorial service was held at Saint Mary's Catholic Church on 28 June 1992. Exley was cremated, and his ashes are buried at Watertown's Brookside Cemetery.

Exley's reputation rests primarily on *A Fan's Notes.* Ironically, its publication brought Exley the fame he despairs of ever knowing at the novel's end, where he concludes: "It was my fate, my destiny, my end, to be a fan." While Exley never achieved the popular or critical success of such contemporaries as Jack Kerouac or Norman Mailer, *A Fan's Notes* earned him a loyal cult following and the respect of his fellow writers James Dickey, William Styron, and John Cheever, among others. At the age of sixty, Exley regretted that his literary output had not been greater, that more time had been devoted to drinking instead of writing. Nevertheless, he managed to turn a troubled life into art and to carve for himself a unique niche in American literature.

★

Exley's papers are at the University of Rochester. Given their autobiographical nature, Exley's own writings are a valuable source of information on his life. Jonathan Yardley's *Misfit* (1997) is a reliable if somewhat unconventional biography. Magazine articles containing biographical information include Mary Cantwell's interview, "The Sad, Funny, Paranoid, Loving Life of a Male American Writer—Frederick Exley," *Mademoiselle* (June 1976), Jane Howard's portrait in *People* (14 Nov. 1988), and Cantwell's posthumous profile in the *New York Times Book Review* (13 Sept. 1992). Obituaries are in the *New York Times* (18 June 1992) and *Washington Post* (29 June 1992).

WILLIAM M. GARGAN

F

FAIRBANK, John King (*b.* 24 May 1907 in Huron, South Dakota; *d.* 14 September 1991 in Cambridge, Massachusetts), widely regarded as the most influential historian of modern China and the virtual founder of modern Chinese studies in the United States.

Fairbank was the only child of Arthur Boyce Fairbank, a lawyer, and Lorena King, a homemaker and minor civic leader. In 1911 the family moved to Sioux Falls, South Dakota, where Fairbank attended public schools for three years. In 1923 he enrolled at a prestigious private school in New Hampshire, Phillips Exeter Academy, from which he graduated two years later as valedictorian. He then matriculated at the University of Wisconsin for two years before transferring to Harvard University, where he earned a bachelor's degree summa cum laude in 1929. Having won a Rhodes scholarship, he studied at Balliol College, Oxford, and was awarded a B.Litt. degree in 1931. Spurred on by diplomatic historian Charles Kingsley Webster at Oxford, Fairbank decided to become a scholar on China.

Initially supported by the Rhodes trust, Fairbank lived in China from 1932 to 1935, mastering the language and traveling extensively throughout the nation. He served as a lecturer at Tsing Hua (Qinghua) University in the academic year 1933–1934 and the following year was a fellow of the Rockefeller-supported General Education Board in Peking (Beijing). In 1936 Oxford University awarded him a D.Phil. degree. His dissertation, much revised and titled *Trade and Diplomacy on the China Coast: The Opening of the Treaty Ports, 1842–1854,* was eventually published in 1954. In 1932 he married Wilma Denio Cannon, a writer, artist, and Orientalist. The couple adopted two children.

In 1936, on his return to the United States, Fairbank joined the faculty of Harvard University as an instructor. There he and his colleague Edwin O. Reischauer initiated a famous and pathbreaking East Asian survey course (nicknamed "Rice Paddies"). During World War II, Fairbank first served in Washington, D.C., on the Far Eastern staff of the Research and Analysis branch of the Office of the Coordinator of Information, renamed the Office of Strategic Services (OSS) in 1942. In August 1942 he was sent to Chungking (Chongking), China, where his task was to find and microfilm Japanese and Chinese publications for the OSS. During 1943 he was a special assistant to the U.S. ambassador in Chungking, essentially a titular post, in which capacity he acted as informal agent of the State Department's Cultural Relations Division. He also purchased Chinese materials for the Library of Congress as its official representative and directed the American Publications Service, which distributed microfilmed American writings to Chinese scholars and libraries. Late in 1943 he returned to Washington to work in the Office of War Information, acting occasionally as deputy director in charge of Far Eastern operations. From October 1945 to July 1946 Fairbank was back in China to direct the U.S. Information Service, administering ten branch offices from a headquarters in

Shanghai and in the process forming a favorable view of the Chinese Communists. He later claimed, "I was committed to viewing 'communism' as bad in America but good in China, which I was convinced was true."

Fairbank returned to Harvard in 1946, where he became full professor two years later. In 1959 he received one of the nation's best-endowed chairs, the Francis Lee Higginson Professorship of History. His publications were prodigious, both in popular and scholarly journals. His book *The United States and China* (1948; revised and enlarged in 1958, 1971, 1979, 1983) was often praised as the best short introduction to China. Fairbank aptly called it "a home run with bases loaded." With Japan expert Reischauer, he wrote *East Asia: The Great Tradition: A History of East Asian Civilization* (1960) and *East Asia: The Modern Transformation* (1965; additional coauthor Albert Craig); both books later appeared in condensed versions. Fairbank's autobiography *Chinabound: A Fifty-Year Memoir* (1982) drew on diary notes of his trips to China. *The Great Chinese Revolution: 1800–1985* (1986) drew strong parallels between imperial China and the regime of Mao Tze-tung (Mao Zedong). *China: A New History* (1992) again focused on problems of state power and dissonance. Other works included anthologies, documentary collections, annotated bibliographies, and collections of his own essays. In 1966, along with Denis Twitchett, he was appointed general editor of the multivolume *Cambridge History of China, 1800–1980.*

Fairbank threw himself into promoting East Asian studies, so much so that he epitomized the academic entrepreneur. In 1956 he became the director of Harvard's East Asian Research Center (renamed in 1977 the Fairbank Center for East Asian Research). It sponsored countless grants, conferences, and publications, including the annual *Papers on China* series. In 1959 he helped spearhead the Social Science Research Council's Joint Committee on Contemporary China and in 1962 the American Council of Learned Societies' Committee on Studies of Chinese Civilization.

Not surprisingly, Fairbank received many honors, among them two Guggenheim fellowships (Japan, 1952–1953; Asia and the USSR, 1960), a $10,000 prize from the American Council of Learned Societies (1960), and the presidencies of the Association for Asian Studies (1959–1960) and the American Historical Association (1968–1969); the latter organization created a John King Fairbank Prize in 1968 to recognize biannually the best North American book on East Asia.

Though he remained at the heart of the academic establishment, Fairbank's public persona was always controversial. In January 1950 Congressman John F. Kennedy attacked Fairbank on the House floor for being instrumental in the fall of Nationalist China. In August 1951 Louis F. Budenz, former editor of the Communist *Daily Worker,* testified before the Senate Judiciary Committee's Internal Security Subcommittee. Budenz named forty-three per-

John King Fairbank, 1966. © BETTMANN/CORBIS

172

sons, Fairbank among them, as belonging to the Communist party in the 1940s. Meeting in mid-March 1952 with the committee in private and public session for close to eight hours, Fairbank denied all charges under oath and expressed deep contempt for international communism. Despite his testimony, his passport to Japan was held up for seventeen months.

By 1950 Fairbank found China possessing "totalitarian tendencies." He supported the initial American effort in the Korean War, including the reunification of all Korea, though he sharply dissented from the strategy advocated by General Douglas A. MacArthur. From 1949 on he endorsed American recognition of Communist China and its representation on the United Nations Security Council. Beginning in 1954, when France lost Dienbienphu, Fairbank endorsed U.S. support for a non-Communist Vietnam. By 1969, however, he was sharply critical of American intervention there. In 1972, after the Nixon-Kissinger accord with the regime of Mao, he returned to China and was one of a select group of scholars who met with Premier Chou En-lai (Zhou Enlai). For a brief time he was euphoric over the People's Republic of China, in 1975 calling Mao "the greatest emancipator of all time." Soon, however, he was writing that "the Chinese path to socialism had led over a cliff," in the process accusing Mao of responsibility for 20 million deaths. In 1977 Fairbank retired from the Harvard faculty. Two years later he had a severe heart attack. He had another heart attack in 1991 and died in Cambridge.

Fairbank's manner was formal and courtly, his wit sardonic. A tireless worker, indeed relentless in pursuing his goal of Chinese studies, he nonetheless exercised paternal care of several generations of China scholars.

★

The Fairbank papers are at the Widener Library, Harvard University. Paul A. Cohen and Merle Goldman, eds., *Fairbank Remembered* (1992), contains the testimony of 127 friends and colleagues. Albert Feuerwerker et al., eds., *Approaches to Modern Chinese History* (1967), is a Festschrift presented to Fairbank on his sixtieth birthday. Paul M. Evans, *John Fairbank and the American Understanding of Modern China* (1988), offers a thorough intellectual and personal biography, in the process analyzing his scholarship. For a more critical treatment, see Steven W. Mosher, *China Misperceived: American Illusions and Chinese Reality* (1990). An obituary is in the *New York Times* (16 Sept. 1991).

JUSTUS D. DOENECKE

FENDER, Clarence Leonidas ("Leo") (*b.* 10 August 1909 in Anaheim, California; *d.* 21 March 1991 in Fullerton, California), inventor who developed some of the most popular electric guitars, the first fretted electric bass, and improved amplifiers.

Fender was born to the farmers Clarence (known as Monty) and Harriet Fender in a barn on their ranch between Anaheim and Fullerton. He attended Fullerton Union High School, graduating in 1928, and went on to attend Fullerton Junior College, where he majored in accounting, and completed his studies in 1930. Though he would eventually achieve fame as an inventor of electrical instruments and amplifiers, he received no formal training in electrical engineering. Electronics had been a hobby of Fender's since age thirteen when his uncle John West had shown him a homemade radio. Upon leaving college Fender took a bookkeeping position with Consolidated Ice and Cold Storage in Anaheim. He married Esther Klosky in 1934. They remained married until her death from cancer in 1979. In 1980 Fender married Phyllis Dalton. He never had children.

While still in high school Fender began building and repairing radios and amplifiers in a small home shop. Throughout the 1930s he continued to do repair work in his spare time and built several public address systems, which he rented out for dances. When Fender lost his job as an accountant for a tire company due to a management switch in 1939, he decided to turn his hobby into his career and opened up a full-scale radio repair shop, Fender Radio Service, in Fullerton. He soon expanded the shop into a retail outlet that, as his newspaper ads stated, specialized

Leo Fender, 1982. AP/WIDE WORLD PHOTOS

"in every branch of sound" and sold radios, phonographs, guitars, and public address systems. Fender also expanded his workforce, hiring the guitarist, street performer, and fellow inventor Clayton ("Doc") Kauffman to help with repairs. Due to the loss of an eye in a childhood accident, Fender was not called for military service in World War II. This allowed him to continue his ultimately revolutionary "tinkering" with sound amplification. In 1943 Fender and Kauffman made their first electric guitar. Kauffman left the company in 1946, the year that Fender began to work full-time at manufacturing guitars and amplifiers. The next year, he changed the name of his company to the Fender Electric Instrument Company.

Fender did not invent the electric guitar. In the early 1930s various jazz musicians and instrument makers experimented with amplifying guitars so that they could "hold their own" in big band ensembles. Most of these guitars were traditionally handcrafted hollow-body guitars with pickups added, though a few instrument makers had experimented with solid-body guitars. Fender, who wanted to make instruments that everyone could afford, decided that he would make solid-body guitars. The solid body not only reduced troublesome feedback problems that occurred with traditional hollow-body electrics at loud, dance-hall volumes, but it also reduced manufacturing time and cost. In the wake of World War II as big band music began to decline in popularity and smaller guitar-based ensembles playing country and blues were on the rise, Fender created a durable, inexpensive electric guitar with a tone that would become classic.

In the 1940s Fender primarily manufactured electric steel guitars and amplifiers, which were in demand by the increasingly popular Western swing bands such as Bob Wills and the Texas Playboys. As important to Fender's success as his ingenuity were his close ties to musicians. Although Fender never learned to play the guitar, he used musicians who lived and played in southern California as a sounding board, giving them prototype guitars and amplifiers to test in the field. He would often bring guitars and amplifiers straight from his workshop to the dance halls. Fender's willingness to work with musicians during his design process was a key reason for his success.

In 1948 Fender hired George Fullerton to manage the company and oversee production, allowing Fender to spend more time in his lab. The same year he began designing what would become the first commercially successful solid-body electric guitar, the Telecaster. With the Telecaster, Fender finally achieved the clean, bell-like tone that he had been seeking. Its tone had distinct highs and deep lows without much mid-range, which he felt muddied the tonal quality. The Telecaster pickups formed the foundation for the Fender sound. The Telecaster went on the market in 1950. Though derisively nicknamed "the canoe paddle" by

Fender's competition, the Telecaster was soon a commercial success.

Never content to rest on his laurels, Fender continued his advances in instrument making. In 1952 he released the Precision Bass, perhaps his most innovative accomplishment. Some earlier attempts had been made to develop electric basses and fretted acoustic basses, but all had retained the upright style of the traditional stand-up bass. Fender turned the music world on its ear by producing a fretted, electric bass shaped like an oversized guitar. The resulting instrument provided the strong sound and ease of playing that made it a cornerstone of postwar bands.

In 1954 Fender began production of what would become the most commercially successful electric guitar design in history, the Stratocaster. The Stratocaster improved on the Telecaster's design in several ways. At the urging of musicians, Fender added contours—a scooped out cut in the back of the guitar and a beveled section in front under the player's arm. These modifications allowed the guitar to fit more comfortably against the musician's body and gave it a unique look. Perhaps the most important addition was a new type of vibrato, or tremolo. Earlier vibratos tended to cause tuning problems. The Stratocaster vibrato sustained notes better than previous designs and allowed the guitarist to vary the pitch more widely without causing tuning problems. Though Fender probably did not foresee it, this quality allowed for the screaming, dive-bombing musical runs popularized by musicians such as Jimi Hendrix. Rock and roll was beginning to make its presence felt in 1954, and the Stratocaster became inexorably linked with the new music. By 1995, Fender had produced more than 1.4 million Stratocasters. In addition to his commercial success, Fender received recognition from both country and rock and roll musicians. In 1981 he received the Academy of Country Music's Pioneer Award and in 1992 he was inducted into the Rock and Roll Hall of Fame in Cleveland.

In 1965 Fender sold his company to CBS and started a consulting firm, CLF Research. He acted as a consultant for CBS-Fender and in 1971 began designing instruments and amplifiers for Music Man. In 1980 Fender and his old friend George Fullerton founded G&L Music Sales.

Fender continued to work on improving guitar and amplifier designs for the rest of his life. His hands-on, empirical style of invention and his willingness to listen to practicing musicians joined with his natural insight to create the instruments that helped define a new musical generation. At the age of eighty-one Leo Fender died at his Fullerton home, possibly from complications of Parkinson's disease. He is buried at Fairhaven Memorial Park in Santa Ana, California.

★

The best overview of Fender's career is Richard R. Smith,

Fender: The Sound Heard 'Round the World (1995). Two longtime associates of Fender's have written personal accounts of the Fender Company: Forrest White, *Fender: The Inside Story* (1994), and Bill Carson with Willie G. Moseley, *Bill Carson: My Life and Times with Fender Musical Instruments* (1998). See also George Fullerton, *Guitar Legends: The Evolution of the Guitar from Fender to G&L* (1994). An obituary is in the *New York Times* (23 Mar. 1991).

J. CHRISTOPHER JOLLY

FENWICK, Millicent Hammond (*b.* 25 February 1910 in New York City; *d.* 16 September 1992 in Bernardsville, New Jersey), Republican politician who won national attention for her aristocratic style and frequent disregard for party labels during terms as a New Jersey assemblywoman and U.S. congressional representative.

Fenwick was the second of three children born to Ogden Hammond and Mary Stevens. Her mother was the heir to a fortune based largely on real estate holdings in Hoboken, New Jersey. Her father was a financier who was also active in the Republican Party. In 1915 Fenwick's mother and more than 1,000 other passengers died on the liner *Lusitania* when it was struck by a German torpedo. In 1925 her father was appointed ambassador to Spain and took his daughter with him, interrupting her education at the Foxcroft School in Middleburg, Virginia. The move proved to be the end of her formal schooling, but she read widely while abroad and acquired a mastery of Spanish, French, and Italian. Returning to the United States in 1929, she took courses at the Columbia University Extension School.

Millicent Fenwick, 1982. AP/WIDE WORLD PHOTOS

She then studied philosophy under Bertrand Russell at the New School for Social Research in Manhattan, and they began a friendship that ultimately foundered because of Russell's hostility toward the United States.

In 1932 she married Hugh Fenwick. They settled in suburban Bernardsville, New Jersey, and had two children, but the marriage soon collapsed and they were divorced in 1938. Simultaneously Fenwick's inherited income faltered in the Great Depression, and she had to look for a job. She found employment at *Vogue* magazine, where she was soon recognized as a talented writer. Along with numerous features, she wrote *Vogue's Book of Etiquette* (1948), which sold more than 1 million copies. "Good behavior," she wrote in her introduction, "is everybody's business and good taste can be anyone's goal."

Post–World War II prosperity revived Fenwick's inherited income and she quit *Vogue* in 1952. She had served on the Bernardsville Board of Education from 1938 to 1947, and she once again became active in local affairs, working as a volunteer for the National Association for the Advancement of Colored People, a prison reform group, and the county's legal aid society. In 1958 she became the first woman elected to the Bernardsville borough council, where she helped build a municipal swimming pool without spending a cent of taxpayers' money.

Elected on the Republican ticket to the New Jersey Assembly in 1969, she pushed for better working conditions for migrant workers and urged a yes vote for the Equal Rights Amendment (ERA). When an opponent said he thought women should just be "kissable, cuddly and sweet-smelling," Fenwick demonstrated her notorious rapier wit. "That's what I thought of men too. I hope you haven't been disappointed as many times as I have."

After two years as New Jersey director of consumer affairs, she was elected to the U.S. House of Representatives in 1974, bucking the post-Watergate Democratic tide. She let neither her age (sixty-four) nor her gender inhibit her from speaking out on many issues. She also revealed that she smoked a meerschaum pipe (as an alternative to cigarettes), an eccentricity that coalesced with her Katharine Hepburn-esque accent to inspire Garry Trudeau, the creator of *Doonesbury,* to put her in the comic strip as the outspoken politico Lacey Davenport.

In Washington, Fenwick got to her congressional office at 6:30 A.M. and frequently stayed until 9:00 P.M. She answered much of her mail in longhand and was often galvanized into causes by a personal story. She instigated a major revision of interstate commerce regulations when a black trucker described the barriers the Interstate Commerce Commission put in the way of someone trying to get started as an independent owner-driver.

She regularly disagreed with her party about issues large and small, opposing, among other things, additional aid to a collapsing Republic of Vietnam and President Gerald Ford's decision to pardon Richard Nixon. At the end of her first year in Congress, the liberal Americans for Democratic Action gave her a 58 rating and a 65 the following year. She voted with the Republicans 44 percent of the time and against them 48 percent. Fenwick decried attempts to label her a liberal, insisting that her support of civil and constitutional rights, including the ERA, was a basically conservative position.

Voters responded to her independence, reelecting her by large majorities. In her subsequent years in Congress, she was especially active in the Helsinki Commission, a body she had proposed to monitor the 1975 Helsinki accords. The commission regularly publicized the Soviet Union's failure to honor the high ideals of this landmark human rights agreement. Some believe this barrage of bad publicity helped to discredit the communist system and thus contributed to ending the cold war.

In 1982 Fenwick ran for the U.S. Senate against Frank Lautenberg, a millionaire businessman. She campaigned with breathtaking candor, telling Jewish war veterans that Nazis should be permitted to march in Skokie, Illinois, and a group of postmasters that something should be done about exorbitant government pensions. She opposed tuition tax credits, the death penalty, and school prayer, three issues that New Jersey Republicans heavily favored. The National Organization for Women refused to endorse her, saying that they preferred a Democratically controlled Senate. Fenwick lost narrowly. President Ronald Reagan then appointed her to the United Nations Food and Agriculture Organization, on which she served until 1987. She died of cardiac arrest at the age of eighty-two in Bernardsville and was buried in St. Bernard's Cemetery there.

Millicent Fenwick's candor, wit, and independence added a new and valuable dimension to women's role in politics. She insisted that women should not cringe at being thought tough or aggressive. At the same time, she put a premium on performance, not power. "Influence [should] come out of the work you've done and the things you've stood for," she said in a speech at an International Women's Year meeting in Trenton, New Jersey.

★

Fenwick's papers are in Rutgers University's Alexander Library in New Brunswick, New Jersey. Her speeches from her terms as New Jersey representative are in the *Congressional Record* (1975–1983). Her book *Speaking Up* (1982) was a political commentary drawn from her speeches, op-ed articles, and congressional newsletter. She also wrote a brief reminiscence of her magazine career that appeared in *Vogue* (Apr. 1992). Peggy Lamson, *In the Vanguard: Six American Women in Public Life* (1979), includes a lengthy chapter on Fenwick. Other good profiles are Vera Glaser, "Millicent Fenwick: At Home in the House," *Saturday Evening Post* (19 Sept. 1975); "Millicent Fenwick," *Current Biography* (1977); "The Very Independent Mrs. Fenwick," *United Mainline Magazine* (Jan. 1982), and William E. Geist, "Millicent Fenwick: Marching to Her Own Drum," *New York Times Magazine* (27 June 1982). A brief treatment is in Joan N. Burstyn, ed., *Past and Promise: Lives of New Jersey Women* (1997). Obituaries are in the *New York Times* and *Washington Post* (both 17 Sept. 1992).

THOMAS FLEMING

FERRER, José (*b.* 8 January 1912 in Santurce, Puerto Rico; *d.* 26 January 1992 in Coral Gables, Florida), stage, screen, and television actor, and film director who won an Academy Award for his portrayal of Cyrano de Bergerac in the 1950 film of the same name.

The son of Spanish-born naturalized U.S. citizens, Rafael (a well-to-do attorney) and Maria Providencia Cintron, Ferrer had two sisters and a half brother. He spent his early childhood years in Puerto Rico—except for a stay on the U.S. mainland when he was only seven months old for successful treatment of a cleft palate. In 1918 his family moved permanently to the mainland, and the young Ferrer attended New York City public and private schools. A precocious achiever, at age fourteen he deferred entrance to Princeton at that university's recommendation and spent a

José Ferrer. © OSCAR WHITE/CORBIS

year at a Swiss boarding school. In 1933 he graduated from Princeton with a B.A. degree, having studied architecture and participated in college theater. To accommodate his parents he then "endured" study (1933–1934) in Romance languages at Columbia University.

Ferrer's professional theatrical career began during the summers of 1934 and 1935. In September 1935 he made his Broadway debut with a one-line part. Subsequently, he gained experience on Broadway, in summer stock, and touring—both as a performer and backstage. In 1940 he played the lead in a well-received Broadway revival of *Charlie's Aunt*. After further stints at acting, directing, and stage managing, on Broadway and touring, Ferrer scored as Iago in a much-touted 1943 production of *Othello* on Broadway. He continued to act and direct in New York City and on tour. His performance in a splendid 1946 Broadway revival of Edmond-Eugène–Alexis Rostand's *Cyrano de Bergerac* won him a Tony Award for best dramatic actor.

His theatrical peak came in the early 1950s: Ferrer directed and costarred in a hit revival (1950) of *Twentieth Century;* he produced, directed, and played a lead in the Pulitzer Prize–winning drama *The Shrike* a performance that won him a Tony in 1952; that year he won another Tony for his direction of *The Shrike* and also directed *Stalag 17* and *The Fourposter;* and in 1953 he directed the comedy hit *We're No Angels*.

In subsequent years, such consistent success eluded Ferrer. He did direct a well-received drama, *The Andersonville Trial,* in 1959, but otherwise his theater career went into what Ferrer described as a "free fall." Three Broadway musicals flopped (1958, 1959, 1963). Although occasionally appearing off-Broadway into the 1970s, he worked mostly—both as a performer and director—in American and English regional theater. Ferrer's last Broadway appearance was replacing the lead in *Man of La Mancha* (1966–1967); he later undertook this function with various touring companies. His last stage appearances were in 1990—in the United States at the Paper Mill Playhouse in Millburn, New Jersey, in the musical *Fanny,* and in England at the Chichester Festival, in a musical version of Eugène Ionesco's *Rhinoceros*.

Like his theater career, Ferrer's film career began well—as *Time* magazine said, he was "a rare bird: a character actor who became a bona fide movie star." Initially he fit movies in between his intense theatrical activity, making his film debut in *Joan of Arc* (1948) as the Dauphin. He earned an Oscar nomination (best supporting actor) for his role, as he later did for his portrayal of the dwarfish Toulouse-Lautrec in the film *Moulin Rouge* (1952). He won an Oscar for best actor for his performance as Cyrano in the 1950 film version of the play. Ferrer had several other acclaimed roles in the 1950s, including the sharp defense

counsel in *The Caine Mutiny* (1953), for which he received a British Academy Award nomination.

Between 1955 and 1962 the ambitious, energetic Ferrer also directed seven films. *The Great Man* (1956), a compelling view of the television industry, was cowritten by Ferrer, who also played a major role. However, overall his films from these years fared poorly commercially and critically; for all their "technical correctness" they were described as snail-paced and deemed to lack warmth, even when Ferrer cast himself (for example, in the 1955 World War II action drama *Cockleshell Heroes* or as the martyred Captain Dreyfus in the 1958 *I Accuse*). His last directorial film effort was the unsatisfactory 1962 remake of *State Fair*.

In the early 1960s his film career lost momentum. Ferrer took parts indiscriminately, both in the movies and on television, to (as he put it) "pay the bills." From 1962 until his death Ferrer appeared in more than fifty movies. Some, such as *Ship of Fools* (1965), a superior filming of the novel, and *Old Explorers* (1990), a unusual comic treatment of old age, had substance. Most did not, being generally low-budget action or thriller productions, such as *Stop Train 349* (1964), *Dracula's Dog* (1978), *The Evil That Men Do* (1985), and *Hired to Kill* (1991).

Such movies made little demand on Ferrer's talent, as did his television work, which included commercial voice-overs, made-for-television movies such as *Samson and Delilah* (1984), miniseries including *The French Atlantic Affair* (1979), and guest appearances on shows such as *Magnum, P.I.* (1981) and *Murder, She Wrote* (1984). He usually played a "heavy" of one sort or another, describing his parts as "roles where I play the villain or . . . go up in flames in the end."

Possessed of versatile, sophisticated intelligence and extraordinary energy, Ferrer could in turn be charming and cold. An acknowledged womanizer, he enjoyed a hedonistic, expensive lifestyle. Ferrer was married four times and had six children: His first wife was the actress Uta Hagen, to whom he was married from 1937 to 1948; they had one child. From 1948 to 1953 he was married to the actress Phyllis Hill. In 1953 he married the popular Irish American singer Rosemary Clooney; before their divorce in 1961, Clooney and Ferrer had five children, including a son, Miguel, who became an actor. (The actor George Clooney is Ferrer's nephew.) Ferrer was briefly remarried to Rosemary Clooney from 1966 to 1967. He married Stella Magee at the end of his life; the couple never revealed their marriage date. He died in Doctors Hospital in Coral Gables, Florida, after a short cancer-based illness. He is buried in San Juan, Puerto Rico.

The five-foot, eleven-inch-tall Ferrer viewed himself as "a regular looking guy" with "short legs and a big head." Although (as one critic said) he was "without leading-man looks," Ferrer's voice was resonant and strong, a distinctive, somewhat gruff baritone that he used to good purpose. A bravura, vigorous, multifaceted talent, he cut a wide swath, especially in the theater, during the 1940s and early 1950s. He was the first actor ever to receive the National Medal of Arts (1985); he also received honorary degrees from Princeton University and the University of Puerto Rico. In 1981 he was named to the Theater Hall of Fame. Ferrer's film and television career never equaled the early success of his career in the theater. He verged on becoming a star and a major force, but his later career was undistinguished.

★

There is a collection of clippings on Ferrer at the Billy Rose Theatre Collection of the New York Public Library of the Performing Arts at Lincoln Center. A detailed overview is Michael Buckley, "Jose Ferrer," *Films in Review* (Feb. 1987): 67–76; (Mar. 1987): 131–145. Also see articles on Ferrer in Gerald Bordman, ed., *The Oxford Companion to the American Theatre* (1984), and Amy Unterburger, ed., *International Dictionary of Films and Filmmakers*, vol. 3, *Actors and Actresses* (3d ed., 1997). He is prominent in Rosemary Clooney's autobiography, *This for Remembrance* (1977). Obituaries are in the *Los Angeles Times* and *New York Times* (both 27 Jan. 1992), London *Independent* and London *Daily Telegraph* (both 28 Jan. 1992), and *Time* (10 Feb. 1992).

DANIEL J. LEAB

FINE, Reuben (*b.* 11 October 1914 in New York City; *d.* 26 March 1993 in New York City), chess grandmaster and Freudian psychiatrist, prolific author in both chess and psychiatry.

Fine was the only child of Jacob Fine, a businessman, and Bertha Nedner, a homemaker. Of Russian-Jewish parentage, Fine was only two years old when his father abandoned the family. He grew up in poor circumstances in the East Bronx, a sensitive, highly intelligent child with an affinity for mathematics and foreign languages. At the age of eight Fine learned chess from an uncle but did not become seriously interested in the game until his graduation from Townsend Harris High School (a school for gifted students) in 1929, when he joined the Manhattan and Marshall Chess Clubs in Manhattan. In his book *Lessons from My Games* (1958), Fine described this as the start of his real passion for chess, which, he wrote, would last for eight years.

Fine found his studies at the City College of New York (CCNY) relatively undemanding and he spent much of his spare time playing chess. He advanced rapidly through the ranks of talented young players, winning Marshall Club championships for 1931–1932 and 1932–1933 and also winning the first of his seven United States Open championships in 1932. In 1933 Fine made the first of his three appearances playing for the American team in the international team tournament. In his formative years, family finances forced Fine to play chess for stakes. During this time he became adept at speed chess (ten seconds per move for each player) and blindfold chess (literally, chess without sight of the board or pieces).

Fine graduated from CCNY with a B.S. degree in 1933 and began to publish technical works on chess, starting with his contributions to the *Chess Review,* which began publication the same year. For several years during the Great Depression he lived the life of a chess professional. Fine made his first trip to Europe in 1935, representing the United States on first board in the international team tournament and gaining his first international success winning the annual Hastings Christmas tournament in 1935–1936. In the United States chess championship tournament in 1936, Fine tied for third place behind Samuel Reshevsky, who would become his chief rival for American chess supremacy. That summer Fine began an extended European tour. From June 1936 until January 1938 Fine played in thirteen tournaments, winning or tying for first place in eight. During this period he competed on equal or better terms with the strongest players of the day.

While living in Amsterdam, Fine met Emma Thea Keesing, a newspaper reporter and daughter of a major Dutch publisher. On 1 September 1937 Keesing became the first of Fine's five wives. (The first four of his five marriages ended in divorce.) For several months that year Fine served as an assistant to world champion Dr. Max Euwe during Euwe's world championship match with the former champion Alexander Alekhine.

In January 1938 Fine returned to the United States with his wife. Having tired of the constant grind of top-level competitive chess, he returned to CCNY and obtained an M.S. degree in education in 1939. In 1938 and 1940 he finished second to Reshevsky in U.S. chess championship tournaments. In both events Fine played Reshevsky in the final round, needing a victory to finish first; he could only draw each game, however, despite having a winning advantage in the latter one. He would never succeed in winning the U.S. championship in four attempts.

Fine participated in only one other international tournament. In the fall of 1938, the Dutch radio company AVRO organized a double-round event with the eight strongest players in the world. By this point Fine had lost his earlier passion for chess. His request to the AVRO organizers to release him from his contract to play was refused. Thus obligated to play, he scored five wins and a draw in his first six games. He eventually tied for first with Paul Keres, but World War II intervened before either player could challenge Alekhine to a match for the world's championship.

In the fall of 1941 Fine began work with the Federal Trade Commission as a translator and editor. After two and one-half years he began research work for the Department of the Navy in May 1944 as part of a team employed to determine likely surfacings of German U-boats and the location of Japanese kamikaze attacks upon American ships. In a final effort to win the U.S. chess championship, he finished second to Arnold Denker in the 1944 event. In 1944 he and his wife Emma were divorced.

Fine played less competitive chess during the late 1940s as he embarked upon a career as a psychoanalyst. He married Sonya Lebeaux in 1946. This marriage produced a son and a daughter, Fine's only children. Fine moved to California, where he enrolled at the University of Southern California, receiving a Ph.D. in clinical psychology in 1948. When invited to play in a 1947 tournament to determine the world champion, which because of chess politics did not take place until a year a later, Fine declined, stating that he did not wish to take time away from his dissertation research.

Fine established a private practice as a psychologist and psychoanalyst in Los Angeles between 1945 and 1948 before returning to New York City, where he was a clinical psychologist for the Veterans Administration and taught at CCNY. He established a private practice in New York and became an internationally respected Freudian psychoanalyst and prolific author, writing twenty books on psychoanalysis, including *A History of Psychoanalysis* (1979), the standard work on the subject. With Theodore Reik, Fine helped organize the National Psychological Association of Psychoanalysis. He was a leading force in the New York Center for Psychoanalytic Training, supervising the training of psychoanalytic candidates. His other psychoanalytic works include *Freud: A Critical Re-evaluation of His Theories* (1962), *The Healing of the Mind: The Technique of Psychoanalytic Psychotherapy* (1971), *The Psychoanalytic Vision* (1981), and *The Meaning of Love in Human Experience* (1985).

A man of strong views and definitive conclusions, Fine's unshaken emphasis on Freudian interpretations extended into his own controversial observations of the struggle manifested on the chessboard. To Fine, chess represented a play substitute for the art of war, underscored by the father-son conflict in which the opponent's king is the target of one's hostile aggression. His monograph on the subject, *The Psychology of the Chess Player* (1967), remains the definitive statement for a Freudian analysis of chess, which Fine applied exhaustively in his assessment of the games of the 1972 world championship match between Bobby Fischer and Boris Spassky. More highly regarded were Fine's many and varied technical writings on chess, which helped to popularize the game and make it accessible to millions. One of the best and most prolific writers on chess from the 1930s to the 1980s, Fine's works include *Basic Chess Endings* (1941), *Chess the Easy Way* (1942), *Practical Chess Openings* (1948), *The World's Great Chess Games* (1952), and *The Middle Game in Chess* (1953).

By the 1970s Fine was living on the Upper West Side of Manhattan; subsequently, he moved to Manhattan's Upper East Side. With an IQ somewhere between 180 and 200, he had many and varied interests, including art, music, history, and mathematics. He also spoke six languages fluently. In the final years of his life Fine was physically limited by a series of strokes, but he continued to write. In January 1993 he suffered a severe stroke and entered Saint Luke's–Roosevelt Medical Center in Manhattan, where he died from complications of pneumonia on 26 March 1993.

Fine was that rare individual who achieved professional distinction in two different fields. A dogmatic and contentious man who had little patience for diverging opinions, his frustration and bitterness in failing to attain the pinnacle in chess cast a sour pall on his relations with officials of the U.S. and international chess federations. Yet his deep passion for chess never truly deserted him. He continued to follow the game, critique it, and occasionally participate in speed chess competitions and exhibition games until the final years of his life. Fine had the ability to convey technical information in clear, dynamic prose that reflected his profound understanding for the game. His passionate belief in the virtues of Freudian analysis and his enormous capacity for literary endeavor led to a prolific output of books, monographs, and articles in psychiatry. He was instrumental in the organization of the Divisions of Psychoanalysis and Psychotherapy within the American Psychological Association, serving as founding president of both divisions. Coming from a modest background, Fine sought to democratize the profession of psychoanalysis by opening access to deserving candidates and improving training facilities for psychologists.

★

Fine's chess notebooks are in the Library of Congress. His *Chess Marches On!* (1945) has some autobiographical information. Fine describes his chess career through the 1940s in *Lessons From My Games: A Passion for Chess* (1958). His unsuccessful attempts to become the U.S. chess champion are detailed in Gene H. McCormick and Andy Soltis, *The U.S. Chess Championship, 1845–1985* (rev. ed., 1997). Bruce Pandolfini, "Reuben Fine: The Man Who Might Have Been King," *Chess Life* (Oct. 1984), contains an interview with Fine emphasizing his chess career and his impressions of his fellow chess masters. Obituaries are in the *New York Times* (28 Mar. 1993), *Chess Life* (June 1993), and *The American Psychologist* 50, no. 1 (Jan. 1995): 38.

EDWARD J. TASSINARI

FINKELSTEIN, Louis (*b.* 14 June 1895 in Cincinnati, Ohio; *d.* 29 November 1991 in New York City), chancellor of the Jewish Theological Seminary for more than three decades and author of scores of books about Judaism.

Finkelstein was one of five children born to Lithuanian immigrants Simon J. Finkelstein and Hannah Brager.

Rabbi Louis Finkelstein. LIBRARY OF CONGRESS

They settled in Cincinnati but later moved to the Browns-ville section of Brooklyn in New York City when he was seven years old. His father, an Orthodox rabbi, supervised his early Jewish education while he attended public high school for his secular studies. His mother was a home-maker. By the age of sixteen Finkelstein already had an extensive knowledge of the Hebrew Bible. After high school he simultaneously attended the City College of New York and the Jewish Theological Seminary. He graduated from the City College in 1915 and in 1918 received his Ph.D. from Columbia University. A year later he was ordained at the Jewish Theological Seminary. He was the first seminary student to graduate earning *hatarat hora'a,* an advanced rabbinic degree that authorized him to render legal deci-sions in matters of Jewish law.

In 1920 Finkelstein took his first position as rabbi of Congregation Kehilath Israel in the Bronx section of New York City, where he officiated for ten years. However, he retained his close association with the Jewish Theological Seminary, returning there a year after his ordination to teach Talmud. On 5 March 1922 he married Carmel Bent-wich, with whom he had three children. Finkelstein's ca-reer as a teacher continued and in 1924 he began teaching theology, becoming a professor of theology in 1931.

As his career at the seminary blossomed Finkelstein be-gan taking on greater administrative responsibility. In 1934 he became the assistant to the president and in 1937, the provost. In 1940 he began a thirty-two-year reign as pres-ident (in 1951 the title was changed to chancellor) of the Jewish Theological Seminary.

During the years that Finkelstein served as provost, Cy-rus Adler, the seminary's president, was ill. Consequently, Finkelstein ran many of the institution's day-to-day opera-tions. When Adler died, Finkelstein had already established his vision of leadership for the seminary: in addition to serving as a training institute for rabbis and teachers, it had to support the idea that religion can impact the quality of American life. His vision called for the institution to grow from a "school of Jewish history" to a "school of religion and ethics, not only for ourselves . . . but for the world at large."

During Finkelstein's tenure the seminary introduced many programs. In the early 1930s the idea of an Institute for Religious and Social Studies was born. Finkelstein de-veloped this idea and in 1938 he established the institute, the seminary's first, with a series of lectures. In 1944 the seminary inaugurated an Inter-American Commission on Judaism to encourage Jews from Latin American countries to attend the school. In 1946 the idea to open a West Coast branch of the seminary, named the University of Judaism, was presented. It was established in 1947, the same year that Camp Ramah, a highly intensive learning and religious camping experience for youth, was founded in Wisconsin. During the 1950s the Cantors Institute and the Lehman Institute of Ethics were created. In 1966 the library was ravaged by a fire and most of the seminary's collection of Judaica was damaged. By 1969 the library had been restored and the collection of Hebrew literature replaced. Always an advocate for interfaith communication, in 1968 Finkelstein announced his last grand initiative before his retirement in 1972, an Institute for Advanced Studies in the Humanities.

Finkelstein used his public relations skills well and he saw to it that the seminary achieved national prominence. On 15 October 1951 Finkelstein, with his bright eyes, flow-ing hair, and thick beard, graced the cover of *Time* maga-zine. In 1944 he arranged for NBC to establish a radio program under the auspices of the seminary to cater to Jews and non-Jews alike. The program succeeded in accom-plishing several of Finkelstein's goals: to heighten the spir-itual level of the community, to promote Judaism, to bring people of all faiths together, and to highlight the seminary. In 1948 the seminary expanded to television, first on CBS and in 1951 on NBC. The program ran under the name *The Eternal Light,* and both the radio and television programs won numerous awards.

Finkelstein's drive to put the seminary in the limelight served him well. He was a close contact and resource to many high-ranking political figures, and in 1957 he secured Chief Justice Earl Warren of the U.S. Supreme Court to spend a Sabbath at the seminary. In addition, in 1940 he was appointed to serve as the official Jewish representative to President Franklin D. Roosevelt's commission on peace. President Dwight D. Eisenhower invited him to give the invocation at his inauguration. In 1963 President John F. Kennedy sent him to Rome as part of an American delegation to the installation of Pope Paul VI.

In addition to his numerous tasks as president of the seminary, Finkelstein managed to make time daily for the study of Jewish texts and for writing. Friends said he rose every morning at 4:00 A.M. to study and write until he went to synagogue at 7:00 A.M. Some of the 337 works he published, including more than 100 books, are *Jews: Their History, Culture, and Religion,* four vols. (1949); *Jewish Self-Government in the Middle Ages* (1924); and *New Light from the Prophets* (1969).

Finkelstein's main interest was study and research into the history and literature of classical Judaism. One area of Finkelstein's expertise was the study of the Pharisees, a Jewish sect in second temple times from which modern tradition developed. His interpretations caused controversy because of his claims that economic and social conditions influenced Pharisaic ideology. In addition, Finkelstein published more than 100 critical investigations of fundamental Jewish documents, searching for the historical and social conditions reflected in liturgical texts such as the *Shema,* the highest prayer in Judaism. In all his work Finkelstein paid fastidious attention to detail, especially to variations in texts.

Even in his retirement, Finkelstein continued writing and studying in his home. When he could no longer walk to synagogue for services, his former students turned his home into a synagogue, assembling the quorum of ten men needed for prayer. Finkelstein died in 1991 of Parkinson's disease.

Finkelstein achieved his goals of widening Jewish life around the country, educating the non-Jewish community about Jews, and transforming the Jewish Theological Seminary into a major institution of Jewish scholarship. All the while, he continued his first love: the study of classic Jewish texts.

★

Finkelstein's manuscripts and personal papers are in the archives of the Jewish Theological Seminary in New York City. Information about Finkelstein's contributions to Judaism can be found in Herbert Parzen, *Architects of Conservative Judaism* (1964), band Marshall Sklare, *Conservative Judaism: An American Religious Movement* (1972). An extensive summary of his career at the Jewish Theological Seminary can be found in Jack Wertheimer, ed., *Tradition Renewed: A History of the Jewish Theological Seminary,* vol. 1 (1997). Additional information can be found in the *Encyclopedia Judaica,* vol. 6 (1971). Obituaries are in the *New York Times* (30 Nov. 1991) and *Time* (9 Dec. 1991).

MOLLY JALENAK WEXLER

FISH, Hamilton   (*b.* 7 December 1888 in Garrison, New York; *d.* 18 January 1991 in Cold Spring, New York), sports hero and military officer who, as a congressman, became a leading conservative and isolationist critic of the New Deal.

Fish, the son of Hamilton Fish, a politician and lawyer, and Emily Mann, a homemaker, was a member of a New York political dynasty that traced its roots back to Peter Stuyvesant, the Dutch governor who surrendered Manhattan to the English in 1664. His grandfather, also Hamilton Fish, was the Empire State's senator and governor before becoming the U.S. secretary of state. His father served in the U.S. House of Representatives, as Speaker of the New York State Assembly, and in the U.S. Treasury Department. Fish's own son later served in Congress. Befitting a member of the Hudson Valley aristocracy, Fish was educated at the Chateau de Lancy in Geneva, Switzerland; at Groton School in Groton, Massachusetts; and at St. Mark's School in Southborough, Massachusetts, before he entered Harvard in 1906 as a member of the storied class of 1910. Strongly built at six feet three inches tall and weighing 200 pounds, he captained the Harvard football team and was named tackle on Walter Camp's "all-time, All-American team." Fish is a member of the College Football Hall of Fame. After graduating cum laude with a B.A., Fish studied law for the 1910–1911 academic year at Harvard and then traveled to tsarist Russia. On returning he won election to the New York Assembly as a Theodore "Teddy" Roosevelt Progressive. During Fish's tenure in Albany (1912–1916), his friend Franklin D. Roosevelt attempted to recruit him for the Democratic Party.

When the United States entered World War I, Fish was commissioned (15 July 1917) a captain in a unit that subsequently became the 369th Infantry, the "Harlem Hellfighters." As the white commander of black soldiers, Fish demonstrated his lifelong commitment to civil rights and black advancement long before a national movement emerged. His unit spent more time in the trenches than any other American regiment and suffered 30 percent casualties. Fish won a Silver Star, the croix de guerre, and a

Hamilton Fish, 1941. © BETTMANN/CORBIS

citation in General Orders. He graduated from the Army Staff College before his discharge as a major (14 May 1919).

Fish's career in national politics began in 1919, after Edward Platt's unexpected resignation created a vacancy in the Twenty-sixth Congressional District. Fish was elected to the House of Representatives in 1920. On his first day in the House, Fish introduced a resolution to create a tomb for America's "unknown soldier." His commitment to his comrades was absolute. He helped found the American Legion and later supported bonus payments for veterans. In 1920 he married Grace Chapin, with whom he had two children. During his first decade in the House, Fish endorsed antilynching legislation, prison reform, German food relief, and prison sentences for those who had betrayed President Warren Harding. Although he supported traditional Republican positions on balanced budgets, high tariffs, and tight money, his several forays at higher office failed. Hardly a model isolationist, he endorsed American membership in the World Court, participation in disarmament conferences, and the Kellogg Pact (1928). Disillusioned during a visit to the Soviet Union, Fish convinced the House to form a special committee to examine domestic communist activity. The investigation found little (one raid netted only lettuce), and its harsh recommendations in 1931 were ignored. But Fish became notable for his "windmilling arms, roof-raising voice and not-quite-legal logic."

The coming of the New Deal transformed Congress from a quiet Republican preserve into a dynamo of action. Fish informed President Franklin D. Roosevelt on 24 February 1933 that Congress would provide "any power that you may need," but he soon viewed the torrent of legislation as dangerous to "individual liberties and human rights." He believed that recognition of the Soviet Union was unwise. When Roosevelt argued that religious freedom still existed in the Soviet Union, Fish scornfully said the president should invite Joseph Stalin to the United States and baptize him in the White House pool. Gradually Fish came to see Roosevelt as a class traitor, and his opinion of the reform administration turned rancid. As the ranking Republican on both the Rules and Foreign Affairs Committees, Fish supported Social Security and the minimum wage, but he also called for withdrawal of American troops from the Far East, naval parity with Japan, a referendum on any war, and nondiscriminatory arms embargoes. Communism and foreign war were his greatest fears. In October 1938 Fish, standing on a platform festooned with swastikas in Madison Square Garden, accused the administration of undermining relations with Germany, Japan, and Italy. He subsequently organized the Committee to Keep America out of Foreign Wars (1939). During Fish's trip to Europe (August 1939), the German foreign minister Joachim von Ribbentrop refused Fish's offer to mediate the Danzig (Gdansk) question. After 1940, certain that President Roosevelt secretly sought to enter the conflict, Fish opposed repeal of the arms embargo and twice voted against conscription.

As a congressman Fish loyally served his constituents, including one named Roosevelt. But during the fall of 1940 both the president and Wendell Willkie found Fish's attitudes appalling and opposed his renomination. On 28 October, Roosevelt explained to an appreciative Democratic crowd that his efforts to aid Great Britain would never have borne fruit if "the decision had been left to [Congressman Joseph] Martin, [Congressman Bruce] Barton, and Fish."

President Roosevelt had practiced the cadence, and the audience loved it. Willkie clearly perceived defeat in their chanted response. Nevertheless, Fish was easily reelected, and in 1941 he led the Republican opposition to a "fascist" Lend-Lease Act that made Roosevelt a "dictator." In response Roosevelt refused to let Fish enter the White House, although some observers believed the reason was not politics but a long-forgotten slight to Roosevelt's mother. The animosity continued despite Fish's goal of "final victory, cost what it may in blood, treasure, and tears." In 1942 one of his aides, George Hill, was convicted of allowing pro-Nazi groups to use his office's franking privileges, yet Fish was still powerful enough to survive politically. Fish's repeated offers to lead black troops again were ignored. In November 1944 disfavor and a district gerrymander finally cost Fish reelection.

In the postwar United States, Fish quietly managed his business holdings and became a prolific author. Publisher of *Today's World* from 1946 to 1947, he was militantly anticommunist, and in 1954 he founded the isolationist American Political Action Committee. Fish sought internal strength for the United States and believed foreign commitments would cause war. He testified before the House against joining the Southeast Asia Treaty Organization (SEATO) in 1955. Fish's first wife died in 1960. In 1967 he married Marie Choubaroff Blackton; they had no children. His second wife died in 1970, and in 1976 he married Alice Curtis Desmond. They had no children and divorced in 1984. His series of anticommunist, anti-Roosevelt volumes culminated in *Tragic Deception* (1983), published when he was ninety-five. Fish lived long enough to watch with "enormous pleasure" the rebirth of American conservatism after 1970. In 1988 he married Lydia Ambrogio. On his 100th birthday the unrepentant aristocrat recalled his vendetta with the president, stating, "I don't hate Roosevelt—but frankly I despise him." Fish died of heart failure and is interred in the family plot at St. Philip's Church in the Highlands in Garrison.

★

Fish's papers are in the Alice Desmond and Hamilton Fish Public Library in Garrison. Fish's beliefs are presented in his autobiography *Memoir of an American Patriot: Hamilton Fish* (1991), which has an epilogue by Brian Mitchell; as well as in his other works *The Challenge of World Communism* (1946), *The Red Plotters* (1947), *FDR: The Other Side of the Coin* (1976), *The American People are Living on Top of a Nuclear Volcano* (1976), and *Tragic Deception: FDR and America's Involvement in World War II* (1983). He also wrote *New York State: The Battleground of the Revolutionary War* (1976). Fish is remembered primarily as an unthinking isolationist, but more nuanced interpretations are in Richard Kay Hanks, "Hamilton Fish and American Isolationism, 1920–1944," Ph.D. diss., University of California, Riverside, 1971; and Anthony C. Troncone, "Hamilton Fish Senior and the Politics of American Nationalism, 1912–1945," Ph.D. diss., Rutgers University, 1993. An obituary is in the *New York Times* (20 Jan. 1991).

GEORGE J. LANKEVICH

FISHER, M(ary) F(rances) K(ennedy)   (*b.* 3 July 1908 in Albion, Michigan; *d.* 22 June 1992 in Glen Ellen, California), author who specialized in, and often combined, a passion for food and autobiographical musings.

Fisher came from a family of journalists; her father, Rex Brenton Kennedy, co-owned and edited a newspaper in Albion. Her mother, Edith Oliver Holbrook, was a homemaker who took pride in her cultured education and background.

When Fisher, the oldest of four children, was two, her father sold his interest in the Michigan paper and took his family to the West Coast. They eventually settled in the southern California town of Whittier, where Rex Kennedy edited and published a newspaper. The Episcopalian Fishers were never entirely accepted in the predominantly Quaker community; their outsider status gave the future writer valuable perspective.

Fisher attended several schools, some public, some private, during her early life, and then as a young adult. She briefly attended Illinois College and Occidental College before meeting and quickly marrying a University of Califor-

M. F. K. Fisher, 1971. AP/WIDE WORLD PHOTOS

nia at Los Angeles graduate student, Alfred Young Fisher, in 1929; they had no children. Fisher enabled his bride to escape from her insular California community when he pursued a doctorate at the University of Dijon. She fell in love with France and its food and studied art at the university.

Returning to the United States in 1932, the Fishers spent three years living at the Kennedy family's second home at Laguna Beach, California. While Al Fisher tried to find work teaching, his wife wrote. The marriage was already weak, however, and when they met the painter Dillwyn Parrish, Fisher fell in love with him.

After much soul-searching and an attempt at living with both men, she settled down with Parrish in Switzerland. In 1937 she divorced Fisher and married Parrish; she also produced her first book about food, the partly historical, partly philosophical work *Serve It Forth*. Within a year Parrish began a fatal struggle with Buerger's disease. The couple returned to the United States and tried a number of medical treatments before settling at a California ranch that they named Bareacres. The couple had no children.

Overwhelmed by pain, Parrish committed suicide in 1941. That same year also marked the publication of Fisher's second book, *Consider the Oyster*, a witty treatise on her favorite bivalve. She continued writing. *How to Cook a Wolf*, a group of essays on coping with wartime food shortages, came out in 1942, and her first autobiographical work, *The Gastronomical Me*, was published in 1943. In it she established two patterns in her work. One was melding memories of food and life. The other was revealing emotions in her life while hiding details about it.

Fisher worked briefly as a Hollywood screenwriter in the early 1940s. In 1943 she gave birth to a daughter. A year and a half later she met and married Donald Friede, a New York editor and publisher. Their daughter was born in 1946, but the marriage did not last. In 1949 Fisher's mother died, and the writer returned home to escape from her emotionally and fiscally insolvent marriage and to care for her ailing father. She and her daughters remained with Rex Kennedy in Whittier until his death in 1953; she obtained a divorce from Friede in 1951. During this period Fisher worked on magazine articles and on her landmark translation of Jean Anthelme Brillat-Savarin's *Physiology of Taste* (1949).

After her father's death, Fisher and her daughters settled in St. Helena in California's Napa Valley, although they journeyed frequently to France. She began a long-term relationship with the *New Yorker* magazine, for which she penned perceptive essays on food and life. Many of these were eventually reprinted in *With Bold Knife and Fork* (1969). In 1954 her first five books were published together

as *The Art of Eating*, a volume considered by many critics to represent her best work.

In 1970 the architect David Pleydell-Bouverie offered to design Fisher a two-room home on his estate in Glen Ellen, California. Aside from sojourns in France and occasional other trips, Fisher lived until her death in what she dubbed "Last House." She spent her last twenty years productively, although arthritis and the Parkinson's disease from which she eventually died slowed her down. Among her later books were *A Considerable Town*, memories of Marseilles (1978); *As They Were*, essays about various places she had known (1983); and *The Boss Dog* (1991), a children's book.

After her death at Last House in 1992, Fisher was cremated and her ashes were scattered by her family. A number of books that Fisher had been working on before her death were issued posthumously, including *Last House* (1995), a collection of essays focusing on the physical and emotional experiences of aging; *Stay Me, Oh Comfort Me* (1993), a group of journals and stories from her young adulthood, and *M. F. K. Fisher: A Life in Letters* (1997), in which correspondence ranging in time from her first marriage until just before her death showcases her moods and qualities, revealing her in turn as testy, courageous, funny, and idealistic.

Fisher was among the first American writers to take food seriously, and although she never enjoyed a best-selling readership, her works spoke to an intelligent audience who shared her perception that the preparation and consumption of what nourishes the body is anything but mundane. Writing of her growing-up years in *To Begin Again* (1992), Fisher noted, "Increasingly, I saw, felt, understood the importance, especially between people who love and trust one another, of a full sharing of one of our three main hungers, which are for food, for love, and for shelter. . . . Since we must eat to live, why not make the best of it and see that it is a pleasure, something more than a mere routine necessity like breathing?" Fisher spent a lifetime making the best of it.

★

The papers of M. F. K. Fisher are housed at Radcliffe University's Schlesinger Library. Aside from her autobiographical works, readers will enjoy the essay on Fisher in Betty Fussell's *Masters of American Cookery* (1983) and the genial heroine worship of Jeannette Ferrary's *Between Friends: M. F. K. Fisher and Me* (1991). Insightful profiles of the author during her life include Maya Angelou's "M. F. K. Fisher" in *People* (24 Jan. 1983) and Molly O'Neill's "Pungent Wisdom from a Kitchen Olympian" in the *New York Times* (28 Feb. 1990). An obituary is in the *New York Times* (23 June 1992). *M. F. K.: A Portrait of M. F. K. Fisher* (1992) is an hour-long documentary video by Barbara Wornum.

TINKY "DAKOTA" WEISBLAT

FLETCHER, Joseph Francis, III (*b.* 10 April 1905 in Newark, New Jersey; *d.* 28 October 1991 in Charlottesville, Virginia), biomedical ethicist who influenced changes in teaching and textbooks dealing with abortion, euthanasia, genetic control, and other fundamental issues.

Fletcher was the older of two children of Joseph Francis Fletcher, II, a businessman, and Julia Davis, a homemaker. Fletcher's mother became sole caretaker of her children when she and his father separated in 1914. Julia Fletcher moved her children from New Jersey to her former home in Fairmont, West Virginia, where young Fletcher particularly enjoyed baseball, swimming, canoeing, and acting in school plays. He revealed an enterprising spirit by undertaking an office job one summer at the Consolidated Coal Company, and the following summer by working as a trapper for another smaller coal mine. He finished his four-year high school in three years, graduating in 1921.

Fletcher's experience with the hardships of coal miners "radicalized" him, as he later put it, by the age of fifteen. Gravitating to leftist literature, he took a special interest in the plays of George Bernard Shaw and the works of H. L. Mencken and Karl Marx. At age sixteen Fletcher entered West Virginia University at Morgantown. Before the year was out, he landed in jail for a night for publicly defending the United Mineworkers Union, which was legally prohibited.

Influenced by the rector of the Episcopal Church in Morgantown, Fletcher decided in his sophomore year to attend divinity school. Fletcher believed he could expand upon his social idealism, which he perceived to be closely linked to Christianity, at divinity school. He graduated from West Virginia in 1925, then entered the Berkeley Divinity School at Yale in Connecticut, earning a bachelor of divinity degree in 1929. Meanwhile, on 5 September 1928 he married Forrest Hatfield; the couple had two children.

After pursuing graduate study in economic history at Yale University, he moved to London, where he studied part-time from 1930 to 1932 at the London School of Economics under the guidance of the writer R. H. Tawney and served as curate at St. Peter's Church. During this period Fletcher developed a deep conviction of the necessity of fusing scholarly pursuits with activism, an approach taken from Marx, who wrote about the imperative of balancing "theory and practice." It was by this principle that Fletcher lived and from which he constructed his most famous works.

In 1932, having received his doctorate of systematic theology from the University of London, Fletcher returned to the United States to teach at St. Mary's Junior College in Raleigh, North Carolina. He also taught labor relations at the University of North Carolina at Chapel Hill. In 1935

Joseph Fletcher. COURTESY OF DR. MARY FAITH MARSHALL

he and his family moved to Cincinnati, where he was the dean of St. Paul's Cathedral from 1936 to 1940 and also the dean of the Graduate School of Applied Religion from 1936 to 1944. In keeping with his philosophy, he promoted the teaching of community involvement as well as pastoral care.

Fletcher also taught both labor history and the Bible at the University of Cincinnati. In 1944 he accepted a position as professor of pastoral theology and Christian ethics at the Episcopal Theology School in Cambridge, Massachusetts, where he taught until 1970. He remained forthright about his socialist leanings, which became increasingly dangerous for him with the advent of the Senator Joseph R. McCarthy era and the tensions leading up to the civil rights movement. Fletcher was summoned to appear before the House Un-American Activities Committee. He survived, with his teaching post intact, the intense protest from his fellow teachers and superiors who felt that his views were too extreme for the time. He rejected efforts to silence those who defended communism, exclaiming: "Don't outlaw them, outthink and outdo them." During an assignment to teach labor history to organizers of the Southern Tenant Farmer's Union, he was cornered by segregationists on two separate occasions and badly beaten each time.

Gradually Fletcher became dissatisfied with the consequences of socialism and cultivated his interest in medicine and ethics. Fearless in the face of controversy, he immersed himself in the problems of euthanasia, contraception, artificial insemination, and sterilization in his 1954 work *Morals and Medicine*. Although Catholics had addressed these issues, Fletcher was the first Protestant theologian to focus on what was later to be termed biomedical ethics. The conservative branches of Judaism and Christianity in particular repudiated Fletcher's defense of each person's moral prerogative to resolve these matters personally. Fletcher argued, however, not for the application of traditional rules of right and wrong to life-altering decisions, but for the consideration, first and foremost, of an individual's well-being.

In 1966 Fletcher published his best-seller *Situation Ethics,* in which he declared that agape—that is, benevolent love and active concern for the good of another—is the "regulative principle" by which one can best decide how to act in a given situation. To make an ethical decision within the confines of legalism or by the abandonment of all principles in antinomianism is to encounter love merely incidentally or, more grievously, not at all.

Fletcher stressed the importance of acting on a case-by-case basis and applying principles with flexibility so as to produce practical benefits for people. Fletcher became estranged from Christian ethics, which he thought too encumbered by doctrine. In 1967 he announced that he was an "unbelieving theologian."

In 1970 he took on a new role as the first professor of biomedical ethics at the University of Virginia at Charlottesville. He wrote *The Ethics of Genetic Control* in 1974 and *Humanhood: Essays in Biomedical Ethics* in 1979. These books, however comprehensive and clear in his argument for utilitarianism, were a fragment of the 160 books and articles he wrote between 1930 and 1988. He worked well past the common age of retirement, and after the death of his first wife, the eighty-six-year-old Fletcher married Elizabeth Hobbs in the summer of 1991. He died of cardiovascular disease and his remains were cremated.

Possessed of a mischievous but personable spirit, Fletcher welcomed debate but rarely left opponents bitter. He motivated people to think about the difficult and emotionally charged ethical issues that affected everyone but had remained largely unaddressed. Fletcher influenced healthcare policy concerning in-vitro fertilization, a patient's right to know the truth of his prognosis, the right to die, recombining DNA, and fetal research.

★

A collection of Fletcher's personal papers is at The University of Virginia, Claude Moore Health Sciences Library. Kenneth Vaux, ed., *Joseph Fletcher: Memoir of an Ex-Radical: Reminiscence and Reappraisal* (1993), includes an autobiographical essay. See also James F. Childress, "Death of a Pioneer in Biomedical Ethics," *Biolaw* (Dec. 1991): U:2245–U:2247, and *Contemporary Authors,* New Revision Series 2 (1984). An obituary is in the *New York Times* (30 Oct. 1991).

ELIZABETH MCKAY

FOOTE, Emerson   (*b.* 13 December 1906 in Sheffield, Alabama; *d.* 5 July 1992 in Carmel, New York), advertising executive, cofounder of one of the nation's largest advertising agencies and later chairman of a second top-ranking agency who, after handling the American Tobacco account for several years, retired from advertising rather than continue to promote cigarettes.

Foote was the youngest of seven children born to James Adonijah Foote, a wholesale cotton and grain dealer, and Ruth Penn. By the time of Foote's birth, two of his six siblings had already died. In 1912 Foote's father moved the entire family to California, where Foote grew up in a section of Los Angeles called Mount Washington. He attended Washington Grammar School, a two-room schoolhouse, before entering Los Angeles High School at the age of eleven. After graduating from high school at the age of fifteen in 1922, Foote worked "for a year or so" at a fine stationery store in downtown Los Angeles. He then studied for a semester in 1923 at the University of California at Los Angeles.

Emerson Foote, 1935. © BETTMANN/CORBIS

With his only college experience behind him, Foote spent the next ten years working at various jobs, including one with a building and loan association and a mutual life insurance company. In 1928 he moved to San Francisco, where he took a position with the McAllister Company, the northern California Chrysler-Plymouth distributor. While with McAllister he was first introduced to the field of advertising.

That first contact with the advertising business was with MacManus, Inc., an agency run by the accomplished advertising executive Theodore MacManus. That agency, which eventually became Darcy-MacManus and Masius, then numbered Chrysler among its clients. George Haig, a representative of the firm, planted the seed that developed into Foote's interest in advertising as a career.

Foote was also encouraged to enter the advertising profession in 1929 by Sabina Fromhold, who later became his wife. Foote had met Fromhold, a copywriter at the H. and S. Pogue Company in Cincinnati, in May of that year. While dining and dancing with Foote at the Palace Hotel Palm Court, Fromhold encouraged him to try the advertising profession, telling him, "I think you would be a good account executive." Three days after their meeting Foote proposed marriage. Because of the Great Depression, however, their wedding waited almost nine years, until 18 April 1938. They subsequently had four children.

Meanwhile Foote had begun his advertising career. In 1931 he became a copywriter at the Leon Livingston Advertising Agency in San Francisco. Within four years his entrepreneurial nature surfaced and he briefly became a principal in his own agency, Yeomans and Foote, in the same city. A year later he moved to New York City to take a position with an agency that had been attracting much attention, J. Stirling Getchell, Inc.

By 1938 Foote had found the position that led to his greatest success and his most profound professional and personal crisis. He became an assistant account executive in the New York City office of Lord and Thomas, a legend in the advertising world. Established in 1881, the most respected people in the field had passed through its offices. When Foote joined, the firm was being run by Albert Lasker, whom many considered the "father of modern advertising." Foote was assigned to the American Tobacco Company's Lucky Strike cigarette account.

Through his work on Lucky Strike, Foote became a confidant of George Washington Hill, the president of the American Tobacco Company. Hill became the model for the character of the tyrannical advertising client in Frederick Wakeman's 1946 novel *The Hucksters,* which was made into a motion picture in 1947. Foote was probably the original of the character Kimberly in the book and film.

Foote quickly rose to be a vice president of the agency and was responsible for the entire American Tobacco ac-

count. In 1941 Foote took over the New York City office as executive vice president and general manager. When Lasker retired in 1942, he sold the agency to his three top executives, Foote in New York City, Fairfax Cone in Chicago, and Don Belding in Los Angeles. Lord and Thomas became Foote, Cone and Belding (FCB). The trio opened their newly named agency in January 1943 with billings of $22.5 million.

Although at thirty-six years of age he was the youngest of the three, Foote was made president of the new firm, at Lasker's suggestion, to appease Hill, who would not deal with anyone but the agency president. Hill, as head of the agency's largest client, exerted a powerful influence. Foote, however, seemed destined for the role of president. According to a later partner, he was "well read, well spoken . . . tall and very distinguished-looking." His relationship with Hill simply ratified a choice that, to them, appeared ordained by nature.

Foote remained president until 1950, during which time the agency created the first radio commercials, jingles, music variety shows, and soap operas. FCB's work established stars, such as Jack Benny, Bob Hope, and Frank Sinatra, along with the fictional character Smokey Bear, who encouraged folks not to start forest fires. The agency also promoted films like *The Best Years of Our Lives* (1946) and *The Secret Life of Walter Mitty* (1947).

By 1948 Hill had retired from American Tobacco Company, and FCB's relationship with that company had deteriorated. FCB voluntarily resigned the $11.5 million account, then its largest, and Foote commented, "If an agency can't do the kind of advertising it believes in, it ought to stop taking commissions." Foote, however, began to doubt whether he had done the right thing in leaving the account. The stress wore on him, and he began treatments for manic-depressive illness and hypertension. In 1950, under pressure from his partners, he resigned from the agency and sold his shares back at a price far below their fair market value.

For the next two years Foote struggled. His former colleagues shunned him. He was treated, he said, "like a dirty shirt" because of his illness. However, Marion Harper, chairman of McCann-Erickson, another top ten agency, did not ignore him. Aware of his treatment for mental illness, Harper offered Foote a position with McCann-Erickson. Joining the company as vice president and general executive in 1952, Foote became president in 1960 and chairman in 1962, a position he held until his resignation in 1964. Foote suffered brief manic relapses while at McCann-Erikson but rose to the presidency and chairmanship despite them. Within a short time of leaving that agency, he openly expressed his opposition to cigarette advertising. Cone described Foote in his memoir *With All Its Faults* (1969): "Foote and [Don] Belding would loom large in the story of [the agency's] early years and its continuing character and personality, for he is an individual with extraordinary talent for advertising and firm convictions about its use."

Foote served on President Lyndon B. Johnson's Commission on Heart Disease, Cancer, and Stroke from 1964 to 1965. He was the first chairman of the National Interagency Council on Smoking and Health from 1964 to 1976; chairman of the Campaign to Check Population Explosion from 1967 to 1969; director of the National Liberty Corporation in Valley Forge, Pennsylvania, from 1969 to 1973; chairman of the board of DeMoss Associates, Inc., from 1969 to 1973; and adviser to the government of India on family planning. He was a trustee or director for numerous nonprofit organizations, including the Menninger Foundation, the American Cancer Society, the Environmental Fund, and the Population Institute. He chaired the advisory board of the Rutgers Center for Alcohol Studies and was vice chairman and executive committee chairman of the Afro-American Purchasing Center. Awarded the Clement Cleveland medal for his cancer work in 1953, he received a National Volunteer Leadership Award from the American Cancer Society in 1974.

Foote's wife died in 1985. Foote died of complications following an operation for appendicitis. He is buried in Lake Carmel, New York. At the time of his death Foote, Cone and Belding was ranked as the largest advertising agency in the United States and the eighth largest in the world with billings of $5 billion.

★

Foote's papers and unpublished autobiography are held by his son James A. Foote, a resident of Old Greenwich, Connecticut. Bart Cummings, *The Benevolent Dictators: Interviews with Advertising Greats* (1984), contains a lengthy interview with Foote. Fairfax M. Cone, *With All Its Faults* (1969), is his partner's memoir. Obituaries are in the *Chicago Tribune* (8 July 1992), *New York Times* (9 July 1992), and *Advertising Age* (13 July 1992).

RICHARD L. TINO

FORD, Ernest Jennings ("Tennessee Ernie") (*b.* 13 February 1919 in Bristol, Tennessee; *d.* 17 October 1991 in Reston, Virginia), singer and entertainer whose recording of "Sixteen Tons" became an instant classic in country music.

Ford was one of two children born to Clarence Ford, a post office worker, and Maude Ford, a homemaker. A deeply religious family, the Fords regularly sang in their Methodist church's choir. Ford played trombone in the band at Bristol High School. After graduating in 1937, he began working as an announcer at a local radio station and attended Intermont College in Virginia from 1937 to 1939, though he did not earn a degree. In 1939 he took singing lessons at

"Tennessee Ernie" Ford, 1985. AP/WIDE WORLD PHOTOS

the Cincinnati Conservatory of Music. Ford was working as an announcer and disc jockey at a Knoxville, Tennessee, radio station when the United States entered World War II in 1941. He enlisted in the U.S. Army Air Corps and served as a bombardier and flight instructor. He flew combat missions as a navigator but was stationed most often at the air base in Victorville, California. In 1942 he married Betty Jean Heminger; they had two children. Ford was discharged from the military in 1945 with the rank of first lieutenant.

Settling permanently in California, Ford resumed his radio career. While working on the country-and-western music station KXLA in Pasadena, California, he became friends with the veteran bandleader Cliffie Stone. Blessed with a rich bass-baritone voice, Ford soon became a regular singer on Stone's popular radio program, *Hometown Jamboree*. Stone also put Ford in contact with Capitol Records, which signed the promising young crooner to a recording contract. In 1949 Ford recorded "Mule Train" and "Smokey Mountain Boogie"—both of which reached the top ten on the country-and-western music charts. His career took off the following year when he came out with a trio of top-ten singles—"Anticipation Blues," "I'll Never Be Free" (with Kay Starr), and "The Cry of the Wild Goose"—and his first number-one hit, "Shotgun Boogie."

From 1950 to 1955 Ford had his own radio shows on the CBS and ABC networks. He also recorded "Mister and Mississippi" (1951), "Blackberry Boogie" (1952), "River of No Return" (1954), and "The Ballad of Davy Crockett" (1955), all top-ten hits. His "Davy Crockett" was the theme song for the popular Walt Disney television show of the same title. Ford scored his greatest success in 1955 with "Sixteen Tons," a song written by Merle Travis. In simple but compellingly memorable lyrics, "Sixteen Tons" recounts the woes of a proud but disheartened miner who realizes that even after years of back-breaking labor, he has nothing to show for his exertions: "I owe my soul to the company store." This plaintive tune catapulted Ford to national fame. The recording sold 2 million copies in the first nine weeks after its release, remained at the top of the charts for months, and eventually sold more than 20 million copies worldwide. Ford once described the song as an "everlasting hit. It seems that young marrieds and even high school kids know it. It caught on to every working man in the world, I guess." In 1963 Ford's 1956 album *Hymns* became Capitol Records' best-selling record of all time. *Hymns* is one of the few platinum-selling religious recordings.

As he grew older Ford devoted himself increasingly to gospel music. He recorded "The Old Rugged Cross," "Rock of Ages," "Faith of Our Fathers," and many other famous Christian hymns. "Of all the singing I do, hymns, spirituals, and gospel songs not only give me great pleasure but seem to be something that truly needs to be done. People may get all steamed up about big new love songs that come along, but let's not forget that hymns and spirituals are the finest love songs of them all." Ford's religious songs found a wide audience. By the end of the 1960s he had sold more than 10 million gospel records, netting him six Gold Record awards from the Recording Industry Association of America (RIAA).

During the late 1950s and into the mid-1960s Ford hosted several popular television variety shows, including the *College of Musical Knowledge* (1954), the *Tennessee Ernie Ford Show*, (1955–1957 and 1961–1965), and the *Ford Show* (1956–1961). For Americans of that era, Ford's wholesome, homespun demeanor and unpretentious charm had an irresistible appeal. He would introduce his shows with the trademark folksy line "Bless your little pea-pickin' hearts, this is Ole Pea-Picker here." His shows included a mix of pop and country music, and he usually closed his program by singing a hymn.

Ford's popularity led to guest appearances on numerous television shows, including *I Love Lucy, This Is Your Life, Hee Haw,* and the variety shows hosted by Steve Allen,

Rosemary Clooney, Perry Como, Danny Thomas, Jack Benny, Andy Williams, Red Skelton, Jim Nabors, Mike Douglas, and Dinah Shore. In his career, Ford recorded more than eighty albums, among them *Civil War Songs of the North* (1961), *Civil War Songs of the South* (1961), *Long, Long Ago* (1963), *Favorite Hymns, The Very Best of Tennessee Ernie Ford* (1963), *Great Gospel Songs near the Cross* (1964), *Tennessee Ernie Ford's Country Hits* (1964), *World's Best Loved Hymns* (1965), *God Lives!* (1966), *America the Beautiful* (1970), and *Ernie Sings and Glen Picks* (1975).

Ford was the first country-music singer to perform in London's Palladium Theatre. Queen Elizabeth II, who had a special liking for "Shotgun Boogie," included herself among his fans. He was also part of the first group of country singers ever to tour the Soviet Union. Ford received many prestigious awards for his career achievements. *Motion Picture Daily* cited his TV show as the best program of the 1956–1957 season. Ford received a Grammy Award for "Great Gospel Songs" in 1964; he was nominated seven other times for Grammys. He also received two Emmy nominations for his work on television. President Ronald Reagan presented him with the Medal of Freedom in 1984, and he was elected to the Country Music Hall of Fame in 1990. After his first wife's death, Ford married Beverly Woodsmith in 1989. He died of a liver ailment and is buried in Alta Mesa Cemetery in Palo Alto, California. His place as a pop-culture icon of the post–World War II years is secure, and it is likely that his signature song, "Sixteen Tons," will continue to be enjoyed by music lovers for generations to come.

★

Ford's autobiography is titled *This Is My Story, This Is My Song* (1963). There is one full-length biography, Ted Hilgenstuhler's *Tennessee Ernie Ford* (1957). He is also covered in Patrick Carr, ed., *The Illustrated History of Country Music* (1979). There are obituaries in the *New York Times* (18 Oct. 1991) and *Current Biography Yearbook* (1992).

IRINA BELENKY

FOSTER, Vincent William, Jr. (*b.* 15 January 1945 in Hope, Arkansas; *d.* 20 July 1993 in Fort Marcy Park near McLean, Virginia), lawyer and President Bill Clinton's deputy White House counsel, whose death sparked political controversy and gave rise to a number of conspiracy theories questioning the official verdict of suicide.

One of three children born to Vincent William Foster, Sr., a well-to-do real-estate broker and developer, and Alice Mae Waddle, a homemaker, Foster knew the future president Bill Clinton from childhood, and the two remained lifelong friends.

Foster attended Hope High School, where he was pres-

Vincent Foster, deputy counsel, in an official White House photo, 1993. ASSOCIATED PRESS WHITE HOUSE

ident of the student body and, like Clinton, a delegate to Boys State. After graduating in June 1963, Foster attended Davidson College, a small liberal-arts school in North Carolina, and earned a degree in psychology in June 1967. While at Davidson, Foster met Elizabeth ("Lisa") Braden, a student at Sweet Briar College in Virginia. On 20 April 1968, during Foster's first year at Vanderbilt University Law School, in Nashville, Tennessee, the couple married. They had three children.

As the Vietnam War escalated, Foster joined the Arkansas National Guard and transferred to the University of Arkansas at Fayetteville School of Law. In 1971 he graduated first in his class and earned the highest score in the state on his bar examination. He immediately joined Little Rock's prestigious Rose Law Firm, where his specialty was commercial litigation, and within two years he was made a partner. Among his colleagues at Rose was the future First Lady Hillary Rodham Clinton.

Respected in legal circles, Foster served a term as the president of the Pulaski County Bar Association and worked with the Arkansas Legal Services Corporation. He also took an interest in the Arkansas Repertory Theatre, serving on its board and raising funds for it.

When Clinton became the President in January 1993,

Foster surprised many by giving up his lucrative practice (he reported his income as $295,000 for 1992) to assume the post of deputy White House counsel. Foster apparently believed that public service was important and worth the financial sacrifice. In Washington, D.C., Foster almost immediately found himself in the midst of controversy as first Zoë Baird, then Kimba Wood, Clinton's first two nominees for attorney general—each of whom Foster had vetted— were forced to withdraw after each admitted she had hired illegal aliens as domestics. Foster, who was supposed to be Clinton's "integrity cop," apparently felt he had failed his boss.

On 8 May 1993 Foster delivered the commencement address at the University of Arkansas School of Law. He told the graduates that following their bar exams their most difficult test would be "not what you know but what is your character," and he warned that "no victory, no advantage, no fee, no favor . . . is worth even a blemish on your reputation."

But Foster's reputation would soon be tarnished. During confirmation hearings of former Rose partner Webster Hubbell as the associate attorney general, Hubbell's membership in the formerly all-white Country Club of Little Rock became an issue. On 19 May Hubbell told the Senate Judiciary Committee he would resign from the club. Foster, who was also a member, had little choice but to do the same.

On the same day, a new storm broke. A week earlier David Watkins, the head of White House administration, had approached Foster with the suspicion that "mismanagement and corruption" had occurred in the White House travel office. Foster assigned the associate White House counsel William H. Kennedy III (formerly of Rose), to investigate. On 19 May, Watkins fired all seven members of the travel-office staff, precipitating what came to be called "Travelgate." When a Little Rock travel agency run by friends of the Clintons was put in charge of White House travel, it was seen, as the *Washington Post* put it, as a case of "White House cronies sacking longtime employees" in order to give lucrative business to friends. Charges also arose over alleged misuse of the Federal Bureau of Investigation (FBI) in connection with the probe. Kennedy, but not Foster, was eventually reprimanded for mishandling the investigation. Foster apparently felt Kennedy had been unfairly treated and that he (Foster) had failed to protect his friend Bill Clinton from the political consequences of Travelgate.

Between 17 June and 19 July the *Wall Street Journal* published a series of articles and editorials critical of Foster and other former members of the Rose Law Firm in the Clinton administration. It accused the "Rose clique" of engineering the firing of the FBI director William Sessions and it sarcastically complimented Foster for his successful arguments in defense of Hillary Clinton's role as the chair of a task force on healthcare reform.

On 20 July 1993 after participating in a 9:00 A.M. staff meeting, Foster attended a Rose Garden ceremony at which President Clinton announced the nomination of Louis Freeh as the director of the Federal Bureau of Investigation. Afterward Foster talked to Chief Counsel Bernard Nussbaum, who complimented him on his work in vetting Freeh and Judge Ruth Bader Ginsburg, who appeared certain of confirmation by the Senate as a Supreme Court justice. After eating lunch at his desk, Foster left his office at about 1:00 P.M. and was never seen alive again. Shortly after 6:00 P.M. a body, later identified by the U.S. Park Police as that of Foster, was discovered in Fort Marcy Park, Virginia.

On 23 July President Clinton delivered a eulogy at Foster's funeral in Little Rock. Later in the day Foster was buried at the Memory Gardens Cemetery in Hope.

Almost immediately questions about Foster's death were raised. Initially no suicide note was found, but six days after Foster's death a note, torn into twenty-seven pieces with a twenty-eighth piece missing, was found in a briefcase that had been searched by Nussbaum four days earlier. In the note Foster acknowledged mistakes made from "ignorance, inexperience, and overwork," but contended he had "not knowingly violate[d] any law or standard of conduct." He accused the FBI and the editors of the *Wall Street Journal* of lying about Travelgate and closed with the statement that "I was not meant for the job or the spotlight of public life in Washington. Here ruining people is considered sport."

By 5 August 1993 the Park Police officially ruled Foster's death a suicide. However, press reports that documents had been removed surreptitiously from Foster's office by White House staffers led the attorney general Janet Reno in January 1994 to appoint Robert Fiske as special counsel to reopen the investigation. On 30 June 1994 Fiske released a report affirming that Foster had committed suicide in Fort Marcy Park. Nonetheless on 29 July 1994 the Republican-controlled Senate Banking Committee held a one-day hearing on Foster's death, but eventually released a report agreeing with Fiske's conclusions. Meanwhile, Congress renewed the independent-counsel law (which had been allowed to expire) and in August 1994 Kenneth Starr was appointed as independent counsel to investigate the so-called Whitewater affair and other matters. Although Starr eventually endorsed the conclusions of the Park Police, Special Counsel Fiske, and the Senate Banking Committee that Foster died by his own hand in Fort Marcy Park on 20 July 1993, conspiracy theorists, led by the journalist Christopher Ruddy, refused to accept these findings. While most of these critics stop short of openly charging that Foster was murdered, all suggest that a "cover-up" occurred to obscure the "fact" that he did not die a suicide in Fort Marcy Park.

★

There is extensive coverage of the Foster affair in James B. Stewart, *Blood Sport: The President and His Adversaries* (1996). Christopher Ruddy, *The Strange Death of Vincent Foster: An Investigation* (1997), and Ambrose Evans-Pritchard, *The Secret Life of Bill Clinton: The Unreported Stories* (1997), both contain some biographical information on Foster, but their major focus is on Foster's death and both question the official version of his suicide. Dan E. Moldea, *A Washington Tragedy: How the Death of Vincent Foster Ignited a Political Firestorm* (1998) is a painstaking effort to debunk the theories of Ruddy and Evans-Pritchard but contains little on Foster's life. David Von Dreble, "The Crumbling of a Pillar in Washington: Only Clinton Aide Foster Knew What Drove Him to Fort Marcy," *Washington Post* (15 Aug. 1993), provides a brief biographical sketch. Peter J. Boyer, "Life After Vince," *New Yorker* (11 Sept. 1995), is based on the author's interview with Foster's widow. Initial reports of Foster's death, sketches of his career, and obituaries are in the *New York Times, Washington Post,* and *Arkansas Democrat Gazette* (all 21–24 July 1993).

ROMAN ROME

FOXX, Redd (*b.* 9 December 1922 in St. Louis, Missouri; *d.* 11 October 1991 in Los Angeles, California), nightclub and television entertainer notorious for his off-color comedy albums and the star of one of television's most successful comedy series.

Foxx was born John Elroy Sanford, one of two sons of Fred Sanford, an electrician, and Mary Carson, a radio preacher and domestic worker. His father left home when he was four years old. His mother then moved to Chicago, where she worked as a domestic for the vice president of the Chicago White Sox baseball team. There, John Elroy acquired the nickname "Chicago Red" because of his ruddy hair color and skin tone. While attending DuSable High School in Chicago, he met Lamont Ousley and Steve Trimel, and together they formed a washtub band they called the Bon Bons. The three ran way from home together in 1939; they took a freight train to Weehawken, New Jersey, and from there they went to New York City, where they sang and performed on street corners. They appeared on *Major Bowe's Amateur Radio Show* and won second prize, which was a week's booking at a Newark, New Jersey, nightclub.

Foxx worked as a busboy, a cart pusher in the garment district, and a dishwasher in Harlem, New York, during the early 1940s, when he began using the last name "Foxx" after the baseball star Jimmie Foxx. Work was scarce, and Foxx was arrested and jailed for minor offenses, mostly for theft of food and for loitering. (During this time, "Chicago Red" met a man in a pool hall named Malcolm Little,

Redd Foxx (*right*) with *Sanford and Son* cast member Desmond Wilson. AP/WIDE WORLD PHOTOS

whose nickname was "Detroit Red." Later, Chicago Red's friend Detroit Red took the name Malcolm X.) Although Foxx was rejected by the U.S. Army for service in World War II, the Bon Bons broke up during the war. After the war Foxx worked in a tramp band act at the Apollo Theatre in Harlem. In the mid-1940s he married Eleanor Killebrew; the marriage ended in divorce in 1951.

One of his first jobs in the 1940s was performing mime and singing at a club called Mimo's on Seventh Avenue in Harlem. This led to a job as the master of ceremonies at a nightclub called Gamby's in Baltimore. Foxx stayed at Gamby's for two years, developing his stand-up comedy act. He returned to New York in 1945 and worked at clubs for $5 per night. He teamed with Slappy White in 1947, and their act met with enough success that Foxx was soon earning $450 per week. In 1952 the duo was invited to California to perform with Dinah Washington. The job lasted only a month, but Foxx stayed on the West Coast. He was performing in Los Angeles and supplementing his income by working as a sign painter in 1955 when Dootsie Williams, the owner of Dooto Records, persuaded him to record a comedy album. *Laff of the Party* became the first of some fifty raunchy recordings that gained Foxx notoriety and widespread popularity, although they had to be albums sold under the counter at many outlets. The year *Laff of the Party* was released, Foxx married Betty Jeanne Harris; they had a daughter and later divorced (in 1974). Foxx quit the Dooto label over a contract dispute but was forbidden by his contract to record with anyone else. Frank Sinatra, the owner of Reprise Records, bought out Foxx's contract and signed him. All told, the albums Foxx recorded sold between 10 and 20 million copies, but he felt that he never received proper payment.

Foxx became known to a national television audience in 1964, after NBC television host Hugh Downs saw him perform in San Francisco, where he was reportedly earning $1,250 per week. Although NBC executives were concerned about Foxx's "blue" humor, he was invited to appear on the *Today Show,* and in short order he was in demand as a guest on the *Tonight Show* and other talk and variety programs including those hosted by Joey Bishop, Merv Griffin, Mike Douglas, and Steve Allen. Clubs throughout the United States clamored to offer Foxx bookings; when he performed in Las Vegas, Nevada, he was earning $4,000 per week.

In 1968 he was signed to open for Aretha Franklin at Caesars Palace. When she failed to appear on opening night, he entertained for an hour and forty minutes. Booking agents from the Hilton were so impressed with Foxx that they signed him to a contract worth $960,000. With this security he moved from Los Angeles to Las Vegas.

Foxx broke into movies in 1970, portraying a junk dealer in *Cotton Comes to Harlem.* The television producer Norman Lear admired his performance and tagged Foxx for the title role of an American adaptation of a British television comedy called *Steptoe and Son.* Foxx gave the new situation comedy its title, *Sanford and Son,* naming the lead character—Fred G. Sanford, a junk dealer living in the Watts section of Los Angeles—after his brother. The show, which premiered on NBC on 14 January 1972, centered on the comic disputes and foibles of Fred and his son, Lamont. The show's comedic hook occurred when Fred was losing an argument or felt that his son's ambition would cause him to leave the junk business: he would feign a heart attack and cry out to his dead wife, "I'm coming Elizabeth, I'm coming." Lamont and another character, Reverend Trimel, were named after Foxx's childhood friends in the washtub band who ran away from home with him. Additionally, Slappy White and LaWanda Page, who had worked with Foxx in decades past, were cast as regular characters on the show, which ran from 1972 to 1977 and was a top-ten hit. After the second season Foxx moved back to Los Angeles from Las Vegas. In the mid-1970s he married Yun Chi Chong; they divorced in the late 1980s.

Foxx was nominated for six Emmy Awards during the run of *Sanford and Son.* The show made an important contribution toward the representation of African Americans on television, with Foxx playing a lead character who was a small businessman, not a butler or a maid. However, Foxx's salary demands threatened the show; at one point he asked for $25,000 per week plus $1, to equal and best the salary of Carroll O'Connor for his portrayal of Archie Bunker in CBS's leading comedy, *All in the Family*. After *Sanford and Son* ended, Foxx worked in a few short-lived television shows, including one that reprised the Fred Sanford character, and he continued to work at Las Vegas nightclubs.

In 1983, Foxx's extravagant lifestyle—which included a fleet of cars and several houses—caught up with him, and he filed for bankruptcy. In 1989 the Internal Revenue Service claimed that he owed $2.9 million in back taxes and seized his personal possessions. But 1989 also afforded Foxx the opportunity for a television comeback; that year, Eddie Murphy cast Foxx, Richard Pryor, and Della Reese in the movie *Harlem Nights*, and although the film was not a commercial success, Foxx and Reese stole the movie. Their on-screen chemistry inspired the creation of a television series titled *The Royal Family*, which began taping in 1991. In July 1991 Foxx married his fourth wife, Kahoe Cho. On 11 October 1991, shortly after the season premiere of *The Royal Family*, Foxx suffered a fatal heart attack during a rehearsal at Paramount Studios in Los Angeles. He is buried at Palm Memorial Gardens in Las Vegas.

Redd Foxx will be remembered for *Sanford and Son*, but his career lasted over fifty years. He was instrumental in the creation of the comedy album and was an inspiration to many comedians.

★

Foxx provides autobiographical information in his *Redd Foxx, B.S. (Before Sanford),* edited by Joe X. Price (1979), and *The Redd Foxx Encyclopedia of Black Humor* (1977). Dempsey J. Travis chronicles his life and career in *The Life and Times of Redd Foxx* (1999). *Current Biography Yearbook* (1972) contains an entry on Foxx. The genre of "black comedy," and Foxx's contributions to it, are reviewed in Mel Watkins, *On the Real Side: Laughing, Lying, and Signifying—the Underground Tradition of African-American Humor That Transformed American Culture, from Slavery to Richard Pryor* (1994). Obituaries are in the *Los Angeles Times* (12 Oct. 1991), and *Washington Post* and *New York Times* (both 13 Oct. 1991).

ANTHONY TODMAN

FRANCE, William Henry Getty (*b.* 26 September 1909 in Washington, D.C.; *d.* 7 June 1992 in Ormond Beach, Florida), NASCAR founder and head who helped turn stock car racing from a disorganized regional pastime to one of the nation's fastest-growing sports.

France was one of three children of William H. France, a banker, and Emma Graham, a homemaker. Attending

Bill France, founder of NASCAR, is awarded the Patrick Jacquemart Trophy for his contributions to auto racing, 1984. ASSOCIATED PRESS

Gage Primary School and Columbia Junior High School in Washington, D.C., France took to car racing at a young age, watching races at the Baltimore-Washington Speedway in nearby Laurel, Maryland. While a student at Central High School, France and a friend built their first race car, a wood-body, canvas-covered vehicle with a Model T engine.

On 23 June 1931 France married Anne Bledsoe, a nurse he had met at a dance; they had two sons. In 1934 the Frances left Washington, D.C., for Miami. They stopped to go swimming at Daytona Beach, Florida, and decided to stay. (The story that France ended up in Daytona Beach because his car broke down there is almost certainly apocryphal; he would have been capable of fixing a breakdown.)

France took a job as a mechanic at a local garage and got involved in the local racing scene. An Englishman, Sir Malcolm Campbell, had been using Daytona Beach's broad, flat sands to set speed records, but by the late 1930s he had moved his operation to Utah. City leaders were looking for ways to keep speed fans coming to Daytona Beach and France, who soon owned his own service station, teamed with another local man to promote an annual race over the beach and the city's streets.

From the time he took over the Daytona Beach race in 1938, France wanted to make it the national championship of stock car racing, but he lacked an organization of race promoters to make that a reality. In 1947 after organizing a handful of Southern races as the National Championship Stock Car Circuit, France decided there was a future in a league with rules that would allow it to name a champion, award prize money and keep records. That December France gathered promoters from across the region at Daytona Beach's Streamline Inn to incorporate NASCAR, the National Association for Stock Car Automobile Racing. He was its president.

Like many benevolent dictators, the six-feet, five-inch tall, 260-pound France brought stability where there had been chaos. NASCAR's simple structure and France's absolute control and determination to make his rules stick helped him keep unruly drivers and track promoters in line. "There were track operators who said they'd put up a certain amount of money and then it wouldn't be there after the race," France said in 1983. "One of the aims of NASCAR was to have a purse that would be paid when the race was over." By racing "stock" cars—cars that looked the same as those that fans saw on the auto showroom floor—NASCAR tapped into post-World War II consumer desire and a natural sponsorship market. Attendance and purses boomed and by the early 1990s, NASCAR's top-level Winston Cup series was drawing 3.3 million fans a year and offering its champion a $1 million bonus.

In the early 1950s France started work on his other great innovation: Daytona International Speedway. By 1949 he had realized that Daytona Beach's booming growth would inevitably mean an end to racing on the beach and began searching for a new site. Inspired by the stock car circuit's first asphalt track in Darlington, South Carolina, France built the speedway on drained swampland due west of Daytona Beach, about three miles from the beach and the city center, selling $300,000 in stock and borrowing another $600,000 to make his vision a reality. Opened in 1959, Daytona International Speedway was two-and-a-half miles around, with banked turns and long straightaways that allowed drivers to reach the previously unheard-of speed of 140 miles per hour, and a massive grandstand with a view of the entire track. It became the model for future superspeedways.

Throughout the 1950s and 1960s France resisted all efforts to loosen his control of NASCAR. He turned back two attempts to unionize drivers, one by the Teamsters and one by the drivers themselves. He was equally tough with the corporations whose sponsorships were the sport's lifeblood, tinkering with the rules and closing loopholes to keep races competitive. When France outlawed Chrysler's hemi engine, decreeing that the powerful hemispherical combustion chamber gave Chrysler cars an unfair advantage and thus made the race less competitive, the automaker made good on a vow to leave stock car racing, taking with it its star driver Richard Petty. France stood firm, though, and Chrysler and Petty soon returned. In 1972 France turned over everyday control of his empire to his sons Bill Jr., who became NASCAR's president, and Jim, who became the president of International Speedway Corporation, which owned the Daytona Beach, Darlington, and Talladega, Alabama, tracks.

For the rest of his life, France remained a forceful presence in racing. He and his wife, who was also his business partner, kept offices at NASCAR's Daytona Beach headquarters well into the 1980s. In his final years France suffered from Alzheimer's disease; he was in poor health for the last two years of his life, and his death came shortly after that of his wife. He died of natural causes in Ormond Beach and is buried there in Hillside Cemetery.

As founder and for a quarter-century head of NASCAR, France was almost single-handedly responsible for making NASCAR's Grand National (later Winston Cup) series the world's most popular auto-racing circuit. With a background in both racing and race promoting, France was an honest broker between drivers and promoters who otherwise never could have worked together, while his Daytona International Speedway set the blueprint for the massive superspeedways that followed, feeding a seemingly ever-growing appetite for stock car racing.

★

France and his life are featured prominently in a pair of books about NASCAR by Peter Golenbock: *American Zoom: Stock Car Racing—From the Dirt Tracks to Daytona* (1993) and *The Last Lap: The Life and Times of NASCAR's Legendary Heroes* (1998). Stories and memories of France also are in the *Charlotte Observer* (8 June 1992) and the "Motorsports" column in the *San Diego Union-Tribune* (14 June 1992). Bill Nelly wrote a remembrance of France in *AutoWeek* (15 June 1992), and a detailed obituary is in the *Atlanta Journal-Constitution* (8 June 1992).

Tim Whitmire

FREUND, Paul Abraham (*b.* 16 February 1908 in St. Louis, Missouri; *d.* 5 February 1992 in Cambridge, Massachusetts), constitutional scholar and distinguished teacher at the Harvard Law School.

Freund, the son of Charles Freund and Hulda Arenson, demonstrated his academic abilities when, at the age of eleven, he graduated from the Wyman School and entered high school in St. Louis. Interviewed by the *St. Louis Post-Dispatch,* he admitted to a love of poetry and expressed interest in becoming a lawyer but confessed that "supreme happiness could come if he could only grow up to be a big-

Paul Freund, 1970. AP/WIDE WORLD PHOTOS

league baseball player." His lifelong love of sports followed naturally from his membership in the "Knothole Gang," a group of children who, as tradition has it, watched the Cardinals through the holes in the wooden fence that surrounded the field.

In 1928 Freund graduated from Washington University. He went on to study at Harvard Law School, where he was elected president of the editorial board of the *Harvard Law Review* and in 1931 earned his bachelor of laws degree. Serving as Felix Frankfurter's graduate assistant, he completed his doctorate the following year. Frankfurter, in turn, selected Freund to clerk for Justice Louis D. Brandeis for the 1932 Supreme Court term.

Like many of the talented young lawyers of the era, Freund took advantage of the employment opportunities created by the New Deal. From 1933 to 1935 he served on the legal staff of the Treasury Department and the Reconstruction Finance Corporation, and from 1935 to 1939 as special assistant in the office of the Solicitor General. During his time in the Department of Justice he prepared briefs or argued a number of landmark cases before the Supreme Court, including *United States* v. *Carolene Products* (304 U. S. 144, 1938), *Electric Bond & Share Co.* v. *S. E. C .* (303 U. S. 419, 1938), and *Tennessee Power Co.* v. *T. V. A.* (306

U. S. 118, 1939). He returned to the Solicitor General's office from 1942 to 1946, successfully defending the federal government's wartime regulation of prices and wages.

In the meantime Harvard Law School appointed Freund to its faculty, first as a lecturer (1939) and then as professor (1940), and assigned him responsibility for teaching constitutional law and conflict of laws. Freund's professional experience, extensive knowledge of history, enduring love of literature, and mastery of the law itself made for a winning combination in the classroom. Viewed by both students and colleagues as the quintessential teacher, he was named Fairchild Professor in 1950, Royall Professor in 1957, and Carl M. Loeb University Professor in 1958, the last appointment providing opportunities to teach Harvard undergraduates as well as law students.

Freund was, in his own words, "by temperament and conviction preeminently a teacher." This sense of himself, along with his having recently agreed to serve as editor in chief of the multivolume *History of the Supreme Court,* known as the *Holmes' Devise*, explains his decision to decline appointment as solicitor general of the United States, a position that has traditionally served as a stepping stone to the Supreme Court. Disappointed, President John F. Kennedy remarked, "I'm sorry. I hoped you would prefer making history to writing it."

The demands of overseeing the *History of the Supreme Court* and the standards Freund imposed on himself as editor of the series and as author of the volume on the New Deal Court proved formidable. Although he published a number of articles about the Supreme Court under Chief Justice Charles Evans Hughes, he eventually delegated completion of both projects to others.

Over the course of his career Freund published more than 100 articles, primarily in law reviews, along with three collections of essays. Convinced that the Constitution requires compromise, he dismissed absolutist approaches and explored instead its complexities, ambiguities, and tensions. Quoting Lord Acton, one of his favorite authors, he insisted, "when you perceive a truth, look for the balancing truth."

Freund questioned whether one could identify the "original intent" of the Framers and argued instead that, "like a work of artistic creation, the Constitution endures because it is capable of responding to the concerns, the needs, the aspirations of successive generations." Similarly, he challenged the practice among judges of drawing selectively from history to justify results that should have been reached on other grounds.

His academic career included appointment as Pitt Professor of American History and Institutions at Cambridge University (1957–1968) and fellow at the Center for Advanced Study of Behavior Sciences in Palo Alto, California (1969–1970). He also served as director of the Salzburg

Seminar in American Studies. In 1975 the National Endowment for the Humanities chose him as Jefferson lecturer.

Appointed by Chief Justice Warren Burger to chair the Federal Judicial Center's Study Group on the Caseload of the Supreme Court, Freund assumed much of the responsibility for the controversial report issued in 1972. The committee's recommendations included the establishment of a National Court of Appeals to screen all petitions for certiorari and appeal, creation by law of a nonjudicial body to investigate and report on complaints of prisoners, and increased staff support for the Supreme Court. None of the group's recommendations was adopted.

Freund retired from Harvard Law School in 1976 but remained active. In addition to his scholarly work, he chaired the Judicial Selection Commission of the United States Court of Appeals, First Circuit, from 1977 to 1979. Over the course of his life he received twenty-one honorary degrees as well as awards from the American Bar Foundation, the Federal Bar Council, the Thomas Jefferson Memorial Foundation, the American Law Institute, and the Civil Liberties Union of Massachusetts. He died of cancer in 1992.

A modest, gentle man who never married or had children, Freund believed deeply that the law should be studied with a recognition of the impact it has on individuals' lives. His own knowledge of the humanities and affinity for literature enabled him to convey this to his students through an apt quotation, a reference to history, and, above all, his own example. "I never knew anyone kinder or more considerate than Paul," observed his colleague James Vorenberg. "He was incapable of meanness." A brilliant scholar, Freund's greatest legacy lies nevertheless in the influence of his teaching on his students.

★

Freund's papers are deposited in the Harvard Law School Archives but are not yet cataloged. His published works include *On Understanding the Supreme Court* (1949, 1977); *Constitutional Law: Cases and Other Problems* (4th ed. 1977); *The Supreme Court of the United States: Its Business, Purposes and Performance* (1961); *Religion and the Public Schools* (1965); and *On Law and Justice* (1968). Memorials are in *The American Scholar* (spring 1993), *Harvard Law Review* (Nov. 1992), and *The New Yorker* (24 Feb. 1992). Obituaries are in the *Boston Globe, New York Times,* and *Washington Post* (6 Feb. 1992).

CHRISTINE L. COMPSTON

G

GAINES, William Maxwell (*b.* 1 March 1922 in New York City; *d.* 3 June 1992 in New York City), founding publisher of *Mad* magazine and creator and publisher of EC Comics, including *Weird Science* and *Tales from the Crypt*.

Gaines was one of two children of Max C. Gaines, who published the first comic books in the 1930s, and Jessie Postlethwaite, an elementary school teacher. He was an unruly and unorthodox child; he became an atheist at the age of twelve and took up magic as a hobby. After graduating from James Madison High School, he majored in chemistry at Polytechnic Institute in Brooklyn, New York, from 1941 to 1942, but dropped out and joined the Army Air Corps during World War II. While serving as the base photographer at De Ridder Army Air Corps Base in Louisiana, he married Hazel Grieb in 1944; they had no children.

After his discharge in 1945 as a private first class, Gaines enrolled at New York University (NYU) and majored in education. In 1947 he and Grieb divorced. Shortly thereafter his father was killed in a boating accident. Gaines took over Educational Comics (EC), the current family business, while finishing his studies, graduating from NYU in 1948. At first Gaines was happy to allow EC's managers to run the company, which published children's comics devoted to religion and science, but slowly he became more involved. When the artist and writer Al Feldstein submitted a portfolio of sexy young female characters as examples of those in the then-popular teenage comics, Gaines's attention was caught as it never had been by the illustrated books of Bible stories put out by EC.

Gaines and Feldstein became friends, and together they became passionate creators of the comic book as an art form. They assembled a stable of artists, and Gaines became the editor in chief. In 1950 Gaines changed the name of the company to Entertaining Comics and premiered a new line, beginning in that year with *Tales from the Crypt* and *The Vault of Horror,* two of the first horror comics ever published. *Weird Science* and *Weird Fantasy,* both science fiction comics, were the next new titles, followed by *Shock SuspenStories* and *Crime SuspenStories,* and another horror title, *The Haunt of Fear.* Gaines and Feldstein wrote stories that were gory, gruesome, and darkly humorous. But these comics were often morality tales as well, which focused on aspects of social inequality. Later in 1950 Gaines hired Harvey Kurtzman, an artist and writer who created two new comic books, *Two-Fisted Tales* and *Frontline Combat.*

Gaines's "new trend" comic books were an unqualified financial success, especially the horror and crime comics, which allowed him to run EC in a very unorthodox style. The staff lavished loving care on stories of vampires and rotting corpses, artists were encouraged to develop unique styles (in an industry that usually treated them as factory workers), and the war comics had a decidedly pacifist bias. Plots had surprising twists and "good" did not always triumph.

Bill Gaines in his *Mad* magazine office, 1989. JACQUES M. CHENET/
CORBIS CORPORATION (BELLEVUE)

Meanwhile, Kurtzman was developing another new idea, one that would bring comic books back to their humorous roots. In 1952, with Gaines's encouragement and backing, Kurtzman premiered the first issue of *Mad*. Like the other EC comics, *Mad* was a thirty-six-page color comic book that cost a dime. The early issues parodied other comic books, television, movies, and other aspects of American culture. The writing and art was wildly experimental, incorporating images found in other sources, chunks of type from foreign newspapers, and covers that mimicked other kinds of books and magazines. For example, Alfred E. Neuman, *Mad*'s gap-toothed mascot, was originally an image swiped from popular postcards of the time. Within four issues, *Mad* had found its own fanatical following and had become a financial success. When *Mad*'s parodies of Madison Avenue offended advertisers, Gaines simply discontinued advertising in *Mad*.

Meanwhile, however, parents became worried about the blood and carnage churned out in the hundreds of horror and crime comics that were now choking the newsstands and began to organize against comic books. In 1954 Fred-

eric Wertham, an influential liberal psychiatrist, published *Seduction of the Innocent*, the result of seven years of research at "mental hygiene" clinics. The book detailed Wertham's observations of the ravages of comic books on youth: not only as dangers to literacy but also stories of children carrying out crimes, even committing suicide and murder, after reading comics.

Gaines's comics quickly became targets. Parents and demagogues continued the anticomics crusade, which culminated in federal hearings on the issue. In April 1954, at the Foley Square Federal Court House in Manhattan, Gaines testified before the Subcommittee to Investigate Juvenile Delinquency of the Committee on the Judiciary. He was the only speaker in defense of comics and was pilloried by the press.

Despite attempts by EC to organize other comic book publishers against censorship, the industry instead devised the Comics Code Authority, based largely upon the current production code then used by the motion picture industry. The code outlawed much of EC's current content. Although Gaines continued publishing his comic books, distributors refused to deliver them to retail outlets.

As sales flagged, Kurtzman convinced Gaines to change the format of *Mad* from a comic book to a magazine, which he thought would allow more creative freedom. Gaines capitulated, and then realized that since *Mad* was now technically a magazine, it was exempt from the Comics Code. While Gaines battled problems with the rest of his publications, Kurtzman developed the new *Mad* into a twenty-five-cent, black-and-white, advertisement-free magazine that premiered in 1955. Also in that year Gaines married Nancy Siegel, who had been working in *Mad*'s subscription department. They had three children.

By 1956 the only publication remaining in the EC line was *Mad*, which was a success not only with teenagers but also with many adults. When Kurtzman left to develop a color magazine for Hugh Hefner, Gaines appointed Al Feldstein the new editor of *Mad*. Feldstein refined what Kurtzman had begun and *Mad* grew steadily more popular.

In 1961 Gaines sold ownership of *Mad* to Premier Industries, which changed hands several times and in 1969 became part of Warner Communications, later Time Warner. Throughout the ownership changes Gaines remained the publisher and retained full authority over the content of *Mad*.

During the 1960s *Mad*'s circulation rose, reaching a high of 2.4 million in 1972. It was also printed in seventeen foreign editions. Gaines let his hair and beard grow long and took the staff, writers, and artists on annual trips to places all over the world, including Italy, Greece, Kenya, Japan, Thailand, and Morocco. In 1971 Gaines and Siegel divorced. He became a gourmet and wine-lover and also assembled important collections of Statue of Liberty objects and airship models.

In the 1980s Gaines began a serious relationship with Anne Griffiths. They married in 1987; they had no children. *Tales from the Crypt,* a horror series based on the old EC comic books, premiered in 1989 on the HBO cable network and became a successful original series. Also in the 1980s and 1990s, all of the original EC comics were reprinted in hardcover compendiums.

Gaines died at home of natural causes on 3 June 1992. His ashes were scattered over the Statue of Liberty and in the wine cellar of his favorite restaurant in Paris, among other places.

Beginning in the 1950s, William Gaines provided noncommercial, widely distributed publications that were wildly original, vivid experiments in the emerging new medium of comic books. The original EC comics are still regarded by collectors and connoisseurs as the best of their time and among the best ever published. *Mad* magazine became a rite of passage of American adolescence, a place where youngsters could confront the gap between traditional values and ideals and the ruses and corruption they encountered in the contemporary world.

★

Frank Jacobs, a regular contributor to *Mad,* is the author of the only biography, *The Mad World of William M. Gaines* (1972). Maria Reidelbach, *Completely MAD: A History of the Comic Book and Magazine* (1991), details the history of EC and *Mad.* The entire run of EC comics, including those written by Gaines, has been reprinted in hardcover, annotated editions by Russ Cochran. Vincent P. Norris, "Mad Economics: An Analysis of an Adless Magazine," *Journal of Communication* (winter 1984), analyzes *Mad*'s unorthodox financial practices. *Seduction of the Innocent* (1954), Frederic Wertham's diatribe against comics, contains illustrations of EC comics, while *The Mad Morality* (1970) by Vernard Eller, a minister, is a theological defense of *Mad.* An obituary is in the *New York Times* (4 June 1992), along with an editorial (5 June 1992).

MARIA REIDELBACH

GALLO, Julio Robert (*b.* 21 March 1910 in Oakland, California; *d.* 2 May 1993 near Tracy, California), vintner and wine industrialist who, together with his brother Ernest, founded the Gallo wine empire, changing Americans' drinking habits and revolutionizing the field of wine making.

Gallo was one of three children of Guiseppe ("Joseph") Gallo, a wine maker, and Assunta ("Susie") Bianca, a homemaker. His parents immigrated to the United States from the Piedmont region of Italy, bringing their families' wine-making traditions with them. The Gallos lived in many towns in California, from Hartford to Livermore to Escalon, eventually settling in Modesto in 1922. After various unsuccessful business ventures, the Gallos, along with Julio's uncle, Mike, founded the Gallo Wine Company in

Julio Gallo.

1906, laying the foundation for what would become one of the largest wine empires in the United States. Julio spent his formative years learning the wine-making business from the ground up. He attended Modesto High School from 1925 to 1929 but spent the bulk of his time in the vineyards. Prohibition significantly affected the winery's sales, sending Julio's father into a depression that culminated with a murder-suicide when Joe Gallo shot his wife and then himself in 1933. Julio and his older brother, Ernest, were named guardians to their younger brother, Joseph. Julio married Aileen Lowe on 8 May 1933; they had three children: Robert, Susann, and Phillip.

After their parents' deaths, the Gallo brothers decided to capitalize upon the business their father had started. They were granted their first winery permit on 22 September 1933. Julio was in charge of wine making and overseeing the vineyards, and Ernest was in charge of marketing and sales. Starting with only $5,900 between them, the brothers worked incessantly. They convinced banks to loan them money, growers to cede them grapes on credit, and transporters that they would get paid after the winery sold its product. Through the combination of Julio's amiable personality and Ernest's business instincts, their winery slowly became the largest in California.

Their original product was modestly priced dessert wines. Realizing that the average American in the 1930s and 1940s preferred beer to wine, they hired advertising agencies to convince the public that wine was for general consumption, not just for special occasions. Market research helped by showing target areas and audiences. In order to appeal to a broad range of tastes, the winery ultimately produced many different kinds of wines, including sherry, port, Chablis, and Burgundy—overall a total of sixteen brands. By the 1990s, Gallo had captured almost one-third of the entire American wine market.

There were setbacks over the years. Not all of their releases were received well, and because of the limited number of top personnel at the winery, Julio worked seven days a week. The stress of entrepreneurship eventually took its toll: in 1941, Julio suffered a nervous breakdown and was hospitalized for four months, and he had a relapse in 1942. In 1958 his son Phillip took his own life. Julio and his wife sought solace in each other, their two remaining children, and numerous grandchildren.

The Gallos had perhaps their biggest marketing success in the 1950s when they released Thunderbird. This combination of lower-grade grapes with either pear or apple juice appealed to many for both its sweet taste and inexpensive price. It was so successful that the winery followed with Ripple in 1960 and later introduced Night Train Express. These labels sold well but stigmatized the Gallo winery for years as "street wine" producers. To counteract that image, the Gallos introduced new champagne lines—Eden Roc, André, and Tott's—and, in 1967, their Boone's Farm wine label. But the lower-end image haunted them, so the winery launched its Hearty Burgundy and Chablis products, which were promoted as affordable table wines and packaged in volumes up to a gallon. In the late 1970s, another Gallo "jug wine," the Carlo Rossi brand, was quite successful, and in 1984, Bartles and Jaymes wine coolers (bottled like beer, in a six-pack) were hugely popular. Their battle with image continued, however, until 1991 when the winery released Estate Chardonnay and effectively moved into the upscale varietal grape market.

The 1970s were a time of strife for the Gallos as César Chávez and the United Farm Workers brought suit and a great deal of media attention to the plight of migrant laborers. The suit was settled through negotiations, a boycott of grapes and Gallo wine ended, and the Gallos' grape pickers joined the Teamsters; Julio and Ernest were both firm believers in unions. The Gallos also established a growers relations department, which focused on methods of improving grape production. These changes, combined with the winery's insistence that its growers keep up to date with viticultural developments, placed it at the forefront of the industry. The Gallos were also heralded for other changes: they developed a colored bottle they called "Flavor-guard," which blocked ultraviolet rays and thereby extended the shelf life of a wine (1957); they used modern advertising, thereby making wine a national beverage; they manufactured their own glass, thereby cutting costs (the Gallo Glass Company was founded in 1958); they pioneered new training methods and point-of-sale displays; and they introduced stainless steel wine-making vats and computers for wine blending. Julio played a key role in all of these developments. His brother Ernest said, "More than any man alive, Julio was responsible for upgrading the quality-control and sanitary practices of the California wine industry." His efforts were also noted by *Time* magazine, which named Julio and Ernest "Kings of Wine" in its November 1972 cover story, and by the American Society of Enologists, which awarded Julio its Merit Award in 1975.

In 1986 Ernest and Julio filed a trademark infringement suit against their brother Joseph. Joseph, a cheese maker, was using the Gallo name on his product. He countersued the same year. After many years and bitter feuds, Joseph was ordered by the court to cease using the name Gallo. This case effectively estranged Joseph from his brothers.

Julio spent the last years of his life at the Gallo of Sonoma winery attempting to create an even more upscale brand of wine, and in this pursuit he also made significant financial contributions to the viticulture and enology departments at Fresno State University and the University of California at Davis. He died from a cervical spine fracture caused by a car accident and was buried in the Saint Stanislaus Cemetery in Modesto, California.

To Julio Gallo, the most important thing was the land. He spent years of his life cultivating the soil, plucking grapes by hand, and studying growing times to make the best wine possible. His technological contributions to the field enabled other vintners to improve all aspects of their product. As it says on his tombstone, Gallo was first and foremost a "Winemaker Who Loved The Land."

★

Julio and Ernest Gallo collaborated with Bruce B. Henderson on *Ernest and Julio: Our Story* (1994), presenting every aspect of their lives from their grandparents' immigration to America up to and including Julio's death (included as a postscript). Ellen Hawkes wrote *Blood and Wine: The Unauthorized Story of the Gallo Wine Empire* (1993) with the intention of exposing the hypocrisy of the lawsuit between the brothers. She contends that Joseph was railroaded into giving up his share of the family fortune, and that Ernest and Julio rewrote history to hinder Joseph from sharing any of the Gallo fame. An obituary is in the *New York Times* (4 May 1993).

SHARON L. DECKER

GANN, Ernest Kellogg (*b.* 13 October 1910 in Lincoln, Nebraska; *d.* 19 December 1991 on San Juan Island, Washington), pilot and author of more than twenty-five fiction and nonfiction works including *The High and the Mighty* (1952) and *The Aviator* (1981).

Gann was the son of George Kellogg Gann and Caroline Kupper. He graduated from Culver Military Academy in Culver, Indiana, in 1930, and then attended Yale Drama School from 1930 to 1932. He left before finishing his degree and traveled around the world, settling for a short time in New York City, where he was an assistant to Leon Leonidoff, the director of Radio City Music Hall. During this time, he also earned money as a barnstormer pilot. Gann, whose nickname throughout his life was "Ernie," married Eleanor Michaud in 1933; they had three children. Their marriage ended in divorce, and he married Dodie Post, also a pilot, in 1966.

Gann's first book, *Sky Roads* (1940), was written while he was a pilot for American Airlines, but it was not until

Ernest Gann, 1957. AMERICAN STOCK/ARCHIVE PHOTOS

World War II, when he was in active combat with the U.S. Army Air Forces, Air Transport Command, that he wrote his first important work, *Island in the Sky* (1944). The tense plot revolves around an airline pilot who makes a successful crash landing in the frigid landscape of northern Canada and the brave men who rescue the passengers and crew. The overpowering forces of nature are a paradigm for the human drama that unfolds.

Hollywood recognized Gann's talent for writing screenplays. Shelly Winters starred in *The Raging Tide* (1951), adapted by Gann from his novel *Fiddler's Green* (1950). Clark Gable played the leading role in *Soldier of Fortune* (1954), which was adapted from the novel of the same name (1954). John Wayne starred in Gann's adaptation of *Island in the Sky* in 1953 as well as in *The High and the Mighty,* released in 1954 with a screenplay Gann adapted from his acclaimed 1952 novel of the same name. In *The High and the Mighty,* two pilots struggle to keep a crippled plane airborne after it loses one of its engines. Through Gann's well-developed characterizations of the pilots and passengers, the readers and viewing audience explore the various ways in which people react in a crisis. Wayne's costars Claire Trevor and Jan Sterling, as well as the director, William Wellman, were all nominated for Academy Awards. Gann's script won the National Association of Independent Schools Award in 1954.

In his autobiography, *Fate Is the Hunter* (1961), adapted into a screenplay in 1964, Gann recounted the ways in which airline pilots responded to life-threatening situations. In doing so, he put his audience at the razor's edge of death-defying moments in flight. He wanted his audience to appreciate every living moment, for fate can intervene at any time to steal life away. While most of Gann's important works were drawn from his experiences as a pilot, he also won rave reviews for his renderings of life at sea in his novels *Twilight for the Gods* (1958) and *The Song of the Sirens* (1968).

One of his last adaptations from novel to screenplay was drawn from *The Antagonists* (1971). This novel was the source for the four-part television miniseries *Masada,* which aired on ABC in 1981. Peter O'Toole, Peter Strauss, and Giulia Pagano played the starring roles. *Masada* was a historical account of the courageous Jewish revolt lead by Eleazar ben Yair against the Roman general Flavius Silva in A.D. 70, and the martyrdom of 960 men, women, and children who chose to die rather than surrender to the Romans.

While Gann viewed fate as a hunter, he also examined the various ways in which people faced their destinies. Gann's heroes died with dignity; the survivors faced overwhelming odds with integrity. The film *The Aviator* (1985), adapted from his novel, starred Christopher Reeve and Rosanna Arquette as a pilot and a young woman who face incredible odds after a plane crash. The movie, however, was not a commercial success.

Gann's last book, the nonfiction *Black Watch: The Men Who Fly America's Secret Spy Planes* (1989), was dedicated to the pilots who fly for the air force and for the Central Intelligence Agency. Gann had flown a number of Douglas planes including the DC-2, DC-3, C-54, and C-87. In 1981, at the age of sixty-nine, he flew a U-2 at an altitude of 71,200 feet. As a result, when he described the feeling of soaring above the clouds, he was able to bring his readers along with him, giving them the sense of the danger, thrill, and exhilaration of flying.

Gann's honors include the Pacific Northwest Booksellers Award (1973), the Aviation Journalist of the Year Award (1975), and the Inspirational Award of the Western Aerospace Association (1977). The last years of his life were full and creative; among other activities he was an artist and showed his work in Seattle. He died of kidney failure at the age of eighty-one at his home on San Juan Island.

In his best-selling books Gann grappled with the concept of fate and questioned whether men and women could control their destinies. Gann felt that luck was a key ingredient for survival, but his protagonists were self-reliant and that often made the difference between life and death. Through his writings, readers and movie audiences have the vicarious opportunity to explore historical events, life at sea, and, most importantly, the world of men and women in flight.

★

Fate Is the Hunter (1961) is a fast-paced autobiography about the early years of Gann's flying experiences. His other autobiography is *A Hostage to Fortune* (1978). For insights into Gann's life as a pilot and as a writer see Russell Munson, "Gentleman of Adventure: Ernest K. Gann," *Flying* 119 (Dec. 1992): 72–80, and "Ernest K. Gann," in Nicholas O'Connell's collection of interviews *At the Field's End* (1998). Notable reviews of Gann's work include "In the Company of Eagles," *New Yorker* (29 Oct. 1966); Brian Garfield, "Duel in the Sky," *Saturday Review* (24 Dec. 1966); Edward Garside, "The Complete Sailor: The Song of the Sirens," *New York Times Book Review* (27 Oct. 1968); "The Antagonists," *New York Times Book Review* (14 Feb. 1971); and David Myers, "Gentlemen of Adventure," *New York Times Book Review* (22 Jan. 1984). An obituary is in the *New York Times* (21 Dec. 1991).

JANE FRANCES AMLER

GARRISON, Jim (*b.* 20 November 1921 in Denison, Iowa; *d.* 21 October 1992 in New Orleans, Louisiana), district attorney who made international headlines for his investigation into the assassination of President John F. Kennedy.

Garrison, born Earling Carothers Garrison, was one of two children of Earling R. Garrison, occupation unknown, and

Jim Garrison, 1967. ASSOCIATED PRESS AP

Jane Ann Robinson. When Garrison was two, his parents divorced, and his mother, who raised him and his younger sister, Judith, became a schoolteacher. In 1928 the family moved to New Orleans, where Garrison attended elementary school and Forrier High School, from which he graduated in 1940. In January 1941 he joined the U.S. Army. Serving with distinction in World War II as a combat pilot, flying observation aircraft during bombing missions, Garrison flew thirty-five missions and received the European Theater Campaign Medal with two battle stars. In 1946 he enrolled in Tulane University Law School, and he was admitted to the Louisiana bar in 1949. After working for the Federal Bureau of Investigation briefly, Garrison reenlisted in the army for service in Korea but was discharged for "physical disability." At some undetermined time he legally changed his name to Jim Garrison.

In 1951 Garrison began working for the Orleans Parish district attorney's office. In 1957 he ran unsuccessfully for assessor, and in 1960 he lost a race for district judge. He was appointed assistant city attorney in 1959. He married Leah Elizabeth Ziegler (date unknown). They had five children. In 1962, despite his underdog status, Garrison, taking full advantage of a televised debate to gain public recognition and newspaper endorsements, won the district attorney's race. A huge man, six feet, seven inches tall and weighing close to 250 pounds, Garrison earned the sobriquet "the Jolly Green Giant." He gained considerable publicity and popular support through several raids against the wide-open vice activities in the New Orleans French Quarter.

In the fall of 1966 Garrison and Senator Russell B. Long discussed the assassination of President John F. Kennedy during a plane flight to New York. Long expressed grave reservations about the Warren Commission's conclusion that Lee Harvey Oswald had acted alone in killing Kennedy. After reading several books and articles that detailed flaws in the commission's investigation, Garrison decided to launch his own inquiry. He was certain that a conspiracy to murder the president had been hatched in New Orleans. Employing the considerable investigative and subpoena resources of the district attorney's office, he interrogated witnesses and focused his attention on several suspects. In February 1967 one of those suspects, David William Ferrie, died suddenly from natural causes. Garrison exploited the death, claiming it was a suicide.

On 1 March 1967 Garrison ordered the arrest of the New Orleans business and civic leader Clay L. Shaw for conspiracy to murder Kennedy. The arrest caused a sensation. Not only did Garrison publicly criticize the official government version of the assassination, but he also backed up his accusations with a legal prosecution. At the preliminary hearing to determine whether or not Shaw would be indicted under Louisiana criminal law, Garrison produced a witness, Perry Raymond Russo, who testified that he had observed Shaw, Ferrie, and Oswald discussing the assassination of the president at a party in New Orleans. The object of substantial publicity in the press, Garrison became an international celebrity and appeared on numerous radio and television programs. Claiming that he had "solved" the mystery behind Kennedy's assassination, he promised to reveal the truth at Shaw's trial.

During Shaw's trial in New Orleans, January through March 1969, Garrison produced a number of witnesses and medical experts who testified about inconsistencies in the lone assassin thesis. Though he rarely attended the trial, he assured that the famous Zapruder film of the assassination was shown many times. In addition to Russo, his witnesses against Shaw included a convicted heroin addict and a man who claimed that aliens spied on him. The jury took less than an hour to reach its verdict of not guilty. Garrison had simply failed to prove his case against Shaw. Highly critical of Garrison from the beginning, the national press and media denounced the investigation as a fraud and the prosecution of Shaw as a travesty of justice.

In 1973 Garrison lost his bid for reelection to the district attorney's position, but in 1978 he was elected to a seat on the Fourth Circuit Court of Appeals of Louisiana. He wrote three books, *A Heritage of Stone* (1970), *The Star Spangled Contract* (1976), and *On the Trail of the Assassins* (1988). The last detailed his investigation of the assassination and the prosecution of Shaw. The book attracted the curiosity of movie director and producer Oliver Stone, whose 1991 film *JFK* ignited a fierce national debate. The film, in which Kevin Costner plays Garrison and Garrison appears in a cameo role as Earl Warren, portrays Garrison in a sympathetic manner and argues forcibly for an assassination conspiracy. Garrison died of undisclosed causes on 21 October 1992. He is buried in New Orleans.

Garrison's prosecution of Shaw has received justified condemnation, for he produced no credible evidence that implicated Shaw in a conspiracy to assassinate President Kennedy. Garrison's flamboyant, publicity-seeking harangues to the press about his "solution" to the assassination have also been justifiably criticized. Yet Garrison did produce evidence of an assassination conspiracy at the Shaw trial, and his claims of a government cover-up of critical evidence in that case have been substantiated in the several million pages of documentary records released between 1993 and 1998. In its depiction of Garrison as a lone defender of the truth against the malevolent powers in the federal government, the film *JFK* rehabilitated Garrison in the public eye. Nevertheless, it received a barrage of criticism from journalists and scholars. Garrison and his investigation into the Kennedy assassination remain the subjects of fierce debate among researchers.

★

No collection of Garrison manuscripts is known to exist. The records of his investigation and of the Shaw trial are in the National Archives and Records Service, College Park, Maryland; and in the New Orleans Public Library Louisiana Room. Garrison's books are *A Heritage of Stone* (1970), *The Star Spangled Contract* (1976), and *On the Trail of the Assassins* (1988). Critical studies of Garrison include Milton E. Brener, *The Garrison Case* (1969); James Kirkwood, *American Grotesque* (1970); and Patricia Lambert, *False Witness: The Real Story of Jim Garrison's Investigation and Oliver Stone's Film* JFK (1998). Sympathetic studies include James DiEugenio, *Destiny Betrayed* (1992), and William Davy, *Let Justice Be Done: New Light on the Jim Garrison Investigation* (1999). An obituary is in the *New York Times* (22 Oct. 1992).

MICHAEL L. KURTZ

GATES, John (*b.* 28 September 1913 in New York City; *d.* 23 May 1992 in Miami Beach, Florida), American Communist Party leader and editor of the *Daily Worker* who renounced the Party in 1958.

Gates was born Sol Regenstreif on the Lower East Side of Manhattan. His parents, Joseph Regenstreif and Rosie Snapf, were Jewish immigrants from the Galicia region of

John Gates (*left*), editor in chief of the *Daily Worker,* a paper affiliated with the Communist party, is ordered out of his office by a Treasury agent, 1956. © BETTMANN/CORBIS

Poland. His father was a waiter at Ratner's Restaurant on Delancey Street. His mother was a homemaker. In 1917 his father bought a candy store and moved the family to West Ninety-eighth Street, near Central Park. Six years later the family relocated to the Bronx, where Gates's father operated a large ice-cream parlor. Gates graduated from DeWitt Clinton High School in January 1930, at age sixteen, and immediately entered the City College of New York.

The seminal event in Gates's early life was the Great Depression, which he believed was the inevitable result of the capitalist system. Attracted by communist and socialist doctrines, he joined the Young Communist League in March 1931 and quit City College in early 1932 to work full-time for the Communist Party. Over the next four years he helped organize steelworkers in Warren and Youngstown, Ohio. Before leaving for the Midwest, Gates changed his name to John Gates. He selected his new name at random, out of a newspaper. "There was no compelling reason to change the name except that it was the thing to do in those days," he wrote in his 1958 autobiography, *The Story of an American Communist.* "This was not to hide anything but to symbolize a change in a way of life."

In February 1937 Gates joined a contingent of several hundred young men from the United States who were volunteering to fight against the fascists in the Spanish Civil War. He fought in several battles and was named a commissar in the Abraham Lincoln Brigade, the highest rank of any American who served in Spain. In 1937 Gates was

elected to the National Council of the Young Communist League in absentia. After the fascists won, Gates returned to the United States in December 1938.

Ten days after Pearl Harbor, on 17 December 1941, Gates enlisted in the U.S. Army and was posted to the Aleutian Islands in Alaska, where unlike his action-filled experience in Spain, the only enemy he battled was boredom. In March 1945 he volunteered for the paratroopers and was sent to France. He was honorably discharged on 17 January 1946 as a first sergeant in the famed 101st Airborne Division. Shortly before he enlisted, Gates met Texas native Lillian Ross, an education director in the New York City branch of the Young Communist League. They were married on 5 February 1945, in Bennettsville, South Carolina. After the war they lived in the Borough of Queens in New York City. They had no children.

When the Soviet Union expanded its dominion over Eastern Europe and the cold war began, the American Communist Party lost the relative respectability that it had accrued as a result of the alliance with the USSR during World War II. In June 1947 Gates was appointed the editor in chief of the party's newspaper, the *Daily Worker.* Although not an experienced journalist, he proved a capable editor, and his influential position put him in the line of fire when the specter of communism grew to dominate the postwar national agenda.

On 20 July 1948 a federal grand jury indicted John Gates and eleven other leaders of the Communist Party, under Title I of the Smith Act. This 1940 legislation made it illegal to organize a political party to teach and advocate the violent overthrow of the U.S. government. The indictment did not allege that the defendants had committed any overt revolutionary act, only teaching and advocating. The trial opened on 17 January 1949 in the Manhattan federal court building. Gates later remarked that the "anti-Communist hysteria was so intense, and most Americans were so frightened by the Communist issue, that we were convicted before our trial even started." They were indeed found guilty after a raucous trial that lasted nine months. The defendants each received a five-year prison term and a $10,000 fine. Gates remained free while the case was appealed, until 4 June 1951, when the U.S. Supreme Court, in a 6 to 2 decision, upheld the constitutionality of the Smith Act. He served his sentence in a federal penitentiary in Atlanta. Released on 1 March 1955, he returned to New York City and his post as editor in chief of the *Daily Worker*.

During his imprisonment, Gates had begun to question his commitment to the Communist Party. By 1956 thousands of Party members were quitting in the wake of the Soviet suppression of the revolt in Hungary and Soviet leader Nikita Khrushchev's speech revealing some of Joseph Stalin's atrocities. Gates was also repulsed by revelations of the Soviet Union's treatment of Jews. For him, "the Jewish question has been the acid test of the democratic-mindedness and humanity of societies," and the Soviet disclosures were the "most shameful blot on its record."

Over the next two years, Gates led a faction within the party that sought to institute reforms. He believed the basic reason for the party's failure was its "worshipful and imitative relationship to the Soviet Union." The party, he said, must reject unquestioned acceptance of the Soviet interpretation of Marxist theory and formulate its own more democratic policies corresponding to conditions in the United States. Gates's ideas were promulgated in a Draft Resolution of 1956, but the American Communist Party leadership briefly accepted it but then backtracked, dooming the reforms to failure. For Gates, the last straw was the decision of the party's leadership in December 1957 to suspend the *Daily Worker*. "When the *Daily Worker* went, I would go with it," he had decided. He resigned from the party on 9 January 1958.

After his resignation Gates became a research assistant for the International Ladies Garment Workers Union in New York City, helping union members with workers compensation and jobless claims. He retired in 1987 and moved with his wife to North Miami Beach. He died in 1992 at the Miami Heart Institute of heart disease and stroke. His remains were cremated.

John Gates was not a big man (he was five-feet, eight-inches tall and slender), but throughout his life, his calm, cool demeanor in all types of confrontational situations gave him a commanding presence. His story is representative of what happened to a generation of Americans whose lives were transformed by the Great Depression of the 1930s. The desire for change that led him to the Communist Party did not end with his resignation in 1958. "I am no longer a Communist," Gates wrote in 1958, but "American life does need basic changes and there have always been plenty of problems requiring radical solutions, even in 'good times'."

★

Gates's autobiography, *The Story of an American Communist* (1958), provides a detailed and comprehensive account of his life up to 1958. His role in the Communist Party is discussed in David A. Shannon, *The Decline of American Communism: A History of the Communist Party of the United States Since 1945* (1959), and Joseph R. Starobin, *American Communism in Crisis, 1943–1957* (1972). Obituaries are in the *New York Times* (21 May 1992) and *Los Angeles Times* (26 May 1992).

KENNETH R. COBB

GEHRINGER, Charles Leonard ("Charlie") (*b.* 11 May 1903 in Fowlerville, Michigan; *d.* 21 January 1993 in Bloomfield Hills, Michigan), baseball player who was considered the premier second baseman of his generation and who was inducted into the Baseball Hall of Fame in 1949.

Gehringer was one of three children born on a family farm sixty miles north of Detroit. His parents' full names are unknown. He loved baseball so much as a boy that he and his brother carved out a diamond on their farm so they could play every day. Gehringer was devoted to his mother, Teresa, who had diabetes. He lived with her until he was forty-three and did not marry until after her death because he felt his responsibility for her care left no room for a wife in his life.

Gehringer was a star third baseman for his Fowlerville High School team, and he played both baseball and football during 1923, the only year he attended the University of Michigan. The lean, five feet, eleven inch, 185-pound youngster, who threw right-handed and batted left-handed, impressed the Detroit Tigers' player-manager Ty Cobb during a 1924 tryout at Navin Field. Cobb did not take time to change his uniform before he rushed Gehringer to the front office to sign a contract. Gehringer said Cobb, with whom he spent many hours of long train rides discussing the secrets of hitting and baserunning, became like a second father to him.

Gehringer played in the last five games of the 1924 season and batted .462. After a successful 1925 minor league season in Toronto, where he hit .325 with 25 home runs and 108 runs batted in (RBIs), he played in the final eight games for the Detroit Tigers. In 1926 Gehringer became a team regular, beginning a string of sixteen years as their starting second baseman.

Charlie Gehringer, 1934. AP/WIDE WORLD PHOTOS

An intense-looking man with his cap fixed tightly on his head, Gehringer was known as much for his silence and lack of color as for his legendary fielding and batting skills. He was nicknamed the "Mechanical Man" by the Yankee pitcher Lefty Gomez, who said of him: "They wind him up at the start of the season and he never runs down. All I know is that whenever you played the Tigers, you would look up and he would be on base." His Detroit manager Mickey Cochrane explained, "Charlie says 'hello' on Opening Day, 'goodbye' on Closing Day, and in between hits .350 and fields for a .980 average."

Gehringer covered second base with a smooth, seemingly effortless style. Possessed of quick hands and an encyclopedic memory of opposing batters, he positioned himself so astutely that he rarely made diving catches and his plays did not appear spectacular. As a defensive player he led American League second basemen in fielding percentage nine times, led or tied in assists a record seven times, and was the leader in putouts three times.

Gehringer's offense was as impressive as his defense. Because of his controlled batting swing, he was difficult to strike out, and in sixteen full seasons his strikeouts ranged from sixteen to forty-two. The 1929 season exemplifies the Mechanical Man's all-around playing excellence. That year Gehringer led the league in stolen bases, doubles, triples, hits, runs scored, games played, putouts, and fielding av-

erage while batting .339. On 14 August 1929 the Tigers' management and fans celebrated Charlie Gehringer Day at the ballpark, and Gehringer responded in turn. He handled cleanly ten chances in the field, slugged a home run, smacked three singles, and stole home to help the Tigers beat the visiting New York Yankees. A smart and powerful hitter, Gehringer slapped the ball to all parts of the field and was consistently among the league's leaders in extra bases with doubles and triples. Although not a home run hitter, he did slug ten or more home runs in eleven seasons, ending with a career high of twenty in the 1938 season.

As further proof of his consistency, the Mechanical Man played seven seasons with 200 or more hits and seven seasons with over 100 RBIs. In thirteen seasons he batted over .300, and his lifetime batting average of .320 mirrors his lifetime World Series average (twenty games) of .321. He played every inning of the first six All-Star Games (1933–1938) and at the beginning of the twenty-first century was still the career leader with a .500 batting average (ten for twenty). Gehringer was on first base and scored when an aging Babe Ruth hit the first All-Star home run in 1933. In 1937 Gehringer's .371 average made him the oldest player to win his first batting title, and he was voted the American League's Most Valuable Player. He led the Detroit Tigers to their first World Series championship in 1935 and to pennants in 1934 and 1940. From 1924 to 1942 he played in 2,184 games; collected 2,839 hits; scored 1,774 runs; drove in 1,427 runs; slugged 184 home runs, 574 doubles, and 146 triples; and fielded .976. His highest major league salary was $35,000.

Gehringer enlisted in the U.S. Navy in 1943 and served for three years as a fitness instructor. In 1949 he was elected to the Baseball Hall of Fame. Echoing the priorities he established earlier in his life, he did not show up for his summer induction ceremony at Cooperstown, New York, instead marrying Josephine (maiden name unknown) in California. They had no children. In 1951 Gehringer became the Detroit Tigers' vice president and general manager. In 1953 he relinquished the general manager duties, but he remained vice president until 1959.

After suffering a stroke in December 1992, Gehringer entered a nursing home near his home. He died there less than a month later and is buried in Holy Sepulchre Cemetery in Southfield, Michigan. Before his death in 1993 he was the oldest living member of the Baseball Hall of Fame.

Although taciturn and undemonstrative, Gehringer is famous for two baseball quotes: "Show me a good loser and I'll show you an idiot," and "Us ballplayers do things backward. First we play, then we retire and go to work." During his entire career blacks were excluded from major league baseball. But in 1929, after the Negro League pitcher Bill Foster shut out the Tigers in an exhibition game, Gehringer said, "If I could paint you white I could get $150,000 dollars for you." When asked who was the best pitcher he ever saw, he picked another Negro League legend, Satchel Paige. In 1976 Gehringer established the Charlie Gehringer Golf Classic, an annual tournament benefiting charity, in which he and his wife played each year until his death. At the time of baseball's centennial celebration in 1969, a special committee of baseball writers named Gehringer the game's greatest living second baseman.

★

Gehringer's career reminiscences can be found in Lee Allen and Tom Meany, *Kings of the Diamond* (1965); Martin Appel and Burt Goldblatt, *Baseball's Best: The Hall of Fame Gallery* (1970); Tom Meany and Paul McFarlane, *TSN Daguerreotypes of Great Stars of Baseball* (1971); Ken Smith, *Baseball's Hall of Fame* (1978); and fill seventeen pages in Richard Bak, *Cobb Would Have Caught It: The Golden Age of Baseball in Detroit* (1991). Obituaries are in the *New York Times* (23 Jan. 1993) and the *Detroit Free Press* (23 Jan. 1993).

MARK A. BLICKLEY

GEISEL, Theodor Seuss ("Dr. Seuss") (*b*. 2 March 1904 in Springfield, Massachusetts; *d*. 24 September 1991 in La Jolla, California), author and illustrator of forty-seven children's books and creator of fabled characters, including the title characters of *Horton Hatches the Egg!* (1940), *The Cat in the Hat* (1957), and *How the Grinch Stole Christmas!* (1957).

Geisel was the only son of first-generation German Americans Theodor Robert Geisel, a brewery owner before Prohibition forced the brewery's closure in 1920, and Henrietta Seuss, a spunky, six-foot-tall homemaker. "Ted," as young Geisel was called, had an older sister to whom he was devoted in childhood. A younger sister was born in 1906 but died of pneumonia eighteen months later; Geisel never forgot the image of her tiny casket in the music room of the three-story home at 74 Fairfield Street in Springfield. Yet most of his childhood was happy, rich with family encouragement for his loopy, lopsided drawings of animals and his flair for nonsense and exaggeration. He gave credit for "Seussian" rhymes and rhythms to his mother, who recited poems and read him bedtime stories. Geisel's father, a champion marksman and member of the city parks board, instilled in his son a drive for perfection and led behind-the-scenes tours of the Springfield Zoo, which would influence the work of "Dr. Seuss."

Also evocative for Geisel were the bustle and clatter of Springfield streets in the early 1900s: the rattle of trolleys, ice wagons, and grocers' delivery vans, the horse-drawn carriages, three-wheeled bicycles, and horn-honking Hudson Six motor cars. A fascination with inventions characterized this western Massachusetts city, and Geisel carried such tinkering into his writing—adding new letters to the al-

Theodor Geisel ("Dr. Seuss"). LIBRARY OF CONGRESS

phabet in his 1955 book, *On Beyond Zebra*. Names of Springfield citizens and streets appear in his work, including his first children's book: *And to Think That I Saw it on Mulberry Street* (1937).

After graduating from Central High School in 1921, Geisel entered Dartmouth College, a train ride north to Hanover, New Hampshire. He struggled for grades as a literature major, preferring his hours on the staff of the school's comic magazine *Jack-O-Lantern*. His easiest course was German, widely spoken in Springfield prior to World War I. While he managed to graduate with a B.A. in 1925, he was stripped of the *Jack-O-Lantern* editorship in his senior year for drinking bootleg gin with friends on Easter weekend. This ignominy led to the subterfuge of submitting cartoons using only his middle name, Seuss.

That autumn Geisel found himself at Oxford University's Lincoln College. It was one of many times that his rampant imagination skittered beyond the truth. He had boasted to his father that he had won a scholarship to Oxford; in fact, he had only applied. But having made a proud announcement in the Springfield newspaper, Geisel's father helped pay the tuition. Geisel was not prepared for serious study. While he failed to earn a degree, he met a charming, willful Wellesley graduate, Helen Marion Palmer, who was five-and-a-half years his senior. After watching him doodle in a Chaucer notebook, she blurted: "You're crazy to try to be a professor. What you really want to do is draw!" They were married in New Jersey in 1927, and she remained his booster, editor, prod, and shield until her suicide in La Jolla, California, in October 1967.

The couple's early years were heady ones, spent in New York City. Geisel sold cartoons and satire to the popular *Judge* magazine, where he first used the pseudonym "Dr. Seuss" by adding the degree he did not get at Oxford to his mother's maiden name. He was hired by the Standard Oil Company of New Jersey to illustrate advertisements for Flit insect spray, vital in American households before air-conditioning. The slogan "Quick, Henry! the Flit!" entered the lexicon, allowing the Geisels plentiful funds for foreign travel. It was before the stock market crash of 1929 and the Great Depression, an era of speakeasies, optimism, and outrageous practical jokes among the young creative set in New York. Such humor and their shared sense of privacy helped mask the Geisels' anguish that Helen could not have children. Their charade included an imaginary child, Chrysanthemum-Pearl, whose outlandish feats were legend and to whom the second Dr. Seuss tale, *The 500 Hats of Bartholomew Cubbins* (1938), was dedicated.

But the launching of Dr. Seuss as artist and writer was not smooth, and Geisel's confidence wore thin. In 1937, after twenty-seven publishers had rejected his rhyming story of *Mulberry Street*, he decided to return to his apartment and burn the manuscript. En route, on Madison Avenue, he met a Dartmouth classmate who had just been named juvenile editor at Viking Press; within the hour, a contract was signed. From then on, Geisel swore that he owed his success to luck.

After *Mulberry Street* and *The 500 Hats* the new firm of Random House published all of Dr. Seuss's works, and its founder, Bennett Cerf, became a lifelong friend. Cerf, who called Geisel the only true genius among his authors, even went along with his dogged attempt at an adult cartoon book, *The Seven Lady Godivas,* which failed both in 1939 and when it was reissued fifty years later. ("When I tried to draw naked ladies they ended up looking ridiculous," Geisel said.) He returned to children's books until 1940, when war headlines from Europe provoked him into drawing savage political cartoons for the liberal New York tabloid *PM.* A lifelong Democrat, he skewered Hitler, Mussolini, and Hirohito as well as American isolationists, such as Charles Lindbergh. After the Japanese attack on Pearl Harbor, Geisel, then forty years old, signed on as a U.S. Army captain and was assigned to director Frank Capra's Signal Corps film unit in Hollywood. Throughout World

War II he made propaganda documentaries and recruitment cartoons with a team that included composer Meredith Willson ("The Music Man"), historian Paul Horgan, and the pioneering animator Chuck Jones, with whom he later collaborated to bring *How the Grinch Stole Christmas!* and *Horton Hears a Who!* to television.

A brief fling with Hollywood filmmaking in the 1950s was a disaster—Geisel always worked best alone—and *The 5,000 Fingers of Dr. T.,* his tangled attempt at musical fantasy, did not become a cult classic for years. Irked with movies, the Geisels bought an abandoned observation tower on a La Jolla hilltop and built their home around it. There, in a tile-roofed studio overlooking the Pacific, Geisel wrote every Dr. Seuss book from *If I Ran the Zoo* (1950) to *Oh, the Places You'll Go!* (1990).

After a 1954 article in *Life* magazine lamented the illiteracy of American youth, Dr. Seuss was challenged to write and illustrate a reader with a vocabulary of only 225 words. The hard-fought result was *The Cat in the Hat* (1957), an immediate success that led to a series of Beginner Books and changed the way Americans learned to read. *The Cat in the Hat* was fun and feisty; critics and teachers applauded its hypnotic merit. Children seized on it instead of their bland primers. That December, he followed with *How the Grinch Stole Christmas!* Two Seuss classics appeared in 1960: *One Fish Two Fish Red Fish Blue Fish* and *Green Eggs and Ham,* the charming result of a bet with Cerf that he could not write a book using only fifty different words. Rollicking couplets, such as this one from *How the Grinch Stole Christmas,* became instantly recognizable as "Seussian":

The Grinch hated Christmas! The whole Christmas season!
Now, please don't ask why. No one quite knows the reason.
It could be his head wasn't screwed on just right.
It could be, perhaps, that his shoes were too tight.
But I think that the most likely reason of all
May have been that his heart was two sizes too small.

Geisel won Academy Awards for *Hitler Lives?* (1946) and *Design for Death* (1947), and an Emmy Award for *Halloween is Grinch Night* (1977, 1982), as well as honorary degrees from a dozen universities, including Princeton in 1985, where the senior class rose to chant the full text of *Green Eggs and Ham.* Yet he grew increasingly shy of crowds and fearful of public speaking. He remained happiest during long hours in his studio, striving to meet his own rigorous standards to get words and meter right.

Less than a year after Helen's death in 1967, Geisel married Audrey Stone Dimond, who was seventeen years his junior and the recently divorced wife of a former best friend in La Jolla, and abruptly changed the direction of his writing. Over editorial arguments at Random House, he took on tough issues: environmental threat in *The Lorax* (1971); the arms race in *The Butter Battle Book* (1984); and, on his eighty-fifth birthday, the medical establishment in *You're Only Old Once!* (1986). By then he was battling cancer. In 1984 he received a Pulitzer Prize for his "special contribution over nearly half a century to the education and enjoyment of America's children and their parents." The Pulitzer brought a flurry of media exposure for the tall, thin, white-bearded author. Still he lived simply, refusing to complicate his life with a fax machine, word processor, or electric typewriter. He had no back-up artists or writers; one secretary in La Jolla handled fan mail. He firmly refused all efforts at franchising Dr. Seuss, whether toys, T-shirts, or theme parks.

Geisel's final book, *Oh, the Places You'll Go!,* was a valedictory, a summing-up of optimism and courage. He exulted that he had finally made the adult best-seller list of the *New York Times*, where the book remained for more than two years and reappeared annually at graduation time. It was the closest he came to an autobiography, since he was unable to manage either facts or prose.

Geisel died of cancer at his home in La Jolla, a frugal millionaire, stretched out on the same threadbare couch where he had flung himself over the years when ideas would not come at his desk or drawing board. He was cremated and his ashes placed in a sealed box in Audrey's living room; there was no funeral or grave marker. Tributes came from throughout the English-speaking world: "Dr. Seuss, Modern Mother Goose, Dies at 87," was the front-page headline of the *New York Times*. He was eulogized in the U.S. Senate. Read-aloud vigils were held on college campuses as fan clubs formed to remember the man who spoke to their fears and dreams.

Dr. Seuss, who sold more than 400 million books in his lifetime, was a unique mentor for four generations of Americans, championing children's rights before that phrase was familiar and revolutionizing the way children learn to read. His forty-seven books are recognized for their whimsical, tongue-twisting honesty and ebullient art, as he sought to stretch young imaginations and make the incredible credible.

★

Geisel's papers, manuscripts, and drawings are in the Special Collections of the Geisel Library at the University of California, San Diego. A biography by Judith Morgan and Neil Morgan, *Dr. Seuss & Mr. Geisel* (1995; reissued in paperback, 2000), has extensive footnotes. His work and its lasting effect are discussed in Barbara Bader, *American Picturebooks from Noah's Ark to the Beast Within* (1976). A revealing profile by E. J. Kahn appeared in the *New Yorker* (17 Dec. 1960). Dr. Seuss's contributions to the English language were cited in two reference books published in 1992: *The Oxford Companion to the English Language* and *Bartlett's Familiar Quotations* (16th ed.). Lengthy obituaries ran in the *San Diego Tribune* (25 Sept. 1991), and the *San Diego Union* and the *New York Times* (26 Sept. 1991). Dr. Seuss was the only American among six authors of twentieth-century children's literature featured in a BBC series, *An Awfully Big Adventure* (1998).

JUDITH MORGAN
NEIL MORGAN

GETZ, Stan(ley) (*b.* 2 February 1927 in Philadelphia, Pennsylvania; *d.* 6 June 1991 in Malibu, California), one of the greatest jazz improvisers, known as a creator of beautiful melodies on the tenor saxophone for forty-seven years.

Getz was the first of two sons born to Al Getz, a journeyman printer, and Goldie Yampolski, a homemaker. The family moved from Philadelphia to the Bronx in New York City when Getz was six. He quickly established himself as a musical prodigy and was chosen for the prestigious, classical All-City High School Orchestra at the age of fourteen. A year later in 1943, Getz dropped out of James Monroe High School to join Jack Teagarden's big band, becoming the family breadwinner because his father had trouble earning a living. He joined Stan Kenton's band in 1944 and became a heroin addict during this period. He also worked

Stan Getz. AP/WIDE WORLD PHOTOS

for Jimmy Dorsey and Benny Goodman before joining the renowned "Four Brothers" sax section (with Zoot Sims, Serge Chaloff, and Herbie Steward) of Woody Herman's band of that era, known as his Second Herd (1947–1949). During these formative years he discovered the music of his idol, the saxophonist Lester Young, and mastered big band dynamics and the complex grammar of bebop, the cutting-edge jazz idiom of the 1940s. After absorbing these influences he found his distinctive melodic voice with Herman and became a major star at twenty-one with his 1948 solo on "Early Autumn."

Getz married Beverly Byrne, a singer with Gene Krupa's band, in 1946, and the couple had two sons and a daughter before divorcing in 1956. Three days later he married a Swedish woman, Monica Silfverskiold, with whom he had a daughter and a son. They were divorced in 1987. Getz also fathered an illegitimate son in 1958.

Getz loved playing in big bands. But he appeared with them only sporadically after 1948 because his genius as an improviser—as a creator of fresh and beautiful melodies placed him thereafter as the leader of his own small groups, usually quartets. His rapport with his listeners was particularly strong because he added to his gift for melody a mastery of a wide range of sound—whispers, cries, shouts, purrs, wails. Getz's personal timbre was unique, a poignant ache that penetrated to the listener's marrow. In a profession noted for creative burnout, Getz maintained the highest aesthetic standards throughout a career that spanned more than four decades and produced roughly 300 records. Despite years of personal torment and turmoil, his playing on all but a handful of these occasions shines at the highest level.

His first great small-group recordings were made in a quintet with the guitarist Jimmy Raney (1951–1953). In 1954 he was jailed for six months on a drug offense and thereafter gave up heroin. He soon became an alcoholic, however, and did not attain sobriety until many years later.

Getz signed with Norman Granz's record labels and his Jazz at the Philharmonic tours in 1952 and recorded many outstanding albums for the record companies during a twenty-year period. In October 1957 alone, Getz made six recordings with such stars as Ella Fitzgerald, Gerry Mulligan, Roy Eldridge, Oscar Peterson, and J. J. Johnson. Getz's greatest triumphs for Granz's labels occurred between 1962 and 1972, after Getz returned to the United States from a three-year sojourn in Denmark. Five performances stand out. Getz considered the first, *Focus* (1962), his masterpiece. In it, he created the best marriage of jazz and classical music to date as he improvised brilliantly over Eddie Sauter's classical suite for a small string orchestra. In the second, *Jazz Samba* (1962), he took an obscure Brazilian music genre, bossa nova, and made it a force that stirred millions worldwide. *Jazz Samba* is the only jazz re-

cording to become No. 1 on the pop charts, and it made Getz a rich man at age thirty-six. It also earned him his first Grammy Award for the single "Desafinado." He followed this in 1964 with *Getz-Gilberto,* a collaboration with the Brazilian giants Antonio Carlos ("Tom") Jobim, João Gilberto, and Astrud Gilberto that included "The Girl from Ipanema"; the album won him three Grammys and made it to number two on the pop charts. The fourth and fifth great recordings of the period, *Sweet Rain* (1967) and *Captain Marvel* (1972), were created with the pianist Chick Corea, considered by Getz to be the best musician with whom he had ever performed. Other fine performances from the Granz years include *Stan Getz and Bob Brookmeyer Quintet* (1961), *The Dizzy Gillespie–Stan Getz Quintet* (1953), *West Coast Jazz* (1955), *For Musicians Only* (1956) with Dizzy Gillespie and Sonny Stitt, *Stan Getz and J. J. Johnson at the Opera House* (1957), and *Nobody Else but Me* (1964) with Gary Burton. From 1972 to 1980, Getz recorded for Columbia, which did not handle him well. Only three recordings from that association stand out: *The Master* (1975) featuring Albert Dailey, *The Peacocks* (1975) with Jimmy Rowles, and *Another World* (1978) featuring Andy LaVerne. Getz fared far better between 1980 and 1991 with the record companies Concord and Polygram.

In the quartet format Getz preferred, he was backed by a pianist, a bassist, and a drummer. Getz looked for inspiration mainly from the pianist, who carried the strongest melodic and harmonic load. Throughout his career Getz hired an outstanding array of pianists—Corea, Dailey, Rowles, and LaVerne, mentioned above, as well as Horace Silver (whom Getz discovered playing in a Hartford, Connecticut, bar), Joanne Brackeen, Jim McNeely, Lou Levy, Richie Beirach, and the man he called "the other half of my heart," Kenny Barron.

Getz suffered from depression and attempted suicide at least twice. For many years he tried to medicate his condition with drugs (alcohol was by far the main culprit). Tragically, Getz never found the support and personal resources to break his cycle of depression and alcoholism until he was well into his fifties. He thus felt trapped for decades in a hellish prison of frustration—a frustration that too often boiled over into destructive rage. When he found the tools to combat his demons in the early 1980s, he fought a long and difficult, but ultimately successful, battle.

Getz's life had a happy and dignified ending. During his last five years he was clean and sober, treated those around him with decency, and made amends to many whom he had hurt. He created glorious music for the albums *Anniversary* (1987), *Serenity* (1987), *Apasionado* (1990), and *People Time* (1991), all with Kenny Barron; and *You Gotta Pay the Band* (1991) with Abbey Lincoln. He also bravely battled the liver cancer that finally killed him. He was cremated, and his ashes were scattered in the

Pacific Ocean near Marina Del Rey, California. Getz was awarded his fifth Grammy posthumously for his solo on "I Remember You" from *Serenity*.

Getz possessed an incredible devotion to his gift, his art, and his audience. No matter how damaged, sick, or hungover he may have been, he always managed to pull himself together and provide music of the highest order. As he wrote in the liner notes for *Another World*:

My life is music. And in some vague, mysterious, and subconscious way, I have always been driven by a taut inner spring which has propelled me to almost compulsively reach for perfection in music, often—in fact, mostly—at the expense of everything else in my life.

The words of his friend, the comedian Spike Milligan, provide Getz with a fitting epitaph: "Of suffering, beauty is born; I feel this might be the essence of Stan Getz. Like Van Gogh—he suffers, but my God look what he gave us."

★

Sources include the full-scale biography *Stan Getz: A Life in Jazz* (1996) by Donald L. Maggin and three short, perceptive analyses of Getz's work: Richard Palmer, *Stan Getz* (1988); Alain Tercinet, *Stan Getz* (1989); and Ron Kirkpatrick, *Stan Getz: An Appreciation of His Recorded Work* (1992). See also Arne Astrup's comprehensive *Revised Stan Getz Discography* (1991). Obituaries are in the *New York Times* (7 June 1991), *San Francisco Chronicle* (7 June 1991), *Time* (17 June 1991), *Down Beat* (Aug. 1991), and *Rolling Stone* (8 Aug. 1991).

DONALD A. MAGGIN

GILBERT, Felix (*b*. 21 May 1905 in Baden-Baden, Germany; *d*. 14 February 1991 in Princeton, New Jersey), historian and educator who specialized in the Italian Renaissance, international diplomacy, and intellectual history.

Gilbert was the second child of William Henry Gilbert, an English medical doctor, and Cecile Mendelssohn-Bartholdy, a homemaker. His father, who directed a sanatorium patronized by upper-class patients, died when Felix was an infant. His mother, a descendant of the famous Jewish composer (for whom Gilbert was named) and relative of the wealthy Oppenheim banking family, then took her two children to Berlin. As Gilbert recalled in his memoirs, he was raised in a comfortable, cultivated world of servants and foreign travel. Even the upheaval caused by World War I and the chaos that followed failed to disturb the family's well-being.

Receiving an excellent education at a Berlin gymnasium (secondary school), Gilbert continued his studies at the University of Heidelberg after the war. But the rampant inflation of the early 1920s compelled him to leave school and find gainful employment. From 1923 to 1925 Gilbert worked in the historical section of the German foreign ministry, where he helped edit the official collection of diplomatic documents concerning the origins of World War I. He attended classes at the University of Berlin in the evening.

Improved economic conditions permitted Gilbert to resume full-time study. By then he had developed a strong interest in both foreign policy and Renaissance Italy. Under the direction of the renowned scholar Friedrich Meinecke, he completed a doctoral dissertation on the nineteenth-century Prussian historian Johann Gustav Droysen. Published in 1931, it was followed two years later by his edition of Droysen's political writings.

Gilbert spent most of 1932 and 1933 exploring the Florentine archives. But his academic career was blighted when the Nazis came to power and began placing restrictions on Germany's Jews. Consequently, in October 1933 Gilbert left his homeland for Great Britain where his sister lived. He resided in London for almost three years, learning English and discussing politics with fellow German refugees.

To improve his circumstances, Gilbert accepted a teaching position at Scripps College in Claremont, California, emigrating to the United States in August 1936. A year later he moved to Princeton, New Jersey. There, at the Institute for Advanced Study, he served as an assistant to Edward Mead Earle, who specialized in diplomatic history. Gilbert helped plan and administer seminars, one on American foreign policy, the other on national security. Out of these discussions emerged *Makers of Modern Strategy: Military Thought from Machiavelli to Hitler* (1943), to which he contributed a chapter dealing with Machiavelli's ideas about war.

Naturalized as an American citizen that same year, Gilbert served his new country through his work with the Office of Strategic Services (OSS). He was assigned to the Central Section of the Research and Analysis Branch where he evaluated information from Nazi-controlled Europe. Stationed first in Washington, D.C., Gilbert was later assigned to London, Paris, and, at war's end, Wiesbaden, Germany. While working as an analyst for the German section of the European Research Branch of the OSS in Wiesbaden in 1945, he sought to revive university education along democratic lines. His wartime experience enabled him to publish *Hitler Directs His War* (1950), an annotated edition of the secret records of the German dictator's daily military conferences. After being demobilized, he spent a year as a research analyst with the U.S. State Department. Returning to the academic world in 1946, Gilbert joined the faculty of Bryn Mawr College in Pennsylvania. There he spent sixteen years, rising from lecturer to full professor. He married one of his graduate students, Mary Raymond, on 21 April 1956; they had no children. A popular course that he taught on modern Europe was later transformed into a textbook, *The End of the Eu-*

Felix Gilbert. © BETTMANN/CORBIS

his scholarship on the author of *The Prince.* His *Niccolò Machiavelli e la vita culturale del suo tempo* (*Niccolò Machiavelli and the Cultural Life of His Time,* 1964) brought together essays written over the previous quarter century. *Machiavelli and Guicciardini: Politics and History in Sixteenth-Century Florence* (1965) depicted the two writers as humanists, one the originator of modern political theory, the other the founder of modern historical writing.

Gilbert also devoted considerable attention to historiographical questions. In collaboration with John Higham and Leonard Krieger, he published *History* (1965), contributing a chapter on the interaction of European and American historical thought. In 1971, with Stephen R. Graubard, he edited *Historical Studies Today,* a series of essays written by prominent historians about trends in their various fields. His own contribution dealt with the aims and methods of intellectual history. Gilbert also produced *The Historical Essays of Otto Hintze* (1975), which collected the essential writings of a German scholar whose work he esteemed.

In retirement, Gilbert again focused on the Italian Renaissance. His book *The Pope, His Banker and Venice* (1980) explored the intricate economic diplomacy practices in early sixteenth-century Italy. Gilbert's final study, *History: Politics or Culture? Reflections on Ranke and Burckhardt* (1990), surveyed the contributions made by two major nineteenth-century historians who held divergent points of view.

To honor their teacher and friend, several of Gilbert's former students published *History: Choice and Commitment* (1977). This extensive collection of his articles, book reviews, and addresses demonstrated his extraordinary erudition. The American Historical Association recognized his many accomplishments in 1985 when it conferred upon Gilbert its first Award for Scholarly Distinction.

Suffering from amyotrophic lateral sclerosis, Gilbert died at his home in Princeton and was cremated.

Of medium height, gray-haired, and bespectacled, Gilbert was shy and decorous in public. But with students and colleagues he displayed warmth and charm. A noticeable German accent did not prevent him from becoming a highly effective classroom lecturer. Gilbert's knowledge of subjects that ranged from the Italian Renaissance to Nazi Germany, his tireless capacity for research, and his fresh ideas enabled him to publish extensively, thereby exerting considerable influence within the historical profession.

★

Gilbert's papers are housed at the Hoover Institution in Palo Alto, California, but remain closed until 2018, as per his widow's request. His official wartime correspondence is available in the records of the Office of Strategic Services held by the National Archives and Records Administration. In *A European Past: Memoirs, 1905–1945* (1988), Gilbert recalls his family, education, and early career. His student years are described in "The Historical

ropean Era, 1890 to the Present (1970). With Gordon A. Craig, he edited and contributed to *The Diplomats, 1919–1939* (1953), a collection of essays concerning European and American ambassadors as well as the conduct of policy by foreign ministers. It focused on the transformation of international relations under pressure from both democracy and totalitarianism. On his own, Gilbert produced *To the Farewell Address: Ideas of Early American Foreign Policy* (1961), which traced the international and intellectual origins of U.S. diplomacy. It concluded with an examination of George Washington's message to his countrymen in 1796, stressing how his words fused realism and idealism. The book earned Gilbert the Bancroft Prize from Columbia University.

In 1962 he accepted an appointment at the School of Historical Studies of the Institute for Advanced Study. Gilbert remained there until 1974 when he retired as professor emeritus. Even in retirement, however, he actively pursued

Seminar of the University of Berlin in the Twenties," in Hartmut Lehmann and James J. Sheehan, eds., *An Interrupted Past: German-Speaking Refugee Historians in the United States after 1933* (1991). A study by Barry M. Katz, of Gilbert's activities during World War II, "German Historians in the Office of Strategic Service," appears in the same volume. An extensive bibliography of his writings is given in *History: Choice and Commitment* (1977). For an overview of Gilbert's attainments, see Hartmut Lehmann, ed., *Felix Gilbert as Scholar and Teacher* (1992). Appreciations are presented in *Journal of the History of Ideas* 52 (Apr.–June 1991), *Renaissance Studies* 5 (Dec. 1991), and *Proceedings of the American Philosophical Society* 137 (Mar. 1993). An obituary is in the *New York Times* (16 Feb. 1991).

JAMES FRIGUGLIETTI

GILLESPIE, John Birks ("Dizzy") (*b.* 21 October 1917 in Cheraw, South Carolina; *d.* 6 January 1993 in Englewood, New Jersey), virtuoso improviser on trumpet and a major figure in jazz history who led the bebop and Latin jazz revolutions.

Gillespie was the son of James Gillespie, a bricklayer and part-time bandleader, and Lottie Powe, a homemaker; he was the youngest of seven children to survive infancy. Gillespie was bathed in music as a child as he listened to rehearsals of his father's band and absorbed ecstatic gospel

Dizzy Gillespie at the JVC Jazz Festival, 1989. AP/WIDE WORLD PHOTOS

music at nearby churches. He fell in love with the trumpet while playing in a school band at age twelve and was soon practicing several hours each day. When the young Gillespie saw how deeply comedy and music moved people, it stirred in him the desire to be a performer, to mount a stage and transform the emotions of an audience. His professional performances joined music with showmanship, in the tradition of idols such as Fats Waller and Cab Calloway.

His father's death when Gillespie was ten threw the family into poverty. Facing years of manual labor at age fifteen because his hometown black school ended at the ninth grade, he was fortunate to win a full scholarship at the Laurinburg Institute, an all-black North Carolina boarding school. There he found economic security and the opportunity to spend almost limitless hours honing his skills on trumpet and piano. He used the piano to explore chordal harmony and began the harmonic innovations that became a key aspect of bebop. Gillespie was almost entirely self-taught musically; one consequence of this was that he allowed his cheeks to puff out—something professionally trained trumpeters are taught not to do—when he played. In later life, his cheeks became a visual symbol, a trademark, but he discounted their importance in his playing.

Gillespie was an accomplished musician when he left Laurinburg at the age of seventeen to join his family in Philadelphia, where they had recently moved to escape the grinding poverty and racist environment of South Carolina. Too poor to buy a case—he carried his trumpet in a paper bag—the nickname "Dizzy" began in 1935 when the pianist Bill Doggett said, "That little dizzy cat's from down south carries his horn around in a paper bag [*sic*]." Gillespie's constant clowning, such as dancing in the trumpet section and wearing an overcoat and gloves to a May audition, solidified the use of the nickname in the months following. Within a year, he was featured in a local band at $45 a week, a princely sum in 1936. At this time, he came under the influence of Roy Eldridge, the fiery star who was the first to develop a trumpet style not fully indebted to the reigning king, Louis Armstrong.

Gillespie's big break came in 1937 when, because he sounded like Eldridge, Teddy Hill hired him to fill the trumpet chair recently vacated by Eldridge in New York City. Gillespie was happily married to Lorraine Willis from May 1940 until his death in 1993, and he maintained several strong and affectionate long-term friendships. He and his wife spent their last twenty-five years in a large, comfortable home in Englewood, New Jersey; they had no children.

From 1938 to 1945, while employed mostly by big bands led by Cab Calloway, Charlie Barnett, Earl Hines, and Billy Eckstine, Gillespie created the bebop revolution with saxophonist Charlie Parker, drummer Kenny Clarke, pianist

Thelonious Monk, and guitarist Charlie Christian (who died in 1942). Their main venues were two famous Harlem clubs, Minton's Playhouse and Monroe's Uptown House, where they developed their ideas in extended jam sessions.

Frustrated with the prevailing swing aesthetic of the late 1930s, which did not allow them to express their emotions with the rhythmic and harmonic materials at hand, Gillespie and his cohorts radically transformed those materials through their new language of bebop. The most fundamental changes were rhythmic. They replaced swing's insistent time-keeping beat of the bass drum with a shimmering, fluid pulse, played on a cymbal. An even more important development was that the drummer, with his free hand and his feet, was enjoined to create polyrhythmic effects to complement and comment upon the lines that his bandmates were playing.

Before bebop, jazz harmony (with a few exceptions such as the music of Duke Ellington and Art Tatum) was at about the level of mid-nineteenth-century classical music. Beboppers, however, were determined to use any and all combinations of notes available in Western music, and they opened harmonic floodgates. Between 1938 and 1945 they moved jazz harmony from Johannes Brahms to Béla Bartók and beyond. Gillespie, the most systematic thinker among the revolutionaries, became the main architect of the new harmonies and rhythms as he wrote down and codified them for his colleagues. Among their outstanding small-group bebop CDs are the two Media 7 series (*Dizzy Gillespie,* volumes 1–8, and *Charlie Parker,* volumes 1–5), *Jazz at Massey Hall 1953* (which won a 1995 Grammy as one of the great recordings of all time), and *Max & Dizzy, Paris 1989.*

The bebop revolution was a group effort, but Gillespie almost single-handedly created Afro-Cuban or Latin jazz. Like the American variety, Latin jazz can be viewed as an overlay of European harmony on an African rhythmic base, except that Latin rhythms are more purely African and much more complex. Gillespie relished this rich percussive stew, and after 1947, when he hired the phenomenal Cuban conga player Chano Pozo, he made a Latin repertoire and Latin musicians central to his music. His last great group, the United Nation Orchestra, consisted of three Brazilians, three Cubans, a Panamanian, a Dominican, a Puerto Rican, and six Americans. It won him a 1991 Grammy for the CD *Live at Royal Festival Hall.*

From 1946 to 1950, Gillespie led one of the greatest of all big bands. With it he proved that the complexities of bebop and Latin jazz could be adapted to the big band idiom in powerful and wildly exciting arrangements. Television diminished the big band audience after 1950, however, and Gillespie led such groups only sporadically during the rest of his career. Along with the United Nation Orchestra, his most notable large aggregation was the orchestra with which he toured the Middle East, Greece, and South America for the State Department in 1956. Outstanding musicians who performed in Gillespie's big bands were Milt Jackson, Ray Brown, John Lewis, Chano Pozo, Kenny Clarke, James Moody, Max Roach, Lee Morgan, Quincy Jones, Paquito D'Rivera, Arturo Sandoval, Phil Woods, Benny Golson, J. J. Johnson, Melba Liston, and Danilo Perez. Key big band recordings are *Dizzy Gillespie: The Complete RCA Victor Recordings, Dizzy In South America 1956* (volumes 1 and 2), and *Live at Royal Festival Hall.*

During the last four decades of his career Gillespie usually led quartets and quintets, using such outstanding sidemen as Moody, Lalo Schifrin, Kenny Barron, Mike Longo, Brown, Leo Wright, and Jon Faddis. He also toured extensively with Norman Granz's Jazz at the Philharmonic groups and recorded many times for Granz's labels. His playing reached a peak in the mid-1970s when his still-dazzling technique was matched by a hard-earned emotional maturity. Important CDs from this period are *Dizzy Gillespie's Big 4* (1974), with Brown, and the Grammy winning *Oscar Peterson and Dizzy Gillespie* (1975). Gillespie was a prolific composer whose outstanding songs included "Manteca" and "Tin Tin Deo," with Walter ("Gil") Fuller and Chano Pozo; "A Night in Tunisia," with Frank Paparelli; "Anthropology," with Charlie Parker; "Con Alma"; "Kush"; and "Swing Low, Sweet Cadillac." In 1990 the singer Jeanie Bryson, born in 1958, alleged that she was Gillespie's illegitimate daughter. In the mid-1990s she initiated a lawsuit to claim part of his estate.

One of the few jazzmen of his generation to become an international pop icon, Gillespie was a master of public relations. He played with an upward-swept trumpet after his horn was bent accidentally in 1953, and the new shape became his logo, recognizable throughout the world. His mock run for the U.S. presidency in 1964 garnered him wide publicity, and his warm and humorous personality guaranteed him many appearances on the *Tonight Show with Johnny Carson* and other highly visible showcases. Gillespie loved to teach and generously shared his gifts with great musicians and grade-school children alike.

Plunged into depression by the assassination of Martin Luther King, Jr. in 1968, Gillespie, born a Methodist, found solace in the Baha'i faith, which he joined later that year and adhered to deeply for the rest of his life.

Gillespie performed at a consistently high level until early 1992 when he was felled by the pancreatic cancer that would kill him a year later. Between 1980 and 1992 he received ten honorary degrees, bringing his total to seventeen, and in 1989 he won a Lifetime Achievement Grammy Award. France made him a Commandeur D'Ordre des Artes et des Lettres in 1989, and he received a Kennedy Center Honor, America's highest artistic award, in 1990.

Gregarious and energetic, Gillespie possessed a tremendous drive to define and achieve his goals. He was a dedicated teacher, preaching his musical gospel to professional musicians and schoolchildren alike. He loved to perform and was not daunted by the rigors of the road, where he spent more than half of his professional life. More than eight thousand people attended his memorial service at the Cathedral of St. John the Divine in New York City, where Mayor David Dinkins called him the "eighth wonder of the world," and Wynton Marsalis, the director of the Lincoln Center Jazz Program, said, "We've lost one of the true giants, not just of music, but of humanity." In a letter read at the ceremony, President Bill Clinton wrote, "America and the world have lost one of the creative geniuses of the twentieth century."

★

To Be, or Not . . . to Bop, Memoirs (1999), is a re-released edition of Gillespie's 1979 autobiographical work with Al Fraser. Biographies include Alyn Shipton, *Groovin' High: The Life of Dizzy Gillespie* (1999) and four valuable shorter works: Raymond Horricks, *Dizzy Gillespie* (1984), Barry McRae, *Dizzy Gillespie, His Life & Times* (1988), Tony Gentry, *Dizzy Gillespie* (1991), and Leslie Gourse, *Dizzy Gillespie and the Birth of Bebop* (1994). Valuable information is also in Carl Woideck, *Charlie Parker: His Music and Life* (1996). Obituaries are in the *New York Times* (7 Jan. 1993), London *Sunday Times* (10 Jan. 1993), *People* (18 Jan. 1993), *Village Voice* (19 Jan. 1993), *New Yorker* (25 Jan. 1993), and *New Republic* (8 Feb. 1993).

DONALD L. MAGGIN

GISH, Lillian Diana (*b.* 14 October 1893 in Springfield, Ohio; *d.* 27 February 1993 in New York City), stage and screen actress who appeared in such landmark films as *Birth of a Nation* (1915) and *Intolerance* (1916).

Gish was the older of two daughters of James Lee Gish, a traveling salesman, and Mary Robinson McConnell, a homemaker. Her sister, Dorothy Gish, was born in 1898 in Dayton, Ohio. James Gish's addiction to alcohol forced Mary to become the breadwinner. On an afternoon in 1902, while Mary was working, Lillian and Dorothy watched furniture men remove most of their possessions because James, who had sneaked away from the premises, had stolen their money. To help pay the rent, Mary took in boarders. A touring actress living with them suggested that Lillian be allowed to play a small role in a stock production of *In Convict's Stripes* at a theater in Risingsun, Ohio.

Over family objections, the three Gishes crisscrossed the United States, playing in popular melodramas of the day. During the summer of 1912, when they were living in Baltimore, Lillian chanced to see fellow trouper Gladys Smith, now known as Mary Pickford, on a motion picture screen in *Lena and the Geese*. When Mary Gish learned that "Little

Lillian Gish, in a portrait from *The Lily and the Rose,* 1915. © BETTMANN/CORBIS

Mary" and her golden curls were earning $175 per week, she suggested that her daughters try to find work in the "flickers" in New York City.

Mary Pickford introduced Lillian and Dorothy to Biograph studio director D. W. Griffith. He improvised a story about a robbery and started the camera rolling. What he failed to mention was the gunshots he would add. As the sisters ran around the room, their emotions were filmed. Because the camera responded to their extraordinary beauty, Griffith immediately cast them in *An Unseen Enemy* (1912). This initial effort was a hit, and the sisters were given a $5-per-day contract. Lillian appeared in eleven more short films that year, including *The Musketeers of Pig Alley* and *The New York Hat.*

At the end of each shooting day, Lillian would remain at Griffith's side, watching him clip sections of film together to form a smooth narrative. She was learning and mastering every aspect of filmmaking. As her popularity increased, her salary rose to $50 a week. The training in two-reelers served her well. She soon played the imperiled Southern heroine of Griffith's *The Birth of a Nation* (1915), a sweeping Civil War and Reconstruction story told in an unprecedented twelve reels. Although condemned in some quarters for its racist point of view, this film galvanized the entire country and firmly established the motion picture as a mature art form. The next year, Gish's expressive beauty earned her a brief but iconic role in Griffith's epic *Intolerance,* another landmark of the cinema.

In the summer of 1917, the three Gishes, in a black-sailed ship under cover of darkness, went to England and France during wartime to film Griffith's *Hearts of the World* (1918). Lillian played another fragile heroine in *Broken Blossoms* (1919) and fled memorably across an ice-choked river in *Way Down East* (1920). *Orphans of the Storm* (1922), her last collaboration with Griffith, was her sixty-second film.

Knowing she could not make an effective transition into the Charleston Era as a dancing flapper, Lillian appeared in period classics that showcased her timeless vulnerability: *The White Sister* (1923), *Romola* (1924), *La Bohème* (1926), *The Scarlet Letter* (1926), and *Annie Laurie* (1927). Aware of her own popularity, and refusing to allow Metro-Goldwyn-Mayer studio chief Louis B. Mayer to "allow a scandal to be arranged" in an effort to revive her career, she left Hollywood in 1928 after completing *The Wind.* An unsuccessful early sound film, *One Romantic Night* (1930), made her rethink her life and career. She returned to the theater. Shepherding her theatrical comeback was the drama critic George Jean Nathan, with whom she had a ten-year relationship.

Despite personal coaching from Eugene O'Neill, a friend of Nathan's, her 1928 attempts to star in O'Neill's *Marco Millions* (1927) and *Strange Interlude* (1927) were rejected by Theatre Guild director Phillip Moeller, who still viewed Gish as the girl on the ice floes in *Way Down East.*

Producer Jed Harris, another friend of Nathan's, provided Gish the opportunity to make her mature theatrical debut, as Elena in his production of *Uncle Vanya* (1930). Her Ophelia in Guthrie McClintic's production of *Hamlet,* starring John Gielgud (1936), was highly successful. Other plays that decade included Phillip Barry's *The Joyous Season* (1934), Sean O'Casey's *Within the Gates* (1934), Zoë Akins's *The Old Maid* (1936), Maxwell Anderson's *The Star Wagon* (1937), and Howard Lindsay and Russell Crouse's *Life with Father* (1939). In the 1940s, however, Gish's reluctance to take a chance on an unknown playwright led her to reject the role of Amanda Wingfield in Tennessee Williams's *The Glass Menagerie.* Fiercely isolationist, Gish nevertheless withdrew her association with the America First Committee when the Chicago box-office receipts of *Life with Father* significantly dropped. Six months later, the Japanese bombed Pearl Harbor.

Returning to the screen in 1943 with *Top Man* and *Commandos Strike at Dawn,* she later played supporting roles in David O. Selznick's *Duel in the Sun* (1946) and *Portrait of Jennie* (1948). Gish made her television debut that same year in a Philco Television Playhouse production of Sidney Howard's *The Late Christopher Bean.* Other television work included Jim Bishop's *The Day Lincoln Was Shot* (1956) and Joseph Kesselring's *Arsenic and Old Lace* (1968).

For two decades, she was an active presence on stage, appearing in Horton Foote's *The Trip to Bountiful* (1953), T. S. Eliot's *The Family Reunion* (1958), Tad Mosel's *All the Way Home* (1960), and George Bernard Shaw's *Too True to Be Good* (1963). Her last stage performance was in *A Musical Jubilee,* which opened in New York in 1975. Her forays into film included Vincente Minnelli's *The Cobweb* (1955), Charles Laughton's *The Night of the Hunter* (1955), John Huston's *The Unforgiven* (1960), and Walt Disney's *Follow Me, Boys!* (1966). Her last film performance was opposite Bette Davis in the 1987 film *The Whales of August.*

A year after her sister Dorothy's passing in 1968, Lillian Gish's *The Art of Film,* a compilation of scenes from major American silent films, with an emphasis on her work with D. W. Griffith, premiered at Columbia University's Mc-Millan Theatre. The program was seen at 387 colleges across the United States, in addition to three worldwide tours. Gish received an honorary Academy Award in 1971 and the American Film Institute's Lifetime Achievement Award in 1984. The Gish Film Theater was dedicated at Bowling Green State University in Ohio in 1976, and in 1990 a documentary version of her autobiographical book *An Actor's Life for Me* was televised as part of the *American Masters* series on PBS.

Gish's romantic involvements were unconventional. In the mid-1920s a relationship with the producer Charles Duell during the filming of *The White Sister* caused her to seek legal counsel when Duell tried to sue her for breach of contract. Her association with George Jean Nathan was complex in nature. She never married.

Only her death, a few months short of her 100th birthday, put a closing to a career that spanned the century. Gish passed away in her sleep at her East Fifty-seventh Street apartment, where she had lived alone for many years. She was laid to rest alongside her mother and sister at St. Bartholomew's Episcopal Church on Park Avenue in New York City.

"[A death at home and burial beside her family] was what she wanted," James Frasher, her longtime manager told the press. "She *was* film. Film started in 1893, and so did she."

★

Gish-related material can be found at the New York Public Library's Library for the Performing Arts and the Jerome Library at Bowling Green State University in Bowling Green, Ohio. Gish wrote several autobiographical works. *Lillian Gish: The Movies, Mr. Griffith, and Me,* written with Ann Pinchot, was published in 1969. *Dorothy and Lillian Gish,* a collection of reminiscences edited by James E. Frasher, was published in 1973. *An Actor's Life for Me* (1987), coauthored by Selma G. Lanes, was written for a young audience and covers her years as a child actor. Biographies include Albert Bigelow Paine, *Lillian Gish: A Life on Stage and Screen* (1932), Charles Silver, *Lillian Gish* (1999), and Stuart Oderman, *Lillian Gish: A Life on Stage and Screen* (1999). An obituary is in the *New York Times* (1 Mar. 1993).

STUART ODERMAN

GLEASON, Thomas William ("Teddy") (*b.* 8 November 1900 in New York City; *d.* 24 December 1992 in New York City), labor leader and president of the International Longshoremen's Association.

Gleason was the oldest of thirteen children born to Thomas William Gleason, a dockworker, and Mary Ann Quinn, a homemaker. His parents were second-generation Irish Catholic immigrants who lived on Manhattan's West Side. He was called "Teddy" to distinguish him from his father and his grandfather, both namesakes. Teddy's formal education was limited. He attended Saint Alphonsus Roman Catholic School only to the seventh grade, leaving in 1915 to help support his large family.

Gleason joined his father and grandfather on the docks of the port of New York, then the busiest harbor in the world. Working by his father's side at the Charles Street Pier on Manhattan's West Side, the center of longshore-

Teddy Gleason, 1965. ARCHIVE PHOTOS

men's employment, Gleason's pay was little (thirty-five cents per hour), his hours were long, and the conditions were horrendous.

At this time longshoremen "shaped up" for work. They appeared at the shipping company's docks and waited to be chosen by the company for work that day. Employment was never guaranteed, and often workers were hired for short periods and had to shape up as many as four times a day. To secure work, the longshoremen were forced to pay many hiring bosses a "kickback," further reducing their meager wages.

Gleason told a *Newsweek* reporter in 1962 that the docks of New York had been like "the Barbary Coast." In protest he joined the young International Longshoremen's Association (ILA) in 1919 and became active in dockworkers' struggles. The ILA was, Gleason later recalled, "a gang of rebels," the only group working to better the workers' conditions.

Because of his union activity and his visibility as a union man, Gleason found regular employment difficult. In 1923 he married Emma Martin, and they quickly had three children. In 1932 the industry formally blacklisted Gleason for his union activity. His family was forced to move into an apartment with only one bed in an Irish working-class neighborhood, and Gleason took work in a Brooklyn sugar factory.

In 1933, with the help of New Deal legislation favorable to unions, Gleason once again found work on the docks. In 1934 he rose to business agent of the Checkers' Local, and later he became local president. He worked closely with the international leadership and continued to negotiate successful contracts for his local. In 1947 the ILA president Joseph Ryan appointed Gleason full-time organizer for the ILA.

By all accounts Gleason and Ryan had a stormy relationship. Ryan fired him from the ILA at least three times, hiring him back on each occasion because of rank-and-file protest. By 1951 Gleason led a dissident group within the ILA that organized a general strike on the docks of New York in 1951. The strike prompted the New York State Crime Commission's investigation of corruption on the waterfront and inspired the film *On the Waterfront* (1954). In 1953, in response to public cries of corruption, the American Federation of Labor (AFL) expelled the ILA.

Ryan resigned as president of the now independent union. Gleason backed the next president, William Bradley, and assumed the top organizer post, which Bradley created for him. Gleason steered the union through tough times. He fought off the rival AFL union, the International Brotherhood of Longshoremen, through his able bargaining with employers. Using money borrowed from the United Mine Workers, Gleason held the union together. Then in 1956, tired of the instability in the industry, the New York Shipping Association signed a contract with the ILA, making it the sole union for East Coast longshoremen. In 1959, convinced that Gleason had cleaned up the union, George Meany, the president of the new federation formed by the 1955 merging of the AFL and the Congress of Industrial Organizations, welcomed the ILA into the AFL-CIO.

By 1961 Gleason had risen to power within the ILA as executive vice president of the national union, president of the ILA's Atlantic Coast District, and president of the Checker's Local, one of the largest in the ILA. Gleason led the union in its 1962 strike, in which the issues were work-gang size and automation. With the aid of federal mediation, the strike was settled in 1963, when both sides agreed to submit these issues to a federal two-year study. That same year Gleason, then president, announced he would open the union's books for auditing and he would take away the locals' right to honor all picket lines. Gleason, who was described as a "fireplug of a man," at five feet, six inches tall and about 180 pounds, declared that only "responsible" picket lines and strikes would be honored and that he would decide what was responsible.

Two issues dogged the ILA after 1962, the tradition of not handling cargo going to communist nations and automation. In 1963, when President John F. Kennedy announced that the United States would sell excess wheat to Russia, Gleason was in a bind. The wheat was going with or without the ILA. In the end the ILA agreed to handle the cargo providing that at least 50 percent of the ships were American, which because of the maritime laws essentially meant using union labor, and that none of the ships be Russian. In 1964, when one company was shipping only 38 percent of its cargo on American ships, Gleason called a boycott. President Lyndon B. Johnson stepped in, and the government honored the 50 percent rule.

In the 1964 contract talks the issue of crew size and automation once again proved the sticking points. Just four days before a strike the parties reached a settlement. Gleason called the contract "the best ever made in the history of the ILA." The work-gang was reduced from twenty to seventeen, shrinking the workforce, and in exchange the union members received an annual income guarantee whether they worked or not. The workers also gained hourly wage increases, and the union won an increase in their automatic dues checkoff, called a "double dues checkoff." Because of the dues issues the workers rejected the contract and went out on a twenty-day strike. Gleason eventually convinced the rank and file to accept the original conditions. On the issue of automation Gleason relented and allowed the use of containers. Containerization and laborsaving technologies eventually destroyed the union. Using containers and technology, shipping companies employed fewer and fewer workers. Yet Gleason's union members did well. In exchange for accepting containerization,

workers received their annual incomes. At the end of his service as president, Gleason watched his union decline. Clearly technology was inevitable, and Gleason was powerless to stop it. In the end he chose to take care of his members.

In 1964 Gleason was appointed to the President's Maritime Advisory Committee and advised a number of governmental bodies on maritime issues. In 1969 he became a vice president and an executive board member of the AFL-CIO. He retired from labor in 1984. After suffering from a heart condition for a number of years, he died in New York City at age ninety-two. He was buried in New York City.

★

Gleason's papers are in the ILA Collection at the Robert F. Wagner Labor Archives, Taminent Library, New York University. He is mentioned in a number of histories of the industry, including Maud Russell, *Men Along the Shore* (1966); Bruce Nelson, *Workers on the Waterfront* (1988); Calvin Winslow, ed., *Waterfront Workers* (1988); Joshua B. Freeman, *Working-Class New York* (2000); and Andrew Gibson and Arthur Donovan, *The Abandoned Ocean* (2000). An obituary is in the *New York Times* (26 Dec. 1992). An oral history is in the ILA Collection at the Robert F. Wagner Labor Archives, Taminent Library, New York University.

RICHARD A. GREENWALD

GOBEL, George Leslie (*b.* 20 May 1919 in Chicago, Illinois; *d.* 24 February 1991 in Encino, California), comic performer, monologist, and musician who rose to fame during the 1950s as the host of a prime-time television comedy-variety hour.

Gobel was born George Leslie Goebel. His father, Herman Goebel, was a grocery store owner, and from an early age George delighted in performing imitations of the customers who came into the shop, some of whom appreciated these renditions more than others. His mother, Lillian MacDonald, had been a music teacher, and she encouraged him to learn to play the guitar and sing. When his church choir was invited to perform on a Chicago radio station, Gobel was featured as a soloist. Soon after, the twelve-year-old was signed to a contract with the NBC Radio. "Little George Gobel" (he was only five-feet, five-inches-tall as an adult) appeared regularly on the NBC Blue Network's country-and-western variety program, *National Barn Dance*.

As he matured, Gobel's soprano voice deepened. As a result, the teenager redirected his career toward radio acting, gaining parts in the soap operas and Westerns that originated from Chicago during the 1930s. He attended Roosevelt High School throughout this period, and upon graduation in 1937 he set off to become a country-and-western musician and storyteller, appearing on regional radio stations in the Midwest and South. He married Alice

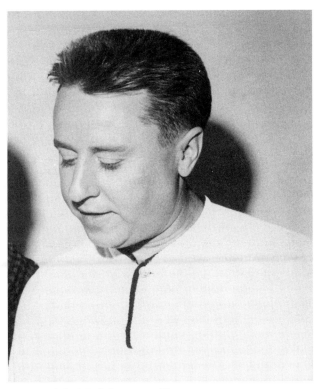

George Gobel, 1954. © BETTMANN/CORBIS

Humecki in 1942, and they eventually had three children. An amateur pilot, Gobel enlisted in the U.S. Air Army Corps in 1943. He served mainly as a flight instructor in Oklahoma until he was discharged as a first lieutenant in 1945.

In his radio act Gobel had always flavored his guitar picking with witty stories. But in the years immediately following World War II, he decisively shifted the focus of his work toward stand-up comedy, though his guitar usually remained in hand. He emerged as a stand-up comic, developing material on the rough-and-tumble Chicago nightclub circuit. His engagements encompassed a range of venues, from the city's most elegant hotels to barrooms where heckling was an expected part of the evening's entertainment. He credited his nightclub experiences for his success in reaching the mass, heterogeneous audience of the 1950s. For his act, Gobel punctuated short guitar riffs with humorous anecdotes and stories in a patter that did not quite qualify as joke telling. His signature was his unflinching poker face, which remained implacable, even when the house roared with laughter. This distinctive style helped earn him the nickname "Lonesome George."

Television was expanding rapidly in the 1950s, and Gobel became a frequent guest on such popular network programs as the *Garry Moore Show* and the *Colgate Comedy Hour*. At a time when nightclubs were becoming increasingly identified with risqué "blue" material, Gobel's act

was family fare, just the kind that television advertisers were looking for. He signed an exclusive contract with NBC Television in 1952. However, it took the network more than a year—and two failed situation comedy pilots—to find an acceptable vehicle for the offbeat comedian. "Maybe it's because I sometimes used a guitar and sang, they thought of that homespun or bucolic nonsense. I'm really a city boy at heart."

The *George Gobel Show*, a comedy-variety hour, premiered on NBC's Saturday lineup in the fall of 1954. It won both a large audience and critical acclaim. Comedy-variety was generally dominated by the frenetic pace that had been established by such comedians as Milton Berle, Martha Raye, Jerry Lester, and the team of Dean Martin and Jerry Lewis. Gobel's deliberate, almost leisurely timing was refreshing for segments of the audience who had grown weary of early television's "Hellzapoppin' " style. Moreover, many new viewers in the Midwest and South, who were getting television service for the first time, found Gobel's homespun style recognizable and friendly. The *New York Times* praised Gobel's "low pressure, off-beat humor." He won both an Emmy and a Peabody Award during that first season.

If Gobel's personal style was quirky, the form of his comedy-variety program was not. It started with the star delivering a stand-up monologue, followed by the introduction of the week's guest star and perhaps a song. The hour then moved into a series of sketches, most of which explored the banalities and aggravations of middle-class married life, as experienced by George and his television wife, Alice. Some of Hollywood's best writers were attracted to the staff, including Hal Kanter, Norman Lear, and Ed Simmons. Simmons, who went on to produce the *Carol Burnett Show,* called the year he spent writing for Gobel's show "a writer's dream": "You could see your commas on the screen. He had a rhythm that was totally different. . . . And he had a sense of humor. A lot of comics don't have any sense of humor." By 1956, Lonesome George Gobel was among the highest paid performers on television, earning more than $7,000 per weekly episode. The network further capitalized on his popularity by giving him a regular position on the *Eddie Fisher Show*, which aired on alternate weeks from his own.

Through the late 1950s and early 1960s, Gobel appeared in several Broadway plays (notably *Let It Ride,* 1958) and Hollywood movies (including *I Married a Woman,* 1958). But his television popularity ultimately declined as abruptly as it had risen. Although Gobel's show was highly rated during most of its run, it faced heavy competition in 1957 after NBC switched it from its Saturday night time slot to a weeknight slot. Upon the expiration of his five-year contract with NBC, the network cancelled the show. CBS picked it up for the 1959–1960 season, but then cancelled it in less than a year. The writer Hal Kanter recalled that Gobel, already something of a drinker, began to drink even more heavily around this time.

After the cancellation of his show, voice-overs for television commercials became a mainstay of Gobel's work. In the 1970s, he reemerged on national television as a regular on the game show *Hollywood Squares*. This led to a role in a situation comedy, *Harper Valley P.T.A.*, but the series was quickly cancelled. He appeared in some Broadway revivals in the 1980s, but Gobel never again achieved the stardom he had known during the heyday of his comedy-variety hour. He died in Los Angeles of a stroke following coronary by-pass surgery and was buried at San Fernando Mission Cemetery in Mission Hills, California.

Gobel's meteoric rise from obscurity to national stardom in early television comedy-variety reflects the experience of a number of 1950s performers, including Sid Caesar and Milton Berle. The medium's insatiable appetite for new material, as well as the fickleness of audiences and network programmers, tended to burn out comedy-variety performers. Perhaps none fell so far so quickly as Gobel.

★

Several relevant interviews are archived at the Steven H. Scheuer Collection in Television History at Syracuse University Library, Syracuse, New York: they are interviews by David Marc with the writers Everett Greenbaum (1996) and Hal Kanter (1997) and by Bernie Cook with the writer Ed Simmons (1997). Gobel's life and early career are profiled in *Current Biography 1955*. Obituaries are in the *Los Angeles Times* and *New York Times* (both 25 Feb. 1991).

DAVID MARC

GOODSON, Mark (*b.* 24 January 1915 in Sacramento, California; *d.* 18 December 1992 in New York City), the most successful creator and producer of game shows in the history of television.

Goodson, the "king of television game shows," was the only child of Abraham and Fanny Gross Goodman, Jewish immigrants from Russia. Although lacking formal education themselves, and suffering the financial woes of the Great Depression, they encouraged and helped their son to work his way through the University of California at Berkeley. He graduated in 1937, cum laude and a member of Phi Beta Kappa, intending to become an attorney. Hard times, however, dictated a job before law school.

He found work through a friend as an announcer at KFRC, a San Francisco radio station, taking on the surname "Goodson." Within two years Goodson had created and produced his first game show, *Pop the Question*, which required contestants to throw darts at balloons as a way of selecting categories, though this stunt could only be de-

Mark Goodson. ARCHIVE PHOTOS

scribed to the radio audience. In 1941 Goodson moved to New York City, hoping to break into network radio. He found work in radio direction, creating a program called *Appointment with Life,* a dramatic radio series based on the supposed case histories of a marriage counselor. He also wrote and directed the dramatic spots on the radio variety hour hosted by Kate Smith. From 1944 to 1945 he directed the U.S. Treasury Department radio show *The Treasury Salute.*

In 1946 in New York he formed a corporate partnership with Bill Todman, a salesman and accountant who could take care of the business end of a company that would specialize in game show production, freeing Goodson to focus on creative work. The company's first major sale was a radio quiz, *Winner Take All,* which in 1946 pioneered the use of live, on-air contestant telephone calls. But the money in the broadcasting business was moving toward television, and by the 1950s Mark Goodson–Bill Todman Productions turned its attention to this new medium. The two men took equal credits on screen for a Goodson–Todman Production, but Todman's role was strictly in the front office. After Todman's death in 1979, the studio was renamed Mark Goodson Productions.

Mark Goodson–Bill Todman Productions ultimately supplied more than five hundred game series to the ever-expanding medium of television. Goodson's extraordinary portfolio of national hits included such programs as *What's My Line?* (1950–1967), *I've Got a Secret* (1952–1967), *To Tell the Truth* (1956–1967; 1969–1977), *Concentration* (1958–1973), *Password* (1961–1975), *Family Feud* (launched in 1976 and still on the air in 200), *Beat the Clock* (1950–1958), and *The Price Is Right* (launched in 1956 and still on the air in 2000). In all, he produced more than 42,000 half-hour episodes of such shows. At the end of the twentieth century, not a day had gone by on American television since 1950 without a Goodson program having aired. Many of the shows were licensed for production in various languages, gaining distribution around the world.

The technique underlying Goodson's dominance of the genre lay in his emphasis on amusing gimmicks and snappy patter, as opposed to the excitements and tensions of big cash awards. Contestants on *What's My Line?*, for example (where four panelists tried to guess the professions of contestants by asking them yes-or-no questions), could not win more than $50 (and were often given that much even if they failed to win it). Instead, the show depended on the entertaining chatter of its panelists, including such New York raconteurs as the publisher Bennett Cerf and the gossip columnist Dorothy Kilgallen.

If the *What's My Line?* panel seemed in dress and manner as if they had just stopped by for some parlor-room fun after taking in a Broadway show, contestants on *Beat the Clock* were more likely to be outfitted in cheap plastic raincoats in anticipation of throwing cream pies; the idea behind this Goodson daytime show, built around physical comedy, was to pull off a series of stunts as precious seconds ticked away on a giant clock. Plenty of eggs were broken and balloons popped. Once again, cash prizes were not large enough to be a factor in the show's popularity.

Goodson made forays into other areas of show business, producing such television shows as *The Rebel*, a Western, and *The Richard Boone Show*, a weekly series of original dramas performed by Boone's repertory company. Other business interests, fueled by the immense profits of Goodson's game-show factory, included extensive real estate holdings and ownership, through Goodson Newspapers, Inc., of more than twenty small city dailies and weeklies. A generous philanthropist, Goodson gave millions of dollars to charities and nonprofit institutions. A wing of the Cedars-Sinai Medical Center in Los Angeles bears his name.

Goodson received numerous Emmy awards over the years, including one for lifetime achievement in 1990. In 1993 he was inducted into the Hall of Fame of the Academy of Television Arts and Sciences. He was wed three times (to Bluma Neveleff in 1941, to Virginia McDavid, and to Suzanne Waddell) but each marriage ended in divorce. He had two children with Bluma and one with Virginia. He maintained dual residences in New York City and Los Angeles for most of his life. He died in New York of pancreatic cancer. He is buried in Hillside Cemetery in Culver City, California.

As a result of his "all for fun" strategy, Goodson was the only major game show producer to survive the quiz show scandals of the late 1950s. Nearly every other game show on television was knocked off the air when it was discovered, in congressional hearings, that producers were "fixing" the outcomes of their big-money quizzes to capture high ratings. Emerging clean from the investigations, Goodson had a virtual lock on the genre for the balance of the twentieth century, introducing new programs and reviving and recycling his trademark properties into updated versions, some of which eclipsed the success of the originals. It was not until years after his death that network game shows once again attracted serious public attention, but this revival was directly tied to the introduction of million-dollar prizes. No one has ever been able to effectively duplicate the Goodson formula on a comparable scale.

*

The University of California, Los Angeles, Film and Television Archive maintains the Mark Goodson Collection of six hundred kinescopes of television game shows produced by Goodson–Todman Productions between 1950 and 1967. Goodson provided the introduction to David Schwartz and Fred Wostbrock, *The Encyclopedia of TV Game Shows* (3d ed., 1999). See also Mark Duka, "From *What's My Line?* to *Child's Play*, the Game's the Thing for Him," *New York Times* (5 Dec. 1982), and Maxene Fabe, *TV Game Shows* (1979). Obituaries are in the *New York Times* and *Los Angeles Times* (both 19 Dec. 1992). Goodson discusses his career as a game show producer with host Steven H. Scheuer in the video recording *All About TV*, produced by WNYC-television in New York (1985). Gil Fates talks about Goodson in an interview with David Marc (1999 sound recording held at the Steven H. Scheuer Television History Collection, Syracuse University Library, Syracuse, New York).

DAVID MARC

GOREN, Charles Henry (*b.* 4 March 1901 in Philadelphia, Pennsylvania; *d.* 3 April 1991 in Encino, California), champion and theorist of contract bridge whose numerous books and syndicated newspaper column helped to create a popular following for the game.

Goren was one of two children of Jacob Goren, a writer, and his wife Rebecca, a homemaker, both Jewish immigrants from Russia. Goren excelled academically and was involved in a wide variety of extracurricular activities at Philadelphia's Central High School, which awarded him a diploma in 1918. After working briefly as a furniture salesman, he studied law at McGill University in Montreal, Canada, receiving his LL.B. in 1922 and his LL.M. in 1923. At McGill he learned to play whist and auction bridge. He was admitted to the Pennsylvania bar in 1923, then practiced law in Philadelphia.

After Harold S. Vanderbilt invented contract bridge in

Charles Goren, 1961. © BETTMANN/CORBIS

accurate evaluation of the strength of the thirteen cards one is dealt and the clear conveyance of that information to one's partner through established bidding conventions. The earliest contract bridge theorists wrestled with the enigma of hand evaluation. Culbertson's method, the honor trick count, was popular but flawed. Work and Goren preferred a point-count method, whereby high cards are assigned progressive numerical values. Several point counts are possible, and to be useful they must also make quantitative allowances for suit distribution; it can be advantageous to have few cards in a given suit because an opponent's otherwise winning card can be trumped once the hand is void in that suit. Goren, after experimenting with refinements of Work's point count, finally settled on the simplest: Ace = 4, King = 3, Queen = 2, Jack = 1, Void = 3, Singleton = 2, and Doubleton = 1. With 40 high-card points in the deck, an average hand is 10, a borderline opening bid hand is 12 or 13, and a mandatory opening bid hand (using Goren's strategy) is 14.

Goren's reputation as a bidding theorist was firmly established by his first book, *Winning Bridge Made Easy: A Simplified Self-Teaching Method of Contract Bidding Combining All the Principles of the New Culbertson System with the Principal Features of the Four Aces System* (1936). With the success of this book he quit practicing law in 1936 to devote himself full-time to bridge and writing. His other books include *Better Bridge for Better Players: The Play of the Cards* (1942), *Contract Bridge Made Easy: A Self-Teacher* (1948), *The Fundamentals of Contract Bridge* (1950), *Contract Bridge for Beginners* (1953), *New Way to Better Bridge* (1958), *An Evening of Bridge* (1959), *Elements of Bridge* (1960), *The Sports Illustrated Book of Bridge* (1961), *Goren's Easy Steps to Winning Bridge* (1963), *Bridge Is My Game: Lessons of a Lifetime* (1965), *Bridge Players Write the Funniest Letters* (1968), *Charles H. Goren Presents the Precision System of Contract Bridge Bidding* (1971), *Precision Bridge for Everyone* (1978, with C. C. Wei), *Play as You Learn Bridge* (1979), and *Introduction to Competitive Bidding* (1984, with Ronald P. Von der Porten).

Three of his books became standard instructional texts, each appearing in many editions: *Contract Bridge Complete* (1951), *Contract Bridge in a Nutshell* (1946), and *Point Count Bidding in Contract Bridge* (1949). Especially by virtue of *Contract Bridge Complete* (published as both *Bridge Complete* and *New Bridge Complete*), the phrase "according to Goren" became for bridge players more authoritative than "according to Hoyle." The tenth edition of *Contract Bridge Complete* (1985) replaced Goren's standard four-card major bidding system with the five-card major system that had come to be preferred by most experts. This was considered an important concession and kept Goren in the mainstream of bridge theory. He also wrote books on subjects other than bridge: *Complete Canasta* (1949, with Ralph

1925, and especially through Ely Culbertson's whirlwind publicity campaign in the late 1920s to supplant auction bridge with contract, Goren became fascinated with the game. He read the books of his fellow Philadelphian Milton Work, an auction bridge expert then engaged in establishing the theory of contract. Impressed by Goren's diligence, talent, and enthusiasm, Work hired him as his assistant. By 1931, Goren was playing in tournaments.

Goren won the first of his forty-three national bridge championships in 1933, his first major national championship in 1937, and his only world championship, the Bermuda Bowl, in 1950. He won each of the major national events at least once. Perhaps most amazing are his eight wins and two seconds in the prestigious Reisinger Board-a-Match Team Championships. His favorite partner was Helen Sobel.

Bridge is a communication game. Much depends on the

Michaels), *Canasta Up-to-Date* (1950), *New Canasta and Samba* (1951), *Hoyle Encyclopedia of Games* (1961), *Go with the Odds: A Guide to Successful Gambling* (1969), and *Modern Backgammon Complete* (1974).

Goren began writing a daily newspaper column in 1944, succeeding Culbertson at the *Chicago Tribune*. With Alex Dreier he cohosted the national television show *Championship Bridge* from 1959 to 1964. Along with Vanderbilt and Culbertson, he was one of the three original members elected to the American Contract Bridge League Hall of Fame in 1964.

Because of his health, he retired from playing tournament bridge in 1966 and became a virtual recluse, living mostly with his nephew Marvin Goren in Encino, California. After his eyesight began to fail in the 1970s, he relied more on ghostwriters and coauthors. Omar Sharif and Tannah Hirsch ghostwrote his newspaper column. He died at home of a heart attack and is buried in Trevose, Pennsylvania, near the residence of his other nephew, Norman Goren.

Goren never married and had no children. To say he was married to the game of bridge is not farfetched. Fans called him "Mr. Bridge." He was hard-working, friendly, tolerant, and cultured. He played golf, frequented the theater, and loved classical music. In recognition of all his accomplishments, McGill awarded him an honorary LL.D. in 1973.

★

The best source of further information is the archives of the American Contract Bridge League (ACBL). Feature stories are in *Sports Illustrated* (16 Sept. 1957), *Time* (29 Sept. 1958), and *Current Biography* (March 1959). Details of Goren's tournament victories are in the ACBL's *Official Encyclopedia of Bridge* (5th edition, 1994). Obituaries are in the *New York Times* (12 Apr. 1991) and *Contract Bridge Bulletin* (May 1991 and June 1991).

ERIC V. D. LUFT

GRAHAM, Bill (*b.* 8 January 1931 in Berlin, Germany; *d.* 25 October 1991 near Vallejo, California), America's leading promoter of live rock music.

Graham was born Wolfgang Wolodia Grajonca to Russian-Jewish refugees who immigrated to Weimar, Germany, in the late 1920s. His father, Jacob, an engineer, died in a construction accident two days after his birth, leaving his mother, Freida, to care for him and his older sisters. In 1939, as Nazi-era legislation increasingly restricted Jewish life in Germany, Freida dispatched her two youngest children, Graham and his sister Tolla, to Lyons, France, on a student-exchange program. After the invasion of France in 1940, Graham and Tolla, along with sixty-three other children, were evacuated from Lyons via Red Cross transport.

Bill Graham, 1973. AP/WIDE WORLD PHOTOS

The severely malnourished, thirteen-year-old Tolla died of pneumonia during the evacuation. The eleven-year-old Graham, weighing forty pounds, made it to America and was placed in a Pleasantville, New York, orphanage operated by the Jewish Foster Home Bureau.

As Graham later recalled of his time in the orphanage, "On the weekend the families would come up to the cottages, looking at us as though they were picking out a pet . . . and all of us wanted to be taken by somebody. Nine weeks passed. Finally on the last weekend of November, a family came, a couple with a boy who was two years older than I was . . . I was taken by them and began my life in New York City." His foster parents, Alfred Ehrenreich, an insurance salesman, and his wife, Pearl, a homemaker, brought him to their home on Montgomery Avenue in the Bronx, where neighborhood children taunted the German-speaking refugee with chants of "Nazi go home!" while goose-stepping in front of his new home.

Young Graham soon learned English with the help of his foster brother, Roy, and attended P.S. 104 and P.S. 82. He graduated from DeWitt Clinton High School. While in high school he became a jazz and Latin music devotee, regularly attending the Palladium and the Apollo Theatre to hear live performances by Tito Puente and Cab Calloway. In 1949, at the age of eighteen, he changed his surname to "Graham" to sound more American. In 1950 he got a job as a singing waiter at Grossingers Resort in the Catskill Mountains. Graham became a U.S. citizen on his twenty-first birthday in 1952.

During the Korean War, Graham was drafted into the U.S. Army. He received a summary court-martial for insubordination during basic training but went on to see action as an artillery spotter in Korea, where, displaying courage under fire, he earned the Bronze Star and Purple Heart. After the war he drove a taxicab part-time and earned a B.A. degree in business administration from City College of New York in 1955. He drifted west to California, working as a statistician for the Southern Pacific Railroad and the Allis-Chalmers industrial firm. Bored by dead-end jobs, he returned to New York City, studied drama briefly at Lee Strasberg's Actors Studio, and in 1964 moved back to San Francisco.

In 1965 Graham became the unofficial business manager for the radical improvisational street theater group the San Francisco Mime Troupe. His responsibilities included hanging promotional posters, driving trucks, and other grunt work. Writing about this emerging art scene, Oliver Trager states that, since Graham "was someone bereft of roots and displaced by the terrible consequences of history, it is easy to fathom why the Mime Troupe's highly political sense of community and call to higher purpose appealed to [him]. Here was a group of people attempting to engender a better society through expression of art as they saw it with no compromises . . . and no money." When the Mime Troupe was charged with obscenity after a commedia dell'arte performance of *Il Candelaio,* Graham put to work his innate street smarts, managerial skills, and chutzpah. Securing the help of the bohemian collective that called itself the Family Dog, which had begun sponsoring highly popular dances in San Francisco halls, Graham organized a fund-raising dance benefit for the Mime Troupe's mounting legal fees. The benefit was held at the Longshoreman's Hall and featured performances by Jefferson Airplane, the saxophonist John Handy, and the Beat poets Allen Ginsburg and Lawrence Ferlinghetti. "We expected a few hundred people; thousands showed up," Graham recalled. "There were people with huge hats and loud colors and baggy pants and costume jewelry and army coats. . . . We had big barrels filled with vodka and juice. My eyes were opened. There's a new world and a new society and a new spirit." Many have referred to this night, 6 November 1965, as the birth of the San Francisco music scene.

A second benefit was held on 10 December 1965, this time at the 1,100-seat Fillmore Auditorium in San Francisco's black ghetto. It was an even bigger success, and Graham soon left the Mime Troupe to promote live rock music full-time. The Fillmore quickly emerged as an incubator for the nascent local music scene. It nurtured acts such as the Quicksilver Messenger Service, the Grateful Dead, and Big Brother and the Holding Company. Graham found his métier here and in the process discovered a gold mine. Together with the rival promoter Chet Helms of the Avalon Ballroom, Graham introduced and popularized electric-light shows and concert posters of original psychedelic art, which later became highly collectible artifacts of the era. Graham also began to integrate performances with black jazz, blues, and gospel acts playing the opening sets. Keith Richards of the Rolling Stones recalled: "Back then, it was a brave move to mix up soul acts with the most extreme of white music at the time. Bill was the first to do it on a regular basis." Examples of double bills included the jazz trumpeter Miles Davis opening for the Grateful Dead or the blues guitarist Buddy Guy preceding the Who. Non-rock acts such as the comedian Lenny Bruce, the Staple Singers, and Rahsaan Roland Kirk were introduced to his growing audiences. The Chicano guitarist Carlos Santana said that "the Fillmore was what Jimi Hendrix would call an electric church . . . it was like a sanctuary from Vietnam. Going to the Fillmore in those days was a real healing thing." On 11 June 1967 Graham married Bonnie McLean. They had two sons but the marriage did not last.

With his ever-present clipboard in hand Graham directly oversaw all aspects of his productions. He was a hard-driving entrepreneur—demanding, outspoken, and at times ruthless and violent. His caustic, confrontational demeanor did not endear him to all. As the first to make serious money from the new hippie music, he was severely criticized by some members of the counterculture for being just a "dollar and cents" man.

The growing popularity of the Fillmore Auditorium led Graham to seek a larger venue. In August 1968 he bought the Carousel Ballroom on Market Street and renamed it the Fillmore West. Earlier that spring he had opened a New York City spin-off, the Fillmore East, in a seedy former vaudeville theater on Manhattan's Second Avenue. For the next three years these were America's leading venues for cutting-edge live-rock performance. Then, in 1971, Graham abruptly closed both Fillmores. The counterculture, Graham asserted, had become too commercialized; his critics pointed to him as a major culprit in this process. Graham later retorted: "When we began the original Fillmore, I associated with the employed musicians. Now more than not, it's with officials and stockholders of large corporations—only they happen to have long hair and play guitar."

Graham retired briefly and then in 1972 opened the 5,400-seat Winterland Arena in San Francisco. He was now at the helm of the emerging phenomenon of mega rock concerts in huge stadiums and parks. He had become, as Bruce Lambert put it in the *New York Times,* "the central figure in organizing, producing, and marketing rock music across the nation and around the world in all forms from live concerts to records, film, video and TV." Twenty years after his first show Graham reflected: "I came to realize what I could do with my life. I am not an artist. But I had found a means of expression." Graham confounded his critics by being at the forefront in organizing and staging live benefit concerts for myriad social and political causes. In 1968 he raised money for the Columbia University students' legal defense fund, packed Kezar Stadium when the San Francisco school board cut afternoon athletic programs, and ran the famine relief concert Live Aid (1985) and two tours for Human Rights Now/Amnesty International (1986, 1988). He raised money for AIDS research and the Haight-Ashbury free medical clinic. According to Jann Wenner, publisher of *Rolling Stone,* "he and his company [Bill Graham Presents] undoubtedly did more free concerts, benefits, charitable fund-raising and community work than any other performer or business people in Rock 'n' Roll."

Graham produced several history-making concerts. At Watkins Glen, New York, his Summer Jam in July 1973 drew a record crowd in excess of 600,000. He also promoted the first American rock concert in the Soviet Union (4 July 1987 at Moscow's Izmajlovo Stadium), which featured Santana, the Doobie Brothers, James Taylor, and Bonnie Raitt. Graham had bit parts in such Hollywood movies as *Apocalypse Now* (1979), *The Cotton Club* (1984), and *Gardens of Stone* (1987); he played Lucky Luciano in *Bugsy* (1991) and was the executive producer of Oliver Stone's *The Doors* (1991).

The guitarist Peter Townshend of the Who said that Graham "changed the way rock evolved. Without him I would not be here. His Fillmore promotions produced a model for halls around the world in which audiences would sit, listen, and applaud as well as scream and dance. Rock became music in that process."

Graham's tragic end came when he was taking a helicopter from a Huey Lewis and the News concert at the Concord Pavilion in Concord, California, back to his Marin County estate, Masada. Flying in a storm, the Bell Jet Ranger crashed after hitting a 200-foot-high Pacific Gas and Electric transmission tower. Graham, his longtime companion Melissa Gold, and the pilot, Steve Kahn, were all killed instantly. A free live memorial concert in San Francisco's Golden Gate Park was attended by 300,000 people; the Rebirth Brass Band led a New Orleans–style jazz funeral procession to kick off Graham's final show. Buried in San Francisco, he was posthumously inducted into the Rock and Roll Hall of Fame in 1992.

★

Graham's posthumously published autobiography, *Bill Graham Presents: My Life Inside Rock and Out* (1992), is a lively collection of oral interviews and anecdotes. John Glatt, *Rage and Roll: Bill Graham and the Selling of Rock* (1993), is an exhaustively researched, lucid account, especially of the sex and drug indulgences of a rock-and-roll life; the extensive bibliography on the literature of the era (books, magazine articles, government documents) is useful. Charles Perry, *The Haight-Ashbury: A History* (1984), and Oliver Trager, *The American Book of the Dead: The Definitive Encyclopedia of the Grateful Dead* (1997), offer biographical details in the larger context of the San Francisco pop-music scene. In an extended article filled with personal remembrances by many whose lives Graham touched, see M. Goldberg, "Rock's Greatest Showman," *Rolling Stone* (12 Dec. 1991). Irwin Stambler's article on Graham in his *Encyclopedia of Pop, Rock, and Soul* (1974) contains much early history. An obituary is in the *New York Times* (27 Oct. 1991), and there were many articles published in the *San Francisco Examiner* and *San Francisco Chronicle* in the days following his death.

JEFFREY S. ROSEN

GRAHAM, John (*b.* 8 May 1908 in Seattle, Washington; *d.* 29 January 1991 in Seattle, Washington), architect who designed the first regional shopping center and the Seattle Space Needle.

Graham was one of three children born to John Graham, an architect, and Hallie Corrine Jackson, a homemaker. His father had moved to Seattle from his native Liverpool, England, in 1900 and started an architectural firm that became one of the largest on the West Coast.

Graham attended the Moran School but graduated from Queen Anne High School in Seattle in 1927. He owned and sailed small boats during his childhood, and during the summer after his high school graduation he worked on a ship that sailed between Seattle and Nome, Alaska. He then entered the University of Washington at Seattle to study naval architecture.

During his other summer vacations Graham worked at his father's firm, John Graham and Company, as a draftsman. In his sophomore year he won an award of the Beaux Arts Institute of Design in New York and transferred to the Yale University School of Architecture, where he won further awards.

After graduating from Yale with a B.F.A. in 1931, Graham spent a year working in his father's firm. He then joined the statistical merchandising division of Allied Stores, a national department store chain. Graham later transferred to the chain's flagship store in Seattle, the Bon Marché, which his father's firm had designed in 1916. He was assistant general merchandise manager for merchandise control systems and later became divisional merchandise manager for the main-floor accessory departments. During the four years Graham worked at the department store he spent evenings and weekends designing office buildings and department stores at his father's firm.

In 1937 Graham moved to New York City, where he and William Painter set up the architectural firm Graham and Painter and specialized in department store designs. After the United States entered World War II, Graham attempted to join the U.S. Navy but was declared ineligible for service because of an old arm injury. Instead he designed housing for defense industry workers during the war and built housing projects in New Jersey, Maryland, and Washington, D.C. While in the District of Columbia, Graham met Marjorie Belle Clark, a merchandising specialist at the Office of Price Administration. They married on 20 February 1943 and subsequently had three children.

After the war Graham returned to Seattle and took over direction of his father's firm. Later renaming it John Graham Associates, he expanded its operations by adding offices in New York City; Honolulu, Hawaii; and Toronto, Canada. Under Graham's leadership the firm pioneered new commercial complexes that became known as regional shopping centers. Differing from older shopping centers, they were on a much larger scale, were set well back from public roads in the middle of an extensive parking space, and attracted one or more major department stores to "anchor" the rest of the specialty stores in the mall.

In April 1950 the first regional shopping center in the world, the Northgate Mall, opened near Seattle's Route 5, anchored by a Bon Marché department store. At the direction of James B. Douglas, the department store owner who commissioned the mall, Graham minimized the ornamentation. Many architects criticized it as a collection of unadorned boxes resembling Boeing aircraft factories. Douglas responded: "Some centers spend a lot more on frills, but they'll never get their money back. The main thing is that Northgate make money." Northgate was a financial success from the time it opened, taking in twice the expected sales revenues and undergoing several expansions. Graham subsequently added more color and variation to the architecture of his later malls, including the Bergen Mall in Paramus, New Jersey; Westchester Plaza in New Rochelle, New York; Cottonwood Center in Salt Lake City, Utah; Gulfgate in Houston; and Wellington Square near Toronto.

Graham constructed his first-generation shopping centers as open-air malls. He and his developers believed it would be too expensive to enclose them, which would add the costs of heating, ventilation, and air-conditioning. In 1956, however, the architect Victor Gruen designed an enclosed mall for Northland Center in Detroit that, owing to its popularity, became the model for the nation's second generation of regional shopping centers. Graham subsequently enclosed his early malls in later renovations. He also expanded the concept of shopping centers to include office buildings, hotels, and other institutions, as exemplified by the Lloyd Center in Portland, Oregon.

During 1959 Graham designed the Ala Moana Shopping Center in Honolulu, which included a building with a revolving restaurant on its top floor. Graham later applied this concept to the Seattle Space Needle, which he designed in collaboration with the architects Victor Steinbrueck and John Ridley for the 1962 Seattle World's Fair. The Seattle Space Needle was commissioned by the hotel executive Eddie Carlson, who formulated the idea after a visit to a Stuttgart television-tower restaurant. Carlson asked the architects to model the structure on a teak native carving in his home. They devised a three-legged skeletal tower rising 600 feet with a revolving restaurant and observation deck on top.

The Kings County commissioners, who controlled most of the World's Fair development, initially rejected the proposal. Carlson, Graham, and the builder Howard Wright then purchased a 120-foot square plot of land within the fairgrounds and erected the tower as a private venture. *Life* magazine reported on its construction weekly with extended photo essays. The Space Needle became the most popular structure at the fair and continued operating after the fair closed. The best-known feature of the Seattle skyline, it is shown in *The Parallax View* (1974) and other films. Most media viewers, however, know it from the title logo and background balcony shots of the popular 1990s television comedy *Frasier*. The Seattle Landmarks Preservation Board designated the Space Needle a historic landmark on 15 April 1998.

In 1986 Graham sold his firm to a nationwide architectural firm, the DLR Group. The firm operated under the name DLR John Graham Associates until 1998, when it was renamed the DLR Group. Graham died of heart disease at the Swedish Medical Center in Seattle. He is buried at Mount Pleasant Cemetery, Seattle.

Graham's fame as an architect is based primarily on two accomplishments, his design of the Seattle Space Needle and his conception and development of the first regional shopping center. The latter dominates the American suburban landscape as strongly as the former dominates the Seattle skyline. The architectural historian Meredith Clausen noted that Graham's success "was acknowledged only reluctantly by the architectural community," since "his approach to design was economic, not artistic." The fact that both Northgate and the Seattle Space Needle were located in a remote and relatively ignored region allowed later shopping center designers like Gruen and Benjamin Thompson to overshadow Graham's reputation as an innovator.

★

Graham's papers are in the Seattle Museum of History and Industry. For discussions of the Space Needle see Harold Mansfield, *The Space Needle Story* (1976); and Don Duncan, *Meet Me at the Center: The Story of Seattle Center from the Beginnings to the*

1962 Seattle World's Fair to the 21st Century (1992). Many of Graham's Seattle projects are also mentioned in John Graham and Company, *The First 80 Years* (1980); Roger Sale, *Seeing Seattle* (1994); Walt Crowley, *National Trust Guide, Seattle: America's Guide for Architecture and History Travelers* (1998); and Richard C. Berner, *Seattle in the 20th Century*, vol. 3, *Seattle Transformed: From World War II to Cold War* (1999). The best works on Graham and the evolution of modern shopping centers are Meredith Clausen, "Northgate Shopping Center—Paradigm from the Provinces," *Journal of the Society of Architectural Historians* 43 (May 1984), 144–161; and Meredith Clausen, "Shopping Centers," in *Encyclopedia of Architecture: Design, Engineering & Construction,* edited by John A. Wilkes (1988–1989). Northgate is discussed in Geoffrey Baker and Bruno Funaro, *Shopping Centers: Design and Operation* (1951); "Markets in the Meadows," *Architectural Forum* 90 (March 1949): 114–124; and Victor Gruen and Lawrence P. Smith, "Shopping Centers: The New Building Type," *Progressive Architecture* 33 (1952): 1–109. An obituary is in the *New York Times* (1 Feb. 1991).

STEPHEN G. MARSHALL

GRAHAM, Martha (*b.* 11 May 1894 in Allegheny, Pennsylvania; *d.* 1 April 1991 in New York City), dancer, choreographer, teacher, and leading member of the pioneering generation of dancer-choreographers who established American modern dance as a serious form of artistic expression.

Graham was one of four children (one of whom died in childhood) of George Greenfield Graham, a physician, and June Beers, a homemaker. She grew up in the prosperous city of Allegheny, at the confluence of the Allegheny, Monongahela, and Ohio rivers, which was later absorbed into the city of Pittsburgh. Her father, who specialized in mental disorders, gave Graham her first inkling that inner thoughts and feelings could be physically expressed and understood when he caught her in a childish deception and explained: "The body doesn't lie."

Physically she took after her mother, who was pretty and petite; like her father, Graham was an observant Presbyterian. She retained a profound religious sensibility throughout her life and expressed it in her work. Her sister Mary's asthma led the family to move away from smoke-polluted Pittsburgh to Santa Barbara, California, where the clean sea air would benefit her. Mary's health improved, but the most profound effect was on Graham, who became aware of a liberating social climate removed from the strict Eastern world that had circumscribed her life. She was an excellent student, and her father wanted her to go to college. In 1913 he took her for an outing to Los Angeles as a present for her graduation from Santa Barbara High School. They saw Ruth St. Denis dance, and Graham was, in her own words, "chosen" for her future career. Her fa-

Martha Graham. AP/WIDE WORLD PHOTOS

ther wanted her to attend prestigious Vassar College in the East, but she persuaded him to allow her to attend Cumnock Junior College in Los Angeles, where the curriculum emphasized "expression" as well as academic study.

During her years at Cumnock (1913–1916), the first Denishawn (Ruth St. Denis and Ted Shawn) dance school was established in Los Angeles, and it was there that she took her initial dance classes in 1916. Her idol St. Denis largely ignored her, but Shawn encouraged her. During the next several years Graham began to teach at Denishawn (in Los Angeles and, after 1920, in New York City) and Shawn choreographed a romantic drama set in ancient Mexico, *Xochitl* (1921), around her. She had a smoldering quality that lent itself to the exotic repertory of the company, which drew on the myths of Asia and the Americas for subjects. At Denishawn she also met the composer Louis Horst, who, as her longtime musical director and adviser, would contribute much to her artistic success.

In New York City, dissatisfied with the progress of her artistic career, Graham joined the cast of John Murray Anderson's 1923 edition of the *Greenwich Village Follies* on Broadway; she also taught at the Anderson-Milton professional school for a time. During this transitional period the director Rouben Mamoulian recruited her to teach at the Eastman School of Music in Rochester, New York, where she prepared students for weekly performances from 1924 to 1925. From among these students she drew her first small performing ensemble, three young women who joined her on Broadway at the Forty-eighth Street Theater on 18 April 1926 for a program of eighteen dances choreographed by Graham. It was the start of her independent career. She was not even thirty-two years old.

In 1927 she founded the Martha Graham School of Contemporary Dance in New York City. Two years later she introduced her all-female dance company Martha Graham and Dance Group, and presented her first works free of the Denishawn influence, shedding its aesthetic of the exotic and embracing instead the hard-edged realities of blunt emotions. Audiences were not quick to embrace those realities, however, and her work was often subjected to ridicule. Small wonder, perhaps, that her first non-solo work, *Heretic* (1929), pitted a lone dancer in white against a "jury" of twelve stern figures clad head-to-toe in black. Overall, the work of this period concentrated on plotless dances that were geometrically structured, stark in costuming and makeup, and devoid of theatrical glamour; emphasizing spare, percussive gestures, they had an astringent, minimalist beauty. *Primitive Mysteries* (1931), which examined the ceremonial rite of passage of a young aspirant into a group, was the most powerful work of the first two decades. Revived thirty years later, it still astounded audiences with its formal rigor and stark, unadorned costuming. In three sections, it explored the emotional climates of joy, suffering, and glorious acceptance.

Of this period Graham later said: "I went on stage with a whip in my hand." Her dancers were not selected for having any particular body type but were generally of sturdy stock. "We never dieted," recalled Sophie Maslow, a member of that early ensemble. To study with another dance teacher was regarded as disloyalty to the aesthetic ideals of the group. If anyone took a class elsewhere, they didn't speak openly of it. They were ideologically motivated. Most held daytime jobs, rehearsed in the evenings, and were paid $10 per performance. Graham's finances remained precarious throughout her lifetime.

During the years she worked exclusively with female dancers (1926–1937), nearly half of the dances she created were solos. (This form would diminish to a trickle in the latter stages of her career.) Her most publicized solo concert occurred in the White House on 26 February 1937, when, with Louis Horst at the piano, she danced a short program as part of an after-dinner entertainment. First Lady Eleanor Roosevelt then commented on the evening in her syndicated newspaper column, "My Day." It was the most widely reported concert of Graham's early career and drew attention to the special position she held in the emerging world of modern dance.

In the spring of 1938 the ballet-trained Erick Hawkins took classes in Graham's studio and was invited to join her at Bennington College in Vermont for the six-week Summer School of the Dance, culminating in the Bennington Festival that took place during the last week of the session. When she choreographed *American Document* (1938), she gave Hawkins a major role in it. Soon two other male dancers, Merce Cunningham and John Butler, were added to the ensemble, which now became the Martha Graham Company. The inclusion of men opened up a new range of dramatic possibility that fueled her creative efforts until the end of her life. By putting aside the instructional "whip" in favor of the more familiar—and at times amusing—cudgels of the battle of the sexes, Graham also found wider acceptance among the theatergoing public. A popular cartoonist of the era, Helen Hockinson, portrayed two plumpish matrons emerging from a Graham concert, conversing animatedly: "Either she's getting worse or we're getting better, because I liked it."

During the late 1930s and 1940s, Graham peered into the human heart with a relentlessness that resulted in a body of work unmatched in the field. In this "American" period she examined the work of the poet Emily Dickinson in *Letter to the World* (1940) to find the solitary comfort of the dedicated artist. She expressed the defiant triumph of passion in *American Document*, in which recited passages from Solomon's "Song of Songs" were contrasted with the rebuking words of the Puritan preacher Cotton Mather. She took a lighthearted look at the alternating female roles of virgin and temptress in the street-theater presentation *El Penitente* (1940). The choice between free and fettered emotional companionship in *Every Soul Is a Circus* (1939) found her coming down on the side of the fettered commitment. *Appalachian Spring* (1944), her signature piece, with the music of Aaron Copland, emerged triumphantly from the tangled emotions of this period. It told of the hopes of a young married couple, inheriting their own land and facing the future standing together. Meanwhile, at the age of fifty, Graham had found the mature love of her life; Hawkins danced the Husbandman onstage and was her lover offstage. They married in 1948 and divorced six years later in 1954.

Graham's imagination was cosmic in scope, and her choice of heroines evolved from American historical figures to personages of classical myth and the Bible. What remained constant was the imagination of a woman who conceived of her life experiences as being archetypal and who sifted through history for correspondent lives to develop whatever aspect of experience she wished to explore. The martyred Joan of Arc in *Seraphic Dialogue* (1955) reflected Graham's own steadfastness and faith in her work despite personal and professional disappointments. The evening-long *Clytemnestra* (1958) detailed the process of a soul achieving peace beyond the world of the living.

In 1969, at the age of seventy-five, health problems forced her to retire from the stage. She reclaimed her company in 1973, no longer as a dancer but as director of the Martha Graham Center of Contemporary Dance. Increasingly limited by arthritis, she continued to choreograph, but the fire of her imagination was severely diminished. The pieces she produced for her company lacked the emotional heat that had been one of the major hallmarks of her mature work. *Acts of Light* (1981), for example, was essentially a demonstration of her dancers' physical prowess.

Despite her waning creative powers, during the final years of her life Graham had the satisfaction of receiving virtually every award that can be bestowed on an American artist. In 1976 President Gerald Ford awarded her the nation's highest civilian honor, the Presidential Medal of Freedom; she was a Kennedy Center Honors recipient in 1979, and in 1985 she was one of the first to be honored with the National Medal of Arts. Her honors in the artistic world stem from the fact that her modern dance technique is the most widely taught technique in the world.

Graham's final work as a choreographer, the *Maple Leaf Rag* (1990), is a humorous one. In it she created a wryly dolorous role representing herself as an anxiously pinwheeling figure in an enormous skirt who crossed in front of the stage. Behind her, dancers in bright-colored costumes gamboled insouciantly to Scott Joplin's music and even quoted overwrought, dramatic gestures from her repertory. The "high priestess" of modern dance impishly left with a choreographed smile. She died of pneumonia and cardiopulmonary arrest shortly before her ninety-seventh birthday.

In six-and-a-half decades onstage, Graham created a whole vocabulary of dance movement out of her need to express the intensity of her perceptions about life. She created the most widely taught modern dance technique and continually revised and expanded it to meet her creative needs as she progressed through her long performing career. As a result, various versions of the Graham technique exist and are perpetuated by teachers in slightly differing forms. What these teachers all agree on is the use of the floor as a source of energy and on the importance of the disciplined breathing that Graham characterized as contraction and release of energy.

Graham's company was the cradle out of which a family of choreographers emerged to build on her work and carry its principles into the next generation. Among them were Merce Cunningham, Paul Taylor, Erick Hawkins, Anna Sokolow, John Butler, Pearl Lang, May O'Donnell, and Stuart Hodes. She always identified herself as a dancer first, and secondarily as a choreographer. Ironically, it is Graham the choreographer and teacher, not the dancer, who is most honored.

★

Graham's autobiography *Blood Memory* was posthumously published in the fall of 1991. This somewhat meandering book with occasional informative passages appears to have been prepared from tape-recorded interviews late in her life when memory can be deceiving. It contains errors of memory or transcription that suggest she never reviewed the final manuscript. Agnes de Mille, a longtime admirer, prudently published *Martha: The Life and Work of Martha Graham* in 1991, after Graham's death. It reveals much about her personal life that was scanted in the autobiography. Don McDonagh, *Martha Graham: A Biography* (1973), was the first comprehensive look at her life and career. Ernestine Stodelle, *Deep Song: The Dance Story of Martha Graham* (1984), is a respectful but somewhat florid account of her creative life. The July 1991 memorial issue of *Dance* magazine contains an excellent anthology of articles about Graham. An obituary is in the *New York Times* (2 Apr. 1991).

DON McDONAGH

GRAHAM, William Patrick ("Billy") (*b.* 9 September 1922 in New York City; *d.* 22 January 1992 in West Islip, New York), professional boxer and leading welterweight contender, known as the "Uncrowned Champion" for his performance in a championship bout in 1951 that he lost in a controversial and highly disputed decision.

Graham was one of four children born to William Graham, a candy store owner and later tavern proprietor, and Mary Hogan, a homemaker. Born and raised on Manhattan's Lower East Side, Graham became interested in boxing at an early age, receiving a pair of boxing gloves from his father and learning to box at a nearby Catholic Boys' Club. Graham had several hundred amateur bouts, fighting at boys' clubs, church athletic associations, and political smokers. In one such bout at about the age of thirteen he won a three-round decision over a young fighter named Walker Smith, who as Sugar Ray Robinson would be considered by many to be the finest fighter pound for pound who ever lived.

Graham was an indifferent student who spent two years at Gramercy Park High School before dropping out. After being rejected three times by a New York City Golden Gloves physician because he had a heart murmur, he turned professional in 1941, fighting in the lightweight division (at that time, lightweights ranged from 126 to 134 pounds). Managed by Irving Cohen and Jack Reilly, Graham was undefeated in his first fifty-eight bouts before suffering his first loss in September 1945. A superb boxer and defensive stylist, Graham—handicapped by several hand fractures—lacked only a knockout punch.

Billy Graham, during a fight against Joey Giardello, 1959. © BETTMANN/
CORBIS

During World War II, Graham served in the U.S. Coast Guard on antisubmarine patrol. After being released from the service, he resumed his boxing career in April 1944. For a time beginning in December 1945, he was plagued by a circulatory ailment that affected his right foot. He overcame this handicap and advanced slowly through the ranks of the lightweight division, being rated the tenth leading lightweight in the world in 1946. In 1950 Graham—a five-foot, eight-inch boxer fighting in the welterweight division (a division ranging from 135 to 147 pounds)—won and lost two close decisions against Gerardo Gonzalez, better known as Kid Gavilan, a leading contender for the welterweight title, then held by Sugar Ray Robinson. When Robinson gained the middleweight title from Jake LaMotta on 14 February 1951, he relinquished the welterweight crown, and Graham met Gavilan for the title on 29 August 1951. After fifteen hard-fought rounds, the majority of the sports writers present and most of the highly partisan crowd believed that Graham had won, but Gavilan was awarded a split decision victory. A near riot ensued after the decision was announced and the police were needed to restore order. Writing thirty years later in *Only the Ring Was Square* (1981), matchmaker Teddy Brenner claimed that one judge who voted for Gavilan revealed in a deathbed confession that he had been ordered by "the boys" to do so. It was

generally thought that Cohen's refusal to give a percentage of Graham's contract to the underworld boxing czar Frankie Carbo influenced the decision in favor of Gavilan.

Despite the defeat Graham remained a leading contender for the welterweight title and actively campaigned for a rematch. He fought Gavilan a fourth and final time, again for the title, on 5 October 1952 in Havana, but was decisively defeated in a fifteen-round decision.

Controversy continued to follow Graham's ring career. On 19 December 1952, his narrow split-decision loss to young middleweight Joey Giardello was reversed by Bob Christenberry, head of the New York State Athletic Commission, who—upon examining the officials' scorecards—altered the scoring of one judge, thus giving Graham the victory. Giardello's managers sued to have the decision reversed, and on 17 February 1953 the New York State Supreme Court judge Bernard Botein ruled that the commission was not legally authorized to alter the original verdict, thus again declaring Giardello the winner. Subsequently, Graham would win a twelve-round decision over Giardello on 6 March 1953.

After 1953 Graham began losing to lesser fighters and was dropped from the ratings. He retired in 1955 with a career record of 102 wins, 15 losses, and 9 draws, with 26 wins by knockout. He was never knocked out and suffered no official knockdowns. Graham's meticulous preparation and thorough professionalism were lauded by such prominent sportswriters as Jimmy Cannon, Red Smith, Frank Graham, Sr., A. J. Liebling, and W. C. Heinz. After Graham had retired from the ring, Heinz would model Eddie Brown, the protagonist of his boxing novel *The Professional* (1958), after Graham.

Always a tremendously popular fighter with a friendly personality, Graham was hired as a salesman and manufacturer's representative for a liquor company in 1955. He worked as a salesman and representative for various distillers for thirty-five years until his retirement. For a time, he was a member of the New York State Athletic Commission and refereed and judged bouts. He enjoyed big band music and fashionable clothing.

On 2 October 1948, Graham married Lorraine Hansen. They had four children. With the help of a GI loan in 1950, he bought a modest home in West Islip on Long Island.

In 1985, after the publication of Brenner's book, the New York State Athletic Commission reviewed the events surrounding the 1951 bout between Graham and Gavilan, but in the end the decision stood. In the final years of his life, Graham began to receive belated recognition for his boxing accomplishments. He was elected to the Ring Magazine Hall of Fame in 1986 and chosen for the International Boxing Hall of Fame in 1992. That same year the Boxing Writers of America nominated him for the James J. Walker Award for long and meritorious service to boxing.

On 22 January 1992 Graham died of cancer at his home. He is buried in Pinelawn Memorial Park in Farmingdale, New York.

Graham was an excellent fighter who fought the finest fight of his life in the most important fight of his career, yet was denied the championship that many thought he clearly deserved. A modest man and a gentleman in a profession of scoundrels, Graham was a boxer whose skills were best appreciated by boxing purists in a time when the advent of television made most fans clamor for crude sluggers with little finesse. Highly regarded by the boxing fraternity, friendly and approachable to writers and fans alike, and universally respected by his opponents, Graham was perhaps best described in the words of A. J. Leibling: he was "as good as a fighter can be without being a hell of a fighter."

★

James B. Roberts and Alexander G. Skutt, *The Boxing Register* (2d ed., 1999), contains details of Graham's boxing career and basic biographical information. Graham's last fight was memorably recounted by A. J. Leibling in "Next to Last Stand-Maybe," reprinted in his book *The Sweet Science* (1956). Years after Graham had retired, W. C. Heinz renewed acquaintances with him and relived some of his past fights in "The Uncrowned Champion," a chapter in Heinz's *Once They Heard the Cheers* (1979). The background to the disputed Gavilan fight is in Teddy Brenner, as told to Barney Nagler, *Only the Ring Was Square* (1981). *Ring* magazine provided the best coverage of boxing in the years that Graham was a professional, and reported on his fights for the title (Nov. 1951 and Dec. 1952). Graham related his own frank assessment of a fighter's life in Billy Graham, as told to Lester Bromberg, "You Don't Get Rich Fighting," *Sport* (Aug. 1952). W. C. Heinz, "Punching Out a Living," *Collier's* (2 May 1953), described Graham's training in preparation for his final bout with Giardello. Obituaries are in the *New York Daily News* and *Newsday* (both 23 Jan. 1992), and *Ring* magazine (June 1992).

EDWARD J. TASSINARI

GRANGE, Harold Edward ("Red") (*b.* 13 June 1903 in Forksville, Pennsylvania; *d.* 28 January 1991 in Lake Wales, Florida), college and professional football player and broadcaster who came to prominence in the "Golden Age of Sport" in the 1920s and became a football legend.

Grange was one of four children of Lyle Grange, a lumber camp foreman and police officer, and Sadie Sherman, a homemaker who died when Grange was five years old. After his wife's death Lyle Grange moved with his children from Pennsylvania to Wheaton, Illinois, thirty miles west of Chicago, where he had relatives. After a brief but unsuccessful stint as a house mover, the elder Grange became a police officer in Wheaton.

Red Grange. COURTESY PRO FOOTBALL HALL OF FAME

As a youngster "Red," so nicknamed for the color of his hair, quickly realized he could run faster than his playmates. When he entered Wheaton High School in 1918, his athletic ability became evident. In addition to scoring seventy-five touchdowns during his career as the school's football halfback, he was a state track champion in the sprints and broad (later the "long") jump, captain of the basketball team, and a good enough baseball player to receive an offer to sign a contract with Connie Mack's Philadelphia Athletics. Grange, arguably the most humble and modest of all celebrities, said many years after his retirement that his speed was "God-given." "I could always run fast," he said, "Some guys were meant to get nineties and hundreds in chemistry and Latin. I could run. That's just the way God distributed things."

In 1922, at a time when many colleges did not offer athletic scholarships, Grange matriculated at the University of Illinois because as a state school, it was less expensive than private schools such as the University of Chicago and Northwestern University. In addition, this was a time when most high school athletes stayed within their state's boundaries when choosing a college.

At first Grange did not even plan to play football for the university's team, the Fighting Illini, but his fraternity brothers in Zeta Psi coaxed him into going out for the freshman team—a varsity career was limited to just three seasons in those days. Grange, who would make jersey number 77 famous in his college and professional careers, was asked about the significance of the legendary double digits. "Nothing special," said the unassuming Grange, "they gave number seventy-six to the guy ahead of me and number seventy-eight to the guy behind me." He made an immediate impression when the freshman team scrimmaged with the varsity in the fall of 1922. It became clear that he was the fastest football player at Illinois, freshman or varsity, and his elevation to the varsity the next year was an anticipated event.

Grange's varsity debut was spectacular—in the 24–7 victory over Nebraska, he gained 208 yards and scored three touchdowns. One of his scores came early in the game on a zigzagging, sixty-six-yard return of a punt. Grange lived up to his outstanding start through the rest of his sophomore season. He would score at least one touchdown in each of the remaining six games (in the 1920s the average football schedule consisted of six or seven games), twelve in all for the season. He would gain a minimum of 140 yards rushing in each game, peaking with 251 against Northwestern in a game in which he scored three touchdowns. That year his offensive production was 1,260 yards. Not only was Grange a thrilling runner, he was an adequate passer and punter, a reliable receiver, a dangerous returner of kicks, and a fine defensive back. He made consensus All-America.

Grange's junior year in 1924 made him a household name and a legend. He became one of the glamorous athletes who—along with baseball's Babe Ruth, boxing's Jack Dempsey, golf's Bobby Jones, tennis's "Big" Bill Tilden, and swimming's Johnny Weissmuller—gave the 1920s its reputation as the Golden Age of Sport.

Illinois had already played two games, defeating both Nebraska and Butler, when the team played the Michigan Wolverines at home for the dedication of the state-of-the-art Memorial Stadium on the Champaign-Urbana campus. Michigan was also undefeated, having outscored two opponents for a combined 62–0. At the coin toss before the game, the Michigan captain asked the Illinois captain, "Which one is Grange?" "Seventy-seven," came the reply. The supremely confident Wolverines sent the opening kickoff right to Grange. Through a broken field, Grange sprinted ninety-five yards for a touchdown. The game was just seconds old and Grange was just getting started. With the game still in the first quarter, Grange added three more touchdowns on long, twisting runs of sixty-seven yards, fifty-six yards, and forty-four yards. Later in the game, he added a fifth score and even threw a touchdown pass. When the day was done, Grange and the Illini had humbled Michigan with a score of 39–14. It was the game that earned his storied nickname, the "Galloping Ghost," from famed

sportswriter Grantland Rice, for his ghostlike elusiveness and speed. (Having earned money and maintained peak physical condition by delivering fifty- and one-hundred-pound blocks of ice while in high school, Grange had previously earned the nickname the "Wheaton Iceman.")

Later that season Grange turned in an outstanding performance against the University of Chicago, then a Big Ten power. He gained 300 yards and scored three touchdowns, the last on an eighty-yard run to tie the underdog Chicago team with a score of 21–21. Again, he was consensus All-America.

While Grange's fame spread nationally, his greatness was not accepted by all. Football in the eastern states was elitist, and Grange had never performed against an eastern team nor played in the East. Two weeks before the end of his intercollegiate career, on 31 October 1925, Illinois played the University of Pennsylvania Quakers in Philadelphia. With three touchdowns and 363 yards, Grange led his team to a 24–2 victory over the Quakers. It was one of only two losses that year for the strong Pennsylvania team. For the third time, each of his varsity seasons, Grange was a consensus All-America choice.

Rumors swirled around campus during the last few weeks of his senior season. Would Grange turn pro? The National Football League (NFL) was a struggling five-year-old operation at the time and was lightly regarded; it consisted mostly of Midwestern "town teams" playing before crowds numbered in the hundreds. College coaches discouraged players from "playing for pay." But immediately after his last game, a 14–9 victory over Ohio State, Grange—through his representative, Charles C. ("Cash & Carry") Pyle, a local theater manager—signed a contract with the NFL's Chicago Bears. It was headline and newsreel news. The deal, worth $100,000 (twice what Babe Ruth made at the time), called for Grange and the Bears to play a series of exhibition games after the Bears regular NFL season ended. Grange, who left Illinois without a degree, later summed up the public's reaction to his turning pro: "I probably would have been more highly thought of if I had joined the [Al] Capone gang," Chicago's notorious Prohibition-era mob.

Nevertheless, Grange, at six feet and 180 pounds, was a drawing card as a professional. In his first game, on Thanksgiving Day 1925, Grange drew a crowd of 40,000 to Wrigley Field despite blustery weather as the Bears played a scoreless tie against the Chicago Cardinals. The next important stop was New York City's Polo Grounds. So great was the demand for tickets to the Bears-Giants game that fans stormed the gates when all tickets were sold out. Seventy-five thousand spectators (the largest crowd to see a pro football game up to that time) went to see the game—many without the benefit of tickets. That game, which the Bears won 19–7, is credited with saving the first-year Giants franchise and establishing the NFL. Throughout late 1925 and early 1926, the Bears and Grange toured the South and finished the season on the West Coast. In sixty-six days they played nineteen games. Grange, Pyle, and Bears player-coach-owner George Halas each made a reported $100,000.

Ever the promoter, Pyle wanted his own franchise in the NFL for the 1926 season, but it was not granted. Pyle and Grange then formed the rival American Football League. Grange was the star attraction of the New York Yankees, who played in Yankee Stadium. Although Grange played quite well, the new league lasted just one year before going broke. But in 1927 Grange and Pyle were allowed to take their Yankees franchise back to the NFL.

That season Grange suffered a knee injury that robbed him of some of his speed and much of his elusiveness. After the injury, Grange said, "I was just another halfback." He sat out the 1928 season and then rejoined the Bears, with whom he played from 1929 through 1934. Although he was no longer the Galloping Ghost, he was still an offensive threat and regarded as the NFL's premier defensive back.

After his playing career ended, Grange coached for a few years and then built a successful insurance brokerage in Chicago. He also began working in sports broadcasting and was the first successful athlete-turned-announcer.

On 13 October 1941, Grange married Margaret ("Muggs") Hazelberg, one of the first commercial airline flight attendants; they had no children. Grange and his wife moved to Miami in 1954 and to a new community, Indian Lake Estates, in central Florida in the late 1950s. Grange was a frequent interview subject until his death from complications of pneumonia at the age of eighty-seven. His remains were cremated.

Grange was one of the most humble celebrities of the twentieth century. He once said his biggest football thrill occurred when Earl Britton, his noted blocking back, beat Iowa with a late-game, fifty-five-yard field goal. "I held the ball," said the self-effacing football immortal. Grange is credited with popularizing college football during the post–World War I era, and with almost single-handedly gaining acceptance for the fledgling National Football League. He was one of the first and few to be inducted in both the College Football Hall of Fame (1951) and the Professional Football Hall of Fame (1963)—a charter inductee of both organizations.

★

Grange wrote an "as-told-to" autobiography with Ira Morton titled *The Galloping Ghost: The Autobiography of Red Grange* (rev. ed., 1981). See also the biographies *Red Grange: Football's Greatest Halfback* (1952), by Gene Schoor, and *Grange of Illinois* (1956), by James A. Peterson. John M. Carroll, *Red Grange and the Rise of Modern Football* (1999), uses Grange's career to make larger

points. See also William F. Heffelfinger, as told to John D. McCallum, *This Was Football* (1954), and Allison Danzig, *Oh, How They Played the Game: The Early Days of Football and the Heroes Who Made it Great* (1971), both histories of football. An obituary is in the *New York Times* (19 Jan. 1991).

JIM CAMPBELL

GRUCCI, Felix James, Sr. ("Pops") (*b.* 28 May 1905 in Bellport, New York; *d.* 9 January 1993 in Patchogue, New York), fireworks creator and businessman whose company, Fireworks by Grucci, created spectacular pyrotechnics displays in the United States and abroad.

Grucci was one of nine children of James Grucci, a grocer, and Maria Lanzetta. As a youth he worked in his father's grocery on Long Island, New York, but he soon joined his maternal uncle, Anthony Lanzetta, in the fireworks business. In so doing he became the third generation of the family to enter the Suffolk Novelty Fireworks Company, which his maternal grandfather, Angelo Lanzetta, had pioneered. In the 1920s the family relocated the company to Florida, where Grucci and Anthony Lanzetta produced impressive displays in the Miami area. Al Capone, who had witnessed their handiwork, commissioned a huge Saint Valentine's eve display in 1929. The show never took place, however, because the local authorities refused to issue the necessary permits.

By 1931 Grucci and his uncle returned to suburban Bellport, where Grucci established the New York Pyrotechnics Company. The firm got off to a slow start because of the Great Depression, but Grucci persevered. By day he devoted his energies to fireworks, and at night he played the drums in a band to generate an income. In 1938 he married Concetta Di Dio, with whom he had three children. When the United States entered World War II, the struggling company rebounded thanks to government contracts. The expertise that had created dazzling fireworks displays in peacetime was harnessed to produce flares, simulated grenades, and aerial bombs in wartime. The most unusual devices that emerged from the Grucci factory during the war were simulated atomic bombs commissioned by the War Department. Detonated on Long Island and in upstate New York, the bombs were used to gauge the dispersal of radiation and the impact of a simulated mushroom cloud on observers. According to his wife, this constituted Felix Grucci's "single most important achievement." After the war Grucci was credited with a number of firsts in the pyrotechnics industry. His stringless shells, perfected in 1954, constituted a major advance in safety because they eliminated the burning fragments that cascaded to the earth after twine-wrapped shells exploded. In 1960 Grucci synchronized a fireworks display with the music of the New

Felix "Pops" Grucci, 1969. COURTESY OF FIREWORKS BY GRUCCI, INC.

York Philharmonic Orchestra, and his fireworks illuminated the skies as the Boston Pops Orchestra saluted the U.S. bicentennial in 1976. In 1978 the *Guinness Book of World Records* included Grucci for creating a 720-pound Fat Man II explosive that was detonated in Florida.

By the 1970s Grucci's entire immediate family was involved in the company. The Grucci family skyrocketed to success when its firm became only the second American company to enter the International Fireworks Competition in Monte Carlo in 1979. Armed with well over 1,000 pyrotechnical devices, Grucci, accompanied by several family members, headed to Monaco, where new challenges awaited. Chief among them was a lack of a sufficient number of firing tubes, which ruled out firing the shells electrically. Rising to the occasion, the Gruccis trained volunteers to assist them in hand-firing the shells. As breathtaking images of Niagara Falls and the American flag filled the sky, it seemed that everyone in Monte Carlo was looking up.

As the last shells exploded, Monte Carlo erupted in pandemonium. People cheered, and automobile and boat horns bellowed in the most impressive salute ever rendered in the fourteen-year history of the competition. Tears welled up in the eyes of the usually stoical Grucci. Assessing

the magnitude of the Gruccis' triumph in Monte Carlo, *Newsday* declared: "In 1979, the Gruccis were indelibly etched in fireworks history. The Gruccis became the first American family to win the Gold Medal for the United States at . . . Monte Carlo. . . . This is the Super Bowl, the Olympics of all fireworks competitions. The Gruccis consider this one of their greatest accomplishments, and the New York press dubbed them as America's First Family of Fireworks" (28 June 1998).

After fifty years in the business, the company, which had once survived by putting on displays for Fourth of July celebrations and Italian feasts on Long Island, was now a world-class firm with a new name, Fireworks by Grucci, Inc. Still headquartered in Bellport, the company thrilled audiences around the country with its handiwork. In the 1980s Fireworks by Grucci produced displays for the Winter Olympics at Lake Placid, New York (1980), the inaugurations of President Ronald Reagan (1981 and 1985), and the centennial of the Brooklyn Bridge (1983).

Six months after the Gruccis' artistry illuminated the skies over the historic Brooklyn Bridge, tragedy struck in the form of a series of explosions at the Bellport plant. In November 1983 the unexplained explosion of fireworks valued at $700,000 leveled the plant, killing Grucci's son

James, chief executive officer of the company, and a nineteen-year-old niece. Two dozen people were injured, and 100 homes in the vicinity were badly damaged and were subsequently ordered to be evacuated. Within four minutes the work of a lifetime vanished in what eyewitnesses described as a mushroom cloud. Felix Grucci, who was on the fringe of the company's thirteen-acre compound, received minor injuries. The indomitable Grucci, who was only two years away from his eightieth birthday, vowed to rebuild.

Using fireworks scrounged from various sources, the family fulfilled a contract for a 1983 New Year's Eve display in New York City's Central Park. Preparing a display for the closing ceremonies of the Los Angeles Olympics, the Gruccis resumed their operation in the spring of 1984 at a more isolated location in East Moriches, Long Island. When neighbors, including residents of a nearby nursing home, objected, the Gruccis purchased a 131-acre site in the Long Island Pine Barrens. Environmental concerns relating to the potential impact of fireworks manufacturing and testing upon the underground water supply caused Suffolk County to offer the Gruccis a smaller parcel in Yaphank in exchange for the Pine Barrens property. In 1985 Grucci presided over the opening of a state-of-the-art facility in Yaphank, where the closest homes were nearly a mile away and ten-foot-high sand barriers protected the plant's storage facilities. Shells produced there were used in the July 1986 extravaganza in New York Harbor celebrating the centennial of the Statue of Liberty. On this occasion the family worked with two other companies to produce an elaborate show with synchronized patriotic music, but the Gruccis provided the computer program that choreographed the fireworks.

In 1989 the Gruccis produced the display marking the inauguration of President George Bush, and four years later they produced a similarly impressive show for President William Jefferson Clinton's inauguration. This extravaganza took place less than a week after Grucci died of Alzheimer's disease in a Patchogue, Long Island, hospital. He is buried in Woodland Cemetery in Bellport.

Commenting on his passing, *Time* magazine called him the "patriarch of pyrotechnics," adding, "During his reign, the clan's productions rose to world class, with visual choreography worthy of Broadway." The *New York Times* observed: "There are fireworks and there are Grucci fireworks. Felix Grucci . . . was America's master of ooh's and ah's." Although Fireworks by Grucci was not the largest company of its type in the United States, the *New York Times* noted, "As its name suggests, it has a certain stature." Grucci was responsible for many innovations in pyrotechnics, which he had made safer and more spectacular. This was the real legacy of the man who received worldwide recognition yet remained a down-to-earth Long Islander.

He dwelled in a modest house and to his dying day retained his memberships in the Bellport Fire Department, the Knights of Columbus, and the Italian-American Service Club of Brookhaven.

★

A substantial biographical article is in *Contemporary Newsmakers 1987* (1987). Additional information about Grucci's life and career is in George Plimpton, *Fireworks: History and Celebration* (1984), and Plimpton's "First Family of Fireworks," *New York Times Magazine* (29 June 1980). Grucci's business career is discussed in *Newsday* (1 July 1988; 28 June 1998); the *Wall Street Journal* (5 Sept. 1990); and the *New York Times* (13 July 1975; 29 July 1979; 30 Dec. 1979; 11 Jan. 1981; 28 Nov. 1983; 30 Dec. 1983; 17 Sept. 1985; 4 June 1986). He is commemorated in the *New York Times* (13 Jan. 1993). Obituaries are in the *New York Times* (12 Jan. 1993), *Newsday* (12 Jan. 1993), and *Time* (25 Jan. 1993). The present article is partly based on the author's interview with Concetta Di Dio Grucci (June 2000).

MARILYN E. WEIGOLD

GUTHRIE, A(lfred) B(ertram), Jr. (*b.* 13 January 1901 in Bedford, Indiana; *d.* 26 April 1991 near Choteau, Montana), novelist, short story writer, essayist, and poet widely acclaimed for his writing on the American West, best known for *The Big Sky* (1947), the finest novel written about the mountain man.

Guthrie moved with his family to the small ranch town of Choteau, Montana, when he was six months old, his father taking a job as principal of the Teton County High School. Both of Guthrie's parents were highly educated by the standards of the time: his father, Alfred Bertram Guthrie, graduated from Indiana University at Bloomington, while his mother, June Thomas, a homemaker, graduated from Earlham College, a Quaker school at Richmond, Indiana. The high plains country on the eastern slope of the Rockies, where Guthrie enjoyed hunting and fishing, remained his center of the universe, even though he might be as far away as Kentucky or Massachusetts. This love for the West became the focal point in his writing, and is also reflected in his lifelong concern with protecting the environment.

Guthrie was the third of nine children, six of whom died at very early ages. Although reared in the rather rigid fundamentalism of the frontier Methodist Church, after graduation from college Guthrie rejected his religious background and adopted a kind of pantheistic view of deity in nature.

In 1915 Guthrie began a summer job as printer's devil with the weekly *Choteau Acantha,* a newspaper his father had briefly owned. He also played on the high school basketball team and pitched for the town baseball team in summers. Graduating from Teton County Free High School in 1919, he enrolled at the University of Washington in

A. B. Guthrie. LIBRARY OF CONGRESS

about the rise and fall of the fur trapper, the mountain man, in the second quarter of the nineteenth century. Feeling that no novel had treated this period in American history truthfully, Guthrie wanted to base his portrait on actual documents of the time. After three chapters, however, he realized he was not creating what he wanted, and set the work aside. A major turning point in his life came in 1944, when he was awarded a Nieman Fellowship, a program instituted to provide journalists a free year of unrestricted study at Harvard University. While in Cambridge he completed two-fifths of the manuscript under the direction of Professor Theodore Morrison. Concluding his work at Harvard, he was granted a fellowship at the Bread Loaf Writers' Conference in Vermont, and there in August 1945, publisher William Sloane read the manuscript and offered Guthrie a $5,000 advance. Returning to the *Leader,* Guthrie completed his manuscript in off-hours, and *The Big Sky* was published in 1947. That same year he resigned from the *Leader* to devote himself full time to his writing.

The Big Sky received both critical and popular acclaim, and Guthrie was an overnight success. Most major reviews gave near-lavish praise, and Guthrie's picture was on the cover of the *Saturday Review of Literature.* The book centers on three main characters, all mountain men: Boone Caudill, Jim Deakins, and Dick Summers, between the years 1830 and 1843. All contribute to the destruction of the beaver, eventually depriving the trapper of a livelihood. This expressed Guthrie's theme that "each man kills the thing he loves." The second novel in the series, *The Way West* (1949), is about a wagon train of settlers moving from Missouri to Oregon in 1845. Dick Summers reappears as the scout and guide for the wagon train. It became a Book-of-the-Month-Club selection, and in May 1950 Guthrie received the Pulitzer Prize for this novel.

Although the remaining novels in this series did not receive the acclaim of the first two, Guthrie continued to be regarded as one of America's premier western novelists. *These Thousand Hills* (1956), a story of cattle ranching in Montana in the 1880s, was criticized for its predictable and melodramatic plot. Still, Twentieth Century–Fox purchased movie rights for $100,000. These first three novels of the series were made into movies, but Guthrie did not feel that they accurately conveyed his intentions. *Arfive* (1971), perhaps the most autobiographical of the novels, deals with life in a small Montana town from the turn of the twentieth century to World War I. The central character, Benton Collingsworth, a school principal, closely resembles Guthrie's father. *The Last Valley* (1975) continues the *Arfive* story, focusing on the problems of a small-town newspaperman from about 1920 to 1940. *Fair Land, Fair Land* (1982) is the last of the series. It goes back to earlier times, treating roughly the years from 1845 to 1870, which were omitted between *The Way West* and *These Thousand*

Seattle. Unhappy with the gray skies of Seattle, the next year he transferred to the University of Montana at Missoula, where he was much happier. There he joined a fraternity, became its president, majored in journalism, and graduated with honors in 1923. Jobs were scarce, and Guthrie took temporary work wherever he could find it, in Montana, Mexico, California, and New York. Then, in July 1926, he obtained a job as cub reporter with the *Lexington* (Kentucky) *Leader,* an association that lasted twenty-one years, with Guthrie moving through the ranks of reporter, editorial writer, city editor, managing editor, and finally executive editor.

On 25 June 1931 he married Harriet Helen Larson, whom he had known since childhood in Choteau. They had two children. Guthrie wrote his first novel in 1936. A combination mystery and cowboy story, it was, by Guthrie's own admission, a contender for the worst novel ever written. But it was a beginning, and eventually it was published as *Murders at Moon Dance* (1943).

Guthrie's major contribution to literature was to be a series of six novels treating the opening, settlement, and development of the West. After the publication of *Murders at Moon Dance,* Guthrie made a brief beginning on *The Big Sky,* the first novel in the series. He wanted to write a novel

Hills. The story centers on Dick Summers, and is a requiem for the fate of the mountain man as his life comes to a close.

In addition to this series of novels, Guthrie wrote numerous newspaper editorials and magazine articles. He also authored other books: *The Big It* (1960), a collection of short stories; *The Blue Hen's Chick* (1965), an autobiography; *Once Upon a Pond* (1973), animal fables for children; *Wild Pitch* (1973), *The Genuine Article* (1977), *No Second Wind* (1980), and *Playing Catch-Up* (1985), murder mysteries set in a small Montana town; *Four Miles From Ear Mountain* (1987), a book of poems; *Big Sky, Fair Land: The Environmental Essays of A. B. Guthrie, Jr.* (1988), a collection of socio-environmental essays; *Murder in the Cotswolds* (1989), a murder mystery set in England; and *A Field Guide to Writing Fiction* (1991). In 1949 Guthrie was awarded an honorary doctorate of literature by the University of Montana and in 1951 he went to Hollywood to write the screenplay for *Shane* (1953), for which he received an Academy Award nomination. In 1953 the Guthries sold their home in Lexington and returned to Montana. By mutual agreement, Guthrie and his wife divorced in 1962, but he remembered his married life with fondness.

On 3 April 1969, Guthrie married Carol Bischman Luthin. The marriage was a happy one, with his wife inspiring him to be productive. On rugged land twenty-five miles northwest of Choteau, they constructed their year-round home, which they fondly called The Barn because the outside of the structure was modeled after the actual barn on the property of the home in Choteau where Guthrie had spent his childhood. The Teton River ran through his land and from his window he could see Ear Mountain; both of these landmarks made frequent appearances in his writing. In 1972 he was given the Western Literature Association's Distinguished Achievement Award. In 1977 he received a doctorate of literature from Montana State University. He continued to write and publish until his death. He succumbed to lung failure at his home at the age of ninety. As he had requested, his body was cremated and his ashes were scattered over Ear Mountain and the land nearby.

Guthrie's six novels on the opening and development of the West established his reputation as one of America's foremost western novelists. Perhaps his major talent was his ability to evoke poetically the epic sweep and spiritual qualities of the western land without forsaking realistic details and historical accuracy.

★

Collections of Guthrie's manuscripts and personal papers are in the Margaret I. King Library at the University of Kentucky and in the Beinecke Library at Yale University. Guthrie's autobiography, *The Blue Hen's Chick* (1965), is packed with personal anecdotes and information up to the early 1960s. Thomas W. Ford, *A. B. Guthrie, Jr.* (1981), is a book-length biographical-critical study of Guthrie. John R. Milton, "The Historical Inheritance: Guthrie and Manfred," in Milton's *The Novel of the American West* (1980), discusses the first five of Guthrie's novels on the American West. Fred Erisman, "A. B. Guthrie, Jr.," in *Fifty Western Writers: A Bio-bibliographical Sourcebook* (1982), edited by Fred Erisman and Richard W. Etulain, includes a brief biographical sketch. Wayne Chatterton, "A. B. Guthrie, Jr.," in *A Literary History of the American West* (1987), edited by J. Golden Taylor et al., is a biographical-critical essay. David Petersen, "The Evolution and Expression of Environmental Themes in the Life and Literature of A. B. Guthrie, Jr.," in his *Big Sky, Fair Land: The Environmental Essays of A. B. Guthrie, Jr.* (1988), discusses Guthrie's lifelong concern with environmental issues. Richard W. Etulain and N. Jill Howard, "A. B. Guthrie, Jr.," in their *A Bibliographical Guide to the Study of Western American Literature* (2d ed., 1995), lists secondary sources about Guthrie. Martin Kich, "A. B. Guthrie, Jr.," *Western American Novelists,* vol. 1 (1995), is a bibliography of primary and secondary sources. David Petersen, "A. B. Guthrie, Jr.: A Remembrance," in *Updating the Literary West* (1997), edited by Thomas J. Lyon, et al., is a reflection on some events in Guthrie's life after his marriage to Carol Luthin in 1969. Obituaries are in the *New York Times* and *Houston Chronicle* (both 27 Apr. 1991). A television documentary, "A. B. Guthrie's Vanishing Paradise," funded in part by the Montana Committee for the Humanities, an affiliate of the National Endowment for the Humanities, aired on PBS in 1985. The program, available on videocassette, features interviews with Guthrie, and comments by critic Thomas W. Ford.

THOMAS W. FORD

H

HABIB, Philip Charles   (*b.* 25 February 1920 in Brooklyn, New York; *d.* 25 May 1992 in Puligny-Montrachet, France), career diplomat whose professionalism and negotiating skills influenced U.S. policy in Asia and the Middle East and won him the personal confidence of every secretary of state and president from Lyndon B. Johnson to Ronald Reagan.

The son of Alexander Habib, a grocer, and Mary Spiridon, Habib attended the University of Idaho, receiving a B.S. degree in 1942, and he earned a Ph D. in agrarian economics at the University of California at Berkeley in 1952 in pursuit of a career in forestry. Between degrees he married Marjorie W. Slightam. The couple had two daughters. Habib also served in the army from 1942 to 1946, rising to the rank of captain.

Habib joined the State Department in 1949 and served at American embassies in Canada (1949–1951), New Zealand (1952–1954), Trinidad (1958–1960), and the Republic of Korea (1962–1965). His service in Vietnam changed his life and established his diplomatic career. As minister-counselor in Saigon (1965–1966), he was the chief political adviser to Ambassador Henry Cabot Lodge, Jr. Upon returning to Washington, D.C., Habib served as the deputy assistant secretary of state for East Asian and Pacific affairs (1967–1969) and became the highest-ranking diplomatic official specializing in Vietnamese affairs. In March 1968 Habib had a profound impact on ending American involvement in Vietnam. Still a low-level bureaucrat, he risked his career by shocking Secretary of Defense Clark Clifford and a distinguished group of senior presidential advisers known as the "wise men" with a pessimistic assessment that it would take at least five years for any substantial progress to occur in creating a viable noncommunist South Vietnamese government. His powerful argument influenced President Lyndon B. Johnson's decision to end the escalation of the ground war, halt the bombing of North Vietnam, and begin peace talks. Habib served as a member of the U.S. delegation to the Paris peace negotiations (1968–1971). As ambassador to the Republic of Korea (1971–1974) and assistant secretary of state for East Asian and Pacific affairs (1974–1976), Habib became the State Department's leading authority on Asian affairs.

In 1976 Habib became undersecretary of state for political affairs, the highest career position in the State Department, and shifted his focus to Middle East affairs. After suffering a near-fatal heart attack, one of several that eventually took his life, Habib officially retired from the State Department in 1978 but agreed to serve as special adviser to Secretary of State Cyrus Vance the following year.

Habib handled a number of difficult tasks for the Jimmy Carter and Ronald Reagan administrations with great skill. Under President Carter, Habib helped conduct the landmark Camp David accords between Egypt and Israel in September 1978, for which he received the President's Award for Distinguished Federal Service (1979). He also carried out the unpleasant task of explaining to the sultan

Philip Habib. ARCHIVE PHOTOS

of Oman why President Carter had used his country without prior consultation as a base for the aborted U.S. hostage rescue operation into Iran in April 1980. Habib continued his service as a diplomatic troubleshooter for the Reagan administration in the Middle East, the Philippines, and Central America. His upbringing as a Lebanese Maronite Christian in a predominately Jewish neighborhood in New York City provided him with an acute understanding of the complexities of ethnic strife in the Middle East and influenced his efforts to reduce tensions in the region. In 1981 his shuttle diplomacy averted an Israeli-Syrian confrontation over Lebanon. After the June 1982 Israeli invasion of Lebanon, Habib negotiated a cease-fire that permitted the Palestinian Liberation Organization to leave West Beirut. He then mediated a cease-fire between Lebanon and Israel. Though the agreement collapsed and Israeli troops ultimately remained in Lebanon for nearly two decades, Habib won international acclaim as America's preeminent diplomat and received the Presidential Medal of Freedom from Reagan in 1982.

As special envoy to the Philippines in 1986, he convinced the Reagan administration that President Ferdinand Marcos could no longer govern his country. Habib then persuaded the Filipino leader to resign in favor of Corazon Aquino, the widow of a Marcos political opponent who claimed victory in a disputed presidential election early that year, and to go into exile. In 1987 Habib tackled problems in Central America, negotiating a cease-fire and free elections in Nicaragua. He pressed the Reagan administration to fight communism on the isthmus by pursuing a two-track policy of diplomacy and military strength but was ignored. He resigned without protest, thus ending his diplomatic career.

During his retirement Habib served as a trustee of the American University in Beirut (1983–1992) and chaired the Pacific Forum of Honolulu (1980–1991). The University of California at Berkeley recognized Habib's distinguished diplomatic career by appointing him Regent's Lecturer at both its Institute of International Studies and Institute of East Asian Studies (1982). Habib was also a senior research fellow at Hoover Institution at Stanford University (1980–1992). In addition, he remained an active alumnus of the University of Idaho, establishing the Philip Habib Endowment for the Study of Environmental Issues and World Peace.

A shining example of professionalism in public service, Habib told the truth, regardless of how unwelcome, to senior officials of five administrations and maintained their respect by keeping his dissent on policy hidden from the public and following orders. His cheerful disposition, optimism, intelligence, integrity, honesty, perseverance, knowledge, and humor contributed to his high standing as a shrewd and tough negotiator. Colleagues praised Habib for his love for the foreign service and his work ethic. Henry Kissinger, secretary of state under presidents Richard Nixon and Gerald Ford, described him as "one of my heroes" who "was every secretary of state's idea of a great foreign-service officer." George Shultz, one of President Reagan's secretaries of state, called Habib "America's top diplomatic professional" with a style that was "direct, forceful, and no-nonsense." Habib's fellow career diplomat Richard Holbrooke characterized him as the "optimal diplomat without peer." Leslie Gelb, a former State Department and Pentagon official, considered Habib the "most outstanding foreign officer of his generation."

★

Without the aid of a collection of personal papers or a full-length biography, one must rely primarily on Habib's superiors to reconstruct his diplomatic career. Alexander M. Haig, Jr., *Caveat: Realism, Reagan, and Foreign Policy* (1984); Ronald Reagan, *An American Life* (1990); and George P. Shultz, *Turmoil and Triumph: My Years as Secretary of State* (1993), praise Habib's service during the Reagan administration, especially regarding the Middle East. See also Philip C. Habib, *Diplomacy and the Search for Peace in the Middle East* (1985); Steven L. Spiegel, *The Other Arab-Israeli Conflict: Making America's Middle East Policy from Truman to Reagan* (1985); Stanley Karnow, *In Our Image: America's Empire in the Philippines* (1989); and William M. LeoGrande, *Our Own Backyard: The United States in Central America, 1977–1992* (1998).

For Habib's involvement in the Vietnam War, see Clark Clifford, *Counsel to the President: A Memoir* (1991), and Jeffrey Kimball, *Nixon's Vietnam War* (1998). An obituary is in the *New York Times* (27 May 1992).

DEAN FAFOUTIS

HALDEMAN, H(arry) R(obbins) (*b.* 27 October 1926 in Los Angeles, California; *d.* 12 November 1993 in Santa Barbara, California), advertising executive who became chief of staff to President Richard M. Nixon and who was deeply implicated in the Watergate affair.

H. R. Haldeman was the first of three children born to Harry Francis Haldeman, a successful businessman, and Kathcrine Elizabeth Robbins, a homemaker. He graduated from Harvard School, a private high school in the San Fernando Valley, in 1944. Between 1944 and 1946 he attended the University of Redlands and the University of Southern California while participating in the U.S. Naval Reserves' V-12 program. He next entered the University of California at Los Angeles, earning a B.S. degree in business administration in 1948. While at UCLA he became friends with John D. Ehrlichman, who later joined him as a member of

H. R. Haldeman, 1973. ASSOCIATED PRESS AP

the Nixon administration and was Haldeman's codefendant in the criminal trial resulting from the Watergate cover-up.

In 1949 Haldeman joined the J. Walter Thompson advertising agency as an account executive, and on 19 February of that year he married Joanne Horton. The couple had four children. By 1959 Haldeman had risen to vice president and was manager of the Thompson agency's Los Angeles office.

During the 1950s Haldeman was slowly drawn to Republican leader Richard M. Nixon. Although Haldeman's grandfather was a founder of the Better America Federation, an early anticommunist organization, Haldeman claimed not to have been attracted to Nixon because of ideology. Haldeman later stated in *The Ends of Power* (1978) that it was not, as had been widely reported, because of Nixon's anticommunism, but because Haldeman felt his fellow Californian was "a fighter."

In 1952 Haldeman's offer to work on Nixon's vice presidential campaign was ignored, but in 1956 he worked for Nixon's reelection as an advance man. In 1960 he took a leave of absence from the Thompson agency to work full time as the chief advance man during Nixon's unsuccessful campaign for the presidency. In 1962, when Nixon ran unsuccessfully for the governorship of California, Haldeman managed his campaign. After this debacle, many people thought that Nixon was finished politically, but he came back to gain his party's nomination for the presidency in 1968. With the Democratic party in disarray over President Lyndon Johnson's handling of the Vietnam War, Haldeman, aided by his former schoolmate Ehrlichman, directed Nixon's victorious campaign.

In January 1969 Haldeman became chief of staff in the new Nixon administration. Haldeman was fiercely loyal to the president, and his vigorous efforts to protect the chief executive soon earned him the hostility of the press, which portrayed him as the arrogant "keeper of the gate" who severely limited access to the Oval Office. His German origins and crew cut led to such labels as the "Iron Chancellor," the "Prussian Guard," and the "Berlin Wall."

During Nixon's reelection campaign in 1972, Haldeman remained at his post in the White House, leaving the direction of the Committee to Reelect the President (CRP or CREEP) to former attorney general John Mitchell. In *The Ends of Power,* Haldeman argued that Mitchell was distracted from his duties by the apparent emotional and mental problems of his wife, Martha. Without firm direction from the top, CREEP operatives carried out what Ronald L. Ziegler, Nixon's press secretary, called a "third-rate burglary attempt" on the night of 17 June 1972, when five men were apprehended inside the Democratic National Committee headquarters in the Watergate apartment and office complex in Washington, D.C. The effort to cover up the connection between the burglars and the Nixon campaign eventually led to the resignation of the president on 9 August 1974.

In the meantime, as a result of congressional and judicial investigations into the Watergate affair, Haldeman was forced to resign on 30 April 1973. In March 1974 he was indicted by a grand jury, and on 1 January 1975 he was found guilty of conspiracy, obstruction of justice, and three counts of perjury in connection with his role in the Watergate cover-up. In June 1977, after the U.S. Supreme Court refused to hear his appeal, Haldeman entered a minimum-security federal prison in Lompoc, California. His sentence of two and a half to eight years was reduced to one to four years by Judge John J. Sirica because Haldeman admitted his "guilt and feelings of remorse." An editorial in the *New York Times* (5 October 1977) disagreed with Sirica's ruling, suggesting that Haldeman's "admission of guilt" was made only to get a reduced sentence. Haldeman, paroled on 20 December 1978 after serving eighteen months, returned to Los Angeles and rebuilt a career in business and real estate. Seven months after his release from prison, he became a vice president with the David H. Murdock Development Company in Los Angeles. In 1986 he moved to Santa Barbara and managed his own real estate investments and a chain of Sizzler Family Steak Houses in Florida.

While still in prison Haldeman published *The Ends of Power* to give his view of the Watergate affair. However, in his preface to the work, Haldeman stated that this was not the book he had hoped to write, for his original goal had been to deal with the accomplishments of the Nixon presidency. To some extent the posthumously published *Haldeman Diaries: Inside the Nixon White House* (1994), which covers Haldeman's entire time at the center of power, is an effort to show that Watergate was only one facet of the Nixon years.

Haldeman's post-Watergate relations with his old boss were strained as the result of Nixon's May 1977 television interview with David Frost. First Ehrlichman and then Haldeman publicly criticized the version of Watergate that Nixon gave to Frost. When some 250 former members of the Nixon administration gathered at Nixon's home in San Clemente, California, on 4 September 1979, the *New York Times* noted that Ehrlichman and Haldeman, the only two who had criticized the former president, were "conspicuous by their absence." The *Times* also pointed out that neither man appeared at a reunion of Nixon's 1972 campaign workers held in Washington, D.C., on 6 November 1982.

However, in his afterword to *The Haldeman Diaries,* the historian Stephen E. Ambrose suggests that by 1990 Haldeman had come to regret some of the negative things he had said earlier about Nixon. Indeed, when the Richard Nixon Library and Birthplace was dedicated on 19 July 1990, the *New York Times* duly noted that Haldeman was

in attendance. Three years later Haldeman died at his home in Santa Barbara of an abdominal tumor after an illness of one month. He is buried in Santa Barbara.

Although Haldeman suggested that he was not guilty of any specific crime in connection with the Watergate affair, many of his critics argue that he played a fundamental role in the cover-up. As he admitted in *The Ends of Power,* his fervid loyalty to Nixon and his demand that all members of the White House staff serve the president without question certainly helped create an atmosphere that made both Watergate and its cover-up possible.

★

Haldeman's *The Ends of Power* (1978), written with Joseph DiMona, provides some biographical information but is mainly concerned with giving Haldeman's perspective on the Watergate affair. *The Haldeman Diaries: Inside the Nixon White House* (1994), gives a chronological record of Haldeman's activities as chief of staff from 21 January 1969 to 30 April 1973. Carl Bernstein and Bob Woodward, *All the President's Men* (1974), and Theodore White, *Breach of Faith: The Fall of Richard Nixon* (1975), deal with Haldeman's involvement in the Watergate cover-up. A brief biographical sketch is in *Current Biography 1978.* Peter Haldeman, "Growing up Haldeman," *New York Times Magazine* (3 Apr. 1994), gives a son's view of the travails of his father. Obituaries are in the *New York Times, Washington Post,* and *Los Angeles Times* (all 13 Nov. 1993). An oral history interview is in the California State Archives, Sacramento, California.

ROMAN ROME

HALE, Clara McBride ("Mother Hale") (*b.* 1 April 1905 in Elizabeth City, North Carolina; *d.* 18 December 1992 in New York City), social activist best known for her founding of the not-for-profit Hale House, a treatment center for drug-addicted babies, located in New York City's Harlem.

Hale was one of four children of James McBride, a dockworker, and Elizabeth McBride, who owned a boarding-house. Soon after Hale's birth the family moved to Philadelphia, where her father was murdered when Hale was still an infant. Left with few resources, her mother worked as a cook and took in boarders. She too died, when Hale was sixteen years old. Nevertheless, Hale graduated from Philadelphia High School and then obtained employment as a domestic worker.

A few years later she married Thomas Sam Hale. They moved to New York City, where Thomas opened a floor-waxing business. Because the income from their business was not sufficient, Hale obtained employment cleaning theaters. In 1932, when she was twenty-seven years old, her husband died of cancer, leaving her with three children to raise. In need of money, Hale cleaned homes during the day and theaters at night. Troubled about leaving her chil-

Clara Hale. AP/WIDE WORLD PHOTOS

dren without adult supervision, Hale decided to stay home and take care of other people's children. She worked hard and in 1940 became a licensed foster parent, taking in foster children for $2 a week per child. Hale retired in 1969 after caring for more than forty children.

That same year, Hale's daughter, Dr. Lorraine Hale, encountered a heroin-addicted woman in a Harlem park with a two-month-old baby. Lorraine gave the woman her mother's address. By the end of that day Hale was caring for the mother and child in her home. Within six months Hale had twenty-two drug-addicted infants. For a year and a half, Hale's three children provided financial and moral support. Hale and her daughter became the institutional founders of Hale House, and later Lorraine Hale became the director.

In 1970 Percy E. Sutton, then president of the Borough of Manhattan, helped Hale find and renovate a Harlem brownstone at 154 West 122d Street. The vacant five-story building was rebuilt and had a floor for play and preschool activities, a nursery for detoxified babies, and a floor where new arrivals were kept during the withdrawal period. In 1975 Hale House was officially licensed as a child-care facility. It was the only black voluntary child-care agency in the United States. In the 1980s the program drew national attention as drug-addicted babies languished in municipal hospitals. Hale House took the children at birth, reared them until their mothers completed a drug-treatment program, and then reunited the children with their families.

They were able to reunite the children 90 percent of the time.

Mother Hale, who earned her affectionate nickname from her children, loved to talk about her work. A woman of small stature, she had a gentle touch, tremendous energy, and great confidence and charm. She was a woman of boundless maternal love committed to social justice. As a result of her dedication to childcare, President Ronald Reagan in his 1985 State of the Union address honored Hale as a true American heroine. In 1986 the State of New York agreed to finance a new Harlem project that provided temporary apartments for recovering drug addicts and their children. The state also agreed to pay the operating costs of Hale House.

Throughout the Abraham Beame and Edward Koch mayoral administrations in New York City, Hale House won waivers from state regulations barring group nurseries for children under the age of five years. However, David Dinkins, elected mayor of New York in 1989, refused to make an exception for Hale House. His administration decided that the city was doing better than Mother Hale was in providing foster care for children. In the fall of 1990 the city threatened to shut down the Hale House group nursery home and to stop sending children there. In October 1990 Mayor Dinkins complied with state regulations and withdrew funding and support from the Hale House program.

Hale refused to give up. Children continued to come, brought by desperate parents, police officers, churches, and other groups. To finance their care without government funding, Hale House increased its private fund-raising. In 1991 it received tens of thousands of dollars in private donations. In 1990 and 1991 Hale House expanded its programs to include housing and education for mothers after detoxification, training for youth, and a home for mothers and infants infected with AIDS. Even in her last days, Hale continued to care for the children. In 1992, at the age of eighty-seven, Mother Hale died of complications from a stroke at Mount Sinai Hospital in New York City. She was cremated. Her daughter, Dr. Lorraine Hale, continued to run Hale House.

In 1985 Hale received an honorary doctorate of humane letters from the John Jay College of Criminal Justice of the City University of New York. In 1987 she received two of the Salvation Army's highest honors, the Booth Community Service Award and the Leonard H. Carter Humanitarian Award. In 1982 the New York chapter of the Urban League gave Hale the League Building Brick Award.

Mother Hale, who was a Baptist, dedicated most of her life to caring for abandoned, unloved, and orphaned children. She was a nurturing and loving woman whose gentle maternalism made her a rare individual, one who lived according to the conviction that every child deserves the love and dignity he or she is inherently due as a human being. Her outstanding work in nurturing and childcare made her a national icon, and she left her loving imprint on the lives of thousands of children. Her work will always be remembered.

★

Bob Italia wrote a juvenile biography titled *Clara Hale: Mother to Those Who Needed One* (1993). Useful background information about Hale's life is in *Current Biography 1985*. Hale's career is discussed in Mary Ellen Snodgrass, *Late Achievers: Famous People Who Succeeded Late in Life* (1992), and Mary R. Holley, *Notable Black American Women* (1991). See also Alessandra Stanley, "Hale House Fights City Hall on Babies' Care," *New York Times* (20 Sept. 1990), and Lorenzo Carcatera, "Mother Hale of Harlem Has Saved 487 Drug-Addicted Babies with an Old Mirage Cure: Love," *People* (5 Mar. 1984). Obituaries are in the *New York Times* (20 Dec. 1992), *Los Angeles Times* (21 Dec. 1992), and London *Daily Telegraph* (21 Dec. 1992).

NJOKI-WA-KINYATTI

HALEY, Alex(ander) Murray Palmer (*b.* 11 August 1921 in Ithaca, New York; *d.* 10 February 1992 in Seattle, Washington), author best known for his collaboration with Malcolm X on *The Autobiography of Malcolm X* and for *Roots: The Saga of an American Family*.

Haley was the son of Simon Alexander Haley, a professor of agriculture, and Bertha George Palmer, a music teacher. He was born while his father was studying for a master's degree at Cornell University and his mother took courses at the Ithaca Conservatory of Music (later Ithaca College). Six weeks after his birth, Haley's parents took him to Henning, Tennessee, where he grew up in the household of his maternal grandmother, Cynthia Murray Palmer. It was on her porch that Haley heard stories about his furthest back relative, "the African," which later led to his search for his family's history in Africa and the United States.

Haley graduated from high school at age fifteen and entered Alcorn A&M College in Lorman, Mississippi. He soon transferred to Elizabeth City State Teachers College in North Carolina. In 1939, after two years and a mediocre academic record, Haley's father urged him to join the U.S. Coast Guard, whose three-year enlistment period was shorter than the four-year commitment of the other branches of the armed services. His father assumed that he would mature in three years, complete his college education, and become a schoolteacher. But Haley remained in the Coast Guard for twenty years, starting as a cook and rising to the position of chief journalist by the time that he retired in 1959. He married Nannie Branch in 1941; they had two children. The marriage ended in divorce in 1964, and Haley married Juliette Collins that same year; they had one child and divorced in 1972. Haley married Myra Lewis

Alex Haley. AP/WIDE WORLD PHOTOS

in 1976, from whom he was separated at the time of his death.

While in the Coast Guard, Haley read voraciously and wrote prolifically, mainly letters to everyone he knew as a way to pass the time aboard ship. Because he received so much mail, fellow sailors asked him to write love letters for them. Apparently, the love letters were very effective. He charged a dollar a letter and had so much business that he soon earned more writing love letters than his military salary. He decided to become a writer and started submitting love-confession stories to magazines such as *Modern Romances* and *True Confessions* but without success. He would write for eight years before he sold his first story.

As chief journalist of the Coast Guard, Haley edited its publication *The Outpost* and did public relations work, such as writing speeches and working with the press on search-and-rescue stories. When he retired from the Coast Guard, Haley moved to New York City, where he sought a public relations job. He sent out his resume to about twenty-five of the largest advertising and public relations agencies. He put his picture on each resume and got only two replies, thanking him for his interest. He did not receive a single interview, which he attributed to sending in his picture and resultant race prejudice.

Haley was determined to become a writer and eked out a meager existence in a small room in Greenwich Village. He was down to eighteen cents and two cans of sardines when he received a small check from a magazine for one of his stories. He saved the eighteen cents and the cans of sardines, which he later framed as a reminder of his lowest point. He basically wrote men's adventure stories before landing an assignment from *Reader's Digest* for a story on Elijah Muhammad, leader of the Nation of Islam, a fast-growing organization that was making inroads among the black masses and about which most Americans knew very little. Haley studied the organization and interviewed Elijah Muhammad. He concluded that the Nation of Islam was "anti-white, anti-Christian, resentful, militant, disciplined" and that it would continue to grow unless the government and the Christian churches removed the legitimate grievances of African Americans.

In January 1963 Haley and Alfred Balk published an article in the *Saturday Evening Post*, "Black Merchants of Hate," on the Nation of Islam. He seemed to be fascinated by the organization, especially its charismatic leader of the New York City temple, Malcolm X. Haley earned his major journalist break when *Playboy* magazine commissioned him to interview the great jazz trumpeter, Miles Davis. The piece, which was published in September 1962, inaugurated the *Playboy* Interview as a feature of the magazine. For his second assignment, *Playboy* asked him to interview Malcolm X, who did not believe that *Playboy* would run the interview without toning down his rhetoric, but he was pleasantly surprised by the feature. The interview influenced the editor in chief at Doubleday to contract for Malcolm X to tell his life story to Haley. After reviewing the manuscript, Doubleday refused to publish it. Grove Press released *The Autobiography of Malcolm X* in 1965, and the book sold more than six million copies by 1977.

For many critics, *The Autobiography of Malcolm X* was Haley's most successful literary work. Haley sensitively helped Malcolm X tell the story of his early life in poverty and his transformation from Malcolm Little, a street hustler and thief, to Malcolm X, the proud and defiant minister in the Nation of Islam. Malcolm X called the American dream a nightmare for African Americans, who did not know their true identity and were victims of democracy and Christianity. Malcolm X and the Nation of Islam preached racial separatism and depicted white people as devils, the natural enemies of black people. During the last stage of his life, after his break with Elijah Muhammad and the Nation of Islam in 1964 and a year before his assassination, Malcolm

X became more universal in outlook and less pessimistic about a future for African Americans in the United States.

It appears that Haley was very much affected by the doctrine of the Nation of Islam, especially its racial separatism and disavowal of the United States as a place for African Americans. He sought to use his family's genealogy as a source of pride and an example of the historical bond between African Americans and the United States. He initially planned to call the book "Before This Anger," a chronicle of how his family rooted itself in the United States for over two hundred years. Two weeks after he completed the manuscript for *The Autobiography of Malcolm X*, Haley visited the National Archives in Washington, D.C., and searched through the U.S. Census Reports for his grandmother's father, Tom Murray. He remembered his grandmother telling him that she had been born on the Murray Plantation in Alamance County, North Carolina. After hours of searching and some frustration, Haley found the name of his great grandfather, Tom Murray. He became convinced that his family, indeed African Americans, had a past and a heritage—one that was just not well documented.

As a child, he had heard his grandmother and her sisters talk about their family and "the African." They said he had been brought from Africa to a place called "Naplis," that he tried to escape four times, and that a foot was cut off after the last attempt. His owner, John Waller, who called him Toby, then sold him to his brother, William Waller. The African insisted that the other slaves call him Kunta Kinte. He had a daughter, Kizzy, who he taught the names of objects in his native language. He called a guitar a *ko* and referred to a nearby river as the Kamby Bolongo. He also told her that he was about seventeen rains (years) when he went out from his village to chop wood for a drum, was captured, taken to America, and sold into slavery. This story was passed down through Haley's family for seven generations.

Haley spent about eight years researching his family's history and some four years writing *Roots: The Saga of an American Family*, published in 1976. From talking with African linguists and historians, he determined that Kunta Kinte was probably Mandinkan in origin, from the Gambia in West Africa. *Reader's Digest* provided Haley with a monthly stipend and travel expenses for his journey to Africa. He later published an essay on his research and a condensed version of the book in the magazine. One of the most controversial parts of the book was Haley's meeting with a griot, an oral historian, in the village of Juffure, Gambia. The griot recounted the story of the Kinte clan and the disappearance of the son of Omoro and Binta Kinte, Kunta, who had gone out of the village to chop wood. A British Broadcasting Corporation documentary aired in 1997 carried charges of plagiarism and fraud in feeding the griot information that Haley wanted to hear before their meeting.

Haley had to contend with much criticism, accusations of plagiarism, and several lawsuits as *Roots* became a phenomenal success. The book appeared in thirty-seven different languages and sold 5.5 million copies by 1992. The American Broadcasting Company aired *Roots,* a twelve-hour miniseries, over eight nights in January 1977. More than half the country watched at least one episode of the series, which won nine Emmy awards. Its stunning success led to *Roots: The Next Generations,* a fourteen-hour miniseries broadcast in February 1979, which took Haley's family story from 1882 to his search for "the African." He later worked on the miniseries *Palmerstown,* the story of a friendship between a black boy and a white boy in the segregated South, which aired in 1980. Haley defended *Roots* against two major copyright infringement lawsuits, one by Margaret Walker Alexander, author of the novel *Jubilee,* and the other by Harold Courlander, author of the novel *The African.* The court dismissed Alexander's case, while Haley settled Courlander's suit out of court for $650,000. He stood by his own work and indicated that any material resembling passages from *The African* appeared inadvertently, the result of relying on other researchers.

The Pulitzer Prize committee gave Haley a special award in 1977 for *Roots* because it could not place the book in the category of fiction or history. The committee cited the work for its "important contribution to the literature of slavery." The National Book Awards that same year gave Haley special recognition because *Roots* did not accommodate the category of history but transcended it. Haley maintained that the names, dates, places, and events were all true. The dialogue, thoughts, and emotions were inventions based on as much fact as possible. Doubleday published the book under the nonfiction category, and Haley preferred to call it "faction," a combination of fact and fiction. Most major historians, however, labeled the book a historical novel.

Much in demand on the lecture circuit, Haley earned about $250,000 a year from an exhausting schedule of speeches. He spent two months on a freighter as a way to find the time to write his next book, a novella called *A Different Kind of Christmas,* about a slave escape on the underground railroad. From his book royalties, magazine articles, and lecture fees, Haley kept homes in Seattle, Washington; Knoxville, Tennessee; and a 127-acre farm near Norris, Tennessee. His boyhood home in Henning, Tennessee, became the site of the first black heritage museum in the state. Haley died of a heart attack in Seattle, where he was scheduled to give a lecture at the Bangor Naval Submarine Base. At the time of his death, he was working on a book and miniseries, *Queen,* based on the life of his paternal grandmother. The miniseries aired in February 1993, and the book was posthumously published with the assistance of David Stevens. Haley, who is buried on the front lawn of his boyhood home, was also working on a biography of Madame C. J. Walker, the black founder of a cosmetics company and the first female millionaire in the United States, and a book on Henning, Tennessee.

Although Haley had earned millions of dollars, he left a debt of $1.5 million, most of which his estate settled through an auction in October 1992. The manuscripts for *Roots* and *The Autobiography of Malcolm X* brought $71,500 and $110,000 respectively. The Jewett Family Foundation purchased Haley's Pulitzer Prize and donated it to the Henning museum. Some personal letters, household furnishings, personal effects, and other manuscripts were also sold. The Playboy Foundation bought the notes, recordings, and manuscripts for his *Playboy* Interviews and gave them to the Schomburg Center for Research in Black Culture in New York City. The U.S. Coast Guard commissioned the 282-foot cutter *Alex Haley* in July, 1999, the first military vessel named for a journalist.

Through *Roots,* Alex Haley brought renewed pride to African Americans and sparked an interest in genealogy among all Americans. He hoped that families would seek and preserve their own histories to strengthen the family bond and to give everyone a sense of belonging. He also affirmed the close bond between African Americans and the United States as he dedicated *Roots* "as a birthday offering to my country within which most of *Roots* happened," during the nation's Bicentennial.

★

In 1991 Haley gave a collection of his manuscripts, correspondence, rewrites, research notes, newspaper articles, and trial materials relating primarily to *Roots* to the University of Tennessee at Knoxville, where they are housed in the Special Collections at the Hoskins Library. The Schomburg Center for Research in Black Culture of the New York Public Library houses documents from the *Playboy* Interviews and miscellaneous Haley material, including correspondence with Malcolm X. The newsreel *A Conversation with Alex Haley* (San Francisco, Calif.: California Newsreel, 1992) contains important biographical information. Murray Fisher's introduction and interview of Alex Haley in *Alex Haley: The Playboy Interviews* (1993) provides insight into his life by one of his literary collaborators. See also Arlene Clift-Pellow, "Alex Haley," in Jessie Carney Smith, ed., *Notable Black American Men* (1999). An obituary is in the *New York Times* (11 Feb. 1992).

ROBERT L. HARRIS, JR.

HARKEN, Dwight Emary (*b.* 5 June 1910 in Osceola, Iowa; *d.* 27 August 1993 in Cambridge, Massachusetts), cardiologist who pioneered early surgical techniques on the human heart and created intensive care units for critically ill patients.

Dwight Emary Harken was the son of Conreid Rex Harken, the town doctor in Osceola, and Edna Emary. Dwight's academic prowess took him away from Iowa to Harvard University, where he earned a B.A. degree in 1931 and an M.D. in 1936. Dwight married his childhood sweetheart, Anne Hood, in 1934; they had two children.

After Harvard, Harken interned at Bellevue Hospital in New York City at the height of the Great Depression, earning just $15 a month. His father refused to help the young couple unless they returned to Osceola, but they survived on Annc's salary as employment manager at Stern's Department Store. Dwight subsequently won a New York Academy of Medicine fellowship to study in London, worth $1,800. There he studied with the famous British surgeon A. Tudor Edwards, developed a special interest in cardiac care, and began devising surgical techniques for hcart infections.

With the outbreak of World War II, Harken served in the U.S. Army Medical Corps in the European theater of operations. With the rank of lieutenant colonel, he joined the Massachusetts General Hospital Medical Unit, head-

Dwight Harken. © BETTMANN/CORBIS

quartered in London. He was one of the youngest men in the Medical Corps qualified in thoracic surgery. In the brutality of wartime conditions, Harken began to distinguish himself as a bold and innovative surgeon.

Faced with massive casualties and desperate conditions, Harken was among a handful of military doctors willing to experiment with new and risky techniques that would not pass muster in a stateside hospital. The result was a number of medical advances that could not have arisen in more pristine conditions. Harken was the first to operate on the human heart, an organ previously considered untouchable—too complex and delicate to endure a surgical incision. But Harken had little choice. Many of his patients had shrapnel or unexploded bullets lodged in their hearts. Removing shell fragments would almost surely be fatal, but leaving a foreign object in the heart was equally dangerous. Indeed, his advances would have been impossible without the war and the resulting stream of young, strong, wounded men. Looking for a surgical technique to stem the flow of casualties, Harken began to experiment with animals. His goal was to improve his skill to the point where he could cut into the wall of a live human heart, insert a finger, locate the shrapnel and remove it.

His first test group consisted of fourteen animals, all of which died. His technique improved markedly with the second group, producing a survival rate of 50 percent. In the third test group, only two of fourteen animal subjects died. Emboldened by his progress, Harken was ready to try the technique on humans. During the remainder of the war, he successfully removed bullets, shrapnel, and shell fragments from the hearts of more than 130 soldiers without a fatality. Harken was the first to have consistent success with this kind of procedure and, by his work, single-handedly shattered the taboo on heart surgery. "We discovered that the heart wasn't such a mysterious and untouchable thing after all," he said later.

After the war Harken accepted an appointment at Tufts University for two years before returning to his alma mater, the Harvard School of Medicine, where he taught for twenty-two years, from 1948 to 1970. During those years he was also chief of thoracic surgery at the Harvard-associated Peter Bent Brigham Hospital in Boston and at Mount Auburn Hospital in Cambridge.

Harken set out to apply his technique to address defective heart valves. Just as with military casualties, a small hole was cut in the side of a beating heart and a finger was inserted to widen the narrowed valve. In 1948 Harken and Charles Bailey, a Philadelphia surgeon, operating independently but acting within days of each other, tested a technique to correct mitral stenosis, a condition where the mitral valve is narrowed and will not open properly, typically stemming from rheumatic fever. Early results were less than promising, with the majority of patients dying. Gradually, however, surgeons were able to improve the technique. The procedure, known as closed-heart surgery, became quite safe over time, with Harken and Bailey gaining joint recognition as creators of the technique. In 1960 Harken furthered his pioneering work, becoming the first doctor to successfully perform a totally artificial aortic heart valve replacement. He also developed and implanted the first device to assist the heart's pumping and the first internal pacemaker.

Harken was also an innovator in broader dimensions of health care, including systemic care regimes, psychological aspects of care, public health, and medical education. In 1951 Harken opened the world's first intensive care unit at Brigham Hospital. Convinced that low survival rates could be ameliorated, Harken provided extra staffing and equipment to monitor patient vital signs during the critical hours after surgery. He created a systematic response that could be applied quickly if and when difficulties arose. This approach proved to be an important medical innovation with utility in the care of all patients in life-threatening conditions. Survival rates skyrocketed and intensive care protocols were adopted worldwide.

In the same year Harken began to focus on the emotional and psychological needs of patients. He brought together four of his cardiac patients to form a support group. This effort grew into what is now Mended Hearts, Inc., an international support group for patients, families, and caregivers with branches in 260 cities.

Harken was an early critic of tobacco smoking, cofounding Action on Smoking and Health, a leading proponent of the link between smoking and lung cancer. Harken helped found Heart House, a Washington, D.C.–based center for information on heart disease and treatment that later became the headquarters of the American College of Cardiology, of which Harken was a past president. He also helped found the American Board of Thoracic Surgery and was a former president of the Association for the Advancement of Medical Instrumentation. He wrote or edited more than 200 scientific articles and several books and served on the boards of eight academic and health journals. Harken died of pneumonia in a Cambridge hospital at the age of eighty-three, leaving behind a legacy as the father of heart surgery and the originator of the intensive care unit.

★

There is no full-scale biography of Harken but judging from his foreword in *To Mend the Heart: The Dramatic Story of Cardiac Surgery and Its Pioneers* (1980) by Lael Wertenbaker, Harken prompted the writing of the book and collaborated closely with Wertenbaker. The book is not solely about Harken but is one of the few sources of personal information about him. Harken's professional story is chronicled adequately elsewhere, including Stephen L. Johnson, *The History of Cardiac Surgery, 1896–1955*

(1970), and the documentary *Pioneers of Heart Surgery* (1997), produced for the PBS television program *Nova*. Obituaries are in the *New York Times* and *Washington Post* (both 30 Aug. 1993).

Timothy Kringen

HAWKINS, Erskine Ramsay (*b.* 26 July 1914 in Birmingham, Alabama; *d.* 11 November 1993 in Willingboro, New Jersey), trumpet player and composer who was one of the most successful African American big band leaders of the twentieth century.

Hawkins was one of five children. His mother, Cary Ann, taught at Birmingham's Ramsay High School, and his father, Edward Hawkins, was killed in action in France while with the American Expeditionary Force in World War I. The young Hawkins began playing drums when he was seven years old and later turned to the trombone. At thirteen he started to play the trumpet.

The core of what came to be the Erskine Hawkins Orchestra consisted of a group of boys who attended Tuggles Institute and Industrial High School in Birmingham. Several of these youths were recruited by the president of the Alabama State Teachers College and offered scholarships, with room and board, to attend the Montgomery school. They entered college in 1930 and became the nucleus for the 'Bama State Collegians, a dance orchestra that soon attracted considerable attention. A booking agent arranged for them to play at Chicago's Grand Terrace Ballroom, and in 1935 the band got another break on its way to the big time when it played at New York City's Harlem Opera House. At this time the college musicians received one dollar each for performing. The rest of the money they earned went to the school, helping to sustain it during the Great Depression.

Hawkins graduated in 1934 with a bachelor's degree and accepted a position teaching music and drama for a year. In 1935 he married Florence Browning. They had no children. Hawkins then moved the band to a professional level. A showman and fine musician, Hawkins was prevailed upon to become the band's leader, and the band adopted its new name. By 1937, when the manager-booker Moe Gale, who owned Harlem's famed Savoy Ballroom, took them on as clients, Hawkins and his group were beginning to attain national recognition. In 1938 Erskine Hawkins and His Orchestra made its first official appearance. That same year the band received a recording contract, and the sale of records helped to extend the group's success, as did the use of a radio wire three times a week.

The most important influence on Hawkins himself was the trumpeter Louis Armstrong, who met the performer for the first time backstage at the Apollo Theater in Harlem.

Erskine Hawkins. ARCHIVE PHOTOS

From that time, whenever Hawkins was in New York City, Armstrong shared the Savoy's stage with him.

The band's popularity ensured that Hawkins could retain a regular personnel of musicians, including the baritone saxophone player Haywood Henry, who stayed with Hawkins until the band split up in 1953, the trumpeter Sam Lowe, and the pianist Avery Parrish. Lowe and Parrish were two of the band's major arrangers. Other members included Dud Bascomb on trumpet and Bob Range on trombone. Even through the mid-1940s, when many other big bands, both white and African American, broke up or shrank to a much smaller format, Hawkins's organization stayed intact.

The band's musical style was blues-inspired, down-home jazz, but it could still swing. In 1938 "Tuxedo Junction" was a great favorite of American servicemen during the early part of World War II. This number became the theme song that identified Hawkins's orchestra but was also a hit for other bands. In 1940 "Tuxedo Junction" (the name taken from a Birmingham suburb that served as a mass-transit transfer point) was number one on the *Billboard Magazine* chart for the Glenn Miller Band, number seven on the chart for Erskine Hawkins Orchestra, and number fifteen for Jan Savitt. The Miller cover's higher rank on the charts may well be explained by the aptness of the white public to more readily embrace a song performed by a white artist or group.

The opening notes of the song had for many years been used as a "sign-off" by the bands at the Savoy Ballroom. According to one version of the song's development, on an evening when the bandleader Chick Webb was late in com-

ing on the stand, Hawkins and his group improvised on the notes, working them into an effective, swinging number. Another version has it that, in need of one more tune to fill out the allotted time in a recording session, the band took the sign-off tag and embellished it to reach the necessary length. Modern dance groups in the 1940s used the number, and in the 1980s, equipped with words, it became a hit song for the vocal group Manhattan Transfer.

Hawkins played several instruments but mainly the trumpet. He was given the nickname the "Twentieth-Century Gabriel" (after the biblical archangel who is to blow the trumpet on Judgment Day) because of his ability to play an astonishing number of consecutive high notes. He was also a composer, his credits including "Tuxedo Junction," "Dolomite," "Norfolk Ferry," "After Hours," "Tippin' In," and "Midnight Stroll," some in collaboration with other band members. The music produced by the Hawkins band maintained a jazz emphasis but in its later years took on a rhythm-and-blues flavor.

In the 1950s, responding to financial pressures, Hawkins broke up his band. He continued to perform with a smaller group while occasionally assembling the big unit for special events. During the 1960s and 1970s he led small groups in New York clubs and hotels while also appearing at festivals. He visited Europe in 1979 and in 1986 sailed on the SS *Norway* for the Fifth Annual Floating Jazz Festival.

At the height of his career Hawkins helped other entertainers on their climb to success. These included the vocalists Delores Brown, Ida James, and Della Reese and the rhythm-and-blues pianist Ray Charles. In 1978 Hawkins was one of five inductees into the Alabama Jazz Hall of

Fame. In 1989 he received the Lifework Award for Performing Achievement from the Alabama Music Hall of Fame. Typifying the expression, "jazz keeps you young," Hawkins continued to play into the 1990s, spending a total of twenty-three years at the Concord Hotel in New York State's Catskill Mountains. He died of heart failure at the age of seventy-nine. He is buried in Birmingham.

In a fashion similar to that of his contemporary, the trumpeter Harry James, Hawkins combined an outstanding performing technique with an understanding of the commercial demands of the business and a feeling for jazz. Hawkins retained the loyalty of his audience, even as its members changed over the years, by being moderately adaptable in the music that he played. Rarely seen without a trumpet in his hand, either playing it or conducting with it, Hawkins throughout his career put forth the same effort whether he was playing for a small or large audience. This attitude, coupled with danceable swing numbers, provided him with lifelong success and made him a role model for numerous trumpet players.

★

Roger D. Kinkle, *The Complete Encyclopedia of Popular Music and Jazz, 1900–1950* (1974), contains ample biographical coverage and a discography. Leonard Feather and Ira Gitler, *The Biographical Encyclopedia of Jazz* (1999), provides a lengthy biographical sketch, as does Ian Carr, Digby Fairweather, and Brian Priestley, *Jazz: The Rough Guide* (1995). Gene Fernett, *Swing Out: Great Negro Dance Bands* (1970), contains a brief chapter on the Hawkins band. George T. Simon, *The Big Bands* (4th ed. 1981), contains good, brief coverage of Hawkins and a section on Moe Gale. Gunther Schuller, *The Swing Era: The Development of Jazz, 1930–1945* (1989), supplies an analysis of Hawkins's style. An obituary by the music critic Peter Watrous is in the *New York Times* (13 Nov. 1993). *An Introduction to Erskine Hawkins: His Best Recordings 1936–1947,* Best of Jazz: The Swing Era CD 4060, contains recordings of the 'Bama State Collegians and the Hawkins orchestra. *Erskine Hawkins: Tuxedo Junction,* Masters of the Big Bands series, Bluebird CD 61069–2, features numbers originally appearing on the Bluebird label, recorded 1938–1945.

BARRETT G. POTTER

HAYAKAWA, S(amuel) I(chiye) (*b.* 18 July 1906 in Vancouver, British Columbia, Canada; *d.* 27 February 1992 in Greenbrae, California), author, semanticist, college president, and U.S. senator. He wrote *Language in Action* (1941), and as president of San Francisco State College (1968–1972), he ended a Vietnam-era strike that had paralyzed the college, launching his term in the U.S. Senate (1977–1982).

Hayakawa was one of four children born to Ichiro Hayakawa, an importer and exporter, and Tora Isono, a homemaker. Ichiro Hayakawa had left his native Japan as a

S. I. Hayakawa. CORBIS CORPORATION (BELLEVUE)

seaman at the age of eighteen, returning two years later to marry Tora. Soon afterwards they emigrated to western Canada.

After attending public schools in Alberta and Manitoba, Hayakawa, whose family called him "Don," finished high school in Winnipeg, Manitoba, in 1923. Graduating from the University of Manitoba with a B.A. in 1927, he moved to Montreal, Quebec, to take graduate courses at McGill University. Supporting himself with secretarial work and driving a taxi in Montreal, he finished his M.A. in English literature in 1928. In 1929 his parents returned to Japan, but Hayakawa emigrated to the United States that year. He received a fellowship to begin doctoral studies at the University of Wisconsin-Madison, where his dissertation, a study of the writing of Oliver Wendell Holmes, earned him a Ph.D. in 1935.

The following year Hayakawa received an appointment as an English instructor at the University of Wisconsin. On 29 May 1937 Hayakawa married Margedant Peters, one of his students, and considered moving west. But marriages between Asians and Caucasians were not then recognized in California, so the Hayakawas stayed in Madison. They had three children. Hayakawa adapted his dissertation to a textbook anthology, *Oliver Wendell Holmes: Representative Selections,* on which he collaborated with Howard Mumford Jones. The book, his first, appeared in 1939.

In 1939 Hayakawa moved to Chicago, where he taught English at the Armour Institute of Technology, which became the Illinois Institute of Technology. He was promoted to associate professor in 1942. A factor in his promotion was Hayakawa's highly successful book *Language in Action,* published by Harcourt, Brace in 1941. The book was enthusiastically reviewed and was distributed by the Book of the Month Club, greatly increasing public awareness of general semantics. Dealing with the function and meaning of language, general semantics was originally articulated by the Polish linguist Alfred Korzybski in his *Science and Sanity* in 1933. Hayakawa often acknowledged that he was strongly influenced by Korzybski's teaching and writing. Hayakawa's *Language in Thought and Action,* a revision of his 1941 text, was the most successful of his many books. In 1943 he became editor of *Etc., A Review of General Semantics,* the journal of the International Society for General Semantics, of which he was later president (1949–1950).

Hayakawa was an associate professor at the Illinois Institute until 1947, when he began five years as a lecturer at the University of Chicago. In 1955 he accepted an appointment as professor of English at San Francisco State College, which was renamed San Francisco State University shortly thereafter.

In 1954 Hayakawa became a U.S. citizen. A *nisei* (son of native Japanese), he had remained a Canadian citizen until 1954 because, even as a Canadian citizen, he was subject to the tight U.S. immigration quota for Japanese when he moved to Wisconsin. U.S. citizenship was not required to teach in the California State College system, but it was a distinct asset to his later political aspirations.

In 1954 Hayakawa edited *Language, Meaning, and Maturity,* a synthesis of articles that had appeared in *Etc.* In 1959 he edited *Our Language and Our World.* That same year he began a series of lectures at the University of Montreal's Institute of Experimental Medicine and Surgery, and two years later he taught at the Menninger Psychiatric Clinic in Topeka, Kansas.

Hayakawa achieved his greatest public attention when he became acting president of San Francisco State University in 1968 during a long strike led by the Black Student Union. His actions in opposition to this strike made it clear that he was a man of definite opinions and was willing to articulate them.

The most famous episode occurred in the fall of 1968, shortly after Hayakawa succeeded Robert R. Smith, the second president to resign that year in the face of the boisterous strike led by the Black Student Union, whose principal demand was the establishment of a large, autonomous black studies department. Hayakawa was a member of the presidential search committee, and although he was sympathetic to the black students' desire for representation, he opposed the strike, saying that a few hundred students, to

advance their own interests, were depriving 17,500 others of their educations. Many members of the faculty were unenthusiastic about the strike, but Hayakawa was one of the few who actively objected. Because of Hayakawa's stance, Glenn Dumke, chancellor of the state university system, with the backing of Superintendent of Public Instruction Max Rafferty, San Francisco mayor Joseph Alioto, and Governor Ronald Reagan, invited him to serve as acting president. Hayakawa accepted the job on the condition that he could call for police support if he needed it. He assumed office on 28 November and announced that classes would resume 2 December, at the end of Thanksgiving recess.

The first week was predictably tumultuous. On the first day of classes student demonstrators parked a sound truck near the administration building, an action the new president had forbidden. Hayakawa, wearing a brightly colored knit tam-o-shanter, confronted them, climbing on the truck and pulling wires out of their amplifier. Television cameras recorded the performance of the five-foot, six-inch-tall man with a trim athletic build and a small mustache. Even though he had to start Christmas vacation a week early to stall the demonstrations, Hayakawa was suddenly a celebrity to people who had never heard of semantics. In January the American Federation of Teachers struck. Finally in late March, when Hayakawa gave the Black Student Union a student-controlled black studies department, the campus returned more or less to normal.

Hayakawa had become the folk hero of California's conservative establishment. He retired from San Francisco State in 1973, became a Republican, and on 2 November 1976 was elected to the U.S. Senate. As a senator, Hayakawa was plain-spoken, predictably conservative in his social and economic policies, hawkish in his support of South Vietnam, and much interested in a constitutional amendment bill to make English the official language of the United States. His voting record on other issues was unpredictable, and he was reported to have narcolepsy, which caused him to doze if proceedings were dull. These qualities combined with a political swing to the left in California politics cost him reelection in 1982. He retired to Mill Valley, north of San Francisco. Hayakawa died of a stroke in the Marin County General Hospital in Greenbrae.

★

Hayakawa's papers regarding his presidency of the university are in the San Francisco State University archives. His congressional papers are in the Hoover Institution at Stanford University. Substantial biographical essays are in *Current Biography 1977* (1978); and Helen Zia and Susan Gall, eds., *Notable Asian Americans* (1995). Shorter entries are in *Contemporary Authors,* vol. 137 (1972); and *Who's Who in America* (1991–1992). An account of his first year as president of San Francisco State University is

Dikran Karagueuzian, *Blow It Up! The Black Student Revolt at San Francisco State College and the Emergence of Dr. Hayakawa* (1971). Obituaries are in the *New York Times* (28 Feb. 1992) and the *Los Angeles Times* (28 Feb. 1992).

DAVID W. HERON

HAYEK, Friedrich August von (*b.* 8 May 1899 in Vienna, Austria; *d.* 23 March 1992 in Freiburg, Germany), Nobel laureate in economics (1974), whose many publications included the influential, pro–free enterprise book *The Road to Serfdom* (1944).

Hayek was the eldest of three sons of August von Hayek, a physician who shifted his interests to botany and became an honorary professor in that discipline at the University of Vienna, and Felicitas von Juraschek, a homemaker. The family was partly of Czech descent; Hayek's parents, although brought up as Catholics, were nonbelievers as adults. During World War I Hayek served on the Italian front (1917–1918) as a junior artillery officer in the Austro-Hungarian army. He later stated that the experience of serving in a multi-ethnic army, with its complex organizational problems, inspired his interest in economics. In 1918, eight days after the war ended, Hayek entered the University of Vienna, where he studied philosophy, law, and economics. He received his doctorate in law (1921), with specialization in economics, and a second doctorate in political science (1923), with specialization in political economy, while studying under Ludwig von Mises, an older economist with whom Hayek is usually connected because of their similar viewpoints. Under von Mises's influence, Hayek abandoned his early socialism in favor of the free-market approach for which he became famous. From 1921 to 1926 Hayek worked under von Mises as his legal consultant at the Austrian Office of Accounts, a temporary government agency set up to fulfill the terms of the post–World War I settlement. During 1923–1924 Hayek, on leave of absence from his government post, was a graduate student in economics at New York University.

In 1926 Hayek married Helene ("Hella") von Fritsch; they had two children. In the following year, he and von Mises founded the Austrian Institute for Business Cycle Research (later renamed the Institute for Economic Research); Hayek was director. From 1929 to 1931 he was also a lecturer in economics at the University of Vienna. His first book, *Monetary Theory and the Trade Cycle,* in German, appeared in 1929 (the English translation was published in 1933). After attending the London Conference on Economic Statistics in 1928, Hayek was invited to lecture at the London School of Economics; from 1931 to 1950 he was Tooke Professor there. Numerous books on economics, mostly technical, were published during these years. In 1938 he became a naturalized British citizen. Hayek became a close personal friend of John Maynard Keynes, despite strong differences on economic matters. During World War II, when the London School of Economics was evacuated to Cambridge, Hayek decided to write a nontechnical book explaining his economic views. *The Road to Serfdom,* published in 1944 and arguably the most important nontechnical book on economics of the twentieth century, gives in fewer than two hundred closely argued pages the case for free enterprise. His thesis was that "big government," which Hayek saw as synonymous with socialism, often results from wartime economic mobilization and leads to loss of freedom and inefficiency. The book became an international best seller and was favorably reviewed even by Keynes. A few months after the book's publication, Hayek was elected to the British Academy. In 1945 an abridged edition of *The Road to Serfdom* appeared in *Reader's Digest* in the United States. Two years later Hayek founded the Mount Pelerin Society, an organization of pro–free enterprise scholars that became very influential and still exists.

Hayek's *Individualism and Economic Order,* which pointed out the difficulties in allocating goods and services without a free price system, appeared in 1949. In the same year, the breakup of his marriage caused a severe depression, which resulted in his leaving England. He married Helene Bitterlich in 1950. That year he was also appointed professor of social and moral science at the University of Chicago, where he inspired the famous "Chicago School" of economics later associated with another Nobel laureate

Friedrich von Hayek. LIBRARY OF CONGRESS

in economics, Milton Friedman. Major books published in those years included *The Counter-Revolution of Science* (1952), a critical study of the origins of "social engineering." In collaboration with four other scholars Hayek edited *Capitalism and the Historians* (1954), which argues against the Marxist theory that the Industrial Revolution "immiserated" England's working class. *The Constitution of Liberty,* which Hayek considered his most important book, appeared in 1960. This restatement of the nineteenth-century "classical liberal" argument asserts that society is too complicated for a planned economy to succeed.

Two years later the aging, homesick Hayek, who was becoming increasingly deaf, left Chicago to become professor of economics at the University of Freiburg in Breisgau in West Germany. By this time he was a major influence on the West German minister of economics and then chancellor, Ludwig Erhard, and later on the British prime minister, Margaret Thatcher. Retiring from Freiburg in 1968, Hayek moved to Salzburg in his native Austria, where he held a visiting professorship at the university until 1974. He had already begun to receive honorary degrees from universities around the world, but shortly after his return to the city of Freiburg in 1974, he was surprised to be awarded the Nobel Prize in economics for his work in the theory of business cycles and his advocacy of the free-market system as an answer to the problems of allocation of goods and services. Hayek continued to publish books on economics, political science, and philosophy such as *Law, Legislation and Liberty* (3 volumes, 1973–1979) and received honorary degrees from universities around the world, to which he traveled despite his increasing age and deafness. In 1984 Queen Elizabeth II awarded Hayek the Companionship of Honour, and in 1991 George Bush awarded him the Presidential Medal of Freedom, America's highest civilian award. Germany and Austria honored him with similar awards, and both Pope John Paul II and Mikhail Gorbachev praised Hayek's achievements.

In his last years Hayek showed signs of returning to his ancestral Catholicism. He died in Freiburg of a heart attack and is buried at Neustift Cemetery in his native Vienna. This "old Whig," as he called himself, with moustache and spectacles, is reputed to have both looked and acted like a courtly, although somewhat shy, European gentleman.

★

Hayek's papers are divided between the family archives in London and the various universities and institutes with which he was affiliated. His complete works in twenty volumes have been published jointly by Routledge (London) and the University of Chicago Press. Autobiographical notes, together with oral history interviews, are published in Stephen Kresge and Leif Wenar, eds., *Hayek on Hayek: An Autobiographical Dialogue* (1994). John Gray, *Hayek on Liberty* (1984), summarizes his ideas and includes an extensive bibliography of Hayek's works. *Hayek: A Commemorative Album,* compiled by John Raybould (1998) is a brief illustrated biography. An obituary is in the *New York Times* (24 Mar. 1992).

STEPHEN A. STERTZ

HAYES, Helen (*b.* 10 October 1900 in Washington, D.C.; *d.* 17 March 1993 in Nyack, New York), actress who was widely regarded as the "First Lady of the Stage" in tribute to her long and successful career and the dignity and generosity with which she conducted her offstage life.

Hayes was the only child born to a traveling salesman, Francis Van Arnum Brown, and his wife, Catherine Estelle ("Essie") Hayes, a homemaker and sometime actress. While Essie pursued her stage aspirations in repertory touring shows, Hayes was brought up largely by her beloved grandmother "Graddy" Hayes, who had considerable influence on the child. She was entranced by her Irish grandmother's animated storytelling and mimicry and by the stage plays and silent films to which she was taken. She was enrolled at the age of five at the Sacred Heart Academy and in Miss Minnie Hawks's dancing classes and studied subsequently at the Cook School, the John Eaton School, and in New York City at the Dominican Academy. Later in her career, the Sacred Heart nuns tutored her when she returned to Washington between New York theatrical engagements. It was in Hawks's recitals, in the Belasco Theatre near the White House, that "Helen Brown," and then "Helen Hayes Brown," first appeared in public—a newspaper rating her turn as among the "biggest hits of the afternoon."

After an apprenticeship with Washington's Columbia Theatre stock company, Helen Hayes Brown debuted on Broadway with the actor-producer Lew Fields in the musical *Dutch* one month after her ninth birthday. She was an immediate sensation and continued with the show on tour. For Vitagraph Studios in New Jersey, she appeared in short silent films, which at the time were generally disdained by other Broadway performers. More roles at home with the Columbia Players and the Poli Theatre Players followed, with Helen, now appearing as "Helen Hayes," playing children and adolescents, sometimes in a new show each week. In 1917 she graduated from Sacred Heart Academy, made another film, appeared on Broadway in *The Prodigal Husband,* toured with that show, and opened in Rochester, New York, in the title role of *Polyanna,* which she then toured with across the country. Newspaper reviews of her performances at this time were almost all ecstatically positive. More New York appearances followed, as well as a season with a new repertory company at the "Theater of Presidents" (the National Theater), three blocks from the White House. It was there that Hayes had seen her first

Helen Hayes. AP/WIDE WORLD PHOTOS

play. Like many child actors of her time, she played male as well as female roles.

Hayes moved easily from youth roles to ingenue performances and became popular as a sweet, coquettish maiden. Estelle Hayes Brown became her daughter's fulltime chaperone, coach, companion, and career guide, as Helen began formal acting lessons with several distinguished New York mentors, including Frances Duff Robinson and Constance Collier. She studied interpretive dance with Florence Fleming Noyes and—perhaps in part for its press value—took boxing lessons. As her acting developed, Hayes combined a certain studied grace with her winsome personality, her exceptional powers of observation, and her ability to bring honest emotion to the stage. An actors' strike in 1919, in which Hayes did not participate, closed most New York theaters. It was not until 1924 that an enlightened Hayes rebelled against her producers and joined the new Actor's Equity union. Over the ensuing years she became increasingly active in support of a host of humanitarian projects, patriotic endeavors, and charities.

At the age of twenty Hayes received her first star billing in *Bab*. She then began to appear on Broadway or on tour almost every year for decades. She sparkled as the sweet yet impish darling in light romantic comedies, many tailored to her talents. Among her successes were *To the Ladies* (1922), *We Moderns* (1924), *Dancing Mothers* (1924), and *Young Blood* (1925). She next moved into classic theater, effectively in the eighteenth-century Irish-born playwright Oliver Goldsmith's *She Stoops to Conquer* (1924) and less successfully in the nineteenth-century Irish dramatist

George Bernard Shaw's *Caesar and Cleopatra*. Critics found her Cleopatra to be too much of a contemporary flapper. The following year, however, Hayes appeared as Maggie Wylie in the turn-of-the-century Scottish playwright and novelist James M. Barrie's *What Every Woman Knows*, creating a role to which she returned frequently over the years, always with success. In 1927 she portrayed the doomed heroine of *Coquette* in a spectacular three-year run on Broadway and on tour. By that time she was widely acclaimed as one of America's leading young players in both comedy and serious drama.

From the late 1920s onward, while constantly appearing in live theater, Hayes also pursued a rigorous schedule in radio as the star and eventually the producer of several series of performances. She reprised her great stage successes on the air and essayed new scripts and classical roles as well. It was for a radio show that she was dubbed the "First Lady of the American Theater," a title she bore with dignity for the next sixty years.

On 17 August 1928 Hayes married the playwright Charles MacArthur, author with Ben Hecht of *The Front Page*, which opened to acclaim on Broadway that same year. MacArthur already was established as a well-known journalist, screenwriter, and bon vivant in Manhattan literary and artistic circles—a surprising match for the still young and somewhat naive Hayes. MacArthur was as iconoclastic and erratic as Hayes was idealistic and disciplined. Alcohol and depression later haunted him, yet he proved to be the one great love of Hayes's life. Their daughter, Mary MacArthur, appeared with Hayes in *Alice Sit by the Fire* (1946) at the Bucks County Playhouse in New Hope, Pennsylvania. She appeared again with her mother in a summer-stock tryout of *Good Housekeeping* in 1949, and during this run Mary fell ill and died suddenly of polio. Hayes's grief led her into the crusade against the disease as patron of the Mary MacArthur Fund, which worked in synergy with the March of Dimes.

In 1931 Hayes made her screen debut in an adaptation of the melodramatic play *The Lullaby*, a performance which earned her the Academy Award in 1932 for best actress. At this time the MacArthurs acquired a handsome showboat gothic house on Broadway Street in suburban Nyack, which became Hayes's residence for the rest of her life. The house was a mecca for celebrities, and Hayes often drove her own automobile to nearby New York City for her performances. In 1932 she had another film success with *A Farewell to Arms*, in which she played opposite Gary Cooper. The following year she made four more films, starring opposite Ramon Navarro, Robert Montgomery, John Barrymore, and Clark Gable. She was not, however, particularly comfortable either in Hollywood or in front of the cameras, and she returned eagerly to Broadway to score a triumph in the title role in the American dramatist Maxwell

Anderson's *Mary of Scotland* in 1934. The following year she created perhaps her greatest stage success as another queen in *Victoria Regina*. Numerous awards and an invitation to the White House ensued in the wake of her astounding portrait, which moved from maiden princess to elderly monarch. She reputedly played the final scenes with apple slices in her cheeks to complete the appearance of advanced age. Although Hayes's command of her technique and her audiences was unfailing, she claimed to have suffered from stage fright all her life. She apparently was able not only to disguise her anxiety but also to convert her nervous energy into dramatic power.

Hayes and Charles MacArthur adopted James Gordon MacArthur soon after his birth in December 1937. After several childhood theatrical appearances, he studied at Harvard and then pursued a successful career in film and notably in television. In 1939 Hayes appeared in *Ladies and Gentlemen,* a play written by her husband with Ben Hecht. As a patriotic gesture during World War II, she played Harriet Beecher Stowe in *Harriet* on Broadway and on tour, from 1943 to 1945. In 1947 the Antoinette Perry ("Tony") Awards were established in New York and Hayes won the first award ever given for best actress for her performance in *Happy Birthday.*

Other comedies and serious plays followed, along with prestigious awards and humanitarian efforts, which included frequent public appearances at charity events and public ceremonies at which she received countless trophies, statuettes, plaques, inscribed paperweights, "keys," and other awards from associations, clubs, and cities. The United States Mint issued a Gold Medallion bearing her portrait and the words "First Lady of the Stage." Her company was solicited by various U.S. presidents and royal figureheads, including Queen Elizabeth II, who received her on the royal yacht *Britannia*. She was awarded the Presidential Medal of Freedom, the nation's highest civilian honor, and in 1951 she authored, with Lewis Funke, *A Gift of Joy,* the first of several inspirational works.

On 21 April 1956 Hayes's beloved husband died, having battled alcoholism and depression in the wake of his daughter's death seven years earlier. Helen buried her grief in her work, fulfilling an obligation to appear opposite Ingrid Bergman in the film *Anastasia* (1956). She continued to appear on the stage occasionally until 1971, when she made her final live theatrical appearance at Catholic University in Washington, D.C., in the American playwright Eugene O'Neill's *Long Day's Journey into Night.*

She made appearances in television and films, winning an Academy Award as best supporting actress in 1971 for *Airport*. A Broadway theater was named for her and, when it was razed, another theater was named in her honor. Her likeness, painted by Furman Finck, was received by the National Portrait Gallery in Washington, D.C. The former

Rockland County Hospital, established in 1900 in West Haverstraw, New York, was renamed the Helen Hayes Hospital in 1974 in recognition of her nearly fifty years of "voluntary support and leadership of its mission." She did more than 600 broadcasts of a radio show for senior citizens, received some thirty honorary degrees, and made countless public appearances. Despite short hospital stays, Hayes was indefatigable into her nineties. She finally succumbed to congestive heart failure on 17 March 1993 in Nyack, and is buried there in Oak Hill Cemetery. She lived and died a devout and practicing Roman Catholic.

During her long and remarkable career, Hayes met the demands of the melodramatic style of the early twentieth century and pleased Broadway audiences for more than fifty years. She had noteworthy award-winning successes in radio, television, and film. She maintained a public persona of impeccable repute, gave of herself unsparingly to myriad public causes, and was an inspiration through her life, her acting appearances, and her books. Singularly energetic and able to rebound from setbacks with the grace of bearing and iron will that enabled the diminutive and sylphlike woman to achieve her greatest success impersonating commanding and formidable monarchs, her motto was "You rest, you rust."

★

While Hayes's performances were her signal artistic creation, she also wrote or coauthored a number of books, including *Star on Her Forehead* with Mary Kennedy (1949), *A Gift of Joy* with Lewis Funke (1965), *Twice over Nightly* with Anita Loos (1972), *A Gathering of Hope* (1983), *Our Best Years* with Marion Glasserow Gladney (1984), *Where the Truth Lies* with Thomas Chastain (1988), and *My Life in Three Acts* with Katherine Hatch (1990). Books about Hayes include Kenneth Barrow, *Helen Hayes, First Lady of the American Theater* (1985), and Donn B. Murphy and Stephen Moore, *Helen Hayes: A Bio-bibliography*. The latter lists more than 1,300 articles, published photos, and other bibliographic references to Hayes.

DONN B. MURPHY

HAZLITT, Henry Stuart (*b.* 28 November 1894 in Philadelphia, Pennsylvania; *d.* 9 July 1993 in Fairfield, Connecticut), journalist and author who wrote extensively in favor of a free market economy, including the popular title *Economics in One Lesson.*

Hazlitt was born to Stuart Clark, who died when Hazlitt was still a baby, and Bertha Zauner. Hazlitt started school at Girard College in Philadelphia, a school for poor, fatherless boys. When he was nine years old, his mother remarried. The family then relocated to Brooklyn, New York, where Hazlitt was enrolled at Public School 11. In 1912, upon graduation from Boys' High School, he entered City

Henry Stuart Hazlitt. FOUNDATION FOR ECONOMIC EDUCATION

College of New York. He dropped out after a few months, however, to look for work after his stepfather died.

After trying various low-paying, menial jobs, Hazlitt discovered that if he learned typing and shorthand, he could secure a better-paying position. For several weeks he attended a secretarial school and, with his newfound expertise, in 1913 finally found a position that he liked—as a reporter with the *Wall Street Journal.* His job was to prepare reports on small companies.

The job at the *Journal* made Hazlitt realize how little he knew about the world of business and economics. Being an avid learner, he began a rigorous self-study program, concentrating on philosophy and economics, and soon caught up with much of what he had missed by dropping out of college. One of the books he read, *The Common Sense of Political Economy* (1910) by Philip Wicksteed, made a special impression on him. The book was the first English exposition of the Austrian school of economics, which had laid the foundation for the modern theories of free markets.

Hazlitt soon began his prolific book-writing career with *Thinking as a Science* (1915) at the age of twenty-two. By this time he had left the *Wall Street Journal* and was writing editorials for the *New York Evening Post.* He worked for the *Post* until 1917, when the United States entered World War I and Hazlitt enlisted in the Army Air Corps.

Before Hazlitt had a chance to go overseas, the war ended and he returned to his routine of reading and writing. In 1922 he published his second book, *The Way to Will Power.* By this time he had been employed for a year with the *New York Evening Mail* as a financial editor, a post he held until 1923. During the next ten years, Hazlitt changed jobs five times, working for various periodicals including *American Mercury,* for which he served as editor in 1933, taking over for H. L. Mencken. He wrote on a wide variety of subjects—from politics and economics to philosophy and literature. *A Practical Program for America,* which he edited in 1932 in the midst of the Great Depression, shows how the scholars of free market economics influenced him. In that book he prescribes the repeal of all barriers to free trade as the way to economic recovery.

Hazlitt married Frances S. Kanes in 1936. They had no children. Two years earlier, he had joined the editorial staff of the *New York Times,* a relationship that would last for twelve years. He mostly wrote about economic issues. He wrote reviews of Ludwig Von Mises's *Socialism* and Friedrich von Hayek's *The Road to Serfdom.* Both men were prominent scholars of the Austrian school, to which Hazlitt was very much attuned.

At the same time that the laissez-faire economics of the Austrian school was slowly developing, almost every government in the world seemed to have embraced the teachings of John Maynard Keynes, the English economist who provided the intellectual support for President Roosevelt's New Deal policies. To Hazlitt, Keynesian policies were nothing but short-run fixes benefiting special interests. In his view, such policies would eventually bring about chronic inflation and recession and would damage the spirit of entrepreneurship and economic freedom. Hazlitt set out to educate the general public about free market economics and warn of the perils of government intervention in 1946, publishing *Economics in One Lesson,* which soon became a best-seller.

The next venue for Hazlitt's regular commentary on current business and economic issues was *Newsweek.* He joined the magazine's staff in 1946 and was given his own column, "Business Tides." There were also other, albeit less regular, venues for Hazlitt's teachings. In *Will Dollars Save the World?* (1947) he explained why the Marshall Plan would not be ideal for economic growth without inflation in Europe. In *The Great Idea* (1951), he contrasted the weaknesses of socialism with the merits of capitalism. From 1950 to 1954 he edited *The Freeman,* the flagship publication of the Foundation for Economic Education, of which he was a founding trustee. In *The Failure of the "New Economics": An Analysis of the Keynesian Fallacies* (1959), he presented a devastating review of Keynes's famous book *The General Theory of Employment, Interest, and Money* (1936).

By the late 1950s this slim, courtly, humble, and witty writer had become a national champion of free enterprise and human liberty. In 1958, Grove City College in Pennsylvania conferred upon him an honorary doctorate degree. Two years later the Freedom Foundation awarded him a Medal of Honor.

Hazlitt stayed with *Newsweek* until 1966. At the age of seventy-five he decided to retire from active journalism, but he continued writing books until he was ninety years old. In 1986 he was admitted to Carolton Chronic Convalescent Hospital in Fairfield, Connecticut. After nearly seven years in residence at this facility, he died in 1993, two years after the death of his beloved wife, Frances.

Hazlitt was one of the early champions of free enterprise. Through his lucid writings, he promoted the principles of free market economics among the American public and influenced conservative economic thinking in the United States in the late twentieth century.

∧

Hans F. Sennholz, ed., *The Wisdom of Henry Hazlitt* (1993), is the best source of information on Hazlitt's life, career, and thought. It contains three tributes (one of which provides an annotated bibliography) and many of Hazlitt's own articles. In "Henry Hazlitt: In One Lesson," *National Review* (31 Dec. 1985), W. F. Rickenbacker gives an account of the events that led to the publication of *Economics in One Lesson*. Obituaries are in the *New York Times* (10 July 1993) and *National Review* (9 Aug. 1993).

MOJTABA SEYEDIAN

HEALY, Timothy Stafford (*b.* 25 April 1923 in New York City; *d.* 30 December 1992 in Elizabeth, New Jersey), Jesuit priest, scholar, president of Georgetown University in Washington, D.C., and president of the New York Public Library.

Healy was the eldest of four children of Margaret Dean Vaeth, a teacher and homemaker, and Reginald Stafford Healy, a petroleum engineer and executive of a small oil company. Reginald Healy was also the host of the radio shows *Captain Tim's Stamp Club of the Air* and, with wife Margaret, *At Home with the Healys*. Timothy grew up in Manhattan and graduated from the Jesuit-run Regis High School in 1940.

At the age of seventeen Healy joined the Jesuit order and spent two years of novitiate training as well as his first two years of college at St. Andrew-on-Hudson in Poughkeepsie, New York. He earned a B.A. degree in 1946 and an M.A. degree in 1948 at Woodstock College in Maryland, and taught English and Latin at Fordham Preparatory School in the Bronx, New York, from 1947 to 1950. He then went to Louvain, Belgium, for four years of theology studies at the Facultés St. Albert. There he was ordained a priest in 1953 and earned a licentiate in sacred theology in 1954. After a year of prayer, study, and ministry at the In-

Timothy Healy, 1981. AP/WIDE WORLD PHOTOS

stituto del Santo Duque in Valencia, Spain, he taught English and was director of alumni relations at Fordham University from 1955 to 1962, earning another M.A. degree in 1959. He next enrolled at Oxford University in England, where he studied under Dame Helen Gardner, wrote a dissertation on John Donne, and was awarded a doctorate of philosophy in 1965.

For the next twenty-seven years Healy held positions of major leadership. He returned to Fordham as an associate professor of English, but within a few months, upon the arrival of Leo McLaughlin, S. J., as president, Healy was appointed executive vice president. The 1960s were exciting years at Fordham, as its academic reputation soared due to McLaughlin and Healy's initiatives, such as an experimental liberal arts college and the hiring of high-salaried administrators and professors like Margaret Mead and Marshall McLuhan. But there was not enough money to pay for all the creativity and daring. When McLaughlin separated from Fordham in 1969, Healy also moved on. In a dramatic job change, he swapped the Roman collar of a Jesuit university administrator for a coat and tie and became the vice chancellor for academic affairs at the City University of New York (CUNY). Healy from the start embraced "open enrollment," a policy that guaranteed a seat somewhere in the CUNY system to every New York City high school graduate. He wrote and spoke of the university's "long identification with the nation's greatest city, its years in service to the urban poor through more than five great immigrant waves" and of CUNY's "tradition of gathering to itself a multiplicity of nations, races, creeds, and people and taming them to tolerate each other, at least in order to learn." By 1975 enrollment in City University's twenty colleges reached 253,000 with minority enrollment overall rising from twenty-three percent to forty-six percent.

In 1976, this time changing tie for Roman collar, Healy became president of Georgetown University, the oldest Catholic university in the United States. His thirteen years at the Jesuit university were a time of growth and prosperity for Georgetown: new buildings, an increase in endowment from $37.7 to $227.7 million, an increase in the quality of the faculty and student body and the number of minority students (up to twenty percent), the creation of off-campus student-run service programs, and numerous Rhodes scholars. There was also a fair share of controversy: a lawsuit regarding university recognition of a gay student group (after eight years, he decided not to appeal a court decision wanting both to "pull the community back together" and to restore Georgetown's eligibility for District of Columbia tax-exempt bonds); a $600,000 donation from a Libyan government accused of terrorism (Healy returned the money to the Libyan embassy in person); the John Thompson–led basketball program (although he found basketball games boring, he supported Thompson on campus and off, including Thompson's opposition to National Collegiate Athletic Association rules deemed unfair to blacks); the closing of the dental school and other graduate programs; and the question of how to define and safeguard Georgetown's Catholic identity. When Healy left Georgetown in 1989 at the conclusion of the university's bicentennial anniversary celebration, its undergraduate colleges, along with its medical and law schools, ranked among the most selective in the nation, and the university as a whole had joined Notre Dame as a Catholic university in the top tier of research universities.

Although now sixty-six years old Healy was selected in 1989 to succeed Vartan Gregorian as president of the New York Public Library, the second largest library (after the Library of Congress) in the nation. He was once again wearing civilian clothes. A group of New York writers, including Jimmy Breslin, Gay Talese, and Joseph Heller, publicly asked whether a Catholic priest could be trusted with this assignment. For Healy, their challenge was another chance to display his wit in rebuttal. He used his powers of persuasion and fund-raising skills both to ward off severe budget cuts by city officials and to increase the library's endowment from $170 to $220 million. He increased access to the library's holdings and improved services at its four noncirculating research libraries, but he was even more pleased ("I want to see the library serve the poor") to have five-day-a-week service restored to all eighty-two branch libraries scattered around the neighborhoods of Manhattan, Staten Island, and the Bronx. He oversaw expansion of the Andrew Heiskell Library for the Blind and Physically Handicapped as well as planning for the new Science, Industry, and Business Library. At the height of his powers at the end of 1992, returning from a vacation in Arizona, Healy collapsed of a heart attack in Newark Airport and was pronounced dead at Elizabeth General Medical Center. His grave is in the Jesuit cemetery at Georgetown University.

Healy was just under six feet tall and slightly overweight despite a daily swim. He met people with sass and joy in his eyes, beneath bushy brows, his smile ready to escalate to shared laughter. Profiles written about him invariably mention his way with language (sometimes salty) as raconteur and conversationalist; his reading over and over again of Virgil's *Aeneid* in Latin as his way of purging anger; his inability to quit smoking cigarettes; his hobbies which included skeet shooting, deep-sea fishing, and doing crossword puzzles (especially at meetings he was not running); his insistence, in every position he held, on teaching a poetry seminar every semester on Monday mornings; and his love of good food and meals with friends. Robert Mitchell, a fellow Jesuit and close friend, said at Healy's funeral: "Tim's presence could fill a room, and life was better when he was around."

Healy published two books on John Donne. He wrote scores of articles, ranging from the scholarly to op-ed pieces. He served as chairman of both the American Council on Education and the National Association of Independent Colleges and Universities. As a Catholic leader in higher education, Healy stood with Theodore Hesburgh of Notre Dame as preeminent.

His *New York Times* obituary erred in saying: "In New York, as in Washington, Father Healy led a divided life." Whatever position he held or clothes he wore, Healy's personality and style never varied, nor did his passions: education, teaching and learning, poetry, reconciling scholarship and faith, service to city and nation, and the education of the urban poor, especially African Americans. For him there was no division between his university and library vocations: "The Public Library is the people's university," he said. "A university is a place of teaching, a library is a place of learning. But they are both in the same trade: the transmission of ideas."

At the many ceremonies in his memory, the famous, friends and colleagues, former students, all praised not so much the man's accomplishments as the man himself and what he gave to each of them personally. A fellow teacher who watched and admired him over many years said: "Tim Healy was above all a priest and a teacher. . . . His lasting influence can be found in the shaping impact he had on the lives of the young men and women he so generously taught and cared for."

★

Healy's books are *John Donne: Selected Prose* (edited with Dame Helen Gardner; 1967) and *Ignatius His Conclave* (1969). His papers are at the New York Public Library on Fifth Avenue and Forty-second Street; the Georgetown University Library; the CUNY Archives at La Guardia Community College in Queens; and the Fordham University Library in the Bronx (including an oral history). See also Robert A. Mitchell, "Education Was IIis Line," *America* (30 Jan. 1993), a homily at the Healy funeral liturgy; and "Celebrating the Life of Timothy S. Healy," *Biblion* (fall 1993), tributes delivered at a memorial service in Bryant Park, behind the main branch of the New York Public Library (28 Apr. 1993). Obituaries are in the *New York Times* and *Washington Post* (both 1 Jan. 1993).

JAMES N. LOUGHRAN

HEARST, William Randolph, Jr. (*b.* 27 January 1908 in New York City; *d.* 14 May 1993 in New York City), heir to the Hearst publishing empire founded by his father as well as publisher, editor, and Pulitzer Prize–winning reporter.

Hearst was the second of five sons born to the publishing mogul William Randolph Hearst, Sr., and his wife Millicent Veronica Willson. Hearst's childhood was marked by wealth and social privilege. As a child he split his time between the family's luxurious apartment on New York's Riverside Drive and his grandmother's home in Pleasanton, California. The Hearst family fortune had its beginnings in the late nineteenth century when Hearst's grandfather George Hearst, a silver-mining tycoon, was elected a U.S. senator from California and took ownership of the *San Francisco Examiner* newspaper, supposedly as payment for a gambling debt.

At an early age Hearst showed an interest in his father's newspaper business by working as a fly boy (a boy who takes off the sheet from the tympan as the pressman turns it up) at the presses of the *New York Mirror* while on summer vacation from the military school he attended in San Rafael, California. In 1925 he entered the University of California at Berkeley and joined the Phi Delta Theta fraternity, but he left after only two years of liberal arts study to pursue a career in journalism. In 1928, at the young age of twenty, Hearst joined the staff of the *New York American,* one of his father's newspapers, as a police reporter, but soon was promoted to a managerial position as assistant city editor.

In 1936 Hearst was made publisher of the *New York American* by the Hearst Corporation management, undoubtedly with the approval of his father. The magazine, because of company financial problems, soon merged to

William Randolph Hearst, Jr., *c.* 1940s. © BETTMANN/CORBIS

form the *New York Journal-American*. Hearst played a prominent role in the reorganization of the family's newspaper properties during the Great Depression of the 1930s, a time in which 40 percent of the company's holdings were sold. He also modernized the newspapers by emphasizing more local news stories, objective reporting, a new layout, and a revamping of the editorial policies.

Hearst was a World War II correspondent in Europe from 1943 to 1945. His father often edited his reports from the front before they were published. At the end of the war, having finally won the confidence and approval of his father, he was appointed publisher of two Sunday newspaper supplements, *Puck—the Comic Weekly* and the flagship *American Weekly,* while still acting as publisher of the *New York Journal-American.*

On 29 July 1948 Hearst married the society gossip columnist Austine McDonnell. They had two sons, William Randolph III and Austin, both of whom were to follow him into the family business, William Randolph III as publisher of the *Examiner* and Austin as president of Hearst Entertainment and Syndication. Hearst's previous two marriages, to Alma Walker in 1928 and Lorelle McCarver in 1933, had ended in divorce with no children.

In the 1940s, after the release of the popular 1941 Orson Welles film *Citizen Kane,* William Randolph Hearst, Sr., was criticized for his scandalous relationship with the actress Marion Davies. Hearst valiantly protected the honor and privacy of his mother while publicly defending his father as well, especially against what he considered to be an unfair and inaccurate portrayal of his father in the movie, which neither he nor his father ever saw.

In August 1951 William Randolph Hearst, Sr., died. Hearst and his four brothers were among the thirteen trustees who gained voting control of the company following his father's death, although not a majority control, which followed the directives of the elder Hearst's will by leaving managerial control in the hands of his longtime business associates and appointees. Hearst was then named president of Hearst Consolidated Publications and vice president of Hearst Publishing Company. In 1955 he became chairman of the executive committee of the privately held Hearst Corporation and succeeded his father as editor in chief of the Hearst newspapers, a position his father had held for more than fifty years.

In January 1955 Hearst was given permission to visit Moscow, along with the International News Service columnists Frank Conniff and J. Kingsbury-Smith. Their goal was to observe and write about daily life in the Communist capital of the Soviet Union. In Moscow, Hearst planned to report on a diverse range of subjects including Soviet attitudes toward Americans, religious issues, and the working conditions of Soviet women. Hearst scored a journalistic coup while in Moscow when he and his colleagues conducted interviews with important Soviet officials including Defense Minister Georgi Zhukov, Foreign Minister V. M. Molotov, and Communist party secretary Nikita Khrushchev. The series of eight articles that Hearst, Conniff, and Kingsbury-Smith wrote about the interviews and visit were well received by the American public and published widely. The series gave Americans their first indication of what post-Stalin Soviet leadership was going to be like.

In 1956 Hearst won the Pulitzer Prize in international reporting for the Moscow series, an award made ironic by the fact that it was Joseph Pulitzer, his father's primary rival in the publishing business for many years, who had established the prize. In 1957 Hearst won the Overseas Press Award for the Moscow reporting and in 1960 published his book about the trip, *Ask Me Anything: Our Adventures with Khrushchev.*

For more than forty years Hearst wrote the "Editor's Report" column that appeared each week in the Sunday edition of the Hearst newspapers. Politically Hearst carried on where his father left off. Hearst was bitterly anticommunist and supported Senator Joseph McCarthy's redbaiting tactics even after they had been discredited.

In 1991 he published his memoir, *The Hearsts: Father and Son,* a book in which he wrote openly about his complex relationship with his father and the history of the Hearst family. In 1974 Hearst was subjected to the media spotlight when his niece Patricia Hearst was kidnapped and held for ransom by the radical terrorist group the Symbionese Liberation Army. While she was held captive she joined the group and was later arrested for bank robbery and imprisoned. Though Hearst was fond of nightlife and socialized regularly with celebrities, the Patty Hearst episode caused him to retreat from public life. He died at age eighty-five of cardiac arrest in New York City. He is buried in the Hearst family mausoleum at Cypress Lawn Memorial Park in Colma, California.

Hearst's career as a journalist and publisher spanned more than sixty years, a period of time in which he presided over the decline of much of the corporate empire his father had built. Although much of his professional life was spent in the shadow of his flamboyant and domineering father, Hearst's own influence on the world of publishing and journalism remains significant. "I don't need a title," he once said, referring to his last name. "My father gave me one when I was born."

★

The William Randolph Hearst, Jr., papers are held at the Bancroft Library, University of California at Berkeley. Hearst's memoir, written with Jack Casserly, is *The Hearsts: Father and Son* (1991); extensive biographical material is also in Judith Robinson, *The Hearsts: An American Dynasty* (1991). See also *Current Biography 1955*; Debra Gersh, "A Journalism Legend Revisited," *Editor and Publisher* 124, no. 50 (1991): 14–20; and "William Randolph Hearst, Jr.," in Perry J. Ashley, ed., *American Newspaper Publishers, 1950–1990* (1993). Obituaries are in the *New York Times* and *San Francisco Examiner* (both 15 May 1993).

RICHARD STRINGER-HYE

HEIDELBERGER, Michael (*b.* 29 April 1888 in New York City; *d.* 25 June 1991 in New York City), chemist who is generally considered to be the father of immunochemistry.

Heidelberger was the son of David Heidelberger, a merchant and salesman, and Fanny Campe, a homemaker. The Heidelbergers had lost a child before the birth of Michael, who was followed by a brother two years later. Heidelberger's education was obtained entirely in New York City. After graduating from a public elementary school, he attended the Ethical Culture High School. He then obtained his B.S. (1908), A.M. (1909), and Ph.D. (1911) degrees in chemistry from Columbia University.

Through Samuel Meltzer, the family's physician and a staff member at the Rockefeller Institute for Medical Research, Heidelberger met Rockefeller biochemists Phoebus

A. Levene, Walter Jacobs, and Donald D. Van Slyke. They advised him to go abroad for a postdoctoral year to extend his training, recommending the laboratory of Richard Willstätter in Zurich, Switzerland. After his year with Willstätter, Heidelberger accepted a position as an assistant to Jacobs at the Rockefeller Institute in 1912.

At first Jacobs and Heidelberger carried out chemotherapeutic research on polio, but without success. They next turned to African sleeping sickness, which was caused by a microorganism known as a trypanosome. Other investigators had shown that some organic arsenic compounds were effective against trypanosomes, but these chemicals had serious toxic side effects. The Rockefeller chemists synthesized new arsenicals in an effort to find one that was a safer, more effective therapeutic agent. A compound that they called Tryparsamide was shown in clinical trials to be superior to any of the previously used drugs against sleeping sickness. The Belgian government, grateful for a drug that successfully treated a disease that was a serious problem in its African colonies, awarded the Order of Leopold II to Jacobs, Heidelberger, and their coworkers.

With a war on in Europe, Heidelberger enrolled in an officer's training course in the summer of 1915. At about this time he also met Nina Tachau, whom he married in June 1916. The couple had one child, a son Charles, who went on to become a noted oncologist. After the United States entered the war in 1917 Heidelberger served as a first lieutenant in the Army Sanitary Corps, and was assigned to the Rockefeller Institute, much of which had been given over to training army physicians in laboratory techniques.

After the war Jacobs and Heidelberger continued their chemotherapeutic research, this time focusing on bacterial infections. Their efforts yielded little in the way of practical results, and the two chemists soon turned to other projects. Heidelberger went to work with Van Slyke, who was chemist to the hospital of the Rockefeller Institute. One of Heidelberger's duties was to prepare the oxyhemoglobin needed for Van Slyke's study of the equilibrium between oxygen and hemoglobin. During the course of this work, which involved keeping the materials at low temperature, Heidelberger designed the first refrigerated centrifuge.

During the two years that Heidelberger worked with Van Slyke he received his introduction to immunology through collaboration with the noted immunologist Karl Landsteiner in research on the immunological properties of hemoglobin. Oswald Avery, microbiologist of the pneumonia team at the institute, asked for Heidelberger's chemical assistance on the "soluble specific substance" of the pneumococcus bacillus, which seemed to hold the key to the immunological response of the blood to the microorganism. The more that Heidelberger purified the substance, the less nitrogen it contained, which was surprising because at the time, all immunologically active substances

Michael Heidelberger, accepting the Emil von Behring Prize for his work on disease immunization, 1954. AP/WIDE WORLD PHOTOS

were thought to be proteins. The Rockefeller group was soon able to demonstrate that the capsular substance of the pneumococcus, which provoked the immunological response, was a carbohydrate, not a protein. These studies established that polysaccharides played a crucial role in immunology and opened a field of research that was to occupy Heidelberger for many years.

In 1927 Heidelberger accepted the post of chemist at Mount Sinai Hospital. The following year he moved to Columbia University as an associate professor of medicine (changed to biochemistry in 1929) and as chemist at Columbia Presbyterian Hospital. Heidelberger and his colleagues at Columbia provided the first solid evidence of the chemical nature of antibodies, unequivocally demonstrating that antibodies were proteins, namely gamma globulins. They also developed quantitative analytical micromethods for studying the antibody-antigen reaction.

During World War II Heidelberger became involved in an attempt to find a way to protect and cure animals infected with anthrax and to study the toxic principle of the castor bean. Based on an experiment involving student volunteers, Heidelberger recommended to the army that some 8,500 men at a training camp for aviators in South Dakota be vaccinated with pneumococcal polysaccharides in an effort to immunize them against pneumonia, with an equal number receiving saline solution as a control. Within two weeks there were no more new cases of pneumonia of the types vaccinated against in the immunized group, but an average of one new case a week in the control group from weeks three through sixteen.

After World War II Heidelberger suffered a personal loss with the death of his wife Nina from cancer in 1946. She had been active in the cause for world peace, and Heidelberger became more involved in this effort himself after her death. His research interests became focused principally on the relations between chemical constitution and immunological specificity. In 1948 his title was changed from professor of biochemistry, the position he had held since 1945, to professor of immunochemistry.

In 1955, a year before he was to reach the mandatory retirement age at Columbia, Heidelberger accepted an invitation from Selman Waksman to be a visiting professor of immunochemistry in Waksman's Institute of Microbiology at Rutgers University. Columbia gave him a year's terminal leave with pay so that he would not have to resign, and made him emeritus professor of immunochemistry in 1956. In that same year he married his second wife, Charlotte Rosen, who shared his love of music. Heidelberger was an excellent clarinet player, and Charlotte was an accomplished violist and violinist.

Heidelberger left Rutgers in 1964 to become an adjunct professor of pathology at the New York University School of Medicine. He continued to work in the laboratory on immunochemistry until close to the time of his death, following a stroke, at the age of 103. He is buried in New York.

Heidelberger's work played a crucial role in the development of immunochemistry. He demonstrated that carbohydrates could serve as antigens to provoke immune responses, and provided the first chemical insight into antibodies by showing that they were proteins. His contributions to science and medicine were recognized through fifteen honorary degrees and forty-six medals, citations, and awards, including the National Medal of Science in 1967 and the prestigious Albert Lasker Award twice, in 1952 and 1978.

★

An extensive collection of Heidelberger's personal papers resides in the History of Medicine Division of the National Library of Medicine, Bethesda, Maryland. Heidelberger published his "Reminiscences" in three parts in *Immunological Reviews:* 81 (1984): 7–19; 82 (1984): 7–27; and 83 (1985): 5–22. Useful sources of biographical information are Elvin A. Kabat, "Michael Heidelberger, April 29, 1888–June 25, 1991," *Journal of Immunology* 148, no. 1 (1992): 301–307, and M. Stacey, "Michael Heidelberger, 29 April 1888–25 June 1991," in *Biographical Memoirs of Fellows of the Royal Society* 39 (1994): 179–197. An obituary is in the *New York Times* (27 June 1991). An oral history interview with Heidelberger is at the History of Medicine Division of the National Library of Medicine.

JOHN PARASCANDOLA

HEINZ, Henry John, III (*b.* 23 October 1938 in Pittsburgh, Pennsylvania; *d.* 4 April 1991 in Lower Merion Township, Pennsylvania), heir to the H. J. Heinz Company fortune and three-term Republican senator from Pennsylvania.

Heinz was the only child of H. J. Heinz II, who was known as "Jack" to distinguish him from the dynasty's founder, H. J. Heinz, and Joan Diehl, a homemaker. Heinz grew up both in Fox Chapel, Pennsylvania, near Pittsburgh, and in San Francisco, where his mother lived with her second husband, the U.S. Navy captain Monte McCauley, whom she married in 1942. Heinz graduated from Phillips Exeter Academy in New Hampshire in 1956 and, following in his father's footsteps, attended Yale University. He graduated with a B.A. degree in history in 1960. With an eye toward his future in business, he earned an M.B.A from the Har-

Senator Henry J. Heinz III, 1984. AP/WIDE WORLD PHOTOS

vard School of Business Administration in 1963. Enlisting in the air force, he served a tour of duty with the reserves and received an honorable discharge in 1969 with the rank of staff sergeant. Tall, good-looking, and athletic, he particularly enjoyed tennis and downhill skiing. He was also patrician or, as his Senate colleagues later described him, reserved. Nonetheless, he worked summers in tomato fields and canning factories and later took a position as a sales representative for International Harvester in Australia and then a position in banking in Geneva, Switzerland. In Geneva he met his future wife, Maria Teresa Thierstein Simoes-Ferreira (who was raised in Mozambique and was fluent in five languages). When she moved to New York City as a consultant to the United Nations in 1966, she and Heinz wed. They had three sons. Returning to the family business in 1965, Heinz worked his way up from an entry-level desk job to associate manager in 1966, then to general manager of the grocery product marketing division in 1968.

At the same time Heinz became increasingly involved in local Republican politics. He served as an aide in the Republican senator Hugh Scott's reelection campaign in 1964, attended the 1968 Republican National Convention as a Nelson A. Rockefeller delegate, and chaired Pennsylvania's Republican Party Platform Committee in 1970. Although he tried his hand at teaching, lecturing at the Carnegie Mellon Graduate School of Industrial Administration in 1970–1971, Heinz was convinced that he could make his own mark and make a difference in politics.

When Congressman Robert J. Corbett of Pennsylvania's Eighteenth Congressional District died in April 1971, Heinz seized the moment. He quickly moved his family to Fox Chapel and declared his interest in running for the vacant position. Although his Democratic opponent, the wealthy businessman John E. Connelly, was favored to win in a district where Democrats outnumbered Republicans by 16,000, Heinz won by a landslide, becoming the youngest and one of the wealthiest members of the Ninety-second Congress. He won reelection easily in 1972 and 1974. Heinz supported progressive social programs at home and urged withdrawal from Vietnam and normalization of relations with Cuba. The liberal Americans for Democratic Action (ADA) consistently rated him in the sixtieth percentile, and the conservative Americans for Constitutional Action (ACA) rated him below the tenth percentile.

In the tense post-Watergate climate Heinz declined to run against the popular Pennsylvania governor Milton J. Shapp in 1974, but he ran for the seat held by the retiring senator Hugh Scott in 1975. Heinz admitted that he had accepted illegal campaign contributions from the Gulf Oil Corporation in 1971 and 1972, and his popularity plummeted for the first time. Despite pouring millions of dollars of his own money into his campaign, mostly for television commercials, he barely won the Senate seat. Nevertheless,

he was reelected in 1982 and 1988 with more than 60 percent of the vote.

Heinz retained the family home in Fox Chapel, but the family lived in the former Russian embassy in the Georgetown section of Washington. As a senator, Heinz was known as a liberal to moderate Republican who championed the cause of the elderly, the protection of the environment, and the rescue of the dying industries of Pennsylvania's rust belt. As in his early years in the House of Representatives, he voted more often against than with his Republican colleagues.

Heinz was active in civic and philanthropic affairs in the Pittsburgh area. He was chairman of the H. J. Heinz Charitable and Family Trust, a fellow of the Carnegie Museum of Art, a member of the board of the Children's Hospital of Pittsburgh, and a cofounder of the Pittsburgh Penguins hockey team. He also sat on the boards of Harvard University's Graduate School of Business Administration and the University of Pittsburgh's Graduate Schools of Public Health and Public and International Affairs. Temple University awarded him an honorary doctor of laws degree, the Jaycees gave him the Man of the Year Award, and B'nai B'rith presented him with the National Americanism Award.

In April 1991 Heinz was on his way to Philadelphia for hearings on Medicare fraud. The pilot of his corporate jet radioed for help when it appeared that the plane's landing gear was stuck, and a Sun Oil helicopter that was in the area volunteered to fly close and check. Heinz was killed when the plane and the helicopter collided above a schoolyard in Lower Merion Township, near Philadelphia. Nine people died in the crash—five in Heinz's plane, two in the helicopter, and two children in the schoolyard below. Other children were badly burned. Heinz was buried in the family mausoleum in Homewood Cemetery in Pittsburgh. Teresa Heinz turned down the offer to fill her husband's Senate seat but continued his philanthropy, founding the Teresa and H. John Heinz III Foundation and supporting the Senator John Heinz Pittsburgh Regional History Museum. In 1995 she married Massachusetts Democratic senator John Kerry. Senator Heinz is memorialized in the John Heinz Neighborhood Development Program, supported by the U.S. Department of Housing and Urban Development, and the John Heinz National Environmental Center in Philadelphia.

The media often spoke of Heinz as a possible future Republican presidential candidate. Despite good looks and vast wealth, Senator Heinz probably undermined his chances by voting his conscience rather than following the party line. His political colleagues did not warm up to him, but he was an important figure in his home constituency, particularly in western Pennsylvania. His hopes for a bright future died in that fiery, tragic plane collision.

★

Heinz's papers are archived at the Carnegie Mellon University libraries. This collection includes legislative papers, audiovisual materials, photographs, and memorabilia documenting his political career. Some Heinz papers and memorabilia are also housed in the Senator John Heinz Pittsburgh Regional History Center library. Heinz's obituary and the news release on the accident are in the *New York Times* (5 Apr. 1991). There is a video documenting the Heinz family history from QED Communications, WQED Pittsburgh, *Heinz: The Story of an American Family* (1992).

PAMELA ARMSTRONG LAKIN

HEPBURN, Audrey Kathleen (*b.* 4 May 1929 in Brussels, Belgium; *d.* 20 January 1993 in Tolochenaz, Switzerland), beloved film star and fashion icon of the postwar era who later made a series of inspirational UNICEF missions for the starving children of Africa.

Born Audrey (Edda) Kathleen van Heemstra Hepburn-Ruston, she was the only child of Baroness Ella van Heemstra of Holland and the Anglo-Irish businessman Joseph Hepburn-Ruston, an avid member of Oswald Mosley's infamous British Union of Fascists (BUF). Her grandfather,

Audrey Hepburn. ARCHIVE PHOTOS

Baron Aernoud van Heemstra, was a familiar figure at the court of Queen Wilhelmina and the governor of the Dutch colony of Surinam. His beautiful mini-castles in Arnhem and The Hague were the most idyllic of Hepburn's many residences in early girlhood, a time when her parents' incessant arguments produced chaotic moves back and forth between Belgium, England, and the Netherlands.

Baroness Ella sent Hepburn at age five to a boarding school in Kent as a "shock" cure for chronic introversion. Then and later, her passion was dance, but the budding young ballerina's training was cut short when World War II began. In late 1939, convinced the Germans would soon bomb London but would never attack Holland, her mother took her "for safety" back to Arnhem—just nine miles from the German border and one of the first towns invaded by the Nazis.

Caught in Arnhem for the next six years, Hepburn endured the hardships of occupation and the disastrous Allied paratroop drop chronicled in Cornelius Ryan's *A Bridge Too Far*. Her own schoolgirl efforts on behalf of the Dutch underground included hiding messages in her shoes and ferrying them by bicycle. By late 1944 the Germans had looted Holland of all crops and livestock, leading to what would be remembered as the *Hongerwinter* (hunger winter). By the time the war ended in 1945, Hepburn was too weak to dance, suffering—like millions of youngsters—from malnutrition, anemia, and edema. She would never forget that her first food came from an UNRRA team (United Nations Relief and Rehabilitation Administration, forerunner of the United Nation's Children's Fund, or UNICEF) accompanying Arnhem's liberators.

In 1946 the now-penniless Baroness Ella and her daughter returned to England, where their disgraced husband and father had been interned for his Nazi sympathies throughout the war. Hepburn (who never finished secondary school) had obtained a scholarship to the famous Marie Rambert ballet school, but Rambert soon told her bluntly that she lacked the talent for a ballet career. Hepburn turned to the London stage, landing a hoofer's job in *High-Button Shoes* (1948) and two cabaret shows in which she stood out as "the girl with the *eyes*." She was soon offered a film contract by Ealing Studios.

Small parts in such English films as *The Lavender Hill Mob* (1951) led to a movie in France, *Nous irons à Monte Carlo* (*Monte Carlo Baby*, 1952), during which the author Colette spotted her filming in a hotel lobby and instantly offered her the title role in a forthcoming (1951) Broadway adaptation of her 1945 novel *Gigi*. Simultaneously, a screen test for Paramount netted Hepburn the starring role in William Wyler's *Roman Holiday* (1953).

Hepburn was a hit in both productions; equally so in her second stage play, *Ondine* (1954), in which she developed an intense romance—onstage and off—with costar

Mel Ferrer. In the same amazing week in 1954 she won an Oscar for *Roman Holiday* and a Tony for *Ondine*. On 24 September of that year she and Ferrer married; they had one son, Sean, born in 1960.

Hepburn's whimsical, elegant, pixie persona was soon in demand in Hollywood, where she would be one of the last major stars to be nurtured by the studio system. The critic Molly Haskell has pointed out that "she [came] at a historical moment just before feminism, easy divorce, and the sexual revolution," and Hepburn's onscreen persona would remain discreet to the end. As Stanley Kauffman put it, reviewing *Love in the Afternoon* (1957), "The sign of her preparing to take the plunge was when she removes a glove."

In Billy Wilder's *Sabrina* (1954), the designer Hubert de Givenchy gave her the look that became legendary: clothes that emphasized rather than camouflaged her slender figure. From then to the end of her career, Givenchy designed nearly all her high-fashion film costumes as well as her private wardrobe, propelling her onto every best-dressed list in the world. *Vogue*—and every other fashion publication on two continents—recorded every minute change of her appearance. *Funny Face* (1957), her Gershwin-based musical with Fred Astaire, was a song-and-dance landmark of the 1950s but also "the best fashion show ever recorded on film," wrote Rex Reed.

Hepburn's look caused a revolution, but she was an unlikely revolutionary. "I never thought I was pretty," she told the designer Ralph Lauren. She felt too skinny, too flat, and too tall. She was self-conscious about her uneven front teeth, yet during *Roman Holiday* declined the studio's offer to cap them. Nor would she let them pluck her thick eyebrows.

Her fashion image derived largely from that "ideal" figure, admired by millions if not to everyone's taste. "If I wanted to look at bones, I could always have my foot X-rayed," said one producer. "Structurally, she has all the curves of a piece of melba toast—viewed from the side," wrote *McCall's*. Billy Wilder's was the most legendary observation: "If that girl had tits, she could rule the world." She would rule it anyway, marching straight into the middle of the 1950s bosom boom and pioneering a look of her own. Hepburn's vital statistics were the same from age twenty-three to the end of her life: 32–20–35. Anita Loos noted that her hat size (21) was bigger than her waist.

By 1960 Hepburn could have virtually any film part she wanted. A case in point was Holly Golightly in *Breakfast at Tiffany's* (1961), a role she won over the objection of its author, Truman Capote, who had written it for Marilyn Monroe. Jack Warner loved Hepburn for turning *The Nun's Story* into his surprise blockbuster of 1959.

The only role she ever wanted badly was Eliza Doolittle in *My Fair Lady* (1964), the last great Broadway musical to receive lavish screen treatment. Warner owned the film rights, and Hepburn was his first and only choice for Eliza. But columnists nationwide loudly lamented the "injustice" to Julie Andrews, who originated the role on the stage, and Eliza became Hepburn's worst nightmare: She was misled to believe she would sing the songs and trained hard to do so, even as the soprano Marni Nixon was being hired to dub Hepburn's singing voice.

The previous year, her spectacular teaming with Cary Grant in *Charade* had produced a whole new mystery-comedy genre. The offbeat marital saga *Two for the Road* (1967) with Albert Finney, the thriller *Wait Until Dark* (1967), and the soulful *Robin and Marian* (1976) with Sean Connery proved her dramatic skills and flexibility. She received Oscar nominations five times, yet her favorite director, Stanley Donen, declared: "Audrey was always more about fashion than movies or acting."

Hepburn was the most beautiful film- and fashion-statement of her era. She was a ballet dancer who never performed a full ballet. She was the world's highest-paid film actress, who never studied acting. She graced more covers of *Life* than any other star except Marilyn Monroe, but no other film goddess except Greta Garbo ever seemed so remote from Hollywood. She starred in a mere twenty films over forty years. But when, in *Breakfast at Tiffany's*, she sang "Moon River" in her breathy, melancholy little voice, she broke the hearts of audiences around the world. No one thought a new feminine ideal could emerge from World War II, wrote Cecil Beaton. "It took the rubble of Holland, an English accent, and an American success to launch a wistful child who embodied the spirit of a new day."

Hepburn seemed to define every new feminine vogue of the 1950s and 1960s. And she came to represent not just a new look but a new kind of femininity—the European opposite of the blond American sex goddess. She was second only to Jacqueline Kennedy in the degree of flattery-by-imitation she inspired. The opera diva Maria Callas and millions of others looked to Hepburn as a model: the vulnerable but paradoxically sophisticated waif. She influenced the way women looked and acted, then and for decades to come. Her posthumous force in fashion continued through the 1990s—her look and look-alikes more à la mode than ever, dominating the runways of Calvin Klein, Givenchy, and Lauren anew.

Public adulation never spoiled her and southern California never lured her. Her actress-friend Leslie Caron said that Hepburn "conducted her life as discreetly as the way she dressed," closely guarding her personal and family life. Hepburn lived in Switzerland during her marriage to Ferrer, which ended in divorce on 5 December 1968. A little more than a month later, on 18 January 1969, she married an Italian psychiatrist, Dr. Andrea Dotti. The couple lived in Rome. Over the years she had had numerous miscarriages, but with Dotti she had a second son, Luca, in 1970. She and Dotti divorced in 1982.

Hepburn's true soul mate was a fellow Dutchman, the actor Robert Wolders, the widower of the film star Merle Oberon. As a child he had suffered under the Nazis in Rotterdam while Hepburn was doing the same in Arnhem. She and Wolders never married but lived together for her last thirteen years in the Swiss village of Tolochenaz near Geneva.

In 1988, with the crucial moral and logistical support of Wolders, Hepburn launched the dynamic UNICEF work that consumed her for the rest of her life, and which brought her full circle from her own traumatic childhood in war-torn Holland. As UNICEF's goodwill ambassador, she used her celebrity and the media coverage it attracted to speak for millions of starving children around the world, voiceless victims of war and drought. In 1992, Hepburn brought the tragedy in Somalia and emergency relief efforts there to the forefront of world attention. "I don't believe in collective guilt," she said, "but I believe in collective responsibility."

Two weeks after returning from the physically and emotionally exhausting UNICEF trip to Somalia, she was diagnosed with colon cancer. She died less than three months later and left a humanitarian legacy far beyond stardom. She is buried on her estate in Tolochenaz.

★

Audrey Hepburn wrote no autobiography or extensive correspondence except to family and a few close friends. A small museum containing selected items is located on the grounds of her home in Tolochenaz, not far from her gravesite there. UNICEF Geneva has all her goodwill ambassador speeches and statements on file. Biographies include Barry Paris, *Audrey Hepburn* (1996); Warren G. Harris, *Audrey Hepburn: A Biography* (1994); Caroline Latham, *Audrey Hepburn* (1984); and Ian Woodward, *Audrey Hepburn* (1984). An excellent account of the behind-the-scenes making of *My Fair Lady* is found in André Previn, *No Minor Chords: My Days in Hollywood* (1991). Cogent assessments of Hepburn's career and impact are in Molly Haskell, "Our Fair Lady Audrey Hepburn," *Film Comment* (March–April 1991); Frank Thompson, "Audrey Hepburn," *American Film* (May 1990); Elizabeth Wilson, "Audrey Hepburn," *Sight and Sound* (March 1993); and Isaac Mizrahi et al., "That Girl with the Eyes," *Interview* (Aug. 1990). An obituary is in the *New York Times* (21 Jan. 1993). Hepburn's early films and related biographical material can be found at the Dutch Film Archives in Amsterdam and The Hague Film House. Excellent video documentaries are Robert Wolders, *Audrey Hepburn in Her Own Words* (1993), and Wombat Productions, *Audrey Hepburn Remembered* (1993).

BARRY PARIS

HERMAN, William Jennings ("Billy") (*b.* 7 July 1909 near New Albany, Indiana; *d.* 5 September 1992 in Palm Beach Gardens, Florida), baseball player, manager, and coach best known as a hard-hitting second baseman and All-Star team member in the 1930s; ranked as one of the National League's fifty greatest players.

Herman was the ninth of ten children of a farming family. Named after the three-time Democratic presidential nominee William Jennings Bryan, Herman was occasionally given the additional nickname "Bryan." He attended New Albany High School and pitched his church team to a league championship, for which he won a trip to Pittsburgh to see the first two games of the 1927 World Series. On 31 August 1927 he married Hazel Jean Steproe. Although he first followed his southpaw father as a pitcher, the five-foot, eleven-inch Herman began his minor league career as a second baseman for Vicksburg, Mississippi (Cotton States League), and Louisville, Kentucky (American Association), in 1928. After stints with Dayton, Ohio (Central League), and again with Louisville from 1929 through 1931, he embarked on a fifteen-year major league career in August 1931, when the Chicago Cubs purchased his contract from Louisville for $50,000. At second base Herman replaced the player-manager Rogers Hornsby, who was suffering from

Billy Herman, 1941. ASSOCIATED PRESS AP

ailing feet and legs. Herman played in only twenty-seven games in 1931, but his .327 batting average earned him a salary of $7,000 for 1932. He was only the tenth player to make 200 hits in his first major league season. With the Cubs he played in three World Series, 1932, 1935, and 1938. Herman played on the day of Babe Ruth's famous "called" home run against Charlie Root in the 1932 World Series and cast his vote against the myth. When Ruth pointed after taking two strikes, Herman claimed, he was pointing in a warning fashion at Root rather than at the centerfield stands.

Soon after the 1941 season opened the Cubs were in New York to play the Giants. Herman received a phone call in his Commodore Hotel room on 6 May at 2:30 A.M., from the Cubs owner Larry MacPhail, who announced that he had traded Herman to the Brooklyn Dodgers. Herman went first to the Polo Grounds to pick up his gear and then headed directly to Ebbets Field, where he was four for four in his first game, a good start to his major contribution to Brooklyn's first pennant in twenty-one years. During spring training with the Dodgers in 1942 Herman and his teammates Hugh Casey, Larry French, and Augie Galan spent an evening with Ernest Hemingway, first at Hemingway's gun club and then at his home in Havana, Cuba. Each left with an autographed copy of *For Whom the Bell Tolls* (1940) as well as vivid memories of heavy drinking with their host. Hemingway challenged Casey to box and, after being whipped by the burly pitcher, challenged him to a duel the following day either with pistols or swords. Herman reported that the next morning a sobered Hemingway, who came with his wife to the ballpark, expressed embarrassment over his behavior.

Herman volunteered for the U.S. Navy after the 1943 season and played service ball first with Johnny Mize, Walker Cooper, and "Schoolboy" Rowe on a Great Lakes team coached by Mickey Cochrane. Starting in 1944 he played in an army-navy league in Honolulu, Hawaii, with Stan Musial, Bob Lemon, and "Cookie" Lavagetto. Herman returned to spring training with the Dodgers in 1946. He played for the Dodgers until he received another late-night phone call in his hotel room on 15 June at 2:00 A.M. from Branch Rickey; he had been traded to the Boston Braves. Again in proof of his zest for the game, Herman organized his affairs and arrived in Boston in time to play in a doubleheader that same day. On 6 September 1946 he and three other players were traded to the Pittsburgh Pirates for Bob Elliott, who became the National League's most valuable player in 1947, and the catcher Hank Camilli.

During his major league career Herman played in 1,922 games, made 2,345 hits, slugged 486 doubles, scored 1,163 runs, and had 839 runs batted in while compiling an im-

pressive .304 lifetime batting average. He batted .433 in ten All-Star games, a major league record at the time of his retirement, and he held National League records at his position for the most years leading in putouts (seven), the most putouts in a doubleheader (sixteen on 28 June 1933), and the most seasons handling at least 900 chances (1932–1933, 1935–1936, 1938). Herman was named to the National League All-Star team ten times, seven times while with Chicago (1934–1940) and three while with Brooklyn (1941–1943). In 1943 he was named to the *Sporting News* Major League All-Star team.

Herman served as player-manager for the Pittsburgh Pirates in 1947 and for Minneapolis (American Association) in 1948. He played for Oakland, California (Pacific Coast League), in 1950. He also managed Richmond, Virginia (Piedmont League), in 1951; the Boston Red Sox from 1964 to 1966; Bradenton, Florida (Gulf Coast Rookie League), in 1968; and Tri City (Northwest League) in 1969. The major league teams he managed won 189 games and lost 274, perennially finishing in the second division. His major league coaching assignments included stints with the Brooklyn Dodgers from 1952 to 1957, the Milwaukee Braves in 1958 and 1959, the Boston Red Sox from 1960 to 1964, the California Angels in 1967, and the San Diego Padres in 1978 and 1979. The Oakland Athletics hired him as a scout from 1968 through 1974. He retired from baseball in 1975 and was inducted into the Hall of Fame the same year.

Herman had a reputation as one of the best players of his day. An excellent hit-and-run man and a driving force on four pennant winners, Herman was lauded by Casey Stengel as "one of the . . . smartest players ever to come into the National League." Attempting to establish the American Baseball Guild to address labor concerns within baseball following World War II, Robert Murphy advocated a strike by the Pittsburgh Pirates and tried to organize the Boston Braves. Herman was named one of three Braves players to meet with the owner Lou Perini to discuss the guild's platform, then he was chosen as one of six player representatives to join the owners in the landmark meeting of the Joint Major League Committee on 27 August 1946.

Herman and his first wife divorced in 1960. He wed Frances Ann Antonucci on 23 May 1961. They had one son. After 1968 he was a resident of Palm Beach Gardens, where he died of cancer.

Herman had a superlative career and is remembered as one of the best second baseman ever to put on a major league uniform. In 1935 he was voted the National League's second baseman of the year and Player of the Year. His abilities as a slugger in the regular season and especially in the All-Star games still command respect decades after his retirement, and his dedication to the game continues to inspire new generations of ballplayers.

★

For further information on Herman see Gene Karst and Martin J. Jones, Jr., *Who's Who in Professional Baseball* (1973); Donald Honig, *Baseball When the Grass Was Real: Baseball from the Twenties to the Forties Told by the Men Who Played It* (1975); *The Sporting News Hall of Fame Fact Book* (1983); Charles F. Faber, comp., *Baseball Ratings: The All-Time Best Players at Each Position* (1985); Richard M. Cohen and David S. Neft, comps., *The World Series: Complete Play-by-Play of Every Game, 1903–1985* (1986); David L. Porter, ed., *Biographical Dictionary of American Sports: Baseball* (1987); David Quentin Voigt, *Baseball: An Illustrated History* (1987); and William Marshall, *Baseball's Pivotal Era, 1945–1951* (1999). An obituary is in the *New York Times* (7 Sept. 1992).

JIM CASTAÑEDA

HERSEY, John Richard (*b.* 17 June 1914 in Tientsin, China; *d.* 24 March 1993 in Key West, Florida), writer whose reporting in World War II helped awaken the nation to the horrors of nuclear warfare and whose postwar fiction and journalism grappled with contemporary moral issues and the effect of major events on the lives of ordinary people.

One of two sons born to Grace Baird, a missionary, and Roscoe Monroe Hersey, a secretary for the Young Men's Christian Association, Hersey spent the first ten years of his life in China. He learned to speak Chinese before he spoke English, but he said later that he could recall very little of his early life abroad. He attended the Tientsin Grammar School and then its American School until the family returned to the United States in 1924, settling in Briarcliff Manor, a suburb north of New York City. From 1927 to 1932, Hersey was at Hotchkiss, a private school in Lakeville, Connecticut. Entering Yale in the autumn of 1932, he was, according to a classmate, "an aesthete" who played varsity football—a tall, thin athlete who wrote poetry. As an upperclass student he was chief music critic and vice chair of the *Yale Daily News*. He graduated with a bachelor's degree in 1936 and sailed for England to attend Clare College, Cambridge, as a Mellon fellow, although he did not take a degree.

Back home in 1937, he spent a "marvelous summer" in Stockbridge, Massachusetts, as personal secretary and—in his word—"factotum" to the novelist Sinclair Lewis. In the autumn he was hired as a reporter for *Time* magazine by the publisher Henry Luce, himself the son of missionary parents and a graduate of Hotchkiss and Yale. By 1939 Hersey had become a favorite of Luce's and *Time*'s chief correspondent in the Far East, where he interviewed such luminaries as the Chinese general and politician (later president) Chiang Kai-shek and the Japanese general Masa-

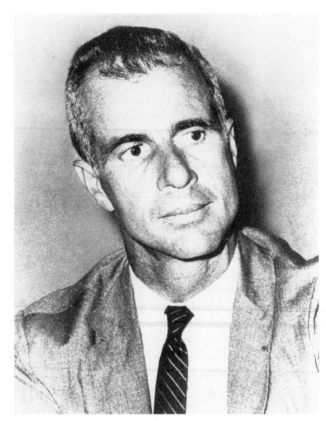

John Hersey. AP/WIDE WORLD PHOTOS

haru Homma. On 27 April 1940, Hersey married Frances Ann Cannon, with whom he had three sons and a daughter. The marriage ended in divorce in February 1958. Hersey married Barbara Day Adams Kaufman on 2 June 1958; they had one daughter.

Hersey was in New York writing *Time*'s coverage of the war in Europe when the Japanese bombed Pearl Harbor on 7 December 1941, precipitating the entry of the United States into World War II. He applied for a commission in the navy but ended up as a war correspondent for *Time* and *Life* with a noncombatant's officer rank equivalent to that of first lieutenant. While awaiting assignment to the Pacific, he wrote *Men of Bataan* (1942), a tribute to General Douglas MacArthur's ill-fated defense force in the Philippines.

By October, Hersey was in the Solomon Islands at Guadalcanal, where he received a letter of commendation from the secretary of the navy for helping medical corpsmen remove the wounded under fire. On one occasion, he accompanied a Marine patrol along the Mataniko, a stream on the coast of Guadalcanal where they were caught in a Japanese ambush. He described the action in spare prose reminiscent of the style of the American novelist Ernest Hemingway for *Life* and then in *Into the Valley: A Skirmish of the Marines* (1943), which a wartime publishers' council cited as "imperative" home-front reading. From May to September 1943, he reported on the U.S. Army engagements in North Africa and Italy. By the time he returned home that fall, he had survived injuries from two plane crashes in the Pacific and two in the Mediterranean. He was grateful, he wrote, that in each accident his notebooks, which he kept sheathed in condoms, were undamaged.

In 1944, Hersey published his first novel, *A Bell for Adano,* based on the experiences of a New Yorker, Major Joppolo (a character derived from the real-life figure Major Frank E. Toscani), who became the military governor of a small Sicilian town. It was an instant best-seller and the winner of the 1945 Pulitzer Prize for fiction. Translated into French, Russian, and Swedish, among other languages, the book was adapted into a hit Broadway play in 1944 and a Hollywood film the following year.

Hersey's assignments for *Time* and *Life* took him to Moscow and Eastern Europe in August 1944 and to China and Japan at the war's end. In May 1946, he visited Hiroshima for the *New Yorker* to interview survivors of the first atomic bomb blast nine months earlier, on 6 August 1945. "A Noiseless Flash"—his calm, clear recital of what happened to six men and women that fateful morning— filled all sixty-eight pages of editorial space in the 29 August 1946 issue of the magazine, creating a publishing sensation. Newsstand copies sold out in a matter of hours. Newspapers across the country and in Europe requested reprint rights, and the Book-of-the-Month Club mailed free reprints to its entire mailing list. Published as *Hiroshima* (1946), the prize-winning book sold more than 3 million copies and remained in print for the next fifty years.

In 1946, after a bitter break with Luce, Hersey turned to freelance writing—notably for the *New Yorker* and the *Atlantic Monthly*—and to books. Over the next forty years, he produced more than a dozen novels and a half dozen works of nonfiction, all of which proceeded from his belief that his writing (especially fiction) must be directed to the ethical understanding of modern social problems and contemporary events. As he put it in the *Atlantic Monthly* (November 1949), imaginative literature is a "clarifying agent" that comes closer than any other literary form to providing "an impression of the truth." His books appeared after months of exhaustive research and were filled with facts and telling detail, yet in the eyes of many reviewers, the end results were closer to journalism than to art, and his characters were stick figures too thinly drawn to make them real. Few critics faulted his craftsmanship: his plotting and use of language were much admired, but as his writing became increasingly experimental, allegorical, and sometimes mystical in form, the later novels were dismissed as didactic and simplistic or were viewed simply as disappointing.

His second novel, *The Wall* (1950), was conventional in form, generally well received by reviewers, and a commercial success. An account of the German razing of the Warsaw ghetto in 1943, it was dramatized on Broadway (1950) and filmed for television (1982). The first of the experimental novels was *The Marmot Drive* (1953), an allegorical account of a New England town's effort to destroy invading woodchucks that reviewers found puzzling and unconvincing. Hersey then wrote *A Single Pebble* (1956), centering on cultural differences, and two best-selling books— *The War Lover* (1959), a parable of humanity's propensity for violence, and *The Child Buyer* (1960), satirizing the government and educational reformers. Less artistically and commercially successful were the futuristic *White Lotus* (1965), in which Chinese captors enslave American whites, and *Too Far to Walk* (1966), which examined contemporary college-age youth—a theme to which Hersey returned in *The Walnut Door* (1977). He explored the relationship of two couples caught in a hurricane on board a yacht in *Under the Eye of the Storm* (1967). In nonfiction he offered true stories of human survival under adverse conditions in *Here to Stay* (1963), and attacked the American justice system as fundamentally racist in *The Algiers Motel Incident* (1968), which recounts the trial of white policemen charged with the death of three black men during the Detroit riots of 1967.

A liberal Democrat, Hersey worked actively in Adlai Stevenson's presidential campaigns in 1952 and 1956. His growing interest in public education in the fifties and sixties led him to service on several local, state, and national commissions that sought to address educational problems. He was an outspoken critic of America's role in the war in Vietnam from 1964 onward and one of the organizers of the March for Peace in Washington, D.C. (1965). From 1945 on, he was an active member of the Authors League of America (serving as its president from 1975 to 1980), the Authors Guild, and the American Academy of Arts and Letters, which he served as secretary (1961–1978) and chancellor (1981–1985). He was master of Pierson College at Yale (1965–1970)—the first nonacademic to hold that appointment. He taught classes in writing and literature (1965–1985), first as a lecturer and after 1975 as a full professor of English. In the early 1980s he reduced his teaching load to a weekly writing seminar for selected students.

In this later period he produced four novels: *The Conspiracy* (1972), an imaginary account of an assassination attempt on the Roman emperor Nero; an anti-utopian novel, *My Petition for More Space* (1974); *The Call* (1985), based on the lives of American Protestant missionaries in early-twentieth-century China; and a fictionalized history of a Stradivarius violin, *Antonietta* (1991). Hersey's first short story collection, *Fling and Other Stories,* appeared in 1990. His nonfiction included *Letter to the Alumni* (1970), a memoir of student unrest over the war in Vietnam in his last year at Yale; *The Writer's Craft* (1974), which brought together essays by such writers as Gustave Flaubert, e. e. cummings, and Virginia Woolf; and *The President* (1975), a critical appraisal of Gerald Ford. Hersey subsequently merged that book with an earlier *New Yorker* profile of Harry Truman in *Aspects of the Presidency: Truman and Ford in Office* (1980). He revisited Hiroshima in 1985 for the *New Yorker* and three years later wrote "A Mistake of Terrifically Horrific Proportions," a powerful introductory essay for John Armor and Peter Wright's *Manzanar* (1988), a book featuring Ansel Adams's photographs of a detention center for Japanese Americans in World War II. His last nonfiction books were *Blues* (1987), a celebration of deep-sea fishing, and *Life Sketches* (1989), a fifty-year compilation of biographical profiles he had written for various magazines. He also completed his second collection of short stories, *Key West Tales* (1993), which was published a few weeks after his death. Hersey died of cancer at home in Key West. He is buried on Martha's Vineyard, Massachusetts.

Throughout his long career, Hersey was virtually ignored by academic critics, who viewed him as a gifted journalist rather than an accomplished writer of fiction. Little changed with his death. In postmortem evaluations, the consensus seemed to be that *Into the Valley* and *Hiroshima* might have continuing historical or literary interest. The novels, on the other hand (including *A Bell for Adano* and *The Wall*), were already considered dated by the end of the century and were unlikely to attract an audience from a new generation of readers.

★

Hersey's papers are at Yale University, New Haven, Connecticut. The principal collection is in the Beinecke Rare Book and Manuscript Library, and the research materials for his novel *The Call* (1985) are in the Divinity Library Special Collections. There is no autobiography or biography of Hersey, and in later years he gave no interviews. See his reflections on combat journalism in the foreword to the reprint edition of *Into the Valley* (1989), his accounts of his experiences as secretary to Sinclair Lewis and as a writer for Henry Luce in *Life Sketches* (1989), and his reflection on his years as a Yale professor in *A Letter to the Alumni* (1970). See also his article "Hiroshima: The Aftermath" in the *New Yorker* (15 July 1985), which has been added to all subsequent editions of *Hiroshima*. Brief studies of his writing include two books by Nancy Lyman Huse: *John Hersey and James Agee: A Reference Guide* (1978) and *The Survival Tales of John Hersey* (1983). There are also two books by David Sanders: *John Hersey* (1967) and *John Hersey Revisited* (1991). See also David Sanders, "John Hersey: War Correspondent into Novelist," in *New Voices in American Studies,* edited by Ray B. Browne, Donald M. Winkelman, and Allen Hayman (1966). Tributes from his college classmates and others are in the *Yale Alumni Magazine* (October 1993). Obituaries are in the *New York Times* (25 Mar. 1993) and *New Yorker* (5 Apr. 1993).

ALLAN L. DAMON

HILLCOURT, William ("Green Bar Bill")   (*b.* 6 August 1900 in Aarhus, Denmark; *d.* 9 November 1992 in Stockholm, Sweden), outdoors writer and professional scout who contributed to numerous revisions of the *Boy Scout Handbook;* wrote a camping advice column for *Boys' Life,* a scout magazine; and was an ambassador for the world scouting movement.

Born Wilhelm Hans Bjerregaard-Jensen to Johannes Hans Bjerregaard-Jensen, a building contractor, and Andrea Kristina Pedersen, a homemaker, Hillcourt joined the Danish scouting movement, *Det Danske Spejderkorps* (DDS), as a boy. In 1920 he attended the first world jamboree of scouts, held in London, which was a gathering of around 8,000 scouts from thirty-four countries. There he first met scouting's founder, Lord Robert Baden-Powell. The Danish contingent so impressed the jamboree lead-

William Hillcourt ("Green Bar Bill"). COURTESY BOY SCOUTS OF AMERICA

ership that Denmark won the honor of hosting the second world jamboree four years later.

After completing his university training with an M.S. degree from the Pharmaceutical College in Copenhagen in 1924, he chose writing over pharmacy and became an assistant editor for the Ferslaw Newspapers in Copenhagen. One of his first jobs was to cover the second world jamboree in 1924. Ever the adventurer, Hillcourt left the paper the following year and toured Europe before arriving in the United States in February 1926. He later visited the Boy Scouts of America (BSA) national office while in New York City, where Chief Scout Executive James West offered the precocious Dane a position in the BSA Supply Service, which was in charge of scouting materials such as uniforms, camping equipment, and handbooks. Hillcourt's first two months on the job were reportedly spent watching up to three movies a day in Times Square theaters to improve his command of colloquial English.

Hillcourt served as the managing editor of *Scouting,* a magazine for adult leaders, from 1927 to 1931. During this time he challenged the BSA's failure to implement the patrol method, where six to eight boys worked together, as the fundamental building block of the scouting program. As a corrective, he wrote the first *Handbook for Patrol Leaders* in 1929; its basic nature endured through numerous revisions. Hillcourt then became a contributing editor to *Boys' Life,* a magazine for BSA youth, in 1932. During this time he took the sobriquet "Green Bar Bill" for his long-running camping advice column. Hillcourt superimposed the name "Bill" on the two green bars of the patrol leader identification badge, probably because the bars represented the essence of boy leadership within the patrol, a concept to which Hillcourt was fundamentally committed. His column was immensely successful because it was relevant and easily understandable; it helped build both self-confidence and teamwork in literally millions of young men. Hillcourt married Grace Constance Brown, chief scout executive West's personal secretary, on 3 June 1933; they had no children. Soon after, they moved from New York City to Schiff Scout Reservation in New Jersey. At nearby Mendham, New Jersey, Hillcourt formed Troop 1 and served as scoutmaster. From there he could witness firsthand the patrol method in action. Hence, the advice he offered in his *Boys' Life* columns came from direct interaction with his intended audience. Concerned that adult leaders needed to be as knowledgeable of the patrol method as their scouts, in 1936 Hillcourt helped revise the *Handbook for Scoutmasters.*

At Schiff that same year, Hillcourt served as senior patrol leader for the first Wood Badge training course held in the United States; Wood Badge was a British adult leader training program based on the patrol method. Hillcourt received the coveted Wood Badge beads in 1939, the same

year in which he became a naturalized United States citizen. Earlier, he had legally changed his name to William Hillcourt, recollecting that when "they started pronouncing it 'beer garden,' I decided the time had come to change it." While implementation of the BSA Wood Badge program was interrupted by World War II, Hillcourt ultimately served as scoutmaster in 1948 for the first two American courses offered to nonprofessional scouters. He also wrote the course training materials. During World War II, Hillcourt was a special instructor for the U.S. Army's Second Service Command Tactical School. Returning to civilian life, Hillcourt became the BSA national director of *Scoutcraft,* a position he held until 1954, when he became the assistant to the director of program resources. The need for more specialized scoutcraft knowledge resulted in his coauthoring the first *Scout Field Book* (1944) with James West. From 1956 until his official retirement from the BSA in 1965, Hillcourt was the director of program resources. During this period of increasing scout enrollment he was responsible for writing the sixth and seventh editions of the *Boy Scout Handbook* in 1959 and 1965. When the scouting movement foundered in the antiestablishment climate of the Vietnam-Watergate era, the near-octogenarian Hillcourt came out of retirement and, without remuneration, revised the BSA handbook in a 1979 edition. His uncompromising call for a renewed focus on outdoor activity, scoutcraft, and the patrol method helped to reinvigorate a lethargic program.

Between 1910 and 1990, more than 33 million copies of the *Handbook* were printed, making it one of the world's most popular books. But because Hillcourt wrote as a paid BSA employee, his "royalty" compensation amounted to only six free copies of the *Handbook* for every 400,000 sold. His most popular non-BSA publication is the definitive biography of scouting's founder. *Baden-Powell: The Two Lives of a Hero* (1964), written with the cooperation of Lady Baden-Powell, remained in print at the beginning of the twenty-first century.

Hillcourt's passion for the ideals espoused by the scouting movement knew no bounds. He attended most world jamborees and all BSA national jamborees through 1989. Hillcourt never tired of meeting with the boys and adults who were already his friends through scouting. Even the youngest of scouts had no fear of reprimand for calling a man old enough to be his grandfather by the name "Green Bar Bill." With a twinkle in his eye, an endearing grin, and decades of stories to tell, Hillcourt, next to Lord Baden-Powell, was the most beloved figure in scouting. His contributions were recognized by five Freedoms Foundation George Washington Honor Medals; a Medal of Merit from the DDS; the Silver Buffalo, the BSA's highest honor; the Silver Wolf from the British Scouts Association; the Youth of the Americas award, for inter-American scouting; and the Bronze Wolf, World Scouting's highest honor. Despite these and other honors, however, he typically wore his scout uniform unadorned in the same humble manner in which he carried himself. Yet Hillcourt relished every opportunity to speak out for the importance of the scouting movement in developing responsible youth. When he passed away from natural causes, Hillcourt was on an around-the-world trip. He is buried next to his wife in St. Joseph's Cemetery in Mendham.

Friend, mentor, adviser, teacher, writer, prankster, storyteller, and lover of the outdoors, "Green Bar Bill" Hillcourt helped define the world scouting movement through decades of selfless service to youth. In doing so he earned the title "Scoutmaster to the World."

★

Hillcourt was in the process of writing an autobiography when he passed away. Lawrence van Gelder, "A Work of Love For 'Boy Scout,' 78," *New York Times* (4 Feb. 1979), offers an insightful look at Hillcourt during a controversial time for the BSA. Obituaries are in the *New York Times* and *The Post-Standard* (Syracuse, New York) (both 14 Nov. 1992).

WILLIAM E. FISCHER, JR.

HOLLEY, Robert William   (*b*. 28 January 1922 in Urbana, Illinois; *d*. 11 February 1993 in Los Gatos, California), biologist, biochemist, and Nobel laureate in physiology or medicine (1968) for his research into the genetic code and its function in protein synthesis.

Holley was one of four sons of Charles Holley and Viola Wolfe, who were both educators. He attended public schools in Illinois, California, and Idaho and graduated from Urbana High School in 1938. He studied chemistry at the University of Illinois and received his B.A. degree in 1942. His graduate work at Cornell University led to a Ph.D. in organic chemistry in 1947. A few years earlier he participated in the first chemical synthesis of penicillin. Various appointments eventually led to a professorship of biochemistry and molecular biology in 1964 at Cornell. It was then on to the Salk Institute for Biological Studies in La Jolla, California, as a resident fellow from 1966 to 1993 and the American Society Professor of Molecular Biology.

Because of Holley's biochemical training and his basic interest in living things, one could have anticipated further painstaking research into the molecular structure of the cell. Work on amino acids and peptides led to the biosynthesis of proteins. Thus the alanine transfer ribonucleic acid (tRNA) was discovered. There followed a period of a few years that were spent working with RNA, first concentrating on the isolation of RNA, and then working on the determination of the structure of RNA. The nucleotide sequence was completed at the end of 1964. His classic paper

Robert Holley. LIBRARY OF CONGRESS

on the subject, "Sequences in yeast alanine transfer ribonucleic acid," appeared in the *Journal of Biological Chemistry* in 1965. Because of this achievement Holley was awarded the Nobel Prize in physiology or medicine in 1968.

The process by which every individual—black, white, blonde, brunette, dull, or smart—acquires countless inherited characteristics depends on a complex chemical code—the genetic code stored in the cell's DNA, which dictates the synthesis of proteins. Many of these proteins are enzymes that control the biochemical reactions that regulate inherited characteristics (including eye color, skin color, and intelligence) that make every individual different. Our genes (DNA) form messenger RNA, which in turn forms proteins. Proteins are then used as building blocks. Holley was largely responsible for deciphering the genetic code.

At the Nobel presentation ceremony, Professor Peter Reichard, a member of the Nobel Committee for Physiology or Medicine of the Royal Caroline Institute, remarked on that year's prize for medicine, which was shared by Dr. Robert Holley, Dr. Har Khorana, and Dr. Marshall Nirenberg. In the past, no connection between genes and nucleic acid could be seen. Previously, nucleic acid research was considered dull, exclusive, and of interest to only a few scientists. But nucleic acid research came of age in 1944 with the American scientist Oswald T. Avery transferring a hereditary property from one bacterium to another with the aid of pure nucleic acid, signifying that genes are made up of nucleic acids. Avery's discovery launched the new science of molecular biology. To emphasize the importance of this new area, Professor Reichard stated that the 1968 prize to Holley and his corecipients was the fifth prize in medicine since 1958 to be awarded to molecular biologists.

What is the mechanism for the translation of the code within the cell? This question was successfully challenged by Holley, who was one of the discoverers of a special type of nucleic acid that was called transfer-RNA. This nucleic acid has the capacity to read off the genetic code and to transform it to the protein alphabet. In 1965 Holley wrote its chemical structure. His work represented the first determination of the complete chemical structure of a biologically active nucleic acid. This was an awesome piece of research and from this was built piece by piece the puzzle of what is now the human genome. Humans could finally begin to understand the causes of numerous diseases and possibly treat them.

Holley married Ann Dworkin, a mathematics teacher, on 3 March 1945. They had one son. The family enjoyed the outdoors, especially the mountains and the ocean. Holley died of lung cancer in 1993 at the age of seventy-one.

At the end of his Nobel lecture in 1958 Edward Tatum mused that in some of the future developments in molecular biology there would be a solution of the genetic code, and that it would occur in the lifetime of some of his audience. Little did he realize that this was to be achieved less than three years before the first letters of the code were deciphered. Because of Holley and his co–Nobel recipients, the nature of the code and much of its function in protein synthesis were known within less than eight years. At that moment, they had written the most exciting chapter in modern biology.

★

The Robert Holley Papers, covering the years from 1942 to 1989, are kept in the Division of Rare and Manuscript Collections, Cornell University Library. See also entries in *Current Biography Yearbook* (1967) and in several editions of standard bibliographical works, including *American Men and Women of Science* and *Who's Who*. Obituaries are in the *New York Times* (14 Feb. 1993) and *The Scientist* 7, no. 6 (22 Mar. 1993).

JOHN E. FISHER

HOLM, Hanya (*b.* 3 March 1893 in Worms, Germany; *d.* 3 November 1992 in New York City), seminal figure in American modern dance and a Broadway choreographer of distinction.

Holm was born Johanna Eckert, the daughter of Valentin Eckert, a German wine merchant, and Marie Mörschel, an amateur scientist who held several patents. Johanna had one sibling. Her parents gave their physically active daughter a progressive education in a convent school in Mainz, Germany. As well as gaining respect for knowledge, an iron self-discipline, and a craving for perfection, she was awakened to a love of music. From 1917 to 1920 she sought additional music training at Dalcroze Institutes in Frankfurt am Main and Hellerau, where she earned a teaching certificate. Through the Dalcroze method she learned to value spontaneity and improvisation. Holm married the painter-sculptor Reinhold Martin Kuntze in 1917. When they divorced in February 1921, Holm retained custody of their son.

A solo concert by Mary Wigman, a pioneer of German modern dance, inspired Holm to change her allegiance from music to dance. She was accepted as a student at the Wigman School in 1920 and after one year became an assistant teacher. She assumed the stage name "Hanya Holm." Petite, blonde, articulate, and keenly intelligent, Holm became an indispensable member of the faculty and in 1929 became codirector of the Wigman Central Institute in Dresden.

Holm danced in the original Wigman company from 1923 to 1928 and also took charge of the organizational

Hanya Holm. MARCUS BLECHMAN

details on the group's many European tours. When the company disbanded, Holm took advantage of two opportunities for choreography and direction, the staging of Euripides' *Bacchae* in Ommen, Holland, in the summer of 1928 and the choreography of Igor Stravinsky's *L'histoire du soldat* (1918) in Schauspielhause, Dresden, in 1929. In May 1930 she directed the dancing chorus for Wigman's epic *Totenmal* (1930), created for a dance congress in Munich.

Wigman's solo tour of the United States in 1930–1931 inspired the formation of a branch Wigman School in that country. Holm arrived in New York on 25 September 1931 to serve as the chief teacher. Contracted with the responsibility for promoting the Wigman method in the United States, she successfully adapted German dance training to American needs and the American temperament. An invitation to teach at the premier U.S. dance institution, the Bennington Summer School of Dance (1934–1942), recognized her as one of four major American modern dance artists along with Martha Graham, Doris Humphrey, and Charles Weidman.

The rise of fascism in Germany compromised Holm's position in New York, as the Wigman School came under suspicion of Nazi affiliation. In 1936 Holm broke her ties to Wigman and put her own name on the school and the company with which she had been touring. She brought her son out of Germany and began an independent personal and professional life, living in an apartment above her school on the corner of Waverly Place and West Eleventh Street in Greenwich Village. Holm became a citizen of the United States in 1939.

Holm often gave lecture demonstrations that captivated audiences while explaining the building blocks of dance creation. In 1936 she presented her first full program of dances and a year later created one of America's dance masterpieces. *Trend,* a work of epic proportions about social destruction and rebirth, was chosen the best group choreography of 1937 by the *New York Times* critic John Martin. In 1939 she created two other works in response to the crisis in Europe, *They Too Are Exiles* and the award-winning *Tragic Exodus.* Her lighthearted satire *Metropolitan Daily* (1938) was the first dance televised in the United States. Other notable works are *Dance of Work and Play* (1938), *From This Earth* (1941), and *Namesake* (1942). Some dances touched deep universal themes, and others were lyrical celebrations of movement. In 1941 Holm established a summer program of instruction and dance production at Colorado College, where she continued to choreograph for the concert stage after she disbanded her company in 1945 and turned to Broadway.

In 1948 Holm scored three successes as a choreographer in the high-stakes arena of commercial theater: "The Eccentricities of Davey Crockett," one of three independent sections of *Ballet Ballads* (1948); José Ferrer's production of the Karel Čapek and Josef Čapek play *The Insect Comedy* (1933); and Cole Porter's *Kiss Me, Kate* (1948). The Porter production won her a New York Drama Critics Award. In 1950 she choreographed another Porter show, *Out of This World* (1950). Eight other musicals followed. The most memorable were *The Golden Apple* (1954), for which she won three awards, *My Fair Lady* (1956), for which she was again recognized with a Drama Critics Award, and *Camelot* (1960). Holm built a reputation for clever, imaginative detail and for crafting dance that sprang in seemingly spontaneous fashion from story and song.

Perhaps Holm's immigrant status allowed her a holistic view of dance culture that embraced several genres and appealed to many different audiences. She directed the world premiere of Douglas Moore's opera *The Ballad of Baby Doe* at the Central City Opera House in Colorado in 1956 and staged Christoph Gluck's opera *Orpheus and Euridice* in Vancouver and Toronto in 1959. She choreographed a musical film, *The Vagabond King* (1956), and several television specials. In the last decade of her life she choreographed four dances for the Don Redlich Dance Company, one of which, *Jocose* (1982), toured the world with Mikhail Baryshnikov's White Oak Project in 1994 and 1995.

Witty, human, and uncompromising, Holm was a legendary teacher. She was a strict disciplinarian who inspired students to use their instincts. She mentored many dance artists, whom she equipped to discover their own styles. Her theory-based teaching method has been an important influence in college and university dance programs. For her contributions to musical comedy and the concert dance, Holm was honored with the Capezio Award (1978), the American Dance Festival Scripps Award (1984), and the *Dance Magazine* Award (1990).

Holm moved comfortably in elite social circles and could be playful and irreverent with friends. A frequent guest in homes of the wealthy, she often gathered with Broadway luminaries and attended glittering parties at the Stork Club. She was also embraced by the old-money social elite of Colorado Springs during the forty-three summers she directed her dance institute there. Never abandoning her German accent, she had a seemingly endless repertoire of aphorisms that heightened the fun of her conversation and intensified the profundity of her meaning. In 1956 she purchased a town house on West Eleventh Street, where she lived until her death from pneumonia at the age of ninety-nine. She is buried in Wilkes-Barre, Pennsylvania.

★

Holm's papers are in the Jerome Robbins Dance Division in the New York Public Library for the Performing Arts, Astor, Lenox, and Tilden Foundation. Her only biography, Walter Sorell's *Hanya Holm: The Biography of an Artist* (1969), is marred by sentimentality. The distinguished dance critic John Martin praised Holm's successful adaptation of German training to American rhythm in his *Introduction to the Dance* (1939). Margaret Lloyd gives Holm's early choreography and her teaching lengthy consideration in *The Borzoi Book of Modern Dance* (1949). Recent discussion on her teaching, choreography, and importance to American dance culture can be found in Jack Anderson, *Art Without Boundaries* (1997), and Claudia Gitelman, "Finding a Place for Hanya Holm," *Dance Chronicle* 23, no. 1 (2000). Two journals that devote issues to essays, photographs, and a chronology of her works are "Hanya Holm: A Pioneer in American Dance," *Choreography and Dance* 2, pt. 2 (1992); and "Hanya Holm: The Life and Legacy," *Journal for Stage Directors and Choreographers* 7, no. 1 (spring/summer 1993). An obituary is in the *New York Times* (4 Nov. 1992). A documentary videotape is *Hanya: Portrait of a Dance Pioneer* (1984).

CLAUDIA GITELMAN

HOPPER, Grace Brewster Murray (*b.* 9 December 1906 in New York City; *d.* 1 January 1992 in Arlington, Virginia), naval officer, mathematician, and computer expert.

Hopper was one of three children of Walter Fletcher Murray, an insurance broker, and Mary Campbell Van Horne, a homemaker. Her father urged his children to obtain a college education and then work for a year to prove they could support themselves. Hopper graduated from Hartridge School in Plainfield, New Jersey, in 1923 and then studied physics and mathematics at Vassar College, earning a B.A. in 1928. On 15 June 1930 she married Vincent Foster Hopper. They had no children and were divorced in 1945. Hopper continued her studies at Yale University, earning an M.A. in 1930 and a Ph.D. in 1934. She taught mathematics at Vassar from 1931 to 1943.

After the Japanese attack on Pearl Harbor on 7 December 1941, Hopper wanted to serve the federal government. At thirty-five years of age she was too old to enlist in the U.S. Navy, and she weighed only 105 pounds instead of the required 121 pounds. Obtaining waivers, however, she joined the Women's Reserve of the Naval Reserve and attended the Naval Reserve Midshipman's School for Women in Northampton, Massachusetts, from which she graduated first in her class. On 27 June 1943 she was commissioned a lieutenant junior grade and was billeted to the Bureau of Ordnance Computation Project at Harvard University.

At Harvard, Howard Aiken, who was working on a doctorate, had written a paper on how a calculating machine could be built. Advised to do so, he contacted the International Business Machines Corporation (IBM) and in 1939 signed a contract to build the Mark I computer, which

Grace Hopper. LIBRARY OF CONGRESS

used punched cards and performed three additions every second. With the Mark I, calculations that would have taken six months to do by hand could now be done in a day. Upon reporting to Harvard's Cruft Laboratory, Hopper was assigned to make the calculations, using the Mark I computer, for firing naval guns, rockets, and atomic bombs. Under Aiken's direction she also wrote a book describing how to operate the Mark I. Once, when the machine shut down, Hopper, shining a flashlight at the electric relays, found a moth in between them and ejected it—the first case of "debugging" a computer.

The Mark I computer used only one language, and code numbers told it how to perform a particular calculation. New programs called for new codes, which were punched holes on paper tape. In the summer of 1945 work began on building the Mark II computer. Completed in three years, it was five times faster than the Mark I.

The maximum age at which women could transfer to the regular navy after World War II was thirty-eight. Hopper was forty when the war ended. She declined an offer to teach at Vassar, choosing to remain at Harvard as a research fellow in engineering science and applied physics. She also remained in the Naval Reserves. In 1949, however, she joined the Eckert-Mauchly Computer Corporation in Philadelphia as senior mathematician. There she agreed that computers could be adapted to service businesses and participated in their development. First came the Electronic Discrete Variable Automatic Computer (EDVAC), a small binary machine, and the Universal Automatic Computer (UNIVAC), which used high-speed magnetic tape instead of punched cards. Hopper provided program languages that could be used by persons who were not mathematicians or "computer nuts." Remington Rand bought Eckert-Mauchly and then merged into the Sperry Company (later UNYSIS), but Hopper remained with the company until 1971. For Remington Rand she served as director of automatic programs development.

Although IBM built scientific computers, the company needed program language development. In 1954 IBM produced an automatic programming language in FORmula TRANslation (FORTRAN), useful to scientists but not to businesspeople. Meanwhile Hopper originated the idea that computer programs could be written in English if computers used symbols that stood for the letters of the alphabet. These programs were known as compilers. She developed Flowmatic, a language useful to businesses for tasks such as automatic billing and calculating payroll. Of the three main languages used by American computers in 1957, Hopper's was the only one that used English commands.

At the Western Joint Computer Conference held in San Francisco in March 1959, military as well as civilian representatives sponsored efforts to produce a composite computer language. The result was Common Business Oriented Language (COBOL), applicable to both UNIVAC II and RCA's 501 computer. The Department of Defense advised U.S. businesses to use COBOL, which worked on almost any business computer.

Advised by the chief of the Bureau of Naval Personnel that she should retire from the Naval Reserve because she was sixty years old, Hopper sadly did so, with the rank of commander, on 31 December 1966. Shortly after, the National Bureau of Standards, the Office of Management and Budget, and the General Services Administration, who set the standards for federal information processing, called on Hopper to standardize different versions of COBOL for the navy, and she happily returned to duty on 1 August 1967. Among other accomplishments, she produced the navy manual *Fundamentals of COBOL* (1969). In 1973 she was promoted to captain. Her literary output totaled six books or articles, and one of her best achievements was advising teachers on how to convey computer literacy to all students. She also published over fifty papers on software

and program languages, including the instructions for using the computers and compilers that she created.

Of the many awards Hopper received, she especially valued the first, the Naval Ordnance Development Award of 1946. Other awards came from UNIVAC and the Legion of Merit. In 1973 she was the first woman and the first American designated a Distinguished Fellow of the British Computer Society. President Gerald Ford awarded her a U.S. Medal of Freedom. She was also a prime instigator in the creation of a computer center at Brewster Academy, a small private school in Wolfeboro, New Hampshire, where she had spent her summers as a youth. On 15 December 1983 President Ronald Reagan attended her promotion to commodore. On 27 September 1985 the Regional Data Automation Center in San Diego was named for her, and on 8 November 1985 she became a rear admiral, the third female admiral in the U.S. Navy. She was the first woman to receive the National Medal of Technology, presented to her by President George Bush. She retired from the navy in 1986. In spite of her seventy-nine years, she became a senior consultant for Digital Equipment Corporation and represented the firm to schools and businesses. Affectionately known to subordinates as "Amazing Grace, Grandmother of the Computer Age," she died of natural causes at the age of eighty-five. At her request, she was buried in Arlington National Cemetery, Virginia, with full military honors. In 1994 the navy announced that a guided missile destroyer would be named the USS *Hopper*.

★

An excellent short biography is Charlene W. Billings, *Grace Hopper: Navy Admiral and Computer Pioneer* (1989). Nancy Whitelaw, *Grace Hopper: Programming Pioneer* (1995) is written for young readers and contains clear definitions. Among many short sketches are Amy C. King and Tina Schalach, "Grace Brewster Murray," in *Women of Mathematics,* ed. by Louise S. Grinstein and Paul J. Campbell (1987); and Robert Slater, *Portraits in Silicon* (1987). An obituary is in the *New York Times* (3 Jan. 1992).

PAOLO E. COLETTA

HOWE, Irving (*b.* 11 June 1920 in New York City; *d.* 5 May 1993 in New York City), literary critic, historian, socialist, editor, and translator of Yiddish literature.

Howe was born Irving Horenstein, the son of David Horenstein, at various times a grocer, peddler, and dress-factory presser, and Nettie Goldman, a dress trade operator. In 1934, while still a student at DeWitt Clinton High School in the Bronx, Howe became active in left-wing but strongly anti-Stalinist politics. After graduating from high school in 1936, he entered City College of New York (CCNY), where, though a dilatory student, he took a serious interest in literary criticism, especially that of Edmund Wilson. Although

Irving Howe. AP/WIDE WORLD PHOTOS

he was still Horenstein in class and is so called in the CCNY yearbook for the graduating class of 1940, he began to use the Trotskyist party name Hugh Ivan and, for speeches and articles, Irving Howe. Although an English major, he graduated with a bachelor of social sciences in 1940.

In 1941 Howe married Anna Bader. Living in Greenwich Village, Howe became managing editor of *Labor Action,* the weekly paper of the Workers Party. Under Howe's leadership the paper consistently opposed American entry into and prosecution of the war against Germany and Italy. But in mid-1942 Howe was drafted into the army. He entered the army at Camp Upton, Long Island, New York, and was sent to Alaska in 1944. He spent sixteen months at Fort Richardson, near Anchorage. After serving for three and a half years, he reached the rank of sergeant before his discharge early in 1946. He then legally changed his surname to Howe. He divorced Anna that year and moved back to the Bronx. He resumed writing for *Labor Action* and for *New International,* the Trotskyist "theoretical" journal, but he began also in 1946 to write on Jewish topics for *Commentary* and on literary subjects for *Partisan Review,* which shared Howe's paradoxical devotion to both Leon Trotsky and T. S. Eliot. During 1946 Howe took some graduate courses at Brooklyn College, but he earned no degree.

In 1947 Howe married archaeologist Thalia Filias, with whom he had two children. He worked for a time as assistant to Hannah Arendt at Schocken Books and to Dwight Macdonald at *Politics* magazine, where he wrote under the pseudonym Theodore Dryden. For four years, starting in 1948, Howe reviewed nonpolitical books for *Time* magazine, a publication typically scorned by people of Howe's political persuasion. In 1948, after moving to Princeton, New Jersey, Howe became acquainted with the town's numerous literary inhabitants, including Delmore Schwartz and Saul Bellow.

In his first public involvement in "Jewish" issues, Howe in 1949 entered the controversy over awarding the Bollingen Prize for poetry to Ezra Pound, who had spoken on behalf of fascism and against Jews during the war. At the same time Howe published with B. J. Widick *The UAW and Walter Reuther* (1949). His career as a literary critic burgeoned with two books on American writers well outside his New York milieu, *Sherwood Anderson* (1951) and the pioneering *William Faulkner* (1952). Largely for financial reasons, Howe accepted a post teaching English at the newly formed Brandeis University, where his job interview was conducted in Yiddish. During his tenure at Brandeis (1953–1961), Howe established a reputation as a superbly gifted teacher.

Although he had abandoned Trotskyism by 1948 and had resigned from the Independent Socialist League in 1952, Howe remained a committed socialist and did not give up on Marxism until 1960. In 1954 he founded *Dissent* magazine to promote "democratic" socialism, more as an animating ethic than as a political program. For the next forty years he spent two days a week editing the magazine without remuneration. Also in 1954 he published, with the Yiddish poet Eliezer Greenberg, the first in a series of groundbreaking anthologies adorned with brilliant introductions designed as acts of critical salvage of the destroyed culture of Eastern European Jewry. *A Treasury of Yiddish Stories* (1954) was dedicated "To the Six Million." Howe turned to Yiddish literature in belated response to the Holocaust during World War II.

Now writing on all his three tracks: socialist, literary, and Jewish, with the abundance of a major industry, Howe published in 1957 *Politics and the Novel,* his first major collection of literary essays, and *The American Communist Party: A Critical History,* with Lewis Coser However, his personal life was less than happy, and in 1959 he and his wife divorced. In 1961 Howe moved to California to teach at Stanford University, a place he soon disliked partly, so it was reported, because nobody there understood his Jewish jokes. When a job offer came from Hunter College in the City University of New York, he accepted it with alacrity and in 1963 returned to what he called his natural habitat. In 1964 he married Arien Hausknecht, a member of the New School (New York) faculty in psychology.

The 1960s was a decade of controversy for Howe. In 1963 he organized a tumultuous public forum to debate Arendt's *Eichmann in Jerusalem* (1963), the book that blamed European Jews for having significantly and willingly participated in their own destruction. He was active in the dissent against the Vietnam War but also against its antidemocratic, New Left opponents. His critiques of the "authoritarians of the left" were collected in a volume of essays on the politics of democratic radicalism entitled *Steady Work* (1966). By now a famous, respected, and honored literary critic, Howe published his only book-length study of an English novelist, *Thomas Hardy* (1967).

In the 1970s Howe became a sharp critic of the new generation of militant feminists and also of the professors who, in universities and professional organizations, exploited literature for partisan political purposes. At the same time he continued his collaboration with Greenberg in establishing a canon of the essential works of secular Jewishness. *A Treasury of Yiddish Poetry* appeared in 1969 and *Voices from the Yiddish*, a collection of nonfiction writing, in 1972. In 1970 he was named distinguished professor at the City University of New York and in 1971 received both the Bollingen and Guggenheim Fellowships. In 1972, with indefatigable energy and in defiance of the expectations of friends, Howe plunged into work on a massive history of the immigrant Jewish world of New York. For four years he pored over memoir literature in English and Yiddish, studies of immigrant experiences, the Yiddish and American press, historical studies, personal interviews, and works of fiction to produce a work of social and cultural history that could "lay claim to being an accurate record."

Howe timed the appearance of *World of Our Fathers: The Journey of the East European Jews to America and the Life They Found and Made,* a masterwork of historical writing, in 1976 to coincide with the bicentennial celebration of American independence. He proclaimed that the history of the 2 million East European Jews who came to the United States starting in the 1880s was a distinctly American story and a part of American history. The book sketches the world of the shtetl and its demise and the trials of departure from the Old World and arrival in the new. It then examines life on "the East Side," with emphasis upon social and political movements. The third part of the volume deals with the literary culture of Yiddish. Written with the assistance of Kenneth Libo, the huge volume of more than 700 pages was a best-seller and a selection of the History Book Club.

World of Our Fathers won the National Book Award for History and the Francis Parkman Prize and prompted the election of Howe as a member of the American Academy of Arts and Letters in 1979. The book's popularity threatened to make Howe into an institution, but he was determined to make a full and honest reckoning with his past.

This he did in *Leon Trotsky* (1978), *A Margin of Hope* (1982), and *Socialism and America* (1985). In all three Howe tried to tell the truth about his radical socialist past. The second is an autobiography that tells little of his life and loves but much about his career as a public intellectual. Still its dedication reflected yet another change in Howe's private life. *World of Our Fathers* was dedicated to his third wife, whom he divorced about 1978. The 1982 book was dedicated to Ilana Wiener, an Israeli expatriate who became his fourth wife in about 1980.

Howe retired from the City University of New York in 1986 but continued to write voluminously. He was named a MacArthur Fellow in 1987. For the third time in his career he went into combat against literary radicals, now called "theorists," who saw little intrinsic value in literature and used it mainly as an instrument of their political ambitions. Slowed by illness in his last years, he died of a ruptured aorta in New York City.

Howe's career was the story of three loves. He began as a passionate believer in the capacity of socialism to end war and injustice but eventually was forced to acknowledge its almost universal failure as a political movement. Nevertheless, he transformed socialism into a myth of considerable power as an ethical instrument of social and political criticism. He was stirred belatedly into Jewishness by the Holocaust and undertook a heroic effort to save a language and a literature that were almost destroyed by Nazism. Although he endowed the idea of secular Jewishness with a special twilight beauty, he ceased to believe in its future long before he died. Literature proved the most powerful and compelling of his three loves. He defended its autonomy against Stalinists and Trotskyists in the 1940s, against "guerrillas with tenure" in the 1960s, and against theorists in the 1980s. Among American men of letters in the twentieth century, he was the exemplar of intellectual heroism and tenacious idealism.

★

Howe's *A Margin of Hope: An Intellectual Autobiography* (1982) is almost as impersonal as its subtitle suggests but is of great value. Edward Alexander, *Irving Howe—Socialist, Critic, Jew* (1998), the only book-length study of Howe, is primarily a biography of his mind. Useful discussions of particular aspects of Howe's work are in Edward Alexander, *Irving Howe and Secular Jewishness: An Elegy* (1995). Journal articles include Alvin Rosenfeld, "Irving Howe: The World of Our Fathers," *Midstream* 22 (October 1976): 80–86; and Sanford Pinsker, "Lost Causes/Marginal Hopes," *Virginia Quarterly Review* 65 (spring 1989): 215–230. Several personal memorials and tributes are in "Remembering Irving Howe," *Dissent* 40 (fall 1993): 515–549. An obituary is in the *New York Times* (6 May 1993).

EDWARD ALEXANDER

HUMPHRY, (Ann) Wickett (*b.* 16 June 1942 in Belmont, Massachusetts; *d.* 2 October 1991 near Bend, Oregon), college professor and vocal right-to-die advocate who cofounded the Hemlock Society in 1980.

Wickett Humphry was the only child of Arthur J. Kooman, a banker, and Ruth Fenderson, a former Peace Corps volunteer and Shakespearean scholar. She was born and raised in Belmont, a residential suburb of Boston. She graduated from Boston University in 1964 and went on to receive a master's degree in 1973 from the University of Toronto and a doctorate from the University of Birmingham in England in 1977. She was an adjunct professor of English language and literature at Putney College in London, England (1976–1978), and later at Occidental College (1978–1979), and the Art Center College of Design (1978–1981), both in Los Angeles, California. She met Derek Humphry, a British journalist and social activist, while studying in England. The two wed on 16 February 1976.

Humphry's first wife, Jean Edna Crane, had suffered from breast cancer and had died in March 1975 at age forty-two in a suicide assisted by her husband. Shortly after their marriage, Wickett and Derek Humphry published *Jean's Way* (1978). The work, a chronology of Humphry's twenty-two-year marriage to Jean, recounts the circumstances leading up to the detection of her cancer and the facts surrounding her assisted suicide using a strong mixture of secobarbital and codeine prepared by her husband.

While living in Los Angeles in 1980 and crusading for new laws to enable physicians to aid voluntary suicide victims without fear of prosecution, the Humphrys established the Hemlock Society, the first such organization in North America. The Hemlock Society, dedicated to what the Humphrys called "assisted suicide" and "self-deliverance" for the dying, is named after the cup of poisonous herbs from which the fifth-century B.C.E. Greek philosopher Socrates was forced to drink by his enemies. Many critics of the Hemlock Society point out the irony that Socrates was indeed a victim of "involuntary" euthanasia. Yet by 1990 the once minuscule Hemlock Society had grown to nearly 30,000 members in fifty-one U.S. chapters. Its growth was the subject of dissension, but the obscure organization saw its controversial message become more widely accepted as a result of the AIDS epidemic.

In early 1980 the Humphrys printed and edited the *Hemlock Quarterly* and the *Euthanasia Review*. In 1986 they published *The Right to Die: Understanding Euthanasia,* an extensive history of euthanasia and a widely used reference book. Two years later the Hemlock Society privately published *Double Exit,* an ostensibly fictionalized account of an elderly couple's assisted suicide. The couple was, in fact, Wickett Humphry's parents. Ann Wickett and Derek Humphry had illegally impersonated physicians to procure deadly doses of a foreign-made barbiturate (Vesparex). According to accounts from the American Life League's Pro-Life Encyclopedia, the two aided the parents in swallowing the lethal drug. Although Wickett Humphry's ninety-two-year-old father may have been ready to die, she knew that her seventy-eight-year-old mother, who had struggled against forced feeding, was not. This firsthand experience of her parents' death may have been a turning point in her activist support for mercy killings.

The Humphrys moved the Hemlock Society's headquarters from Los Angeles to Eugene, Oregon, in 1988. The regret of her role in her parents' death, along with the news of her own breast cancer in 1989 and her husband's subsequent "abandonment" (her word) of her, led Wickett Humphry to question mercy killing publicly. She saw it not as a sympathetic remedy for suffering but as a "deadly deception" that often led to additional suffering. As her aversion to the Hemlock Society mounted, she formed a covert friendship with the head of the anti-euthanasia forces, Rita Marker, an outspoken opponent of Derek Humphry. Wickett Humphry confided not only her dissatisfaction with the policies and philosophies of the Hemlock Society and her belief that society-backed legislation might be too dangerous as it would allow anyone of any age to enter a euthanasia clinic, but also her attitudes toward her marriage and bitter divorce.

By 1989 the Humphrys were engaged in public accusations. Wickett Humphry blamed her husband for deserting her when she was diagnosed with breast cancer and claimed that he had labeled her "mentally incompetent" and threatened to expose her involvement in her mother's death. He countered with assertions that the marriage had been rocky for years and that Wickett Humphry had told him that she had attempted suicide in the early 1970s. He contended that he had not left her because of the cancer, which he publicly announced was in remission in 1990. As the Humphrys' bitter public divorce escalated, public opinion began affecting the image of the Hemlock Society. To counter such negativism, the society's board removed the couple from their leadership positions in January 1990. Although Derek Humphry was replaced by a national president when it was determined that his efficacy as a spokesman for the "humane right to die" had been undermined by his wife's assertion of his abandonment, the board reappointed him to perhaps a far more important role, executive director. Wickett Humphry was not reappointed.

Wickett Humphry continued to undergo chemotherapy and breast reconstruction and to endure the psychological impact of the disease, and she felt more isolated than ever. On 1 October 1991 at age forty-nine, on the verge of receiving her pilot's license after winning a battle with the U.S. Federal Aviation Administration over the effects of the drugs she was taking for her cancer, she set into motion the events that led to her death. According to obituary accounts, Wickett Humphry spent the morning on her correspondence. As time passed, her mood apparently shifted and she hastily left her home, the fifty-acre Windfall Farm, about twenty-five miles north of Eugene. She drove 100 miles into the Oregon wilderness, where she parked, saddled her horse, and rode another three miles up a trail veering off into the forest. Her body was found on 8 October 1991 near the Three Sisters Wilderness. Her suicide by an overdose of barbiturates was confirmed the next month by the state medical examiner. Conflicting reports of Wickett Humphry's disease, said to be in remission; her mental state; and the possible collapse of a $6 million lawsuit against her ex-husband and the Hemlock Society continued to stoke the fires of euthanasia advocates and opponents.

Ironically, it was the son whom she had given up for adoption as the result of a failed relationship in the early 1970s and who had finally located her in the fall of 1991 who helped recover his mother's ashes from a mortuary in Bend. In accordance with her wishes, Wickett Humphry was cremated and her friends scattered her ashes at night near the pond at her farm.

Ann Wickett Humphry's suicide raised more questions than it answered, including the extent to which euthanasia proponents might go to extinguish another person's life. Initially, Wickett Humphry and her husband were in agreement ideologically that "an individual's right to live and die in the manner of his or her best choice is the ultimate civil liberty." By 1989, she acknowledged that she was exhausted by the "world of death and dying," fearful of giving physicians a "license to kill," and concerned that the right to die could become the "pressure to die." Derek Humphry continued to espouse a person's right to assisted suicide and to advocate the passage of laws to protect patients' and physicians' rights in such matters.

Derek Humphry's 1991 best-seller, *Final Exit: The Practicalities of Self-Deliverance and Assisted Suicide for the Dying,* immediately generated a heated national debate that was intensified by Wickett's action. One physician hailed it as the possible "landmark book on the subject of self-deliverance and assisted suicide." Still, a major opponent of the movement was heard most dramatically. The day before her death, Wickett Humphry had accused her ex-husband of "applying unwelcome pressures" after her diagnosis of cancer. A typewritten note left for him read in part: "You got what you wanted. . . . You have done everything conceivable to precipitate my death." Was her own "final exit" aimed at "pulling the plug on her ex-husband's right-to-die movement," as her critics have claimed? Or was she pleading for someone like Rita Marker, who wrote the 1995 book *Deadly Compassion: The Death of Ann Humphry and the Truth About Euthanasia,* to take up her new crusade against the "deadly deception" of mercy killings?

★

Rita Marker, *The Death of Ann Humphry and the Truth About Euthanasia* (1995), gives an insight as to why Wickett Humphry changed her feelings about euthanasia after her own involvement in her aging but not terminally ill parents' deaths. A biographical sketch, "Wickett, Ann 1942– ," *Contemporary Authors,* vol. 122 (1988), also provides information. Robert Reinhold, "Right-to-Die Group Is Shaken as Leader Leaves His Cancer-stricken Wife," *New York Times* (18 Feb. 1990), gives an inside look at the once obscure Hemlock Society. For an article about Wickett Humphry's disappearance and suicide, see "Advocate for Suicide Group Found Dead," *New York Times* (10 Oct. 1991), and Garry Adams's article in the *Los Angeles Times,* "A Bitter Legacy: Angry Accusations Abound After the Suicide of Hemlock Society Co-founder Ann Humphry" (23 Oct. 1991). In "A Fight to the Death," *New York Times* (9 Dec. 1991), author Trip Gabriel looks at a videotape of Wickett Humphry made on 1 October 1991, just days before her suicide. A compassionate and protective letter by Wickett Humphry's only child, Robert W. Stone, can be read in *Vanity Fair* (Mar. 1992).

ELLEN O'CONNELL BRASEL

HUTCHINSON, G(eorge) Evelyn (*b.* 30 January 1903 in Cambridge, England; *d.* 17 May 1991 in London, England), ecologist and limnologist who pioneered the development of the scientific basis of ecology.

Hutchinson was born into academia, the son of Arthur Hutchinson, a professor of mineralogy at Cambridge University and the master of Pembroke College, and Evaline Demezy Shipley, a feminist writer and activist. He was first educated by his parents along with his younger brother and sister and was encouraged to pursue scientific studies by his father and his uncle, the Cambridge vice chancellor Sir Arthur Shipley, who was a zoologist, embryologist, and noted contributor to *Cambridge Natural History.* At about the age of five Hutchinson began gathering fish and insects from local waters for his own aquariums and became intrigued by the fact that different animals live in different waters. He attended St. Faith's School in Cambridge from 1912 to 1917 and Gresham's School in Holt, Norfolk, from 1917 to 1921. At age fifteen he published a paper about a swimming grasshopper in *Entomologist's Record and Journal of Variation* (1918). Entering Emmanuel College, Cambridge University, in 1921, he received a B.A. degree in 1924 and a master's degree in 1928, both in zoology.

In 1925 Hutchinson took a Rockefeller Fellowship to the Stazione Zoologica in Naples to study octopus endocrinology, but the work was unsuccessful. In 1926 he became a zoology lecturer at the University of the Witwatersrand in Johannesburg, South Africa, but after two years he was dismissed for "incompetence," like all his predecessors, by the professor in charge. Publications later described the situation there as unstable. Hutchinson then began his first major work in limnology, the study of lakes and other freshwater bodies, researching the geology, chemistry, and biology of South Africa's dry lakes with Grace Pickford, a Cambridge graduate who was in the country on a scientific fellowship. The couple married in 1928 and divorced five years later. They had no children.

Hutchinson moved to the United States in 1928 when he went to Yale University in New Haven, Connecticut, as a zoology instructor. He got this position in an unusual manner when, after applying late for a fellowship, he was offered an instructorship instead. This position led to his illustrious forty-three-year career at Yale. Promoted to an assistant professor in 1931, an associate professor in 1941, and a full professor in 1945, he was named the Sterling Professor of Zoology in 1952. From 1947 to 1965 he was the director of graduate studies in zoology, and he retired as the Sterling Professor emeritus in 1971.

In his early years at Yale, Hutchinson published twenty-seven papers based on limnological work performed mostly in Africa. In 1932 he was named biologist for the Yale North India Expedition, which led to important publications on high altitude lakes and his first book, *The Clear Mirror: A Pattern of Life in Goa and in Indian Tibet* (1936). On the voyage home Hutchinson met his second wife, Margaret Seal, with whom he shared deep interests in art, music, and religion. Their 1933 marriage lasted until her death in 1983. They had no children.

Hutchinson returned to Yale in 1933 and began the stream of research, writing, and teaching that continued to almost the end of his life. Constructing a bold, theoretical approach to ecology, he helped transform it from a descriptive, classificatory, and intuitive endeavor into a formal science of hypothesis testing and mathematical methods. He taught his students to consider all of the processes that exist in ecological systems and brought together diverse scientists and mathematicians to try to answer ecological questions. Besides limnology, Hutchinson's enormous range of interests led him to contribute to several other fields, including biogeochemistry, radioecology, paleoecology, systems ecology, and population ecology. Before 1947 he taught about the relation between carbon dioxide and Earth's temperature and the expectation of global warming, a concept that was not discussed much by scientists before the late 1960s. One of his best-known contributions was his quantitatively oriented conception of the ecological niche, first discussed in a 1957 paper entitled "Concluding Remarks" in *Cold Spring Harbor Symposia on Quantitative Biology*. His multileveled

approach became known as the "Hutchinson research school" and inspired generations of students, many of whom became leading ecologists and teachers themselves.

A gifted writer, Hutchinson authored nine books, nearly 150 articles, and many opinion columns over almost six decades. His four-volume *A Treatise on Limnology* (1957–1993) revolutionized the subject with its breadth of coverage on the geography, physics, and chemistry of lakes (1957); biology and plankton (1967); botany (1975); and lake invertebrates, published posthumously (1993). His other books include three collections of essays, *The Itinerant Ivory Tower* (1953), *The Enchanted Voyage and Other Studies* (1962), and *The Ecological Theater and the Evolutionary Play* (1965); and a textbook, *An Introduction to Population Ecology* (1978). For many years he also wrote a regular, widely read column called "Marginalia" on broad issues of science and society for *American Scientist*. A 1947 column on the English author Rebecca West's *Black Lamb and Grey Falcon: A Journey through Yugoslavia* (1941) led to their lifelong friendship. In 1957 Hutchinson published *A Preliminary List of the Writings of Rebecca West, 1912–1951*, a bibliography of West's works, and he later curated a collection of her papers at Yale's Beinecke Library.

Hutchinson's scientific accomplishments brought him membership in many important societies, including the National Academy of Sciences, the American Academy of Arts and Sciences, the American Philosophical Society, the Linnean Society of London, and the Royal Entomological Society, and foreign membership in the Royal Society. His scientific awards included the Leidy Medal (1955); the Naumann Medal (1959); the Eminent Ecologist Award of the Ecological Society of America (1962); the Tyler Award, which is often referred to as the Nobel Prize for conservation (1974); the Frederick Garner Cottrell Award (1974); the Franklin Medal, whose previous recipients included Thomas Edison and Albert Einstein (1979); the Daniel Giraud Elliot Medal (1984), and Japan's Kyoto Prize (1986). A naturalized American since 1941, he refused to accept the Medal of Science in 1973 in protest of President Richard Nixon but was awarded that medal posthumously in 1991. Although he never earned a Ph.D. in the traditional sense, he received honorary doctorates from Harvard University, Princeton University, the University of Pennsylvania, and Cambridge University. At least twenty-two species have been named for him along with a lake in Ontario and a research laboratory at the University of the Witwatersrand.

Hutchinson spent his last years in failing health. In 1985 he married Anne Twitty Goldsby, a former biology teacher, who died in 1990. In 1991 he returned to England for a visit and died in London. His ashes were buried on 18 October 1991 at Christ Church in New Haven, Connecticut.

Considered a true polymath by many people, Hutchinson understood the complexity of environmental issues and with his students gave ecology an intellectual basis decades before most of the world was aware of environmental problems. He was a slim man, about five feet, ten inches tall; he was handsome when he was younger, but developed drooping eyes and rounded shoulders by his forties. A shy and deeply reserved man with a warm sense of humor, he was also a brilliant teacher who inspired students with his passion for science and his impeccable scholarship. One of the fathers of ecology, Hutchinson was also one of America's foremost scientists.

★

The main collection of Hutchinson's papers is in the Biology Collection of the Kline Science Library at Yale University. His papers related to Rebecca West, including her letters to him, are in the General Collection of Rare Books and Manuscripts, Beinecke Library, Yale University. Hutchinson's letters to West are in the Special Collections Department of McFarlin Library, University of Tulsa, Oklahoma. His partial autobiography, *The Kindly Fruits of the Earth: Recollections of an Embryo Ecologist* (1979), traces his personal life and scientific development to 1930. A biographical essay with a partial bibliography is in Emily J. McMurray, ed., *Notable Twentieth-Century Scientists* (1995). Hutchinson's "Concluding Remarks," *Cold Spring Harbor Symposia on Quantitative Biology* 22 (1957): 415–427, was reprinted in *Bulletin of Mathematical Biology* 53 (1991): 193–213. Vivid articles that combine tribute, biography, and scientific analysis are L. B. Slobodkin, "George Evelyn Hutchinson: An Appreciation," *Journal of Animal Ecology* 62, no. 2 (1993): 390–394; Ruth Patrick, "George Evelyn Hutchinson," *Proceedings of the American Philosophical Society* 138 (Dec. 1994): 529–535; and Lawrence B. Slobodkin and Nancy G. Slack, "George Evelyn Hutchinson: 20th-Century Ecologist," *Endeavour* 23, no. 1 (1999): 24–30. A special issue of *Limnology and Oceanography* 16 (Mar. 1971): 167–477, dedicated to Hutchinson at his retirement includes a "phylogenetic tree of intellectual descendants," a complete bibliography to 1971, photographs, and biographical material. Obituaries are in *Time* (3 June 1991), the *Times* (4 June 1991), London *Independent* (12 June 1991), and London *Daily Telegraph* (17 Aug. 1991).

MADELEINE R. NASH

I-J

IBA, (Payne) Henry ("Hank") (*b.* 6 August 1904 in Easton, Missouri; *d.* 15 January 1993 in Stillwater, Oklahoma), college basketball coach and athletic director who was among the most respected in the United States and who won two National Collegiate Athletic Association (NCAA) basketball titles while coaching at Oklahoma State University (OSU).

Iba was one of five children of Henry Burkley Iba, a traveling salesman, and Zylfa Dell Payne, a refined homemaker who brought her Kentucky traditions with her when she moved to Easton. At Easton High School, Iba was a member of the debating team and was acknowledged as the best player on the school's basketball team. After graduating in 1923, he attended Westminster College in Fulton, Missouri, where he had an athletic scholarship to play basketball, football, and baseball, and to run track. In his four years at Westminster, Iba participated on seven league championship teams. He lettered four times each in basketball and baseball and two times in football. He made the all-state basketball team four times and led the state in scoring in 1926. Playing as an end, he made all-state in football for his 1926 team.

In 1927 Iba took a teaching and coaching position at Classen High School in Oklahoma City, Oklahoma. As Classen's basketball coach, Iba stressed fundamentals and defense. On offense, Iba slowed the game and stressed close-to-the-basket shots and accuracy. In his first year he took Classen to the state finals, only to lose 22–17. Iba also

coached baseball and won several tournament championships. In the 1928 basketball season, Iba's Classen Comets won the state championship and competed in the finals of the national high school tournament, which they lost.

After the academic year, Iba attended summer school at Marysville State Teachers College in Marysville, Missouri, where he finished his B.S. degree in physical education. After another championship year at Classen, Iba landed a college job at Marysville State University, where he served as head basketball coach and assistant football coach. It was in Marysville that Iba met his future bride, Doyne Williams. They married on 25 August 1930 and eventually had one son, Henry Williams ("Moe") Iba, who also became a successful basketball coach.

Iba's trademark was defense and ball control. The game's tempo was slow. Iba developed a pattern offense that included approximately fifty plays, with someone guaranteed an open shot if the pattern were correctly run. His first year at Marysville was an undefeated one (31–0). Three more years of winning records and winning tournaments followed before Iba accepted a new position—head basketball and head baseball coach at Oklahoma A&M College (now Oklahoma State University) in Stillwater.

Assuming his new position in 1934, Iba took charge of a losing basketball team whose last winning season had been in 1928. He managed to turn the program around in just one year. His team posted a 9–9 record, a statistic that Iba had predicted before even playing the first game. In

Henry Iba, 1970. © BETTMANN/CORBIS

1935, in addition to his coaching duties, Iba was named the college's athletic director. That year, his basketball team won a share of the Missouri Valley conference by tying Drake and Creighton in conference wins.

A host of good years followed. Iba's teams became contenders for national laurels. His 1945 team won the NCAA title and his 1946 team repeated the feat. Iba became the first college coach to win back-to-back basketball titles. Subsequently, he continued his career in Stillwater until his retirement in 1970. Although he never won another NCAA basketball crown, his overall record was a dazzling 767 career victories and only 338 losses. His victories placed him fourth (as of 2000) on the list for wins as a college coach. Only Dean Smith, Adolph Rupp, and Jim Phelan had more wins.

As athletic director of OSU, Iba also made his mark. By 2000 the university had won thirty-five NCAA championships in various sports: twenty-five of those came during Iba's tenure as athletic director. Iba also supervised the modernization of OSU's athletic facilities.

In a fitting climax to a successful career, Iba was named to coach the United States basketball team in the Olympic games of 1964, 1968, and 1972. He became the only American to coach basketball in three Olympics. His teams won gold medals in 1964 and 1968 but had to settle for the silver after losing to the Soviet Union in 1972's final game—a contest marred by last-second controversial rulings that al-

lowed the Soviet team three chances in which to take the last shot of the game. The Soviets finally scored on the third try and won the game with the score of 51–50. Iba also served as the honorary coach of the gold medal–winning Olympic basketball team under Bobby Knight in 1984.

Iba was best known as an innovator in "hard-nosed" man-to-man defense and in ball control and pattern offense. He also believed in iron discipline for his teams both on and off the court. He was an honest, ethical coach and administrator who served as a role model for college basketball players and coaches everywhere.

Iba won many awards during his career. He was the NCAA coach of the year in both 1945 and 1946. He was inducted into the Basketball Hall of Fame in 1968. In 1976 the Basketball Hall of Fame trustees gave him the John W. Burn Award for outstanding contributions to basketball and to athletics. In 1982 Iba won OSU's Henry G. Bennett Distinguished Service Award for contributions to OSU and to the state of Oklahoma. He was selected for both the Oklahoma Hall of Fame and the Missouri Hall of Fame.

After his retirement in 1970, Iba continued to live in Stillwater and became a sports consultant for OSU and many other universities. He died of heart failure at the age of eighty-eight. He is buried in Fairlawn Cemetery in Stillwater.

Iba will always be remembered as one of the most successful college basketball coaches of all time. He excelled as both player and coach, and remained number four on the list of coaches with the most career wins at the end of the twentieth century. As a coach Iba was known for building a defensive team and slowing down games. The play of his national championship teams of the 1940s as well as his other teams over his thirty-five years as OSU's athletic director attest to his great coaching abilities. Under his direction OSU became known as a university with excellent and ethical athletic leadership.

★

A collection of Iba's personal papers is maintained by the Media Division of the OSU athletic department in Stillwater, Oklahoma. John Paul Bischoff wrote Iba's full-length biography, *Mr. Iba: Basketball's Aggie Iron Duke* (1980). The biography stresses Iba's career but does not develop his family history. Also containing material on Iba are Tom C. Brody, "Who Says You Can't Win Them All," *Sports Illustrated* (Apr. 1964); Tom C. Brody, "The Man Who Said Control the Ball," *Sports Illustrated* (Dec. 1967); and Neil D. Isaacs, *All the Right Moves: A History of College Basketball* (1975). For a look at the coach and his Olympic basketball teams of 1964, 1968, and 1972, see *The United States 1964 Olympic Book* (1965); *The United States 1968 Olympic Book* (1969); and *The United States Olympic Book* (1973). Other books that consider Iba's career are Alexander M. Weyand, *The Cavalcade of Basketball* (1960), and Philip Reed Rulon, *Oklahoma State Uni-*

versity Since 1890 (1975). Obituaries are in the *Saturday Oklahoman & Times* and *Tulsa Tribune* (both 16 Jan. 1993).

JAMES SMALLWOOD

IRWIN, James Benson   (*b.* 17 March 1930 in Pittsburgh, Pennsylvania; *d.* 8 August 1991 in Glenwood Springs, Colorado), astronaut and the eighth man to walk on the moon.

Irwin was the elder of two sons born to James Benson, a plumber, and Elsie Strebel, a homemaker. His family moved to Florida, Oregon, and then to Salt Lake City, Utah, where Irwin attended East High School. Irwin later wrote that his first date in high school was with the daughter of Utah's governor. In 1951 he graduated from the U.S. Naval Academy at Annapolis and won a commission in the Air Force but not the test pilot's training that he hoped to get. In December 1952 he married Mary Etta Wehling, a young woman that he had met in Texas, but the marriage ended in divorce in the summer of 1954. He endured years of persistence at desk jobs while hoping for another chance at test pilot training. Also in the 1950s, he did graduate work at the University of Michigan in aeronautical and instrument engineering, for which he was awarded a master's degree in 1957.

After a training flight to California, Irwin met Mary Ellen Monroe in San Jose, and the two were married on 4 September 1959. There was a religious difference, as Mary was a devoted Seventh Day Adventist and Irwin was a Baptist. He proposed that their children's religious training be decided by gender: their sons would go to his church and their daughters would go to hers. Over the next decade the couple had five children.

After three years as a project officer in Ohio, Irwin transferred to test pilot school at Edwards Air Force Base in California, graduating in 1961. Irwin admitted that as a test pilot, he was something of a show-off. Flying five feet above railroad tracks in the face of oncoming trains and buzzing fishing boats were among the stunts to which he admitted performing on training flights. In 1963 he attended special training courses in aerospace studies.

Irwin first applied to be an astronaut in 1963 but was rejected twice before he was accepted in 1966, just a month away from the age limit. Irwin wrote that the first rejection was due to the fact that he was recovering from a serious airplane accident that occurred during a training flight, which had left him with two broken legs and a serious concussion. The second time the agency was more interested in scientists than test pilots. Irwin was a member of the support crew for the Apollo 10 mission and was the backup lunar module pilot on Apollo 12, but his only completed mission was Apollo 15, which took him to the lunar surface on 30 July 1971.

On the Apollo 15 mission, Irwin and Colonel David R. Scott were the first astronauts to get a sound sleep on the moon because they could take off their space suits while inside the lunar module. Their sixty-six-hour, fifty-four-minute stay on the moon's surface set a record. They were the first astronauts to use a battery-operated moon vehicle known as the Lunar Rover, which operated at a speed of six miles per hour and allowed them to venture as many as three miles from the lunar excursion module, and collect 175 pounds of rock samples, including a rock that many believe to be the most important sample from any of the Apollo missions. This crystalline sample, known as the Genesis Rock, tested at 4.15 billion years of age—just 100 million years newer than the estimated age of the solar system. It was believed to be part of the original lunar crust. The third member of the crew, Major Alfred M. Worden, piloted the Apollo command module in lunar orbit while the other two astronauts were on the surface.

While religion had been important to him as a young man, Irwin later wrote that he had fallen away from the church up until the time that he went to the moon. Once there, he experienced a religious feeling of omniscience. He wrote that he knew what orders would be coming from Houston seconds before they arrived.

After returning from the moon, it was discovered that the three Apollo 15 astronauts had made a deal with a German stamp dealer to carry stamps to the moon for resale when they returned to earth. The astronauts were reprimanded and the stamps were confiscated. A decade later a court victory forced the government to return the stamps to the three astronauts. Irwin apologized for poor judgment, and left NASA and the Air Force on 1 July 1972. At the time of his retirement, he had attained the rank of colonel. A speech to 50,000 Christians at the Houston Astrodome launched Irwin on a second career as an evangelist. Shortly afterward he established the High Flight Foundation, a nonprofit religious organization, with the Baptist minister William H. Rittenhouse. Irwin traveled the country speaking in churches and raising money for his organization. In 1973 he wrote a book with William A. Emerson, Jr., on his religious and astronautics experiences, *To Rule the Night: The Discovery Voyage of Astronaut Jim Irwin,* which was revised several times to cover his experiences after leaving the program.

In his postflight years, Irwin led six expeditions to Mount Ararat to find Noah's ark. In 1982, he suffered a fall that nearly killed him. Despite a flurry of publicity in 1984, when the party found a "boat-shaped formation," no hard evidence of the ark's existence was found by Irwin. His quest was ended by Turkish bureaucrats who thought the expeditions might be a cover for espionage, and in 1985 Irwin wrote with Monte Unger *More Than an Ark on Ararat.*

A thin and earnest-looking man with dark hair, known

James Irwin. ASSOCIATED PRESS AP

to friends as Jim, Irwin wrote that he resembled the character Alfalfa from the *Our Gang* film comedies. He later remarked that at five feet, eight inches, he was the shortest of the three astronauts on Apollo 15.

During the grueling days on the moon, Irwin and Scott had both experienced irregular heart rhythms. The astronauts were unaware of this problem, although it was being monitored at mission control. Less than two years later, at the age of forty-three, Irwin suffered a serious heart attack while playing handball. He suffered a second major heart attack in 1986 while jogging. A third heart attack was the cause of death in 1991, making him the first of the twelve lunar landing astronauts to die. He died at Valley View Hospital in Glenwood Springs and is buried at Arlington National Cemetery in Arlington, Virginia.

★

Irwin's autobiography, *To Rule The Night* (1973), is a good source of information. There is also extensive coverage of Irwin and the Apollo 15 mission in *A Man on the Moon* by Andrew Chaikin (1994). An obituary is in the *New York Times* (11 Aug. 1991).

TERRY L. BALLARD

JACOBY, James Oswald ("Jim") (*b.* 4 April 1933 in New York City; *d.* 8 February 1991 in Dallas, Texas), contract-bridge champion, developer of bidding methods, and author.

Jacoby was the elder of two sons of Oswald ("Ozzie") Jacoby and Mary Zita McHale. His father, an actuary, was one of the best contract-bridge players of all time. His mother was a homemaker except during World War II, when, like many other women, she worked outside the home to help the war effort.

Jacoby entered the University of Notre Dame in 1949 but left during his junior year to study briefly at Southern Methodist University in Dallas, then volunteered for the U.S. Army. He served as a private, mostly at Fort Meade, Maryland. In 1955 he returned to Notre Dame and received a bachelor's degree in English in 1957. He married Judith Mudd in La Plata, Maryland, on 14 June 1958. They had one son.

One reason it took Jacoby seven and a half years to get his college degree was that he began playing bridge obsessively shortly after he arrived at Notre Dame. Playing with Ben Fain, George Heath, Paul Hodge, and his father, in 1955 he won his first major bridge title, the Chicago Trophy (after 1965 called the Reisinger Board-a-Match Team Championship). He won the Reisinger twice more, in 1970 and 1977. Altogether he finished first twenty times in national or international competition. He won the North American Men's Pairs in 1956; the Vanderbilt Knockout Teams in 1965, 1967, 1971, and 1982; the Master Mixed Teams in 1968; the North American Men's Teams in 1968, 1972, and 1973; the Spingold Knockout Teams in 1969; the World Mixed Teams in 1972; the Grand National Teams in 1981 and 1986; the North American Swiss Teams in 1985; and the World Team Olympiad in 1988. He shared five of these twenty victories with his father.

Perhaps the most notable of his victories was his membership in the team that twice won the Bermuda Bowl, the irregularly scheduled world bridge team championship. After the once-dominant U.S. team had lost the championship to Italy for ten years in a row, Ira G. Corn, Jr., a wealthy Texas entrepreneur, decided to buy the services of the brightest young American bridge experts to bring the Bermuda Bowl back to the United States. In 1968, along with Bobby Wolff, Billy Eisenberg, Bobby Goldman, and Michael Lawrence, Jacoby was a founding member of

Corn's professional bridge team, the Aces. Joe Musumeci joined as coach later that year and Bob Hamman joined as a player early in 1969. The Aces won the Bermuda Bowl in 1970 and 1971, then finished second to Italy in 1973.

Throughout his four and a half years with the Aces, Jacoby was partnered mostly with Wolff. Prompted by Goldman and Eisenberg to improve the accuracy of their bidding, Jacoby and Wolff invented a version of the strong-club bidding system, called the "Orange Club" because the Aces wore orange jackets. Strong-club systems are very popular, especially in Europe and Asia, but can be difficult to master. The main features of this variant are that an opening one-club bid shows at least 17 high-card points, responses show controls, and an opening one-no-trump bid shows either 13–15 or 16–17 high-card points. Jacoby and Wolff used this system when they won the world championships; later, Wolff played it with Hamman.

Jacoby won the Sally and Harry Fishbein Trophy in 1968 for the best individual performance at the American Contract Bridge League (ACBL) summer national championships. He won the Barry Crane Trophy in 1988 for the most ACBL master points accumulated in a year. At the time of his death, his total of 25,226 ACBL master points was fifth on the all-time list.

Jacoby worked as a stockbroker but generally earned his living from bridge and backgammon. His uncanny last-minute triumphs at backgammon earned him the nickname "Hero." He enjoyed most sports and frequently attended the opera. He often served on the ACBL board of governors.

Many of Jacoby's accomplishments were family projects. He and his father invented Jacoby transfer bids and Jacoby artificial two-no-trump responses. Both of these conventions became indispensable to serious bridge players by the 1980s. With his father he cowrote *Win at Bridge with Jacoby and Son* (1966), *Win at Bridge with Jacoby Modern* (1970), *Improve Your Bridge with Oswald Jacoby* (1983), and *Jacoby on Card Games* (1986). With his mother he cowrote *The New York Times Book of Backgammon* (1973). His father, likewise an expert in backgammon, wrote the introduction. He published *Jacoby on Bridge* (1987) under his own name, but his mother copyedited it and his father's influence is obvious on every page. Beginning in the late 1960s, Jim cowrote "Jacoby on Bridge," the Newspaper Enterprise Associates syndicated column that his father began in 1950. After Ozzie's death in 1984, he continued the column alone until his own death.

Jacoby died at Doctors' Hospital in Dallas of a rapidly metastasizing osteosarcoma that had been diagnosed only a week earlier. He is buried in Calvary Hills Cemetery in Dallas, near his parents.

Jacoby's bridge accomplishments were always overshadowed by those of his father, but that never seemed to bother him. In contrast to his father's well-known impatience, Jacoby was calm and easygoing, almost to the point of laziness. Yet he did not always take criticism of his bridge game well. His apparent lack of seriousness disguised a tremendous talent and a vigorous competitive spirit. Opponents would sometimes underrate him and suffer the consequences of that misjudgment. Partners enjoyed playing with him because of his imperturbable and reassuring manner at the table.

★

The archives of the ACBL are the best source of further information. Jacoby's memoir of his father in *Jacoby on Bridge* also reveals much about himself. Bob Hamman's autobiography, *At the Table* (1994), contains many insights into Jacoby's life and character. A feature story is in the *Contract Bridge Bulletin* (Mar. 1997). Obituaries are in the *New York Times* (10 Feb. 1991) and *Contract Bridge Bulletin* (Mar. 1991).

ERIC V. D. LUFT

JANEWAY, Eliot (*b.* 1 January 1913 in New York City; *d.* 8 February 1993 in New York City), political economist, author, syndicated columnist, and presidential adviser and critic.

Janeway, the son of Meyer Joseph Janeway, a physician, and Fanny Siff, graduated from Cornell University in Ith-

Eliot Janeway. © OSCAR WHITE/CORBIS

aca, New York, in 1932 with a B.A. degree in philosophy. He then pursued graduate work at the London School of Economics in England, returning to the United States in 1935 without another degree.

Janeway began his writing career at the age of twenty-four when he penned a series of articles for the *Nation* in which he predicted that the United States would experience an inventory recession in 1937 and 1938. The American economy had risen steadily from the depths of the Great Depression in 1932, and conventional economic wisdom held that it would continue to do so for the foreseeable future. Seeing things differently, Janeway proposed that the federal government initiate a massive investment program in infrastructure to moderate the impact of the "coming" recession. Both his forecast and his policy recommendation were ignored, and the United States, as he predicted, experienced a first in its economic history, a recession imbedded within a depression.

The series of articles in the *Nation* attracted the interest of the administration of President Franklin D. Roosevelt and brought Janeway a modicum of influence with its policy-making councils. Another interested reader, Henry R. Luce, the publisher of such periodicals as *Time, Life,* and *Fortune,* admired Janeway's insights into economics and hired him to write part-time for those magazines. Janeway also worked directly for Luce, writing a private weekly economic and political advisory letter. On 29 October 1938 Janeway married Elizabeth Hall, a novelist and essayist. They had two sons.

From 1940 to 1942 Janeway served as the business editor of *Time* magazine, where his articles appeared on a regular basis. In 1941 he wrote *Smashing Hitler's International: The Strategy of a Political Offensive Against the Axis* with Edmund Taylor and Edgar Snow. In 1944 he became the business trends consultant for *Newsweek,* and for the next four years he continued to publish articles that linked economics and politics in interesting and provocative ways. In 1948 he put his journalism career on hold while he wrote his first solo book, *The Struggle for Survival* (1951). Subtitled *A Chronicle of Economic Mobilization in World War II,* this scholarly book was a study of how the United States mobilized its economy to become the decisive weapon that turned the tide in World War II. During the 1950s Janeway started two weekly economic advisory newsletters that formed the core of the Janeway Publishing and Research Corporation, a business he operated from his five-story townhouse on East Eightieth Street in Manhattan. During this period he became an informal adviser and fund-raiser for Senator Lyndon B. Johnson.

Janeway first became acquainted with Johnson in the late 1930s, when Johnson was a member of the House of Representatives. Over the years Janeway became close to Johnson and urged him to run for the presidency in 1956.

Janeway was an active fund-raiser for Johnson during the 1960 Democratic presidential primary. After Johnson became president in November 1963, Janeway began to disagree with him on many points of economic policy, but an irrevocable break between the two came in 1965 over Johnson's handling of the Vietnam War. Janeway did not disapprove of the war exactly, just its financing. "I was not arguing against the war itself," he once told an interviewer, "that is not my field of expertise." What Janeway found objectionable was the lack of financing for the war. "I said that putting it [the war] on the back of the economy without raising taxes and instituting controls would bring disaster," a position he elaborated in detail in *The Economics of Crisis: War, Politics, and the Dollar* (1968).

In the 1960s and 1970s Janeway became a syndicated columnist for the Chicago Tribune–New York News Syndicate. A tireless worker, he usually began his day at about 9:00 A.M., reading a dozen newspapers, magazines, and trade publications, and finished his day around 3:00 A.M., reading history, economics, biographies, or novels. He never actually wrote his articles or books, preferring instead to dictate everything. "I don't think of myself as a writer," he once said. "I'm a talker who reduces some of what he says to writing."

In these decades Janeway began to write a series of personal finance and investment books in addition to publishing his newsletters, writing a syndicated column, and making frequent appearances on television talk shows and the lecture circuit. He was at the top of his game. Yet for all his personal success, Janeway was never sanguine about the prospects of the world as a whole. Years earlier his continually gloomy predictions as a stock market forecaster had earned him the nickname "Calamity Janeway" among Wall Street pundits. Seen through the fractured lenses of two world wars and the most protracted economic downturn the Western world had experienced, his view of the future was always apprehensive. The financial advice he gave in such works as *What Shall I Do with My Money?* (1970), *You and Your Money* (1972), and *Musings on Money* (1976) reflected this anxiety.

In his last book, *The Economics of Chaos* (1989), ostensibly a critique of Reaganomics, Janeway created a complex yet compelling economic history of the United States and the policy lapses of just about every president from George Washington to Ronald Reagan. Following in the intellectual footsteps of the maverick American economist Thorstein Veblen, Janeway reiterated his belief that the nexus of technology, ideas, and social institutions did more to shape the patterns of economics than market activity and the interplay of demand and supply. He was particularly harsh in his criticism of mainstream economists and the politicians who trust without questioning the theories they expound. In his judgment, basing economic policies on irrelevant and often inaccurate hypotheses was a surefire formula for disaster. Janeway once mused that the "practitioners of the 'dismal science' do best when they live up to their reputations," a conviction he held until his death. He died of diabetes and heart problems in 1993.

★

Janeway's *The Economics of Chaos* (1989) is a tour de force that reveals much about his thinking process. See also Norman King, *The Money Messiah$* (1983). Additional insights can be found in S. Wellisz's review of Janeway's *The Economics of Crisis* in *Commonweal* (12 July 1968) and C. Welles, "Eliot Calamity Janeway: An Old Bear Who's Largely Bull," *Esquire* (21 Nov. 1978). The best available on-line source of information about Janeway is the Gale Literary Databases. Obituaries are in the *Chicago Tribune* (9 Feb. 1993) and the *New York Times* (9 Feb. 1993).

JAMES CICARELLI

JOHNSON, D(aniel) Mead (*b.* 2 March 1914 in Philadelphia, Pennsylvania; *d.* 21 January 1993 in Palm Beach, Florida), president of Mead Johnson and Company from 1955 to 1968.

Johnson was the son of Edward Mead Johnson, Jr., a pharmaceuticals executive, and Katheryn Josephine Moran. His grandfather Edward Mead Johnson, Sr., was the founder of Mead Johnson and Company. Upon the founder's death

D. Mead Johnson. COURTESY OF MEAD JOHNSON NUTRITIONALS

in 1934, the company was headed by Johnson's uncle, Lambert D. Johnson, Sr., with Edward Mead Johnson, Jr., serving as vice president of sales and advertising until his death in 1930 at the age of forty-two.

Though born in Philadelphia, Johnson spent most of his life in Evansville, Indiana. His introduction to the family's heritage and responsibility came at the age of twelve, when his first job at Mead Johnson and Company was to clean the rabbit cages in the laboratory. Although he was the founder's grandson, Johnson was shown no favoritism. He was expected to work for his $12 a week. He attended the Tennessee Military Institute in Sweetwater from 1927 to 1932, graduating as valedictorian. In 1936 Johnson enrolled at Johns Hopkins University in Baltimore, where he majored in business administration and chemistry until World War II interrupted his education. He enlisted in the American Field Service and served with the British Eighth Army in the African, Indian, and Burmese campaigns, receiving citations of valor from both the British and French governments. After a bad fall aggravated an old back injury, Johnson was discharged in October 1943 and resumed his education. At Johns Hopkins, he was elected president of the student council and was a winner of the Carlyle Barton Cup as the outstanding senior-year student. He received a B.S. degree in economics.

Starting as a sales representative in one of Mead Johnson's divisions in New York City, Johnson soon moved up the corporate ladder through a series of vice presidencies. In 1955 Johnson became president of the company, the third member of his family to head the firm and, at forty-four, its youngest president.

Under his direction, Mead Johnson and Company grew from a moderate-size manufacturer specializing in baby formulas to a global nutritional pharmaceutical company. Annual sales more than tripled under his leadership, and profits rose from $3.2 million to $8.2 million per year. In 1967 Mead Johnson and Company merged with Bristol-Myers. Johnson remained chief executive of Mead Johnson and joined its board of directors and executive committee. He was also made senior vice president of Bristol-Myers.

Although he held high positions, Johnson never lost touch with his employees. He liked to go through each plant, stopping occasionally to chat with the workers. One colleague remembered him and noted: "You got a feeling the moment you watched him at work, intense, serious and full of drive. Here was a man with pride of accomplishment, a pride in his job and his company, in its growth, development and security of the 1,850 employees and their families."

Through the D. Mead Johnson Foundation, monies were contributed to capital building funds of civic organizations. In addition to these contributions, the company contributed extensively to scholarship funds, professional organizations, and welfare activities around the globe. Johnson was a member of the John Hopkins University board of trustees from 1953 to 1955 and was also a trustee of the Tennessee Military Institute; he also served as a director of the Health Information Foundation, the Citizen Nation Bank, the Chicago and Eastern Illinois Railroad, and First National Bank.

In 1968 Johnson resigned as head of Mead Johnson and Company and retired to Palm Beach, Florida, where he built an 8,000-square-foot beachfront mansion. In retirement he became a founder and principal supporter of Evansville (Indiana) Future, Inc., a community group that worked to bring the city out of its federally designated classification as a depressed area. Evansville was the community Johnson grew up in and he was determined to see it through its difficult times.

Johnson married Elizabeth Jane Baumer. They had one son, Edward Mead Johnson III. They were later divorced and Johnson married Valerie Ellis Anderson, who had three children from a previous marriage. His hobbies included deep-sea fishing and cars.

Johnson died at the age of seventy-eight at his home at 1515 North Ocean Boulevard in Palm Beach. He was re-membered by Jesse Newman, the president of the Palm Beach Chamber of Commerce, as "a gregarious, wonderful man. He had excellent taste. He had a keen sense of business acumen." Upon his death, the Johns Hopkins University received a gift of $1 million for the D. Mead Johnson Chair in Chemistry. W. Paul Torrington, a top executive of Mead Johnson and Company, remembers Johnson as a wise leader who hired the best people he could get and used their collective knowledge to build the business. "Mead was a marvelous guy, brilliant." He recognized and embraced the need for change in organization. He said, "it's futile to restore normality; normality is only the reality of yesterday. This job is not to impose yesterday's norm on a changed today, but to change the business, its behavior, its attitudes, its expectations—as well as its products, its markets, and its distribution channels—to fit the new realities and the new opportunities."

★

An article on Johnson can be found in *Biography Index* 18 (1993). Obituaries are in the *Evansville Daily News Society, Evansville Courier, Evansville Press,* and *Palm Beach Post* (all 22 Jan. 1993), and *New York Times* (23 Jan. 1993).

YAN TOMA

K

KAUFFMAN, Ewing Marion (*b*. 21 September 1916 in Garden City, Missouri; *d*. 1 August 1993 in Kansas City, Missouri), self-made billionaire and philanthropist who founded the Fortune 500 pharmaceutical company Marion Laboratories and was the owner of the Kansas City Royals baseball team.

Kauffman was one of two children of John Samuel Kauffman, a mathematics whiz and insurance salesman, and Effie Mae Winders, a teacher and homemaker. He was named for Anna Ewing Cockrell, the wife of the Missouri senator Brigadier General Francis Marion Cockrell, and for John Marion Winders, his maternal grandfather. A brilliant child and an Eagle Scout who finished everything he started, Kauffman swam twice a day and once swam 240 feet under water without coming up for air. He was a member of Mensa, a prestigious group of intellectuals with IQs above the genius level, which he joined in childhood.

As a child Kauffman suffered from endocarditis, a heart ailment that kept him bedridden at the age of eleven. He passed the time with books, reading the Bible, biographies of American presidents and frontiersmen, and the works of Lloyd C. Douglas, including *Magnificent Obsession* (1929) and *Dr. Hudson's Secret Journal* (1939).

Kauffman attended Westport High School in Kansas City, graduated from Kansas City Junior College in 1936 with a degree in business, and entered the U.S. Navy in 1941. Before he left to serve in World War II, he married Marguerite Blackshire. After the surrender of Japan, he worked as a pharmaceuticals salesperson for Lincoln Laboratories in Missouri, where he outsold everyone in the company. Rather than rewarding him, however, the company cut back his territory. Frustrated, he decided to found his own company. Kauffman began Marion Laboratories in his basement in 1950 with $5,000 seed money, his poker winnings from his time in military service. That first year, Marion Laboratories made $36,000 in gross sales and $1,000 profit. One of the firm's products was the calcium tablet OS-CAL, which was developed because of its apparent therapeutic properties in healing broken bones. Meanwhile Kauffman adopted two children. After his wife died in 1960, Kauffman married Muriel McBrien in February 1962; they had one child.

By the time Kauffman was in his fifties, his company was worth billions and was one of the prestigious Fortune 500 companies because of excellent sales associates and hands-on product development by Kauffman. In 1989 Marion Laboratories merged with Merrell Dow Pharmaceuticals to form Marion Merrell Dow, with Kauffman serving as chairman emeritus until 1993. Kauffman always regarded the pharmaceutical company as the financial operation that made it possible for him to pursue his philanthropic interests.

Kauffman was on vacation in Europe with Muriel in 1969 when he suffered a stroke. The renowned heart surgeon Michael DeBakey advised Kauffman to cut out cig-

Ewing M. Kauffman. © BETTMANN/CORBIS

arettes, limit his consumption of coffee, and take up a hobby as part of a rehabilitation regimen. Kauffman, a die-hard baseball fan, purchased the Kansas City Royals Baseball Club as an American League expansion franchise. The Royals soon had a state-of-the-art stadium, complete with fountains in the outfield behind the fences, built as a present for his wife. Kauffman, who was known by associates as Mr. K, started the Baseball Academy in Kansas City to help young athletes from other sports who wanted to play baseball after college. Second baseman Frank White was a graduate of this academy.

In his twenty-five years as owner, Kauffman built the Royals into a championship team. In 1980 the Royals won their first American League pennant and went to the World Series. They lost to the Philadelphia Phillies but fought hard and made the Series quite dramatic. The Kansas City Royals won the pennant again in 1985 under manager Dick Howser and continued on to win the World Series. Kauffman called the 1985 World Series victory his "greatest thrill." His star manager and his greatest franchise player, George Brett, were celebrated all over the world. Brett, whose batting average was over .300, won three American League batting titles in three separate decades, a singular feat. Mr. K started a program called the Royal Lancers, in which people from all walks of life sell season tickets not for money but for perks, such as trips to spring training

and passes to the stadiums around the league. Kauffman was inducted into the Royals Hall of Fame in May 1993, and in June of that year, Royals Stadium was officially renamed Kauffman Stadium.

Kauffman established the Ewing Marion Kauffman Foundation, which embraces the idea of helping young people reach their goals in life. Whether it is providing financing for medical school for deserving students or helping talented young high school and college athletes to realize their dreams of playing professional baseball, the foundation has touched the lives of many young men and women. President George Bush recognized Kauffman for his philanthropic efforts by naming him the sixteenth Point of Light in the president's "Thousand Points of Light" tribute. In 1991 Kauffman received the Good Neighbor Award from the Harry S. Truman Foundation and was inducted into the Academy of Distinguished Entrepreneurs, sponsored by Babson College in Massachusetts. This honor has been extended to only fifty people.

Kauffman not only left a pharmaceutical legacy, allowing for the advancement of medicine, but he also left a baseball legacy through the Kansas City Royals and a philanthropic legacy through the Ewing Marion Kauffman Foundation, which continued to help young people after Kauffman's death from natural causes in 1993.

★

Anne Morgan's authorized biography, *Prescription For Success: The Life and Values of Ewing Marion Kauffman* (1995), is both insightful and regaling, and covers Kauffman's life from both a business and personal standpoint. An obituary is in the *Kansas City Star* (2 Aug. 1993).

BURTON E. ROCKS

KAUFMAN, Irving Robert (*b.* 24 June 1910 in New York City; *d.* 1 February 1992 in New York City), lawyer, government official, and federal judge who presided over the Rosenberg espionage trial.

Kaufman was one of five children of Herman Kaufman, who owned a tobacco humidifier manufacturing company, and Rose Spielberg. After graduating from DeWitt Clinton High School in the Bronx, New York, in 1925, he entered Fordham College, also in the Bronx, at the age of fifteen. Although he was Jewish, his fellow students called him "Pope Kaufman" for his excellence in the school's required "Christian Doctrine" courses. He received a B. A. degree in 1928 and his law degree from Fordham Law School in 1931, graduating at the top of his class. Kaufman practiced law in New York City before becoming assistant United States attorney from 1936 to 1940, largely handling insurance disability fraud cases. He returned to a wide-ranging, lucrative, and politically tinged private practice where one

Irving Kaufman. ARCHIVE PHOTOS

partner, Gregory F. Noonan, was his former boss as U. S. attorney, and another, Edward P. F. Eagan, later became chairman of the New York State Athletic Commission.

In 1947 and 1948 Kaufman served as special assistant to United States attorney general Tom Clark, organizing a new Justice Department section on lobbying. He also became friends on a first-name basis with Federal Bureau of Investigation (FBI) director J. Edgar Hoover. "Hoover was like Jesus Christ to him," observed an FBI official. Kaufman filtered and approved all candidates for positions in the U. S. attorney's office and the federal bench in New York for Clark and the Truman White House. In October 1949 President Harry S. Truman nominated Kaufman to a federal judgeship. He took his seat the next month.

Kaufman's greatest renown came from his presiding over the 1951 espionage trial of Julius and Ethel Rosenberg. The case took place against the backdrop of the Iron Curtain and the mid-twentieth century American anticommunist zealotry. Kaufman sentenced the Rosenbergs to death in the electric chair after a jury found them guilty of having conspired to deliver atomic bomb secrets to the Soviet Union during World War II. Describing their crime as "treason" and "worse than murder," Kaufman claimed that it had "caused . . . the Communist aggression in Korea, with the resultant causalities exceeding 50,000." No such

evidence, however, had been presented or existed. The espionage statute, Kaufman asserted, left him no choice but to act as he did. Despite exhaustive appeals, his ruling was not overturned. The Rosenbergs remain the only American civilians ever to be executed for espionage.

Kaufman had decided on the sentence before the jury handed down its verdict, perhaps even before the trial began. He held ex parte (private) conversations with prosecutors and other Justice Department, FBI, and Atomic Energy Commission officials about the sentence, and even with the Justice Department about future litigation strategies before the Supreme Court. Such conversations, although not totally uncommon at the time, violated judicial canons of ethics. Kaufman asked the prosecution to ascertain the Justice Department and FBI's recommendation. When the chief prosecutor told him, after a telephone call made in his presence at a public function the night before the sentencing, that officials remained divided, Kaufman said he should refrain from making any recommendation. Kaufman announced in court that he would not ask prosecutors for a recommendation, and he told the press that he had sought "spiritual guidance" for his decision and engaged in a solitary struggle of conscience. Later that day, he passed on to Hoover a message that the FBI had done a "fabulous job on this case." For over twenty years Kaufman used the FBI as a "private complaint bureau," criticizing legal efforts to reopen the case and attempting to stifle the appearance of material favorable to the Rosenbergs.

In 1961 Kaufman was promoted to the Court of Appeals for the Second Circuit by President John F. Kennedy. He had almost received appointments in 1957 and 1959, orchestrating the campaigns himself and having strong bipartisan support both times. As an appellate judge, Kaufman's experience as a trial lawyer and a trial judge filtered through everything he did. Facts, he noted, are "the bedrock of decision-making" and "work to limit the reach of judicial values." But the relationship among facts, law, and the "judge's individual character, unconscious though it may be, [is] of the essence" of judging.

Kaufman was a resolute defender of First Amendment rights. In 1971 he voted to release the Pentagon Papers detailing the evolution of the American involvement in Vietnam. In 1972 in *Russo* v. *Central School District No. 1,* he upheld a public school teacher's right to abstain from reciting the Pledge of Allegiance. "Patriotism that is forced is false patriotism, just as loyalty that is coerced is the very antithesis of liberty," Kaufman wrote. "Tolerance of the unorthodox and unpopular is the bellwether of a society's spiritual strength," he noted in *International Society for Krishna Consciousness* v. *Barber* (1981), while striking down a regulation which restricted religious solicitation on New York state fairgrounds. The exercise of First Amendment liberties, he wrote in 1984, "may do harm that the state is powerless to recompense. Yet this is simply the price that must be paid if we are to maintain a viable democracy."

As chief judge from 1973 until 1980 Kaufman reduced the backlog of cases by strict scheduling of appeals and by assigning staff counsel to meet with opposing lawyers to try to settle the case before oral argument. In 1987 he took senior status. Kaufman wrote over 300 articles on nearly all aspects of the legal system, imploring for court, sentencing, and prison reform and improving the juvenile justice system. He emphasized the duty of judges to make their decisions understandable to laypeople. "We're not writing just for ourselves but for the public," he said. Kaufman served as chairman of the President's Commission on Organized Crime from 1983 to 1986 and received the Presidential Medal of Freedom in 1987.

Judge Learned Hand wrote: "Irving Kaufman—a thoroughly competent lawyer, but interested primarily, if not completely, in recognition of Irving Kaufman." He liked prominent cases for their notice and insisted on a punchy first paragraph in his opinions to grab the reader's attention. Kaufman played the media well, never issuing opinions on Friday and having his clerks drop off copies in the press room. In 1979, with his term as chief judge due to expire, he unsuccessfully lobbied the Senate to raise the age maximum for chief judges to seventy-five. Kaufman quoted Lincoln's comment about Chief Justice Salmon Chase that "Chase always knew he was indispensable to the country but just could not understand why the country did not realize it."

Short and with heavy jaws, a prickly personality, and a reputation as a stern taskmaster, Kaufman exerted his authority in court quickly and effortlessly. "He looks like a cross between a rabbinical student and an Army sergeant," Julius Rosenberg said upon first seeing him. Kaufman never escaped from the shadow of the Rosenberg case. He kept on his desk a card with quotations from the trial and, noted one friend, was "haunted by the thought that his obituary will read, 'Rosenberg Judge Dies.'" Kaufman wanted to be remembered instead for his staunch civil libertarianism and for issuing in *Taylor* v. *Board of Education* (1961) the first order desegregating Lincoln Elementary School in New Rochelle, New York, a predominantly black public school, on the grounds that the district had been drawn to keep the school nearly entirely black. On 23 June 1936 he married Helen Rosenberg after working in her father's law firm (she was not related to Julius or Ethel Rosenberg); they had three sons. Kaufman died of pancreatic cancer at the age of eighty-one.

★

Kaufman's papers are in the Library of Congress. Tributes include *Proceedings of a Special Session to Commemorate Twenty-*

Five Years of Federal Judicial Service by the Honorable Irving R. Kaufman (1 Nov. 1974), 508 F.2d lxiv and *In Memoriam: Honorable Irving R. Kaufman, Judge, United States Court of Appeals* (2 June 1992), 972 F.2d cvii. On the Rosenberg case, sources include Ronald Radosh and Joyce Milton, *The Rosenberg File: A Search for the Truth* (1983); Louis Nizer, *The Implosion Conspiracy* (1973); John Wexley, *The Judgment of Julius and Ethel Rosenberg* (rev. ed., 1977); Curt Gentry, *J. Edgar Hoover: The Man and the Secrets* (1991); and Vern Countryman, "Out, Damn Spot: Judge Kaufman and the Rosenberg Case," *New Republic* (8 Oct. 1977). Other sources include the *New York Times* (14 Apr. 1940, 9 Aug. 1948, and 6 Apr. 1951); Jeffrey B. Morris, *Federal Justice in the Second Circuit* (1987); Gerald Gunther, *Learned Hand: The Man and the Judge* (1994); Sheldon Goldman, *Picking Federal Judges: Lower Court Selection from Roosevelt Through Reagan* (1997); Oliver Pilat, "Rosenberg Case: Judge Kaufman's Two Terrible Years," *Saturday Evening Post* (8 Aug. 1953); and Irving R. Kaufman, "The Anatomy of Decisionmaking," *Fordham Law Review* (Nov. 1984). An obituary is in the *New York Times* (3 Feb. 1992).

ROGER K. NEWMAN

KAYE, Sylvia Fine (*b.* 29 August 1913 in Brooklyn, New York; *d.* 28 October 1991 in New York City), lyricist, composer, producer, writer, and teacher best known for writing humorous material performed by her husband, the comedian and actor Danny Kaye.

Fine Kaye was the eldest of three children of Samuel Fine, a dentist, and his wife, Bessie, a homemaker. They lived in the Flatbush section of Brooklyn, New York. Attracted to music at an early age, Fine Kaye started taking piano lessons at age seven and by age ten was taking music theory and harmony. She attended Thomas Jefferson High School in the Brownsville–East New York section of Brooklyn, taking two subways from her house to school. Superior academics at Jefferson convinced her parents to send her there even though she lived closer to Erasmus High School. Skipping three years ahead in school, Sylvia was president of her class and assistant editor of the school newspaper, the *Liberty Bell,* for which she wrote a weekly humor column, and also wrote for the school musical. She graduated in 1929. Her future husband—then known as David Kaminski—attended Thomas Jefferson too, but they did not meet until later.

She took courses at the Brooklyn branch of Hunter College, an academically respected women's college in Manhattan, but graduated in 1933 from Brooklyn College, with a B.A. degree in music. While in college, she wrote both the lyrics and music for George Bernard Shaw's *Arms and the Man*. Her cousin, the novelist Irwin Shaw, wrote the libretto. She also wrote the music for the Brooklyn College alma mater and penned a humor column for the college

Sylvia Fine Kaye with her husband Danny Kaye, 1950. © BETTMANN/CORBIS

paper, gleaning inspiration from Dorothy Parker and Ogden Nash.

After graduation she gave piano lessons and worked for Keit-Engle, a music publishing house where she wrote songs, none of which were published. She was also a writer for *Ed Sullivan's Headliners* (1934), a musical short film. During the summer of 1939 she worked in Stroudsburg, Pennsylvania, at Camp Tamiment, a summer resort known for attracting young theatrical hopefuls. Each week she wrote new numbers for the skits performed by Imogene Coca, Max Liebman, and Danny Kaye. Fine Kaye began writing specialty material for Kaye, including a Yiddish version of Gilbert and Sullivan's *Mikado*. She was able to try out her songwriting skills when she wrote two numbers for *The Straw Hat Review* featuring Coca and Kaye, which opened on Broadway in September 1939 and closed after ten weeks.

She married Danny Kaye in a civil service 3 January 1940 in Fort Lauderdale, Florida, and they held a religious ceremony in a Brooklyn synagogue later that year. Their only child was born in December 1946. The couple spent their married life living on both coasts, having a house in Beverly Hills, California, and an apartment in Manhattan. Danny Kaye often said that he was "a wife-made man" and that he had "a Fine head on his shoulders." This spoke

volumes about the working relationship of this husband-and-wife team. Fine Kaye was the writer of Kaye's material, critiquing his performances almost ruthlessly while refining his unique talent to pure gold.

In 1940 Fine Kaye became a nightclub performer, accompanying her husband at La Martinique in New York City, where she wrote the music and lyrics for the material he presented. Cole Porter's musical *Let's Face It* (1941) included Kaye in the cast and offered the opportunity for Fine Kaye to introduce some of her material in the show. Her song "Melody in 4-F" proved to be a showstopper.

When Kaye was commissioned to make the film *Up In Arms* (1944) in California, Fine Kaye signed with Samuel Goldwyn as a writer of special material for Kaye. In 1952 she and her husband formed Dena Productions, organized to be a complete moviemaking operation. *Knock on Wood* (1954) was its first production.

Having written more than 100 songs for her husband, she coproduced and wrote film scores for *The Inspector General* (1949), *Knock on Wood* (1954), and *The Court Jester* (1956), all featuring Kaye. She wrote the words and music for songs in several of Kaye's films, including *Wonder Man* (1945), *The Kid from Brooklyn* (1946), and *The Secret Life of Walter Mitty* (1947). Her songs ranged from fast-paced, tongue-twisting patter numbers such as "Anatole of Paris" and "The Nightmare Song" from the opera *Iolanthe* to the tender "Lullaby in Ragtime" from the film *The Five Pennies* (1959). Cole Porter described her song "All About You" (from *Knock on Wood*) as "a perfect love song." Two of Fine Kaye's songs were nominated for Academy Awards: "The Moon is Blue" (1953), with music by Herschel Burke Gilbert, and "The Five Pennies," both lyrics and music by Fine Kaye. She was associate producer in the latter production.

In the 1970s, Fine Kaye taught classes in musical comedy at the University of Southern California (1971) and at Yale University (1975). In 1979 she produced and narrated the Peabody Award–winning PBS television program *Musical Comedy Tonight,* which was based on her course. As executive producer for the television production *Danny Kaye: Look-in at the Metropolitan Opera* (1975), Fine Kaye won an Emmy for Outstanding Children's Entertainment Special. She also produced and edited *Assignment Children* (1955), a UNICEF short film starring her husband.

Longtime supporters of the arts in Los Angeles as well as in New York, the Kayes were grand patrons of the Los Angeles Music Center, contributing more than $1 million; Fine Kaye continued to be a major financial supporter after Kaye's death in 1987. After his death, Fine Kaye presented Hunter College with a $1 million gift to renovate its 660-seat theater as the Sylvia and Danny Kaye Playhouse, which reopened in 1990. The couple also endowed the orchid collection at Brooklyn Botanic Garden. Brooklyn College awarded her an honorary doctorate of humane letters in 1985 for outstanding achievements in television and motion-picture production and her contribution to music. She endowed the Sylvia Fine Chair in Musical Theater there in 1991.

Fine Kaye died at age seventy-eight of emphysema. A memorial bench to Danny Kaye and Sylvia Fine Kaye is in Kensico Cemetery in suburban Valhalla, New York.

A child of immigrant parents, Fine Kaye made significant contributions in the area of musical comedy and the arts. Her philanthropic support of theater education continues to leave a legacy to future students of the arts.

★

Fine Kaye's musical-comedy collection is in the Library of Congress, Music Division, Washington, D.C. Additional biographical material is at the New York Public Library, Research Division, Jewish Division. There is no book-length biography of Fine Kaye; however, a great deal of biographical information is included in her husband's biography by Martin Gottfried, *Nobody's Fool: The Lives of Danny Kaye* (1994). An obituary is in the *New York Times* (29 Oct. 1991). An oral history tape of American Jewish Women of Achievement, housed in the Jewish Division of the New York Public Library, contains an interview with Fine Kaye.

CONNIE THORSEN

KEELER, Ruby (*b.* 25 August 1909 in Halifax, Nova Scotia, Canada; *d.* 28 February 1993 in Rancho Mirage, California), dancer and actress known for her starring roles on Broadway and in Warner Brothers musicals.

Keeler was born Ethel Hilda Keeler, the second of the five children of Ralph Keeler, a grocer, and Elnora ("Nellie") Leahy, who also worked in the family-owned grocery store. In 1913 the family moved to the East Side of New York City, where Keeler's father drove a truck for the Knickerbocker Ice Company and her mother became a homemaker. Keeler attended a Roman Catholic grammar school and later the Professional Children's School. She also received private dancing lessons in exchange for teaching dance classes for elementary schoolchildren.

Keeler danced briefly in the chorus of George M. Cohan's *The Rise of Rosie O'Reilly* in 1923, then joined a hotel floor revue. After winning first prize in a dance contest, she worked in Manhattan at the El Fey nightclub run by Texas Guinan. Her dancing attracted the attention of the Broadway producer Earl Lindsay, who cast her in *Bye Bye Bonnie* in 1927. She then appeared in *Lucky* and *The Sidewalks of New York* that same year, and in 1928 Florenz Ziegfeld signed her as the chief tap dancer for *Whoopee!* Before starting rehearsals, Keeler went to Hollywood to appear in live musical prologues for Loew's theaters and to make a pro-

Ruby Keeler in a publicity shot for *Anchors Aweigh*. THE KOBAL COLLECTION

motional film for Fox Movietone sound equipment. A cute, full-faced brunette with short, bobbed hair, Keeler projected a wide-eyed look of natural innocence and naïveté that contradicted her nightclub experience.

While in Hollywood Keeler met the singer Al Jolson, who was then Broadway's biggest star. Jolson, twenty-three years older than Keeler and twice divorced, began courting her. They married in suburban Port Chester, New York, on 21 September 1928 and adopted a son in 1935. After her honeymoon Keeler joined rehearsals for *Whoopee!* but, at Jolson's request, left the show before it opened. Ziegfeld offered Keeler a leading role in his next production, *Show Girl,* which opened in New York on 2 July 1929. She left the show soon after it opened, again at Jolson's insistence, to live at his Hollywood home. After she moved there, however, Jolson spent most of his time in New York, starring in Broadway shows and having affairs with other women.

Warner Brothers asked Keeler to play the lead female role in *42nd Street* (1933), a major musical involving complex dance numbers choreographed by Busby Berkeley. Keeler was the star dancer in the "Shuffle Off to Buffalo" and "42nd Street" production numbers. Critics and the public loved her work with her costar Dick Powell, although she later described herself as "a scared rabbit in *42nd Street*" and recalled, "I knew I wasn't an actress but figured all I had to do was say lines like, 'What?' 'Who?' 'When?' "

Warner Brothers paired Keeler and Powell in several other musicals, often with choreography by Berkeley and songs by Harry Warren and Al Dubin, including *Gold Diggers of 1933* (1933), *Footlight Parade* (1933), *Dames* (1934), and *Flirtation Walk* (1934). The movies had almost interchangeable plots but were wildly successful with audiences seeking fantasy to escape from the Great Depression. A later documentary filmmaker noted, "She represented all that was grand, all that was enjoyable in life at a time when life wasn't that great." Keeler's naive innocence was perfectly complemented by Berkeley's kaleidoscopic, surreal, and frequently erotic dance numbers. Keeler later recalled, "With Berkeley directing, I never knew whether I'd be sprouting out of a flower or dancing on a piano."

In 1935 Keeler and Jolson appeared in their first and only movie together, *Go into Your Dance*, a First National production. Its success led the studio to suggest a sequel, but Jolson declined, fearing he'd lose top billing as part of a husband-and-wife team. Keeler later recalled: "Al was called the greatest entertainer in the world. I know that was true because he told me so—many times."

Keeler was paired again with Powell in *Shipmates Forever* (1935) and *Colleen* (1936). Her final musical was *Ready, Willing and Able* (1937), in which Keeler and her partner Lee Dixon danced on the keys of a giant typewriter. She insisted that this was her favorite dance scene despite the fact that "it was difficult jumping from key to key doing wing-and-taps, and I'd get charley horses in my legs from dancing on those footstools."

Jolson argued with Warner Brothers concerning his contract terms, left the studio, and took Keeler with him. Her next film, *Mother Carey's Chickens* (1938) for RKO Studios, was a drama and did not do well at the box office. *Sweetheart of the Campus* (1941), which Keeler made for Columbia, was also unsuccessful. She said, "It was so bad I had no regrets about quitting."

Keeler and Jolson separated in 1939 and divorced on 27 December 1940. A year later, on 29 October 1941, Keeler married John Homer Lowe, a prominent Los Angeles businessman and real estate developer. Keeler retained custody of her adopted son and had four children with Lowe. When Columbia Studios prepared to film *The Jolson Story* in 1946, Keeler's feelings about Jolson were still so strong that she refused to allow use of her name in the movie. She told the producer Sidney Skolsky, "I don't want my children to grow up and know I was married to a man like that."

For the next three decades Keeler focused her attention on raising her family and made only occasional guest appearances on television and the stage. Among them were *The Greatest Show on Earth* in 1964, *Hooray for Hollywood* in 1964, a summer stock revival of *Bell, Book and Candle*

in 1968, *The Rowan and Martin Special* in 1973, and *Glitter* in 1984. Keeler also appeared as an uncredited extra in the movie *They Shoot Horses, Don't They?* (1969) and had a brief cameo in *The Phynx* (1970).

Although Keeler had not starred in any films for several decades, her work gained attention in the late 1960s. College students began a craze for Berkeley films, whose dance numbers were then viewed as psychedelic or "the MTV of the 1930s." The New York Museum of Modern Art sponsored a Berkeley film festival in 1965, and Keeler appeared as a guest lecturer in New York, San Francisco, and London. She charmed audiences by stating disarmingly: "It's amazing. I couldn't act. I had that terrible singing voice, and now I can see, I wasn't the greatest tap dancer in the world either."

Lowe died in 1969, and shortly afterward the producer Harry Rigby asked Keeler to join a revival of the 1925 musical *No, No Nanette*. She was initially reluctant, but her children persuaded her to accept. "We didn't want her to turn into a golf widow," her son later said. "We thought the show would give her something to do." The show was choreographed by Berkeley and also starred Patsy Kelly, Keeler's long-time friend. Keeler played the role of Sue and tap danced in two show-stopping numbers, "I Want To Be Happy" and "Take a Little One-Step." Keeler's son also joined the production as assistant stage manager.

The show opened on Broadway in New York City on 19 January 1971 and was a huge success. Critics singled out Keeler for special attention, and ABC's John Schubeck called her "the entertainment comeback of the century." She won the Catholic Actors Guild's George M. Cohan Award in 1971 and the Harvard Hasty Pudding Award in 1972.

Keeler stayed with the show during its entire two year Broadway run of 871 performances. She subsequently starred in its nationwide tour for another two years but dropped out after developing a cerebral aneurysm in 1974. Initially paralyzed, she spent several months in physical therapy learning to walk and talk again. She never danced professionally after her stroke, but she appeared in a Disney video series, *Just You and Me, Kid,* volume 4 (1985), about parent-child relationships. She also had a cameo in *Beverly Hills Brats* (1989).

Keeler remained in the public eye, giving lectures about Berkeley films on cruise ships and appearing as a spokesperson for the National Stroke Association, which established the Ruby Keeler Fellowship Memorial after her death from cancer. She is buried at Holy Sepulchre Cemetery in Orange County, California.

Keeler is a major figure in the pantheon of American movie musical stars, and her fame is matched only by Fred Astaire, Ginger Rogers, and Gene Kelly. Unlike the other three dancers and virtually every other movie star, Keeler was not driven by a need to achieve fame. Her friend Theresa Lane noted, "She got big in spite of herself." Keeler began performing only to help her family escape poverty and, once this goal was achieved, could discard her stardom without any regrets. She gave her highest priority to creating her own happy family and finally succeeded during her second marriage.

★

The Billy Rose Theatre Collection of the New York Public Library for the Performing Arts at Lincoln Center has a file of magazine and newspaper clippings about Keeler. Interviews with Keeler are in John Gruen, *Close-Up* (1968); and Cass Werner Sperling and Cork Millner, *Hollywood Be Thy Name: The Warner Brothers Story* (1994). Nancy Marlow-Trump, *Ruby Keeler: A Photographic Biography* (1998), is the only book-length study. Keeler is discussed in David Shipman, *The Great Movie Stars: The Golden Years* (1970); Don Dunn, *The Making of* No, No Nanette (1972), which discusses the nostalgia craze; Sidney Skolsky, *Don't Get Me Wrong—I Love Hollywood* (1975), which describes the incident regarding *The Jolson Story;* Tony Thomas, *That's Dancing!* (1984); Herbert G. Goldman, *Jolson: The Legend Comes to Life* (1988); Rusty E. Frank, *Tap! The Greatest Tap Dance Stars and Their Stories, 1900–1955* (1994); and Ollie Mae Ray, "Biographies of Selected Leaders in Tap Dance," Ph.D. diss., University of Utah (1976). Obituaries are in the *New York Times* and the *Washington Post* (both 1 Mar. 1993) and *Variety* (8 Mar. 1993). Chuck Stewart directed a documentary video, *Ruby Keeler: The Queen of Nostalgia* (1998).

Stephen G. Marshall

KEMENY, John George (*b*. 31 May 1926 in Budapest, Hungary; *d*. 26 December 1992 in Lebanon, New Hampshire), mathematician and president of Dartmouth College who was a codeveloper of the Dartmouth computer time-sharing system and a cocreator of the BASIC computer programming language.

Kemeny was one of two children of Tibor Kemeny, a commodities export-import broker, and Lucy Fried, a homemaker. For three and a half years, while in gymnasium (secondary school) in Budapest, Kemeny had the good fortune of studying with an excellent mathematics teacher who, he later stated, was qualified to teach at the college level. Since the Kemenys were Jewish, Tibor felt threatened after the Nazis marched into Vienna. He left for the United States in 1938 and sent for his wife and children in 1940. John Kemeny, who had not heard a word of English before 1939, attended George Washington High School in New York City from 1940 to 1943. He graduated first in his class of about 1,000 students but stated that the mathematics instruction in high school was woefully inadequate.

In February 1943, at the age of sixteen and a half,

Kemeny entered Princeton University, where he studied both mathematics and philosophy. The United States was deeply involved in World War II at that time, and both the students and the younger faculty were subject to the draft. Consequently, Kemeny's undergraduate mathematics teachers were senior members of the department and all luminaries in their specialties.

In 1945 Kemeny became a naturalized U.S. citizen. His undergraduate work was interrupted when he was drafted into the U.S. Army. He spent one and one-half years (1945–1946) working under the direction of Richard Feynman as an assistant in the Theoretical Division of the Manhattan nuclear project at Los Alamos, New Mexico. There he met a fellow Hungarian, John von Neumann, and had his first contact with the ideas that led to the development of the modern computer. Kemeny was a member of a team of some twenty people whose task was to run seventeen IBM bookkeeping machines in three shifts for twenty-four hours a day, six days a week. They were to solve partial differential equations numerically by feeding about fifty punched cards into a machine, getting a partial result, and manually feeding the new cards into the next machine. It took two to three weeks to get a solution in this manner, but no faster alternative existed.

Kemeny returned to Princeton in 1946 to resume his undergraduate studies and to work as a teaching and research assistant. Elected to Phi Beta Kappa, the national honor society, he received his B.A. summa cum laude in 1947. While continuing his studies in mathematics and philosophy at the graduate level, Kemeny was selected to serve as a research assistant to Albert Einstein at the Institute for Advanced Study at Princeton. Kemeny stated that, although Einstein was very good at mathematics, he needed an assistant because he was not up to date on current mathematical research. In addition, the computations that Einstein was working on were extremely long, and if he and his assistant came up with the same answer, Einstein could be fairly sure it was correct.

Kemeny received his Ph.D. in 1949 at the age of twenty-three. His supervisor was America's most eminent logician, Alonzo Church. The title of his thesis was *Type-Theory versus Set Theory*. Kemeny had enough credits for a master's degree in philosophy, but because of his work with Einstein he did not have time to study for the general examination. In 1950 Kemeny married Jean Alexander; they had two children.

Kemeny accepted his first full-time teaching position as an assistant professor of philosophy at Princeton in 1951. He taught both philosophy and mathematics at Princeton until 1953, when he was invited to become a full professor in the Mathematics and Philosophy Departments at Dartmouth College. At that time the Mathematics Department at Dartmouth was not considered a center of excellence,

John G. Kemeny inspecting a switch panel in the nuclear plant that released radiation during the accident at Three Mile Island, 1979. © BETTMANN/CORBIS

since it recently had been decimated by the retirement of most of its senior members. Kemeny was expected to create a new mathematics program, which he did with great enthusiasm.

In 1955, at the age of twenty-nine, Kemeny became the chairman of the Mathematics Department, a position he held until 1967. He proceeded to build the department to prominence. He also served as a consultant to the Rand Corporation starting in 1953. His experience at Rand was the beginning of his serious interest in computers. During the summer of 1956 Kemeny noticed that many well-known mathematicians at Rand spent hours waiting for their turns at the computers to debug their programs. He sent a memo to the administrators suggesting that someone should devise a way to interrupt the computers to allow other users to test their programs, but no changes were instituted for quite some time.

Kemeny thought that knowledge of computing must be an integral part of a liberal education, but the existing languages were too difficult for the layperson to learn. With Thomas Kurtz, a colleague in the Dartmouth Mathematics Department, Kemeny created a new computer language, Beginners All-Purpose Symbolic Instruction Code (BASIC). First successfully run in 1964, BASIC was designed to be easy for beginners, to be interactive, to give clear and friendly error messages, to have simple editing procedures, and not to require technical knowledge of computer hardware or the operating system. A simple computer language

was not enough, and Kemeny and Kurtz devised the Dartmouth Time-Sharing System, one of the earliest methods for allowing multiple users to share the same mainframe computer. After the success of the time-sharing system in 1964, most Dartmouth undergraduates were required to learn and use BASIC and to have facility with the computer. Kemeny stated that one undergraduate in one afternoon on a 1970 time-sharing computer could solve all the differential equations his group had solved at Los Alamos in a year and still allow 100 other users to access the computer.

Kemeny was disturbed by the fact that mathematics was the only subject a student could study for fourteen years and not learn anything that had been done after 1800. To rectify this situation, Kemeny and J. Laurie Snell created a new undergraduate course called finite mathematics that included such topics as logic, matrix algebra, and probability.

In 1970 Kemeny became the thirteenth president of Dartmouth College. Almost immediately he initiated major reforms, including the admission of women, the recruiting of minorities, and a trimester system to facilitate a more efficient use of the facilities. Kemeny loved teaching and insisted that the board of trustees allow him to teach two courses a year during his presidency.

In 1979 President Jimmy Carter appointed Kemeny chairman of the Presidential Commission on the Accident at Three Mile Island, which became known as the Kemeny commission. The commission was to report on the most serious nuclear accident in the history of the United States, which had occurred on 28 March 1979 at the nuclear power plant at Three Mile Island in the Susquehanna River near Harrisburg, Pennsylvania. Radioactive gas had leaked into the building; fortunately, very little was released into the atmosphere. The final report of the commission was highly critical of federal regulators and the nuclear power industry for lax safety standards.

Kemeny resigned as president of Dartmouth in 1981 to return to full-time teaching and research. He wrote or co-authored twelve books, including *A Philosopher Looks at Science* (1959); with Kurtz, *BASIC Programming* (1967); with Snell and Gerald L. Thompson, *An Introduction to Finite Mathematics* (1957); and *Man and the Computer* (1972). In addition Kemeny published, often jointly, many technical papers in logic, philosophy, and mathematics and nontechnical articles for the *New York Times Magazine, Scientific American,* the *Nation,* and the *Encyclopedia Britannica.* Kemeny was the recipient of numerous honorary degrees and awards, including the Institute of Electrical and Electronic Engineers (IEEE) Computer Pioneer Medal in 1986.

Kemeny lived most of his life in Etna, New Hampshire. He died suddenly of a heart attack in Lebanon, New Hampshire, and was buried in the Dartmouth Cemetery in Hanover. Kemeny is deservedly remembered for his early recognition of the importance of the computer to society in general and for advocating its accessibility to the layperson.

★

Kemeny's presidential papers are in the Dartmouth College Library. Jean Kemeny has his other papers. Kemeny's *Man and the Computer* (1972) contains a vivid description of his early work with computers. Nardi Reeder Campion, "True Basic," *Dartmouth Alumni Magazine* (May 1993), is an homage to the personal side of Kemeny. Obituaries are in the *New York Times* (27 Dec. 1992), *Boston Globe* (27 Dec. 1992), and *Manchester Guardian* (4 Jan. 1993).

HOWARD ALLEN

KENDRICK, Alexander (*b.* c. 1911 in Philadelphia, Pennsylvania; *d.* 17 May 1991 in Philadelphia, Pennsylvania), print and broadcast journalist and author who served as CBS bureau chief in London and was known for his reporting of international events in the World War II and postwar years.

Kendrick was likely born in 1911, although sources are not definitive about the year. His parents were Russian immigrants who never learned to read or write English. Kendrick was one of four children; he had two brothers and a sister. He grew up in South Philadelphia and attended school there, graduating with honors from Central High School in about 1930.

Alexander Kendrick, 1950. © BETTMANN/CORBIS

Kendrick then worked for the *Philadelphia Public Ledger* for two years. After it folded, he moved to the *Philadelphia Inquirer,* which assigned him to its Washington bureau. At one point, all three Kendrick brothers worked for the *Inquirer;* one of them, Richard, was employed there for thirty-five years. In the late 1930s Kendrick won $4,000 in the Irish Sweepstakes and took a year off from the *Inquirer* to travel around the world. On this trip, he worked for a time on the *Honolulu Star-Bulletin.* On vacation in Russia, he met his future wife, Sarah Kunitz, a New York librarian. They had no children.

In 1940, while he was still employed with the *Inquirer,* Kendrick won a Nieman fellowship to Harvard for the 1940–1941 academic year. The recipients of this prestigious award were allowed to select from any of the available courses of study. Kendrick took classes in government, economics, and history. Other journalism awards made to Kendrick during his career came from the Overseas Press Club, the National Press Club, and the Society of Professional Journalists.

At the beginning of World War II, Kendrick covered the infamous Murmansk Run, the route of Allied freighters attempting to deliver supplies to the Soviet Union. He also reported war and political news from Russia. In August 1945 he was assigned to Washington, where he covered the end of the war. Subsequently, he reported from Vienna on Eastern Europe, Africa, and the Middle East.

Kendrick met the CBS vice president Edward R. Murrow in Rome soon after the war. He then joined Murrow as a radio and television correspondent at CBS, an affiliation that lasted until his retirement in 1975. In this capacity, Kendrick traveled widely, reporting on postwar politics and on the creation of the state of Israel in 1948. He was named London bureau chief and served in this capacity until 1965.

At this point Kendrick returned to Washington and continued reporting. The year 1969 marked the appearance of his biography, *Prime Time: The Life of Edward R. Murrow,* a thoroughly readable and authoritative source. *Prime Time* is enhanced by Kendrick's familiarity with his subject and by his understanding of Murrow's philosophy of communication. He illustrates Murrow's insistence that, while the media made it possible to distribute the message, that message had to be worth dispensing: "Otherwise, [Murrow] said, 'all you have is a lot of wires and lights in a box.'" The biography also presents Murrow's fascinating confrontation with Senator Joseph R. McCarthy, the U.S. senator who dominated the 1950s with his accusations of Communist infiltration of American institutions. Eric Goldman in the *New York Times Book Review* called the biography a "richly informed, incisive, pungent book, admiring and affectionate but not forgetting the Murrow canon that candor is a high form of devotion."

In 1974 Kendrick's second book, *The Wound Within: America in the Vietnam Years, 1945–1974,* appeared. This analysis presents an account of both the war and the war's effects on the United States. Quincy Howe, in a review of the book in *Commonweal* in 1975, wrote that *The Wound Within* "expands instant news analysis into instant history, bringing to bear on the recent past the immediacy of personal experience and on the immediate present the perspective of the veteran journalist."

Dan Rather, in his autobiography *The Camera Never Blinks: Adventures of a TV Journalist* (1977), written with Mickey Herskowitz, presents Kendrick as a man and a journalist of integrity. Rather was sent to London in 1965 to succeed Kendrick as bureau chief. Fred Friendly, president of CBS, made it clear that Rather would be following in a line of excellence that began with Ed Murrow and continued with Kendrick. Rather characterized Kendrick as an avid and careful reader who would never move on a story until he had done his homework. He also described his predecessor as kind and helpful, and as a "classic" foreign correspondent, a "straight talker, even blunt."

Kendrick retired in 1975, living in Philadelphia. He continued to keep abreast of international politics and became a staunch Phillies baseball fan. His wife, Sarah, died in 1981. Kendrick died a decade later at Hahnemann University Hospital, after suffering a heart attack.

In this day of "fast fare" reporting and instant biographies, Kendrick stands for journalistic quality. Dan Rather named him as one of Edward R. Murrow's "scholar-correspondents," a thoroughly prepared and appropriately objective reporter.

★

Biographical information on Alexander Kendrick's life and career is not abundant. The best discussion of him from both a personal and professional standpoint is in Rather's *The Camera Never Blinks* (1977). Reviews of *Prime Time* are in the *New York Times Book Review* (28 Sept. 1969) and *Times Literary Supplement* (14 May 1970). Reviews of *The Wound Within* are in the *New York Times* (24 Aug. 1974) and *Commonweal* (17 Jan. 1975). Obituaries are in the *New York Times* and the *Philadelphia Inquirer* (19 May 1991).

MARY BOYLES

KENDRICKS, Eddie James (*b.* 17 December 1939 in Union Springs, Alabama; *d.* 5 October 1992 in Birmingham, Alabama), tenor with the rhythm and blues (R&B) group the Temptations in the 1960s who struck out on a solo career in the 1970s.

Kendricks was one of five children born to Johnny and Lee Bell Kendrick (different spelling). Accompanied by his

Eddie Kendricks, 1960. CORBIS CORPORATION (BELLEVUE)

close childhood friend, Paul Williams, Kendricks left Alabama in 1956 and headed for Cleveland. The two boys followed in the tradition of southern black musicians who migrated in order to pursue their artistic dreams. Kendricks hoped to follow in the path of the "doo wop" groups that were gaining popularity in the 1950s. With that in mind, he and Williams combined efforts with two other young musicians, Kell Osbourne and Willy Waller, to form the Cavaliers. Minus Waller, they moved to Detroit to capitalize upon the burgeoning R&B scene in that city. There the trio became the Primes. In a clever act of showmanship they teamed with a female group for local bookings. The Primettes, as they were called, went on to become the Supremes.

In 1960 Kendricks and Williams merged with Otis Williams, Melvin Franklin, and Elbridge Bryant of the Distants, and the new group became the Elgins. They signed with the Motown label that year and soon thereafter were renamed the Temptations. With the replacement of Bryant (who left in 1963) by David Ruffin in 1964, the five musicians who constituted the classic lineup for the Temptations were in place. While the group survived many personnel changes in previous and subsequent years, the five remained together between 1963 and 1968 and were responsible for creating one of the most celebrated Motown acts.

R&B groups were plentiful on the Motown label, but the Temptations, aptly named indeed, possessed a special and compelling quality. They were athletic and dashing, yet romantic and seductive. Their dance moves as well as their harmonies were precise, smooth, and confident. According to Joe McEwen and Jim Miller in *The Rolling Stone Illustrated History of Rock and Roll,* "they could outdress, outdance, and outsing any competition in sight." (Kendricks was also in charge of the Temptations' wardrobe.) Kendricks's skillful and clear falsetto lent a distinctive quality to the Temptations' music, although he preferred to think of himself as a "roaming tenor." His voice punctuated the blend of gospel styles with pop sounds, and he communicated emotions richly and convincingly. The Temptations' first major hit, "The Way You Do the Things You Do," featured Kendricks and reached eleventh on the pop charts for 1964. Other hits such as "My Girl" (1965), "Get Ready" (1966), "I'm Gonna Make You Love Me, " a collaboration with Diana Ross and the Supremes (1968), and "Just My Imagination (Running Away with Me)" (1971) were marked by Kendricks's characteristic vocal touch. In 1968 Ruffin was voted out of the band after failing to show for a concert; he was replaced by Dennis Edwards.

As the 1960s unfolded and turbulent events affected cultural trends, popular music responded to audiences' desire for a more aggressive sound that included social commentary. Under the guidance of their second producer, Norman Whitfield (their first producer was Smokey Robinson), the Temptations responded to the popularity of "psychedelic soul" with hits such as "Ball of Confusion (That's What the World Is Today)" (1970) and "Psychedelic Shack" (1970). Although the group was at the height of its popularity, Kendricks did not like the direction the band was heading. "I don't dig those weird, freaky sounds," he stated. Far more comfortable with the group's original sound, Kendricks decided to leave the Temptations in 1971 after "Just My Imagination," the final hit recorded in the former style. In addition to creative differences within the group, there was increasing conflict and resentment among members.

Kendricks moved to the West Coast, determined to go alone. His solo career was patchy and proceeded down a variety of paths. His first two albums, *All by Myself* (1971) and *People . . . Hold On* (1972), failed to make a mark. His first solo hit was in 1973 with "Keep On Truckin'" from the album *Eddie Kendricks.* The single sold over 3 million copies and was number one on both the R&B and pop charts. *Boogie Down!* (1974) also produced a hit single. Another album in 1974, *For You,* demonstrated a change in style that submerged Kendricks's voice in a sea of vocal harmonies and gave rise to his third hit single, "Shoeshine Boy." *The Hit Man* (1975), *He's a Friend* (1976), *Going Up in Smoke* (1976), and *Slick* (1977) failed to produce any memorable singles. His next two albums, *Vintage '78* (1978) and *Something More* (1979) surrendered to the disco fad. Thus, Kendricks's years away from the Temptations witnessed prolific recording and a relatively successful solo career. Although his years on his own did not generate many hits, he was critically acclaimed as a performer. A review in the *New York Times* of a 1978 concert at the Apollo Theatre in Harlem noted his "impressive authority" and skill at giving "each word just the right emphasis while maintaining the illusion of a casual, almost speech-like delivery."

Kendricks returned to the Temptations for a reunion tour and album in 1982, when he reestablished the close musical and personal bond he had shared with former Temptation David Ruffin. The two performed at Live Aid in London and Philadelphia, toured with pop duo Hall and Oates and were featured on their album *Live at the Apollo* (1985). The ex-Temptations' album *Ruffin and Kendricks* (1988) was a nostalgic and successful collaboration representing the culmination of many years of creative partnership and complex friendship. The two were rivals who competed for the lead in the Temptations, but they were deeply connected. As one observer noted, their relationship was "impenetrable to outsiders and linked in steel," as was reflected in the intensity and excellence of their musical performances. They reunited once again with the rest of the Temptations in 1989 when the group was inducted into the Rock and Roll Hall of Fame. Ruffin died of a drug overdose on 1 June 1991.

Kendricks, who had been married to a woman named Patricia, by whom he had one daughter, suffered from his own medical problems in 1991 and had a lung removed due to cancer. He believed his illness was caused by thirty years of smoking. He succumbed to the disease on 5 October 1992. He is buried in Elwood Cemetery in Birmingham.

Kendricks was a southern African-American musician who migrated north in a period marked by expanding civil rights activism. He and the Temptations were part of a significant moment in American music history when different traditions and forms combined to create a sound that appealed across racial barriers. They were players in the trend that defined and excited a generation of young Americans. Kendricks was a gifted singer and fine performer who demonstrated flexibility and willingness to adapt to prevailing trends. While his solo career met with uneven results, the Temptations, however, would always be a powerful force in his creative and personal life: between 1963 and 1971 he was featured in twenty of their pop and R&B hits. It was with the Temptations that he achieved his first major success, and it was there that he celebrated his musical finale.

★

The Temptations are the subject of two books, both of which chronicle Kendricks's role in the group and on his own: Otis Williams with Patricia Romanowski, *Temptations* (1988), and Tony Turner with Barbara Aria, *Deliver Us from Temptation: The Tragic and Shocking Story of the Temptations and Motown* (1992). Other relevant accounts appear in Gerri Hirshey, *Nowhere to Run: The Story of Soul Music* (1984, rev. ed. 1994), and in Joe McEwen and Jim Miller, "Motown," *The Rolling Stone Illustrated History of Rock and Roll* (1976). Entries on Kendricks appear in *The African-American Almanac* (1994), *The Encyclopedia of Pop, Rock, and Soul* (1989), and *The Rolling Stone Encyclopedia of Rock and Roll* (1983). An obituary is in the *New York Times* (7 Oct. 1992).

LIANN E. TSOUKAS

KIRSTEN, Dorothy (*b.* 6 July 1910 in Montclair, New Jersey; *d.* 18 November 1992 in Los Angeles, California), lyric soprano, specializing in Puccini roles, who sang for thirty years with the Metropolitan Opera and was the first opera star to appear on the cover of *Life* magazine.

Kirsten was one of four children of George William Kirsten, a building contractor, and Margaret Irene Beggs, an organist and music teacher. The family had a musical background. Her grandfather, James J. Beggs, was a conductor and a bandmaster for Theodore Roosevelt's presidential campaigns as well as Wild Bill Cody's Buffalo Bill Band. Her great aunt Catherine Hayes, an opera singer, was known as the "Irish Jenny Lind."

Dorothy Kirsten, 1978. © IRA NOWINSKI/CORBIS

Early in life Kirsten knew she wanted to be on the stage, either as an actor or singing on Broadway. In high school she took classes in drama, dancing, and voice and continued piano lessons with her mother. To finance her dream of a career on Broadway, Kirsten left high school when she was sixteen to work as a demonstrator of Singer sewing machines and for the New Jersey Bell telephone company as a troubleshooter. She traveled to nearby New York City for dance lessons, believing in the importance of dance for body movement, and for voice lessons with Louis Darnay. During this time Eddie Albert and Grace Albert were studying voice at the same studio and befriended Kirsten. In 1938 they set up an audition for her at the Hearst radio station WINS that resulted in her first professional engagement as a singer. Her show was a fifteen-minute spot, five days a week, paying $5 a show, and featured songs from musicals and operettas.

J. E. "Dinty" Doyle, a columnist with the *New York Journal-American,* wrote flattering reviews of her voice that led to jobs on the *Kate Smith Show* and with the Ted Straeter Singers. But Doyle's biggest boost to Kirsten's career was introducing her to Grace Moore, a star of the Metropolitan Opera. On 30 March 1938 Moore told her to prepare two arias from *La Bohème,* Mimi's aria from Act I and Musetta's aria from Act II, and present herself at Moore's apartment to sing for her. Kirsten had never sung opera and until this moment had no plans to do so. The closest she had come to opera was operettas. Kirsten's audition was a success and Kirsten had found a mentor. Moore provided the financing for Kirsten to study in Rome with Maestro Astolfo Pescia. She sailed to Italy in March 1939. With Pescia's training, Kirsten's voice developed; her range was enlarged as was her volume.

The political situation in Europe, however, was becoming more serious, and Pescia's students began to leave Italy. For Kirsten, leaving was difficult. She sold all of her possessions, including clothing, to get passage money. Later Moore brought Pescia to the United States and Kirsten continued studying with him. Moore also arranged Kirsten's debut as a professional concert singer on 8 August 1940, in Newtown, Connecticut. She was a success. Moore also recommended her to the Chicago Opera Company. Kirsten auditioned for Henry Weber, General Director, who immediately engaged her for two seasons of supporting *comprimario* roles. Kirsten wrote in her autobiography that "Those days of learning in Chicago were probably the hardest work I have ever experienced while studying to be an opera singer."

Kirsten's operatic debut was in Chicago on 9 November 1940, playing the role of Poussette in Jules Massanet's *Manon*. Her performance was singled out by the critics. That year she played Flora in *La Traviata,* and Alisa in *Lucia di Lammermoor*. In total Kirsten sang seventeen different minor roles. The most exciting moment for Kirsten during her first season at Chicago was appearing with Grace Moore in *L'Amore dei Tre Re*. For the second year of her contract she was given larger roles: Nedda in *Pagliacci*, Musetta in *La Bohème,* and Michaela in *Carmen*. In 1941 Kirsten began classes with Ludwig Fabri, a strict disciplinarian. For one year he only allowed her to sing scales during the lessons. The second year he introduced arias by Mozart. Kirsten acknowledged that Fabri gave her "fine vocal technique" and focus, and worked with him until his death.

In the spring of 1942 Kirsten made her New York opera debut as guest artist with the San Carlo Opera at the Center Theater as Michaela in *Carmen,* and a week later in the lead role of Mimi in *La Bohème*. From that point concert dates, opera roles, and appearances on the radio, including the *Telephone Hour* and the *Prudential Family Hour*, followed. During the 1942–1943 season, in addition to singing with the Chicago Opera Company, she sang concerts in thirty-eight states. From September 1943 to September 1944 Kirsten had her own radio program, *Keepsakes*. In 1944 Kirsten sang with a number of orchestras and was engaged by the New York City Center Opera Company for roles in *Faust, La Traviata, La Bohème* and *Manon Lescaut*. Kirsten's debut at the Met was 1 December 1945, as Mimi in *La Bohème*. Before the performance Moore presented

Kirsten with a small ermine muff; she used it in Act IV that night and never sang as Mimi without it. Kirsten never forgot Moore's help and many kindnesses. When Moore died in an airplane crash in 1947 Kirsten sang Schubert's "Ave Maria" at the funeral.

Kirsten performed at the Met for the next thirty years, playing fourteen starring roles. She sang a total of 281 performances; most were Puccini operas. Kirsten was conscious of conserving her voice and would only sing roles she felt were right for her. She became a specialist in Puccini roles; she sang the part of Cio-Cio San in *Madama Butterfly* sixty-eight times at the Metropolitan Opera. In an interview with John Rockwell for *Opera News,* Kirsten stated that she liked Puccini's music best and that "it's the sexiest in the business."

A non-Puccini role she excelled in was Louise in the Gustave Charpentier opera of the same name. During the summer of 1947 she studied the role in Paris with the composer. She dedicated her first performance to Grace Moore since this was one of Moore's great roles. For the April 1966 gala celebration to bid farewell to the old Metropolitan Opera House, Kirsten sang "Depuis le Jour" from *Louise*.

In addition to engagements at the Met, Kirsten also sang for twenty-five years with the San Francisco Opera. She appeared in a number of opening-night performances and in the American premieres of Francis Poulenc's *Les Dialogues des Carmelites* and William Walton's *Troilus and Cressida*. She managed to achieve international fame, yet she only appeared on two tours outside of the United States. One was sponsored by the United States State Department in 1962; Kirsten, the first American soprano to sing in the Soviet Union, sang to huge, enthusiastic audiences. She made her second tour as a fill-in for the ailing Renata Scotto, who was to sing Mimi in the Met's tour of Japan. Although Kirsten officially retired from the Metropolitan Opera on 31 December 1975 at age sixty-five, with a gala performance of *Tosca,* she continued to sing when needed. In 1979 she flew in from California at the last minute to replace the ailing Leonie Rysanek in *Tosca*.

Kirsten's career also included radio, Broadway, television, and film. She never lost her affinity for singing popular music and appeared on the *Kraft Music Hour* with Al Jolson and Nelson Eddy, and *The Railroad Hour* with Gordon MacRae. For two years she starred with Frank Sinatra, who always called her "Diva," on *Light Up Time,* which aired five times a week. She sang everything from Cole Porter to Puccini; duets with Sinatra included "Old Fashioned Walk" and "People Will Say We're in Love." In her autobiography Kirsten states, "I learned more about how to sing a ballad or a popular song from Frank Sinatra than from anyone." She also appeared on Broadway and television and in two films, *Mr. Music* (1950) with Bing Crosby and *The Great Caruso* (1951) with Mario Lanza.

Kirsten described her recording career as a "big faux pas." She signed with Radio Corporation of America (RCA) in 1964 for five years, but RCA was not recording complete operas at that time. Columbia made promises and lured her away from RCA. The operas promised by Columbia never materialized, and Kirsten saw RCA pressing opera after opera with other sopranos singing her roles.

In January 1943 Kirsten married Edward MacKayes Oates, an executive with CBS. They first met when he was on staff at WINS when she was beginning her radio career. They divorced in 1949. Her second marriage, in 1951, was to Dr. Eugene R. Chapman, obstetrician and later Assistant Dean of the Medical School at University of California at Los Angeles (UCLA). He died in January 1954. In July 1955 she married Dr. John Douglas French, first director of the Brain Research Institute at UCLA. After it was discovered that he had Alzheimer's disease, she devoted the rest of her life to raising money to find a cure. She set up the French Foundation for Alzheimer's Research and, in 1985 the 148-bed Center for Alzheimer's Disease in Los Alamitos, California, was opened. She continued her efforts to combat Alzheimer's disease after French's death in 1989. Kirsten had no children.

A glamorous and gifted lyric soprano, Kirsten had a second successful career working to find a cure for and to ease the suffering of those with Alzheimer's disease. She was an individual who knew her own strengths and never forgot those, such as Grace Moore, who helped her become much more than a Broadway singer. Kirsten suffered a stroke on 5 November 1992 and died at the UCLA Medical Center.

★

A collection of Kirsten's scrapbooks, programs and videotapes is housed in Boston University's Mugar Library. Another primary source of information is Kirsten's autobiography, *A Time to Sing* (1982). Included in the book is a discography by Stanley A. Bowker. Books with significant chapters or sections on Kirsten include Lanfranco Rasponi, *The Last Prima Donnas* (1982); Schuyler Chapin, *Sopranos, Mezzos, Tenors, Bassos, and Other Friends* (1995); and Peter G. Davis, *The American Opera Singer: The Lives and Adventures of America's Great Singers in Opera and Concert, from 1825 to the Present* (1997). Periodical articles include Kirsten's reflections on her trip to the Soviet Union in "Diary of a Soprano," *Musical America* 82 (Apr. 1962): 56–57; an interview with John Rockwell, "Kirsten on Puccini," *Opera News* 6 (Mar. 1971): 21–23; and her farewell to the Met, "Farewell, Not Goodbye," *Opera News* 3 (Jan. 1976): 12–13. Tributes include Richard Dyer, "A Distinguished Voice Against Alzheimer's," *Boston Globe* (19 Nov. 1985), and Bruce Burroughs, ". . . al Fine," *The Opera Quarterly* 9.3 (Spring 1993): 215–18. Obituaries are in the *Los Angeles Times* and *New York Times* (both 19 Nov. 1992); *Washington Post* (20 Nov. 1992); London *Times* (21 Nov. 1992); and *Opera News* (30 Jan. 1993). An oral history interview with Sybil D. Hast, "La Voce Lirica-Spinto" (1990), is at the University of California at Los Angeles.

MARCIA B. DINNEEN

KORESH, David (*b.* 17 August 1959 in Houston, Texas; *d.* 19 April 1993 near Waco, Texas), leader of the Branch Davidian religious sect whose investigation by the federal government led to a controversial fifty-one day siege, ending in a deadly inferno.

Koresh was born Vernon Wayne Howell, the illegitimate son of fourteen-year-old Bonnie Clark, a high school dropout, and Bobby Howell, who left Clark shortly after the boy's birth. Koresh was raised primarily in Garland, a suburb of Dallas, where his mother worked cleaning building sites and married Roy Haldeman, a carpenter and bartender. Clark had a son named Roger with Haldeman, six years Koresh's junior. Koresh struggled in school, likely suffering dyslexia, and he afterward described himself as a teased, lonely child. He had ability with machines and enjoyed playing electric guitar. He left Garland High School during twelfth grade and worked in carpentry. He played in local rock bands and lived briefly in Los Angeles, seeking stardom.

As a boy, Koresh was introduced by his maternal grandmother to Seventh-Day Adventism. He felt religion deeply,

David Koresh, *c.* 1993. REUTERS/ARCHIVE PHOTOS

memorizing long biblical passages by age twelve and spending hours in passionate, sometimes tearful prayer. He later claimed to have conversed with God in his teens. Seventh-Day Adventism failed to satisfy Koresh's zeal, and in 1981, at age twenty-one, he joined a splinter community called the Living Waters Branch Davidian Seventh-Day Adventist Association. There were approximately 100 Branch Davidians residing at a rural compound named Mt. Carmel, outside Waco, Texas.

Mt. Carmel was founded in 1935 by an exiled Seventh-Day Adventist. The group shared the Adventists' trust in Christ's imminent return but believed that the church must first be purified. They sought to found a community of 144,000 true believers in Palestine, the eventual site, they believed, of God's earthly kingdom. Although membership typically numbered in the dozens, the group proselytized vigorously, and some 900 people lived at Mt. Carmel for a period during 1959. When Koresh joined, the community had a nearly fifty-year history of biblical literalism and acceptance of their leaders as living prophets.

When Koresh arrived, the sect was led by a sixty-seven-year old woman named Lois Roden. Impressed by Koresh's biblical command and devotion, Roden came to believe that he had been sent as Mt. Carmel's next prophet. The two began a sexual relationship, believing themselves ordained to bear children. Although Roden never conceived, by 1983 she recognized Koresh as her successor. That year, Koresh proclaimed himself the seventh, and final, messenger sent to herald Christ's return. This was a novel interpretation of traditional Seventh-Day Adventist belief in three divine messengers, foretold in the Book of Revelation, each of whom had played roles in the church's founding. Koresh preached of seven messengers, forging a powerful link between himself, Mt. Carmel's earlier leaders (the fourth, fifth and sixth messengers, he claimed), and the origins of Seventh-Day Adventism.

In January 1984 Koresh married Rachel Jones, the fourteen-year-old daughter of a lifelong Mt. Carmel resident. That spring, following a leadership dispute, Koresh moved with forty followers to Palestine, Texas. His preaching matured there, notably following a January 1985 trip to Israel, when he received a revelation at Mt. Zion. In an inspiration he called the "Cyrus message," Koresh saw himself ordained to follow King Cyrus of Persia, whose defeat of Babylon is chronicled in Isaiah. Koresh was called to vanquish modern Babylon, identified as the forces of government-at-large. Like Cyrus, he called himself a "messiah." He began taking multiple wives, many of whom were young teenagers, and taught that he should produce twenty-four children to fulfill scriptural prophecy. Koresh and his legal wife had one son, Cyrus, in early 1985, and two daughters, Star and Bobbie, in 1987 and 1990. He had twelve children with other women.

Lois Roden died in November 1986. Following a struggle with Roden's son, Koresh assumed leadership of Mt. Carmel in the summer of 1988. During this time, the basis of Koresh's final scriptural interpretations emerged, an apocalyptic extension of traditional Davidian beliefs, centered upon the Book of Revelation. Revelation speaks of a book bound with "seven seals" that must be opened by "the Lamb," a reference traditionally thought to mean Jesus Christ. Koresh developed elaborate scriptural logic demonstrating that "the Lamb" was instead a second Christ and preached that he was this figure. According to Revelation, opening the seals will bring the end of time and the triumph of God's kingdom. For Koresh, each seal would be opened through a literal event; it was his task to lead Mt. Carmel through the seals to Judgment Day. Together with the Cyrus message, these interpretations bred a unique radical millenarianism.

Mt. Carmel at this time was a large complex of white wooden buildings, including a chapel, gymnasium, living quarters, and offices, standing in acres of open field. Some 130 people resided there, ranging from infants to octogenarians. The community was diverse: roughly half were foreigners, from Australia, Canada, Israel, Mexico, the United Kingdom, and the Philippines, forty-five were African Americans, and twenty-five were Asian or Hispanic. They included dropouts like Koresh and several who held graduate degrees. Although children were schooled at Mt. Carmel, many adults held jobs in the surrounding area, and most visited Waco routinely. Koresh's leadership was founded on a seemingly inexhaustible ability to interpret scripture. Although he often preached in a tee shirt and jeans, sprinkled his sermons with coarse language, and sometimes struggled against stuttering, his biblical command and repeated revelations convinced followers that he was a true prophet. Acquaintances found Koresh friendly though not overly charismatic, but at Mt. Carmel, where his preaching resonated with half a century's devotion, his presence was literally inspirational.

Koresh led daily morning and evening services and sometimes taught Bible study for eight or more hours. Beginning in 1989, he preached celibacy for all residents except himself and enforced separate living quarters for men and women. That same year, he legally changed his name from Vernon Howell to David Koresh; "Koresh" is Hebrew for "Cyrus." He and a few followers amassed a paramilitary arsenal, to buttress their apocalyptic views and, through gun show sales, as a source of income. They stockpiled hundreds of weapons, including two dozen machine guns and a fifty-caliber cannon. Their transactions were legal, although their practice of converting semiautomatic firearms into automatic weapons was not.

The federal Bureau of Alcohol, Tobacco and Firearms (BATF) began investigating Koresh in June 1992, suspecting trafficking in illegal explosives. On 25 February 1993, the BATF obtained a search warrant for unregistered firearms. Three days later, about 9:30 A.M., some seventy BATF agents and three military helicopters stormed Mt. Carmel to serve the warrant. Koresh learned of the action minutes beforehand, and a three-hour gunfight ensued, claiming the lives of four agents and six Davidians. Koresh was wounded in the wrist and torso. A noontime truce allowed the BATF to collect casualties and retreat. That afternoon, the Federal Bureau of Investigation (FBI) relieved the BATF. Responsibility for the first gunfire was never established.

Inside Mt. Carmel, the assault held powerful significance. Events of past years had convinced the Davidians that they had progressed through the first four seals of Revelation. Opening of the fifth seal, as given in the Bible, would occur through the slaying of God's faithful, clearing the land for Christ's return in seals six and seven. The raid thus appeared to confirm Koresh's central preachings: Babylon had attacked Cyrus and the apocalypse had dawned.

A siege ensued, with 118 Davidians inside Mt. Carmel. FBI negotiators initially believed they could persuade Koresh to leave, but beyond releasing eighteen children in exchange for radio broadcasts of his preaching, he remained unmoved, claiming that God told him to wait. The standoff drew national attention, and pressure for resolution mounted quickly. Progress was hampered by poor coordination between the FBI's negotiators and hostage rescue team, who sometimes worked at cross-purposes. Indeed, the FBI inherited a tactical mess: Mt. Carmel was the Davidians' home and spiritual core; no government "rescue" could possibly outweigh Koresh's promise of salvation. Seventeen Davidians left during the standoff, mostly women and children whom Koresh instructed to leave.

As the siege dragged through its seventh week, U.S. Attorney General Janet Reno, persuaded by allegations of child abuse, authorized an assault to drive out the Davidians. During the same days, negotiations by religious scholars appeared to coax Koresh toward an alternative interpretation of Revelation, one enjoining a peaceful exit. Koresh began a biblical manuscript and announced he would surrender upon its completion. But officials doubted his intentions, citing previous broken agreements, and the assault occurred at 6:00 A.M. on 19 April, when specially equipped tanks smashed holes in the buildings and injected tear gas through the compound's walls. The maneuver continued for six hours, when fire ignited inside Mt. Carmel. Strong winds whipped the flames into a massive blaze. Fire trucks arrived within thirty minutes, but the dry wooden structures were consumed. Nine Davidians escaped. Seventy-four died inside, incinerated beyond recognition. Koresh and twelve others died of bullet wounds to the head, apparently self-inflicted. He was thirty-three years old.

Koresh was buried by relatives in an unmarked plot at the town cemetery in Tyler, Texas.

The events at Waco ignited nationwide controversy. Many viewed Koresh as a delusional con artist, polygamist, and statutory rapist and saw the Davidians as brainwashed cultists. The government was also pilloried. Congressional investigators faulted the BATF for not employing a less confrontational strategy, such as detaining Koresh while away from Mt. Carmel and serving the warrant in his absence. It came out that Koresh had invited agents to examine his weapons the previous summer, but they had neglected the offer, and the allegations of child abuse were disproven. It was charged that the BATF, facing budget curtailment, sought a dramatic operation, and it was shown that the raid proceeded despite clear knowledge that surprise had been lost. The final FBI assault, meanwhile, had no fire contingency, despite Koresh's apocalyptic rhetoric. Responsibility for the blaze appeared to fall upon the Davidians: film showed simultaneous ignition in three sections of the compound, recordings captured Davidians discussing the pouring of fuel in the final moments, and investigation cleared the FBI of using incendiary weapons. Surviving Davidians disputed this finding, and other evidence indicated that FBI actions could have inadvertently resulted in fire. Seven Davidians were convicted in 1994 of aiding voluntary manslaughter in the BATF deaths. A civil suit brought by surviving Davidians cleared the government of wrongful-death charges in 2000.

Poor planning and profound misunderstanding lay at the core of the Waco debacle. Compounding a weak investigation, the BATF launched a provocative invasion. Their failure set the stage for FBI frustration. Trained as tacticians not theologians, agents could never meaningfully engage Koresh nor comprehend the Davidians' beliefs. Pressure tactics only confirmed the conviction of people believing themselves to be fulfilling scriptural imperative. David Koresh was a polygamist and statutory rapist, and his arsenal included banned weaponry. Such crimes require investigation. Yet when they occur within a quiet community of long-established religious conviction, the First Amendment—indeed, the entire Bill of Rights—demands far greater care than was evident in the outcome at Waco.

★

Excellent studies of Koresh and the events at Mt. Carmel are given by Dick J. Reavis, *The Ashes of Waco* (1995), and James D. Tabor and Eugene V. Gallagher, *Why Waco?* (1995). The latter examines the Davidians' beliefs, while the former details the standoff, including evidence that the FBI may have inadvertently started the fire. The *Frontline* documentary *Waco: The Inside Story* (1995) examines the fifty-one day siege through interviews of BATF and FBI officials and provides extensive film footage. *The Dallas Morning News* has compiled its stories on the Davidians, accessible through the paper's Internet site. Scholarly essays may be found in James R. Lewis, ed., *From the Ashes: Making Sense of Waco* (1994), and Catherine Wessinger, ed., *Millennialism, Persecution, and Violence* (2000).

DAVID DIAZ

KOSINSKI, Jerzy Nikodem   (*b.* 14 June 1933 in Lodz, Poland; *d.* 3 May 1991 in New York City), Holocaust survivor, novelist, essayist, and critic.

When the Germans invaded Poland in 1939 Kosinski's parents, Mojzesz Lewinkopf, a translator of technical manuals for textile factories, and Elzbieta Liniecka, a concert pianist, placed their six-year-old son with a peasant woman near the Soviet border in hopes that their young Jewish son would have a better chance of surviving the Holocaust. The woman died, however, and Kosinski had to fend for himself for the next five years until he was recognized by a family friend at a Soviet camp for displaced children; reunited with his family, he met his adopted brother, Henryk, his only sibling.

Kosinski graduated from Stefan Zeromski High School in Lodz in June 1950. He received his master of political science degree in 1953 and his master of history degree in

Jerzy Kosinski. © JERRY BAUER

1955, both from the University of Lodz. From 1955 to 1957 he taught at the Polish Academy of Sciences in Warsaw. He also enlisted as a sharpshooter in the Polish army and studied in the Soviet Union. Meanwhile, photography became Kosinski's chief avocation, although fellow members of the Polish Photographic Society criticized his pictures of female nudes for lacking social import. In a grand hoax, Kosinski fabricated letters of recommendation from four nonexistent professors who urged that he be given a visa to the United States to accept a fictional foundation grant.

Arriving in New York City in 1957, Kosinski attended Columbia University with the support of a Ford Foundation grant (which he received after his arrival in the United States), earning his Ph.D. in sociology in 1964. During this period Kosinski published two books (under the pen name Joseph Novak) analyzing life in the Soviet Union under communism, *The Future Is Ours, Comrade* (1960) and *No Third Path* (1962). Allegations emerged that these books were actually penned by the Central Intelligence Agency as part of an anti-Soviet propaganda campaign, but no proof has ever surfaced to substantiate the charges. These two volumes brought Kosinski to the attention of Mary Weir, the wealthy widow of a steel magnate. They married on 11 January 1962 and divorced in 1966, two years prior to her death from brain cancer. They had no children.

With the success of his nonfiction, Kosinski turned his attention to fiction. *The Painted Bird* (1965), often considered his finest novel, traces a lost boy's struggle to survive during World War II in a surrealistic and gothic setting often compared to the art of Hieronymus Bosch. The novel is semiautobiographical, including a scene in which the protagonist drops a missal during Mass and becomes mute after being thrown into a dung heap as punishment. Kosinski became a U.S. citizen in 1965. He published both the nonfiction book *The Art of the Self* and the novel *Steps* in 1968; the latter won the National Book Award. Also in 1968 Kosinski met Katherina ("Kiki") von Fraunhofer, his constant companion whom he married on 15 February 1987. This marriage, too, was childless. Kosinski and von Fraunhofer narrowly escaped untimely deaths at the hands of Charles Manson's followers in Los Angeles in 1969: they were to visit Sharon Tate the weekend she and her houseguests were murdered, but Kosinski and von Fraunhofer remained in New York City when their baggage was misdirected from Paris. In the late 1960s and early 1970s Kosinski taught at Wesleyan, Princeton, and Yale Universities.

Kosinski's third novel, *Being There* (1971), tells the story of Chance, a man of little intellect who becomes an important political figure through the power of television. With these successes under his belt he served as president of PEN from 1973 to 1975. In addition, the 1970s witnessed the publication of four other novels: *The Devil Tree* (1973), *Cockpit* (1975), *Blind Date* (1977), and *Passion Play* (1979).

Pinball was published in 1982. These novels address the brute force of modern times in experimental and fragmented forms. Hal Ashby made *Being There* into a movie starring Peter Sellers, which was released in 1979; Kosinski won the best screenplay award from the Writers Guild of America. He played the role of Grigory Zinoviev in Warren Beatty's *Reds* (1981). Throughout these years Kosinski developed a reputation for eccentricity based upon his visits to South Bronx cockfights and Manhattan sex clubs, his penchant for strange disguises, and his appearances on Johnny Carson's *Tonight Show.*

On 22 June 1982 Geoffrey Stokes and Eliot Fremont-Smith published "Jerzy Kosinski's Tainted Words" in the *Village Voice* and accused the author of relying heavily on editorial assistants. The charges intimated that Kosinski was not really the author of his own works. Although the allegations were later discredited, Kosinski wrote *The Hermit of 69th Street* (1988) as a refutation against the attack and as a justification of his art; in it, the protagonist Kosky ("Kosinski without the 'sin,'" according to Kosinski) is accused of "telling stories." The novel ends with Kosky drowned at the hands of anonymous thugs.

Kosinski, who lived in an apartment on West Fifty-seventh Street in New York City, also had an apartment in New Haven, Connecticut, and an efficiency apartment in Crans, Switzerland. He enjoyed an extensive social life with the New York City jet set, as well as photography, skiing, and polo. Kosinski's health deteriorated as a consequence of an irregular heartbeat and medicine that left him groggy. After a party in New York City at the home of the writer Gay Talese in honor of Senator William Cohen of Maine, Kosinski committed suicide by tying a plastic bag over his head and lying down to die in his bathtub. His death thus proved true his 1979 statement that "I'm not a suicide freak, but I want to be free. If I ever have a terminal disease that would affect my mind or my body, I would end it." His body was cremated in accordance with his wishes. Beyond his writing work, Kosinski helped establish Amerbank, a Polish-American bank in Warsaw that opened one week after he died.

Critical debate still rages over Kosinski's literary merits. Nonetheless, he was one of the first to write about the Holocaust in fiction. Furthermore, although many readers trace a waning in artistic strength through the course of his career, *The Painted Bird, Steps,* and *Being There* place him on a highly elevated position from which to decline.

★

Biographies of Kosinski include Norman Lavers, *Jerzy Kosinski* (1982), and James Park Sloan, *Jerzy Kosinski: A Biography* (1996). Collections that address both Kosinski's life and literature include Tom Teicholz, ed., *Conversations with Jerzy Kosinski* (1993), and Barbara Tepa Lupack, ed., *Critical Essays on Jerzy Kosinski* (1998).

Gloria L. Cronin and Blaine H. Hall, *Jerzy Kosinski: An Annotated Bibliography* (1991), is an excellent source for additional materials. John Taylor, "The Haunted Bird: The Death and Life of Jerzy Kosinski, *New York* (15 July 1991), provides a moving obituary, as does the *New York Times* (4 May 1991). *Jerzy Kosinski on Fiction: Lecture on Fiction as a Personal and Social Protagonist* is a 1972 sound recording released by the Center for Cassette Studies.

TISON PUGH

KURTZMAN, Harvey (*b.* 3 October 1924 in Brooklyn, New York; *d.* 21 February 1993 in Mount Vernon, New York), cartoonist best known for creating *Mad* magazine.

Kurtzman was one of three children of David Kurtzman, a jeweler, and Edith Sherman, a homemaker. His father died when Kurtzman was young. His mother married Abe Perkes, an engraver. Kurtzman became interested in comics at an early age, and he scoured his neighbors' discarded newspapers to find comics not included in the paper his family received. He was a bright student and graduated in 1939 from the High School of Music and Art, a special New York City public school in Manhattan for the most artistically talented students in the city. At the school he met and became friends with several other artists who became lifelong collaborators.

After graduation Kurtzman worked for Louis Ferstadt, a portrait painter who also drew for comic books. At night Kurtzman attended the Cooper Union for the Advancement of Science and Art in Manhattan, but he dropped out after a year. While working for Ferstadt, Kurtzman learned the skills of the comic book trade, including drawing, inking, and coloring.

Drafted into the army in 1942, Kurtzman was assigned draftsman duties and served his term in the United States, where he continued to moonlight as a cartoonist. After World War II he moved back to New York City and formed the Charles William Harvey Studio with his high school classmates Will Elder and Charles Stern. They pursued commercial drawing and illustration work.

During the 1940s Kurtzman's first regular client was Marvel Comics, publisher of *Superman* and many other well-known comics. The editor Stan Lee purchased a series of one-page humorous comics called "Hey Look!" that he included in many superhero comic books. The ongoing work changed Kurtzman's life as he came to know many of the best cartoonists of the time. He also met Adele Hasan, a proofreader, whom he married in 1948. They had four children.

The "Hey Look!" comics impressed William Gaines at EC Comics when Kurtzman approached him for work in 1949. Kurtzman began drawing for EC's horror and science fiction comics, and when he demonstrated that he could write as well as draw, Gaines made him the editor of two new war comics, *Two-Fisted Tales* and *Frontline Combat*. Kurtzman wrote, edited, and produced some art and covers for the comic books, developing a close working relationship with the artists Elder, Wally Wood, Jack Davis, and John Severin, considered among the best in their field. Kurtzman's war comics were unlike any other in that they avoided stereotypes of good and evil and were heavily researched. Although Kurtzman was shorter than average and physically unimpressive, he was intensely charismatic, inspiring many artists to achieve their best work while working for him.

In 1952 Kurtzman, inspired by college humor magazines and the desire to earn more money, proposed to Gaines a new comic book that would lampoon the comics themselves. The first issue of *Mad* was published in October, and the cover read "Tales Calculated to Drive You MAD—Humor in a Jugular Vein." This first issue spoofed crime, horror, and science fiction comics, and the art was by Kurtzman's war comics team. By the fourth issue *Mad* reached its audience and began a steady climb in popularity.

Soon Kurtzman's satiric range included other aspects of American life, fine art, television, and advertisements. When some ad parodies offended *Mad*'s advertisers, Gaines simply decided to eliminate ads from the comic book, ensuring Kurtzman's ability to take aim where he wished.

For two and a half years Kurtzman pushed the limits of what a comic book could be aesthetically and conceptually. *Mad*'s covers mimicked composition books, racing forms, mail-order catalogs, and *Life* magazine. The work inside incorporated photographs, incomprehensible text from foreign newspapers, and some of the best artwork appearing in comics. In 1955, having taken the form as far as he could, Kurtzman, with Gaines's backing, transformed *Mad* from a ten-cent comic book to a twenty-five cent, typeset, illustrated magazine, black and white, but on better paper with better printing. The boy who became Alfred E. Neuman first appeared in *Mad* magazine in 1955. Kurtzman, ever the scavenger of popular culture, found the face on an old postcard along with the motto "What, me worry?"

After four successful issues, Kurtzman was hired by Hugh Hefner to start a new, all-color humor magazine called *Trump*. Although successful, *Trump* lasted only two issues, after which Kurtzman founded *Humbug*, a magazine funded by Kurtzman and his crew of artists. From 1960 to 1965 Kurtzman and his assistants Terry Gilliam and Gloria Steinem produced *Help!*, a magazine that pioneered the photo funny and included the first published work of the underground cartoonists R. Crumb, Jay Lynch, and Gilbert Shelton.

From the 1960s into the 1980s Kurtzman and Elder contributed to *Playboy* the ongoing satirical cartoon "Little Annie Fanny," the most lavishly produced comic strip in the United States. Kurtzman taught cartooning at the School of Visual Arts in Manhattan, New York, and continued to produce a number of comic books. In 1967, inspired by his autistic son Peter, Kurtzman helped found Clear View School for emotionally handicapped children in suburban Briarcliff Manor, New York. He remained involved with this school over the years. Kurtzman continued to create cartoons, which he collected in *Kurtzman Komix* (1976) and, with Elder, *Goodman Beaver* (1984). Kurtzman died from complications of liver cancer on 21 February 1993 at his home in suburban Mount Vernon, where his ashes were scattered.

Kurtzman was among the most innovative cartoonists of the 1950s and was one of the best cartoonists of the twentieth century. *Mad* was a new kind of humor that reflected the exaggerations and hypocrisies of mass media and society during a time that demanded conformity. *Mad* was available to children and adults nationwide and was one of the few antidotes to the cultural status quo. *Mad*'s format was a model to the underground comics of the 1960s, which were also black and white, without ads, and scorned the Comics Code. Although Kurtzman was not well known to the public at large, he influenced several generations of cartoonists, including Crumb and the Pulitzer Prize winner Art Spiegelman.

★

Kurtzman wrote an autobiography, *My Life as a Cartoonist* (1988). In his role as a teacher and comics historian he authored *From Aargh! to Zap! Harvey Kurtzman's Visual History of the Comics* (1991). The entire run of *Mad* comics has been reprinted in hardcover and annotated by Russ Cochran as *Mad* (1987). An excellent guide to Kurtzman's work is Glen Bray, *The Illustrated Harvey Kurtzman Index, 1939–1975* (1976). Maria Reidelbach, *Completely Mad: A History of the Comic Book and Magazine* (1991), contains a detailed description of the beginnings of *Mad*. An obituary is in the *New York Times* (22 Feb. 1993).

MARIA REIDELBACH

KUSCH, Polykarp (*b.* 26 January 1911 in Blankenburg, Germany; *d.* 20 March 1993 in Dallas, Texas), experimental physicist, educator, and academic administrator who won the Nobel Prize in physics in 1955 for his precision measurement of the magnetic moment of the electron that, along with related discoveries, furnished a fundamental piece of evidence leading to decisive advances in the theory of quantum electrodynamics.

Kusch was born to John Matthias Kusch and Henrietta van der Haas. His father was a Lutheran missionary who named his son after Saint Polykarp, a second-century

Polykarp Kusch, 1964. AP/WIDE WORLD PHOTOS

bishop and martyr whose feast day is 26 January, the day of Kusch's birth.

In 1912 the Kusch family came to the United States, moving to various locations in the Midwest before settling in Cleveland, where his father, after an unsettled period, secured a position with a book publisher. Kusch attended public schools in Cleveland and became a naturalized American citizen in 1922 at the age of eleven. After his high school graduation in 1927, he matriculated at Cleveland's Case School of Applied Science (later named Case Western Reserve University), intending initially to study chemistry and chemical engineering. His interests soon changed to physics and he graduated with a bachelor of science degree with a major in physics in 1931. Later in life he observed: "From the start I felt more adapted to physics than to something like engineering. To me engineering was a matter of cook books and heavy economic motivations."

Receiving a teaching assistantship from the University of Illinois, Kusch did graduate work in physics, receiving an M.S. degree in 1933 and a Ph.D. in 1936. His experimental work at Illinois involved optical spectroscopy under the direction of his dissertation adviser, F. Wheeler Loomis, an accomplished physicist in spectroscopic measurements of molecules. Optical spectroscopy was an area of classical physics that emphasized accurate measurements; within this field Kusch pursued a career with a special focus on precision. After obtaining his doctoral degree, Kusch joined the physics department at the University of Minnesota as a research assistant. There he became expert in a sphere of spectroscopic measurement known as mass spectroscopy. Unlike optical spectroscopy, in which atoms or molecules at rest interact with light of various frequencies, the mass spectroscopic technique directs a current of electrically charged atoms or molecules through a strong magnetic field, which causes the charged particles to bend to a greater or lesser degree, depending upon their mass. A detector such as a photographic film permits clear measurement of the particles because of their differences in deflection, even for particles having nearly the same mass—for example, isotopes of the same element.

Upon the recommendation of his Minnesota supervisor to the outstanding physicist I. I. Rabi (Nobel Prize, 1944), Kusch joined Rabi's group at Columbia University in New York City as an instructor in 1937. Rabi had pioneered development of the still more advanced spectroscopic method based on magnetic resonance. The essential foundation of this technique is that atomic particles having a spin angular momentum will precess (rotate about an axis as a consequence of external force) in a laboratory magnetic field somewhat analogous to the way a spinning top will precess in the earth's gravitational field. The precession frequency depends upon the frequency of the imposed oscillating magnetic field and on the spin frequency of the particle. In addition, the method requires the resonant absorption of short-wavelength or very high frequency radio waves that act upon the atomic particle. However, generators with the required radio frequencies and power in the microwave region of the electromagnetic did not exist at the beginning of Kusch's work at Columbia. The essential devices were developed during World War II by large scientific groups at Massachusetts Institute of Technology, Harvard, Columbia, and elsewhere, in connection with the construction of military radar systems. These wartime activities, although unrelated to fundamental nuclear research, were to make suitable instrumentation available later for Kusch's advanced postwar discoveries at Columbia.

During the war he spent a part of his time at the Westinghouse Electric Corporation (1941–1942), Columbia (1942–1944), and Bell Telephone Laboratories (1944–1946). The general thrust of his research at each of these locations was the development of improved radio frequency generators of variable high or microwave frequencies.

In 1946 Kusch returned to Columbia University as an associate professor of physics. He was promoted to full professor in 1949 and served as chairman of Columbia's physics department from 1949 to 1952.

In 1947 Kusch, with the assistance of a graduate student

and future colleague, Henry M. Foley, measured the magnetic moment of the electron. This was found to be larger by about one part in 1,000 from the value calculated by the English theoretical physicist Paul A. M. Dirac (Nobel Prize, 1933). Though a very small difference, this important result, coupled with the experimental investigations of Willis E. Lamb, Jr., on the structure of the hydrogen atom (also performed at Columbia University), led to Kusch and Lamb's sharing the Nobel Prize in physics in 1955.

In addition to his research, Kusch emerged as an exceptional teacher and academic executive. Besides serving as department chairman, Kusch was promoted to academic vice president and provost of the entire university from 1969 to 1972. In 1972 he took a position as professor of physics at the University of Texas in Dallas, where he retired as professor emeritus in 1982. Kusch's interests extended beyond physics to humanitarian concerns including problems of hunger, the plight of Soviet Jews wishing to emigrate, and the human costs of the Vietnam War.

In 1959 Columbia honored Kusch with its Great Teacher Award. Throughout his career he taught classes to freshmen and sophomore students. He made a point of preparing his undergraduate lectures as carefully as his advanced graduate seminars and his intricate experiments. He also received honorary degrees from eight colleges and universities, including the University of Illinois in 1961 and Columbia University, where he spent the years of his greatest scientific productivity, in 1983.

On 12 August 1935, while a graduate student at the University of Illinois, Kusch married Edith Starr Roberts, with whom he had three daughters. His wife died in 1959. The following year he married Betty Jane Pezzoni, with whom he had two daughters. Kusch suffered a series of strokes and died at his home in Dallas at the age of eighty-two.

The importance of Kusch's accomplishments was summarized by the presentation speech at the time of the Nobel award: "Your discoveries led to a re-evaluation and reshaping of the theory of the interaction of electrons and electromagnetic radiation, thus initiating a development of utmost importance to many of the basic concepts of physics."

★

Kusch's papers include "The Magnetic Moment of the Electron," *Physical Review* 74, no. 3 (1948): 250–263, with Henry M. Foley; and "Hyperfine Structure by the Method of Atomic Beams: Properties of Nuclei and of the Electron," *Science* 123 (1956). Richard P. Feynman, *QED: The Strange Theory of Light and Matter* (1985), is a reasonably accessible layperson's exposition of quantum electrodynamics theory that emerged in large part from the experiments of Kusch, his associates, and others. John S. Rigden, *Rabi: Scientist and Citizen* (1987), is a biography of I. I. Rabi, Kusch's mentor and senior colleague at Columbia; it furnishes an excellent description of the scientific environment in which Kusch did his Nobel Prize–winning research. An obituary is in the *New York Times* (23 Mar. 1993).

LEONARD R. SOLON

KUTNER, Luis (*b.* 9 June 1908 in Chicago, Illinois; *d.* 1 March 1993 in Chicago, Illinois), lawyer, author, and human rights advocate known for establishing the living will and co-founding Amnesty International.

Kutner was the son of Russian Jewish immigrants and had one sister. Health problems kept him out of school until he was nine. Comparing himself to the fictional protagonists Studs Lonigan and Augie March, Chicagoans of his era, Kutner wrote that he too sought most any job, from playing the piano at a hotel restaurant to stints as a professional wrestler, while working his way through high school and then the University of Chicago, which he entered at age fifteen, and finally its law school. Short assignments as a reporter for the *Chicago Herald and Examiner* and as an investigator for the Chicago Crime Commission, for which he observed judges to see if they carried out duties impartially, influenced his future career and, overcoming a youth of poverty, provided persistent inspiration.

Luis Kutner with the petition he would present to Eleanor Roosevelt for the release of William Oatis, an American detained in Communist Czechoslovakia on charges of espionage, 1952. © BETTMANN/CORBIS

During legal studies he served as a clerk for the famous attorney Clarence Darrow and was inspired by Roscoe Pound, dean of the Harvard Law School. His relationship with Pound grew through mutual concern for human rights, which was then a new notion in international law. In 1930 Kutner began practice on his own, inspired by deep concern for the indigent, many of whom were made so by the Great Depression. He wrote to federal judges James Wilkerson and Charles Woodward of his willingness to provide counsel and won releases in his first year for more than 100 men incarcerated illegally. Fees barely paid his expenses, but it was this pro bono work that attracted the attention of several small corporations, his main clients in later years. By 1934 he had achieved enough local renown to run for the U.S. House of Representatives as the youthful opponent of a political machine. Despite losing the race, Kutner credited the effort and resulting publicity with finally assuring a steady stream of clients.

Also in the 1930s Kutner began to develop the concept that became the "living will" four decades later. At that time, to refuse care to a critically ill patient was regarded as tantamount to euthanasia. Brain-damaged and other patients were sustained by doctors despite a family's request, written or otherwise, because the Hippocratic oath required it. Kutner felt that incapacitated individuals should have the right to guide their own medical care by means of a previously prepared document. With his gift for language and his abiding compassion, Kutner helped during years of effort to win the passage of federal and state legislation on the rights of critically ill patients.

Kutner was responding in part to medical advances that could prolong the life of patients suffering from what were previously fatal illnesses or injuries, and in part to an incident that touched him personally. The *New York Times* reported in Kutner's obituary that he had watched a close friend, Dr. George Thilo, die slowly and painfully as the result of a violent attack by muggers. Thilo had expressed to Kutner his wish not to be kept alive by "heroic measures." Public support of such restraint on the part of doctors came mainly from the Euthanasia Society, founded in the United States in 1938, which had had no success in changing prevailing opinion until Kutner voiced his new approach to what had been known as "voluntary euthanasia."

Kutner conceived the living will as a revocable trust established by an individual over his or her own body. In 1967 he wrote the first living will. His concept became universal in the United States, though some debate whether individuals understand what is covered in their living wills or what is meant by durable powers of attorney for health care. Among many developments, in 1975 the Euthanasia Society reactivated itself as the Society for the Right to Die, and in 1976 California became the first state to pass legislation allowing a living will. In 1990 the federal Patient Self-Determinations Act went into effect. It requires health-care providers to inquire whether patients have prepared an advance directive as to their terminal care.

The other great cause Kutner championed, a worldwide code of habeas corpus, did not become law. The concept was originally developed to prevent secret confinement of an accused person. Kutner sought to have that right enforced by the United Nations, which would compel states to reveal where and why a prisoner was being held and why he or she had not been formally charged, given a trial, or released. Kutner headed during the 1970s and 1980s the Committee for International Due Process of Law, also known as World Habeas Corpus. The European Convention on Human Rights embraced the code, but Secretary of State Dean Acheson in the Truman administration called it "unworkable."

Despite the lack of progress on the code, Kutner's commitment to the extension of human rights was influential. Kutner himself represented many world political and cultural figures held in questionable circumstances, among them Cardinal József Mindszenty, who was detained in Hungary in the late 1940s; the journalist William N. Oatis, who was imprisoned in Czechoslovakia in 1952 and freed through the assistance of, among others, Eleanor Roosevelt, then a member of the U.S. delegation to the United Nations; and the American poet Ezra Pound, whose radio broadcasts from Rome of Fascist propaganda resulted in his 1945 arrest and trial for treason, followed by confinement to an American mental asylum for twelve years. In 1961 Kutner joined Peter Benenson, also of Russian-Jewish descent, in founding the human rights organization Amnesty International in London. In his long career Kutner also served as U.S. consul to Ecuador, Guatemala, Venezuela, Haiti, and Ghana. He was eighty-four when he died of heart failure; his wife of fifty-nine years, Rose, and a son survived him.

Despite all his accomplishments, Kutner is not as well known as other attorneys, such as Abe Fortas, Arthur Goldberg, Abner Mikva, and Louis Nizer, of his era. His interests may have been too wide-ranging, his humor a touch quirky. For example, he titled one somewhat dry but useful law handbook of 1970 *Legal Aspects of Charitable Trusts and Foundations: A Guide for Philanthropoids.* His plays, such as *The Trialle of William Shakespeare; Beinge a Playe in 3 Acts to Be Rede and/or Performed* (1974), have received only limited production. An acquaintance from Chicago described Kutner as a gentleman of his city's Gold Coast, who most always wore an ascot and took tea on Friday afternoons at the Ritz. In addition to the great issues of his legal career, he was enthusiastic about poetry, music, and art. In books such as *The Intelligent Woman's Guide to Future Security* (1970) and *Due Process of Rebellion* (1974) and in other writings he expressed a range of progressive thought before its time. But although the world now has thousands of death-with-dignity and human rights organizations, Kutner's efforts have not received their due.

★

Most of Kutner's writings are out of print, but many remain available in law libraries. His semiautobiographical career guide to and history of the law *I, the Lawyer* (1966), though written mainly for young adults, offers insights into the author's passion for justice. See also Marjorie B. Zucker, ed., *The Right to Die Debate: A Documentary History* (1999). Development of the living will is chronicled in an article in the *Indiana Law Journal* 44 (1967): 547–548. Myrna Oliver, "Controlling the End," *Los Angeles Times* (23 May 1988), and Diane E. Hoffmann, Sheryl Itkin, and Catherine J. Tompkins, "The Dangers of Directives or the False Security of Forms," *Journal of Law, Medicine and Ethics* 24, no. 1 (1996): 5–17, offer overviews of contemporary complications surrounding death and legislation. *The Human Right to Individual Freedom: A Symposium on World Habeas Corpus* (1970), edited by Kutner, contains an introduction by Roscoe Pound, contributions by international authors, and Kutner's paean, "The Ultimate for Unity of Mankind." Obituaries are in the *New York Times* (4 Mar. 1993) and the London *Times* (5 Mar. 1993).

ALEX T. PRIMM

L

LAND, Edwin Herbert (*b.* 7 May 1909 in Bridgeport, Connecticut; *d.* 1 March 1991 in Cambridge, Massachusetts), inventor of instant photography and the plastic sheet polarizer, founder of the Polaroid Corporation, scientific researcher on color vision, and confidential U.S. government adviser on spy planes and satellites from the 1950s onward.

Land was one of two children of Matha Goldfaden and Harry M. Land, a scrap-metal dealer and real-estate investor whose Jewish parents had fled persecution in tsarist Russia. Young Edwin and his family settled in Norwich, Connecticut, after World War I. His older sister, Helen, pronounced his name "Din," creating Land's lifelong nickname.

Land was fascinated by science, particularly optics, from childhood. He first encountered light polarizers at the age of thirteen at a Connecticut summer camp named Mooween. A major influence was the textbook *Physical Optics,* by Robert W. Wood of Johns Hopkins University (whom Land finally met in the 1930s). Land graduated from Norwich Academy in 1926, having already pushed far beyond what his high school physics instructor could teach him. He attended Harvard for only a semester, then moved to New York City to begin experiments in optics.

During more than two years in the city, studying intensely at the New York Public Library and experimenting in various Manhattan basements, Land succeeded in making a plastic sheet polarizer with billions of tiny crystals per square inch. This device was suitable for automobile headlights, visors, and windshields, to control nighttime glare and improve visibility. Until that time polarizers of light, used for nearly a century for basic scientific research, were made of expensive crystals like calcite or tourmaline. When Land returned to Harvard in 1929, after applying for the first of 535 U.S. patents, the physics department gave him his own laboratory in which to perfect his invention. On 10 November 1929 Land married Helen (Terre) Maislen of Hartford, Connecticut; the couple had two daughters.

After describing the sheet polarizer at a physics department seminar in 1932, Land again left Harvard, still without a degree, in order to go into the business of making and selling the polarizers he had invented. This enterprise evolved into the Polaroid Corporation in 1937. The company expanded rapidly during World War II, drawing on its pioneering in polarizers to develop and manufacture devices that would cut battlefield glare, improve the accuracy of gun-aiming at night, and maintain the night vision of pilots and sailors. As a diversion from this intense work, and to prepare for peacetime, he led the team that developed one-step, or instant, photography. This was first demonstrated publicly at a meeting of the Optical Society of America in 1947 and placed on the market in 1948. The invention of instant photography, at first delivering pictures in sixty seconds, emerged just as the major U.S. automakers were deciding against installing Land's polarizer system in new cars. Polarizers would, however, become essential to

Edwin Land. ARCHIVE PHOTOS

such products as sunglasses, windows, and displays for digital watches and calculators.

Before he was forty years old, Land had launched two entire industries, sheet polarizers and instant photography. The first was destined for niche markets, the other for mass consumers. With the protection of hundreds of patents, Land led Polaroid's development of successive generations of instant photography. The first photographs were in sepia. Black-and-white followed in 1950. Land and his team continually made the film more sensitive, so that by 1959, Polaroid marketed a variety that could take indoor sports pictures without a flash and deliver a print in fifteen seconds. Color went on the market in 1963, followed in 1972 by an entirely new system, called SX-70, in which the positive and negative were not peeled apart. Resembling a large playing card, SX-70 pictures allowed the customer to see the images "emerge" before their eyes. This basic technology was still in use thirty years later. The convenience of even the first instant photography led to sales of hundreds of thousands of cameras within a few years. The company grew so fast that it was the archetypal science-based industry of its day. Sales multiplied almost 200 times between

1950 and 1970. The reaction on Wall Street was to bid the price of Polaroid shares to ninety times earnings, a record at the time. But only a few years later, amid the struggle to introduce SX-70, Wall Street reversed its judgment and slashed the stock price 90 percent in about a year.

Land devoted little of his time to conventional corporate management, which he left to others, preferring to operate in his lab in an old brick building at Main and Osborn Streets in Cambridge, Massachusetts. During his more than sixty years in the laboratory, in which projects eventually grew to cost hundreds of millions of dollars, Land worked with small groups of collaborating researchers. He recruited and challenged them with such a torrent of new ideas that his coworkers often hoped that his attention would shift elsewhere. But they also found that when they got stuck, they could spend hours with him and go away with new ways to crack the nut.

To keep Polaroid from being swallowed up in a world of such giants as Eastman Kodak, Land not only emphasized patents but also imposed a culture of general secrecy. His concern with secrecy made him an ideal adviser to President Eisenhower and his successors on the subject of obtaining overhead photographs of the missiles and aircraft of the Soviet Union. Reconnaissance information was vital not only for finding targets or warning of dangers but also for obtaining information about the true strength of the Soviet military. This information, in turn, allowed the United States to rein in its own military development during the cold war, and also to monitor, in great detail, compliance with disarmament treaties. As with his instant-photography coworkers, Land often was called on to resolve seemingly impossible technical problems. His usual response was to give the engineers and scientists long lists of things to try. The effect was to restore optimism.

Although Land preferred to remain out of the public eye—he almost never appeared on television, for instance—he frequently spoke to the press and in smaller venues. Of medium height, with a shock of black hair parted on the right and penetrating dark eyes, the shy Land trained himself to be a dramatic public speaker and demonstrator before employees, shareholders, scientists, and officials. He was a fanatic experimentalist. He enjoyed every one of the hundreds or thousands of steps along a pathway—with a goal he spelled out in advance—to create "something well worth having." In 1963 he told a reporter for *Life* magazine that "every creative act is a sudden cessation of stupidity." But he was not merely an empiricist, trying one thing after another. In 1980 he declared, "We use bull's-eye empiricism: we try everything, but we try the right thing first!"

Land knew decades of success, but the spectacular failure of an instant movie system Polaroid introduced in the late 1970s ended his leadership of the company he founded. When Land stepped down as chairman of Polaroid in 1980 under pressure from his board of directors, he defiantly maintained from the stage of Symphony Hall in Boston that the most valuable equity is ideas and shared competences that are built up in carrying out one innovation after another, in a world where one must innovate or die.

He received many honors, including the Presidential Medal of Freedom (1963) and the National Medals of both Science (1968) and Technology (1988); he was inducted in 1977 into the National Inventors Hall of Fame. Land and his wife used much of their wealth in large and small philanthropies, including many millions for three projects in Cambridge: a science building at Harvard, the House of the American Academy of Arts and Sciences, and the Rowland Institute for Science on the Charles River. With gifts to the Massachusetts Institute of Technology, he pushed to increase the amount of time college students spent doing experiments, starting in their freshman year. Land died at the age of eighty-one. He is buried in Mount Auburn Cemetery in Cambridge.

More than a half century after his invention of the plastic sheet polarizer, Edwin Land remained a symbol of restless innovation. When he started out as a youth in the 1920s, it was often said that the frontier was closed. But Land defied the big companies and the notion that the heroic inventor had disappeared. Almost alone, he lived the innovator's high-wire life. He was determined to use science for unexpected, significant new things that thousands or millions would use, thereby launching viable businesses. Thanks to Land's unquenchable energy, millions of people all over the world had the fun of looking at photographs they had just taken, of people and places and events they were enjoying. Skilled in convincing huge numbers of people that innovation could be useful and pleasant, he was ready to walk through the minefields of finance, patents, and public relations, knowing that once an invention is born, the next must already be underway.

★

For an overview of Land's published work, see Mary McCann, ed., *Edwin H. Land's Essays*, 2 vols. (1993), especially "Polaroid and the Headlight Problem," which was his first published article; "Basic Research in the Small Company," dating from 1946; "A New One-Step Photographic Process," a 1947 article that describes the development of instant photography; and "The Retinex Theory of Color Vision," which spells out his evolving ideas on this subject. A full biography is Victor K. McElheny, *Insisting on the Impossible: The Life of Edwin Land, Inventor of Instant Photography* (1998). Accounts of Land's career also appear in Francis Bello, "The Magic That Made Polaroid," *Fortune* (Apr. 1959); Philip Siekman, "Kodak and Polaroid: An End to Peaceful Co-

existence," *Fortune* (Nov. 1970); and Sean Callahan, "If You Are Able To State a Problem, It Can Be Solved," *Life* (27 Oct. 1972). An obituary is in the *New York Times* (2 Mar. 1991).

VICTOR K. McELHENY

LANDON, Margaret Dorothea Mortenson (*b.* 7 September 1903 in Somers, Wisconsin; *d.* 4 December 1993 in Alexandria, Virginia), author best remembered for her novel *Anna and the King of Siam* (1944), which inspired a variety of adaptations including the Rodgers and Hammerstein musical *The King and I.*

Landon was the eldest of three daughters born to Annenus Duabus and Adelle Johanne Estberg. Her father worked at the Curtis Publishing Company in Chicago as an office manager and also, for a time, in the business department of the *Saturday Evening Post.* Her mother was a homemaker. Landon spent most of her childhood in suburban Evanston, Illinois. Her English teacher at Evanston Township High School once told her, "You have the gift of words. Do something with it!" Although she was always interested in writing, she was also drawn to sports as a child and pursued this interest through her college years as the captain of the women's baseball, basketball, and tennis teams at Wheaton College, where she earned her B.A. degree in 1925.

Upon graduation she taught English and Latin in Bear Lake, Michigan, but soon realized she disliked teaching and gave it up after what she called "an agonizing year." She married Kenneth Perry Landon, whom she had met at Wheaton College, on 16 June 1926. Following their wedding Kenneth was assigned as a missionary by the Presbyterian Board of Foreign Missions to serve in Siam (now Thailand). After a year in Bangkok learning Siamese, they spent most of the next ten years in Trang, where Margaret served as the principal of the Trang Girls' School. She found very little time to write anything other than a mission newsletter and correspondence. The Landons took a break from mission work in 1931 while Kenneth earned his master's degree at the University of Chicago, but they returned in 1932 and remained in Trang until 1937. Three of their four children were born in Siam.

While abroad, Landon became fascinated by the story of Anna Leonowens, a widowed Welsh woman who went to Siam in 1862 to teach King Mongkut's many children and his favorite concubines. For the next five years Leonowens taught them English and indoctrinated them with Western ideals of democracy. One of her pupils, Prince Chulalongkorn, demonstrated the influence of her teaching when he became king by abolishing the custom of prostration before superiors and by freeing his slaves. Leonowens wrote two books based on her experiences: *The English Governess at the Siamese Court* (1870) and *The Romance of the Harem* (1872), both of which were banned by the Siamese government after an unsuccessful attempt to prevent their publication. Even Dr. Edwin Bruce McDaniel, a friend of Landon's in Siam who had introduced her to the story of Anna, kept his copies hidden. After returning to the United States, Landon remarkably found copies of both obscure books while browsing through used bookstores in Chicago.

When the Landons returned to the United States in 1937 Landon took up her writing more seriously, enrolling in night school classes at Northwestern University's Medill School of Journalism. One of her assignments evolved into her first published magazine article, "Hollywood Invades Siam," for which she was paid $15.

Landon became increasingly interested in writing about Anna Leonowens. Muriel Fuller, a former college roommate who worked in publishing, suggested that Landon combine the autobiographical elements of both of Leonowens's books and omit the dull descriptions. Landon also relied on personal letters, diaries, and interviews with Leonowens's granddaughter Avis S. Fyshe. The result was a work that Landon described as "seventy-five percent fact, and twenty-five percent fiction based on fact." She began writing *Anna and the King of Siam* in 1939 in Richmond, Indiana, where her family lived through 1941. In 1942 the Landons moved to Washington, D.C., where Kenneth went to work for the State Department. Margaret finished her book in July 1943 only hours before her youngest child was born.

The manuscript was rejected by two publishers and was almost rejected by the eventual publisher, John Day, because an editor dismissed it as "Sunday school stuff" that no one would want to read. But another editor (a friend of Landon's) sold the chief editor on the book's merits. *Anna and the King of Siam* was published in 1944 and became a best-seller. It was dedicated to Landon's sister Evangeline, who was tragically killed in a car crash in 1941.

Anna and the King of Siam inspired a number of adaptations. A film version, *Anna and the King*, starring Irene Dunne and Rex Harrison, was produced by Twentieth Century-Fox in 1946. On 29 March 1951 the Rodgers and Hammerstein musical *The King and I* opened on Broadway, starring Gertrude Lawrence and Yul Brynner. A film version of the musical followed in 1956 (Twentieth Century-Fox) with Deborah Kerr and Yul Brynner. In 1999 Walt Disney released an animated version of *The King and I*. Although another version of *Anna and the King* appeared in 1999 starring Jodie Foster, the screenwriters claimed that their story was based more closely on Leonowens's books than on Landon's novel.

Landon went on to write a less successful second novel,

Never Dies the Dream (1949), about a missionary who runs a school in Bangkok in the 1930s. She worked for many years on a textbook for high school students on Southeast Asian history entitled *Pageant of Malayan History,* but the manuscript remained unfinished.

Landon cited poor health and family responsibilities as reasons for not writing more. She suffered from rheumatic fever for two years after the publication of her first book. Only a few months after her husband's death, she died of a stroke at a retirement home in Alexandria. She is buried next to her husband in Wheaton Cemetery in Wheaton, Illinois.

Margaret Landon was critical of her own work and often lacked confidence in her writing ability. A perfectionist, she rewrote some sections of her books as many as twenty times and was also a meticulous researcher. Had it not been for her work, the life of Anna Leonowens would likely have faded into obscurity. Instead, the Welsh schoolteacher was immortalized, not only in Landon's book but also in one of the most beloved musicals of the twentieth century as well as numerous film adaptations. As a result, the Western world gained a better understanding of Eastern culture and society.

★

A collection of personal papers, correspondence, and manuscripts of both Margaret and Kenneth Landon as well as secondary source material is in the Special Collections Department of Wheaton College, Wheaton, Illinois. The original manuscript of *Anna and the King of Siam* and related material is in the Manuscripts Division of the Library of Congress, Washington, D.C. Biographical information is in *Contemporary Authors* (vols. 13–14) and *Current Biography 1945*. Obituaries are in the *Washington Post* (5 Dec. 1993) and the *New York Times* (6 Dec. 1993).

ARLENE R. QUARATIELLO

LANDON, Michael (*b.* 31 October 1936 in Forest Hills, New York; *d.* 1 July 1991 in Malibu, California), film and television actor, writer, producer, and director, best known for his roles on the television series *Bonanza* (1959–1973) and *Little House on the Prairie* (1973–1983).

Born Eugene Maurice Orowitz, Landon was the son of Eli Orowitz, a movie publicist and theater manager, and Peggy O'Neill, a Broadway actress. His parents doted on his sister while Peggy, mentally unstable, continually harassed her son. He later referred to her as "a stabber, a kicker and a wacko." His mother abused him and threatened suicide several times. On one occasion Landon rescued her from drowning despite his inability to swim. He often escaped to a nearby cave, where he hoarded canned goods while fantasizing about the adventures of his favorite comic-book characters. Years later, in 1976, Landon produced a tele-

Michael Landon, 1989. THE KOBAL COLLECTION

vision movie, *The Loneliest Runner,* a candid look back at childhood anxieties.

The family moved to Collingswood, New Jersey, when Landon was four years old. As an elementary school student, shy, polite Landon (nicknamed "Ugey") excelled at school and pleased his teachers but had few friends. Deciding to become popular, he reversed his behavior by becoming streetwise and boisterous: picking fights, failing classes, and performing dangerous stunts. At Collingswood High School, Landon discovered the javelin. Although small in stature he could throw farther than his peers, and his coach, Maurey Dickinson, recognized his prowess. That summer Landon diligently practiced with a borrowed javelin. After viewing the movie *Samson and Delilah,* he adopted "long tresses" in the belief that it increased his power to throw the javelin. He went on to win regional and state championships, including the longest throw recorded that year in national high school competition. Named an All-American, he was offered several college scholarships and elected to attend the University of Southern California (USC) because of its renowned track team. Landon's high school graduation, however, was deferred by detentions. Before he could receive his diploma, the principal demanded that he sit outside the school to atone for his 200 outstanding detentions. Even though the school year had

officially ended in June, Landon sat outside during school hours for thirty days before he was granted his diploma.

After one stint in a high school drama production, Landon confidently enrolled in the drama department at USC. He thought that if he could win an Olympic medal throwing the javelin, the publicity would make him a star like Buster Crabbe. Unfortunately, early in the track season, teammates attacked him and cut his hair. Stripped of his confidence, he threw the javelin shorter distances and tore his shoulder ligaments, ending his dream of Olympic glory. Disillusioned, he dropped out of college after only one semester. He embarked on a series of odd jobs: loading freight cars, babysitting, and making ribbons. One day an actor acquaintance asked Landon to be his partner in an audition at Warner Brothers. He complied by crying profusely at the audition, recalling childhood memories. He began attending studio acting classes, where he met such future stars as James Garner, Steve McQueen, and Sal Mineo.

In 1955 Landon became engaged to Dodie Fraser, who had a seven-year-old son. Although apprehensive, he and Fraser were married in 1956 in Mexico. About this time, he chose a stage name at random, calling himself Michael Lane. Since there was a duplicate name in the Screen Actors Guild listings, he assumed the name Michael Landon. His early appearances were on live television productions of *Playhouse 90* and *Studio One.* The film *I Was a Teenage Werewolf* (1957) was his first commercial success. The producer David Dortort, impressed by Landon's film work, cast him as "Little Joe" on *Bonanza* (1959–1973), a turning point in his career. However, as the ratings soared, his marriage to Dodie soured. In 1960 the two were divorced.

Landon and Marjorie Lynn Noe were married on 12 January 1961. He adopted Noe's daughter and the couple had four children together. Landon sought professional power and control by writing and directing some *Bonanza* episodes, enabling the family to move to a palatial Beverly Hills, California, mansion. When his teenage stepdaughter was involved in a life-threatening auto accident in 1973, Landon was devastated. He confided, "I promised God that if He would let her live, I would do something useful with my life, something to make the world a little better because I'd been there." She survived her injuries, and Landon subsequently produced two wholesome series "before sincerity got clobbered on television by terminal irony."

In December 1981, Landon and his second wife were divorced. He was often linked with other women, and he arrived in Thailand to film the television movie *Love Is Forever* (1983) with his then partner, Cindy Clerico. The two married in 1983; they had two children.

Landon starred in, wrote, and directed two successful series, *Little House on the Prairie* (1973–1983) and *Highway to Heaven* (1984–1989). The ambitious actor also supervised *Father Murphy,* a frontier television drama (1981–

1984). He played Charles Ingalls, a Minnesota farmer, on *Little House,* and Jonathan Smith, a probationary angel who personified compelling humanism on *Highway to Heaven.* He also wrote and directed a film for television, *Where Pigeons Go to Die* (1991), which was nominated for two Emmy Awards. Although the effort did not win either award, Landon tenaciously proceeded with a new pilot, *Us,* which CBS aired on 20 September 1991, after Landon's death. With Landon as the middle figure in the three-generational drama, he personified the prodigal son, always seeking parental approval.

Neither his fictional characters nor Landon himself were faultless. Michael Leahy wrote in a March 1985 *TV Guide* article: "The moralist who talked incessantly about the need for 'strong family values' was the temperamental artist on his third marriage to a woman twenty years younger." However, the real and imaginary men strove for a kind of perfection, both in themselves and in the world they inhabited. His characters contended with drought, poverty, pride, disease, and despair but acknowledged the triumph of faith. Landon brought laughter, tears, reason, and realization to his vehicles. Behind the scenes the actor often hired disabled actors and espoused several charitable causes, especially those devoted to children. He was an avid fundraiser for Down's Syndrome Parents of Los Angeles and hosted a celebrity gala for the charity every year. He was also active in Free Arts for Abused Children, an organization that introduced creative arts to child abuse victims. In addition to writing parts in his scripts for the blind, crippled, and hearing impaired, he hired many disabled actors for his shows and also contributed to cancer research efforts.

Landon died of pancreatic cancer at his Malibu home and was buried in Hillcrest Memorial Gardens in Los Angeles. Five hundred mourners attended the funeral including former president Ronald Reagan, Nancy Reagan, Melissa Gilbert, Brian Keith, and Landon's first wife, Dodie. Friends recalled Landon as a complex, diversified individualist, stubborn and sensitive, kind but rough, innovative yet traditional. Landon believed his heartening television projects could make a difference, and they did: through his television work he became a fighter and father figure to generations of Americans. Tom Ito wrote that Landon, although ahead of his time, had "the creative courage and ability and talent to put together beautiful pieces of entertainment . . . all wrapped around the nucleus of human understanding: the longing that everybody had for having their own dreams come true, for having a good life, for having a world in which people cared about each other." A direct quote from Landon was: "Remember me with smiles and laughter, for this is how I will remember you all. If you can only remember me with tears, then don't remember me at all."

★

Landon's life has been recorded in several biographies, including Harry Flynn and Pamela Flynn, *Michael Landon: Life, Love and Laughter* (1991); Aileen Joyce, *Michael Landon: His Triumph and Tragedy* (1991); Cheryl Landon Wilson with Jane Scovell, *I Promised My Dad: An Intimate Portrait of Michael Landon by His Eldest Daughter* (1992); Tom Ito, *Conversations with Michael Landon* (1992); and Jill C. Wheeler, *A Tribute to the Young at Heart—Michael Landon* (1992). An extensive article about Landon by Ken Tucker is in *Entertainment Weekly* (11 July 1997). An obituary is in the *New York Times* (2 July 1991).

JOAN LIZZIO

LARSON, (Lewis) Arthur (*b.* 4 July 1910 in Sioux Falls, South Dakota; *d.* 27 March 1993 in Durham, North Carolina), law professor and presidential speechwriter best known as the chief theoretician of Eisenhower-era Republicanism.

Larson, who never used his first name, was the third of five children of Lewis Larson and Anna Bertia Huseboe, both of whom were second-generation Americans of Norwegian descent. Although the first generation of Larsons in South Dakota had been farmers, Larson's father studied law and became a family court judge. His mother was a homemaker. As a result Larson grew up in a comfortable, middle-class milieu in which family life, the Lutheran Church, and the local Young Men's Christian Association were the leading formative experiences. Larson's parents were self-described "party of Lincoln Republicans," though never very partisan ones. Larson matured into a tall, blond, handsome, and well-liked young man who distinguished himself in high school and at Augustana College in Sioux Falls as a champion debater. Larson lost only three debates in high school and college, once for the national championship and twice to teams led by an aspiring actress named Florence Newcomb, whom he married on 31 July 1935. They had two children.

Larson graduated from Sioux Falls High School in 1927 and from Augustana College with a B.A. degree in 1931. He then enrolled at the University of South Dakota Law School. During his first and only year there, he won a Rhodes Scholarship and continued his law studies for the next three years at Pembroke College, Oxford University. In addition to working toward a degree in jurisprudence at Oxford, he became very active in the university's Political Union and was elected to two of its highest offices, librarian and treasurer. In the course of discussing and debating politics and public policy with other union members, Larson was exposed to the moderate conservatism or "middle way" later championed by such leading British conservatives as R. A. Butler and Harold Macmillan. Larson earned a B.A. degree in jurisprudence with first class honors in 1935.

Arthur Larson with a chart linking the John Birch Society with other extremist groups. ARCHIVE PHOTOS

After returning home from England in 1935 Larson practiced law briefly in Milwaukee, Wisconsin, and then became a legal academic at the University of Tennessee Law School and Cornell Law School, specializing in the areas of workers' compensation and social insurance law more generally. His most important work in those fields was a two-volume treatise *The Law of Workmen's Compensation,* which was first published in 1952 and immediately became the standard reference work on that subject. These interests and accomplishments led to his appointments as dean of the University of Pittsburgh Law School in 1953 and as undersecretary of labor in 1954. Larson first came to the attention of the general public in June 1956 when his book *A Republican Looks at His Party* was published. This work defines Eisenhower or "modern" Republicanism as a moderate conservatism that accepted with qualifications many New Deal public policies but sought to keep those policies and the growth of the government more generally within boundaries. The book was an instant success, in large part because President Dwight D. Eisenhower strongly endorsed it. Eisenhower immediately put Larson to work writing speeches for his successful reelection campaign that year.

Once the campaign was over Eisenhower appointed Larson the director of the U.S. Information Agency (USIA), where he was responsible for explaining to the other nations of the world what the United States stood for in the mid-1950s. In October 1958 at Eisenhower's request, Larson moved to the White House staff to supervise speechwriting in the increasingly important area of arms control and disarmament, a field in which Larson remained active for many years. That work led directly to his appointment as head of the World Rule of Law Center at Duke University Law School. He joined that faculty in the fall of 1958 and remained there for the rest of his career.

Over the next decade Larson played a major role in the intense debate within the Republican Party about its future direction. In his 1959 book *What We Are For,* Larson argued that the party should stay on the centrist, modern Republican path. When the 1964 Republican National Convention rejected that advice and chose the more conservative senator Barry Goldwater as its presidential nominee, Larson endorsed and campaigned for Goldwater's Democratic opponent Lyndon Johnson. Four years later Larson attracted heavy press attention when he published a book about the Eisenhower presidency, *Eisenhower: The President Nobody Knew* (1968), which revealed that Eisenhower had privately disagreed with the Supreme Court's school desegregation ruling in 1954. The book also disclosed Eisenhower's privately expressed doubts about Richard Nixon's leadership abilities, revelations that apparently cost Larson whatever chance he might have had to play an important part in Nixon's administration. During the 1970s Larson faded steadily from public view. He died of heart failure on 27 March 1993 in Durham, North Carolina, and is buried there.

In his memoirs Larson wrote with characteristic clarity, "Modern Republicanism's heyday was also mine." One of the leading spokespersons for what he saw as the sensible center, Larson's rise from and eventual return to obscurity reflected the Republican Party's move toward the center during the 1950s and its rightward retreat from that position in the three decades that followed.

★

Larson's papers are in the Eisenhower Presidential Library. See also his posthumously published memoir *A Twentieth-Century Life* (1997). With Lex K. Larson he wrote *Larson's Workers' Compensation Law,* 12 vols. (1952–1997). The Duke Law Journal contains "A Tribute to Arthur Larson" (1980): 385–415. An obituary is in the *New York Times* (1 Apr. 1993).

DAVID L. STEBENNE

LAZAR, Irving Paul ("Swifty") (*b.* 28 March 1907 in New York City; *d.* 30 December 1993 in Beverly Hills, California), talent agent and host of famous post–Academy Awards parties.

Lazar was the oldest of four brothers. His parents, Samuel Mortimer and Stari DeLongpre were Russian-Jewish immigrants. His father was a "butter and egg man." Born Samuel Lazar on New York City's Lower East Side, he

Swifty Lazar. CORBIS-BETTMANN

changed his name to Irving Paul when he was thirteen years old because he thought it sounded more theatrical. When he was eight, his family moved to the Brownsville section of Brooklyn. In this tough neighborhood, Lazar, who at his tallest was about five feet, four inches tall, learned to punch first and run fast.

Lazar attended Commercial High School in New York City. After graduating from Fordham University in the Bronx in 1926, he earned a law degree from Brooklyn Law School in 1931. While in law school, he made his first deal: He convinced a professor to teach a cram course, hired representatives at all the local schools to recruit students, and took a commission for every student they brought in.

Lazar worked briefly for a private law firm and as an assistant district attorney in Brooklyn. In 1932 he set up a private practice and specialized in foreclosures, a lucrative business during the Great Depression. Through a friend who worked as a booking agent for the Music Corporation of America (MCA), Lazar met Ted Lewis, the vaudeville star, who introduced him to many great performers of the day, including Jack Benny, George Burns and Gracie Allen, and Sophie Tucker. In 1936 Lazar was hired as an attorney for MCA. He occasionally acted as an agent on the side. His first client was a little-known comedian named Henny Youngman. Enjoying both the game of making deals and hobnobbing with celebrities, Lazar gave up legal practice and was hired by MCA to book bands into nightclubs. MCA represented many of the great musicians of the day, including Tommy Dorsey, Harry James, Gene Krupa, and Benny Goodman.

In March 1942, at the age of thirty-five, Lazar enlisted in the U.S. Army. By his own account, he was not suited to military life. A fanatically fastidious man, his germ phobia made shared quarters and latrines unbearable. In July he entered Officer Candidate School in Miami, and on completion of training, reported to the Special Services Division at Mitchell Field on Long Island, New York. There, he learned that the commander of the Army Air Force (AAF) in Washington, D.C., General Hap Arnold, was looking for a Special Services Officer to produce a benefit show for the AAF Emergency Relief. Irving Berlin's *This Is the Army* had been a huge success for the ground forces; the AAF wanted a similar production. Lazar convinced Moss Hart, the renowned playwright and director, to develop the show. *Winged Victory* opened on 20 November 1943. The stage and subsequent film versions earned $4 million for the Emergency Fund.

In 1945 Lazar returned to MCA, and he moved to Hollywood, California in 1946. He worked for a year for Eagle Lion film studios. In 1947 he opened the Irving Paul Lazar Agency in Beverly Hills. Until the 1970s, he represented directors, writers, choreographers, composers, and lyricists: everyone but actors, whom he considered too demanding.

He specialized in bringing East Coast talent into the film industry. Through Moss Hart, Lazar met, and eventually represented, George S. Kaufman, Edna Ferber, Maxwell Anderson, Ira Gershwin, and Cole Porter, among others. Through Ira Gershwin, he gained Harold Arlen, Comden and Green, Lerner and Loewe, and Rodgers and Hammerstein, to name a few.

Lazar was aggressive and persuasive in negotiating high-priced deals for his clients. He sold movie rights for Broadway shows before they opened. If the play flopped, the studio would still have to pay. He frequently represented multiple clients in a single deal. For *The Seven-Year Itch* (1955), he represented George Axelrod, the author; Charles Feldman, the producer; and Billy Wilder, the director. He collected his 10 percent from each of them. In the 1980s this became a standard practice called "packaging." He also often interjected himself into deals where he had no clients. Other agents considered it poaching, but he claimed everyone was paid. As legend and Lazar tell it, his good friend Humphrey Bogart bet him that he couldn't make three deals for him by dinner. When he did, Bogart dubbed him "Swifty," a nickname that stuck, despite Lazar's dislike of it.

In 1962 Lazar, fifty-six years old and never married, met a thirty-one-year-old model, Mary Van Nuys, on a plane to Paris. They were married in January 1963. In 1967 the Lazars hosted their first post–Academy Award party. Originally consisting of a group of friends at their home in Beverly Hills, the party moved to successively larger venues, eventually winding up at the celebrity haunt Spago in 1985. An invitation-only affair, it became the Hollywood event of the year.

By the 1970s the movie business had changed. The studio moguls were gone, and lawyers and businessmen ran the studios. This was not Lazar's world. Rather than retire, he switched gears and became a literary agent. He had sold books to publishers in the past; Vladimir Nabokov, for example, was one of his clients. Now, it became his main business. Among others, he represented Larry McMurtry and Bette Bao Lord. The celebrity memoir became his specialty. He convinced actors, including Lauren Bacall, Kirk Douglas, Michael Caine, and Cher that they had stories to tell, and then he sold the stories to the publishers.

Lazar continued to work well into his eighties. In 1992 Mary Lazar was diagnosed with bone cancer and died a few months later. Lazar, eighty-six years old with failing health, went ahead with his post–Academy Award party, but afterward his condition declined rapidly. With his kidneys failing, Lazar discontinued dialysis treatment and died on 30 December 1993. He and his wife are buried in Westwood Memorial Park in Los Angeles.

Lazar believed in the American dream: A child of the ghetto can rise to fame and fortune if he works hard. Lazar, the Brooklyn street kid, cultivated an image of the wealthy sophisticate with his impeccable, tailor-made wardrobe and art-filled homes. He defined himself by the important people he knew. His friends were his clients, and his clients friends. In *Will Success Spoil Rock Hunter?* (1956) George Axelrod immortalized him in the character of Irving "Squeaky" LaSalle, and he is mentioned in the Comden and Green Song "Drop That Line" in *Bells Are Ringing* (1960). For better or worse, he was a Hollywood icon.

★

In the last year of his life, Lazar wrote his autobiography, *Swifty: My Life and Good Times* (1995), in collaboration with Annette Tapert. Although it is wise to question Lazar's version of events, the book is an entertaining chronicle of the life of a true old Hollywood character. An article about Lazar's life, written by Annette Tapert, is in *Vanity Fair* (Apr. 1994). A tribute by Larry McMurtry is in the *Los Angeles Times* (7 Jan. 1994). Other articles are in the *New York Times* (2 Nov. 1980) and the London *Independent* (19 Mar. 1994). Obituaries are in the *New York Times* and Long Island *Newsday* (both 1 Jan. 1994).

SARA STEEN

LEE, Pinky (*b.* 1908 in Saint Paul, Minnesota; *d.* 3 April 1993 in Mission Viejo, California), burlesque and vaudeville comedian who went on to star as the host of television's first comedy-variety series for children.

As a young boy, Pinky Lee—born Pincus Leff—dreamed of becoming a lawyer, but the dream was dashed when his schoolmates made fun of his lisp. Pinky soon turned his lisp into part of a comedy act, however, and by the 1930s he was touring on the burlesque and vaudeville circuits. In 1932 he married Bebe Dancis. The couple had two children.

Lee became an established comic character: a cute, wide-eyed, goofy comedian who sang, danced, and performed in variety skits. His clothes were part of the character. He dressed in a mismatched checkered suit, baggy pants and a too-small, roll-brim, checkered hat. By 1947 his lisp had become such a valued part of his character that he insured it with Lloyds of London for $50,000.

As vaudeville disappeared, the multitalented Lee adapted his act for variety shows. He starred at Earl Carroll's Theatre in Hollywood, and in the late 1940s he performed at London's Palladium. Films provided another showcase for his talents. He appeared in *Lady of Burlesque* (1943), *Earl Carroll's Vanities* (1945), *Blonde Ransom* (1945), *That's My Gal* (1947), and *South Caliente* (1951).

In 1949 the comic began working in the new medium of television. He first appeared on *Hollywood Premiere*, a short-lived series of half-hour programs. Like all other television in those days, everything on the show was done live. The program was produced in Hollywood and shown via

Pinky Lee impersonating Teddy Roosevelt, 1956. © BETTMANN/CORBIS

kinescope on the eastern and midwestern NBC networks. In 1951 Lee starred in *The Pinky Lee Show,* a loosely structured situation comedy set in a vaudeville theater. The series, in which Pinky appeared as a fumbling stagehand, lasted for seven months. He then appeared in a musical situation comedy produced by Larry White, called *Those Two.* As host, Pinky portrayed a piano accompanist madly in love with a nightclub singer, first played by the actress Vivian Blaine, later played by the actress Martha Stewart. The series, which ran on Monday, Wednesday, and Friday, from 7:30–7:45 P.M., was used to fill the remainder of the half hour in which NBC aired its nightly news program. The show was canceled in April 1953, but the producer White's young son had other ideas. He kept telling his father he missed Pinky Lee and pestered him to bring the character back.

On 4 January 1954, *The Pinky Lee Show* premiered nationally on NBC as the first variety show for children. Lee opened his shows by driving a miniature car onto a stage with a live audience of children, and went into a silly introductory song-and-dance number that started with the greeting "Yoo hoo, its me! My name is Pinky Lee!" The comedian would then spend the next twenty-six minutes frantically playing games, telling stories, and wreaking havoc that involved everyone in the studio—series regulars, puppets, and the studio audience. Another appeal of the show was Lee's talent as a master improviser, and he often surprised staff members and the audience alike with his antics. All was not silly, however; he also had a regular segment of the show called "Mr. and Mrs. Grumpy," in which he portrayed "Pinky the Clown," a part he performed with much pathos. In one memorable segment the Grumpys moved away, leaving the lonely Pinky behind. It is said that both the studio audience and the television crew were moved to tears.

Lee loved performing for children, and the feeling was mutual. He was more like a mischievous older brother than the usual authoritative adult. Parents complained that Lee was overexciting kids with his breakneck pace and causing them to adopt his peculiar mannerisms, but kids had no complaints.

During his burlesque and variety show days, Lee had often told vulgar jokes, which made people wonder if he was the right person to host a children's show. "I guess a few parents may have been apprehensive when I first decided that entertaining kids was for me," he said in a 1955 interview. He admitted that he didn't know what he was getting into, but the national show immediately became a huge hit. His live show was broadcast from Los Angeles and appeared Monday through Friday from 5:00 to 5:30 P.M.

The second season Lee agreed to NBC's request that he add a Saturday morning show to his already punishing schedule. On 20 September 1955, while on the air, Lee collapsed in front of his studio audience. The children laughed, thinking this was another one of his skits. Instead it was a case of exhaustion and a serious sinus infection. Lee's doctor told him to take time off, move to a drier climate, and start taking care of himself. Lee reluctantly moved to Tucson, Arizona, to recuperate. While he was off the air his show fell in the ratings. One reason for this was his absence; another was the growing popularity of the *Mickey Mouse Club* on ABC. On 9 June 1956 *The Pinky Lee Show* was canceled.

Lee recovered enough to take over as host of *The Gumby Show,* a children's show that aired in 1957. Lee welcomed the audience and viewers to his Fun Shop, where he presented the adventures of Gumby and his friends. Gumby was a green clay action character created by a combination of live animation and stop-motion photography. The series, which only lasted a season, would be revisited about thirty years later as the comedian Eddie Murphy, in bright green costume, re-created the character Gumby on *Saturday Night Live* sketches.

After *The Gumby Show* was canceled, Lee brought back his old slapstick comedy routines, playing in Las Vegas, Nevada, for three years. In 1964 and again in 1966 he hosted a local *Pinky Lee Show* for children at KABC in Los Angeles. In 1970 he appeared at the University of Colorado in a nostalgic show put on for college students. He was moved to tears by the three-minute ovation given him by the nineteen- to twenty-four-year-old students who remembered him fondly from their childhood. In later years, when the mood suited him, Lee toured the country in vaudeville-style revues; including the musical *Sugar Babies* in 1989. On 3 April 1993 he suffered a fatal heart attack.

Lee, who had been lambasted by the critics for his "low" humor in his early career, felt vindicated in his later years with the revival of vaudeville-style routines and the popularity of slapstick humor displayed by the likes of the Three Stooges. He said that his kind of broad and slapstick humor was just what the country needed.

★

Background about Pinky Lee's life and career can be found in Robert L. Smith, *Who's Who in Comedy* (1992). Jeffery Davis, *Children's Television* (1995), describes Pinky Lee's children's show and traces his influences on later comedians and children's programming. Tim Brooks and Earle Marsh, *The Complete Directory to Prime Networks and Cable TV Shows* (1999), provides insight into the early days of television and Pinky Lee's place in television history. A description of Lee's life after *The Pinky Lee Show* was canceled can be found in L. Botto, "Now You See Them, Now You Don't," *Look* (7 Sept. 1971). An obituary is in the *New York Times* (7 Apr. 1993).

JULIANNE CICARELLI

LE GALLIENNE, Eva (*b.* 11 January 1899 in London, England; *d.* 3 June 1991 in Weston, Connecticut), actress, director, and producer who founded the first classical repertory theater in America.

Le Gallienne was the only child of an English novelist and poet, Richard Le Gallienne, and a Danish journalist, Julie Nørregaard. She grew up in Paris, France, and attended the Collège Sévigné. Inspired by performances of Sarah Bernhardt, she studied acting at the Royal Academy of Dramatic Art and made her acting debut in London in 1914. The next year she sailed for New York. In 1918, while performing in a company with Ethel Barrymore, she formed her first important lesbian relationship with the notorious actress Alla Nazimova. From 1920 to 1925 she starred on Broadway and toured the country in Arthur Reichman's *Not So Long Ago* and Molnar's *Liliom* and *The Swan*.

At the age of twenty-seven and at the height of her fame, she turned her back on stardom and dared to challenge the male-dominated Broadway system of long runs, high prices, and typecasting. Supported by wealthy patrons such as Otto H. Kahn and the reclusive lesbian Alice De Lamar, she established America's first classical repertory theater, the Civic Repertory Theatre (1926–1935). Associated with

Eva Le Gallienne. CORBIS-BETTMAN

it was a school for apprentices that included Robert Lewis, Burgess Meredith, Arnold Moss, Howard da Silva, John Garfield, May Sarton, and J. Edward Bromberg.

At the end of the first season she had filled her theater to an average 78 percent capacity and had produced six out of eight critical successes. In November 1929 she was on the cover of *Time* and for two years she earned a place on the *Nation's* "Roll of Honor." By her third season she was playing to 91 percent capacity. During the company's ten years she staged thirty-seven plays in New York and toured the most successful ones during the summer. The most popular offerings included *The Cradle Song* (1927), *Hedda Gabler, Peter Pan, Romeo and Juliet,* and *The Cherry Orchard* (all 1928), *Camille* (1931), and *Alice in Wonderland* (1932). Her 1926 production of Anton Chekhov's *The Three Sisters* was its English-language premiere in New York.

Her popularity took a turn in the 1930s. With her focus on the classics, especially on the plays of Ibsen, she limited her following. Also, theatergoers had become more aware of her lesbianism. The influential and homophobic critic George Jean Nathan dubbed the Civic Repertory Theatre "the Le Gallienne sorority," while countless cruel jokes and rumors began to circulate about activities at the theater.

In 1937 Margaret Webster moved into Le Gallienne's professional and private life. Together they, along with Cheryl Crawford, founded the American Repertory Theatre in 1946. Le Gallienne starred in *Henry VIII* (1946), *What Every Woman Knows* (1946), *John Gabriel Borkman* (1946), and *Alice in Wonderland* (1947), directing the latter two shows as well. Although they received considerable financial support and strong testimonials from Broadway luminaries, the company could not withstand union demands, the high cost of producing plays in repertory, and the many complaints over play selection. Accusations of communism leveled at both Webster and Crawford hurt ticket sales.

Le Gallienne's life and career went steadily downhill. In 1951 her relationship with Webster ended, and except for sporadic successes her theater career was over. When not acting or directing she turned her energies to translating the plays of Ibsen and the tales of Hans Christian Andersen, as well as writing a biography of Eleonora Duse (*The Mystic in the Theatre: Eleonora Duse,* 1966) and her own autobiography *With a Quiet Heart* (1953). In the summers she often taught acting at Lucille Lortel's White Barn Theatre in Connecticut. One of her young students was Peter Falk. During long stretches of inactivity she turned to alcohol for escape.

In 1957 Le Gallienne appeared as Queen Elizabeth in Tyrone Guthrie's production of Schiller's *Mary Stuart,* which was a stunning success. The attention brought her television roles as well as a five-year affiliation with the National Repertory Theatre (1961–1966), where she either acted in or directed the great plays of Shakespeare, Ibsen, Chekhov, Sheridan, Molière, and Euripides. In 1968 she joined the APA–Phoenix Theatre for one season, performing in *Exit the King* and directing *The Cherry Orchard.* Between 1957 and 1975 the once-prominent actress appeared in only 117 Broadway performances.

Le Gallienne returned to Broadway in 1975 with Ellis Rabb's revival of *The Royal Family.* Although intended for only a two-week engagement at the Kennedy Center in Washington, D.C., the successful production went on to the Brooklyn Academy of Music and to Broadway, had a twenty-three week national tour, and finally became a television special.

Behind her public role as a famous actress, director, and producer, Le Gallienne led a private life troubled by her personal struggle with lesbianism. For more than fifty years she lived in shadows. Like many lesbians of her generation, she viewed herself as a man trapped in a female body. Because she was unwilling to hide behind a convenient marriage or to camouflage her relationships in order to boost her career, her sexuality became a nemesis that created her great need for privacy. Acting was a way of publicly expressing her personal feelings. She could reveal her soul when she performed. Some have said that her struggle with

her sexuality drained her creative energy, others have said it was the very source of it. Regardless, it profoundly influenced her art, coloring her selection of scripts, casting choices, management decisions, style of acting, and ultimately her critical reception.

During her long career Le Gallienne earned a Tony Award for lifetime achievement (1964), an Emmy for her role in the television broadcast of *The Royal Family* (1977), the American National Theatre and Academy's National Artist Award (1977), and an Academy Award nomination for best supporting actress in the film *Resurrection* (1980). At the age of eighty-two she received another Tony nomination for her performance in *To Grandmother's House We Go* (1981). She did not win, but the *New York Times* paid tribute: "She has no equal on Broadway. It is easy to fall in love all over again with Eva Le Gallienne, her face, her voice, her poise, and her beauty." In 1986, President Ronald Reagan awarded her the National Medal of Arts. When *American Theatre* magazine celebrated the silver anniversary of the nonprofit-theater movement in America, they featured Le Gallienne and proclaimed that her efforts in the 1920s, 1930s, and 1940s "presaged a changing role for the theatre a generation in advance." Along with Tyrone Guthrie, John Houseman, and Zelda Fichandler, she was credited for being one of the artists who "played a part in shaping America's nonprofit theatre." She died at her home in Weston of natural causes at the age of ninety-two.

★

The Billy Rose Theatre Collection of the New York Public Library contains clippings, photographs, and taped interviews with her associates. Hundreds of letters she wrote to Mercedes de Acosta are in the Rosenbach Museum in Philadelphia, Pennsylvania. The Civic Repertory Theatre Collection is housed at the Beinecke Library, at Yale University in New Haven, Connecticut. Her autobiographies include *At 33* (1934) and *With a Quiet Heart* (1953). There are two biographies of Le Gallienne: Robert A. Schanke, *Shattered Applause: The Lives of Eva Le Gallienne* (1992), and Helen Sheehy, *Eva Le Gallienne: A Biography* (1996). Another source is Schanke's reference book *Eva Le Gallienne: A Bio-Bibliography* (1989). See also George Jean Nathan, "The Theatre," *American Mercury* 14 (May 1928): 122; Peter Zeisler, "Toward Brave New Worlds," *American Theatre* 3 (Nov. 1986): 5; and the *New York Times* (16 June 1974 and 16 Jan. 1981). An obituary is in the *New York Times* (5 June 1991).

ROBERT A. SCHANKE

LEINSDORF, Erich (*b.* 4 February 1912 in Vienna, Austria; *d.* 11 September 1993 in Zürich, Switzerland), conductor who led world-class ensembles, including the New York Metropolitan Opera and the Boston Symphony Orchestra.

Leinsdorf, who legally changed his name from Landauer in 1934, was born to Ludwig Julius Landauer, a salesman,

Erich Leinsdorf. © UNDERWOOD & UNDERWOOD/CORBIS

and Charlotte Loebl, a homemaker and trained musician. Leinsdorf received his first music lessons from his mother when he was five years old. From the age of eleven he studied piano with Paul Emerich and Hedwig Kammer-Rosenthal, and at thirteen he began to study cello with Lilly Kosz. He also had private lessons in theory and composition with Paul Pisk, a student of Arnold Schoenberg. Leinsdorf attended the University of Vienna in 1930 and earned his diploma from the State Academy of Music in Vienna in 1933.

Leinsdorf served as rehearsal and solo pianist for Anton von Webern's choral group Singverein der Sozialdemokratischen Kunstelle in 1933. After a successful audition, Leinsdorf became Bruno Walter's assistant at the Salzburg Festival in 1934. Impressed by Leinsdorf's talent, Arturo Toscanini invited him to be his assistant in the following year. Leinsdorf worked for both Walter and Toscanini at Salzburg from 1935 through 1937. By 1937 Leinsdorf had already established a name in Italy as a conductor of opera. With the recommendations of Toscanini and the soprano Lotte Lehmann, Leinsdorf was invited to be an assistant conductor to Artur Bodanzky, the director of German repertoire at the New York Metropolitan Opera.

Leinsdorf made his New York debut at the Metropolitan Opera on 21 January 1938 with a performance of Richard Wagner's *Die Walküre* (1856) that was successful and acclaimed. In the same period Leinsdorf was engaged as assistant to Fritz Reiner of the San Francisco Opera. In his debut in San Francisco on 19 October 1938, Leinsdorf con-

ducted the San Francisco Opera's first performance of Claude Debussy's *Pelléas et Mélisande* (1902).

In 1938 the *Anschluss* in Austria, which led to its annexation by Adolf Hitler's Germany, prevented Leinsdorf from returning home. On 3 August 1939 he married Anne Frohnknecht, with whom he had five children. The marriage ended in divorce in 1968. Leinsdorf became an American citizen in 1942.

When Bodanzky fell ill before the Metropolitan Opera's 1939–1940 season, Leinsdorf was given charge of the Wagner repertoire. Upon Bodanzky's death on 23 November 1939, Leinsdorf was instantly named his successor as principal conductor of German operas. He met the challenge with competence and talent. In his first season as the principal conductor he presented fifty-five performances, directing not only the Wagnerian repertoire but also Richard Strauss's *Der Rosenkavalier* (1911), Debussy's *Pelléas et Mélisande,* and Christoph Gluck's *Orpheus and Eurydice* (1762).

Leinsdorf's demanding policies in matters of repertoire and rehearsal time made him some enemies. He left the Metropolitan Opera in 1943 to succeed Artur Rodzinski as music director of the Cleveland Orchestra. However, his induction into the U.S. Army in December 1943 interrupted his tenure there. He was assigned to Camp Lee, Virginia, and was discharged for medical reasons in 1944. He then returned to the Metropolitan Opera as a guest conductor from 1944 to 1945. In 1947 he was appointed music director of the Rochester Philharmonic Orchestra, to which he attracted national attention through a series of recordings for Columbia Records. In 1956 Leinsdorf served as music director of the New York City Opera, where he presented the American premieres of Frank Martin's *The Tempest* (1952–1954) and Carl Orff's *The Moon* (1939). He returned to the Metropolitan Opera as a guest conductor and musical consultant to Rudolf Bing from 1957 to 1962.

In 1962 Leinsdorf accepted his most prestigious post as music director of the Boston Symphony Orchestra, replacing Charles Munch. Leinsdorf expanded the Boston Symphony's repertoire by introducing less traditional programs, such as world premieres of Samuel Barber's *Piano Concerto* (1962) and Elliott Carter's *Piano Concerto* (1964–1965). He founded the Boston Symphony Chamber Players in 1964 and was also in charge of the famous summer concerts at Tanglewood, Massachusetts, where he directed the American premiere of Benjamin Britten's *War Requiem* (1962). On 5 August 1968 Leinsdorf married Vera Graf, an Argentina-born former violinist of the New York City Opera Orchestra.

Tired of endless managerial tasks, Leinsdorf retired from the Boston Symphony in 1969 and devoted himself to engagements as guest conductor. He made appearances with virtually every major orchestra in the United States and Europe. His only stable position after leaving Boston was as principal conductor of the Radio Symphony Orchestra of West Berlin from 1978 to 1980.

In 1981 Leinsdorf published *The Composer's Advocate: A Radical Orthodoxy for Musicians,* which offers a detailed guide to interpretations for conductors. He urged conductors to study all the works of a composer before performing any. In another book, *Erich Leinsdorf on Music* (1997), he criticized modern performers' inability to sight-read and prepare quickly for performances.

Leinsdorf's many recordings include *Ariadne auf Naxos* (1971); *Salome* (1969); *Turandot* (1960); *Die Walküre* (1962); *Lohengrin* (1966); *Aïda* (1971); the complete symphonies of Mozart with an ad hoc orchestra, the Philharmonic Symphony Orchestra of London; and a complete set of the Beethoven piano concertos with Arthur Rubinstein and the Boston Symphony (1963–1967). From 1959 to 1972 eight of Leinsdorf's albums received Grammy Awards from the National Academy of Recording Arts and Sciences. He served on the National Endowment for the Arts and was a member of the American Academy of Arts and Sciences. Rutgers University, Columbia University, Baldwin-Wallace College, and Williams College awarded him honorary doctorates.

Small-framed and compact, Leinsdorf was described by Milton Mayer as "aggressively bald between ear flaps of black hair; long face, large ears, huge hands. He still speaks with an accent, and his conversation is spiced with some of the choicest wit heard from a conductor since the days of Sir Thomas Beecham." His wide interests outside of music included reading, writing, photography, and collecting rare stamps and vintages. His last concert appearance as a guest conductor was with the New York Philharmonic in January 1993. Leinsdorf died of cancer at the age of eighty-one.

Famous for his remarkable memory, wide repertoire, and thorough professionalism, Leinsdorf was regarded as a supreme orchestral technician, whose performances achieved high technical finish representing the German tradition—precise, disciplined, and objective. That tradition also created a kind of impersonal interpretation. His performance was always predictable. His limitations were reflected in music demanding great rhythmic vitality or dramatic effect, when he usually showed his fine workmanship but lacked artistic attraction. Leinsdorf was internationally known for reviving neglected music and for exploring new works. He had a special interest in the original versions of works, conducting *Leonore,* the first version of Ludwig van Beethoven's *Fidelio* (1805), and the first version of Strauss's *Ariadne auf Naxos* (1912).

★

Leinsdorf's autobiography, *Cadenza: A Musical Career* (1976), is a witty book with sharp opinions. David Ewen, *Famous Modern Conductors* (1967), and David Ewen, comp. and ed., *Musicians since 1900: Performers in Concert and Opera* (1978), include Leinsdorf. Joshua Leinsdorf wrote a biographical essay, "Maestro Erich Leinsdorf," *Music Clubs* (1994), that reveals some lesser-known aspects of his father's personal life. William Weaver, "Erich Leinsdorf in Manhattan," *Architectural Digest* (Oct. 1993), is an interesting and descriptive article about Leinsdorf's home in New York, his personal taste, and his experience. Sandra Hyslop, "In Memoriam: Erich Leinsdorf," *Symphony* (1994), contains speeches of friends and colleagues at a memorial gathering on 14 October 1993 in New York. Obituaries are in the *New York Times* (12 Sept. 1993), *Boston Globe* and *Los Angeles Times* (both 13 Sept. 1993), and *Billboard* (25 Sept. 1993).

DI SU

LERNER, Max (*b.* 20 December 1902 near Minsk, Russia; *d.* 5 June 1992 in New York City), educator, lecturer, syndicated columnist, and internationally recognized liberal journalist.

Max Lerner was the younger son of six children (two of whom did not survive) of Benjamin and Bessie Podel Lerner, keepers of a general store. Shortly before Max's birth,

Max Lerner, 1949. © BETTMANN/CORBIS

his father left for America. By 1907 the entire family had passed through Ellis Island and eventually settled in New Haven, Connecticut, with Lerner acquiring U.S. citizenship through the naturalization of his father. Lerner graduated from Hillhouse High School in 1919 with an outstanding academic record and won a scholarship to Yale University. Elected to Phi Beta Kappa in his junior year, he graduated in 1923. He aimed to be a professor of literature until a sympathetic faculty advisor cautioned that his Jewishness would preclude his ever getting a position at an Ivy League college. Opting for the law, he gained admission to Yale Law School in the fall.

In the intervening summer of 1923, he participated in a workshop in Woodstock, New York, sponsored by the International Student Forum, where he was impressed by the group's dedication to making a better world. Exposure to the actual law curriculum soon raised doubts about the attractiveness of a legal career. During Christmas break he first read Thorstein Veblen's *Theory of the Leisure Class.* He found a means of learning more about Veblen in a graduate fellowship program at Washington University in St. Louis. There he used Veblen's ideas as the basis for the M.A. thesis he wrote in 1925. In 1948, he reminisced, "Among all the thinkers who sought to analyze the nature and consequences of this new business imperium of the West . . . Veblen is easily the towering figure. His critique of our civilization is as unsparing as the Marxian, and at the same time more subtle because it is an analysis in depth, with a psychology, an anthropology, and a theory of civilizations."

Lerner earned his doctorate at the newly established Robert Brookings Graduate School of Economics and Government in Washington, D.C., in 1927. His contacts at Brookings helped place him in New York City as an editor and contributor to the *Encyclopaedia of the Social Sciences* project.

The 1930s were productive years for Lerner, with articles and reviews appearing in the *New Republic,* Ivy League law journals, and the prestigious *New York Herald-Tribune* Sunday book review section. He also taught at Sarah Lawrence College (1932–1935) and at Harvard (1935–1936), where as lecturer in government, he taught constitutional law and political theory. In 1936 he accepted a post as political editor at *The Nation.* Personality clashes and policy disagreements with top management led to Lerner's departure in 1938.

Academia beckoned again that fall. Lerner was pleased to accept a professorship in government at Williams College, where he remained until 1943. He was lured back to Manhattan to become editorial director of *PM,* an independent newspaper without advertising. Shortly after the demise of *PM* in 1948, he became a columnist for the *New York Post,* where he stayed for the rest of his life.

Lerner's marriage to Anita Marburg, a graduate student

colleague at Brookings, on 20 July 1928 ended in divorce on 30 July 1940. His second marriage, to Genevieve Edna Albers on 16 August 1941, lasted over fifty years. There were three daughters from his first marriage, three sons from his second.

Throughout his professional careers, Lerner frequently held several positions concurrently, sometimes as a commuter, to lecture in various parts of the country or to take part in national radio and television shows. An inspiring teacher, he held endowed chairs for some of his numerous academic positions: at Brandeis University (his longest association, 1949–1973), at the University of Notre Dame (1959–1960; 1982–1984), and at the United States International University in San Diego (1974–1977). Abroad, he spent several summers in the Salzburg Seminar in Austria and served as Ford Foundation Professor in parts of South Asia. A prolific writer, Lerner also wrote scholarly introductions to new editions of the works of Machiavelli, Justice Oliver Wendell Holmes, and Thorstein Veblen.

As a prominent political commentator for three quarters of the twentieth century, Lerner took positions on almost every domestic and foreign issue before the public. From his leftist perspective, he was skeptical about the New Deal, sometimes regarding it as a possible precursor of the corporate state, at other times as too timid in its response to the Depression. In 1940–1941, he praised Roosevelt's policy of support for Britain but recognized the president's circuitous methods. In the early years of the cold war he criticized the Truman Doctrine but approved the Marshall Plan. Objecting to the United States becoming the world's policeman, he nevertheless supported the containment policy as applied in Korea and (at first) in Vietnam. He upheld the right of Jews to migrate to Israel but urged both sides to accept the internationalization of Jerusalem. By the 1960s he had become a fairly consistent mainstream Democrat, warmly endorsing Adlai Stevenson and Presidents Kennedy and Johnson.

Lerner became alarmed by what he considered the excesses of the New Left and the so-called counterculture. He preferred assimilation to black power and a return to civility in public discussion. He deplored aspects of the sexual revolution that led to broken homes and one-parent families. He considered himself a firm believer in the First Amendment but regarded as incomprehensible the notion that it protected flag-burning. The relief that Lerner found in the presidency of Ronald Reagan reflected Lerner's shifting views.

Lerner's magnum opus, published in 1957, was *America as a Civilization: Life and Thought in the United States Today,* an ambitious and unusual attempt to analyze its subject by drawing on the insights of cultural anthropology as well as on other traditional academic disciplines. Reviewers were in general agreement that the breadth of the study made it a herculean accomplishment. Some critics, while complimentary about the scope of the book, found it lacking in originality and interpretive depth. A second edition contained a final chapter called "Afterword: The New America (1957–1987)." After describing the complexities of the problems facing America in the coming new century, Lerner closed with an act of hope, if not of faith, when he wrote, "If America's center fails to hold, it will leave the world's fate to hands less gentle and more guilt-stained than the American."

Lerner's involvement in so many notable projects and works of scholarship has been attributed to his remarkable energy, his love of teaching, and his need to support two families. More difficult to explain was the womanizing, known to his family as well as associates, which occurred throughout most of his adulthood.

For much of the last decade of his life Lerner was plagued with heart disease and cancer. He finally succumbed to a stroke and died at the age of eighty-nine in Mount Sinai Hospital in Manhattan. He is buried in Sag Harbor, New York.

★

The Max Lerner Papers are deposited at the Manuscripts and Archives Division of the Sterling Library, Yale University. Lerner never completed a planned autobiography but a manuscript of a chapter to be called "From Minsk to Manhood" was published as the first chapter in a full-scale biography by Sanford Lakoff, *Max Lerner: Pilgrim in the Promised Land* (1998). Most of Lerner's books were compilations of his newspaper columns, book reviews, and other published articles. They sometimes contain autobiographical materials. His works include: *It Is Later than You Think: The Need for a Militant Democracy* (1938, rev. 1943); *Ideas Are Weapons: The History and Uses of Ideas* (1939); *Ideas for the Ice Age: Studies in a Revolutionary Era* (1941); *Public Journal: Marginal Notes on Wartime America* (1945); *Actions and Passions: Notes on the Multiple Revolution of Our Time* (1949); *The Unfinished Country: A Book of American Symbols* (1959); and *The Age of Overkill: A Preface to World Politics* (1962). For Lerner's account of his battle with cancer, see *Wrestling with the Angel: A Memoir of My Triumph over Illness* (1990). Evaluation of Lerner's work may be found in Sanford Lakoff, "The Mind and Faith of Max Lerner," *Social Research* 61 (1994): 245–268, and Daniel Bell, *The End of Ideology: On the Exhaustion of Political Ideas in the Fifties* (1961): 95–102. For an interesting comparative study of Lerner and the historian Henry Steele Commager, see Michael Kammen, "They Made American History a Public Matter with Numerous Books and Considerable Patter," *Reviews in American History* 27 (Dec. 1999): 636–645. An obituary is in the *New York Times* (6 June 1992).

CHARLES E. LARSEN

LEWIS, Reginald Francis (*b.* 7 December 1942 in Baltimore, Maryland; *d.* 19 January 1993 in New York City), founder of the first African-American law firm on Wall Street and chief executive of the foods company Beatrice International Holdings.

Lewis was the son of Clinton Lewis, a small business owner, and Carolyn Cooper, a waitress and department store clerk. His father joined the navy when Lewis was an infant and later abandoned the family. When he was six, his parents divorced. Lewis and his mother then lived with his maternal grandparents. He was impressed by his grandfather's tales of his life in France as a soldier during World War I. These conversations led to his appreciation of French culture and language as an adult. In 1951 his mother married Jean Fugett, Sr., a postal employee, who also worked at the Department of Defense. The extended Lewis family expanded to include three half brothers and two half sisters.

Lewis grew up in a middle-class segregated section of Baltimore. He displayed initiative and business sense at an early age, and at age ten he had his first job delivering the *Baltimore Afro-American* newspaper. He was quite successful and so committed that he hired his mother to do the job when he went to summer camp.

Reginald Lewis, chairman and CEO of TLC Group, L.P., 1987. AP/WIDE WORLD PHOTOS

His education began in Catholic grade school, and after being denied admission to a Catholic high school, he went to Paul Lawrence Dunbar High School, a segregated school in Baltimore. Lewis was an outstanding athlete and leader, joining the football, baseball, and basketball teams. He graduated in 1961. Turning down an offer to play professional baseball with the Washington Senators, he attended Virginia State College, a black public institution in Petersburg, Virginia, on a football scholarship. He played quarterback but left the team after his freshman year due to a shoulder injury, causing him to lose his scholarship. Lewis then concentrated on his studies and held a variety of jobs to pay his tuition. He graduated with a degree in economics in 1965. Many students at that time went to military service, but Lewis was medically ineligible because he had diabetes.

Shortly after graduation he entered a summer school program at Harvard Law School. According to Lewis he did not submit an application to Harvard (although he later completed one). But by using his persuasive ability, appearing at formal social events, and securing a school loan from the dean of admissions, he became a full-time matriculated student. His senior thesis subject was on financial takeovers. He graduated in 1968. On 16 August 1969 Lewis married Loida Nicolas, a law graduate of the University of the Philippines. They had two daughters. Lewis moved to New York in 1968 to join the prestigious law firm of Paul, Weiss, Rifkind, Wheaton, and Garrison. He specialized in corporate and securities law. In 1970 he was admitted to the New York bar and helped found the firm of Wallace, Murphy, Thorpe, and Lewis. By 1973 Lewis had cofounded another firm, Lewis and Clarkson, which was the first African American law firm on Wall Street. It specialized in corporate law and venture capital transactions.

Lewis soon gained a reputation as a skilled financial analyst and business adviser, nearly overshadowing his success as a corporate lawyer. His next goal was to purchase a company, restructure it, and sell it again at a profit. After a couple of unsuccessful attempts in the mid-1970s he formed The TLC Group, standing for The Lewis Company, as an institutional holding company in 1983. Later that year he engineered a leveraged buyout of the McCall Pattern Company for an estimated $24.5 million. TLC used only $1 million in cash from investors, borrowing most of the funds from Bankers Trust Company. By 1986 Lewis had doubled McCall's profits, and his company had earned a place in the top ten of the *Black Enterprise Magazine* list of the top 100 black-owned businesses in the United States.

In 1987 he sold the firm for $95 million and negotiated a restructuring that gave him a share of over 80 percent of McCall's total equity. He earned himself and his partners a ninety-to-one return on their original investment and received a personal profit of $50 million. TLC also retained ownership of a manufacturing plant, 20 percent of McCall's stock, and a seat on the board of directors. A year later McCall filed for bankruptcy, and its new owners sued Lewis for fraud, claiming that he caused the company's insolvency, but the suit was dismissed for lack of evidence.

Lewis's greatest triumph came next. Beatrice International Foods was a multinational firm consisting of sixty-four companies in thirty-one foreign countries, whose product line consisted of processed meats, dairy products, and beverages. With the assistance of Michael Milken and the investment bank of Drexel, Burnham, Lambert, and using high yield debt commonly known at the time as "junk bonds," he bought Beatrice in a leveraged buyout transaction from Kohlberg, Kravis Roberts for $985 million in 1987. He restructured TLC Beatrice International, retaining fifteen core companies. Lewis then assumed management of the company, moving his family to Paris in order to supervise the transition. By 1989 TLC Beatrice was profitable, and in 1991 its net income surpassed $50 million. It soon generated revenue of over $2 billion per year.

Forbes magazine estimated Lewis's net worth at $400 million in 1992. He lived in New York and Paris and became an important philanthropist. In 1992 his $3 million contribution to Harvard Law School led to the establishment of the Reginald F. Lewis Center for International Studies. He also gave several million dollars to other educational, civic, and cultural institutions.

That same year Lewis learned that he had inoperable brain cancer and devoted himself to preparing a succession plan for TLC. The public was not notified for nearly one year, until he was hospitalized and in a coma. He died in New York on 19 January 1993. At the time of Lewis's death in New York City, his family owned 55 percent of TLC.

Reginald Lewis succeeded in the world of corporate finance and venture capitalism. He often spoke of being measured by his performance instead of his race. His contributions serve as an example not only to minority groups but also to all Americans.

★

The best source available is a posthumously published autobiography written with Blair S. Walker, *"Why Should White Guys Have All the Fun?" How Reginald Lewis Created a Billion-Dollar Business Empire* (1995). Profiles and essays appear in John N. Ingham and Lynne B. Feldman, *African-American Business Leaders: A Biographical Directory* (1994), and Gene N. Landrum, *Profiles of Black Success: Thirteen Creative Geniuses Who Changed the World* (1997). Further information is also located in *American National Biography* (1999), Peter M. Gareffa, ed., *Newsmakers: The People Behind Today's Headlines* (1988), and a revised edition of the same volume edited by Louise Mooney (1993). The history of TLC Beatrice is succinctly reviewed in "TLC's Final Act," *Black*

Enterprise Magazine 30 (Sept. 1999): 117–126. Obituaries are in the *New York Times* and *USA Today* (both 20 Jan. 1993).

ANTHONY TODMAN

LOEB, Henry, III (*b.* 9 Dec. 1920 in Memphis, Tennessee; *d.* 8 Sept. 1992 near Forrest City, Arkansas), segregationist mayor of Memphis at the time of the 1968 sanitation workers' strike during which Dr. Martin Luther King, Jr., was assassinated.

Loeb was the elder of two sons of William Loeb, the owner of a chain of laundries in Memphis, and Ethel Lob, a homemaker. The family was prosperous and locally prominent. After graduating from Phillips Academy in Andover, Massachusetts (1939), and Brown University (1943), Loeb served in World War II as commander of a PT boat in the Mediterranean, reaching the rank of lieutenant. He returned to join the family business and in 1951 married Mary Gregg, a former queen of the Memphis Cotton Carnival; they had three children.

Disagreements with his brother, combined with an interest in politics, caused Loeb to leave the laundry business. He entered public service with an appointment to the Memphis Park Commission in 1951. Handsome, charming and outspoken, he easily attracted attention with his six-

Henry Loeb, 1968. AP/WIDE WORLD PHOTOS

foot, six-inch frame. In 1950 the Jaycees voted him Outstanding Young Man of the Year, and in 1952 he was elected local commander of the American Legion. He gained a reputation as a political maverick by supporting Dwight D. Eisenhower in 1952 when Memphis was still a "yellow-dog Democrat" town.

Elected to the City Commission in 1955, he became commissioner of public works, pursuing potholes vigorously. He oversaw the city's sanitation department with such zeal that he began referring to himself as a "garbageman." Loeb quickly gained a high profile for open conduct of business, becoming the scourge of politicians who engaged in sweetheart deals or worse.

In 1959 he challenged the incumbent mayor, Edmund Orgill, who subsequently dropped out of the race for medical reasons. Thus Loeb became mayor almost by default. A fiscal and racial conservative, he reflected the views of those who had elected him. In 1960 the newly elected Loeb and the city commissioners heard an appeal from a group of black community leaders to desegregate the city's parks and museums. After listening to their presentation, Loeb said one word, "No," and swiveled his chair around to show them his back.

In October 1963 Loeb terminated his campaign for reelection and resigned as mayor, his mother's death necessitating his return to the family business. But he ran again in 1967 when the weak mayor-commission form of city government was scheduled to change to a mayor-council arrangement. Ever charismatic, he won with the support of the city's white voters in a highly charged, racially polarized campaign.

Early in his new term he converted from Judaism to Episcopalianism, the religion of his wife and children. From a political standpoint, it seemed an attempt to perfectly reflect the old-line Memphis establishment that supported him.

The new administration faced a serious operating deficit, and Loeb began an economy crusade. Six weeks into the term the city sanitation workers went out on strike, maintaining that their working conditions, pay, and benefits were unjustifiably inferior to those of white city workers. State and municipal laws forbade strikes by public employees. Loeb took refuge in those laws, as well as in the city deficit, to rebuff the workers, enjoying the support of both local newspapers and the white business establishment.

Loeb refused to believe that the sanitation workers struck of their own free will. Bitterly antiunion, he was convinced that they were the unwitting pawns of the American Federation of State, County, and Municipal Employees, which was trying to persuade the city to recognize the union as the bargaining agent for the striking workers. The union and the black leadership contended that inequities required redress.

But the mayor never wavered. Because the strike violated state law, Loeb maintained that he would not address the workers' grievances until they went back to work. This was a bit disingenuous. Although the law forbade the workers to strike, it did not prevent the city from negotiating with striking workers. Furthermore, in line with his belief in "open conduct of business," Loeb required that all strike negotiations be carried on publicly, with nothing going on behind closed doors. Throughout the negotiations, reporters scribbled and TV cameras blinked on and off. This made it extremely difficult for either side to make concessions without losing face.

Loeb was never a race-baiting extremist. Rather, he suffered from a "plantation" mentality that favored the status quo. During the strike he made sure that the families of the men on strike received food stamps, and he worked out an arrangement with the power company to ensure that strikers' homes would not have their power cut off. He continued to maintain that he would meet with the strikers to listen to their grievances if they went back to work. But he refused to give credence to the union. Likewise, he turned back conciliation efforts by political moderates, members of the clergy, and friends. Relentlessly stubborn and lacking a broader vision, he never understood that the striking workers wanted more than just higher wages and a union dues checkoff. He did not grasp that what he perceived as a labor dispute had become a civil rights issue.

Dr. Martin Luther King, Jr., planning a "Poor Peoples' March" on Washington, was attracted to the sanitation workers' strike as pertaining to his larger mission. On a Memphis visit to help bring attention to the strike, King was gunned down and killed by James Earl Ray as he stood on the balcony of his room at the Lorraine Motel. The assassination triggered extensive rioting in Memphis and other cities across the country. Loeb called it "the saddest day in Memphis history." Ironically, Loeb had been on the verge of winning the strike deadlock. More and more sanitation workers, dispirited by the strike's dragging on for two months, had gradually returned to work. But in the wake of King's death, Loeb was forced by the pressure of local and national media, as well as an urgent phone call from President Lyndon B. Johnson, to settle the strike, largely on the union's terms. Although Loeb was denounced in the press and from pulpits across the country, he never admitted any regret or wrongdoing in the way he handled the strike.

Loeb's local popularity among the white population of Memphis never diminished despite his connection to the King assassination. As late as 1980, a political adversary said of him, "I hate to admit it, but I don't believe there's anybody in Memphis who could beat him, even now."

He did not run for re-election in 1971 or any year thereafter and later moved with his wife to a farm in Arkansas. In 1988 he suffered a stroke that left him unable to speak. He died four years later of colon cancer and is buried in Memorial Park Cemetery in Memphis.

★

The papers of Henry Loeb III in the Memphis/Shelby County Archives include his terms as commissioner of public works (1956–1960) and mayor (1960–1963, 1968–1971). The best record of the sanitation workers' strike, including the death of Dr. Martin Luther King, Jr., is Joan Turner Beifuss, *At the River I Stand* (1985). Extensive coverage of the strike as well as much coverage of Loeb during his terms as mayor appeared in the Memphis newspapers, the *Commercial Appeal* and *Memphis Press-Scimitar*. The *New York Times* carried a profile of Loeb (17 Apr. 1968) soon after Dr. King's death. Some years after his retirement, *Memphis* magazine ran a lengthy two-part profile by Jackson Baker (Jan.–Feb. 1980). The *Memphis Flyer* carried a major retrospective (17–23 Sept. 1992) following Loeb's death. Obituaries are in the *New York Times* and the *Atlanta Constitution* (both 12 Sept. 1992). An interview with Fred Davis, one of the first black Memphis City Council members, whose first term of office was concurrent with Loeb's second term as mayor, provided valuable insights.

NATALIE B. JALENAK

LORDE, Audre Geraldine (*b.* 18 February 1934 in New York City; *d.* 17 November 1992 in Christiansted, St. Croix, Virgin Islands), African American lesbian feminist and poet who also used the pseudonym Rey Domini.

Born Audrey Geraldine Lorde, she was the youngest of four daughters of Linda Belmar and Frederic Byron Lorde, natives of the West Indies who lived in New York City and whose longing for home figured strongly in Lorde's perception of herself as an outsider. Her parents both worked to support the family, her father first as a laborer, then in real estate. Her mother also worked as a laborer and then became a homemaker. Lorde read and wrote at an early age but did not speak until she was five years old. She claimed that the sadness and silence of her parents—particularly her mother—influenced her choice to express herself in verse. Poor eyesight and a spunky attitude led to her placement in parochial schools. She attended Hunter College High School where a classmate was Diane Di Prima, who later helped to launch Lorde's first books. Her first published poem was in *Seventeen* magazine, after her high-school teacher criticized it as too romantic.

Lorde worked her way through Hunter College with a series of jobs, working in factories, as an X-ray technician, medical clerk, arts-and-crafts supervisor, social worker, and ghostwriter. She spent a year (1954) at National University in Mexico, where she had a significant early lesbian affair.

Audre Lorde. LIBRARY OF CONGRESS

Upon her return to New York City she threw herself into the gay-girl culture of Greenwich Village, which was then largely white. She also had some contact with the Harlem Writers Guild, which she found homophobic. Both of these groups, while important to her sense of self, also served to reinforce her feeling that she was an outsider.

After graduating with a B.A. degree from Hunter in 1959 she went on to earn an M.L.S. degree from Columbia University in Harlem in 1961. She worked as a librarian through the 1960s, first in the suburban Mount Vernon Public Library (1961–1963) and then as head librarian of the Town School Library in New York City (1966–1968). During these years she also surprised her friends by marrying an attorney, Edward Ashley Rollins, on 31 March 1962. This marriage ended in 1970 and she never spoke or wrote about it. She had two children from that union who gave her a central and defining role, that of mother.

In 1968 Lorde's first book, *The First Cities,* was published. That year she also received a National Endowment for the Arts (NEA) grant to teach a six-week poetry work-shop at Tougaloo College in Mississippi where she met her future longtime companion, Frances Clayton. The experience of working with serious young black students and living in the tense atmosphere of the Deep South during the civil rights era proved profoundly moving, and she wrote most of the poems for her next book, *Cables to Rage* (1970), during this brief stay. After her return to New York City she taught courses on poetry at City College and on racism at John Jay and Lehman Colleges in addition to writing and giving public lectures. She received a Creative Artists Public Service Grant in 1972 and her third book, *From a Land Where Other People Live,* published in 1973, was nominated for a National Book Award. She received the 1974 Creative Arts Public Service Book Award for Poetry for her fourth book, *New York Head Shop and Museum,* a political, rhetorical work that marked a departure from her earlier poetry. In 1975 she was named Woman of the Year by Staten Island Community College.

Her friendship with Adrienne Rich, a fellow feminist and lesbian poet, led to Lorde's first publication with a major publishing house. W. W. Norton brought out *Coal* in 1976, adding some new poems to a compilation of previously published work and introducing her to a much broader public. In *The Black Unicorn* (1978), Lorde examined African mythology and its relevance and relationship to the dispersal of her people.

Although Lorde identified herself first and foremost as a poet, she is also remembered as a fierce black feminist. Books such as the nonfiction *Sister Outsider* (1984) and the essay "The Master's Tools Will Never Dismantle the Master's House" became core readings in many women's studies curricula. She is also known to the wider public for her writings on her fourteen-year struggle with various forms of cancer: *The Cancer Journals* (1980) and *A Burst of Light* (1988). In *The Cancer Journals* she urged women who had also undergone mastectomies to see themselves as warriors and to bear their scars proudly. In the last decades of her life she traveled and spoke throughout the world. She cofounded the Kitchen Table: Women of Color Press with Barbara Smith in 1981. She also was a founder of Sisters in Support of Sisters in South Africa and a featured speaker at the first national march for gay and lesbian liberation in Washington, D.C., in 1979.

In 1981 Audre Lorde received a second NEA grant. She also returned to Hunter College, where she was a professor of English from 1980 to 1987 and Thomas Hunter Professor from 1987 to 1988. In 1985 Hunter dedicated the Audre Lorde Women's Poetry Center. Lorde received the Walt Whitman Citation of Merit in 1991, which accompanied her new title of poet laureate of New York State.

She received honorary doctorates from Hunter, Oberlin, and Haverford Colleges, and served on the board of the Feminist Press in New York City. She spent the last years of her life in the Caribbean, settling with her companion, Gloria I. Joseph, in St. Croix, Virgin Islands, There, Lorde was known by her African name, Gamba Adisa, meaning "warrior: she who makes her meaning clear."

Always an imposing presence, in her later years, with close-cropped, salt-and-pepper hair, she lost weight, but never stature. To the end she continued to write and speak out against racism, homophobia, and sexism. The original breast cancer metastasized and spread throughout her body. She died of liver cancer in St Croix.

★

Biographies of Lorde are in Darlene Clark Hine, *Black Women in America: An Historical Encyclopedia* (1993), and Valerie Smith, Lea Baechler, and A. Walton Litz, eds., *African-American Writers* (1991). She is also included in the *Dictionary of Literary Biography*, vol. 41 (1985) and numerous volumes of the *Contemporary Authors* series. An obituary is in the *New York Times* (20 Nov. 1992). A film, *Litany for Survival: The Life and Work of Audre Lorde*, was produced by Ada Griffin and Michelle Parkerson in 1994; Griffin and Parkerson spent eight years collaborating with Lorde in the creation of this film.

PAMELA ARMSTRONG LAKIN

LORENTZ, Pare (*b.* 11 December 1905 in Clarksburg, West Virginia; *d.* 4 March 1992 in Armonk, New York), documentary filmmaker best known for films produced under the sponsorship of U.S. government agencies during the 1930s.

Baptized Leonard MacTaggart Lorentz, he was one of two children born to Pare Hanson Lorentz, a printer, and Alma MacTaggart Ruttencutter, a professional singer. From Clarksburg, the family moved to Buckhannon, West Virginia, where his father opened a printing shop in 1909. Lorentz graduated from Buckhannon High School in 1922 and enrolled at Wesleyan College. A year later he transferred to the University of West Virginia, where he edited the *West Virginia Moonshine,* the student humor magazine, and was elected president of the Southern Association of College Editors. Lorentz left the university before graduating and in 1925 accepted a job in New York City as editor of the trade journal *Edison Mazda Lamp Sales Builder.* A year later he left *Edison* to become the movie critic for *Judge* magazine and assumed his father's given name, Pare.

Concerned about the control of content exerted in Hollywood by the Motion Picture Producers and Distributors of America, founded by Will Hays and popularly known as the Hays Office, and by film censors in several states, Lorentz joined attorney Morris L. Ernst in writing *Censored: The Private Life of the Movies* (1930). From 1931 to 1932 Lorentz was a movie critic for the *New York Evening Journal* and wrote for several other publications including *Vanity Fair, Town and Country,* and *McCall's.* In August

1931 he married the actress Sarah Richardson Bates, who went by the stage name Sally Bates. The couple had two children.

After President Franklin D. Roosevelt took office in 1933, Lorentz tried to find funding to make a short film about the effects of the Great Depression. Unsuccessful, he instead collected news photographs, wrote captions and text, and published *The Roosevelt Year: A Photographic Record* (1934).

In 1934 Lorentz was offered a job writing a syndicated column, "The Washington Side Show," for King Features, which was owned by William Randolph Hearst. This took him to Washington, D.C., where he discussed his ideas for photographing the changes proposed under the New Deal, such as the Tennessee Valley Authority, with acquaintances in the Department of Agriculture. One of these was Rexford Guy Tugwell, who headed the Resettlement Administration. After Lorentz was fired by Hearst for writing a column that was supportive of Secretary of Agriculture Henry A. Wallace, Tugwell hired him as a technical consultant to produce a series of films.

The first of these was *The Plow That Broke the Plains* (1936). Lorentz traveled with a crew filming images of the dust bowl conditions created by drought and questionable farming practices in the Great Plains. He hired the eminent composer and critic Virgil Thomson to write the score and then edited the film and wrote a narration. Lorentz intended to produce a film that not only informed people but was also compelling enough to be shown in commercial theaters. In spite of opposition from Hollywood, Lorentz managed to book the film into the Rialto Theatre in New York City. Favorable popular and critical response led to wider distribution throughout the country.

Lorentz's next film, *The River* (1937), which looked at life in the Mississippi River valley, followed the river's source in Minnesota to the Gulf of Mexico. Lorentz and his crew captured dramatic flood footage that demonstrated the need for soil conservation and flood control. Again, Virgil Thomson wrote the score. To gain acceptance for the film, Lorentz showed it in the river valley communities from New Orleans to St. Louis and beyond. Then, after a successful opening in New York City, Paramount Pictures agreed to distribute it. In 1938 *The River* was named best documentary film at the International Film Festival in Venice. The poetic narration, accompanied by stills from the film, was published as *The River* (1938).

With the support of President Roosevelt, in August 1938 the United States Film Service was created to coordinate distribution and exhibition of films produced by government agencies. Lorentz was appointed head of this organization. He had been developing ideas for a film about unemployment but encountered funding difficulties. When CBS offered him the opportunity to produce a radio program for the Columbia Workshop, a radio anthology program, Lorentz adapted those ideas for the radio script *Ecce Homo.* A film version was never completed.

Meanwhile, Lorentz began work on a film for the Public Health Service based on Paul de Kruif's 1938 book *The Fight for Life,* detailing the problems of childbirth and the unemployed. Wanting the film to be as accurate as possible, Lorentz sent the actors who would play key roles to train at the Chicago Maternity Center. Most of the film was shot there, with clinic workers and Chicago tenement dwellers appearing throughout the film. *The Fight for Life* (1940), Lorentz's first feature-length film, premiered to good reviews. National distribution rights were awarded to Columbia Pictures. The film won the National Board of Review Award for best documentary film.

Lorentz supervised two other Film Service productions, *Power and the Land* (1940), directed by Joris Ivers, and *The Land* (1941), directed by Robert J. Flaherty.

By 1940 opposition to government-sponsored films was growing. Some in Hollywood resented what they now as competition. Some members of Congress questioned the use of government funds for film production. For many, growing concern about international tensions overshadowed domestic concerns. After a series of congressional hearings, funds for the Film Service were eliminated in 1940.

Lorentz returned to *McCall's* as national defense editor and worked briefly on short films at RKO studios. In May 1942 he accepted a commission in the U.S. Air Corps and spent the war years producing briefing films for pilots and documenting the work of the Air Transport Command. After the war Lorentz served as chief of films, theater, and music in occupied countries for the Civil Affairs Division of the War Department, and was responsible for the War Department's film *The Nuremberg Trials* (1946).

Back in New York City, he formed Pare Lorentz Associates and served as president and treasurer from 1947 to 1978, consulting on film projects and lecturing at colleges and universities. In 1949 he married Elizabeth Meyer.

Lorentz received several honorary degrees and awards, including the International Documentary Association Career Achievement Award (1985) and the Washington Film Council Award of Honor (1986). He died from cancer at age eighty-six in Armonk.

Retrospective festival screenings of Pare Lorentz's films demonstrate his contribution to the development of the documentary film genre. While produced to inform the public of specific government programs during the New Deal era, these documentaries present a clear point of view regarding social, economic, and environmental concerns. Their persuasive power, however, comes from the dramatic impact of the visual images and the subtle integration of poetic narration, music, and sound.

★

The Pare Lorentz Collection of books, papers, and films is at the Polk Library, University of Wisconsin at Oshkosh. His personal papers are at the Franklin D. Roosevelt Library, Hyde Park, New York. Lorentz's autobiography is *FDR's Moviemaker: Memoirs and Scripts* (1992). *Lorentz on Film* (1975) contains biographical notes and a selection of his movie reviews. Robert L. Snyder's biography, *Pare Lorentz and the Documentary Film* (1968), places Lorentz's films within a historical context. Erik Barnouw discusses these films in *Documentary: A History of the Non-Fiction Film* (1983). An obituary is in the *New York Times* (5 Mar. 1992).

LUCY A. LIGGETT

LOY, Myrna (*b.* 2 August 1905 in Raidersburg, Montana; *d.* 14 December 1993 in New York City), actress whose long career in films ranged from depicting exotic vamps to embodying the ideal American wife.

Born Myrna Adele Williams, Loy was the daughter of David Franklin Williams and Della Mae Johnson. Her father was a rancher who served as a member of the Montana House of Representatives and later worked in real estate and banking. Her mother was a singer. In 1912 the family moved to Helena, Montana, where Loy's brother was born.

Myrna Loy in a publicity photo for the film *Lucky Night,* 1939. © BETTMANN/CORBIS

Four years later, during a family trip to California, Loy became convinced that she would become an actress. She began taking dancing lessons and performed in a Helena fund-raising event. In 1918, after her father died in the influenza epidemic, Loy, her mother, and her brother moved permanently to California.

Loy attended the Westlake School in Los Angeles for two years and graduated from Venice High School in 1923. That summer, while she was dancing in the chorus at Grauman's Chinese Theater, her photograph came to the attention of Rudolph Valentino and his wife, Natacha Rambova, who took personal charge of Loy's screen test. The test won her bit parts in a number of films, including *Pretty Ladies* (1925) and *Ben-Hur* (1926). Around this time she changed her name to Myrna Loy.

After Loy signed a contract with Warner Brothers, her roles became steadily larger, although she was often consigned to playing vamps, gun molls, mistresses, and wicked women of vaguely Asian background. She could be spotted briefly in the landmark film *The Jazz Singer* (1927) and was occasionally rewarded with a title role, as in *The Girl from Chicago* (1927) and *State Street Sadie* (1928). She could also be seen in such movies as *The Desert Song* (1929, as the native girl Azuri), *Show of Shows* (1929), and *Under a Texas Moon* (1930). After Warner Brothers failed to renew her contract, Loy moved to Fox Studios, where her roles, while more prominent, still obliged her to play mostly treacherous or heartless women in such films as *Body and Soul, A Connecticut Yankee,* and *Hush Money,* all released in 1931. She was kept busy throughout that year, appearing in *Rebound* and *Consolation Marriage* on loan to RKO Studios and also taking a small but sympathetic part opposite Ronald Colman in Samuel Goldwyn's film version of Sinclair Lewis's novel *Arrowsmith* (1925).

Signed by Metro-Goldwyn-Mayer (MGM) in 1932, Loy continued to play mostly nasty roles, turning up that year in, among others, *The Wet Parade, Emma,* and most preposterously, *The Mask of Fu Manchu,* in which she was the sadistic daughter of the monstrous Dr. Fu. On loan to RKO, she was an evil Asian murderess in *Thirteen Women* (1932), a manipulative "other woman" in *The Animal Kingdom* (1932), and a worldly vamp in *Topaze* (1933). At Paramount, she was featured in her first classic film, playing the man-crazy Countess Valentine in Rouben Mamoulian's witty, sparkling musical comedy *Love Me Tonight* (1932), which starred Maurice Chevalier and Jeanette MacDonald.

At MGM, Loy's star continued to rise until she was playing a variety of roles in major releases. As the size of her roles increased, Loy's innate warmth, intelligence, and sophistication came to replace her wicked, vampish persona, and she was entirely sympathetic in such films as *When Ladies Meet* (1933), *Penthouse* (1933), and *Manhattan Melodrama* (1934). A major breakthrough in her career came in 1934, when she was cast opposite the suave, dapper William Powell in *The Thin Man,* the first in a series of popular comedy-mysteries featuring the society detective Nick Charles and his wife, Nora. Quipping, hard-drinking, and clearly in love with each other, Nick and Nora gave a new dimension to the depiction of marriage in movies. *The Thin Man* was so successful that it spawned five sequels as well as a number of lesser imitations. In real life, Loy gave her own approval of marriage by becoming the wife of the film producer Arthur Hornblow, Jr., on 27 June 1936.

By the end of the 1930s and into the 1940s, Loy was MGM's leading female actress, often costarring with the rugged Clark Gable. In 1936 a nationwide poll conducted by the newspaper columnist Ed Sullivan crowned them king and queen of Hollywood. In *Wife vs. Secretary* (1936), *Test Pilot* (1938), and *Too Hot to Handle* (1938), her lady-like ways complemented his brash masculinity. Still, her most compatible costar and onscreen husband remained William Powell, whose suavity matched her wry wit and sophistication, not only in the *Thin Man* movies but also in *The Great Ziegfeld* (1936), in which she played actress Billie Burke; *Double Wedding* (1937); *I Love You Again* (1940); and *Love Crazy* (1941). In real life, however, marriage for Loy was not as congenial—in 1942 she divorced Hornblow and six days later married John D. Hertz, Jr., an advertising executive and heir to the Hertz Rent-a-Car fortune. For the next few years, during World War II, Loy left the screen to work with the Red Cross, arranging entertainment for wounded servicemen. On 3 January 1946, having divorced Hertz in 1944, Loy married a third time, to Gene Markey, a writer and producer whose previous wives included the actresses Hedy Lamarr and Joan Bennett.

In 1946 Loy had one of the best roles of her career in Samuel Goldwyn's production of *The Best Years of Our Lives.* As Milly, the loving, supportive wife of a banker and returning war veteran, Al Stephenson (Fredric March), she enhanced this sensitive drama and was especially moving in the scene in which she welcomes her husband home. The film won seven Academy Awards, including one as Best Picture, and Loy received the Brussels World Film Festival prize for the best performance by an actress. Her subsequent roles in such movies as *The Bachelor and the Bobby-Soxer* (1947), *Mr. Blandings Builds His Dream House* (1948), and *Cheaper By the Dozen* (1950) took advantage of her screen image as a wise, capable woman. *Mr. Blandings* in particular gave Loy a choice role as the patient wife of hapless new homeowner Cary Grant.

In real life Loy was becoming more active in public affairs. In 1945 she attended the San Francisco conference at which the United Nations was created and later served as a tireless U.S. representative to UNESCO. A lifelong fighter for liberal causes, she attacked fascism in the 1930s, and in the 1940s and 1950s she spoke openly against Senator Joseph McCarthy and the House Un-American Activities Committee, which sought to rout communists in the entertainment industry. In 1950 she divorced Markey and on 1 June 1951 married her fourth husband, Howland Sargeant, then assistant secretary of state for public affairs. They divorced in 1960 after several years of separation.

Loy continued to make occasional appearances in films, playing supporting roles in *The Ambassador's Daughter* (1956), *Lonelyhearts* (1959), and *From the Terrace* (1960), in which she had an uncharacteristic role as a battered, alcoholic wife. She also turned up as Doris Day's solicitous aunt in *Midnight Lace* (1960) and as Charles Boyer's eccentric wife in *The April Fools* (1969). In the 1960s and 1970s she toured in many plays, including *The Marriage-Go-Round, Barefoot in the Park,* and *Don Juan in Hell,* and she appeared in a 1972 Broadway revival of Clare Boothe Luce's *The Women.* She also starred in numerous television productions. During this period she remained active in government and politics. She was appointed chairman of the Advisory Council of the National Committee Against Discrimination in Housing, and she worked assiduously for many years on the presidential campaigns of Eugene McCarthy, Adlai Stevenson, and Robert Kennedy.

Late in her career Loy took supporting roles in *Airport 1975* (1974) *The End* (1979), and *Just Tell Me What You Want* (1980) while continuing to appear in television plays, most notably *Summer Solstice* (1981), opposite Henry Fonda. She also received many honors. In 1980 the National Board of Review of Motion Pictures presented her with its first David Wark Griffith Award "in grateful recognition of her outstanding contribution to the art of screen acting." She received a Kennedy Center Honor in December 1988 and a Lifetime Achievement Academy Award in March 1991. She died during surgery in New York City in 1993 and was buried in Forestvale Cemetery in Helena.

During a career that spanned more than five decades, Myrna Loy was much more than just a piquantly beautiful star. From her early roles as a seductive vamp to her many years as the onscreen essence of womanly warmth and sophistication, she radiated a special charisma that enchanted moviegoers. She was also a dedicated public servant and a fervent champion of the causes in which she believed.

★

The Myrna Loy Center, established over twenty years ago in Loy's hometown of Helena, offers extensive programs in the performing arts. *Myrna Loy: Being and Becoming* (1987), written with James Kotsilibas-Davis, is her autobiography. Karen Kay, *Myrna Loy* (1977), and Lawrence J. Quirk, *The Films of Myrna Loy* (1980), cover most of her life and career. References to Loy can also be found in biographies of Clark Gable, William Powell, Louis B. Mayer, and Irving Thalberg. Obituaries are in the *New York Times* (15 Dec. 1993) and *Variety* (27 Dec. 1993).

TED SENNETT

LUDWIG, Daniel Keith (*b.* 24 June 1897 in South Haven, Michigan; *d.* 27 August 1992 in New York City), shipping tycoon who developed new methods of financing and constructing ships and amassed the world's largest fleet of tankers.

Ludwig was the only child of Daniel F. Ludwig, a ship captain, and Flora Ludwig. Ludwig was obsessed with privacy and shunned the press, so details about his early life are limited and based almost entirely on a single interview he gave in 1957. He claimed he began business activities at the age of nine by purchasing a sunken boat, which he salvaged, repaired, and chartered at a profit. Ludwig dropped out of public school in the eighth grade, and after his parents separated a year later in 1912, he moved with his father to Port Arthur, Texas. He worked at a ship chandler's firm and studied marine engineering at night school. Returning to Michigan a year or two later, he worked at the Morse Fairbanks marine engine company for three years.

Ludwig quit Morse Fairbanks in 1916 to go into business for himself. With a loan cosigned by his father, he

Daniel Keith Ludwig. LIBRARY OF CONGRESS

bought a derelict excursion boat, sold its boiler and machinery, and converted it into a barge. He purchased other small barges and tugboats and began chartered operations, hauling molasses from New York to Canada for A. L. Kaplan. Ludwig later concentrated on hauling lumber products with his tugboats.

After the end of World War I, Ludwig sold some of his tugboats, purchased a surplus tanker from the War Shipping Board, and began hauling fuel oil for a refinery in Massachusetts. His purchase of a second, larger tanker required additional capital, so he took on a partner, who subsequently took over control of the business and left Ludwig with only a few tugboats.

Ludwig formed the American Tanker Corporation in 1925 with capital supplied by owners of a chain of gasoline stations in Massachusetts. The firm purchased other surplus tankers from the War Shipping Board to supply gasoline stations and other customers. Ludwig suffered extensive back injuries in 1926, when an explosion occurred on one of the gasoline tankers. He swam extensively, the only sport or hobby he participated in, to relieve the chronic back pain he experienced for the rest of his life. Although six feet tall, Ludwig's back injuries caused him to stoop and walk with a slight limp. Otherwise, he kept himself in excellent health, avoiding smoking and drinking. He kept trim and lean by eating sparingly, with a taste for buttermilk and bananas.

Ludwig married Gladys Madeline Jones, a chorus girl, on 29 February 1928. They had one daughter in 1936, but Ludwig denied paternity and obtained a divorce in April 1937. That same year Ludwig married Gertrude Virginia ("Ginger"), who had two children from a previous marriage.

During the 1930s Ludwig concentrated on oil tankers, using a converted coal ship to haul oil on a charter basis from one port to another. When the economy began to revive in the late 1930s, he prospered by focusing on oil shipping. Ludwig set up operations as National Bulk Carriers in 1936 and innovated the ship financing process. He purchased ships by borrowing from banks, using charter leases as well as the physical ship as collateral. He financed conversions of dry bulk ships, which hauled grain and ore and whose trade had fallen during the economic autarky of the 1930s, into oil tankers, which met growing demands for domestic and foreign oil. He also acquired shipbuilding facilities in Virginia.

During World War II, Ludwig's major shipbuilding operations were taken over by the U.S. Navy. He kept control of one small facility that produced tankers requisitioned by the government, but which were returned to him at the end of the war. Ludwig pioneered in several new techniques, principally welding rather than riveting hulls and sideways rather than traditional bow-first launches.

Ludwig owned one of the world's largest tanker fleets at the end of the war, and foreseeing a growing postwar demand for oil, he built ever-larger tankers. He negotiated with the Japanese and Japan's occupation government to build a new shipyard in Kure that, benefiting from low rents, low labor costs, and minimal government restrictions, constructed giant tankers at half the cost of those made in shipyards in the United States. The absence of union rules and government regulations allowed experimentation in new building methods, and Ludwig adapted an assembly-line, high-efficiency method of production. His efforts helped Japan become one of the world's largest shipbuilders during the third quarter of the twentieth century.

Ludwig also took advantage of postwar legislation that allowed registration of ships under foreign "flags of convenience," such as Liberia and Panama, to further reduce sailors' pay, labor union membership, and governmental regulations. One of his business subordinates, Steve Bollenbach, described Ludwig as "the meanest man I've ever worked for."

As the demand for oil skyrocketed during the 1960s and 1970s, so did the demand for oil tankers and Ludwig's fortunes. He used his excess cash to diversify into real estate, public utilities, and banking, obtaining control of businesses in more than two dozen countries. Most striking and most unprofitable, he invested $1 billion in a pulp and paper development project during the late 1970s. With the cooperation of Brazilian officials and bankers then seeking foreign investment, Ludwig purchased 4 million acres of rain forest, a tract approximately the size of Connecticut, along the Jari River in Brazil's Amazon basin. Ludwig razed the virgin rain forest and planted masses of melina (*gmelina arborea*), a fast-growing evergreen tree imported from Southeast Asia. Ludwig told an interviewer, "I always wanted to plant trees like rows of corn." Although melina grew rapidly in its native land and in the laboratory tests set up by Ludwig's scientists, it failed to adapt to the Brazilian environment. Ludwig lost over a billion dollars on the project before bailing out in 1981. *Time* magazine commented: "Not many men have lost a billion dollars and managed to remain billionaires. Daniel Ludwig . . . did just that."

Ludwig refrained from any other major business ventures after the Jari debacle, concentrating his efforts during the 1980s on promoting cancer research. In 1971 he founded the Ludwig Institute for Cancer Research in Zurich, Switzerland, and it eventually established research centers in ten countries. Johns Hopkins University awarded Ludwig an honorary doctorate in 1980. He spent his final years, like the rest of his life, in relative anonymity. He employed a public relations firm to keep his name out of the press and once attacked a photographer who attempted to photograph him on his daily walk to his New York City office.

Ludwig died of heart failure at the age of ninety-five.

The bulk of his estate was willed to various medical schools and cancer research institutes. Ludwig had taken particular care to ensure that the daughter of his first wife would obtain no inheritance. He had had samples of his blood tested and placed in cold storage in 1982 and again in 1988 in anticipation of the inevitable probate litigation.

Ludwig became one of the richest men in the world by transporting oil at a time when the American economy shifted its energy base from coal to petroleum. He was also an early proponent of globalization and multiplied his fortune by taking advantage of low-cost labor and minimal government regulations at Japanese shipyards and foreign-registry of his ships. He was less successful in his personal life, and one of his lawyers described him as "a billionaire with trailer-park problems."

★

Ludwig is the subject of a biography by Jerry Shields, *The Invisible Billionaire, Daniel Ludwig* (1986), which supersedes the chapters dealing with him in Kenneth Lamott, *The Moneymakers* (1969); and Jacqueline Thompson, *The Very Rich Book* (1981). Modesto da Silveira, *Ludwig, imperador do Jari* (1981), has not been translated into English. For his role in shipping and oil see George Rosie, *The Ludwig Initiative: A Cautionary Tale of North Sea Oil* (1978); Charles Coombs, *Tankers, Giants of the Sea* (1979); Tomohei Chida and Peter N. Davies, *The Japanese Shipping and Shipbuilding Industries: A History of Their Modern Growth* (1990); and René De La Pedraja, *The Rise and Decline of U.S. Merchant Shipping in the Twentieth Century* (1992). The Amazon River basin project is described in Loren McIntyre, "Jari," *National Geographic* 157 (May 1980); and Clayton E. Posey et al., *Plantation Forestry in the Amazon: The Jari Experience* (1997). His relationship with his disowned daughter is mentioned in Ruth G. Davis, "Bad Blood," *New York* 28 (9 Oct. 1995). Obituaries are in the *New York Times* (29 Aug. 1992) and the *Washington Post* (29 Aug. 1992). Vivienne King wrote and produced a documentary film, *Mr. Ludwig's Tropical Dreamland* (1979).

STEPHEN G. MARSHALL

LURIA, Salvador Edward (*b.* 13 August 1912 in Turin, Italy; *d.* 6 February 1991 in Lexington, Massachusetts), microbiologist whose research on the genetics of viruses and bacteria earned him the Nobel Prize in 1969.

Born Salvatore Luria and nicknamed "Salva," Luria belonged to a middle-class branch of an old and proud Jewish family. His father, David Luria, an accountant, and his well-read mother, Esther Sacerdote, a homemaker, encouraged a refined intellectualism. Salva's older brother was an early role model. As Fascism developed in Italy, Luria responded to the liberal socialism of a rebellious high school literature teacher. His lifelong friend, Ugo Fano, inspired an interest in physics and pure science. Not a passionate student, Salva chose medical school and graduated from the University of Turin in 1935, unenthusiastic about treating patients.

Luria served his internship in the medical histology laboratory of Giuseppe Levi, where he learned experimental techniques and maintained (as he would throughout life) an active interest in literature. Attempting to combine the strengths of medicine and physics, Luria then joined a radiology laboratory. During this time he served for eighteen months (and he reported, ineptly) in the Italian army.

Looking to prepare for a career in science, Luria affiliated in 1937 as a radiologist with the physics laboratory of Enrico Fermi at the University of Rome. During this period Luria was exposed to the German physicist Max Delbrück's ideas regarding the molecular nature of the gene. The bacteriologist Gio Rita introduced Luria to bacteriophage viruses and to related laboratory techniques. Just when Luria won an Italian government fellowship to travel to Delbrück's laboratory in Berkeley, California, the Fascist racial laws (which among other laws, excluded Jews from any government position and most other positions of responsibility) were passed and Luria's fellowship disappeared.

While his family stayed, suffered, and survived the Fascist era and the war, Luria was eager to cut his ties to the past and create a new future. He emigrated first to Paris in 1938 and worked at the Institute of Radium on the effects of radiation on bacteriophage. Paris provided ample opportunity for him to exercise his interest in radical socialist politics. After enduring the fall of Paris to the German army on 14 May 1940, Luria departed by bicycle, making his way toward Lisbon with the help of expatriate Italians. Having obtained a U.S. visa in Marseilles, he entered New York Harbor on 12 September 1940 with $52 and the clothes on his back.

Enrico Fermi, then at Columbia University, helped Luria obtain a Rockefeller Foundation fellowship to continue his research at Columbia's College of Physicians and Surgeons. Luria applied immediately for citizenship, using the opportunity to adopt the Spanish variant of his name and transposing the truncated "e" to a new middle name: Edward. (Naturalization followed in 1947.) In December 1940 he met Delbrück at a conference in Philadelphia, Pennsylvania, and began a collaboration that was to last many years. Later their collaboration included Alfred Hershey. The three formed the core of the "phage group" that received the Nobel Prize in 1969. The field of study using the viruses that infect bacteria yielded valuable information on the subcellular mechanisms of mutation and reproduction. Delbrück was at Vanderbilt University, but they were able to work closely during summers at the Cold Spring Harbor Laboratory, alongside such leading geneticists as Hermann Muller and Barbara McClintock.

In 1941, with T. F. Anderson, Luria used one of the first

electron microscopes to obtain a picture of bacteriophage. This significant achievement and others won for Luria a Guggenheim fellowship that he used to join research teams at Vanderbilt and Princeton.

In January 1943 Luria joined the faculty of Indiana University, where he proved to be an enthusiastic and popular professor. In the laboratory he demonstrated spontaneous mutations in bacteria, and Delbrück worked out the mathematical explanation for these events. Luria discovered the reactivation of bacteriophage killed by radiation, opening the field of DNA repair studies. His first graduate student at Indiana in 1947 was James Watson, who later elucidated the molecular structure of the gene and was awarded the 1962 Nobel Prize. Renato Dulbecco, also associated with Luria at Indiana, won the 1975 Nobel Prize for his work on the cultures of viruses and tumor cells.

Luria married Zella Hurwitz, then a graduate psychology student, on 18 April 1945. Their only child was born in 1948. In 1950 the Lurias moved to the University of Illinois, which was building a strong biochemistry and genetics program based on the research of Irwin Gunsalus and Sol Spiegelman. Luria continued his work on bacteriophage, discovering the restriction modification phenomenon, which was to become the foundation of genetic engineering.

In 1951 Luria was refused a passport as a result of his outspoken political activism. His socialism and commitment to justice and equality drew him to many causes, and he affiliated with like-minded intellectuals. He opposed McCarthyism and nuclear testing and supported organized labor and civil rights. He was still on the blacklist of the National Institutes of Health and actively opposing the Vietnam War when he learned of winning the Nobel Prize in 1969. He felt that his life in the Midwest contributed significantly to his personal sense of identity as an American intellectual.

The Midwest period came to an end in 1958 with a sabbatical year at the Massachusetts Institute of Technology (MIT), which offered him a faculty position in 1959. Luria was given the authority to build a strong biology department at MIT, while Zella joined the faculty at Tufts University. Luria was director of the Center for Cancer Research at MIT from 1974 to 1985, although he retired from most other official duties in 1978. The Lurias' extensive involvement in the Boston and Cambridge communities was based as much on social and political interests as on scientific interests.

Luria's writings, aside from scores of specialized scientific papers, drew a wide readership. His early textbook *General Virology* (1953) went through four editions. *Life: The Unfinished Experiment* (1973), a book written for the general public, won the National Book Award for science. *A View of Life* (1981), a beginning biology text written with

Salvador Luria. ARCHIVE PHOTOS

Stephen Jay Gould and Sam Singer, was an admittedly unsuccessful attempt to reap the royalties that come from popular school titles. His autobiography, published in 1984, was a successful attempt to write a more literary than scientific narrative.

Luria died of a heart attack at his home in suburban Lexington, on 6 February 1991. Through his original experiments and as a prolific and persuasive writer and teacher, Luria contributed heavily to the growth and synthesis of the discoveries that formed the prevailing paradigm of molecular biology.

★

The personal papers of Salvador Luria are housed at the American Philosophical Society in Philadelphia, Pennsylvania. Luria's autobiography, *A Slot Machine, A Broken Test Tube: An Autobiography* (1984), is a personal memoir containing as much motivational revelation as scientific explication. A biographical article by Tom Crawford is in Emily J. McMurray, ed., *Notable Twentieth Century Scientists*, vol. 3 (1995). Obituaries are in the *New York Times* (7 Feb. 1991) and *Genetics* 131 (May 1992): 1–4.

MICHAEL F. HAINES

LYNES, (Joseph) Russell, Jr. (*b*. 2 December 1910 in Great Barrington, Massachusetts; *d*. 14 September 1991 in New York City), longtime editor of *Harper's* magazine, noted authority on cultural taste, and social historian.

Lynes was born to Joseph Russell Lynes, an Episcopal clergyman, and Adelaide Sparkman, a homemaker, in the rectory of St. James's Church in Great Barrington. He attended public schools in his hometown and in Jersey City, New Jersey, before entering the Cathedral Choir School in New York City in 1920. In 1925 he enrolled at the Berkshire School in Sheffield, Massachusetts, from which he graduated in 1928. He then entered Yale University, in New Haven, Connecticut, and earned a bachelor of arts in English in 1932.

For four years following his graduation from Yale, Lynes worked as a clerk at the publishing agency Harper and Brothers. On 30 May 1934 he wed Mildred Akin, and they subsequently had two children. In 1936 Lynes moved from his office in Manhattan up the Hudson River to Poughkeepsie, New York, to take a position as the director of publications at Vassar College, at that time an all-female institution. A year later he and his wife moved from Poughkeepsie to Bryn Mawr, Pennsylvania, to become assistant principals of the Shipley School, a boarding school for girls. Beginning in 1940 the couple shared duties as principals of that institution. During his four-year tenure at Shipley, Lynes also served from 1942 through 1944 as an assistant chief of the civilian training branch of the U.S. Army Services Forces in the War Department.

In 1944 Lynes moved back to Manhattan and joined *Harper's* magazine as an assistant editor. By 1947 he was a managing editor, a post he held until 1967, when he became a contributing editor. From 1947 through 1957 Lynes published more than 100 essays in a variety of popular and scholarly journals on topics ranging from art and museums to architecture and cultural taste. Yet no other piece gained him more attention than "Highbrow, Lowbrow, Middlebrow," published in *Harper's* in February 1949.

In that article Lynes argued that social status and economic power no longer determined a person's "taste," defined as the strange distinction separating those who know good "culture" from those who do not. While the article was widely read, a firestorm of discussion erupted two months later following a reprint of Lynes's argument as a cartoonish chart in *Life* magazine. In either form Lynes suggested that Americans could be grouped according to their tastes in art, music, dress, drink, and general cultural preferences. This was a unique piece of commentary because never before had so prominent a critic defined so starkly the cultural distinctions of such a wide audience. At the time and years later Lynes explained that he was "just

poking fun at intellectual pretensions." Indeed he illustrated that judging people on their appearances rather than their intelligence was ridiculous. Yet his article and the chart that followed seemed to backfire. It became popular to categorize oneself and everyone else by Lynes's pithy labels.

In 1954 Harper Brothers published Lynes's first serious attempt at cultural history, a book entitled *The Tastemakers*. While the volume included Lynes's infamous essay, it also took a long-term view of changes in popular taste from the period immediately following the Civil War to contemporary times. The book received favorable reviews, giving Lynes scholarly respectability and making him a pioneer in the fields of cultural studies and popular culture.

Lynes published a number of books that illustrated his rhetorical flair for diminishing the stature of the wealthy but tasteless. Earlier works such as *Snobs: A Guidebook to Your Friends, Your Enemies, Your Colleagues, and Yourself* (1950), *Guests: Or, How to Survive Hospitality* (1951), and *Confessions of a Dilettante* (1966) took brief and humorous looks at people for whom image was everything and substance was trivial. He returned to the theme of social observation in his last book, *Life in the Slow Lane: Observations on Art, Architecture, Manners, and Other Such Spectator Sports* (1991). As the title suggests, Lynes had an interest in matters beyond merely critiquing his neighbors. He was a Renaissance man, whose writing style and varied interests helped shape *Harper's* magazine into an intelligent, mainstream periodical that enjoyed great prominence in the 1940s, 1950s, and 1960s.

Lynes also became a noteworthy expert on the history of American art museums. In *Good Old Modern* (1973), he chronicled the origins and early history of the Museum of Modern Art in New York City. The book remains one of the best volumes on the personalities and dynamics of the museum's founding and development. Lynes had the distinct honor of being the only nonacademic asked to contribute to *The Lively Audience: A Social History of the Visual and Performing Arts in America, 1890–1950* (1985), a series of scholarly monographs on American culture. His reputation as an intelligent critic with broad expertise in the American arts was further advanced in *The Art-Makers: An Informal History of Painting, Sculpture, and Architecture in Nineteenth-Century America* (1982) and *More Than Meets the Eye: The History and Collections of Cooper-Hewitt Museum, the Smithsonian Institution's National Museum of Design* (1981).

Lynes died of heart failure in New York City. Known as the "dean of social sciences at the house of Harper" and characterized as "the maestro of an unpretentious brand of social commentary which is civilized and stimulating," Lynes wrote as an expert for the educated public. He emerged as a popular critic in an era that fell between a period dominated by the "custodians of culture," as historian Henry May called them, and the self-imposed obscurity of deconstructionist and postmodernist critics of a later era. Lynes appeared on a number of television shows to speak about American art and culture, and for many years he also contributed regular columns, "Russell Lynes Observes" in *Architectural Digest,* "The State of Taste" in *Art in America,* and "After Hours" in *Harper's.*

★

Yale University's Beinecke Rare Book and Manuscript Library holds a collection of Lynes's papers. Lynes's books *Confessions of a Dilettante* (1966) and *Life in the Slow Lane* (1991) are good collections of essays from the many periodicals that published his work. J. Brooks, "Highbrow, Lowbrow, Middlebrow, Now," *American Heritage* (June/July 1983), is an interview with Lynes. An obituary is in the *New York Times* (16 Sept. 1991).

RAYMOND J. HABERSKI, JR.

M

McCLINTOCK, Barbara   (*b.* 16 June 1902 in Hartford, Connecticut; *d.* 2 September 1992 in Huntington, New York), geneticist whose groundbreaking work in the field using maize made her the sole winner of the 1983 Nobel Prize in physiology or medicine for the discovery of "mobile genetic elements."

McClintock was the third of four children of Thomas Henry McClintock, a physician, and Sara Handy, a homemaker. From McClintock's earliest years her relationship with her mother was strained, so between the ages of three and six she was sent to live with an aunt and uncle in rural Massachusetts. There she acquired a love of nature that lasted throughout her lifetime. In 1908 McClintock and her family moved to Brooklyn, New York, where her father forbade his children's teachers to assign them homework. Consequently McClintock was able to pursue many outside interests, including playing the piano and ice-skating.

In 1919 after graduating from Erasmus Hall High School in Brooklyn, New York, McClintock enrolled at Cornell University in Ithaca, New York. She became the president of the freshmen women and also played the tenor banjo in a jazz group until she found that those activities took too much time away from her studies. At that time she also realized that her independent spirit could only be kept alive if it were unfettered by close emotional relationships, and she decided that marriage did not fit into her plans.

McClintock developed a keen interest in cytology while working privately with Professor Lester Sharp (who would later become her thesis advisor) on Saturdays. Her performance was noticed and, as a result, she was invited to take graduate-level genetics courses during her junior year. In 1923 she received a B.S. degree and began graduate school at Cornell. Her major was cytology with minors in genetics and zoology. Although the fruit fly (*Drosophila melanogaster*) was the organism of choice for experiments in many laboratories at that time, corn or maize (*Zea mays*) was selected at Cornell. While a graduate student, McClintock modified a technique originally developed by John Belling, a botanist at the Florida Agricultural Experiment Station, that permitted her to apply the preparation of slides to detailed chromosomal studies of maize.

After she earned an M.A. degree in 1925 and a Ph.D. in 1927, McClintock was appointed as an instructor in Cornell's botany department. Remaining in this position until 1931, she was particularly concerned about the relationship between linkage groups and specific chromosomes in corn. At that time McClintock's mentor Rollins A. Emerson, along with Charles R. Burnham and other young scientists such as Marcus Rhoades, George Beadle, and Harriet Creighton, formed a small but important group of individuals studying the sequence of genes.

In 1931 McClintock and Creighton, who had been McClintock's student, published a study proving that a correlation existed between genetic and chromosomal cross-

Barbara McClintock. AP/WIDE WORLD PHOTOS

over. This work later became the cornerstone of modern genetic research. From approximately 1931 to 1933 McClintock was a fellow of the National Research Council. For the next year or so after that she was a fellow with the Guggenheim Foundation, which enabled her to go to the Kaiser Wilhelm Institute in Berlin. She soon returned, however, because she was concerned about Adolf Hitler's rise to power. McClintock's next position was as a research associate with Cornell from 1934 to 1936. During this time she became interested in the mutagenic effects of X-rays on corn that had been demonstrated by Lewis Stadler at the University of Missouri at Columbia. Stadler sent her some irradiated strains of corn, and McClintock identified ring chromosomes and hypothesized the existence of a telomere, a structure at the tip of a chromosome that ensured its stability. As a result of this association, Stadler brought McClintock to the University of Missouri, where she remained from 1936 to 1941 as an assistant professor of botany.

In 1942, under the auspices of the Carnegie Institution of Washington and with an invitation obtained by Rhoades, McClintock became a staff member at Cold Spring Harbor, the institution's center for genetics research, on the North Shore of Long Island in New York. There she conducted the work that led to her discovery of "jumping genes,"

which decades later, in 1983, earned her the prestigious Nobel Prize in physiology or medicine for her pioneering work with "mobile genetic elements."

In 1967 McClintock became a distinguished service member at Cold Spring Harbor, a position she held until her death in 1992. She also served as a visiting professor at the California Institute of Technology in Pasadena, California, in 1954, as a special consultant to the Agricultural Science Program of the Rockefeller Foundation from 1963 to 1969, and as Andrew D. White Professor-at-Large at Cornell from 1965 to 1974.

McClintock's life was filled with accolades, including the American Association of University Women Achievement Award in 1947 and honorary degrees from over fifteen colleges and universities. She also received the Kimber Genetics Award presented by the National Academy of Sciences in 1967; the National Medal of Science in 1970; the Lewis S. Rosenstiel Award for Distinguished Work in Basic Medical Research in 1978; the Thomas Hunt Morgan Medal from the Genetics Society of America in 1981; the Wolf Prize in Medicine in 1981; the Albert Lasker Basic Medical Research Award in 1981; the MacArthur Prize in 1981; the Louisa Gross Horwitz Prize for Biology or Biochemistry from Columbia University in 1982; the Charles Leopold Mayer Prize from the Académie des Sciences, Institut de France, in 1982; the Albert A. Michelson Award in 1984; and the National Women's Hall of Fame Award in 1986.

McClintock was a member of many learned societies as well, including the American Association for the Advancement of Science; the American Academy of Arts and Sciences; the American Philosophical Society; the American Society of Naturalists; the Genetics Society of America (of which she was vice president in 1939 and the first female president in 1945); the National Academy of Sciences; and Sigma Xi. McClintock was chosen as the honorary vice president of the Sixteenth International Congress of Genetics held in Ontario, Canada, in 1988; a foreign member of the Royal Society of London; and an honorary fellow with the Indian Society of Genetics and Plant Breeding among other memberships and honors. On 2 September 1992 McClintock died of natural causes at the age of ninety.

Enthusiastic, intense, dedicated, and shy, McClintock was a very private person in what became her very public world. While not working in the field that won her renown, she enjoyed playing the banjo, studying Eastern religions and forms of meditation, and—while she worked in Cold Spring Harbor—accompanying the local children home from the school bus speaking to them about nature. Her closest friends believed her mystical insight and "touch of genius, alloyed with sheer grit, determination and tenacity" made her "short in size, but great in stature" in a field that did not gladly receive women.

★

McClintock's papers are at the Kroch Library of Cornell University and at the Archives of Cold Spring Harbor Laboratory. She is mentioned in the papers of Lewis John Stadler 1927–1955 (C#2429), Ernest R. Sears 1928–1991 (C#3892), and Lewis E. Atherton 1865–1974 (C#3603, folders 559 and 561), all archived at the University of Missouri at Columbia; and in the University of Missouri at Columbia Citations from 1966 to 1968 (C#2549). Evelyn Fox Keller, *A Feeling for the Organism* (1983), and Mary Kittredge, *Barbara McClintock* (1991), focus on all facets of McClintock's life. Sharon Bertsch McGrayne, ed., *Nobel Prize Women in Science* (1993); Martha J. Bailey, *American Women in Science: A Biographical Dictionary* (1994); Emily J. McMurray, ed., *Notable Twentieth-Century Scientists* (1995); and Pamela Proffitt, ed., *Notable Women Scientists* (1999), contain short biographies. Robert Cooke, "Nobel Winner Remembered," *Newsday* (18 Nov. 1992), pays tribute to McClintock. Obituaries are in *Newsday* (3 Sept. 1992), the *New York Times* (4 Sept. 1992), and *Nature* (24 Sept. 1992).

ADRIANA C. TOMASINO

McCONE, John Alex (*b.* 4 January 1902 in San Francisco, California; *d.* 14 February 1991 in Pebble Beach, California), director of the Central Intelligence Agency (CIA) who pressed the search for Soviet nuclear missiles in Cuba and warned Presidents John F. Kennedy and Lyndon B. Johnson of the dangers of intervention in the Vietnam War.

John McCone, director of the CIA, leaving the White House after a National Security Council meeting, 1962. © BETTMANN/CORBIS

McCone, the son of Margaret Enright, a homemaker, and Alexander J. McCone, an industrialist, spent most of his early years with his parents and sister in Los Angeles, where the family relocated when he was a child. After finishing Los Angeles High School he entered the University of California at Berkeley, where he received a bachelor of science degree in mechanical engineering in 1922. After graduation and a stint as a boilermaker and riveter, McCone worked as a construction engineer at Llewellyn Iron Works in Los Angeles. He rose though management ranks to become superintendent in 1929, when Llewellyn was absorbed by Consolidated Steel Corporation. McCone became executive vice president and director of Consolidated Steel in 1933.

McCone left Consolidated Steel in 1937 and, with Stephen Bechtel, formed Bechtel-McCone Corporation in Los Angeles. McCone took the position of president of the corporation, an engineering firm that designed and built power plants and oil refineries in North and South America and the Middle East. In 1938 he married Rosemary Cooper; they had no children.

With the onset of World War II, Bechtel-McCone expanded into shipbuilding and aircraft production. A separate entity, California Shipbuilding Corporation, formed in 1941 with McCone as president and director. California

Shipbuilding was enormously profitable, earning $44 million during the war on an investment of $100,000, which raised suspicions of war profiteering among congressional investigators. McCone refuted the profiteering allegations and won the trust of President Harry S. Truman, who appointed McCone to his Air Policy Committee in 1947. Bechtel-McCone was disbanded in 1945, and California Shipbuilding liquidated in 1946. McCone bought the Joshua Hendy Iron Works in 1945, expanded its operations into Pacific Ocean shipping, and renamed it Hendy International Corporation in 1969. He retained his ties to the company as its president, chairman, or director throughout his years of government service.

As a member of Truman's Air Policy Committee from 1947 to 1948, McCone focused on military aspects of air policy. In 1948 he was named special deputy to Secretary of Defense James V. Forrestal, and he served as undersecretary of the air force from 1950 to 1951. During this period McCone emerged as a leading proponent of a strong U.S. strategic missile program. He formed a close personal relationship with General Dwight D. Eisenhower, then commander of the North Atlantic Treaty Organization (NATO) forces in Europe, with whom he worked on matters of strategic air power and NATO's nuclear capability. McCone, a Republican, left the Truman administration in 1951 and supported Eisenhower for president in 1952.

President Eisenhower offered McCone the position of secretary of the air force, but McCone declined in order to devote himself to private business. In 1954, however, he accepted Eisenhower's appointment to the Wriston commission, chaired by Brown University president Henry Wriston. This commission developed a program for the rehabilitation of the U.S. Foreign Service, then demoralized by charges of disloyalty from Senator Joseph R. McCarthy and his followers. In 1958 McCone, a devout Catholic, attended the funeral of Pope Pius XII as President Eisenhower's personal representative.

McCone returned to full-time government service in 1958 as chairman of the Atomic Energy Commission (AEC), a position he held to the end of the Eisenhower administration. As AEC chairman, McCone repaired relations with the Democratic-controlled Joint Congressional Committee on Atomic Energy, which had been strained under his predecessor, Admiral Lewis Strauss. McCone gave the committee regular intelligence briefings on Soviet nuclear capabilities, one of his major concerns. He frankly acknowledged his personal opposition to Eisenhower's unilateral moratorium on atmospheric nuclear testing, which he believed hampered the development of strategic weapons necessary for the defense of the United States. McCone insisted on the inclusion of effective safeguards against cheating in any nuclear test ban treaty with the Soviet Union. By the time he returned to private life in January 1961, McCone's tough-minded, principled positions had earned him the respect of defense experts in both political parties.

After an invasion force of Cuban exiles—organized, supplied, and directed by the U.S. Central Intelligence Agency (CIA)—was defeated at the Bay of Pigs by troops loyal to Fidel Castro in April 1961, President John F. Kennedy appointed McCone to head the CIA. McCone had little taste for covert operations and proceeded to reorient the CIA toward the collection and analysis of intelligence gathered by satellites and high-flying reconnaissance aircraft. Responsibility for covert operations was put under a White House "Special Group" headed by the president's brother, Attorney General Robert F. Kennedy. As CIA director McCone was an ex-officio member of the Special Group, and he took a dim view of proposals to assassinate Castro. As a Roman Catholic, McCone declared that he could not countenance assassination, so plans were developed to kill Castro without McCone's knowledge. McCone's first wife died in 1961. In 1962 he married Theiline Pigott; they had no children.

In 1962 CIA U-2 aircraft detected Soviet surface-to-air missiles (SAMs) in Cuba. Defense and State Department experts concluded that the SAMs were defensive, but McCone suspected that the SAMs were in Cuba to protect intermediate-range ballistic missiles (IRBMs) capable of raining nuclear warheads on the cities of the eastern United States. McCone pressed the search for the IRBMs, and in October 1962 U.S. aircraft located offensive missile emplacements in western Cuba and IRBMs on Soviet ships en route to Cuba. The U.S. government strongly objected, and the missile crisis of October 1962 resulted in the removal of the IRBMs from Cuba and the restoration of the CIA's credibility.

McCone advised President Kennedy in 1963 against supporting a coup by South Vietnamese generals against President Ngo Dinh Diem. The CIA director raised moral and practical objections to the likely assassination of Diem. McCone warned that Diem's removal would lead to instability in South Vietnam and would require massive U.S. military intervention to prevent a Communist takeover. After the assassinations of Diem and Kennedy in the fall of 1963, President Lyndon B. Johnson faced a worsening situation in Vietnam. McCone advised the new president that victory would require relentless heavy bombing of North Vietnam, which Johnson rejected in favor of tentative escalation. With Johnson consistently ignoring the CIA's realistic assessments of enemy strength in Vietnam, McCone resigned his post in 1965. White-haired, trim, and athletic, McCone cut an imposing figure. An avid golfer, he had a high-toned, clubhouse affability that appealed to Presidents Eisenhower and Kennedy, though not Johnson.

As a private citizen McCone consulted with President Richard Nixon on Vietnam and with President Jimmy Carter on Cuba. In 1987 Ronald Reagan awarded him the Presidential Medal of Freedom, citing his reputation for integrity, hard work, and unbiased analysis. McCone died in 1991 of cardiac arrest and was buried in Carmel, California.

★

The University of California in Berkeley holds a major collection of McCone's papers for the period 1957–1991. Papers pertaining to McCone's chairmanship of the Atomic Energy Commission, 1958–1961, are in the Dwight D. Eisenhower Library in Abilene, Kansas. McCone is mentioned in the major histories of the United States in the 1950s and 1960s. Most useful is Ray S. Cline, *The CIA: Reality vs. Myth* (1981; also published as *The CIA Under Reagan, Bush & Casey: The Evolution of the Agency from Roosevelt to Reagan,* 1981). See also Bruce Wetterau, *The Presidential Medal of Freedom: Winners and Their Achievements* (1996). Obituaries are in the *New York Times* and the *Los Angeles Times* (both 16 Feb. 1991). An interview with McCone by Harry Kreisler is in *Reflections, [with] John A. McCone,* Television Service, University of California, Berkeley (1988).

NEILL MACAULAY

McGEE, Gale William (*b.* 17 March 1915 in Lincoln, Nebraska; *d.* 9 April 1992 in Bethesda, Maryland), U.S. senator from Wyoming who, in his later post as ambassador to the Organization of American States, was an architect of the Panama Canal Treaty of 1978.

McGee was one of three sons of Garton Wilson McGee, an automobile salesman, and Frances Alice McCoy, a homemaker. In 1919 the family moved to Norfolk, Nebraska, where McGee attended public schools, graduating from Norfolk High School in 1932. Active in student government, debate, and public speaking, he graduated from Nebraska State Teachers College (now Wayne State University) in 1936. After teaching high school in Crofton and Kearney, Nebraska, McGee received an M.A. degree in history from the University of Colorado in 1939 and began a career as a university history professor, teaching at Nebraska Wesleyan University (1940–1943), Iowa State College (now Iowa State University, 1943–1944), and the University of Notre Dame (1944–1945). While teaching at

Gale McGee at a rally in support of Israel, 1967. ARCHIVE PHOTOS

Notre Dame, a Selective Service physical exam disclosed that he had diabetes, making him ineligible for active duty during World War II. In 1947 McGee received a Ph.D. in history from the University of Chicago, where his studies had concentrated on U.S.–Latin American relations. Meanwhile, in 1946, McGee had accepted a teaching position in the department of history at the University of Wyoming. He married Loraine Baker on 11 June 1939, and they had four children.

At the University of Wyoming, McGee quickly became a popular teacher whose lectures were renowned for their substance, humor, and flamboyant style—he spoke at length on complex issues without ever using a note. McGee also headed the university's Institute for International Affairs, a post he used to bring such figures as Henry Kissinger to the relatively isolated campus. Although still an untenured junior faculty member, he assumed a leadership role in a 1951 faculty dispute with the conservative University of Wyoming board of trustees over the issue of academic freedom.

In 1951 he directed *The Struggle for Men's Minds,* a series of broadcasts for Voice of America. From 1952 to 1953 McGee took a leave of absence to work with the Council on Foreign Relations in New York City to study the Soviet Union, and his brief tenure with the council placed him in contact with prominent national and world leaders. Upon his return to Wyoming, McGee and his wife organized a study tour of the Soviet Union and Eastern Europe in 1954, and McGee soon found himself in demand throughout the state and across the country as a public speaker on international issues. He was briefly involved with a weekly radio program, *History Behind the Headlines,* and both he and Loraine wrote newspaper articles about their trips abroad. Reluctantly, because of suspicions about his political ambitions, the university trustees granted McGee a leave of absence in 1955–1956 to serve as a legislative assistant to Senator Joseph C. O'Mahoney of Wyoming, a popular New Deal Democrat.

In his first attempt to secure an elected office, McGee narrowly defeated the incumbent U.S. senator, Republican Frank A. Barratt, in 1958. In the election 3,000 former students served as McGee's core supporters while the history professor campaigned against the "isolationist mindset" represented by his opponent. McGee's campaign was aided by endorsements from O'Mahoney, the American Federation of Labor–Congress of Industrial Organization (AFL–CIO), and former president Harry S. Truman, who visited the state to campaign for him. McGee advocated federal aid to education, the development of the West's mineral resources, and the banning of state right-to-work laws.

In a state in which blacks comprised less than 1 percent of the electorate, McGee was a moderate on civil rights issues and integration. Offered a seat on the Senate Committee on Foreign Relations following his election victory, McGee declined, noting that such an assignment would be "political suicide" in a state where his opponents accused him of knowing "more about the world than he does about Wyoming." Instead, he accepted Senate Majority Leader Lyndon B. Johnson's appointment to the Appropriations committee (the sole freshman senator to be so honored), and for the next eighteen years McGee skillfully used his influence on this committee to secure federal funding for Wyoming. Only after winning reelection in 1964 did McGee feel comfortable taking a place on the Foreign Relations committee, the last member of the Senate to hold positions on both the Appropriations and Foreign Relations committees. McGee also served on the Commerce committee and the Western Hemisphere Affairs subcommittee, and he chaired the Post Office and Civil Service committee, where he authored the Postal Reorganization Act of 1970, which created an independent U.S. Postal Service. In 1960 McGee was selected by his Democratic colleagues in the Senate as one of two "young" men with great potential. The other was Senator John F. Kennedy.

McGee supported the Great Society programs of the Johnson administration, including the Office of Equal Opportunity, the expansion of Social Security benefits, and open housing legislation. His liberalism on domestic issues, moderate stand on civil rights issues, and opposition to state "right to work" laws put him at odds with his generally conservative Wyoming constituency. He also supported conservation measures, including the banning of clear-cutting timber in the national forests and the imposition of fuel conservation measures. McGee favored beef import quotas, the "oil depletion allowance," and unrestricted access to firearms, all issues dear to most Wyomingites.

His support of the Vietnam War and huge Department of Defense appropriations earned McGee a reputation as one of the Senate's leading "hawks." He viewed the war in Vietnam as a test of American resolve in a key cold-war battleground. He authored *The Responsibilities of World Power* (1968) and argued that a strong military and a tough stand against the expansion of communism were required for world leadership. He stated that "events of World War II placed us in a position of leadership. This was not sought after, but since it fell upon us, we must fulfill the responsibilities of this leadership." McGee supported U.S. foreign aid, American involvement in the United Nations, and assistance to Israel. He urged caution and moderation during the Watergate hearings and impeachment proceedings against President Richard M. Nixon in the early 1970s. McGee's brand of moderate liberalism and his attention to bread-and-butter issues in his home state enabled him to win reelection in 1964 and 1970. In both races his opponent was John Wold, a mineral-industry entrepreneur and one-term member of the U.S. House of Representatives.

McGee was defeated in his 1976 bid for a fourth term in the Senate by the conservative Republican Malcolm Wallop. In 1977 President Jimmy Carter appointed McGee to serve as ambassador to the Organization of American States, where he labored successfully to secure Senate approval of a new and more equitable Panama Canal Treaty, which called for the eventual transfer of the canal to Panama. In 1978 McGee accompanied President Carter to Panama for the signing of the controversial treaty. Although reappointed ambassador to the OAS by President Ronald Reagan in 1981, McGee left government service to establish a consulting firm later that year specializing in international affairs. From 1987 to 1989 he was a senior consultant at Hill and Knowlton in Washington, D.C.

McGee was an avid fly fisherman and bird hunter. A gifted and forceful public speaker, he was known for his rugged good looks, charm, and taste for bright neckties and flashy sport coats. Following a brain aneurysm in 1991, he died of pneumonia in Bethesda. He is buried in Oak Hill Cemetery in Washington, D.C.

McGee was one of the most influential senators to ever represent the "Cowboy State." An articulate and well-informed spokesman for a strong military and assertive foreign policy during the height of the Cold War, McGee was enthusiastic in his advocacy for U.S. involvement in the Vietnam War, much to the consternation of many of his former colleagues in the academe. As a proponent of a liberal domestic agenda, McGee earned the support of conservative Wyomingites through his relentless support of the oil and mineral industries. His election defeat in 1976 after three terms came as a result of a growing conservatism in his home state and an adverse reaction to his support of the Vietnam War on the part of his Democratic constituents.

★

McGee's papers are located in the American Heritage Center at the University of Wyoming, which has also published Mark S. Shelstad, ed., *The Gale McGee Papers: A Guide* (1997). See also Ann Kelly, *Gale W. McGee* (Ralph Nader Congress Report, 1972), and "A Freshman's Washington Merry-Go-Round," *Pageant* (May 1959). Obituaries are in the *New York Times, Washington Post,* and Casper, Wyoming, *Star Tribune* (all 10 Apr. 1992).

MICHAEL J. DEVINE

McGOWAN, William George (*b.* 10 December 1927 in Ashley, Pennsylvania; *d.* 8 June 1992 in Washington, D.C.), business entrepreneur and chairman and chief executive officer of MCI Communications Corporation.

A native of a small coal mining and railroad town southwest of Wilkes-Barre, Pennsylvania, McGowan grew up in an Irish Catholic family with three brothers and a sister.

William McGowan, announcing a lawsuit against AT&T for false advertising. © BRAD MARKEL/GAMMA-LIAISON

His father, Andrew J. McGowan, Sr., a railroad engineer, and his mother, Katherine Evans, a schoolteacher, both placed a strong emphasis on education. McGowan graduated from Hanover Township High School in 1945, attended the University of Scranton for one year, and then joined the army in 1946. After a three-year stint as a medic in Germany, he was honorably discharged as a sergeant and entered Kings College in Wilkes-Barre on the GI Bill, graduating with a B.S. degree in chemistry in 1952. After college McGowan entered the Harvard School of Business Administration, graduating as a Baker Scholar with an M.B.A. in 1954. For the next thirteen years he worked primarily as a management consultant and venture capitalist, specializing in saving companies in distress and financing emerging technology companies. In 1967 McGowan traveled around the world on a mission for the United Nations Educational, Scientific, and Cultural Organization (UNESCO) to see how venture capital might spur the growth of small businesses in developing nations. When he returned in 1968 he discovered a developing business in need of financial expertise.

With venture capital, a business plan, and strong finan-

cial contacts, McGowan rescued an Illinois company, Microwave Communications, Inc. (MCI), which sought a license to build a private line microwave telephone system between Chicago and St. Louis. McGowan realized that to compete successfully, a telephone system would have to be nationwide. He headquartered the company in New York City to be close to the sources of investment capital, then he established seventeen locally financed, affiliated, regional companies, each covering the area between major cities in its part of the country. When all the affiliates were put together, they created a national network of independently franchised companies. At the center of the MCI affiliates was McGowan's new company, Microwave Communications of America, established in August 1968.

More critical to the company's success than McGowan's cash or business acumen was the decision of the Federal Communications Commission to grant MCI the license to build the microwave system. On 14 August 1969 the Commission, in a 4–3 vote, approved MCI's application. It was the first time that the federal government had licensed a long-distance competitor to the American Telephone and Telegraph Company (AT&T), a change that AT&T's attorneys immediately challenged in court. For the next sixteen years, until AT&T divested its local operating companies from its long-distance business in 1984, MCI and AT&T were locked in a series of fierce regulatory and legal battles over the issue of competitive telecommunications.

McGowan's personality perfectly matched the qualities needed for such a war. McGowan radiated his Irish background, Harvard training, and unbridled optimism. Like the leprechaun of Irish folklore, he spoke with twinkling eyes, lively gestures, and a bit of blarney. He exuded a confidence born of his extraordinary ability to process mounds of new information, to synthesize data, and to present the material with clarity, precision, and accuracy. He inspired others to join him in the crusade against monopoly and for equal access to long-distance calling. McGowan also looked the part. His wrinkled, bulldog-like jowls and quick, combative tongue left no doubt that the fight was worth every minute and every dollar invested. McGowan's natural brashness, impish grin, dogged determination, intense desire to win against overwhelming obstacles, aggressive sense of humor, and relish for verbal combat, all at the expense of the archenemy AT&T, came to personify MCI: smart, pugnacious, feisty, and competitive.

After raising more than $30 million in an initial stock offering in 1972, McGowan moved MCI's headquarters from New York and its financial connections to Washington, D.C., to be closer to the federal regulators that could make or break the fortunes of the company. The move proved to be prescient. From 1973 until 1980 McGowan defined competition in telecommunications and led the move to break up the Bell Telephone System. So much of MCI's resources were tied to litigation that wags called the company a law firm with an antenna on the roof. McGowan won the first legal case in December 1973 when a federal judge ordered AT&T to provide MCI with interconnections to the Bell network. AT&T bitterly fought MCI's right to market long-distance service, legally in a series of cases at the Federal Communications Commission between 1975 and 1978 and unilaterally by refusing to provide MCI with interconnections to the Bell System.

AT&T's actions served to bolster McGowan's mantra that the telephone giant was a harmful monopoly impeding advances in telephony. In March 1974, at McGowan's urging, MCI filed a civil antitrust suit against AT&T. The following November, using much of the material MCI had assembled, the Department of Justice filed a similar antitrust suit. On Friday, 13 June 1980 the jury of the *MCI* v. *AT&T* trial found that the defendant had violated the Sherman Antitrust Act and awarded MCI damages of $600 million. Trebled to $1.8 billion, the monetary award was the largest in the history of American law. Some eighteen months later, AT&T and the Department of Justice reached a settlement in the government's antitrust case. AT&T would divest itself of the Bell operating companies, separating the long-distance business from the local access networks.

McGowan embodied MCI. His vision and determination drove the MCI cause. His biting wit proved effective in the press and in the courtroom. His optimism rallied MCI's troops when all seemed lost. He was also a shrewd businessman. Under his leadership MCI grew to become an $8 billion company. It was the first telephone company to market its services, the first to aggressively advertise, and the first to widely integrate new technologies—such as digital switching, microwave transmission, fiber optic cable, electronic mail, and computer software— to create intelligent networks that enabled the advent of the Information Age. Aside from creating fresh opportunities for communications lawyers, he created new industries. McGowan opposed MCI's entering the equipment manufacturing business as AT&T had done. He asked vendors to build to his advanced specifications. This policy helped establish a second telephone equipment industry to compete with AT&T. With MCI struggling to attract customers in the early 1980s, McGowan engineered an alliance with IBM, giving his company instant credibility in the business community. When interest rates rose above 18 percent, McGowan successfully turned to a new kind of financing, junk bonds, which enabled MCI to continue its growth to become the second largest long-distance carrier in the country. Although McGowan liked to portray himself and MCI as a David against the AT&T Goliath, he and MCI were more like Joshua before Jericho. They sounded their horns so persistently that the walls of AT&T's monopoly finally came tumbling down. These same tactics later eroded the defenses of the international telephone monopolies.

McGowan married Sue Ling Gin on 3 July 1984. They had no children. McGowan was a workaholic. MCI was his business, his passion. Years of fifteen-hour days, living on cigarettes and coffee and forsaking exercise, finally took their toll. Just days after his fifty-ninth birthday in 1986, he suffered a heart attack. In April 1987 McGowan received a heart transplant at the Presbyterian University Hospital in Pittsburgh. By June he had returned to his office and was back on a regular basis by Labor Day. McGowan's humor remained, but those who knew him best recognized that he lacked the energy of the old McGowan. Four years later, while waiting to begin one of his regular early morning exercise sessions at the Georgetown University Hospital, he collapsed and died of another heart attack at the age of sixty-four. He is buried in St. Mary's Cemetery in Hanover Township, Pennsylvania.

McGowan and the company he built, MCI Communications Corporation, reshaped the telecommunications industry in the United States and fundamentally changed the way Americans phoned long distance. Because of McGowan, telephone service shifted from a comfortable monopoly to a highly competitive industry in the last quarter of the twentieth century. Because of the changes brought to telecommunications by McGowan and MCI, long-distance calling had gone from the uncommon to the commonplace.

★

There is no biography of McGowan. For someone with a high public profile, McGowan was a very private man and released little about his private life. He wrote almost nothing for publication. The MCI archives are at the Hagley Museum and Library in Delaware and include a transcript of an extensive McGowan oral history completed in 1988. Books about MCI and its fight for competitive telecommunications and equal access include works by two journalists: Steve Coll, *The Deal of the Century: The Breakup of AT&T* (1986), and Larry Kahaner, *On the Line: How MCI Took on AT&T—And Won!* (1986). An excellent economic history that includes the impact of MCI on AT&T's divestiture is Peter Temin with Louis Galombos, *The Fall of the Bell System: A Study in Prices and Politics* (1987). The definitive work on MCI and McGowan is Philip L. Cantelon, *The History of MCI, 1968–1988: The Early Years* (1993). An obituary is in the *Washington Post* (9 June 1992).

PHILIP L. CANTELON

McKISSICK, Floyd B. (*b.* 9 March 1922 in Asheville, North Carolina; *d.* 28 April 1991 in Durham, North Carolina), civil rights leader who served as national director of the Congress on Racial Equality (CORE) during the 1960s.

McKissick was the son of Magnolia Thompson and Ernest Boyce McKissick, both employed by the North Carolina Mutual Life Insurance Company in Durham, but worked in Asheville. Ernest McKissick later worked at a hotel in Asheville. After graduating from high school in Asheville in 1939, McKissick attended Morehouse College, an all-black, all-male school in Atlanta. At Morehouse, McKissick was active in civil rights issues and joined both the National Association for the Advancement of Colored People (NAACP) and CORE. During this period he married Evelyn Williams, with whom he had four children.

After McKissick graduated from Morehouse, he fought in World War II, serving as an army sergeant in the European theater. He returned to North Carolina after the war and participated in CORE's first Freedom Ride in 1947. The Freedom Rides sent an interracial group of men to the Upper South, where they attempted to ride buses to compel enforcement of a Supreme Court ruling that declared segregation in interstate travel unconstitutional. Following violence and arrests, the event brought CORE national attention.

In 1951 McKissick entered law school at North Carolina College (later North Carolina Central University), a segregated state institution in Durham. During this period

Floyd McKissick. AP/WIDE WORLD PHOTOS

McKissick and a small group of fellow students brought a successful lawsuit against the law school at the University of North Carolina at Chapel Hill (UNC) that resulted in the institution's integration, though McKissick never attended UNC. After graduating from North Carolina College, McKissick established a legal practice in Durham, where his work included efforts to integrate public facilities, including labor unions and schools. In addition McKissick successfully represented his daughter in her attempt to gain admission to an all-white public school and he successfully defended students who participated in North Carolina's sit-in movement during the early 1960s.

Despite these legal victories, McKissick noted that desegregation often only contributed to the increased harassment of blacks. Later he recalled that his own children, like other blacks, had "patches cut out of their hair, pages torn out of books, water thrown on them in the dead of winter, ink down the front of their dresses" when they entered recently integrated schools.

McKissick was not alone in his frustration with the pace of integration. By the mid-1960s tensions between older and younger members of the civil rights movement reached a boiling point. While older members contended that the movement should be an integrated coalition of blacks and whites, younger people questioned the inclusion of whites, maintaining that they did not understand the problems that affected blacks in the United States, particularly poor urban blacks who occupied the lowest rung on the nation's economic ladder.

By 1965 McKissick and his counterpart on the Student Non-Violent Coordinating Committee (SNCC), Stokely Carmichael, were striving to convert their respective organizations to strategies of separatism and, if necessary, violent confrontation. In January 1966 McKissick replaced James Farmer as the national director of CORE. In June 1966 McKissick became a significant figure in a key debate on the future of the civil rights movement when he joined forces with Carmichael and Martin Luther King, Jr., to organize a civil rights march through Mississippi, called the Meredith March, with the goal of enrolling unregistered blacks to vote. During a planning meeting McKissick and Carmichael suggested that marchers should meet any resistance with civil disobedience. King and the NAACP leader Roy Wilkins staunchly refused to support the march if it advocated civil disobedience. Aware that King's support of the march was essential to its success, McKissick and Carmichael backed down, but the three men did agree that white participation would be deemphasized at the march.

Despite this compromise, the march became a staging ground for the wider debate within the civil rights movement. Was the movement to be interracial, nonviolent, and dedicated to integration, or would it embrace civil disobedience, separatism, and black nationalism? The answer was voiced by Carmichael and applauded by McKissick on 16 June, when Carmichael, speaking at a rally in Greenwood, Mississippi, shouted "Black Power!" to the assembled crowd, which responded loudly and positively. Shortly thereafter King called a meeting to discuss the slogan, which he opposed, fearing it would confuse white allies, isolate the black community, and further prejudice racist whites against blacks. McKissick and Carmichael argued that the civil rights movement needed a rallying call that would mobilize the black community. King triumphed when, to ensure his continued participation in the march, McKissick and Carmichael agreed to refrain from using the slogan for the remainder of the march.

Although muted temporarily, the Black Power slogan was far from dead. CORE, under McKissick's leadership, formally endorsed the slogan at its annual convention in July. McKissick proclaimed: "1966 shall be remembered as the year we left our imposed status as Negroes and became Black Men. 1966 is the year of the concept of Black Power." For McKissick, Black Power meant racial pride, solidarity, and black leadership of institutions—all contributing to tangible progress for African Americans.

McKissick attempted to make this vision a reality in his native North Carolina after he retired from CORE in 1968 to pursue his next project. Drawing on his legal, business, and political experience, McKissick approached the Department of Housing and Urban Development (HUD) with a plan to build a new community called Soul City in rural Warren County. His goal was to bring opportunities to people residing in a rural, economically depressed area to prevent them from fleeing to urban ghettos in search of employment. McKissick obtained approximately $19 million in a bond issue guarantee from HUD and a loan of $500,000 from the First Pennsylvania Bank.

With these resources, in 1969 McKissick created a community with an infrastructure capable of sustaining a population of about 700 people. Soul City was one of fourteen new communities created under the Urban Growth and Development Act and was notable for building the largest regional water system in the nation during the 1970s. By the early twenty-first century Soul City's population reached about 1,400 people, and its industries included a Purdue chicken hatchery, the only recreational facility in Warren County, and a medical center. In 1980 McKissick returned to practicing law, and he was appointed a district court judge in 1990. He died of lung cancer one year later in Durham.

Speaking about Soul City in a 1973 interview, McKissick commented, "I'm doing what I advocated, I'm doing right now the same thing I was doing since I've been twelve years old and since I've been talking about it, even though I've gone through a civil rights movement." From his activities at Morehouse to his integration of the University of North Carolina Law School, his leadership of CORE, and the establishment of Soul City, McKissick strove to bring legal, political, and economic autonomy to black people accompanied by a sense of self-determination and pride.

★

Material on McKissick and CORE is in Clayborne Carson, *In Struggle: SNCC and the Black Awakening of the 1960s* (1981); Allen J. Matusow, *The Unraveling of America: A History of Liberalism in the 1960s* (1984); August Meier and Elliott Rudwick, *CORE: A Study in the Civil Rights Movement, 1942–1986* (1973); Robert Weisbrot, *Freedom Bound: A History of America's Civil Rights Movement* (1990); and Terry Anderson, *The Movement and the Sixties: Protest in America from Greensboro to Wounded Knee* (1995). An obituary is in the *New York Times* (30 Apr. 1991). The author gratefully acknowledges Floyd B. McKissick, Jr., who offered time, patience, and good-humor during a valuable telephone interview.

DEBORAH GERSHENOWITZ

McMILLAN, Edwin Mattison (*b.* 18 September 1908 in Redondo Beach, California; *d* 7 September 1991 in El Cerrito, California), physicist who won the Nobel Prize in chemistry for his work on the transuranic elements and was codiscoverer of neptunium and plutonium.

McMillan was the only child of Edwin Harbaugh McMillan, a physician, and Anne Marie Mattison, a homemaker. When McMillan was a year and a half old, the family moved to suburban Pasadena, California. As a youth McMillan built many gadgets and took advantage of his proximity to the California Institute of Technology by attending public lectures. In 1924, after graduating from Pasadena High School, he attended the California Institute of Technology. His undergraduate work was first-rate, as demonstrated by his election to Sigma Xi, a scientific research honor society, and Tau Beta Pi, an engineering honor society. While still an undergraduate he published his first paper in chemistry on the X-ray study of alloys of lead and thallium. His faculty collaborator was Linus Pauling, the future double Nobel Prize laureate in chemistry and in peace, who suggested that McMillan publish the paper. McMillan received his bachelor of science degree in 1928. A year later he received his master of science degree, then he transferred to Princeton University to work on his doctoral degree in physics, which he obtained in 1932.

The work for his doctorate, carried out under E. U. Condon, famous for the Franck-Condon Principle, examined the generation of a molecular beam of hydrogen chloride nuclei in a nonhomogeneous electric field. This molecular beam method enables one to measure the magnetic moment of a proton, a particle of relative mass and charge

Edwin McMillan. LIBRARY OF CONGRESS

While in the process of completing his apparatus for the measurement of the magnetic moment of the proton, McMillan discovered that Otto Stern had published his results on the experiment. So McMillan began to study the hyperfine structure and published several papers in that area. Simultaneously he grew increasingly interested in the activities of the adjacent Radiation Laboratory. Nuclear physics was changing rapidly with the discoveries of the neutron by James Chadwick in 1932, the positron by C. D. Anderson in 1932, and induced radioactivity. Immediately McMillan recognized the efficacy of the cyclotron.

In 1934 McMillan joined the staff of Lawrence's Radiation Laboratory as a research associate. Beginning in 1935 he was simultaneously an instructor of physics at the University of California at Berkeley. Described as a fine teacher, he rose to assistant professor in 1935, to associate professor in 1941, and to full professor in 1946. The last two promotions were in absentia. From the beginning of their association, Lawrence recognized McMillan's inventiveness and his profound practical and analytical skills. McMillan was a meticulous and versatile experimenter. Discoveries seemed to spring from his work. He made the first substantial verification of the theory that a gamma ray striking a nucleus would yield an electron pair, one negative, one positive. In 1934 McMillan and M. Stanley Livingston discovered radioactive oxygen-15. In 1940, with Samuel Reuben, he discovered beryllium-10, and with Philip Abelson he succeeded in the separation of a product of 2.3-day activity (beta decay) from fissionable uranium-239. McMillan was rightly convinced that the product was produced by transmutation rather than fusion and was, therefore, a new element. He deduced that this was not an element of the manganese family, which was the consensus among chemists, but rather that the product was more like the rare earth elements. Using his chemical expertise, he completed the separation and proved conclusively that this was a transuranium element, the first, and named it neptunium. The daughter product of neptunium, for which the name plutonium was reserved, was expected to be an alpha-active isotope. Although McMillan and Abelson detected some alpha activity, it was too weak to measure. World War II interrupted his research, and all of his work on element 94 was left to Glenn J. Seaborg. A team headed by Seaborg completed the work on element 94, leading to a joint Nobel Prize in 1951. Element 94, plutonium, became the principle material for atomic bombs.

During World War II, McMillan directed the field tests of America's first airborne radar at the Massachusetts Institute of Technology. He also researched sonar at the Navy Radio and Sound Laboratory in San Diego, California, and he was an assistant to J. Robert Oppenheimer at Los Alamos. McMillan worked on both the Hiroshima-type and the Nagasaki-type atomic bombs.

of one and plus one respectively. While at Princeton University, McMillan published several papers on research he completed without a collaborator. One paper dealt with the isotopic composition of lithium in the Sun. In 1932 he won a richly deserved and highly regarded National Research Council (NRC) fellowship to support his research at any university or research institute in the country. That year McMillan accepted an invitation to work with Ernest Orlando Lawrence, who was then exploring the potential of the cyclotron, at the University of California at Berkeley. A cyclotron is a circular accelerator capable of generating particle energies of very high magnitude. The charged particles generated at a central source in a vacuum are accelerated incrementally in a plane at right angles to a fixed magnetic field by an alternating electric field of frequency equal to the frequency of revolution. The particles spiral outwardly with increasing energy.

On 7 June 1941 McMillan married Elsie Walford Blumer, whose sister, Mary Kimberly, was married to Ernest Lawrence. They had three children.

After the war McMillan concentrated on accelerators. As particles were accelerated numerous times, they fell out of phase with the accelerating pulse and slowed down. In a flash of insight McMillan determined the conditions that would keep the particles accelerated. He called the device a synchrotron, an accelerator in which the charged particles are accelerated around a fixed circular path by a radio-frequency (rf) potential and held to that path by a time-varying magnetic field. Thus the particles had "phase stability." This instrument became the standard of high-energy physics. Later McMillan learned that Vladimir I. Veksler, a Soviet scientist, had a similar idea and published papers on it. They shared in the recognition of their parallel work, which had happened frequently in science.

McMillan taught both undergraduate and graduate physics courses from 1946 to 1954 and supervised fifteen graduate students to Ph.D. degrees. He ceased teaching when he was appointed associate director of the Radiation Laboratory in 1954. He became deputy director after Lawrence's death in August 1958. Subsequently he became director of the renamed Lawrence Radiation Laboratory and served for fifteen years, until his retirement in 1973. He retired from Berkeley in 1974, but he participated in the laboratory's work until he suffered a stroke in 1984.

McMillan was an active participant on various scientific policy committees and program advisory committees to several laboratories. He served on the General Advisory Committee to the Atomic Energy Commission, was elected to the National Academy of Science in 1947, and was a fellow of the American Physics Society. He received the Research Corporation Scientific Award in 1951; the Nobel Prize in 1951; and the Atoms for Peace Award in 1963. In 1990 he received the nation's highest civilian award, the National Medal of Science. Even though he received numerous other awards and honorary degrees, he maintained his humility.

McMillan died on 7 September 1991 at his home in El Cerrito, California, after years of declining health. He died of complications from diabetes just eleven days shy of his eighty-fourth birthday. He is buried in El Cerrito.

McMillan was one of the world's great scientists. His interests were expansive, varying from the rocks and shells on the beach to elementary particles to mathematics to the composition of the Sun. His discoveries had a profound effect on various fields of study, from anthropology (carbon-14 dating) to the study of fundamental particles (synchrotron) to defense and unlimited energy (plutonium discovery). He was a great teacher, modest and witty. He enjoyed gardening, smoked a pipe, and drove a 1957 Thunderbird.

★

McMillan's works are listed in National Academy of Sciences, *Biographical Memoirs* 69 (1996): 214–241. For further information see *Current Biography 1952*. Obituaries are in the *New York Times* (9 Sept. 1991) and *Physics Today* 45 (1992): 2, 118.

SAMUEL VON WINBUSH

MACMURRAY, Fred(erick) Martin (*b.* 30 August 1908 in Kankakee, Illinois; *d.* 5 November 1991 in Santa Monica, California), film and television star whose career spanned forty-five years and eighty-five feature films.

MacMurray, the only child of Frederick MacMurray, a violinist, and Maleta Martin, a homemaker, was born during his itinerant father's one-night concert engagement in Kankakee. The family soon moved to Beaver Dam, Wisconsin, then to Gilroy, California, which MacMurray's father used as a base while making concert tours up and down the West Coast. By the time MacMurray was five, his father had taught him to play the violin, his parents had separated, and he had moved back to the Midwest with his mother, where they lived a hardscrabble life for the next thirteen years. His mother was a poorly paid stenographer but managed to send Fred to a military academy in Quincy, Illinois. After his grammar schooling they returned to Beaver Dam.

As a student at Beaver Dam High School, MacMurray played baritone horn in the American Legion band. Between terms he worked at a pea-canning factory, earning

Fred MacMurray. THE KOBAL COLLECTION

enough money to buy a saxophone, which he played in his own three-piece ensemble, Mac's Melody Boys. He suffered from severe stage fright, never quite overcoming it, even during his later, deceptively laid-back acting career. The youngest in his class, he graduated at age sixteen, a "ten-letter man" who also had the school's highest scholastic average. He was awarded the American Legion Medal for his accomplishments and attended Carroll College in Waukesha, Wisconsin, on an American Legion athletic scholarship. But he was so busy playing football and working as a musician six nights a week that he had little time to study, and he abandoned college in 1926 to move to Chicago. He nurtured an interest in becoming a newspaper cartoonist by enrolling as a night student at the Chicago Art Institute, supporting himself by selling golf clubs in a department store and playing tenor sax with Jack Higgins' Royal Purples, a dance band out of Loyola University

In 1928 MacMurray drove his mother and aunt to Los Angeles to visit relatives. A strapping, handsome lad—six feet, three inches tall, with black hair, brown eyes, and a prominent chin dimple—he was a natural for Central Casting, where he registered and occasionally got a day's work as an extra, including the 1929 film *Girls Gone Wild*. He took a host of jobs to "keep the wolf from the door," scraping paint off old cars and working as a freelance musician with the George Olsen Orchestra, the Gus Arnheim Orchestra, and the Warner Hollywood Theatre Orchestra. It was during the Warner stint that MacMurray's first big career break occurred. He joined the renowned vaudeville band California Collegians, which featured his talents as vocalist, saxophonist, and clown.

The Collegians signed MacMurray to go to New York City and join them onstage in the Broadway cast of *Three's a Crowd* (1930), which starred Libby Holman, Fred Allen, and Clifton Webb. During the course of each performance, the flirtatious Holman crooned "Something to Remember You By" to a self-conscious MacMurray. The band subsequently appeared in *The Third Little Show* (1931) and in the Jerome Kern hit *Roberta* (1933), in which MacMurray spoke a few lines and understudied for the lead, Bob Hope. On 20 June 1936 MacMurray married Lillian LaMonte, a dancer he had met in the show; they adopted two children. After the Broadway run MacMurray joined the road tour, and when he got back to New York he secured an appointment with the head of the Paramount movie studio's talent department, who arranged for a screen test, which was sent to Hollywood. Word came back to "send him out," and MacMurray was signed to a standard seven-year contract. It was several months, though, before he did any acting.

His inauspicious debut was in *Friends of Mr. Sweeney* (1934); his second film was *Grand Old Girl* (1935), made while MacMurray was on loan to RKO. Back at Paramount, the film that catapulted him to stardom was the romantic comedy *The Gilded Lily* (1935), the first of five films in which he costarred with Claudette Colbert. He stayed at Paramount for eleven years, with occasional work at other studios, annually grossing for Paramount between $30 and $40 million in four or five pictures a year. Although late in his acting career he was regarded as an icon of out-to-lunch affability, MacMurray established his movie stardom in films that were sexy little delights, films in which he starred with more of Hollywood's glamorous leading ladies than did any other male star of the era. He made four movies with Carole Lombard, three with Barbara Stanwyck, and several each with Madeleine Carroll and Irene Dunne. Other costars of the period included Sylvia Sidney (*Trail of the Lonesome Pine*, 1936), Gladys Swarthout (*Champagne Waltz*, 1937), Alice Faye (*Little Old New York*, 1940), Jean Arthur (*Too Many Husbands*, 1940), Mary Martin (*New York Town*, 1941), Rosalind Russell (*Take a Letter Darling*, 1942), Marlene Dietrich (*The Lady Is Willing*, 1942), and Joan Crawford (*Above Suspicion*, 1943).

His busy schedule continued into the mid-1940s. In 1943 MacMurray was the year's highest paid actor, with an income of $420,000. The man who fifteen years earlier had been subsisting as a movie extra was becoming one of Hollywood's richest citizens, amassing a fortune through shrewd investment and thrift.

Charm and understatement characterized MacMurray's acting style, on display in a wide range of roles during the Paramount years, including screwball comedies, Westerns, musicals, and historical dramas. It was shocking, therefore, when the director Billy Wilder cast the actor against type as the murderous insurance salesman in *Double Indemnity* (1944). MacMurray's sympathetic portrayal of a rotter prompted Wilder to offer him another "heel" role sixteen years later in *The Apartment* (1960), as Shirley MacLaine's boss and seducer. Both roles were among MacMurray's most memorable.

In 1945 his Paramount contract expired and he signed with Twentieth Century–Fox, where he subsequently made a series of uninspired films. He was announced for, but never played, the role for which James Dunn eventually won an Academy Award in *A Tree Grows in Brooklyn* (1945). Incredibly, MacMurray was never nominated for an Academy Award or Emmy. His costar in the 1945 musical fantasy *Where Do We Go from Here?* was June Haver, seventeen years younger than he and being groomed to succeed Betty Grable at the studio. Haver's career came to a well-publicized halt when, after the death of her fiancé, she, a devout Catholic, entered a convent. She remained there for seven months, then left in 1953, which was also the year MacMurray's wife died. On 28 June 1954 Haver became the Presbyterian actor's second wife and they adopted twin daughters. They lived in a colonial-style Georgian home in Brentwood, California. Their marriage lasted until MacMurray's death and by all accounts was a happy union.

Long before MacMurray's film career slowed down in the mid-1950s, he hosted the radio show *Hollywood Hotel* (1934–1938) and starred in the radio comedy drama *Bright Star* (1952–1953). By the time his film career was in a slide he was making approximately twenty appearances a year as a regular on the *George Gobel Show* and as a guest on the Bob Hope, Jack Benny, Dinah Shore, Lucille Ball, and Ed Sullivan programs. In 1958 he starred in a television drama, *One Is a Wanderer*, based on a James Thurber short story.

MacMurray made two to three pictures annually in the 1950s, several of them "B" Westerns, but only one film has stood the test of time: *The Caine Mutiny* (1954), in which he plays the morally weak character who instigates the mutiny but ducks responsibility for it. Walt Disney rescued MacMurray's film career, making him a top-grosser once more by starring him in a series of domestic comedies starting with *The Shaggy Dog* (1959), then the truly funny *Absent-Minded Professor* (1961) and its mediocre sequel, *Son of Flubber* (1963). All told, MacMurray made seven films for the Disney organization.

As he aged, the metamorphosis of Fred MacMurray, sex symbol, into asexual paterfamilias, reached its apogee in his being cast as the wise patriarch in the weekly television series *My Three Sons*, which ran from 1960 to 1972 first on ABC, then on CBS. (Twenty years later it was still running in syndication.) In retrospect, television historians ascribe sociological significance to the fact that the show was one of the first to feature a nontraditional household (all-male); feminist critics view the series as misogynistic. MacMurray viewed it as a cash cow, and the shooting schedule that he insisted on, whereby all of his scenes were done first—no matter who else was available—in sixty-five days, was dubbed the "MacMurray method" and adopted later by other stars in the industry, to the scriptwriters' dismay.

After the show ended MacMurray went into semiretirement on his 2,300-acre California ranch, raising Angus cattle. Both he and his wife were fine cooks and he collected cookbooks. He also enjoyed fishing, sketching, and golf. In 1977 he won the Artistry in Cinema Award presented by the National Film Society (defunct as of 1982) of Canada and in 1986 the Golden Boot Award of the Motion Picture and Television Fund Foundation. He died of pneumonia at St. John's Hospital and Health Center in Santa Monica, after having been admitted for cancer treatment. He is buried in Holy Cross Cemetery in Culver City, California.

For a movie star MacMurray led an unusual life, free from scandal and without much publicity. A genial family man whose affable personality and simple, unpretentious manner belied a fierce personal ambition and solid acting ability, Fred MacMurray is securely ensconced in the American popular-culture memory.

★

The clipping file on MacMurray at the New York Public Library of Performing Arts's Billy Rose Theatre Collection is of tremendous value to the film scholar and fan. There is no biography, although there is an entry about him in virtually every biographical dictionary of film actors. One of the best appears in David Shipman, *The Great Movie Stars*, vol. 1 (1989). An extensive appreciation of seven American male stars, including MacMurray, is James Robert Parish, *The All-Americans* (1977); its filmography is the most reliable. Two magazine interviews reveal personal tidbits not mentioned elsewhere: Pete Martin, "I've Been Lucky," *Saturday Evening Post* (24 Feb. 1962); and Dan Navarro, "The MacMurrays At Home: A Double Portrait," *American Classic Screen* (Mar.–Apr. 1979): 13–16. For a unique perspective—that of costar William Frawley—on *My Three Sons*, the book to read is Rob Edelman and Audrey Kupferberg, *Meet the Mertzes: The Life Stories of I Love Lucy's Other Couple* (1999). An obituary is in the *New York Times* (6 Nov. 1991).

HONORA RAPHAEL WEINSTEIN

McPARTLAND, James Dugald ("Jimmy") (*b.* 15 March 1907 in Chicago, Illinois; *d.* 13 March 1991 in Port Washington, New York), jazz cornetist and bandleader known as one of the founders of the "Chicago School" of jazz.

McPartland was one of four children of James McPartland, a sometime boxer and baseball player who was also a music teacher, and his wife, Jeannie Munn, a schoolteacher. His brother Dick was also was a musician. The family was dysfunctional, although sometime after the parents divorced, they reconciled and moved into a somewhat better section of Chicago from that in which they had been living. This was the area served by Austin High School, famed in the history of Chicago jazz. Although young McPartland graduated from John Hay Grammar School, he quit high school after two years and devoted his time to music. Jimmy and Dick had both been taught the violin by their father. As the boys grew older they took up other instruments, with Jimmy playing the cornet by age fifteen, perhaps because it was louder than other instruments used in jazz.

Jimmy and Dick joined with other classmates to form a band. Because the musical group members attended Austin High School, they became known as the Austin High Gang and learned music by listening to records in a restaurant they frequented. For a time they used the name Blue Friars, which included, along with McPartland on cornet, Bud Freeman (tenor sax), Frank Teschemacher (clarinet), Dick McPartland (guitar), and Dave Tough (drums). In 1924 the seventeen-year-old McPartland replaced the famous cornetist Bix Beiderbecke in a jazz group called the Wol-

Jimmy McPartland, 1982. AP/WIDE WORLD PHOTOS

the number with a collective improvisation, followed by a series of solos backed by the rhythm section and perhaps other lead instruments, and closed with the musicians jamming together. The nucleus of the Chicagoans was the Austin High Gang, including McPartland on cornet.

Late in 1942 McPartland enlisted in the U.S. Army and engaged in heavy fighting in the 462nd AAA Automatic Weapons Unit during the early days of the Normandy invasion in 1944. He requested a transfer to another unit and became an emcee for a USO camp show. While serving in this capacity in Belgium, he met a British pianist, Margaret Marian Turner. The cornetist had reservations about the abilities of a female jazz pianist, especially one from Britain. However, they got along well and were married in Aachen, Germany, on 3 February 1945. Subsequently McPartland helped his wife with her playing while she influenced his appreciation of more modern forms of jazz.

Following his military discharge, the cornetist performed at the International Jazz Festival in Paris in 1949 and after returning to the United States led a series of groups, some of which included his wife. In 1953 he began appearing regularly in New York City and often played at Nick's Club. The following year he spent several months leading his own band at New York's Metropole, visited England, and appeared as a guest on the British Broadcasting Corporation radio. In the 1950s McPartland also took up acting. He performed in a television fantasy, *The Magic Horn* (1956), about a jazz musician. This resulted in a role in *Showboat* at the Jones Beach Theatre, and a recorded version of *The Music Man* (1958). From 1965 to 1966 he joined Tony Parenti at Jimmy Ryan's Club.

The McPartlands were divorced in 1967; they had no children. (They would remarry two weeks before his death.) However, they had continued to work together even as Marian built a career for herself so that she was not restricted to performing her husband's style of music. She would later gain fame as the host of the longest-running National Public Radio program, *Piano Jazz,* which began in 1979.

McPartland continued to be active into the 1980s. He and Marian appeared together at the Newport Jazz Festival in 1978. Their last concert was in 1990 at the University of Chicago. Throughout his career McPartland played the instrument given to him by Bix Beiderbecke and often worked with such musicians as Bud Freeman and other Chicago-style players. The McPartlands, with Jimmy as leader, also performed at the final night of the "new" Eddie Condon's Club in New York City on 31 July 1985. Condon was perhaps the nation's foremost publicist of Chicago-style jazz during his lifetime.

Jimmy McPartland and Bud Freeman, who had grown up and performed together for many years, both of whom were members of the Austin High Gang and staunch pro-

verines, at which time Beiderbecke personally chose a Conn Victor cornet for McPartland. Both instrumentalists played in a clean, lyrical style. From 1926 to 1927, McPartland played with Art Kassel and in late 1927 joined Ben Pollack's band. The cornetist was busy with freelance recording from the late 1920s into the early 1930s and played with Russ Columbo from 1931 to 1932. Following his stint with Columbo he was in bands conducted by Smith Ballew, Harry Reser, and Horace Heidt. In 1935 Jimmy and Dick McPartland led a Chicago band called the Embassy Four. Between 1936 and 1939 Jimmy led another group, under his own name, mainly in Chicago, and returned to New York City for a time in 1941. He primarily directed combos, although he had a "big band" in 1939 and joined Jack Teagarden from 1941 to 1942.

While associated with Pollack, McPartland met the Williams sisters, Dorothy and Hannah, a song-and-dance team. He married Dorothy in 1930. They had one child and were divorced in 1932.

In the late 1920s, a recording session held by a group known as the McKenzie-Condon Chicagoans made four sides that showed what in the near future would become Chicago-style jazz. The musicians became famous individually and henceforth often worked together. In a typical "Chicago School" performance, the instrumentalists opened

ponents of Chicago-style jazz, died within two days of each other in 1991. McPartland died from lung cancer in suburban Port Washington, New York. The funeral was held in Chicago with memorial services at St. Peter's Church in Manhattan and the University of Chicago. He was cremated and his ashes are interred at Arlington Cemetery, Elmhurst, Illinois.

★

McPartland left his memorabilia to the University of Chicago. There is no full-length biography; Marian McPartland graciously provided information to the author of this article. Chip Deffaa, *Voices of the Jazz Age* (1990), Max Jones, *Talking Jazz* (1987), and Whitney Balliett, *American Musicians: Fifty-six Portraits in Jazz* (1986), contain extensive interview coverage on the cornetist. Ian Carr et al., *Jazz, The Rough Guide* (1995), and Roger D. Kinkle, *The Complete Encyclopedia of Popular Music and Jazz: 1900–1950* (1974), contain biographical and discographical material. William Howland Kenney, *Chicago Jazz: A Cultural History, 1904–1930* (1993), puts Chicago jazz in its cultural context. An obituary by John S. Wilson is in the *New York Times* (14 Mar. 1991); a eulogy by John McDonough is in *Down Beat* (May 1991). One recording that clearly delineates some differences between types of jazz is *Dixieland Now (Chicago) and Then (New Orleans),* featuring Jimmy McPartland's Chicago Rompers and Paul Barbarin's New Orleans Stompers, recorded during the 1950s. Another LP recording, *The McPartlands: Live at the Monticello* (1972), is an excellent example of his music. Other discs are listed in Kinkle and Carr, et al. A highly recommended videotape is *Jazz at the Top: Remembering Bix Beiderbecke, with Jimmy McPartland, Marian McPartland, Joe Venuti, and Their Friends* (1976).

BARRETT G. POTTER

MALESKA, Eugene Thomas (*b.* 6 January 1916 in Jersey City, New Jersey; *d.* 3 August 1993 in Daytona Beach, Florida), educator, legendary crossword puzzle editor for the *New York Times,* and the only person to have a New York City school named for him during his lifetime.

Maleska was the son of Matthew Michael Maleska and Ellen Kelly. His father worked for the Central Railroad Company in New Jersey. Raised in Bergen County, New Jersey, he attended Regis High School in New York City and Montclair State Teachers College in New Jersey, where he received a B.A. degree in 1937 and an M.A. degree in 1940. He did some graduate work at Columbia University from 1943 to 1946, and he received a doctorate in education from Harvard University in 1955.

Maleska discovered his first crossword puzzle in 1932. He was traveling home from high school on the commuter train, when he found a copy of the *New York Daily News* on the seat next to him. He saw the puzzle and was hooked for life. He began to keep notebooks of words and defini-

tions, and eventually he created his own puzzles. His first success came while he was an undergraduate, trying to catch the attention of a student named Jean Merletto. He saw her working on the crossword in the *New York Herald-Tribune,* so he constructed a puzzle for her. The one-across clue was "Most beautiful girl on campus." The answer was "Jean." They were married on 23 March 1940. Their friends called them "Big Gene" and "Little Jean," and both became schoolteachers. They had two children.

While in college Maleska began submitting his puzzles to the *Tribune.* The *Tribune* rejected his first forty puzzles, because they were so well crafted that they thought he was using other puzzle writers' clues. In 1940 Maleska was accepted as a regular contributor at $1.50 a puzzle. At the time, the *New York Times* did not publish crossword puzzles, considering them "a primitive form of mental exercise." In 1942 the *Times* published its first puzzle in the Sunday magazine. Maleska's puzzles were included almost from the start.

From 1937 to 1940, Maleska taught Latin and English at a junior high school in suburban Palisades Park, New Jersey. In 1940 he began his more than thirty-year career in the New York City public school system. He was an English teacher at Frederick Douglass Junior High School in Manhattan from 1940 to 1946. He was the assistant to the principal at P.S. 169 in 1946, and in 1952 he became the principal of P.S. 192. He took a year off to study at Harvard University from 1954 to 1955 and was the principal of Junior High School 184 from 1955 to 1958.

During this time, Maleska had dozens of crossword puzzles published in the *Times.* Over the years he pioneered many changes in construction, including the use of nonprimary definitions, such as "nutcracker's suite," for "nest" and "meter man" for "poet," rather than the straight-from-the-dictionary clues of the past. One of his puzzles had the first multiple-word answer ever printed in the *Times.* The answer was "hard-shelled crab." It "crawled across the page," he said in an interview in 1991. "That just opened up the idea for phrases like 'in a rut' or 'all the way,' and then titles. You could have whole titles. It could be a quotation." He also developed new puzzle forms, including the "Stepquote," the "Diagonogram," and the "Cryptoquote."

From 1958 to 1964, Maleska was the coordinator, then superintendent, in charge of teacher recruitment for the New York City public school system. He was the assistant superintendent of schools in District 8 of the Bronx from 1964 to 1966. Between 1966 and 1970 he was the associate program director for the Center for Urban Education in New York City, but he resumed his position as assistant superintendent of District 8 from 1970 until 1973, when he retired. That year, Intermediate School 174 in the Bronx was renamed the Eugene T. Maleska Intermediate School in his honor. He was the first person to have a New York City school named for him during his lifetime, and he will be the last, due to a subsequent law.

Maleska also taught at the college level. He was an instructor at Hunter College in New York City from 1947 to 1951, taught in the summers of 1960, 1961, and 1962 at the University of Vermont, and was a lecturer at the City College of New York from 1952 to 1962. In 1962 he wrote *The Story of Education* with Carroll Atkinson. This book became a standard text in education courses for many years.

In 1977 Maleska was appointed crossword puzzle editor of the *New York Times*. There had only been two other editors before him, Margaret Farrar and Will Weng. From 1977 until his death in 1993, Maleska selected more than 7,000 puzzles for the daily paper and Sunday magazine. He estimated that he pored through more than 40,000 clues per year to choose which puzzles to publish, and that he made about seven mistakes a year. Explaining the popularity of crossword puzzles, he said, "The biggest reason puzzles are popular is they're a cheap way to kill time. People attack them because they love words. Nature abhors a vacuum and so does a human being. You see those blanks there, and you leap in."

Maleska wrote and edited a number of books throughout his life. In addition to numerous crossword puzzle compilations, he wrote a collection of poetry, *Sun and Shadow* (1961), and the puzzle-related books *A Pleasure in Words* (1981), *Across and Down: Inside the Crossword Puzzle World* (1984), and *Crosstalk: Letters to America's Foremost Crossword Authority,* published posthumously in 1993.

Jean Maleska died in 1983. On 9 February 1985, Maleska married Annrea Neill Sutton, a portrait painter. The marriage ended in divorce. In 1991 he married Carol Atkinson, the widow of his *The Story of Education* coauthor, Carroll Atkinson. A heavy smoker and cigar lover all his life, Maleska was diagnosed with throat cancer. "After fifty-five years of devotion to Lady Nicotine," he said about the choice to have surgery in early 1993, "I traded my voice for my life." Maleska died of throat cancer at his home in Daytona Beach.

At six feet, four inches, Eugene Maleska was an imposing figure, but he was often described as charming and personable. His puzzles continued to be published in compilations well after his death, and working on the *New York Times Sunday Magazine* puzzle was a weekend tradition for many. He was called a "cruciverbalist" (maker of crossword puzzles), but he found the word pretentious. He preferred the term "crossword constructor." "My main purpose is to entertain," he said in a December 1991 interview in the *Minneapolis Star-Tribune.*

★

There are no biographies of Eugene Maleska, but his books

A Pleasure in Words (1981), *Across and Down: The Crossword Puzzle World* (1984), and *Crosstalk* (1993) contain biographical information. Articles about his crossword puzzle career include David Streitfeld, "Getting Down (And Across); The Crossword Gurus and Their Square Dance," *Washington Post* (13 Mar. 1987); Boo Browning, "Word Weaver Is a Puzzler," *San Diego Union-Tribune* (4 Sept. 1990); and Amanda Gardner, "He Who Causes Cross Words: The Answer Is Cruciverbalist, Not Sadist," *Minneapolis Star-Tribune* (31 Dec. 1991). Obituaries are in the *New York Times* and the *Bergen Record* (both 5 Aug. 1993).

Sara J. Steen

MANKIEWICZ, Joseph Leo (*b.* 11 February 1909 in Wilkes-Barre, Pennsylvania; *d.* 5 February 1993 in Mount Kisco, New York), one of the most celebrated writer-directors in U.S. cinema, known for such classics as *The Ghost and Mrs. Muir* (1947), *A Letter to Three Wives* (1949), and *All About Eve* (1950).

Mankiewicz was the youngest of three children born to the German immigrants Franz Mankiewicz, a secondary schoolteacher, and Johanna Blumenau, a homemaker. Mankiewicz's father wanted to become a college professor, so the family moved to New York City in 1913. After graduating from Stuyvesant High School at age fifteen, Mankiewicz immediately enrolled at Columbia University. He received a B.A. in English in 1928, when he was only nineteen. The fact that he grew up in and was educated in the

Joseph Mankiewicz in a publicity shot for *Guys and Dolls,* 1955. The Kobal Collection

New York City area may explain his decision to settle in suburban Westchester County, where he lived from 1951 until his death.

Like others of his generation, Mankiewicz embarked on the grand tour after graduation, unaware that a visit to Berlin would change his life. Mankiewicz's fluency in German and the contacts of his brother Herman Mankiewicz, then head of Paramount's scenario department, landed him a job providing English translations for the intertitles in German films scheduled for release in Britain and the United States. On his return to the United States in 1929 Mankiewicz took a similar position at Paramount, writing titles for sound films to be shown in theaters still unequipped for talkies. The written word became Mankiewicz's passport to Hollywood, and soon it became his signature. Unlike his brother Herman, known primarily as the coauthor of the *Citizen Kane* (1941) screenplay, Joseph Mankiewicz enjoyed a career that spanned four decades, during which he won two Oscars two years in a row for the script and direction of both *A Letter to Three Wives* and *All About Eve*.

Paramount realized Mankiewicz had a gift for language, and he quickly progressed from titling to screenwriting, receiving dialogue credit for eight films and screenplay credit for eight more. Mankiewicz's best Paramount films were comedies: *Million Dollar Legs* (1932) with W. C. Fields; *If I Had a Million* (1932), an anthology film for which he wrote, among other episodes, the celebrated "Rollo and the Roadhogs" with W. C. Fields and Alison Skipworth; and *Diplomaniacs* (1933), featuring the comedy team of Bert Wheeler and Robert Woolsey. In 1934 Mankiewicz married Elizabeth Young, a stage actress. They had one son. Mankiewicz and Young divorced in 1937.

In 1934, after five years at Paramount, Mankiewicz moved to Metro-Goldwyn-Mayer (MGM), where he functioned primarily as a producer. During his eight years at MGM (1934–1942) he produced eighteen films, including *The Philadelphia Story* (1940), in which Katharine Hepburn scored a personal triumph after being labeled "box-office poison"; and *Woman of the Year* (1942), the first of nine films that Hepburn made with Spencer Tracy. Mankiewicz was the producer of *Three Comrades* (1938), but when the star, Margaret Sullavan, complained about F. Scott Fitzgerald's script, which she found unactable, Mankiewicz agreed and rewrote considerable portions of it. Dismayed, Fitzgerald was forced to admit that good novelists do not necessarily make good screenwriters. In 1939 Mankiewicz married Rosa Stradner, an actress, with whom he had two sons.

In 1943 Mankiewicz's desire to direct as well as produce and write brought him to the studio with which he has been most identified, Twentieth Century–Fox, then headed by Darryl F. Zanuck, whose obsession with well-written scripts equaled Mankiewicz's. Significantly all the films Mankiewicz directed at Fox with the exception of *No Way Out* (1950), a powerful indictment of racism, were adaptations. *Dragonwyck* (1946), *The Ghost and Mrs. Muir,* and *House of Strangers* (1949) were based on novels; *Somewhere in the Night* (1946), *A Letter to Three Wives,* and *All About Eve* originated as short stories; *The Late George Apley* (1946), *Escape* (1948), and *People Will Talk* (1951) derived from plays; and *Five Fingers* (1952) originated from a work of nonfiction. In 1951 Mankiewicz moved from Hollywood to Bedford, New York.

After he left Fox in 1952 Mankiewicz was still drawn to stage and literary properties. He adapted and directed Shakespeare's *Julius Caesar* (1953); *Guys and Dolls* (1955), a faithful recreation of the Broadway classic; *The Quiet American* (1957), adapted from Graham Greene's 1956 novel; *Suddenly, Last Summer* (1959), based on Tennessee Williams's 1958 one-act play; *The Honey Pot* (1966), a modern reworking of Ben Jonson's *Volpone* (1605); and his last film, *Sleuth* (1972), which Anthony Shaffer adapted from his own stage success. Even Mankiewicz's original screenplay, *The Barefoot Contessa* (1954), with its impotence subplot, owed much to Ernest Hemingway's novel *The Sun Also Rises* (1926). Mankiewicz's wife, who suffered from periods of depression, committed suicide in 1958.

While *Cleopatra* (1963) might be called an original screenplay, other writers in addition to Mankiewicz were involved, and even the credits acknowledged Plutarch, Suetonius, and Appian. Unfortunately, the romantic escapades of the stars, Elizabeth Taylor and Richard Burton, during the shooting received more attention than the film, which was for the most part historically accurate. In 1962 Mankiewicz married Rosemary Matthews, who had been his production secretary during the filming of *Cleopatra.* That marriage produced a daughter.

Mankiewicz, a stocky man with piercing blue eyes, once hoped to be a playwright. He brought great theatricality to his films, even having characters deliver lengthy monologues on camera or narrate large portions of the film in voice-overs. His most famous film, *All About Eve,* portrays theater people living as if life were a play in which discourse takes the form of witty repartee. In 1991 Mankiewicz was honored by the Academy of Motion Picture Arts and Sciences. In his tribute Michael Caine, who costarred in *Sleuth* with Sir Laurence Olivier, called Mankiewicz "the most civilized man I ever met in the cinema." "Civilized" is equally applicable to his films. Mankiewicz died of heart failure shortly before his eighty-fourth birthday.

★

Kenneth L. Geist, *Pictures Will Talk: The Life and Films of Joseph L. Mankiewicz* (1978), includes many details about Mankiewicz's personal life. Bernard F. Dick, *Joseph L. Mankiewicz*

(1983), is a critical study that drew on Twentieth Century–Fox production files. Sam Staggs, *All About "All About Eve"* (2000) documents the making of Mankiewicz's most popular film. An obituary is in the *New York Times* (6 Feb. 1993).

BERNARD F. DICK

MARCELLO, Carlos (*b.* 6 February 1910 in Carthage, Tunisia; *d.* 2 March 1993 in Metairie, Louisiana), reputed crime boss of Louisiana who has been linked to the assassination of President John F. Kennedy by some conspiracy theorists, though none have produced any credible evidence of his involvement.

Marcello's Sicilian parents migrated to the French protectorate of Tunisia, where in 1909 his father, Giuseppe Minacori, left his pregnant wife, Luigia Farrugia, and sailed to New Orleans. He secured work on a sugar plantation where his wife and infant son, Calogero, joined him in October 1910. In the United States the Minacoris changed their last name to Marcello and anglicized their first names, Giuseppe becoming Joseph and Luigia becoming Louise, and gave their son Calogero the Spanish name "Carlos."

Carlos Marcello leaving a federal court in New Orleans, 1980. © BETTMANN/CORBIS

Joseph Marcello acquired land and became a vegetable farmer in Jefferson Parish, across the Mississippi River from New Orleans. He and Louise, who helped him with the family farm, became naturalized American citizens, and their eight children born in Louisiana were citizens by birth. For some reason Carlos Marcello was never naturalized, an oversight that would later plague him.

Marcello dropped out of school at fourteen years of age and soon ran afoul of the law. As the result of an aborted robbery, he entered prison for the first time in May 1930 to serve nine to fourteen years, but he was pardoned four years later by Louisiana governor O. K. Allen.

In 1935 Marcello opened a bar in the Jefferson Parish town of Gretna, from which he reputedly sold drugs. On 6 September 1936 he married Jacqueline Todaro, the daughter of a reputed underboss of the New Orleans Mafia; the couple had four children. In March 1938 Marcello was arrested for selling twenty-three pounds of marijuana to an undercover federal agent and sentenced to a year and a day in federal prison.

During the early 1940s Marcello reportedly began distributing illegal slot machines in Jefferson Parish for Frank Costello, a reputed Mafia chief in New York City. By the end of 1945 Marcello was said to be a partner in a posh Jefferson Parish casino controlled by Costello. When Silvestro "Silver Dollar Sam" Carollo, reputed head of organized crime in Louisiana, was deported in May 1947, Marcello apparently replaced him with Costello's blessing.

On 25 January 1951 Marcello was called before Senator Estes Kefauver's Special Committee to Investigate Organized Crime in Interstate Commerce; however, Marcello invoked the Fifth Amendment to avoid answering questions. He was sentenced to six months for contempt of Congress, but the conviction was overturned on appeal. However, in February 1953 he was ordered deported as an undesirable alien—an order he would fight for four decades.

On 24 March 1959 Marcello appeared before a committee headed by Senator John L. McClellan that was investigating links between labor racketeering and organized crime; again he "took the Fifth." The committee's chief counsel was Robert F. Kennedy, who in 1961 became attorney general of the United States in the administration of his brother John F. Kennedy. As part of an effort to break the power of corrupt labor leaders and Mafia bosses, Robert Kennedy arranged Marcello's deportation to Guatemala in April 1961. Kennedy accomplished this in a move that was arguably illegal; he used the existence of a bogus Guatemalan birth certificate, which Marcello had obtained through bribery, to get Guatemala to accept Marcello. Marcello's lawyers accused the government of "kidnapping" and using fraudulent documentation to effect the deportation, and the American Civil Liberties Union protested the government's "totalitarian tactics." Two months later, under circumstances never fully explained, Marcello slipped back into the United States and successfully avoided deportation for the rest of his life.

In *Mafia Kingfish: Carlos Marcello and the Assassination of John F. Kennedy* (1989), John H. Davis suggests that Marcello's "humiliation" at the hands of Robert Kennedy provided the "motive" for the assassination of President Kennedy. However, Davis's "case" against Marcello, based on circumstantial evidence and a good deal of speculation, remains unproved.

On 22 September 1966 Marcello was one of thirteen alleged Mafia leaders from seven states arrested in a Queens, New York, restaurant. Marcello avoided testifying before a New York grand jury and on 1 October 1966 returned to New Orleans, where he became involved in an altercation at the airport and was indicted on charges of assaulting an FBI agent. In October 1970, after years of legal wrangling, Marcello entered a federal prison facility and served six months for the assault.

Despite trouble with federal officials, Marcello's position in Louisiana appeared secure. According to David Chandler (*Life,* 10 April 1970), Marcello avoided paying most state and local taxes and bribed or influenced officials to use public funds to drain and improve some 6,000 acres of swampland he owned, thereby turning Marcello's "$1 million investment in a Louisiana swamp into a real estate bonanza worth $60 million."

However, Marcello finally overreached. Joseph Hauser, a convicted swindler, "cooperated" with the FBI in an undercover investigation of Marcello. He gained Marcello's confidence, and the two set out to obtain state insurance contracts by bribing Louisiana officials. As part of a "sting" operation known as "Brilab," the FBI bugged Marcello's office and telephones from February 1979 to February 1980 and taped his conversations.

On 30 March 1981 Marcello and four other defendants went on trial for conspiracy, racketeering, and mail and wire fraud in connection with the insurance scheme. On 3 August 1981 Marcello was convicted. Two days later he was indicted on new charges stemming from an attempt to bribe a federal district judge, who was to preside over a racketeering case in Los Angeles involving associates of Marcello.

In January 1982 Marcello was sentenced to seven years in the Brilab case. In April he received ten years in the California bribery case. Despite efforts to fight both convictions, Marcello was ordered jailed on 15 April 1983. As his sentences were to run consecutively, Marcello, at seventy-three, faced the prospect of seventeen years in prison.

However, in June 1989 Marcello's Brilab conviction was overturned and in October, Marcello—who appeared to be suffering from Alzheimer's disease—was released on good behavior after serving six years on the bribery charge. At that time the five-foot, three-inch Marcello, known as the

"Little Man," was estimated by federal authorities to be worth $30 million. Upon his release, he returned to his home in suburban Metairie. Marcello lived there quietly until he died in his sleep at the age of eighty-three. No cause of death was released, and he was buried in a private funeral in Metairie.

At the height of his career Marcello perhaps wielded more power in Louisiana than any individual since Huey Long. If he was involved in the assassination of John F. Kennedy, however, he took this secret to his grave.

★

Although John H. Davis, *Mafia Kingfish: Carlos Marcello and the Assassination of John F. Kennedy* (1989), contains considerable biographical information on Marcello, the author's primary intent is to convince the reader, through circumstantial "evidence," that Marcello was behind the assassination of President John F. Kennedy. "Carlos Marcello: King Thug of Louisiana," *Life* (8 Sept. 1967), and a follow-up article by David Chandler, "The 'Little Man' Is Bigger Than Ever," *Life* (10 Apr. 1970), emphasize Marcello's power and influence with Louisiana politicians at the height of his career. Jim Amoss and Dean Baquet, "Carlos Marcello," a three-part series in the *New Orleans Times-Picayune*'s *Dixie Magazine* (14, 21, and 28 Feb. 1982), provide a good biographical overview. Obituaries are in the *New York Times* and *New Orleans Times-Picayune* (both 3 Mar. 1993).

ROMAN ROME

MARK, Herman Francis (*b.* 3 May 1895 in Vienna, Austria; *d.* 6 April 1992 in Austin, Texas), chemist known for pioneering work with polymers, important long-chain constituents of plastics and natural substances.

Mark was one of the three children of Herman Carl Mark, a Viennese surgeon, and Lili Mueller. His father was a Jewish convert to Lutheranism, and his mother was a Lutheran. Mark was raised comfortably in Vienna, one of the world's most cosmopolitan cities. Mark loved museums, music, and sports, especially soccer, skiing, skating, and mountain climbing. Between 1910 and 1914 he attended seminars and talks at the University of Vienna given by leading scientists, including Albert Einstein, Ernest Rutherford, and Marie Curie—"all of whom," he remembered, "made deep and unforgettable impressions on a young mind."

After enlisting in the armed forces of the Austro-Hungarian Empire in 1913, Mark served with distinction on the front lines during World War I, was wounded three times, was captured by the Italians in 1918 and was held prisoner for eleven months. He ended the war the most highly decorated company-grade officer in the Austrian army. Returning to Vienna in 1919 Mark took up the study of chemistry, a field in which he had become interested while recovering from wounds. He earned his Ph.D. degree at the University of Vienna in 1921. He married Marie Schramek on 19 August 1922; they had two children.

After a period of postdoctoral work at the University of Berlin, Mark joined a new research group at the Kaiser Wilhelm Institute for Physical Chemistry that was devoted to investigating the nature of fibrous substances such as cellulose, wool, and silk. The great question of the day concerned the molecular nature of such materials: were they made of aggregates of smaller bits and pieces, or did they involve giant molecules (macromolecules)? Mark's work in the late 1920s helped to prove that these natural fibers consisted of enormously lengthy and flexible molecular threads, long chains of atoms with unique properties. In many substances they appeared to be made of identical subunits joined end-to-end; in this case they were called polymers.

At the end of 1926 Mark became a research director for I. G. Farbenindustrie, Germany's largest chemical corporation. His job was to find ways to make polymer-based commercial products and stronger and more durable materials. Financially secure and happy, Mark spent the next six years furthering his studies. At Farben, Mark gathered a research group that took a multifaceted approach to problems. He used every new technique available, pioneering the application of X-ray diffraction, electron diffraction, and spectroscopy to fiber studies, and bringing together physicists, organic chemists, physical chemists, and chemical engineers to attack problems from many angles. It was a productive approach. The Mark group developed ways to align, stretch, crystallize, and spin long-chain molecules into new forms; for example, they used cellulose as a raw material to create industrial quantities of cellulose acetate (a substitute for silk). Mark discovered ways to create artificial rubber and developed an industrial process for producing polystyrene.

Then came the rise of Nazism. In 1932 Mark was informed by a superior at Farben that because he was Austrian (hence a foreigner) and because his father had been born Jewish, it was unlikely despite his fine work that he would receive promotions or advancement. Mark thanked him for his frank comments and began looking for other jobs. His first step took him back to Vienna, where in the summer of 1932 he began teaching as professor of physical chemistry at the University of Vienna. During the next few years he created the world's first comprehensive educational program for polymer science, devising the curriculum and writing important textbooks. However, he was once again forced to flee the Nazis. The day after Hitler's takeover of Austria in March 1938, Mark was arrested, interrogated for several days, and stripped of his passport. It took a year's salary in bribes to retrieve it. Mark and his family escaped from Vienna to Zurich, then to Canada, where he took a position as head of research for a paper company.

In 1940 Mark accepted a faculty position at the Polytechnic Institute of Brooklyn, where he would remain for the next several decades and retired as dean emeritus in 1990. At Brooklyn he became an influential teacher and continued his productive research. He founded the Polymer Research Institute in 1942 and became its first director. It quickly became a leading world center for research into a field that proved extremely important in postwar development, and which attracted a number of leading scientists. Mark's research during these years moved polymer science from a descriptive phase, in which the molecular structure of various polymers was discovered and manipulated, into a more theoretical phase, in which he helped to develop methods of predicting the behavior of different polymers. Now his field was moving rapidly, with new plastics, fibers, paints, and other materials the result.

Mark's influence was changing, too. Rather than doing basic research, he became important as a communicator in the fast-growing field. Many of the valuable advances in polymer research after 1945 were due to Mark's ability to spread what he called the "polymer gospel." To help spur worldwide communication he founded the *Journal of Polymer Science;* served as editor of the *Journal of Applied Polymer Science;* and was associate editor of the *Journal of Applied Physics,* the *Journal of Chemical Physics,* and the *Textile Research Journal.* He wrote about twenty books on polymer chemistry as well as more than five hundred articles for journals. He also organized a once-a-month Saturday morning conference on polymers in New York City that attracted hundreds of scientists. His open, friendly, enthusiastic manner made him an ideal proselytizer. Mark died after a short illness in Austin, Texas, where he was living with his son Hans.

The rapid development of polymers, especially plastics and synthetic fibers, in the latter half of the twentieth century had a profound effect on society. Virtually no one in developed nations goes a day without using a device made from or dependent upon these materials. Herman Mark as much as any single person made this possible.

★

Mark wrote a short autobiography, *From Small Organic Molecules to Large: A Century of Progress* (1993), published posthumously. Obituaries are in the (London) *Independent* (18 Apr. 1992) and (London) *Times* (2 May 1992). An oral history interview with Mark conducted in 1986 can be found at the Chemical Heritage Foundation.

THOMAS HAGER

MARSHALL, Thurgood (*b.* 2 July 1908 in Baltimore, Maryland; *d.* 24 January 1993 in Bethesda, Maryland), lawyer and jurist who was chief counsel for the National Association for the Advancement of Colored People and the first African American to sit as a justice on the U.S. Supreme Court.

Marshall was the son of William C. Marshall, a dining room steward at an all-white club, and Norma Arica Williams, a teacher. Marshall attended public schools in segregated Baltimore, where the 1896 U.S. Supreme Court decision in *Plessy* v. *Ferguson* legitimized the separation of the races and placed the Court's imprimatur on state-mandated Jim Crowism. As a young man, he had to address racism in the streets with his fists. "Son," Marshall's father admonished, "if anyone ever calls you a nigger, you not only got my permission to fight him—you got my orders to fight him." He graduated from Frederick Douglass High School, then attended Lincoln University, a predominantly black school in Pennsylvania. In 1929 he married Vivian "Buster" Burey. After graduation in 1930, he entered the predominantly black Howard University Law School. He had been denied admission to the University of Maryland Law School because of his race, but Marshall was able to "remedy" this slight in 1935, when he won a lawsuit in the Maryland Court of Appeals that ordered the Law School to admit black students.

At Howard, Marshall was exposed to the teachings of Charles Hamilton Houston, who encouraged his students to think of lawyers as social engineers. For Houston, lawyers should "shape litigation into a vehicle for sustained social protest, choosing a case to argue not only on the basis of an individual's need but also on the basis of the needs of a cause." Marshall adopted the Houston definition of attorney as public interest lawyer. After graduating first in his class from Howard Law School in 1933, Marshall prac-

ticed law in Baltimore, then in 1934 went to work for the NAACP under Houston, who was the NAACP's first full-time salaried special counsel. When Houston stepped down in 1938, Marshall became the director of the NAACP's newly created Legal Defense and Education Fund. He won fourteen civil rights cases before the U.S. Supreme Court while with the NAACP. After the University of Maryland desegregation case in 1935, Marshall successfully argued the unconstitutionality of excluding black voters from primary elections (Smith v. Allwright, 1944), racial restrictions in housing (Shelley v. Kraemer, 1948), and, in two cases in 1950, separate-but-equal facilities in state universities (Sweatt v. Painter and McLauren v. Oklahoma State Regents).

His most famous case before the Supreme Court was *Brown* v. *Board of Education of Topeka* (1954), which overturned the separate-but-equal racial segregation policy in public schools and signaled the end of the era of segregation in all public facilities. In February of the following year his wife died, and in December he married Cecilia "Cissy" Suyat; they had two children.

In 1961 Marshall was nominated for the Second Circuit of the U.S. Court of Appeals by President John F. Kennedy. As shown in the Senate confirmation hearings, there was great consternation in the legislature and in the nation about the appointment of an African American to the federal appeals bench. Senators such as North Carolina's Sam Ervin and South Carolina's Strom Thurmond, cognizant of Marshall's legal successes against Jim Crowism in the federal courts, did not believe that Marshall had the intelligence or the temperament to serve as a federal appeals court judge.

Furthermore, Attorney General Robert F. Kennedy tried to block the appointment. One tense conversation between the two ended when Kennedy started talking about the trouble with "you people." Marshall broke off the conversation, saying, "I never like anybody [calling] me 'you people,' because I know what they're talking about." Marshall rejected the offer, stating to Kennedy that the "trouble with you is that you are different from me. You don't know what it means, but all I've had in my life is nothing. It's [rejection] not new to me. So goodbye." President Kennedy, however, pressed for the appointment, and after nearly a year of delay and attacks by southerners in the Senate, Marshall was confirmed.

Marshall's appointment in 1961 by President Lyndon B. Johnson to the position of U.S. solicitor general was seen as an action of "racial preference" by many (as was Kennedy's appointment of Marshall to the Court of Appeals) who believed that Marshall *really* was fundamentally inferior and unfit to serve on the federal courts. After President Lyndon Johnson appointed Marshall to the U.S. Supreme Court in 1967, Marshall, the first African American to sit on the Court, was depicted, even by his brethren, as a person who was appointed because of his race. Behind his back

Thurgood Marshall, 1967. CORBIS CORPORATION (NEW YORK)

some even referred to Marshall as the "house nigger." But for Marshall there was always the belief that the law would, in the end, open the doors to equal opportunity for blacks and other minorities in America. "If we are ever to become a fully integrated society," wrote Marshall in a dissent in 1978, "one in which the color of a person's skin will not determine the opportunities available to him or her, we must be willing to take steps to open those doors."

Marshall believed that a task of judges, when adjudicating concrete cases before them, was to try to ensure that all persons have the possibility of living in a "just and humane society." He believed that all persons have the right to be free of all forms of capricious discrimination; that all persons must have access to decent education, decent housing, and decent jobs; and that all persons have a significant interest in the Fourteenth Amendment's due process clause to be free from governmental interference in their personal lives. He also believed that, in order to maintain and protect these valued liberties, the courts had to be available to all persons, regardless of their financial status. Again and again he was very critical of a Court majority that ignored the peculiar circumstances of the impoverished. This meant that the Supreme Court justice's role in a constitutional republic was to give meaning to the evolving words of the Constitution in such a manner as to provide justice to the weak and the underclasses who needed its protections. For the justices of the Supreme Court to ignore their legal and constitutional oaths to provide justice for both the rich and the poor was an unforgivable lack of fundamental fairness. Unfortunately, such decisions by the Court majority while Marshall served on the Supreme Court were not uncommon, and he spoke out, in conference and in his dissents.

For example, in *San Diego Independent School District* v. *Rodriguez* (1973), the Court upheld the constitutionality of using local property taxes to finance schools, thereby enabling school districts with high property tax bases to provide better schools than poorer districts. Marshall, however, dissented, believing that state policies that have the effect of discriminating on the basis of wealth were subject to judicial scrutiny. In his opinion, the Constitution provided the "right of every American to an equal start in life." Equality of opportunity was a value he had seen as primary when fighting the NAACP battles in federal courts. As a Supreme Court justice, Marshall continued to argue for its primacy, finding it in the language of the Constitution.

Although Marshall often said he would never retire from the Court, failing health prevented him from staying on until a new presidential administration could appoint another liberal to his seat. In June 1991, about a month before his eighty-third birthday, he announced his retirement for health reasons. A reporter asked him what was wrong, and Marshall replied, "I'm old. I'm getting old and coming apart." His retirement took effect in October.

Just days before his death in January 1993, Marshall was scheduled to swear in the newly elected Democratic vice president, Al Gore, but his health prevented him from doing so. He died of heart failure at the Bethesda Naval Medical Center and was buried in Arlington National Cemetery.

Known as "Mr. Civil Rights," Marshall fought battles against racism and segregation at a time when black legal advocates confronted extreme danger. "You know," said an elderly African American cabdriver, "Marshall was like Joe Louis for us. He was the black man who was always there to inspire you. The white folk would send up their best against him, and he would knock them out time after time." Marshall was the consummate lawyer, in his own words "a man of the law." Law mattered for him more than any other societal norm. One of his clerks said, he "is someone who deeply believes in the law. . . . He has faith that the law matters—that it is a real thing you can point to and say, 'This is the right answer' or 'This is the wrong answer.'"

★

Marshall's letters and papers are located at the Madison Building of the Library of Congress in Washington, D.C. Biographies of Marshall are Howard Ball, *A Defiant Life: Thurgood Marshall and the Persistence of Racism in America* (1999); Michael D. Davis and Hunter R. Clark, *Thurgood Marshall: Warrior at the Bar, Rebel on the Bench* (1992); Roger Goldman and David Gallen, *Thurgood Marshall: Justice for All* (1992); and Carl T. Rowan, *Dream Makers, Dream Breakers: The World of Justice Thurgood Marshall* (1993). For information on Marshall's civil rights cases before he became a Supreme Court justice, see Jack Greenberg, *Crusaders in the Courts: How a Dedicated Band of Lawyers Fought for the Civil Rights Revolution* (1994); and Mark Tushnet, *The NAACP's Legal Strategy against Segregated Education, 1925–1950* (1987) and *Making Civil Rights Law: Thurgood Marshall and the Supreme Court, 1936–1961*. Articles of interest on Marshall's views of the law and justice are: Kevin T. Baine, "Wit, Wisdom, and Compassion of Justice Thurgood Marshall," *Hastings Constitutional Law Quarterly* 20 (spring 1993): 497–502; Lucius J. Barker, "Thurgood Marshall, the Law, and the System: Tenets of an Enduring Legacy," *Stanford Law Review* 44 (summer 1992): 1237–1247; Susan Low Bloch, "Thurgood Marshall: Courageous Advocate, Compassionate Judge," *Georgetown Law Review* 80 (1993): 2003–2009; and Juan Williams, "Marshall's Law: The Triumph of Thurgood Marshall," *Washington Post Magazine* (7 Jan. 1990). An obituary is in the *New York Times* (25 Jan. 1993).

HOWARD BALL

MAYNARD, Robert Clyve (*b.* 17 June 1947 in Brooklyn, New York; *d.* 17 August 1993 in Oakland, California), African American journalist, newspaper editor, publisher, and syndicated columnist best remembered for opening and advancing opportunities for minority journalists.

Robert C. Maynard. AP/WIDE WORLD PHOTOS

Maynard was the youngest of six children born to Samuel Christopher Maynard, a part-time lay preacher who owned a small trucking firm, and Robertine Isola Greaves. His parents had emigrated from Barbados to the United States in 1919. Maynard attended, but did not graduate from, Boys' High School in Brooklyn, developing an enduring love for writing from an early age. While Maynard cut school classes, he spent time at the *New York Age,* a black-owned weekly paper. At the age of sixteen, he dropped out of high school to become a writer for the *Age.*

In 1956 Maynard moved to Greenwich Village in Manhattan. There he continued to work for the *Age* and became a freelance writer at the age of nineteen. He met such famous writers as James Baldwin and Langston Hughes, who encouraged him in his literary efforts. He also worked as a reporter for the *Afro-American News* in Baltimore. At this time, Maynard worked at odd jobs while searching unsuccessfully for full-time journalistic work. Although his freelance work got him a few interviews, Maynard was rejected when his race became known. In 1961 the *York Gazette and Daily* in Pennsylvania hired him as a police and urban affairs reporter. He worked hard and eventually was as-signed to cover the civil rights movement in the South. In 1966 Maynard was awarded a one-year Nieman fellowship to study journalism at Harvard University. After finishing, he returned to the *Gazette* to work as a night editor.

Maynard became the first black national correspondent for the *Washington Post* in 1967. That same year, he wrote a five-part, five-city series on racial unrest, which won him a national reputation. In 1972 he covered the Watergate scandal and, with *New York Times* reporter Earl Caldwell, codirected a Ford Foundation program for minority journalists at Columbia University. (The Ford Foundation ended its support of Columbia's training program in 1974 to Maynard's disappointment.) While continuing to write for the *Washington Post,* Maynard began to work part-time as a senior editor at *Encore,* a new monthly. That same year, the *Washington Post* appointed Maynard to an eighteen-month term as ombudsman of the newspaper and named him associate editor. He remained at the *Washington Post* for ten years, serving as a reporter and editorial writer. In January 1975 Maynard married Nancy Hicks, a *New York Times* reporter. Their union produced two sons. Maynard also had a daughter from an earlier marriage.

Maynard was selected to serve as one of three questioners at a 1976 presidential campaign debate between Gerald Ford and Jimmy Carter. The following year, Maynard took a leave of absence from the *Post* and went to Berkeley, California, where he and Nancy cofounded a journalism program known as the Institute for Journalism Education at the University of California. Maynard served as its chair until 1979. In December 1993, the Institute became the Robert C. Maynard Institute for Journalism Education.

The mammoth Gannett newspaper organization hired Maynard in 1978 as an affirmative action consultant. In 1979 he became the editor of the *Oakland Tribune,* then owned by Gannett, becoming the nation's first black director of editorial operations for a major daily newspaper. In this post Maynard hired minority journalists, including the first openly gay columnist. In 1983 he bought the *Oakland Tribune,* becoming the editor, publisher, and president as well as the first African American to own a major metropolitan newspaper. During a decade of leadership, the newspaper won hundreds of awards for editorial excellence as well as a Pulitzer Prize in 1990 for its coverage of the Loma Prieta earthquake and its coverage of the Oakland Hills fire.

Maynard began a weekly syndicated newspaper column in the 1980s. His views were broadcast through regular television appearances on *This Week with David Brinkley* and *The MacNeil-Lehrer NewsHour.* In 1992 Maynard suffered a recurrence of a cancer that had first been diagnosed and treated in the late 1980s. That same year the family decided to sell the *Tribune* to the Almeda Newspaper Group. Maynard returned to work for the Institute and continued to promote the cause of racial equality and equal opportunities for minorities. He also wrote an autobiography, *Letters to My Children* (1995), and continued to contribute articles. He died at his home in Oakland of complications from prostate cancer at the age of fifty-six. He was buried in Washington, D.C., at the Rock Creek Church Cemetery.

Maynard, a Democrat and a Lutheran, was active in many professional organizations, served on the board of directors of the Associated Press, the American Society of Newspaper Editors, the National News Council, the Oakland Chamber of Commerce, and the Pacific School of Religion. He was a member of the Pulitzer Prize committee and received honorary degrees from six institutions of higher learning. Among other affiliations, Maynard was a member of the Council on Foreign Relations, the Rockefeller Foundation, and the steering committee of the Reporters' Committee on Freedom of the Press.

Although fully committed to journalism, Maynard had other interests. Earl Caldwell called him a "Renaissance man" and noted his love of books, cooking for dinner parties, classic cars, photography, languages, and collecting fountain pens.

A lifelong newspaperman, Maynard was one of the nation's most respected and successful minority journalists. Noted for his cheerful personality and confidence, Maynard was described by Paul Cobb as being to journalism what Jackie Robinson was to baseball. Throughout his lengthy career, Maynard was regarded as an excellent, influential, and popular journalist. His enduring legacy lies in his dedication to the cause of racial equality and equal opportunities for minorities. Maynard once said, "This country cannot be the country we want if its story is told by only one group of citizens." His serious, concerned, and determined demeanor complemented his attitude toward his work. Maynard was a charismatic leader, editor, and publisher who cared deeply about the news and the role of the press in society. He believed that newspapers should be used as instruments of social change and reform.

★

Maynard's autobiography is *Letters to My Children* (1995). There is no full-length biography. Useful biographical information appears in *Current Biography Yearbook* (1986): 352–355, and *Contemporary Authors* 115 (1985): 295–298. Maynard's journalistic career is discussed in Jessie C. Smith, *Notable Black American Men* (1999): 778–780, and Pamela Noel, "Robert Maynard: Oakland's Top Newsman," *Ebony* (June 1985). The most complete obituary appears in the *Washington Post* (19 Aug. 1993). Other obituaries are in the *Los Angeles Times* and *New York Times* (both 19 Aug. 1993) and the *San Francisco Chronicle* (21 Aug. 1993).

NJOKI-WA-KINYATTI

MERRIAM, Eve (*b.* 19 July 1916 in Philadelphia, Pennsylvania; *d.* 11 April 1992 in New York City), poet, author, playwright, and educator whose more than fifty books for children and adults were acclaimed for their wit, wordplay, and incisive social commentary.

The youngest of four children, Merriam was born Eva Moskowitz to Max Moskowitz and Jennie Siegel, Russian immigrants who owned a chain of women's clothing shops. She grew up in Germantown, Pennsylvania, a suburb of Philadelphia. From childhood Merriam loved to read, write, and recite poetry; she avidly read the childhood classics and was particularly fond of the "tongue-twisting verses" (as she called them) of the Gilbert and Sullivan operettas she attended as a child. As a mature writer she described the remarkably visceral response to poetry that she experienced all her life: "I find it difficult to sit still when I hear poetry or read it out loud. I feel a tingle in the tips of my fingers and in my toes, and it just seems to go right from my mouth all the way through my body. It's like a shot of adrenalin or oxygen when I hear rhymes and wordplay." Driven by a compulsive need to write, Merriam's prolific career began at age seven, when she began to write poetry. Although she received encouragement from her teachers and frequently published poems in her high school magazine and weekly newspaper, the adolescent Merriam did not plan to become a writer. She graduated from Germantown High School in 1933.

Merriam attended Cornell University, in Ithaca, New

Eve Merriam. ©LAYLE SILBERT

York, but transferred to the University of Pennsylvania in Philadelphia, where she graduated with an A.B. degree in 1937. After briefly pursuing graduate studies at the University of Wisconsin and Columbia University, she was hired in 1939 as a radio scriptwriter for CBS, and from 1942 to 1946 she conducted a weekly poetry program on New York City's WQXR. These jobs were followed by brief editorial stints at *Deb* and *Glamour* magazines. On 15 October 1939 Merriam married her first husband, Erwin Edwin Spritzer (they divorced on 10 March 1946). By the mid-1940s Merriam began to win recognition. In 1946 her first book, *Family Circle,* won the prestigious Yale Younger Poet's Prize. The contest was judged by Archibald MacLeish, whom Merriam had idolized since college days, when as a student she slept with a copy of one of his books under her pillow. She was also influenced by MacLeish's philosophy that poetry "should not mean but be." In 1949 she won a *Collier's* prize for fiction.

Merriam married Martin Philip Michel on 27 May 1947. They had two sons (her only children). She divorced Michel on 17 July 1960 and married twice more (to Leonard Case Lewin on 1 August 1963 and, after their divorce on 5 June 1980, to Waldo Salt, an Academy Award–winning screenwriter, on 22 October 1983). A highly productive author who wrote for all age groups and in a variety of genres, Merriam prided herself on her ability to support herself and her family by writing. Her career as a freelance writer spanned the years from 1949 until her death in 1992. During the 1960s, her most productive decade, Merriam published thirty books, including biographies, nonfiction, picture books, and poetry for children as well as poetry and nonfiction with a strong feminist slant for adults. Her first volume of children's verse, *There is No Rhyme for Silver,* was named a Junior Literary Guild Selection in 1962.

Throughout the 1970s and the 1980s Merriam continued her prodigious output of poetry and juvenile nonfiction. Reviewers of her books for children praised her celebration of the music and magic of poetry through lively wordplay and freshness of voice, qualities that would become her literary trademark. Merriam's "How to Eat a Poem" (1962) playfully illustrates her lifelong devotion to the sound and sensuality of language: "Don't be polite. / Bite in. / Pick it up with your fingers and lick the juice that may run down your chin. / It is ready and ripe now, whenever you are." The books of poetry and nonfiction she wrote for adults express her views about feminism and equality of the sexes. These include *The Double Bed from the Feminine Side* (1958), *After Nora Slammed the Door: American Women in the 1960s—the Unfinished Revolution* (1964), and, as editor, *Growing Up Female in America: Ten Lives* (1971).

Through articles, interviews, readings, and lectures, Merriam energetically promoted techniques that could be used at home or in the classroom to encourage children's enjoyment and appreciation of poetry. "Whatever you do," she advised teachers in an article published in 1985, "find ways to read poetry. Eat it, drink it, enjoy it, and share it." She was a member of the Bank Street College of Education's field project staff in Manhattan (1958–1960) and taught creative writing at City College of the City University of New York (1965–1969). She also taught drama at New York University in the 1980s. She received the prestigious National Council of Teachers of English Award for excellence in poetry for children in 1981.

While Merriam's writing for children garnered mostly favorable reviews, one of her books, *The Inner City Mother Goose* (1969), intended for an adult audience, proved highly controversial. Drawing on the historical origins of many traditional nursery rhymes as social commentary, Merriam sought to use the form to draw attention to the dire conditions in American inner cities. (A typical line: "Jack be nimble Jack be quick / Snap the blade and give it a flick.") When the book was published it was denounced by public officials and civic organizations who claimed the book glorified crime and incited violence. Merriam described it as "just about the most banned book in the country," yet it sold over 100,000 copies, inspired a Broadway musical in 1971, and was reissued in an expanded and newly illustrated edition in 1996.

In the 1970s Merriam began to write for the theater. Her most talked-about and successful play was *The Club,* which was produced off-Broadway in 1976 at the Circle-in-the-Square. The play was set in a private club and featured a cast of women dressed as men in formal Edwardian attire exchanging sexist banter and songs. It won ten Obie Awards. Another play, *Out of Our Father's House* (based on her book *Growing Up Female in America*), was presented in New York City in 1977 and at the White House in 1978, and it was shown on public television. Merriam wrote a total of eight plays, most of which were either published or performed. She served on the Tony Awards nominating committee and was an officer of the Dramatists Guild and Authors League.

During her last decade Merriam's output barely flagged. She published numerous volumes of juvenile poetry and children's picture books. Reviews of the books she published in the 1980s, such as *Fresh Paint: New Poems* (1986), *Blackberry Ink: Poems* (1985), and *A Sky Full of Poems* (1986), comment on her inventive language, humor, appealing imagery, and continued ability to make children "think and wonder and laugh." Merriam remained active well into her seventies, writing and taking dance lessons and long walks around Manhattan. She died of cancer at age seventy-five at St. Vincent's Hospital in Manhattan. Her ashes were scattered under a tree that was dedicated to her memory on the northwest corner of Washington Square Park in Greenwich Village.

Merriam was a gifted poet and a talented writer of prose and plays who reached a remarkable range of readers, from toddlers to sophisticated Broadway audiences. She also identified herself as a "lifelong feminist" who wrote, often satirically, about the social inequalities that plagued postwar American society. But above all she was a passionate and effective advocate for the elemental joys of poetry. Through her belief that "poetry must be fun," she brought children and poetry together.

★

Merriam's papers are in the Kerlan Collection at the University of Minnesota at Minneapolis; the de Grummond Collection at the University of Southern Mississippi in Hattiesburg; and the Schlesinger Library at Radcliffe College. Merriam's article "Some Pearls from Eve Merriam on Sharing Poetry with Children" was published in *Learning* 85 (Sept. 1985): 78–81. Helen Heffer, *A Checklist of Works By and About Eve Merriam* (1980), is an unpublished master's thesis (University of Maryland). For interviews see Kathleen Betsko and Rachel Koenig, *Interviews with Contemporary Women Playwrights* (1987), and Jeffrey S. Copeland, *Speaking of Poets: Interviews with Poets Who Write for Children and Young Adults* (1993). See also Glenna Sloan, "Profile: Eve Merriam," *Language Arts* 58 (Nov.–Dec. 1981): 957–963; and Elizabeth Kamarck Minnich, "An Appreciation of Eve Merriam," *Ms.* (Nov.–Dec. 1992). An obituary is in the *New York Times* (13 Apr. 1992). Jacqueline Schachter's interview with Merriam, available on videocassette, was produced by Temple University Office of Television Services in 1974 as part of the Profiles in Literature series. An audiocassette, *Sharing Poetry with Children, by Eve Merriam,* was released by the Children's Book Council in 1983 as part of the Prelude Children's Book Council Mini-Seminars on Using Books Creatively, series 7.

CHRISTINE STENSTROM

MEYENDORFF, John (*b.* 17 February 1926 in Neuilly-sur-Seine, France; *d.* 22 July 1992 in Montreal, Canada), Eastern Orthodox theologian, pastor, teacher, and ecumenical leader.

Meyendorff, whose given name was Jean, was one of three children of Russian émigré parents, barons of Baltic German aristocratic lineage who had fled the Bolshevik Revolution. His father, Theophile Meyendorff, was an artist who painted portraits and miniatures on ivory. His mother, Catherine Schidlovsky, assisted her husband by establishing contacts for him.

Meyendorff attended various schools in Paris and Biarritz, where the family spent most of World War II. He enrolled simultaneously at the Orthodox Theological Seminary of Saint Serge, in Paris, and at the Sorbonne, which awarded him the License ès-lettre degree and a Diplome

d'Etudes Superieures degree, respectively. At Saint Serge he studied with luminaries of the Russian Orthodox diaspora, including Father Georges Florovsky. After graduating from Saint Serge in 1949, he taught there until 1959 and also worked for the Centre National de la Recherche Scientifique while preparing his doctorate for the Sorbonne. Meyendorff married Marie Mojaysky on 26 January 1950; the couple had four children. He completed one year of military service, largely with the Train des Equipages, in October 1952.

In 1959 two of Meyendorff's seminal works were published: *Défense des saints hésychastes* a two-volume French translation of a treatise, best known as the *Triads,* by the fourteenth-century Byzantine theologian Saint Gregory Palamas, and Meyendorff's thesis, an analysis of Palamas titled *Introduction à l'étude de Grégoire Palamas* (1959, published as *A Study of Gregory Palamas,* 1964). Gregory, the archbishop of Thessalonica, was a defender of the Byzantine theological and cultural movement known as *hesychasm.* (The term *hesychasm,* whose varied meanings were explored by Meyendorff, describes inner silence and the practice of contemplative prayer. Practiced by the early Christian fathers of Egypt, Palestine, and Asia Minor, *hesychasm* has been described as a method for achieving spiritual concentration and the ultimate vision of God.) The *Triads,* in particular, have been called pioneering works. In them, Gregory distinguishes between the "essence" (which is unknowable) and "energies" (knowable) of God, thus providing a dogmatic basis for *hesychasm* in Orthodox theology, since God enters into a direct relationship with humankind through these energies.

Meyendorff further established his authority on the subject with a number of shorter studies published between 1953 and 1955, later collected in *Byzantine Hesychasm: Historical, Theological, and Social Problems* (1974). Meyendorff's works, which were written in French, English, and Russian and published in eight languages, established his reputation as an internationally recognized Orthodox theologian. His other works include *St.Gregoire Palamas et la Mystique Orthodoxe* (1959; published in English as *St. Gregory Palamas and Orthodox Spirituality,* 1994), and *L'Eglise orthodoxe hier et aujourd'hui* (1960, published as *The Orthodox Church: Its Past and Its Role in the World Today,* 1962, 1995). *Orthodoxie et Catholicité* (1965, published as *Orthodoxy and Catholicity,* 1966), is a collection of essays devoted to problems of Christian unity, examining issues that have emerged between the Orthodox Church and Roman Catholicism and Protestantism. *Christ in Eastern Christian Thought* (1969), explores the Orthodox perspective on Christology. *Byzantium and the Rise of Russia* (1981), examines the relationship between Byzantium and the early history of Russia, and the history of *hesychasm* as it relates to the authority of the ecumenical patriarchate in Constantinople (modern Istanbul). Other published works include *Byzantine Theology* (1974), and *Marriage: An Orthodox Perspective* (1975). *Witness to the World* (1987), collects editorials written for the *Orthodox Church,* a newspaper, between the late 1960s and early 1980s.

Ordained to the priesthood in February 1959 at the Cathedral of Saint Alexander Nevsky in Paris, in the fall of that year Meyendorff emigrated to the United States and joined the faculty of Saint Vladimir's Orthodox Theological Seminary (then in New York City and subsequently in its suburbs) as a professor of church history and patristics. In doing so, he followed in the steps of Florovsky and Alexander Schmemann, prominent Orthodox theologians of the Russian diaspora. He later served as the seminary librarian, director of studies, and editor of *Saint Vladimir's Seminary Quarterly* and the *Orthodox Church*. In 1967 he became a professor of history at Fordham University in New York City, where he taught Byzantine history and patristics in the college and graduate school part-time until 1992. Meyendorff also taught courses at Columbia University and at Union Theological Seminary in New York City. In 1953 he became a cofounder and the first general secretary of Syndesmos, an international organization of Orthodox youth movements.

Meyendorff was instrumental in negotiations that resulted in the granting of autocephaly to the Metropolia in 1970. The Metropolia, comprised chiefly of Russians, Carpatho-Russians, and other linguistically or ethnically related Orthodox Christians, became the Orthodox Church in America (OCA); subsequently, the Romanian, Albanian, and Bulgarian jurisdictions joined the OCA. Autocephaly was necessary to regularize the canonical situation that had resulted from the break in relations with the Russian Orthodox Church after the Communist Revolution, when the formerly united Orthodox Church in the United States and Canada split into multiple ethnic jurisdictions, all under foreign patriarchates. Meyendorff represented the Metropolia (and later the OCA) on the Central Committee of the World Council of Churches (WCC), serving as moderator of the WCC Faith and Order Commission from 1967 to 1975. It was during this period that Meyendorff was naturalized as a U.S. citizen.

Shortly after his arrival at Saint Vladimir's, Meyendorff was tapped as a senior fellow by Harvard University's Dumbarton Oaks Byzantine Research Center in Washington, D.C., commuting there biweekly until 1967; he remained a lifelong member of its Senior Fellows Committee. During a sabbatical year in 1978, he served as the acting director of studies, and also as a parish priest for a mission parish in Reston, Virginia. He served as a priest in Saint Vladimir's seminary chapel and as a rector of Christ the Saviour Church in New York City. Meyendorff was named dean of Saint Vladimir's Orthodox Seminary in 1984, following the death of Schmemann, and continued in this position until shortly before his death. He was coeditor of *Christian Spirituality: Origins to the Twelfth Century* (1986), a volume in the World Spirituality series. His last published book, *Imperial Unity and Christian Divisions: The Church 450–680 A.D.,* appeared in 1989.

For years a target of official hostility by the former Soviet Union, the emergence of glasnost and perestroika in the mid-1980s allowed Meyendorff to make regular visits to Russia, where he lectured at seminaries and established fruitful relations with church leaders, including the Russian patriarch Aleksy II. As the chairman for external affairs of the OCA, Meyendorff's extensive knowledge of Western Orthodoxy and understanding of the perils faced by the Russian Church under communism won him the trust of many leaders in the Russian Church. Despite some opposition in Russia to his ecumenism, in 1991 Meyendorff was awarded the Order of Saint Vladimir by Aleksy II during the latter's visit to the United States. He retired in 1992 in order to write books and translate some of his earlier work into Russian.

Meyendorff received honorary degrees from Notre Dame University, the General Theological Seminary in New York, and the Leningrad (now Saint Petersburg) Theological Academy. He became a corresponding fellow of the British Academy in 1977. He regularly attended the International Congress of Byzantine Studies. An eloquent and passionate defender of Eastern Orthodoxy, as well as a gifted teacher and confessor, Meyendorff worked constantly for Orthodox jurisdictional unity in America, and saw the creation of the OCA as a step in that direction. He died of pancreatic cancer while vacationing in Labelle in Canada's Laurentian Mountains. He is buried at Oakland Cemetery in suburban Yonkers, New York.

★

Saint Vladimir's Seminary houses archives relating to Meyendorff's years as dean. See "Memories of Father John," *O.N.E.* (Orthodox New England) (Oct. 1992), and "Protopresbyter John Meyendorff (1926–1992)," *The Orthodox West* (summer 1992), which includes an interview with Meyendorff on his retirement as dean of Saint Vladimir's Seminary. A brief biographical sketch may be found in Gerald H. Anderson, ed., *Biographical Dictionary of Christian Missions* (1998). Obituaries include Dimitri Obolensky, "John Meyendorff (1926–92)," *Sobornost* 15, no. 2 (1993): 44–51, and "In Memoriam: Fr. John Meyendorff, History Professor Dies at Age 66," *The Ram News* (Fordham University) (1 Oct. 1992).

JONATHAN G. ARETAKIS

MILLER, Roger Dean (*b.* 2 January 1936 in Fort Worth, Texas; *d.* 26 October 1992 in Los Angeles, California), country singer and songwriter best known for the classic truck-driving anthem "King of the Road" and for his humorous, mid-1960s hits, including "Dang Me" and "Chug-a-Lug."

Miller was the only child of Jean Miller, a farmer, and Laudene Holt, a homemaker. After his father died of spinal meningitis when Miller was an infant, he was raised by his uncle, Elmer D. Miller, in Erick, Oklahoma. Elmer was a small-time farmer who sharecropped cotton. Miller joined the family picking cotton and raised enough money to buy his first guitar when he was twelve years old. Miller's cousin, Melva Laure Miller, was married to Sheb Wooley, who became famous in the 1960s for the novelty hit "Purple People Eater." Wooley also lived in Erick and taught Miller his first chords on the guitar.

Miller left school after completing the eighth grade and worked in various jobs, including as a ranch hand and as a performer in local rodeos. In 1952 he enlisted in the U.S. Army and served in the Korean War. By this time Miller was an adept guitarist, and he played the fiddle, banjo, piano, and drums. Shortly before his discharge, he was sent back to the United States to serve in a Special Services unit as a musician. After the war, while stationed in Atlanta, Miller played fiddle in the Circle A Wranglers, a band that previously featured another army enlistee, Faron Young. Miller served with a sergeant who was a brother of Jethro Burns of the famous country comedy duo Homer and Jethro. The sergeant encouraged Miller to go to Nashville, Tennessee, after his discharge and arranged for Miller to

Roger Miller, 1966. ARCHIVE PHOTOS

audition with RCA Records. Although his audition did not result in a recording contract, Miller soon found work as a backup musician. He played the fiddle for the country comedienne Minnie Pearl and toured as a drummer with Young and Ray Price.

Miller, a short, wiry man with a puckish face, first achieved success as a songwriter in the late 1950s. He placed "Invitation to the Blues" with Price, who scored a number-three hit on the country chart with it. The song was later a pop hit for Patti Page. Miller also wrote "Half a Mind" for Ernest Tubb and "Billy Bayou" for Jim Reeves. In 1960 Miller finally signed with RCA as a solo artist. A year later, a country ballad he wrote with Bill Anderson called "When Two Worlds Collide" reached number six on the country chart.

Despite his success, Miller was frustrated by the limitations he faced both as a performer and as a songwriter in Nashville. In late 1963 he signed with Smash Records, a small label affiliated with the Mercury label. Using his advance money, Miller relocated to Los Angeles. A year later Miller broke through with the hits that launched his career as a smooth-voiced, humorous pop vocalist; "Dang Me" went to number one on the country chart and number seven on the pop chart, and "Chug-a-Lug" was number three on the country chart and number nine on the pop chart. Miller won an unprecedented five Grammy Awards in 1964 and went on to win a total of eleven throughout his career. That career Grammy record remained until it was finally broken by Michael Jackson in 1983. In February 1965 Miller released his big-rig anthem "King of the Road," which topped the country and adult contemporary charts and reached number four on the pop charts. That year four more singles made the country top ten, including "Engine Engine #9," which rose to number two on the country chart and number seven on the pop chart. In addition, "England Swings," a humorous commentary on the success of the Beatles and other "British invasion" groups, reached number one on the adult contemporary chart, number three on the country chart, and number eight on the pop chart.

Miller's successes on the country and pop charts continued throughout the late 1960s, as he alternated smooth ballads with more tongue-in-cheek material. He also continued to write songs for other singers, most notably the 1966 Andy Williams hit "In the Summertime," which gained Miller a spot on Williams's television variety show. Between 1966 and 1967 Miller hosted a short-lived show of his own on NBC, the *Roger Miller Show*. Miller's major hits from that period include "Husbands and Wives," which reached number five on the country chart and number twenty-six on the pop chart in 1966, and the classic "Little Green Apples," which made the country and pop charts in 1968.

By the end of the 1960s, Miller had become addicted to

amphetamines, which affected the quality of his work. Miller's pop career faded in the early 1970s, although he continued to place songs regularly in the country top thirty. He last appeared on the country chart in December 1973 with "I Believe in Sunshine," which barely made the top twenty-five. A year later he wrote and performed songs for the Disney animated version of *Robin Hood* (1974). Miller then dropped out of the music scene for nearly a decade. In 1982 the singer Willie Nelson, an old friend from Miller's early days in Nashville, invited Miller to join him on the aptly titled *Old Friends* album. The title song, written by Miller, was a number-nineteen country hit. Soon after, Rocco Landesman, a producer of stage musicals, suggested that Miller write the music and lyrics for *Big River,* a stage adaptation of Mark Twain's book *The Adventures of Huckleberry Finn* (1884). The show opened on the road but in 1985 reached Broadway, where it won for Miller a Tony Award for best musical score. The play ran for two and a half years on Broadway, and later Miller briefly acted in the role of Finn's father in the road company version of the show. "River in the Rain," a ballad from the show, was a minor country hit as well.

Big River revitalized Miller's performing career. In the late 1980s he developed a nightclub act that he successfully took on the road, performing at supper clubs and also with many small symphony orchestras. Miller settled in Santa Fe, New Mexico, with his third wife, Mary Margaret Arnold, whom he had married on 14 February 1978, and seemed to enjoy his newfound fame. However, he was diagnosed with throat cancer in late 1991 and succumbed to the illness in October 1992. He is buried in Los Angeles. Miller was posthumously elected into the Country Music Hall of Fame in 1995.

Miller was a talented comic vocalist whose gentle twang betrayed his country roots but whose vocal style was subdued enough to win him a mainstream audience. Although Nashville executives found his voice "unusual," it was the perfect vehicle for expressing his often ironic, slightly skewed version of the world. His success as a crossover artist on the pop chart was mainly thanks to his easygoing vocals and amusing songs.

★

Articles in the popular press and biographies in standard reference works discuss Miller's life and career. Obituaries are in the *Los Angeles Times* (26 Oct. 1992), *New York Times* (27 Oct. 1992), and *Billboard* (7 Nov. 1992).

RICHARD CARLIN

MILLS, Wilbur Daigh (*b.* 24 May 1909 in Kensett, Arkansas; *d.* 2 May 1992 in Searcy, Arkansas), influential Democratic congressman (1939–1977) who played a crucial role in tax and welfare policies as chairman of the Ways and Means Committee from 1958 to 1974.

Wilbur Mills was born in Kensett, Arkansas, to Ardra Pickens Mills and Abbie Daigh, who owned a country store. Ardra was also a prominent local banker and one of the town's elite citizens. Wilbur had two younger siblings. After finishing high school, Mills attended Hendrix College and graduated in 1930. He then entered Harvard Law School, where he had trouble adjusting to the social environment, but after a rocky start his grades improved. He left Harvard in 1933, before graduating, in order to work as a cashier for his father during the Great Depression. Soon after, Mills was admitted to the state bar. One year after returning to Kensett, he launched his political career by winning election as probate judge for White County. Mills surprised the long-time incumbent Foster White through an effective campaign that focused on ending corruption and reducing public spending. Fulfilling his campaign promises, he devoted his first year to cutting the county debt. On 27 May 1934 Mills married his high school sweetheart, Clarine ("Polly") Billingsley. The couple had two daughters.

In 1938 Mills was elected to Congress by the Second District of Arkansas, which had a largely white and rural population. The district was one of the poorest in the United States, with voters having low incomes and little education; unions were virtually nonexistent until 1960. Immediately upon entering Congress, Mills earned a reputation as a workhorse, rarely attending parties and spend-

Wilbur Mills. AP/WIDE WORLD PHOTOS

ing up to twelve hours a day in the office. The norms of Congress at this time encouraged deference to senior members and specialization. Mills adhered to both customs by voting along party lines, defending key Democratic provisions, and mastering the intricacies of taxation. He supported the anticommunist campaign at home and abroad as well as federal spending on Social Security, highway development, and unemployment assistance. At the same time, Mills was a fiscal conservative who insisted that government had to provide services prudently to avoid tax hikes and deficits. Like most southern Democrats, he opposed civil rights legislation. Most white constituents in his district opposed federal intervention in this issue.

Speaker of the House Sam Rayburn, a Democrat from Texas, took Mills under his tutelage and in 1942 placed him on the Ways and Means Committee, which had jurisdiction over Social Security, income taxation, welfare, and trade. In 1950 Mills gained the attention of policymakers by working closely with the Social Security Administration's Wilbur Cohen and Robert Ball and Chief Actuary of Social Security Robert Myers. Mills helped craft the Social Security Amendments of 1950, which extended coverage to millions of farm and domestic workers and established the pay-as-you-go finance system. As chairman of a Joint Economic Committee subcommittee on fiscal policy, Mills introduced Congress to a community of policy experts who supported using tax policy to foster economic growth.

Following the death of Jere Cooper, a Democratic representative from Tennessee, Mills became chairman of the House Ways and Means Committee in 1957. Moving forward with a proposal to extend unemployment compensation benefits in 1958 through an unorthodox financial scheme, Mills suffered an embarrassing defeat. But after his difficult start, Mills solidified his position by not releasing legislation from his committee until he knew it would pass. While this caution resulted in a successful record, it also frustrated fellow lawmakers who felt that Mills blocked legislation.

There were several additional means through which he enhanced his power. In 1958 and 1959, for example, Mills gained widespread praise for holding groundbreaking hearings on reforms to close tax loopholes. To increase his influence, Mills eliminated Ways and Means subcommittees while making effective use of the "closed rule," which banned floor amendments to committee legislation. Mills teamed up with the Wisconsin congressman John Byrnes, the ranking Republican on Ways and Means, to design bipartisan compromises. Finally, the chairman used "members bills," small provisions in the tax code granted to particular congressmen, in exchange for their support of future legislation.

Unlike many others who held the chairmanship, Mills gained a reputation as a fiscal expert. He worked closely with policy experts such as Robert Myers and Laurence Woodworth, head staff for the Joint Committee on Income Taxation. Two of his most important relationships were with Wilbur Cohen, a key policymaker in the Social Security Administration, and Stanley Surrey, a leading income tax policymaker who served as assistant secretary of Treasury throughout the 1960s. Those who testified during Ways and Means hearings frequently found themselves being grilled by the chairman on the minutia of their proposals. His reputation as a fiscal expert helped blunt the impact of his opposition to civil rights, although his stance proved damaging at those times when he was a potential candidate for Speaker of the House, a justice on the Supreme Court, or president of the United States. Within the tax community, however, Mills had influence in policymaking that extended beyond the formal prerogatives of his position.

Between 1958 and 1974, the fiscally conservative Mills played an important role in many key pieces of legislation. He struggled to balance the demands for macroeconomic policy and social welfare with the need for budgetary restraint. In 1964, Mills changed his position and supported legislation that reduced taxes by more than $10 billion. He changed positions after President Lyndon Johnson agreed to cut spending and to make the tax cuts permanent. Similarly, after years of opposing Medicare on the grounds that it threatened Social Security, Mills crafted the final Medicare and Medicaid legislation in 1965. The program's jerrybuilt design was an intentional effort by Mills to overcome the opposition of physicians and to protect the fiscal soundness of Social Security. The final legislation creating Medicare and Medicaid, designed by Mills in a surprise last-minute compromise, was more expansive than anything the Kennedy or Johnson administrations had proposed. When President Johnson pushed for a tax surcharge to fund the war in Vietnam and to curb inflation, Mills bottled up the legislation for two years until Johnson agreed in 1968 to accept steep spending cuts in his domestic programs. In 1969, Mills helped guide loopholes-closing tax reform through both chambers of Congress.

In 1972, Mills tried his hand at presidential politics. Although a handful of pundits were optimistic about a moderate southerner in the Democratic primaries, Mills fared poorly in New Hampshire. He dropped out of the race soon after. During the campaign, Mills's technocratic reputation suffered when he reversed his position on a number of key policies, including his decision to support revenue sharing and an expansion of Social Security. These uncharacteristic reversals—based on obvious political motivations, and accompanied by revelations of suspicious campaign contributions—fueled intense criticism of the chairman. Mills was also the target of a congressional reform movement in the 1970s that aimed to open the legislative process to the public and to weaken powerful committees such as Ways and Means. Meanwhile, Mills gradually succumbed to alcoholism and addiction to the painkillers he took for severe back problems beginning in the late 1960s.

Scandal ultimately brought Mills down. In October 1974, the U.S. Park Police pulled over a speeding car in which Mills was a passenger. After the car stopped, a woman jumped out and ran into the Tidal Basin. Mills followed to pull her out. A cameraman who heard the police radio reports captured the arrest on film. The media soon revealed that Mills was having an affair with the woman, a local stripper whose stage name was "Fanne Fox, the Argentine Firecracker." The story accelerated a shift in coverage within the media toward the private lives of politicians. The contrast with his professional persona before the incident made the scandal even more shocking. Although Mills was reelected in November, he could not seem to control himself. He staggered onto the stage of Fanne Fox's first public appearance in a Boston strip club before a roomful of stunned reporters. The following day, the Democratic Caucus stripped Ways and Means of many of its key powers, including the ability to make committee assignments for the party, and it forced Mills to resign as chairman. After leaving Congress in 1977, Mills spent the rest of his life working for a prominent Washington, D.C., law firm and appearing around the country to speak about the dangers of alcohol abuse. Mills died in Arkansas and is buried in Kensett Cemetery.

Wilbur Mills was one of the last giants from a political era dominated by powerful congressional committee chairmen. Mills embodied an era when specialized expertise was valued in American culture, so much that the chairman of the Ways and Means staked his reputation on his fiscal expertise and not just on his ability to broker deals. His career reflected that system's virtues—namely its ability to produce bipartisan compromises and federal programs with limited budgetary impact—as well as its problems, such as the way it curtailed public participation and favored senior legislators. Legislative moderates such as Mills gradually disappeared from both parties in the next two decades. Contrary to the prevailing wisdom about an "imperial presidency," Mills's career is representative of an era when Congress was extremely powerful in shaping policymaking from inception to implementation.

★

The collection of Mills's professional and personal papers is held at Hendrix College in Conway, Arkansas. The House Ways and Means Papers are stored at the National Archives in Washington, D.C. The two books that cover Mills's career are John Manley, *The Politics of Finance: The House Committee on Ways and Means* (1970) and Julian E. Zelizer, *Taxing America: Wilbur D. Mills, Congress, and the State, 1945–1975* (1998). An obituary is in the *New York Times* (3 May 1992).

JULIAN E. ZELIZER

MILSTEIN, Nathan (*b.* 31 December 1903 in Odessa, Russia; *d.* 21 December 1992 in London, England), violin virtuoso whose elegant musicality influenced twentieth-century violin playing.

Milstein was one of the seven children of Maria Bluestein and Miron Milstein. His father was a successful importer of woolens and English and Scottish tweeds, as well as an enthusiastic Tolstoyan who followed the moral teachings of the great Russian novelist. Nathan Milstein, who was Jewish, recalled that the family spoke only Russian while he was growing up; he regretted that he never learned Yiddish. Milstein's mother was a homemaker who hired and supervised her children's tutors and governesses. She recognized Nathan's early interest in music and gave him his first violin hoping it would keep him out of mischief. Milstein admitted that he was an unruly child and was continually getting into trouble. Once he saw that he could garner praise from adults and his childhood friends by playing the violin, he began to practice in earnest. He was further motivated to take his musical studies seriously when he went to hear some of the world's greatest violinists, including Jan Kubelik, Bronislaw Huberman, and Eugène-Auguste Ysaÿe, who performed regularly in Odessa.

In 1909 Milstein began to study with Odessa's most prestigious violin teacher, Pyotr Stoliarsky, who was his teacher for six years. The ten-year-old Milstein was pro-

Nathan Milstein. © HULTON-DEUTSCH COLLECTION/CORBIS

jected into the limelight with his performance of Aleksandr Glazunov's Violin Concerto, as a last-minute replacement for the soloist who became ill. Glazunov himself, director of the St. Petersburg Conservatory, was guest conducting the Odessa Orchestra at the time and was deeply impressed by the boy's intelligence, virtuosity, and interpretive genius.

In 1916 having heard Milstein perform in Odessa, Leopold Auer, the renowned Hungarian violinist and teacher, invited the eleven-year-old to come to St. Petersburg (then Petrograd) to study with him. Auer had trained such notable performers as Jascha Heifetz, Mischa Elman, Toscha Seidel, and Efrem Zimbalist. After a year with Auer, Milstein began to give concerts throughout Russia with his sister Sara as his accompanist. They gave their first concert together in 1919 in Kiev, where he met the young pianist Vladimir Horowitz. He and Horowitz not only became fast friends, but Milstein moved in with Horowitz's family and lived with them for three years. The two musicians began to tour Russia to rave reviews. After the Bolshevik Revolution, Soviet authorities decided to send the duo to Europe to show the world the beneficent effects of the revolution on Russian cultural life. Although Milstein was allowed to move to Paris in 1926, he insisted on working informally with his greatest musical influence, Ysaÿe, at Ysaÿe's seaside estate on the Belgian coast. After a few months Ysaÿe declared that he had nothing more to teach Milstein, who was already a fully-formed artist at the age of twenty-two.

During his three years in Paris, Milstein gave many concerts with Horowitz and met a variety of other musicians. He became friendly with the great Russian bass Fyodor Chaliapin, claiming that after he heard Chaliapin's performance of *Boris Godunov* as a youth in Odessa he had chills for ten days. He made his American debut in October of 1929 with the Philadelphia Orchestra under the direction of Leopold Stokowski. Critics immediately recognized his virtuosity and remarked on the unique way in which he combined a flawless technique with an endearing warmth and keen intelligence. A commentator in the *New York Herald Tribune* described him as "an artist of sensitive perception and adaptability."

Although Milstein lived in a variety of countries throughout his life, it was while he was living in Burgenstock, Switzerland, on Lake Lucerne, that he was introduced by Horowitz to the great Russian pianist and composer Sergei Rachmaninoff. Milstein and Rachmaninoff frequently played together informally. Milstein credited Rachmaninoff with teaching him how to discover the presence of cultural elements and detect the influence of other composers in a particular musical text.

In the early 1930s Milstein also became close friends with Igor Stravinsky and Sergei Prokofiev and, as a result of these friendships, he championed Stravinsky's Violin Concerto and both of Prokofiev's violin concerti. He later recorded the Prokofiev Second Concerto for EMI twice— once with Vladimir Golschmann and once with Carlo Maria Giulini.

Because of World War II Milstein moved to the United States, where he became a citizen in 1942. In 1945 he met and married Therese Kauffman, with whom he would have one daughter, Maria Bernadette. At the end of World War II Milstein acquired the famous "Goldman Stradivarius"(so named for its previous owner, the New York City collector Henry Goldman), one of a small number of extant instruments crafted by shopkeeper Antonio Stradivari in the late seventeenth/early eighteenth century. He renamed the prized acquisition Maria-Theresa after his wife and daughter. While giving over 100 concerts worldwide a year, Milstein maintained homes in New York City (a triplex on Park Avenue and Fifty-eighth Street); Gstaad, Switzerland; Paris (on Cours Albert 1st), and London. One of his closest friendships in New York City was with the violinist he most admired and loved, Fritz Kreisler.

Milstein left behind a legacy of recordings, sometimes rerecording pieces two and even three times. He began recording many classic concerti beginning in the late 1940s and early 1950s. His first recording of the Tchaikovsky Violin Concerto with the Chicago Symphony Orchestra and Frederick Stock for Columbia Records rivaled Jascha Heifetz's best-selling RCA recording. Milstein's early 1950s Capitol recordings of Johann Sebastian Bach's sonatas and partitas established him as the definitive interpreter of those masterpieces. He rerecorded all of them with Deutsche Grammophon in 1976, earning him a Grammy from the National Academy of Recording Arts and Sciences, and the Diplome d'Honneur at the Montreux International Awards.

As successful as his Columbia recording of the Tchaikovsky concerto was with Stock, he recorded it again in the early 1950s with conductor William Steinberg and the Pittsburgh Symphony to great critical acclaim. Critics and the public grew to cherish his impeccable technique and brilliant burnished tone. He recorded the Tchaikovsky concerto yet again in the 1970s with the Vienna Philharmonic and Claudio Abbado for Deutsche Grammophon. Capital-EMI asked him to record both the Brahms and Beethoven concerti with the Pittsburgh Symphony and Steinberg and, several years later, to rerecord the Brahms concerto with first the Philharmonic Orchestra and then the Vienna Philharmonic. Milstein also recorded such staples of the violin repertoire as Édouard Lalo's *Symphonie Espagnole* and the Mendelssohn concerto (twice), along with both concerti of Prokofiev, and two of Mozart's concerti. His three recordings of the Glazunov concerto are unrivaled even by Heifetz. Though he did not make as many recordings as Isaac Stern or Jascha Heifetz, he is one of the most recorded major violin virtuosi in the history of recorded music.

Not only was Milstein a consummate musician, he was also a talented painter. In fact, he confessed that on the days he was giving concerts he spent most of his time painting rather than practicing. He also told record producer Dorle J. Soria that his philosophical approach to life in general was to treat every activity as a form of recreation: "If I write a letter to my wife—I write on only one side—I draw a picture on the back. That is recreation. But if the drawing is not good, I must write the letter over." Soria reported that when he was relaxing with friends Milstein was "a brilliant, amusing and non-stop talker." His conversation was stimulating because he was an avid reader, who quoted from the works of his revered favorite writers: Anton Chekhov, Tolstoy, and Boris Pasternak.

Milstein brought to violin playing an elegance and warmth that few musicians have achieved. As prodigiously gifted a technician as Jascha Heifetz or Zino Francescatti, he also combined the genial grace of Fritz Kreisler with the flawless pyrotechnics of Heifetz. Although he always favored emotional expression over virtuoso display, he nevertheless avoided sentimentality in his pristine but ardent playing. He died in London.

★

The only book-length treatment of Nathan Milstein in English is *From Russia to the West: The Musical Memoirs and Reminiscences of Nathan Milstein* (1990) by Milstein and Solomon Volkov. Though not entirely reliable with respect to dates and places (Milstein was eighty when writing it), the book demonstrates the range of Milstein's intelligence, the energy of his imagination, and his marvelous wit. His description of prerevolutionary life in Odessa, Kiev, and Saint Petersburg is informative and highly entertaining. An obituary is in the *New York Times* (22 Dec. 1992).

PATRICK MEANOR

MITCHELL, Joan (*b.* 12 February 1926 in Chicago, Illinois; *d.* 30 October 1992 in Paris, France), artist who was a major nonobjective painter through the 1950s and in the years following the heyday of abstract expressionism.

Joan Mitchell's father, James Herbert Mitchell, was a physician who became president of the American Dermatological Association and an amateur artist; her mother was a poet and coeditor of the journal *Poetry*. Her father took Joan and her sister (her only sibling) to outings in the country to make watercolor sketches, and he introduced Joan to the treasures of the Art Institute of Chicago. Joan lived in an apartment overlooking Lake Michigan and summered on the lake's western shore; it has been suggested that her memory of the water's flow influenced the rhythms of her paintings' surfaces. She attended a progressive private grammar and high school in Chicago, the Francis W. Parker School. In 1941 she won a regional title in figure skating, and in 1942 she placed fourth in the Junior Division of the U.S. Figure Skating Competition. From 1942 to 1944 Mitchell attended Smith College in Northampton, Massachusetts, majoring in English; from 1944 to 1947 she studied at the School of the Art Institute of Chicago. She spent the summers of 1945 and 1946 painting in Guanajuato in Mexico and met the Mexican painters José Clemente Orozco and David Alfaro Siqueiros.

In the winter of 1947, Mitchell moved to New York, settling in Brooklyn with her former high school classmate, the filmmaker Barney Rosset, Jr. There she came to know the work of the abstract expressionist painters Jackson Pollock and Arshile Gorky. In 1948 she traveled to Paris and studied Romanesque art before proceeding to Guernica in Spain and to Czechoslovakia. She married Rosset in late 1949 in France. Returning to New York, she settled on West Eleventh Street. In Greenwich Village, Mitchell mixed with artists who met at the Cedar Tavern, and she became a member of the Eighth Street Club, founded by the abstract expressionist painters Franz Kline, Willem de Kooning, and others. In 1952 she divorced Rosset, whom she continued to help when he became the publisher of the Grove Press. She became a friend of Kline and the poet Frank O'Hara, who dedicated poems to her. Mitchell's first solo exhibition was held in New York's Stable Gallery, where she continued to show through the 1950s. From 10 March to 28 April 1957 she was part of a group show at the Jewish Museum curated by the noted Columbia University art historian Meyer Schapiro. The show was entitled "Art of the New York School: Second Generation."

In the summer of 1955 in Paris, moving in the Montparnasse art milieu, Mitchell met the Montreal-born artist Jean-Paul Riopelle, then prominent in European avantgarde painting, with whom she began a twenty-five-year relationship. In 1959 she lived with Riopelle in Paris, and thereafter, although showing in New York and visiting the United States, she painted only in France. She moved in the summer of 1961 to the Cap d'Antibes on the Mediterranean coast of France. In 1960 she contributed silk screens to a book of poems by John Ashbery. Through her stay in France until her death she showed at the Galerie Jean Fournier in Paris. In July 1967, using a trust fund that had been established by her maternal grandfather, the steel engineer Charles Louis Strobel, she bought an estate in Vetheuil, northeast of Paris. The cottage on the property had once been Monet's house. (Mitchell insisted that she felt no special affinity to that artist.) Her reputation in the United States grew steadily: in February 1988 the College Art Association of America awarded her its newly established Distinguished Artist Award for Lifetime Achievement.

In Mitchell's paintings nothing is recognizable as an identifiable object. She worked on a very large scale, with heights of canvases sometimes exceeding seven feet, and sometimes she butted together up to four panels. Avoiding the acrylics favored by many nonobjective painters after 1960 (Helen Frankenthaler, for one), she worked steadily in oils, a medium that would reveal the actual working out of the image. Sometimes she presented a central massing of the paint, with a thinning out at the peripheries (*Lucky Seven*, 1962, Hirshhorn Museum and Sculpture Garden). But more often the paint would be bunched up in pools and dribbles and strips, with these bunches separated by ample spaces and applied on a broad, light-colored field (*Hemlock*, 1956, Whitney Museum). Her paintings can bring to the mind of the aware observer rhythms of nature such as the growth of crops in fields, the scattering of leaves, and the growth of trees. In a general way, the paintings allude to landscapes and processes of nature rather than to machines and aspects of life in cities. Through her loose, improvisational handling of the paint, Mitchell is related to the gestural approaches of such abstract expressionists as Kline and de Kooning, but the tenor of her work is lighter and more lyrical, less forceful and violent. Some of her paintings became, for her, a reference to events experienced in the past (*George Went Swimming at Barnes Hole, but It Got Too Cold*, 1957, Albright-Knox Art Gallery, Buffalo). These coded references do not negate the landscape aspect but become another of the multiple layers of the work. Some of the paintings, then, become a means of psychological recall, enabling the artist to recapture through colors and forms the sensations that had been produced in the past.

The art historian and critic Barbara Rose visited Mitchell in Vetheuil. She found that the artist spent several months on a single painting—very different from the rapid execution of Pollock, Kline, de Kooning, and Philip Guston. She had music playing while she painted, worked in a spartan environment ("the most memorable piece of furniture was a pool table"), and habitually dressed like "the last Beatnik."

In 1984 Mitchell was diagnosed with cancer of the jaw. Her death in a Paris hospital eight years later was brought on by lung cancer.

Although she painted in France for most of her career, Mitchell is regarded as an American painter, one who, during the domination of such impersonal approaches as pop art, minimal art, post-painterly abstraction, and photorealism, produced a personal, more muted variation of gestural abstract expressionism in the tradition of Kline, Pollock, and de Kooning.

★

Klaus Kertess, *Joan Mitchell* (1997), has by far the most extensive information on the artist, with a long, informative essay, biographical chronology, exhibition history, and ample bibliography.

See also Robert Miller Gallery, *Joan Mitchell: Paintings, 1956 to 1958* (1996), and Musée d'Art Moderne de la Ville de Paris, *Joan Mitchell: Choix de peintures, 1970–1982* (1982), which contains several short essays in French and one in English by Barbara Rose reporting on a meeting with the artist; paintings are illustrated in both color and black-and-white. The artist's work beyond her paintings is examined in Susan Sheehan Gallery, *Joan Mitchell: Prints and Illustrated Books—a Retrospective* (1993), with an essay by Susan Sheehan.

ABRAHAM A. DAVIDSON

MIZE, John Robert ("Johnny") (*b.* 7 January 1913 in Demorest, Georgia; *d.* 2 June 1993 in Demorest, Georgia), baseball player best known as a power hitter who led the National League in home runs four times, had a lifetime batting average of .312, and compiled a .562 slugging percentage during a fifteen-year major league career.

Mize was born in Habersham County, Georgia, the son of Edward Mize, a local merchant and salesman, and Emma Loudermilk, a homemaker. His parents separated when Mize was young, and he moved in with his grandmother in Demorest. When he was fifteen he was asked to play on the baseball team at nearby Piedmont College: "They told my [high school] coach to let me take a subject in college

Johnny Mize after joining the New York Yankees, 1949. AP/WIDE WORLD PHOTOS

so I could play ball for them. And I played ball for them, but they never came up with a subject," he recounted in a 1991 interview. After playing three years of college baseball while still in high school, Mize graduated from Tipton High School in 1930.

Signed to a professional contract with the St. Louis Cardinals that same year, Mize quickly became a star in the minor leagues. The Cincinnati Reds purchased his contract for $55,000 in 1931. A torn hip muscle, however, sent him back to the Cardinals. Misfortune struck again: he tore a muscle in his other hip. About to quit baseball altogether, despite batting .336 during six minor league seasons, Mize decided to give it one more try after successful surgery on both hips.

On 16 April 1936, Mize made his first major league appearance with the Cardinals. His first big-league at bat resulted in a strikeout, but his rookie season was generally sensational. He hit nineteen home runs, batted .329, and drove in ninety-three runs. His slugging percentage was a healthy .577. Over the next four years his slugging percentage was .595, .614, .626, and .636. The first six years he played with the Cardinals, Mize batted over .300 and averaged twenty-six home runs a year. In 1940 he led the league in runs batted in.

Apart from his hitting skills, Mize was a slow but smooth-fielding first baseman. Graceful despite his hulking size of six feet, two inches, and 215 pounds, Mize earned the nickname "the Big Cat" for the way he pounced on bad hops at first base, as well as for the balance of his batting stance and the way in which he effortlessly avoided brush-back pitches.

At the end of the 1941 season, Mize unsuccessfully sought to renegotiate his contract with the St. Louis general manager Branch Ricky. Ricky wanted Mize to take a cut because his batting average was down from previous seasons. Mize, who had led the league in hitting, in home runs, and in runs batted in, asked to be traded, and before the start of the 1942 season he found himself wearing a New York Giants uniform.

New York, under its recently appointed manager, Mel Ott, exchanged three players and $50,000 to bring Mize to the Giants. As a straightaway hitter, Mize worried that the Polo Grounds—a huge park marked by a distant center-field fence and a right field power alley—was the worst place he could have been traded to, but he quickly learned to adapt his hitting style to fit the park's dimensions. Mize reached the pinnacle of his baseball success as a New York Giant. His first year in New York saw him lead the league in runs batted in (110) and in slugging percentage (.521).

In 1943 Mize was summoned into World War II military service, and he spent three years in the navy. He returned to the Giants for the 1946 season. However, during an exhibition game he was hit by a pitch and broke a bone

in his hand. The injury limited him to 101 games that season, but he managed to hit .337 with a slugging percentage of .576. The next year, at age thirty-five, he hit fifty-one home runs to become the only National League lefty to hit fifty or more homers in a season. He also knocked in 138 runs, thus leading the league in both categories. He batted .302 that year. It marked the fourth time in his career that he had edged over .600 in slugging percentage. Despite these achievements he was not selected the league's Most Valuable Player—he finished third in the voting behind Bob Elliott and Ewell Blackwell. In 1948 he led the league in homers again with forty and drove in 125 runs. But for the first time in his major league career his batting average fell below .300.

In 1948 Leo Durocher arrived as the new Giants manager. Mize's slowness, due to his size, and the fact that the Giants were overloaded with power hitters led Durocher to cut his playing time. During the early part of the 1949 season he was traded to the New York Yankees and their new manager, Casey Stengel, for $10,000.

Stengel, who referred to Mize as "a slugger who hits like a leadoff man," was delighted to have a quality backup first baseman. But after only six days as a Yankee, Mize separated his shoulder diving to tag first base. He played sparingly that season, and for the next four years he was a part-time player. His most important contribution was as a pinch hitter. In 1951, 1952, and 1953 Mize led the American League in pinch hits. From 1949 through 1953 Mize played in five World Series; the Yankees won all five. The 1952 World Series against the Brooklyn Dodgers represented the high point of Mize's career. In game three, replacing first baseman Joe Collins, Mize homered; in game four his home run proved to be the winning hit; in game five he hit a three-run homer, marking the first time a player had homered in three consecutive World Series games. For the seven-game series, Mize finished with three home runs, six runs batted in, and a .400 batting average and was named the Series' Most Valuable Player. In 1953, at age forty, Mize played the last season of his career, as a successful pinch hitter in a year in which the Yankees achieved their fifth consecutive championship. As Mize neared retirement, the New York sportswriter Dan Parker penned a fitting ode in tribute to the big first baseman: "Your arm is gone, your legs likewise. But not your eyes, Mize, not your eyes."

Mize was a unique slugger, one who rarely struck out while hitting for a high average, and he has been rated the fifth-best first baseman of all time (behind Lou Gehrig, Bill Terry, Jimmy Foxx, and George Sisler). Mize, who threw right-handed and batted left, is the only man in major league history to hit fifty home runs in a single season while striking out less than fifty times. He accomplished that feat in 1947, hitting fifty-one homers and striking out only forty-two times. He remains the only player to hit three homers in a game on six different occasions. He also homered, at least once, in all fifteen of the ballparks in use during his playing days.

Mize accomplished a number of other impressive statistics during his fifteen-year baseball career. In his first nine years he hit over .300 each year. In 1939 his .349 batting average led the league. He finished his career with a .312 lifetime batting average. He led the National League in home runs four times and finished with a career total of .359. He led the National League in runs batted in three times. His career slugging percentage of .562 is eighth on the all-time list. He played in nine All-Star games. Finally, he holds the World Series records for pinch-hit at bats and pinch hits. He was inducted into the Baseball Hall of Fame in 1981.

After his retirement as a player, Mize worked in the Giants organization as a scout. In 1961 he served as a coach for the Kansas City Athletics. He also worked briefly as a special batting instructor for the Bradenton Braves of the Florida Winter League. His retirement years were first spent in Deland, Florida, where he operated a liquor store and an orange grove near his twelve-acre homestead.

On 14 July 1957, Mize's first wife, the former Jane Adams, whom he had married in August 1937 and with whom he had two children, died from burns suffered in a fire at their home. On 23 October 1957, Mize married Marjorie Pope, a Deland radio news writer. The two owned and operated orange groves for a number of years.

In 1974 they moved to Demorest and settled in Mize's grandmother's house, his boyhood home. In December 1982, he underwent successful triple-bypass surgery. Mize spent his retirement playing golf, attending baseball card shows, signing autographs, and contributing time and money to charitable causes. On 2 June 1993, Mize died of cardiac arrest in his sleep at home. He is buried at Yonah Cemetery in Demorest.

Mize won fame as much for his humility as for his exploits in the batter's box. "As a player," he commented to one reporter on induction day at the Hall of Fame, "I never broke a bat after striking out. A guy couldn't be blaming a poor old bat for what happened, could he?"

★

A scrapbook collection and memorabilia on Mize's professional career are at the National Baseball Hall of Fame and Museum in Cooperstown, New York. There are brief autobiographical accounts in Donald Honig, *Baseball Between the Lines: Baseball in the 40's and 50's, as Told by the Men Who Played It* (1976); Noel Hynd, *The Giants of the Polo Grounds: The Glorious Times of Baseball's New York Giants* (1988); and Roger Kahn, *The Era: 1947–1957, when the Yankees, the Giants, and the Dodgers Ruled the World* (1993). Newspaper articles discussing Mize's career are J. G. Taylor Spink, "The Big Cat Still Winning Blue Ribbons at Forty," *Sporting News* (8 July 1953); Dick Young, "Writers' Dislike of Mize Kept Him Out of Hall," *New York Daily News* (13 Mar. 1981); George Vecsey, "Welcome to the Hall," *New York Times* (3 Aug. 1981); and David Craft, "John Robert Mize," *Sports Collectors' Digest* (25 Sept. 1987). A special tribute to Mize is Leo Trachtenberg, "At the Age of Eighty, Johnny Mize Passes Away: A True Yankee Great," *Yankees Magazine* (1993). Obituaries are in the *St. Louis Post-Dispatch* (3 June 1993), *New York Times* (3 June 1993), and *Northeast Georgian* (8 June 1993).

CHARLES F. HOWLETT

MOORE, Garry (*b.* 31 January 1915 in Baltimore, Maryland; *d.* 28 November 1993 in Hilton Head Island, South Carolina), radio and television performer and writer, principally known as the host of popular television series, including the *Garry Moore Show,* and prime-time game shows, such as *I've Got a Secret* (1952–1964) and *To Tell the Truth* (1969–1976). At the height of his career, he starred in two television series and a daily radio program, all broadcast nationally by CBS, and over the course of his career he appeared in more than 3,000 episodes of these and other shows.

Born Thomas Garrison Morfit, of a blue-blooded family, Moore was a high school dropout. His early determination to become a writer disappointed his father, Mason P. Morfit, an attorney. (Little is known about his mother, who apparently was not married to his father.) Moore left school at age eighteen to join the Vagabonds, a local amateur the-

Garry Moore. © BETTMANN/CORBIS

ater company, for which he wrote sketches for the troupe's musical comedy revues. He collaborated with Zelda Fitzgerald, wife of the famous novelist F. Scott Fitzgerald, who wrote songs and other musical material for the Vagabonds. The two later collaborated on several one-act plays, but these were never produced. As consolation for her young—and jobless—collaborator, Zelda used family connections to get him a position as a writer with WBAL, the leading Baltimore radio station.

In an echo of American show business folklore, Moore was put in front of a live microphone one evening when a comedian failed to appear for a scheduled performance. Although the twenty-year-old was "astonished to find people laughing" at his jokes, the station manager hired him on the spot to be a radio comedian. His aspirations, however, remained literary, and in 1938 he moved to KWK, a St. Louis station, in hopes of becoming a newswriter. His reputation, however, proceeded him, and the station assigned him to do on-air comedy segments, but he quit in less than a year.

After brief unemployment Moore received a major break that would shape the rest of his career. NBC signed him as a writer and performer for *Club Matinee,* a daily, live morning variety show airing nationally from Chicago on the Blue Network. Still known as Garry Morfit, he decided to hold a national on-air contest to select a more mellifluous radio name. A Pittsburgh listener won $50 and a trip to Chicago for her entry, "Garry Moore."

The success of *Club Matinee* prompted the network to bring Moore to New York. After doing a similar daytime show, *Everything Goes,* he was teamed by NBC with the star Jimmy Durante for a daily radio series. *The Durante-Moore Show* was a major success in prime-time radio, quickly becoming one of the highest-rated shows of 1942. Durante's famous tag line, "Dat's my boy!" was first heard in reference to Garry Moore. After four years Moore left the show and hosted several other variety hours and game shows on network radio.

CBS was starting up its television operations in the late 1940s, and the network began a formal relationship with Moore that would last for twenty years. Always sporting a bow tie and a smile, Moore's easygoing, guy-next-door persona was, "made for television." His prescience in understanding the nature of the medium came through in a 1952 interview. "Above and beyond everything else," he told *Theater Arts* magazine, "we're selling a mood, not formalized entertainment." He also understood the changing nature of entertainment technology in the television era. He was an early user of the TelePrompTer for announcing on-air commercials, which he refused to rehearse.

Indeed, Moore's daytime TV variety show was generally acknowledged on Madison Avenue as among the best possible ways to reach homemakers with product advertisements. Sponsors had to be turned away for lack of time.

His prime-time variety show, broadcast from New York during a period when most such shows were originating from Hollywood, was the vehicle that brought a number of Broadway stars to the home screen, including Carol Burnett and Dorothy Loudon, who were both *Garry Moore Show* regulars. He introduced innovative weekly "segments" into the comedy-variety show, which distinguished it from other productions. These included "Candid Camera with Allen Funt," which later spun off into a separate series, and "That Wonderful Year," which examined the music and fashion of a particular year in American pop culture history each week.

Betsy Palmer, who was a panelist for many years on Moore's prime-time game show, *I've Got a Secret,* attributed his success to a lack of artifice. "The thing about TV—and especially live television—was that you really showed who you were. There was no pretending. And this came through. Somebody told me that I would never make it in New York because I didn't have a gimmick. And I said, 'That will be my gimmick, that I don't have one.'" When Garry Moore was asked by Palmer why he had hired her, he responded, "I've been watching you for a year. I was sure that I would find a chink in your armor. I couldn't believe that you are what you are. You are."

In 1976, during his seventh year as host of the daily afternoon game show, *To Tell the Truth,* Moore publicly identified himself as a recovering alcoholic in the hope of inspiring other sufferers to fight the condition. The following year he was forced to retire when he was diagnosed with throat cancer. He survived that illness, and enjoyed sailing, his favorite pastime, during much of his retirement. He maintained homes in South Carolina and Maine. His first marriage, to Eleanor Borum Little, produced two sons. Eleanor died in 1974. The following year Moore married Mary Elizabeth ("Betsy") De Chant. In 1993 Garry Moore died of emphysema.

★

The author's and other audio interviews with Judy Crichton, Gil Fates, Betsy Palmer, et al., are available at the Steven H. Scheuer Television History Collection at the Syracuse University Library, New York, and have provided material for the present article. Print sources with information about Moore include *Current Biography 1954* and Horace Newcomb, *Encyclopedia of Television* (1997). An obituary is in the *New York Times* (29 Nov. 1993).

DAVID MARC

MOSCONI, William Joseph ("Willie") (*b.* 27 June 1913 in Philadelphia, Pennsylvania; *d.* 16 September 1993 in Haddon Heights, New Jersey), arguably the best tournament billiards player of all time, who did much to polish the image of the sport.

Mosconi was one of six children born to Joseph Mosconi, an ex-boxer and poolroom operator, and Helen O'Reilly, a homemaker. Young Mosconi was introduced to the game of pool early on, but not in the way that would have seemed most likely. Pop Mosconi was not in favor of his son learning the game, at least not at the tender age of six. He wanted him to be a dancer, like the youngster's uncles. Willie's father kept the pool cues and balls locked up to prevent the boy from playing the game, but this could not keep the youngster from playing his own type of pool. The innovative Mosconi simply gathered the roundest potatoes he could find in his mother's pantry, aligned them as billiard balls, and, using a broomstick for a cue, played on.

Eventually his father relented, and Mosconi learned the game so rapidly he was dubbed "the child prodigy of pool" at age seven, and later "the juvenile champion." By the time he was in his teens, he was an accomplished player.

As Mosconi was growing up, so was the game of pool or billiards. The sport peaked in the 1920s, when it was

Willie Mosconi at the world pocket billiard championship, 1935. © BETT-MANN/CORBIS

estimated that 500,000 commercial pool tables were in use in the country. The Depression years of the 1930s saw the emergence of the pool hustler, a skilled shooter with a little con artist thrown in. The hustler would "lemonade" (poolroom jargon for disguising one's true ability) in order to sucker an unsuspecting opponent into a game for money. With unemployment high, desperate men would risk what little they had for a chance, albeit a slim one, at a larger payoff. Mosconi maintained that he never hustled. ("Hustlers shoot pool," the old saying goes, but "gentlemen play billiards.") Although his name was known to hustlers, there is no hard evidence that Mosconi was ever anything but a supremely competent gentleman billiards player. (Billiards, played with the same equipment as pool, is a more restrictive game that requires certain banks and caroms and is limited to certain pockets on the table; a true billiards table sometimes has no pockets. Pool is a more wide-open game with fewer constraints.)

Mosconi attended South Philadelphia High School, but before he graduated his father enrolled him at Banks Business College in Philadelphia. At the same time, he was becoming very well known as a billiards player. In 1933 Mosconi, age nineteen and considered one of the two best players in the country, signed on to do a nationwide tour with Ralph Greenleaf, considered the other top player at the time. Said to have "movie-star good looks," Mosconi always dressed impeccably, keeping his suit coat on and his tie tightly knotted while he played. A sure sign of his arrival as a star was that, after defeating Greenleaf a considerable number of times on their first national tour, the older player refused future bookings against the youngster.

Mosconi, a modest man, once said without any braggadocio, "In the early Thirties in Chicago, I would attract a crowd of fifteen hundred for a Saturday-night exhibition, while George Halas's Chicago Bears [of the National Football League] would draw twelve hundred to Wrigley Field on Sunday."

Continuing to elevate his game, Mosconi also is credited with burnishing the image of billiards to the point of respectability by the 1940s, disassociating it from smoky basements and dingy pool halls crawling with drunks and hustlers. Up until this time, the neighborhood poolroom was considered a male refuge, so much so that vaudeville comics would get a sure laugh by reporting a bogus newspaper headline: "Pool Room Burns Down; 5,000 Men Homeless."

Mosconi married Ann Harrison in 1940. They had two children. Ann later took the two children and left Willie while he was serving (stateside) in World War II. The couple divorced in 1945 and Willie gained custody of the children.

During the fifteen years from 1941 to 1956 Mosconi won the world pocket-billiards championship thirteen times. Not even Willie Hoppe, an earlier legendary player, dominated the sport to such an extent. About this time a running feud developed between Mosconi and Rudolph Wanderone, known then as "New York Fats," "Brooklyn Fats," or "Broadway Fats." Wanderone was an unabashed hustler, and a loud one at that. He constantly taunted Mosconi but continually declined Mosconi's invitation to play. This period was not all billiards all the time for Mosconi. On 11 February 1953 he married Gloria "Flora" Marchini. The couple had one child.

In 1961 Mosconi served as technical adviser for the acclaimed Paul Newman–Jackie Gleason film *The Hustler*. (He also made a cameo appearance.) Much to Mosconi's chagrin, Wanderone began calling himself "Minnesota Fats," claiming that the Gleason character (and the protagonist in Walter Tevis's novel of the same name) was modeled after himself. Mosconi, upset by Fats's bogus claims, asked Wanderone if he "had ever even been to Minnesota?"

In 1978 Wanderone at last accepted Mosconi's invitation, and a head-to-head match was arranged for ABC's *Wide World of Sports,* with Howard Cosell as the announcer. Mosconi won handily. The match was a study in contrasts, the nattily-dressed Mosconi versus the rumpled, disheveled Wanderone. For Mosconi it was more than just defeating Minnesota Fats. It was billiards (Mosconi never used "pool" to describe his game) defeating pool. Mosconi, as always, used a rapid-fire, extremely accurate approach to his game on this telecast. His wife, Flora, once likened his quick, graceful moves around the billiard table to that of a ballet dancer. Fats kept up a steady stream of chatter to distract and irritate Mosconi, but to no avail.

During the time he thoroughly dominated the game, Mosconi set a record by running 526 straight balls in a 1954 exhibition in Springfield, Ohio. In 1956, in Kinston, North Carolina, he shot a perfect game, sinking 150 balls without a miss. His opponent, Jimmy Moore, looked on in amazement.

At the age of eighty, on the afternoon of 16 September 1993, Mosconi died of a heart attack at his home in suburban Haddon Heights, New Jersey. He is buried in St. Mary's Cemetery in Bellmawr, New Jersey.

Mosconi used skill and a courtly manner to become accepted as a gentleman. During his long and storied career, his name was as synonymous with his sport as Babe Ruth's was with baseball. Mosconi's dominance of pocket billiards could rightfully be called Ruthian.

★

Mosconi's life is discussed in his autobiography, written with Stanley Cohen, *Willie's Game* (1993) and in his 1959 book *Willie Mosconi on Pocket Billiards.* See also George Fels, "Where the Boys Were," *Sports Heritage* (March–April 1987) and Gene Brown, ed., *The New York Times Encyclopedia of Sports,* vol. 11 (1979). An obituary is in the *New York Times* (18 Sept. 1993). At the height of his career Mosconi was featured in a documentary film, *The Willie Mosconi Story* (1948).

JIM CAMPBELL

MOTHERWELL, Robert   (*b.* 24 January 1915 in Aberdeen, Washington; *d.* 16 July 1991 in Provincetown, Massachusetts), painter, printmaker, writer, and educator who was a major figure in the abstract expressionist movement.

Motherwell was the first of two children born to Robert Burns Motherwell and Margaret Hogan Motherwell and raised on the Pacific Coast. His father was a prominent banker and provided educational opportunities largely unknown to the other abstract expressionist artists. As a child, Motherwell suffered from severe asthmatic attacks and was sent to Moran Preparatory School in Atascadero in the dry climate of southern California, where he developed a love for the broad spaces and bright colors that later characterized some of his abstract paintings. His later concerns with themes of mortality can also be traced to frail health as a child. From 1932 until 1937 he studied literature, philosophy, and psychology at Stanford University in California, and discovered in French symbolist poetry an expression of

Robert Motherwell. ARCHIVE PHOTOS

moods dispensing with traditional narrative that he believed to be the fountainhead of modern art. A number of his later paintings are tributes to such writers as Charles Baudelaire and Stéphane Mallarmé. As a postgraduate student of philosophy at Harvard University from 1937 to 1939, Motherwell found further justification for abstraction in the writings of John Dewey, Alfred North Whitehead, and David Prall. Motherwell decided to become an artist after seeing modern French painting during a trip to Paris in 1938 and 1939, but in order to satisfy his father's demands for a secure career, he first studied art history from 1940 to 1941 under Meyer Schapiro at Columbia University in New York. Through Schapiro, he met the European surrealist artists exiled in New York during World War II. Their use of automatic techniques as a means of registering subconscious impulses had a lasting effect on Motherwell and coordinated with his interest in Freudian psychology and symbolist poetics. Motherwell also developed a profound interest in the previous generation of modern artists, particularly Hans Arp, Paul Klee, Henri Matisse, Joan Miró, Piet Mondrian, and Pablo Picasso.

In 1941 Motherwell traveled with the surrealist Roberto Matta to Mexico, where he developed a lifelong interest in Hispanic cultures. In Mexico, Motherwell created his first preserved works and married the Mexican actress María Emilia Ferreira y Moyers in 1941. Returning to New York City, which remained his home base for the next twenty-eight years, Motherwell met his fellow abstract expressionist artists, including William Baziotes, Jackson Pollock, Lee Krasner, Willem de Kooning, and Hans Hofmann. Motherwell was invited along with Baziotes and Pollock as the only Americans to submit works to an international collage exhibition by Peggy Guggenheim, founder of the Art of This Century Gallery, the most important gallery to show early works of the abstract expressionists. This event began Motherwell's lifelong interest in collage, a medium in which he was one of the major practitioners since Picasso. Motherwell had his first one-person exhibition at Art of This Century Gallery in 1944. That same year he began to edit the Documents of Modern Art series, volumes published over the next four decades that brought the writings of modern artists to the American public and thus expressed Motherwell's belief in the ideational basis of modern art.

During the late 1940s and early 1950s, Motherwell's works were exhibited with increasing frequency, including the seminal "Fourteen Americans" show at the Museum of Modern Art in New York City. Motherwell also spent much of his time lecturing and teaching, becoming the unofficial spokesperson for the abstract expressionists, a position for which his educational background and broad understanding of modern art had prepared him. His involvement in teaching included the founding of an informal art school in a loft on East Eighth Street in New York City

(with Baziotes, David Hare, and Mark Rothko) called "The Subjects of the Artist," which closed in 1949. He also held positions at Black Mountain College in North Carolina in 1950 and Hunter College in New York City from 1950 to 1958 and from 1971 to 1972.

In 1948, Motherwell made a decisive discovery for his career in the course of creating his *Elegies to the Spanish Republic.* The design of the *Elegies* consists typically of black organic ovals squeezed by stiff vertical bars against a white ground, and Motherwell invented it in the context of a small black-and-white ink drawing to accompany a poem by the art critic and poet Harold Rosenberg. The motif, which Motherwell subsequently explored in approximately 140 large canvases, maintains the spontaneity of the original ink sketch even when enlarged to an enormous scale. In the chance discovery of the Elegy forms, constituting the paintings for which he is best known, Motherwell felt that he had uncovered elements essential to his personality and to the condition of the modern world. The *Elegies,* whose black-and-white tonalities suggest life-and-death contrasts, are rich in associations of archetypal imagery that include figures, body parts, architecture, and forms in nature, but they are sufficiently generalized to create a somber and mournful mood rather than yield specific representation. The *Elegies* express a nostalgia experienced by many of Motherwell's generation for the lost cause of the Spanish Civil War, which had come to represent a loss of innocence in the world. The series was further inspired by the Spanish poet Federico García Lorca's powerful poetic meditation on death, *Lament for Ignacio Sánchez Mejías.*

Motherwell divorced his first wife in 1949. During the 1950s, as Motherwell developed the *Elegies,* he married Betty Little. Their two daughters, Jeannie and Lise, were born in 1953 and 1955. In this decade, Motherwell's work received increasing international exposure, including the seminal exhibition "Modern Art in the United States: Selections from the Collection of the Museum of Modern Art, New York." During this period, Motherwell developed different types of art to embody various moods. The *Elegies,* severe in their concentration on black and white and in their ever-growing scale, were the vehicles for his most profound emotions, while small oil paintings occasioned by the birth of his daughters, the *Je t'aime* series, expressed more intimate feelings. His collages from the 1960s began to incorporate such materials from studio life as cigarette packets and labels from artists' supplies, so as to become records of daily experiences. The coastline near the artists' colony of Provincetown, where Motherwell began to spend his summers in 1962, inspired works such as *Beside the Sea,* a suite of sixty-four pictures in which he splashed oil paint against rag paper with the full force of his arm—a physical equivalent of the action of sea spray on the bulkhead in front of his studio.

In 1957 Motherwell divorced Betty Little and in 1958 married the color-field painter Helen Frankenthaler, a marriage that formed one of the best-known artistic couples of the era until their 1971 divorce. In 1967 Motherwell began a series of paintings with the generic title *Opens* as a personal response to the color-field paintings made by younger abstract painters during the 1960s. Representing the more contemplative strain of his art, an "open" typically consists of a surface of a single color onto which Motherwell drew three sides of a rectangle in charcoal lines, a motif he used frequently until 1974. The *Opens* responded to the graceful simplicity of Chinese calligraphy, which profoundly interested Motherwell. These paintings also provided abstract equivalents to the views-through-open-windows favored by European painters like Matisse as metaphors for the relationship between the interior world of feelings and the exterior world of the senses. In addition to his paintings, drawings, and collages, Motherwell's first important print was published in 1961 by Tatyana Grossman's Universal Limited Art Editions and marked him as one of the leaders of the American printmaking renaissance of the 1960s. Motherwell subsequently produced an important body of printed work, notably *A la pintura* (1972), a limited-edition book of twenty-four unbound pages printed in letterpress, etching, and color aquatint, the imagery of which was inspired by the poetry of Raphael Alberti—thus uniting Motherwell's longstanding interest in the relationship between modern art and literature.

Beginning in the 1960s, Motherwell was given numerous retrospective exhibitions of his art. The first, at the São Paulo Bienal and Pasadena Art Museum in 1961, was followed by a major retrospective at the Museum of Modern Art, which traveled to museums throughout Europe. Other retrospective exhibitions occurred in Mexico City (1975); Düsseldorf and Stockholm (1976); Vienna, Paris, and Edinburgh (1977); London (1978); Barcelona and Madrid (1980); Buffalo, New York; Los Angeles; San Francisco; Seattle; Washington, D.C.; and New York City (1983); and Mexico City and Fort Worth, Texas (1991). In 1970 Motherwell moved his studio from New York to a stone carriage house in suburban Greenwich, Connecticut, and in 1972 married photographer Renate Ponsold. During this same period, Motherwell received significant international awards that indicated his leadership in the cultural community. These include the Grande Medaille de Vermeil de la Ville de Paris (1978); the Gold Medal of Honor, Pennsylvania Academy of Fine Arts (1979); the Medal of Merit from the University of Salamanca (1980); the Mayor's Award for Art and Culture from the City of New York; the MacDowell Colony Medal of Honor (1985); election to the American Academy of Arts and Letters (1986); the Medalla de Oro de Bellas Artes in Madrid (1985); and the National Medal of Arts at the White House (1990).

In 1977 Motherwell received a commission for the largest painting of his career, the *Reconciliation Elegy* (3.05 × 8.27 meters) for the lobby of the East Wing at the National Gallery of Art in Washington. While the work is grand in conception, the execution is somewhat stiff. Because of the extremely large size of the work, Motherwell could not create it spontaneously on the canvas surface but rather was compelled to scale-up the design from smaller studies. In contrast to the stylized *Reconciliation Elegy,* one of Motherwell's most significant series of late paintings and drawings was the *Hollow Men.* While the title of these works was taken from T. S. Eliot's poem of despair for Cassius's plight in Shakespeare's *Julius Caesar,* Motherwell's paintings evoke a different spirit: the artist's desire to slice through superficiality and reveal the essence of his art. As such, the *Hollow Men* incorporates both the style of the *Elegies* and that of the *Opens.* The organic forms of the *Elegies* are now translucent rather than solid, and consequently more exposed. The somber black tonalities that had dominated these forms have been pushed into the background. Thus, in the shapes of the *Hollow Men,* Motherwell revealed more of his fragile automatic drawing, which he believed was the essence of his artistic personality. Despite the changes that the art world underwent at the end of the century in the context of movements that ranged from pop art to neo-expressionism, Motherwell continued to trust in the power of modern abstraction to communicate the artist's deepest feelings, and the *Hollow Men* stands as one of his final assertions of that belief.

Motherwell died of a stroke on Cape Cod. He is buried in Provincetown.

★

Motherwell's papers are in the Dedalus Foundation, New York City. Motherwell's writings are gathered in *The Collected Writings of Robert Motherwell,* edited by Stephanie Terenzio (1992). Books on Motherwell include H. H. Arnason, *Robert Motherwell* (rev. ed. 1982); Mary Ann Caws, *Robert Motherwell: What Art Holds* (1996); Jack Flam, *Motherwell* (1991); and Robert Saltonstall Mattison, *Robert Motherwell: The Formative Years* (1987). An obituary is in the *New York Times* (18 July 1991).

ROBERT SALTONSTALL MATTISON

MURPHY, George Lloyd (*b.* 4 July 1902 in New Haven, Connecticut; *d.* 3 May 1992 in Palm Beach, Florida), actor who appeared in more than forty films, primarily as a song-and-dance man, and who assumed a leadership role in the Screen Actors Guild. He served in the U.S. Senate from 1964 to 1970.

Murphy was the youngest of three children born to Michael Charles Murphy and Nora Long. Murphy's father was the

George Lloyd Murphy as Republican senatorial candidate, 1970. © COR-BIS/BETTMANN-UPI

track coach at the University of Pennsylvania as well as an Olympic coach who worked with the famed athlete Jim Thorpe. Two years following the death of his father in 1913, Murphy and his family moved to Detroit to live with his mother's parents. In 1917 his mother died, and Murphy received a partial athletic scholarship to attend the Peddie School in Hightstown, New Jersey. He subsequently attended the Pawling School in Pawling, New York, from which he graduated in 1921.

Although he was less than a stellar student, Murphy's family connections and athletic talents secured his admission to Yale College in the fall of 1921. However, Murphy enjoyed the collegiate party and sport scene more than his studies, and in 1924 he departed Yale without graduating. After working in a variety of jobs, including as a miner in Pennsylvania where he was injured in a mine car accident, Murphy ended up in New York City, where he was employed as a runner for a Wall Street brokerage firm. While living and working in New York, Murphy met the dancer Julie Johnson (real name Juliette Henkel), who taught him to dance. Johnson and Murphy formed a dance act, performing in cocktail lounges, nightclubs, and vaudeville. They were married on 28 December 1926. The marriage produced two children and lasted forty-seven years until Johnson's death in 1973.

Murphy made his Broadway debut in 1927, and the couple received their big break in 1929 when they took over the lead roles in the popular musical *Hold Everything*. Mur-

phy moved on to a successful solo career in the Broadway romantic comedy productions *Of Thee I Sing* (1933) and *Roberta* (1934).

In 1934, Murphy made the transition from Broadway to Hollywood, portraying Eddie Cantor's younger brother in *Kid Millions*. In the 1930s and 1940s, Murphy appeared in over forty films, most of them musicals, capitalizing upon his dancing background in New York. Among Murphy's musical films are: *After the Dance* (1935); *Top of the Town* (1937); *Little Miss Broadway*, with Shirley Temple (1938); *Broadway Melody* (1940), with Fred Astaire; *Little Nellie Kelly* (1940), with Judy Garland; *For Me and My Gal* (1942), which also featured Judy Garland and Gene Kelly; and *Step Lively* (1944). Among his non-musical credits and dramatic roles are: *Public Menace* (1935); *London by Night* (1937); *Risky Business* (1939); *The Navy Comes Through* (1942); *Bataan* (1943), with Robert Taylor; *The Arnelo Affair* (1947); *Big City* (1948); *Battleground* (1949); and *Walk East on Bacon!* (1952).

A longtime Democrat, in 1939 Murphy converted to the Republican Party, increasingly taking an active role in both Hollywood and national politics. As a member of the board of directors of the Screen Actors Guild from 1937 to 1953 and serving as its president (1944–1946), Murphy was noted for his efforts to combat racketeering and earn better working conditions for screen actors. However, some of his most controversial actions were taken in his support of the House Un-American Activities Committee investigations into the role of the Communist Party in Hollywood. In his 1979 autobiography, Murphy asserted that he was proud of his role in the Hollywood anticommunist crusade: "Whatever the reasons, the communist party became a major threat in the motion picture industry. Fighting communism was not easy, nor was it pleasant, but it had to be done. It still has to be done—and not only in Hollywood" (p. 296).

While blacklisted performers were unhappy with Murphy, he was honored by the industry, receiving a special Academy Award in 1951 for "services in interpreting the film industry to the country at large." Retiring from acting in 1952, he served as a public relations spokesman for Metro-Goldwyn-Mayer. In 1958, he joined Desi Arnaz and Lucille Ball at Desilu Productions, serving as vice president, before moving on to the Technicolor Corporation as vice president and director of operations in 1966.

Meanwhile, Murphy continued his active involvement with the Republican Party, serving as chair of the California state central committee in 1953 and directing the 1953 and 1957 inaugurations of President Eisenhower and providing programming for the 1952, 1956, and 1960 Republican national conventions. In 1964 Murphy ran for the U.S. Senate, narrowly defeating Democratic candidate Pierre Salinger, former press secretary to President John Kennedy, even while President Lyndon Johnson was overwhelmingly carrying the state over his Republican rival, Barry Goldwater.

While he proved to be a successful fund raiser for the national Republican Party, Murphy's senatorial career was controversial. His colleagues sometimes criticized him for being uninformed, while his voting record was conservative on issues such as civil rights and federal aid to education. Murphy also maintained a hawkish position on the Vietnam War, insisting that American troops were being prevented from achieving victory. What appeared to be his ultra-conservative record led to a split between Murphy and his Republican senatorial colleague from California, Thomas H. Kuchel.

Running for reelection in 1970, Murphy's campaigning was limited by a 1966 operation for a malignancy on his vocal cords. Although the operation was successful, he required electronic amplification whenever he spoke. Murphy's campaign was also the target of conflict-of-interest allegations arising from his continuing service as a paid consultant for Technicolor during his Senate tenure. Murphy's reelection bid was defeated by the Democratic challenger John V. Tunney, son of the former heavyweight boxing champion, Gene Tunney.

Following his defeat, Murphy remained active in politics and public relations work. In 1973, after the death of his wife, Murphy retired to Florida, where he wrote his autobiography. In 1982, he married the socialite and former model Bette Blandi. Murphy died from leukemia at the age of eighty-nine and was buried in Palm Springs, Florida.

Murphy's film career as a dancer and dramatic performer spanned two decades and forty films. His political career in Hollywood with the Screen Actors Guild and on the national level with the Republican Party in the Senate produced a controversial legacy. For example, as a union representative, he worked to secure better working conditions, while supporting the existence of a blacklist for those with alleged communist connections. He is also noted for fostering the political career of his fellow actor Ronald Reagan, who told the *Los Angeles Times,* "When I was beginning in show business he was a star who became a very good friend and a great help to me. . . . He was a wonderful man and he and I got very close together in those terrible days when there was a communist thrust in the film business."

★

Murphy's autobiography, *Say . . . Didn't You Used to Be George Murphy?,* with Victor Lasky (1970), is a valuable source for the actor's personal and political perspectives. Obituaries are in the *New York Times* and *Los Angeles Times* (both 5 May 1992).

RON BRILEY

MURRAY, Arthur (*b.* 4 April 1895 in New York City; *d.* 3 March 1991 in Honolulu, Hawaii), dance teacher and entrepreneur who founded a successful chain of dancing schools and a mail-order program of dance instruction.

Murray, born Murray Teichman, was the eldest of five children born to poor Jewish Austrian immigrants who had come to America in 1894. His father, Abraham Teichman, sold bread from a pushcart until his mother, Sara Schor, opened her own bakery on New York City's Lower East Side.

Murray was a sickly, painfully shy child, who desperately wanted to escape the surrounding poverty. He turned to social dancing as a means of meeting girls and becoming more popular. To practice his dancing, he frequently sneaked into wedding receptions, which were held in neighborhood public halls. He quit Morris High School in the Bronx at the age of seventeen to study draftsmanship at Cooper Union in the hope of becoming an architect, but when he won a waltz contest at a local settlement house in 1912, he left school, convinced he could make a living from dancing.

Murray left his first job as a part-time dancing instructor at Grand Central Palace, a large exhibition hall in New York City, to become a full time instructor at G. Hepburn

Arthur Murray teaching film star Anita Stewart the "hesitation waltz." © BETTMANN/CORBIS

Wilson Dance Studios, where he spent four hours each day teaching such new dance crazes as the bunny hug, grizzly bear, and one-step. At the same time, for six hours a day, he took dance instructor lessons at Castle House, run by the famous dancers Irene and Vernon Castle. There, in 1914, he met the Baroness de Kuttleston, who asked him to be her teaching partner at a resort hotel in Asheville, North Carolina. Murray accepted, and at the baroness's suggestion, he changed his name to Arthur Murray to escape the American public's animosity toward German-sounding names because of World War I.

In 1917 Arthur had a falling-out with the baroness, and he moved to Atlanta, where he enrolled in the Georgia School of Technology, in his spare time teaching dancing at the Georgia Terrace, the leading hotel in Atlanta. Here he organized dance classes for children, which by 1920 had outgrown the hotel with more than 1,000 children enrolled. Arthur opened his first dance studio nearby, and soon adults also began to take lessons, giving Murray the chance to mingle with the rich and the famous, including Enrico Caruso, who took lessons while touring with the Metropolitan Opera.

One day Murray had an idea inspired by his architectural and terpsichorean background. A person, he reasoned, should be able to learn to dance from following a footstep diagram. Soon he established the Arthur Murray Correspondence School of Dancing. The dance course by mail cost $10 and was quickly successful because of Murray's natural advertising acumen; he promoted the school with such ads as "How I Became Popular Overnight" and "Thirty Days Ago They Laughed at Me." In 1923 the young entrepreneur left Atlanta, moving to New York to conduct his mail-order business from a mid-Manhattan office, at the same time opening a dance studio in the city. The following year he had a radio show on which he danced with partners and promoted his correspondence school. At the show, he met Kathryn Kohnfelder, a teacher from Jersey City, New Jersey. When the couple married in 1925, the mail-order business was netting over $35,000 a year.

The couple had twin girls in 1926 and bought a home in Mount Vernon, New York, but after Kathryn suffered bouts of severe depression and attempted suicide, they moved around between New York and California, settling back in New York in 1938. While the Great Depression had brought an end to the mail-order business, the dance-franchise business flourished. By 1946 the Murrays did a gross business of $12,000,000, with branch schools in all the major American cities.

In 1950 they entered the world of television with a fifteen-minute show on CBS where they taught dancing.

The Arthur Murray Party, hosted by Kathryn, ran for eleven years and featured dance contests, dancing instruction, comedy sketches, and guest appearances, helping to launch the careers of such notables as Johnny Carson and Merv Griffin. The show's signature, "To put a little fun in your life—try dancing," became a popular phrase, and the show's popularity increased the number of dance studio franchises to 500.

In 1952 Murray sold most of his franchises for $5 million but stayed on as manager of the chain until the 1960s, when the Federal Trade Commission (FTC) investigated the company's high-pressure sales tactics and bogus contest promotions. In 1960 the FTC ordered the Murray Studios to stop such aggressive business methods as signing people for lessons while promising that the lessons would make them irresistible to others. In May 1964, Murray was arrested for disregarding a subpoena ordering him to appear before a grand jury that was investigating reports of fraudulent practices by dance studios. Although not charged, Murray resigned as president of Arthur Murray, Incorporated, two months later. He and his wife moved to Hawaii, where he became a financial adviser to his close friends, who reported that he helped them increase their stock holdings fivefold. In 1983 a tennis injury forced him into permanent retirement. He died from pneumonia at the age of ninety-five and was buried in Honolulu.

Murray was an ordinary-looking man, with a bald head, receding chin, and slight stutter. But he created such an image of personal charm and magnetism that the rich and famous filled his studios, including Eleanor Roosevelt, Jack Dempsey, Katharine Hepburn, and Tallulah Bankhead. Murray exemplified the class of the ballroom dancer. He claimed that a man should be able to treat his partner like a china doll, guiding her and gliding gracefully around a room. He was no fan of the disco craze or the rock-and-roll style of dancing alone, which, he claimed, were forms of exhibitionism. He combined the skill of dancing with a sharp sense of business and great advertising ability. Although tainted by government investigations and accusations of extreme frugality, he has left his imprint on the American scene, his name synonymous with the grace and sophistication of the ballroom dancer.

★

Kathryn Murray wrote a biography of her husband, *My Husband, Arthur Murray,* with Betty Hannah Hoffman (1960), which is filled with personal anecdotal details about the couple. An interesting article about Murray's financial "footwork" is in the *New York Times* (21 Sept. 1980). Obituaries are in the *New York Times* and *Atlanta Constitution* (both 4 Mar. 1991).

JOHN J. BYRNE

N

NEMEROV, Howard (*b.* 1 March 1920 in New York City; *d.* 5 July 1991 in University City, Missouri), poet, teacher, novelist, critic, and recipient of numerous major literary prizes; poet laureate of the United States.

The oldest of three children of Gertrude Russek and David Nemerov, Nemerov was raised in a New York environment of servants, private school, and childhood summers in Deal, New Jersey. His mother's family owned Russek's, an elegant department store of which his father became president. His parents were also philanthropists. Nemerov's younger sisters were Diane Arbus, the noted photographer for whom he later wrote a memorial poem ("To D——, Dead by Her Own Hand," *Gnomes and Occasions,* 1973), and Renee, a sculptor. Raised in an affluent but sometimes troubled family, Nemerov was a high achiever in academics and sports at Fieldston, a notable Ethical Culture Society school in the Bronx, from which he graduated in 1937. Entering Harvard College, he continued to excel but felt that as a Jew he was not fully accepted. This underlying feeling of estrangement along with depression lingered through most of Nemerov's life despite his eventual national recognition and many prestigious awards, the first of which was the Bowdoin Prize (1940), for an essay on Thomas Mann that received Mann's praise. During this same period some of his short stories were published in the *Harvard Advocate.*

After graduating from Harvard in 1941, Nemerov flew fifty missions with the Royal Canadian Air Force (1941–

1944) and another fifty-seven with the Eighth U.S. Army Air Force (1944–1945). He was a fighter pilot who became a "flying officer" in the RCAF, a first lieutenant in the U.S. Air Force. These experiences are reflected in numerous poems, including those in "War in the Air," the second section of *War Stories Long Ago and Now* (1987), in which the poem "Models" speaks of survivors who "aged decades in a year." With his nineteen-year-old English bride, Margaret ("Peggy") Russell, whom he married on 26 January 1944, Nemerov spent a short time writing in New York City. Then from 1946 to 1948, he taught English to returning GIs at Hamilton College in Clinton, New York. He also became associate editor of the literary magazine *Furioso* in 1946. Nemerov's long academic career was centered on small, avant-garde Bennington College in Vermont (1948–1966) and larger, urban Washington University in St. Louis, Missouri (1962–1991), where he became Edward Mallinckrodt Distinguished University Professor (1976–1990). Nemerov was also associated with the University of Minnesota (1958–1959), Hollins College in Roanoke, Virginia (1962–1963), Lawrence University in Appleton, Wisconsin (1964), Brandeis University in Waltham, Massachusetts (1963, 1966–1968), Tufts University in Medford, Massachusetts (1969), and Yale University in New Haven, Connecticut (1983).

Simultaneously, Nemerov's writing was published in such periodicals as *The Virginia Quarterly, Poetry,* and *Story.* Of his more than two dozen book-length publications,

Howard Nemerov. CORBIS CORPORATION (BELLEVUE)

about half are poetry. The first of these, *The Image and the Law,* with its poems of death, appeared in 1947 to the mixed reception that marked most of his early work. Some of Nemerov's other volumes of poetry are *Mirrors and Windows* (1958), the winner of the Blumenthal Prize; *New and Selected Poems* (1960), which contains Nemerov's favorite and longest poem, "Runes"; *The Blue Swallow* (1967), which won the first Theodore Roethke Memorial Prize; and *The Collected Poems of Howard Nemerov* (1978), which was awarded both the Pulitzer Prize and the National Book Award in 1978 and the Bollingen Prize in 1981.

Beginning as a poet evocative of T. S. Eliot and W. H. Auden, Nemerov wrote increasingly about nature and was often compared to Robert Frost. Yet he was a sophisticated observer of the contemporary American scene. Known as a superb craftsman able to write in any form and meticulously attentive to language, Nemerov was praised for his intelligence and wit. His writing embodied the apparent contraries of aloofness and romanticism, erudition and simplicity, serious concerns and humor. Calling himself a "writer of fictions in verse and prose," Nemerov also wrote three novels, *The Melodramatists* (1949), *Federigo; or, The Power of Love* (1954), and *The Homecoming Game* (1960). The last, dramatized as a comedy by Howard Lindsay and

Russel Crouse, also served as the basis of the 1960 film *Tall Story.* Another of his works, the slim autobiographical *Journal of the Fictive Life* (1965), is a Freudian analysis of himself and the writing of fiction. In it he explains, "My passion is to know. And since I cannot know I must imagine." Nemerov also authored two short story collections *A Commodity of Dreams* (1959) and *Stories, Fables, and Diversions* (1971); two verse plays, *Endor* (1961) and *Cain* (1962); many essays; and a considerable amount of criticism.

Among Nemerov's many prominent awards were a National Institute of Arts and Letters grant (1961) with election to that body in 1965, a Guggenheim Fellowship (1968–1969), an Academy of American Poets Fellowship (1970) with chancellorship from 1976, as well as election to both the American Academy of Arts and Letters and the American Academy of Arts and Sciences, and more than a dozen honorary doctorates. Another significant honor was the National Medal of Arts awarded at the White House (1987). A consultant in poetry to the Library of Congress from 1963 to 1964, Nemerov was named poet laureate of the United States for 1988–1990, the third recipient of this office.

A reserved, tall, good-looking man with close-cropped hair (though he sported a mustache as a pilot), Nemerov was considered a demanding yet supportive teacher. He and Peggy were married forty-seven years and had three sons—David, Alexander Michael, and Jeremy Seth. He died of cancer; a private family funeral service followed, with burial in St. Louis. At the memorial service in Graham Chapel of Washington University, the poet Richard Wilbur spoke the eulogy. There are memorial plaques at the University and in the St. Louis Walk of Fame.

A prolific man of letters, Nemerov was a poet whose perceptions, moral concepts, and imagination were expressed with clarity and wit. A teacher and versatile writer who "wore his intellect lightly," Nemerov received many awards for his contributions to literature.

★

A collection of Nemerov's papers is at Washington University in St. Louis. His *Journal of a Fictive Life* (1965, 1981 with a new preface) is a Freudian self-analysis with reflections on writing and imagination. Patricia Bosworth, *Diane Arbus, a Biography* (1984), includes details of Nemerov and his sister's childhood and family life. Some full-length books are William Mills, *The Stillness in Moving Things: The World of Howard Nemerov* (1975), an analysis of his themes, vision, language; Ross Labrie, *Howard Nemerov* (1980), a biocritical study; Diane L. Potts, *Howard Nemerov and Objective Realism* (1994), a study of "the influence of Owen Barfield," a British philosopher with whom Nemerov corresponded for more than twenty years. A chapter by Miriam Marty Clark in *Contemporary Jewish-American Dramatists and Poets: A Biocritical Sourcebook* (1999) assesses Nemerov's family background, literary themes, and critical reception. Obituaries are in the *New York Times* and *Washington Post* (both 7 July 1991).

RACHEL SHOR

NEUMANN, Vera Salaff ("Vera") (*b.* 24 July 1910 in Stamford, Connecticut *d.* 15 June 1993 in North Tarrytown, New York), textile designer known for her highly successful lines of home furnishings and signature brightly-colored scarves.

Neumann, popularly known as "Vera," was the only child of Meyer Salaff, a businessman, and Fanny Shenkow, a homemaker. She was educated at the Cooper Union for the Advancement of Science and Art and the Traphagen School of Design, both in New York City. She considered a career as an art teacher but instead became a fashion designer. Disillusionment set in, however, when she was asked to steal designs.

She moved to Greenwich Village and set up a small studio, where she designed children's furniture and murals for Childhood, Inc. On 11 February 1943 she married George Neumann, a refugee from Austria who had a background in business administration and an interest in textiles; his parents had owned Hungary's largest textile screen printing business. They had two children. In 1945 Vera, her husband, and their friend F. Werner Hamm formed a partnership and went into the textile-printing business. Vera did all of the designing and color separating and helped her husband with the printing. George Neumann mixed and tested dyes and paints and created new formulas. Hamm was their purchasing agent and sales manager. Their first order—from B. Altman, the prominent Manhattan department store—was for 1,000 place mats in three

designs. Early in her career Vera created her distinctive, simple signature paired with a drawing of a ladybug, symbol of good luck.

After this early success, the Neumanns moved into a spacious loft on West Fifty-seventh Street in Manhattan, where they began to expand their line from place mats to tablecloths. Soon Vera created an allover pattern of leaves in greens and browns that sold immediately to Schumacher, the largest drapery house in New York. Her distinctive style consisted of abstracted silhouetted motifs in vivid colors—red, blue, yellow, green—underlined with black lines and with attention paid to the background white space around the motifs. Designs like her classic fern fronds were revolutionary during the 1940s because they used just a few colors that, when overprinted with one another, caused three-dimensional effects.

As their business grew, Vera, her husband, and Hamm moved to a converted Georgian mansion in suburban Ossining, New York, in 1947 to set up Printex Corporation of America. In 1949 the company began an association with Schumacher Fabrics that would last for more than thirty years. For Schumacher she designed decorative fabrics, wallpapers, and rugs. Three famous designs were "Jack in the Pulpit," "Framed Fruits," and "Nature Study," a collage of leaf forms.

Neumann found inspiration almost everywhere. For a formal drapery pattern she was asked to do for the Commemorative Group of Textiles in Colonial Williamsburg, Virginia, she used authentic reproductions of colonial carriages on a background she adapted from endpapers of old books. Other inspirations included keys, Swiss chalets, old clocks, fish nets, cookie molds, jars full of candies, beaded curtains, and objects she discovered on her many trips

Vera Neumann, 1950. AP/WIDE WORLD PHOTOS

abroad. Sometimes her prints were abstract, as in one of her favorites, "Jorongo," which was shown in the 1952 Good Design Collection at the Museum of Modern Art in New York.

Neumann's method of working was to first sketch or paint the design in watercolor, then develop it so that no lines of demarcation would show when the design repeated all over a piece of fabric. A single drapery fabric might require screens for five or six separate colors, and the overlapping colors created effects of even more shades. She transformed sunflowers and blue skies of Portofino, or dolls and other toys, into abstracted motifs that retained the character of the original objects.

After home furnishings and signature scarves, Neumann added women's blouses and tops, casual shifts, and pants into her repertoire. She designed bright, colorful tops to be worn with custom-matched pants in solid colors. Imaginative Vera accessories in 1953 included a felt pocket worn by Swedish shopkeepers which she converted into a colorful bib to be worn over a dress, and casual hats like the "Doll's Cap" and the "Pixie Tip."

Early in the 1950s, the renowned architect Marcel Breuer designed a "Scarves by Vera" showroom on Fifth Avenue in New York. He also designed George and Vera Neumann's home in Croton-on-Hudson, only a few miles from their Printex plant in Ossining. During their marriage the Neumanns also collected art by modern artists including Pablo Picasso, Ben Shahn, Josef Albers, and Alexander Calder.

George Neumann died in 1960. Vera continued the business and in 1967 sold it to the Manhattan Shirt Company for $5 million, making her one of the country's richest businesswomen. She retained the presidency of the Vera Companies subsidiary and was the only woman on the board of directors of Manhattan Industries. The Vera Companies included Linens by Vera, Scarves by Vera, and Vera Sportswear. In 1969 she began her association with Burlington Industries, for which she designed an enormously successful line of sheets and pillowcases and later bedspreads, blankets, draperies, bath towels, shower curtains, and other bath accessories. In 1970 a large, mirrored showroom opened on the twenty-ninth floor of 417 Fifth Avenue at West Thirty-seventh Street, the former location of the Metropolitan Opera. The showroom was an impressive design by Breuer, with stark walls and corridors where Vera garments, fabrics, and murals could be displayed.

In 1972 Neumann received the Trailblazer Award of the National Home Fashions League and the 1972 Total Design Award from the National Society of Interior Designers. That same year she was honored by a retrospective exhibition entitled "Vera: The Renaissance Woman" at the Smithsonian Institution in Washington, D.C. Cooper Union gave her its Outstanding Alumna Award.

During the 1970s prominent clients of Vera Companies were Burlington Industries for bedding, Dritz-Scovill for needlepoint, and Mikasa for chinaware. Later in the decade, Neumann's use of colors in home furnishings evolved to deeper colors for backgrounds of her prints, including dark red, navy blue, hunter green, and even black. In 1974 she designed a popular black-and-white sheet for Burlington, but she still considered her bold use of primary colors to be "her contribution to the textile industry." Also in 1974, the young fashion designer Perry Ellis joined Neumann in Manhattan Industries to create clothing from her fabric paintings.

In 1976 Neumann marked her long working relationship with Schumacher by creating eight fabrics and wallpapers for the firm, which also revived the fern pattern she had designed in the late 1940s. She became the first designer of note to create arrangements of dried flowers and silk flowers for home decor. Sales of Vera designs reached more than $100 million and her merchandise was sold in more than 1,200 stores. By 1979 her companies employed 500 people. Her new linen lines were launched twice a year, in May and November. Popular designs for Burlington bed linens included "Shadow Fern," "Sunset," and "Daisy Spray." One reason for the great sales success of sheets was that shoppers usually purchased them on impulse. Typically, each collection of Vera home furnishings was half new designs and half reissues. Vera was the number-one designer of domestics merchandise in 1979.

Drawing from impressions absorbed during trips to China, Neumann used Oriental colors and themes for her June 1979 collection of napkins and table mats. Recognized as an artist, Neumann had the honor of having her designs exhibited in galleries and museums. She was a longtime supporter of the Fashion Institute of Technology in New York, which dedicated the "Vera Neumann Room" in her honor.

By 1980 there were Vera showrooms around the United States and printing facilities in New Jersey, West Virginia, Puerto Rico, and Japan, in addition to Ossining. Neumann remained active in the business until shortly before her death from cardiac arrest after surgery at Phelps Memorial Hospital in North Tarrytown, New York.

★

Neumann's works are archived at the Fashion Institute of Technology. Her early work was described in *American Artist* (Sept. 1953). She was interviewed for *American Fabrics and Fashions* (summer 1979). In-depth analysis of Neumann's creative working methods appeared in *American Artist* (May 1980). An obituary is in the *New York Times* (17 June 1993).

THERESE DUZINKIEWICZ BAKER

NEWELL, Allen (*b.* 19 March 1927 in San Francisco, California; *d.* 19 July 1992 in Pittsburgh, Pennsylvania), pioneer of research into artificial intelligence (AI).

Newell was the second child of Robert R. Newell, a radiologist, and Jeanette Levalley, a homemaker. Graduating from Lowell High School in 1945 after a career marked more by his ability in football than by intellectual pursuits, Newell enlisted in the U.S. Navy. Assigned to the chore of making maps of the radiation emitted during the Bikini Atoll nuclear tests, Newell realized that he loved doing scientific work. He accordingly, after his discharge in 1946, enrolled at Stanford University, where he copublished an article on X-ray optics. In December 1947 Newell married his high school sweetheart, Noel McKenna. They had one son. Newell earned a bachelor's degree in 1949 and began studying mathematics at Princeton University in New Jersey.

At Princeton, Newell's interests soon turned away from theoretical math and toward experimentation. Consequently, he took a leave of absence from Princeton and went to work for the newly formed Rand Corporation in Santa Monica, California. One of the papers he wrote during this period, "Observations on the Science of Supply" (*Technical Report D-926,* Rand Corporation, 1951), focuses directly on the weakness of theoretical models to comprehend the realities of production and distribution systems. While working over the next few years on a Rand study of the U.S. Air Force early warning system, Newell and a colleague, Cliff Shaw, solved a basic problem: how to use a computer to simulate radar images on an early warning screen. Their achievement represented a major step not only toward Newell's ultimate work in artificial intelligence (AI) but also toward the development of modern video games.

In September 1954 Newell experienced what he later described as a "conversion experience." At a Rand seminar he learned that computer systems could not only create images but recognize them as well. His reaction was embodied in a classic paper, "The Chess Machine: An Example of Dealing with a Complex Task by Adaptation" (*Proceedings of the Western Joint Computer Conference,* 1955), which embodied nearly all the key features of what became known as an expert system: aspiration levels, "good enough" moves, generation of subgoals, and a coherent symbol system with which to represent the playing surface. Newell moved to the Carnegie Institute of Technology (now Carnegie-Mellon University) in Pittsburgh, where he developed for Rand the logic theory machine in 1956. He worked with the Nobel Prize winner Herbert Simon toward a Ph.D., which Newell received in 1957. Perhaps the culmination of this fertile period was his invention of Information Processing Languages (IPL), the first list-processing languages. These languages introduced lists, associations, frames, streams, and associative retrieval, without which the achievements in AI of the next decade might have been impossible. His 1961 manual for the IPL-V was

the first to advocate "top-down" programming. Another prime goal of AI research had been reached: a language that "relies heavily on heuristic methods similar to those that have been found in human problem solving activity."

Newell continued his dual role as Carnegie researcher and Rand employee until 1961, when he became a full-time professor in charge of developing Carnegie-Mellon's School of Computer Science. His own doctoral degree had been awarded in industrial administration because no appropriate title for his work existed at that time. Working closely with Shaw and Simon, he produced the effective chess-playing program he had theorized earlier. Although it was no IBM Deep Blue—a ten-year-old once beat it—it provided the experimental validation that Newell always demanded from theoretical schemas. In 1972 he and Simon finally put all their accumulated insights into a book, *Human Problem Solving,* which remained a standard in its field into the twenty-first century.

Newell believed that the physical architecture of the computer was not the key to machine intelligence, although he acknowledged that the development of massively parallel computing systems made the kind of processing he was designing far simpler. He and Gordon Bell coauthored a book on such systems, *Computer Structures: Readings and Examples* (1971). Again pushing theoretical insights toward their practical applications, Newell collaborated on L*, a new language based on the insights of his book, and a new type of menu system called ZOG, which ultimately was used on the aircraft carrier *Carl Vinson* in 1982.

During this period Newell also tackled a Xerox PARC project analyzing cognitive skills, the heart of which was embodied in the acronym GOMS: goals, operators, methods, and selection. His exposition of this project in *The Psychology of Human-Computer Interaction* (1983), which he wrote with Stuart K. Card and Thomas P. Moran, was a key step in the attainment of Newell's ultimate goal, a broad-based theory of cognition. His first real breakthrough in this direction was Soar, a cognitive architecture capable of solving problems and learning in a human way. Other models of cognition focus on verbal memory, sense perceptions, or the creation of concepts, but Soar focuses on problem solving. As Simon said, "The Soar program is a production system."

After Newell's death the Soar project continued at Carnegie-Mellon University, the University of Southern California, the University of Michigan, and other centers of research on artificial intelligence. Soar works effectively because of two innovations, "chunking" and the use of a "weak" method of problem solving. With its memory defined as a set of relatively discrete chunks rather than as an unbreakable whole, the system can adapt to new information or concepts without rebuilding the entire memory. By relying on a problem-solving formula that is relatively weak, the system becomes less "stubborn," turning away from time-wasting problems and trying to resolve them a different way. Invited to deliver the William James Lectures at Harvard University in 1987, Newell sketched out the advantages of the Soar system. He also used Soar as the model in his final book, *Unified Theories of Cognition* (1990).

When the American Association for Artificial Intelligence was founded in 1979, Newell was elected its first president, and he also headed the Cognitive Science Society. A month before his death he received the National Medal of Science. In 1975 he and Simon received the A. M. Turing Award from the Association for Computing Machinery, which established an annual award in Newell's honor after his death. Newell's other honors included awards from the American Federation of Information Processing Societies (1971), the American Psychological Association (1985), the Institute of Electrical and Electronics Engineers (1990), the Franklin Institute (1992), and honorary degrees from the University of Pennsylvania and Groningen University. Newell died of cancer in 1992.

With his muscular build and six-foot, one-inch frame, Newell stood out among computer scientists, who are often more dedicated to intellectual, rather than physical, development. He was renowned for his work ethic, often working through the night to solve a problem. As he said in 1991, "There is no substitute for working hard—very hard." One of his few leisure pursuits was watching football games on television on the weekends, a reminder of his high school avocation. A man of prodigious energy and endurance, focused on the impalpable workings of the brain, Allen Newell was a rare combination.

★

For more information on Newell see Pamela McCorduck, *Machines Who Think* (1979), and J. Laird and P. Rosenbloom, "In Pursuit of Mind: The Research of Allen Newell," *AI Magazine* 13, no. 4 (1992): 17–45. An obituary is in the *New York Times* (20 July 1992).

HARTLEY S. SPATT

NEWHALL, Beaumont (*b.* 22 June 1908 in Lynn, Massachusetts; *d.* 26 February 1993 in Santa Fe, New Mexico), historian of photography, curator, educator, and author.

Newhall's parents, Herbert William Newhall, a physician, and Alice Lillia Davis, a photographer and homemaker, were both descended from the first settlers of New England. His only sibling, Ruth, died of typhoid fever in 1912 at the age of seventeen. He was privately educated until 1917, when he entered the Lynn public schools, eventually enrolling in Lynn Classical High School. In 1925 Newhall attended Phillips Academy in Andover, Massachusetts, to prepare for Harvard.

In his 1993 autobiography *Focus,* Newhall traced his interest in photography to the German experimental film *Variety* (1925), which he saw at age eighteen. He became fascinated with the technical aspects of the movie, particularly the camera work and special effects. He even hoped to go to Hollywood and become a film director, but his parents preferred that he attend Harvard, which he did, "in order not to disappoint them." Newhall studied art history (there were no courses in photography or motion pictures at that time) and earned a bachelor of arts degree, cum laude, in 1930. He won a scholarship to Harvard's Graduate School of Arts and Science, and in 1931 received a master's degree in art museum management. He reentered Harvard in the fall of 1933, intending to study for a Ph.D. in art history, but after two years, to his "amazement and embarrassment," he failed his oral examinations. Newhall met Nancy Wynne Parker, an artist, in 1933. They were married on 1 July 1936, in her hometown of Swampscott, Massachusetts. Their union produced no children.

In 1935, after two short-lived docent jobs at the Philadelphia Museum of Art and the Metropolitan Museum of Art, Newhall was hired by the Museum of Modern Art (MOMA) in New York City as librarian. The following year Museum Director Alfred Barr, Jr., asked him to curate the first major exhibition of photography. Newhall immediately saw this as an opportunity to elevate the appreciation of photography, "the most exciting and the most expressive art of our time," to the level of painting, sculpture, and music. Newhall's historical overview "Photography 1839–1937" opened on 17 March 1937. Its success led the museum to create a department of photography in 1940, the first such department at any art museum, and to appoint Newhall the curator of photography.

In August 1942, after the United States entered World War II, Newhall enlisted as a first lieutenant in the Army Air Forces. He served overseas for two-and-a-half years in the Third Photo Intelligence Detachment, stationed in Egypt, Tunisia, and Italy. Newhall's wife Nancy acted as curator of photography at the MOMA during his absence.

Newhall returned from service in October 1945 and resumed his position at the museum until 1947, when the trustees appointed the photographer Edward Steichen over him as director of the department of photography. Describing the situation many years later, Newhall wrote, "Since Steichen's interest was in photojournalism and mine was in photography as an art, I resigned from the museum."

In 1947 Newhall was awarded a Guggenheim fellowship to revise his 1937 exhibition catalog into a full-length book. Published in 1949, *The History of Photography* concentrated on the artistic development of the medium. Universally praised for its scholarship and elegant style, it became the standard text on the subject. Newhall received a

Beaumont Newhall, curator of Eastman House. © ARTHUR ROTHSTEIN/CORBIS

second Guggenheim fellowship in 1975, which enabled him to publish a fifth edition in 1982.

In 1948 Newhall was appointed the first curator of photography at the new George Eastman House museum of photography in Rochester, New York. Ten years later he became director. Under Newhall's leadership, and with his deep knowledge of the subject, he built an unsurpassed collection for the institution and guided its development into the world's finest museum of photography.

Newhall's scholarly output over the years contributed immeasurably to the field of photography. He wrote more than 600 articles and catalogs and 30 books, among them *The Daguerreotype in America* (1961), *Latent Image: The Discovery of Photography* (1967) and *Airborne Camera* (1969). In 1952 he founded the magazine *Image* to document the progress of the art and science of photography and cinematography. He cofounded the quarterly *Aperture* and was a contributing editor to the periodical *Art in America from 1958 to 1965*. Newhall also found time, between 1956 and 1969, to write 234 newspaper columns about food, the "Epicure Corner," for the Brighton-Pittsford (New York) *Post*.

After Newhall retired from George Eastman House in 1971 he started a major program in photography at the University of New Mexico in Albuquerque and taught there for thirteen years. With his tall frame (six feet, three inches) and high, intelligent forehead, Newhall was a legendary figure on campus, long remembered for the generosity of time he made for his students.

In the summer of 1974, while vacationing in Grand Teton National Park in Wyoming, Beaumont and Nancy Newhall went rafting down the Snake River. Without warning, a huge tree, undermined from the unusually high water, crashed upon the raft and struck Nancy. She died on 7 July 1974 from the injuries she had received. Over the course of their thirty-eight-year marriage Nancy had been Newhall's partner and collaborator as well as a noted photographer and author in her own right.

Newhall spent his life studying, writing about, and promoting photographers and photography, and beginning in the 1970s he began exhibiting his own work. *In Plain Sight,* a book of his photographs, was published in 1983. Newhall married Christi Yates on 22 May 1975 and moved to a house and garden in the foothills of the Sangre de Cristo Mountains in Santa Fe, New Mexico. Officially divorced in 1985, they continued to share the house until he died there from complications of a stroke. His remains were cremated.

"We may and can play an important part in fostering the appreciation of photography, but our quest for perfection, our passion for the expression of feeling in a photograph, are things that in general will be no more appreciated than the great chamber-music performers," Newhall wrote Nancy in one of his letters during their long wartime separation. Although Newhall foresaw the challenge that lay before him, he could not anticipate how his own talents and achievements would one day foster the appreciation of photography that he so desired.

★

The Beaumont and Nancy Newhall papers and photographs, 1943–1993, are at the Getty Research Institute in Los Angeles. A smaller collection of personal and business papers is at the Center for Creative Photography at the University of Arizona. Newhall's autobiography *Focus* (1993) provides a detailed and comprehensive account of his life. Newhall wrote further autobiographical information in the introduction to his book *In Plain Sight: The Photographs of Beaumont Newhall* (1983). Obituaries are in the *New York Times* and *Los Angeles Times* (both 27 Feb. 1993), and London *Independent* (9 Mar. 1993).

KENNETH R. COBB

NIKOLAIS, Alwin Theodore (*b.* 25 November 1910 in Southington, Connecticut; *d.* 8 May 1993 in New York City), choreographer, designer, composer, and pioneer of multimedia dance.

Nikolais was the youngest of five children who survived infancy of John Nikolais, a Russian immigrant, and German-born Martha Heinrich. His parents had a successful bakery and retail business in Southington. Nikolais showed an aptitude for theater and music from an early age, and after his graduation from high school he found employment in a wide range of musical and theatrical enterprises in New England. By 1934 he was codirector, with Michael Adrian, of the Southington Drama Center. At the same time, he returned to a childhood interest in puppetry and created a successful marionette theater, which, with support

Alwin Nikolais. TOM CARANAGLIA

from the Works Progress Administration (WPA), toured Connecticut. The WPA also engaged him to direct stage movement for the Negro Ensemble of the Federal Theater Project.

The future choreographer became interested in modern dance in 1933 when he saw a performance of the great German dance pioneer Mary Wigman in New Haven, Connecticut. He studied at the Bennington College Summer School of Dance in 1937, 1938, and 1939, where he was influenced by the American choreographer Martha Graham, the musician Louis Horst, and the writer and critic John Martin. In May 1939, Nikolais created his first major ballet, in collaboration with Truda Kaschman: *Eight Column Line* (music by Ernest Krenek, designs by A. Everett Austin) premiered at Avery Memorial Theater in Hartford, Connecticut. He toured the United States and Mexico with a small company, Dancers en Route, but later gave up performing to concentrate on choreography, music composition, and theater design.

Nikolais served with the United States Army in Europe from 1942 to 1946. After the war he concentrated his dance study with Hanya Holm, a former assistant to Mary Wigman and her most prominent representative in the United States. He became Holm's teaching assistant in her New York City studio and at her summer institute at Colorado College in Colorado Springs. In 1948, on her recommendation, he was appointed resident director of the Playhouse at the Henry Street Settlement on Manhattan's Lower East Side, where he formed the Playhouse Dance Company (renamed the Nikolais Dance Theatre in 1951). Under his direction, the Playhouse increased arts education and enrichment programs in its ethnically diverse neighborhood and became a focus of interest for the New York dance community. In 1949 Nikolais met Murray Louis, a dancer who became his companion and artistic partner in a union that lasted for forty-three years, until Nikolais's death. The pair shared houses both in Greenwich Village and in Southampton, Long Island, New York. When either artist was on tour, the men kept in touch with one another through regular correspondence.

As Nikolais developed his own dance aesthetic, he turned away from the dramatic and psychological content prevalent in dance of the 1940s to explore abstract possibilities of movement. *Masks, Props, and Mobiles,* which premiered at the Henry Street Playhouse on 1 December 1955, fully realized his point of view and was acknowledged by the press as a conquest of dance abstraction. One section, "Web," was later developed and titled *Tensile Involvement.* It became a signature Nikolais work, performed by the Nikolais Dance Theatre and then by the Nikolais/Murray Louis Dance Company until its demise in 1999.

Nikolais became nationally prominent in 1956 when *Kaleidoscope* was performed at the American Dance Festival in New London, Connecticut. Critics recognized the ballet as a reinvigoration of modern dance, although some were disturbed by the dancers' lack of emotion. Throughout his career Nikolais was criticized for masking dancers with unusual costuming and stage properties. In response to charges of dehumanization, he contended that his total theater represented a new humanism by showing men and women interacting with universal mechanisms, rather than in domination of them.

With the premiere of *Prism* on 27 December 1956 at the Henry Street Playhouse, Nikolais began developing novel lighting techniques. His innovations with saturated color, low side lighting, and projections of light onto dancers and cyclorama became stock-in-trade for dance, theater, and multimedia productions. In creating works for television, he pioneered the use of chroma-key blue technology for dance. It became a widely used technique for superimposing images. After 1958 he created electronically manipulated sound as an integral part of all his ballets.

Nikolais created eleven large-scale works in the decade following *Kaleidoscope* and *Prism*. The most successful were *Cantos* (1957), *Allegory* (1959), *Totem* (1960), and *Sanctum* (1964), which all opened at the Henry Street Playhouse; and *Vaudeville of the Elements* (1965), which was commissioned by the Walker Arts Center in Minneapolis and premiered at the Tyrone Guthrie Theatre there. Although he pursued nonliteral communication, his works were not without content. Human evolution and folly were frequent concerns. Often he used humor to draw audiences into unsettling experience. *Tent* (1968) begins with the jolly construction of a world—the tent—in which the dancers awaken to life and ultimately annihilate themselves and their world. After the success of *Tent* and *Imago* (1963) in Paris in 1968, the Nikolais Dance Theatre was booked to perform in major opera houses and theaters in North and South America, Europe, and Asia.

Nikolais continued to choreograph prolifically for his own theater, as the training of his dancers was so specific to his choreographic method and philosophy that no other New York City companies performed his works. Among his most important works of the 1970s and 1980s are *Scenario* (1971), *Foreplay* (1972), and *Crossfade* (1974), which all premiered in New York City; *Temple* (1974), which premiered in Madrid, Spain; *Guignol* (1977) and *Gallery* (1978), which premiered in New York City; *Countdown* (1979), which premiered in Mexico City; *Mechanical Organ* (1980, reworked in 1982), which premiered in Charleston, South Carolina; *Persons and Structures* (1984), which premiered in New York City; and *Graph* (1984) and *Crucible* (1985), both of which premiered in Durham, North Carolina. He continued to choreograph in the late 1980s while being treated for cancer, but during his illness the quality of his work diminished.

Expanding upon a European conceptual approach to dance training, Nikolais had wide-ranging influence as an educator. He gave his students the means for technical mastery without imposing a movement vocabulary, stimulating their own artistry with improvisation and choreographic opportunity. Many of his company members and students became respected teachers and choreographers with differing and distinctive styles.

In 1978 he established a school in Angers, France, at the behest of the French Ministry of Culture. Two years later the ministry commissioned *Schema* for the Paris Opera. For his influence on the dance community in France he was made a Commander of the Order of Arts and Letters (1982) and a Knight of the Legion of Honor (1984). In the United States he received all major dance awards, including the *Dance Magazine* Award (1967), the Capezio Award (1982), and the Samuel H. Scripps American Dance Festival Award (1985), as well as Kennedy Center honors and the National Medal of Arts (both in 1987).

Known as "Nik" by everyone from his most prestigious acquaintances to students, Nikolais's relaxed assurance and articulate speech inspired admiration and confidence. He avidly collected artifacts from around the world, often scouring flea markets and bazaars. He cooked, built furniture, and even cobbled together his charming country house in Southampton. He sketched, and he wrote eloquently, but except for a few essays his writing has not been published. He succumbed to prostate cancer at the age of eighty-two and is buried in Père Lachaise Cemetery in Paris.

★

Nikolais's extensive archives will be available at Ohio University Libraries, Athens, Ohio, beginning in 2003. *The World of Alwin Nikolais,* a five-volume video record of his choreography, is distributed by Nikolais/Louis Foundation for Dance in New York City. No full-scale biography has been written, but Nikolais figures in all accounts of late twentieth-century American modern dance. A monograph edited by Marcia B. Siegel, "Nik: A Documentary," was published by *Dance Perspectives* (spring 1971), and his essay "No Man from Mars" is contained in Selma Jeanne Cohen, *The Modern Dance: Seven Statements of Belief.* An obituary is in the *New York Times* (10 May 1993). A documentary film by Christian Blackwood, *Nik and Murray* (1987), was produced for PBS television as part of the *American Masters* series.

CLAUDIA GITELMAN

NIXON, Pat(ricia)   (*b.* 16 March 1912 in Ely, Nevada; *d.* 22 June 1993 in Park Ridge, New Jersey), first lady of the United States from January 1969 to August 1974.

Nixon was born Thelma Catherine Ryan in Ely, a small mining town in the mountains of eastern Nevada, the first

Pat Nixon. LIBRARY OF CONGRESS

daughter and third child of William ("Will") Ryan, a miner, and Katharina ("Kate") Halberstadt, a homemaker. Her father, proud of his Irish heritage, called her "Pat" because she was born on the day before St. Patrick's Day. Later, when she enrolled in junior college, she made Patricia her formal name. Pat's mother, a widow, also raised a daughter from her previous marriage. A son from that previous marriage was reared by his paternal grandparents. In 1913 the Ryans moved to southern California, settling in Artesia, a town south of Los Angeles. Will Ryan took up vegetable farming and became known locally as the "cabbage king." But the family experienced much hardship. Their house had no electricity, and the children worked long hours on the farm. In 1925 Kate Ryan died of cancer, and since Kate's oldest daughter had left home for junior college the year before, Pat took charge of running the household, caring for her father and brothers in addition to attending school. She graduated from Excelsior Union High School in June 1929.

Will Ryan died in May 1930. Nixon worked at various jobs in town to save money for college. In the fall of 1931 she enrolled at Fullerton Junior College while holding down a job at the National Bank of Artesia. But after a year of study she was asked to drive some family friends to Connecticut and took the opportunity to move to New York City. There she worked for two years as a secretary,

an X-ray technician, and a store clerk to continue saving for college. Nixon returned west in 1934 and entered the University of Southern California on a scholarship. She studied merchandising, performed odd jobs, including bit parts for the RKO and MGM movie studios, and graduated cum laude in 1937.

In September 1937 Nixon began teaching typing, bookkeeping, and stenography at Whittier High School in nearby Whittier, California. She also acted in local theater. In 1938, at the auditions for George S. Kaufman and Alexander Woolcott's play *The Dark Tower,* she met Richard Milhous Nixon, a twenty-five-year-old Whittier lawyer. Nixon courted her for two years, and they married on 21 June 1940. They had two daughters.

In 1942 Richard Nixon enlisted in the U.S. Navy, and while he served in the South Pacific, Pat Nixon worked for the Office of Price Administration in San Francisco. Richard Nixon returned to the United States in 1945, and for a while the couple lived in Middle River, Maryland. In September 1945 a group of southern California Republicans recruited Richard Nixon to run for Congress, and the Nixons moved back to Whittier in January 1946. Even though she was a new mother, Pat Nixon worked as her husband's office manager on the campaign, the beginning of her career as a political wife. Richard Nixon won the election, and the family moved to Washington, D.C., in early 1947.

Richard Nixon's political star rose quickly. He won election to the Senate in 1950 and to the vice presidency in 1952 and 1956. More than most politicians of his day, Richard Nixon showcased his family as part of an effort to project a wholesome image. Pat Nixon frequently appeared by her husband's side, and she granted interviews to women's and general-interest magazines. In 1952 she contributed a ghostwritten article to the *Saturday Evening Post* about her husband, "I Say He's a Wonderful Guy."

In 1950 Richard Nixon used Pat Nixon's traditional, conservative profile as a foil to that of his opponent, the liberal congresswoman Helen Gahagan Douglas, an outspoken and ambitious career woman. He invoked Pat in his famous "Checkers" speech, which he delivered in September 1952 after allegations of financial impropriety threatened to force his withdrawal as General Dwight D. Eisenhower's vice presidential running mate. Protesting that he had not misspent campaign funds, Richard Nixon said: "Pat doesn't have a mink coat. But she does have a respectable Republican cloth coat. And I always tell her that she'd look good in anything." Liberal sophisticates mocked the performance, but Republican voters identified with what seemed an upstanding young couple.

During Richard Nixon's vice presidential years, Pat Nixon became known as the epitome of the reliable suburban housewife: attractive, five feet, five inches tall, with a slim figure and strawberry blonde hair, but decidedly unstylish with a simple, ordinary wardrobe. Unlike her controversial husband, she was unfailingly soft-spoken and restrained with her opinions, especially political ones, a trait she continued to exhibit as first lady. Conservative women's groups awarded her honors, including Outstanding Homemaker of the Year in 1953, Mother of the Year in 1955, and the Nation's Ideal Wife in 1957.

Privately Pat Nixon was not happy with her husband's high political profile. Over the years she urged him not to run for office, but he did not heed her wishes. She invariably swallowed her reservations and threw herself into his campaigns. Richard Nixon ran unsuccessfully for president in 1960 and for governor of California in 1962, and after each loss she harbored relief as well as disappointment. "Politics was not what I would have chosen for him," she once told an interviewer.

After spending the mid-1960s practicing law in New York City, Richard Nixon was elected president of the United States in November 1968. As first lady Pat Nixon assumed a traditional role, receiving coverage from newspaper society pages for redecorating the White House living quarters and entertaining guests. She meticulously carried out social duties, such as writing thank-you notes. She protected her privacy, declining offers to write a syndicated column and requests that she hold regular press conferences.

Pat Nixon did undertake some public projects, but they were always uncontroversial. In 1969 she encouraged Americans to volunteer to aid the needy, and in 1971 she helped promote new federal parks. More unconventionally, she traveled extensively, accompanying the president on his breakthrough trips to China and the Soviet Union. Pat also traveled without her husband. She attended the inaugurations of several world leaders and visited Peru in 1970 in the wake of an earthquake. Every year from 1968 to 1971 the Gallup poll found her one of the nation's most admired women. Richard Nixon continued to use his family to show the public, especially the so-called "Middle Americans," whose votes he fervently pursued, that he possessed all-American values.

As women's liberation swept the nation, Pat Nixon became a target of criticism. To many observers she seemed to have submerged her interests to her husband's career. Feminists derided her as "Plastic Pat." To the dismay of liberals, she could be dismissive of feminism, stating at one point that "women have equal rights if they want to exercise them."

The Nixons' marital relationship also seemed anachronistic during the sexual revolution. Both maintained proper, almost Victorian demeanors, and they kept separate bedrooms in the White House, even when television couples no longer did so. They never showed much tenderness toward each other in public. After his second inauguration as president, Richard Nixon wrote in his diary that he was pleased that "Pat did not kiss me" and that, on an occasion such as the inaugural ceremony, "displays of affection" were not "quite fit."

Starting in 1973, after Richard Nixon's reelection as president, the Watergate crisis consumed his presidency. The revelation of presidential burglaries, cover-ups, and other abuses of power threw his future into doubt. Pat Nixon stood steadfastly by her husband, publicly defending him when confronted. Although she had not known that the president had recorded his White House conversations, when she learned of the taping she thought he should destroy the tapes, viewing them as private, "like love letters." Still the crisis distressed Pat Nixon greatly. She withdrew into solitude, eating less and less. Until the end she did not believe her husband should resign the presidency. When in August 1974 her daughter Julie Nixon Eisenhower told her that Richard Nixon had decided to step down, Pat questioned, "But why?"

On 9 August 1974 the nation watched President Richard Nixon deliver his resignation speech and then join hands with Pat Nixon before leaving the White House for the last time. They repaired to San Clemente, California, where they kept a low profile for several years. Soon Richard Nixon began his campaign to revive his reputation for history, efforts in which Pat played little overt role.

Pat Nixon suffered various health problems after leaving the limelight. In 1976 she suffered a major stroke, which, it was said, occurred while reading Bob Woodward and Carl Bernstein's book about the end of the Nixon presidency, *The Final Days* (1976). Among the book's revelations were reports from people close to the Nixons that they maintained for many years a sexless and to some degree loveless marriage. In 1979 the Nixons began the process of selling their home in San Clemente and began a move to New York City that was completed in 1980. In 1981 the Nixons again moved, this time to Saddle River, New Jersey. In 1983 Pat had a second stroke. A heavy smoker who refrained from lighting up in public, she also was plagued by emphysema. She died of lung cancer on the morning of 22 June 1993 in her home in Park Ridge. She is buried at the Richard M. Nixon Library and Birthplace in her husband's native Yorba Linda, California.

Pat Nixon was perhaps the last of the old-style first ladies, seen by the public as mainly a wife, mother, and social figure without influence on the president's politics or policies. Despite the criticism she received from feminists for hewing to this role, it generally kept her free of the scandal and hostility that plagued her husband. To her death she remained a symbol of both traditional domesticity and long-standing, silent suffering.

★

Julie Nixon Eisenhower, *Pat Nixon: The Untold Story* (1986), written by Nixon's daughter, is the most thorough work on Nixon although clearly told from a loyal and loving daughter's point of view. Lester David, *The Lonely Lady of San Clemente: The Story of Pat Nixon* (1978), is short and breezy. Many biographies of Richard Nixon contain biographical information on Pat as well. Roger Morris, *Richard Milhous Nixon: The Rise of an American Politician* (1990), excellent and thorough if quite critical of Richard Nixon, covers only through 1952. Stephen E. Ambrose's three-volume *Nixon* (1987–1991) is reliable though more encyclopedic than analytical. Bob Woodward and Carl Bernstein, *The Final Days* (1976), has some information on Pat Nixon's last year in the White House. Two good works on presidential couples that include lengthy sections on the Nixons are Gil Troy, *Affairs of State* (1997), and Carl Sferrazza Anthony, *First Ladies: The Saga of the Presidents' Wives and Their Power* (1990). Obituaries are in the *Los Angeles Times* (23 June 1993), *New York Times* (23 June 1993), and *Washington Post* (23 June 1993).

DAVID GREENBERG

P-Q

PAGE, Ruth Marian (*b.* 22 March 1899 in Indianapolis, Indiana; *d.* 7 April 1991 in Chicago, Illinois), ballet dancer, choreographer, and ballet company director whose dancing combined cosmopolitan flair with innovative technique.

Page was the second of three children born to Lafayette Page, a surgeon, and Marian Heinly, a pianist. As a young child, she began taking dancing lessons with Anna Stanton in Indianapolis. In her family home, Page met noted musical and artistic houseguests and entertained family visitors with "fancy dancing" (dancing with a scarf). Her first exposure to classical ballet was during high school, when her mother took her to New York City for one week of classes at Elizavetta Menzeli's "Knickerbocker Conservatory, School of Ballet, Fancy, Stage and Society Dancing." Young Page was inquisitive and serious, as revealed in her journals. In 1915 she entered Tudor Hall School for Girls in Indianapolis, where she wrote essays on topics such as Serge Oukrainsky and Serge Diaghilev's Ballets Russes; she graduated in 1916.

After visiting Page's home, the Russian ballerina Anna Pavlova recommended Page for classical training with her troupe. Pavlova sent Jan Zalewski, a Polish dancer, to Indianapolis to give the teenager daily lessons. Page described a "communication gap" with Zalewski, perhaps the result of Page's ignorance at that time of French ballet terms. In July 1915 she continued instruction with Zalewski in Chicago at Midway Gardens. From 1918 to 1919 Page, accompanied by her mother, traveled with the Anna Pavlova Company on a South American tour. Page wrote her friend Eleanor Shaler, who had considered a dancing career, "Are you glad you went to college (Vassar), or do you think you would have rather gone on dancing, and 'gone to perdition' with me?"

In 1917 Page entered Miss Williams' and Miss McClellan's French School for Girls, a finishing school in New York City, and resumed courses in 1919, following the Pavlova tour. She studied ballet with Adolph Bolm, learning his specialty—character dance—which became instrumental to Page's career. He encouraged her to create her first choreographies, stressing movement. In 1917 she danced in Bolm's "poem-choreographic," "Falling Leaves," in Victor Herbert's revue *Miss 1917* at the Century Theatre in New York City. She then starred in John Alden Carpenter's *The Birthday of the Infanta* in 1919 at the Chicago Grand Opera Company.

When Page went to London to appear at the Coliseum in 1920, Bolm insisted she study with Maestro Enrico Cecchetti, an eminent Italian professor of ballet and master of mime. Her mother did not approve of Cecchetti's requirement that female pupils kiss him on the cheek before and after each class, fearing that her daughter would contract germs. Page mused, "I survived."

On 6 December 1921, Page performed "The Girl with the Flaxen Hair" at the Apollo Theatre in New York City. In March 1922 Page's career turned to the Broadway stage

Ruth Page, 1982. Nancy R. Schiff/Archive Photos

with Bolm in *Danse Macabre,* the first danse-film (cinema in the dance genre) with synchronized sound, which premiered at the Rialto Theatre. She was première danseuse in Irving Berlin's *Music Box Revue* in New York City from 1922 to 1923, and on the show's U.S. tour from 1923 to 1924.

In December 1923 Page first met lawyer Thomas Hart Fisher for tea at the Russian Tea Room in Chicago. They married on 8 February 1925, and Fisher was Page's confidant and business manager until his death in 1969. They had no children. During their honeymoon in Paris, Page, missing dance, left for Monte Carlo to audition for Diaghilev's Ballets Russes. Diaghilev arrived late, and Page worried his delay might affect her warm-up. However, she danced well enough to be accepted as the first American woman in the Ballets Russes company. Carefree, Page wrote Fisher,

> Diaghilev is still furious, he found out about Balanchine's teaching us a dance, and he thinks it was awful of me . . . I'm afraid Diag. will be my enemy for life, but I really don't care much—I never would have dreamed that it would have made the slightest difference to him.

Page contended that Diaghilev resented Balanchine teaching her a dance, as well as using his studio and pianist. The Diaghilev-Page relationship ended in April.

Once back in Chicago, Page resumed dancing for Bolm in rehearsals for a role she had desired, the Queen of Shemakhan in *Le coq d'or,* performed at the Teatro Colón in Buenos Aires, Argentina. In 1925 and 1926 she performed numerous roles as principal dancer for Bolm in the newly established Chicago Allied Arts. Page reflected contemporary life in her choreography and dancing as the Flapper in *The Flapper and the Quarterback* in 1925.

In 1928 Page danced at the Japanese emperor Hirohito's coronation. In subsequent years, her career in Chicago demonstrated her intuitive creativity. She and the Austrian expressionist dancer Harald Kreutzberg formed an American and Far East tour from 1933 to 1934. Beginning in 1935, for two decades, Page worked with Bentley Stone, her partner and choreographic collaborator. As codirectors of the Dance Section of the Chicago Federal Theatre Project/Work Projects Administration (WPA), they presented Page's most memorable work on an American theme, *Frankie and Johnny,* and formed the Page-Stone Ballet in 1938. Page was ballet director and principal dancer for the Ravinia Opera in Highland Park, Illinois, in 1926; the Metropolitan Opera in New York in 1927; the Chicago Civic Opera from 1934 to 1936; and the Chicago Opera in 1941 and 1942. She was the choreographer and ballet director of the Chicago Lyric Opera from 1954 to 1969 and led an independent ballet company, Ruth Page's Chicago Opera Ballet, from 1956 to 1966. Page celebrated her first year as director of the Lyric Opera with a double-bill presentation of *The Merry Widow* in Chicago and in New York City. Page's "The Nutcracker" ballet, debuted in Chicago in 1965, became an annual holiday event. She directed the Ruth Page Foundation School of the Dance, which continued under Larry Long. She was the artistic director of the

Chicago Ballet from 1974 to 1977 and a guest choreographer for Les Ballets des Champs-Élysées (1948), London's Royal Festival Ballet (1953), and (Leonide Massine's) Ballet Russe de Monte Carlo (1952).

Page was the author of *Page by Page* (1978) and *Class Notes on Dance Classes Around the World, 1915–1980* (1984). She married the French stage designer and director André Delfau in 1983. The recipient of several honorary degrees, Page also received the *Dance Magazine* Award in 1980 and 1990, and the Illinois Gubernatorial Award in 1985. For Ruth Page, dance was life. She remained focused on the art throughout her later years. She continued barre practice and took daily classes into her eighties. True to her art, Page once wrote, "Next to performing, class is the most important thing in a dancer's life." Page died in her home in Chicago of respiratory failure.

★

Page's correspondence, housed in the Dance Collection of the New York Public Library, has been cataloged by her biographer, Andrew Mark Wentink, in "The Ruth Page Collection: An Introduction and Guide to Manuscript Materials through 1970," in *Bulletin of Research in the Humanities*. Page's *Page by Page* (1978), edited and introduced by Wentink, is an honest autobiography. John Martin wrote a personal biography of her life in *Ruth Page: An Intimate Biography* (1977). Page's *Class: Notes on Dance Classes Around the World, 1915–1980* (1984), edited with additional notes by Wentink, provides a record of international dance education, classwork technique, and selected profiles of ballet impresarios, including Adolph Bolm, Enrico Cecchetti, Bentley Stone, Cia Fornaroli Toscanini, and Larry Long. Page describes her assemblage of "*Die Fledermaus* for television" in *Dance Magazine* (Dec. 1986). An obituary is in the *New York Times* (9 Apr. 1991). Franz Lehar's "*The Merry Widow*" (1983), choreographed by Page, is available on color video, in Louise Spain, ed., *Dance on Camera: A Guide to Dance Films and Videos* (1998).

SANDRA REDMOND PETERS

PAPP, Joseph (*b.* 22 June 1921 in New York City; *d.* 31 October 1991 in New York City), Pulitzer Prize-winning producer, theatrical director, and founder and artistic director of the New York Shakespeare Festival.

Papp was born Josef Yosl Papirofsky in the Williamsburg section of Brooklyn, New York. He was the second of four children born to Samuel Papirofsky, a trunk maker from Poland, and Yetta Miritch, a seamstress from Lithuania. His parents were poor Jewish immigrants, and he was raised during the Great Depression. As an enterprising youth, he shined shoes, sold penny pretzels, shoveled snow, and plucked chickens, working at many odd jobs to add to the family's resources. While attending Brooklyn's Eastern District High School, he served as editor of the student

Joseph Papp during an interview in his office, *c.* 1981. BERNARD GOTFRYD/ARCHIVE PHOTOS

newspaper, led the debate team, sang in the glee club, and performed in school plays, while working nights at a laundry. He acknowledged the influence of his high school English teacher Miss McKay, who read from *Julius Caesar,* and the social climate of the 1930s (Papp was a communist from the age of fifteen to his early thirties) in having contributed to his desire to create a free Shakespeare theater. He graduated from high school in 1938. Plans for college never materialized.

In 1942 Papp enlisted in the U.S. Navy, where he was first assigned to an aircraft carrier with the mission of depth-bombing German submarines. In 1945 he was assigned to Special Services, an entertainment unit that flew from island to island in the Pacific performing for the troops. Following his discharge from the service with the rank of chief petty officer, he was an actor and managing director of the Actors' Laboratory Theater in Hollywood, where he learned the politics of nonprofit theater. In 1950, after the school had been closed under pressure from the House Un-American Activities Committee, Papp toured as an assistant stage manager with the National Company production of Arthur Miller's *Death of a Salesman.* Returning to New York City in 1952, he was a director of the Equity Library Theater, and from 1952 to 1960 a stage manager for CBS television's live drama anthology *Studio One* and the celebrity game show *I've Got a Secret.* When called before the House Un-American Activities Committee in 1958, he invoked the Fifth Amendment and was fired by CBS, but he was reinstated after an arbitration ruling.

While working at CBS in 1953 Papp organized the Elizabethan Workshop, later renamed the Shakespeare Workshop, in a church on Manhattan's Lower East Side with a group of enthusiastic actors who had a passion for the English classics. In 1954 he was granted a provisional charter for a nonprofit theater, one that would encourage and cultivate interest in the works of Shakespeare and the Elizabethans; the proposal included building a theater styled after an Elizabethan playhouse. In 1955 he produced *Much Ado About Nothing, As You Like It, Romeo and Juliet, Two Gentlemen of Verona,* and *Cymbeline.* He moved outdoors to the East River Park amphitheater in 1956 with productions of *Julius Caesar* and *The Taming of the Shrew.* In 1957 he debuted his Mobile Theater with a presentation of *Romeo and Juliet,* mounted on a thirty-five-foot platform trailer truck. The Mobile Theater traveled from one New York City park to another; and when the truck broke down on the shores of Turtle Pond in Central Park, he left it there, staging *Romeo and Juliet, Two Gentleman of Verona,* and *Macbeth* that same season. Thus began the tradition of free Shakespeare in Central Park.

That fall *Macbeth* was transferred indoors to the Heckscher Theater, at 104th Street and Fifth Avenue, which became the indoor home of the Shakespeare Workshop through 1964, as Papp continued to alternate his stages according to the season. In the summer of 1964 a new and specially built Mobile Theater toured New York City's five boroughs, presenting *A Midsummer Night's Dream* in thirty-nine parks and playgrounds. A Spanish-language Mobile Theater extended his free theater outreach to yet another audience with a tour of *La zapatera prodigiosa* (The Shoemaker's Prodigious Wife) and *El retablillo de don Cristóbal* (Puppet Theater of Don Cristóbal), two plays by Federico García Lorca. As a producer, much of Papp's time was spent fundraising from foundations, private individuals, and city officials. And long before anyone was using expressions like "multiculturalism" or "nontraditional casting," he was sending multicultural productions on summertime tours of the New York City neighborhoods.

In 1957 Papp received his first Obie Award "for bringing Shakespeare back to life in a small Eastside playhouse with virtually no budget." In 1958 he received a Tony Award for distinguished service to the theater. In 1959 Papp feuded successfully with the New York City parks commissioner Robert Moses, who wanted to put an end to free admission to performances in the park. In 1962, with the granting of a permanent charter, the Shakespeare Workshop officially changed its name to the New York Shakespeare Festival (NYSF), whereupon Papp left CBS to devote full time to his enterprise.

In 1962 the NYSF moved into the Delacorte Theater, a permanent open-air amphitheater at the same site on Turtle Pond, opening with *The Merchant of Venice* with George C. Scott in the role of Shylock. During the same season Papp directed *King Lear,* and in 1963 *Antony and Cleopatra,* starring Colleen Dewhurst, and *Twelfth Night.* He continued to direct on occasion: *Twelfth Night* (1958, 1963, 1969), *Hamlet* (1964, 1967, 1968, 1983), David Rabe's *In the Boom Boom Room* (1973), Thomas Babe's *Buried Inside Extra* (1983), and *Measure for Measure* (1985). He also directed the CBS television productions of *The Merchant of Venice* (1962), *Antony and Cleopatra* (1963), and *Hamlet* (1964).

In 1967 Papp acquired and renovated the landmark Astor Place Library at 425 Lafayette Street, turning the site into the year-round headquarters for the New York Shakespeare Public Theater—with offices, rehearsal facilities, and a six-theater complex space for the presentation of winter repertory programs of contemporary plays. The first theater to open was the Anspacher, ushering in the 1967 season with a production of the rock musical *Hair.* As the initial offering in a subscription series, the show signaled Papp's commitment to new playwrights and contemporary plays of social significance. The second offering was a modern-dress version of *Hamlet,* an experimental theater piece with rock interludes, which Papp directed. Though both productions met with cries of indignation, Papp announced that he was not interested in middle-class Broadway audiences, but in youthful audiences concerned with contemporary issues.

Charles Gordone's *No Place to Be Somebody* premiered at the Public Theater in 1969 and won the Pulitzer Prize for drama in 1970, bringing recognition to the NYSF and to a minority playwright. In 1973 a Pulitzer was awarded to Jason Miller's *That Championship Season,* produced at the Public Theater in 1972. And after nearly two seasons of superior productions, critics concluded that the New York Shakespeare Festival had become the most powerful and artistically the most promising theater of the day.

In 1972 *That Championship Season* (which also won that year's Tony for most promising playwright) was transferred to Broadway to join productions that had been launched by the NYSF in 1971: *Two Gentlemen of Verona* (which won a Tony for best musical) and *Sticks and Bones* (which won a Tony for best play). When *Much Ado About Nothing* opened in November 1972, Papp boasted four commercial ventures on the Great White Way. Although he never produced a show directly for Broadway, seventeen NYSF plays were transferred, including *For Colored Girls Who Have Considered Suicide when the Rainbow Is Enuf* (1975), *The Pirates of Penzance* (1981), *The Mystery of Edwin Drood* (1985), *Cuba and His Teddy Bear* (1986), *and Serious Money* (1988). *A Chorus Line* (1975) ran for fifteen years, providing a regular subsidy and long-term relief from financial stress.

In 1973 Papp broadened his institutional base, taking over the management of the prestigious Lincoln Center Theater, comprising the Vivian Beaumont and the Forum (later renamed the Mitzi E. Newhouse) theaters, where his policy of presenting new works by American playwrights alienated repertory theater subscribers. He opened his first season with David Rabe's *In the Boom Boom Room* (1973) but was forced to turn to the classics and box-office stars midway through the second season. Henrik Ibsen's *A Doll's House* (1975) with Liv Ullmann was the first such production to sell out. Plagued with a never-ending struggle to cover the annual deficit, he left in 1977 to devote himself to the development of new plays and television productions at the Public Theater.

In 1982 he introduced the Festival Latino de Nueva York; in 1983 he initiated an exchange with London's Royal Court Theatre; and in 1986 he developed the short-lived Belasco Project to present Shakespeare on Broadway for schoolchildren. In 1987 he inaugurated the Shakespeare Marathon, a celebration of his lifelong passion for the Bard, with a production of *A Midsummer Night's Dream* at the Anspacher. The goal of the marathon was to mount productions of all the plays of Shakespeare within a time frame that Papp expected to be six years; he did not live to see the project to the end. He appointed JoAnne Akalaitis to succeed him, shortly before losing a four-year battle with prostate cancer on 31 October 1991. He died at his home in Greenwich Village and was buried on Staten Island, New York, at Baron Hirsch Cemetery, one of the oldest Jewish cemeteries in the Northeast. The New York Shakespeare Public Theater was rededicated to Papp on 23 April 1992 (the date believed to be Shakespeare's birthday) and renamed the Joseph Papp Public Theater.

Among his many awards, Papp received a Special Tony in 1976 for distinguished achievement in the theater; Equity's Paul Robeson Award in 1977; and in 1988, as first recipient, the William Shakespeare Award for Classical Theater from the Folger Shakespeare Library. In 1990 he was awarded a Tony for his courageous stand against censorship, after he turned down $323,000 from the National Endowment for the Arts by refusing to sign an obscenity clause issued in the wake of the controversial Robert Mapplethorpe exhibition, which had been funded by the NEA.

Described as a man of boundless energy, Papp was known for his volatile temper, his occasional intimidation of playwrights, and bullying of directors, but praised as a hands-on powerhouse of a producer and play-doctor; a dynamic force in the renaissance of New York theater; and one of the most influential and productive men in contemporary American theater. He was married four times and had five children. His first three marriages ended in divorce. His first marriage was to Betty Ball in 1941; the couple had one daughter. His second marriage was to Sylvia Ostroff, with whom he had one son. His third was to Peggy Bennion (1951), with whom he had one daughter and one son (who died of AIDS in 1991). In 1976 he married Gail Merrifield, who survived him at his death. Papp

also had one daughter with Irene Ball, whom he met while in the service.

In his forty years of service to the nonprofit NYSF, Papp distinguished himself as a producer, director, theatrical innovator, scholar, advocate of controversy, and champion of the arts. He was one of the most important forces in the theater of his day. During his lifetime, he produced some 450 plays and directed more than 40. Under the auspices of the Public Theater, he nurtured minority playwrights such as Adrienne Kennedy, Alice Childress, Charles Gordone, Ntozake Shange, Derek Walcott, Aishah Rahman, and David Henry Hwang as well as others among theater's greatest contemporary playwrights, including Václav Havel, David Mamet, David Rabe, Caryl Churchill, John Guare, Sam Shepard, David Hare, and Larry Kramer. Papp's productions provided opportunities for fledgling actors, among them George C. Scott, Colleen Dewhurst, James Earl Jones, Al Pacino, Kevin Kline, Raul Julia, Meryl Streep, and William Hurt; and featured New York's first female Hamlet (Diane Venora, 1984) in modern times, under his direction.

★

The entire New York Shakespeare Festival Newsclippings Collection (thirty-two reels of microfilm) was donated after Papp's death to the Billy Rose Theatre Collection at the New York Public Library for the Performing Arts, Lincoln Center. Helen Epstein's official biography, *Joe Papp: An American Life* (1994), provides details to journalistic literature, such as the annotated bibliographies: Barbara Lee Horn, *Joseph Papp: A Bio-Bibliography* (1992), and Brenda Coven and Christine E. King, *Joseph Papp and the New York Shakespeare Festival: An Annotated Bibliography* (1988). Stuart W. Little, *Enter Joseph Papp: In Search of a New American Theater* (1974), examines Papp's many roles, as producer, director, fund-raiser, and public champion of the arts; and the principles that enabled the festival to become a success. An obituary is in the *New York Times* (1 Nov. 1991).

BARBARA LEE HORN

PARKS, Bert (*b.* 30 December 1914 in Atlanta, Georgia; *d.* 2 February 1992 in La Jolla, California), radio and television game show host and actor best known as the master of ceremonies for the *Miss America Pageant*.

Parks was born Bert Jacobson, the younger of two sons of Aaron Jacobson, a merchant, and Hattie Spiegel. Between 1926 and 1932 young Bert attended Marist College, a prep school run by a Catholic order. His introduction to the entertainment world came while he was still in school through local singing gigs, which led him to change his name. He landed his first broadcasting job at the age of sixteen with WGST in Atlanta, earning $7 a week. By the time he left the station two years later he had graduated to

Bert Parks. CBS Photo Archive/Archive Photos

was discharged from the army in 1945. By this time he had risen to the rank of captain on the staff of General Joseph "Vinegar Joe" Stillwell and had won a Bronze Star. Settling in suburban Greenwich, Connecticut, Parks and his wife had three children.

In 1946 Parks became the host of the CBS radio quiz show *Break the Bank,* and he added *Stop the Music* in 1948. The latter show was so popular that it beat the perennial National Broadcasting Company (NBC) favorite, the *Fred Allen Show,* in its time slot. In 1949 the Federal Communications Commission (FCC), upset about what it considered the questionable morality of giveaway shows, started an investigation that for a time threatened to drive them from the air. But the investigation soon blew over, much to the chagrin of Fred Allen, who lamented the rise of "scavengers" over "entertainers." Parks took the shows on to television, where he had a phenomenal run during the first half of the 1950s in *Balance Your Budget* and *Double or Nothing.* Parks appeared on radio through the American Broadcasting Corporation and on television with the Canadian Broadcasting Corporation. The key to the success of these shows was not the game itself, which was rudimentary in the extreme, or the prize money, which was meager by later standards, or the stage presence of the contestants, who were stolidly middle class and, by all appearances, in awe of the new medium of television. Rather the shows' appeal lay with the looks and personalities of the emcees.

Darkly handsome, his greased-down hair suggesting the Hollywood stereotype of a Latin lover, Parks had what the *TV Guide* critic John Crosby called a "smile to read by," all of which added a sense of glamour and excitement to the rather drab stage sets of the time. Always ebullient, ever solicitous, Parks considered it his job to put his guests at ease, particularly the women. A film of one of the *Break the Bank* programs shows him gushing continually about "how wonderful" it was to be on television. He was in essence a gatekeeper between an old-style Middle America, with its rock-solid Protestant values, and the post–World War II world of consumerism. Ipana toothpaste and Vitalis hair cream were his early sponsors. Parks had no undue modesty about his contribution. As he told the *New York Post* in a 1964 interview, "If I dropped out of a show it was through." He even turned down *The $64,000 Question* in 1955 because he feared the amount of prize money would draw attention away from the host.

In the late 1950s, however, Parks's star as a game show host began to dim. His frenetic style was wearing less well with viewers and advertisers, who now leaned toward a more low-key approach. That and the general disfavor game shows encountered in the wake of the Charles Van Doren scandal (in which it was revealed that some quiz show contestants were given the answers beforehand)

chief announcer and doubled his salary. In 1933 Parks went on to New York City, where, lying about his age, he auditioned for a staff announcer's position at Columbia Broadcasting Corporation (CBS) radio. He was promptly hired and at eighteen became the youngest network announcer in the country. Remaining with CBS until 1939, Parks, in addition to announcing, acted on the radio Western *Bobby Benson.* His big break came with the *Eddie Cantor Show,* in which he served as straight man and occasionally as vocalist in addition to staff announcer. By the close of the 1930s Parks was also emcee for the *Xavier Cugat Show* and announcer for the *Camel Caravan* series.

Love and war added a new dimension to Parks's life. He enlisted as a private in the U.S. Army in 1942, and a year later he married Annette Liebman, a Columbia University student whom he met on a blind date. Soon thereafter he was shipped overseas, where he served as an infantryman in the China-Burma-India theater. For the next two years he was involved in reconnaissance operations establishing underground radio communications behind Japanese lines, including three months in enemy territory operating a wire recorder. Ever the showman, he found time for announcing on the weekly army radio programs. Parks

forced Parks into an unwanted retirement for ten months. He staged a comeback with the more subdued *Bid 'n' Buy* in 1958, followed by two more television shows, *County Fair* and *Masquerade Party,* plus a radio show, *Bert Parks Bandstand*. But by this time Parks had found his lasting claim to fame. In September 1955 he began his long association as host of the *Miss America Pageant*. The pageant had been televised from Atlantic City, New Jersey, for the first time the year before, but in his debut as host Parks introduced the signature song *There She Is,* with which he serenaded the winning contestants through 1979.

Parks's explanation for the pageant's appeal was simple. Frank Deford, in his book *There She Is: The Life and Times of Miss America* (1978), quoted him:

> It's corny. Let's face it. It's corny and it's basic and it's American. But in this sick, sad world a little fairyland is welcome and refreshing. . . . There are a lot of nice people out there beyond the big slick areas—and these are good, straight people for the most part. . . . They have a great longing for normalcy, as so many of us do, Miss America buys them a piece of that dream.

For a quarter of a century Parks's slick homeyness was the one constant presence in the *Miss America Pageant*. His bronzed visage, accentuated by his crisp tuxedo, stood in sharp contrast to the all-American appearances of the contestants, but this enhanced the image of the young women as symbols of small-town innocence. With his rendition of *There She Is,* partly Las Vegas lounge act, partly paean to an idealized version of American womanhood, Parks evoked both sexual desire and avuncular concern, feelings no doubt shared by much of the audience.

By the 1960s Parks was living in Hollywood, Florida, and indulging in his favorite pastimes, boating, swimming, and golfing. Although his salary as emcee never exceeded $18,500, Parks's *Miss America Pageant* connection led to numerous career opportunities. He had no regular television shows after 1962 but instead turned his attention to acting, appearing in the summer circuit tours of *Mr. President* and *Damn Yankees*. He also had television guest star roles in *Burke's Law, Ellery Queen,* and *The Bionic Woman*. But his turn on Broadway in the title role of Meredith Wilson's *The Music Man* in 1960–1961 gave Parks his greatest satisfaction. He appeared in 330 performances to generally positive reviews. *Newsweek* praised him as "expert and thoroughly likeable." Parks considered this chance to act, sing, and dance on stage "the single greatest experience of my life." His role as a city slicker who injects a measure of excitement into a small American town was not really much of a stretch. It was after all a role he had been playing all those years on radio and television, especially in the *Miss America Pageant*.

Despite the phenomenal popularity of the pageant, which placed consistently among the year's top shows in the Nielsen ratings, by the late 1960s its version of the American dream was vigorously challenged. As *Sports Illustrated* noted, feminist critics assailed it for what they considered its "image of sex, virginal prettiness, glory of war, mindless conformity, acceptance of racism, and competitive spirit." It received unwanted publicity when female protesters showed their ire by burning bras on the boardwalk in Atlantic City. The pageant director, Albert A. Marks, tried to make the pageant more contemporary. He allowed "soft rock" in the performance numbers and shortened hemlines for the contestants. The latter drew a wail of protest from Parks, who thought miniskirts made it harder to pay the proper homage to America's queen. As the show's emcee, he bore much of the brunt of the criticism. One writer called him a "high camp figure of dated views and purpose." During the 1970s rumors of Parks's dismissal were heard from time to time, and he had a short stint as television emcee on *Circus!* But not until Parks's sixty-fifth birthday did Marks decide that the personality, age, and image of the emcee required a change. Parks, who learned of his firing from a reporter, was bitterly disappointed, and his firing became a minor cause célèbre. The *Tonight Show* host Johnny Carson launched a "Bring Back Bert" campaign, and a former president of the National Organization of Women offered to assist him in an age discrimination suit.

Parks meanwhile basked in his newfound role of discarded icon. Larry Flynt, editor of *Hustler,* offered him $10,000 to reveal his sexual fantasies, but Parks wisely turned him down. Meanwhile Parks guest starred on television and served as host for a number of lesser pageants, in which he was the center attraction. In 1990 he appeared in the Marlon Brando movie *The Freshman,* spoofing his image as *Miss America* emcee by serenading a Komodo dragon with *There She Is* in the climactic scene. He also belted out a campy version of Bob Dylan's *Maggie's Farm,* an improbable coming together of Middle America and the counterculture that won him rave reviews. His real experience as emcee, however, ended on a sour note. Invited back in 1990 for the seventieth anniversary of the *Miss America Pageant,* he rambled on about how the contestants should be called "ladies" and lost his place while announcing the names of previous winners, a gaffe that was all too evident on national television. It was his last major appearance. Parks died of lung disease on 2 February 1992 in La Jolla, California. At the very least, the normalcy that he had always championed was with him to the end of his days.

★

Segments from Parks's quiz shows and the *Miss America Pageant* are at the New York Museum of Television and Radio. Interesting interviews are in the *New York Post* (6 Sept. 1964) and the *New York Herald Tribune* (22 Feb. 1959). Frank Deford, *There She Is: The Life and Times of Miss America* (1978), provides useful background material on Parks. He is profiled in *Current Biography 1973*. See also A. R. Riverol, *Live from Atlantic City: The History of the Miss America Pageant Before, After, and in Spite of Television* (1992); Sarah Banet-Weiser, *The Most Beautiful Girl in the World: Beauty Pageants and National Identity* (1999); and Ann-Marie Bivans, *Miss America: In Pursuit of the Crown: The Complete Guide to the Miss America Pageant* (1991). Informative articles are in the *New York Herald Tribune* (2 July 1958); the *New York World Telegram and Sun* (2 July 1958); the *New York Sunday News* (18 Feb. 1962); and *Variety* (16 Sept. 1972). Obituaries are in the *New York Times* and the *Los Angeles Times* (both 3 Feb. 1992).

BILL MORALES

PARNIS, Sarah Rosen ("Mollie") (*b.* 18 March 1899? in New York City; *d.* 18 July 1992 in New York City), philanthropist and fashion designer whose designs were worn by several first ladies.

Parnis, the eldest daughter of Austrian immigrants Abraham and Sarah Parnis, grew up on the Lower East Side of Manhattan. Her early years were spent in poverty, and at the age of eight Parnis worked odd jobs to help her parents and four siblings. Her earliest jobs included tutoring English to immigrants for twenty-five cents an hour.

Parnis informally entered the fashion industry when Leonard Livingston asked her out to a football game. Excited about the date, Parnis begged her mother to buy her a dress. After the game Livingston decided they should go dancing and, unaware that Parnis was wearing the only dress she owned, suggested that she go home and change. Undaunted, Parnis went into her room, and by changing the neckline and adding a lace collar and an artificial flower, she turned the dress into a completely new outfit, her first Parnis creation. The couple went dancing that night and continued dating throughout high school. They married in 1930 and had one son.

After graduating from Wadleigh High School, Parnis entered Hunter College and took courses in pre-law. During her sophomore year she found a summer job as an assistant saleswoman at a blouse manufacturer. Parnis enjoyed the position so much she never returned to college, a decision she later regretted. At the age of eighteen, young and eager, she made suggestions to the designers. When the firm opened another department, the designers gave Parnis the opportunity to design blouses. Her next job was at a dress house, where she designed dresses while working in the showroom.

In 1933 Parnis and her husband decided to venture into the fashion industry together. With $10,000 they started

Mollie Parnis, 1964. © BETTMANN/CORBIS

their own partnership named Parnis-Livingston. Although she could not sketch, cut, or drape, Parnis created the designs while Livingston dealt with the finances. The first year of business was a success, and according to Parnis, Parnis-Livingston sold over $1 million in volume. With business faring well, Parnis hired other designers but continued to oversee operations as the fashion director. Parnis-Livingston designs were recognized as fashionable, classic dresses made of superior fabrics for the well-to-do woman. Never a trendsetter, Parnis made dresses that were timeless and could be worn over and over. In fact she encouraged women to avoid fashion fads.

During the 1940s and 1950s Parnis's designs sold at stores such as Bloomingdale's and Bergdorf-Goodman. Parnis-Livingston competed against major fashion designers, including Parnis's sister Jerry Parnis. Mollie Parnis's dresses became so popular that they were known by her name alone. Her designs reached the height of popularity in 1955, when her client, First Lady Mamie Eisenhower, and another woman appeared at a reception wearing the same blue-green silk taffeta Parnis-Livingston evening gown. When asked about the incident, Parnis casually replied: "I do not sell directly to any wearer. Nor do I usually make one of a kind, that's what makes this country a great democracy."

Parnis closed Parnis-Livingston in 1962 after the death of her husband and partner. For three months she was out of the fashion business. When a friend told her that she stood out from other New York widows because she worked, Parnis was motivated to reopen her business, renaming it Mollie Parnis, Incorporated. In 1979 she introduced a cheaper line targeted to the working woman called Mollie Robert after her son, Robert Livingston. Other lines quickly followed, including a "couture" line, which she simply called Mollie Parnis, and her inexpensive line, Mollie Parnis Studio. She attempted to retire in 1984 but quickly returned to work, creating her first loungewear collection at Chevette Lingerie, which was owned by her sister Peggy.

Throughout her career Parnis designed for First Ladies Lady Bird Johnson, Mamie Eisenhower, Pat Nixon, and Betty Ford. Parnis was also known as a great hostess, entertaining members of high society, journalists, and politicians. Her Park Avenue duplex became one of the most popular salons in New York City, renowned for her election night parties. Sadly the parties ended for Parnis in 1979, when her son, Robert, died.

A noted designer and art collector, Parnis was also known for her philanthropic activities. She donated money to fashion schools and founded the Council of Fashion Designers of America. A 1967 visit to Jerusalem after the Six-Day War inspired Parnis to start a foundation to clean up the streets of Jerusalem. She expressed her idea to the mayor of Jerusalem, Teddy Kollek, and soon the successful project was implemented. After Parnis told the New York City mayor John Lindsay about the Jerusalem project, Lindsay appointed her as the chair of the Dress Your Neighborhood project in New York City. Parnis even had an office in city hall. Each year the project awards $50,000 to underprivileged neighborhood organizations that have improved their surroundings.

Despite her success, Parnis regretted her decision not to finish college. She once lamented that she wished she had become a journalist. As a tribute to the memory of her son, Robert, who also shared her love for journalism, she founded the Livingston Journalism Award in 1980. The Livingston award is a cash prize given to journalists under the age of thirty-five for outstanding achievement in print, broadcast, and news media reporting. Parnis died of congestive heart failure.

Throughout her life Parnis demonstrated that hard work, discipline, and courage lead to achievement. As a young woman with limited means, she knocked down barriers as an entrepreneur in an era when few women appeared in the workplace. With a shrewd business sense and an astute understanding of fashion, she created an empire with her husband and expanded it after his death. Although she became a member of high society and mingled with the wealthy, she never forgot her modest beginnings. An entrepreneur, designer, and philanthropist, Parnis redefined fashion and the role of women.

★

Parnis's accomplishments in fashion and her philanthropic activities are discussed in *Current Biography 1956* (1957). Marylin Bender, *The Beautiful People* (1967); Barbra Walz and Bernadine Morris, *The Fashion Makers* (1978); Barbaralee Diamonstein, *Fashion: The Inside Story* (1985); Colin McDowell, *McDowell's Directory of Twentieth Century Fashion* (1987); and Elinor Slater and Robert Slater, *Great Jewish Women* (1994). Obituaries are in the *New York Times* (19 July 1992), the *Wall Street Journal* (20 July 1992), and *Time* (3 Aug. 1992).

SABINE LOUISSAINT

PARSONS, James Benton (*b*. 13 August 1911 in Kansas City, Missouri; *d*. 19 June 1993 in Chicago, Illinois), U.S. District Court judge, Northern District of Illinois from 1961 to 1993 and the first African American appointed to an Article III (life tenure) U.S. District Court.

Parsons, the son of James Benton Parsons and Maggie V. Mason, found the rhythm of his life through his parents' professions. His father, an evangelist with the Disciples of Christ Church, traveled extensively, moving the family, including his three siblings, around the Midwest plains until settling finally in Decatur, Illinois. Parsons's mother, a teacher, composer, and musician, influenced her son's lifelong love of music. In Decatur, Parsons played out his secondary education studying piano and eventually extended his talents to the organ, French horn, trumpet, and cello.

After high school Parsons worked at the Decatur *Herald Review* to finance his education at Millikin University. He received his B.A. in political science from Millikin in 1934. Parsons also continued his musical studies at the Conservatory at Millikin University. Unable to afford law school after his graduation, he accepted a position at Lincoln University in Jefferson City, Missouri, where he taught classes in political science and later headed the music department from 1938 to 1940. He then taught music at Bennett College (a women's institution) and at a public school in North Carolina. Parsons continued his musical career when he enlisted in the U.S. Navy in 1942, and he served as a bandmaster for a black navy band that entertained troops in the Pacific during World War II. He received his master's degree in political science from the University of Chicago in 1946. In 1949 he earned his J.D. from the University of Chicago Law School.

James Benton Parsons, 1961. AP/WIDE WORLD PHOTOS

Upon receiving his degree and passing the bar, Parsons became a partner in the law firm Gassaway, Cross, Turner and Parsons. Shortly thereafter, Parsons became an assistant corporation counsel for the city of Chicago. In 1951 he accepted a position as an assistant U.S. Attorney for Northern Illinois. During his tenure with the U.S. Attorney's office, Parsons worked in the Criminal Division investigating and trying draft dodgers and conscientious objectors. Among his selective service cases was one involving the failure of the son of Elijah Mohammed, the leader of the Church of Islam (Black Muslims), to register with Selective Service. Parsons made a deal with Elijah Mohammed that he would not prosecute his son and would recommend to the Selective Service board that the members of the Church of Islam be allowed to apply for religious deferments. By that evening more than 1,500 draft dodgers had registered.

On Christmas Eve, 1952, Parsons married Amy Margaret Maxwell. They later adopted a son. In 1960 Parsons ran as a Democrat and was elected judge for the old Superior Court of Cook County, Illinois. A year later President John F. Kennedy appointed Parsons to the U.S. District Court, Northern District of Illinois. Nominated on 10 August 1961, he received his commission on 30 August 1961, thus becoming the first African American with a life-tenure federal judgeship. While on the bench, Parsons was a strong proponent of individual rights and liberties. In 1969, in the case of *Miller* v. *Gillis,* Parsons upheld the right of students to "present themselves physically to the world in a manner of their own individual choice" and struck down a school hair and dress code as a violation of the Equal Protection Clause of the U.S. Constitution. The next year, in *United States* v. *Plasch*, Parsons sparked controversy when he ordered striking air traffic controllers back to work, but temporarily prohibited the FAA from taking any disciplinary action against the controllers. Although the U.S. Court of Appeals upheld his order, other appellate courts struck down similar orders.

Parsons served as Chief Judge of the U.S. District Court, Northern District of Illinois from 1975 until 1981, when he took senior status, a form of semiretirement. During this time Parsons continued to hear cases and again stood up for the rights of ordinary citizens when he upheld a Chicago Ordinance known as the Tenant's Bill of Rights in *Chicago Board of Realtors* v. *Chicago* (1987). Calling the ordinance "harsh and revolutionary," he still upheld it on the grounds that constitutionally it was a reasonable attempt by the city to promote the health, safety, and welfare of its citizens. In 1988 Parsons dealt with the question of whether the Chicago Public Building Commission could prohibit the display of a crèche and a menorah on the Daley Center Plaza. In this case, *Grutzmacher* v. *Public Building Commission of Chicago* (1988), Parsons held that the Daley Center Plaza was a traditional public forum and the Commission could not exclude these displays simply because they were religious expressions.

Parsons also engaged in political and advisory work during his career. President Lyndon Johnson appointed him to serve on a Presidential Crime Commission. He was also a member of the Illinois Commission on Education for Law and Justice of the Illinois Board of Education, and a member of the Federal, National, American, and Cook County Bar Associations. Parsons also served on the advisory boards of the Boy Scouts of America, the Illinois Masonic Hospital, and the Citizenship Council of Metropolitan Chicago. He founded and was honorary chair of the Chicago Conference on Religion and Race. In 1992 Parsons stepped down from the bench and, after a lengthy illness, he died in Chicago on 19 June 1993.

Parsons's appointment as the first African American U.S. District Court judge is only part of his significance in American life. From a young age Parsons confronted and challenged racism. He quit his first job as a waiter when his boss spoke to him in racist terms, and he and his college friends enlisted in the armed forces during World War II as a challenge to the navy to make them officers. While on the bench he sparked controversy with his unusual methods, especially his habit of taking his court (staff, lawyers, and jurors) to the site of the actual dispute. Ideologically, he was a supporter of individual rights over the power of government, a fact that resulted in a high reversal rate in his later years as the appellate courts became weighted with conservative judges. To the end he was a firm believer in democracy and due process.

★

Judge Parsons's papers are available at the National Archives and Records Center in Chicago, Illinois. An interesting, if rambling resource on Parsons's life and career is *The Unfinished Oral History of District Judge James Benton Parsons,* Collins T. Fitzpatrick, Interviewer (May 1996), which is available at the William J. Campbell Library of the U.S. Courts, Chicago. An obituary is in the *New York Times* (22 June 1993).

KATE GREENE

PASTERNAK, Joseph Herman ("Joe") (*b.* 19 September 1901 in Szilágy-Somlyó, Hungary; *d.* 13 September 1991 in Beverly Hills, California), film producer whose pictures combined a romantic vision of life with glossy production values and a substantial amount of classical music.

Pasternak was the middle son in a family of nine children born to Samuel Pasternak, shammes, or sexton, of the synagogue in Szilágy-Somlyó, and Roza Janovitz, a homemaker. After attending the village school Pasternak supplemented the family income through numerous entrepreneurial schemes, and while his father served in World War I, Pasternak assumed his father's duties at the synagogue.

In 1921, with the support of an uncle in the United States, he emigrated to Philadelphia, where he worked in a belt factory. Moving to New York City, he found better pay as a cafeteria busboy. He gave extra portions to theater ushers, who in turn gave him free admission to movies.

Joe Pasternak, 1964. AP/WIDE WORLD PHOTOS

Pasternak's growing love for films led him to invest his savings in a sham course in becoming a movie star. In 1923 he took his "diploma" to Paramount's Astoria studio in the borough of Queens in New York City, but he could find work only as a dishwasher in the studio canteen. However, he became personal waiter to prominent stars and directors. Given a chance to act, Pasternak failed; but the director Allan Dwan made him his third assistant director.

In 1926, despite promotion to first assistant director, Pasternak lost his job when Paramount began closing the Astoria facility. By this time, however, he had become a naturalized U.S. citizen, and undeterred, he set out to find film work in California.

After several months of unemployment, Pasternak and a partner shot a shoestring two-reel comedy, which he himself directed. *Help Yourself,* about a well-meaning busboy, was technically amateurish; but it attracted the interest of the director Wesley Ruggles, who made Pasternak his assistant at Universal Pictures.

In 1928 Carl Laemmle, head of Universal, dispatched Pasternak to Germany, where he worked with Paul Kohner in overseeing the studio's European productions. From assistant director in Hollywood he became a producer in Berlin, and from 1929 to 1936 he made at least thirteen pictures, mostly light romantic comedies with music. Among the most successful were *Fraülein Paprika* (1931) and *Pardon, Tévedten! (Scandal in Budapest,* 1933), both with the Hungarian actress Franciska Gaál.

On 22 February 1931 Pasternak married his secretary, Margaret Fladder (also spelled Fladez), the daughter of a German-American film exhibitor in Berlin. They had no children.

The burning of the Reichstag in Berlin in 1933 led Pasternak to move production first to Vienna and later to Budapest. In 1936, when Universal shut down European filming, he returned to the United States, bringing with him the director Hermann Kosterlitz (Henry Koster). Four of his brothers and sisters accompanied him, but Pasternak's father and other family members were unwilling to leave and later died in the Holocaust.

Pasternak and Koster arrived in New York on 24 February 1936; on 14 March, Carl Laemmle lost control of Universal Pictures. In Hollywood the new management, facing insolvency, sought to dissolve its contracts with Pasternak and Koster. By sheer perseverance the two forced the company to let them make one film. The picture was *Three Smart Girls* (1936) with Deanna Durbin. Its success—and that of the nine other Durbin-Pasternak films—saved the studio from financial collapse.

While producing Durbin's second film, *One Hundred Men and a Girl* (1937), Pasternak again fought the studio, this time about including long interludes of classical music conducted by Leopold Stokowski, whom the studio regarded as "box office poison." Although the film was a success, the strain of production contributed to Pasternak's divorce from Margaret on 21 July 1937.

In 1938 Pasternak contacted Marlene Dietrich, whom he had met in Berlin. Although Dietrich had been declared "box office poison," Pasternak saw her potential for comedy and persuaded her to take the role of a saloon-keeper in the western *Destry Rides Again* (1939) with James Stewart. The film's popularity reignited Dietrich's career and led her to make two more films with Pasternak.

Disagreeing with Universal about the handling of Deanna Durbin and discontented with his contract, Pasternak left the studio in 1941 to join MGM, where Louis B. Mayer offered him command of his own unit. At first Pasternak adhered to his taste for smaller musical films without large production numbers, but he soon gave way to MGM's lavish style. He produced several celebrated musicals, including *Anchors Aweigh* (1945), in which Gene Kelly dances with the animated mouse Jerry; *In the Good Old Summertime* (1949), with Judy Garland and Van Johnson; and *Love Me or Leave Me* (1955), with Doris Day and James Cagney. Pasternak also promoted the careers of such stars as Kathryn Grayson, June Allyson, Margaret O'Brien, Jane Powell, and Esther Williams; and whenever possible he found parts for classical musicians like Lauritz Melchior

and José Iturbi. On 9 January 1942, while working on his first MGM film, Pasternak married the dancer and actress Dorothy Darrell. The couple had three children.

Pasternak's 1943 film *Song of Russia*, about an American conductor in love with a Soviet girl, was produced as a patriotic gesture for an ally in World War II; but it later excited suspicions of communist conspiracy in the House Un-American Activities Committee, which began hearings in May 1947. Pasternak himself escaped notoriety and continued to make pictures.

In 1949 Mayer brought Mario Lanza to MGM and entrusted his career to Pasternak. Lanza proved a singer and actor of great talent but difficult temperament. Pasternak shepherded him through four pictures, including the fictionalized but immensely successful biographical film *The Great Caruso* (1951). The strain of managing Lanza and dealing with the studio upheavals that ousted Mayer in 1951 jeopardized Pasternak's marriage. Dorothy sought a divorce in 1952, but the couple reconciled before the decree became final.

As the studio system declined Pasternak continued to make one to two pictures a year but, despite hits like *Where the Boys Are* (1960) and *The Courtship of Eddie's Father* (1962), he found himself out of touch with filmgoers' tastes. As he said later, "We were growing older, and the audiences were growing younger." The failure of his 1962 film *Jumbo*, even with musical numbers by Busby Berkeley, signaled the end of the old-fashioned Hollywood musical. In 1965, however, Pasternak produced a successful Elvis Presley film (*Girl Happy*) and another (*Spinout*) in 1966. In 1967, after more than twenty-five years at MGM, he left the studio to make his last film, *The Sweet Ride* (1968) at Twentieth Century–Fox.

In addition to his films Pasternak produced three telecasts (1964–1966) of the annual Oscar presentations for the Motion Picture Academy. He also published a popular recipe collection, *Cooking with Love and Paprika* (1966).

In retirement Pasternak worked for charities, including the American Parkinson Disease Association and the Masquers Club of Los Angeles. When approached by friends to make another picture, he would reply, "I couldn't make a problem film if I tried." He died of complications from Parkinson's Disease in Beverly Hills, California, and is buried in Los Angeles.

Joe Pasternak's life often seems a fairy-tale success story, though darkened by childhood poverty, the Holocaust, and uncertain studio politics. His eighty-seven known films—he claimed to have made 105—present a world without such dark presences. ("Some of them," he said, "even lacked a plot.") They celebrated things he often associated with memories of prewar Budapest: youthful idealism and good-natured families, festive cabarets, charming artists, sophisticated but innocent romances, and especially, music.

"The only messages in my films," he said to an interviewer in 1985, "were the kind thoughts the audience took home."

★

The Academy of Motion Picture Arts and Sciences, Beverly Hills, California, maintains an archive on Pasternak. He published an autobiography, written with David Chandler, *Easy the Hard Way* (1956). Pasternak and his family were featured in human-interest articles for *Colliers* (5 May 1951) and *Saturday Evening Post* (6 Feb. 1954). See also *Films in Review* (Feb. 1985) and *The Annual Obituary 1991*. Pasternak's spiritual beliefs were the subject of a brief interview in Terrance A. Sweeney, *God &* (1985). Obituaries are in the *Daily Variety* (16 Sept. 1991), *Los Angeles Times* (17 Sept. 1991), *New York Times* (18 Sept. 1991), and London *Times* (20 Sept. 1991).

ALAN BUSTER

PEALE, Norman Vincent (*b.* 31 May 1898 in Bowersville, Ohio; *d.* 24 December 1993 in Pawling, New York), popular American preacher and author who inspired millions with his inspirational message, typified in his best-selling book *The Power of Positive Thinking* (1952).

Peale was the oldest son of Charles Clifford Peale, a Methodist preacher, and Anna Delany, a homemaker. Norman and his two brothers grew up in a conservative Methodist atmosphere in Bowersville. Peale's mother was involved in her husband's ministry and managed the family finances. Peale's father was an easygoing and straightforward man, who stressed to his sons that simplicity was the way to reach people. As a boy, Peale often had feelings of insecurity and was sensitive to criticism. He prayed about these things and forced himself to take a number of sales jobs to help him deal with his inferiority complex.

In 1916 Peale graduated from high school in Bellefontaine, Ohio. He earned a bachelor's degree from Ohio Wesleyan University in 1920 and became a reporter for the *Detroit Journal*, but he quickly became disenchanted and decided to follow his father into the ministry. He attended the School of Theology at Boston University from 1921 to 1924 and was ordained by the Methodist Church in 1922. He preached his first sermon on 3 April 1922 at the Methodist church in Walpole, Massachusetts. Not an abstract thinker, Peale was critical of the program at Boston University, suggesting that there was too much philosophy and theology and not enough practical studies. Even though he remained politically conservative all his life, he became an adherent of the liberal religious tradition that focused on the social gospel. He graduated in 1924 with a bachelor of sacred theology degree and a master of arts degree in social ethics. He later studied at Syracuse University and received a doctor of divinity degree in 1931. He was awarded an honorary doctor of divinity degree from his undergraduate alma mater, Ohio Wesleyan University, in 1930.

Norman Vincent Peale. LIBRARY OF CONGRESS

After ordination in 1922, Peale became a student pastor at the Berkeley Church in Berkeley, Rhode Island, where he served until his graduation from Boston University in 1924, when he was assigned to St. Mark's Church in Brooklyn, New York. He was soon assigned to work with a new church they wished to plant, King's Highway Church. During his three years at St. Mark's the congregation grew from 40 to 900. In 1927 he became the pastor of the University Methodist Church in Syracuse, New York, where he was one of the first pastors to have his own radio program.

On 20 June 1930 Peale married Ruth Stafford. Ruth was Peale's emotional support throughout his career (despite his positive and joyful exterior, Peale continued to struggle with his childhood fears and feelings of inferiority). She was an essential sounding board for his ideas and the administrative aide for his many projects. Peale gave her tremendous credit for his work. He and Ruth had three children. A medium-sized man, bespectacled and jovial, with a warm smile, Peale maintained strong emotional bonds with his family, and although he lived in Manhattan most of his life, he kept strong ties to his home state of Ohio.

In 1932 Peale made a decision that would set the course for much of the rest of his life. He changed denominations from Methodist to Dutch Reformed in order to become the pastor of the Marble Collegiate Church on Fifth Avenue in Manhattan, founded in 1628. Under Peale's leadership, the church became one of the premier churches of New York City, experiencing substantial growth during the Great Depression and World War II. Peale's dynamic sermons, which were televised during the 1950s, generated standing-room-only conditions and long lines of people outside the church hoping for a chance to hear Peale preach.

Peale's message was a combination of Fundamentalism and New Thought modernism. True to his father's advice, Peale offered a message that was positive and simple. It emphasized practical Christianity through self-examination, prayer, and gaining control over one's life by visualization. He proclaimed that people could empower themselves through this manner of positive thinking. In order to address "everyday issues facing people," Peale endeavored not to use biblical language or religious terms in his message, and he proudly stated that he was not an intellectual. He believed that the power of God was released through the power of thought. Tim Stafford in *Christianity Today* has suggested that Peale was "the first example of nondenominational, entrepreneurial, communications-savvy, pragmatic, populist religion that rose out of the fundamentalist-modernist split." Others have characterized Peale's message as a potpourri of his conservative Methodist background, Dutch Reformed tradition, modern psychology, and metaphysics.

Through a variety of sermons, broadcasts, and publications, Peale brought his message to millions. Following World War II, Peale founded an inspirational leaflet called *Guideposts,* published weekly and aimed primarily at businessmen. In the 1950s it became a monthly magazine with a subscription base that eventually reached 5 million. Peale and his wife also hosted a television show called *What's Your Trouble?* from 1952 to 1968. His radio program *The Art of Living* was broadcast on NBC Radio for fifty-four years. Peale also wrote forty-six books, including *The Art of Living* (1937), *You Can Win* (1938), *A Guide for Confident Living* (1948), and *This Incredible Century* (1991). But it was *The Power of Positive Thinking* (1952) that became one of the best-selling religious books in history, remaining on the best-seller list for three years. The book contains a number of inspirational messages and anecdotes, and a variety of religio-psychological catchphrases such as "visualize, prayerize, actualize." It encourages people to free their "inner powers," and proclaims to help people turn "self-doubt into self-esteem" and "obstacles into opportunities" using imagery, self-talk, and the power of prayer. At the time of Peale's death, the book had been translated into forty-one languages and had sold more than 20 million copies.

In the 1940s, responding to the needs of his congregation, Peale and Dr. Smiley Blanton (a former student of Sigmund Freud) founded one of the first clinics to provide counseling through a combination of religion and psychiatry. In 1951 the clinic expanded to train religion-based counselors and programs, and became the American Foundation for Religion and Psychiatry, for which Peale served as president.

All of this made Peale one of the most well-known and popular clergymen in America and gained him the moniker "the Minister to Millions." Yet he had critics as well. On the one hand his liberal theology caused conservatives to criticize his message; on the other hand he drew ire from liberals because of his conservative politics. Carol V. R. George, one of Peale's biographers, points out that Peale's desire to increase the numbers at his congregation led him to remain reticent on topics such as sin, guilt, suffering, and atonement as well as social issues such as racism. Many accused him of "watering down" the Christian message into a humanistic philosophy that focused more on humans than on God. Peale was hurt by the criticism that he was unscholarly. Liberals also criticized him for his support of Prohibition, his anti-New Deal stance, and especially for his public opposition to presidential candidate John F. Kennedy because of his concerns about possible papal influence.

Peale retired as senior pastor from the Marble Collegiate Church in 1984 and devoted himself to lecturing at business seminars as a motivational speaker, spending much of his time traveling to speaking engagements. That same year President Ronald Reagan awarded him the Medal of Freedom and his autobiography, *The True Joy of Positive Living,* appeared. Peale remained vital and active until his death. He died in his sleep at his farm in Pawling on 24 December 1993, having suffered a stroke about two weeks earlier. He is buried in Pawling.

Despite the criticism that Peale ignored important biblical themes such as sin and atonement, and that he did not take the problem of suffering seriously, Peale's message resonated with the culture of the mid–twentieth century. While his message was more human-centered than God-centered, and more of a philosophy than a religion, he inspired millions of people and gave them hope. His influence on the self-help movement, on motivational speakers such as Dale Carnegie and Zig Zigler, and on preachers such as Robert Schuller and the "prosperity gospel" cannot be denied. Peale perhaps impacted American religion and culture more than any other speaker or preacher of the twentieth century.

Peale's autobiography, *The True Joy of Positive Living* (1984), was published the year he retired. Perhaps the best biography of Peale is by Carol V. R. George, *God's Salesman* (1992), a scholarly book that utilizes interviews with Peale and people who worked with him. It recounts his life using personal anecdotes and examines his influence within its historical, cultural, and religious context. *Norman Vincent Peale: Minister to Millions* (1958) and *One Man's Way* (1972) are overtly sympathetic biographies by Arthur Gordon. For more concerning the context of Peale's influence on American religion, see *Twentieth-Century Shapers of American Religion* (1989), edited by Charles H. Lippy. Tim Stafford judiciously details many of the criticisms of Peale's message in "Half-Full Christianity—God's Salesman: Norman Vincent Peale and the Power of Positive Thinking," *Christianity Today* 37 (1993): 35–36. Obituaries are in *Christian Century* 111 (1994): 41; *Christianity Today* 38 (1994): 56; the *New York Times* (26 Dec. 1993); and the *Wall Street Journal* (27 Dec. 1993). The film *One Man's Way* (1963) portrays Peale's life and successes.

MARKUS H. MCDOWELL

PERKINS, Anthony (*b.* 4 August 1932 in New York City; *d.* 12 September 1992 in New York City), actor best known for his portrayal of Norman Bates in Alfred Hitchcock's 1960 thriller *Psycho*.

Perkins was the only child of the actor Osgood Perkins and Janet Rane. Osgood had created the role of the newspaper editor Walter Burns in the original 1928 stage production of *The Front Page* and appeared in several films. When Osgood died of a heart attack in 1937, five-year-old Perkins was left in the care of his mother. She took Perkins to suburban Brookline, Massachusetts, where she had family, and worked as a bookkeeper for various New England theater companies and as the executive director of the American Theatre Wing's Boston Stage Door Canteen.

In 1947, at age fifteen, Perkins made his stage debut in *Junior Miss* at the Brattleboro Summer Theatre in Vermont. Over the next five years he appeared in stock productions of *Kiss and Tell, Sarah Simple,* and *My Sister Eileen,* among others, and also acted in high school plays at the Browne and Nichols School in Cambridge, Massachusetts, from which he graduated in 1950.

That same year he was accepted into the theater department at Rollins College in Winter Park, Florida. Two significant events occurred while he was there. First, he narrowly escaped being implicated in a gay-bashing scandal that involved his circle of male friends and resulted in several student expulsions. The incident taught Perkins the necessity of hiding his homosexuality. Second, he took time off to make his screen debut in George Cukor's *The Actress* (1953). Unfortunately, the film failed at the box office.

Anthony Perkins, 1985. BERRY BERENSON/THE KOBAL COLLECTION

In 1953 Perkins transferred to New York City's Columbia University to be near the theater. (He never graduated.) After landing parts in the live television shows *Studio One* and *The Big Story,* he was hired to replace John Kerr on Broadway in Robert Anderson's hit play *Tea and Sympathy,* opposite Joan Fontaine. During his run as Tom Lee, the effeminate student accused of homosexuality by his peers (a situation Perkins knew well), he caught the eye of the Hollywood director William Wyler, who cast him as the socially-conscious Quaker son of Gary Cooper in *Friendly Persuasion* (1956). The film was a hit, earning Perkins an Academy Award nomination for best supporting actor.

Signing a seven-year contract with Paramount Pictures in 1955, the six-foot, three-inch, lanky actor was publicized as the new James Dean. (Dean had died in 1955.) He appeared in a series of mediocre films, including *The Tin Star* (1957) with Henry Fonda, *Desire Under the Elms* (1958) with Sophia Loren, *The Matchmaker* (1958) with Shirley Booth, and most notably *Fear Strikes Out* (1957), in which he played the emotionally troubled baseball player Jim Piersall. The shooting of *Fear Strikes Out* was difficult for Perkins, who was not naturally athletic, and who was fearful of growing gossip of his romance with another leading man. While critics praised his performance in the film, it was a financial disappointment.

Disillusioned, Perkins returned to Broadway in 1957, starring opposite the actress Jo Van Fleet in *Look Homeward, Angel,* Ketti Frings's adaptation of the Thomas Wolfe novel. The play won him high praise, including a Tony Award nomination. In 1958 he was hailed as "possibly the most gifted dramatic actor under 30 in the country."

Back in Hollywood, he starred in *Green Mansions* (1959), *On the Beach* (1959), and *Tall Story* (1960). He returned to Broadway in the musical *Greenwillow,* the composer Frank Loesser's first flop. Then Alfred Hitchcock cast him as the murderous boy-next-door in *Psycho.* A box-office smash, the film was the high point of the careers of everyone involved.

His once-wholesome image smashed, Perkins made a series of disappointing European films—*Goodbye Again* (1961) with Ingrid Bergman, *Phaedra* (1961) with Melina Mercouri, Orson Welles's *The Trial* (1963)—and returned to the stage in the lackluster comedies *Harold* (1962) and Neil Simon's *Star-Spangled Girl* (1966).

Approaching the age of forty and no longer on Hollywood's A-list, Perkins began considering alternatives. He directed some regional theater and a troubled off-Broadway production of Bruce Jay Friedman's *Steambath* (1972), and he cowrote the screenplay of *The Last of Sheila* (1973) with Stephen Sondheim. But it wasn't enough.

In 1973 he surprised the world by marrying the twenty-four-year-old photographer Berry (née Berinthia) Berenson, granddaughter of the legendary couturiere Elsa Schiaparelli and sister of the model Marisa Berenson. Having spent the previous few years living with a man, Perkins attributed his change in sexual orientation to psychotherapy. The marriage assuaged many of his private insecurities and lasted nearly twenty years, until his death. He and Berenson had two sons in 1974 and 1976, respectively.

Although he still hit occasional professional heights, such as his run on Broadway in Peter Shaffer's acclaimed drama *Equus* (1975–1976), Perkins's career was now spotty at best. Films like *Mahogany* (1975), *Twice a Woman* (1979), and *ffolkes* (1979) did little to revive his appeal. Finally, in 1983 he reluctantly agreed to resurrect Norman Bates for *Psycho II.* Despite his initial ambivalence, the sequel's success cheered the actor, who negotiated a deal to star in and direct *Psycho III.* A more visually stylish and atmospheric film than the earlier sequel, *Psycho III* (1986) drew paltry crowds, shattering Perkins's self-confidence.

Drug arrests in 1984 and 1989 (for marijuana and LSD possession) helped fuel the rumors of weird behavior and illness that plagued him in his last years. In 1990 a supermarket-tabloid headline declared that Perkins had tested positive for HIV, the virus that causes AIDS. He and his wife denied the report, yet Perkins did nothing to refute it.

He spent the next two years mostly in seclusion. "There are many who believe that this disease is God's vengeance," he wrote towards the end of his life, "but I believe it was sent to teach people how to love and understand and have compassion for each other. I have learned more about love, selflessness, and human understanding from the people I have met in this great adventure in the world of AIDS than I ever did in the cutthroat, competitive world in which I spent my life." He died of AIDS-related complications in his Los Angeles home, surrounded by a small group of friends and his family. His remains were cremated.

The public's identification of Perkins with the psychopathic Norman Bates remains one of the most vivid examples of the effects of typecasting, both negative and positive, on an actor's life. While the role crippled Perkins's potential as a romantic leading man, it immortalized him as a pop cultural icon.

★

A biography of Perkins is Charles Winecoff, *Split Image* (1997). An obituary is the *New York Times* (14 Sept. 1992).

CHARLES WINECOFF

PERRY, Harold Robert (*b.* 9 October 1916 in Lake Charles, Louisiana; *d.* 17 July 1991 in New Orleans, Louisiana), the first African American Roman Catholic bishop in the United States in the twentieth century.

Perry, one of the eight children of Frank Perry and Josephine Petrie, was born into a French-speaking family with a long Catholic tradition. His father was a rice mill worker and his mother was a domestic servant. At age fifteen, he entered Saint Augustine Seminary in Bay St. Louis, Mississippi, to study with the Society of the Divine Word fathers, a German Catholic religious fraternity with a long tradition of ministry to blacks in the South. Ordained as a Divine Word father in 1944, he served parishes in Louisiana, Arkansas, and Mississippi, until being named rector of his alma mater, Saint Augustine Seminary, in 1958.

At that time, the Divine Word fathers' integrated seminary was unique in American Catholicism. Relatively few seminaries accepted black applicants, and many dioceses declined to ordain black men. Many parochial schools refused Negro students, and Negroes and whites were frequently segregated during the celebration of Mass, particularly in the South.

Despite this hostile environment, Perry—a soft-spoken man known for his personal gentleness and his ability to work with both black and white Catholics—continued to be a pioneer in church leadership roles. In 1962 he was elected provincial of the Southern Province of the Society of the Divine Word, the first black man to serve as a major religious superior in the United States. He also served for

Harold Robert Perry. LIBRARY OF CONGRESS

many years as chaplain to the Saint Peter Claver Society, a fraternal organization largely focused on the needs of black Catholics, and as a board member of the National Council for Interracial Justice. He was among the religious leaders called to the White House to consult with President Lyndon Johnson at the height of the civil rights crisis in the summer of 1964.

Perry's ordination to the rank of bishop was a national event. Perry's cousin, Father Jerome LeDoux, described the 1966 ordination, held in Saint Louis Cathedral in New Orleans at a time of tense race relations in the South, as "the ecclesiastical equivalent of Jackie Robinson's introduction into the major leagues." Protesters outside the cathedral that day carried signs proclaiming, "God does not recognize Negro priests, bishops" and "We don't want a nigger bishop."

Archbishop Philip M. Hannan of New Orleans called Perry a pioneer who, "as with all pioneers, suffered from it." A fellow black bishop, John H. Ricard, noted that at the time of Perry's ordination, there were almost no black leaders in government or in the Catholic Church. "Bishop Perry took the brunt of the resistance," said Ricard. By the time of Perry's death, there were a dozen African American Catholic bishops in the United States.

Perry himself did not believe in militancy, and he was uncomfortable in the limelight. Still, in a low-key manner, Perry helped the church come to grips with the ramifications of the civil rights struggle, and while still a parish priest, he worked to integrate his Lafayette diocese parish in Broussard, Louisiana, which was a center for black Catholic life in the United States.

"As a priest, I have found the most success in approaching the problem of race relations through kindness, charity and Christian love," Perry said in a 1965 interview. In that same interview, he acknowledged the need for nonviolent demonstrations to draw attention to racism. "God's justice is at stake more than the fact that Negroes have not received their due," he said. "No matter whether a person is of high station or low, if he is deprived of his rights as a human being, God's justice is offended."

During a time when Malcolm X and other black leaders began calling for racial separatism, Perry professed his belief in unity between blacks and whites, both inside and outside the church. "Integration expresses in one term the unity that God intended for the whole human race. This is traditional Catholic teaching," he said. LeDoux noted, "Father Perry served in a quiet, unassuming, nonthreatening manner which stirred the impatience of some activists but moved most people to admiration."

As bishop, Perry consulted six times with Pope Paul VI and served on a number of committees for the National Conference of Catholic Bishops, where he was instrumental in the formation of the Campaign for Human Development, the domestic antipoverty effort funded by U.S. Catholics. He also was on the board of the Urban League. As the only American black bishop, he frequently spoke at national conferences. His duties in the Archdiocese of New Orleans included service as pastor of the National Shrine of Our Lady of Prompt Succor in New Orleans and Our Lady of Lourdes. He was also vicar of religious life for the archdiocese, supervising the reforms that took place throughout Catholic orders as a result of Vatican II.

A regular patron of the fine restaurants of New Orleans, Perry often ministered to the staffs there by hearing confessions from the kitchen help and waiters. He was a supporter of the reforms of Vatican II, which included a renewed emphasis on ministry with the poor and involvement of priests, brothers, and nuns in addressing social ills.

In 1985, beset by failing health and afflicted by Alzheimer's disease, Perry retired. He died six years later and was buried in New Orleans at Saint Louis Cemetery. At Perry's 1991 funeral mass, Hannan commented, "There are no pickets tonight. There are only mourners and loving, devoted friends and supportive members of the flock of Christ."

★

Perry's career is recounted extensively in the *Clarion-Herald,* the newspaper of the Catholic archdiocese of New Orleans, particularly in issues marking his ordination as bishop (7 Oct. 1965), the observance of his tenth anniversary as a bishop (22 Jan. 1976), and his death (1 Aug. 1991). Other obituaries and commentary on Perry's life are in *Commonweal*, "Looking Ahead, Black Catholic Bishops" (4 Oct. 1985); *Washington Post*, (19 July 1991); *Chicago Defender*, "Rites for First Black Catholic Bishop," (20 July 1991); *New Orleans Times-Picayune*, "Perry's Humility Remembered," (23 July 1991); and *Jet Magazine*, "First Black Catholic Bishop Named in Twentieth Century Dies," (5 Aug. 1991).

PETER FEUERHERD

PHILBRICK, Herbert Arthur (*b*. 11 May 1915 in Rye, New Hampshire; *d*. 16 August 1993 in North Hampton, New Hampshire), FBI informant whose testimony was key to the landmark convictions of eleven top leaders of the American Communist Party in 1949 and whose book about his undercover life became a best-seller.

Philbrick was one of two children, and the only son, of Guy Philbrick, a conductor for the Boston & Maine Railroad, and Alice May Shapleigh, a nurse. He spent his early years in northern New Hampshire, and the family moved to Boston before he was ten years old. He attended high school in Somerville, Massachusetts, and his social life revolved around the Baptist church there. He worked at odd jobs to attend night school at the Lincoln Technical School of Northeastern University in Boston, earning a civil engineering degree in 1938. He married Eva Luscombe on 3 September 1939 and they later had five girls. Unable to find

Herbert Philbrick, 1949. AP/WIDE WORLD PHOTOS

engineering work, he took an advertising job with Holmes Direct Mail Service. Seeking new clients in 1940, he called on the Massachusetts Youth Council in Cambridge.

Philbrick got involved in the council's pacifist work but suspected it was secretly run by communists. He contacted the Federal Bureau of Investigation (FBI) and agreed to inform. Over the next nine years he was in a series of suspect groups. In 1942 he took a job in Boston as assistant advertising director for a movie theater chain and joined the Young Communist League. In 1943 he joined American Youth for Democracy, and a year later he joined the Communist party. Throughout, he taught Sunday school at the First Baptist Church in Wakefield, Massachusetts, and read the Bible to avoid succumbing to Communist propaganda. Initially he did not even tell his wife of his secret work.

On 6 April 1949 Philbrick's undercover life became national news. He appeared as a surprise witness in the trial of eleven communists charged with violating the 1940 Smith Act by advocating the violent overthrow of the U.S. government. Philbrick wore a red, white, and blue bow tie when he took the stand in U.S. District Court in Manhattan. He was thirty-three years old, clean-cut, and bespectacled, prompting *Time* magazine to say he seemed more like a "carefully dressed clerk than a secret government agent." Philbrick, then living in Melrose, a Boston suburb, testified that party officials taught that the revolution would come at some unknown time: "We were instructed that the revolution will not take place next week or next month or two o'clock Wednesday afternoon, but will take place under two circumstances: In case of a heavy depression, or in case of a war. . . . It would result in the overthrow of the capitalist class and the dictatorship of the proletariat." The defendants denied the charges and their lawyers challenged Philbrick, who swore, "I never received any money from the FBI except for my actual expenses." The jury convicted party general secretary Eugene Dennis and his codefendants. Philbrick's testimony was the nation's first on current Communist Party activities at the local level.

Afterward, Philbrick worked in Boston as the advertising manager of Maintain Store Engineer Service. He obeyed FBI instructions not to discuss the case pending appeal. He turned down several publishing offers until 1951, when the U.S. Supreme Court upheld the verdict. In 1952 he published a series on his undercover life in the *New York Herald Tribune* and also a best-seller, *I Led Three Lives: Citizen, "Communist," Counterspy*. Reviewing the book, the *New York Times* said, "Mr. Philbrick writes clearly and briskly, but without humor or charm. His book has no sensational interest. Its genuine importance lies in its description of the typical behavior of American Communists." The biographer Oliver Pilat said in the *Saturday Review* that the book had "considerable documentary value" but "does not provide details of actual espionage by anybody." Philbrick disparaged "amateur red hunters, ambitious politicians, demagogues, and rabble-rousers."

In February 1952 Philbrick publicly criticized Senator Joseph R. McCarthy, the Wisconsin Republican, as exaggerating Communist strength and injuring innocent liberals. Philbrick, then of suburban White Plains in Westchester County, New York, said he merely wanted to sell ads for the *Herald Tribune* and lead a "normal life." But anticommunism became Philbrick's lifelong career. FBI files show the bureau paid him $6,823 for services and $359.38 for expenses through the trial's resolution. In May 1951 the FBI helped arrange Philbrick's job at the newspaper and his book deal. Philbrick submitted drafts of the book and series to the FBI, editing them at the bureau's request. The series ran in seventy-five newspapers in 1952 and earned Philbrick $17,287. In February 1953 Philbrick sold a thirty-nine-episode television version of *I Led Three Lives,* which the *Times* said "relied too much on trite preachment and corny melodrama." Philbrick earned $141,015 in royalties from the show and $24,525 from the book, according to uncontested testimony in his former lawyer's successful 1958 suit for commissions. In the early 1950s Philbrick began a biweekly column on communism for the *Herald Tribune,* "Red Underground." The paper canceled it in 1958, and Philbrick ran a country store in Rye Beach, New Hampshire, until the mid-1960s. He still spoke and wrote widely on "the deadly menace of Communism," appearing around the country with Dr. Fred Schwartz's Christian Anti-Communist Crusade through 1965.

Philbrick won more than fifty civic awards, including a 1954 Freedoms Foundation citation, but drew claims that he recklessly impugned people's loyalty. In March 1957 Minnesota's Democratic senator Hubert H. Humphrey complained to the FBI that Philbrick insinuated he was a communist. The National Farmers Union dropped its slander suit in 1957 only after Philbrick retracted claims about the group. In 1967 Philbrick moved to Washington, D.C., and ran the United States Anti-Communist Congress, which described Vietnam War protests, racial unrest, and flag burnings as evidence of a Communist plot.

Philbrick's crusade weighed on his home life. At a 1961 meeting of Constructive Action, an anticommunist group, he met Shirley Joy Brundige. They had a daughter out of wedlock in 1963. On 10 August 1967, two days after divorcing his first wife, Philbrick and Brundige married. They ran the private U.S. Press Association in Washington, D.C., distributing conservative editorials. In 1976 the couple and their daughter moved to Rye Beach. He continued to track communism, keeping his phone and address unlisted and traveling under aliases. The year before he died at his North Hampton home of cancer, Philbrick said he never slept through the night and that because of the communist threat "we remain in grave danger." Philbrick is buried at Rye Center Cemetery in Rye.

To some observers, Philbrick was a self-sacrificing hero of the cold-war era. To others he represented excesses of a time when dissent was suspect. His testimony figured in other trials: he was called before the House Un-American Activities Committee in 1951 and 1953 and before the Senate Internal Security Subcommittee in 1952. In July 1957 the U.S. Supreme Court effectively ended Smith Act prosecutions, barring surprise witnesses and holding that to be criminal, speech must incite specific violence and not merely advocate political belief.

★

More than 1,600 pages of previously secret FBI files on Philbrick are available from the FBI under the Freedom of Information Act. His book, *I Led Three Lives,* is out of print but available through libraries. The most comprehensive magazine article is "The Fourth Life of Herbert Philbrick," *Yankee* (Feb. 1992). The 1949 New York Smith Act trial was extensively covered by the *New York Times.* Obituaries are in the *Boston Globe* and *New York Times* (both 18 Aug. 1993), and in the Manchester (New Hampshire) *Union-Leader* (20 Aug. 1993).

Seth Rosenfeld

PHOENIX, River Jude (*b.* 23 August 1970 in Madras, Oregon; *d.* 31 October 1993 in Los Angeles, California), Academy Award–nominated actor who advocated vegetarianism, environmental responsibility, and protection of animal rights.

Named River Jude Bottom after the river of life in Hermann Hesse's *Siddhartha* (1922), River Phoenix was born in a small house on an Oregon peppermint farm, where his parents, John Lee Bottom and Arlyn Dunetz, were working. Out of sync with mainstream society and embodying nonconformist hippie idealism, the bohemian parents, with their infant son in tow, spent the first two years after his birth trekking across the country from commune to commune. They considered themselves seekers and believed psychedelic drugs would aid their inner spiritual journey.

In 1972 the Bottoms abandoned drugs in favor of religion and joined the controversial Children of God. The antiestablishment beliefs of the group appealed to the couple, who began using the surname Phoenix (changed officially in 1989) to symbolize their rebirth into the church. They settled in Colorado Springs, Colorado, at one of the group's largest communes.

After two years the family took to the road to spread the church's teachings and recruit new members in Texas, Mexico, Puerto Rico, and finally Caracas, Venezuela, where the family, which now included River's sister Rain and brother Joaquin (who went by the name "Leaf" for many

River Phoenix. THE KOBAL COLLECTION

years), settled in 1976. With almost no financial support from the Children of God, the penniless missionaries often lacked adequate food and shelter. River (who had learned basic guitar chords) and Rain, ages five and three, respectively, sang for money on the streets and passed out religious literature.

Weary from hunger and poverty and troubled by proclamations from the Children of God's egotistical leader, who encouraged using sex to recruit new members, the Phoenix clan returned to the United States at the end of 1978 and settled in Florida. The family, with the addition of daughters Liberty and Summer, became devout vegans who neither ate meat nor used leather or any product that exploited animals.

The Phoenix children were bright, but without formal education they lacked the basic knowledge that other children their age possessed. Nonetheless, they were gifted in the arts, and encouraged by their success in local talent contests, the Phoenix family next headed to Hollywood in the family Volkswagen. Arlyn found a secretarial position in the NBC casting department and made an appointment with Iris Burton, a leading talent agent for children. River's wholesome good looks helped land him jobs in commercials, including those for Ocean Spray, Mitsubishi, and Saks Fifth Avenue. Despite the precious money it provided

the family, River quickly decided that commercials were too "phony," and so, with the family's approval, he stopped doing them.

In 1982 River and Rain landed small singing roles on the television series *Fantasy*. This exposure led to River's role as the singing, guitar-playing youngest brother on the CBS show *Seven Brides for Seven Brothers* (1982). After that show's cancellation, he made guest appearances on the television shows *Hotel, It's Your Move,* and *Family Ties* (1984) and in the miniseries *Celebrity* (1984) and *Robert Kennedy: The Man and his Times* (1985). He played the lead in a one-hour drama, *Backwards: The Riddle of Dyslexia* (1984) and had a key role in *Surviving: A Family in Crisis* (1985).

His first movie role came in 1985, playing a comic teenage inventor in *Explorers*. But it was his next performance, in the coming-of-age story *Stand by Me* (1986), that launched him as a teen idol and raised his profile among directors and casting agents. After playing Harrison Ford's son in *The Mosquito Coast* (1986), when he began dating the actress Martha Plimpton, River began taking nearly back-to-back movie roles, starring in three movies released in 1988: *A Night in the Life of Jimmy Reardon, Little Nikita,* and *Running on Empty*. Although uneasy with his heartthrob image, the lithe, five-foot, eleven-inch actor with blue eyes and sandy brown hair adorned dozens of teen magazines and received thousands of fan letters each week.

In 1988 at age seventeen, he was nominated for a best supporting actor Academy Award for his portrayal of the son of political radicals hiding from the FBI in *Running on Empty*. Much sought after by directors, he then took small parts in Steven Spielberg's *Indiana Jones and the Last Crusade* (1989) and in *I Love You to Death* (1990) as well as a starring role in *Dogfight* (1991).

River valued privacy and retreated to Gainesville, Florida, where his family lived, when he was not filming. There Phoenix enjoyed relative anonymity and was able to focus on his band, Aleka's Attic, which he formed with his sister Rain and a few friends. The band had a loose contract with Island Records but only released one song—on *Tame Yourself*, a fund-raising compilation for P.E.T.A. (People for the Ethical Treatment of Animals). In addition to a concern for animals, River and the other Phoenix family members were outspoken about protecting the environment, especially the destruction of the rain forests.

Persuaded by costar Keanu Reeves, Phoenix took the role of Mike Waters, a narcoleptic gay prostitute in Gus Van Sant's dark 1991 drama *My Own Private Idaho*. His gritty performance earned him best actor awards at the Venice Film Festival and from the National Society of Film Critics. After a smaller role in *Sneakers* (1992), he returned to his musical roots in Peter Bogdanovich's *The Thing Called Love* (1993), singing all of his character's songs in his role as a struggling Nashville singer. (One of the songs,

"Lone Star State of Mind," was actually written by Phoenix.) His final completed movie was *Silent Tongue* (1993), a Western directed by Sam Shepard.

On a break from shooting his next film, the nearly completed *Dark Blood,* the twenty-three-year-old actor, along with girlfriend Samantha Mathis (his *The Thing Called Love* costar) and siblings Rain and Joaquin, visited the Viper Room, a Los Angeles nightclub. Within a few hours a convulsing River collapsed on the sidewalk outside and was then rushed to nearby Cedars Sinai Medical Center. He was declared dead twenty minutes later. The coroner's report confirmed rumors that his death was the result of a drug overdose. Fans around the world mourned his shocking death. *Dark Blood* was never finished, and his upcoming role in the film adaptation of the Anne Rice novel *Interview with the Vampire* (1994) was recast. Following a memorial service, he was cremated and his ashes were scattered on his family's ranch in Gainesville. After his death many struggled to reconcile his healthful public image with accounts that his experimentation with drugs had begun in his early teens. The length and severity of his substance abuse are disputed.

River Phoenix was one of the most talented actors of his generation. He infused his roles with a rare mixture of innocence and wisdom. His life was guided by the idealistic principles espoused by his tight-knit family, and his career choices often reflected artistic integrity rather than commercial success. His acting gifts and social activism have been somewhat overshadowed by his highly sensationalized death.

★

Biographies include John Glatt, *Lost in Hollywood: The Fast Times and Short Life of River Phoenix* (1995); Brian J. Robb, *River Phoenix: A Short Life* (1997); and John L. Barker, *Running on Empty: The Life and Career of River Phoenix* (1998). Obituaries are in the *Los Angeles Times* and *New York Times* (both 1 Nov. 1993). A lengthy article also appeared in the London *Independent* (5 Dec. 1993).

CARRIE C. MCBRIDE

PICON, Molly (*b.* 28 February 1898 in New York City; *d.* 5 April 1992 in Lancaster, Pennsylvania), greatest attraction of the Yiddish musical theater for more than sixty years, during the most cataclysmic period of Jewish history.

Picon, born Margaret Pyekoon on New York's Lower East Side, was the first of two daughters of Clara Ostrow (later Ostrovsky), who had fled pogroms near Kiev, Ukraine, Russia, and Louis Pyekoon (later Picon), a needleworker who abandoned a wife and three children in Warsaw to emigrate to the United States, where he married Clara.

Molly Picon in a promotional portrait for the Yiddish musical *My Malkele,* c. 1930s. ARCHIVE PHOTOS

Professing disappointment that his wife gave birth to only daughters, he abandoned his American family after the birth of Picon's sister.

The Picons moved to Philadelphia, Pennsylvania, at the turn of the century, and Clara got a job as wardrobe mistress at the Columbia Yiddish Theater. To supplement the family's income, Clara encouraged her daughter, an eager performer who charmed audiences from the start, to sing on trolley cars. Picon's stage debut was in 1903 as "Baby Margaret," winning a children's amateur night contest at the Bijou Theater. Although she attended the Northern Liberties School by day, Molly was a theatrical trouper by night, playing child parts in Yiddish productions and entertaining in nickelodeon theaters. When she was fourteen years old, she appeared in a Philadelphia stock presentation of George M. Cohan's *Broadway Jones.* That was followed by a season barnstorming as Topsy in *Uncle Tom's Cabin.* Her formal education ended in 1915 when she quit William Penn High School after her sophomore year. For the next sixty-five years she devoted herself to show business full-time.

In 1917 Molly joined Ted Riley's vaudeville act, *The Four Seasons.* She toured with them for a year then was left stranded in Boston, where she reverted to the Yiddish theater by joining a musical comedy troupe managed by Polish-born Jacob Kalich, whom she married on 29 June 1919. During the course of their fifty-six year marriage, Kalich was his wife's manager, producer, and frequently her director and librettist. Their relationship was an extraordinary welding of personal and professional lives. Picon's only pregnancy ended at seven months in 1920 with the stillborn birth of a daughter. Severely depressed, Picon agreed to allow her husband to groom her for a Yiddish stage career by taking her on a two-year tour of the sources of Yiddish stage art in Eastern Europe. The trip combined a belated honeymoon with the opportunity for Picon to improve her Yiddish as she established a reputation as an actress, singer, and comedian in Paris, Łódź, Warsaw, Vienna, Prague, and Bucharest.

Back in the United States, Picon made her debut in New York on Second Avenue, on the Jewish Broadway, in her husband's musical play *Yonkele* on 24 December 1923. The diminutive actress—five feet tall and barely 100 pounds—played an adolescent yeshiva boy. The audience adored her, and over the course of her career she repeated the role almost 3,000 times.

After her debut she starred for six seasons in a series of operettas written by Jacob Kalich and the famous composer Joseph Rumshinsky; Picon wrote the lyrics. By 1926 Kalich owned David Kessler's Second Avenue Theater, where most of the productions were presented. Picon's scintillating manner and gamin sprightliness—a novelty among Yiddish theater divas—made her the "Sweetheart of Second Avenue" in *Tzipke, Shmendrick, Gypsy Girl, Molly Dolly, The Little Devil, Mamale* (*Little Mother*), *Raizele, Oy Is Dus a Madel* (*You're Some Girl!*), and *The Circus Girl*. Audiences were thrilled to see her because they never knew what to expect of the multitalented woman. She played eight instruments, sang in a dozen languages, toe-danced, performed acrobatic feats, walked a tightrope, did sleight-of-hand, rode a horse, and roller-skated. Her style, which owed as much to American showbiz as to Jewish folk theater, revolutionized the tastes of American Jewish audiences and in turn greatly influenced American mainstream theater.

After the Wall Street crash, the Kalichs lost all of their money and the lease on their theater, so Molly welcomed the opportunity for the next three years to play the major American vaudeville circuits. She and her husband also toured Europe, Palestine, South Africa, and South America. By 1940 they had been traveling 30,000 to 50,000 miles in a season, interspersing the performing jaunts with long runs in the Jewish theaters of New York.

In the early 1930s Picon experimented with various performance venues, reaching out to both English- and Yiddish-speaking audiences. Her first American musical,

Birdie, directed by Monty Woolley, closed in Brooklyn in 1933 before its Broadway opening. She made her radio debut in 1934 on WMCA doing five programs a week. She and her husband, broadcasting in both Yiddish and English, were popular radio attractions into the 1960s. Picon made her film debut in European productions. The Austrian Yiddish films *Judenmadel* (1921) and *Hutet Eure Tochter* (1922) have not survived. Another Viennese production, Goldin and Kalich's *Ost und West* (*East and West,* 1923), has become the oldest surviving Yiddish film. Her first American film was *A Little Girl with Big Ideas* (1929). Picon became a motion picture star with the release of two feature-length Yiddish musical films made in Poland and produced by American promoters: *Yidl Mit'n Fidl* (*Yidl with a Fiddle,* 1936) and *Mamale* (*Little Mother,* 1938), based on her husband's stage production. These films were made on the eve of the destruction of European Jewry; they document a vanished world. Most of the actors, as well as the dozens of shabby, poverty-stricken Jews who appear as extras in the films, were murdered by the Nazis.

Picon, the star of thirty-five downtown musical shows, made her Broadway debut in an English-speaking part on 16 April 1940 in *Morning Star,* which closed after eight weeks, even though the *New York Times* critic called Picon "darling" in the role. *Oy Is Dus A Leben* (*Oh What a Life,* 1942), written in both Yiddish and English and directed by Jacob Kalich, did much better; it ran for 139 performances at the Molly Picon Theater on Seventh Avenue and Fifty-ninth Street. It retold Picon's life from the time she was a child actress until she became a Yiddish theater star.

During World War II, Molly gave many performances in army camps, seamen's canteens, and military hospitals. At this time she and her husband adopted the first of their four foster children, a Belgian Jewish war orphan. After the war the Hebrew Actors Union and the American Jewish Labor Committee wrote the State Department requesting permission to send Molly Picon and Jacob Kalich to entertain Jews who had survived Nazi persecution. In 1946 the Kalichs spent five months in Europe; they were among the first performers to comfort the remnants of European Jewry in displaced-persons camps.

After the stresses of wartime tours, as well as thirty years of ceaseless trouping, the Kalichs bought a country home in 1947 in Mahopac, New York. It became their oasis, "Chez Shmendrick." In 1949 Molly had one of her biggest successes in Kalich and Rumshinsky's musical *Abi Gezunt* (*As Long as You're Healthy*). It was not until 1961 that Molly achieved Broadway success in Jerry Herman's first musical, *Milk and Honey.*

Molly made her first appearance on American television in 1949 as hostess of the *Molly Picon Show,* a variety series on ABC. Highlights of her later television work were playing Jerry Lewis's mother in a remake of *The Jazz Singer*

(1959), a recurring role on *Car 54, Where Are You* (1961–1963), and appearances on *Dr. Kildare* and *Gomer Pyle*.

During the 1950s and 1960s Picon and Kalich kept Yiddish theater alive when the audience was disappearing and the theaters were being demolished. Between arduous United Service Organizations (USO) tours of Korea and Japan, bond rallies for the State of Israel, and new plays written for her by her husband—*Sadie Is a Lady* (1950), *Mazel Tov, Molly* (1950), *Farblondjete Honeymoon* (*Snafued Honeymoon*, 1955), *Kosher Widow* (1959)—Molly began to play nightclubs, hotels, college auditoriums, and the "straw-hat circuit." The concerts, one-woman shows, and autobiographical revues, performed into the 1980s, introduced her to young people whose great-grandparents had applauded her.

As opportunities to perform in Yiddish productions waned, Molly was featured in films: Frank Sinatra's mother in *Come Blow Your Horn* (1963)—for which she was nominated for an Academy Award for best supporting actress—Yente the Matchmaker in *Fiddler on the Roof* (1971), and a madam in *For Pete's Sake* (1974), which starred Barbra Streisand. In her last two films, *Cannonball Run* (1981) and *Cannonball Run II* (1984), Molly played Mrs. Goldfarb.

Jacob Kalich died on 16 March 1975; soon thereafter Molly sold Chez and rented a house in Cortland, New York. She later moved to Manhattan to live with her sister, also a widow. In 1975 Picon was honored at the Hundredth Anniversary of the Yiddish Theater at the Museum of the City of New York. Restaurateur Abe Lebewohl built an addition to his fabled New York City eatery, the Second Avenue Deli, in 1980, naming the room in honor of the actress and filling it with Picon memorabilia. In 1981 she was elected to Broadway's Theater Hall of Fame and in 1985 was one of the first three Yiddish theater stars to receive a "Goldie"—named for Abraham Goldfaden, the father of Yiddish theater—awarded by the Congress of Jewish Culture.

Picon suffered from Alzheimer's disease during the last few years of her life and died at her sister's home. She was buried alongside her beloved husband in Mt. Hebron Cemetery in Flushing in the borough of Queens, New York, in a section known as the Hebrew Actors' Cemetery, maintained by the Society of the Yiddish Theatrical Alliance.

Beyond the entertainment value of Molly Picon's performances, she played an important role in preserving Yiddish language and culture and introducing them to mainstream American audiences. The revitalization of *Yiddishkeit,* a late twentieth-century phenomenon, owes much to her indefatigable efforts.

★

During their lifetimes, Picon and Kalich donated a tremendous amount of material related to their careers to the American Jewish Historical Society and the Yiddish Scientific Institute (YIVO), both of which are located in the new Center for American Jewish History in Manhattan. The Museum of the City of New York has, in its theater archives, a modest collection of clippings, posters, programs, and correspondence but also fifty of her costumes, warehoused in New Jersey for museum exhibitions. The New York Public Theatre Research Division has clipping files and scrapbooks.

Picon kept diaries and drew upon them for two autobiographies: *So Laugh a Little* (1962), as told to Eth Clifford Rosenberg, and *Molly!: An Autobiography,* written with Jean Bergantini Grillo (1980). The first is an amusing if unreliable resource; the other is indispensable but with occasional lapses in accuracy.

Sidney Skolsky, *Times Square Tintypes* (1930), a collection of snappy celebrity sketches, includes a gossipy one about the "ghetto girl." Lila Perl, *Molly Picon: A Gift of Laughter* (1990), is written for children. Joann Green's essay about Picon in *Jewish Women In America: An Historical Encyclopedia,* vol. 2 (1998), includes information not available elsewhere. Carolyn Starman Hessel, ed., *Blessed Is the Daughter* (1999), a book for young adults, contains a perceptive essay about Picon.

Quite unlike anything else written about Molly Picon is Sandra Shipow, "Depression-era trends in popular culture as reflected in the Yiddish theatre career of Molly Picon," *Theatre Studies: The Journal of the Ohio State University Theatre Research Institute* 30 (1983–1984): 43–55. The clever, if startling, insights about Picon's appeal to Depression-era audiences are memorable. An obituary is in the *New York Times* (7 Apr. 1992).

HONORA RAPHAEL WEINSTEIN

PORTER, Sylvia Field (*b.* 18 June 1913 in Patchogue, New York; *d.* 5 June 1991 in Pound Ridge, New York), journalist whose daily syndicated newspaper columns reached some 40 million readers worldwide, and author of twenty-one books in addition to *Sylvia Porter's Income Tax Guide,* issued annually since 1960, and *Sylvia Porter's Money Book* (1975), which sold over 1 million copies.

Porter was one of two children born to Russian-Jewish immigrants Louis Feldman, a physician, and Rose Maisel. The family moved to Brooklyn, New York, where Porter's father practiced medicine until his death in 1925. Porter's mother, who later changed the family name to Field, supported the family as a proprietor of a dry cleaning emporium, as a real estate sales woman, and as a successful milliner. Their home life was intellectual and cultural. "We rather thought that intelligence added to womanliness," Porter's brother noted. Porter never forgot her mother's pronouncement, "You! You will have a career."

Porter attended New York City's P.S. 69 and graduated from James Madison High School in three and a half years with an A average. At age sixteen she entered Hunter Col-

Sylvia Porter. © PETER JONES/CORBIS

lege in New York City expecting to major in English and history. However, family financial difficulties brought on by the 1929 stock market crash caused her to switch to economics. In 1931, while she was still in college, she married Reed R. Porter, a financier. Elected to Phi Beta Kappa in her junior year, Porter graduated magna cum laude in 1932. Later she took courses at New York University's business school.

After graduation, Porter started working at the Wall Street investment counseling firm of Glass and Krey. In anticipation of America's abandonment of the gold standard, she converted $175,000 of the firm's gold coins to British pounds in Bermuda and then to United Kingdom bonds, earning the company a profit of $85,000. From her work on Wall Street, Porter gained knowledge of bond markets, business cycles, and currency movements. She turned her knowledge into a weekly column on government securities for the *American Banker* at age twenty-one. Later this knowledge became the base for her own information service on government bonds.

In 1935, using the byline S. F. Porter to mask the fact that she was a woman, Porter began to write occasional columns for the *New York Post.* Soon a regular columnist, she became the paper's financial editor in 1936. By 1937 her columns were nationally syndicated in 450 papers. She published her first book, *How to Make Money in Government Bonds,* in 1939. Her second book, *If War Comes to the*

American Home (1941), received favorable reviews, and in 1942 her *New York Post* editor, T. O. Thackrey, decided her gender was an asset and changed her byline to Sylvia F. Porter. Her third book, *The Nazi Chemical Trust in the United States,* came out in 1942. She and Reed Porter divorced in 1941, and in 1943 Porter married G. Sumner Collins, a newspaperman. They had one child in addition to Collins's son from a previous marriage. In 1944 Porter founded a newsletter, *Reporting on Governments,* and sold subscriptions for $60 a year. Her annual income in 1960 was more than $250,000.

In 1965 Porter began to contribute to such periodicals as *Ladies Home Journal,* for which she later became a contributing editor, and *Woman's Home Companion. Reader's Digest* printed her articles in condensed form. She appeared on the lecture circuit, radio, and television, and ABC's *Good Morning America* featured Porter regularly. However, she experienced reverses; her 1983 venture into magazine publishing, *Sylvia Porter's Personal Finance,* failed when the stock market crashed in 1987.

Sylvia Porter's Money Book (1975), the eighth of Porter's books, was updated in 1976 and again in 1979, when it was renamed *Sylvia Porter's New Money Book for the 80's.* Many of her books appeared on the *New York Times* best-seller lists. Her last book was *Sylvia Porter's Planning Your Retirement* (1991). J. K. Lasser, a tax expert, collaborated with her on her financial handbooks, and she sought help from specialists on others. Her ability to make complex economic and financial issues, which she called "bafflegab," accessible to nonexperts made her popular with consumers and small investors. Although one academic critic called her approach "eye-dropper" economics, public acceptance attested to her success.

Porter's books were generally well received by critics, even in professional journals. R. Badger, a commentator for *American Economic Review* said of her government bond book, "Portions of the book could be used for reference purposes in courses on investment." A *New York Times* reviewer held that, in her *If War Comes to the American Home,* "Facts, figures, broad word-pictures and succinct arguments are all presented with conversational ease." The *Library Journal* critic S. A. Singer wrote that *Sylvia Porter's New Money Book for the 80's* was "very definitely worth reading" and urged libraries to purchase it even if they owned the first edition. Discussing this same book, the *Saturday Review* critic Ted Morgan said Porter "has a bargain-basement mentality" but added she is "good at reminding people of their rights in their various capacities as workers, veterans, and retired people."

A brusque, tough competitor, a crusader on behalf of those with low incomes, and a liberal Democrat, Porter was also short-tempered. She attacked President Franklin D. Roosevelt's secretary of the treasury, Henry Morgenthau, Jr., for his handling of the bond market, questioning whether his actions were the result of his "obstinacy, stupidity or sheer ill advice." In an interview in *People* (29 October 1979), she castigated the administration of President Jimmy Carter for being "inept, . . . lacking in leadership and geared to reacting instead of acting." She won many academic and nonacademic awards, including fourteen honorary degrees. In 1964 she received the U.S. Internal Revenue Service's Meritorious Public Service Certificate.

By 1976 Porter's portfolio ran to seven figures, and she had worldwide fame. Standing at five feet six inches tall, she was a handsome woman who took pride in her sense of style and fine wardrobe. Porter said, "All I want from money is dignity and independence." Her wealth provided these and much more.

Porter's second husband died in January 1977. On 2 January 1979 she married James F. Fox, a public relations counselor. Porter divided her time between her Fifth Avenue apartment in New York City and her thirty-two-acre estate in Pound Ridge, New York. She golfed, swam, and hiked for exercise, played the piano, attended the opera and ballet, and read, particularly murder mysteries. She was fond of flowers in her home. An inveterate cigarette smoker, she died of emphysema at her home in Pound Ridge and was cremated.

★

Information on Porter is in *Current Biography Yearbook 1980* (1981); "Sylvia and You," *Time* (28 Nov. 1960); and "Super-Sylvia," *Ladies Home Journal* (Jan. 1976). An obituary is in the *New York Times* (7 June 1991).

HAROLD L. WATTEL

POUSETTE-DART, Richard Warren (*b.* 8 June 1916 in Saint Paul, Minnesota; *d.* 25 October 1992 in New York City), one of the original participants in the development of abstract expressionism, whose work demonstrated his belief in the spiritual nature of art.

Pousette-Dart was one of three children of Nathaniel Pousette, a painter who supported his family through publications on art and editorial work for the *Distinguished American Artists* series, and Flora Louise Dart, a poet and musician. His parents combined their names upon their marriage as a gesture of equality. In 1918 they moved to suburban Valhalla in Westchester County, New York, where their home became a gathering place for artists, writers, and musicians. From this diverse cultural milieu Pousette-Dart understood art and life to be inseparable. He decided early on to be an artist, spending much time in his father's studio. However, his philosophical beliefs about the nature of art seem to have been grounded more on his mother's observations.

Richard Pousette-Dart in his studio in Suffern, New York, 1962. COPYRIGHT © BY FRED W. McDARRAH

Pousette-Dart began drawing by the age of eight. By ten he had filled a notebook with drawings, which he later described as abstractions. He graduated in 1935 from the Scarborough School, a private school in Scarborough-on-Hudson, New York, and in 1936 entered Bard College in Annandale-on-Hudson, New York. He left during his first year and moved to Manhattan in 1937. Pousette-Dart assisted Paul Manship, a sculptor and friend of his father's, while he painted and sculpted on his own in the evenings. The next year he worked in a photographic studio as secretary and bookkeeper. Two brief marriages in 1938—to Blanche Grady, a dancer, and then to Lydia Modia, an artist—ended in annulment. In 1939 Pousette-Dart left his job to devote himself to his art. He visited the American Museum of Natural History as often as the Metropolitan Museum of Art, because his interests were diverse, from medieval stained glass to Native American artifacts. During this period he would write down his thoughts in notebooks, a practice he continued throughout his life. Even at this early date Pousette-Dart could be found using allusive, metaphorical language in his observations on art.

The Artists' Gallery in New York City held Pousette-Dart's first solo exhibition in 1941, followed by three more at the Willard Gallery in 1943, 1945, and 1946. At his first Willard show he met a poet, Evelyn Gracey, whom he married on 2 June 1946. They lived on East Fifty-sixth Street, near the East River. The couple had two children. At this time Pousette-Dart became associated with a disparate group of fiercely independent painters who, despite great variation in style, nonetheless shared many of the same aesthetic and cultural concerns. Critics dubbed them abstract expressionists. Although Pousette-Dart stayed away from the raucous socializing and fights, he participated in the group shows and events. His work was included in Peggy Guggenheim's now famous group exhibition in 1944 at her gallery, Art of This Century, notable for being one of the first public displays of this new trend. He was also included in Howard Putzel's 1945 exhibition, *A Problem for Critics*. In 1947 Guggenheim gave Pousette-Dart a solo exhibition. Her gallery space was large enough to display his seminal work *Symphony Number 1, The Transcendental* (1942). Measuring 90 feet by 120 feet, this work is noteworthy for being the first large-scale abstract expressionist painting. In 1948 Pousette-Dart moved to the perceptive modern art dealer, Betty Parsons, who gave him a solo show that year and nearly annually thereafter, his final one in 1967.

In April 1950 Pousette-Dart joined his colleagues for the three-day, roundtable discussions held at Studio 35, a pivotal moment in the history of abstract expressionism in that they attempted to define their commonalities of purpose and establish their differences from mainstream abstractionists. Pousette-Dart and the others shared an interest in mythic, ideographic, and biomorphic imagery drawn from myriad sources, including African and Native American art forms and their own unconscious as a means to communicate larger cultural truths about society. They also sought an authenticity of form and expression stemming from personal experience. "The authenticity of painting," stated Pousette-Dart in his 1951 talk at the School of the Museum of Fine Arts in Boston, "lies in the pure form and inner life which springs from the artist's realization and experience." He added, "We must go to [paintings] and look at them, and within them find reflected our own experience."

The following month Pousette-Dart and the other abstract expressionists signed an open letter protesting the Metropolitan Museum of Art acquisition policy that favored mainstream American modernists. The resulting publicity culminated in a now famous group portrait called "The Irascibles" that was published in the 15 January 1951 issue of *Life* magazine. Pousette-Dart's stance in this photograph, positioned at the edge of the group, presaged his decision later that year to move his family to Eagle Valley Road in Sloatsburg, New York. In 1954 they moved to Christmas Hill Road in Monsey, New York, followed by a move in 1958 to Suffern, New York. Although he later maintained a small apartment in Manhattan, Pousette-Dart kept his home and studio in Suffern for the rest of his life, because he preferred to work apart from the pressures of the New York City art scene.

In his paintings from the 1940s Pousette-Dart employed a cubist infrastructure (a kind of grid) out of which his forms—circles, fishes, eyes, amoebae-like shapes, eggs—would emerge as shifting, translucent forms. His process was slow—as many as forty layers of oil paint—which made for compositions controlled more by intellect than by the unconscious. "Layering," as he wrote in one of his notebooks, "is an analogy to life itself." During the next decade, he began to use color more expressively and spread his forms across the canvas. By the 1960s Pousette-Dart had reduced his imagery to circular, holistic forms set in fields of color, evoking a sense of the cosmos. Although Pousette-Dart's outward style changed, his basic intent—his quest for the transcendent in art—remained the same.

Throughout his life Pousette-Dart remained connected to the New York art scene. He received many awards, starting with a 1951 Guggenheim Fellowship. He also taught in various New York schools, first at the New School for Social Research (1959–1961), followed by the School of Visual Arts (1964), Columbia University (1968–1969), and Sarah Lawrence College in Bronxville (1970–1974). In 1980 he began teaching at the Art Students League in New York City, which he continued until his death. Bard College, which had awarded him an honorary doctorate of humane letters in 1965, made him the Milton Avery Distinguished Professor of Arts in 1983. In 1974 he joined the Andrew

Crispo Gallery, moving in 1980 to the Marisa del Re Gallery.

Pousette-Dart also had many museum exhibitions. The Whitney Museum of American Art held his first retrospective in 1963, followed by a solo show in 1974. The Museum of Modern Art organized an extensive traveling exhibition of his work in 1969. Late in life he was honored with two retrospectives, at the Fort Lauderdale Museum of Art in 1986 and the Indianapolis Museum of Art in 1990. The latter museum commissioned bronze doors from Pousette-Dart for the facade of its new pavilion, which were installed in time for the opening of his retrospective. On 25 October 1992, six months after the four-venue Indianapolis show closed, Pousette-Dart died of colon cancer at his apartment in New York City.

Pousette-Dart remained a fierce individualist, who so firmly believed in his artistic vision that he worked in isolation to keep it free of commercialism. His paintings were for him a portal, communicating to the viewer the spiritual nature of the universe. In his statement for the Whitney's 1958 show, *Nature in Abstraction,* Pousette-Dart wrote, "A work of art for me is a window, a touchstone or doorway to every other human being. It is my contact and union with the universe." He added, "Art transcends, transforms nature, creates a nature beyond nature, a supra nature, a thing in itself—its own nature, answering the deep need of man's imaginative and aesthetic being."

★

Pousette-Dart's notebooks are in his estate. The following exhibition catalogues are particularly useful: Sam Hunter, ed., *Transcending Abstraction: Richard Pousette-Dart, Paintings 1939–1985* (1986); Robert Hobbs and Joanne Kuebler, *Richard Pousette-Dart* (1990); and Lowery Stokes Sims, *Richard Pousette-Dart* (1997). Two general sources on abstract expressionism containing useful discussions of Pousette-Dart are Stephen Polcari, *Abstract Expressionism and the Modern Experience* (1991), and April Kingsley, *The Turning Point: The Abstract Expressionists and the Transformation of American Art* (1992). For the bronze doors, see Stephen Polcari and David Finn, *The Portal* (1998). A significant article is Gail Levin, "Richard Pousette-Dart's Emergence as an Abstract Expressionist," *Arts Magazine* 54 (Mar. 1980): 125–129. An unpublished interview of Richard and Evelyn Pousette-Dart, conducted by Stephen Polcari on 9 March 1992, is in the Archives of American Art, Washington, D.C. An obituary is in the *New York Times* (27 Oct. 1992).

LEIGH BULLARD WEISBLAT

PRICE, Vincent Leonard, Jr. (*b.* 27 May 1911 in St. Louis, Missouri; *d.* 25 October 1993 in Los Angeles, California), art connoisseur and actor in 100 motion pictures, best known for his roles in horror films.

Price was the youngest of four children of Vincent Leonard Price, president of the National Candy Company of St. Louis, and Marguerite Cobb Willcox, a homemaker. An early interest in art led Price, at the age of twelve, to purchase a Rembrandt etching for $37.50. Throughout grammar and high school at the exclusive St. Louis Country Day School, Price acted in school plays and musicals.

Price entered Yale University in 1929. Along with studying, he frequented theaters and art galleries and joined the Yale Glee Club. He graduated in 1933 with a B.A. in English (with an art history minor). After a year of teaching English at the Riverdale Country School in New York City, Price left the United States in 1934 to study art history at London University's Courtauld Institute. He never finished his thesis on Albrecht Dürer. In 1935, on a dare, Price auditioned for, and was cast in, *Chicago* at London's Gate Theater. That same year he was cast as Prince Albert in *Victoria Regina*. His performance was praised, and he rapidly became a celebrity. The play moved to Broadway in December, where Price continued his role opposite Helen Hayes. Later, Price would credit Hayes with teaching him the craft of acting. When the play began a national tour in the summer of 1937, Price stayed in New York to broaden his acting range through summer-stock productions. He met the actress Edith Barrett when the two starred in *Parnell,* and they were married less than a year later, on 23 April 1938. Their son, Vincent Barrett Price, was born on 30 August 1940.

Vincent Price. THE KOBAL COLLECTION

Late in 1938 Price joined Orson Welles's Mercury Theatre, which was devoted to producing classics on Broadway. After appearing in *Shoemaker's Holiday* and *Heartbreak House,* Price grew disenchanted with Welles's undisciplined style of production and left that summer for Hollywood. He soon signed a generous contract with Universal Pictures, and before the year was over he had made *Service De Luxe* (1938), a romantic comedy with Constance Bennett. This film, as well as *The Private Lives of Elizabeth and Essex* (1939) and *The House of the Seven Gables* (1940), established Price as a matinee idol. In 1941–1942, Price appeared on Broadway in *Angel Street* to rave reviews. The Prices decided to divide their time between Hollywood and New York City. Though for the rest of his life Price would travel back and forth, he considered Hollywood his home.

In 1943 Price and his fellow actor George Macready opened The Little Gallery, an art shop in Beverly Hills. Despite the fact that it closed in a year, Price's reputation as an art connoisseur was cemented, and he would later sit on the board of trustees of the Los Angeles County Art Museum and spread his enthusiasm for the arts throughout the nation.

In the 1940s, under contract to Twentieth Century Fox, Price appeared in a number of memorable films, such as *The Song of Bernadette* (1943), *Laura* (1944), and *Dragonwyck* (1946). Price was also in demand on radio, performing on such programs as *Suspense* and *The Saint.* In 1948 Vincent and Edith were divorced. Price married the costume designer Mary Grant on 28 August 1949; their only daughter, Mary Victoria Price, was born on 27 April 1962.

In 1951 Price donated ninety pieces from his personal art collection to East Los Angeles College, with which he had been affiliated since he had given an art lecture there in 1948. This donation became the foundation of the Vincent Price Gallery, the first hands-on, "teaching art collection" in a U.S. community college. Price remained integrally involved with the gallery until his death.

Price moved easily from drama to comedic character roles in films such as *Champagne for Caesar* (1950) and *His Kind of Woman* (1951). His performances were usually praised by critics, but it wasn't until he appeared in his first true horror film, *House of Wax* (1953), that he achieved stardom. Along with appearing in such classics as *The Ten Commandments* (1956) and *The Fly* (1958), Price appeared onstage in West Coast theaters and toured the nation in *Don Juan in Hell.* He also appeared in numerous television shows, including *Playhouse 90* and the quiz show *$64,000 Challenge* in 1956, where he won the top prize in the category of art. That appearance is credited with linking him to art in the mind of the public. At the request of the U.S. government, from 1957 to 1972 he served on the Indian Arts and Crafts Board, which promoted Native American products. Price's autobiographical journey through art, *I Like What I Know* (1959), was a critical and popular success.

In 1960 American International Pictures (AIP) and the director Roger Corman made *House of Usher,* starring Price. The film's success resulted in Price working on twenty-two more films for AIP over the next fourteen years, six of which were based on the works of Edgar Allan Poe, most notably *The Pit and the Pendulum* (1961), *The Raven* (1963), and *The Masque of the Red Death* (1964). These low-budget films mixed humor with menace, garnered generally good reviews, and made money. Some, like the "shockumentary" *Taboos of the World* (1965), Price merely narrated. Others, like *Witchfinder General* (1968) and *The Abominable Dr. Phibes* (1971), though still within the horror genre, allowed Price to exhibit his fine dramatic range.

From 1962 to 1966, Price worked for the department-store chain Sears, Roebuck selecting original works of art for the Vincent Price Collection, which aimed to bring "fine art at reasonable prices" into the homes of middle-class people. Also for Sears, Price and his wife edited *A Treasury of Great Recipes* (1965). This cookbook, featuring recipes from restaurants in nine nations, was a best seller and added culinary expertise to Price's reputation as a Renaissance man.

During the 1960s and 1970s, Price continued to appear on television programs, including *The Lucy Show, The Brady Bunch,* and *Batman,* usually as a "wacky" villain, a self-parody of his earlier roles. Price also appeared on game shows, most notably more than 900 times on *Hollywood Squares.* Price's wit made him a hit on talk shows, especially the *Tonight Show,* where he once demonstrated how to cook a fish in a dishwasher. In 1966 Price began to write an art column for the *Chicago Tribune,* which was soon nationally syndicated.

While filming *Theater of Blood* (1973), Price met and fell in love with the actress Coral Browne. Mary and Vincent divorced in April 1974, and Price married Browne on 24 October. Starting in 1977 Price toured the country for a year and a half in *Diversions and Delights,* a one-man play about Oscar Wilde. Most critics and fans agree that it was the performance of his career. Although it closed after a short time on Broadway, Price would go on to perform it throughout the 1980s in more than 250 cities worldwide.

Price's voice was so recognizable that he was often hired for voice-over work. He appeared on Alice Cooper's album *Welcome to My Nightmare* (1975) and Michael Jackson's *Thriller* (1983). In 1986 Disney hired him as the voice of Professor Ratigan, the villain in *The Great Mouse Detective* (1986). After narrating the director Tim Burton's animated short *Vincent* (1982), about a boy who idolizes Vincent Price, the two men became friends, and in 1990 Price had a cameo in Burton's feature film *Edward Scissorhands,* as Edward's inventor. From 1981 to 1989 Price hosted *Mystery!*

for PBS, introducing British mysteries to the American television audience. It was perhaps the ultimate incarnation of his lifetime of personas: menacing, yet urbane. Price died of lung cancer and Parkinson's disease. He was cremated and his ashes scattered off Point Dume, near Santa Monica, California.

★

Price's papers are held at the Library of Congress, Manuscript Division, Washington, D.C. Price's *I Like What I Know* (1959) covers his early years. Victoria Price, *Vincent Price: A Daughter's Biography* (1999) is an exhaustively detailed biography. Lucy Chase Williams, *Complete Films of Vincent Price* (1995) examines his films and contains a lengthy biography. See also Lawrence French, Steve Biodrowski, and David Del Valle, "Vincent Price: Horror's Crown Prince," in *Cinefantastique* 19, no. 1/2 (1989): 40–84. Obituaries are in the *Los Angeles Times* (26 Oct. 1993) and the *New York Times* (27 Oct. 1993).

KEVIN LAUDERDALE

QUESADA, Elwood Richard ("Pete") (*b.* 13 April 1904 in Washington, D.C.; *d.* 9 February 1993 in Jupiter, Florida), innovative commander of tactical aviation units during World War II and first administrator of the Federal Aviation Agency.

Quesada was one of three children of Lope Lopez Quesada, a Spanish-born consultant on currency engraving to the U.S. Treasury Department, and Helen A. McNamara, an executive secretary. He grew up in Washington, D.C., and attended Technical High School, where he excelled at sports and was named all-district football quarterback. After a brief period at the Wyoming Methodist Seminary in Wilkes-Barre, Pennsylvania, he transferred to the University of Maryland on a football scholarship. He subsequently matriculated to Georgetown University, although family lore holds that he never graduated.

Quesada enlisted as a cadet in 1924 in order to quarterback the Army Flying School's football team at Brooks Field, Texas. Although a broken leg put an end to his gridiron career, he completed the aviation training program, won his wings, and was commissioned in 1925 as a second lieutenant in the Air Reserve.

Following a brief and unsuccessful attempt to play professional baseball and a stint as a government employee, Quesada went on active military duty in September 1927 as an engineering officer at Bolling Field, Washington, D.C. Nine months later he made the first of what would become a series of productive associations with senior officials when he became aide to Major General James Fechet, then chief of the Air Corps. Quesada gained widespread public attention when Fechet selected him to copilot the *Question Mark,* a Fokker trimotor that set an endurance

Lt. General Elwood Quesada after President Eisenhower named him administrator of the new Federal Aviation Agency, 1958. © BETTMANN/ CORBIS

record in January 1929 by staying aloft for 150 hours and forty minutes, thereby demonstrating the potential of aerial refueling.

Quesada served as an assistant military attaché in Cuba from October 1930 to April 1932, then returned to Bolling Field. The pattern of forming close relationships with influential officials continued and Quesada became aide (in turn) to Trubee Davidson, the assistant secretary of war for air; General Hugh Johnson, the head of the National Recovery Administration; and Secretary of War George Dern. His one significant operational assignment came between February and June 1934, when he served as chief pilot of the Newark-Cleveland route when the Army Air Corps briefly took over operation of the nation's commercial air mail service.

The years from 1936 to 1940 brought academic and diplomatic duties for Quesada. He graduated from the Air Corps Tactical School and the Army Command and Staff College. For two and half years he served as technical adviser to the Argentine air force. Returning to Washington from Buenos Aires in October 1940 he became an intelligence analyst in the office of the chief of the air corps.

In July 1941 Quesada embarked on the first of what would become a series of operational assignments when he took over the Thirty-third Pursuit Group at Mitchel Field, New York. His overseas duty began early in 1943, with leadership of the Twelfth Fighter Command in North Africa. Over the next eight months Quesada became a strong advocate of tactical air power while participating in the Tunisian, Sicilian, Corsican, and Italian campaigns.

In October 1943 Quesada took over the Ninth Fighter Command in England and prepared for the invasion of Europe. His force of 1,500 P-38s, P-47s, and P-51s supported the D-Day landings in France in June 1944, then worked closely with General Omar Bradley's First Army in a series of interdiction campaigns during the drive into Germany. During these months of heavy fighting, Quesada earned a reputation as a hard-driving, no-nonsense commander. "His friends liked to say he had a strong personality," one former staffer commented; "his enemies said he was a son-of-a-bitch of the first order." Certainly, Quesada's army superiors valued his aggressive, innovative approach to tactical air support. A number of air force generals, wedded to strategic aviation, were less appreciative of his outspoken behavior.

Quesada returned to the United States in April 1945 to prepare for assignment to the Pacific theater. The war ended, however, before his scheduled departure, giving him time for his family. Quesada had married Kate Davis Pulitzer Putnam, granddaughter of the publisher Joseph Pulitzer, during the war; With Putnam he had two stepdaughters and two sons.

In 1948 Quesada was promoted to lieutenant general and given command of the Tactical Air Command in the newly independent United States Air Force. He soon clashed with General Hoyt Vandenberg, the air force chief of staff, over the low priority accorded tactical aviation. Bitterly disappointed, Quesada retired in October 1951.

Quesada spent 1951 to 1953 as vice president of Olin Industries, a defense contractor, then three years as vice president of the missile division of Lockheed Aircraft Corporation. In 1957 U.S. president Dwight D. Eisenhower selected him to chair the Airways Modernization Board, where he worked to integrate civilian and military aircraft into a modern air traffic control system. After helping to draft the law for a new Federal Aviation Agency (FAA), Quesada become the organization's first administrator in November 1958.

Quesada brought to the FAA the same aggressive qualities that he had displayed during the war. Intent on enhancing aviation safety, he clashed with the Air Line Pilots Association over the mandatory retirement age for pilots (which he set at sixty), and with industry over a requirement for airborne radar. Quesada set the tone for a federal agency whose main task would be the vigorous enforcement of safety regulations in the jet age.

Quesada retired in January 1961. He went on to head a firm to develop L'Enfant Plaza in Washington, D.C., and to become co-owner of the Washington Senators baseball team. He died of heart failure in a Jupiter hospital. He is buried in Arlington National Cemetery in Arlington, Virginia.

★

Quesada's papers are in the Library of Congress and the Dwight D. Eisenhower Presidential Library. His wartime service is detailed in Thomas Alexander Hughes, *OVER LORD: General Pete Quesada and the Triumph of Tactical Air Power in World War II* (1995). For his FAA years, see Stuart I. Rochester, *Takeoff at Mid-Century: Federal Civil Aviation Policy in the Eisenhower Years, 1953–1961* (1976). An obituary is in the *New York Times* (10 Feb. 1993).

WILLIAM M. LEARY

R

RAUH, Joseph Louis, Jr. (*b.* 3 January 1911 in Cincinnati, Ohio; *d.* 3 September 1992 in Washington, D.C.), civil rights activist, labor lawyer, and a fixture in Democratic party politics who personified post–World War II liberalism.

Rauh was born into a prosperous family of German Jewish ancestry in Cincinnati. He was the youngest of three children. His mother was Sarah Weiler, a homemaker; his father, Joseph Rauh, was a shirt manufacturer who had emigrated from Germany. He attended Harvard, earning an A.B. magna cum laude in 1932. He then attended Harvard Law School, graduating first in his class in 1935. After law school, he went to work as a Supreme Court clerk, first for Justice Benjamin Cardozo and then for his former law school professor Felix Frankfurter. He also worked as counsel to a number of New Deal agencies, such as the Lend-Lease Administration. In 1942 he accepted an army commission as a lieutenant and joined General Douglas MacArthur's staff as a lend-lease expert. He transferred to the Pacific later in the war, rising to the rank of lieutenant colonel, and he was eventually awarded the Distinguished Service Medal. He was married in September 1935 to Ollie Westheimer, with whom he had two sons.

After the war, he returned to Washington, D.C. He became legal adviser to various unions, including the United Auto Workers (UAW) and the Brotherhood of Sleeping Car Porters. He also aided those hounded by McCarthyism, most notably the playwright Arthur Miller and the writer Lillian Hellman. But he is best remembered for his activism for civil liberties and civil rights. And in this he had a near revolutionary zeal.

In 1947 Rauh joined with Eleanor Roosevelt, the labor leader Walter Reuther, the economist John Kenneth Galbraith, the historian Arthur Schlesinger, Jr., the theologian Reinhold Niebuhr, and former vice president Hubert Humphrey to create Americans for Democratic Action (ADA). The ADA was created as a liberal base to defend the Democratic Party from the growing conservative movement and to prevent liberalism's hijacking by communists. He was ADA chair from 1955 to 1957 and remained active throughout his life. In 1992, he was an ADA vice president.

In 1948 Rauh was hired by Walter Reuther, then the president of the UAW, to be the union's Washington counsel. At the time the UAW was the most powerful union in the United States. As the union's point man on lobbying and legislative matters, Rauh was at the center of national policy debates surrounding issues of economic reform and racial policy.

Rauh used his position with the union and the ADA to push for a civil rights agenda in the 1948 Democratic party platform. He continued to push his party in this direction for the rest of his life. He shared his sense of mission with his client Walter Reuther and often acted as a liaison between the powerful labor leader and the civil rights movement. For example, in 1963 Rauh arranged for $160,000 in bail for civil rights activists being held in jails in Birming-

Joseph L. Rauh, Jr., 1958. CORBIS CORPORATION (BELLEVUE)

ham, Alabama—including the Reverend Martin Luther King, Jr. Rauh contacted Reuther, who provided the bulk of the funds and pressured other unions for the rest.

Reuther and Rauh did not always see eye to eye. During the summer of 1963, members of the Student Nonviolent Coordinating Committee (SNCC), working together with local activists, attempted to register African American voters in Mississippi, where opposition to civil rights led to the murders of three of the activists. SNCC had steady opposition from the all-white Mississippi State Democratic party, so they registered the new voters into the newly chartered Mississippi Freedom Democratic Party (MFDP). They planned to challenge the all-white party at the upcoming Democratic party national convention in 1964. Joe Rauh agreed to serve as the MFDP's counsel at the convention. The Democratic incumbent Lyndon Johnson believed the challenge would embarrass him, and he asked for Reuther's help. Reuther demanded that Rauh decline to serve as attorney for a group that many Democrats viewed as too radical. Rauh replied, "I am acting not as your general counsel, but as a private citizen. I've got a private law practice. If you want to fire me, Christ's sake, be my guest." Reuther, according to Rauh, was so mad "you could fry an egg on his heart." But he did not fire him. In the end, the delegates from the MFDP walked out after

Reuther worked behind the scenes with other liberals to engineer a compromise favorable to Johnson.

Although Rauh continued to work for his union clients and he backed Johnson in strenuously lobbying Congress for the 1964 Civil Rights Act and the Voting Rights Act of 1965, the Vietnam War also drove a wedge between Rauh and Johnson. On matters of civil rights, Rauh thought Johnson "near perfect." But as the war dragged on, he and fellow liberals such as Martin Luther King, Jr. began to advocate peace. Starting in 1968, Rauh began to advocate a negotiated settlement and created a group to further that cause called "Negotiate Now!" He endorsed Eugene McCarthy for president later that year because of McCarthy's peace platform.

Rauh gave up his law practice late in life but continued to remain active in politics. He kept up a strenuous speaking schedule and never gave up the opportunity to vocally attack the Reagan and Bush administrations—especially the choices for the Supreme Court. He had a profound belief in the future. "I'm proud of our laws," he said, "what our generation has done is bring equality in law. The next generation has to bring equality in fact." Several months after Rauh's death from heart failure, President Bill Clinton awarded him the Presidential Medal of Freedom. Rauh is buried in Washington, D.C.

★

Rauh's papers are on deposit at the Library of Congress. There are no biographies of Joseph Rauh, but he receives prominent mention in a number of important works. See David J. Garrow, *Protest at Selma: Martin Luther King Jr. and the Voting Rights Act of 1965* (1978); Arthur M. Schlesinger, *Robert Kennedy and His Times* (1978); William H. Chafe, *Never Stop Running: Allard Lowenstein and the Struggle to Save American Liberalism* (1993); Kevin Boyle, *The UAW and the Heyday of American Liberalism, 1945–1968* (1995); Nelson Lichtenstein, *The Most Dangerous Man in Detroit: Walter Reuther and the Fate of American Labor* (1995); and David J. Garrow's biography of King, *Bearing the Cross: Martin Luther King Jr. and the Southern Christian Leadership Conference* (1986). Oral histories are on deposit at the LaGuardia-Wagner Archives, City University of New York. An obituary is in the *New York Times* (5 Sept. 1992).

RICHARD A. GREENWALD

RAY, Aldo (*b.* 25 September 1926 in Pen Argyl, Pennsylvania; *d.* 27 March 1991 in Martinez, California), gravel-voiced American screen actor who portrayed tough guys with soft hearts in the 1950s and 1960s.

Ray was born Aldo Da Re, the first of five children born to Silvio Matteo Da Re, an Italian immigrant who worked as a laborer, and Maria De Pizzol, a homemaker who was born in Brazil but grew up in Italy. When Ray was an

Aldo Ray. THE KOBAL COLLECTION

infant his family moved from Pennsylvania to Crockett, California, about forty miles northeast of San Francisco, where Silvio Da Re found work in a sugar refinery. After graduating from John Swett High School in 1944 Ray enlisted in the U.S. Navy and became a frogman during the last year of World War II. He served in the Pacific, including in the invasion of Okinawa. After the war, from 1946 to 1948, Ray attended Vallejo Junior College, where he was a star athlete in football and swimming. Upon receiving his associate of arts degree he studied political science at the University of California at Berkeley from 1948 to 1950 but left without graduating.

Ray moved back to Crockett and successfully campaigned for election as constable (sheriff). In 1950 he drove his brother to an audition as an extra in a film called *Saturday's Hero*. The director David Miller asked Ray to read for a part. Instead, Ray delivered one of his campaign speeches. The studio executives, who loved his gravelly voice, declared him a natural actor and offered him a part in the movie. The head of Columbia Pictures, Harry Cohn, wanted Ray to change his name to John Harrison, but Ray agreed only to drop the first syllable of his last name and to anglicize the spelling of the last syllable. In 1951 Ray married Shirley Green; they had one daughter and were divorced in 1952.

After *Saturday's Hero*, Ray's contract was renewed, and he was cast opposite the established actress Judy Holliday in *The Marrying Kind* (1952). Ray was acclaimed an instant success. A role in *Pat and Mike* (1952), with Spencer Tracy and Katharine Hepburn, followed by Ray's portrayal of Sergeant O'Hara in *Miss Sadie Thompson* (1953), with Rita

Hayworth, led to *Battle Cry* (1955), in which Ray portrayed a World War II soldier who returned home an amputee. This role called for a wide range of emotions, from a brash and harsh soldier to a sensitive and loving husband. It was rumored that Cohn had wanted Ray to play the lead opposite Deborah Kerr in *From Here to Eternity* (1953), but the director Fred Zinnemann insisted the role be given to Montgomery Clift. Perhaps Ray's career would have taken a different direction had he won the part. In 1954 he married Jean Marie Donnell, an actress known as Jeff Donnell. They divorced in 1956.

Ray's all-American, wholesome good looks, athletic build, and blond hair were a dramatic contrast to Humphrey Bogart's dark, dour character in *We're No Angels* (1955), which demonstrated that Ray could play comedy roles. His next major role was in *God's Little Acre* (1958). Later that year he played the sadistic yet complex Sergeant Croft in *The Naked and the Dead*, based on the 1948 book by Norman Mailer, arguably Ray's most memorable role. His last major film was *The Green Berets* (1968), with John Wayne, in which Ray was typecast as still another sergeant, this time during the Vietnam War. In 1960 Ray married Johanna Bennett, with whom he had two sons. They were divorced in 1967.

When his career took a downward turn after *The Naked and the Dead,* Ray decided to try filmmakers in Europe, but he was offered only minor roles. Returning to California, he made almost fifty B films over the next seventeen years, all beneath his talents. In the last interview before his death, Ray stated: "In some ways the tough soldier role locked me in. There were no sophisticated roles for me. I never seemed to get past master sergeant, although I always thought of myself as upper echelon."

Mired in debt and unable to secure major roles in films, Ray returned to his hometown of Crockett in 1983. He worked occasionally in minor films and television, including a small part in *Falcon Crest* in 1985. Ruefully Ray later worked in a nonunion film and was forced to resign from the Screen Actors Guild in 1986. Though Ray continued to work until 1989, he was plagued by illness. Admitted to the Veterans Administration Hospital in Martinez, California, in February 1991, he died of throat cancer and complications from pneumonia at the age of sixty-four. He was cremated, and his ashes were scattered into the water beneath the Golden Gate Bridge in San Francisco.

Ray never became a big Hollywood star, but he was not just a supporting actor, at least for the first ten years of his career. Although he showed early promise in comedy and romantic roles, directors never explored that promise. Consequently he was locked into portrayals of military men whose complexity was never allowed to develop.

★

An excellent, factual article on Ray is in Bob King, ed., *Films of the Golden Age* 13 (summer 1998): 74–84. Biographical sketches are in many indices of performing arts, including Barbara McNeil and Miranda C. Herbert, eds., *Performing Arts Biography Master Index* (1981), and Dennis La Beau, ed., *Theatre, Film, and Television Biographical Master Index* (1979). Obituaries are in Deborah Andrews, ed., *The Annual Obituary 1991* the *Los Angeles Times* and the *New York Times* (both 28 Mar. 1991), *Newsweek* and *Time* (both 8 Apr. 1991).

ELAINE MCMAHON GOOD

REASONER, Harry (*b.* 17 April 1923 in Dakota City, Iowa; *d.* 6 August 1991 in Norwalk, Connecticut), broadcast journalist and news anchor who brought a wry wit and graceful urbanity to network news across four decades.

Reasoner was born in Dakota City, Iowa, in the heart of the agricultural prairie, the only child of two teachers. His father, Harry Ray Reasoner, became superintendent of a rural school district. His mother, Eunice Nicholl, had family in nearby Humboldt, a community established by abolitionists in 1863, where Reasoner spent most of his childhood.

From an early age Reasoner wanted to be a writer, and he developed an interest in journalism as a way of learning his craft. Like his parents, he saw his career as a civic responsibility. The Midwestern "middle," he was convinced, had long been the strength and the direction of the country. When his family moved to Minneapolis in 1934, Reasoner's moderate views were welcomed at West High School, where his rugged good looks and amiable self-deprecation made him well liked. Graduating in 1941, he wrote for the *Minneapolis Times* before deciding to continue his education, first at Stanford University and then at the University of Minnesota, where he resumed his work with the *Times*.

In 1943 Reasoner was drafted into the U.S. Army but remembered the experience because of a leave he won in 1944 to speak at the Republican Party convention after winning a national first-voter contest on what the party's postwar policy should be. He enjoyed the spotlight, he said, "once I was sure the crowd wasn't coming at me." He began writing what would be his only novel, *Tell Me About Women,* a thinly disguised autobiographical account of two army buddies "of distinctly sedentary type" and their halfhearted pursuit of women who "knew all about themselves" and "had more self-assurance than anyone, except God, ought to have." The book was published in 1946, the year of Reasoner's discharge from the army. It hardly cemented his literary reputation but encouraged him to press ahead with his writing for the *Minneapolis Times.* Later that year he married a Minneapolis girl, Kathleen "Kay" Carroll. They had seven children.

Reasoner's work as a drama critic for the *Times* lasted

Harry Reasoner, 1980. © BETTMANN/CORBIS

less than two years. He panned the musical *Up in Central Park* and was fired on the theory that "you couldn't criticize a New York show or they'd stop coming." He had his revenge when the *Minneapolis Times* later "slipped and fell and had to be destroyed." His two years in public relations, working for Northwest Airlines, was pleasant enough, but he drifted back into news writing with WCCO radio in Minneapolis in 1950. The following year he was back in government service as chief editor at the U.S. Information Agency's Far East production center in Manila. He traveled throughout Asia during this assignment and was getting well-rounded, but he found that the work didn't pay. While home on leave he looked up Sig Mickelson in New York, a former professor of his at the University of Minnesota who was now president of CBS News. Mickelson told Reasoner to get experience in broadcast journalism if he wanted to work at the network.

Reasoner became news director at KEYD-TV in Minneapolis in 1954, doing the 6:00 and 10:00 news, while producing half-hour weekly documentaries that included a look at racial prejudice in Minneapolis. Reasoner began writing little end-pieces on the Saturday and Sunday evening news that showed his characteristic wit and capacity for droll cultural commentary. It led him to the opportunity to work as a summer replacement on the assignment desk at CBS in New York for $157.50 a week. His thirty-five-year career in network news had begun.

Initially Reasoner rose quickly through the ranks. In 1957 he was made the first full-time CBS television correspondent. Reasoner did news and features for *Douglas Edwards with the News,* the network's nightly news show. "The challenge was to illuminate the story for television," Reasoner recalled, "without corrupting it for journalism." The key was to remember that "even with the pictures, the writing was still important." He covered the first fumbling days of the U.S. space program and thought he did "my best work ever" in reporting the desegregation of Little Rock's Central High as a battle between "old custom and new conscience." He covered the visit of Soviet premier Nikita S. Khrushchev to the United States in 1959 and President Dwight D. Eisenhower's Far East tour the following year. Nevertheless, by the fall of 1960 his career was on hold. In West Virginia, he had gone to bed before finding out that Hubert H. Humphrey had ended his presidential campaign after his defeat in a crucial primary to John F. Kennedy. He "sulked and behaved badly" when Charles Kuralt, twelve years younger, was promoted over him to host the weekly *Eyewitness to History.* As a result of his attitude and major faux pas, Reasoner was assigned a backwater job of writing and reading two ten-minute radio broadcasts a day on CBS radio. He feared he would always be a journeyman.

Reasoner perfected his distinctive broadcast style on radio. A ten-day story on the hijacking of a Portuguese ocean liner was written in the style of a soap opera. Ernest Hemingway's obituary was delivered in Hemingway's style. Jack Gould of the *New York Times* wrote that Reasoner's dry humor and individuality were the best things on radio. CBS executives took notice. Reasoner was made anchor of the WCBS-TV evening news in New York. The show's popularity soared and with it Reasoner's reputation. For two years he hosted *Calendar,* the forerunner of the *CBS Morning News,* and beginning in the fall of 1963 he became a frequent substitute for Walter Cronkite on the fledgling *CBS Evening News.* His documentaries for *CBS Reports* included "The Fat American," "The Taxed American," "The Teen-Age Smoker," and "The Harlem Temper." His prime-time work with writer Andy Rooney between 1963 and 1965 included "An Essay on Doors," "An Essay on Bridges," and "The Great Love Affair," which was about the American romance with the automobile.

The Reasoners gave up their home in Weston, Connecticut, in February 1965, when Harry succeeded Dan Rather as CBS White House correspondent. However, Reasoner had a distaste for Washington's insularity and thought covering the president represented a lot of time wasted. His critics complained he wasn't aggressive enough, and CBS felt that the position did not play to his strengths. Don Hewitt approached Reasoner and Mike Wallace to cohost *60 Minutes,* a magazine news program that went on the air in September 1968 against the most popular show on television, *Marcus Welby, M.D.* Reasoner specialized in soft news. Wallace gave the show its edge. Neither thought it would last. When Reasoner left the show in December 1970 to coanchor the *ABC Evening News,* Hewitt's brainchild was well on its way to becoming the most popular news show in the history of television.

Leaving CBS was the most wrenching experience Reasoner had ever had, but "I wanted to be an anchorman once before I died and the only tiger in the zoo." Reasoner's appearance beside Howard K. Smith nearly doubled the audience for ABC News by 1973. Two years later Reasoner was anchoring alone. But ABC remained in third place among the networks and Reasoner blamed it on his laziness. He had found that daily anchoring was a grinding job that took daily meticulous devotion. By the fall of 1975 he was "tired of introducing reports from interesting places I would never have a chance to see." The ABC evening news had lost its momentum and network officials teamed Reasoner with Barbara Walters, hired from NBC's *Today Show,* to boost ratings. It attracted publicity but not viewers.

When Reasoner returned to CBS News in June of 1978 he feared he had grown "soft on a lot of money" and wondered whether "I could do what I used to do." The 33 million weekly viewers of *60 Minutes* gave him his answer. The show annually appeared as one of the top ten programs on the air throughout the 1980s. Reasoner left it at the end of the 1990–1991 season to become, at the age of sixty-seven, editor emeritus. His veteran colleague Mike Wallace called him the heart and soul of the show. The success at CBS the second time around proved bittersweet. Reasoner had long neglected his personal life and his marriage ended in divorce in 1981. He married Lois Parker Weber seven years later; they had no children. A long-time smoker, he survived surgery for lung cancer in 1987 and 1989. In 1989 he finally completed his journalism degree at the University of Minnesota. He was sixty-six. Two years later, on 6 August 1991, he died of cardiopulmonary arrest after emergency surgery to remove a blood clot from his brain. Reasoner was buried at Union Cemetery in Humboldt, Iowa.

For years Reasoner had been, next to Walter Cronkite, the most trusted newsman in America. Don Hewitt, the executive producer of *60 Minutes,* observed that "Harry Reasoner was not the only broadcaster from the Midwest, but he was the only broadcaster who brought the Midwest with him to television." He said his long-time associate had "that Iowa sense of what's important." His work won five Emmy Awards and a Peabody Award for outstanding achievement in news. At his death, Rooney and Hewitt affirmed Reasoner's central role in celebrating the power of good writing in broadcast journalism. Reasoner saw journalism as the effort of men and women to bring order out of chaos, not by exhortation or evangelism, but by trusting audiences to do what they ought with information they needed to know.

★

Reasoner's memoir of his days in broadcast journalism is *Before the Colors Fade* (1981). A collection of his early broadcast essays appeared as *The Reasoner Report* (1966). His novel *Tell Me About Women* was republished in 1964. A speech he gave at Memphis State University on "The News Media—A Service and a Force, The Changing Challenge to Journalism," is reprinted in Phineas J. Sparer, *The World Today* (1975). His reflections on the news business also appear in Sally Bedell, "What Made ABC's Harry Reasoner Switch Back to CBS?" *TV Guide* (27 Jan. 1979). A biographic article on Reasoner, written by Tommy V. Smith, appears in *Encyclopedia of Television News* (1999). A summary of his first decade at CBS is described in *Current Biography 1966*. For context on his work as a network news anchor, there is Barbara Matusow, *The Evening Stars: The Making of the Network News Anchor* (1983). For his many roles at CBS News, there is Gary Paul Gates, *Air Time: The Inside Story of CBS News* (1978). Don Hewitt and Mike Wallace described Reasoner's importance in the development of *60 Minutes* when they were interviewed on the Cable News Network's *Larry King Live* on 21 May 1996. Reasoner's work on *60 Minutes* is also analyzed by Axel Madsen, *60 Minutes: The Power and Politics of America's Most Popular TV News Show* (1984), and Richard Campbell, *60 Minutes and the News: A Mythology for Middle America* (1991). An obituary appears in the *New York Times* (7 Aug. 1991).

BRUCE J. EVENSEN

REMICK, Lee Ann (*b.* 14 December 1935 in Boston, Massachusetts; *d.* 2 July 1991 in Los Angeles, California), actress whose all-American beauty and natural acting style graced such films as *Anatomy of a Murder* (1959) and *Days of Wine and Roses* (1962) and the television miniseries *Jennie: Lady Randolph Churchill* (1975).

Remick was the younger of two children of Frank Edwin Remick, a Harvard-educated clothier, and Margaret Waldo, a stage actress. She spent her earliest years in Quincy, Massachusetts, where her father managed his family's specialty apparel store. When Remick was seven, her parents separated, and she and her brother went to live with their mother in New York City. Her mother enrolled Remick at Miss Hewitt's Classes (now the Hewitt School), an exclusive day school for girls on Manhattan's Upper East Side. Groomed for a career in the performing arts, she attended after-school classes in ballet, modern dance, music, speech, and theatrical costume and scene design.

Although ballet was the great passion of her childhood, Remick gravitated toward the theater as she grew older. In

Lee Remick. THE KOBAL COLLECTION

the spring of 1952 she answered an advertisement for dancers for summer stock at the Music Circus in Hyannis, Massachusetts, lied about her age, and ended up performing in ten different shows in ten weeks. In the fall of that year Remick met playwright Reginald Denham at Sardi's restaurant and was given a chance to read for the part of a sarcastic teenager in *Be Your Age*, a comedy co-written by Denham and Mary Orr. When she was cast in the Broadway role in 1953, Remick was nearly expelled from Miss Hewitt's Classes for breaking school rules forbidding participation in professional productions during the academic year. After lengthy deliberations, she was allowed to remain in school and to act in the play. *Be Your Age* closed after only five performances, but the job gained Remick an agent and a number of new auditions before her graduation.

To be near work opportunities Remick matriculated at Barnard College in Manhattan in the fall of 1953. She tried to juggle a full course load, theatrical and television auditions, and dance and voice lessons, but the effort only wore her to a frazzle. As a result she left school after one semester to begin acting professionally. Over the next five years Remick honed her craft in the live dramas that abounded in New York City during the "Golden Age" of television. She appeared in a variety of roles on such anthology programs as *Armstrong Circle Theater, Playhouse 90, Robert Montgomery Presents,* and *Studio One,* working with Richard Kiley, Viveca Lindfors, Paul Muni, and other accomplished actors.

A May 1956 performance in "All Expenses Paid" on *Robert Montgomery Presents* brought Remick to the attention of director Elia Kazan, who cast her in the film *A Face in the Crowd* (1957), a cautionary tale of the power of radio and television media. Remick's work in the small but showy role of a seductive drum majorette resulted in a seven-year, one-picture-per-year contract with 20th Century–Fox. Remick married William Arthur Colleran, a television director, on 3 August 1957. They had two children.

After moving to Los Angeles Remick appeared in *The Long Hot Summer* (1958) and *These Thousand Hills* (1959) for Fox. Her first major role came in a Columbia picture, *Anatomy of a Murder* (1959), when she replaced Lana Turner, who was fired by director Otto Preminger after a wardrobe dispute. Remick got along with the notoriously difficult Preminger, and as the flirtatious Laura Manion, whose husband is on trial for killing her alleged rapist, she more than held her own in a cast that included James Stewart and George C. Scott as opposing lawyers. During a pivotal scene in which the strikingly beautiful, blue-eyed blonde removed her glasses and shook down her hair on the witness stand, film historian David Thomson wrote, "the jury audience wavers like chaff in a sensual breeze."

Remick's early portrayals of kittenish characters seemed to bring her to the brink of major stardom, but she resisted efforts to promote her as an American Brigitte Bardot. After *Anatomy of a Murder,* Remick avoided sexpot roles in favor of more challenging parts in pictures directed by Elia Kazan and Blake Edwards. Kazan put her intuitive, unmannered style to good use as a young widow with two children who falls in love with the Tennessee Valley Authority official (Montgomery Clift) sent to take her family's land in *Wild River* (1960). Under Edwards's direction she ably played a bank teller menaced by a psychopathic extortionist in *Experiment in Terror* (1962), and gave her most memorable film performance as a wife drawn into alcoholism by her husband (Jack Lemmon) in *Days of Wine and Roses* (1962). For this last role, which Remick thoroughly researched at Alcoholics Anonymous meetings, jails, and rehabilitation centers, she earned her only Academy Award nomination.

Despite her string of artistic successes, Remick's film career began to stall by the mid-1960s. The "lost, lovely ladies" she played won praise from critics, but her movies had little box-office appeal. The well-bred Remick's aversion to self-promotion also put her at a disadvantage in the fiercely competitive atmosphere of Hollywood.

Although she received fewer scripts and experienced a drop-off in the quality of her pictures, Remick continued to turn in first-rate performances. Most notable were her portrayals of the long-suffering wife of a wandering ex-convict (Steve McQueen) in *Baby, the Rain Must Fall* (1965), and the promiscuous, estranged spouse of the title character (Frank Sinatra) in *The Detective* (1968). Among Remick's other films of the decade are *Sanctuary* (1961), *The Wheeler Dealers* (1963), *The Hallelujah Trail* (1965), *No Way To Treat a Lady* (1968), and *Hard Contract* (1969).

In 1964 Remick returned to New York City to make her Broadway musical debut in *Anyone Can Whistle,* a satirical paean to nonconformity, written by playwright Arthur Laurents and composer Stephen Sondheim. As Fay Apple, a nurse at an asylum called the Cookie Jar, she received rave reviews for her acting, singing, and dancing, but the critics were not as kind to the avant-garde show, and it closed after only nine performances. Shortly thereafter Remick relocated to Manhattan and sought more theatrical opportunities. In 1966 she originated the role of a blind woman terrorized by drug smugglers in Frederick Knott's dramatic thriller *Wait Until Dark.* The play became an enormous hit and Remick, who prepped for her part at the Lighthouse (New York Association for the Blind), was nominated for a Tony Award.

Following a separation of several months, Remick and her husband divorced in November 1968. That same year she met William Rory ("Kip") Gowans, a British assistant director, during the filming of *Hard Contract.* They married in December 1970, and Remick moved to London. They had no children.

Of the twelve films Remick made during her British residency from 1970 to 1982, only the blockbuster supernatural thriller *The Omen* (1976), in which she played the mother of the anti-Christ, and the Ismail Merchant-James Ivory art house production of Henry James's *The Europeans* (1979), in which she was a fortune-hunting German baroness, garnered much attention. As a consequence, she rediscovered television as a vehicle for her talents. With the motion picture industry having tilted more toward the youth market in the 1970s, the made-for-TV movie and its offshoot, the miniseries, provided Remick with opportunities to appear in adaptations of contemporary novels and historical biographies geared to an adult audience.

After picking up Emmy award nominations for supporting parts in *The Blue Knight* (1973) and *QB VII* (1974), the first two American miniseries, Remick landed the plum role of Jennie Jerome, the American beauty who became the mother of British statesman Winston Churchill, in the British-made *Jennie: Lady Randolph Churchill.* The elaborate, seven-part costume drama, in which Remick aged from eighteen to sixty-seven, aired in Britain in 1974 and on PBS the following year. Although she bore no resemblance to the flamboyant Jennie physically or emotionally, Remick received almost universal acclaim for her performance. "The somewhat cool Miss Remick obviously likes the very warm Jennie," wrote *New York Times* critic John J. O'Connor, "and the mixture of actress and characterization is most attractive." In addition to winning the Best Actress award from the British Academy of the Film and Television Arts (BAFTA) for *Jennie,* Remick captured a Golden Globe award and her third Emmy nomination.

A flood of small-screen work followed and Remick was earning $500,000 to $750,000 per television movie by 1980. She was at her best in characterizations of real-life figures, including Kay Summersby, the British driver and alleged lover of General Dwight D. Eisenhower in *Ike* (1979); Margaret Sullavan, the troubled actress and wife of producer Leland Hayward in *Haywire* (1980), for which she received another Emmy nomination; and especially, Frances Bradshaw Schreuder, an unbalanced heiress who conspired with her son to murder her father in *Nutcracker: Money, Madness, Murder* (1987). Remick, who had moved back to Los Angeles in 1982, also portrayed first lady Eleanor Roosevelt in *Eleanor: In Her Own Words* (1986), a one-woman show. Among her other notable television credits are *Wheels* (1978), *The Women's Room* (1980), *The Letter* (1982), and *A Gift of Love: A Christmas Story* (1983).

Shortly after completing the telefilm *Dark Holiday* (1989), Remick was diagnosed with kidney and lung cancer. She battled the disease for two years, undergoing surgery and experimental treatments, but her health continued to fail and she was prevented from taking on any major projects. Remick made her last acting appearance in the A. R. Gurney play, *Love Letters* in Beverly Hills, in 1990, and in the last stages of her illness, she attended the dedication of her star on the Hollywood Walk of Fame in April 1991. Remick died at her home in Los Angeles and her remains were cremated.

At her death, commentators praised Lee Remick's talent, versatility, and professionalism, but most lamented the fact that she never reached the level of film stardom attained by her idols Bette Davis and Katharine Hepburn and contemporaries Audrey Hepburn and Elizabeth Taylor. The modest Remick probably would not mind such comments. As she once said: "I don't quite know what stardom means. It was never something I went after, as such. I love to work . . . and I love trying to do the best. I suppose stardom means power, basically—and I'm not too good at that."

★

There are clipping files on Remick at the Margaret Herrick Library of the Academy of Motion Picture Arts and Sciences in Beverly Hills, California, and in the Billy Rose Theatre Collection at the New York Public Library for the Performing Arts, Lincoln Center. Barry Rivadue, *Lee Remick: A Bio-Bibliography* (1995)

includes a biographical sketch, a detailed inventory of Remick's film, stage, and television performances, and an annotated list of newspaper and magazine articles on her life and career. Lillian Ross and Helen Ross, *The Player: A Profile of an Art* (1962), contains a short autobiographical piece assembled from interviews of Remick. David Thomson, *A Biographical Dictionary of Film* (1994), contains a useful entry on Remick. Michael Buckley, "Lee Remick," *Films in Review* (Nov. 1988), is a substantial portrait which includes Remick's own commentary on her work. Important tributes are by Charles Champlin in the *Los Angeles Times* (3 July 1991) and Andrew Sarris in the *New York Observer* (30 Sept. 1991). Obituaries are in the *Los Angeles Times* and *New York Times* (both 3 July 1991) and in *Variety* (8 July 1991).

RICHARD H. GENTILE

RESHEVSKY, Samuel Herman (*b.* 26 November 1911 in Ozorkov, Poland; *d.* 4 April 1992 in Suffern, New York), chess grandmaster and author who gained international fame touring Europe and the United States as a young boy and became the leading American player and a world championship contender for nearly three decades.

Reshevsky was the sixth child of Jacob Reshevsky (originally Rzeszewski), a linen merchant, and Shaindel Eibeschitz, who were Orthodox Jews. At the age of four or five, Reshevsky learned chess while watching his father play and almost immediately developed an unusual talent for the game, quickly defeating other players in his native village. Impoverished by World War I, his family moved to Łódź where Reshevsky's chess skill was recognized. At the age of six, he toured Poland, giving small chess exhibitions. During 1919 and 1920, at the age of eight, he toured Europe giving exhibitions against twenty or more players, winning the vast majority of his games, attracting considerable publicity, and enriching his family.

Invited to the United States by American chess aficionados, Reshevsky arrived in New York City with his family on 3 November 1920, where the city's chess-playing community had arranged a series of exhibitions. In his first public performance, Reshevsky scored nineteen wins and one draw, playing twenty opponents simultaneously at the U.S. Military Academy in West Point, New York, on 10 November 1920. This and subsequent exhibitions were widely reported in the American press.

In 1921 and 1922 Reshevsky went on a national tour of the United States that lasted nearly eighteen months. In October 1922, at age ten, he played in his first tournament. Although his results were only fair, his victory over David Janowski, once a challenger for the world championship, stunned the chess world.

Child welfare authorities had been monitoring the strain imposed on Reshevsky by his exhibitions and his lack of

Samuel Reshevsky at the International Chess Congress, 1937. © HULTON-DEUTSCH COLLECTION/CORBIS

formal schooling. In October 1922 legal action was initiated against Reshevsky's parents, who were charged with improper guardianship. The case was dismissed after it was proven that Reshevsky was receiving religious education at a rabbinical school. Following a court recommendation, a sponsor outside the Reshevsky family was designated to report to the court periodically on his behalf.

While on tour in Chicago, the businessman and philanthropist Julius Rosenwald took an interest in Reshevsky and offered to finance his education, providing that he would curtail his chess exhibitions. Reshevsky's family settled in Detroit, where six months of private tutoring enabled him to enter Northern High School. In 1925 Reshevsky became a naturalized American citizen. On graduation from high school in 1929, he entered the University of Detroit to study accounting. After two years, he transferred to the University of Chicago, graduating in 1933 with a bachelor's degree in accounting.

Meanwhile, Reshevsky began to play chess more frequently, after his family relocated to Chicago in the early 1930s. After several excellent results in Western Chess Association championships, Reshevsky easily won a tournament in Syracuse, New York, in 1934 that featured many of the leading American chess masters. Returning to Europe in 1935, he won two English tournaments, in one of which he defeated the Cuban player José Raoul Capablanca, a former world champion.

In 1936 Reshevsky recovered from two early losses to win the U.S. championship. He repeated that performance

on five other occasions (1938, 1940, 1942, 1944, and the final time in 1969). By the end of the 1930s, Reshevsky was recognized as one of the finest players in the world. His style was characterized by a fierce will to win, technical virtuosity, uncommon tenacity in defending inferior positions, and icy calm in the face of time pressure. On 24 June 1941, Reshevsky married Norma Mindick; they had three children.

For a time during the 1940s, Reshevsky devoted more attention to his accounting profession and abstained from tournament chess. In 1946 he returned to compete in the first "over-the-board" match (that is, in person rather than by radio communication) between the United States and the Soviet Union, held in Moscow, and later that year decisively won the U.S. championship. In Reshevsky's only opportunity to directly compete for the world's championship, he tied for third place behind Mikhail Botvinnik in a five-man tournament in 1948.

Reshevsky conducted a national exhibition tour in 1950, after which he stated that he would concentrate on chess full-time. During the cold war in the late 1940s and early 1950s, he emerged as the leading player outside the Communist bloc and was recognized as the unofficial champion of the "Free World" by winning two matches against the Polish-born Argentine grandmaster Miguel Najdorf. The peak of his career occurred in the United States–Soviet Union team match held in Moscow between 29 June and 5 July 1955. While the United States suffered a 25–7 defeat, Reshevsky won his individual match from world champion

Botvinnik, scoring one win and three draws. He was lionized in a widely publicized 4 July reception at the American Embassy, and was photographed with the Soviet leaders Nikita Khrushchev and Nikolai Bulganin. During this period of his chess career, Reshevsky was supported by a yearly stipend raised by a group of wealthy chess patrons. His efforts to challenge Botvinnik and other leading Soviet players to an extended match were unsuccessful, however.

Reshevsky's preeminent position in American chess was challenged by Bobby Fischer in the late 1950s. A 1961 match between the two players ended in a contentious and controversial draw when Fischer withdrew after eleven games due to a dispute with match sponsors over the starting time for the twelfth game. Throughout the 1960s Reshevsky continued to compete internationally and in American events. One of his finest triumphs was in Buenos Aires in 1960, when he tied for first with Victor Korchnoi. Fischer was among the also-rans. Reshevsky also continued his quest for the world championship, participating in qualifying tournaments and matches during the 1960s and 1970s. During the 1960s, he became a contributor to the *New York Herald Tribune* and *New York Times* and wrote several chess books, including an account of the 1972 world championship match between Fischer and world champion Boris Spassky.

Reshevsky suffered an apparent heart attack between rounds of a tournament in 1976. Yet he continued to live the life of a chess professional, competing, giving exhibitions and chess lessons, writing books and articles, conducting correspondence games, and playing more frequently than in his heyday decades earlier. Intermittently during his chess career, he had also worked as an accountant, a life insurance salesman, and a financial analyst. In October 1983 Reshevsky was reunited with his two oldest rivals: Reuben Fine, America's second great player in the 1930s, and Botvinnik, on the occasion of the latter's visit to New York City. In 1986 Reshevsky was inducted into the U.S. Chess Federation Hall of Fame.

Reshevsky's final serious chess competition took place in Moscow in June 1991, when he drew a short match against the former world champion and old rival Vassily Smyslov, whom he had first played in 1939. On 4 April 1992, while attending Sabbath services, Reshevsky suffered a fatal heart attack. He died at Good Samaritan Hospital in Suffern, New York.

A devoutly religious man, Reshevsky's strict adherence to his Orthodox Jewish beliefs often created difficulties for tournament organizers and opponents, as well as self-imposed hardships. He was a diminutive man (barely over five feet tall), blunt, terse, with a rather cold personality to those outside his close friends and family, and he viewed chess pragmatically as a profession. His exploits as a child prodigy served to popularize chess and attract countless adherents to the game but also robbed him of a normal childhood.

★

Biographical information on Reshevsky, together with a selection of his best games to that point, can be found in his *Reshevsky on Chess* (1948), a book which may have been completely ghost-written. Edward Lasker, *Chess Secrets* (1951), contains reminiscences of Reshevsky. A recent attempt to amass all his games, details of his chess career, and extensive biographical information is Stephen W. Gordon, *Samuel Reshevsky: A Compendium of 1,768 Games, with Diagrams, Crosstables, Some Annotations, and Indexes* (1997). Reshevsky was profiled in *Time* (20 Oct. 1952). A Reshevsky interview, given to Hanon Russell in 1991, appears in *Chess Life* (Nov. 1991). An obituary is in the *New York Times* (7 Apr. 1992).

EDWARD J. TASSINARI

REVELLE, Roger Randall Dougan (*b.* 7 March 1909 in Seattle, Washington; *d.* 15 July 1991 in San Diego, California), oceanographer and pioneer in the study of global warming, noted also for his leadership in academic, scientific, and government circles on environmental, population, and natural resource policy.

Revelle's father, William Roger Revelle, was a lawyer, but after the family's move from Seattle to Pasadena, California, in 1917, he spent most of the remainder of his career as a junior high school teacher. Ella Robena Dougan, his mother, also taught for a short time. Both parents were graduates of the University of Washington. He had one sibling.

While a boy, Revelle attended schools in Pasadena, California. Upon entering Pomona College at the age of sixteen in 1925 his initial interest was in journalism, but he was soon inspired to study geology. After completion of his bachelor of arts degree in 1929 he pursued graduate study in geology, first at Pomona College for a year, and then for a year at the University of California at Berkeley. He then accepted an appointment to study at the Scripps Institution of Oceanography in La Jolla, California, where he completed his doctoral studies in 1936.

While an undergraduate he met Ellen Virginia Clark, a member of the Scripps newspaper publishing family, and they were married on 22 June 1931. Remaining together until his death, they had four children. The Scripps family was the great benefactor and namesake of the Scripps Institution of Oceanography, with which Revelle was closely affiliated during most of his career. He was influential in developing Scripps into one of the world's outstanding oceanographic research institutes. Following completion of his doctorate at the Scripps Institution, Revelle spent a year at the famous Geophysical Institute in Bergen, Norway,

Roger Revelle. AP/WIDE WORLD PHOTOS

after which he returned to Scripps in 1937 as an instructor. He became an assistant professor there in 1941.

Revelle's initial research during the 1930s was on sediments of calcium carbonate in the Pacific Ocean and chemical buffering relationships in sea water, research that was later to be extended to the interaction of atmospheric gases—carbon dioxide, in particular—with sea water. This area of research, with which he remained involved throughout his professional life, led to the publication in 1957, with Hans E. Suess, of the first influential paper on the anthropogenic, or human, sources of carbon dioxide and the potential for the creation of a "greenhouse effect" in the earth's atmosphere.

Revelle became committed to oceanography early in his career, although the science of the oceans was much better developed at that time in Europe than in the United States. Over the course of his career, Revelle became one of the most influential figures in the world in the development of oceanography, perhaps as much because of his eventual status as a "statesman of science" as because of his scientific accomplishments.

Realizing early in his career that knowledge of seamanship would be an advantage when studying the oceans, he obtained a small boat operator's license while a young faculty member at Scripps. A few months before the bombing of Pearl Harbor in 1941, Revelle began active duty in the

U.S. Navy, where he would remain for seven years. He used his special expertise to advise the military about the oceans and to help develop the navy's research function. By 1944 he had been promoted to the rank of commander.

Revelle is credited with conceiving and organizing both the initial and the first follow-up research missions surrounding the first postwar atomic tests by the United States in 1946 on the Bikini Atoll in the Marshall Islands. The experience and contacts he developed during these years in the navy, working with government and military officials as well as with many influential scientists, served him well as a promoter and leader in the development of environmental and science policy.

In 1948 Revelle returned as associate director and professor of oceanography at the Scripps Institution. In 1950, after some internal opposition to a physical oceanographer becoming head of Scripps, he assumed its directorship. The next decade was the period of his most creative scientific work. He was the organizer and leader of a number of ocean research expeditions that contributed to a change in prevailing views of the ocean floor and to development of the theory of plate tectonics.

When the University of California set out to found a new campus in southern California, Revelle was the primary leader in convincing the Board of Regents to establish the new campus at San Diego, next to the Scripps Institution. It was widely assumed, because of his extensive involvement and influence in founding the new University of California at San Diego, that he would become its first chancellor in 1961. That was not to be, however, and the disappointment led him to embark upon what his colleague and long-time friend, Walter Munk, has called a "fourteen-year exile."

In 1961 Revelle took a leave of absence from Scripps to become the first science adviser to serve in the U.S. Department of the Interior, where he was active in advising government officials during the initial stages of the environmental movement. He, for instance, advised Interior Secretary Stewart L. Udall and President John F. Kennedy to support the controversial views of Rachel Carson, detailed in her 1962 book *Silent Spring*. They both did so, and the book is widely recognized as the most important early stimulus to the environmental movement.

After almost two years in Washington Revelle returned to Scripps in 1963, but the following year he founded the Center for Population Studies at Harvard University, where he became the director and professor of population policy. While at Harvard he expanded his work on world population, food resources, and environmental pollution, as well as fulfilling his role as a key adviser on scientific and environmental issues to government and scientific leaders in India and Pakistan.

During the 1992 U.S. presidential campaign, and again

during the campaign of 2000, Revelle was credited by candidate Albert Gore with having inspired Gore's interest in the environment through a course taught by Revelle at Harvard. Revelle remained at Harvard until 1976, when he returned to the University of California at San Diego to teach science, technology, and environmental policy.

Because of the wide recognition of Revelle's contribution to the issue of global warming, his service to a vast array of government and scientific panels and commissions tends to be overlooked. Recognition was accorded, however, in the many awards he received, among them the Tyler Prize in Ecology in 1984, the Balzan Foundation Prize in 1986 for overall contributions on matters of the oceans and atmosphere, and the National Medal of Science in 1990, the latter conferred by President George Bush. He was elected to membership in the prestigious National Academy of Sciences in 1957, and he served a term as president of the American Association for the Advancement of Science in the 1970s. Revelle died at the age of eighty-two of complications from a heart attack. His remains were cremated and his ashes scattered at sea off the coast of La Jolla.

★

The Roger Randall Dougan Revelle Papers (1928–1979) are in the archives of the Scripps Institution of Oceanography, La Jolla, California. Among Revelle's publications, two are especially informative concerning the work he did on the greenhouse effect and global warming. The first of these is Roger Revelle and Hans E. Suess, "Carbon Dioxide Exchange Between Atmosphere and Ocean and the Question of an Increase of Atmosphere CO_2 During the Past Decades, Tellus 9, no. 1 (1957): 18–27. The second is Roger Revelle, "Carbon Dioxide and World Climate," *Scientific American* 247, no. 2 (1982): 35–43, which was highly influential in informing a broad audience of the potential impact of the greenhouse effect. A tribute by Walter H. Munk is in the *Proceedings of the National Academy of Science, U.S.A, 1997,* vol. 94 (8275–8279). An obituary is in the *New York Times* (17 July 1991).

W. HUBERT KEEN

RIDGWAY, Matthew Bunker (*b.* 3 March 1895 in Fort Monroe, Virginia; *d.* 26 July 1993 in Pittsburgh, Pennsylvania), U.S. Army officer who served as commander of the Eighty-second Airborne Division and the Eighteenth Airborne Corps in World War II, commander of United Nations forces in the Korean War, and chief of staff of the United States Army.

Ridgway was the son of an army artillery officer, Thomas Ridgway, a native of Staten Island, New York, and Ruth Starbuck Bunker, of Garden City, Long Island, New York. He had one sister. In 1901, after his father returned from a tour in China, the family moved from Long Island to a series of army postings, including Fort Walla Walla, Washington, and Fort Snelling, Minnesota.

Matthew Ridgway. LIBRARY OF CONGRESS

Between 1907 and 1912, young Matt Ridgway attended schools in North Carolina, Virginia, and Boston. He was admitted to West Point on 14 June 1913. He graduated at roughly the middle of his class of 139 in May 1917. After graduation, he was sent to Eagle Pass, Texas, on the Mexican border, where he commanded an infantry company.

Shortly before his West Point graduation, he married the first of three wives, Julia Caroline Blount, with whom he had two daughters. On 16 June 1930, the couple divorced, and Ridgway subsequently lost touch with his daughters. A few days after the divorce was final, the young officer married Margaret ("Peggy") Wilson Dabney. In 1936 he adopted Peggy's daughter. Peggy divorced him in June 1947. In December 1947 he married Mary Princess ("Penny") Anthony, a descendant of Susan B. Anthony, whom Ridgway admired for her love of the outdoors and the strenuous life. Their son was born in 1949. He was hit by a train and killed during a canoe portage at the age of twenty-one.

In September 1918 the army ordered Ridgway to West Point, where he served as a Spanish instructor until 1925. The new academy superintendent, General Douglas MacArthur, appointed him director of athletics. This prominent position helped him earn prime assignments to the Fort Benning infantry school in Georgia, and from there to the Fifteenth Infantry Regiment in Tianjin, China.

After China, Ridgway resumed troop duty with the Ninth Infantry Regiment in San Antonio, Texas, where the brigade commander, Major General Frank R. McCoy, took notice of him and invited him on a high-level military political mission to conduct and supervise elections in Nicaragua. Ridgway's fluent Spanish made him an obvious choice and he jumped at the chance to go to Central America, even though he had to abandon his plans to try out for the 1928 Olympic pentathlon.

When he returned from Nicaragua, Ridgway took the new, much revised infantry course at Fort Benning, finishing first in his class. He held a variety of staff, school, and politico-military assignments through the 1930s, graduating from the Command and General Staff School at Fort Leavenworth, Kansas, in 1935, and from the Army War College in 1937. These school assignments placed him in line for generalship if war came. In 1939, he accompanied General George C. Marshall on an important military mission to Brazil, and Marshall soon appointed him the army's desk officer for Latin America.

Despite some cloak-and-dagger work in Latin America, he loathed the desk job. By the end of January 1942, General Marshall assigned him to be General Omar Bradley's assistant division commander for the Eighty-second Division, a position that carried with it Ridgway's first star. Within seven more months he would get command of the famed Eighty-second Division, and with it his second star. In twenty-five months, he had risen from major to major general.

Shortly after Ridgway took command of the Eighty-second, the outfit was converted into an airborne division, requiring Ridgway to train his men in an entirely new technology that the army had never before used in combat. The Eighty-second Airborne fought valiantly under Ridgway's command in the big airborne operations during the invasions of Sicily and Normandy. On 6 June 1944 (D day) Ridgway became the first Allied major general on French soil—the only one to drop in by parachute. But the air corps tended to scatter troops when they dropped them in both operations, so that the soldiers were insufficiently concentrated to carry out their missions without sustaining heavy casualties.

Ridgway was given command of the Eighteenth Airborne Corps in recognition of his combat victories against significant odds and despite serious technological obstacles during the Normandy campaign. But Ridgway had yet to prove himself at high command—late in 1944 Supreme Commander General Dwight D. Eisenhower rated him thirty-one out of his thirty-two corps commanders. Eisenhower reevaluated his opinion of Ridgway after the Battle of the Bulge, writing General Marshall early in 1945 that Ridgway was one of the three top corps commanders in the European theater.

Ridgway commanded several more successful operations in the war against Germany, including Operation VAR-SITY, a drop on the far side of the Rhine River and the envelopment of the Ruhr River, in which his forces took 317,000 German prisoners. At the end of the war he successfully managed the Eighteenth Airborne Corps "dash to the Baltic" from central Germany—a logistical tour de force designed to cut the Red Army off from Denmark. During that operation, he won an Oak Leaf Cluster to the Silver Star for venturing out onto a bridge over the Elbe River that was under fire from German 88s, in order to encourage the engineers to finish the bridge in record time (he had been awarded the Silver Star for gallantry in the airborne invasion of Holland in September 1944). He was promoted to lieutenant general on 4 June 1945.

Postwar life offered a rich succession of posts between 1945 and 1950: commander of U.S. forces in the Mediterranean; U.S. Army representative to the United Nations Military Staff Committee; representative to the Inter-American Defense Board; and commander in chief, Caribbean theater. As deputy chief of staff for administration, he became the Pentagon point man on the Korean War.

On 22 December 1950, General Walton H. Walker, commander of the U.S. Eighth Army in Korea, was killed in an auto crash. Ridgway rushed from Washington to Korea to assume the command. Many knowledgeable observers believed that superior Chinese forces would soon push the UN forces off the Korean peninsula. Instead, Ridgway reorganized the Eighth Army's potentially disastrous retreat and advanced north to (more or less) the current border between the Koreas, a feat that was described by the army chief of staff General Maxwell Taylor as "the finest example of military leadership in this century." Shortly after President Harry S. Truman fired Douglas MacArthur for insubordination as commander in chief, Far East, in April 1951, he gave Ridgway the job. The appointment brought a promotion to full general on 11 May 1951.

Ridgway was less successful in the political military jobs he held in the 1950s, especially in his management of the Korean truce talks. But President Truman, eager to maintain the prestige that General Eisenhower had brought to the command of NATO forces in Europe, appointed General Ridgway to that critical position in 1952.

Eisenhower had lobbied against the appointment because he felt that Ridgway lacked political sensitivity. As president, Eisenhower kicked Ridgway upstairs to the office of army chief of staff (in July 1953) and then declined to reappoint him in 1955 after Ridgway publicly opposed Eisenhower's "New Look" defense policy, which limited defense expenditures and built up the air force at the expense of the army.

Ridgway's significant accomplishments as chief of staff include his steadfast defense of the army when it was attacked by the Republican senator Joseph McCarthy and his successful protest against American intervention in Indochina in 1954. He retired from the army as a four-star general and as America's top soldier in 1955 and worked until 1960 as director of the Mellon Industrial Research Institute in Pittsburgh—one of the predecessors of Carnegie Mellon University.

In the 1960s he became famous for his criticism of President Lyndon B. Johnson's decision to send combat troops to Vietnam. He was later invited to the White House (in March 1968) as one of the "wise men" who advised Johnson to negotiate a withdrawal. He actively supported Ronald Reagan for president in 1980, and he traveled with Reagan on his controversial trip to the German Army burial ground at Bitburg in 1985. Ridgway died of cardiac arrest on 26 July 1993 in Pittsburgh, Pennsylvania, at the age of ninety-eight and was buried with full military honors in Arlington National Cemetery in Arlington, Virginia.

Although he was not strong as a military politician, Ridgway was an excellent commander because he combined impressive personal courage with managerial and logistical skill. He was an excellent chief of staff because of his recognition of the limitations of American power. When the Eisenhower administration made it clear that that military expenditures would be limited, Ridgway understood that such limits on American military power dictated an avoidance of commitments to large-scale ground wars. Ridgway is remembered as a great commander because of the war in Indochina that he tried to prevent, as much as for the battles that he won in Europe and Korea.

★

Matthew Ridgway authored two books: *Soldier* (1956) and *The Korean War* (1967). His extensive collection of papers, photographs and oral histories may be found at the U.S. Army Military History Institute in Carlisle, Pennsylvania. George C. Mitchell's *Matthew B. Ridgway: Soldier, Statesman, Scholar, Citizen* (1999) is the authorized biography. Other biographies include Jonathan Soffer, *General Matthew B. Ridgway: From Progressivism to Reaganism* (1998); Clay Blair, *Ridgway's Paratroopers: The American Airborne in World War II* (1985), and *The Forgotten War: America in Korea, 1950–1953* (1987); and Roy Appleman, *Ridgway Duels for Korea* (1990). For additional bibliographic information, see Paul M. Edwards, *General Matthew B. Ridgway: An Annotated Bibliography* (1993). Obituaries are in the *New York Times* and *Washington Post* (both 27 July 1993).

JONATHAN M. SOFFER

RIDING, Laura (*b.* 16 January 1901 in New York City; *d.* 2 September 1991 in Sebastian, Florida), poet and literary critic best known for her avant-garde poetry of the 1920s and 1930s and a poetics, developed alone and in collaboration with the English writer Robert Graves, that contributed to the development of the New Criticism.

Born Laura Reichenthal, Riding was the daughter of Nathaniel S. Reichenthal, an Austrian Jew who immigrated to the United States in the 1880s, and Sarah ("Sadie") Edersheim. She had an older half sister and a younger brother. Both parents worked in the garment industry; the family lived in a tenement apartment in Brooklyn, New York, where Riding attended public school. She was influenced early by her father's fervent socialism and his determination that life could be improved through education and political activism. According to Riding's biographer, her father taught her "to read the newspapers with an eye for the capitalist subtext."

After graduating from Brooklyn Girls' High School, Riding entered Cornell University on a full scholarship in 1918. On 2 November 1920 she married Louis Gottschalk, her European history instructor, and discontinued her Cornell studies; in 1923 she moved to Louisville when Gottschalk was appointed assistant professor at the University of Kentucky, and although she took classes at this institution she eventually abandoned her undergraduate career. The couple had no children.

In the early 1920s Riding, who had started writing poetry at Cornell, began submitting her work to literary journals. From the beginning, her poems revealed a distinctive intelligence concerned with the articulation of consciousness; they derived less from traditional poetic images and diction than from philosophical inquiry. Because of this, Riding came to the attention of the Fugitives, a group of writers and thinkers centered at Vanderbilt University in Tennessee. From 1922 to 1925 in their journal *The Fugitive,* they published work by Robert Graves, Hart Crane, and Riding, among others. The group, which included the poets John Crowe Ransom, Allen Tate, and Robert Penn Warren, was dedicated to a reexamination of cultural and poetic practice, and they hailed Riding's innovative, densely textured, ironic verse, awarding her their top prize for poetry in 1924.

Divorced from Gottschalk in May 1925, Riding returned to the East Coast and was briefly enmeshed in the literary life of Greenwich Village. That December she left for Europe at the invitation of Graves, who had admired her work in *The Fugitive* and contacted her about a possible collaboration. Marking this new stage of her career was the publication of her first book of poems, *The Close Chaplet,* in 1926. In 1927 Laura Reichenthal changed her surname to Riding.

Riding spent thirteen years with Graves, who was married throughout the time of their association. Critics have described their influence on each other alternately as vital and "vampiric." Together they founded the Seizin Press in England in 1927. After Riding attempted suicide in 1929 (an action she later described as an effort not to kill herself but to break the bonds of the past), Graves moved with her to Majorca, Spain, where they relocated their publishing venture. They remained in Majorca until the outbreak of the Spanish civil war in 1936, when they relocated to London. The Seizin Press, which continued in operation until 1939, published important early modernist works and counted Gertrude Stein among its authors.

Riding and Graves's critical collaborations *A Survey of Modernist Poetry* (1927) and *A Pamphlet Against Anthologies* (1928), and Riding's *Contemporaries and Snobs* and *Anarchism Is Not Enough* (both 1928), laid the groundwork for the New Criticism by advocating the organic integrity of literary works and emphasizing the personal authority of the writer. William Empson acknowledged the influence of *A Survey* in his famous work *Seven Types of Ambiguity* (1930). In *Contemporaries and Snobs*, Riding expounded on her belief that poetry "changes accidental emotional forms into deliberate intellectual forms." She denounced the "professionalization" of poetry achieved by traditional literary criticism, which contextualized literature into a social and historical framework at the expense of the individual work: "More and more the poet has been made to conform to literature instead of literature to the poet—literature being the name given by criticism to works inspired by or obedient to criticism." She asserted that "poetry invents itself" and that the poem is a self-referential entity.

While in Europe, Riding edited with Graves a critical series titled *Epilogue*; on her own she published nine volumes of poetry and several works of fiction. In 1938 her *Collected Poems* was issued; in the preface to this work she introduced her poems as "an uncovering of truth." The early poem "Incarnations" is a representative piece; it begins, "Do not deny, / Do not deny, thing out of thing. / Do not deny in the new vanity / The old, original dust."

After Riding and Graves returned to the United States in 1939 their association ended. Riding married Schuyler B. Jackson, with whom she had begun a correspondence while in Spain, on 20 June 1941, and thereafter used the authorial signature Laura (Riding) Jackson. They had no children. Educated at Princeton, Jackson was a onetime poetry reviewer for *Time* magazine. He had praised her 1938 *Collected Poems* as written "in a language in which every word carries its fullest literate meaning."

Riding's commitment to language as revelatory of truth ultimately led to her renunciation of poetry in 1941. She explained in 1962, during a reading of her poems broadcast by the BBC (the statement was published in 1972 in Riding's *The Telling,* a book she described as her "personal evangel") that poetry, "with its overpowering necessities of patterned rhythm and harmonic sound-play," inevitably distorted truth. Moving to Wabasso, Florida, in 1943, Riding and Jackson undertook an ambitious linguistic study, and operated a fruit-shipping business until 1950. After Jackson's death on 4 July 1968 Riding lived alone and simply; she completed the study, which was published post-

humously in 1997 as *Rational Meaning: A New Foundation for the Definition of Words.* Her early works, which had fallen out of favor and out of print, saw a revival in the 1980s and 1990s, and in 1991 Riding received the Bollingen Prize from Yale University for her achievement in poetry. She died of a heart attack on 2 September 1991 at the age of ninety. Riding was cremated and her ashes buried in Wabasso.

In 1969 the critic Michael Kirkham, in *The Poetry of Robert Graves,* detailed Riding's seminal influence on Graves's later work. In *The Word "Woman" and Other Related Writings* (1993), Riding claimed that Graves's archetypal study *The White Goddess* (1948) was a distorted appropriation of her thought; she castigated the estranged Graves for having "sucked, bled, squeezed, plucked, picked, grabbed, dipped, sliced, carved, lifted [*The White Goddess*] out of the body of my work."

Riding is frequently described by critics as a cultural outrider who prefigured later movements and literary styles. In a review in the *New York Times* (28 November 1993) Carol Muske wrote that Riding's work in linguistics "anticipat[ed] (in spirit if not substance) contemporary language theory." In London's *Sunday Telegraph* (19 July 1992) the critic Anthony Thwaite suggested that in her "abrupt, enigmatic style" and "angular, piercing, sometimes uncanny" poetic forms Riding recalls such later poets as Sylvia Plath and John Ashbery; and the editors of Riding's *The Word "Woman"* envision her early writings as heralding the contemporary feminist movement.

Riding's singular commitment to truth, forged out of the cultural dislocations following World War I, led to work that has been characterized as difficult, obscure, and even impenetrable, and inevitably was vulnerable to the attacks brought against New Criticism generally: that the understanding of literary works solely as independent entities risks their irrelevance with respect to the larger cultural and historical context. Riding's denouncement of "relativist" constructs makes her poetry and prose difficult to place, and her commitment to the universal and immutable can leave the individual reader at sea. Personal eccentricities and a relentless compulsion to challenge critical appraisals of her work and life opened her to charges of megalomania. Riding, who once described herself as "embodying finality," approached neither life nor art with equanimity.

★

Riding's papers can be found in the Laura (Riding) Jackson and Schuyler B. Jackson Collection at the Cornell University Library, Ithaca, New York. A full-length biography is Deborah Baker, *In Extremis: The Life of Laura Riding* (1993). Richard Perceval Graves, *Robert Graves: The Years with Laura, 1926–1940* (1990), details her most important personal and professional collaboration. Joyce Piell Wexler, *Laura Riding's Pursuit of Truth,* is a critical approach to her work (1979). Jeanne Heuving, "Laura (Riding) Jackson's 'Really New' Poem," in *Gendered Modernisms: American Women Poets and Their Readers* (1996), edited by Margaret Dickie and Thomas Travisano, discusses Riding's "utopian vision of a new human universality." Obituaries are in the *New York Times* and the Florida *Vero Beach Press-Journal* (both 4 Sept. 1991).

MELISSA A. DOBSON

RIZZO, Frank Lazzaro (*b.* 23 October 1920 in Philadelphia, Pennsylvania; *d.* 16 July 1991 in Philadelphia, Pennsylvania), police commissioner and mayor of Philadelphia who was both praised as an effective crime fighter and denounced for ostensibly promoting police brutality.

Frank Rizzo was the oldest of four children of Italian immigrants Teresa Erminio, a homemaker, and Raffaele Rizzo. His father began working in Philadelphia as a tailor and then joined the city's police force for a long career as a patrolman, whetting his son's interest in law enforcement. A restless youth, Rizzo dropped out of Southern Philadelphia High School in 1938 and joined the U.S. Navy. Rizzo's naval career was cut short in 1939 when he was

Frank Rizzo, 1980. © LEIF SKOOGFORS/CORBIS

discharged for medical reasons after being diagnosed with diabetes.

Upon his return home the family moved out of its south Philadelphia immigrant neighborhood to more comfortable quarters on Mount Pleasant Avenue in northwest Philadelphia and Rizzo took a job at Midvale Steel, manufacturing war equipment. The death of his mother in 1942 devastated Rizzo, who vowed to settle down and marry a woman who could provide the kind of close-knit family home life like the one in which he had been raised. On 18 April 1942, only five weeks after his mother's death, Rizzo married Carmella Silvestri. They had two children. Joining his father on the Philadelphia police force in 1943, Rizzo worked as a foot patrolman back in the south Philadelphia neighborhood where he had grown up. Unlike his easygoing father, who seldom made arrests, Rizzo—a 250-pound, six-foot, two-inch patrolman—was a hard-driving, career-striving, macho tough guy who was an effective street cop. Tagged "Fearless Frank" by his fellow patrolmen, he earned the second nickname of "The Cisco Kid," a popular television cowboy of the time, and also a reputation for honesty. In 1951 Rizzo was promoted to sergeant by the reform administration of the new mayor Joseph Clark. In 1952 he was made acting captain of his unit.

Assigned to an African American district, Rizzo was criticized by black activists for his tough crackdown on the numbers rackets and street crime, but became deputy police commissioner in 1964. Two years later—after several police officers had been shot by African American activists and black power advocate Stokely Carmichael had threatened publicly "to wage the war tactics of guerrillas against the police"—Rizzo invaded a safe house and found a cache of explosives and firearms. He was credited with putting Carmichael and the organization he belonged to, the Student Nonviolent Coordinating Committee, out of business in Philadelphia.

In 1967 the newly elected Democratic mayor James Tate decided to take the "law and order" issue away from the Republicans by appointing Rizzo as police commissioner. Rizzo, a lifelong Republican, then became a Democrat. The tough commissioner cracked down on violent groups such as the African American Revolutionary Action Movement (RAM), which was stockpiling weapons and explosives for a threatened war against white America. After Rizzo's raids RAM faded as a threat. An Associated Press photo of the bare-buttocked Black Panther revolutionaries being strip-searched by the Philadelphia police in 1970 was broadcast across the nation and had positive and negative consequences for the commissioner. Liberals and African American activists used it as an emblematic photo to confirm their charges of Rizzo as a "racist" and anti-black. On the other hand, the Republican president Richard Nixon was impressed by the Philadelphia police department's ability to prevent the kinds of riots—accompanied by burning, looting, and vandalism—that swept Los Angeles, Detroit, and Newark during the 1960s. Nixon made a public relations trek through Philadelphia in 1968 and praised Rizzo's record as a standard for urban police departments.

By 1970 Rizzo's frequent appearances in Washington, D.C., and the national publicity surrounding his hard line against revolutionary violence had made him, as his biographer, S. A. Paolantonio, wrote, "America's Number One Crime Fighter." Both the Democratic and Republican parties maneuvered to get him on their mayoral tickets, knowing he would carry the white urban working-class vote. President Nixon had hoped to convince Rizzo to join the Republicans, but Rizzo took the Democratic nomination in 1971 and won the mayoral election over his socially prominent opponent, W. Thatcher Longstreth.

Rizzo's first term, from 1972 to 1976, was a perilous time for urban America. White flight was spurred by the violent urban riots of the 1960s. At the same time, urban manufacturers and other businesspeople were moving to lower-tax suburbs or to the South. Philadelphia suffered massive job losses for which the mayor was blamed by his political opponents. Despite the lack of support from his own party, Rizzo handily won reelection in 1975.

In 1976 Rizzo's second term began inauspiciously when he pushed a huge tax increase through the city council. The increase was used to pay for Rizzo's generous wage settlements with city employees, including money spent to settle teachers' strikes. In addition, the newly elected Democratic president, Jimmy Carter, who had publicly repudiated Rizzo as a Democrat, cut Philadelphia's share of federal general revenue sharing, putting even more pressure on the city budget. Philadelphia also lost federal jobs when Carter moved many of them south of the Mason-Dixon line. To add insult to injury, Carter and Congress refused to appropriate federal funds to make Philadelphia the "Bicentennial City" for the 1976 Independence Day celebration.

Finally, although whites and the "little people" (as Rizzo called them) felt safer with the "big man" in office, African American activists and liberals continued to criticize the mayor for his allegedly racist law enforcement policies. His critics mounted a mayoral recall campaign, which fizzled when the courts ruled against it, declaring that many of the petition signatures were forgeries or belonged to unregistered voters. Rizzo's bad relations with the press contributed toward the expanding press image of Rizzo as "a racist and nasty bully." Annoyed by his treatment, Rizzo filed a $6 million libel suit against the *Philadelphia Inquirer,* which had satirized him in a Sunday column. The suit was dismissed, but when a union struck the *Inquirer* and blocked the delivery of newspapers, Rizzo refused to call out the police to break the boycott and strike. As a result, the city's press permanently turned against Rizzo.

Facing a two-term limit, Mayor Rizzo sought unsuccessfully to change the city charter so that he could run for another term. After sitting on the sidelines for a term, he ran for mayor twice in the 1980s. In 1983 he lost the Democratic primary to Wilson Goode, who went on to become the city's first African American mayor. But Goode's administration stumbled badly in 1985 when it bombed MOVE, a black nationalist cult group, burning down sixty-one homes and killing several of the cultists. After Goode's inept handling of the MOVE crisis and the crack cocaine epidemic that raced through inner-city ghettos, Rizzo's tough cop policies again won the appreciation not only of whites but also of an increasing number of African American leaders.

In the 1980s Rizzo worked hard to redeem his reputation. He ran one of the most popular call-in radio shows in Philadelphia. Like many politicians, such as Presidents Nixon and Carter, the mayor looked better in his post-public years than in his years of public service. He also worked hard with African American political leaders and clergy and persuaded many of them that they had misunderstood his law-and-order policies. Rizzo had always showed great personal warmth to his fellow cops, and now he extended that attitude to the larger African American community by marching in anti-drug and anti-crime campaigns. Rizzo ran again for mayor in 1987 and his partial redemption showed in the election returns, with Rizzo making sizable inroads in black voting districts.

Rizzo made a political comeback in 1991 when he overcame the Republican leadership's opposition to win the party's mayoral primary against long odds, and was set to oppose Democrat Ed Rendell. While gearing up for the campaign, Rizzo died of a heart attack. He is buried in Holy Sepulchre Cemetery in Cheltenham Township, Pennsylvania.

Controversial in life, Rizzo remains controversial in death, scorned by some for his tough law enforcement policies and revered by others for making his city a safer place to live. Rizzo was a flawed yet public-spirited giant and a populist with a warm personal touch. He was a larger-than-life presence on the urban political scene during the riot-torn 1960s and the troublesome decades that followed.

★

Information on Frank Rizzo prior to his death can be found in Fred Hamilton, *Rizzo* (1973), while S.A. Paolantonio offers a standard, authoritative biography on the mayor two years after his death in *Frank Rizzo: The Last Big Man in Big City America* (1993). Ruminations on the Byzantine nature of urban Philadelphia politics can be found in Stephen Goode, "Back on the Mayor Go-Around," *Insight* (22 July 1991) and a handy summary of the

Rizzo story as told by Paolantonio is John J. Dilulio, Jr., "Philadelphia Story," *Washington Monthly* (July–Aug. 1993).

MELVIN G. HOLLI

ROACH, Harold Eugene ("Hal") (*b.* 14 January 1892 in Elmira, New York; *d.* 2 November 1992 in Los Angeles, California), pioneering film and television producer, writer, and director best known for introducing film audiences to Harold Lloyd, Laurel and Hardy, and Our Gang.

Roach was one of two children of Charles H. Roach, an Irish-Catholic insurance and real estate broker, and Mabel Bailey, who ran the boardinghouse in which the family lived. Bored with school, Roach left home at the age of sixteen. He headed west and embarked on a four-year odyssey down the Pacific Coast, working a series of fairly rugged jobs (as gold prospector, mule skinner, and construction worker) from Alaska to Southern California. By 1912, at the age of twenty, he arrived in Los Angeles. Having acquired an authentic western wardrobe during his wanderings, Roach found himself readily employable as a "dress" extra in movie Westerns. During the next two years,

Hal Roach, 1970s. NANCY R. SCHIFF/ARCHIVE PHOTOS

Roach rose from bit player to assistant director. In 1914 Roach and an acquaintance named Dan Linthicum founded the Rolin (*Ro*ach and *Lin*thicum) Film Company. Lacking a distributor to market its product to theaters, Rolin's first year produced little more than a stack of unsold films and a sea of red ink. Linthicum dropped out of the partnership.

Just as things were beginning to look hopeless for Rolin, Roach secured a distribution contract with the Pathé Exchange. Although Roach had intended for Rolin to produce everything from dramatic feature-length pictures to short comedies, Pathé was only interested in the latter, particularly those starring another Roach acquaintance, the comedic actor Harold Lloyd. Thus by this twist of fate, rather than by design, Roach became a specialist in slapstick comedy. For the remainder of the 1910s, Rolin's output was almost exclusively centered on the increasingly popular films of Harold Lloyd, many of which were personally directed by Roach. Under Roach, Lloyd's first screen persona, the Chaplin-derivative "Lonesome Luke," was replaced in 1917 by his "Glass Character," the bespectacled All-American boy-next-door, which brought Lloyd enduring fame.

The success of Lloyd's comedies gave Rolin financial stability. Roach brought his parents to California and made his father Rolin's secretary-treasurer. In 1920 the company moved from rented facilities in Hollywood to a new studio in the Los Angeles suburb of Culver City and changed its name from Rolin to the Hal E. Roach Studios.

In 1922 Roach inaugurated the "Our Gang" series, which charted the day-to-day comic adventures of a group of unaffected, working-class children. An immediate success, "Our Gang" became one of the longest-lived short-comedy series in movie history, produced by Roach from 1922 to 1938 and by MGM from 1938 to 1944. Renamed "The Little Rascals" for television syndication, the series remains a perennial favorite.

In 1921 Harold Lloyd began starring in feature-length pictures, joining the ranks of Charlie Chaplin and Buster Keaton, at the apex of film comedy. The Hal E. Roach Studios enjoyed its silent-era zenith with the release of *Safety Last* (1923), in which the hapless Lloyd is forced to climb the side of a tall building, at one point dangling from the hands of a giant clock. However, Lloyd soon decided to follow Chaplin's lead and set up his own independent production firm. After Lloyd's departure, Roach's output for much of the remainder of the 1920s was a mix of modestly successful short-comedy series, occasional feature-length Westerns and comedies, and the ever-reliable "Our Gang" series.

In 1927 two events lifted the studio out of its doldrums: Roach switched his distribution from the foundering Pathé to the industry's rising star, Metro-Goldwyn-Mayer

(MGM), and he teamed second-tier comedian/director Stan Laurel with a supporting comic named Oliver Hardy. Laurel and Hardy would become Roach's most successful stars since Harold Lloyd. The team remained with Roach until 1940, when they departed for other studios due to creative differences between Roach and Laurel.

Roach was married twice. His first marriage, to Margaret Nichols, produced two children: Hal, Jr., who died in 1972, and Margaret, who died in 1963. After Margaret's death in 1940, Roach wed Lucille Prin in 1942. This union produced four daughters and lasted until Lucille's death in 1981.

Although Roach won two Academy Awards for best short subject, for Laurel and Hardy's *The Music Box* (1932) and Our Gang's *Bored of Education* (1936), the tide in the 1930s was turning against independent short-comedy producers. The rise of double features left little revenue or time on a theatrical program for a twenty-minute short. In 1936 Roach decided to concentrate on feature-length pictures and to phase out short-film production. Laurel and Hardy, alone among Roach's short-film stars in their ability to carry a feature-length picture, were joined by a new breed of sleek and sophisticated comedies, such as *Topper* (1937); adventure films, such as *One Million B.C.* (1940); and serious dramas, notably *Of Mice and Men* (1939).

This new policy, however, resulted in fewer films being released per year. While most of Roach's films were at least modestly successful, none provided the type of box-office bonanza necessary to keep the studio going on such a slender output. By 1941 the studio was in serious financial trouble. Roach ceased feature production and instituted a series of "streamliners," forty-five minute "featurettes" that fit nicely as the second half of a double-feature program. The "streamliner" policy was just beginning to pay off when the United States entered World War II. Roach, who had joined the U.S. Army Signal Corps Reserves in the 1920s along with a number of other studio executives, was called into active military service at age fifty. Roach terminated "streamliner" production and leased the whole studio facility to the Army Air Force's First Motion Picture Unit for the production of training films. Ironically, Roach was never able to arrange a transfer to his own studio, nicknamed "Fort Roach," and spent the war working at other film facilities in the Eastern United States.

After the war, Roach had a difficult time obtaining financing to resume production. Too deeply in debt to continue after the production of only four more "streamliners" in 1947 and 1948, the studio seemed doomed when the arrival of television brought new hope. Beginning with relatively modest productions for the new medium (including commercials, one of which starred a young Marilyn Monroe), Roach was able to begin full-scale series production in 1951, funded by the proceeds from television distribution of the old "Our Gang" comedies.

By 1955 Roach's studio was the largest single producer of filmed television series. His television output included *My Little Margie, Racket Squad, The Stu Erwin Show,* and *Screen Director's Playhouse.* With the future of the company seemingly assured, Roach decided to retire, selling the studio in 1955 to his only son, Hal Roach, Jr. At this point, however, the major Hollywood studios decided to commence television production. The majors could afford to lavish more money and care on their television programs, making Roach's shows look cheap by comparison. Roach's production costs (and debts) rose, and series output diminished. The studio ceased production in 1959 and began a liquidation of assets in 1960. The studio facility saw some use by independent filmmakers renting space until 1963, when it was demolished to make room for an industrial/commercial development.

Because his son still owed him a substantial amount of the 1955 studio purchase price, Hal Roach, Sr., had a major stake in the company's remaining assets: its library of old movies and television series. Roach served as an associate producer on the remake in 1966 by Raquel Welch of *One Million Years B.C.*, before finally selling all interests in Hal Roach Studios to a group of Canadian investors in 1971. This new ownership later pioneered the controversial "colorization" process for black-and-white movies. Roach had nothing to do with the development of "colorization" and regretted that his name was associated with it.

Roach remained active and vigorous during the last two decades of his life. In 1984 he received a special Academy Award for lifetime achievement, and in 1992 the Academy Awards ceremony included a special tribute to his accomplishments. Not one to enjoy dwelling on past glories, Roach instead loved to look ahead, to speculate on the future of the industry, and to plan new projects. He lived long enough to serve as a consultant during the early planning stages of a new, feature-length version of *The Little Rascals* (1994).

After he reached the age of 100 on 14 January 1992, Roach's health began to decline rapidly. He died of pneumonia at the University of California, Los Angeles Medical Center. His body was returned to Elmira for burial in Woodlawn Cemetery. His epitaph reads, "After leaving Elmira he found success in Hollywood and motion pictures, but always loved his hometown and has returned."

Hal Roach's life and career spanned most of the twentieth-century history of the motion picture. He watched the industry progress from silent films photographed by hand-cranked cameras to computer-generated images and surround sound. He introduced the movie-going public to some of its most beloved comedians and developed a style of comedy that, in emphasizing character and situation over mechanical slapstick, laid the groundwork for the most successful of the later television situation comedies.

★

The business records of the Hal E. Roach Studios are in the Special Collections Department at the University of Southern California. While no biography of Roach exists, the studio's story is told in Richard L. Ward, "A History of the Hal Roach Studios" (Ph.D. diss., Univ. of Texas at Austin, 1995), and William K. Everson, *The Films of Hal Roach* (1971). A brief studio and series profile may be found in Leonard Maltin, *The Great Movie Shorts* (1972). Roach's better-known film series have been extensively documented in Leonard Maltin and Richard Bann, *Our Gang: The Life and Times of the Little Rascals* (1977), Tom Dardis, *Harold Lloyd: The Man on the Clock* (1983), and Randy Skretvedt, *Laurel and Hardy: The Magic Behind the Movies* (1987). An obituary is in the *New York Times* (3 Nov. 1992).

RICHARD L. WARD

ROBINSON, Earl (*b.* 2 July 1910 in Seattle, Washington; *d.* 20 July 1991 in Seattle, Washington), political activist, musician, conductor, teacher, and composer, best known for his compositions "Joe Hill" (1936) and "Ballad for Americans" (1940).

Robinson was the oldest of three children born to Morris John Robinson, a manager for a local Sears store, and Hazel Beth Hawley, a homemaker. He grew up in Seattle, expecting and expected to follow in his father's footsteps in business. His father got him a summer job at Sears, but his real love was music. After graduating from West Seattle High School, he enrolled at the University of Washington in 1928, planning to study business. His grades were so low in his first semester that he was required to complete an extension course before being readmitted as a full-time student. He enrolled in a course on harmony, excelled, and switched his major to music when he returned the following year. He graduated in 1933 with a B.A. in music.

Following graduation he worked as a musician on a ship sailing the Pacific. The trip gave him experience as a working musician and began his political education. On a visit to the American sector in Shanghai he saw a sign saying "No Chinamen or dogs allowed." It made such an impression on him that fifteen years later he quoted it to explain to people how China could become communist.

In 1934 he went to New York City to find work and continue his study of music. There he was introduced to labor politics and joined the Communist Party after a policeman clubbed him during a demonstration. He also joined a communist theater group but never found his way to the prestigious Juilliard or Eastman schools, choosing instead to take "theater out to the struggling people."

In 1935 he won a competition in musical composition sponsored by the American composer Aaron Copland. The prize of a year-long study with the master began a long relationship with Copland. In the mid-1930s, Robinson worked at Camp Unity in New York, sponsored by the Communist Party. It was there in the summer of 1936 that he wrote music for Alfred Hayes's lyrics "Joe Hill," arguably his most famous composition. During these years he also composed scores for films.

In 1937 he married Helen Wortis. Robinson admitted that he was far from an ideal husband. He reported telling his wife before they married that the Communist movement and his music would always come before their marriage. It was a testimony of her love, he said, that she married him anyway. They had two sons, one born in 1938 and another adopted in 1947.

Robinson received national recognition on 5 November 1940 when Paul Robeson performed his composition "Ballad for Americans" on a CBS radio broadcast. The song is a tribute to the American people composed for a 1939 musical revue, titled *Sing for Your Supper*, sponsored by the Federal Theater Project. Robeson's performance was so popular that he repeated it on New Year's Eve. These performances, along with his work in the communist theater group, brought Robinson to the attention of the Federal Bureau of Investigation (FBI), which maintained surveillance on him for more than thirty-five years, beginning in 1939 or 1940. FBI files indicate that he was considered for "custodial detention" following the broadcasts. A short film version of "Ballad for Americans" was used at the 1940 political conventions of both the Republican and Communist parties.

In 1940 Robinson received a coveted Guggenheim fellowship, which he used to compose music for Carl Sandburg's long poem *The People, Yes*. He was invited to the White House for the first time in December 1941. Expecting a large gathering, he found himself at a small dinner, seated next to President Franklin Roosevelt and across from Eleanor Roosevelt and Winston Churchill. He had never supported the president, but he later said, "They reminded me of my father and mother." Mrs. Roosevelt subsequently invited him to perform at numerous events, and Robinson worked for Roosevelt's 1944 reelection campaign. His composition "Lonesome Train," commemorating Abraham Lincoln, was widely used on the radio to mark President Roosevelt's death.

Robinson went to Hollywood in 1943. His first significant film score was for *The Roosevelt Story* in 1946. After the war he composed "Same Boat, Brother," for the ceremony celebrating the founding of the United Nations. His career suffered during the 1950s when promoters were reluctant to hire left-wing performers. Robinson was denied a passport in 1952 and was called to testify before the House Un-American Activities Committee on 11 April 1957. When asked by a committee member if he had ever written a song praising America, he responded by singing "The House I Live In," originally performed by Frank Sinatra in the Oscar-winning movie of the same name.

With his career languishing, he began teaching high

school in New York City in 1957. In the early 1960s his wife died following a long illness. He married Ruth Martin on 5 May 1965. They were divorced in 1973. During the 1960s and 1970s he continued to compose a wide variety of music, including "Ride the Wind" (1974), a cantata about Supreme Court Justice William O. Douglas, and an opera, *David of Sassoun* (1978). He also taught music at the University of California, Los Angeles.

Later in his life Robinson lost interest in the political struggles that occupied his earlier days. He developed a fascination with New Age philosophies, becoming involved in Transactional Analysis and *est* in the early 1970s. Several years later he became interested in communicating with the dead, using these experiences with "channeling" to provide material for his compositions. His music became less political and more introspective. Robinson commented that these new interests did not detract from his earlier work; rather, he said, they simply allowed him to expand into other aspects of life. By the time of his death, however, he seems to have abandoned his former political stance, with its emphasis on oppression and struggle, in favor of a belief that each of us chooses what happens to us.

Robinson had long maintained that he would live to the age of 140 and then decide whether he wanted to stay here or "move to a new address." However, he died in an automobile accident in Seattle. His remains were cremated.

Comprising more than five hundred compositions in a career spanning half a century, Robinson's music documents the working-class struggles and aspirations of his generation.

★

The primary collection of Robinson's papers, including his musical manuscripts and videos, is held by the University of Washington Archives. *Ballad of an American: The Autobiography of Earl Robinson* with Eric A. Gordon (1998), presents one of the most thorough examinations of his life and work. While not free of bias and lacking serious analysis of the importance of his music, it does provide a compelling portrait of the man and an introduction to his music. The most informative obituaries appeared in the *Seattle Times* (21 July 1991) and *Seattle Post-Intelligencer* (22 July 1991). Betty Jean Bullert's documentary *Earl Robinson: Ballad of an American: A Documentary* (1994) is another thorough examination of Robinson.

KEN LUEBBERING

ROBINSON, Roscoe, Jr. (*b.* 28 October 1928 in St. Louis, Missouri; *d.* 22 July 1993 in Washington, D.C), first African American four-star general in the U.S. Army and a highly decorated combat commander honored for his professional conduct and distinguished leadership in the military.

Robinson was one of three children of Roscoe Robinson, who worked in a steel foundry, and Lillie Brown, a home-

Roscoe Robinson, 1982. AP/WIDE WORLD PHOTOS

maker. He graduated from Charles Sumner High School in St. Louis, Missouri, where he served as class president in 1946. Too young to be drafted into the army during World War II, he attended St. Louis University for a year, then received an appointment to the U.S. Military Academy at West Point, New York. Robinson received a B.S. degree in military engineering in 1951, becoming only the sixteenth African American graduate in the 150-year history of West Point. After graduation he was commissioned as a second lieutenant in the U.S. Army. He was assigned to the Associate Infantry Officer Course and the Airborne Basic Course, then served as a platoon leader in the 188th Airborne Infantry Regiment of the Eleventh Airborne Division until 1952. On 1 June 1952 he married Mildred Sims; they had two children.

Robinson began his tour of duty in Korea in 1952 in an all-black unit. He served as a platoon leader, a rifle company commander, and a battalion S-2 in the Thirty-first Infantry Regiment, Seventh Infantry Division. Although the black units serving in Korea were often in dangerous and exposed positions, he led his unit with distinction in difficult circumstances. During this year of combat he was awarded the Combat Infantryman's Badge and the Bronze Star Medal. Upon returning to the United States in 1953 he served in the Eleventh Airborne Division, and in 1954 he became an instructor in the Airborne Department of the Infantry School at Fort Benning, Georgia. Completing the Infantry Officers Advanced Course in 1957, Robinson, now a captain, reported to the U.S. Military Mission in Liberia. Robinson was one of the first African Americans to serve in an unsegregated unit.

The 1960s proved to be fruitful for Robinson. He completed a two-year tour of duty with the Eighty-second Airborne Division serving as S-4, Second Battle Group, 504th Airborne Infantry Regiment and then as Company Commander of "E" Company of the 504th. He expanded his career by graduating from the Army Command and General Staff College in 1963 and was awarded a master's degree in Public and International Affairs from the University of Pittsburgh in 1964. Although his three-year (1965–1967) assignment to the U.S. Army Office of Personnel Operations as personnel management officer was one in which he had major responsibilities for vital logistic assignments related to the Vietnam War, he felt that he should be doing real soldiering. He was promoted to lieutenant colonel in 1966 and was posted to Vietnam, where he served as G-4 and then as Battalion Commander in the Seventh Cavalry Regiment, First Infantry Division. For his service and leadership in Vietnam during a period of close and intense combat, he was the recipient of two Silver Stars, the Distinguished Flying Cross, eleven Air Medals, and the Legion of Merit. Robinson completed the National War College in 1969. His service for this decade concluded with his serving at Headquarters Pacific Command in the G-5 Plans Directorate and as executive officer to the chief of staff in Hawaii. He received his second Legion of Merit Award.

Upon his promotion to full colonel in 1972, Robinson assumed command of the Second Brigade, Eighty-second Airborne Division at Fort Bragg, North Carolina. In July 1973 Robinson was promoted to the rank of brigadier general, and was made deputy command general, then commanding general, U.S. Army Garrison, Okinawa Base Command. In 1976 Robinson returned to Fort Bragg to become the first African American to command the renowned Eighty-second Airborne Division, a post he referred to as one of the highlights of his career. Robinson had served as a young officer in this unit. In 1978 he was made deputy chief of staff operations, U.S. Army Europe and the Seventh Army.

On 1 June 1980, Robinson was promoted to lieutenant general and became Commanding General of the U.S. Army, Japan IX Corps. On 30 August 1982 President Ronald Reagan nominated Robinson to become the Army's first African American four-star general. From September 1982 to September 1985 Robinson served as the military representative to the North Atlantic Treaty Organization (NATO), the first African American to do so. After thirty-four years of service Robinson retired from the army in November 1985. At his retirement Robinson received two Distinguished Service Medals and the Defense Distinguished Service Medal.

After his retirement Robinson served on the boards of various companies, including McDonnell Douglas Corporation, Comsat, Giant Food Inc., Metropolitan Life, and Northwest Airlines. In 1987 he was named to oversee the work of a panel to review the Korean War performance records of certain African American army units that were criticized at the time. In May 1993 Robinson was recognized with the Distinguished Graduate Award presented by the U.S. Military Academy's Association of Graduates. In 1995 officials at Fort Leavenworth in Kansas dedicated a bust of Robinson at the Buffalo Soldier Memorial Park.

On 7 April 2000 Robinson's wife, children, alumni, cadets, former colleagues, and distinguished guests attended the dedication of the Roscoe Robinson, Jr. Auditorium at West Point. Giving remarks, his son, Major Bruce Robinson, stated that his father was "a man who loved people, his family, and his troops."

In his thirty-four years of active duty, Robinson built a reputation as a dedicated and talented soldier. A close friend and classmate, General Edward Meyer, characterized Robinson as "a selfless leader who respected his soldiers and was respected by them in turn." Fellow four-star army general and friend Colin Powell stated that Robinson "was one of the pioneers who worked for racial change in the army. . . . He was a soldier worthy of praise" and "a mentor, a teacher, an inspiration, and a perfect example of the professional soldier." Robinson died of leukemia at Walter Reed Army Medical Center in Washington, D.C. He is buried in Arlington National Cemetery.

Robinson's philosophy can be simply stated in his own words: "I think that what you're doing and how you go about doing it is much more important than who is doing it." Becoming the first African American four-star general was a struggle for Robinson. He fought the battle of racial prejudice in the army, a fight for which he received no medals but paved the way for others to follow.

★

Robinson's papers have been donated to the Library of Congress. Good sources for biographical information are the *Annual Obituary Index* (1993), Walter L. Hawkins, *African American Generals and Flag Officers: Biographies of over 120 Blacks in the United States Military* (1993), and Jesse Smith and Joseph Palmisano, *The African American Almanac,* 8th ed. (2000). Information on his career is found in various issues of the *Army Times* and in the *National Technical Information Service Technical Report No.*

ADA195006 (23 Mar. 1988). Additional information on Robinson can be found at the United States Military Academy Library, West Point, New York. Obituaries are in the *New York Times, Washington Post,* and *St. Louis Post-Dispatch* (all 23 July 1993).

JOYCE K. THORNTON

RODDENBERRY, Eugene Wesley ("Gene") (*b.* 19 August 1921 in El Paso, Texas; *d.* 24 October 1991 in Santa Monica, California), writer and producer who created the *Star Trek* television and film series.

Roddenberry was the oldest of three children born to Eugene Edward Roddenberry, a lineman for a local electric company, and Caroline Glen Golemon, a telephone operator. Because the employment prospects in El Paso were limited, the Roddenberrys moved to California in 1923, and Roddenberry's father became an officer with the Los Angeles Police Department (LAPD) in July 1923.

After graduating from Franklin High School in Los Angeles in the winter of 1939, Roddenberry enrolled at Los Angeles City College (LACC) in February 1939. He studied the police curriculum and served as the president of the LACC Police Club. In his second year at LACC, Roddenberry joined the Civilian Pilot Program, a U.S. Army initiative to recruit pilots in anticipation of World War II. He received his pilot's license on 17 September 1940 and his

Gene Roddenberry, 1987. AP/WIDE WORLD PHOTOS

associate of arts degree from LACC on 26 June 1941. On 18 December 1941, less than two weeks after the Japanese attack on Pearl Harbor, Roddenberry reported for duty.

Roddenberry served in the U.S. Army Air Corps from 1941 to 1945. On 20 June 1942, while he was stationed at Kelly Field in San Antonio, Texas, Roddenberry married Eileen Rexroat, whom he had met while attending LACC. They had two children. Roddenberry received his officer's commission on 5 August 1942, and one month later he headed to Hawaii for his first military assignment.

Roddenberry flew a B-17 Flying Fortress on eighty-nine missions, including a stint on the sweltering island of Guadalcanal in 1942. Serving in the South Pacific as a second lieutenant, he earned the Distinguished Flying Cross and the Air Medal. While still in the military he began to submit his writing to periodicals for publication. After the war Roddenberry and his wife moved to Jamaica on Long Island, New York. Roddenberry became a commercial pilot for Pan American World Airways and moved to River Edge, New Jersey, in 1946. He also took writing courses at the University of Miami and Columbia University.

Roddenberry routinely piloted flights from New York to Johannesburg, South Africa, and Calcutta, India. In June 1947, while returning from Calcutta, Roddenberry was involved in a terrible plane crash in the Syrian Desert. The Pan American Clipper he had boarded as a passenger lost two of its four engines and crash-landed in the Syrian Desert on 18 June 1947, killing fourteen people. Roddenberry led the rescue effort and received a commendation from the Civil Aeronautics Board for his bravery. Because of his family and his increasing concern about the safety of the airplanes he was flying, Roddenberry resigned from Pan American on 15 May 1948 to write full-time.

In August 1948 Roddenberry and his family moved in with his parents in Temple City, a suburb of Los Angeles. His writing career stalled because there was little television production occurring in Hollywood at that time. At his brother's request, Roddenberry joined the LAPD and served as a police officer from 1949 to 1953. He honed his writing skills by reading science fiction and listening to radio dramas such as *Dragnet.*

Roddenberry landed a job in 1953 as the technical adviser to *Mr. District Attorney,* a drama syndicated by Frederick W. Ziv. As he reviewed scripts, Roddenberry became convinced that he could write just as well, and in March 1954 he sold an episode of the program to Ziv Productions. He soon received permission from his police superiors to do "freelance writing" to supplement his income. For three years Roddenberry moonlighted as a writer under the pseudonym Robert Wesley. His work appeared on programs such as *Science Fiction Theater* and *Space Patrol.* On 7 June

1956 he resigned from the LAPD with secure writing prospects.

From 1956 to 1962 Roddenberry wrote dozens of stories and scripts for Screen Gems, a television production company. Roddenberry's marriage was not happy, and he routinely had affairs with other women. At Screen Gems he met Majel Leigh Hudec, an actress known as Majel Barrett, and they soon began an affair.

On 11 March 1964 Roddenberry completed a treatment of his *Star Trek* idea. He teamed up with Oscar Katz of Desilu Productions to sell *Star Trek* to the NBC network, which paid Roddenberry $435,000 to shoot a pilot, "The Cage." NBC did not broadcast it at the time, but the network bought the show in February 1966.

Star Trek debuted on 8 September 1966 on NBC to mixed responses. Most reviewers appreciated the intent of the first episode, "Man Trap," but found the show too cerebral. Despite a positive reception from science fiction fans, the initial ratings were mediocre. As the season progressed, however, a more loyal audience began watching and writing fan mail to NBC. With a $500,000 weekly budget, full-color, otherworldly sets complemented space scenes of the majestic starship *Enterprise*. Fans also liked the show's characters, including Captain James Tiberius Kirk (played by William Shatner), Dr. Leonard Horatio ("Bones") McCoy (played by DeForest Kelley), and Mr. Spock (played by Leonard Nimoy). The depiction of human civilization surviving into the twenty-fourth century also inspired a cold war audience.

Star Trek continued for two more seasons, totaling seventy-nine episodes, before it was canceled on 2 September 1969. By that time, however, Roddenberry had made a legendary impression. *Star Trek,* which featured the first interracial kiss on television, had shown viewers a world in which humanity had largely overcome its prejudices and destructive tendencies. Roddenberry's personal life also changed dramatically. He and Eileen divorced on 26 December 1969. He married Majel Barrett on 29 December 1969. They had one child.

Star Trek fan conventions began in 1972 and the attendees ushered in the explosive popularity that the series continued to have. From 1973 to 1974 Roddenberry worked as the executive consultant to an animated version of the series. Soon after, Paramount returned *Star Trek* to television in syndicated reruns. The program became a classic.

Roddenberry brought his work to the large screen with *Star Trek: The Motion Picture,* which premiered on 6 December 1979. Although the film received poor reviews, it grossed $80 million. The sequel, *Star Trek II: The Wrath of Khan* (1982), was both a critical and financial success. Other sequels followed: *Star Trek III: The Search for Spock* (1984), *Star Trek IV: The Voyage Home* (1986), *Star Trek*

V: The Final Frontier (1989), and *Star Trek VI: The Undiscovered Country* (1991).

Roddenberry's work inspired several spin-off series, including *Star Trek: The Next Generation* (1987–1994), on which he consulted; *Star Trek: Deep Space Nine* (1993–1999); and *Star Trek Voyager* (1999–). *The Next Generation* characters also revived the *Star Trek* film series in *Star Trek: Generations* (1994), *Star Trek: First Contact* (1996), and *Star Trek: Insurrection* (1998).

Roddenberry was an imposing man who stood six feet, three inches tall. He had graying brown hair and bright blue eyes, lending him an air of gentle but uncompromising authority. William Shatner once said that Roddenberry's "stature was superseded by his towering imagination." Roddenberry died at the Santa Monica Medical Center on 24 October 1991 after suffering a heart attack in his doctor's office. His remains were cremated. On 21 April 1997 some of his ashes were transported aboard the *Lunar Prospector* spacecraft and launched into the earth's orbit, where they would remain for up to ten years. Although he never escaped the bonds of Earth in his lifetime, Roddenberry was a visionary who led millions into space. Because of his optimism about the future of humanity, *Star Trek* grew from an ambitious dream into a worldwide phenomenon. Appropriately, Roddenberry was often called "the Great Bird of the Galaxy."

★

Roddenberry's authorized biography is David Alexander, *Star Trek Creator: The Authorized Biography of Gene Roddenberry* (1994). A less-flattering portrait is Joel Engel, *Gene Roddenberry: The Myth and the Man behind Star Trek* (1994). The firsthand account of the *Star Trek* universe is Stephen E. Whitfield and Gene Roddenberry, *The Making of Star Trek* (rev. ed. 1991). Obituaries are in the *Seattle Times* (25 Oct. 1991) and the *New York Times* (26 Oct. 1991).

LEROY GONZALEZ

ROOSEVELT, James (*b.* 23 December 1907 in New York City; *d.* 13 August 1991 in Newport Beach, California), six-term Democratic congressman from the Twenty-sixth Congressional District of California, serving in the Eighty-fourth through Eighty-ninth Congresses (1955–1965).

Roosevelt was the second of the six children of Franklin Delano Roosevelt and (Anna) Eleanor Roosevelt. His father was the thirty-second president of the United States, serving from 1933 to 1945. His mother was a niece of Theodore Roosevelt and a distant cousin of her husband. She became a well known political activist and humanitarian.

Roosevelt was born in the first house his parents had all to themselves. He attended schools in New York and St. Albans School in Washington, D.C. He graduated from

James Roosevelt, 1962. © BETTMANN/CORBIS

the Groton School in Massachusetts in 1926 and Harvard University in 1930, and then attended the Boston University Law School.

While still a junior at Harvard, Roosevelt managed his father's presidential campaign in Massachusetts in 1932, when he reportedly made 200 speeches. Because of his distribution of federal patronage in the state following his father's election to the presidency, *Time* magazine dubbed him the "czar of Massachusetts patronage."

In 1930 Roosevelt began his business career as an insurance broker in Boston, where he organized Roosevelt & Sargent in 1935, earning as much as $250,000 per year during his early years in the business. He served as president of the company until January 1937. In 1936 Roosevelt set aside his business interests long enough to campaign for his father's reelection to the presidency. He then joined the White House staff as a $6,000-per-year executive assistant, a move presaging his own political ambitions. In 1937 he was promoted to the position of secretary to his father, where he served in 1937 and 1938 as liaison between the president and heads of various federal agencies.

He worked in the motion picture business from November 1938 until November 1940 and was made a vice president of Samuel Goldwyn Inc. He produced the 1940 and 1941 films *Pastor Hall* and *Pot o' Gold*. (James Stewart, the star of *Pot o' Gold*, called it his worst movie.)

In November 1940 Roosevelt enlisted for active service as a captain in the U.S. Marine Corps. He commanded a battalion in the Gilbert Islands in August 1942 and was awarded the Navy Cross for saving three men from drowning in heavy surf. He also fought at Guadalcanal and in 1943 was awarded the Silver Star for gallantry during a raid on Makin Atoll (Butaritari) in the Pacific. He served in the Solomon and Gilbert Islands and at Kiska in the Aleutian Islands. Roosevelt was promoted to colonel on 13 April 1944, was released from active duty in August 1945, and was promoted to brigadier general in the Marine Corps Reserve.

Following the war Roosevelt rejoined Roosevelt & Sargent as an executive vice president and opened an office in Los Angeles. In June 1946 he served as chairman of the board of Roosevelt & Haines, Inc., an insurance brokerage. He was also on the board of trustees of the American Center in Denver.

Continuing his interest in politics, in 1946 Roosevelt became chairman of the California Democratic Party, which then criticized him for political involvements that raised questions about his party loyalty. He lost his Democratic Party chairmanship for attempting to persuade General Dwight D. Eisenhower to oppose President Harry S. Truman for the 1948 Democratic presidential nomination. In Truman's hotel room during a campaign stop in Los Angeles, the president reportedly told Roosevelt, "If your father knew what you are doing to me he would turn over in his grave."

Roosevelt was selected as a delegate to the Democratic national conventions in 1948 and 1952. In 1950 he was the unsuccessful Democratic candidate for the governorship of California, challenging the incumbent governor Earl Warren. Four years after his defeat for the governorship of California he was elected to Congress, where he represented California's Twenty-sixth District for the next eleven years.

While in Congress, in 1965 Roosevelt was defeated by Samuel Yorty in a nonpartisan primary for the office of mayor of Los Angeles. In August 1965 President Lyndon B. Johnson appointed Roosevelt to be the United States representative to the United Nations Economic and Social Council (UNESCO). He resigned from Congress on 30 September 1965 to accept the position. In 1966 he was criticized for having become a board member of a mutual fund sponsored by the International Overseas Services Management Company, on the ground that this compromised his position with the United Nations. He resigned his United Nations post in December 1966 and became president of the International Overseas Services Management Company. This Switzerland-based company collapsed when several of its members were accused of fraud. The Securities and Exchange Commission dismissed a lawsuit against Roosevelt after he signed a 1973 court order pledging not to violate any securities laws. He admitted to no wrong-doing in the affair.

The independent Roosevelt lost additional support and credibility within his party in 1972 when he played a prominent role in the Democrats for Nixon movement. The same year he moved to Orange County and became a lecturer at the University of California, Irvine, and at Chapman College. He also worked as a business consultant and served on the Orange County Transportation Commission, where he was chairman in 1986. In 1984 he endorsed the California Republican governor Ronald Reagan for president.

In 1983 Roosevelt launched the National Committee to Preserve Social Security and Medicare, a well-funded non-profit lobbying organization that sought to safeguard the social security benefits put in place by his father half a century earlier. The organization called itself an advocacy group for the elderly. In March 1987 Roosevelt traveled to Washington to defend his organization against charges that it used scare tactics to solicit millions of dollars by mail from the elderly and for sending mailings to elderly people that looked as though they were federal government correspondence.

Roosevelt published three books: *Affectionately, F.D.R.: A Son's Story of a Lonely Man* (1959), coauthored with Sydney Shalett; *My Parents: A Differing View* (1976), coauthored with Bill Libby; and *A Family Matter* (1980), coauthored with Sam Toperoff. He was married four times. His first marriage to Betsey Cushing (daughter of the neurologist Harvey Cushing) on 4 June 1930 ended in divorce in March 1940. They had two children. His marriage to Romelle Theresa Schneider on 14 April 1941 ended in divorce in June 1955. They had three children. On 1 July 1956 he married Gladys Irene Owens, with whom he had one child. They were divorced in September 1969, and the following month, on 3 October 1969, he married Mary Lena Winskill, with whom he had one child.

The last surviving child of Franklin and Eleanor Roosevelt, James Roosevelt died on 13 August 1991 at eighty-three years of age at his home in Corona del Mar, California, from complications resulting from a stroke and Parkinson's disease. He is buried at the Pacific View Memorial Park in nearby Newport Beach. He was survived by his fourth wife.

Roosevelt had been honored in 1981 with the Humanitarian of the Year award by the National Conference of Christians and Jews, and with the National Americanism Award of the Anti-Defamation League of B'nai B'rith.

★

There are scores of articles and brief sketches of the life of Roosevelt in anthologies, newspapers, and magazines. A few of the representative items are in *Who's Who in America*, 45th edition (1988–1989); *The New York Times Biographical Service* (Aug. 1991); *Biographical Directory of the American Congress, 1774–1996*

(1997); *Time* (8 July 1946); "Democrats in the Smoke-filled Room," *New Republic* (12 July 1948); Crocker Coulson, "Geezer Sleaze," *New Republic* (20 Apr. 1987). Obituaries are in the *New York Times* and the *Los Angeles Times* (both 14 Aug. 1991).

NORMAN E. TUTOROW

ROSS, Steven Jay (*b.* 17 September 1927 in Brooklyn, New York; *d.* 20 December 1992 in Los Angeles, California), corporate executive who played a lead role in development of cable television and home video and created the Time-Warner entertainment and telecommunications giant.

Ross was born in the Flatbush section of Brooklyn. His father ran a successful home building business, but the Great Depression left the family virtually penniless. They moved from their home on Carroll Street to a small apartment on Newkirk Avenue. To get a job as an oil burner salesman, Ross's father changed the family name from the Semitic Rechnitz to Ross in 1932. Ross attended the neighborhood school, P.S. 152, then Erasmus High School. When his father had recovered sufficiently from the depression years he moved the family to Manhattan. There Ross won an athletic scholarship to attend the private, largely Jewish Columbia Grammar School. Over six feet tall and athletic, he played varsity football, basketball, and baseball, and managed the swimming team. He was elected president of the student council, served on the junior prom committee, and was co-winner in the senior class vote for "most popular."

Immediately on graduating in June 1945 he enlisted in the U.S. Navy. He later liked to tell friends he lied about his age to get in; in fact, he was eligible to enlist, though not yet subject to the draft. Similarly, he later claimed his hearing problems came from participating in combat, but his service on the USS *Hopping* included only seven days at sea, most of those spent taking the ship to Florida, where it was decommissioned. (Ross often embellished stories about his accomplishments, though he was reticent about elements of his life: for example, nowhere does he provide the names of his mother and father.) He was discharged from the navy in 1946.

On the advice of the headmaster at Columbia Grammar, Ross used the college tuition offered by the GI Bill of Rights to enroll at the newly opened Paul Smith College in Lake Placid, New York. It offered only a two-year program. While playing football in the fall of 1947, he badly broke his arm, requiring the insertion of a steel plate to set it properly. Ross later claimed that the arm injury ended his professional career with the Cleveland Browns.

Graduating in 1949, Ross landed in New York's garment district, working first as a stockroom boy and then as a salesman for a sports slacks manufacturer. He then went to work for an uncle selling children's bathing suits. In 1954

Steven Ross, 1989. ASSOCIATED PRESS FILES

he married Carol Rosenthal, whose father owned The Riverside, an expanding funeral home on Manhattan's Upper West Side. The couple had two children. Ross refused an initial offer to work for his father-in-law, fearing he would have to do embalming. But when it turned out the offer was to work in administration, he accepted.

Ross soon recognized that the funeral home did not make good use of one of its principal assets, the limousines used to drive mourners to and from burial sites. He began to rent out the limousines. With five partners, he soon created Abbey Rent-a-Car. And because cars require a place to park, Ross soon formed an alliance with New York's largest parking lot operator, Kinney Service Corporation, by giving it a quarter ownership in Abbey in exchange for free parking. In 1961 he merged with Kinney, envisioning development of a broad service company. Under the Kinney umbrella, he brought together parking, car rentals, funeral homes (now a chain), and his brother-in-law's office-cleaning service. In the first year under his leadership, Kinney had revenues of $17 million; Ross took it public after just five months.

In 1966, reflecting his ambition to make Kinney into a one-stop service company, Ross changed the name to Kinney National Service, Inc. He brought in a new cochief, William V. Frankel, the son of the founder of National Cleaning Contractors. He then went on an acquisitions spree, including a top talent agency, Ashley Famous Agency, in 1967, Panavision and National Periodical Pub-

lications (distributor of *Mad* magazine) in 1968, Warner–Seven Arts in 1969, and the Elektra record label in 1970. He also acquired along the way a bank in New Jersey, a printing business, a painting and plumbing contractor, a comic book publisher (*Superman, Batman, Wonder Woman*), and a data processing firm, among others. Ross put Ashley in charge of Warner; it was soon turning out hit films (such as *Klute, A Clockwork Orange,* and *The Exorcist*) and thus restored the legendary Warner Brothers name. Ashley also expanded Warner Brothers production and distribution of television programs. Characteristically, Ross gave Ashley extraordinary autonomy in running the studio. Ross combined this with a pattern of paying his managers average salaries but stunning bonuses—sometimes only loosely linked to performance.

The Warner investment (which included the successful music labels Reprise and Atlantic) led Ross to consider the opportunities in entertainment and telecommunications. By 1973 he had sold off profitably most of the pieces of Kinney (though he retained part ownership), investing the monies in two cable television companies. He refocused Kinney as a "leisure and entertainment company"; in 1972 he had renamed the company Warner Communications Inc., and he remained president of the company for eighteen years. Recognizing the potential markets in both video and cable, he launched Warner Home Video in 1979 and began a joint cable venture with American Express. In the meantime, he had failed with a New Jersey animal park, Jungle Habitat, and acquired Knickerbocker Toys, Ralph Lauren perfume and cosmetics, Music Television (MTV), Nickelodeon, and a major interest in the Pittsburgh Pirates. He also bought the New York Cosmos soccer team, reviving it by paying millions to the incomparable Pelé to join the roster.

In 1975 on a family trip to Disneyland, Ross observed that the new Atari video games got much attention from youngsters. In 1976 Warner acquired Atari for $28 million. The timing was perfect; it caught the huge wave of popularity of Pac-Man and other video games. By 1982 Atari accounted for half of Warner's $4 billion in revenues. But Ross's hands-off management style meant he failed to see a catastrophic deterioration of Atari sales; by the end of the year the company was hemorrhaging. Atari would cost Warner more than $1 billion before Ross could sell it off. In 1983 he buried tons of discarded Atari games in the desert near Alamogordo, New Mexico.

Atari was one of only three crises—personal and business—that Ross faced in the early 1980s. In 1974 he had separated from Carol. In 1978 they divorced. In November 1979 Ross married Amanda Mortimer Burden. The marriage was short-lived: they divorced in 1981. In October 1982, with 300 guests looking on in the Plaza Hotel ballroom, he married Courtney Sale; they had one child.

Typical of his lavish style, the guest list included Quincy Jones, Cary Grant, Barbara Walters, Steven Spielberg, and a roster of other stars. Even as he celebrated his marriage, Ross was wrestling with another serious threat: he and other Warner executives were being investigated for bribery and fraud in conjunction with a minor investment in the Mafia-controlled Westchester Premier Theater in Tarrytown, New York. Ross avoided indictment, but two other Warner executives were convicted.

Ross recognized that Warner, struggling with Atari losses and legal threats, was a potential takeover target, its share price having tumbled from $60 to $21. Rupert Murdoch began buying up shares; by December 1983 he owned 7 percent of Warner, making him its largest shareholder. Ross feared Murdoch's advances; he turned to Herbert J. Siegel, president of Chris-Craft Industries. They soon constructed an intricate deal, giving Warner a big stake in Chris-Craft's television stations. The deal thwarted Murdoch, but Siegel was not the compliant ally Ross had anticipated. Siegel challenged Ross's leadership. Ross turned on Siegel, eventually stripping him of most representation on the board of directors. But Siegel's presence forced Ross to divest the miscellaneous businesses in the Warner portfolio (such as Eastern Mountain Stores, the Franklin Mint, and Showtime) and fire some of Ross's closest cronies. Soon Warner was focused on its critical components: the Warner Brothers studio, its cable television systems, and its music labels. Siegel was particularly outraged by Ross's employment contract, which made him the highest-paid American business executive, averaging $14 million annually.

By the mid-1980s the core assets at Warner were rapidly gaining value. Ross again looked to acquisitions for growth. In 1986 he joined with Time to invest in Turner Broadcasting. In 1987 he added Chappell & Company, the world's largest music publishing company, to the Warner stable. In 1989 he bought Lorimar Telepictures, a leading television production company. His company was now worth more than $4 billion and had ended 1988 with net income of $423 million. At about the same time he began discussing the possibility of a merger with Time, Inc. Worried about the potential decline of print media, Time was looking for a merger partner but had already failed in several earlier efforts. And Ross had the brilliant insight that made the merger so exciting: differing media platforms could be brought together within one company, permitting the same content to be used in different ways and the different platforms to be used to promote the others. After lengthy, tense negotiations, a deal seemed to be set, only to fall apart literally at the last moment. Ross could not accept language that implied Time was "acquiring" Warner; nor would he accept the implication that he would be only a transitional chief executive. He clearly intended to run the merged companies. But in January 1989 the negotiations resumed. At a critical meeting in Ross's apartment in February the agreement was largely worked out, and the $14 billion merger went forward. Remarkably, Time never looked closely at Ross's background and never asked to see an 800-page assessment of the Westchester Theater investigation. Perhaps even more amazing, the merger gave Ross a guarantee of the chairmanship for ten years, an immediate payout of $193 million plus salary, options for at least 1.8 million shares, and bonuses that could have reached hundreds of millions of dollars. Even his stunning success of producing annual returns on investment of 24 percent from 1973 to 1990 seems an insufficient basis for such compensation.

Ross's leadership of Time-Warner was cut short by prostate cancer that was diagnosed in November 1991. Doctors were unable to control the disease. Though he would not visit his Manhattan office for more than a year because of the illness, Ross still exercised remarkable influence. Most importantly, in February 1992 he engineered the firing of his heir apparent, Nicholas J. Nicholas, Jr., and had his own candidate, Gerald M. Levin, installed as president. Ross died in University Hospital in Los Angeles and was buried at "The Springs" in East Hampton, New York.

Steven Ross was a remarkable individual. Six feet, two inches tall, with a broad smile and a mane of silver hair, he loved socializing and, many thought, helping people. Yet he had a volcanic temper and was unable to share authority. He had a remarkable circle of famous friends, particularly in the entertainment industry, and he loved to live—and entertain—lavishly. He owned a Park Avenue duplex, a tasteful home in East Hampton, an estate in Acapulco, and a residence in Los Angeles. He treated guests and business associates to lavish entertainment and gifts. Even his funeral, described in great detail by Connie Bruck for the *New Yorker,* was a lavish affair. Yet he seems never to have received an honorary degree, and his civic participation was limited, serving only on the board of directors for sports medicine of Lenox Hill Hospital in New York City, for the New York Convention and Visitors Bureau, for the Museum of Television and Radio, and for the New York State Alliance to Save Energy.

★

Richard M. Clurman, *To the End of Time: The Seduction and Conquest of a Media Empire* (1992), provides much of Ross's business history, focusing on the process that led to the Time-Warner merger. Connie Bruck, "The World of Business: Strategic Alliances," *New Yorker* (6 July 1992), and Bruck's "The World of Business: A Mogul's Farewell," *New Yorker* (18 Oct. 1993), cover the merger, the ousting of Nicholas, and the lavish funeral for Ross. An obituary by Kathryn Harris is in the *San Francisco Chronicle* (21 Dec. 1992).

FRED CARSTENSEN

RUFFIN, Davis Eli ("David") (*b.* 18 January 1941 in Whynot, Mississippi; *d.* 1 June 1991 in Philadelphia, Pennsylvania), singer and member of the vocal group the Temptations who was inducted into the Rock and Roll Hall of Fame in 1989.

Ruffin, the son of Eli Ruffin, a strict Baptist minister and gospel singer, and Ophelia Davis, was born near Meridian, Mississippi. Ruffin's mother died of complications from childbirth soon after he was born. His father married Earline Johnson, a schoolteacher, in 1942. As a child Ruffin sang both in church and with his older siblings, his sister Rita Mae and his brothers Quincy and Jimmy, who also achieved solo fame.

As a teenager Ruffin moved to Memphis, Tennessee, where he attended a high school for one year. In Memphis he joined a gospel group, the Dixie Nightingales, for two years. He also worked briefly as a racehorse jockey in Arkansas. In 1958, after moving to Detroit with his godfather Eddie Bush, Ruffin became a drummer and singer for the Voice Masters. In 1960 and 1961 he released unsuccessful solo singles for the Anna and Check-Mate labels, both of which were later absorbed into Motown. In February 1961 Ruffin married Sandra Kay Barnes. They had three children.

David Ruffin, 1960. Corbis Corporation (Bellevue)

Both David Ruffin and Jimmy Ruffin were familiar with members of the five-man Detroit vocal group the Temptations, which had released several singles without any hits. At one of their performances David brought down the house when he joined the group onstage, spun around, threw the microphone in the air, and collapsed in a split. He was asked to join the group at Christmas in 1963.

In 1964, immediately after Ruffin joined the Temptations, the group had its first hit, "The Way You Do the Things You Do," produced and co-written by William "Smokey" Robinson and featuring Eddie Kendricks on lead vocals. Their next hit was written particularly for Ruffin's rougher, gospel-edged voice. In 1965 "My Girl" was a crossover smash, climbing to number one on both the pop and the rhythm and blues charts. Ruffin became the group's dominant vocalist, singing lead on a string of their most successful and enduring songs, such as "Ain't Too Proud to Beg," "Beauty Is Only Skin Deep," "(I Know) I'm Losing You," "I Wish It Would Rain," and "I Could Never Love Another," all of which reached number one on the rhythm and blues chart and the top fifteen on the pop chart.

Tall, thin, and always wearing his trademark thick-rimmed glasses, Ruffin was a charismatic showman whose soulful, raspy voice expressed tremendous emotion and stretched from baritone to gospel-inflected tenor. Ruffin was also responsible for suggesting that the group employ a four-headed microphone stand onstage, which, along with their famous "Temptation Walk" (a coordinated line dance in which all the Temptations would high-step, sway, and swivel), become the group's trademark. With their sweet harmonies and slick choreography, the group appeared on many television shows and in 1968 shared a television special with Motown's top female group, the Supremes.

Ruffin's vocal prowess and natural showmanship made him the group's focal point, which the other four members sometimes resented. He had been in a drug rehabilitation program in 1967, and his erratic and sometimes egotistical behavior coupled with his sizable entourage served to alienate him from the rest of the group. He missed rehearsals and performances, and he suggested that the group change its name to David Ruffin and the Temptations, as some other Motown groups, like Diana Ross and the Supremes, had done. Ruffin insisted on driving separately in a mink-lined limousine. Some people alleged abuse when Ruffin's live-in girlfriend, the singer Tammi Terrell, collapsed onstage in 1967 from a brain tumor. Ruffin was fired from the group in mid-1968 when he chose to be with a girlfriend on her opening night rather than with the Temptations on theirs.

Complaining about being underpaid and overcontrolled, Ruffin tried to leave Motown, but the company, which had a contract, sued to keep him. The company delayed the release of his first solo hit, "My Whole World Ended (the Moment You Left Me)," which eventually reached the top ten on both the pop and the rhythm and blues charts in 1969. He continued to record regularly for Motown throughout the 1970s, including cutting an album with his brother Jimmy. But Ruffin felt that the label concentrated on Ross, Marvin Gaye, and Stevie Wonder and did not actively promote his records. Suspecting that this was punishment for trying to leave, he called it "economic peonage." His only other significant hit single during this time was "Walk Away from Love" in 1975, and he later began performing as a duo with another former Temptations member, Eddie Kendricks. Ruffin and his wife divorced in 1977. He also had a son with a live-in companion, Genna Sapia.

The nostalgia boom of the early 1980s generated renewed interest in the Temptations, and Ruffin and Kendrick, who had shortened his name, briefly rejoined the group in 1982 for a *Reunion* album and tour. The longtime fans Daryl Hall and John Oates invited the duo to join them in 1985 at the reopening of the Apollo Theater, a concert that was released as a live album, and at the July Live Aid concert. In January 1989 the Temptations were inducted into the Rock and Roll Hall of Fame.

Ruffin started smoking crack cocaine, which affected his asthma, forcing his hospitalization for respiratory failure and squashing his many comeback attempts. The 1980s were a litany of legal and drug-related problems. Ruffin was fined and jailed in 1982 after the *Reunion* tour for failing to file a tax return for 1976, and his house was foreclosed. He was arrested in 1986 for receiving and concealing a stolen handgun and in 1987 for cocaine possession. In 1988 he was convicted of using cocaine, and after moving to Philadelphia, Pennsylvania, in the summer of 1989, he tested positive for cocaine, a probation violation, and was sent to rehab.

In 1991, after a successful month-long tour of England with Kendrick and Dennis Edwards, Ruffin collapsed in a Philadelphia crack house after sharing ten vials with a friend in under half an hour. He was rushed to the hospital, where he died. His body was positively identified only through Federal Bureau of Investigation (FBI) fingerprints. Although the cause of death was ruled an accidental overdose of crack cocaine, Ruffin's family and friends suspected foul play, claiming that a money belt containing the proceeds from the tour ($40,000) was missing from his body. He had only $53 in his pocket. Michael Jackson paid for Ruffin's funeral in Detroit. The service at New Bethel Baptist Church featured performances by Stevie Wonder, Aretha Franklin, and the surviving Temptations. Ruffin is buried in Woodlawn Cemetery in Detroit. Although to many it seemed Ruffin spent more time in courtrooms than

in concert halls in his later life, Ruffin's rough but romantic voice made him one of America's finest soul singers.

★

Ruffin's companion Genna Sapia has self-published *Memoirs: David Ruffin—My Temptation* (1998) about their life together. Ruffin's strained relationship with Motown is covered in Nelson George, *Where Did Our Love Go? The Rise and Fall of the Motown Sound* (1985). Numerous reminiscences about Ruffin and the Temptations by the group's bass singer Melvin Franklin, a distant cousin of Ruffin, are in Don Waller, *The Motown Story* (1985). *Temptations* (1988), by the group's founder Otis Williams with Patricia Romanowski, provides a firsthand, though frequently anti-Ruffin, view of the early days of both Motown and the group. Tony Turner, the road manager for many of the later tours, details Ruffin's drug use in *Deliver Us from Temptation* (1992), written with Barbara Aria. An article on Ruffin is in *Contemporary Musicians: Profiles of the People in Music,* vol. 6 (1992). Of the many tributes to Ruffin, the most notable are by the music critic Tom Moon in the *Philadelphia Inquirer* (3 June 1991); Richard Harrington in the *Washington Post* (9 June 1991); and the singer Daryl Hall, "Last Thoughts on David Ruffin: Remembering a Great Temptation," *Musician* (Sept. 1991). Obituaries are in the *Philadelphia Inquirer,* the *Boston Globe,* the *Los Angeles Times* (all 2 June 1991), the *Detroit Free Press,* the *Chicago Defender,* the *New York Times* (all 3 June 1991), and the *Michigan Chronicle* (5 June 1991).

JOHN A. DROBNICKI

RYAN, John William ("Jack") (*b.* 12 November 1926 in New York City; *d.* 13 August 1991 in Los Angeles, California), inventor of the technology for the Barbie doll, the best-selling toy of the twentieth century.

Ryan was the younger of two sons of James Ryan, a prosperous building contractor, and Lily Urquhart Croston. Ryan insisted early in life on being called Jack. In fact most who met him as an adult never knew his birth name. After graduating from the prestigious Barnard School in 1943 in Riverdale, New York, where he was called "professor" by his classmates, Ryan went to Yale College, where he was active in the Dramatic Association ("Dramat"), the Pistol Club, and the Naval Reserve Officers' Training Corps. He served in the Pacific for a short time during World War II and in 1946 returned to Yale, where he was known as an "engineering genius."

Upon receiving his engineering degree in 1948, Ryan moved to Los Angeles to work in the Missile and Radar Division of the Raytheon Company, a weapons manufacturer. He helped design the Hawk (surface-to-air) and the Sparrow (air-to-air) missiles for the Korean War.

In 1955 Ryan approached the Mattel Toy Company with an idea for a toy transistor radio. The owners were im-

Jack Ryan and his wife, Zsa Zsa Gabor, at their wedding in 1975. ARCHIVE PHOTOS

pressed with his knowledge of engineering and technology and tried to lure him to Mattel. A savvy businessman, Ryan refused until his contract gave him a percentage of every toy he invented, which eventually made him a multimillionaire. He joined Mattel in 1955 and remained there for nineteen years, becoming corporate research director in 1956. While the Barbie doll was not Ryan's idea, he did invent the technology that allowed her to "twist-'n-turn" and to talk. The doll became the best-selling toy of the twentieth century. Ryan subsequently designed the technology for over thirty-five Mattel toys, including Chatty Cathy, Hot Wheels cars, the Thunderburp cap gun, and the Tommy Burst detective gun.

Ryan left Mattel in 1974 to form his own company for "interdisciplinary invention." He continued as a consultant for Mattel, eventually holding over 1,000 patents worldwide with sales of $16 billion by 1988.

In 1962 Ryan bought a five-acre estate in wealthy Bel Air, a neighborhood of Los Angeles, that had been owned by the silent-screen star Warner Baxter. Ryan had the eighteen-bedroom Tudor house remodeled as a medieval castle, complete with a moat and a dungeon decorated in black fox fur. At any given time in the 1960s and 1970s the castle was occupied simultaneously by eighteen to twenty people, including his wife of the moment, daughters, mistresses, colleagues, and ten young men from the University of California at Los Angeles (UCLA) who received room and board in return for maintaining the estate.

When Ryan married the actress Zsa Zsa Gabor in 1975 he had already been thrice-divorced. Gabor refused to live at the castle and remarked that "Jack's sex life would have made the average *Penthouse* reader blanch with shock." The marriage lasted seven months.

The short, barrel-chested Ryan was known to his friends as a generous and fun-loving if somewhat blunt and outspoken man who loved to entertain lavishly and to dress in fantasy costumes. He organized charity events for such organizations as the Thalians, a movie star organization that raises funds for emotionally disturbed children, and the Hollywood Motion Picture and Television Museum, of which Ryan was a director. He served on the Board of Scientific Advisors at the UCLA Crump Institute of Medical Engineering and was chairman of the Harvard-Yale-Princeton Alumni Association of Southern California.

In 1989 Ryan underwent bypass surgery before suffering a massive stroke from which he never recovered. He died at home of the stroke's debilitating effects two years later and was buried in Los Angeles.

Ryan's engineering and inventive technical skills ranged from missiles to toys and had a major impact on American society and abroad. Shortly after his death a London newspaper, the *Independent,* in describing Ryan's influence on millions of children worldwide through the Barbie doll and the thirty-five other toys he developed, wrote, "He was responsible to some extent for the forming of their life-attitudes, their farthest-reaching ambitions and fantasies, and perhaps also their greatest fears and anxieties."

★

Ryan's personal life is mentioned in Zsa Zsa Gabor's autobiography, *One Lifetime Is Not Enough* (1991), and M. G. Lord, *Forever Barbie: The Unauthorized Biography of a Real Doll* (1994), which includes considerable anecdotes regarding Ryan's sojourn at Mattel. Obituaries are in the *Los Angeles Times* (19 Aug. 1991), the *New York Times* (21 Aug. 1991), *Time* (2 Sept. 1991), and Deborah Andrews, ed., *The Annual Obituary 1991* (1992).

ELAINE MCMAHON GOOD

S

SABIN, Albert Bruce (*b*. 26 August 1906 in Białystok, Russia [now Poland]; *d*. 3 March 1993 in Washington, D.C.), virologist who developed the live-virus oral vaccine that helped make possible the global eradication of polio.

Sabin was one of four children of Jacob Sabin, a silk weaver, and Tillie Krugman. In 1921, leaving behind an impoverished life in tsarist Russia, the family immigrated to the United States and settled in the Jewish section of Paterson, New Jersey, and Sabin's father went to work in the textiles industry. After receiving a crash course in English from two of his cousins, Sabin attended Paterson High School, graduating in 1923.

Sabin entered New York University to study dentistry under the auspices of an uncle who had offered to finance his education if he entered that profession. But guided by William H. Park, his professor of bacteriology, Sabin switched his academic focus to medicine two years later. He subsequently supported himself through scholarships and by working as a laboratory technician. He was also influenced in his choice of careers by Sinclair Lewis's novel *Arrowsmith* (1925), about an idealistic doctor, and Paul De Kruif's *Microbe Hunters* (1926), a classic of scientific biography. In 1974 Sabin told National Public Radio that, in reading these texts, his "imagination was fired by what had been done and by the possibilities of things yet to be done."

After receiving a B.S. in 1928, Sabin entered the New York University medical school. Distinguishing himself as a researcher, he developed a rapid typing system for the identification of pneumococci, the viruses that cause pneumonia, and published papers in major medical journals. He became a U.S. citizen in 1930. Upon obtaining his M.D. degree in 1931, Sabin undertook his residency in pathology, surgery, and internal medicine at Bellevue Hospital in New York City. That year, a major epidemic of poliomyelitis, familiarly known as polio, a highly infectious disease that can impact the spinal cord and lead to paralysis or death, hit the city. Park, who had become director of the New York City Department of Health Bureau of Laboratories, recruited his former protégé to take part in the ongoing research into this disease, also called infantile paralysis, which had been growing as a threat since 1916, the year of the first large epidemic in the United States. Sabin wrote the first of his many papers on polio in 1931. During Sabin's internship a fellow researcher at Bellevue, William Brebner, died after being bitten by a laboratory monkey. Sabin isolated and identified Cercopithecine herpesvirus 1, commonly known as B virus, a fatal infection transmitted by rhesus monkeys. This contribution was one of several Sabin made to the understanding of nonpolio pathogens during his polio research.

Sabin was awarded a National Research Council Fellowship in 1934 and spent the following year on the staff at the Lister Institute of Preventive Medicine in London. Returning to New York City, he joined the staff of the prestigious Rockefeller Institute for Medical Research, now

Albert Sabin, 1969. AP/WIDE WORLD PHOTOS

Rockefeller University. In his application to the institute Sabin stated that his interest was in "filterable viruses with special reference to the study of the mechanism of immunity." He spent the next four years at Rockefeller, which by the mid-1930s was the center for virus research in the United States, a status largely attributed to Thomas M. Rivers, who became a strong supporter of Sabin's research career. In 1935 Sabin married Sylvia Tregillus, with whom he had two daughters.

Sabin's focus at Rockefeller soon narrowed to polio, a disease whose visibility in the United States increased dramatically with President Franklin D. Roosevelt's ascendancy to the presidency in 1933. Roosevelt, whose infection with the virus in 1920 had left him partially paralyzed, spearheaded a massive fund-raising campaign—which became known as the March of Dimes—through the National Foundation for Infantile Paralysis, founded in 1937 to help victims of polio and to support scientists and institutions in finding a cure. Sabin was among the researchers the foundation supported.

Although it is an ancient disease, polio epidemics were unknown in the western hemisphere until the early twentieth century, when, ironically, improvements in public hygiene prevented infants from developing a natural immunity to the disease. By the 1930s the mode of transmission of poliovirus was largely a mystery. This, combined with the quick onset of symptoms, the disease's preference for children, and the fact that polio struck entire communities, turning the summer months into "polio season," caused widespread fear bordering on national paranoia. Although most people who contracted polio made a full recovery, the disease killed a number of people and paralyzed even more. Iron lungs, wheelchairs, steel braces, and aluminum crutches became visible reminders of its ravages.

At Rockefeller in 1936 Sabin, working with Peter Olitsky, became the first to cultivate poliovirus in vitro. Laboratory production of the virus in large quantities was considered the first step in developing a vaccine, which would introduce into the body a modified form of the virus to provoke an antibody response. But Sabin and Olitsky's finding presented new problems. Using human embryonic tissue, they found that poliovirus thrived in nerve cells but not in kidney, liver, skin, or any other types of cells. This reinforced what other research, based on pathology reports, had suggested, that polio attacked nerve cells exclusively. Since viruses grown in nerve-cell culture could cause a fatal reaction if injected into humans, the finding appeared to confirm that development of a vaccine against polio was unfeasible and in fact delayed such development for decades.

In 1939 Sabin joined the staff of the Children's Hospital Research Foundation at the University of Cincinnati, where he also worked as an associate professor of pediatrics at the College of Medicine. His continuing research into poliovirus was interrupted during World War II. Commissioned a major in the U.S. Army Medical Corps, Sabin saw active duty in the Pacific theater from 1943 to 1945, combating the threat to American soldiers from endemic illnesses overseas. In his research into arboviruses, or insect-borne pathogens, he isolated the virus causing sandfly fever, a nonfatal epidemic disease affecting troops in Africa, and he developed a vaccine for dengue, a debilitating illness prevalent in the South Pacific. A vaccine Sabin developed against Japanese encephalitis was administered to about 70,000 U.S. troops prior to the invasion of Japan. He was discharged from the army in 1946 with the rank of lieutenant colonel.

Sabin then returned to Cincinnati and what he called his "thirty-year war against polio." The postwar period from 1945 to 1955, the start of the American baby boom, marked an increase in polio outbreaks that culminated in the worst epidemic, in 1952, when 58,000 cases were reported. In addition the postwar period was the most fruitful for polio research. In the 1940s researchers at Johns Hopkins University discovered that polio was caused by more than one type of virus. In 1949 John Enders and his research team discovered that poliovirus could indeed be grown in nonnervous system tissue in the laboratory (Enders later won a Nobel Prize for this). In fact poliovirus could grow in cell and tissue cultures of almost any kind of human cell. In their 1936 research Sabin and Olitsky, it turned out, had used a strain of the virus that was resistant to growth in any but nervous system cells.

After the Enders discovery, the scientific community immediately rallied to the development of a polio vaccine. Scientific thinking soon cohered around two different approaches: a live attenuated vaccine, advocated by Sabin and others, and a killed-virus vaccine that a researcher eight years Sabin's junior, Jonas Salk, was working on at the University of Pittsburgh. This divergence led to one of the most famous rivalries, both personal and professional, in twentieth-century medicine and eventually enabled the first global disease-eradication initiative in history.

In 1946 Sabin was promoted to full professor of research pediatrics at the University of Cincinnati and chief of infectious diseases at the Children's Hospital Research Foundation. Through his research in the late 1940s, Sabin showed that poliovirus was present in the intestinal tracts as well as the central nervous systems of victims, indicating that the pathogen did not enter humans through the respiratory tract, as previously thought, but through the mouth. This finding informed his conviction that an oral live-virus vaccine was the most efficacious way to combat the disease. While at Cincinnati, Sabin worked twelve-hour days and expected the same from his staff. Though he was considered a demanding taskmaster, he also had a lighter side. Sabin, an avid pipe smoker, enjoyed inviting reporters into his laboratory to show off a research monkey he had trained to smoke a cigar.

Upon Salk's announcement in 1953 that he had developed a killed-virus polio vaccine, Sabin, who had a reputation in the scientific community as a fierce and articulate debater, became an outspoken opponent against its production. Speaking before the American Medical Association, the National Foundation for Infantile Paralysis Committee on Immunization, and ultimately the U.S. Congress in October 1953, Sabin criticized the Salk vaccine as unsafe and maintained that a field trial of the vaccine scheduled for 1954, in which thousands of children would be inoculated, was dangerously premature. He maintained that the killed-virus vaccine was ineffective in conferring long-term immunity, requiring frequent reinoculation and leaving open the possibility that people would reach adulthood without permanent immunity. He also petitioned Salk in private on various occasions not to go forward with the trials, which he considered scientifically irresponsible and doomed to failure. But the fear of polio had reached a pinnacle in the 1950s, and expedience won out over caution. Sabin's concerns proved valid, however. In April 1955, after the Salk vaccine was declared safe, 204 people contracted polio following inoculation, and eleven eventually died. The vaccination program was temporarily halted, but it started up again after the problem was assessed as an aberration. By 1960 the Salk vaccine had in fact virtually ended the epidemic scare in the United States, and Salk was hailed as the hero who had conquered polio.

Sabin nevertheless persevered in his efforts to develop a live-virus vaccine, and based on his arguments against the Salk vaccine, the National Foundation for Infantile Paralysis continued to support him with research grants. By 1954 his oral vaccine, an attenuated live strain of all three types of poliovirus, was ready for field tests, and between 1954 and 1957 it was administered to volunteers at the federal penitentiary in Chillicothe, Ohio. A major trial of the Sabin vaccine, involving 6 million children and adults, took place in the Soviet Union in 1959.

Field trials of the Sabin vaccine were first conducted in the United States in April 1960, and in August 1961 the vaccine was approved by the U.S. Public Health Service. Throughout the 1960s millions of children received the vaccine in mass weekend inoculation drives that became known as "Sabin Sundays." Local physicians administered the free vaccine orally in a cherry-flavored liquid. By the mid-1960s, after the American Medical Association recommended its use over the Salk vaccine, the Sabin vaccine became the polio vaccine of choice throughout the world.

Sabin's vaccine had several advantages over Salk's. It was less expensive to produce, easier to administer because it was not injectable, did not require booster shots, and conferred "intestinal immunity," which can spread throughout populations and protect even those who are not vaccinated. It was this "herd immunity" concept that made the Sabin vaccine a valuable tool in regions of the world without an organized public health program.

Sabin retired from the University of Cincinnati in 1970. In that year President Richard Nixon awarded him the National Medal of Science "for numerous fundamental contributions to the understanding of viruses and viral diseases, culminating in the development of the vaccine which has eliminated poliomyelitis as a major threat to human health." Sabin's first wife died in 1966, and in 1970 he married Jane B. Warner. They divorced in 1971, and in 1972 Sabin married Heloisa Dunshee de Branchis. His second and third marriages produced no children.

Much of Sabin's postpolio research concerned the relationship between viruses and cancer. He served as president of the Weizmann Institute of Science in Rehovoth, Israel, from 1970 until 1972, but he was forced to leave that post to undergo heart bypass surgery. He was a consultant to the National Cancer Institute of the U.S. Public Health Service in 1974, distinguished professor of biomedicine at the College of Medicine of the University of South Carolina from 1974 to 1982, and consultant to the National Institutes of Health Fogarty Center for Advanced Studies in Washington, D.C., from 1984 to 1986. Sabin's hair turned white in middle age, and in his later years he grew a beard, reinforcing the shrewd academic demeanor he projected throughout his career.

In the early 1980s Sabin developed a nasal aerosol vaccine against measles, which like his polio vaccine was easier to administer than the previously available injectable vaccine. In 1983, while working on the vaccine, Sabin contracted a rare paralyzing illness, Guillain-Barré syndrome, giving him a new perspective on perhaps the most brutal aspect of the disease he had spent the better part of his life trying to wipe out. Although he recovered, other health problems led to his complete retirement in 1988. Sabin died in 1993 of congestive heart failure at Georgetown University Medical Center in Washington, D.C. He was eighty-six years old. President Bill Clinton hailed him as "one of the great heroes of American medicine." Salk, who died two years later, issued a statement calling Sabin's death "a great loss" and acknowledging that "the effect of his contributions toward the control of polio will endure long in the future." Sabin is buried at Arlington National Cemetery.

Scientific advance, like all human achievement, is cumulative, and Sabin's role in conquering polio impacted later medical research. In 1993 Sabin's colleague, Bernard N. Fields, then chairman of the Department of Microbiology and Molecular Genetics at Harvard Medical School, told NPR that Sabin had a profound effect on how viruses are taught and studied:

In the era where we're still trying to understand how HIV causes AIDS, the questions that Albert Sabin asked remain

as fresh as they were thirty, forty, and fifty years ago. . . . Many of us still assign some of his papers from the 1940s for reading among our students, so that they can understand how a fresh and brilliant mind came to understand how a virus like polio actually gets into the body.

Widespread use of the Sabin polio vaccine throughout the 1970s and 1980s revealed a risk that Sabin persisted in denying. His vaccine in rare cases, about 1 in every 2.4 million doses of vaccine, caused polio. Critics attributed Sabin's stance to stubbornness and egoism. Salk denounced the Sabin vaccine in a 1973 editorial in the *New York Times,* urging return to the injectable vaccine. Sabin, into his eighties, continued to denigrate the Salk vaccine as "pure kitchen chemistry." Some scientists believed that the ill will between the two prevented either from winning the Nobel Prize. In the 1980s the Centers for Disease Control began advocating the use of both vaccines for maximum protection against polio.

In 1988 the World Health Organization (WHO), in the first program of its kind, launched an initiative to eradicate polio from the globe by the end of the year 2000. Although the western hemisphere was declared polio free in 1994, the disease remained endemic in sub-Saharan Africa and central Asia at the beginning of the twenty-first century. But officials at WHO continued to believe in global eradication of polio by 2005 and vaccination against polio becoming obsolete by 2010. Sabin's vaccine was replaced with a stronger version of the injectable Salk vaccine in 2000, and medical historians concluded that both vaccines played essential roles in the triumph over polio.

★

Sabin's papers are in the Albert B. Sabin Archives at the Cincinnati Medical Heritage Center. A separate collection of biographical material, clippings, correspondence, and photographs is at the Rockefeller University Archives in New York City. Information about Sabin is in books documenting the history of polio and its eradication, including Greer Williams, *Virus Hunters* (1960); John R. Paul, *A History of Poliomyelitis* (1971); Aaron E. Klein, *Trial by Fury: The Polio Vaccine Controversy* (1972); Jane S. Smith, *Patenting the Sun: Polio and the Salk Vaccine* (1990); and Nina Gilden Seavey, Jane S. Smith, and Paul Wagner, *A Paralyzing Fear: The Triumph over Polio in America* (1998). Obituaries are in the *New York Times* and *Washington Post* (both 4 Mar. 1993).

MELISSA A. DOBSON

SACHAR, Abram Leon (*b.* 15 February 1899 in New York City; *d.* 24 July 1993 in Newton, Massachusetts), educator, scholar, and founding president of Brandeis University in Waltham, Massachusetts. Sachar was an early authority in Jewish studies.

Sachar was the eldest of six children born to Samuel Sachar, who was born in Lithuania and immigrated to the United States in the 1880s, and Sarah Abramowitz, who was born in Jerusalem and came to the United States at the age of seventeen. In 1906 the family left New York City for St. Louis, where Samuel Sachar became a successful realtor and Abram attended Yeatman High School, from which he graduated in 1916. Sachar attended Washington University in St. Louis and received his bachelor's and master's degrees in history together in 1920. Following graduation, he studied history in England at Emmanuel College, Cambridge University. In 1923 Sachar became the first person to be granted a Ph.D. from that university. His thesis was "The Victorian House of Lords." In 1926 he married Thelma Horowitz, whom he had met at Washington University, where she graduated Phi Beta Kappa in 1925 with a major in Romance languages. The couple had three children.

After returning to the United States in 1923, the small-statured (five feet, six inches) Sachar joined the faculty at the University of Illinois, where he taught for the next

Abram Sachar. ARCHIVE PHOTOS

twenty-four years and served on that institution's Hillel Foundation. He was the national director of the National Hillel Foundation from 1933 to 1948 and the chair of the Hillel National Commission from 1948 to 1955. Sachar was a leading authority on Jewish history long before Jewish studies were fashionable in the United States. His books include *Factors in Jewish History* (1927); *A History of the Jews* (1930), which was reprinted six times; *Jews in the Contemporary World: Sufferance Is the Badge* (1939); *The Course of Our Times* (1972); *A Host at Last* (1976, rev. ed. 1995); and *The Redemption of the Unwanted* (1983). In addition Sachar contributed articles and reviews to such publications as the *New Republic,* the *Menorah Journal,* the *Saturday Review of Literature,* and the *New York Herald Tribune.* In 1945 Hebrew Union College awarded him an honorary doctorate of Hebrew letters.

In 1948 Sachar became the first president of the newly opened Brandeis University, the first Jewish-sponsored nonsectarian university in the United States. As the founding president, Sachar envisioned Brandeis becoming the Jewish Princeton University, a nonsectarian place of learning initiated by the Jewish community for the benefit of all faiths. Indeed, in his installation ceremony on 7 October 1948 he pledged that the university would offer "opportunity . . . to all regardless of race, creed, or color." Sachar served as the president of Brandeis until 1968, when he was appointed chancellor. In 1981 he became chancellor emeritus, a position he held for the remainder of his life.

Under Sachar's leadership Brandeis University attained a reputation for academic excellence. Brandeis opened in 1948 with 107 students and 13 faculty members. At the time of Sachar's death in 1993 the institution enrolled 3,700 undergraduate and graduate students and had a full-time faculty of 360. A tireless faculty recruiter, he attracted to Brandeis some of academia's best researchers and scholars.

During his tenure Sachar raised $250 million for the school and saw the university grow into a complex of ninety buildings on 235 acres. He established the School of Near Eastern and Judaic Studies, the largest and most comprehensive program in the discipline outside of Israel. In addition he promoted the Jewish heritage of Brandeis through the Tauber Institute for the Study of European Jewry, the Maurice and Marilyn Cohen Center for Modern Jewish Studies, and the Benjamin S. Hornstein Program for Jewish Communal Services. Sachar became close friends with Richard Cardinal Cushing of Boston, who supported the building of a Catholic chapel alongside the Protestant chapel on the Brandeis campus. Sachar was also a strong advocate for civil rights. In 1966 he signed K. C. Jones, a star of the Boston Celtics basketball team, as the Brandeis basketball coach, thus making Brandeis the first nonblack-sponsored university in the country to name an African American as the coach of a sports team.

Sachar died of respiratory failure on 24 July 1993 at his home in suburban Newton, Massachusetts. He was buried in Temple Israel Cemetery in Wakefield, Massachusetts, but the following spring he was reinterred on the Brandeis campus in front of the international center that bears his name.

★

Sachar is discussed in Israel Goldstein, *Brandeis University: Chapter of Its Founding* (1951). The testimonials published following Sachar's death are the best source of information. See particularly "Abram Sachar: 1899–1993, Valedictory," *Brandeis Review* (1993), and Howard Jeruchimowitz, "First President Abram Sachar Dies at 94," *Justice: The Independent Student Newspaper of Brandeis University* (27 July 1993). An obituary is in the *New York Times* (25 July 1993).

JACK R. FISCHEL

SALANT, Richard S. (*b.* 14 April 1914 in New York City; *d.* 16 February 1993 in Southport, Connecticut), attorney without journalistic training who served as president of CBS News for sixteen years, and was noted for his commitment to ethics in journalism and an independent news media, as well as for numerous innovations in television news.

One of two children of Louis Salant, an attorney, and Florence Aronson, Salant attended Phillips Exeter Academy in New Hampshire, where he edited the student newspaper (his only formal journalism experience) and graduated cum laude in 1931. Salant graduated from Harvard with a B.A. degree magna cum laude in 1935. He made Phi Beta Kappa and wrote an honors thesis on the lunar influence on romantic poets. He then earned a Harvard law degree in 1938 and served on the editorial board of the *Harvard Law Review*. After law school Salant entered government service with President Franklin D. Roosevelt's New Deal administration in Washington, D.C., serving as an attorney with the National Labor Relations Board from 1938 to 1941 and in the solicitor general's office in the Department of Justice from 1941 to 1943.

On 14 June 1941 Salant married Rosalind Robb, with whom he had four children. During World War II he served in the navy from 1943 to 1946, attaining the rank of lieutenant commander. After the war Salant joined the New York City law firm of Rosenman, Goldmark, Colin and Kaye, where he represented the Columbia Broadcasting System (CBS) in various legal matters, including litigation against the Radio Corporation of America–National Broadcasting System (RCA-NBC) over the future of color television broadcasting. Network executives were impressed by his work, and in 1952, in what Salant described as the "best move I ever made," he left the law and became a CBS staff vice president. In 1955 Salant divorced Rosalind Robb,

and on 31 December 1955 he married Frances Trainer, with whom he had one child. In 1961 he was appointed president of CBS News and a member of the CBS board of directors. Salant designated Walter Cronkite as network anchor, and launched the first half-hour network evening news television broadcast, expanding the program from fifteen minutes of airtime. In 1964, when Fred Friendly was appointed CBS News president, Salant briefly returned to duties at CBS corporate headquarters, but came back to head the news division once again following Friendly's resignation in 1966.

Salant presided over CBS News until 1979, an era that included the civil rights movement, the Vietnam War, and the Watergate scandal, an extremely challenging period for the news media. Despite his lack of a journalistic background, Salant enjoyed a reputation as a standard setter for ethics and integrity. He vehemently opposed blurring the line between news and entertainment. The sound judgment of news professionals was, in his view, more important than popularity or ratings. "Our job is to give people not what they want, but what we decide they ought to have," is an oft-quoted Salant axiom. He staunchly defended the independence of CBS News against external and internal interference, refusing to censor or withdraw news stories that might offend major network advertisers; defending controversial news broadcasts, including the 1971 documentary, "The Selling of the Pentagon," and resisting pressure from the Nixon administration over Vietnam and Watergate coverage. Salant made the decision to produce *60 Minutes,* which went on to become the premier news magazine show in broadcast history. He also hired such notable correspondents as Mike Wallace, Roger Mudd, Dan Rather, and Diane Sawyer. He dismissed Howard K. Smith for editorializing in news stories, and arranged the resignation of Daniel Schorr following his release of a classified government document. Salant is also credited with opening up opportunities for women and minorities at CBS News.

Forced by CBS's mandatory retirement policy to leave his post at the age of sixty-five in 1979, Salant was honored with numerous awards, including the George Polk Memorial Award, the Alfred I. Du Pont–Columbia University Award, the George Foster Peabody Award, the Society of Professional Journalism Award, and the International Radio and Television Society Gold Medal. Reluctant to withdraw from active journalism, Salant immediately joined rival broadcast network NBC as vice chairman, with specific responsibilities to strengthen the NBC news division. He failed, however, to attain his primary goal of expanding NBC's evening news broadcast to a full hour. He left NBC in 1983 to become president of the National News Council, an independent industry organization established in the post-Watergate years to restore public confidence in the

Richard Salant, 1973. AP/WIDE WORLD PHOTOS

news media by investigating reader and viewer complaints of unfair, biased reporting. A year later Salant announced the dissolution of the News Council because of a lack of support from major media organizations.

During retirement Salant lectured frequently on broadcast journalism, particularly on quality and ethics issues. He was sharply critical of the new corporate owners of the television networks, who seemed to him to be more interested in profitability than in the social responsibility of network news, and worried that media credibility was jeopardized by the shift towards more entertaining, less serious coverage; the disappearance of in-depth documentaries; and ratings-based editorial decisions. He died of a heart attack while speaking on news media ethics to a senior citizens men's club. Salant is regarded by many as the architect of modern broadcast journalism. His most important contributions include his lasting imprint on the format of broadcast journalism as we know it today. The thirty-minute evening news program is now the standard. The in-depth reporting of *60 Minutes* achieved institutional status in American society, and the program's news magazine format was widely emulated. Many of the correspondents he hired remain household names. His steadfast defense of the First Amendment and the independence of the news media and advocacy of ethical practices continue to serve as a point of reference for broadcast journalists. While his disapproving views on the blending of entertainment and news are often dismissed by some television executives as outdated, Salant's perspective still has sway with practicing journalists and helps shape the debate within the industry.

★

Salant's posthumous memoir, *Salant, CBS, and the Battle for the Soul of Broadcast Journalism* (1999), edited by Susan Buzenberg and Bill Buzenberg, provides valuable insights into Salant's philosophy, values, and career. An in-depth profile, "Never a Newsman, Always a Journalist," *Broadcasting* 96, no. 7 (26 Feb. 1979): 90–94, traces Salant's major career accomplishments. Obituaries are in the *Washington Post* and *New York Times* (both 17 Feb. 1993) and *Los Angeles Times* (18 Feb. 1993).

JERRY BORNSTEIN

SALISBURY, Harrison Evans (*b.* 14 November 1908 in Minneapolis, Minnesota; *d.* 5 July 1993 near Providence, Rhode Island), journalist whose lucid prose and historical perspective made him one of his generation's most distinguished reporters, and whose books and prize-winning dispatches from the Soviet Union, China, and Vietnam often influenced the course of American foreign policy during the cold war.

Called a "journalistic one-man band" by an admiring editor, Salisbury was one of two children of Georgiana Evans, a homemaker, and Percy Pritchard Salisbury, a sales manager for a Minneapolis factory that made bags for grain and flour. He attended the local public schools and graduated in 1925 from North Side High School, where he edited *Polaris,* the school newspaper. Entering the University of Minnesota in Minneapolis, he immediately joined the campus paper, the *Minnesota Daily,* and beginning in 1928 worked professionally as a part-time reporter for *the Minneapolis Journal.* In his senior year he assumed the editor-

Harrison Evans Salisbury. LIBRARY OF CONGRESS

ship of the *Daily,* earning the enmity of the administration and the Board of Regents with editorials and stories sharply critical of the university's policies. In a confrontation that made the front page of the *New York Times,* he was expelled from the university in January 1930, four months shy of graduation, after violating the school's ban on smoking in the vestibule of the library.

The expulsion, Salisbury wrote in his memoirs, was a blessing because it led immediately to a job with United Press (UP) at thirty dollars a week. His first major story—an unsparing account of the Great Depression's impact on Minneapolis—won praise from UP's Chicago office and a demand from the *Minneapolis Journal* that he be fired for slandering the city, foreshadowing the controversy his later reporting often produced. UP killed the story but retained Salisbury, who was moved to Chicago, where he covered the trial of Al Capone. On 1 April 1933, he married Mary Jane Hollis, with whom he had two children; the marriage ended in divorce in 1950. He married Charlotte Young Rand, a writer, on 18 April 1964. Salisbury stayed with UP for eighteen years, moving successively through positions of increasing responsibility and gaining a reputation for clear writing, well-researched stories, and a knack for

scooping the competition. Although company policy prohibited writing for other publications, Salisbury supplemented his meager wages by freelancing under more than a dozen pseudonyms for magazines like *Coronet, Collier's,* and *Esquire.* Assigned to UP's London office in 1942, he was named the bureau chief in 1943 and the foreign news editor a year later. He spent eight months in the Soviet Union at the end of World War II, and on his return to the United States in 1945 wrote a series of articles for *Collier's* that became his first book, *Russia on the Way* (1946).

In 1949 Salisbury joined the *New York Times* as its Moscow correspondent—a difficult assignment because of the Soviets' restrictions on foreign journalists. During a single month in 1951, for example, Soviet censors allowed only six of Salisbury's thirty-four stories to reach New York City. Because the *Times* gave no indication that his prose had been altered or cut by the Soviets, he was often vilified by the paper's readers for glorifying the communist state. He refuted the charges on his return home in 1954 in a fourteen-part newspaper series, "Russia Re-viewed," and in *American in Russia* (1955), which described in detail the terror of Joseph Stalin's regime. He won the 1955 Pulitzer Prize for foreign reporting and later published the uncensored versions of his dispatches from 1949 and 1954 in *Moscow Journal: The End of Stalin* (1961).

Barred from the Soviet Union after 1955, Salisbury reported domestically for the *New York Times,* wrote freelance articles for periodicals like the *Saturday Evening Post,* and expanded a controversial story on Brooklyn's teenage gangs into *The Shook-up Generation* (1958). His vivid accounts of police brutality against civil rights workers in Birmingham, Alabama, in 1960 led to a $6 million libel suit against the *Times* that the newspaper eventually won on appeal four years later.

In 1957 Salisbury won a George Polk Memorial Award for his coverage of several Eastern European states, including Poland and Romania. He was readmitted to the Soviet Union in 1959 and reported favorably on the changes Nikita Khrushchev was bringing to Russia, a theme he pursued in *To Moscow—and Beyond: A Reporter's Narrative* (1960) and *A New Russia?* (1962). He wrote a well-received novel, *The Northern Palmyra Affair* (1962); published two books for young people, *The Key to Moscow* (1962) and *Russia* (1965); and edited *The Soviet Union: The First Fifty Years* (1967).

In his initial administrative assignment for the *Times,* Salisbury was named the director of national correspondence in 1963, and in that role directed the paper's coverage of the assassination of President John F. Kennedy. The following year he was made the assistant managing editor, overseeing a variety of special projects. In 1970 he became the first editor of the *Times's* Op-Ed page. He edited two collections of pieces from that page: *The Eloquence of Pro-*

test: *Voices of the 70's* (1972) and, with David Schneiderman, *The Indignant Years: Art and Articles from the Op-Ed Page of the New York Times* (1973). In 1972 Salisbury became an associate editor of the paper.

Salisbury's own reporting interests had shifted by the mid-1960s to China and Southeast Asia. A thirty-thousand-mile tour, the first of several trips to the Chinese mainland, became the basis for *Orbit of China* (1967); subsequent visits produced *War Between Russia and China* (1969), in which he argued that the ties between these two powers were fraying to a greater extent than most observers in the West realized, and *To Peking—and Beyond: A Report on the New Asia* (1973), describing recent regional economic and political developments.

Salisbury earned notoriety in the mid-1960s for his controversial dispatches from Hanoi during the Vietnam War. The first American reporter to visit North Vietnam in more than a decade, he was present when American planes bombed Hanoi on Christmas Eve, 1966. In a dramatic series of detailed articles, which the *Times* syndicated worldwide, and in *Behind the Lines—Hanoi, December 23, 1966–January 7, 1967* (1967), he wrote that the relentless bombing had only stiffened North Vietnam's resolve to fight on. His eyewitness accounts of collateral bomb damage contradicted the American government's assertion that the air war targeted only military installations and produced only minimal civilian casualties. The government, he suggested, was not telling the truth to the American people.

President Lyndon Johnson was furious, and his administration opened a deliberate campaign to discredit Salisbury as "careless" and "a known Communist sympathizer," allegations picked up and enlarged by editors and columnists who favored a hard line against the North Vietnamese. Salisbury weathered the criticism, but not without cost. He received both the Overseas Press Club award for international reporting and his second George Polk Memorial Award, but was denied a second Pulitzer Prize when the prize jury's four-to-one vote in his favor was overruled by the Pulitzer's governing board. In 1971 he found a measure of vindication as part of the *New York Times* team that published the "Pentagon Papers," giving an inside look at the administration's policymaking during the war.

Salisbury's *The 900 Days: The Siege of Leningrad* (1969) brought him international acclaim—the English writer C. P. Snow called it "a nonfiction masterpiece"—and denunciation by the Russians, who banned it because, they said, it denigrated the Communist Party. In his next book, *The Many Americas Shall Be One* (1971), he called on Americans to renew the nation by restoring the traditional values of the Founding Fathers.

Following his mandatory retirement from the *Times* in December 1973 at age sixty-five, Salisbury continued freelancing from his home in rural Taconic, Connecticut, while maintaining an apartment in Manhattan. He rose nearly every morning at 4 A.M. to write for three or four undisturbed hours, devoting the remainder of the day to research for his next project. It was a regimen that produced fifteen books and numerous essays over the next twenty years, beginning with his second novel, *The Gates of Hell* (1975), the story of a dissident Russian writer (modeled on Aleksandr Solzhenitsyn) that received largely unenthusiastic reviews.

Salisbury fared better with *Travels Around America* (1976), in which he compared the United States on the eve of the bicentennial to the world of his ancestor—a Yankee peddler in the eighteenth century. He completed his second history of Russia, *Black Night, White Snow: Russia's Revolutions, 1905–1917* (1978), and followed it with *Russia in Revolution: 1900–1930* (1978). In addition, he edited *Sakharov Speaks* (1974), by Andrei Sakharov, and *Russian Society Since the Revolution* (1979). In 1980 he wrote the critically acclaimed *Without Fear or Favor: The New York Times and Its Times*. He was a moderator for *Behind the Lines* (1974–1975), a weekly critique of the media, and for *National Town Meeting*, both on PBS. He served as the president of the American Academy and Institute of Arts and Letters (1975–1977) and of the Authors League (1980–1985).

After completing *A Journey for Our Times: A Memoir* (1983) and *Vietnam Reconsidered: Lessons from a War* (1984), Salisbury and his wife spent four months in China retracing the 7,400-mile route Mao Zedong had followed five decades earlier to save the Red Army from Chiang Kai-shek. *The Long March: The Untold Story* (1985) was both a history of that epic journey and a meditation on the changes that had come to China since Mao's death. As he turned eighty, Salisbury published a second memoir, *A Time of Change: A Reporter's Tales of Our Time* (1988), followed by *The Great Black Dragon Fire: The Chinese Inferno* (1989), an account of a devastating forest fire in Manchuria in 1987.

Salisbury was back in Beijing in early June 1989, just in time to observe the events in Tiananmen Square, in which the Chinese government attacked dissident students who were calling for democratic reforms. His first-hand account, *Tiananmen Diary: Thirteen Days in June* (1989), was in bookstores by mid-September. His final books were *The New Emperors: China in the Era of Mao and Deng* (1992), a dual biography of Mao and his successor, Deng Xiaoping; and *Heroes of My Time* (1993), profiles of Robert F. Kennedy, Malcolm X, and Nikita Khrushchev, among others, who had inspired him "by their conduct in times of great peril."

Salisbury died from a sudden heart attack while riding in a car driven by his wife near Providence, Rhode Island. He had a history of heart trouble but had not let it interfere with his demanding schedule of travel and research. To the end of his life, he took great pleasure in being a writer. "There is nothing," he once said, "I would rather do."

★

Salisbury's papers, consisting of more than 200,000 items from 1930 until his death, are in the Rare Book and Manuscript Library at Columbia University in New York City. They include his reporter's notebooks, interview notes, and his bylined newspaper articles, as well as letters from many national and world figures. His memoirs, *A Journey for Our Times* (1983) and *A Time of Change* (1988) are complemented by six published diaries of his wife, Charlotte Salisbury, covering their travels in Russia and Asia from 1966 to 1983: *Asian Diary* (1967); *China Diary* (1973); *Russian Diary* (1974); *China Diary: After Mao* (1979); *Tibetan Diary* (1981); and *The Long March Diary: China Epic* (1986). An obituary is in the *New York Times* (7 July 1993).

ALLAN L. DAMON

SALK, Lee (*b.* 27 December 1926 in New York City; *d.* 2 May 1992 in New York City), child psychologist, educator, author, and social commentator.

Salk was the youngest of three sons born to David Bonn Salk, a designer in the women's-wear industry in Manhattan, and Dora Press, a homemaker. As Lee later wrote, the strong personality of his immigrant mother was pivotal in stimulating the desire for career success and public service in him and his brothers. Jonas, the eldest, was famous for his discovery of the polio vaccine, and Herman became a veterinarian and advocate of international wildlife conservation.

Salk grew up and attended schools in the borough of the Bronx in New York City. After attending Rutgers University in New Brunswick, New Jersey, in 1944 and the University of Louisville in Kentucky, in 1946, Salk did the rest of his university training at the University of Michigan in Ann Arbor. There, he received the A.B. degree in 1949, an M.A. in 1950, and a Ph.D. in 1954. From 1954 to 1957 he was a research associate in the Department of Psychiatry of the Allen Memorial Institute of Psychiatry at McGill University in Montreal. He held a multitude of professional posts in New York from 1957 onward. He was a visiting lecturer in human relations at the University Settlement House in New York City; an instructor of scientific methods in resident-training programs of the Department of Psychiatry at City Hospital in Elmhurst, Queens; the chief psychologist for pediatric psychiatry services at Lenox Hill Hospital in Manhattan; and a professor of psychology in psychiatry and pediatrics at Cornell University Medical College. In addition he served as a consultant to organizations including the American Red Cross, NBC, Girl Scouts of the U.S.A., and the American Foundation for Maternal and Child Health. During the final two years of

Lee Salk, 1986. © JACQUES M. CHENET/CORBIS

his life he served as the first director of prevention services for KidsPeace, a not-for-profit organization dedicated to helping children in crisis, located in Bethlehem, Pennsylvania. At the time of his death, Salk was a clinical professor of psychology and psychiatry at the Cornell University Medical Center in New York City, where he resided. He was also an adjunct professor of child development in the Child Study Center of Brown University in Providence, Rhode Island.

Salk's advocacy of children and families was displayed in his research and in his writing. He won national attention in 1960 for his groundbreaking research on infants' reactions to their mothers' heartbeats. Stimulated by his observations (at the Central Park Zoo in New York City) that Rhesus monkeys tend to hold their newborns close to their heart, against their left breast, Salk noted that human mothers had the same tendency. This tendency was the same for right- and left-handed mothers. He conducted an experiment in a New York City hospital where for four days the sound of a normal heartbeat was played for 102 newborn infants. Comparing these infants to another group of newborns who had not been exposed to the heartbeat sound, he found that the babies who had heard the continuous heartbeat cried less and put on substantially more weight than the other group over the four-day period. Salk concluded that the heartbeat is learned in the womb through imprinting. When imprinting occurs, the organism is relatively free from anxiety, and when the organism is subsequently in the presence of the imprinted stimulus it is again relatively free from anxiety. Hence the babies who heard the heartbeat cried less and ate more. Much of Salk's other research focused on the effects of childhood experiences on later behavior.

In addition to his research, Salk was best known as the author of parenting books and for his use of television and print media to promote a common sense approach to child rearing. His first book, *How to Raise a Human Being,* was published in 1969. In this and the nine books that followed, advocacy of family values is a continuing theme. For twenty years he also wrote a monthly family-oriented column for *McCall's* magazine titled "You and Your Family."

Salk was a fellow of the American Psychological Association and one of the founders of its Division of Child, Youth, and Family Services, for which he served as president from 1979 to 1980. Among the many awards he received during his career were the first Distinguished Contribution Award from the Society of Pediatric Psychology and the American Psychological Association's Distinguished Contribution Award in Clinical Child Psychology. In 1981 he was the recipient of the special National Media Award from the American Psychological Foundation. A tribute to his legacy is the Lee Salk Center, the research-and-development arm of KidsPeace.

In 1990 Salk was diagnosed with esophageal cancer, requiring extensive surgery. With the help of his family he lived happily and productively for two years. During this time he finished his final book, *Familyhood: Nurturing the Values that Matter Most* (1992) and launched a program in child abuse for KidsPeace. Salk had a heart attack while undergoing cancer treatment; he died in New York City.

Salk's world was one of child advocacy, and his proudest accomplishment was that of his role as a parent. His daughter, Pia, followed his lead as a psychologist; his son, Eric, became a physician. *Familyhood* was the embodiment of Salk's life as a father and family member. The introduction to *Familyhood* is a poignant tribute to his wife, Mary Jane Salk, his children (who were from a previous marriage), and his brothers, as they mediated the devastating effects of his illness. The strength of his personal character was displayed in the dedication of the book to his wife, "whose strength, determination, and love turned a ghastly nightmare into a beautiful sunrise."

★

All of Salk's books deal to some extent with his personal ex-

periences and therefore contain much autobiographical material. In addition to those mentioned in the text, see especially *What Every Child Would Like Parents to Know* (1978) and *My Father, My Son: Intimate Relationships* (1982). His pioneering research on the heartbeat is referenced in "The Role of the Heartbeat in the Relations Between Mother and Infant," *Scientific American* (May 1973). Obituaries are in the *New York Times* (4 May, 1992) and *Washington Post* (5 May 1992).

RICHARD E. RIPPLE

SCHUMAN, William Howard (*b.* 4 August 1910 in New York City; *d.* 15 February 1992 in New York City), composer, music educator, and arts administrator.

Schuman was the second child of Samuel Schuman, a bookkeeper who eventually became manager of Oberly and Newell, a large Manhattan printing company, and Rachel Heilbrunn. Both of his parents believed firmly in the attainment of the American dream through hard work and education, and they named their son after William Howard Taft, then the president of the United States. The family enjoyed going to the theater, and they gathered around the piano on Sunday evenings to sing songs from operettas and other popular semiclassics. While in elementary school at Manhattan's P.S. 165, Schuman requested violin lessons so

William Schuman, 1965. AP/WIDE WORLD PHOTOS

he could play in the school orchestra, and his parents arranged for him to study with Blanche Schwarz. Nevertheless, Schuman preferred playing baseball to practicing.

Schuman continued his education at Speyer Experimental Junior High School for Boys, a school for gifted children. At Speyer he developed an interest in theater, and he wrote and produced a play titled *College Chums*. During the summer of 1925 Schuman was invited to travel to France on a program called the Boys' Educational Tour of France. He spent other summers of his teenage years happily at Camp Cobbossee in Winthrop, Maine. There he wrote some of his first musical compositions, including a violin tango titled *Fate* (c. 1926) and numerous popular songs with lyrics by his friend Edward B. Marks, Jr., the son of the music publisher Edward B. Marks.

Attending George Washington High School, Schuman organized a jazz band named Billy Schuman and his Alamo Society Orchestra. He served as its manager, sang vocal solos, and played violin and banjo. During this time Schuman also learned to play the double bass and performed with the school orchestra. Although he had little formal musical training, he learned quickly and was facile on a number of different instruments.

Following his graduation from high school in February 1928, Schuman enrolled in the New York University School of Commerce. He assumed that he would have a career in business, most likely in advertising. This changed on the evening of 4 April 1930, which Schuman considered the marker of his conversion to a life in classical music. On that evening he reluctantly accompanied his sister to a concert of the New York Philharmonic conducted by Arturo Toscanini at Carnegie Hall. He had never heard a symphony orchestra before and was awestruck by the experience. As Schuman recounted later, "I just left and said I knew I would have to spend my entire life in this type of music." He quit New York University the following day and enrolled at the Malkin Conservatory of Music in New York City to study harmony with Max Persin.

Persin encouraged Schuman to learn the principles of harmony through the study of the music itself and did not prescribe the use of a specific textbook. This free approach later influenced Schuman's own pathbreaking initiatives in teaching music theory. Persin also encouraged Schuman's continued work in popular music genres. Around this time Schuman met the songwriter Frank Loesser. They eventually collaborated on approximately forty popular songs, including Loesser's first published song "In Love with a Memory of You" (1931).

During the summer of 1931 the entire Schuman family traveled to Europe. Upon his return Schuman began counterpoint studies with Charles Haubiel. He also enrolled in the Juilliard School of Music summer school program, studying harmony with Bernard Wagenaar and orchestra-

tion with Adolf Schmid. Aware that he would need some sort of practical degree to support a creative life in music, Schuman enrolled in Columbia University Teacher's College in 1933. He received a B.S. degree in 1935 and an M.A. degree in 1937. During the summer of 1935 he studied conducting at the Mozarteum in Salzburg.

In the fall of 1935 Schuman assumed his first teaching post at Sarah Lawrence College in Bronxville, New York, attracted to the position in part because of the school's innovative educational philosophy. During his decade at Sarah Lawrence he developed many of the educational principles he later established at Juilliard. Through creative and innovative methods that encouraged individual development, he successfully taught the elements of music to students who had no prior training. Schuman described his theories in a 1938 article, "An Unconventional Case History," published in the journal *Modern Music*.

Schuman's compositional work continued while he pursued his teaching career. He composed his Symphony no. 1 for chamber orchestra in 1935 and entered it into the prestigious Bearns Prize competition at Columbia University. The work was not successful, and Schuman decided to seek guidance from the American composer Roy Harris, whose works he admired. From 1936 to 1938 he studied with Harris, first through Juilliard's summer school and later privately. Schuman married Frances Prince on 27 March 1936. They had two children. In 1937 Schuman composed his Symphony no. 2, String Quartet no. 2, Prelude and Fugue for orchestra, and two choral works. The second symphony won first prize in a 1938 competition sponsored by the Musicians' Committee to Aid Spanish Democracy. Aaron Copland, one of the judges, was impressed with the young composer. Copland introduced the symphony to the conductor Serge Koussevitzky, who performed it with the Boston Symphony in February 1939. Although generally not well received by the critics, this major performance nevertheless sparked interest in Schuman's music. His first major critical acclaim came in 1939 with the Boston Symphony's performance of his *American Festival Overture,* also under the direction of Koussevitzky. Energetic and prolific, Schuman composed both Symphony no. 3 and Symphony no. 4 in 1941. Symphony no. 3, given an acclaimed performance by Koussevitzky and the Boston Symphony in October 1941, is considered one of Schuman's finest works. Among the works he composed in 1942 was a cantata for chorus and orchestra, *A Free Song,* which received the first Pulitzer Prize for Music in 1943. By this time the composer was firmly established as a major presence in American artistic life.

In 1944 Schuman was offered the position of the director of publications at G. Schirmer, the company that published most of his music. Since he was committed to his teaching position at Sarah Lawrence until June 1945, he accepted the position on a part-time basis for the first few months. He formally assumed this appointment on 1 June 1945. Three days later Schuman was invited to apply for the position of president of the Juilliard School of Music. Initially Schuman was reluctant to pursue this opportunity. He saw many problems in the school's educational curriculum and did not think the board would allow him the freedom to make the radical changes he thought necessary. This was not the case, however, and the board unanimously approved his appointment as president beginning 1 October 1945.

Schuman indeed made numerous innovative changes during his seventeen-year tenure as the president of Juilliard. First was the complete amalgamation of the Institute of Musical Art and the Juilliard Graduate School, Juilliard's two predecessor institutions. He established the Juilliard String Quartet in 1946 and the school's dance division in 1951, and he negotiated Juilliard's place as the educational component of Lincoln Center for the Performing Arts, established as cultural center in the mid-1950s. He fostered the creation and performance of new music through the development of commissioned programs and festivals. His establishment of the pathbreaking Literature and Materials of Music curriculum in 1945 for teaching music theory became a model for similar programs throughout the United States and remained in use at Juilliard into the twenty-first century.

On 1 January 1962 Schuman assumed the presidency of Lincoln Center. As only the second president of the newly created complex, following General Maxwell D. Taylor, Schuman faced numerous challenges, including unfinished architectural plans and funding shortages. Among his important initiatives during his six-year tenure, he established an educational outreach program that eventually became the Lincoln Center Institute, and he developed the Film Society of Lincoln Center and the Chamber Music Society of Lincoln Center. Schuman suffered a heart attack in April 1968, prompting him to resign from the Lincoln Center presidency as of 31 December 1968. He remained active as a composer and served as a consultant to many arts organizations. Schuman died at the age of eighty-one from complications following hip surgery.

Schuman was prolific as a composer throughout his years in demanding administrative posts. His output included ten symphonies, the last of which was commissioned for the American bicentennial celebrations; five string quartets; two operas, *The Mighty Casey* (1953) and *A Question of Taste* (1988); choreographic works for Antony Tudor and Martha Graham; as well as numerous solo, chamber, vocal, and choral works. He received many commissions, honors, and awards throughout his lifetime, including more than twenty-three honorary degrees, Guggenheim Fellowships, and the first Brandeis University

Creative Arts Award in Music in 1957. He was honored by the Kennedy Center in 1989 "for an extraordinary lifetime of contributions to American culture through the performing arts." His children established the William Schuman Music Trust, which encourages dissemination and performances of his music.

Schuman's music and his artistic and educational innovations have had a profound impact on American musical life. His fellow composer Morton Gould stated: "He used his creative juices not only to write his music, but to stimulate the music of his time and the things around him. . . . He triggered all the things that have become part of our musical way of life."

★

Schuman's papers are at the New York Public Library for the Performing Arts, and his musical manuscripts are at the Library of Congress. Major works about Schuman are Flora Rheta Schreiber and Vincent Persichetti, *William Schuman* (1954); Christopher Rouse, *William Schuman, Documentary* (1980); and K. Gary Adams, *William Schuman: A Bio-bibliography* (1998), which includes citations for hundreds of journal articles and dissertations about Schuman and his music published through 1994 as well as a complete list of Schuman's own writings. An obituary is in the *New York Times* (16 Feb. 1992). An unpublished oral history was compiled by Sharon Zane for the Lincoln Center for the Performing Arts Oral History Project (1990).

JANE GOTTLIEB

SCHUYLER, James Marcus (*b.* 9 November 1923 in Chicago, Illinois; *d.* 12 April 1991 in New York City), Pulitzer Prize–winning poet, novelist, dramatist, and member of the New York School of poets.

Schuyler was the only child of Marcus James Schuyler, a writer and newspaper owner in suburban Downers Grove, Illinois, and Margaret Daisy Connor. In 1926 the family moved to Washington, D.C., where Marcus Schuyler began working for the *Washington Post*. Schuyler remembered his father as a "jolly, well-read . . . enchantingly wonderful man" whose one significant vice was gambling, a problem that led to his parents' divorce in 1929. At this point Schuyler's maternal grandmother, Ella Slater Connor, came to live with them. An important influence on young Schuyler's creative development, Granny Connor became the model for a character in his first novel, *Alfred and Guinevere* (1958).

In 1931 Schuyler's mother married Fredric Berton Ridenour, a stern man who disapproved of Schuyler's love of reading. Two years later a half-brother, Fredric, was born. The family moved to Buffalo, New York, in 1935, and then to the small town of East Aurora, New York, in 1937. Schuyler felt alienated in this traditional suburban com-

James Schuyler. © CHRIS FELVER

where they entertained guests such as Truman Capote and Tennessee Williams. When Auden returned to Ischia, Schuyler worked as his secretary for several months.

Returning to New York City in September of 1949, Schuyler immersed himself in the contemporary art scene, working first at the Kleeman Gallery and later at the Museum of Modern Art (1957–1961), where he eventually became a curator of traveling exhibitions. He was an editorial associate and critic for *Art News* (1955–1965) and an editor and contributor to the little magazine *Locus Solus* (1961–1962). In 1951 Schuyler met Frank O'Hara and John Ashbery, two of the most important New York School poets. He became close friends with them, as well as with a host of other New York artists.

Given to bouts of mania and depression, Schuyler had the first of many breakdowns in 1951. He entered the Bloomingdale mental hospital in suburban White Plains, New York, where he stayed for several months. Throughout the rest of his life he was in and out of hospitals, dependent on medication and on the kindness of friends for support. (In one case, he lived with the painter Fairfield Porter and his wife Anne Porter for twelve years.) At Bloomingdale, Schuyler began writing his first poems, which were later published in *New World Writing* (1952).

Hanging out in such artists' haunts as the Club and the Cedar Tavern in Greenwich Village, Schuyler became a collaborator with many other poets, painters, actors, directors, and musicians. In 1953 his short play *Presenting Jane* was produced by the Artists' Theater in Greenwich Village, with Elaine de Kooning providing hand-painted sets. During a car trip, Schuyler and Ashbery began their collaborative absurdist novel, *A Nest of Ninnies* (1969), which they would work on sporadically for the next seventeen years. Together with the author and composer Paul Bowles, Schuyler wrote *A Picnic Cantata,* which was released by Columbia Records in 1955.

By 1960 Schuyler was becoming known as a poet. His work appeared in Donald Allen's landmark anthology, *The New American Poetry: 1945–1960,* and his first volume, *Salute* (with prints by Grace Hartigan), was published by the Tiber Press. Influenced by the early poetry of O'Hara and Ashbery—and through them by Dada and Surrealism—Schuyler experimented with techniques of collage and fragmentation in this volume.

Schuyler's subsequent volumes, beginning with his first commercially published work, *Freely Espousing* (1969), tend to be more autobiographical, intimate, and objective than his early abstract work. These are poems of memory, desire, and appreciation, which present subtly detailed portraits of places and objects. The tone of the "intimist," as the poet Barbara Guest once called Schuyler, who attends to the still moments of daily life, continues through his succeeding volumes: *The Crystal Lithium* (1972), *Hymn to Life* (1974),

munity, where his interest in books and art were out of place. Moreover, he had become aware of his homosexuality early in life, which led to further estrangement. Encouraged by a perceptive English teacher, Schuyler had decided by the age of fifteen that he would become a writer.

In 1941 Schuyler entered West Virginia's Bethany College, where he had an unsuccessful and incomplete academic career. In 1943 he left Bethany to join the U.S. Navy, where he did convoy duty in the North Atlantic. On a visit to New York City, Schuyler met Chester Kallman, a poet and lover of the distinguished writer W. H. Auden. After going AWOL, Schuyler was discharged from the Navy as "undesirable" when his homosexuality was revealed. He stayed in New York City, working as a clerk for the Voice of America at NBC.

Hoping to fulfill his dream of becoming a writer, Schuyler sold a farm he had inherited from his paternal grandmother and traveled to Italy in 1947 with his lover, Bill Aalto. Schuyler enrolled at the University of Florence, and the couple later spent the winter of 1948 house-sitting for Auden in Forio d'Ischia, an island in the Bay of Naples,

the 1981 Pulitzer Prize–winning *The Morning of the Poem* (1980), and *A Few Days* (1985).

In a near-fatal 1977 incident, a fire broke out in Schuyler's rooming-house bedroom, caused by the poet smoking in bed. He was kept in intensive care and then, suffering from continuing mental and physical distress, moved for a time to a nursing home. In 1979 concerned friends came up with the idea of Schuyler living at the Chelsea Hotel, an eclectic Victorian building on West Twenty-third Street that had been home to many artists including Thomas Wolfe, Dylan Thomas, and O. Henry. An assistant volunteered to come each morning to help with his medication, meals, and errands. While the poet was writing some of his finest work, friends assisted him in applying for grants and fellowships. Among others, he received awards from the National Endowment for the Arts (1972), the Guggenheim Foundation (1981), the American Academy of Arts and Letters (1982), and the Ingram Merrill Foundation (1988). Schuyler was a fellow of the Academy of American Poets (1983), and a recipient of the prestigious Whiting Award (1985).

Influenced by a former assistant, Tom Carey, the poet was confirmed as an Episcopalian in 1989, "after a lifetime as a non-practicing Presbyterian." In 1991 he was discovered semiconscious in his room in the Chelsea, having suffered a stroke. He was transferred to the intensive-care unit at Saint Vincent's Hospital, where he remained for a week until his death at the age of sixty-seven. A funeral service was held at the Church of the Incarnation on 16 April. His ashes were buried in the small cemetery on the grounds of Little Portion Friary in Mount Sinai, New York.

Compared to his more boisterous colleagues in the New York School, Schuyler and his poetry seem reserved and reflective. His shyness and lack of self-promotion may in part explain his lesser renown. He will be remembered for his domestic meditations on friendship, art, and natural beauty. While the poet's life lacked the usual workaday pressures, his writing responds to different, perhaps more primal, pressures of memory, feeling, and desire. His poems record moments of serenity in spite of suffering, everyday moments that most people fail to see: "It's the shape of a tulip. / It's the water in the drinking glass the tulips are in. / It's a day like any other."

★

Schuyler's papers from 1947 to 1991 are held in the Mandeville Department of Special Collections at the University of California, San Diego. *The Diary of James Schuyler,* edited by Nathan Kernan (1997), includes a valuable introduction and chronology. Book chapters on Schuyler include Geoff Ward, "James Schuyler and the Rhetoric of Temporality" in his *Statues of Liberty: The New York School of Poets* (1993) and David Lehman, "James Schuyler: things as they are" in his *The Last Avant-Garde: The Making of*

the New York School of Poets (1998). *Denver Quarterly* 24 (spring 1990), a special issue edited by Donald Revell, is devoted to Schuyler's work and includes essays, interviews, and previously unpublished poems. The poet's *Selected* and *Collected Poems* were published in 1988 and 1993, respectively. An obituary is in the *New York Times* (13 Apr. 1991).

MARK SILVERBERG

SCHWARTZWALDER, Floyd Burdette ("Ben") (*b.* 2 June 1909 in Point Pleasant, West Virginia; *d.* 28 April 1993 in St. Petersburg, Florida), college football coach who revived the Syracuse University program after World War II.

Schwartzwalder was one of three sons of Michael Schwartzwalder, a nurseryman, and Hattie Stewart, a homemaker. During his childhood his brother gave him the nickname Ben. He was an outstanding high school wrestler and football player in Huntington, West Virginia, and he attended the University of West Virginia on a football scholarship. A snub-nosed, firm-jawed, powerfully built young man standing five feet, nine inches tall and weighing 152 pounds, Schwartzwalder competed in football and wrestling at West Virginia and graduated with honors and a B.S. degree in 1933. With the hope of becoming a high school football coach, Schwartzwalder earned

Floyd "Ben" Schwartzwalder, 1959. AP/WIDE WORLD PHOTOS

an M.A. degree in physical education from West Virginia in 1935. He married Ruth Simpson, who was known as Reggie, in 1934. They had two daughters.

With aid from Dean Carl Schott, his mentor at the University of West Virginia, Schwartzwalder held a series of coaching positions at high schools in Sisterville, Weston, and Parkerville, West Virginia. From 1941 to 1942 he taught and coached at McKinley High School in Canton, Ohio. After the United States entered World War II, Schwartzwalder joined the U.S. Army and served with the 507th Parachute Infantry of the famed Eighty-second Airborne Division. He became a company commander and earned the rank of major. During the D-Day invasion in 1944, Schwartzwalder parachuted into Normandy and was wounded. After recovering he fought in the Battle of the Bulge and parachuted across the Rhine River. Among other citations, Schwartzwalder was awarded the Bronze Star and the Silver Star.

In 1946 Schwartzwalder began his collegiate coaching career at the tiny Muhlenberg College in Allentown, Pennsylvania. He posted a record of twenty-five wins and five losses there in three seasons, and his 1946 team defeated Saint Bonaventure in the Tobacco Bowl. Syracuse University, a perennial eastern power that had fallen on hard times in football after World War II, hired Schwartzwalder in 1949. Years later Schwartzwalder remarked: "The alumni wanted a big-name coach. They got a long-name coach." He struggled through his first season (1949) with a four and five record but managed to convince the Syracuse chancellor William P. Tolley to increase the number of football scholarships from twelve a year to eventually reach twenty-five a year. Beginning with the 1950 season Schwartzwalder led Syracuse to twenty-two consecutive winning seasons, coached in seven bowl games, and had an overall college coaching record of 178–96–3.

Schwartzwalder's teams were known for their intensive conditioning and toughness as well as for a pounding ground attack run from an unorthodox, unbalanced line. The former Syracuse halfback Jim Brown, one of the finest runners in the history of football, recalled that he found practices with the National Football League Cleveland Browns a welcome relief from Schwartzwalder's training regimen, which included rope climbing and endless running. Schwartzwalder, who recalled running six miles a day before breakfast as a World War II paratrooper, believed thorough conditioning was a key to success in football. Using a finely tuned running game, he produced some of the most talented and feared offensive backs in college football. Beginning with Brown in the mid-1950s, Syracuse became known for its running backs. After Brown, Schwartzwalder coached the 1961 Heisman Trophy winner Ernie Davis, Floyd Little, Jim Nance, and Larry Csonka. Brown, Davis,

and Little made jersey number forty-four a legend at Syracuse.

During Schwartzwalder's twenty-five years as coach at Syracuse, his teams were awarded the Lambert Trophy, signifying the best eastern team, in 1952, 1956, 1959, and 1966. The 1959 squad was Schwartzwalder's finest, posting an eleven and zero record, winning the national championship, and capping off the season with a 23–14 victory over Texas in the Cotton Bowl. Syracuse dominated the opposition as few other teams had, averaging 451.5 total yards and 39 points a game while holding opponents to just 96.2 yards a game and only 19.3 yards rushing. Schwartzwalder was named national collegiate coach of the year.

Schwartzwalder became a legend at Syracuse not only because of his football victories but also for his absentmindedness. He once attended a morning football practice wearing his blue chambray pajama bottoms, thinking he had changed into slacks. The longtime Syracuse coach Roy Simmons, Sr., recalled that Schwartzwalder could "get lost in a phone booth." Schwartzwalder's wife, Reggie, pointed out, however, that Ben's forgetfulness was a fault he used to his advantage. "He simply refuses to clutter up his mind with anything but football," she said. Players remembered Schwartzwalder as a hard but fair coach both on and off the field. In 1957, when Syracuse played Texas Christian in the Cotton Bowl in Dallas, for example, Schwartzwalder threatened to pull out of the event if the bowl committee followed through with its plan to segregate Syracuse's black halfback Brown from the team hotel.

Schwartzwalder's coaching career came to an end at Syracuse in the wake of racial tension and a boycott of spring football practice by black players in 1970. The Syracuse All-American Brown charged in a 1970 news conference that black players had been the victims of racial epithets and unequal treatment and that money was given illegally to white players. The boycott ended with Schwartzwalder suspending seven players and one leaving the team. He refused to take them back. In the ensuing controversy surrounding the boycott, Syracuse's performance on the field suffered. Schwartzwalder's teams managed only a 18–24–1 record from 1970 to 1973. Schwartzwalder was forced to retire after the 1973 season, but he remained close to the Syracuse football program until he died of a heart attack in St. Petersburg. He is buried at the Onondaga County Veterans Memorial Cemetery in New York.

Inducted into the College Football Hall of Fame in 1982, Schwartzwalder was known as a hard-nosed, nononsense coach who emphasized rigorous conditioning and toughness. He developed some of the best running backs in college football history.

★

A file on Schwartzwalder is in the Syracuse University Archives. Joseph English and Eleanor English, "Floyd Burdette (Ben) Schwartzwalder," in *Biographical Dictionary of American Sports: Football,* edited by David L. Porter (1987), is informative. The best summary of his early career is Mal Mallette, "Football's Absent-Minded Professor," *Saturday Evening Post* (29 Oct. 1960). Also see "Coach Ben," *Time* (31 Oct. 1960). Obituaries are in the *New York Times* (29 Apr. 1993) and the *Syracuse Record* (3 May 1993).

JOHN M. CARROLL

SERKIN, Rudolf (*b.* 28 March 1903 in Eger, Bohemia, now Cheb, Czech Republic; *d.* 8 May 1991 in Guilford, Vermont), pianist best known for his interpretations and recordings of central European classics, teacher at and director of the Curtis Institute of Music in Philadelphia, and cofounder and later president and director of the Marlboro Festival in Vermont.

Serkin was the fifth of eight children born to Mordko Serkin, a Russian basso, cantor, and merchant, and Augusta Schargel, a homemaker. Serkin's father introduced all his children to the piano and the violin, and Rudolf Serkin preferred the piano. He progressed prodigiously under the tutelage of his childhood teacher Camilla Taussig. His first public performance, at age five or six, took place in the town of Franzensbad near Eger. At age nine Serkin, who was called Rudi, played for the Viennese pianist Alfred

Rudolph Serkin, *c.* 1960s. © BETTMANN/CORBIS

Grunfeld, who encouraged him to study in Vienna with the distinguished teacher Richard Robert. At age twelve Serkin debuted in Vienna with the Tonkünstler-Orchester under the conductor Oskar Nedbal, performing Felix Mendelssohn's Piano Concerto in G Minor, op. 25. Serkin studied theory and composition with Joseph Marx and harmony and counterpoint with Arnold Schoenberg, one of his most important influences. He had no formal academic schooling.

Serkin flourished in the rich cultural environment of Vienna, where he was welcomed into the home of the patroness Eugenia Schwarzwald, within whose sphere circulated the leading creative thinkers of the day. Blessed with an insatiably curious mind, Serkin developed lifelong interests in art, history, philosophy, poetry, and politics.

As a young pianist Serkin cultivated an extensive and varied repertoire that included compositions by Max Reger, a particular favorite, and a good deal of twentieth-century music. His plans to visit Paris in 1920 for further study with Isidor Phillip were interrupted by unreliable train travel. Stranded in Vienna, Serkin had a chance encounter with the violinist and teacher Adolf Busch that changed his life. Busch directed Serkin to Berlin to study with the venerable Ferruccio Busoni. Busoni, however, thought Serkin too old for lessons and advised him to continue his development solely through performance. Hearing the young Serkin play, Busch quickly selected him as his own sonata partner. In turn Serkin found in Busch a benefactor. He moved in with the Busch family in 1920 and in May 1935 married Busch's daughter Irene, a gifted violinist. They had seven children, one of whom died in infancy. Busch was a caring mentor who profoundly influenced Serkin. His expressive and deeply thoughtful playing resonated with Serkin's own instincts, and the synergy of their partnership drew widespread acclaim.

Serkin made his first appearance in Berlin with Busch in 1921. In the following years he toured extensively, garnering an enviable reputation as a solo and chamber pianist. Serkin moved with the Busch family first to Darmstadt, Germany, in 1922, then to Basel, Switzerland in 1927. They all took Swiss citizenship after Adolf Hitler's rise to power. Basel's location enabled Serkin to travel regularly to Italy to hear performances by Arturo Toscanini, another great musical influence in his life. The combined architecture and passion of Toscanini's art circumscribed the totality of Serkin's own vast and penetrating vision, and their collaboration years later catapulted Serkin to the forefront of the world's leading pianists.

Serkin's appearances in the United States began in 1933 with a sonata recital with Busch at the Coolidge Festival in Washington, D.C. His concerto debut was at Carnegie Hall in New York City on 20 February 1936 with Toscanini and the New York Philharmonic Society. That program included the Mozart Piano Concerto no. 27 in B-flat, K. 595, and the Beethoven Piano Concerto no. 4 in G, op. 58. In 1944 Serkin and Toscanini collaborated again on the same Beethoven concerto, a historic performance with the NBC Symphony Orchestra preserved in a broadcast recording.

Amid the threat of war in 1939 the Busch and Serkin families moved to the United States, where Serkin joined the faculty of the Curtis Institute of Music in Philadelphia as head of the piano department. Serkin's rigorously intellectual approach and discipline profoundly altered the tenor of the institute, strengthening its place as one of the world's foremost music conservatories. Accordingly many of the most gifted young musicians, including his own son Peter Serkin, who like his father was one of the finest pianists of his generation, passed through Serkin's studio. As a teacher Serkin was extraordinarily demanding. He expected no less of his pupils than he did of himself, and he responded harshly to arrogant, shabby, or unprincipled playing. The bedrock of his teaching was the faithful study and interpretation of the printed score, which he regarded as inviolate. Inculcating in each of his pupils the highest standards of pianism, integrity, and stewardship, he served as the institute's director from 1968 until 1976.

In 1950 Serkin, Adolf Busch, Herman Busch, Marcel Moyse, Louis Moyse, and Blanche Honegger Moyse inaugurated the first summer programs at Marlboro College in Marlboro, Vermont. The program was a hybrid: a music school and festival in which a community of like-minded musicians pooled their personal resources and gathered to play chamber music. With personal egos and the business of music left outside the gate, Marlboro was for Serkin the most natural setting in which to make music. Serkin and his wife became U.S. citizens in 1950.

Upon Adolf Busch's death in 1951 Serkin became the artistic director and by consent Marlboro's "sovereign among equals." Serkin applied himself assiduously to the task, molding Marlboro into one of the world's most prestigious summer programs for professional musicians. He engaged distinguished colleagues as regulars and shared in the general work of the community, from serving meals to turning pages. The familial surroundings showcased his boundless generosity toward others and triggered his mischievous wit and proclivity for practical jokes. However, no room existed for joking when it came to making music, and for participants and listeners alike Marlboro was intense and intensely satisfying.

Serkin's career and reputation grew to astonishing proportions. He cared little for celebrity, avoiding interviews and self-promotion, but nonetheless enjoyed box office success, winning audiences all over the world through his sincerity, personal warmth, and exalted musicianship. His success was a product of monumental labor. He practiced for hours on end and toured season after season. Recordings rolled off the presses and accolades poured in, including honorary degrees and memberships, a Presidential Medal of Freedom in 1963, and a National Medal of Art in 1988. He took a year's sabbatical in 1960–1961 to study musical works such as the Haydn quartets and the Bach cantatas—pieces that he as a pianist would never have the occasion to play but that drew his attention simply for their inherent beauty.

Serkin made his home in Guilford, Vermont. He relished his role as a citizen of Guilford and took pride in his achievements as a New England dairy farmer. Illness in the late 1980s forced him to curtail his activities but he rallied to program the last three Beethoven sonatas in his final Carnegie Hall appearance on 8 April 1987 and the *Emperor Concerto* in Cleveland and Chicago in 1988. He died of cancer on 8 May 1991 and was laid to rest in Guilford, Vermont.

Serkin is widely regarded as one of the most important pianists of the twentieth century. He was lean, nervous, "bookish," and bug-eyed behind thick glasses. He was gaunt and pale in later years, with very little hair scattered in untamed white wisps. In contrast were the strength of his playing and his large, powerful hands and thick fingers, which compounded the technical challenges of playing. Notwithstanding his achievements, he was not a "natural" pianist. He regarded making music as a crushing responsibility and a serious business for which musicians could not overprepare. In the grip of a performance he was nervous and ungainly, driven by an elemental inner frenzy. His playing combined a biting tone, foot stomping, and anguished groaning with lofty and incorruptible musical ideals, a keen understanding of musical architecture, taut and unrelenting rhythms, unity, and ruthless logic. He avoided musical effects, pianistic gimmickry, and crowd-pleasing display pieces, choosing in his later years severe and intellectually demanding programs centered around large-scale works of Wolfgang Mozart, Franz Schubert, Johannes Brahms, and especially Ludwig van Beethoven. Serkin remained ever humble in the face of the music he loved and in which he saw human grandeur. He evoked a saintly aura in his approach to music making and he became the musical conscience of generations of listeners and musicians. His many recordings perpetuate his legacy as a divinely gifted artist consumed by music.

★

Archival materials on Serkin are at the Curtis Institute of Music in Philadelphia. Serkin's art is best represented in his Columbia recordings of works of Beethoven, Brahms, Mozart, and Schubert. John Gillespie and Anna Gillespie, "Rudolf Serkin," in *Notable Twentieth-Century Pianists* (1995), couples a chronology of his life with an assessment of his art through reviews. David Dubal,

"Rudolf Serkin," in *The Art of the Piano* (1995), is an engaging essay devoted to details of Serkin's playing. The biography by Tully Potter, *Adolf Busch: The Life of an Honest Musician* (2001), includes information about Serkin. The most important interviews with Serkin are Dean Elder, "Serkin," *Clavier* 9 (Nov. 1970): 8–15, and Robert Silverman, "Serkin," *Piano Quarterly* 26, no. 100 (winter 1977–1978): 3–6. Other important articles include Irving Kolodin, "The Complete Musician," *Horizon* (Sept. 1961): 82–87; Joseph Roddy, "Rudolf Serkin," *High Fidelity* 11 (July 1961): 24–28, 82; and Claude Frank, "Rudolf Serkin: Servant of Music," *Keynote* (Mar. 1983): 12–16. An obituary is in the *New York Times* (10 May 1991).

ROBERT J. CHABORA

SEUSS, DR. *See* Geisel, Theodor A.

SEVAREID, (Arnold) Eric (*b.* 26 November 1912 in Velva, North Dakota; *d.* 9 July 1992 in Washington, D.C.), CBS war correspondent, radio and television commentator, and author, known for the intellectual depth and painstaking eloquence of his commentaries.

Sevareid (who first used his middle name, Eric, as a correspondent in France) was one of four children of Alfred Eric Sevareid, a local banker, and Clare Hougen, a homemaker and the daughter of a Norwegian Lutheran minister. Young Sevareid was a product of his mother's inspiration to read widely, his heritage of Norwegian-Lutheran reticence and morality, and the effect of the vast Dakota wheat fields on his imagination. In his autobiography, *Not So Wild a Dream* (1946), he recalled his Velva (pop. 800) boy-

Eric Sevareid. © BETTMANN/CORBIS

hood in Edenic imagery, as a source of the individualism and spirit of cooperation that enabled American democracy to survive World War II. As an apprentice in the office of the *Velva Journal,* a four-page weekly, he learned what he wanted to do with his life.

When drought brought disaster to farm country and caused his father's bank to fail in 1925, the family moved for a year to Minot, North Dakota, then to Minneapolis, where they lived in a large wooden house in a middle-class neighborhood. Arnold learned how to run the Central High School newspaper before graduating in 1930. Shortly thereafter, at the age of seventeen, he and a school friend, Walter Port, paddled a canoe a spectacular 2,250 miles from Minneapolis to the Hudson Bay and published a newspaper series and book, *Canoeing with the Cree* (1935), about the experience. This thirst for adventure also led him to hitchhike and ride the rails in the summer of 1933 to toil in a California gold mine.

Working his way through the University of Minnesota, he majored in political science but threw most of his energies into the campus *Minnesota Daily*. He also joined an elite political discussion club, the Jacobins, disciples of the charismatic Professor Benjamin Lippincott, known as a Democratic Socialist. Many of the Jacobins were pacifists who, like students throughout the country, demonstrated against compulsory military drill. Sevareid's participation later contributed to his "radical" reputation, and references to it showed up in his FBI file. Emotionally crushed when he did not become the *Daily* editor, he was convinced that the university president had vetoed his selection.

On 18 May 1935, shortly before graduation, Sevareid married Lois Finger, a law student and the beautiful and brilliant daughter of the university track coach. He worked as a cub reporter for the *Minneapolis Star,* during which time he saw the police brutally crush a truckers' strike. He then took a job as a reporter for the *Minneapolis Journal,* where he wrote an exposé of the Silver Shirts, a national network of fascist, Ku Klux Klan–like clubs, but he was fired in the wake of a newspaper strike. Disillusioned, in 1937 he and Lois left for a new life in Paris.

The Paris edition of the *New York Herald-Tribune* recognized his talent and let him write what he wanted. He interviewed Gertrude Stein and covered the notorious murder trial of the serial killer Eugène Weidmann with a style that brought him to the attention of the CBS correspondent Edward R. Murrow in London, who recruited him in 1939 as one of the first "Murrow boys"—the cadre of radio correspondents eventually including William L. Shirer, Larry LeSueur, Howard K. Smith, Winston Burdett, and Charles Collingwood—who covered the outbreak of World War II and who became the stars of postwar CBS radio and TV news.

In April 1940 Lois gave birth to twins and escaped with

them to New York the following month as the German army bore down on Paris. As the city fell, Sevareid wrote: "Paris lay dying, like a beautiful woman in a coma, not knowing or asking why." As France collapsed under the Nazi assault, he escaped to London where, with his hero Murrow, he covered the German blitz. His nerves did not take bombing well. He went on assignments in Mexico in December 1940, returned to the CBS Washington, D.C., office in January 1941, and covered the third Pan-American Conference in Brazil in January 1942, but his eyes were on the war in Europe. In his opinion the media (though the term was not yet current) were too "objective," when they should have been mobilizing public opinion against Nazi Germany. After Pearl Harbor he had a crisis of conscience over whether he should enlist, but he was persuaded to serve as a war correspondent instead.

Sevareid's first war assignment came at government request in 1943, when he flew to China to assess the political-military situation. Over the Burma "hump" the engines of his C-46 gave out, and the twenty passengers, including the diplomat John Paton Davies, parachuted into the jungle. They were rescued by Naga headhunter tribesmen, and Philip Adams, a young British colonial officer, led them on a ten-day trek to safety. Sevareid, who had lost his Lutheran faith at college, served as chaplain to the party; most important, the ordeal helped settle any lingering questions about his own physical courage. When he completed his mission to China he wrote a report exposing the corruption of the nationalist Chinese government, which the War Department forbade him to publish in any form. It foresaw the "loss" of China to the Communists, for which Davies and other China hands were later blamed. When Davies lost his job under Secretary of State John Foster Dulles in 1954, Sevareid defended him in a blistering radio commentary. Sevareid was also one of the first to attack the red-hunting Senator Joseph McCarthy, even though he knew his own buried China report could be used to ruin his career.

Restless away from the front, Sevareid followed the U.S. Army to North Africa, Italy, southern France, and, finally, across the Rhine into Germany. After the war he took a few months to write *Not So Wild a Dream,* an interpretation of the American character as well as an account of his own life. He settled in Seminary Hill in Alexandria, Virginia, covered presidential nominating conventions, commuted to New York for various assignments, and most of all, honed his prose style, finding his voice with original five-minute commentaries—mini-essays—at the end of the 11 P.M. radio news.

But his personal life was falling apart. Lois was manic-depressive and frequently hospitalized. Eric was attentive and tried to be loyal; but he had limited emotional energy and had been concentrating on his career. In 1959 they

moved to Georgetown in the District of Columbia. Then Eric fled to Spain with Belén Marshall, the vivacious daughter, half his age, of a Cuban-born opera singer, who was herself a songwriter and singer. On 16 August 1962 he and Lois divorced, and on 28 February 1963 he married Belén, with whom he had one child. The couple moved into a new house in Washington, D.C., but the worlds of the lively Belén and the scholarly Eric did not mesh. They separated, although they did not divorce until 1973. Eric never justified his treatment of Lois, who died in 1970. In Dan Rather's words, "It remained an object of excruciating guilt for him the rest of his life."

Sevareid's career took on a new dimension with the inauguration of the half-hour CBS-TV *Evening News* with Walter Cronkite in 1962. Though very nervous in front of the camera, Sevareid worked all day to carefully craft two-minute commentaries. Although conservative in his fidelity to American institutions, he was a liberal in the tradition of Franklin D. Roosevelt and Adlai Stevenson and a strong defender of human liberty and the free press. He was unsympathetic to students who trashed their universities but was one of the first correspondents to go to Vietnam and conclude that it was both a losing and an immoral adventure. On 19 April 1972 he said, "If we have reached the dreadful point where the honor of the state and the conscience of the people collide, then what does honor mean anymore? . . . There does come a time when the heart must rule the head. That time is when the heart is about to break." While striving to keep a balance in his language, he was nevertheless relentless in the last days of Watergate, "one of the most destructive political scandals in recent times."

In 1977 Sevareid marked his obligatory retirement at age sixty-five by three commentaries reflecting on his career. He concluded: "There is in the American people a tough, undiminished instinct for what is fair. Rightly or wrongly, I feel that I have passed that test." He went on the lecture circuit, made occasional film cameo appearances, and narrated documentaries. In 1979 he married Suzanne St. Pierre, a CBS producer. They had no children. Always insecure about money, he nevertheless declined a million-dollar offer to do endorsements for an investment house, lest he tarnish his name. A shy man, he loved to retire to trout streams and his cabin in the woods of Warrenton, Virginia. He lacked the will to write another volume of his memoirs; but as long as his words are on record, he will be remembered as speaking both to and for America at its best. Sevareid died in Washington, D.C., from stomach cancer, and his remains were cremated.

★

The Sevareid papers are in the Library of Congress. Sevareid's memoir *Not So Wild a Dream* was published in 1946. His radio commentaries are collected in *In One Ear: 107 Snapshots of Men and Events Which Make a Far-Reaching Panorama of the American Situation at Mid-century* (1952) and *Small Sounds in the Night: A Collection of Capsule Commentaries on the American Scene* (1956). The only complete biography is Raymond A. Schroth, *The American Journey of Eric Sevareid* (1995). See also Stanley Cloud and Lynne Olson, *The Murrow Boys: Pioneers on the Front Lines of Broadcast Journalism* (1996). Sally Bedell Smith's biography of William Paley, *In All his Glory: The Life of William Paley: The Legendary Tycoon and His Brilliant Circle* (1990), is valuable for its pictures of CBS. The best history of broadcast journalism is Edward Bliss, Jr., *Now the News: The Story of Broadcast Journalism* (1991). An obituary is in the *New York Times* (10 July 1992).

RAYMOND A. SCHROTH, S.J.

SHAWN, William (*b*, 31 August 1907 in Chicago, Illinois; *d*. 8 December 1992 in New York City), the editor of the *New Yorker* magazine for more than three decades in the post–World War II period.

Shawn was one of four children (one of whom died in childhood) born to Benjamin ("Jackknife Ben") Chon, owner of a profitable silver, diamond, and cutlery shop in Chicago's meatpacking district. His mother was Anna Bransky, a homemaker. In 1925 Shawn graduated from the Harvard School for Boys, a prestigious Chicago preparatory school. He attended the University of Michigan in Ann Arbor, but left before graduating and worked as a reporter for the *Daily Optic* in Las Vegas, New Mexico. On returning to Chicago he wrote captions and headlines for a photo syndicate. On the day after his twenty-first birthday he married Cecille Lyon, also a journalist. They had three children.

While in Chicago, Shawn followed the lead of his brother Nelson, a songwriter, in changing his surname to "Shawn." Like Nelson, he had musical aspirations, and in 1932 Shawn moved to New York City, hoping to establish himself as a composer. To earn money he began helping his wife out with freelance fact-gathering assignments she had taken from the *New Yorker*, a weekly magazine. The editors were impressed with the thoroughness and quality of Shawn's work and in 1933 he was hired as a full-time reporter for "Talk of the Town," a collection of short pieces at the front of the magazine.

The *New Yorker* had been started in 1925 by Harold Ross primarily as a comic magazine, and its early volumes were filled with pieces by such humorists as Dorothy Parker, Robert Benchley, James Thurber, E. B. White, Frank Sullivan, and Ring Lardner. But by the time of Shawn's arrival its scope was broadening to include serious works of journalism and fiction. Shawn's interest and aptitude was in the former. Although he wrote several short pieces for the magazine (only one of them, a fantasy imagining what would happen if New York City was struck by a frighteningly powerful bomb, was signed with the initials "W. S."), it quickly became apparent that his métier was editing. In 1935 Ross promoted him to the responsibility of devising and coordinating possible subjects for articles. The position had no official title, but Shawn was so good at it that the *New Yorker* writer A. J. Liebling dubbed him "the information man."

In 1939 Shawn became the managing editor and took charge of all journalism in the magazine. As an editor his greatest strength was (and continued to be) the intense and intelligent interest he took in every writer's work; many of his authors remarked over the years how inspirational they found this attentiveness to be. S. N. Behrman, a longtime *New Yorker* contributor as well as a playwright, once remarked of Shawn, "He is a most remarkable incubator. I feel that with his help I could write any piece—or almost any piece."

The timing of Shawn's appointment was propitious, for 1939 marked the start of the European conflict that would become World War II. Under Shawn's direction, correspondents such as A. J. Liebling, E. J. Kahn, Jr., John Lardner, Walter Bernstein, Janet Flanner, Mollie Panter-Downes, and John Hersey sent in dispatches from all corners of the globe. Overall, the magazine's coverage of the war was thorough and distinguished and finally convinced the public at large that the *New Yorker* was more than just a humor magazine. (*Infantry Journal* stated in 1944, "One magazine of general circulation stands high above all others in the accuracy of what it prints about the war—the *New Yorker*.")

The culmination of the *New Yorker*'s World War II journalism was Hersey's "Hiroshima." The article was an editorial triumph for Shawn, who had sent Hersey to Japan to write about the aftermath of the dropping of the atomic bomb. When Hersey produced a manuscript of more than 30,000 words, Shawn felt that its power demanded that it be published in one issue, even though the issue would have room for no other articles or stories. He convinced Ross to go along with this plan and "Hiroshima" essentially *was* the *New Yorker* for 31 August 1946. Published three months afterward as a book, it remained in print into the twenty-first century. In 1999 New York University released a ranking of the top 100 works of journalism of the twentieth century; "Hiroshima" topped the list.

Harold Ross died late in 1951 and early the next year Raoul Fleischmann, the publisher of the *New Yorker*, named Shawn editor. In the first decade of his tenure such writers as Dwight Macdonald, John Updike, and Truman Capote each started a long association with the *New Yorker*, and the magazine also published notable work by J. D. Salinger, Edmund Wilson, Lillian Ross, John Cheever, Saul

Steinberg, and Mary McCarthy. But Shawn instituted no notable changes in format, editorial policy, or design, and in general the *New Yorker* of the 1950s was genteel and placid.

That changed in the early 1960s. Most notably, in an eight-month span between June 1962 and February 1963 the *New Yorker* printed three highly charged social documents: Rachel Carson's "Silent Spring," about the threat of dichlorodiphenyltrichloroethane (DDT) to the environment; James Baldwin's "Letter from a Region in My Mind," about race relations in the United States; and Hannah Arendt's "Eichmann in Jerusalem," about the trial of the Nazi war criminal Adolf Eichmann. All three were later published as books (Baldwin's under the title *The Fire Next Time*), and all three helped establish the reputation of the *New Yorker* as a periodical not only of belles lettres but of political journalism and social commentary. In 1965 the magazine caused even more of a stir with the publication of the full text of Capote's *In Cold Blood*, a "nonfiction novel" about the gruesome murder of a family in Kansas.

Shawn was a quiet man whose eccentricities, phobias, and almost painful shyness became legendary. Increasingly his life was wrapped up in the *New Yorker* and its writers. He did not speak in public, he gave few interviews, and from the 1960s onward he never set foot outside the New York City metropolitan area. But he was also a man of strong convictions. In the late 1960s and early 1970s he—and the magazine—became aligned with two crusades: to preserve the environment and to end the war in Vietnam. In addition to Jonathan Schell's long, passionate anti-Vietnam editorials in "Talk of the Town," the *New Yorker* published Charles Reich's essay in praise of hippiedom, "The Greening of America," and Richard Harris's withering attacks on the Nixon administration. In 1970 in large part because these and other articles offended some conservative longtime readers, the magazine saw its first drop in circulation since the Great Depression.

Shawn was always adamant about not editing the *New Yorker* for its readers, its shareholders, or anyone other than himself, its other editors, and its authors, and so there was no question of his adjusting its contents to stem the tide of subscriber defections. But with Richard Nixon's resignation and the final withdrawal of U.S. troops from Vietnam, the magazine underwent a more organic political disengagement. In the middle and late 1970s it not only recovered its financial footing but experienced a creative revival, publishing such notable articles as Susan Sheehan's "A Welfare Mother" and C. D. B. Bryan's "Friendly Fire," as well as outstanding work from a remarkable roster of writers and artists, including Donald Barthelme, Ann Beattie, Jorge Luis Borges, Isaac Bashevis Singer, Calvin Trillin, John McPhee, Roger Angell, Kenneth Tynan, Garrison Keillor,

Ian Frazier, Pauline Kael, Roz Chast, Jack Ziegler, and Edward Koren.

The 1980s were a difficult time for Shawn. Several *New Yorker* articles were found to have factual errors, which led to minor scandals, and an increasing number of critics chided the magazine for what they saw as its dullness, preciousness, and irrelevance. Meanwhile Shawn, who celebrated his seventy-fifth birthday and began his fiftieth year with the magazine in 1982, showed a marked resistance in addressing the issue of his eventual successor. These and other factors left the *New Yorker* vulnerable to a takeover, and in 1985 the communications magnate S. I. Newhouse purchased the magazine from shareholders. Two years later Newhouse dismissed Shawn and replaced him with Robert Gottlieb. Following his dismissal, he served informally as editorial consultant with the company Farrar, Straus and Giroux. Shawn died of a heart attack in his New York City apartment at Fifth Avenue and Ninety-sixth Street.

Along with Harold Ross, Henry Luce, and a handful of others, William Shawn would be included on any list of the outstanding American magazine editors of the twentieth century. He stands apart from the others in the way his own professional and personal identity merged with that of the publication he oversaw. Although his published works consisted of one signed article and the introduction to four books, the collected issues of the *New Yorker* in the thirty-five years of his editorship stand as Shawn's literary achievement.

★

The *New Yorker* Records at the New York Public Library contain a substantial number of letters and memoranda written by Shawn, as well as original copies of manuscripts edited by him and typescripts of unsigned obituaries and editorials. Three memoirs by longtime *New Yorker* staff writers give varying perspectives on what it was like to know and work with Shawn: *Remembering Mr. Shawn's New Yorker: The Invisible Art of Editing* (1998), by Ved Mehta; *Here But Not Here: A Love Story* (1998), by Lillian Ross; and *Gone: The Last Days of the New Yorker* (1999), by Renata Adler. *About Town: The* New Yorker *and the World It Made* (2000), by Ben Yagoda, is a cultural and critical history of the magazine. An obituary is in the *New York Times* (9 Dec. 1992).

BEN YAGODA

SHIRER, William Lawrence (*b.* 23 February 1904 in Chicago, Illinois; *d.* 28 December 1993 in Boston, Massachusetts), journalist and radio commentator whose newspaper dispatches and pioneering radio broadcasts from Berlin, Germany, and other European capitals in the 1930s alerted the American public to Adolf Hitler and the Nazi menace, and whose postwar book detailing the history of the Third Reich was an international best-seller.

A child of the American Midwest when that region was at its most insular and parochial, Shirer became a cultivated man of the world, fluent in four languages, well-versed in food and drink, and the personification of the fabled foreign correspondent, who had been everywhere, known everyone, and covered the most important stories of his day. He was the middle child and first son born to Seward Smith Shirer, an assistant U.S. district attorney, and Bessie Josephine Tanner Shirer, a homemaker. He idolized his father both as a parent and as a lover of books, music, and the life of the mind. Tragically, Seward died in 1913 at the age of forty-one when a misdiagnosed case of appendicitis led to a rupture. His widow and her three children returned to her family home in Cedar Rapids, Iowa, where Shirer graduated from Washington High School in 1921. Financially strapped and forced to live at home, he entered nearby Coe College, where early on he resolved to become a writer. In the summers of his sophomore and junior years he took his first newspaper job as a sports reporter and feature writer for the *Cedar Rapids Republican.* By his senior year he was the outspoken and controversial editor of the college weekly. Elected to Phi Beta Kappa, he graduated with a B.A. degree in 1925. He worked his way across the Atlantic on a cattle boat, having set out for Europe to escape, in his

words, the "fundamentalism, puritanism and . . . puerility" of the Coolidge era.

Following a summer of travel, Shirer was hired as a copy editor for the Paris edition of the *Chicago Tribune.* He harbored the hope of becoming a novelist, but after several failed attempts at short fiction, he concluded that his writing talents lay elsewhere. Over the next two years he took history courses at the College de France in Paris and in 1927 became a European correspondent for the *Tribune*'s Chicago edition, reporting such stories as Charles Lindbergh's landing at Le Bourget outside Paris that year, and the summer and winter Olympics in 1928. He spent the three years from 1929 to 1932 as the head of the *Tribune*'s Central European bureau headquartered in Vienna, Austria. During that time he traveled to India to cover Mahatma Gandhi, who became, he wrote, a major influence in his life and the subject of a later book, *Gandhi: A Memoir* (1980). He married Theresa Stiberitz, a Viennese-born editor for a London magazine, on 30 January 1931; they had two daughters and divorced in August 1970.

In 1932 Shirer lost both the sight in his right eye in a skiing accident and, weeks later, his job at the *Tribune* in a cost-cutting move. He made a brief stab at freelance writing in Spain, but returned to France in January 1934 to work briefly for the Paris edition of the *New York Herald.* In August 1934 he joined William Randolph Hearst's ill-fated Universal News Service (UNS) in Berlin. Although his assignments for UNS took him through most of Europe, his primary focus was on events in Berlin, Vienna, and Prague, Czechoslovakia, where he observed Hitler's rise to power and where his forthright reporting and dogged investigations tested the limits of Nazi censorship. Joseph Goebbels, the German propaganda minister, ordered Shirer publicly denounced for alleged anti-German sentiments in his accounts of the 1936 Olympics, and he threatened to have Shirer expelled from the country for his wire-service dispatches on anti-Semitism in the Third Reich.

By 1937 the UNS had folded and Shirer was hired by the CBS vice president Edward R. Murrow as a radio newsman based in Berlin, experimenting with transatlantic programming. Initially he and Murrow, who was in London, did no reporting; instead they introduced print journalists, who delivered their own stories over the air. But in March 1938, on the day of the *Anschluss*—the forced union or uniting of Germany and Austria engineered by the Nazis—the Nazi government prohibited radio broadcasts of any kind from Vienna. Shirer, who had been a firsthand observer of the German army's entrance into the city, flew to London that evening for an impromptu, and historic, live broadcast to America. Murrow next organized a round-table of European correspondents, including Shirer, for a half-hour program describing the reaction of other European states to the German invasion. To the surprise of CBS

William L. Shirer. LIBRARY OF CONGRESS

executives, the innovative broadcasts gained a large audience nationwide. William S. Paley, the head of CBS, immediately assigned Murrow and Shirer to regular newscasts that brought live foreign news reports into American homes for the first time—a development that quickly made CBS the nation's leading network for news.

Shirer, still based in Berlin, faced continuous Nazi interference and censorship but managed to score a personal triumph on 21 June 1940, when Hitler arrived at Compiegne in France to arrange the French surrender. All journalists present were required to send their dispatches to Berlin for clearance. When it came time for Shirer to broadcast his account to Berlin, a German radio engineer opened the wrong switch, sending Shirer's message to London by mistake. In minutes, his dramatic reportage was on the air, crossing the Atlantic to the United States and beating the competition (print and radio alike) by more than six hours.

Shirer continued to report from Germany throughout the summer and fall of 1940 but following rumors of his imminent arrest, he and his family returned to America by ship in December. He edited his daily journals into a best-selling book, *Berlin Diary: The Journal of a Foreign Correspondent, 1934–1941* (1941), which was eventually translated into seven languages, with sales in the United States alone exceeding 500,000 copies. Ignoring Murrow's request that he return to London—a move that would cost him Murrow's friendship—Shirer spent most of the war years in New York City as a Sunday-night radio commentator for CBS (1941–1947) and a syndicated columnist for the *New York Herald Tribune* (1942–1948). He returned to Europe in the waning days of the war to cover the Nuremberg trials and gather material for his second book, *End of a Berlin Diary* (1947).

In 1946 Shirer won the George Foster Peabody Award for his radio commentary, but a year later he resigned from CBS in a bitter conflict with Paley and Murrow, claiming they were trying to muzzle him. He joined the Mutual Broadcasting System, where he worked from 1947 to 1949, but was blacklisted in 1950 during the McCarthy era, when his name appeared in "Red Channels," an anonymously-authored booklet that listed the names of alleged communists and sympathizers in the movies, radio, and television. Despite his denial that he had ever been a party member, he was unable to get on-the-air work or to sell his freelance articles to national magazines like *Life, Collier's, Atlantic Monthly,* and *Harper's* that had bought from him in the past.

Shirer now entered the lowest period of his life, surviving through lecture tours on college campuses—the only places, he said, that he was welcome—and the publication of five books. Three were fiction: *Traitor* (1950), loosely based on the life of "Axis Sally," a British turncoat; *Stranger Come Home* (1954) a roman à clef concerning free speech

on radio; and *The Consul's Wife* (1956), a thriller set in a fictitious British colony. Each received a tepid critical reception, reviewers generally agreeing that the novels were closer to journalism than to literature. His nonfiction fared much better. *Mid-Century Journey: The Western World Through Its Years of Conflict* (1952), which examined events in Austria, Germany, France, and Great Britain, was a Literary Guild selection. *The Challenge of Scandinavia: Norway, Sweden, Denmark and Finland in Our Time* (1955) attracted a smaller but respectable audience.

In 1960 Shirer published his blockbuster: *The Rise and Fall of the Third Reich: A History of Nazi Germany* (reprinted with the author's afterword in 1990). Despite its 1,245 pages and $10 price tag, it was an instant best-seller, winning the National Book Award and other literary prizes as well as near unanimous praise from nonacademic reviewers who called it a readable and definitive history. A number of academics acknowledged its literary quality but faulted Shirer's emphasis on the more lurid details of Nazism and his oversimplification of complex events. Published in paperback in 1961, it was frequently reprinted and had sold nearly 20 million copies worldwide by the time Shirer died.

Shirer also wrote two children's books, *The Rise and Fall of Adolf Hitler* (1961) and *The Sinking of the Bismarck* (1962). He devoted seven years of research to the three-volume *Collapse of the Third Republic: An Inquiry into the Fall of France in 1940* (1969), another history popular with readers but dismissed by academics as indiscriminate and unbalanced in its sources and its emphases.

Shirer spent the 1970s and 1980s writing a massive three-volume autobiography, collectively titled *Twentieth Century Journey: A Memoir of a Life and the Times.* Volume one, *The Start, 1904–1930* (1976), reached a wide audience and was generally well received. Volume two, *The Nightmare Years, 1930–1940* (1984), and volume three, *A Native's Return, 1945–1988* (1990), were less successful. His last book, *Love and Hatred: The Troubled Marriage of Leo and Sonya Tolstoy,* was published posthumously in 1994 and dedicated to his second wife, Irina Lugovskaya, whom he married in 1988 (they had no children); and his cardiologist, who had helped him through the cardiac problems that plagued him in his last years.

Shirer died of heart failure during a brief confinement in Massachusetts General Hospital, Boston. He is buried in Lenox, Massachusetts.

When he joined Edward Murrow's CBS news staff in 1937, Shirer was a widely respected foreign correspondent with very limited radio experience. He had previously made only one transatlantic broadcast, a report from Berlin on the German people's reaction to the Hindenburg disaster that May. Burdened with a high, thin, reedy voice, he nonetheless became a popular on-air reporter because of his intelligent commentary and his superior news-gathering skills. Along with the rest of "Murrow's boys" he revolutionized broadcast journalism and established CBS news as the industry leader in the years before and after World War II. His vividly written, often controversial radio reports from Germany and central Europe helped develop an international awareness among American listeners. Mysteriously blacklisted and barred from broadcasting during the first years of the cold war, Shirer's focus on writing led to his most successful book, *The Rise and Fall of the Third Reich*. Professional historians deemed his books readable, but simplistic and historically unbalanced; Shirer's readers believed otherwise and his work continued to sell well until his death.

★

Shirer's papers are divided between the Coe College Library, Cedar Rapids, Iowa, and his family in New York and Massachusetts. Volume one of his autobiography, *Twentieth Century Journey: A Memoir of a Life and the Times: The Start: 1904–1930* (1976), is the most useful—and in many ways, the most revealing—of the three volumes. Shirer also published a brief memoir in a limited edition that did not circulate to the public: *An August to Remember: A Historian Remembers the Last Days of World War II and the End of the World that Was* (1986). See also the posthumous publication, William Shirer, *This is Berlin: Radio Broadcasts from Nazi Germany* (1999). There is no biography. Stanley Cloud and Lynne Olson, *The Murrow Boys* (1996), describe Shirer's years with Edward R. Murrow and CBS. Recordings of World War II radio broadcasts by CBS correspondents, including Shirer, are in the National Archives in Washington, D.C. A transcript of his historic broadcast of the surrender of France in 1940 is reprinted in Louis L. Snyder and Richard B. Morris, eds., *A Treasury of Great Reporting* (1949). An obituary is in the *New York Times* (30 Dec. 1993).

ALLAN L. DAMON

SHUSTER, Joseph E. ("Joe") (*b.* 10 July 1914 in Toronto, Canada; *d.* 30 July 1992 in Los Angeles, California), comic book illustrator best known for creating and drawing the character Superman with Jerry Siegel.

Shuster was the oldest of three children born to Julius Shuster, a Dutch tailor, and Ida Kaklarsky, a Russian singer and actress. The family moved to Cleveland when Shuster was nine. A fragile child, Shuster lifted weights to build stamina, delivered newspapers, and worked in a sign-painting shop to help his family, which was beset by poverty. When not working, he escaped into pulp magazines and the Sunday newspaper comic strips. Despite the objections of his parents, he decided to take up art and wrote and drew his first comic work for the Alexander Hamilton Junior High School student newspaper. In 1931 he met Jerry Siegel, a fellow science fiction enthusiast, at Glenville High School, and the pair soon wrote and illustrated a Tarzan parody, "Goober the Mighty," for the *Glenville Torch*. Shuster graduated from high school in 1932 and his talent won him a scholarship to the Cleveland Art School, which he attended from 1931 to 1933. He paid for additional lessons for a single semester in 1932 from the John Huntington Polytechnical Institute a dime at a time. He did not graduate or receive a degree from either institution.

Shuster and Siegel created numerous comic strips with Shuster drawing and Siegel writing. They sent the strips to the larger newspaper syndicates but generated little interest. To stay busy they produced their own fanzine, *Science Fiction,* beginning in October 1932. Its third issue, in January 1933, introduced "The Reign of the Superman," in which the title character was a villain. Siegel rewrote the character as a hero, a strongman dressed in a muscle shirt and trousers—a man of genius and action but not a superman—for a comic book they tried unsuccessfully to sell to Consolidated Book Publishers of Chicago in 1933.

In 1934 Siegel and Shuster again reworked the character, this time giving him superpowers, and Shuster created the visual image that launched a half-century of imitations. Following the design of Buck Rogers, Shuster placed the character in tights but added a cape and the emblematic *S* on the chest. The city of Metropolis setting was modeled on his childhood memories of Toronto. If the "man of steel" was his fantasy, however, Clark Kent was Shuster's reality. Superman's socially awkward, bespectacled alter ego was based on Shuster himself. The strip met rejection again. The financial situation for the team was so desperate that their work was submitted on the back of unused wallpaper and brown wrapping paper. They did some work that year for the Christmas advertising supplement for the *Cleveland Shopping News.*

In 1935 Shuster and Siegel were finally successful with two comic features, "Henri Duval" and "Dr. Occult," published by Major Malcolm Wheeler-Nicholson for *New Fun Comics* number six (October 1935). The team continued with Wheeler-Nicholson, producing "Federal Men" in *New Comics* number two (January 1936), "Radio Squad" in *More Fun Comics* number eleven (July 1936), and their first great success, "Slam Bradley" in the company's flagship title, *Detective Comics* number one (March 1937).

Harry Donenfeld, who partnered with Wheeler-Nicholson to publish *Detective Comics* (DC), was looking for original material for a new title. He saw Siegel and Shuster's Superman strip and purchased it on the stipulation that they redraw it and produce it as a comic book. Siegel and Shuster signed the standard contract, earning $10 a page for the thirteen-page story, and all rights to the character became the property of DC's subsidiary company, Superman, Incorporated. *Action Comics* number 1 (June 1938)

Joe Shuster at a gym in Cleveland, 1940. © BETTMANN/CORBIS

and the popularity of the character Superman initiated the golden age of superhero comic books. By 1941 *Action Comics* sold over 900,000 issues monthly, while a second title, *Superman,* begun in the summer of 1939, sold 1.25 million issues, together grossing $950,000 a year. On 16 January 1939 McClure's Syndicate, which had originally rejected the strip, debuted it in four newspapers. Two years later the strip ran in over 300 newspapers and reached some 20 million readers.

At first Shuster drew the bulk of the art in a primitive but cleverly laid out style that fit the energy of the character. He deviated from the rigid small panel approach of the period by incorporating larger panels and angular visions of the action. His characters were rounded and fluid and evoked a dynamic sense of speed and movement. The uncluttered style was well suited to the technology of comic book publishing in the late 1930s and became the template for countless imitators.

To meet the burgeoning weekly demand for thirteen comic pages, six daily strips, a full Sunday page, plus artwork for merchandising and advertising, Shuster rented a studio in Cleveland and hired a staff that included his brother Frank Shuster and such recognized names as Paul Cassidy, Wayne Boring, Jack Burnley, John Sikela, Dennis Neville, and Leo Nowack. Suffering from failing eyesight, Shuster still did the layouts, rough sketches, and facial details but let others do the pencils and inks. At the height of his success he shared $500 a story plus a small percentage of the merchandising profits with Siegel. He averaged an estimated $36,000 a year and covered the cost of the studio and artists out of his own pocket.

DC published another Siegel and Shuster idea, Superboy, in *More Fun* number 101 (January–February 1945) but refused to pay the team for its original idea. In 1947 the pair sued to regain the rights to Superman and Superboy and to recover $5 million of revenue lost during their nine years with DC. In the end they settled for a reported $400,000 and signed away all rights. Their names were withdrawn from the strips, and they were in effect released from DC. They went to Vincent Sullivan's Magazine Enterprises to produce *Funnyman* number one (December 1947) and a subsequent newspaper comic strip. When the effort failed late in 1949, Siegel and Shuster dissolved their partnership, although they remained close friends for the rest of their lives. Shuster then moved to New York to live with his brother in Queens.

In 1954 Shuster returned to comic books at Charlton Publishing to illustrate *Crime and Justice, Racquet Squad in Action, Space Adventures, Strange Suspense Stories,* and *This Magazine Is Haunted.* But poor eyesight and a depressed market ended his career. In 1960 Shuster made some rough sketches for a strip called "Stormy Weathers," but no publishers were interested.

The copyright to Superman came up for renewal in 1963, and Shuster and Siegel again tried to reclaim the rights. The case dragged on until 1975, and their effort failed. When Time Warner, which now owned DC Comics, announced the production of a Superman movie in 1976, Siegel and Shuster took their plight to the media. The resulting publicity led to a settlement in 1978 in which Warner Brothers agreed to pay the pair an annual stipend of $20,000 each for the rest of their lives, to give them full medical coverage, and to restore their names to the comic book they had created.

By that time, however, Shuster's personal life was in disarray. He could no longer see well enough to draw. His 1976 marriage to a showgirl, Judy Cantro, ended in divorce two years later. They had no children. In December 1978 Shuster moved to California to be close to Siegel and his wife Joanne. For the remainder of his life Shuster worked odd jobs and lived in obscurity. He died in his apartment on 30 July 1992 from congestive heart failure. He is buried in Los Angeles. In 1992 he was posthumously elected to the Comic Book Hall of Fame.

The people who knew him said that the picture of Joe Shuster in his later years was a sad one. He never reaped any considerable financial reward for creating one of the most prominent icons in American culture. Still, he maintained a positive attitude and felt honored to have his creation be recognized and enjoyed by so many people.

Although Shuster's professional illustrating career lasted only twelve years, it changed the face of American popular culture and mass media forever. Shuster almost single-handedly created the visual style and form of the superhero genre and launched the golden age of mass marketing and production of comic books.

★

Reprints of Siegel and Shuster's work that offer informative introductions include Siegel and Shuster, *Superman: The Dailies* (1998); Siegel and Shuster, *Superman: The Sunday Classics* (1998); *The Golden Age of Superman* (1993); and Siegel and Shuster, *The Superman Archives* (1994–2000). Among the collections that discuss Shuster's work are Mike Benton, *The Comic Book in America* (1989); Ron Goulart, *The Encyclopedia of American Comics* (1990); Ron Goulart, *Over Fifty Years of American Comic Books* (1991); Mike Benton, *Masters of Imagination* (1994); Paul Sassienie, *The Comic Book* (1994); and Les Daniels, *Superman: The Complete History, the Life and Times of the Man of Steel* (1998). Michael Catron's informative obituary in the *Comic Journal* (Oct. 1992) focuses on Shuster's work. Another obituary is in the *New York Times* (3 Aug. 1992).

Patrick A. Trimble

SIEGEL, Don (*b.* 26 October 1912 in Chicago, Illinois; *d.* 20 April 1991 in Nipomo, California), film director and producer respected for his expertise in the action-adventure film genre.

Siegel was one of two children born to Sam and Anne Siegel. An older sister died at age fourteen. Sam Siegel had played mandolin on the vaudeville circuit, and he and his wife founded the Chicago School of Correspondence to teach through the mail how to play musical instruments. Over the next few years the family moved between Chicago

Don Siegel. The Kobal Collection

and New York City. Siegel attended schools in both cities, graduating from DeWitt Clinton High School in the Bronx, New York, in 1929. When his father accepted an offer to be the managing director of the Parker Holiday Company in England, Siegel enrolled at Cambridge University, where he took his preliminary exams on the New Testament. In London he studied at the Royal Academy of Dramatic Art. From England the Siegels moved to Paris, France, but in 1932 Siegel returned to the United States, earning his way playing drums in the ship's orchestra. In Los Angeles, he contacted his uncle Jack Saper, who was a film editor for Warner Brothers. Saper referred him to Hal Wallis, production head at the studio.

Siegel's first job at Warner Brothers was in the film library, screening reels of film to identify bits that could be used as stock shots in other movies. He soon became interested in editing and was given the opportunity to work as an assistant editor, then moved into the insert department, where he was responsible for coordinating the shooting of sequences and montages used as narrative transitions. Under contract to Warner Brothers, Siegel directed second units, learning to adapt to the shooting style of some of Hollywood's most accomplished directors and finding innovative and economical ways to film action sequences, stunts, and background shots.

Eventually Siegel was given the opportunity to direct a

short film. The project he chose was *Star in the Night* (1945), a modern parable of the birth of Christ. It won the Academy Award for the best two-reel short of 1945. This was followed by *Hitler Lives!* (1945), which won the Academy Award for best two-reel documentary. Siegel was then assigned to direct two feature films, *The Verdict* (1946) and *Night unto Night* (1949), featuring Ronald Reagan and Viveca Lindfors. Siegel and Lindfors were married in 1948, had one son, and divorced in 1953.

After his contract with Warner Brothers expired, Siegel directed films at several other studios, gaining a reputation for completing emotionally charged action-adventure films on time and within budget. These included *The Big Steal* (1949), *No Time for Flowers* (1952), and *Count the Hours* (1953) at RKO; *Duel at Silver Creek* (1952) at Universal; and *China Venture* (1953) at Columbia. *Riot in Cell Block 11* (1954), filmed in a cell block at Folsom State Prison in Represa, California, in what Siegel referred to as "documentary style" was praised for its realistic treatment of the serious subject of prison reform and earned the 1954 British Academy Award for best film. After two less successful action films, *Private Hell 36* (1954) for Filmakers and *An Annapolis Story* (1955) back at Allied Artists, came *Invasion of the Body Snatchers* (1956), in which beings from outer space duplicate and inhabit the bodies of residents of a small town. For Siegel, these pods represented people who simply exist—who have no soul, no emotion, no ability to love.

A Spanish Affair (1957), a low-budget film shot on location in Spain, was followed by the more successful *Baby Face Nelson* (1957) starring Mickey Rooney as the psychotic gangster. After two more action films, *The Gun Runners* (1958) and *Edge of Eternity* (1959), came two films featuring popular singers, *Hound Dog Man* (1959) with Fabian and *Flaming Star* (1960) with Elvis Presley. *Flaming Star* carried a strong antiracist message. *Hell Is for Heroes* (1962) carried an equally strong antiwar message. In 1957 Siegel was married to Doe Avedon. They adopted four children but divorced in 1975.

When work on feature films was scarce, Siegel directed and occasionally produced television pilots and episodes as well as feature-film versions of the television series *Crime in the Streets* (1956) and *The Lineup* (1958). *The Killers* (1964), intended by Universal Studios to be the first two-hour film made specifically for television, was in production when President John F. Kennedy was assassinated. Studio executives decided the film was too violent for television and released it as a feature film. *The Hanged Man* (1964) and *Stranger on the Run* (1967) were also made for television. Siegel continued working at Universal, directing *Madigan* (1968), which garnered good reviews, and stepping in to finish a film begun by Robert Totten, *Death of a Gunfighter* (1969).

Coogan's Bluff (1968) was the first of several films Siegel directed starring Clint Eastwood. These included *Two Mules for Sister Sara* (1970); *The Beguiled* (1971), which Siegel considered his best film; *Dirty Harry* (1971); and *Escape from Alcatraz* (1979). When Eastwood directed his first film, *Play Misty for Me* (1971), he cast Siegel as the bartender.

Unhappy with the way the studio promoted *Charley Varrick* (1973)—which earned Walter Matthau a British Academy Award for best actor—and *The Black Windmill* (1974), Siegel asked to be released from his contract at Universal. Two years later he directed *The Shootist* (1976), John Wayne's final film, and the cold war thriller *Telefon* (1977). Siegel had finished editing *Rough Cut* (1980) when he was diagnosed with lymphoma and underwent chemotherapy. He came back to direct Bette Midler in *Jinxed!* (1982). Siegel's third wife, Carol Rydall, acted as his associate on these later films. In retirement Siegel worked on his autobiography. He died of cancer in Nipomo.

For most of his career, Siegel's directing assignments were limited to low-budget, "B" movies that had modest success with audiences and critics at home while earning higher regard abroad. A reassessment of these films reveals Siegel's skill in using limited resources to bring remarkable action sequences and compelling narratives to the screen. He worked closely with scriptwriters, insisted on careful planning before a day's shooting began, and devoted hours to the editing process. It would be tempting to assume that his many films that center on the loner opposed by a hostile society echo his often contentious relationships with studio executives. However, actors who worked with Siegel speak of his willingness to listen to suggestions, his sense of humor, and his thorough knowledge of film and film techniques.

★

A collection of Siegel's correspondence, screenplays, interviews, notes, and manuscripts is at the Mugar Memorial Library at Boston University. His autobiography, *A Siegel Film* (1993), was published after his death. Stuart M. Kaminsky, "A Biographical Study of the Career of Donald Siegel and an Analysis of his Films" (Ph.D. diss., Northwestern University, 1972), and Leonard Maltin, ed., *Don Siegel: Director* (1975), rely on extensive interviews with Siegel and his colleagues. Peter Bogdanovich includes a lengthy interview with Siegel in *Who the Devil Made It* (1997). Critical appraisals of Siegel's films include Alan Lovell, *Don Siegel: American Cinema* (1975), chapters in John Belton, *Cinema Stylists* (1983), and Colin McArthur, *Underworld USA* (1972). An obituary is in the *New York Times* (24 Apr. 1991).

LUCY A. LIGGETT

SIMON, Norton Winfred (*b.* 5 February 1907 in Portland, Oregon; *d.* 2 June 1993 in Los Angeles, California), industrialist and art collector who founded the Norton Simon Museum in Pasadena, California.

Simon was the first of three children of Myer Simon, who sold surplus goods at his discount store, Simon Sells for Less, in Portland, and Lillian Glickman, a homemaker, who died of diabetes in 1921 when Simon was fourteen years old. Myer Simon moved with his children to San Francisco in 1922 and married Lucille Michaels the following year; they had no children.

Simon had a photographic memory and a genius for calculating numbers in his head. He wanted nothing more than to go into business when he graduated from Lowell High School in San Francisco in 1923, at the age of sixteen. At his father's insistence he enrolled at the University of California at Berkeley, but he left after six weeks. He helped his father import and market surplus goods and pursued independent business ventures in San Francisco until 1925, when he set out for Los Angeles. His family followed in 1929. Simon married Lucille Ellis, a social worker, on 3 February 1933. They had two children.

Simon acquired the first block of his corporate empire in 1931 by investing $7,000 in a bankrupt orange juice bottling plant in Fullerton, California. He intended to sell the equipment, but his father persuaded him to operate the plant for a year. The venture was profitable, so Simon kept it going, switching from bottles to cans and from oranges to tomatoes. In 1942 he acquired a controlling interest in additional food-processing plants, most notably Hunt

Norton Simon, 1970. © BETTMANN/CORBIS

Brothers Packing Company in Hayward, California. Simon took charge of the little-known firm and launched an aggressive advertising campaign, "Hunt for the best." Within three years it was a household slogan, and Hunt was among the biggest food-processing companies on the West Coast.

Known as an early corporate raider, Simon targeted undervalued companies, bought enough stock to gain control, and turned them into highly profitable enterprises. His tactics, including shrewd exploitation of wartime shortages, earned him so many enemies that in 1953 *Fortune* magazine dubbed him "the most unpopular businessman in California." Simon insisted that he was merely performing a service for shareholders as he took charge of Ohio Match Company, Wesson Oil, Snowdrift Company, Northern Pacific Railway Company, McCall Corporation, Canada Dry, Knox Glass, and Wheeling Steel. By 1965 Hunt Foods and Industries, Inc., had either merged with or obtained large holdings in twenty-seven companies, giving the conglomerate a $72 million portfolio.

In 1954 Simon began to apply his business acumen and some of his fortune to a new challenge, collecting fine art. He made his first purchase, a $16,000 portrait by the French impressionist Pierre-August Renoir, to decorate his new house in the Hancock Park district of Los Angeles, and he soon became a voracious and extraordinarily savvy collector. He educated himself by consulting the best-informed scholars at great length and at all hours of the night, then made his own decisions and drove hard bargains. His initial fascination with the French impressionists and postimpressionists broadened to encompass early modern art and old master paintings. Spanning the thirteenth through the twentieth centuries, his collection included fine works by Guariento di Arpo, Raphael, Peter Paul Rubens, Jacopo Bassano, Francisco de Zurbarán, Rembrandt, Giovanni Battista Tiepolo, Édouard Manet, Edgar Degas, Vincent van Gogh, and Pablo Picasso.

In 1964 Simon made the largest purchase of his collecting career, the entire inventory of Duveen Brothers, a New York dealership that shaped America's greatest collections of European art from the 1880s to the late 1930s. His acquisition of more than 400 artworks, a 12,000-volume library, and the five-story building that housed them had a market value of $15 million. He paid only $4 million and recouped most of it by selling the library to the Clark Art Institute in Williamstown, Massachusetts, and auctioning off minor artworks and decorative objects.

Simon weathered profound changes in both his professional and personal life from 1968 to 1971. In 1968 he consolidated Hunt Foods and Industries and the companies it controlled into Norton Simon, Inc., and relinquished his administrative position. His emotionally troubled younger son, Robert, fatally shot himself in the head on 29 October 1969, at the age of thirty-one. In December 1969 Simon resigned as a director of Norton Simon, severing his last managerial tie with the conglomerate he had built. To the astonishment of his friends and family, he plunged into national politics in 1970 and ran an unsuccessful campaign for the U.S. Senate. Later that year he and his wife of thirty-seven years were divorced.

Single again, Simon accepted an invitation to escort the actress Jennifer Jones to a social event early in May 1971. The irascible sixty-four-year-old tycoon and the glamorous movie star twelve years his junior seemed an unlikely couple, but their blind date began a whirlwind courtship. They were married aboard a ship off the coast of England on 30 May 1971. The couple had no children. During their honeymoon trip to India, Simon visited the National Museum in New Delhi, where he was smitten with Indian art. Within a few years he acquired about 600 sculptures from India and Southeast Asia.

Simon also played a public role in higher education and visual art. Despite his abbreviated college career, he served as a University of California Regent from 1960 to 1976. Ever the outsider, he challenged funding cutbacks, sympathized with student dissidents, and opposed the firing of the black activist Angela Davis. In search of a home for his growing art collection, he tried to establish a museum with the city of Fullerton, became a founding trustee of the Los Angeles County Museum of Art, and loaned large groups of artworks to educational institutions across the country. His quest ended with a controversial move in 1974, when he took charge of the bankrupt Pasadena Art Museum, including its debt and 7,000-piece collection of modern and contemporary art, and renovated it. When it reopened in 1975, Simon's collection occupied three-fourths of the space. Several months later, he changed the name of the institution to the Norton Simon Museum.

Simon contracted Guillain-Barré syndrome in 1983. Agonizing over the fate of his artistic legacy, he devised a plan to give his collection to the University of California at Los Angeles (UCLA) and considered a merger with the J. Paul Getty Museum but ultimately left his museum intact. It was not given to UCLA. At his death from complications associated with his neurological disorder, his 12,000-piece holding was widely acclaimed as the best private collection of art amassed in the United States since World War II. He is buried in Los Angeles.

★

Papers on Simon's art collection are at the Norton Simon Museum. Suzanne Muchnic, *Odd Man In: Norton Simon and the Pursuit of Culture* (1998), is the only full-length biography of Simon. Profiles include Freeman Lincoln, "Norton Simon—Like Him or Not," *Fortune* (Dec. 1953), and articles in the *New York Times* (31 May 1972), and *Los Angeles Times* (1 Aug. 1971 and 24 June 1990). Obituaries are in the *Los Angeles Times* (4 June 1993) and *New York Times* (4 June 1993).

SUZANNE MUCHNIC

SINGER, Isaac Bashevis (*b.* 21 November 1904 in Leoncin, Poland; *d.* 24 July 1991 in Surfside, Florida), Nobel Prize winner in literature (1978) for his Yiddish novels, short stories, and memoirs that have been translated into English and fifteen other languages, and a writer for the American Yiddish newspaper *Der Forverts* (Jewish Daily Forward).

Singer was also known by the names Yitzchok Bashevis for his works in Yiddish; Y. Varshovsky, a transliteration of a Yiddish name that means "the man from Warsaw"; and D. Segal for his nonfiction in the *Jewish Daily Forward* (the *Forward*). He was the fifth of six children, of whom only four survived childhood. His father, Pinchos Menachem Singer, was a rabbi, and his mother, Basheve Zylberman, the daughter of the rabbi of Biłgoraj, was a homemaker who was literate in Yiddish. His sister Hinde Esther Kreitman, who suffered from epilepsy and depression, and his brother Israel Joshua, also a Yiddish author, played prominent roles in his life and served as models for a number of fictional characters. His father died in 1929. His younger brother, Moishe, the only son to remain an Orthodox Jew, and his mother both died in the Holocaust.

Singer did not have a formal secular education. He was taught the Gemara, Jewish law, by his father and the Bible by his mother, who was learned in Jewish studies. He went

Isaac Bashevis Singer. © JERRY BAUER

to cheder, the orthodox religious elementary school, and in 1921 he attended the Tachkemoni Rabbinical Seminary in Warsaw but did not complete his studies. He was self-taught in German and Polish as well as in philosophy. He ceased to be an observant Jew according to law although he maintained a belief in God. His own ethic he described as "one of protest," whereby "the true protester expresses his protest by avoiding doing evil to the best of his ability."

Singer's more than ten novels for adults, collections of short stories, four memoirs, and even his children's books are set most frequently in the small villages of eastern Europe that he knew as a child. The family moved in 1907 from Leoncin to Radzymin, where his father was head of a yeshiva. In 1908 they left for Warsaw, where even though not officially licensed, his father was regarded as the rabbi of Krochmalna Street, where the family resided at number 10. The cases that most impressed the young Singer are chronicled in what he called a fusion of memoirs and belles lettres, *In My Father's Court* (1966), first published in Yiddish as *Mayn tatn's bes-din-shtub* (1955). The cases the young boy hears are narrated as dramatized stories, and some, such as "Why the Geese Shrieked," were published in collections of stories.

World War I dispersed the family. Israel hid to avoid conscription; Hinde married a diamond cutter and moved to Antwerp; and Singer left for Biłgoraj with his mother and Moishe to avoid starvation in German-occupied Warsaw. Singer studied the Talmud and Hebrew. He also studied the kabala, whose broad concept he described in *Love and Exile* (1984) as "everything is God and God is everything." In this shtetl (rural village) he immersed himself in folklore. After his year at the seminary in 1921 Singer spent a year in Biłgoraj teaching Hebrew, and in 1922 he joined his parents and Moishe in Dzikow, an adjoining village.

Singer's first literary job in 1923 was as a proofreader for *Literarische bleter* (Literary Pages), for which his brother Israel was coeditor. He also began translating works into Yiddish, most notably Thomas Mann's *The Magic Mountain* (1924) and Erich Maria Remarque's *All Quiet on the Western Front* (1928). Singer was interested in the relationship between mind and disease, central to Mann's novel, seeking an explanation for his sister's illness and for his own bouts of depression. Remarque's work appealed to his own pacifist leanings.

In 1925 Singer wrote his first short story about birth and new beginnings, "Of der elter" (In Old Age), for *Literarische bleter* under the name of "Tse." Later that year he published his second story, "Nerot" (Candles), in *Ha-yom* signed Isaac Bashevis, a matronymic that distinguished him from his brother, a more established Yiddish writer. Other stories were penned between 1926 and 1928, one of which, "Ofn Olem hatoye" (In the World of Chaos), yielded "Two Corpses Go Dancing," published in Yiddish in 1943 and in English in 1968 in the collection of short stories *The Séance and Other Stories*. His translation work kept him occupied although not well paid.

In 1932 Singer became coeditor of *Globus*. This literary magazine printed some of Singer's short stories and in 1933, at his own expense, serialized his first novel, *The Satan in Goray*, which countered the tradition of Yiddish writing with its sexuality and satanic possession. Also that year Singer began to write for a Parisian Yiddish paper, *Parizer haynt,* and for the *Forward,* for whom his brother Israel, living in the United States as of 1933, was a journalist. The Warsaw PEN Club published *Satan in Goray* as a book in 1935. Israel arranged for a U.S. visa for his brother, who received a copy of *Satan in Goray* shortly after his arrival in the United States in May. With his brother's influence, Singer received an advance from the *Forward* for a serialized novel, *Der zindiker meshiekh* (Messiah the Sinner), but he developed a writer's block. The completed novel was not well received.

Despite the failure of this novel, in the 1940s Singer was hired as a staff writer for the *Forward* and contributed a column, "It's Worthwhile Knowing." He married Alma Haimann Wassermann, a German-born Jew with two children, on 14 February 1940 in a civil ceremony in New York City. The couple initially lived in Brooklyn and established their last residence at the large and historic Belnord Apartment House on Broadway and Eighty-sixth Street. (Singer had an illegitimate son by Rochel [Ronye] Shapira in 1930.) In 1943 Singer became a naturalized U.S. citizen, and his efforts to obtain the necessary papers are detailed in *Lost in America* (1981), initially published separately and then made the last of the three memoirs of *Love and Exile*. In 1944 Farlag Matones in New York published *Satan in Goray and Other Tales* in Yiddish. Singer began writing short stories again. In 1944 Israel died of a heart attack. This event depressed Singer. His relationship with his brother had been ambivalent, regarding him as a father and mentor but also as a rival. He had difficulty establishing an independent reputation as a writer because Israel Singer's novels were well regarded. The only remaining immediate family connection in the United States was Israel's son Joseph Singer, who translated into English some of Singer's fiction. "The Spinoza of Market Street" was published first in Yiddish and in 1961 in English in *Esquire* 1. "Der kurtser fraytik" (Short Friday) was published in Yiddish in 1945 and in English in 1964 in a collection bearing its title. The most widely known short story, "Gimpel Tam" (Gimpel the Fool, 1957), as well as "The Little Shoemakers" and "The Wife Killer," were published in Yiddish in 1953 and appeared in later collections translated into English.

The 1950s were particularly important for launching Singer's career in the English language. *The Family Moskat,* inspired by his reading of Mann's *Buddenbrooks* (1900), began in 1945 as a three-year serialization in the *Forward* and was aired on WEVD's *Forward Hour*. But Alfred A.

Knopf's publication of the novel in 1950 introduced Singer to a wider American audience. In 1952 Singer wrote "A Tale of Two Lies" for the *Forward*, and it appeared in English in 1961. Another novel, *The Manor*, was serialized in the *Forward* in 1952. In 1953 the English translation of "Gimpel Tam" appeared in the May issue of *Partisan Review*. Following that story's critical acclaim Singer published his stories in other major American magazines, such as *Commentary*, *New Yorker*, *Harper's*, and *Esquire*.

The death in 1954 of Singer's sister, whom Singer saw only once in England after he married and whom he had refused to help financially, ended another difficult personal relationship. His memoir, *Love and Exile*, records the ambivalent feelings he had toward her sexually and psychologically. Her hysteria and suicide attempts and his own depressive states and frequent thoughts of suicide had made him fear a family history of insanity. In 1955 Noonday Press published *Satan in Goray*, and Kval Publishers produced *Mayn tatn's bes-din-shtub* (In My Father's Court). In 1957 the *Forward* serialized *Shadows by the Hudson* (published in book form posthumously in 1998), and Noonday published Singer's first collection of stories in English, *Gimpel the Fool and Other Stories*.

In 1956 the Folksbeine Theatre in Manhattan dramatized segments from the Yiddish version of *In My Father's Court*, the first stage adaptation of one of Singer's works in Yiddish. In 1958 the *Forward* serialized *A Ship to America*, followed by *The Magician of Lublin* in 1959. Noonday published the latter novel in 1960. Singer revealed that he sometimes changed the text in English because Yiddish was an overstated language and English an understated language. He also said that he did not write his works in Yiddish with an English-speaking audience in mind; that would have affected his writing adversely. His Yiddish was considered elegant and grammatically correct.

Farrar, Straus, and Cudahy's purchase of Noonday Press in 1960 initiated a long relationship between the publishing house and Singer. In 1961 the *Forward* serialized *The Slave*. This novel contains many of the conflicts Singer dramatized in his works, including conflicts between the law and the humane treatment of people, rationalism and superstition, and the Jewish rituals and the gentile world. The supernatural plays an important role, as it does in *Satan of Goray* and in most of Singer's short stories. *The Spinoza of Market Street and Other Stories* (1961), his second collection in English, was published by Farrar, Straus, and Cudahy, and in 1962 that house also published *The Slave*. In 1963 Richard Hall adapted "Gimpel the Fool" as a one-act play for the Mermaid Theater in New York City. The following year Farrar, Straus, and Giroux published *Short Friday and Other Stories*. In 1966 the *Forward* serialized *Enemies, A Love Story*, and Farrar, Straus, and Giroux published Singer's first memoir, *In My Father's Court*.

Singer began writing children's literature when he was asked to write Hanukkah stories. In 1966 Harper and Row published *Zlateh the Goat and Other Stories*, inspired by the simple narrative style of the Bible, which Singer said emphasized events and descriptions of characters but did not analyze them within the text. For this collection Singer won his first Newbery Award. In 1967 *The Manor* was nominated for the National Book Award, and on 25 November 1967 his first publication at the *New Yorker*, "The Slaughterer," appeared. That year *The Fearsome Inn*, a children's book that won another Newbery Award, was followed by *Mazel and Shlimazel; Or, The Milk of a Lioness*, the first part of whose title translates as Luck and Bad Luck. In 1968 Farrar, Straus, and Giroux produced *The Séance and Other Stories*, dedicated to the memory of his sister, and the children's collection *When Shlemiel Went to Warsaw and Other Stories*, which won another Newbery Award in 1969. In 1969 *The Estate*, a sequel to *The Manor*, and *A Day of Pleasure: Stories of a Boy Growing Up in Warsaw*, a children's version of *In My Father's Court*, were both published.

The decade of the 1970s began auspiciously for Singer when he won his first National Book Award for *A Day of Pleasure*. In 1970 Farrar, Straus, and Giroux published *A Friend of Kafka and Other Stories* and *Elijah the Slave*, a children's story. *An Isaac Bashevis Singer Reader* came out in 1971 along with another children's book, *The Topsy-Turvy Emperor of China*. Still prolific, Singer wrote *Enemies, A Love Story*; *The Hasidim*; and for children *The Wicked City* in 1972. Two children's books, *A Crown of Feathers and Other Stories*, for which he won his second National Book Award in 1974, and *The Fools of Chelm and Their History*, came out in 1973. The *Forward* serialized *Bal-tshuve* (The Penitent) in 1974. He produced *Passions and Other Stories* in 1975; *Naftali the Storyteller and His Horse, Sus* for children in 1976; and *A Little Boy in Search of God: Mysticism in a Personal Light* in 1976.

During this period Singer's works were adapted for other media. Bruce Davidson's film of *Nightmare and Mrs. Pupko's Beard*, produced for public television, won first prize in its category in 1972. The Yale Repertory Theater produced an adaptation of *The Mirror* in 1973, and *Teibele and Her Demon* opened at the Guthrie Theater in Minneapolis in the spring of 1978.

The crowning award of Singer's career was his receipt of the Nobel Prize for literature on 8 December 1978. In his acceptance speech he said, "The storyteller and poet of our time . . . must be an entertainer of the spirit . . . not just a preacher of social and political ideals." He reiterated his attitude that literature needed to be suspenseful and adventurous. Commenting on a generation that seemed to have lost faith in Providence, he said, "There must be a way for man to attain all possible pleasures, all the powers and knowledge that nature can grant him, and still serve

God—a God who speaks in deeds, not in words, and whose vocabulary is the Cosmos." In Jewish literature, he noted, the poet and the prophet are one and the same. Also that year he was elected to the American Academy of Arts and Letters and a collection of stories, *Old Love,* came out. In 1980 Lester Goran arranged a distinguished professorship at the University of Miami for Singer.

The prestigious prize did not inhibit Singer, who published *The Power of Light: Eight Stories for Hanukkah* (1980); a study of the Baal Shem Tov, *The Reaches of Heaven* (1980); a memoir, *Lost in America* (1981); *The Collected Stories of Isaac Bashevis Singer* (1982); *Isaac Bashevis Singer, Three Complete Novels,* including *The Slave, Enemies, A Love Story,* and *Shosha* (1982); for children *The Golem* (1982); and *The Penitent* (1983). An off-Broadway production of *A Play for the Devil* was performed in 1984. In 1985 Goran worked with Singer in translating the stories that became *The Image and Other Stories.* Also that year the *Forward* serialized *Der veg aheim* (The Way Home). Singer's last collection of stories was *The Death of Methusaleh and Other Stories,* published in 1988. A novel, *The King of the Fields,* also appeared in 1988. Singer was the recipient of the Gold Medal of the American Academy and Institute of Arts and Letters, its highest award, for the film version of *Enemies, A Love Story* (1990), produced and directed by Paul Mazursky. Singer's last novel published while he was alive was *Scum* (1991). In 1998 *Shadows by the Hudson,* a novel about immigrants living in New York and Florida, was published posthumously. Singer always said that he could only write about what he knew personally, the shtetl life of eastern Europe and the immigrant experience.

Singer was a slim, blond, mostly bald man of pallid complexion, but animated in manner, with a penetrating blue-eyed gaze peering out from black-rimmed spectacles and a heavily Yiddish-accented English. He described himself as shy, skeptical, and a loner; yet in public he was charming, affable, and accessible. A frugal person, he was most often seen, regardless of weather, in a dark blue suit, white cotton dress shirt, tie, and black shoes. Singer died of Alzheimer's disease on 24 July 1991 in a nursing home in Surfside, Florida, and was buried in Beth El Cemetery, Cedar Park, in Paramus, New Jersey.

★

The Singer archive is at the University of Texas in Austin. Janet Hadda, *Isaac Bashevis Singer: A Life* (1997), has biographical details. Grace Farrell, ed., *Isaac Bashevis Singer: Conversations* (1992), includes a particularly good interview by Cyrena Pondrom. An obituary is in the *New York Times* (25 July 1991). Roxanne Greenstein interviewed Singer for the videotape *A Conversation with Isaac Bashevis Singer* (1985), produced and written by Richard Hall and distributed by Ergo Media, Inc.

BARBARA L. GERBER

SIRICA, John Joseph (*b.* 19 March 1904 in Waterbury, Connecticut; *d.* 14 August 1992 in Washington, D.C.), lawyer and the leading judge in the Watergate scandal, which led to the resignation of President Richard M. Nixon.

Sirica was one of two sons of Ferdinand ("Fred") Sirica, an Italian immigrant from the village of San Valentino near Naples, and Rose Zinno, a homemaker and native of New Haven, Connecticut. Sirica had a peripatetic childhood as his father, a barber by trade, roamed the country seeking employment. He was educated in the public schools of Jacksonville, Florida; Dayton, Ohio; New Orleans, and Richmond, Virginia. The family finally settled in Washington, D.C., where Sirica received his high school diploma from Columbia Preparatory School in 1921. Skipping college, Sirica entered George Washington University Law School; he dropped out after about a month, however, when he found the courses too onerous. Sirica resumed one of his childhood occupations, selling newspapers. He also practiced boxing, which became a lifelong passion.

He then enrolled at Georgetown University Law School

John Sirica. ARCHIVE PHOTOS

in 1923, supporting himself as a boxing instructor and fighting occasional matches. He earned his LL.B. in 1926 but for a time continued his pugilistic endeavors. Finally at the urging of his mother he gave up boxing, gained admission to the bar, and began his law career in private practice in the District of Columbia. He honed his legal skills defending the poor and watching the courtroom tactics of stellar lawyers.

On 1 August 1930 Sirica became an assistant U.S. attorney for the District of Columbia, a post he served in until 15 January 1934. During this time he developed his competence as a courtroom lawyer. He then returned to private practice, representing such famous clients as the newspaper columnist Walter Winchell. He also became active in Republican party politics as a hardworking presidential campaigner from 1936 through 1952.

During World War II, having failed the naval officer physical exam, Sirica traveled with his friend Jack Dempsey, the former heavyweight champion, on war-bond tours throughout the country. He also had a brief stint as general counsel to the House Select Committee investigating the Federal Communications Commission. In 1949 he became a partner in the well-known Washington law firm of Hogan and Hartson. On 26 February 1952 he married Lucille M. Camalier, daughter of a prominent Washington leather goods merchant. They had three children.

On 2 April 1957, owing to his long service to the Republican party, Sirica was sworn in as a judge on the U.S. District Court for the District of Columbia. He earned the sobriquet "Maximum John" because of the long sentences he handed out. On 2 April 1971 seniority elevated him to the position of chief judge of the District Court. It was in this capacity that he would come to preside over the trials attached to the complex political scandal that became known as Watergate.

Watergate began on 17 June 1972 when a team of burglars masterminded by White House officials invaded the headquarters of the Democratic National Committee located in the Watergate apartment complex in Washington, D.C.; the crisis ended on 9 August 1974 when Richard Nixon became the first president in U.S. history to resign. Seven men were arrested and brought to trial before Judge Sirica in January 1973. Sirica's threat of long sentences and his probing questions eventually led one of the defendants, James McCord, to cave in and implicate high government officials, announcing his change of heart in a March letter to the judge. Slowly but surely the cover-up came apart, and this unraveling led to a constitutional crisis.

On 16 July 1973 in testimony before the Senate Watergate committee, presidential aide Alexander Butterfield revealed President Nixon's elaborate system for the secret taping of his office conversations. Archibald Cox, the special prosecuter assigned to the case, demanded to listen to the tapes that referred to Watergate. Nixon refused to release the tapes, claiming executive privilege. On 29 August 1973 Sirica ordered Nixon to turn the tapes over to him for a hearing to determine which portions should be submitted to a grand jury. Although the White House appealed, Sirica's decision was upheld. A later request for additional tapes by Cox's successor, Leon Jaworski, was upheld by the U.S. Supreme Court. The revelations contained on the tapes proved to be the Nixon administration's undoing.

On 18 March 1974, the day before his seventieth birthday, Sirica stepped down from the chief judgeship as required by federal law. However, he continued to be a judge. In 1984 he halted a controversial gene-splicing experiment and his decision was upheld by the appeals court. (With the exception of the Watergate cases, this was not a common occurrence in his judicial career; his decisions were reversed on appeal more often than most judges.) On 1 October 1986 Sirica retired completely. This allowed him time to pursue more fully his avocations of walking, golf, and other sports. In 1992 he was hospitalized after he had fallen and broken his collarbone; shortly thereafter he died of cardiac arrest in Washington, D.C. He is interred at the Gate of Heaven Cemetery in Silver Spring, Maryland.

Watergate lifted Sirica from obscurity to fame. In 1973 he was named *Time* magazine's "Man of the Year." The controversy that surrounded him and his decisions during this period will continue as long as Watergate is considered and discussed. But if it had not been for his persistence and stubbornness, Watergate would barely rate a footnote in the histories of the time.

★

The John J. Sirica Audio Materials, 1974–1979, are located in the Library of Congress Motion Picture, Broadcasting, and Recorded Sound Division. These consist of recordings of Watergate trial proceedings, speeches, radio and television interviews with Sirica and others, and news broadcasts pertaining to Watergate, as well as Sirica's recorded autobiographical notes. The John J. Sirica Papers, 1932–1986, were transferred to this collection in 1993. Sirica's book *To Set the Record Straight: The Break-in, the Tapes, the Conspirators, the Pardon* (1979) includes an autobiographical prologue. See Carl Bernstein and Bob Woodward, *All the President's Men* (1974), the classic text on Watergate, as well as David William Guard's doctoral dissertation, "John Sirica and the Crisis of Watergate, 1972–1975" (Michigan State University, 1995). Michael Genovese, *The Watergate Crisis* (1999), is another excellent summary. An obituary is in the *New York Times* (15 Aug. 1992).

JOHN MORAN

SISKIND, Aaron (*b.* 4 December 1903 in New York City, *d.* 8 February 1991 in Providence, Rhode Island), documentary and abstract photographer whose nonrepresentational photographs link him to the abstract expressionist art movement.

Siskind was the fifth child of Jacob Siskind and Riva Mystrovitch, Ukrainian Jewish immigrants who settled in New York City's Lower East Side at the end of the nineteenth century. Jacob made his living as a tailor and Riva was a homemaker. Not long after the birth of their sixth (and last) child, the couple moved to the Upper West Side, where Siskind spent the majority of his youth. Due to his gregarious personality, Siskind rarely spent time at home. He was preoccupied primarily with the events of the street and was excited by the political exchanges and debates that abounded in the neighborhood. As a teenager he joined the Junior Young People's Socialist League.

A curious and serious student, Siskind had a great interest in poetry and music. After high school he majored in English at The City College of New York. As a member of his college literary club, Siskind befriended the painters and fellow students Barnett Newman and Adolph Gottlieb, who would later become leading figures of modern American painting. This was the first time Siskind applied his intellectual and creative thoughts to the discussion of visual art. When Siskind graduated in 1926, he accepted a position teaching English to younger students in the New York City public school system. In the spring of 1929 Siskind married Sidonie ("Sonia") Glatter, an artistic and intelligent woman he had met years earlier at the Junior Young People's Socialist League who had also become a teacher in the New York City public school system.

Aaron Siskind, 1990. © BOB ROWAN; PROGRESSIVE IMAGE/CORBIS

It was not until the age of twenty-six that Siskind started taking pictures with a camera he had received as a gift. Siskind experimented by carefully recording scenes of his New York City neighborhood. In 1933, after three years of teaching himself photography, he felt skilled enough to join the Workers Film and Photo League (the Photo League). Like many other artists of the Great Depression, Siskind was attracted to the group's focus on political issues and social reform. Convinced that photography could aid the worker's plight, Photo League members documented the economic and social struggles of New York City's denizens.

By 1937 Siskind's photographic contributions were being publicly acknowledged. Unfortunately, his wife's mental health had deteriorated and she was permanently committed to a mental hospital. Seven years later in the spring of 1945, the marriage was officially terminated through annulment. Siskind's loss was reflected in a series of photographs created in 1938 that document the decay and demolition of the New York Civic Repertory Theatre.

For the next few years, Siskind immersed himself in documentary projects, producing the series *Dead End: The Bowery, Park Avenue North and South* and the acclaimed *Harlem Document,* which was exhibited at the New School for Social Research in New York City. In 1939 he was commissioned to photograph the architecture of Bucks County, Pennsylvania, for a book. The resulting black-and-white photographs demonstrated a focus on visual composition and aesthetic order. From this point on, Siskind paid greater attention to the formal and symbolic elements of the photograph than to the subject matter. Sadly, other Photo League members did not share his new interest in the language of visual composition. After numerous creative disagreements, Siskind resigned from the group in 1940.

Siskind's black-and-white photographs isolate details of exterior objects, creating a flat, abstract picture that only hints at its original source. These unique photographs are not mere documentation of the world but assertions of an individual vision. In 1946 his photographs were included in the Museum of Modern Art's *New Photographers* exhibition, and in 1947 he received his first solo show at the Charles Egan Gallery in New York City.

In 1949 Siskind quit his job as a schoolteacher and took a position teaching photography at Trenton Junior College in Trenton, New Jersey. Still living in Manhattan, he was a member of "The Club," a social group for contemporary artists founded in 1950. Aaron met Cathy Spencer at "The Club" and married her in Edgarton, Massachusetts in the summer of 1952. Also that year, Siskind was offered and accepted a teaching position at the Institute of Design in Chicago. There he worked closely with fellow teacher and photographer Harry Callahan, who would become a lifelong friend.

Throughout the 1950s Siskind continued his exploration of balance and tension between abstract elements, exhibiting his photographs throughout the United States. In 1957 Siskind and Spencer divorced, at which time he concentrated on teaching. The book *Aaron Siskind: Photographs,* with text by the critic Harold Rosenberg, was published in 1958.

On 25 July 1960 Siskind married a third time, to Carolyn Brandt, an aspiring poet with a young daughter. The following year he was appointed the head of the photography department at Chicago's Institute of Design. Throughout the 1960s Siskind traveled frequently to Mexico, Italy, and throughout the United States. In 1964 he received a show at the Art Institute of Chicago and in 1965 a retrospective exhibition of his work organized by the George Eastman House in Rochester, New York, traveled to different American venues. Supported by a Guggenheim fellowship in 1966, Siskind revisited Rome, Italy, in order to "capture the visual layers of history" in photographs. In the late 1960s Siskind participated in numerous conferences, exhibitions, and symposiums.

Siskind had grown increasingly unhappy with the structure of the Institute of Design's curriculum, and in 1970 he retired. One year later, at the age of sixty-seven, he became a professor at the Rhode Island School of Design in Providence.

In 1975 the Center for Creative Photography in Tucson, Arizona, accepted his donation of the Aaron Siskind Archive, which includes negatives, photographic prints, and other documents of his career. In 1976, the same year Siskind was awarded a fellowship from the National Endowment for the Arts and retired from his teaching position, his wife Carolyn died.

In the last years of his life, Siskind kept active in the art world, curating a show of "New Photography" at the Rhode Island School of Design in 1978. Well into the 1980s, in addition to international travel, he continued to meet with students to discuss their work. Siskind died of a stroke in Providence at the age of eighty-seven.

Largely because of Siskind's work, photography has become accepted as a legitimate medium for artistic expression. Like the abstract expressionist painters, he sought a compositional harmony and "one-ness" of the pictorial elements. Siskind's photographs opened up a new avenue for photographic expression. Because of his art, the camera is no longer seen as an objective machine but as a tool for expressing emotion and feeling.

★

A collection of Siskind's negatives, prints, and other personal records are housed in the Aaron Siskind Archive, Center for Creative Photography, in Tucson, Arizona. Carl Chiarenza, *Aaron Siskind: Pleasures and Terrors* (1982), is an in-depth account of Siskind's life up to 1982. Additionally, Thomas Hess's *Places:*

Aaron Siskind Photographs (1971), and Peter Turner, *Aaron Siskind: Photographs 1932–1978* (1979), feature examples of the artist's work. William Morgan, *Bucks County: Photographs of Early Architecture* (1974), displays ninety-three early photographs by the artist. *Harlem Document, Photographs 1932–1940: Aaron Siskind* (1981), with a forward by Gordon Parks, is a compilation of Siskind's early documentary series. An obituary is in the *New York Times* (9 Feb. 1991).

RENEE COPPOLA

SLAYTON, Donald Kent ("Deke") (*b.* 1 March 1924 in Sparta, Wisconsin; *d.* 13 June 1993 in League City, Texas), astronaut who was among the original seven selected for Project Mercury, the program that achieved the first American manned space flights.

Slayton was the first-born child of Charles Sherman Slayton, a farmer and laborer, and Victoria Adelia Larson, a homemaker. He grew up with his four brothers and sisters on the family dairy farm near Sparta. Often an older half brother and half sister stayed at the farm as well. Living through the Great Depression meant hard times for the family, but, as Slayton proclaimed in his autobiography, "Being on a farm, we never worried about starving to death."

In 1942 Slayton graduated from Sparta High School and immediately enlisted in the U.S. Army Air Forces. During

Donald Slayton, 1975. ASSOCIATED PRESS NASA

World War II he completed fifty-six missions over Europe and seven over Japan. After the war he returned to the United States as a B-25 instructor, until discharged from active duty in 1946.

Taking advantage of the GI Bill, Slayton enrolled at the University of Minnesota in 1947. While a student he worked at various part-time jobs and doubled up on his courses. As a result, he graduated in 1949, a year and a half early, with a B.S. degree in aeronautical engineering. He then moved to Seattle to become an engineer for the Boeing Aircraft Company. Although he disliked the work he was doing there, he stuck with it until 1951, when the Korean War intervened. Eager to serve his country once again, he returned to Minnesota as a reservist in the Minnesota Air Guard. While waiting for his call to active duty, he applied for and received a commission as captain in the U.S. Air Force.

From 1952 to 1955 Slayton served as a fighter-squadron pilot and wing-maintenance officer at various posts in California and Germany. While stationed in Germany he met Marjorie Lunney, a secretary from Los Angeles, whom he married on 15 May 1955. Later that year they moved to Edwards Air Force Base in California, where Slayton had been assigned as a test pilot. On 8 April 1957 their only child, Kent Sherman, was born. The family remained at Edwards until 1959, when the National Aeronautics and Space Administration (NASA) selected Slayton as one of the original seven astronauts for Project Mercury.

Along with the other Mercury astronauts, Slayton completed an intense training program as preparation for the rigors of space. After this training NASA assigned him to the fourth space flight, intended as the second to achieve orbit, but Slayton never completed the mission. In May 1962, two months before his launch date, NASA grounded him when doctors identified a recurring irregular heart palpitation known as idiopathic atrial fibrillation. Sorely disappointed, Slayton watched from mission control as other astronauts journeyed into space.

Convinced that he had a better chance of flying as a civilian, Slayton resigned from the Air Force in November 1963 and rejoined NASA as assistant director of flight-crew operations. Three years later NASA promoted him to director. In this position he supervised astronaut training and selected the flight crews for each mission. After learning in July 1970 that his irregular heart palpitation had ceased, Slayton proposed himself for the crew of the Apollo-Soyuz Test Project (ASTP). In January 1973 NASA announced that he would indeed be a member of the crew. He spent the next two-and-a-half years in training, working with simulators, and learning Russian.

On 15 July 1975 Slayton and his fellow astronauts lifted off from a launch pad at Cape Canaveral, Florida. At age fifty-one Slayton had become the oldest astronaut to jour-

ney into space at the time. Unfortunately his parents never lived to see this success. Charles Slayton had died in 1972, followed by Victoria in 1974.

The American and Soviet capsules rendezvoused in orbit on 17 July 1975. The two crews docked their spacecraft, conducted several experiments, and held a joint news conference. Two days later the spacecraft separated and Apollo began its journey back to Earth. During splashdown, a toxic gas was accidentally released into the capsule, causing the astronauts discomfort but no serious harm. While examining Slayton for possible lung damage, doctors found a small lesion on his left lung. At a hospital in Houston, doctors removed the lesion and determined that it was benign. Slayton realized that he had been fortunate. As he stated in his autobiography, "If they'd found it before ASTP, I never would have been allowed to fly."

After recovering from surgery Slayton began to work on the Space-Shuttle program as manager of the Approach and Landing Tests task force. Then in 1978 he became manager of the Orbital Flight Test program for the first four shuttle missions. He officially retired from NASA in 1982. He had stood by NASA for over twenty years, through the good times and bad, from the first manned space flights to the first shuttle missions.

In 1978, having grown apart personally, Slayton and Marjorie decided to separate. In 1983 their divorce became final. On 8 October of that year Slayton married Bobbie Jones-Osborn, a divorced mother whom he had met while they both worked at NASA. In his autobiography, Slayton was characterized by Bobbie as "a wonderful, loving husband and a kind and generous father."

Slayton began working as a consultant for Space Services, Incorporated (SSI) in 1982. He helped design and build its Conestoga rocket, which launched successfully in September 1982 under his supervision. After this success Slayton became president and, eventually, vice-chair of the board for the company. At one point SSI proposed launching cremated human remains into permanent orbit. The idea was later abandoned, but not without causing some damage to the company's reputation.

In 1991 Slayton began to lose his balance. Eventually doctors diagnosed brain cancer as the cause. Slayton died of the disease on 13 June 1993 at his home in League City, a suburb of Houston. He was cremated and his ashes were scattered on his family's farm in Sparta.

Although born in the Midwest, Slayton proved himself a true Texan. After moving to Houston to work for NASA, he remained in Texas for the rest of his life. A rugged outdoorsman, he took full advantage of the considerable fishing and hunting opportunities there. Persistent and dedicated, Slayton proved his devotion by staying with NASA even when they grounded him. By participating in the Apollo-Soyuz Test Project, he helped promote peace and proved that perseverance can breed success.

★

Slayton cowrote several books on the space program and his involvement with it. *We Seven* (1962), written by the seven Mercury astronauts, provides personal insight into the early days of the American space program. *Moon Shot: The Inside Story of America's Race to the Moon* (1994), written by Slayton and Alan Shepard with Jay Barbree and Howard Benedict, covers the space program from its origins to Slayton's historic Apollo-Soyuz mission. His autobiography, *Deke! U.S. Manned Space: From Mercury to the Shuttle* (1994), was written with the assistance of Michael Cassutt. Offering a narrative account of Project Mercury, Tom Wolfe's best-seller *The Right Stuff* (1979) provides a more objective view of the early space program and the astronauts involved with it. Charles Murray and Catherine Bly Cox, *Apollo, The Race to the Moon* (1989), includes discussion of Slayton's key role in that program. Obituaries are in the *New York Times* and *Houston Post* (both 14 June 1993).

BRIAN DANIEL QUIGLEY

SMITH, Joseph (*b.* 31 October 1901 in Scranton, Pennsylvania; *d.* 19 May 1993 at Andrews Air Force Base, Maryland), United States Air Force general who made contributions to the development of modern strategic bombardment, air transport, humanitarian operations, military education, and senior-level military planning.

Smith was one of three children of Jacob Smith, an immigrant from England, and Yetta Kabatchnick, a homemaker. Jacob Smith was a local businessman and alderman. Smith left high school before graduating to help in World War I farm production. He later attended Norwich University in Northfield, Vermont, and entered the U.S. Military Academy in West Point, New York, graduating with a B.S. degree in 1923. First assigned to the Eighth Cavalry in Texas, Smith, a lover of horses, foresaw that the horse cavalry did not have a long future in the age of aviation. In November 1927 he asked to be sent to the Air Corps Primary Flying School in Brooks Field, Texas, transferring to the Air Corps Advanced Flying School at Kelly Field, Texas, in July 1928. He graduated in 1928 with Claire Chennault, the future leader of the Flying Tigers in China during World War II, as his final check pilot. In December 1928 he was sent to Camp Nichols in the Philippine Islands where he flew the MB-1 bomber. The following month Smith officially left the cavalry to join the Army Air Corps (which later became the Air Force), where he was to spend the remainder of his career.

Smith returned to the Air Corps flying school in Brooks Field in March 1931. There he met Anna Pearle Krausse, whom he married on 23 September 1933. They had two

Joseph Smith, 1954. AP/WIDE WORLD PHOTOS

children. From March to May 1934, Smith worked for the legendary Henry H. ("Hap") Arnold in the Air Corps's effort to show both its capabilities and its needs. Successfully flying the hazardous Salt Lake City, Utah, airmail route to Cheyenne, Wyoming, under all conditions in those early airplanes earned Smith the honor of membership in the Air Force's Gathering of Eagles in 1991.

Smith's work with the mail was followed by tours with bombardment units and as an instructor and student in schools such as the Air Corps Tactical School from August 1936 to June 1937. Significantly, in September 1938, he attended the Army's Command and General Staff School at Fort Leavenworth, Kansas, graduating the following June. Smith then returned to his previous duties as the operations officer of the Ninth Bombardment Group at Mitchell Field for a year.

In July 1940 Smith began a series of increasingly important assignments in Washington, D.C., and at Langley Field, Virginia. He served on the staffs of the Air Corps's General Headquarters and of the Air Corps Combat Command. In March 1942, four months after the entry of the United States into World War II, Smith joined the Strategy Section in the Operations Division of the War Department General Staff. In April 1943 he became the senior Air Corps member of the Joint War Plans Committee of the Joint Chiefs of Staff, where he represented Army Air Force interests at the highest levels of strategic planning. In this position, he traveled with President Franklin D. Roosevelt and senior leaders to the Cairo Conference to develop war strategy with America's allies.

In January 1944 Smith left Washington to become the chief of staff of the Third Air Force in Tampa, Florida. In May 1944 the Air Force promoted him to brigadier general. He was sent to India in January 1945 to join the Twentieth Bomber Command. As the war in the Pacific was ending that August, Smith moved to Okinawa as deputy chief of staff of the Eighth Air Force.

When the military demobilized after the war, Smith temporarily returned to Washington in October 1945 as the assistant chief of the air staff for plans. The next month Smith moved to Maxwell Air Force Base, Alabama, to help establish the Air University there. In August 1946 he established and headed the new Air Tactical School at Tyndall Field, Florida.

In November 1947 Smith went to Wiesbaden, Germany, to take charge of the headquarters of U.S. Air Forces in Europe. In June 1948 the Soviets cut off all road, rail, and water links between West Berlin and the Western Zones. The task of supplying Berlin by air devolved upon the U.S. Air Forces in Europe, commanded by Major General Curtis E. LeMay. He entrusted the operation to Smith, who called it Operation Vittles because "We're hauling grub." The first deliveries took place on 26 June 1948, when twin-engine Douglas C-47s made thirty-two flights into Berlin with eighty tons of cargo consisting mainly of powdered milk, flour, and medicine. As the days passed, General Smith increased the use of his aircraft by dispatching planes according to a block system that grouped them according to type, allowing radar controllers on the ground to deal more easily with strings of aircraft having the same flight characteristics. By the end of the first month, Smith was sending 3,028 tons of supplies into West Berlin daily, the largest humanitarian air operation of the twentieth century. The Berlin Airlift lasted for fifteen months, making a total of 276, 926 flights into West Berlin. Smith felt that this was his proudest accomplishment.

That November, while the airlift was still going on, Smith returned to the Air Staff in Washington. He was promoted to major general on 11 September 1949. In November 1951, as the Korean War was still being fought, Smith took command of the Military Air Transport Service at Andrews Air Force Base. He also received his third star, rising to the grade of lieutenant general. He remained at Andrews Air Force Base for the last seven years of his career. During his career, he received the Legion of Merit award with Oak Leaf Cluster, the Distinguished Service Medal with Oak Leaf Cluster, a Bronze Star, and the Medal for Human Action.

The Military Air Transport Service was an outgrowth of the earlier establishment of the Department of Defense and the combining of the navy and air force air transport systems on 1 June 1948. Smith, in an unusually long tenure of seven years, modernized his air fleet and ran several urgent large airlifts. He also had to work with the Civil Reserve Air Fleet, whose civilian airline components carefully monitored how much military transportation he used and how much work he gave to the civilian airlines. But as the demands of the Korean War were ending, Smith's planes moved French soldiers wounded in Indochina from hospitals in Japan to France. In 1956 he had to move United Nations peacekeepers into Egypt and ferry approximately 14,000 political refugees from Hungary to the United States, all actions in aid of peace and humanity. Near the end of his tenure, he again had to modernize his air fleet so that it could move the new larger missiles coming into America's cold war defenses.

Smith retired from the air force on 30 June 1958. He continued his interests in military affairs, serving on the Defense Department's Bolte Board that reviewed promotion and separation laws for the officers of the armed forces. He was a founder of the National Association for Uniformed Services in 1968 to work for better rights and benefits for the members of the military establishment. He died of respiratory and heart failure at the hospital at Andrews Air Force Base where he had spent so much of his career. He is buried in Arlington National Cemetery in Arlington, Virginia.

Smith was a pivotal figure in the development of the jet-age U.S. Air Force. His career spanned the post–World War airplanes to modern, large jet-powered transports and bombers. His ability to start operations such as the Berlin Airlift, which defeated communist efforts to starve West Berlin into submission, and the Hungarian Airlift, which rescued pro-western refugees, showed an important non-combatant role for air power. With his background in bombers and long-distance air transports he also understood the nature of air power in strategic planning and in education. In that area, he helped establish the modern air force school system. From his early love of horses to his concern for the quality of life of the armed forces, Smith's career shows the coming of age of America's defense establishment.

★

One of the best sources about the life of Joseph Smith is the biographical files in the History Office, Air Mobility Command, Scott Air Force Base, Illinois. This command is the successor to the Military Air Transport Service. The Military Air Transport Service itself is described in "MATS: America's Long Arm of the Air," *National Geographic* (Mar. 1957). An obituary is in *Assembly July 1994* (Association of Graduates: West Point, N.Y.): 144. Information about Smith's family came in a brief oral history interview the author conducted with Mrs. Smith on 21 September 2000.

MARTIN K. GORDON

SNELLING, Richard Arkwright (*b.* 18 February 1927 in Allentown, Pennsylvania; *d.* 13 August 1991 in Shelburne, Vermont), four-term Republican governor of Vermont who brought his experiences as a businessperson to the office and helped bolster Vermont's economy.

Snelling was one of six children of Walter Othman Snelling, a scientist, and Marjorie Gharing, a homemaker. He grew up in Allentown and attended the University of Havana in Cuba and Lehigh University in Bethlehem, Pennsylvania, before finally completing his B.A. degree at Harvard University in 1948. He served in the U.S. Army as a private in 1945 and 1946. He sold Electrolux vacuum cleaners to pay his way through Harvard, where he played football and graduated with high honors. On 14 June 1947 Snelling married Barbara Weil. They had four children.

In 1953 Snelling and his wife moved to Burlington, Vermont, where Snelling worked at the Burlington Chrysler Plymouth dealership. In 1957 he founded Shelburne Industries, which made ski equipment. Shortly after this he began his political apprenticeship in the Republican Party.

Snelling acquired some political experience as the chair of Shelburne's planning and zoning boards and as the chair of the Chittenden County Planning Committee. His first significant involvement in politics was in 1956, when he

Richard Snelling, 1983. ASSOCIATED PRESS AP

was the Chittenden County chairman of Robert Stafford's campaign for lieutenant governor. One of the singular features of Vermont election law, aside from governors serving two-year terms, is that candidates for governor and lieutenant governor run separate races, creating a situation in which candidates with different party affiliations can be elected to those offices. For example, the lieutenant governor during Snelling's third term was Madeleine M. Kunin, a Democrat.

Snelling was a member of the Vermont Development Commission from 1959 to 1961, and he served in the Vermont House of Representatives from 1959 to 1960. He launched unsuccessful bids for lieutenant governor in 1964 and governor in 1966, but from 1963 to 1966 he was a member of the state Republican executive committee. He served another term in the Vermont House of Representatives from 1973 to 1977 and was the majority leader for the 1975–1976 term. He also served as a delegate to the Republican National Conventions during this time.

In addition to his political activities, Snelling continued his involvement in business and public service. As the president and chief executive officer of Shelburne Industries, he was active in the Greater Burlington Industrial Corporation and was elected president and chair of its executive committee, serving from 1961 to 1964. He was the chair of the Vermont Aeronautics Board from 1969 to 1972.

Snelling's political and business activities were not unique among the businesspeople involved in American political life. Winning the gubernatorial election on 2 November 1976 marked the emergence of a skilled politician who successfully represented himself to the public as a no-nonsense businessperson who was not political but who wanted to serve. He demonstrated that government could make a difference, an idea some distance from the reigning ideology of the national Republican party, New Federalism. New Federalism called for a smaller national government, one less involved in providing programs that the states could more efficiently provide, while maintaining a strong military. Snelling persuaded utilities in his own state and in other states to cooperate in contracting for Canadian imports, an issue he and Premier René Lévesque began working on in Snelling's first term. He signed legislation that helped the skiing industry and Vermont's tourism economy and that protected the state's water. Over the course of his four terms in office, employment in Vermont climbed 20 percent. In addition he made headway in property tax and education reforms.

Snelling's election as governor also serves as the date from which his involvement in national Republican politics grew. Shortly after his reelection to a second term in 1978 he was chosen as vice chairman of the Republican Governors Association, and he became chairman of the association in November 1979. In national circles Snelling aligned with former president Gerald Ford and encouraged him to run in the 1980 primary. He addressed the Republican National Convention on 15 July 1980 and in the same month characterized the Carter administration as "the greatest failure in the history of the Presidency."

Although Snelling and his wife attended President Ronald Reagan's invitation-only inaugural gala, Snelling emerged in the 1980s as an articulate and forceful critic of Reagan's approach to federalism, passing programs down to the states without providing budgetary support. As the spokesperson for the nation's governors Snelling made a strong case for federal deficit reduction, arguing that higher taxes and cuts in defense and domestic spending would be necessary. He endorsed Proposition One, an initiative to persuade Congress to balance the federal budget by 1990.

By 1984 Snelling was completing a fourth term, a first in the twentieth-century history of Vermont. After announcing that he would not seek a fifth term, he entered the senatorial race against the Democratic senator from Vermont, Patrick Leahy. Both men were popular, and Snelling, a seasoned campaigner and familiar with the ways of Vermont face-to-face politics, unwisely ran a negative campaign and made many wrong moves. Leahy won the November 1986 elections, and Snelling's political career seemed at an end. As if to note that, the University of Vermont awarded Snelling an honorary doctorate of law for his service to the state and the nation.

Snelling did not stay retired, however. He decided to seek a fifth gubernatorial term to undo, as he saw it, the budgetary wreckage of the Kunin years that succeeded his tenure as governor. Elected over Kunin in 1990, he successfully engineered the largest single tax increase in Vermont history to that date to bring the state's budget deficit under control. He died of an apparent heart attack in August 1991, the first governor of Vermont to die in office since 1870. He is buried in Shelburne.

Snelling was a robust and physically active man who flew his own plane and loved to play tennis. He enjoyed sailing and captained his sailboat across the Atlantic in the summer of 1985. The sense of health and vigor that he conveyed made his death that much more surprising and saddening to the people of Vermont. Snelling represented himself as someone who wanted to serve, a characterization that is in fact historically true.

★

For further information on Snelling see Michael Barone, Grant Ujifusa, and Douglas Matthews, *The Almanac of American Politics* (1976, 1978, 1980, 1986, 1988, 1992), and Marie Marmo Mullaney, *Biographical Directory of the Governors of the United States, 1988–1994* (1994). Obituaries are in the *Burlington Free Press* (14 Aug. 1991) and *New York Times* (15 Aug. 1991).

ROBERT B. CAREY

SOLOVEITCHIK, Joseph Baer (*b.* 27 February 1903 in Pruzhan, Poland, now Belarus; *d.* 8 April 1993 in Brookline, Massachusetts), leading figure of the centrist "Modern Orthodox" movement of Judaism who embodied its philosophy of synthesizing the secular and religious worlds and who helped transform American Orthodox Judaism through lectures, teaching, and leadership.

Soloveitchik was born Yosef Dov Halevi Soloveitchik, the oldest of five children of Moses Soloveitchik and Pesia Feinstein. On both sides of his family he was descended from a long line of distinguished rabbis. Through his father he inherited a tradition of rigorous intellectualism, exacting ethical standards, total devotion to the study of Jewish law, and opposition to secular studies and Zionism. From his maternal side he learned a more open approach to the world. Soloveitchik grew up in Khoslavitch in White Russia, where his father was a rabbi and his mother performed the duties expected of a rabbi's wife and was alarmed at the poor quality of his education at the local Jewish school. Her complaints led to his father teaching him Jewish law for the next twelve years while she introduced him to writers such as Henrik Ibsen, Aleksandr Pushkin, and Hayyim Nahman Bialik. During his late teens private tutors taught Soloveitchik secular subjects.

On 20 June 1922 Soloveitchik received certification from the gymnasium (secondary school) in Dubno, Poland, and in 1924 he studied political science at the Free Polish University in Warsaw, where his family was living at the time. With his mother's encouragement he went to Berlin to further his education. In 1926 he studied mathematics, physics, and philosophy at the Friedrich-Wilhelms-Universität and matriculated in the department of philosophy at the University of Berlin. In 1931 he married Tonya Lewit, who received her doctorate in education from Jena University in Jena, Germany. They had three children. In the fall of 1932 he submitted his dissertation on the neo-Kantian philosopher Hermann Cohen. Soloveitchik then left with his family for New York City, where his father had already settled. Soloveitchik received his doctorate on 10 December 1932.

In 1932 Soloveitchik was offered the position of chief rabbi of the Orthodox Jewish community of greater Boston, which he held until his death in 1993. He rented an apartment on Elm Hill Avenue in Roxbury, Massachusetts. Beginning in 1933 he commuted weekly to New York City to teach rabbinics at Yeshiva University, the major institution of higher learning for American Orthodox Judaism. Soloveitchik was horrified by the poor level of Orthodox Judaism, the level of ignorance of the average American Jew who typically attended synagogue for social, not religious, reasons. He was concerned that younger generations seemed to be straying from religiosity. He started over much opposition the coeducational Maimonides School,

Joseph Baer Soloveitchik. AP/WIDE WORLD PHOTOS

the first Jewish day school in New England, in 1937. Soloveitchik also conducted postgraduate Talmudic classes for young scholars. With conditions worsening in Europe at that time, an influx of refugees helped formalize these classes into the Hekhal Rabenu Hayim Halevi and Yeshivath Torath Israel, a school of advanced religious studies. On his father's death in 1941 Soloveitchik succeeded him as head of the Rabbi Isaac Elchanan Theological Seminary of Yeshiva University in New York City. He also lectured at the Yeshiva University Bernard Revel Graduate School in Jewish philosophy. Although he had a small apartment in New York City, Boston remained his home.

On the first anniversary of his father's death Soloveitchik began a tradition of public memorial lectures in Yiddish. These lectures, considered the major Orthodox intellectual event of the year, became an American Jewish institution, attracting about 2,000 attendees at Yeshiva University. He later added a second lecture in honor of his wife and mother after they and his brother died within months of each other in 1967. Soloveitchik was a spellbinding speaker, and his lectures lasted from two to five hours. He also gave weekly talks in Yiddish, Hebrew, and English to more general audiences in New York and Boston.

Soloveitchik served as the honorary president of the Religious Zionists of America (Mizrachi) from 1952 until his death. In 1952 he was also appointed the chair of the Rabbinical Council of America's Halakhah Commission, which made religious rulings for Orthodox Jews. One of his most important rulings found support for Orthodox rabbinic students serving in the military as chaplains. Another stated that Orthodox Jews could serve in organizations with non-Orthodox colleagues on secular matters. His rulings, however, were not without controversy. He refused to rule on the legitimacy of Ethiopian Jews, and he maintained that it was preferable to stay home on the High Holy Days than to pray at a non-Orthodox synagogue.

In 1959 Soloveitchik declined the position of the Ashkenazic chief rabbi of Israel, supposedly because he valued his independence from political concerns. (He had unsuccessfully applied for the position of chief rabbi of Tel Aviv in 1935.) As the American Jewish community's representative to the Secretary of Agriculture's Advisory Committee on Humane Methods of Slaughter in 1959, he sought ways to make Jewish ritual slaughter (*shekhita*) more humane. In 1960 he served as the principal Jewish representative in the Yeshiva University Institute of Mental Health project, undertaken with Harvard and Loyola Universities, to study religious attitudes toward psychological problems.

In the 1960s Soloveitchik successfully battled cancer. However, by the mid-1980s symptoms of Alzheimer's disease became apparent and his activities were increasingly curtailed. Soloveitchik died of heart failure at his home on 8 April 1993. He is buried in Beth El Cemetery in West Roxbury, Massachusetts. Because he was buried on the last day of Passover, only about 5,000 people attended. Still, it was the largest Orthodox Jewish funeral in New England to that date.

Soloveitchik was reverentially known simply as "the Rav," or the ultimate rabbi, teacher, or master, by generations of Yeshiva University students and rabbis. He participated in the ordination of more than 2,000 Orthodox rabbis. Unlike many of his conservatively religious colleagues, Soloveitchik championed secular studies, a more intensive Jewish education for women, and religious Zionism. His analytic prowess at blending Jewish sources and secular knowledge seduced audiences large and small, learned or not.

Soloveitchik was thin and of average height. His thick spectacles were offset by a squared-off beard, which fell about three inches below his chin. Shy and modest, with a tentative public smile, when lecturing he transformed into a captivating, assured, intellectually challenging public speaker in Yiddish, Hebrew, and English.

Soloveitchik carried on his family's tradition or "malady" of not publishing due to an overdeveloped striving for perfection. The most famous of his few, carefully constructed writings are *Ish ha-Halakhah* (Halakhic man,

1944); *The Lonely Man of Faith* (1965); *Kol Dodi Dofek* ("The voice of my beloved knocketh," 1969); and *The Halakhic Mind* (1986). Because his lectures were widely recorded by his audiences, his legacy is in assorted oral discourses, translated by devoted pupils, including Pinchas Peli's *Soloveitchik on Repentance* (1984), Abraham Besdin's *Reflections of the Rav* (1989), and Aaron Rakeffet-Rothkoff's *The Rav* (1999).

Soloveitchik's philosophy falls into an existential vein with its emphasis on modern feelings of alienation, loneliness, conflict, isolation, and helplessness as the basis for human relationships with the divine. "Man is a great and creative being," be explained, "because he is torn by conflict and is always in a state of ontological tenseness and perplexity." Soloveitchik's analysis revolved around certain "types," the best known of which are the halakhic man and the lonely man of faith. Soloveitchik reflected his philosophical concerns. He was a private man whose best friend was his wife, Tonya.

★

The standard biographical source on Soloveitchik is an article by Aaron Lichtenstein, his son-in-law, in Simon Noveck, ed., *Great Jewish Thinkers of the Twentieth Century* (1963). An interesting view of his parents and their family life is provided by his sister in Shulamit Soloveitchik Meiselman, *The Soloveitchik Heritage: A Daughter's Memoirs* (1995). Other biographical sources are Hillel Goldberg, *Between Berlin and Slobodka: Jewish Transition Figures from Eastern Europe* (1989), and Naomi Pasachoff, *Links in the Chain: Shapers of Jewish Tradition* (1997). Studies of Soloveitchik's religious writings and philosophy are Marc D. Angel, ed., *Exploring the Thought of Rabbi Joseph B. Soloveitchik* (1997); Zvi Kolitz, *Confrontation: The Existential Thought of Rabbi J. B. Soloveitchik* (1993); and Reinier Munk, *The Rationale of Halakhic Man: Joseph B. Soloveitchik's Conception of Jewish Thought* (1996), which details Soloveitchik's life in Europe in the introduction. An obituary is in the *New York Times* (9 Apr. 1993).

SHARONA A. LEVY

SPECK, Richard Benjamin (*b.* 6 December 1941 in Kirkwood, Illinois; *d.* 5 December 1991 in Joliet, Illinois), mass murderer whose brutal slaying of eight student nurses transformed the popular perception of murder in America.

The seventh of eight children born to Benjamin Franklin Speck, a farmer and logger, and Mary Margaret Carbaugh, a homemaker, Speck was raised in a strict Presbyterian household. After his father's death in 1947, Speck's mother married Carl August Lindberg, a hard-drinking Texan who worked in the insurance business. Together, they moved with her two youngest children from Monmouth, Illinois, to Dallas, Texas. Prone to violent rages when drunk, Lindberg regularly beat his wife and abused Speck physically

Richard Speck, 1966. AP/WIDE WORLD PHOTOS

and psychologically. A poor student and social outcast, Speck struggled through grammar school and enrolled in Crozier Technical High School, dropping out in 1958 after one semester. He began running with a gang of older delinquents and soon settled into a life of petty crime. By the age of twenty-four, Speck had been arrested forty-one times and had served several stints in jail. He also had held various menial jobs such as working at a 7-Up bottling plant and driving a truck for a meatpacking company.

On 19 January 1962 Speck married fifteen-year-old Shirley Annette Malone. A cruel and irresponsible husband, Speck habitually beat his wife and often forced sex upon her. The couple had already separated and Speck was serving time for disorderly conduct when their daughter was born in 1962. While in jail he acquired a crude tattoo on his left forearm—the infamous "Born to Raise Hell." Following a felony burglary conviction, Speck was sent to the Texas penitentiary at Huntsville from September 1963 to January 1965. Two days after his parole, Speck was arrested for assaulting a woman with a knife and returned to Huntsville until his release in July 1965. In March 1966, the same month Shirley was granted a divorce, an arrest warrant was issued in Speck's name for the burglary of a supermarket. Fearing another prison sentence, he fled to Chicago.

Speck arrived at the home of his sister and her husband and soon traveled to Monmouth, Illinois, where he visited family and friends but spent most of his time loafing in bars and steeping himself in crime. In April 1966 Speck allegedly entered the home of a sixty-five-year-old woman and, after raping her at knifepoint, absconded with money and jewelry. Speck was also a suspect in several burglaries as well as the murder of a barmaid, Mary Kay Pierce. Fearing that the police were closing in, Speck abruptly returned to Chicago. He landed a job as a deckhand with the Inland Steel Company aboard the *Clarence B. Randall* but was soon fired for assaulting an officer. On 11 July 1966 he sought work at the National Maritime Union's hiring hall on Chicago's shabby South Side, but no berths were available.

Disgusted, jobless, and broke, a furious Speck continued drinking heavily, and on the night of 13 July he entered the back door of a townhouse at 2319 East 100th Street near the union hall. The townhouse was the residence of eight student nurses from nearby South Chicago Community Hospital. Corazon Amurao, an exchange student from the Philippines, was the first to encounter Speck. Brandishing a switchblade and a pistol, Speck discovered five more nurses—Merlita Gargullo, Valentina Pasion, Pamela Wilkening, Patricia Matusek, and Nina Schmale—and herded them into a large bedroom, where he bound each with strips torn from a sheet.

Assuring the frightened nurses that he intended no harm, he pocketed their cash, explaining that he needed it to go to New Orleans to ship out. A sixth nurse, Gloria Davy, returned from a date and was likewise bound. Speck chatted aimlessly with his captives until 12:30 in the morning when two more nurses, Suzanne Farris and Mary Ann Jordan (a friend planning to spend the night), returned. When they resisted Speck, his response was swift and brutal. He plunged the knife into Farris's chest and stabbed Jordan eighteen times before strangling her with a stocking. His bloodlust aroused, Speck began dragging the other nurses one by one to different rooms before stabbing and/or strangling them. Only Amurao survived the slaughter by hiding beneath a bed until Speck left.

Amurao was able to provide police with a detailed description of Speck—six feet tall and 160 pounds with slicked-back blondish hair, a severely pockmarked face, a slow Southern drawl, and a "Born to Raise Hell" tattoo on his arm. With the help of a composite sketch, police traced Speck to the union hall and were able to match his fingerprints to those found at the crime scene. Now the target of a massive manhunt, Speck fled to Chicago's Skid Row with the vague hope of hopping a freight train out of town. Instead he checked into the Starr Hotel, where on the night of 17 July 1966 he slashed his arms with a broken wine bottle in a suicide attempt. Bleeding and near death, he was taken to Cook County Hospital where he was arrested after an intern recognized the telltale tattoo.

On 15 April 1967 Speck was found guilty of eight counts of murder. The conviction was due largely to Amurao's dramatic courtroom identification of Speck. Although he was sentenced to die in the electric chair, Speck's life was spared when the U.S. Supreme Court declared the death penalty unconstitutional in June 1971. He was resentenced to Stateville Correctional Center at Joliet, Illinois, for fifty to one hundred years for each murder. On 5 December 1991 Speck suffered a massive heart attack and died at nearby Silver Cross Hospital. His body, which was unclaimed, was cremated and the ashes scattered at an unknown location. Speck never admitted his guilt, steadfastly maintaining that his mind was so clouded by alcohol and drugs he had no memory of that bloody night. A prison-made videotape uncovered in 1996, however, showed a grinning and unrepentant Speck describing the murders in grisly detail.

Richard Speck forever changed the face of modern crime. The sheer brutality and senselessness of the slayings shocked a nation from its complacency and imprinted upon the popular imagination the terrible pockmarked face of a tattooed drifter as the symbol of unbridled evil. A certain American innocence and assurance died along with the eight student nurses. If those innocents could be slaughtered by a stranger for no apparent reason, then henceforth no one could be safe, no security assumed. Richard Speck's legacy was the beginning of America's chilling age of modern mass murders and serial killings.

★

An account of Speck's life and six months in prison awaiting trial, Jack Altman and Marvin Ziporyn, M.D., *Born to Raise Hell: The Untold Story of Richard Speck* (1967), presents an intriguing, though slightly sympathetic, psychological portrait of Speck gleaned from numerous interviews. Dennis L. Breo and William J. Martin, *The Crime of the Century: Richard Speck and the Murder of Eight Student Nurses* (1993), is the best and most thorough account of the life and crimes of Richard Speck. Martin was the assistant state's attorney who prosecuted Speck. Biographical videos include *Great Crimes and Trials of the 20th Century: John Wayne Gacy/Richard Speck* (1993); *Biography: Richard Speck* (1998); *Investigative Reports: Richard Speck* (2000). An obituary is in the *New York Times* (6 Dec. 1991).

MICHAEL MCLEAN

STAGGERS, Harley Orrin (*b.* 3 August 1907 near Keyser, West Virginia; *d.* 20 August 1991 in Cumberland, Maryland), sixteen-term member of the House of Representatives who from 1966 to 1980 served as the chairman of the House Committee on Interstate and Foreign Commerce.

Literally born in a log cabin, Staggers was the fifth of twelve children of Jacob Kinsley Staggers and Frances Winona Cumberledge. His father engaged in various businesses, but none were very successful in supporting his large family. Staggers attended Keyser High School of Mineral County, West Virginia. Because of the family's financial straits, Staggers worked as a child in an area silk mill. His love of football took him to Emory and Henry College in Emory, Virginia, where he played fullback. He was also active in student government. To finish his education, he worked for the Baltimore and Ohio Railroad, eventually becoming a brakeman. Summer employment found him in the wheat fields of Kansas and Oklahoma and for one year he worked in a rubber factory in Akron, Ohio. After graduating with a B.A. degree in 1931, Staggers spent two years as a teacher and coach at Norton High School, deep in the mountains of western Virginia. Returning to Mineral County, he served as the head football coach at Potomac State College from 1933 to 1935. He then did a year of graduate study at Duke University, in Durham, North Carolina, and later took courses at Northwestern, in Chicago.

From 1937 until 1941 Staggers served as the sheriff of Mineral County. He then secured an appointment as right-of-way agent for the West Virginia Road Commission in 1941 and 1942. In the latter year he became the state director of the federal Office of Government Reports (which later became the Office of War Information).

Harley Staggers, 1965. AP/WIDE WORLD PHOTOS

Enlisting in the U.S. Navy in World War II, Staggers was commissioned an officer and served as a navigator in the Naval Air Service in both the Atlantic and Pacific theaters. During his Pacific duties he sustained injuries when his plane crashed on landing. He left the navy as a lieutenant commander in 1946. Just before leaving for overseas duty, Staggers married Mary Veronica Casey on 4 October 1943. They eventually became the parents of six children.

Staggers moved into national politics in 1948 when he defeated the one-term congressman Melvin C. Snyder to represent the Second District of West Virginia. As the cold war heated up Staggers became a consistent hawk in foreign affairs and a foe of domestic communists. Early in his career the Democratic party elected him as an assistant majority whip, and he proved efficient in marshaling votes on key issues. He was a member of the Veterans Affairs Committee and the Post Office and Civil Service Committee. He also chaired the Transportation and Aeronautics Subcommittee of the Interstate and Foreign Commerce Committee. As a staunch anticommunist, in January 1954 Staggers introduced H.R. 6943, which requested the president to appoint a blue-chip commission to find a way to outlaw the Communist party and to make membership in that party a crime.

In February 1962 his H.R. 10019 would have facilitated "action where action is needed most to apprehend members of the Communist conspiracy in this country." The penalty was a fine of $10,000 and a five-year prison term. Among other provisions, this law would deny passports to members of groups identified as communist and disallow tax exemptions for such groups. It would have barred members of such groups from representing workers and making use of the facilities of the National Labor Relations Board. Finally, it would have required such persons to testify under oath and provide documentation demonstrating their innocence, removing their privilege against self-incrimination. The dubious constitutionality of some of these requirements stemmed from Staggers's lack of training in law. Yet in earlier years he had opposed what he perceived to be the excesses of Senator Joseph McCarthy.

In 1966 his colleagues elevated Staggers to chair the powerful Committee on Interstate and Foreign Commerce, and he continued in that post until his retirement. The committee's responsibilities were extremely broad. In addition to trade matters, it held responsibility for communications, transportation, energy production, consumer protection, auto safety, public health, and pollution abatement. Among his accomplishments were actions to remove unsafe toys from the market, the introduction of safety devices in autos, federal funding for cancer research, and a truth-in-packaging law. During the Arab oil embargo, and in the service of his West Virginia constituents, Staggers pushed coal as an alternate energy source. The most publicized activity of his tenure was when he challenged CBS for supposedly fabricating news on hunger in America and Vietnam, as well its general coverage of Vietnam, a war he supported. The charges of contempt of Congress that his committee initiated against Frank Stanton, the head of CBS, were not sustained by the whole House of Representatives.

Staggers was responsible for the legislation that allowed railroads to divest themselves of unprofitable passenger traffic in 1971. But the legislation also created the federally subsidized Amtrak, which guaranteed that both the Baltimore and Ohio and the Chesapeake and Ohio would continue to run through West Virginia. In 1976 Conrail legislation gave further assistance to America's declining rail system. Finally, the Staggers Rail Act of 1980 partly deregulated railroads. As a result several megasystems were created while smaller and weaker companies went out of business.

In some respects Staggers's career seems paradoxical. Willing to strip communists of their rights, he was a supporter of the civil rights movement and voted for the Civil Rights Act of 1964 and the Voting Rights Act of the following year. He supported the Equal Rights Amendment and the amendment that extended voting rights to eighteen-year-olds. He felt that both the District of Columbia and Puerto Rico should become states. At the same time he continued to support U.S. involvement in Vietnam and agreed with the National Rifle Association on gun legislation. The year after he sought to outlaw the Communist party, he recommended creation of a cabinet-level position called Secretary of Peace. These inconsistencies arose from the fact that Staggers was an old-time West Virginia politician who supported the interests and wishes of his constituents, policies that sometimes brought criticism from his colleagues. He was a tough and skilled fighter in Congress who generally used his power on behalf of the underdog. To the end of his career Staggers was an advocate for consumers and minorities. He was a joiner and among his many memberships (Moose, Lions, Elks, Knights of Pythias) his service in World War II took precedence; he belonged to the American Legion, Veterans of Foreign Wars, Disabled American Veterans, and AMVETS. A lifelong Methodist, Staggers was also active as a Sunday-school teacher.

In 1980 Staggers chose not to run for reelection, having served thirty-two years in the House, a longevity record in West Virginia. His son, Harley O. Staggers, Jr., was defeated by Republican Cleve Benedict in the election year that brought Ronald Reagan to the White House. In August 1991, shortly after reaching his eighty-fourth birthday, Staggers fell from a ladder while working on his home. A few days later he drove himself to the hospital in nearby Cumberland. There, complications from the fall led to his death from cardiac and respiratory failure. Staggers is buried in his family's plot in Keyser.

The apparent contradictions in Staggers's political views and service grew out of his personal life experiences and from his consistent support of his West Virginia constituents. His long years of service in the seat of power neither corrupted him nor gave him an inflated sense of his own importance. Perhaps, as Rudyard Kipling said in his poem "If," Staggers could "walk with Kings—nor lose the common touch."

★

The Staggers papers are in the West Virginia Collection of the West Virginia University Library in Morgantown. An obituary is in the *New York Times* (21 Aug. 1991).

ART BARBEAU

STEGNER, Wallace Earle (*b.* 18 February 1909 in Lake Mills, Iowa; *d.* 13 April 1993 in Santa Fe, New Mexico), writer, teacher, and environmentalist, who emerged as the preeminent voice among writers in the American West in the second half of the twentieth century and became a leading spokesman for conservation.

Among the themes that Stegner explored in his writing, he returned most often to the ways in which the past and a sense of place shaped ordinary lives, especially his own. He was the second of two sons born to Hilda Paulson, a homemaker, and George H. Stegner, a "boomer," who worked variously as a gold seeker in Alaska, a farmer in Saskatchewan, and a bootlegger in Utah, living on the margins of society and striving for wealth he never attained.

Stegner had a prairie childhood, growing up in Eastend, Saskatchewan, where in the summer months the family worked a half-section farm and in winter the father took such work as he could find in town. In 1921 the Stegner family moved south to Salt Lake City, Utah, where the father ran a speakeasy from their home. Stegner thrived academically in the public schools but much of the time felt himself an outsider and an object of scorn. Physically puny, he was regularly humiliated by his father, who much preferred his athletically gifted older brother, and his classmates at school routinely bullied him. He found solace in books and in the Boy Scouts, whose outdoor programs gave him a sense of community and of competence. In his senior year of high school, Stegner underwent a startling transformation, growing six inches in height. He was now "big enough," he wrote, "to hold my own in sports" and enjoy "the happiest years I ever knew. . . ."

Following graduation from high school in 1926 Stegner worked his way through the University of Utah, where he starred on the tennis team and became a popular man on campus. Graduating with a B.A. degree in English and

Wallace Stegner, 1979. AP/WIDE WORLD PHOTOS

membership in Phi Beta Kappa (1930), he earned an M.A. degree (1932) and a Ph.D. (1935) in English at the State University of Iowa. Meanwhile he taught at Augustana College in Illinois (1933–1934) and at the University of Utah (1934–1937). On 1 September 1934 he married Mary Stuart Page, a fellow graduate student, with whom he had one son.

After he began teaching and his dissertation was completed, Stegner settled into the disciplined life that marked his career. He went to his desk seven days a week—usually in the morning—for three or four hours of writing. In the afternoon, he taught his classes, and later each day devoted some time (often long hours) to physical activity, cutting firewood if he were in Vermont, working at his garden in Palo Alto, playing tennis or badminton or hiking in the California hills. Evenings were for correcting papers or preparing lectures, and for reading and entertaining.

The result of this rigorously adhered-to routine was a prodigious output of thirty-three books of fiction, history, and biography, dozens of short stories and hundreds of essays on travel, Western history, and later, environmental themes for popular magazines from *Esquire* and *Holiday* to *The Atlantic, The New Republic,* and *American Heritage*— along with articles for scholarly journals and regional reviews. He was West Coast editor for the Boston publisher Houghton Mifflin Company (1945–1953) and editor in chief of *American West* magazine (1966–1968). He was editor or coeditor of a dozen teaching texts, of special collections like *The Letters of Bernard DeVoto* (1975), and new

editions of classics like Mark Twain's *The Adventures of Huckleberry Finn* (1960) and A. B. Guthrie, Jr.'s *The Big Sky* (1965). His literary output, said the critic Malcolm Cowley, was "unequaled" by any other American in the twentieth century.

Stegner's first novel was *Remembering Laughter* (1937), a powerful story about a young, unmarried woman from Norway who comes to live with her sister and sister's husband on an Iowa farm and the tragedy that ensues. It won the Little, Brown Prize for a short novel and confirmed Stegner's belief that he could simultaneously teach and write. The prize also brought him $2,500 (a princely sum in the Great Depression, when his salary as a university instructor was $1,800 a year.) Now a published novelist, he moved on to the University of Wisconsin at Madison from 1937 to 1939. In the summer of 1938 he was invited to join the faculty of the Bread Loaf Writers' Conference in Middlebury, Vermont, in company with Bernard DeVoto and Robert Frost, who became friends and exerted a primary influence on his writing and his life. He returned to Bread Loaf seven more times as an instructor or a visiting lecturer. As the decade ended, he accepted an appointment to Harvard University as a Briggs-Copeland fellow to teach composition (1939–1945), first to undergraduates and then, during World War II, to soldiers in the Harvard-based Army Specialized Training Program.

During this period, his short stories sold well and brought him recognition and prizes, like the three O. Henry Awards he won in 1942, 1948, and 1950. In time he published three collections: *The Women on the Wall* (1956); *The City of the Living, and Other Stories* (1956); and *Collected Stories of Wallace Stegner* (1990), which was nominated for a National Book Critics Circle Award. His three short novels from the pre–World War II years—*The Potter's House* (1938), *On a Darkling Plain* (1940), and *Fire and Ice* (1941)—were each well-crafted but flawed and none sold well. He wrote a popular history of Utah, *Mormon Country* (1942), which was the first of his books to be reviewed by the *New York Times*.

The Big Rock Candy Mountain (1943) brought him critical praise, large sales, and a national audience, although critics continued to call him a regional writer for the next thirty years—a label that he and his supporters considered limiting and unfair. The West and the western landscape occupied a prominent place in his writing, his defenders said, but his fictional concerns were not restricted by region or geography. His preoccupations as a writer centered on individuals and their responsibility to themselves and to society, on friendship and community, and on mankind's relationship to the earth. He was especially concerned with the importance of history, remarking at one point that contemporary American problems flowed from the nation's living in "a present amputated from its past."

Following World War II, Stegner became a professor of English at Stanford University (1945–1969) and founder and director of its creative writing program (1946–1969). He retired as the Jackson Eli Reynolds Professor of Humanities (1969–1971). In 1975 he was appointed the Bissell Professor of Canadian–U.S. Relations at the University of Toronto in Ontario. He held two Guggenheim fellowships (1949–1951; 1959); a Rockefeller fellowship to conduct seminars in the Far East (1950–1951); and a senior fellowship from the National Endowment for the Humanities (1972). He was Montgomery fellow at Dartmouth College in 1980.

His students in the writing program were known as Stegner fellows and from its inception in 1946 included talented writers like Larry McMurtry, Ernest J. Gaines, Eugene Burdick, Robert Stone, Wendell Berry, and T. H. Watkins. Stegner told them that he could not teach them how to write; he could only provide them with a place in which to write in a disciplined way and offer them criticism and support in an environment where they could refine the creative powers they already possessed. Only Ken Kesey, the author of *One Flew over the Cuckoo's Nest* (1962), who conducted a long and bitter personal attack on Stegner, dissented from the consensus that Stegner had played an important part in their creative development. Stegner used Kesey as the model for one of the main characters in *All the Little Live Things* (1967).

Despite the demands of his Stanford writing program, Stegner continued to produce a steady output of work, including two novels, *Second Growth* (1947) and *The Preacher and the Slave* (1950), subsequently published as *Joe Hill: A Biographical Novel* (1969); as well as a second history of Utah, *The Gathering of Zion: The Story of the Mormon Trail* (1964). He developed his environmental concerns first in a biography, *Beyond the Hundredth Meridian: John Wesley Powell and the Second Opening of the West* (1954), and then in *This is Dinosaur: Echo Park and Its Magic Rivers* (1955). He helped to define and defend the goals of a newly invigorated environmental movement in a steady stream of magazine articles, some of which he collected in *Wolf Willow: A History, a Story, and a Memory of the Last Plains Frontier* (1962) and *The Sound of Mountain Water* (1969). He was invited by Stewart Lee Udall, President John F. Kennedy's secretary of the interior, to be his special assistant (1961), and he served a four-year term on the Advisory Board on National Parks, Historic Sites, Buildings, and Monuments and in the final year was its chairman (1962–1966). His most influential statement was his "Wilderness Letter" (1960)—reprinted as "Coda" in *The Sound of Mountain Water*—which helped secure the passage of the Wilderness Act of 1964 and was widely used as a manifesto for conservationists worldwide.

The years from 1972 on may well have been his most productive. *Angle of Repose* (1971), which some consider his masterpiece, won the Pulitzer Prize for fiction in 1972. *The Uneasy Chair: A Biography of Bernard DeVoto* (1974) raised important questions about conservation efforts in the United States. *The Spectator Bird* (1976) garnered the National Book Award in 1977, and *Recapitulation* (1979), an autobiographical novel, looked back at his college years. His last novel, *Crossing to Safety* (1987), an examination of friendships over time; *Collected Stories of Wallace Stegner*; and a compilation of his essays, *Where the Bluebird Sings to the Lemonade Springs: Living and Writing in the West* (1992), were each nominated for the National Book Critics Circle Award.

He was in Santa Fe in March 1993 for an awards ceremony, when the rental car he was driving on a rain-slick road at night was broadsided by another vehicle. He died in the local hospital two weeks later of complications from his numerous injuries. His remains were cremated and his ashes scattered on a hillside near his summer cottage in Greensboro, Vermont.

Shortly after Stegner's death, his daughter-in-law wrote that he was always aware of the road he traveled and of the road that still lay ahead. Such an awareness informed most of what he wrote and taught. A sense of place, landscapes, and history permeates his work. Standing in the front ranks of American writers in the latter half of the twentieth century, Stegner sought to capture the truth of ordinary lives and the intricacies of relationships. His students remained his devoted acolytes long after they left his classroom. His impact on the environmental movement, as both a theorist and an activist, was enormous. He was, as his friends said in tribute, a model of generosity and compassion, of discipline and integrity—the embodiment of the themes that lay at the center of his fiction.

★

Stegner's papers, including an unpublished autobiography, are in the Marriott Library, University of Utah, Salt Lake City. His few published autobiographical essays are in *Wolf Willow: A History, a Story, and a Memory of the Last Plains Frontier* (1962); *The Sound of Mountain Water: The Changing American West* (1969); and *Where the Bluebird Sings to the Lemonade Springs: Living and Writing in the West* (1992). See also "Autobiography: Wallace Stegner" in *Contemporary Authors: Autobiography Series*, v. 9 (1989). Stegner provided interviews and unrestricted access to his papers to his biographer, Jackson J. Benson, *Wallace Stegner: His Life and Work* (1996). His views on writing, history, and the American West can be found in *Conversations with Wallace Stegner on Western History and Literature*, with Richard W. Etulain (1983; revised 1990); Wallace Stegner, *On the Teaching of Creative Writing: Responses to a Series of Questions*, edited by Edward Connery Lathem (1988), from his 1980 term as a Montgomery Fellow at Dartmouth; and James R. Hepworth, *Stealing Glances: Three Interviews with Wallace Stegner* (1998). For Stegner's writings, see Nancy Colberg, *Wallace Stegner: A Descriptive Bibliography* (1990). Critical studies include Forrest G. and Margaret G. Robinson, *Wallace Stegner* (1977); Anthony Arthur, ed., *Critical Essays on Wallace Stegner* (1982); Charles E. Rankin, ed., *Wallace Stegner: Man and Writer* (1996); and Curt Meine, ed., *Wallace Stegner and the Continental Vision: Essays on Literature, History and Landscape* (1997). Former students, colleagues, and family offer reminiscences in Page Stegner and Mary Stegner, eds., *The Geography of Hope: A Tribute to Wallace Stegner* (1996). An obituary is in the *New York Times* (15 Apr 1993)

ALLAN L. DAMON

STURGES, John (*b.* 3 January 1911 in Oak Park, Illinois; *d.* 18 August 1992 in San Luis Obispo, California), film director best known for his action films, particularly Westerns.

Born John Carne, Sturges was two years old when his parents moved from the Chicago suburb of Oak Park to Santa Monica, California. After they divorced, he assumed his mother's maiden name, Sturges. During the Great Depression he attended Marin Junior College near San Rafael, California, where he worked as a stage manager and director at a local theater.

Sturges entered the film industry in 1932 with the help of his older brother, Sturges Carne, an art director at Radio-Keith-Orpheum (RKO) Studios. At RKO he worked in the blueprint department and later became an assistant to the production designer Robert Edmond Jones. One of his as-

John Sturges. ARCHIVE PHOTOS

signments was *Becky Sharp* (1935), the first full-Technicolor feature film. By World War II, Sturges had become a film editor. While serving as a captain in the U.S. Army Air Corps, he directed and edited over forty documentaries and training films, including the feature-length combat documentary *Thunderbolt* (1945), which he codirected with Lieutenant Colonel William Wyler, who was a famous Hollywood film director.

After the war Sturges joined Columbia Pictures as a director of minor films, beginning with *The Man Who Dared* (1946) and including his first Western, *The Walking Hills* (1949) with Randolph Scott. In 1950 he began a five-year association with Metro-Goldwyn-Mayer (MGM) as a contract director. His early films for the studio ranged across several genres, from thrillers (*Mystery Street*, 1950; *Kind Lady*, 1951; *Jeopardy*, 1953) to biographical dramas (*The Magnificent Yankee*, 1950; and *The Girl in White*, 1952). He received his best reviews, however, for his Western *Escape from Fort Bravo* (1953), which starred William Holden as a Union Army captain guarding Confederate prisoners in Indian territory. Sturges's handling of the action sequences, especially a climactic Indian raid, was praised by critics. He followed this film with the suspenseful drama *Bad Day at Black Rock* (1955). A modern-day Western thriller that touched on the subject of racist attitudes, the film starred Spencer Tracy as a one-armed man whose life is threatened when he uncovers a deadly secret in a bleak California town in 1945. The movie made adroit use of the wide CinemaScope screen to suggest the terrifying isolation of the beleaguered hero.

Sturges's subsequent work at MGM and other studios frequently involved hard-bitten men coping with dangerous circumstances. Sometimes they confronted the hazards of war, as in *Never So Few* (1959), *The Great Escape* (1963), and *Ice Station Zebra* (1968). *The Great Escape,* in particular, displayed Sturges's skill at staging action sequences in its rousing story of a mass Allied escape from a maximum-security German prison camp. Most often, however, Sturges's heroes thrived in a Western setting where moral dilemmas led to blistering gun battles—for example, *Gunfight at the O.K. Corral* (1957), *Last Train from Gun Hill* (1959), and *Hour of the Gun* (1967). One of Sturges's most popular Westerns, *The Magnificent Seven* (1960), drew on Akira Kurosawa's Japanese film *Seven Samurai* (1954) to tell its story of seven professional gunmen who are hired by townspeople to rid themselves of bandits.

Sturges's recurring theme of man-against-the-odds also surfaced in his non-Western films. In 1958, taking over from the director Fred Zinnemann, he attempted to turn Ernest Hemingway's novella *The Old Man and the Sea* (1952) into a movie. Despite a stalwart effort by Spencer Tracy to embody Hemingway's tenacious Cuban fisherman in battle with a giant marlin, the story failed to cohere on the screen. Tracy, however, received an Academy Award nomination. There was also little Sturges could do with the turgid screenplay of *By Love Possessed* (1961), based on James Gould Cozzens's best-selling novel about life among upper-crust families in a Massachusetts town.

Sturges directed films intermittently throughout the 1960s and into the 1970s—among them were *The Hallelujah Trail* (1965), *Marooned* (1969), and *Joe Kidd* (1972)—but they were seldom as effective as his earlier efforts. His last film, *The Eagle Has Landed* (1977), was adapted from Jack Higgins's best-selling novel centering on a Nazi plot to kidnap Winston Churchill.

In his last years Sturges, suffering from acute anemia and emphysema, retired to his home in San Luis Obispo He died of a heart attack and was survived by his second wife, Katherine, and by his two children. Never a part of the Hollywood social scene, Sturges took a characteristically straightforward view of his work. "I got in the film business in order to make a living. And I proved fairly good at telling a story on screen. I wound up being a very good producer and director."

Confronted with a hostile and violent world, the men of John Sturges's best films—the gunfighters, the servicemen, and the one-armed stranger—responded with courage and determination. And despite Sturges's casual self-assessment, his skill as a director helped to make them memorable.

★

Sturges's widow donated over forty of his annotated shooting scripts to the Academy of Motion Picture Arts and Sciences in Beverly Hills, California. An article by Sturges, "How the West was Lost," appears in *Film and Filming* (Dec. 1962). A two-part article on Sturges by DuPre Jones, "The Merit of Flying Lead," appears in *Films and Filming* (Jan. 1974 and Jan. 1975). An article on Sturges, written by Glenn Lovell a year after the director's death, can be found in the Knight-Ridder/Tribune News Service (26 Aug. 1993). Obituaries are in the *New York Times* (22 Aug. 1992) and *Variety* (24 Aug. 1992).

TED SENNETT

SULZBERGER, Cyrus Leo (*b.* 27 October 1912 in New York City; *d.* 20 September 1993 in Paris, France), foreign correspondent and foreign affairs columnist for the *New York Times* for almost forty years and author of numerous books on foreign affairs.

Sulzberger was one of two children of Leo Sulzberger, a merchandiser in a cotton import firm, and Beatrice Josephi, a homemaker. Between 1926 and 1930 he attended the Horace Mann School for Boys in New York City. He next attended Harvard College and received a B.S. degree in 1934. Although his uncle Arthur Hays Sulzberger was the publisher of the *New York Times,* his immediate interests after college did not include newspaper reporting. He thought about becoming a poet, a forest ranger, or a mag-

C. L. Sulzberger, 1947. © BETTMANN/CORBIS

azine or book editor—something not connected with the family newspaper. However, to prepare to become a book editor, he took a position with the *Pittsburgh Press* as a reporter and rewrite man. Once employed as a newspaperman, he remained one, and in 1935 he went to work in the Washington Bureau of the United Press reporting on the Federal Reserve System, the Department of the Treasury, and the Department of Labor. In 1938 he left the United Press and wrote his first book, *Sit Down with John L. Lewis.*

Later that year Sulzberger decided to become a foreign affairs correspondent, and he went to Europe, where the Nazis had already taken over Austria and were threatening Czechoslovakia. He stopped first in London, where he worked as a freelance writer, but he soon obtained credentials from the North American Newspaper Alliance and became a stringer for the *London Evening Standard.* He next traveled to Vienna and then Prague, where he met with the Czechoslovakian president Edvard Beneš, who advised him to become a foreign correspondent in the Balkans, an area where there were few or no American reporters.

Sulzberger heeded this advice and in 1938 and 1939 he visited all the Balkan countries as a reporter, writing articles for the *London Evening Standard.* When Mussolini's Italian forces invaded Albania in April 1939, the United Press hired him to cover the invasion, which he did until its conclusion in May. Sometime during the spring of 1939 he also flew to London to meet with his uncle Arthur who asked him to work for the *New York Times.* He refused to join the family firm at this time, but he agreed to become the head of the *Times* Balkan bureau if war erupted.

When Hitler invaded Poland on 1 September 1939, Sulzberger immediately honored his agreement and, during his first three years as a *Times* correspondent, traveled 100,000 miles to thirty countries located in the Balkans, North Africa, and the Middle East, as well as to the Soviet Union and Italy. His experiences during this period were harrowing. Late in 1939 he was arrested as an English spy in German-controlled Slovakia, but was soon released. During the summer of 1940, Axis propagandists started to attack him in their newspapers for his reporting, one calling him a "hate agent." In April 1941 he left Belgrade just ahead of the German invasion and finally arrived in Greece, where the subsequent German advance forced him to escape to Turkey aboard a sponge fisher's boat. In July of that year he went to the Soviet Union to cover its invasion by Germany and won a 1941 Overseas Press Club Award for his reporting on the German-Soviet front.

On 21 January 1942 in Beirut, Lebanon, Sulzberger married Marina Tatiana Lada, a Greek woman whom he had met several years earlier in Athens. The union produced two children. In September 1944 he was made the chief foreign correspondent of the *New York Times* and the head of its foreign service. He was stationed in Paris, which

became his residence for the rest of his life. In this position he traveled around the world visiting many countries and interviewing prominent people, including ministers, presidents, dictators, generals, and royalty. Much of his reporting during his career was based on these types of interviews. His approach emanated from Sulzberger's "great man" view of history—that the prime movers of world events were individuals, not ideologies. Among the many people he interviewed over the years were Charles de Gaulle, Winston Churchill, Dwight Eisenhower, the monarchs of Greece and Yugoslavia, Marshall Josip Tito, Jawaharlal Nehru, John F. Kennedy, Lyndon B. Johnson, Richard Nixon, Nikita Khrushchev, and Zhou Enlai, although it was not until the 1970s that he was finally permitted to visit China. Many of these individuals were willing to talk to him because they knew their views would be reported by a tough but objective correspondent and appear in one of the world's most important newspapers. Sulzberger realized that it was his name and the newspaper behind him that often allowed him access to men and women in power.

In 1951 Sulzberger received a Pulitzer Prize in journalism for his article based on an interview with the Yugoslavian archbishop Aloysius Stepinac, who had been imprisoned in 1946 at the beginning of the cold war. In 1954 he ceased being the *Times's* chief foreign correspondent and became a journalist until his retirement in 1977, writing a column that appeared on the paper's editorial page three times a week and later on the op-ed page.

Along with his activities as a reporter and a columnist, Sulzberger also wrote almost two dozen books over a thirty-year period starting in 1956. Most of them dealt with foreign affairs and included three volumes of memoirs: *A Long Row of Candles* (1969), *The Last of the Giants* (1970), and *An Age of Mediocrity* (1973). Written from working notes made at the time of various interviews, these books say little about Sulzberger but do give some very fine portraits of world leaders and show the author at the scene of momentous world events. Some critics, however, found these books overloaded with minutiae. He died in Paris of natural causes.

Sulzberger's almost forty-year association with the *New York Times* enabled him to cover most of the fronts during World War II and afterward to roam the world interviewing the great and the powerful. He had the ability to arrive in a country and to produce a succinct picture of one of its leaders on the same day. He was a respected, aggressive, and objective reporter who wrote about foreign affairs in an intelligent and perceptive manner, as well as a witness of many of the major events of the twentieth century.

★

The three volumes of Sulzberger's memoirs cited in the text, *A Long Row of Candles* (1969), *The Last of the Giants* (1970), and

An Age of Mediocrity (1973), contain some biographical data, although the greater portion of these works is devoted to his global travels and interviews. His 1980 memoir, *How I Committed Suicide: A Reverie,* conveys his loneliness as a widower and his thoughts on aging. References to his life and career, especially his relations with the publishers and personnel of the *New York Times,* can be found in Gay Talese, *The Kingdom and the Power* (1969); Susan W. Dryfoos, *Iphigene: Memoirs of Iphigene Ochs Sulzberger of the New York Times Family* (1981); Joseph C. Goulden, *Fit to Print: A. M. Rosenthal and His Times* (1988); and Susan E. Tifft and Alex S. Jones, *The Trust: The Private and Powerful Family Behind the New York Times* (1999). The 1944 issue of *Current Biography* contains details of his life up to that date, and there is an obituary in the *New York Times* (21 Sept. 1993).

ALLAN NELSON

SUN RA (*b.* 22 May 1914 in Birmingham, Alabama; *d.* 30 May 1993 in Birmingham, Alabama), influential jazz musician, composer, and orchestra leader.

Sun Ra was born Herman Poole Blount, the son of Cary Blount, a railroad laborer, and Ida Jones. After his parents' marriage failed, his maternal grandmother, Margaret Jones, and his great-aunt Ida Howard raised him. His mother worked at a restaurant near the railroad terminal. Blount often ate in the kitchen there and listened to piano rolls by

Sun Ra, 1990s. JOSEPH A. ROSEN/ARCHIVE PHOTOS

Fats Waller. Other childhood influences included the Tabernacle Baptist Church and the public school where he excelled. At Birmingham Industrial High School, Blount studied under the legendary band director John Tuggle Whatley, who pioneered in securing grants to purchase musical instruments for his students. When Blount formed a band of his own, Whatley bought a bus that enabled his students to tour the South. Blount graduated from high school in 1932 and studied for a year at State Agricultural and Mechanical Institute for Negroes in Normal, Alabama, and in the late 1930s he worked as a professional musician playing around the South and Midwest. A conscientious objector during World War II, he spent a short time in jail and then was excused from service for medical reasons.

In 1946 he moved to Chicago and renamed himself Le Sony'ra, which he legally adopted on 20 October 1952 and which appeared on his passport. In Chicago he backed the rhythm and blues stars Wynonie Blues Harris, B. B. King, Joe Williams, and LaVerne Baker and led the house band at the Club De Lisa, one of the city's better nightclubs. He was also a sideman for Coleman Hawkins and served for a year in Fletcher Henderson's Orchestra, learning from two artists he revered. Throughout this period, Le Sony'ra conducted jam sessions. Though one participant likened these nonstop events to boot camps, musicians flocked to jam with the Arkestra, as it became known. Jam sessions flowed into rehearsals and then into performances, establishing Le Sony'ra's reputation among jazz artists.

By 1952 he had renamed himself Sun Ra and refused to acknowledge his birthplace or date, insisting that he was an extraterrestrial. His name signified the bandleader's deep fascination with outer space and ancient Egypt, through which he intended to reawaken African Americans to historical black achievement. He established his own record label, Saturn, which he occasionally renamed Thoth. He was a voracious reader of W. E. B. Du Bois and several Egyptologists. He decorated stage sets for his concerts with Egyptian hieroglyphics and dressed himself and the band in Egyptian costumes. A second theme was hostility to Christianity, which Sun Ra contended had negated black history and seduced African Americans into a secondary status. In the 1950s Sun Ra issued codebooks that used numerology to make radical reinterpretations of the Bible through Egyptology. He also disliked the use by the Christian civil rights movement of the Exodus myth, which he regarded as misguided because of its use of conventional politics. However flamboyant and controversial, Sun Ra and his philosophy fit into an ongoing black intellectual dialogue about history and civilization.

Sun Ra and the Arkestra initially issued songs on 45 rpm records. Although he recorded virtually everything he played, innumerable albums were not released until years after their creation. His albums, many with hand-painted covers, were sold only by mail order or after concerts and were replaced with new recordings on a monthly basis. Sun Ra moved to New York City in 1961. There his music featured references to space travel, another significant subtheme in African American mythology. He used space travel to express the loneliness of the black musician and to forecast a technological future of electronic instruments (which he introduced to jazz) and computers. For example, he insisted that black youth had to stay in school and study electronics and engineering to prepare them for future space travel. His band appeared under numerous names. The poet Amiri Baraka recalled one day in which Sun Ra and the Myth Science Arkestra marched across 125th Street in Manhattan, announcing the Black Arts Movement of the 1960s by proclaiming, "We Travel in Space Ways." Their most significant venue was Slug's, a sawdust bar on East Fourth Street in lower Manhattan, where the Arkestra held Monday evening sessions until late into the night. The tiny, dark bar was always packed and lit only by films projected against the wall. Each performance was unique, including space music as well as reinterpretations of compositions by Duke Ellington and Jelly Roll Morton.

Baraka called the Arkestra a family "whose life was music." Key members included the baritonist Pat Patrick, the tenor saxophonist John Gilmore, and Marshall Allen, alto saxophonist. For one concert in Central Park, Sun Ra was able to summon more than 100 alumni of his Arkestra. In an interview with the Nigerian journalist Tam Fiofori, Sun Ra offered thanks to his innumerable bands, whether popular or not, for being "truly natural Black Beauty."

His fascination with outer space was reflected in his many recordings. Albums such as *Rocket Number Nine Take Off for the Planet Venus* (1959), *We Travel the Spaceways* (1961), and *The Futuristic Sounds of Sun Ra* (1961) were released on Saturn Records or on ESP Records. Each album of songs about space travel and an imminent technological future was expressed as sermons and spiritual chants. In concerts, the Arkestra danced through the audience in a counterclockwise circle, akin to "ring shouts" once used by enslaved African Americans.

Sun Ra's career blossomed after his move to Philadelphia in 1968, where he maintained a cooperative musical society until his death. In succeeding decades, Sun Ra was constantly in demand for concerts and festivals worldwide; his earlier albums, now collectors' items, were rereleased by Evidence Records. His discography lists more than 500 recordings over a forty-seven-year career. Sun Ra inspired John Coltrane and Pharoah Sanders, among many others, to honor Africa in their compositions. His space imagery recurs in the music of pop performers such as Parliament Funkadelic and Prince. Holistic in his use of sources and instruments, he transformed pop culture into experimental jazz. He died of a heart attack in 1993, the result of a series of strokes that were worsened by his indifference to curative drugs and physical therapy. Sun Ra is not known to have ever married, and he left no survivors.

★

Book-length studies on Sun Ra include John F. Szwed, *Space Is the Place: The Lives and Times of Sun Ra* (1997), and Graham Lock, *Blutopia: Visions of the Future and Revisions of the Past in the Work of Sun Ra, Duke Ellington, and Anthony Braxton* (1999). See also Valerie Wilmer, *As Serious as Your Life: The Story of the New Jazz* (1977). A full discography is Robert L. Campbell, *The Earthly Recordings of Sun Ra* (1994). Articles include Amiri Baraka, "Sun Ra," *African American Review* 29 (1996): 249–251. An obituary is in the *New York Times* (31 May 1993). Sun Ra's performances may be seen in *Sun Ra: A Joyful Noise* (Rhapsody Films, 1980) and *Space is the Place* (Rhapsody Films, 1993). A vast array of his albums are available on compact discs.

GRAHAM RUSSELL HODGES

SWANBERG, W(illiam) A(ndrew) (*b.* 23 November 1907 in St. Paul, Minnesota; *d.* 17 September 1992 in Southbury, Connecticut), biographer best known for his entertaining yet meticulously researched portrayals of colorful American publishing figures and business tycoons.

Swanberg was the son of Charles Henning Swanberg and Valborg Larsen. He received a B.A. in literature from the University of Minnesota in 1930 and took graduate courses there in 1931. He then worked at a variety of jobs before becoming an assistant editor at Dell Publishing Company in New York City in 1935. On 21 March 1936 he married Dorothy Upham Green with whom he would have two children, and that year he was named editor at Dell Publishing. Swanberg remained as editor until 1944, when he spent a year as a writer for the U.S. Office of War Information in Europe. Upon his return to the United States, Swanberg settled in Newton, Connecticut, and in 1945 turned to freelance writing for the remainder of his career. He wrote magazine articles and book reviews before turning to biography in 1956.

Swanberg's favorite subjects were controversial people, and he was known for writing entertaining biographies of colorful American tycoons, including the publishing giants William Randolph Hearst, Joseph Pulitzer, and Henry R. Luce. *Citizen Hearst,* published in 1961, won the Frank Luther Mott–Kappa Tau Alpha Award and was recommended by the Pulitzer advisory committee for the prize for biography. For the first time in forty-six years the advisory committee was overruled by the trustees of Columbia University, and no prize for biography was awarded that year. Allegedly rejected due to its subject matter because Hearst and Pulitzer were newspaper publishing rivals, the book consequently became a best-seller. It was critically acclaimed for giving a balanced, sophisticated view of Hearst, whose excesses Swanberg neither excused nor condemned. In 1961 the *Christian Science Monitor* reviewer E.

W. A. Swanberg, 1973. AP/WIDE WORLD PHOTOS

D. Canham called the work "a big step forward from the several biased biographies which . . . preceded it."

Swanberg's sympathetic presentation of tycoons such as Hearst has been compared to the writing of Theodore Dreiser, who also became the subject of one of Swanberg's biographies in 1965. Like Hearst, Dreiser wanted to make an impression on the times and to extend his influence through his publications. As a biographer Swanberg was drawn to these larger-than-life men. With *Dreiser,* Swanberg was criticized for not dealing directly with the subject's writing, choosing instead to focus on his life as an opinionated social commentator and critic. As Swanberg explained in his "Author's Note" for *Dreiser,* he preferred to "study the whole man. . . . For a quarter-century he waged a violent battle against censorship of art, and his works, if not his words, had a large share in the victory."

Two years after *Dreiser,* Swanberg published *Pulitzer* (1967), which most reviewers considered even better than *Citizen Hearst.* Swanberg's meticulous research particularly impressed reviewers who were happy to see new information gleaned from the Pulitzer papers. The biography was hailed as the first concerning Pulitzer that had real depth and breadth and provided rich detail and insight into the incredible life of the publishing magnate.

Swanberg's success continued with the Pulitzer Prize winner *Luce and His Empire* (1973), as entertaining and informative as his earlier books. However, some reviewers felt Swanberg was not objective enough in his treatment of Henry Luce. They praised the book as interesting and important but felt it had a general tone of hostility rather than criticism of its subject. In his narrative Swanberg made the assertion that without Luce no China lobby, no Senator Joseph McCarthy, and no national hysteria over Asian communism would have existed, a claim many reviewers thought excessive. Others noted Swanberg's impeccable research and predicted the book would be the definitive biography of Luce.

Swanberg wrote ten books in all, the first of which was *Sickles the Incredible,* published in 1956. Sickles, a congressman, was tried for the murder of his wife's lover but became a Union general in the Civil War. Swanberg's other works include *First Blood: The Story of Fort Sumter,* published in 1957, two years before he turned to biography as his sole focus with *Jim Fisk: The Career of an Improbable Rascal* (1959). He won the National Book Award in 1977 for his portrait of the American socialist politician Norman Thomas in *Norman Thomas: The Last Idealist* (1976).

Swanberg's final book, published in 1980, was *Whitney Father, Whitney Heiress,* in which he profiled the New York publisher and diplomat John Hay Whitney and his daughter Dorothy Whitney. While the elder Whitney fit Swanberg's preferred "robber baron" type of character, the daughter, according to Barbara Klaw in *American Heritage,* "grew up, astonishingly enough, with a very unWhitney-like social conscience." Klaw concluded that Swanberg was "obviously intrigued by the duplicity of the father, but his affection [was] reserved for the gentle and honorable daughter."

Swanberg was not an academic and, thus, did not have the academic's respect for the text nor the academic's duty to prove his or her points. His research was praised as thorough and meticulous, yet his entertaining style and ability to present balanced, detailed portraits of colorful public figures made his books best-sellers. Some became classics in the genre of biography. Swanberg died of heart failure in Southbury.

★

Reviews of Swanberg's books are E. D. Canham, "Citizen Hearst," *Christian Science Monitor* (14 Sept. 1961); Barbara Klaw, "Whitney Father, Whitney Heiress," *American Heritage* 31, no. 4 (June/July 1980); J.K. Galbraith, "Whitney Father, Whitney Heiress," *New York Times Book Review* 85, no. 30 (1980): 108; and E. F. Goldman, "Citizen Hearst," *New York Times Book Review* 86, no. 35 (1981). Biographical information and some critical discussion are in *Contemporary Authors,* vols. 5–8 (1962), *The Writers Directory: 1992–1994* (1992), and *Dictionary of Literary Biography,* vol. 103 (1991). Obituaries are in the *New York Times* and the *Washington Post* (both 20 Sept. 1992), and *The Annual Obituary 1992* (1993).

NAN POLLOT

T

TAFT, Robert, Jr. (*b.* 26 February 1917 in Cincinnati, Ohio; *d.* 7 December 1993 in Cincinnati, Ohio), U.S. representative and senator from Ohio, known for his staunch advocacy of conservative policies during the John F. Kennedy, Lyndon B. Johnson, Richard M. Nixon, and Gerald Ford administrations.

The second of four sons born to Robert Alphonso Taft, a U.S. senator from Ohio and two-time presidential contender, and Martha Wheaton Bowers, a homemaker, the younger Taft's career in public service was virtually predetermined. Taft was the great-grandson of Alphonso Taft, President Grant's secretary of war and attorney general, and grandson of William Howard Taft, chief justice of the U.S. Supreme Court and twenty-seventh president. Taft completed his primary schooling in the Cincinnati public schools, proceeding then to Cincinnati Country Day School and the Taft School in Watertown, Connecticut, a preparatory school founded by his great-uncle. Taft matriculated at Yale, where he competed in freshman crew and junior varsity football, majored in English, and joined both the Delta Kappa Epsilon fraternity and the campus literary club. In his junior year Taft got his formal initiation to politics by working on his father's senatorial campaign. He graduated with a B.A. degree in 1939 and on 27 June of that year he married Blanca Duncan Noel, with whom he had four children. He enrolled in Harvard Law School, where in 1942 he earned an LL.B. degree. Taft, an ensign

in the U.S. Naval Reserve, then went on wartime active duty, attended the Naval War College, and participated in Allied operations at Guadalcanal, Sicily, Salerno, Normandy, and Okinawa. His active duty ended in January 1946, when he was discharged as a lieutenant.

In the decade after the war Taft's career followed a path into politics common in his family. As an associate and eventual partner in the firm Taft, Stettinius, and Hollister, he specialized in corporate and adoption law. He gained some political experience as an adviser to his father's presidential bids of 1948 and 1952 and, upon his father's death in 1953, became the presumptive candidate for the vacant Senate seat. He brushed aside overtures from Republican party officials, favoring instead additional political experience within Ohio. In 1954 he easily won the Hamilton County seat in the state House of Representatives, where he emphasized the issues of child welfare, aging, and mental health, while serving on the Finance, Industry and Labor, Welfare and Insurance, and Judiciary committees. Voters returned Taft to Columbus three more times, and his colleagues in the House elected him a majority floor leader for 1961–1962.

Taft entered the national legislative scene in 1962. After briefly considering a run against the incumbent Democratic senator Frank Lausche, Taft chose instead to run for an at-large congressional seat. During the campaign he attacked the Kennedy administration for its advocacy of large government programs as well as for deficit spending and weak foreign policy, especially in its handling of Cuba. In November Taft easily defeated Democratic candidate Richard D. Kennedy. Upon being sworn in he was assigned to the House Banking and Currency and Education and Labor committees; was given positions on the Domestic Finance, Bank Supervision, Insurance, and Labor subcommittees; and was chosen leader of the House Republican freshman class. During his initial term Taft made known his views on important issues, including his support for the Civil Rights Act, vocational training, and extension of the Selective Service Act. He also was opposed to additional offices to administer antipoverty programs and to federal court interference in state reapportionment.

Taft's political fortunes took a downward turn in 1964, when he chose to forgo reelection to the House and run instead for a Senate seat occupied by Democrat Stephen M. Young. In the campaign, Taft's close association with the controversial Republican presidential candidate Barry Goldwater became an issue and the November election saw Taft swept away with the anti-Goldwater tide. Afterward Taft stayed active in national politics, serving as the chair of a Republican committee on government relations that recommended returning federal tax money to states with few conditions.

Taft returned to elective politics in January 1966 when he announced his candidacy for U.S. Representative from Ohio's First District. His opponent, the incumbent Democrat John J. Gilligan, largely supported the positions of the Johnson administration, while Taft ran on business-investment tax credits, cutting non-defense spending, investigating waste in federal poverty programs, and greater openness in foreign policy. His victory in November sent him to Washington once again, where he was assigned to the House Foreign Affairs committee and European Relations and Foreign Economic Policy subcommittees. In the House he continued to campaign against excessive spending and extension of executive military powers, while supporting humanitarian aid to India. Taft faced no serious challenge in 1968 and was easily reelected.

In 1970 Taft once again made a bid for a Senate seat. After defeating the popular governor James A. Rhodes in the Republican primary by a mere 6,000 votes, Taft went on to win a hotly contested general election against businessman Howard Metzenbaum. Assigned to the Senate Armed Services, Labor and Public Welfare, and Banking, Currency, and Housing committees, Taft deviated little from the legislative program he had followed in the House. He continued to pursue his interests in the areas of health, justice, and economic antidiscrimination, authoring legislation to extend the National Labor Relations Act to healthcare workers and advocating amnesty for those who had avoided the draft in opposition to the Vietnam War. He generally supported the Nixon administration's foreign policy positions, favored work programs for those receiving food stamps; advocated tax credits for private education, and pushed for some pro-labor legislation.

Taft's political career came to an end in 1976 when, as a result of the Watergate backlash, he lost his reelection bid to Metzenbaum. Fatigued and frustrated with public life, Taft resigned his seat a month after the general election and returned to the practice of law as a partner in his family's firm. He divided his time between Washington, D.C., and Cincinnati prior to retirement from his legal practice in 1988. In late November 1993 Taft suffered a stroke, fell into a coma, and died little more than a week later at the age of seventy-six. He is buried at the Indian Hill Episcopal Church Cemetery in Cincinnati.

Taft was a low-key champion of conservative issues. Although he was a standard-bearer for a famous American political family, he shunned the spotlight and approached public service as an obligation and, often, as a burden. Toward the end of his career, Taft moderated his conservative views and more frequently championed legislation benefiting labor and minority groups, which both brought him into conflict with Republican colleagues and gained for him enduring recognition from citizens across the political spectrum.

★

Biographical material on Taft appears in Ishbel Ross, *An American Family: The Tafts* (1964); Max Charles Graeber, "An Analysis of the Speaking of Robert Taft Jr. Before Selected Audiences" (M.A. Thesis, Bowling Green State University, 1965); *Current Biography Yearbook 1967; Biographical Directory of the American Congress, 1774–1971* (1971); *Congressional Directory, Ninety-Third Congress, Second Session* (1974); Nelson Lichtenstein, ed., *Political Profiles: "The Nixon/Ford Years"* (1979); and L. Sandy Maisel, ed., *Political Parties and Elections in the United States: An Encyclopedia* (1991). Obituaries are in the *New York Times* and *Washington Post* (both 8 Dec. 1993).

RAYMOND D. IRWIN

TAYLOR, Harold Alexander (*b.* 28 September 1914 in Toronto, Canada; *d.* 9 February 1993 in New York City), educator and public intellectual who attracted national attention for his spirited leadership of Sarah Lawrence College during the McCarthy era.

Taylor was the second of two children born to Elizabeth Henderson Wilson and Charles William Taylor. His British-born father worked as a government employee and lay minister in Canada and his mother was a homemaker.

In 1926 while a student at Riverside Collegiate School in Toronto, Taylor's interest in music led him backstage after a Duke Ellington concert. In answer to the eleven-year-old's question about how to become a great player,

Harold Taylor, 1964. AP/WIDE WORLD PHOTOS

Ellington told Taylor, "Take that clarinet and keep on playing it till it sounds real pretty." A few years later Taylor hitchhiked to New York City where he subsisted on bananas and cereal just so he could hear the great jazz artists of the day. He became an accomplished classical and jazz clarinetist. His dedication to music and musicians and to the arts and artists were elements in a philosophy that emphasized individual freedom and creativity. This philosophy sustained Taylor throughout his life.

At the University of Toronto, Taylor earned an A.B. degree in literature in 1935 and an M.A. degree in philosophy and literature in 1936. In 1938 he was awarded a doctorate in philosophy from the University of London. He supported his studies in England by writing a jazz column and playing in jazz bands, frequently aboard cruise ships. It was on one of these voyages that he met Grace Muriel Thorne, whom he married on 8 November 1940. The marriage produced two daughters and ended in divorce in 1968.

From 1939 to 1945 Taylor taught philosophy at the University of Wisconsin in Madison. For part of this time he also contributed to the war effort as a researcher on a classified project for the Office of Scientific Research and Development of the U.S. Navy. He became a naturalized U.S. citizen in 1947.

In 1945 the thirty-year-old Taylor became the youngest college president in the country when he was chosen to lead Sarah Lawrence College. An exclusive, progressive, liberal arts college for women located in Bronxville, New York, just north of New York City, Sarah Lawrence became the focus of national attention as a celebrated target of the forces of McCarthyism during the early 1950s. Twelve members of the faculty of seventy were subpoenaed to testify about possible links to the Communist party. Assaulted at the national level by the Jenner Committee on Internal Security and the House Un-American Activities Committee and attacked locally by the Westchester County American Legion, Sarah Lawrence students, faculty, and trustees rallied around President Taylor. With a campus composed of such renowned faculty colleagues as the sociologist Helen Merrell Lynd, mythologist Joseph Campbell, classicist Horace Gregory, and poet Stephen Spender—some of whom were themselves staunchly anticommunist—it was no easy task for Taylor to emerge as an activist champion of academic freedom.

Taylor's position gave him a bully pulpit from which to argue the legitimacy of Sarah Lawrence's curricular emphasis on an active, experimental, student-centered approach to liberal arts education and prepared him for his outspoken and eloquent opposition to threats to liberty in culture, politics, and education. The issues of the student revolution in American universities became Taylor's issues. The themes of a radical pedagogy, personal freedom, and institutional transformation were expressed in two early books, *Essays in Teaching* (1950) and *On Education and Freedom* (1954). Taylor returned to these concerns again in *Students Without Teachers: The Crisis in the University* (1969) and *How to Change Colleges: Notes on Radical Reform* (1971).

As the president of Sarah Lawrence College, Taylor often functioned as an intellectual and artistic entrepreneur. Contemporaries marveled at his ability to weave people together in cultural and political causes. Taylor introduced the British poet Stephen Spender to American college audiences. He attracted the writers Randall Jarrell and Mary McCarthy to Sarah Lawrence. Consequently, Jarrell's book *Pictures from an Institution: A Comedy* (1954) and, to a lesser degree, McCarthy's book *The Groves of Academe* (1952) sparkle with satirical reflections of the political and intellectual intrigues of the American professorate derived from Sarah Lawrence under Taylor.

Starting early in their years at Sarah Lawrence, the Taylor family spent the summers in Holderness, New Hampshire, at Brushwood, a commodious cottage on White Oaks Pond. It was there that Taylor did most of his writing. For four decades the house was a gathering place for intellectuals and social activists including Norman Cousins, Rollo May, Gardner Murphy, and Tom Hayden and Jane Fonda.

In January 1959 notice of Taylor's sudden resignation

from Sarah Lawrence appeared in more than 100 newspapers across the country. It sent a shock wave through the campus community. Students and alumni pleaded for him to stay. Taylor argued, however, that being a college president had deteriorated from a position of being first among scholarly and artistic peers to the role of a manager and fund-raiser. His retirement party at the Waldorf-Astoria Hotel in New York City drew more than 1,300 people. Hosted by the CBS vice president Edward R. Murrow, speakers included Eleanor Roosevelt, Archibald MacLeish, Robert Frost, and J. Robert Oppenheimer.

For the next fifteen years Taylor refused repeated offers to return to full-time university teaching or administration. He admitted that his presidency had spoiled him for similar posts. Taylor was determined to make his living as what he termed an "itinerant intellectual," to concentrate on speaking out and writing on world and national cultural issues. His new career was launched almost immediately. In late 1959 and 1960 with support from the Ford Foundation, he spent six months traveling and lecturing in Japan, Indonesia, India, and the Soviet Union. Upon his return to the United States he immersed himself in projects designed to internationalize the experiences of American undergraduates. He elaborated his proposals in a book that was the culmination of two years of study, *The World as Teacher* (1969).

A popular speaker, Taylor addressed hundreds of college audiences. A bibliography of his writings includes more than 500 items. He was a frequent contributor to the *Saturday Review*, the *Herald Tribune*, the *New York Times, Change*, and numerous educational journals.

Taylor served many organizations. He chaired the board of the independent and iconoclastic radio station WBAI (1963–1972), was a member of the League for Industrial Democracy (1964–1980), and was a consultant to the Students for a Democratic Society (SDS). Additionally, he worked for the Eleanor Roosevelt Memorial Foundation, was vice president of the Martha Graham School of Dance (1964–1971), president of the American Ballet Theatre (1965–1967), and president of the Agnes de Mille Dance Theatre (1970–1975).

In 1975 Taylor returned to academe as a Distinguished Professor at Staten Island College of the City University of New York. He was instrumental in the creation of an international studies program, a poetry center, and a high school for international service. In 1982 at his second retirement party, a surprise tribute lightheartedly memorialized him as the "Ideal Passenger" and was presented to him by his "chauffeur," a captain on the Staten Island Ferry. During his retirement years Taylor returned each summer to his beloved Brushwood, where he continued to write.

At the time of his death from natural causes in New York City, he was at work on his autobiography. Taylor is buried in the cemetery in Holderness.

★

Extensive archival materials for Taylor including manuscripts, speeches, correspondence, FBI files, project materials, and notes are housed in the Museum of Education at the University of South Carolina in Columbia, South Carolina. A smaller collection of materials is located in the archives at Sarah Lawrence College in Bronxville. Autobiographical material from an oral history project conducted by Carole Nichols for Sarah Lawrence College can be found at both locations. An obituary is in the *New York Times* (10 Feb. 1993).

JOSEPH G. FLYNN

THOMAS, Danny (*b.* 6 January 1912 in Deerfield, Michigan; *d.* 6 February 1991 in Los Angeles, California), nightclub entertainer, singer, comedian, television and film actor, television producer, and philanthropist.

Thomas was the fifth of ten children born to immigrant parents from the small village of Becheri, Lebanon. He was

Danny Thomas. ARCHIVE PHOTOS

born Muzyad Yakhoob, but when his father later Christianized the names of the family, he became Amos Jacobs. His father, Charles, was a horse farmer, and his mother, Margaret Simon, was a homemaker. When the young Thomas's father lost his horse farm in a card game, the family immigrated to Toledo, Ohio, where his father became a factory laborer. Thomas went to live with his beloved aunt and uncle until he was fifteen.

By the age of twelve Amos was selling soda pop at the Empire Burlesque Theater in Toledo, watching comedians perform. At sixteen he dropped out of high school, his mind set on a show business career. He landed his first show business job as a regular on amateur radio in Detroit on *The Happy Hour Club* in 1932, where he met another regular, Rose Marie Cassaniti, whom he married shortly thereafter in 1936. They had three children. Their eldest child, Margaret Julia ("Marlo"), became a celebrity in her own right.

Leaving his new family, Thomas traveled alone to Chicago, getting jobs as a radio character actor and a saloon entertainer. Ashamed that his family would be embarrassed if they heard he was working in saloons, he changed his name in 1940, adopting his oldest brother's first name, Daniel, and his youngest brother's name, Thomas, to create the stage name Danny Thomas, which would be his for the rest of his life.

By 1942 Thomas was working full time at the 5100 Club in Chicago, where he was a huge success. Abe Lastfogel, owner of the William Morris Agency, saw Danny perform here and signed him to the agency. His career grew as he performed in New York nightclubs such as La Martinique and on Ed Sullivan's *The Night of Stars* at Madison Square Garden. At the start of World War II, Thomas volunteered for military service, but they were not accepting married fathers. President Franklin D. Roosevelt put Lastfogel in charge of organizing USO shows, and Thomas "found" himself in the USO as an emcee with Marlene Dietrich, entertaining U.S. troops in North Africa and Europe. After the war he and his family moved to Beverly Hills, California.

In the late 1940s and early 1950s, Thomas made several motion pictures, including *The Unfinished Dance* (1947), *The Big City* (1948), *Call Me Mister* (1951), *I'll See You in My Dreams* (1951), and his favorite, *The Jazz Singer* (1953), in which he portrayed Al Jolson. He did an early television variety show, *All Star Revue* (which later evolved into *The Colgate Comedy Hour*), alternating with other comedians, such as Milton Berle, Jimmy Durante, and Ed Wynn, but he left unhappily in 1952, after two years, calling television "a workplace for idiots."

In 1953, however, he returned to television in *Make Room for Daddy,* which after three years became *The Danny Thomas Show,* one of the longest running situation comedies in television history. The show lasted for eleven years and was modeled on his own life. The title, suggested by his wife, was a phrase his children had used when he would come home from a road trip because they would have to shift bedrooms to accommodate their father. He would never achieve such acting success as he did on this show, which ended in 1964, even though he tried again in other series, such as *Make Room for Granddaddy* (1970) and *The Practice* (1976), both of which lasted only one season.

In the meantime, however, Thomas had become a successful television producer, first with Sheldon Leonard and then with Aaron Spelling. The series he coproduced with Leonard included *The Real McCoys* (1957–1963); *The Andy Griffith Show* (1960–1968); *The Dick Van Dyke Show* (1961–1966); and *Gomer Pyle, U.S.M.C.* (1964–1970). Those produced with Spelling included *The Mod Squad* (1968–1973) and *The Guns of Will Sonnett* (1967–1969).

Thomas was also well known for his philanthropic work on behalf of St. Jude Children's Research Hospital in Memphis, Tennessee, which he founded in 1962 as a result of a promise he had made in the difficult early days of his career when his wife was urging him to give up show business and get a regular job. He prayed to St. Jude Thaddaeus, the patron saint of hopeless, impossible, and difficult causes, asking the saint to give him a sign, to put him on the right path, promising that if the saint did so, he would build him a shrine. Shortly thereafter, he landed the job at the 5100 Club. Years later, Thomas kept his promise. It is estimated that he raised over $1 billion for the hospital, which is widely regarded as the world's premier institution for the study and treatment of childhood diseases, such as acute lymphocytic leukemia and other pediatric illnesses once categorized as incurable. For his humanitarian work, Thomas received numerous awards, including the Congressional Gold Medal presented to him in 1984 by a former fellow actor, President Ronald Reagan.

Shortly before his death Thomas appeared in a Legends of Comedy Act with Milton Berle and Sid Caesar. He died of a heart attack 6 February 1991 in Los Angeles, at the age of seventy-nine. He had just completed a series of coast-to-coast interviews in connection with his autobiography, *Make Room for Danny,* and had just stopped in Memphis to help celebrate the twenty-ninth anniversary of St. Jude Children's Research Hospital. His body is entombed on the grounds of the hospital.

Thomas brought the art of the storyteller to the arena of nightclub entertainment. He was known for stretching a story, carrying his audience with him in anticipation of the punch line, which, when it arrived, caused roars of delight in his listeners. His television shows were family-oriented, the type of entertainment that could be shared by everyone. This wholesome sense of entertainment extended to his humanitarian efforts, which were devoted to restoring sick, sometimes terminally diagnosed, children back to their families' arms.

★

Danny Thomas's autobiography, *Make Room for Danny,* written with Bill Davidson (1991), is filled with personal anecdotal details. Obituaries are in the *New York Times* (7 Feb. 1991) and the *Atlanta Constitution* (6 Feb. 1991).

JOHN J. BYRNE

THOMAS, Lewis (*b.* 25 November 1913 in New York City; *d.* 4 December 1993 in New York City), physician, scientist, administrator, and essayist, whose collection of "biology-watching" essays, *The Lives of a Cell: Notes of a Biology Watcher* (1974), won a National Book Award.

Lewis Thomas was born in Flushing, Queens, the fourth child and first of two sons of Joseph Simon Thomas, a physician, and Grace Emma Peck, a nurse. Thomas often accompanied his father on house calls to patients, observing the physician's work life and learning the extent to which medicine in the early twentieth century was tentative and intuitive rather than definitive and knowledgeable. He developed two lifelong traits, empathy and curiosity, which directed him toward medicine as both practitioner and researcher and later emerged in his literary writing.

At the age of fifteen Thomas graduated from the Mc-

Lewis Thomas. AP/WIDE WORLD PHOTOS

Burney School, a private day school in Manhattan. He received a B.S. degree in biology from Princeton University in 1933, graduated cum laude from Harvard Medical School in 1937, interned for two years at Boston City Hospital, and completed his residency at Columbia Presbyterian Medical Center in 1941. That year he and Beryl Dawson were married in January; they had three daughters.

As a medical officer in the U.S. Navy from 1942 to 1946, Thomas researched infectious diseases on Guam and Okinawa. Following his discharge he took a series of positions in medical schools at Johns Hopkins University (1946–1948), Tulane University (1948–1950), the University of Minnesota (1950–1954), and New York University (1954–1966), where he served as dean of the School of Medicine (1966–1969). He moved to the Yale University School of Medicine in 1969 and served as its dean from 1972 to 1973. Thomas then joined the Memorial Sloan-Kettering Cancer Center in New York City, where he was president and chief executive officer (1973–1980), chancellor (1980–1983), and finally president emeritus in 1983.

Even as an administrator Thomas remained active as a researcher. He published more than 200 scientific articles on such subjects as endotoxins, virology, and infectious diseases. The New York University dean Dr. Saul Farber described him as "the father of modern immunology and experimental pathology." His contributions to medical science led to a number of awards and honors, including the 1983 Association of American Physicians Kober Medal, the 1986 dedication of Princeton University's molecular biology facility as the Lewis Thomas Laboratory, and the first John Stearns Award for Lifetime Achievement in Medicine from the New York Academy of Medicine in 1991.

While scientific and medical honors accumulated, Thomas also established himself as a literary essayist. From 1971 to 1980 Thomas contributed a monthly column, "Notes of a Biology Watcher," to the *New England Journal of Medicine.* The popularity of the column beyond the medical community led to the compilation of a book, *The Lives of a Cell: Notes of a Biology Watcher* (1974), which was both a popular and a critical success and won the National Book Award for arts and letters that year. A second collection from the column, *The Medusa and the Snail: More Notes of a Biology Watcher* (1979), won the Christopher Award and the American Book Award for Science. After shifting his column to *Discover* magazine in 1980, he published a third collection, *Late Night Thoughts on Listening to Mahler's Ninth Symphony* (1983). His other writing included a memoir in *The Youngest Science: Notes of a Medicine-Watcher* (1983), poetry in *Could I Ask You Something?* (1985), essays on language in *Et Cetera, et Cetera: Notes of a Word-Watcher* (1990), and articles and addresses in *The Fragile Species* (1992).

The Lives of a Cell won the National Book Award after

being nominated by both the arts and letters panel and the science panel, a situation that points to Thomas's unique position as both scientist and writer. He wrote gracefully, even lyrically, often linking scientific and medical issues to social and philosophical issues. He emphasized the interconnectedness of life, using as examples the symbiotic presence of mitochondria in every human cell and the interdependent life cycles of the medusa jellyfish and the nudibranch snail. On the return of astronauts from the moon he asserted in an essay in *Lives of a Cell,* "Most of the associations between the living things we know about are essentially cooperative ones, symbiotic in one degree or another. . . . Every creature is, in some sense, connected to the rest." In *Late Night Thoughts* he described the earth as "a living system, an immense organism, still developing, regulating itself, . . . keeping all its infinite parts connected and interdependent, including us." Some critics found this perspective too optimistic, though Thomas was capable, as in his essays on thermonuclear destruction, of a grimness close to despair. His thorough scientific grounding made his arguments for organicism, the view of the whole earth as a living membrane, seem less a kind of mystical wishful thinking and more a rational and expansive interpretation of evidence.

Thomas's essays, particularly in the later collections, drew on the example of Montaigne by exploring and exposing the workings of the writer's mind. Perhaps in line with his own view of the interconnectedness of things, his essays demonstrated the ability of a scientific specialist to communicate to a general readership about matters that were both narrowly technical and broadly relevant. Many of his awards and honors were for his ability to be at the same time a sharply focused scientist and a richly communicative writer, simultaneously bringing science out of the laboratory into the larger community and bringing the larger community into the laboratory.

In 1988 Thomas was diagnosed with Waldenström's disease, a rare form of cancer. He died at age eighty at New York Hospital in Manhattan on 4 December 1993.

★

Lewis Thomas, *The Youngest Science: Notes of a Medicine-Watcher* (1983), mixes autobiography with medical history. Andrew J. Angyal, *Lewis Thomas* (1989), is the only book-length biographical-critical study of his writing. Profiles include Jeremy Bernstein, "Lewis Thomas: Life of a Biology Watcher," in *Experiencing Science* (1978), and Roger Rosenblatt, "Lewis Thomas," *New York Times Magazine* (21 Nov. 1993). Significant articles on his literary nonfiction include Howard Nemerov, "Lewis Thomas, Montaigne, and Human Happiness," in *New and Selected Essays* (1985); Steven Weiland, "'A Tune Beyond Us, Yet Ourselves': Medical Science and Lewis Thomas," *Michigan Quarterly Review* 24 (spring 1985); Chris Anderson, "Error, Ambiguity, and the

Peripheral: Teaching Lewis Thomas," in *Literary Nonfiction: Theory, Criticism, Pedagogy* (1989); and Alison R. Byerly, "Lewis Thomas (1913–1993)" in *American Nature Writers* (1996). An obituary is in the *New York Times* (4 Dec. 1993).

ROBERT L. ROOT, JR.

TIERNEY, Gene Eliza (*b.* 19 November 1920 in Brooklyn, New York; *d.* 6 November 1991 in Houston, Texas), popular film actress of the 1940s noted for her roles in *Laura* and *Leave Her to Heaven.*

Tierney was one of three children of Howard Sherwood Tierney, a successful insurance broker, and Belle Lavina Taylor, a homemaker. The family moved during her childhood to suburban Fairfield County, Connecticut, where Tierney was raised comfortably, riding horses, going to country club parties, and attending private schools in Connecticut and Switzerland. She spoke French fluently and enjoyed writing poetry.

In 1938 while touring the Warner Brothers Studio during a family vacation in Los Angeles, California, the seventeen-year-old Tierney's high cheekbones, blue-green

Gene Tierney. THE KOBAL COLLECTION

eyes, and sensuous overbite caught the attention of the director Anatole Litvak. He talked her into a screen test, but her father objected to her taking the offer of a standard studio contract. Tierney returned to Connecticut to finish a final year of school and to make her social debut.

She was determined, however, to be an actress. Her father formed a family corporation to promote her work on the New York stage. One early part called on her to carry a bucket of water, spurring a *Variety* reviewer to note, "Miss Tierney is certainly the most beautiful water-carrier I've ever seen!"

While still a teenager in 1939 she signed a film contract with Columbia, then moved to Twentieth Century–Fox in 1940. Her first major film, *The Return of Frank James,* was released that year. When she saw her performance she was shocked at the high pitch of her voice and started smoking heavily to lower it. Elegant, cultured, and stunning, she cut a wide swath through Hollywood, clubbing with directors, actors, and producers. On 1 July 1941, acting against her parents' wishes, she eloped with the designer Oleg Cassini. It caused a rift with her father that was worsened when her father's infidelity led to a divorce from her mother.

Tierney's 1941 films—*Tobacco Road, Hudson's Bay, Belle Starr,* and *Sundown*—quickly established her as a rising young star. The studio worked her hard; in 1942 she appeared in *The Shanghai Gesture* (a critically panned effort by the director Josef von Sternberg that featured Oleg Cassini gowns), *Son of Fury, Rings on Her Fingers, Thunder Birds,* and *China Girl.*

Tierney's exposure to German measles while pregnant in 1943 (she later said she contracted it from a fan who broke quarantine and approached her to compliment her on a role she played) severely affected a daughter, Daria, born later that year deaf and mentally retarded. Tierney's only film of 1943 was *Heaven Can Wait,* directed by Ernst Lubitsch.

In 1944 Tierney's best-remembered film was released. *Laura,* directed by Otto Preminger, contrasted the allure of a supposed murder victim, a beautiful woman about whom every man in the film fantasizes, with the rather more common real girl who appears halfway through the movie. Laura's portrait hanging over a fireplace in the film—it was actually an enlarged and varnished photograph—is enough to make men fall in love. It was a good role for Tierney, effectively contrasting her extraordinary physical beauty with her rather more commonplace acting abilities. Preminger added a dose of decadence and perversity, creating what has since become a classic. Tierney followed in 1945 with *A Bell for Adano* and *Leave Her to Heaven,* in the latter of which she showed greatly improved acting ability playing a frighteningly selfish girl. The role earned her an Academy Award nomination for best actress (she lost to Joan Crawford's work in *Mildred Pierce*).

After Daria's birth Tierney's marriage to Cassini began to founder; it ended in divorce in 1952. Through the 1940s and 1950s she was linked romantically with a string of suitors and reputed lovers that included Howard Hughes, Tyrone Power, Kirk Douglas, Spencer Tracy, William Holden, Clark Gable, and the young John F. Kennedy.

In 1946 and 1947, at the peak of her popularity in Hollywood, she made *The Razor's Edge, Dragonwyck,* and *The Ghost and Mrs. Muir.* But after the birth of a second daughter in 1948 Tierney's roles declined. With the exception of *Whirlpool,* released in 1949, Tierney was relegated to a string of generally second-rate thrillers, comedies, and period pieces.

The combination of a stagnant film career and the breakup of a globally publicized love affair with Ali Khan in 1954 hit Tierney very hard. The occasional depression she had suffered since Daria's birth worsened and in 1955, while filming *The Left Hand of God* with Humphrey Bogart, she had a mental breakdown that required hospitalization. She spent the next several years in and out of mental institutions where, she said, she underwent repeated shock therapy. Reporters found her in 1958 working as a salesclerk in a department store in Topeka, Kansas—part of her treatment at the nearby Menninger clinic, she said. "I can no longer doubt," she wrote, "that the main cause of my difficulties stemmed from the tragedy of my daughter's unsound birth and my inability to face my feelings, trying instead to bury them. I regretted too many things: finding out that a father who taught me that honor was everything was not an honorable man. Marrying against my parents' wishes and proving them right. Twice falling in love with men with whom I had no future."

In 1960 she married a Texas oilman, W. Howard Lee, and tried acting once again. In 1962 she made an effective return to the big screen in Preminger's *Advise and Consent,* but subsequent parts were minor. After *The Pleasure Seekers* in 1964, she did little more than an occasional television appearance, preferring a quiet home life in Houston, where she was active in local politics and charitable causes, including helping retarded children. Following her husband's death in 1981, Tierney spent the last ten years of her life in semiretirement. She died of emphysema and is buried in Greenwood Cemetery in Houston.

Although acclaimed as one of the screen's great beauties, with thirty-five feature films to her credit, Tierney's limited acting ability and personal tragedies prevented her from achieving the stardom accorded to contemporaries such as Ingrid Bergman and Marilyn Monroe. She was gorgeous on screen, always alert and intelligent, but sometimes seemed challenged by long speeches and the demands of expressing emotion. As much as film roles, it is still-photo images of Tierney that live in the memory—rather like the portrait of Laura that bewitches observers before the real girl shows up.

★

Tierney, with Mickey Herskowitz, wrote an autobiography, *Self-Portrait* (1979). A critical appreciation of Tierney's work appears in David Thomson's valuable *Biographical Dictionary of Film,* 3rd edition (1994). Obituaries are in the *Washington Post, New York Times,* and *Los Angeles Times* (all 8 Nov. 1991).

THOMAS HAGER

TOWER, John Goodwin   (*b.* 29 Sept. 1925 in Houston, Texas; *d.* 5 April 1991 near Brunswick, Georgia), Republican senator from Texas and the first cabinet appointee by an incoming president ever to be rejected by the Senate.

Tower was one of two children of Joe Z. Tower, a Methodist minister, and his wife, Beryl Goodwin, a homemaker. After attending public schools in Houston and Beaumont, Texas, Tower enlisted in the navy in June 1943, served with an amphibious gunboat in the western Pacific during World War II, and was discharged as a seaman first class.

Like many servicemen still in their twenties, Tower took advantage of the GI Bill of Rights and attended Southwestern State University (now Southwestern University) in

John Tower. KAPPA SIGMA INTERNATIONAL FRATERNITY

Georgetown, Texas, where he received his bachelor's degree in 1948. While an undergraduate Tower had been active in the Kappa Sigma social fraternity on campus, and thus began a lifelong association with the Greek-letter organization. After graduating he served briefly as a radio announcer and also was a life insurance agent.

Short of stature (he was five feet, five inches tall), Tower married Lou Bullington and in time they became the parents of three daughters. Not interested in following in his father's footsteps, Tower ultimately decided on a college teaching career. A conservative Republican in a state where Democrats flourished, Tower joined the faculty of Midwestern University in Wichita Falls, Texas, in 1951 to teach political science classes. To enhance his credentials, he received a master's degree from Southern Methodist University in 1953, after briefly attending the London School of Economics and Political Science (1952–1953).

Gregarious and available as a speaker for civic clubs and school events, Tower became active in Republican politics at the local level and ran for the state legislature in 1954. He lost, but he impressed state party officials with his campaign tactics and affable personality. In 1956 Tower was a delegate to the Republican National Nominating Convention, and again in 1960.

Lyndon B. Johnson was allowed to seek reelection for senator and also run for vice president on the 1960 Democratic presidential ticket. The election of John F. Kennedy and Johnson in November 1960 (Johnson also had won his senate seat) created a vacancy, which necessitated a special election. Tower had run against Johnson as the Republican "sacrificial lamb" and polled an impressive 41 percent of the votes. In April 1961 he gained a runoff spot in the special election, and in May he won a six-year Senate term by a 10,000-vote margin.

The first Republican senator elected from Texas since Reconstruction, from the outset the feisty Tower made his presence in the Senate known. By 1965 he had sought and gained a place as a minority member on the Senate Armed Services committee, where he began to stake out a position as an expert on military matters. He also wore suits (ordered, some wags said, from Bond Street tailors in London) and custom-made shirts with white collars and blue or striped cloth with French cuffs. On the Washington social scene, he often attended parties where he stated to waiters his preference for a particular brand of Scotch whiskey.

When Senator Barry Goldwater sought the Republican presidential nomination in 1964, Tower was the first fellow senator to endorse his colleague. He campaigned for the Arizona senator and defended Goldwater's belligerent remarks concerning the cold war between the United States and the Soviet Union. Goldwater lost, but Tower entrenched his reputation as a "hard-liner" who favored more funding for the military. He also opposed most of President Johnson's civil rights and welfare legislation.

In 1966 Tower was reelected and moved up in the Armed Services committee until he was the ranking minority member. He cultivated his ties with Texas industrialists and in 1971 was elected the national president (Worthy Grand Master) of the Kappa Sigma fraternity, which had many wealthy, conservative, and influential members in Texas.

Richard Nixon's victory in the 1972 presidential election did not bring Senate control to his party, but Tower was again elected to a six-year term and served on important committees—Armed Services, Commerce, Housing and Urban Affairs, and Banking. When demands for equal rights for women were recognized by Congress with Title IX antidiscrimination legislation, Tower pushed through an amendment that granted college fraternities and sororities an exemption from provisions aimed at gender discrimination. At the time, a Greek-letter official said, "John Tower has saved the fraternity-sorority system from chaos and destruction." In 1976 Tower divorced his wife of twenty-four years and within a year married Lilla Burt Cummings; they had no children.

After Ronald Reagan's election as president in 1980 Republicans took control of the Senate, and Tower became chairman of the Armed Services committee. Meanwhile, Tower made no secret of his desire to serve in Reagan's cabinet as secretary of defense. When he was passed over twice, as a loyal Republican, Tower voted for Reagan's nominees. But his feelings were obviously hurt, and he decided to retire from the Senate after twenty-four years of service in 1984.

Tower returned to Texas and established a lucrative consulting business aimed at serving defense contractors. President Reagan appointed him to serve as a U.S. delegate to the arms-control session in Geneva in 1985 and persuaded Tower to lobby in the Senate corridors for passage of a treaty with the USSR banning medium-range nuclear missiles. Reagan also appointed Tower to head a commission set up to investigate charges of scandal in the administration's handling of the arms swap in Iran, which also involved the Contra forces in Nicaragua that Reagan had strongly supported. The Tower Commission's final report of what came to be known as the Iran-Contra scandal was critical of the White House staff but held Reagan blameless. Tower was divorced again in 1987 after negative publicity concerning his drinking and partying habits.

When George Bush of Texas ran for the presidency in 1988, Tower endorsed his fellow Texan and served as an adviser on military affairs. Reporters correctly speculated that, if elected, Bush would name Tower as his secretary of defense; and in March 1989 the Senate subcommittee held hearings on Tower's nomination, with Democratic

senator Sam Nunn of Georgia in the chair. After highly publicized hearings, where charges of excessive drinking and other misdemeanors were brought against Tower (and angrily denied), the subcommittee voted unfavorably on the nomination, eleven to nine. The full Senate concurred, with a vote of forty-seven yeas and fifty-three nays, thus rejecting Tower's nomination.

Angry and hurt, Tower felt betrayed by his former Senate colleagues. He knew that it was a historic rejection, the only time in history that an appointment from an incoming president had been rejected by the Senate. He became a Washington consultant for defense contractors but nursed resentment of the unfavorable publicity and the denial of a cabinet post. Tower struck back with a book, *Consequences: A Personal and Political Memoir,* published early in 1991 and mainly concerned with the Senate debacle. The *New York Times* reviewer summed up the work as "a predictably venomous account of his humiliation." Several reviewers noted that the book was dedicated to his first wife—"She forgave my transgressions . . . and made my career possible."

To promote sales of the book, Tower agreed to attend events arranged by his literary agent. On one of these excursions Tower, accompanied by his daughter, was headed for Sea Island, Georgia, for a book signing party on 5 April 1991 when the twin-engine Atlantic Southeast Airlines flight crashed and burned. All twenty-three people aboard were killed. Tower is buried in Sparkman-Hillcrest Cemetery in Dallas.

★

A sketch of Tower's life, emphasizing his Senate career, is in the Moffett Library archives at Midwestern State University, Wichita Falls, Texas. His book *Consequences: A Personal and Political Memoir* (1991) was widely reviewed, including in *The Economist* (2 Mar. 1991) and London *Times Literary Supplement* (19 July 1991). A biographical sketch of Tower by George N. Green and John J. Kushma is in Michael Collins and K. E. Henrickson, Jr., eds., *Profiles in Power: Twentieth-Century Texans in Washington* (1993). Lengthy obituaries of Tower are in the *Washington Post* and *New York Times* (both 6 Apr. 1991).

ROBERT ALLEN RUTLAND

TREE, Mary Endicott Peabody FitzGerald ("Marietta")

(*b.* 12 April 1917 in Lawrence, Massachusetts; *d.* 15 August 1991 in New York City), socialite, Democratic party activist, and first woman to serve as a U.S. ambassador to the United Nations.

Mary Endicott Peabody was born into the prestigious Peabody clan. Her paternal grandfather founded Groton School and her maternal grandmother helped found Radcliffe College. Her father, Malcolm E. Peabody, was an

Marietta Tree. ARCHIVE PHOTOS

Episcopal minister and eventually bishop of central New York; her mother, Mary Parkman, was active in community volunteer work. Tree was nicknamed "Marietta" at a young age and remained thus throughout her life. She spent her early years in Massachusetts, Pennsylvania, and Maryland, attending the progressive Shady Hill Country Day School in Chestnut Hill, Pennsylvania, and St. Timothy's School, where she graduated in 1934. Tree was a bright, articulate child who loved school and excelled at making friends. When she graduated a year early, she persuaded her parents to let her spend a year abroad in Italy. She returned determined to make her career as a senator or a diplomat. Her family understood her desire for public service, for the Peabody family had a long history of involvement with government and service; her brother Endicott Peabody was the governor of Massachusetts. Her other siblings were Malcolm, Jr. (whom she called "Mike"), George, and Samuel.

Tree dropped out of the University of Pennsylvania during her junior year to marry Desmond FitzGerald on 2 September 1939. She supported herself at the time by modeling for the John Wanamaker department store in Philadelphia. The married couple had one child, Frances ("Frankie") FitzGerald (who became a Pulitzer prize–winning writer for *Fire in the Lake*), before Desmond went to fight in World War II. To supplement her family's income,

Tree worked as a researcher at *Life* magazine in New York City. Her interest and involvement in civil rights was sparked at work, where she shared an office with Earl Brown, an African-American writer and activist. She moved into higher political circles, beginning with a position as union shop steward at her magazine and eventually becoming vice-chair of the Congress of Industrial Organizations' political action committee.

With her husband abroad in the military and with Tree's newfound interests, the marriage began to dissolve. Marietta was linked romantically with John Huston, the film director, when she and her husband, already in the middle of divorce proceedings (which would be a fait accompli on 25 July 1947), vacationed at the Barbados home of Arthur Ronald Lambert Field Tree, called Ronald. An Anglo-American many years older than Marietta and Desmond, he was an investment banker and the grandson of Marshall Field. Ronald admired Marietta's cool, blonde, slim looks and her quick mind; she, his quiet authority and unquestioned love for her. The combination proved irresistible; the two fell in love and decided to marry once their respective divorces were finalized. Marietta and Ronald Tree married on 28 July 1947 and stayed together until his death in 1976, though their last years were strained. Their one daughter, Penelope Tree, became a fashion model.

Tree continued her political activity, organizing women to work on civil-rights issues and raising money for children's hospitals, when she met a man who would focus the direction of her political calling. Vacationing in the summer of 1952 in Maine, she met Adlai Stevenson, then the governor of Illinois and a presidential candidate.

The relationship between Tree and Stevenson was one part friendship, one part mentorship, and one part thinly veiled flirtation. Stevenson was Tree's greatest advocate; she, in turn, escorted him to parties, teased him about his long list of "ladyfriends," and was his staunchest supporter in his two failed bids to become president. To Tree alone would Stevenson admit how humiliating and painful his 1956 presidential election defeat felt. With Stevenson alone would Tree be truly herself: intelligent, probing, and quick.

Tree began to implement her political and organizing skills for Stevenson in 1952, when she actively sought support for him in New York City's inner circles of rich and influential women. Ushering the Democratic women "volunteers" out of their usual tasks of philanthropy through charity balls or magazine shoots, she brought the elite into the ranks of the activist branch of the Democratic party. She held house parties for Stevenson, and the two came to rely on each other on a more than professional level. Their relationship continued and, four years later, she took an even more active role on Stevenson's campaign, crossing the country so many times that Ronnie Tree implored her to spend even a little time with him. The 1956 election was again unlucky for Stevenson and the two embarked on a world tour, accompanied by various family, friends, and press.

In 1961 Stevenson used his influence as the newly appointed U.S. ambassador to the United Nations to have Tree appointed as the U.S. representative to the Human Rights Commission. For the first year she was there she sat behind the former congressman Sidney Yates, who represented the United States on the U.N. Trusteeship Council. Her responsibilities for the commission included traveling to places of unrest such as Kabul and Teheran and articulating U.S. policy on human rights. Three years later when Yates reentered the political arena, Tree took his place on the Trusteeship Council with the honorific title of U.S. ambassador.

Tree remained close to Stevenson for the rest of his life. On the evening of 14 July 1965 the two were walking in London when he collapsed and crashed his head on the sidewalk. Tree ran to the nearest club to summon a doctor and the American ambassador. She began to administer mouth-to-mouth resuscitation, but it was too late to save him. He died instantly of a heart attack. Tree was devastated but still maintained her composure enough to notice that several confidential State Department documents had spilled from his pockets during his fall and to pick them up before she went to the hospital.

Tree moved back to New York City after Stevenson's death and took up residence in a twenty-room town house that she turned into a salon for politicians, journalists, celebrities, and social activists. She also began a new career by becoming a partner at Llewelyn-Davies International City Planning Consultants, along with John Weeks and Richard Llewelyn-Davies, from 1968 to 1980. She was an able networker, convincing city administrators as well as architects to work with her company. During this time, she and Llewelyn-Davies were both professionally and romantically linked. She followed her tenure with the firm by working for various community-improvement groups in the 1980s. Tree died of cancer at the age of seventy-four. She was cremated and her ashes are buried in the Peabody family plot in Northeast Harbor, Saint Mary's-by-the-Sea in Maine.

Tree left behind an impressive legacy of political activism. She was an enormously influential figure in the Democratic party, bringing women from her social circle into campaigns and political philanthropy. As one of the first women in a high position in the United Nations, she strengthened the U.S. position on human rights while still charming heads of state and the New York City social scene. Her talent at maneuvering through both the social and the political worlds made her a fascinating character.

★

The authoritative biography is Caroline Seebohm, *No Regrets: The Life of Marietta Tree* (1997). Seebohm spent time interviewing many of Tree's family and friends, and she also had access to Tree's correspondence. John Bartlow Martin interviewed Tree extensively for his *Adlai Stevenson and the World* (1978). Porter McKeever, *Adlai Stevenson: His Life and Legacy* (1989), also devotes many pages to the relationship between Tree and Stevenson. Inez Robb wrote an extended analysis of Tree in "The Democrats' 'Golden Girl,'" in the *Saturday Evening Post* (20–29 Oct. 1960). Obituaries are in the *Washington Post* and *New York Times* (both 16 Aug. 1991). The documentary film *The Female Line* (1979), by her sister-in-law Pamela Peabody, focuses on Marietta Tree, her mother, Mary Parkman Peabody, and Tree's daughter Frances FitzGerald. It was a television production that was broadcast nationally and ultimately displeased Tree, who believed her personality was not adequately reflected in it.

JUDITH A. PARKER

TULLY, Alice Bigelow (*b.* 11 September 1902 in Corning, New York; *d.* 10 December 1993 in New York City), singer and philanthropist who made significant contributions to the cultural life of New York City.

Tully was the elder daughter of William J. Tully and Clara Houghton. Her father was a lawyer who served two terms in the New York State Senate. Her mother, a homemaker, was the daughter of Amory Houghton, Sr., the founder and president of Corning Glass Works. Tully and her sister lived a life of considerable privilege. In 1908 William Tully became general counsel to the Metropolitan Life Insurance Company, and the family moved to Manhattan. The Tully sisters were educated in accordance with their social class and status. They attended Mrs. J. D. Randall MacIvor's School and were introduced to museums and the arts. Tully then studied at the Westover School in Middlebury, Connecticut. By the time she left at age sixteen, Tully had developed what would be a lifelong interest in music, especially singing.

Despite the opposition of her parents, Tully trained for a career as a singer, studying with a private teacher in New York. In 1923 she moved to Paris and studied voice with Jean Périer, Thérèse Leschetizky, and Miguel Fontecha. She also studied mime with Georges Wague. Her musical debut was at the Salle Gaveau in Paris on 27 September 1927 and her United States debut at New York's Town Hall on 28 November 1936. Tully also appeared in the operas *Carmen* and *Cavalleria rusticana*.

Tully's years in Paris and her travels through Europe had a profound impact on her professional and personal life. From her studies grew a deep and abiding love for the classical repertoire and a commitment to high standards, which she later applied to the work of contemporaneous

Alice Tully at the opening of the New York City concert hall that bears her name, 1969. AP/WIDE WORLD PHOTOS

composers, singers, and musicians. She also became an ardent Francophile. For her service on behalf of France and the French people, Tully was made a Chevalier de l'Ordre National du Merité in the 1960s and an Officier de la Légion d'Honneur in 1986.

Tully returned to New York following the outbreak of World War II and decided to contribute to the war effort. With her experience as an amateur pilot, she flew submarine scouting missions for the Civil Air Patrol. She then volunteered at the French Hospital in Manhattan as a Red Cross nurse's aid.

In 1950 Tully ended her professional singing career and began to divert her considerable energies to civic and cultural service. Thus began a notable career in philanthropy. In 1957 and for the following twenty-eight years, she provided financial support for performances by the Musica Aeterna Orchestra under the direction of Frederic Waldman at New York's Metropolitan Museum of Art. Musica Aeterna programs featured less frequently performed works from the chamber repertoire. The orchestra also premiered works, some commissioned by Tully, that became part of the modern chamber repertoire.

After her mother's death in 1958 Tully's support of the

arts, music, dance, and the opera made her, in the words of one journalist, "the closest thing we have to a Medici in these egalitarian times." In 1958 at the invitation of her cousin Arthur A. Houghton, Jr., Tully made a commitment to underwrite the construction of a chamber concert hall at Lincoln Center for the Performing Arts. Although Tully originally insisted that her donation be anonymous, she relented after she was assured that the hall would have acoustic integrity and would be both beautiful and comfortable. She contributed much of the $4.5 million needed to construct Alice Tully Hall, which opened on Tully's birthday in 1969 and was completed very shortly thereafter. In addition, she contributed the organ, one of the finest of its kind in the United States. While the construction of the building was in progress, Tully turned her attention to the provision of a suitably expert chamber company to reside in the hall, becoming one of the founders of the Chamber Music Society of Lincoln Center.

Tully supported companies and projects that embodied the artistic principles and standards she believed in. She served on the boards of many organizations, giving generously of her time and energy to the Metropolitan Opera, the Metropolitan Museum of Art, the Alliance Française, the Maison Française, New York University Medical Center, the Humane Society, Save the Children Federation, the Juilliard School of Music, and Lincoln Center. Among her many honors for her contributions to American cultural life were New York City's Handel Medallion in 1970 and New York University's Gallatin Medal in 1976. In 1985 President Ronald Reagan awarded Tully the first National Medal of Arts for her work as a patron.

In addition to her philanthropic work or possibly as an adjunct to it, Tully took an active role in high society. She entertained often in her penthouse apartment overlooking Central Park and attended many society functions. A tall, slender woman with dark brown hair, she was noted for her elegance, wry sense of humor, and great personal charm. With all her honors, Tully had a modest opinion of the importance of her contributions to the enjoyment of and the preservation of classical music.

Tully never married and had no children. In 1992 she became housebound after a stroke. She died at her home of pneumonia at the age of ninety-one. Her remains were cremated.

Tully was a talented philanthropist. Her work was important because she knew what she was supporting, be it an individual or an organization. She brought to her philanthropic efforts deeply cultured interests, an informed sensibility, a vast knowledge of music and musicians, and a realistic approach to fostering what was best in music. Her generosity helped fuel the revival of chamber music and provided the most congenial venue in New York City in which to appreciate it.

★

Albert Fuller, *Alice Tully: An Intimate Portrait* (1999), is a memoir of their friendship. Tully's life is documented in Harold C. Schonberg, "Alice Tully's Busy Life in Music," *New York Times* (24 Oct. 1984), and "Alice Tully," *The New Yorker* (5 Oct. 1987). A major obituary describing her contributions to music is in the *New York Times* (11 Dec. 1993).

ELLEN LOUGHRAN

TWITTY, Conway   (*b.* 1 September 1933 in Friars Point, Mississippi; *d.* 5 June 1993 in Springfield, Missouri), early rock-and-roll star who made his mark as a country crooner, both as a soloist and in a series of duets with Loretta Lynn, in the early- to mid-1970s.

Twitty was born Harold Lloyd Jenkins in rural Mississippi, the son of Floyd Jenkins and Velma McGinnis, poor cotton farmers. He was named for the popular silent film comedian. His father operated a small tugboat that ferried passengers across the Mississippi River between their hometown of Friars Point and Helena, Arkansas. Twitty got his first guitar lessons from his father, and by the age of ten he was already performing on local radio stations. Twitty cited two important influences on his early music: country songs he heard on the jukebox at the local honky-tonk and the singing at the "little Negro church" across the cotton fields from his home. "I would sit on the ditch bank and listen to them sing for two or three hours," he would later recall, and "I'd be singing right along." Like many of his contemporaries, Twitty merged black and white influences in his musical style.

As a teenager Twitty dreamed of being a professional baseball player and was good enough to be approached by the Philadelphia Phillies, who offered him a spot on the team. He also contemplated a career as a minister. However, his dreams were put on hold when he was drafted into the United States Army in 1954, and he remained in the service for three years, stationed primarily in Japan. While he was in the army, another country artist named Elvis Presley was recording his first big hits in a new style that would become known as "rockabilly." In 1955 Twitty married Georgia, known as "Mickey"; they would have four children and later divorce and remarry.

On Twitty's return home in 1957, he heard Elvis's recordings and, inspired by Presley's success, began performing in a similar style. He first signed with Sun Records, Elvis's label, but had little success performing as "Harold Jenkins." He decided that if he was going to be a rock star he needed a rock star's name. Looking on a map, he hit on the names of two local towns: *Twitty,* Texas, and *Conway,* Arkansas. He called his band the Twitty Birds. Under this name he signed with Metro-Goldwyn-Mayer in early 1958, and his first hit came shortly after with "It's Only Make Believe," a song that he cowrote which became a number-one pop hit and a million-seller. Several rockabilly/teen pop singles followed, including his second major hit, 1960's "Lonely Blue Boy" (number six on the pop charts). This success won him the attention of Hollywood and, like Elvis, Twitty appeared in a number of forgettable B films. Twitty's success inspired both the Broadway musical *Bye, Bye, Birdie* (with the character Conrad Birdie modeled on Elvis and Twitty) and Peter Sellers's wicked parody of the rock craze, in his portrayal of the lamebrained rocker "Twit Conway." After the Beatles broke through on the charts in 1963, however, Conway's pop career fizzled.

After an abortive attempt to remake himself as a mainstream pop crooner, Twitty relocated to Oklahoma City, Oklahoma, and formed a new, country-oriented band, the Lonely Blue Boys (later renamed the Twitty Birds like his earlier band). The legendary country producer Owen Bradley signed him to Decca Records in 1967, where he remained for many years. After appearing on his own local TV show, Twitty relocated to Nashville, Tennessee, where by the end of the 1960s he was a major star. His first big

Conway Twitty. © WALLY MCNAMEE/CORBIS

country hit came in 1968 with "Next in Line," which reached number one; it was followed by a string of chart-toppers, including 1969's "I Love You More Today" and "To See My Angel Cry," and the classic 1970 recording "Hello Darlin'." Bradley's productions were typical of Nashville's mainstream values, but Twitty's strong personality helped distinguish his vocals from the blander offerings of some other stars.

The early- to mid-1970s saw Twitty's greatest period of sustained country success. In 1971 he made his first duo recording with the famed country singer Loretta Lynn, whose sassy attitude was a perfect foil to his gruff vocals. They hit number one on the charts with "After the Fire Is Gone," a typical "love-gone-wrong" country ballad. They would continue to work together for several years, scoring more hits with a mix of semiautobiographical material ("Louisiana Woman, Mississippi Man," their second number-one hit from 1973) and humorous numbers (1978's "You're the Reason Our Kids Are Ugly," a number-six country hit). The duo took the Country Music Association's "Vocal Duo of the Year" laurels from 1972–1975, making them second only to George Jones and Tammy Wynette as a popular male-female duo in the country genre.

Meanwhile, Twitty began producing an unprecedented string of solo top country hits, reaching the number-one position thirty-six times between 1970 and 1986 (with most of the hits clustered in the early- to mid-1970s). Including his rockabilly years, he eventually scored fifty-five number-one hits. However, by the early 1980s, Twitty was relying on remakes of previous pop hits—like covers of "Slow Hand," a hit for the Pointer Sisters, and "Heartache Tonight," an Eagles' hit—to keep him on the charts.

Twitty made many investments in real estate, fast food, banks, and baseball teams during the 1970s and 1980s. Most notably, he opened a family theme park, the aptly named Twitty City, in Henderson, Tennessee, in the late 1970s; the park, renamed Music Village, USA, went bankrupt in the mid-1980s. Similarly, his franchised hamburger chain—selling (what else?) Twitty Burgers—was a money loser and eventually folded. In 1985 Twitty divorced his wife, Mickey, for a second time. He married his secretary Dee Henry in 1987; they had no children.

Through the 1980s and 1990s Twitty was a yeoman performer, working the road and becoming a well-known act in Branson, Missouri, a Mecca for country fans from around the world. It was there in June 1993 that he collapsed after a performance from a ruptured blood vessel in his stomach. Rushed to a nearby hospital in Springfield, Missouri, the blood vessel was successfully repaired. However, thirteen hours later, Twitty succumbed to a heart attack brought on by the surgery. He is buried in Nashville.

Twitty's baritone voice had some of the same earthiness of Johnny Cash's, with its hint of hard living that is more typical of the country blues. His gruff, almost conversational style made him appealing to listeners who felt he was singing directly to them. He was also a talented songwriter, specializing in the "lovin', lyin', drinkin', and cheatin'" subjects that have made country music an eternal favorite among its listeners. He portrayed male-female relationships with all of the trials and tribulations that they bring, and his clear-eyed assessments of love's hardships and happiness came through in all of his performances.

★

Wilbur Cross and Michael Kosser wrote an authorized biography of Twitty, *The Conway Twitty Story* (1986). His first wife, Mickey Twitty, wrote *What's Cooking At Twitty City?* (1985), a gossipy memoir. Shirley Wilson wrote a history of the Jenkins family, *From Aaron Jenkins to Harold Jenkins: Conway Twitty's Roots* (1985), which was published by "Conway Twitty Enterprises" for his fans. *Country Fever Presents Conway Twitty: His Life, His Music, His Legacy* (1993), is a short pamphlet biography. An obituary is in the *New York Times* (6 June 1993).

RICHARD CARLIN

V

VALVANO, James Thomas ("Jim") (*b.* 10 March 1946 in New York City; *d.* 28 April 1993 in Durham, North Carolina), noted college basketball coach of North Carolina State University and television commentator.

Valvano was the son of Rocco Valvano, a high school basketball coach on Long Island, New York, and Angelina Valvano, a homemaker. He played basketball at Seaford High School for his father's team and attended Rutgers University in New Jersey, playing basketball and majoring in English and education. During his senior year in 1967, he was captain of a team that took third place in the National Invitation Tournament at Madison Square Garden in New York City.

After graduating, he began coaching at Rutgers, directing its freshman basketball team and assisting its varsity team for two years. Moving to Johns Hopkins University in Baltimore, in 1969 he finished his first season as head coach with a 10–9 record. He then spent three years as head coach at Bucknell University in Lewisburg, Pennsylvania (1972–1975), compiling a winning record (14–12) in the third season. In 1975, when he was not yet thirty years old, he took the top job at Iona College, just outside New York City. Over the next five years his team compiled a record of 94–47 and appeared in the National College Athletic Association (NCAA) tournament twice.

On 27 March 1980 Valvano took the head coaching job that would make him famous, at North Carolina State University in Raleigh. The highlight of his coaching career came on 4 April 1983, in the championship game of the NCAA tournament in Albuquerque, New Mexico. His team, the North Carolina State Wolfpack, was a heavy underdog to the celebrated first-ranked Houston, which was led by future NBA stars Hakeem Olajuwon and Clyde Drexler. With the game tied at fifty-two, and the clock running down to zero, a North Carolina State player named Lorenzo Charles tipped in an errant thirty-foot shot by Dereck Whittenburg, giving the Wolfpack the thrilling victory. In the excitement at the end of the game, Valvano was caught on camera in what would become a famous television shot, running around the court searching for somebody to hug.

Three years later Valvano added the post of athletic director to his list of duties at North Carolina State. His celebrity led to roles as a public speaker and television commentator for college basketball programming. But his career took a negative hit in January 1989 when the Raleigh *News & Observer* ran a story announcing that Simon and Schuster would publish a book alleging wrongdoing in North Carolina State's basketball program. Two days later, the NCAA began investigating the book's allegations.

Later that year Valvano resigned his athletic director post, and the NCAA placed the Wolfpack on probation for two years, also forbidding the team from playing in the NCAA tournament in 1990. On 28 February 1990, ABC News reported allegations of point-shaving involving Val-

Jim Valvano after winning the NCAA basketball championship, 1983. ©BETTMANN/CORBIS

"I want to help every cancer patient I can now," he told Gary Smith of *Sports Illustrated* in 1993. "For some reason, people look to me for hope. I'm feeling half dead, and they're coming up to me in the hospital for hope. I don't know if I can handle that, but it's the only conceivable good that can come out of this."

His television time decreased in the disease's final stages as he spent more time with his wife, the former Pamela Susan Levine, whom he had married on 6 August 1967, and their three children. Valvano died of bone cancer at the age of forty-seven. He is buried in Oakwood Cemetery in Raleigh.

The charismatic, high-spirited Valvano, known in sports circles as a master basketball strategist and an incomparable storyteller, lived a final decade of extreme highs and lows. He is remembered by the wider public for his role in the high-profile events of those years and for his public fight against cancer.

★

Valvano, with Curry Kirkpatrick, wrote the autobiographical account *Valvano* (1991), including stories about his life as a coach. Peter Golenbock, *Personal Fouls* (1989), includes allegations of wrongdoing in North Carolina State's basketball program. "As Time Runs Out," *Sports Illustrated* (11 Jan. 1993), tells the dramatic story of his fight against cancer. Obituaries are in the *New York Times* and *Washington Post* (both 29 Apr. 1993).

JEFFREY A. DIAMANT

VAN FLEET, James Alward (*b.* 19 March 1892 in Coytesville, New Jersey; *d.* 23 September 1992 in Polk City, Florida), career army officer who served in World War I, World War II, and Korea and rose to the rank of four-star general.

vano's players. Less than a month later, he lost his job as coach. His final coaching record at North Carolina State was 209–114, with two Atlantic Coast Conference championships, eight NCAA tournament appearances, and the 1983 championship. The only charge ever proven against his teams was that players sold complimentary sneakers and tickets.

In June 1993 Valvano signed a three-year contract with ABC to become a television basketball analyst. He also worked for the sports network ESPN and in 1992 won a high-profile award for his work as a sports commentator on ESPN's *NCAA Basketball*.

His public image took another dramatic turn in June 1992, when ESPN reported that Valvano had been diagnosed with bone cancer. As his physical condition deteriorated, he stayed in the public eye as a broadcaster for selected games, talking about his condition on the air. He founded the (Jimmy) V Foundation for Cancer Research.

Van Fleet was the youngest of four children born to Medora Roxanne Schofield, a homemaker, and William Van Fleet, a businessman who had served in the Union Army during the Civil War. The family moved from New Jersey to Florida when Van Fleet was an infant. In 1911 he graduated from Summerlin Institute in Bartow, Florida, and entered the United States Military Academy at West Point, New York. Upon graduation in June 1915 he was commissioned as a second lieutenant in the infantry. On 25 December 1915 he married Helen Hazel Moore. The couple had three children. Their only son, James, Jr., became an air force pilot; he was reported missing in action during a bombing mission over North Korea in April 1952 and declared "presumed dead" by the air force in 1954.

Van Fleet's first service was on the Mexican border in Texas during a period of strained relations between the United States and Mexico. After America's entry into World War I, he was assigned in October 1917 to Fort Leavenworth, Kansas, where he helped train future officers and

General James A. Van Fleet, 1952. © BETTMANN/CORBIS

which went to England in January 1944. Van Fleet, who did not use alcohol, was still a colonel because Army Chief of Staff George C. Marshall had apparently confused him with an officer with a similar name who had a drinking problem. The identity problem was resolved after Van Fleet's regiment successfully spearheaded the Fourth Division's landing on Utah Beach on D day, 6 June 1944. His skill in directing his unit during the initial landing earned him a promotion to assistant division commander of the Second Infantry Division and the rank of brigadier general.

In October 1944 Van Fleet was given command of the Ninetieth Infantry Division during the Allied thrust toward Germany. By the end of 1944 he had advanced to the rank of major general, and his division was the vanguard of the Allied counteroffensive during the Battle of the Bulge. In March 1945, after a brief time in England, he was given command of the Third Corps, which led the breakout from the bridgehead at Remagen. His corps advanced rapidly across Germany and had reached the foot of the Austrian Alps when Adolf Hitler committed suicide and the war in Europe came to an end.

The Third Corps returned to Camp Polk (later Fort Polk), Louisiana, to prepare for action in the Pacific, but Japan surrendered before it could be redeployed. In February 1946 Van Fleet moved to Governors Island in New York Harbor, where, after a reorganization of army areas in the United States, he became the deputy commander of the First Army.

In December 1947 Van Fleet returned to Europe as a deputy chief of staff at the headquarters of the European Command in Frankfurt, Germany. On 6 February 1948 President Harry S. Truman named him to command United States forces in Greece, where a civil war between communist and noncommunist elements was under way. On 19 February 1948 the United States Senate confirmed his promotion to lieutenant general. As director of the Joint United States Military Advisory and Planning Group, Van Fleet advised the Greek government and supervised the training of the Greek army, which successfully contained the communist threat.

In August 1950 Van Fleet returned to the United States to assume command of the Second Army. After Truman relieved General Douglas MacArthur as commander of United States and United Nations forces in the Far East in April 1951 in a dispute over the conduct of the Korean War, Lieutenant General Matthew B. Ridgway, who had been the field commander in Korea, replaced MacArthur. Van Fleet succeeded Ridgway as the commander of the United States Eighth Army in April 1951, just as communist forces launched a major offensive, which he soon broke. In June 1951 he went over to the offensive, but Truman accepted a truce and fighting subsided, although an

advanced to the rank of captain. In early 1918, after three months of training with the Sixteenth Machine Gun Battalion, Sixth Infantry Division, he was shipped to France. Here he took command of the Sixth Division's Seventeenth Machine Gun Battalion, which he led during the Meuse-Argonne offensive. He was wounded near Sedan a week before the armistice of 11 November 1918.

After occupation duty in Germany, Van Fleet returned to the United States in June 1919. In 1920 he left the Sixth Division for work with the Reserve Officers Training Corps (ROTC) units at several colleges, including the University of Florida, where he also served as coach of the football team. In February 1925 he returned to field duty as a battalion commander with the Forty-second Infantry in the Panama Canal Zone.

In 1927 Van Fleet became an instructor at the Infantry School at Fort Benning, Georgia, and between 1928 and 1929 he was a student in the school's "advanced course." During the 1930s he alternated between educational duties with reserve officer units and field duty.

The outbreak of World War II found Van Fleet in command of the Eighth Regiment, Fourth Infantry Division,

armistice would not be signed until July 1953. Van Fleet, who relinquished command of the Eighth Army on 11 February 1953, stirred controversy when he alleged that he could have defeated the communist forces had he been permitted to go for victory.

Van Fleet left the army on 31 March 1953 after almost thirty-eight years of infantry service and was given the rank of four-star general. His retirement was interrupted briefly during 1961 and 1962 by temporary service as a consultant to the Department of Defense on guerrilla warfare. Van Fleet again stirred controversy by calling for the firing of Ambassador Adlai Stevenson, the chief delegate to the United Nations, because he had not supported the invasion of Cuba at the Bay of Pigs in April 1961.

After leaving the army, Van Fleet returned to Florida, where he became involved in real estate ventures and a variety of business pursuits. In addition, he served as a director on the boards of a number of corporations, was active in organizations fostering American support of Greece and South Korea, and traveled extensively as a representative of both the United States government and private groups. After the death of his first wife in 1984, Van Fleet married Virginia Skinner-Higgins Wells later that year. They had no children.

Six months after celebrating his 100th birthday, Van Fleet died of natural causes at his ranch in Polk City. He is buried in Arlington National Cemetery in Arlington, Virginia.

Van Fleet was an outstanding combat officer with a reputation for earning the respect and affection of the men he led. His decorations included three Purple Hearts, three Distinguished Service Crosses, four Distinguished Service Medals, three Silver Stars, and three Bronze Stars. A blunt, outspoken man who sometimes stirred controversy, he nonetheless displayed diplomatic skill during his successful effort to prevent the fall of Greece to communist insurgents. He also proved to be an efficient army commander in Korea.

★

Van Fleet's papers are at the George C. Marshall Foundation, Lexington, Virginia. A brief biographical sketch covering his early career may be found in *Current Biography 1948*. Alan Axelrod and Charles Phillips, *Macmillan Dictionary of Military Biography* (1998), gives an overview of Van Fleet's military career. Clay Blair, *The Forgotten War: America in Korea, 1950–1953* (1987), provides an assessment of Van Fleet's performance as an army commander in Korea and discusses his sometimes stormy relationship with General Matthew B. Ridgway. Obituaries are in the *New York Times,* the *Washington Post,* and the *Miami Herald* (all 24 Sept. 1992).

ROMAN ROME

VAUGHN, Richard Smith ("Billy") (*b.* 12 April 1918 in Glasgow, Kentucky; *d.* 26 September 1991 in Escondido, California), conductor and arranger whose smooth orchestral versions of pop and R&B hits made him one of the most successful recording artists of the 1950s and 1960s.

Vaughn was one of four children of Alvis Radford Vaughn, a barber and fiddle player, and Sally Maud McWherter, a homemaker. At the age of three Vaughn taught himself how to play the mandolin, the first of eight or nine musical instruments he would go on to master. In early 1941 Vaughn enlisted in the armed forces and joined the Hundred and Twenty-third Cavalry Mounted Band of the National Guard, where he served for four years. While stationed in Mississippi, Vaughn was able to focus on music and develop his arranging and composing skills. He joined a sextet and the base's big band, which performed at various off-base events. At one of these events Vaughn met a Mississippi high-school girl named Marion Smith. Vaughn and Marion were married on 17 April 1943; they had three children.

When Vaughn was discharged from the service after the end of World War II he decided to pursue a career in music. He enrolled at Western Kentucky State Teachers College (now Western Kentucky University), in Bowling Green, in 1947 and studied composition. He never actually graduated, but in 1992 he was awarded an honorary degree by the university and membership in the inaugural class of its Hall of Distinguished Alumni.

Billy Vaughn. ARCHIVE PHOTOS

In 1952, Vaughn formed a vocal quartet, the Hilltoppers, with three college friends: Jimmy Sacca, Don McGuire, and Seymour Speigelman. Vaughn wrote a song called "Trying," which would become the first of his many hits when Dot Records released the group's recording of it in August 1952. The success of the Hilltoppers led them to radio and television appearances, including Ed Sullivan's *Toast of the Town* (26 October 1952), *American Bandstand,* and the Perry Como and Frankie Laine shows. The group also appeared on the cover of *Cash Box* magazine with a second hit, the million-selling "P.S. I Love You," which went to the top of the charts. The Hilltoppers sold more than 8 million records and were consistently ranked among the top ten vocal groups throughout the 1950s, including America's number one vocal group in 1953.

Vaughn left the Hilltoppers in 1954 to become musical director of Dot Records, which specialized in cover records—new versions of familiar songs. He began to arrange and direct recording sessions for the Fontane Sisters, Pat Boone, Johnny Maddox, Gale Storm, the Mills Brothers, and many other Dot recording artists. It was also at this time that Vaughn established his own group, Billy Vaughn and His Orchestra. Perhaps due to his personality, Vaughn preferred working behind the curtain, and he insisted that his new band be primarily a studio orchestra. Vaughn contributed significantly to the label's chart success. His orchestra recorded dozens of internationally known instrumental hits and was voted the most programmed orchestra in 1955 and again in 1958. Dot Records and Vaughn moved to Paramount Recording Studios in Hollywood, California, when Paramount bought Dot in 1958. Vaughn and his orchestra continued to work with big names like Johnny Mercer.

Between 1954 and 1968 Vaughn recorded more than twenty-five albums of cover instrumentals for Dot. His recording of "Melody of Love" was number two on the charts for twenty-seven weeks in 1954; "The Shifting, Whispering Sands (Parts 1 & 2)" was number five for fifteen weeks in 1955; and "Sail Along Silvery Moon" was number five for twenty-six weeks in 1957. In 1960 "Theme from *A Summer Place*" reached number one on *Billboard* magazine's pop album chart. In fact, several of his hits even outsold the originals, among them "The Shifting, Whispering Sands" (first done by Rusty Draper) and "Melody of Love" (a cover of a French hit, "Melodie d'Amour"). He also released an EP (extended play disc) featuring a version of "Shifting, Whispering Sands" with narration by television commercial voice-over specialist Ken Nordine. He had more pop hits than any other orchestra leader during the rock-and-roll era. Reviews in *Billboard* typically ran: "There's no stopping Billy Vaughn. Each album is an automatic chart-winner and this is no exception."

Vaughn's popularity spread to other countries as well, especially Germany and Japan, where he took his orchestra on tours several times. "Sail Along, Silvery Moon" sold over 1 million records in both Germany and Holland, as did "La Paloma" in Germany. In March 1959 he flew to Europe for the award of three gold records, the first American recording artist to be awarded a gold record in Europe. He also won the first platinum record ever awarded for a record that sold over 3 million copies ("Sail Along, Silvery Moon"). Over his forty-year career Vaughn sold more than 200 million records worldwide. He earned eleven gold and two platinum records as well as trophies and awards from Brazil, Denmark, Germany, Japan, Korea, Mexico, Peru, Sweden, and Switzerland.

After a lengthy battle with cancer Vaughn died on 26 September 1991 at Palomar Medical Center in Escondido.

As an arranger, Vaughn tended to have a consistent, predictable sound. He was most famous for his "twin sax" sound, in which the orchestration usually featured an alto sax for the melody, with a second alto sax a third away; supporting instruments typically included a little heavier orchestration on the sax section, with four tenor saxes for the section. Through this formula Vaughn made his most distinctive contribution to the music industry, adapting the youth-oriented pop hits of the 1950s and 1960s in a way that appealed to the tastes of what was then a mainstream, older audience.

★

Limited items of correspondence and sheet music are in the University Archives at Western Kentucky University, in Bowling Green. There is no full-length biography of Vaughn. Biographical entries are in Irwin Stambler, *Encyclopedia of Popular Music* (1965); Colin Larkin, ed., *The Encyclopedia of Popular Music* (1998), which offers selected discography with ratings; and Reuben Musiker and Naomi Musiker, *Conductors and Composers of Popular Orchestral Music* (1998), which also provides a selected discography. Obituaries are in the *Los Angeles Times* (27 Sept. 1991), *New York Times* (28 Sept. 1991), and *Variety* (7 Oct. 1991).

DI SU

VERA. *See* Neumann, Vera.

W

WAGNER, Robert Ferdinand (*b.* 20 April 1910 in New York City; *d.* 12 February 1991 in New York City), lawyer, diplomat, and liberal Democratic politician who served three terms as mayor of New York City.

Wagner was the only child of Margaret McTague and Robert Ferdinand Wagner, who served in the United States Senate from 1927 to 1949 and advocated for the creation of the Social Security system and the passage of landmark labor laws. His mother died of injuries sustained in an automobile accident when he was only nine years old, so "Young Bob" often accompanied his father to political events and grew up in an atmosphere of liberal Democratic politics.

After the death of his illustrious father in May 1953, Wagner dropped the "junior" from his name. His elder son, who also became prominent in New York City politics, then became known as Robert F. Wagner, Jr.

As a boy Wagner made numerous trips to Europe, especially to Germany where his father was born. After attending prestigious private schools in New York and Connecticut, Wagner entered Yale and graduated in 1933. After postgraduate work at the Harvard Business School and the School of International Relations in Geneva, Switzerland, he attended Yale University Law School, earning his LL.B. in 1937.

In 1937 he won the New York State Assembly seat once held by his father. In the assembly, Wagner sponsored pub-

lic housing programs, sought to establish compulsory health insurance, and worked to improve labor relations. He was twice reelected, but after the entry of the United States into World War II in December 1941, Wagner resigned to join the army air corps. He served in the Eighth Bomber Command and rose to the rank of lieutenant colonel. Meanwhile, on 14 February 1942 Wagner married Susan Edwards of Greenwich, Connecticut, at Saint Patrick's Cathedral in New York City. The couple had two sons.

After his discharge in 1945 Wagner served in a variety of appointed positions in New York City's government. When his father resigned from the Senate in 1949, Wagner announced his interest in succeeding him, but he did not get his party's nomination in a special election to fill the seat. Instead, he ran successfully for the borough presidency of Manhattan, a position he held until December 1953. While in that office Wagner again sought the Democratic nomination for his father's old Senate seat but lost the primary election in August 1952. However, in September 1953 Wagner won the New York City Democratic nomination for mayor and went on to defeat his Republican opponent in November.

In January 1954 Wagner entered the office he would hold for three four-year terms, a feat achieved by only two other men: Fiorello La Guardia before him and Edward I. Koch after him. However, his tenure (1954–1965) came at a time when the city was undergoing major demographic change. Many members of the white middle class were

Robert F. Wagner. ARCHIVE PHOTOS

moving to nearby suburbs, while increasing numbers of poor Puerto Ricans and southern blacks were moving to the city. Thus, Wagner was mayor during a period of tremendous social and economic change.

During his mayoralty, Wagner recognized the right of city employees to form unions and bargain collectively, thereby setting a pattern for municipal labor unions throughout the country. He secured the building of thousands of units of public housing, including many for middle-income families. He helped develop the nation's first municipal law outlawing discrimination in housing based on race (Sharkey-Brown-Isaacs Law of 1957).

However, the influx of poorer people in need of social services led to a rapid increase in the city's expenditures, which began to outpace revenues. Rather than raise taxes, Mayor Wagner resorted to borrowing, saying "a good loan is better than a bad tax." Thus, say his critics, were sown the seeds of New York City's fiscal crisis of the early 1970s. But Wagner's efforts to respond to problems arising from the change in the city's ethnic and racial composition perhaps enabled New York to escape the kind of devastating race riots that tore apart Los Angeles, Detroit, and Newark, New Jersey, during the 1960s, though racial strife did occur in Harlem and Brooklyn in July 1964.

Meanwhile, in 1956, Wagner made another bid for the United States Senate, gaining his party's nomination but losing the general election to his Republican opponent,

Jacob K. Javits. Wagner easily won reelection as mayor in 1957, but four years later he lost the support of the regular Democratic "bosses" of the city's five boroughs. However, he easily defeated their candidate in the party primary and went on to win the general election of 1961. Wagner's victory has been credited with permanently breaking the power of "Tammany Hall"—the old municipal Democratic party machine.

Wagner's first wife died on 2 March 1964. He married his second wife, Barbara Joan Cavanagh, on 26 July 1965. The couple, who had no children, separated in December 1969 and divorced in June 1971. Wagner, a Roman Catholic, secured a church annulment.

After declining to seek a fourth term as mayor, he entered a law partnership in 1966. From May 1968 to March 1969 he was the U.S. ambassador to Spain. After returning to the United States he announced his candidacy for mayor, but was defeated in the Democratic primary in June.

Wagner continued to practice law. On 30 January 1975 he was married for a third time to Phyllis Fraser Cerf, the widow of Bennett Cerf, the cofounder of the Random House book publishing company. They had no children. In March 1977 the New York State Senate confirmed him as a commissioner of the Port Authority of New York and New Jersey, and in June he became the agency's vice chairman.

From 1978 to 1980 Wagner was President Jimmy Carter's special envoy to the Vatican, with which the United States had only informal diplomatic ties. In that capacity he arranged a June 1980 meeting between President Carter and Pope John Paul II and helped plan the pope's 1981 U.S. tour. In 1983 he was appointed to another term as commissioner of the Port Authority and continued as its vice chairman.

Wagner, who had been suffering from bladder cancer, died of heart failure at his home in Manhattan. He is buried in Calvary Cemetery in Queens, New York.

Wagner's legacy to the cultural life of New York City was immense. Not only was he instrumental in preserving Carnegie Hall, the city's premier venue for classical music, he played a major role in the creation of Lincoln Center, the home of the city's foremost performing arts institutions, including the New York City Opera and the Metropolitan Opera. He also helped bring the 1964 World's Fair to Flushing Meadows in Queens, New York.

In the political realm, Wagner deserves credit for taking a leading role in bringing about the final demise of the old Democratic political machine known as Tammany Hall. As Sam Roberts put it in the *New York Times* on 14 February 1991, Wagner's victory in 1961 "redefined the mayoralty and established its pre-eminence over the party."

★

Wagner's personal papers are in the LaGuardia and Wagner Archives at LaGuardia Community College of the City University of New York, in Long Island City. His official mayoral papers are in the New York City Department of Records and Information Services, Municipal Archives. A brief biographical sketch covering his early career may be found in *Current Biography 1954*. *The Administration of Robert F. Wagner* (1960), published by the Office of the Mayor, City of New York, gives an official view of the accomplishments of the Wagner administration from 1954 to 1960. Chris McNickle, *To Be Mayor of New York: Ethnic Politics in the City* (1993), provides an extensive discussion of Wagner's mayoralty. Obituaries are in the *New York Times,* the *Daily News,* and the *New York Post* (all 13 Feb. 1991).

ROMAN ROME

WALKER, Edwin Anderson (*b.* 10 November 1909 in Center Point, Texas; *d.* 31 October 1993 in Dallas, Texas), career U.S. Army officer who resigned his commission in 1961 after being accused of right-wing indoctrination of his troops.

Walker was one of two sons of George Pinckney Walker, a Texas rancher, and Charlotte Thornton, a homemaker. After completing high school at New Mexico Military Institute in 1927 he attended West Point, graduating in the bottom quarter of the class of 1931. Commissioned an artillery officer, he had reached the rank of captain by 1940

Edwin A. Walker, 1961. AP/WIDE WORLD PHOTOS

and earned a reputation as a "hell-for-leather" polo player. During World War II, Walker volunteered for the First Special Services Force, a commando unit that fought in the Aleutians, Italy, France, and Germany. By the end of the war he was a lieutenant colonel with a Silver Star, Bronze Star, and other decorations from the United States, France, Great Britain, and Norway.

Early in the cold war Soviet efforts to destabilize the governments of Greece and Turkey galvanized Walker's opposition to communist expansion. Assigned to Korea in 1951, he chafed under the constraint of limited war, which he believed "hog-tied" the army. Despite a promotion to brigadier general, Walker left Korea harboring suspicion that subversive forces in his own government were responsible for the Korean stalemate.

A 1957 assignment as commander of the Arkansas Military District placed Walker, now a major general, in charge of the state's reserve component. The posting seemed routine, but within months international attention was focused on his command. Arkansas governor Orval Faubus defied a federal court order to integrate Little Rock's Central High School. President Dwight D. Eisenhower federalized the state national guard and placed it and troops from the 101st Airborne Division under Walker's command. The general had reservations about forced integration and believed federalization of the Arkansas National Guard was unnecessary. Unable to persuade his superiors to modify their action, Walker carried out their directives, integrating Central High and maintaining order.

On 4 August 1959, with the integration crisis over, Walker submitted his resignation, claiming that a "5th column conspiracy . . . nullified the effectiveness of my ideas and principles." The resignation was rejected, and Walker was assigned to command the Twenty-fourth Infantry Division in Germany. Between his tour in Korea and assignment to Germany the general embraced the far right, joining the John Birch Society in 1959.

The new commander of the Twenty-fourth Division used the troop information program to expound his anticommunist views and conspiracy theories. *Overseas Weekly,* a sensational publication aimed at military personnel serving abroad, accused Walker of indoctrinating troops with John Birch literature and calling prominent Americans "pink." After President John F. Kennedy ordered an investigation, Walker was relieved of command on 17 April 1961. Two months later he was officially admonished for making derogatory remarks about prominent Americans and trying to influence the way his troops voted. On 1 November 1961 he resigned his commission, forgoing his military retirement pension to free himself from "the power of little men."

Returning to Texas, Walker established a residence in Dallas, where his conservative views found support. Over the next few months he voiced his opinions in various forums and was featured on the cover of the 4 December 1961 *Newsweek* magazine. Alerting Americans to the dangers of communism, he identified New Dealers, Fair Dealers, and New Frontiersmen as part of a conspiracy to liquidate constitutional rights. In April 1962 Walker testified before a special Senate subcommittee investigating charges that the government was muzzling military officers. His testimony provided little support for his accusations and disappointed even his right-wing supporters. Against the advice of conservative senators Barry Goldwater and Strom Thurmond, Walker filed in the Democratic primary for governor of Texas in February 1962. His notoriety could not overcome his lack of financial backing and political experience, and he ran last in a six-man race on 5 May, receiving less than 10 percent of the vote.

In late September 1962 Walker traveled to Oxford, Mississippi, to encourage demonstrators attempting to block the enrollment of James Meredith, a black air force veteran, at the University of Mississippi. Although he disappointed vehement proponents of segregation by refusing to assume leadership of the protesters, Walker was arrested on 1 October and transported to a federal mental facility. Government charges of seditious conspiracy, insurrection, and rebellion were apparently based on an erroneous Associated Press story that Walker had led an attack on federal marshals. Released on bond on 7 October, he received a hero's reception in Dallas. Later, after a grand jury failed to return an indictment, charges were dropped. Walker sued Associated Press for libel and won a $500,000 judgment, which was set aside by the U.S. Supreme Court because Walker was a "public figure" and the story had been written "without malice."

On 10 April 1963 Walker narrowly escaped death when a bullet missed his head by inches. The assailant was not immediately apprehended, but during the Warren Commission's hearings into the assassination of President Kennedy, Lee Harvey Oswald's wife, Marina, testified that her husband had fired at Walker. The conservative Texan did not mourn the president's death. In fact he refused to lower his flag to half-staff. He did, however, frequently fly it upside down to symbolize the distress he believed faced the nation.

Following Kennedy's assassination Walker faded from public view. In 1976 he pleaded no contest to a charge of public lewdness for making sexual advances to an undercover policeman in a Dallas park. The passage of years did not diminish his conviction that communism posed an imminent peril. In an interview with a reporter from *Texas Monthly* in 1990, the eighty-one-year-old general remained as stridently anticommunist as he had been when he was relieved of command in 1961. In November 1993 the old soldier, who had never married, died of lung disease. He is buried at the Center Point Cemetery, near the Texas ranch his family had established in the nineteenth century.

In battle Walker repeatedly demonstrated his willingness to sacrifice his life for his country, but limited war, coexistence with communism, and the expansion of federal power were alien to him. He sacrificed his career rather than compromise his principles. When the army granted him a pension in 1982, it called Walker "a truly dedicated American soldier who firmly believed that insufficient action was being taken within the military establishment to combat the threat of communism." The army's assessment may be accurate, but Edwin A. Walker will be remembered for the right-wing activism that brought him notoriety in the early 1960s. If his behavior did not provide a model for the conspiracy-crazed generals in Stanley Kubrick's 1964 black comedy film *Dr. Strangelove,* it could have.

★

The Edwin A. Walker Papers are in the Barker Texas History Center, University of Texas, Austin. The general's most comprehensive biography is Chris Cravens, "Edwin A. Walker and the Right Wing in Dallas, 1960–1966" (M.A. thesis, Southwest Texas State University, 1991), which provides details about Walker's youth and army career not readily available elsewhere. A cover article, "'I Am a Walking Program,' Says . . . the General," *Newsweek* (4 Dec. 1961) also summarizes his career, his beliefs, and the events that led to his resignation. Kent and Phoebe Courtney's *The Case of General Edwin A. Walker* (1961) delves into his "Pro-Blue" program and the investigation that prompted his resignation. Published by the Conservative Society of America, the book makes no claim of objectivity. The liberal view of his conduct as commanding general of the Twenty-fourth Infantry Division is expounded in an undated document, "The Dismissal of Maj. Gen. Edwin A. Walker: A Special Report by Congressman Morris K. Udall." A more evenhanded assessment is Franklyn A. Johnson, "Edwin A. Walker: Man on Horseback or Modern Major General?," *Vital Speeches of the Day* (15 Feb. 1962). *Facts on File* (1961, 1962, and 1963) provides an overview of the general's public activities during the three most contentious years of his life. R. A. Surrey, *The Law of the Land* (1963), released by Walker's American Eagle Publishing Company, presents his account of his arrest and detention following the demonstration at the University of Mississippi in 1962, and Gary Cartwright's "Old Soldier," *Texas Monthly* (Feb. 1991), reviews his career and describes Walker's physical condition and political outlook not long before his death. Obituaries are in the *Dallas Morning News* (1 Nov. 1993) and *New York Times* (2 Nov. 1993).

BRAD AGNEW

WALKER, Nancy (*b.* 10 May 1922 in Philadelphia, Pennsylvania; *d.* 25 March 1992 in Studio City, California), diminutive, energetic stage comedienne of the 1940s and wisecracking television perennial of the 1970s.

Walker was born Anna Myrtle Swoyer, one of two daughters of Stuart Swoyer, an acrobat, and Myrtle Lawler, a dancer. Her father changed his name to Dewey Barto when he joined the vaudeville team the Three Bartos, and the family took on this name. The descendant of a circus clown, acrobats, and bareback riders, Walker supposedly first crawled onto the stage during one of her mother's performances when she was ten months old. Myrtle Swoyer died in 1930, and Walker grew up traveling on the vaudeville circuit with her father. She was educated on and off between 1929 and 1940 at the Professional Children's School in New York, where she used the first name Nan. She left school shortly before graduation to pursue a career as a singer.

Her big break, and her stage name, came to her at age nineteen when she auditioned for the theatrical producer George Abbott, who was casting a college musical comedy, *Best Foot Forward*. Accidentally introduced as Miss Walker, she presented the producer with a peppy rendition of "Bounce Me Brother with a Solid Four." Abbott saw the potential in her small frame and offbeat looks. He created for her the role of "Blind Date," a comic coed who charmed critics and audiences—if not all of the men at *Best Foot*'s fictional college—when the play opened in October 1941.

Walker went to Hollywood for the film version of the play in 1943; she also made a few other pictures, including *Girl Crazy* in 1943 and *Broadway Rhythm* in 1944. Her

Nancy Walker, 1980. THE KOBAL COLLECTION

looks were not conventional, however, and she was most at home in comic roles on Broadway, where she remained for most of the 1940s and 1950s. Probably her greatest success was as a man-hunting taxi driver romancing one of the sailors in the 1944 musical *On the Town*, but she was praised as well for her work in *Look Ma, I'm Dancin'* (1948) and *Phoenix '55* (1955). The latter was written by the composer and vocal coach David Craig, whom Walker had married on 29 January 1951 after a brief marriage to actor Gar Moore in 1947 or 1948. The Craigs had a daughter in 1953.

Walker worked sporadically as an actress in the 1960s, appearing on television variety shows and gaining particular success on the stage in *Do Re Mi* (1960), a satire about the jukebox business, with Phil Silvers. She also took a turn at directing plays; her Broadway directorial debut, *UTBU*, was produced in 1966. She later admitted that her acting career at this time was stalled. "I couldn't get arrested," she told a *New York Times* reporter in 1973. "I just couldn't get work. And, I must say, neither could Bert Lahr. He was selling potato chips on TV. So I thought, 'Why not commercials?'"

In 1970 she and Craig moved to Los Angeles, and the actress became the television spokesperson for Bounty paper towels. As the eponymous proprietress of Rosie's Diner, Walker successfully extolled the virtues of "the quicker picker-upper." She was happy and not at all defensive about the visibility the commercials brought her. "One minute's work done well is just as important as one hour," she said. "Look, if it were a bad minute, I'd feel terrible, because I get paid very well, and that would be cheating. I'm not cheating anybody. I mean, an artist is an artist no matter what he does."

The role of Rosie led to others. Walker may have been the most visible performer on American television in the early to mid-1970s. She was a semi-regular on *Family Affair* from 1970 to 1971, playing a housekeeper to Brian Keith's bachelor father. She moved on to the role for which she is best known among fans of situation comedy, Ida Morgenstern, the mother of Rhoda, first as a guest star on *The Mary Tyler Moore Show* (1970–1974) and then as a regular on its spin-off, *Rhoda* (1974–1976, with a return in 1977 for a season). A nagging Jewish mother with a heart of gold, Ida was a more fully fleshed-out character than Walker's other television alter ego of the period, the snoopy housekeeper Mildred on the comedy-detective series *McMillan and Wife* (1971–1976).

In 1973 Walker became one of the first women to direct a situation comedy, joining the Directors Guild of America after directing her first episode of *Mary Tyler Moore*. She went on to direct episodes of *Rhoda*, *Alice*, and *13 Queens Boulevard*, as well as one motion picture, *Can't Stop the Music* (1980).

In the 1976–1977 season, Walker quit *Rhoda* and *Mc-Millan* to star in a situation comedy of her own, *The Nancy Walker Show,* in which she played the head of a talent agency who juggles business and family concerns. After its swift cancellation, she moved on in the same season to the equally short-lived *Blansky's Beauties.*

Although she never regained her near-ubiquity of the early 1970s, Walker continued to act on television, appearing as a guest star and occasional regular on programs such as *Fantasy Island, Love Boat, Golden Girls,* and *Mama's Boy.* Her last ongoing role was as the caustic mother (and mother-in-law) of an interracial couple in *True Colors* (1990–1992), a part she played in a wheelchair as her health deteriorated. She died of lung cancer on 25 March 1992 in Studio City and her ashes were scattered over St. Thomas Island.

Walker was in many ways held back by her comic persona and lack of beauty-pageant looks: she was often typecast, first as a plain, funny man hunter, later as a wise and wisecracking middle-aged shrew. Nevertheless, she made the best of her roles and carved out a space for herself as a performer, projecting humor, intelligence, and energy on stage and screen. "I can't tell anyone else how to live," she said in 1975, "but I did the best I could and it's not even over yet."

★

The Billy Rose Theater Collection of the New York Public Library has clipping files on Nancy Walker. Other helpful sources include a *New York Times* profile by John Gruen (14 Oct. 1973), an essay in *Current Biography 1965,* and biographical essays in the Directors Series section of *Films in Review* (Aug.–Sept. 1980) and in *Action* (July–Aug. 1975). Obituaries are in the *New York Times* (26 Mar. 1992) and *Variety* (30 Mar. 1992).

TINKY "DAKOTA" WEISBLAT

WALTON, Sam(uel) Moore   (*b.* 29 March 1918 near Kingfisher, Oklahoma; *d.* 5 April 1992 in Little Rock, Arkansas), retail executive who was the founder and chief executive officer of Wal-Mart Stores.

Walton was one of two sons born to a young farm couple, Nancy Lee and Thomas Gibson Walton. In 1923 the family moved from Oklahoma to Missouri, where Walton's father worked as a farm-mortgage broker and his mother was a homemaker. In his youth Walton lived in several different rural communities in Missouri. Growing up during the Great Depression, the hardworking young Eagle Scout helped out on the family farm by doing chores such as milking the family cow after school and delivering the milk. At Hickman High School in Columbia, Missouri, he was quarterback of the state-champion football team, and in his senior year he was elected president of the student body and voted "most versatile boy."

Sam Walton. AP/WIDE WORLD PHOTOS

After graduating in 1936, Walton entered the University of Missouri at Columbia. He put himself through college by waiting on tables and delivering newspapers. With his outgoing personality and ability to work well with others, Walton made friends easily and became involved in a variety of campus- and church-related activities. His busy schedule garnered him the nickname "hustler," and his classmates elected him the permanent president of the senior class. In 1940 he graduated with a degree in economics. Three days after graduation he went to work as a management trainee for a J. C. Penney store in Des Moines, Iowa.

From 1942 to 1945 Walton served in the U.S. Army Intelligence Corps, achieving the rank of captain. On 14 February 1943 he married Helen Robson of Claremore, Oklahoma, the daughter of a successful banker, and by 1949 they had three sons and one daughter. In 1945 Walton combined $5,000 of savings with $20,000 borrowed from his father-in-law and purchased a struggling Ben Franklin variety store in Newport, Arkansas. As a result of Walton's competitiveness and hard work, the store soon turned a profit. Walton assumed a prominent role in the life of the small town, regularly attending services at the Presbyterian church and serving in various civic organizations. Walton and his family were content in the small community, but in 1950 the landlord of the store, who wanted the now thriving business for his son, refused to renew Walton's lease.

Although disappointed, Walton lost no time in finding another small-town Ben Franklin store to buy, this time in Bentonville, in northwest Arkansas. Walton relocated his family to the tiny Ozark community and renamed the store Walton's 5 & 10. In 1952 Walton opened another variety store in Fayetteville, Arkansas, this one with self-service, a novel retail concept in that day. By 1962 Walton, along with his brother, Bud, owned sixteen units located throughout Arkansas, Missouri, and Kansas, making the business the largest independent variety-store chain in the United States.

Walton kept abreast of developing retail trends, and he became convinced that his business would soon be threatened by a relatively new form of retailing known as discounting. Discounters keep operating costs down by maintaining low overhead expenses and buying goods in volume; they pass those savings on to consumers in the form of low prices in order to generate high overall sales and profits. Walton believed that a full-size discount store could succeed in a small rural market. He asked Ben Franklin's management corps to join him in a small-town discounting venture, but the retail executives refused. "They just couldn't see the philosophy," Walton explained. Undeterred, Walton decided to launch his own discount operation.

Skeptics abounded regarding Walton's discounting idea. As Walton stated in his autobiography, "Nobody wanted to gamble on that first Wal-Mart." Walton financed 95 percent of the venture himself, a move that plunged him deep into debt. He opened his first Wal-Mart store in Rogers, Arkansas, in 1962. In that same year the S. S. Kresge Company opened its first Kmart discount store, and the Dayton Corporation established its Target discount operation.

Walton's store was a resounding success. Consumers flocked to Wal-Mart for its low prices, and Walton began to open additional Wal-Marts in small towns in Arkansas and later in Missouri. During the early years many brand-name manufacturers were reluctant to do business with the discount chain, and the quality of the goods sold in those early Wal-Marts was often inferior. But customers found value in Walton's rock-bottom prices, and the chain grew steadily. In 1969 Walton opened a general headquarters and distribution facility in Bentonville to service his eighteen-store chain. In 1970, needing money to finance his future expansion plans, Walton authorized the public sale of Wal-Mart securities. Two years later Wal-Mart Stores was listed on the New York Stock Exchange.

During the 1970s Walton expanded Wal-Mart by locating his stores close to highly automated distribution centers. That shrewd location strategy ensured that stores could be replenished rapidly with goods. The quality of Wal-Mart's merchandise improved markedly during this period as formerly reluctant manufacturers now solicited Walton's busi-

ness, and Wal-Mart's sales and earnings increased at an annual rate of about 40 percent. Walton continued to open stores in small towns that other retailers ignored. "There's a lot more business in those communities than people thought," Walton observed. In 1974 Sam Walton relinquished his position as chairman of Wal-Mart but returned two years later and reclaimed the leadership post. In 1979 Wal-Mart recorded its first billion-dollar year in sales, becoming the youngest retail firm and the only regional retailer ever to reach that volume.

During the 1980s Walton accelerated his firm's pace of growth through diversification. Determined to keep his business from stagnating, Walton embraced change and flexibility and was willing to experiment with innovative business concepts. In 1983 he introduced one of his most successful departures, Sam's Club, a no-frills wholesale club. In 1987 Walton launched giant stores called Hypermart USA. But operation of the 225,000-square-foot behemoths, which sold everything from car batteries to butter, proved unwieldy, leading to one of Walton's rare setbacks in retailing. In 1988 Walton threw his boundless energy and enthusiasm into another new retail format, the Wal-Mart Supercenter. Walton had great confidence in the 150,000-square-foot combination grocery and discount store, believing correctly that the Supercenter would be the instrument of Wal-Mart's future growth.

In the mid-1980s Walton began to enter urban markets and launched a campaign to expand his firm nationwide. By 1987 Wal-Mart had become the third largest retail firm in the United States, behind Sears and Kmart. In 1988 Walton, then sixty-nine, relinquished the job of chief executive officer to David D. Glass while retaining the title of chairman of the board. During the 1980s Wal-Mart's annual sales grew from $1 billion to over $25 billion and the number of stores increased from under 300 to more than 1,500. Wal-Mart became a national retail chain and passed Kmart to become the nation's second-largest retailer. In 1991 Wal-Mart overtook Sears to become the nation's leading retail firm, with annual sales of $32.6 billion.

Wal-Mart's phenomenal success was based squarely on the business skills and personality traits of Sam Walton. A consummate merchant, Walton diagnosed the rising demand by consumers for brand-name goods at reasonable prices and devised innovative methods for cutting costs and passing the savings on to his customers. In his quest for cost cutting and efficiency, he made bold investments in sophisticated distribution and technology systems. In 1987 Wal-Mart launched its own satellite communications network. The largest privately owned system in the United States, the technology cost $20 million, a sum that astounded the notoriously frugal Walton. "It blows my mind that we spent $20 million for a satellite outfit," he marveled. But his disclaimer belied Walton's unwavering commitment to elaborate marketing and communications systems that allowed his firm to maintain operating costs that were well below other retail firms.

Another advantage that Wal-Mart enjoyed over its competitors was Walton's talent for eliciting amazing loyalty from his workforce. He forged a partnership with his personnel, whom he called "associates," by sharing information with them and giving them a wide range of decision-making responsibilities. He demanded hard work and hired individuals based largely on their stamina and willingness to submit to the rigors of Wal-Mart's grueling pace. At the same time he rewarded employee effort through generous financial incentives, such as profit sharing and stock-purchase plans that made some employees rich, and incentive bonuses, such as rewarding employees if "shrinkage" (the loss of merchandise due to damage or internal theft) was reduced. The amazing buoyancy of the firm's stock in particular imbued Wal-Mart's personnel with a high level of energy and dedication that Walton described as "Wal-Mart fever."

Walton was a charismatic leader with an unassuming, folksy demeanor. He enthralled Wal-Mart's small-town workers and customers alike through spontaneous promotional stunts, such as walking a pig down a Dallas street in 1986 or dancing the hula on Wall Street in 1984 to fulfill a pledge made to his employees when they attained record-breaking profits for the firm. Nowhere was his flamboyant showmanship more in evidence than at Wal-Mart's annual shareholders' meetings. He converted those gatherings into huge pep rallies, complete with songs, awards for outstanding performance, and, of course, favorable price comparisons with competitors.

Walton would typically rise before dawn and work into the evening. By 6:30 A.M. on most days he was in the air piloting his own twin-engine Cessna to visit stores. For many years Walton fulfilled his objective of visiting every store in his chain at least once a year. Even after his empire expanded beyond his ability to maintain that goal, he continued his hectic pace, sometimes visiting two and three Wal-Marts a day. Terming his store visits "the most important thing I do," he would arrive unexpectedly, lead his associates in the Wal-Mart cheer, talk to employees, stress the importance of greeting and helping customers, and genuinely solicit their ideas on ways to improve the firm. Walton was an avid tennis player and quail hunter and usually carried cages for his bird dogs in the back of his 1985 Ford pickup truck. When his favorite bird dog, Ol' Roy, who often accompanied him on store visits, died, Walton mourned the death in an open letter to his employees.

As Wal-Mart's success grew, Walton garnered numerous honors and awards, including being named chief executive of the decade in 1989 by *Financial World* magazine. He refused to take credit for his firm's astounding growth, in-

sisting that his employees were the real source of Wal-Mart's success. The self-effacing Walton was especially dismayed when in 1985 *Forbes* magazine declared that his fortune of $2.8 billion, derived mainly from his 39 percent ownership of Wal-Mart stock, made him the richest man in America. Walton disdained what he saw as a dubious honor and showed far more interest in his firm than in his growing wealth. When, for example, his fortune plunged by $1.8 billion in the stock-market crash of 1987, he shrugged off the loss, saying, "It's paper anyway." Walton held the richest-American distinction until 1989, when, in part to deflect the unwanted publicity that the title had generated, he and his wife divided their fortune with their four children. By 1990 the Walton family fortune was valued at $12.5 billion; in 2000 it was $85 billion.

As Walton's fame and popularity spread, his business increasingly became an object of controversy, especially its impact on Main Street merchants in the small towns that Wal-Mart inhabited. Local retailers complained that they could not compete with Wal-Mart's low prices, and critics blamed Walton's aggressive price-cutting for putting small-town merchants out of business. Walton deflected those criticisms by insisting that he was merely meeting the demands of consumers for quality merchandise at bargain prices.

In 1990 Walton was diagnosed with multiple myeloma, an aggressive form of bone cancer. He had suffered from leukemia since 1982, but that disease was in remission. In 1992 President George Bush presented Walton with the Medal of Freedom, the nation's highest civilian honor. A few days later Walton died at the age of seventy-four. He is buried in Bentonville. At the time of his death, the family fortune was valued at $23.6 billion.

Walton was one of the twentieth century's leading entrepreneurs. Many of his business practices, especially his empowering management techniques based on sharing information and profits with his employees and his use of state-of-the-art distribution and technology systems, have been widely copied. His single-minded focus on providing customers with quality, value, and service transformed the expectations of consumers. Manufacturers and other retailers alike were compelled to incorporate Walton's regimens of cost cutting and efficiency into their businesses in order to compete in the consumer-oriented, value-driven marketplace that Walton himself did so much to create.

★

Walton's autobiography, *Sam Walton, Made in America: My Story* (1992), written with John Huey, senior editor of *Fortune* magazine, is anecdotal and informative but lacking in insight. A journalistic account of Walton's life and achievements is Vance H. Trimble, *Sam Walton: The Inside Story of America's Richest Man* (1990). For a balanced, in-depth account of Walton's role in the birth and development of Wal-Mart, see Sandra S. Vance and Roy V. Scott, *Wal-Mart: A History of Sam Walton's Retail Phenomenon* (1994). One of several journalists who are critical of Wal-Mart's impact on small-town America is Bob Ortega, who wrote *In Sam We Trust: The Untold Story of Sam Walton and How Wal-Mart Is Devouring America* (1998). Of the many magazine articles on Walton and Wal-Mart, two noteworthy examples are Arthur Markowitz, "Mr. Sam: Wal-Mart's Patriarch," *Discount Store News* (18 Dec. 1989), and John Huey, "Discount Dynamo: Sam Walton," *Time* (7 Dec. 1998). Obituaries are in the *New York Times* (6 Apr. 1992) and the *Wall Street Journal* (6 Apr. 1992).

SANDRA S. VANCE

WATSON, Thomas John, Jr. (*b.* 8 January 1914 in Dayton, Ohio; *d.* 31 December 1993 in Greenwich, Connecticut), businessman who led International Business Machines (IBM) into electronic computing and made it one of the most profitable and admired American corporations of the second half of the twentieth century; he later served the Jimmy Carter administration as the ambassador to the Soviet Union.

The eldest of five children, Watson was born the same year his father, Thomas J. Watson, became the chief executive of a newly organized manufacturer of equipment used in

Thomas Watson, Jr. AP/WIDE WORLD PHOTOS

business offices and retail establishments. Leaving his wife, Jeannette Kittredge, to run the household in suburban Short Hills, New Jersey, the forty-year-old executive set about cultivating a reputation for himself and his firm, which in 1924 was renamed International Business Machines. Under a contract that gave him a percentage of the profits, the elder Watson in 1936 became the highest-paid executive in the United States, with an income of $1,000 a day. An ardent supporter of Franklin Roosevelt, he was the president's most trusted confidant among the business community. Though the Watson family never owned more than 5 percent of IBM, T. J. Watson exerted so much influence over its affairs during his forty-two years as CEO that many came to believe he was the proprietor. His portrait hung in every office, and more than thirty top executives reported directly to him.

Aside from the affluence and reputation his father provided, little in Watson's early years suggested he might someday succeed his father at IBM and ultimately surpass his accomplishments in business and public affairs. The younger Watson struggled as a student at the private Short Hills Academy and frequently got into trouble with authorities at the school and in the community. Lonely and often distressed by the domineering manner with which his father treated him and his mother, Watson suffered throughout his teens from periodic bouts of depression that left him bedridden and delirious. He spent time at three prep schools before finally graduating from the Hun School in Princeton in 1933 at age nineteen. Denied entry to Princeton University, he enrolled that fall at Brown University, whose president had once served as minister to his father. Freely spending his monthly allowance of $300, Watson devoted far more time to activities such as skiing and dancing than to his studies.

Upon graduating with a B.A. from Brown without distinction in 1937, Watson spent a summer in Russia and Asia assisting a colleague of his father's in marketing exhibition space for the 1939 New York World's Fair. That fall he joined IBM as a salesman. With his father pulling strings, Watson worked a plum territory in Manhattan, where he lived with his parents in their town house on East Seventy-fifth Street. In 1940 he met his annual quota with a single sale arranged by his father in early January. Embarrassed by such stunts, Watson spent increasing amounts of time carousing and pursuing his passions of sailing and flying. He later characterized his three years as an IBM salesman as "a time of sickening self-doubt."

Determined to escape IBM, Watson joined the National Guard in spring 1940. By the end of that year he had earned his wings and a commission as a second lieutenant in the 102nd Observation Squadron. When Roosevelt mobilized the National Guard in September 1940, Watson moved to Fort McClellan, Alabama, for further training as a military pilot. Transferred to California for shore patrol following the attack on Pearl Harbor, Watson summoned his fiancée, Olive Field Cawley, to Alabama for a hasty wedding in December 1941. A socialite and fashion model who had graced the covers of several magazines by the time she and Watson first met on a blind date in early 1939, Cawley remained married to Watson for the rest of his life. After losing an infant son in February 1943, the couple raised six children.

Admitted to the Command and General Staff School at Fort Leavenworth, Kansas, through the pull of his father, Watson spent most of World War II as special assistant and pilot for Major General Follett Bradley, head of the First Air Force. Watson later credited Bradley with instilling self-confidence in him and turning his life around. Promoted to captain soon after assuming his assignment in June 1942, Watson helped Bradley coordinate shipments of aircraft to the Soviet Union. He spent several months in Moscow while Bradley negotiated with the likes of Joseph Stalin and Winston Churchill. Although stationed for the remainder of the war near Washington, D.C., where he assisted top brass in inspections and other duties, Watson participated in some harrowing flights in the Pacific theater before resigning his military commission as a lieutenant colonel in late 1945.

Watson returned to IBM in January 1946 with a completely different outlook. Focused on succeeding his father as chief executive, he rapidly moved into the top ranks of management. By June he had become one of five vice presidents at the firm, and in October he joined the board of directors. When his most serious rival for the top post died suddenly the following spring, Watson emerged as the obvious leading candidate. Although he would not formally take over full responsibility for IBM until shortly before his father's death in 1956, during the late 1940s and early 1950s he steadily assumed more duties. After a two-year stint as vice president of sales, Watson became executive vice president in September 1949.

In this post Watson embarked on the major initiatives that distinguished his stewardship and transformed IBM from a respected firm of modest size into the most noteworthy corporation of the American century. Convinced that IBM had outgrown the intensely personal management style of his father, Watson created new staff-level positions and moved toward a divisionalized organizational structure. He authorized new laboratories and manufacturing plants in locations such as Rochester, Minnesota, and San Jose, California, far removed from the established facilities in New York that his father favored. Accepting antitrust regulation as inevitable, Watson over the course of several years negotiated a consent decree with the Department of Justice. Signed in January 1956, it called for IBM to sell as well as rent its products.

During these years before his father's death Watson also took key steps in moving IBM from its established technological base in electromechanical punched-card equipment into the world of electronics and stored-program computing. Encouraged by the success of two electronic calculators that IBM introduced shortly after the war, Watson championed the widespread use of emergent technologies, such as magnetic core memory, magnetic tapes, disks, drums, and transistors. With the outbreak of the Korean War, he shepherded a project known as the Defense Calculator, which provided IBM's first standard stored-program computer to some eighteen military contractors and government agencies. Introduced in April 1953 as the IBM 701, it laid the foundations in logical design, assembly, and service that kept IBM at the forefront of advanced computing in engineering and business into the early 1960s. Watson also personally secured a massive contract to build giant computers for Semi-Automatic Ground Environment (SAGE), a U.S. Air Force antiaircraft defense system that supported new ventures in automated manufacture and ultimately proved useful in IBM commercial products.

While embracing these moves into high-end defense work, Watson pressed for IBM to build more modest electronic computers that would substitute for existing punched-card equipment in the established business market. Machines such as the 650-drum computer and the Random Access Memory Accounting Machine (RAMAC), which gave users access to vast amounts of information stored on disks, sold in the thousands. During the late 1950s they became fixtures in business and also at universities, which could rent them at a steep discount.

As Watson relentlessly promoted the new technology within IBM, he subtly realigned the firm's public image in ways that associated it with the broadly felt public enthusiasm for a future paved with technical marvels. In 1954 he launched a comprehensive program of modern design that gave a new, clean look to everything from buildings to machines to sales brochures. World-class architects such as Eero Saarinen designed bold new facilities, including a dramatic laboratory in suburban Westchester County, New York. Named for T. J. Watson, the laboratory housed the new research division IBM created in 1955. Though IBM's most commercially important breakthroughs still emerged from product laboratories located at the manufacturing plants, this research facility carried enormous cachet in scientific and cultural circles.

In imparting a new gloss to IBM, Watson, like his father, did not hesitate to put himself forward as a symbol of the corporation. In June 1955 he appeared on the cover of an issue of *Time* magazine devoted to new technologies and automation. Later in the decade he and his family were featured in cover articles for *Life* and *Sports Illustrated*. The young CEO and his large family, seen skiing at their mountain house in Vermont or sailing off the coast of their island summer home in Maine, personified the energetic jet set, much as their close friends the Kennedys did in the realm of politics. Watson took an active role in philanthropic causes, including the New York United Fund, the Boy Scouts of America, and the United Nations Association. Through organizations such as the American Society of Sales Executives and the Business Advisory Council, he became widely known as a rare liberal voice in business circles.

By the time Watson formally succeeded his father as chairman and CEO in May 1956, four years after he had become president, he had developed the basic strategy and managerial style that characterized his subsequent fifteen years at the helm of IBM. Leaving much of the detailed execution to a trusted set of close associates, Watson concentrated on setting the tone. Typically, this involved grand gestures, as when he declared in January 1958 that all IBM employees would work on a salaried basis. In a move often cited as one of the boldest in the annals of American business, Watson announced in April 1964 that IBM would replace virtually all of its existing products with a new line of computers known as System/360. This venture caused enormous internal turmoil and incurred delays that kept IBM under a cloud of antitrust prosecution for some fifteen years. But the developments it fostered in logical design, programming, and the manufacture of electronic components sustained the firm for another two decades.

While critics and admirers alike regarded IBM as an exemplar of modern bureaucratic management, the image belied the often tempestuous climate in which critical decisions were made. A method known as the contention system openly encouraged disputes among top managers. Watson filled these posts with "sharp, scratchy, harsh, almost unpleasant guys," many of whom he did not like. With his own fiery temper on frequent display, Watson set a tone that could easily overwhelm the faint of heart. "I was a volatile leader," he recalled in his memoirs. "I wanted all the executives of IBM to feel the urgency I felt." That sense of urgency ran deep. Watson later confessed that, upon his father's death, "fear of failure became the most powerful force in my life."

IBM's financial performance during his tenure as CEO branded Watson as anything but a failure. By 1961 annual sales exceeded $2 billion, over two and a half times their level when his father left the firm. By 1970 sales had topped $7.5 billion. The value of IBM stock rose even faster, quintupling during the first five years of his stewardship alone. In 1967 its value surpassed even that of General Motors. *Fortune* magazine called Watson "the greatest capitalist who ever lived."

But the intense pressure to succeed took its toll. Strained relations with coworkers and family members and worries about diminished growth and an antitrust suit filed by the Department of Justice in January 1969 left Watson increasingly distraught. "If I had been a drinker in those days," he later surmised, "I'd have quickly killed myself." After a serious heart attack left him near death in November 1970, Watson decided to relinquish his post as CEO the following year. He did not formally retire as chairman until his sixtieth birthday in 1974, and he remained chairman of the executive committee of the board of directors for another five years after that. Nevertheless, his involvement in the key affairs of the company dwindled. Watson spent much of his time taking extended sailing trips on his new yacht, once venturing far above the Arctic Circle off the coast of Greenland.

With the 1976 election of President Jimmy Carter, Watson fulfilled his longtime ambition to work full-time in public service. Long active in Democratic politics, Watson had spent considerable time in Washington, D.C., while still at work for IBM. In 1960 he chaired a panel on technological change for President Dwight D. Eisenhower's Commission on National Goals. Watson served on several committees during the John F. Kennedy administration, including the steering committee to the Peace Corps and the Advisory Committee on Labor-Management Policy, a group of nineteen leaders from business and labor organizations who advised the president on joblessness. Watson focused on automation. During the Lyndon B. Johnson administration he committed IBM to a program of corporate citizenship that included building a plant in the impoverished Bedford-Stuyvesant district of Brooklyn, New York. Testifying before the Senate Foreign Relations Committee in June 1970, Watson advocated immediate withdrawal from Vietnam. His remarks appeared on the front page of the *New York Times* on 3 June.

Under President Carter, whose secretaries of state and defense both had served on IBM's board, Watson concerned himself primarily with foreign affairs. In the summer of 1977 he began chairing the General Advisory Committee on Arms Control and Disarmament. Two years later he became ambassador to the Soviet Union on the eve of the Soviet invasion of Afghanistan. After leaving this post with the change of administrations in January 1981, Watson spoke frequently in favor of arms control. His 1981 commencement address at Harvard University covered this topic. He helped found the Center for Foreign Policy Development at Brown University.

Watson died within weeks of suffering a serious stroke in suburban Greenwich, Connecticut, where he had made his home since 1946. He is buried in Sleepy Hollow Cemetery in Westchester County. Holding many honorary degrees, he also received the Presidential Medal of Freedom. In November 1999 *Fortune* named him one of the four greatest American businesspeople of the twentieth century.

★

Watson's best-selling memoir, *Father, Son & Co.: My Life at IBM and Beyond* (1990), offers a detailed survey of his career and a startlingly frank assessment of his stormy relationship with his father. Other helpful sources are Robert Sobel, *IBM: Colossus in Transition* (1981), and Emerson W. Pugh, *Building IBM* (1995). Obituaries are in the *New York Times* and *Washington Post* (both 1 Jan. 1994).

STEVEN W. USSELMAN

WEBB, James Edwin (*b.* 7 October 1906 in Granville County, North Carolina; *d.* 27 March 1992 in Washington, D.C.), the second administrator of the National Aeronautics and Space Administration (NASA), during whose tenure NASA developed the techniques necessary to coordinate and direct sending people to the Moon and bringing them safely back to Earth.

Webb was the son of John Frederick Webb, the superintendent of schools in Granville County, and Sarah Gorham. He was educated at the University of North Carolina, where he received an A.B. in education 1928. He then studied law at George Washington University (1933–1936) and was admitted to the bar of the District of Columbia in 1936.

James Webb. © BETTMANN/CORBIS

In 1938 Webb married Patsy Aiken; they had two children.

Webb enjoyed a long career in public service. He went to Washington in 1932 to serve as a secretary to Congressman Edward W. Pou of the Fourth North Carolina District, who was the chair of the House Rules Committee. In 1934 Webb became an assistant in the office of O. Max Gardner, an attorney and former governor of South Carolina. In 1936 Webb had become the secretary-treasurer of the Sperry Gyroscope Company in Brooklyn, New York, and he advanced to vice president before entering the U.S. Marine Corps in 1944. After World War II, Webb returned to Washington as the executive assistant to Gardner, who was by then the undersecretary of the treasury. Webb was soon named the director of the Bureau of the Budget in the Executive Office of the President, a position he held until 1949, when President Harry S. Truman asked Webb to serve as the undersecretary of state. When the Truman administration ended in early 1953, Webb left Washington for a position in the Kerr-McGee Oil Corporation in Oklahoma City.

Webb returned to Washington on 14 February 1961 to accept the position of administrator of the National Aeronautics and Space Administration (NASA). His long experience in Washington paid handsomely during his years at NASA, as he lobbied for federal support for the space program and dealt with competing interests on Capitol Hill and in the White House. His career changed fundamentally after 25 May 1961, when President John F. Kennedy announced that the United States was committed to landing an American on the Moon before the end of the decade. For seven years after Kennedy's announcement, through October 1968, Webb politicked, coaxed, cajoled, and maneuvered for NASA in Washington. The longtime Washington insider proved a master at bureaucratic politics. In the end, through a variety of methods, Webb wove a seamless web of political liaisons that brought continued support for and resources to accomplish the Apollo Moon landing in accordance with the schedule Kennedy had announced. Webb left NASA in October 1968, just as Apollo was nearing a successful completion.

One of Webb's most difficult challenges came in the aftermath of the Apollo 204 fire on 27 January 1967. During simulation tests on the launchpad at Kennedy Space Center in Florida, the astronauts Gus Grissom, Edward White, and Roger B. Chaffee died in a flash fire that broke out in the spacecraft's pure oxygen atmosphere. As shock gripped the nation during the days that followed, Webb told the media: "We've always known that something like this was going to happen sooner or later. . . . Who would have thought that the first tragedy would be on the ground?" The day after the fire Webb appointed an eight-member investigation board to discover the details of the tragedy, and to determine if it could happen again and how NASA could recover.

The members of the board quickly found that the fire had been caused by a short circuit in the electrical system that ignited combustible materials in the spacecraft fed by the oxygen atmosphere. They also found that it could have been prevented and called for several modifications to the spacecraft, including a less oxygen-rich environment. Changes to the capsule followed quickly, and a little more than a year later it was ready for flight.

Webb reported these findings to various congressional committees and took a personal grilling at every meeting. His answers were sometimes evasive and always defensive. The *New York Times* said that, under Webb, NASA stood for "Never a Straight Answer." While the ordeal was personally taxing, whether by happenstance or design Webb deflected much of the backlash over the fire from both NASA as an agency and from the administration of President Lyndon B. Johnson. While he was personally tarnished by the disaster, the space agency's image and popular support were largely undamaged. Webb never recovered from the stigma of the fire, and when he left NASA in October 1968, few mourned his departure.

Recovery from the Apollo 204 capsule fire took more than a year, but in October 1968 astronauts flew the Apollo system in Earth orbit. It appeared that reaching the Moon on Kennedy's timetable was again a possibility. After retiring from NASA, Webb remained in Washington, D.C., and served on several advisory boards, including as a regent of the Smithsonian Institution. He died of heart failure on 27 March 1992 in Washington, D.C.

★

A collection of Webb's papers is in the Lyndon B. Johnson Library, at the University of Texas, Austin, and a duplicate set is in the Harry S. Truman Library in Independence, Missouri. The NASA Historical Reference Collection, NASA Headquarters, Washington, D.C., also has a sizable collection of Webb materials. An excellent biography of Webb is W. Henry Lambright, *Powering Apollo: James E. Webb of NASA* (1995). Webb's NASA career, especially his relationship to Project Apollo, is recounted in several books, including Courtney G. Brooks, James M. Grimwood, and Loyd S. Swenson, Jr., *Chariots for Apollo: A History of Manned Lunar Spacecraft* (1979); Roger E. Bilstein, *Stages to Saturn: A Technological History of the Apollo/Saturn Launch Vehicles* (1980); Andrew Chaikin, *A Man on the Moon: The Voyages of the Apollo Astronauts* (1994); John M. Logsdon, *The Decision to Go to the Moon: Project Apollo and the National Interest* (1970); Walter A. McDougall, *The Heavens and the Earth: A Political History of the Space Age* (1985); and Charles Murray and Catherine Bly Cox, *Apollo: The Race to the Moon* (1989). Obituaries are in the *New York Times* and *Washington Post* (both 28 Mar. 1992).

ROGER D. LAUNIUS

WELK, Lawrence LeRoy (*b.* 11 March 1903 in Strasburg, North Dakota; *d.* 17 May 1992 in Santa Monica, California), orchestra leader, accordionist, and television program host whose "champagne music" epitomized middle-American taste from the 1930s through the 1970s.

Welk was born and brought up on a farm near Strasburg, North Dakota. His Alsace-born parents, Ludwig Welk (a blacksmith) and Christina Schwahn, had immigrated to the United States in 1892. The seventh of eight surviving children, Welk grew up speaking German and attended a local Catholic school run by German Ursuline nuns. As an adult Welk spoke English with a heavy German accent and it was often assumed he had been born outside the United States. His formal education ended at age eleven when a prolonged hospitalization and recuperation from a ruptured appendix put him so far behind his peers that his parents decided not to return him to school. During his recuperation Welk learned to play his father's accordion, and he later convinced his father to lend him $400 (to be repaid by work on the farm) to buy a new, first-rate instrument. As a teenager Welk honed his musical skills by entertaining at local social events.

Lawrence Welk after being selected as "Music Father of the Year," 1956. ASSOCIATED PRESS AMERICAN AIRLINES

In 1924, at age twenty-one, Welk left the farm to begin a career as a professional musician. He joined the Lincoln Boulds Chicago Band, but displeased by meager and often nonexistent paychecks from Boulds, he left and briefly managed his own band. He then joined George T. Kelly's Peerless Entertainers as an accordionist. In 1927, after the dissolution of the group, Welk again formed his own band, first called The Hotsy Totsy Boys and later known as Lawrence Welk and his Novelty Orchestra. The Welk orchestra soon began making regular appearances on WNAX, a Yankton, South Dakota, radio station. The radio exposure earned Welk a wider following and, while based in Yankton, he obtained frequent bookings at ballrooms in the Midwest and West including the Broadmoor Hotel in Colorado Springs, Colorado, and the El Mirador in Phoenix, Arizona. While living in Yankton, Welk met Fern Renner, a nurse, who like Welk was a Catholic of German extraction. The couple married on 19 April 1931 and had three children.

In 1936 the Welks moved to Omaha, Nebraska. De-emphasizing the polkas, waltzes, and other ethnic specialties that had been his musical focus, Welk developed a softer and more genteel sound aimed at middle-class audiences. He eschewed the flashy swing style exemplified by bandleaders such as Benny Goodman and Glenn Miller. A stint at the Saint Paul Hotel in Saint Paul, Minnesota, in 1938 led to a lengthy engagement at Pittsburgh's William Penn Hotel and regular broadcasts over the Pittsburgh radio station WCAE. While performing in Pittsburgh, Welk's bubbly musical style was likened to sipping champagne. The comment inspired Welk to rename his group Lawrence Welk and His Champagne Music Makers and to take as their signature song "Bubbles in the Wine." The female singer who appeared with the orchestra became known as the "Champagne Lady."

In 1939 Welk again moved his base of operation, this time to Chicago, where he spent the next decade as a mainstay at the Trianon Ballroom. Now enjoying a comfortable income, he settled his family into a large house in suburban River Forest, Illinois. Typically Welk would spend a few months of the year on the road; he sometimes substituted for Guy Lombardo and his Royal Canadians, a higher-profile orchestra with a similarly smooth style, at New York's Hotel Roosevelt.

Welk oriented his music towards ballroom dancers rather than record buyers. Although he made a few recordings in the 1940s he was never dependent upon record sales and was thus less affected than other orchestras by the waning popularity of big bands. From 1949 to 1951 many of Welk's national tour dates were broadcast over the radio by the American Broadcasting Company (ABC) and sponsored by the Miller Brewing Company, producer of Miller High Life, the "Champagne of Bottled Beers." An astute promoter of his orchestra, Welk had engineered the Miller sponsorship himself.

Welk's strongest support had always come from his home territory in the Midwest, but by the early 1950s he was finding that his most lucrative bookings were now on the West Coast. In 1951, an extremely successful engagement at the Aragon Ballroom on the pier at Santa Monica, California, led to his being offered a regular television program on the Los Angeles station KTLA. Welk accepted the offer and moved his family from Chicago to Los Angeles.

Television cameras were brought into the Aragon to broadcast performances of Welk's ballroom show, which included both vocal and instrumental numbers, to local Southern California home audiences. In 1955 the Welk program was picked up by ABC television, then a struggling "third network," as a nationwide summer-replacement offering. The nationally televised show moved Welk and his performers out of the ballroom and into a television studio but retained essentially the same format. The summer program was so popular that ABC put Welk on its regular schedule in the autumn of 1955. It quickly became one of the network's leading programs.

For the next sixteen years the *Lawrence Welk Show* was a fixture in ABC's Saturday-night television lineup. Welk offered an eclectic mix of Tin Pan Alley standards, ragtime, romantic ballads, folk songs, hymns, patriotic songs, show tunes, and contemporary hits, all performed in the cheerful yet decorous manner that was Welk's trademark style. In addition to musical numbers the Welk show featured tap and ballroom dancers. He also encouraged his studio audience members to get up and dance. "You have to play what people understand. Our music is always handled crisply. It's rhythmic and has a light beat all the time. Our notes are cut up so they sparkle. And, against the sparkle, we have an undercurrent of smoothness in violin, organ, and accordion," Welk told *Time* magazine.

Of medium height and weight with blue eyes, a large nose, and light brown hair he wore slicked back, Welk was a shy man who had never been comfortable addressing his audiences because of his heavy accent and natural reserve. He presided over his television program in an awkward, deadpan manner that many viewers found a refreshing change from the slick, highly professional style of most other television hosts. Welk's usual response to a vocal or dance performance was a calmly stated "Wunnerful, wunnerful," and this became a popular catchphrase, as did his way of starting up the orchestra's tempo with "Ah one, ah two."

Welk considered his musicians, singers, and dancers his "musical family" and ran his program in a paternalistic fashion. He expected those who worked for him to uphold the program's wholesome values in their private lives. Hostile to the significant changes in popular music and fashion that took place in the 1960s and 1970s, Welk opposed efforts by his performers to make the show sound and look more up to date. Miniskirts, Nehru jackets, and psychedelic colors were never seen on the Welk show. Although carefully selected contemporary songs made it into the Welk repertoire, they were always sung in the Welk house style.

Some performers chafed under Welk's restrictions and left his employ, but most remained with him for years. Welk's long-standing performers included accordionist Myron Floren, singer Jimmy Roberts, saxophonist and vocalist Dick Dale, pianist and bass vocalist Larry Hooper, Irish tenor Joe Feeney, tap dancer Jack Imel, ballroom dancer Bobby Burgess, and "Champagne Lady" singer Norma Zimmer. Since the program's original format never changed, Welk kept the show fresh by frequently adding new young performers to the cast. Later additions included Guy Hovis and Ralna English, a husband-and-wife vocal duo, Tom Netherton, a balladeer, and Anacani, a female vocalist specializing in Latin numbers.

From the beginning the Welk show was generally disliked by critics, who dismissed the musical arrangements as vapid and the singers and dancers as talented but colorless automatons. Welk ignored critics and sought the approval only of the public. He was highly influenced by letters sent in by viewers, and he showcased performers who received the greatest amount of favorable mail. Probably the best-known Welk performers were the Lennon Sisters, a Los Angeles quartet who began appearing on the program as children in the mid-1950s and remained with him until 1968 when, tiring of Welk's domination, they struck out on their own without much success.

In the social upheavals of the late 1960s, *The Lawrence Welk Show* came to be seen by some as a bulwark against the increasing power of untamed youth and degenerate rock-and-roll music; others saw it as a laughable anachronism; and still others considered it the favorite program of reactionaries wishing to turn back the clock. Despite the symbolism heaped upon the show, its contents never became political or didactic. The "champagne music," nonrevealing costumes, and restrained vocal performances spoke for themselves.

In 1971 ABC canceled Welk's show primarily because its audience share, while large, was too old and rural to draw the top advertising prices that the network desired. Ever resourceful, Welk began producing the show on his own and offering it directly to television stations. Under this arrangement the show stayed on the air for another eleven years. The program finally ended in 1982 when Welk, approaching eighty years of age, decided to retire. The Public Broadcasting System later showed reruns of the Welk program repackaged as *Memories with Lawrence Welk* and hosted by former cast members.

Early in his television career Welk placed his finances in the hands of Ted Lennon, uncle of the Lennon Sisters. Over the years Lennon's investments in real estate, including Lawrence Welk Village, a retirement community in Escondido, California, made Welk one of the richest people in show business (a Lawrence Welk Museum operates nearby). Welk also owned a thriving music-publishing business run by his son, Lawrence Jr., which held the rights to many old standards (including the works of the composer Jerome Kern, which the Welk organization bought for $3.2 million in 1970) and contemporary country-and-western hits. In his later years Welk wrote his autobiography and several other books extolling the virtues of hard work, clean living, and patriotism. Welk died of pneumonia at his Santa Monica, California, home. He is buried in Holy Cross Cemetery in Culver City, California.

Welk and his "champagne music" pleased audiences in ballrooms and on radio and television for more than forty years. In terms of public acceptance he is among the leading figures in American popular music of the twentieth century.

★

With the exception of his first book, *Guidelines for Successful Living* (1968), all of Welk's books were written with Bernice McGeehan, including his autobiography, *Wunnerful, Wunnerful!* (1971), *Ah-One, Ah-Two: Life with My Musical Family* (1974), *My America, Your America* (1977), *This I Believe* (1979), and *You're Never Too Young* (1981). Pete Martin, "I Call on Lawrence Welk," *Saturday Evening Post* (21 June 1958), offers a lengthy interview with Welk. Sedulus, "The Enduringly Crummy," *The New Republic* (19 Dec. 1970), is a critique of Welk's musical style. Roger Neal, "Wunnerful, Wunnerful!," *Forbes* (26 Sept. 1983), examines Welk's business enterprises. Obituaries are in the *New York Times* (19 May 1992) and *Newsweek* (1 June 1992).

MARY KALFATOVIC

WELLS, Mary Esther (*b.* 13 May 1943 in Detroit, Michigan; *d.* 26 July 1992 in Los Angeles, California), pop-soul singer and the first solo star of Motown Records, who helped solidify the black-owned record label's crossover appeal to the white mainstream market.

Wells was raised by her mother, who worked as a domestic, and began her singing career in the time-honored fashion of joining her local church choir. By her mid-teens Wells was also performing at school functions, talent contests, and clubs.

At the same time, a musical revolution was brewing in Detroit. In 1959 Berry Gordy, Jr., a former boxer, record-shop owner, and Ford assembly-line worker, founded the Motown Record Corporation. The company's slogan embodied its crossover intentions: "The Sound of Young America," not the sound of only black or white America.

Mary Wells, 1964. © HULTON-DEUTSCH COLLECTION/CORBIS

The strategy worked admirably, with early singles like "Shop Around" by the Miracles and "Please Mr. Postman" by the Marvelettes (both released on Motown's Tamla label) finding success on both the pop and R&B charts.

Although accounts differ as to how Wells and Gordy met, it is certain that in 1960, at age seventeen, Wells pitched Gordy a song she had written, "Bye Bye Baby," hoping he would place it with Jackie Wilson. Instead, Gordy signed Wells to Motown and had her record the song herself. "Bye Bye Baby," released on the Motown label in February 1961, performed respectably for a debut release, reaching the top ten in the R&B charts and just missing the pop Top 40, peaking at number 45. "I Don't Want to Take a Chance," cowritten by Gordy and Motown's head of A&R, William "Mickey" Stevenson, became Wells's first Top 40 entry upon its release in 1961, peaking at number 33 and again hitting the top ten in the R&B charts.

Wells was then teamed with a new songwriter, William "Smokey" Robinson (also a member of the Miracles), who steered her in a new direction. While her first singles had a strong blues element, Robinson aimed for a lighter, more sophisticated touch. In contrast to the girl-group records of the era, designed to appeal to teenagers, Wells's songs took a more mature, adult approach to romance. In "Two Lovers" (1962), for example, Wells was clearly beyond adolescent yearnings for a boyfriend, coolly assessing her "two lovers" who turned out to be the two sides of her man's personality.

For the next three years Wells enjoyed a steady stream of hits. Not only "Two Lovers" but also "The One Who Really Loves You," and "You Beat Me to the Punch" hit the top ten in the pop and R&B charts in 1962. "Laughing Boy," "Your Old Stand By," "You Lost the Sweetest Boy," and "What's Easy for Two Is So Hard for One" (all 1963) hit the top thirty in the pop charts and top ten in the R&B charts. Wells's career at Motown climaxed in 1964 with the chart-topper "My Guy," which gave the Motown label its first number one hit (Motown's previous number one records had been on the Tamla label) and made Wells Motown's first solo star. The song's breezy melody was irresistibly catchy, perfectly matched by her confident yet lighthearted vocal. The worldwide success of the song landed Wells a coveted spot on the Beatles' 1964 United Kingdom tour; the following year Wells released the album *Mary Wells Sings Love Songs to the Beatles*.

Wells had two more Top 40 entries on the Motown label: "What's the Matter with You Baby" and "Once upon a Time," both duets with the Motown singer Marvin Gaye and released in 1964. But when Wells turned twenty-one, at the urging of her then-husband Herman Griffin (a singer and Motown songwriter), she declared her contract with Motown invalid because she had signed when she was a minor. Wells then signed with Twentieth Century–Fox, but her sole Top 40 entry on the label was "Use Your Head" (1964), which reached number 34 (number 13 R&B). "Never, Never Leave Me" (1965), stalled at number 54, though it did reach the top twenty in the R&B charts. Wells subsequently signed to Atco (a subsidiary of Atlantic), Jubilee, and Reprise, but never again recaptured the success she had had at Motown. "Dear Lover" (1966) hit the top ten in the R&B charts, but "The Doctor" (1968) and "Dig the Way I Feel" (1969) were only minor hits. She also appeared in the 1967 film *Catalina Caper*.

Wells divorced Griffin and married Cecil Womack (brother of the musician Bobby Womack) in 1967. She and Womack had three children. Divorced in 1977, Wells subsequently had another child with Cecil's brother Curtis. Wells's career was on hold for most of the 1970s while she raised her children. She returned to performing in the late 1970s, signing with Epic and releasing the album *In and Out of Love* in 1981. She also found work on the rock revival circuit, re-recorded her Motown hits for Allegiance, and released her final album, *Keeping My Mind on Love*, on Motor City in 1990.

The same year, Wells was diagnosed with cancer of the larynx and underwent surgery in August, followed by chemotherapy. The illness left Wells financially destitute. After she lost her house, the Washington, D.C.–based Rhythm & Blues Foundation (an organization founded by the singer

Ruth Brown) raised money for her medical expenses. In 1991 physicians discovered that Wells's cancer had spread to her lungs. She underwent further treatments but died at the Norris Cancer Center at the University of Southern California in Los Angeles. She is buried at Forest Lawn Memorial Park in the Hollywood Hills of Los Angeles.

While Wells's tenure at Motown was brief compared to that of acts like the Supremes, it was her success in the early 1960s that pushed open the doors for other African-American artists and helped eradicate the musical segregation of the era. In contrast to the turbulence of the decade, Wells's songs, and those by other African-American artists, were able to bring people of all races together in celebration rather than strife.

★

There are no biographies of Mary Wells, but a substantial interview appears in Gerri Hirshey, *Nowhere to Run: The Story of Soul Music* (1984). Martha Reeves with Mark Bego, *Dancing in the Street: Confessions of a Motown Diva* (1994) offers further personal insights; Nelson George's *Where Did Our Love Go?* (1985) is a critique of Motown's development; and Gillian Gaar's *She's a Rebel: The History of Women in Rock & Roll* (1992) examines Wells's role as a woman in the music industry. The compact discs *Mary Wells: Looking Back 1961–1964* (1993) and *Mary Wells: The Ultimate Collection* (1998) have useful liner notes by David Ritz. Brief biographies are in *The Rolling Stone Encyclopedia of Rock & Roll* (1983), *The New Rolling Stone Encyclopedia of Rock & Roll* (1995), and Colin Larkin, ed., *The Encyclopedia of Popular Music*, vol. 7 (1998). Obituaries are in the *New York Times* (27 July 1992) and *People* (10 Aug. 1992).

GILLIAN G. GAAR

WILDAVSKY, Aaron Bernard (*b.* 31 May 1930 in New York City; *d.* 4 September 1993 in Oakland, California), political scientist and noted authority on government budgeting and public administration and policy.

Wildavsky was the third child and the only son to live to adulthood of Eva and Sender Wildavsky, who immigrated to the United States from the Ukraine in 1928. His parents had experienced life under tsarist and Bolshevik governments and were committed to the policies exemplified in President Franklin D. Roosevelt's New Deal. His father, a bookbinder by trade, was injured shortly after arriving in the United States, and the money he received under the workman's compensation laws allowed him to buy a small apartment building in Brooklyn. Wildavsky recalled that his first contact with partisan politics came from negotiating housing matters on behalf of his parents with City Hall through the local Democratic club. At fourteen he distributed campaign leaflets for President Roosevelt. Wildavsky indicated, however, that it was his time at Brooklyn College

Aaron Wildavsky. THE INDEPENDENT INSTITUTE

that really led to his intense personal interest and involvement in politics.

Wildavsky attended public schools in Brooklyn, graduating from P.S. 89 and Erasmus Hall High School (1948), where he was, by his own account, an indifferent student. He blossomed as a scholar, however, when he entered Brooklyn College in the fall of 1948. His undergraduate work was interrupted by military service in the U.S. Army (1950–1952), after which he returned to college and graduated Phi Beta Kappa with a B.A. degree in 1954. He was a Fulbright scholar at the University of Sydney in Australia (1954–1955). Upon returning to the United States, he earned an M.A. degree in 1957 and a Ph.D. in 1959, both from Yale University. In 1955 he married Carol Shirk; they had four children. They divorced in 1970 and he later married Mary Cadman.

In 1958 Wildavsky began his academic career at Oberlin College in Ohio. In 1962 he moved to the University of California at Berkeley, where he became chairman of the Department of Political Science from 1966 to 1969. He was the first dean of the Graduate School of Public Policy at Berkeley from 1969 to 1977. At the time of his death, he was Class of 1940 Professor of Political Science and Public Policy at Berkeley. Wildavsky became the president of the Russell Sage Foundation in New York City (1977–1978) but returned to Berkeley within two years.

Wildavsky was a remarkably prolific author in the fields of political science, public policy, and public administration. He wrote or coauthored thirty-nine books and approximately 200 articles, essays, and reviews on a wide range of issues. In 1964 Wildavsky coauthored *Presidential Elections: Strategies of American Electoral Politics* with his longtime friend Nelson W. Polsby, who had been a fellow graduate student at Yale and subsequently a colleague at Berkeley. The book examined why some candidates were successful and others were not and how voter choices were constrained by the rules regulating nominations and elections. This book had a long-term impact on teaching about presidential elections and was revised in seven subsequent editions during presidential election years.

Wildavsky made his mark in public administration with the publication of *The Politics of the Budgetary Process* (1964) and in *The New Politics of the Budgetary Process* (1988 and 1992). Wildavsky analyzed the use of power, strategy, and compromise in incremental budgetary changes that tend to distribute dissatisfaction relatively equally to all parties over time. *Politics of the Budgetary Process* was named by the American Society for Public Administration (ASPA) as the third most influential work in public administration in the previous fifty years.

Wildavsky thought of political analysis as more of an "art" or "craft" than a "science," and he was unmoved by the trend toward more empirical approaches in political science. He saw much of his writing as self-expression. As he wrote, "Every man needs a craft through which he can express himself to the extent of his abilities, and I have found mine." Polsby wrote about him, "He is one of those who writes in order to learn what he thinks, and who embraces the discipline of putting his ideas promptly into words and sentences."

Wildavsky's political views and party affiliation changed over his career from that of a New Deal Democrat to an increasingly conservative Republican by the early 1980s. He believed that most men had "little knowledge and limited moral sensibility," and therefore he had a "deep-seated pessimism about man's ability to control the evil in him." He came to be increasingly uncomfortable with what he considered the rise of radical egalitarianism within the Democratic party. Toward the end of his career, Wildavsky believed that the government had become too responsive to this radical minority's demand for more regulation in the areas of health, safety, and the environment. He was, not surprisingly, distrustful of the value of normative theory—which indicates a preference based on moral or social values rather than on empirical evidence—in public administration. These views elicited criticism from many academic colleagues in a harsh manner he had not previously experienced.

Wildavsky's prominence within political science was recognized by the many honors and awards that he received. Brooklyn College, his alma mater, bestowed an honorary degree on him (1977) as did Yale University (1993). Wildavsky received more awards than any other political scientist of his generation. In 1972 he received the ASPA's William E. Mosher Award, and in 1982 the organization awarded him the Dwight Waldo Award for his contributions to the literature of public administration. He received the Charles E. Merriam Award from the American Political Science Association (1975) in recognition of his contributions applying theory to the practice of politics, the Paul F. Lazarsfeld Award for Research (1981), and the Harold Lasswell award for contributions to the study of public policy (1984). He was president of the American Political Science Association from 1985 to 1986.

Wildavsky died of lung cancer at the age of sixty-three. He is buried in Oakland, California.

Wildavsky possessed a character and scholarly presence that served to enlighten and inspire individuals whether or not they agreed with him. His intellectual contributions were not limited to his prodigious publications but include his work as an excellent teacher with caring concern for his students.

★

Wildavsky's broad-ranging views, including an introspective look at his own scholarly approach, is found in his *Revolt Against the Masses and Other Essays on Politics and Public Policy* (1971). The most thorough and objective evaluation of Wildavsky's contributions to political science is found in L. R. Jones, "Aaron Wildavsky: A Man and Scholar for all Seasons," in *Public Administration Review* 55, no. 1 (Jan.–Feb. 1995). A revealing portrait of Wildavsky is found in Nelson Polsby, "The Contributions of President Aaron Wildavsky" in *PS: Political Science and Politics* 18, no.4 (fall 1985). Eulogies and a complete bibliography of his publications are found in Institute of Government Studies, *Aaron Wildavsky: A Memorial 1930–1993* (1994). An obituary is in the *New York Times* (6 Sept. 1993).

CHARLES L. COCHRAN

WOJNAROWICZ, David Michael (*b.* 14 September 1954 in Red Bank, New Jersey; *d.* 22 July 1992 in New York City), artist, writer, and activist whose passionate, deeply personal work about sexuality, mortality, and the AIDS epidemic made him a lightning rod for debates in the 1980s about federal government funding for the arts.

One of three children of Edward Theodore Wojnarowicz, a merchant seaman (who had two children from a previous marriage), and Dolores McGuinness, a homemaker, Wojnarowicz was two years old when his parents divorced. Specific details of Wojnarowicz's unhappy childhood years are difficult to verify and rely largely on Wojnarowicz's mem-

David Wojnarowicz. PHOTO: TIMOTHY GREENFIELD-SANDERS.

ories which, by his own admission, were often uncertain and embellished in the context of his later literary work.

Following his parents' divorce, Wojnarowicz and his siblings initially lived with their mother, but she was unable to care for them. Thereafter the children lived in an institutional setting, with relatives, and with their father, a physically abusive alcoholic who was often away at sea for weeks at a time. When Wojnarowicz was eight years old his father sent the children back for the final time to their mother, who moved the family to nearby New York City. By the age of eleven, Wojnarowicz had begun working on the streets as a male prostitute. Despite the desperate circumstances of his home life, he attended the High School of Music and Art in Manhattan, but dropped out at the age of sixteen and left home for good. Falling prey to beatings, rapes, and robberies on the streets, he continued to earn a living by hustling and other criminal activities. His health deteriorating, Wojnarowicz finally got off the streets in 1972, seeking shelter at a halfway house where he had previously lived for a short time.

Over the next five years Wojnarowicz traveled, first working on a farm and then later hopping trains or hitchhiking to the West Coast. He settled for a year in San Francisco, where for the first time he lived openly as a homosexual, and started writing and taking photographs.

He returned to New York in 1977, where he began writing monologues based on his street experiences, and then spent the next year in France, staying in Normandy and in Paris, where his sister lived. It was also during 1978 that his father committed suicide. Upon his return from Europe, Wojnarowicz again settled in New York City, where he began his art career in earnest.

While working various jobs as a busboy or janitor to support himself, often at popular music clubs, the dark-haired, gauntly handsome Wojnarowicz began to record his experiences—through writing, photography, and film—with the drug culture and gay community that frequented the abandoned warehouses and run-down piers of Manhattan's West Side. He joined a band called 3 Teens Kill 4—No Motive (taken from a headline in a New York tabloid newspaper), playing children's instruments and tape recordings of found sounds. He also began a series of guerrilla art actions, decorating streets and buildings in Manhattan with stenciled images of burning houses, falling figures, soldiers, targets, and bomber planes.

By the beginning of the 1980s, several dramatic events occurred that would have a profound impact on the direction of Wojnarowicz's career and life. The first was the emergence around 1982 of the East Village art scene, a low-budget, artist-driven movement that would spawn several dozen galleries in the storefronts and tenement buildings of the working-class neighborhood. Although the phenomenon would disappear by the end of the 1980s, the brief but highly visible scene would jump-start the careers of several artists, including Keith Haring. Wojnarowicz began having solo exhibitions of his sculpture and paintings in the East Village as early as 1982 and would go on to show at least a half dozen times at galleries there, including Civilian Warfare and Gracie Mansion. Continuing his work in stencil and with found maps, a motif he would employ throughout his career, he also began producing freehand paintings, often done on surplus grocery-store price signs. Their subjects ranged widely but typically involved iconic images borrowed from pop culture, usually modified and then recontextualized in settings that explored the relationship between violence and eroticism.

The early 1980s also saw the emergence of the AIDS epidemic, which struck at the heart of New York's alternative culture and its large gay community. Wojnarowicz's militant posture regarding the attitude of the government and the general public toward AIDS was crystallized when his closest friend, the photographer Peter Hujar, became ill in 1984. Hujar died in 1987, the same year that Wojnarowicz was himself diagnosed with the disease. Wojnarowicz's long-standing artistic involvement with issues of sexuality and mortality was given an extraordinarily powerful frame by the crisis. His work over the next five years would address itself almost exclusively, if at times obliquely, to AIDS.

Although Wojnarowicz was well known within the art world, he became a national celebrity during the so-called culture wars of the late 1980s. In 1989, the National Endowment for the Arts first rescinded and then eventually restored funding for an exhibition catalog in which Wojnarowicz made pointed personal attacks on a number of national religious and political figures. The following year, *David Wojnarowicz: Tongues of Flame,* a retrospective of the artist's work organized by Illinois State University, was denounced by a member of the U.S. House of Representatives. Wojnarowicz also drew the attention of the Reverend Donald Wildmon, a conservative activist and head of the American Family Association. Wildmon cropped sexually explicit images out of the photo and text works Wojnarowicz was then creating and put them in a pamphlet denouncing the artist, then circulated the pamphlet to politicians, church leaders, and journalists around the country. Wojnarowicz sued the American Family Association for misrepresenting him and damaging his reputation. In 1990, a federal district court judge in New York ruled in the artist's favor.

Over the last few years of Wojnarowicz's life, as his health rapidly deteriorated, he exhibited less but continued to produce work—typically photography and painting, often set into compositionally complex arrangements with excerpts from his writings. A collection of his writings, *Close to the Knives: A Memoir of Disintegration,* was published by Vintage Books in 1991. The following year Wojnarowicz died of AIDS-related complications in New York City. His remains were cremated.

The confluence of volatile political times and the confrontational nature of his art transformed David Wojnarowicz from a little-known downtown New York fringe artist into one of the most visible symbols of the debates of the 1980s regarding homosexuality, government support for the arts, and the AIDS epidemic. Although often remembered for the transgressive qualities of his work, Wojnarowicz was also capable of remarkably delicate conceptual gestures and highly refined formal approaches. His willingness to take on the political and religious establishment mark him as one of the most socially committed artists of the decade; his wide-ranging experiments in painting, photography, film, and writing constitute an essential document of the times in which he lived.

★

There are numerous catalogs, brochures, and articles on David Wojnarowicz. Since his work and life were so closely aligned, readers may find themselves struggling at times to separate fact from fiction, particularly with regard to the artist's early life and his many often harrowing personal experiences. The artist's own memoirs and essays have been collected in *Close to the Knives: A Memoir of Disintegration* (1991); *Memories That Smell Like Gasoline* (1992); and *The Waterfront Journals,* edited by Amy Scholder (1996). In addition, two major catalogs have been produced to accompany exhibitions of Wojnarowicz's work: *David Wojnarowicz: Tongues of Flame* (1990) and Amy Scholder, ed., *Fever: The Art of David Wojnarowicz* (1998). An obituary is in the *New York Times* (24 July 1992).

JEFFREY KASTNER

Y-Z

YATES, Richard Walden (*b.* 3 February 1926 in Yonkers, New York; *d.* 7 November 1992 in Birmingham, Alabama), novelist and short story writer who depicted the thwarted lives of middle-class suburbanites in the period from the Great Depression to the early 1970s.

Yates's literary specialty was the portrayal of social disaster, particularly the miscalculations that ruin marriages and friendships and blight careers. With no desire to be inventive or to romanticize his characters, he set out to chart his own damaged, essentially uneventful life in nine fictional versions. Yates and his sister were children whose parents had divorced in 1929; that fact provided Yates with an early window on clashing personalities and money troubles. His mother, Ruth Maurer, was a trained sculptor of modest talents who cherished illusions about a brilliant career and sacrificed family stability and her own earning capacities for art. His father, Vincent Matthew ("Mike") Yates, a down-to-earth salesman for the General Electric Mazda lamp division, was at odds with his wife's flighty bohemianism. After raising the children on her own in New York City's Greenwich Village, Ruth Yates wanted a prep school education for her son, a demand that his father met with great sacrifice. Their son went to Avon Old Farms School in Connecticut, the dispiriting locale of Yates's *A Good School* (1978). After graduation in 1944, he was drafted into the army, serving as an infantryman in the European theater.

After his discharge Yates spent 1946 to 1948 as a rewrite man for the news information service United Press International. In 1948 he married Sheila Bryant, with whom he had two children. After working from 1949 to 1950 at Remington Rand as a publicity writer, he secured a veterans' disability pension for tuberculosis he had contracted during the war, and he moved to Europe for two years. By 1953 he was in Redding, Connecticut, living unhappily with his in-laws, working as a freelance public relations writer— and absorbing the stultifying atmosphere to be used in his first novel, *Revolutionary Road* (1961). Radically revised from a melodramatic manuscript, the novel is about the plastic and pastel nightmare of suburbia in the mid-1950s. Frank and April Wheeler, a pair of attractive self-deceivers, lose their sense of purpose in life and destroy themselves, all the while epitomizing the illusions of many post–World War II Americans. The book was arguably the high point of Yates's career—an austerely written, devastatingly ironic social study that earned critical praise and was a finalist for the National Book Award.

Yates's *Eleven Kinds of Loneliness* (1962), a collection of stories written in the 1950s, was a strong second book. Regarded as an American equivalent of James Joyce's *Dubliners* (1914), the collection finely hones the desperations of disconnected people: a hospital patient and his cheating wife, a neurotic teacher and her disappointed class, a slum kid confused by middle-class children, a real writer and a taxi driver with ludicrous literary schemes. Chagrin and

Richard Yates. © JERRY BAUER

denial dominate these episodes. One piece about an exacting army sergeant, "Jody Rolled the Bones," won the Atlantic Monthly First award in 1953. Before the impact of his successes, Yates had divorced in 1959 and abandoned the business world for teaching at the New School (1959–1962) and Columbia University (1960–1962). During the 1960s other honors and distinctions rolled in: grants from the Guggenheim Foundation (1962), the National Institute of Arts and Letters (1963), and the Rockefeller Foundation (1967); a job as Robert F. Kennedy's speechwriter (1963); stints as a screenwriter at United Artists (1962) and Columbia Pictures (1965–1966); and a post in the prestigious writing program at the University of Iowa, which lasted from 1964 to 1971.

Meanwhile Yates's drinking and attendant psychological problems resulted in hospitalization at the University of California at Los Angeles's Neuropsychiatric Institute in 1965. His literary output was meager during the decade, and when his war novel *A Special Providence* appeared in 1969 it disappointed everyone, including himself: it was an old-fashioned, overwritten initiation story in the wake of Joseph Heller's surreal satire and Kurt Vonnegut's cosmic fantasies; its hell-and-boredom view of war was lost in the maelstrom of experimentation. He married Martha Speer

in 1968, a union that produced one child and ended in divorce in 1975.

Shocked at being denied tenure at Iowa in 1971, Yates tried another post as distinguished writer-in-residence at Wichita State University (1971–1972), but only achieved relative security when Seymour Lawrence, an editor at Delacorte Press with his own imprint, put him on a salary of $1,500 a month from 1973 until the early 1990s. After a few years living in Greenwich Village, he moved to Boston in 1976 and stayed for ten years. The 1970s and early 1980s became his most productive period. With *Disturbing the Peace* (1975), a harrowing account of a businessman who drinks his way to the madhouse, Yates was back in form— precise and in touch with an age that was fascinated by mental illness and bourgeois conformity. He followed his literary comeback with *Easter Parade* (1976), a short novel that nevertheless has an epic sweep; the story follows the unhappy lives of the two Grimes sisters, go-getting professional Emily and passive Long Island housewife Sarah. Yates traced their mistakes and futile hopes from the late 1930s into the 1970s. He told a woman fan that the book was "my autobiography, sweetheart, Emily fucking Grimes is me." *A Good School* (1978) was cut and tailored from Yates's fragile early life; its young protagonist, Bill Groves, is a struggling misfit in the affluent preppy world of Dorset Academy, a "funny little place" where even teachers and rich kids hang on to dignity by just a thread.

In the 1980s Yates resumed teaching in creative writing programs, first at Boston University (1981) and Emerson College (1984), briefly at the University of Southern California (1989), and finally—when nearing his death from emphysema—at the University of Alabama at Tuscaloosa (1990–1991). His last three books traced his master theme of mere survival in new ways. *Liars in Love* (1981) is a collection of long, reflective short stories about crises in his life, most notably the collapse of his mother's career illusions in the Village during the 1930s and the end of his second marriage. *Young Hearts Crying* (1984) is his most sustained treatment of the writer's vocation—and its destructive side effects. *Cold Spring Harbor* (1986) returns to adolescent feelings of social embarrassment caused by moneyed neighbors and an inept mother. Yates's unfinished novel, *Uncertain Times,* is about his days as Robert Kennedy's speechwriter: it is an unidolatrous look at the energy and optimism of the New Frontier.

Yates was out of step with the literary styles and attitudes of post-1950s America. An exacting realist who disdained postmodern pyrotechnics, a keen observer of neurotic behavior who ignored Freud, he was a literary independent in his time—respected by critics and fellow writers, including Raymond Carver and Ann Beattie, but never as popular as flashier contemporaries. Yet his unsparing vision and meticulous prose recall the classic distinction of Hemingway's taut early stories. Yates was cremated and his remains were given to his daughter.

★

Drafts of Yates's short fiction and assorted correspondence are located in Boston University's Special Collections Division at Mugar Library; the manuscript of *Uncertain Times* is held by his daughter, Monica Yates, a section having been published in *Open City,* no. 3 (1995): 35–71. Yates's writing and life have been fully treated in the only book-length study, David Castronovo and Steven Goldleaf, *Richard Yates* (1996), a volume that includes material from interviews, cultural criticism, analysis of the fiction, and extensive bibliography. A notable review of *Revolutionary Road* by Theodore Solotaroff, which offers a penetrating critique of Yates's views of class in modern America, is in *Commentary* (July 1961). Richard Ford, "American Beauty (Circa 1955)," is a sharply focused appreciation of *Revolutionary Road* on the occasion of its fortieth year in print, *New York Times Book Review* (5 Apr. 2000). Stewart O'Nan, "The Lost World of Richard Yates," is an excellent short survey of Yates's art and problematic place in American letters, *Boston Review* (Oct.–Nov. 1999). An obituary is in the *New York Times* (9 Nov. 1992).

DAVID CASTRONOVO

YERBY, Frank Garvin (*b.* 5 September 1916 in Augusta, Georgia; *d.* 29 November 1991 in Madrid, Spain), best-selling African American novelist.

Yerby was the son of Rufus Garvin and Wilhelmina Ethylyn Smythe Yerby. His father was a hotel doorman in Detroit and Miami. His mother, who raised Yerby, was a teacher, as were his aunts, all of whom influenced Yerby's development. He became interested in writing while a high school student at Haines Institute in Augusta, Georgia. The famed writer James Weldon Johnson, who visited the high school, gave Yerby early encouragement. After graduation from high school in 1933, Yerby matriculated at Paine College in Augusta, where he majored in English and languages and received a B.A. degree in 1937. He studied briefly at the City College of New York before returning to Paine. Yerby earned an M.A. degree in English at Fisk University in 1938, then studied in the education department at the University of Chicago in 1939. He worked for the Federal Writers Project of the Works Progress Administration in Chicago, joining a Muslim religious cult for research purposes.

In June 1939 Yerby took a position teaching in the English department at the Florida Agricultural and Mechanical College in Tallahassee. He then taught for a year at Southern University in Baton Rouge, Louisiana. He married Flora Helen Claire Williams on 1 March 1941, and he said that his wife gave him the drive he needed as a writer. The Yerbys had four children.

Frank Yerby. LIBRARY OF CONGRESS

During World War II, Yerby first worked as a lab technician for the Ford Motor Company in Dearborn, Michigan. He then moved with his family to New York, where he worked in the Ranger engine division of the Fairchild Airplane Manufacturing Company on Long Island from June 1944 until August 1945.

Yerby's first publications were poems, which were printed in *New Challenge,* an African American literary quarterly, as early as 1937. His first fiction, a short story called "The Thunder of God," appeared in *New Anvil,* a left-wing bimonthly, in 1939. In 1944, *Harper's* magazine gave him his first national exposure by publishing his short story "Health Card," which was chosen for an O. Henry Memorial Prize. Critics hailed these stories and others published over the next few years for their sensitive portrayal of African Americans in Georgia. Other short pieces that Yerby wrote in this period about racial discrimination remain unpublished. Yerby's first novel, *The Foxes of Harrow,* published in February 1946, was written with the intent of making money. His aim was accurate, for the book sold over a million copies by the end of its first year in print. Black critics hailed the book as a breakthrough but white critics generally dismissed it as a flowery tale of the Deep South, packed with stock characters and melodramatic turns of plot. The book was reprinted several times and in

1947 was made into a film starring Rex Harrison and Maureen O'Hara.

The racism Yerby and his family experienced while living in New York drove them into exile in France in 1952. In his 1951 novel, *A Woman Called Fancy,* a sympathetic white character states that "blacks and whites can't live together," and then details racist insults endured by intellectual African Americans. Supported by his ample earnings, the Yerbys lived in Nice, sent their children to school in Switzerland, and enjoyed racing cars and skin diving. In 1956, Flora Yerby returned to the United States and filed for divorce, claiming that Yerby had abandoned her the year before. Soon thereafter Yerby married Blanquita Calle-Perez, a Spanish secretary who worked for an American military corporation. Devoted to Yerby, she nursed him through a serious illness and became his assistant and secretary. They visited the United States briefly in 1956, but angered by hostile stares, the interracial couple soon departed for Europe. Yerby rarely returned to his home country again, preferring to live in Spain with his second wife. They had no children.

Yerby churned out twenty-eight novels in the next three decades. In a 1960 article, Yerby explained his devotion to the "costume novel," which was "a certain genre of light, pleasant fiction." Although his novels are often set in an earlier historical period, Yerby maintained that he was not a historical novelist, because, he said, most of his research wound up on the cutting-room floor. He contended that the novelist's primary job is to entertain and stay in contact with the readers; real talent, he said, is never neglected and unread authors simply have not mastered the craft of writing. His rules were to make the protagonist a picaresque, romantic, dominant male, who was physically imposing but emotionally immature. The hero should be incurably polygamous, while the heroine should be sexy and beautiful. Plots should be lean and dramatic. Novelists should stay out of politics and stick to the big themes of God, sex, death, and evil. For most of his career, Yerby used only white heroic figures, a practice that ultimately alienated his African American followers.

Generally, critics derided Yerby's novels, claiming that he often resorted to strokes of fate to untwine apparently insoluble problems in his plots. The *Saturday Review of Literature* in 1946 reviled *The Foxes of Harrow* as one of the "technicolored fantasies" that had been recently popular. As Yerby published a novel almost every year, few of them were even reviewed. The critic Darwin Turner credited Yerby with a vast imagination and an ability to portray emotions and the plight of the poor and oppressed. More significant was the criticism that he avoided difficult racial issues. Turner argued that behind the soap opera clichés in Yerby's books were "ideas . . . bitter ironies, caustic debunking, painful gropings for meaning." Turner and his student James Lee Hill have proposed that Yerby's portrayal of his southern white characters as flawed and picaresque results in a subtle debunking of southern mythology. Because his characters are often mean-spirited, greedy, and bigoted, Turner and Hill interpret Yerby's art as existential and antiheroic. Although he appreciated Turner and Hill, generally Yerby dismissed critics. In a 1984 interview, he retorted that critics "couldn't write if they were paid their weight in Saudi Arabian oil bonds."

Despite his contempt for reviewers, Yerby worried about his reputation. He gradually moved beyond formulaic southern novels to fictionalized histories of ancient Greece, Spain, and the Caribbean and the origins of Christianity and Judaism. His novels *Speak Now* (1969) and *The Dahomean* (1971) were well-received deliberations on African American and African cultures. Yerby published his last novel, *McKenzie's Hundred,* in 1985. His influence on African American letters is found in the popular historical novels of Alice Walker, Terry McMillan, and Robert Dean Pharr. Yerby died of a heart attack in Madrid. At his request, Yerby's widow kept his death a secret for five weeks and he was buried in complete privacy, presumably in Madrid. In addition to his wife, his survivors included his four children and seven grandchildren.

★

Yerby's unpublished stories and papers are held at the library of Boston University. An early glance at Yerby and his career is in *Current Biography* (1946). A fuller sketch plus a bibliography and an interview can be found in *Contemporary Authors: New Revision Series,* vol. 16 (1981). Also see Louis Hill Pratt, "Frank Garvin Yerby," in *Contemporary African American Novelists: A Bio-Bibliographical Critical Sourcebook* (1999), and James Lee Hill, "Anti-Heroic Perspectives: The Life and Work of Frank Yerby," Ph.D. diss., University of Iowa (1976). A key article is Darwin T. Turner, "Frank Yerby as Debunker," *Massachusetts Review* 20 (summer 1968): 569–578. Obituaries are in the *New York Times* (8 Jan. 1992) and London *Times* (11 Jan. 1992).

GRAHAM RUSSELL HODGES

YLVISAKER, Paul Norman (*b.* 28 November 1921 in Saint Paul, Minnesota; *d.* 17 March 1992 in Washington, D.C.), urban planner, government official, foundation executive, and educator.

Ylvisaker was one of five children of Dr. Sigurd C. Ylvisaker and Norma Norem. At the time of his birth, his father, a Lutheran minister, was a professor at Concordia College in Saint Paul. In 1930 the family moved to Mankato, Minnesota, where Sigurd Ylvisaker became the president of Bethany Lutheran College, a position he held until 1950. Ylvisaker attended Immanuel Lutheran Elementary School,

Paul Ylvisaker, 1967. AP/WIDE WORLD PHOTOS

Bethany Lutheran High School, and Bethany Lutheran College, from which he received his A.A. degree in 1940. He went on to Mankato State Teachers College, graduating with a B.S. degree in 1942. Following completion of his undergraduate studies, he taught for a short time at Bethany Lutheran College while taking graduate courses at the University of Minnesota. From 1943 to 1946 he was a staff member of the Blue Earth County Council on Intergovernmental Relations, and at the same time he pursued graduate studies at Harvard University, where he was a Littauer Fellow and where he earned his M.P.A. in 1945. He went on to earn a Ph.D. in political economy and government in 1948. While studying at Harvard, he met Barbara Ewing, a Radcliffe College student, whom he married in 1946; they had four children.

After completing his studies at Harvard, Ylvisaker joined the faculty at Swarthmore College in Pennsylvania, where he earned a reputation for being a fine teacher. He also was highly regarded as a scholar and took leave during the 1951–1952 academic year to serve as a Senior Fulbright Research Scholar in England. While not interested in a political career, Ylvisaker served as the Democratic chair for the town of Swarthmore and as the executive secretary to Philadelphia Mayor Joseph S. Clark from 1954 to 1955. He also worked on Clark's senatorial campaign.

The demands of undertaking this political activity while maintaining his teaching job, coupled with health problems, led Ylvisaker to leave Swarthmore and the Clark organization and accept a position as the executive associate for the Public Affairs Program of the Ford Foundation in New York City. In 1958 he became the associate director of the program and the next year became its director. Before leaving the Ford Foundation in 1967, he spent time in both India and Japan on urban planning projects. In Japan he served as a technical assistant in a United Nations position from 1960 to 1962 and again in 1964. His most important work with the Ford Foundation was the development of what he called the "Gray Areas" program. Ylvisaker used that term to refer to the deteriorating areas of cities between the downtowns and the suburbs. Traditionally, the Ford Foundation had put its money into surveys and scholarship; Ylvisaker convinced them to invest in programs that targeted the physical and social problems of decay. There were two significant features to this program. The first was to combine what had been separate educational, employment, health, and social-welfare efforts into one entity. The other was to bring those who would benefit from the program—the poor and the minorities—into the management of the operation. His work in this field attracted the attention of President John F. Kennedy and Ylvisaker was asked to serve on the federal Task Force on the City, which he later chaired under President Lyndon B. Johnson. In that capacity, Ylvisaker was a major contributor to the development of the federal model cities program.

On 1 March 1967 Ylvisaker was sworn in as New Jersey's first Commissioner of Community Affairs. In his campaign for governor of New Jersey, the Democratic candidate Richard Hughes had promised to establish such a department. Richard Leone, an administrative assistant to Governor Hughes, recruited Ylvisaker for the job. His first year in that office was an eventful one. On 12 July a riot involving African American residents and police erupted in Newark. Governor Hughes asked Ylvisaker to lead an effort to ease tensions. Although the rioting lasted for five days, Ylvisaker played a significant role in bringing it to an end. On 17 July just as the Newark riots were over, violence broke out in nearby Plainfield. Ylvisaker quelled those riots by confronting the rioters and by preventing large-scale police intervention. His tenure in New Jersey was also noted for his successful revitalization of the Hackensack Meadows, in which a former garbage dump was transformed into the Meadowlands complex of sports facilities, with nearby shops and housing. In addition, he established several social reform programs in New Jersey. Nonetheless, a Republican victory in 1969 led to a cabinet housecleaning and a request for Ylvisaker's resignation.

Ylvisaker spent the next year teaching at Yale and from 1970 to 1972 he was a professor of public affairs and urban planning at Princeton University in New Jersey. He left Princeton in September 1972 to become the dean of the Harvard Graduate School of Education, a position he held until 1982. With a decline of federal grants and a shrinking of enrollments, he presided over the downsizing of the school. At the same time he was responsible for committing the school to a public service mission and increasing the ratio of women and minorities among faculty and students. After resigning as dean, he continued to teach at Harvard as the Charles William Eliot Professor of Education, and he served as a senior consultant to the Council on Foundations. He was also a trustee of several private and community foundations. In 1991 his wife died and his own health was deteriorating. He died of a heart attack at George Washington University Hospital in Washington, D.C., at the age of seventy.

Ylvisaker faced health problems most of his life. In addition to suffering a heart attack in 1956, he had diabetes and was legally blind for many years. Although not imposing in appearance—he was short in stature, with blond hair often worn in a brush cut—his passion, commitment, courage, and the moral force of his arguments made him a formidable champion for cities and the urban underclass.

★

Ylvisaker's papers, covering the years 1939–1992, are in the Harvard University Archives. While there are no biographies of Ylvisaker, there is substantial biographical information, along with a collection of speeches and writings, in Virginia M. Esposito, ed., *Conscience and Community: The Legacy of Paul Ylvisaker* (1999). Obituaries are in the *New York Times,* the *Boston Globe,* and the *Newark Star-Ledger* (all 20 Mar. 1992), as well as in the *Journal of the American Planning Association* 58 (summer 1992): 367. Ylvisaker was interviewed for a Ford Foundation oral history project while he was a dean at Harvard. The interviews are located at the Ford Foundation Archives in New York City.

IVAN D. STEEN

ZAPPA, Frank Vincent (*b.* 21 December 1940 in Baltimore, Maryland; *d.* 4 December 1993 in Los Angeles, California), rock-and-roll musician and experimental composer who expanded the possibilities of rock and at the same time redefined the role of the popular musician.

Zappa's father, Francis Vincent Zappa, was an immigrant from Sicily who came to the United States as a child. He married Rose Marie, a first-generation Italian American. Zappa's father became a meteorologist and metallurgist, a professional background with links to the U.S. military that kept the Zappa family moving. His mother was a homemaker. Zappa, the first born, was followed by two brothers and a sister. He was raised as a Roman Catholic, and his early schooling was marked by an almost immediate reaction against the discipline of parochial school. He later attended public schools throughout California. Zappa was twelve years old when he took up the drums, his first musical instrument.

Frank Zappa. ARCHIVE PHOTOS

At age thirteen Zappa discovered a composition by Edgard Varèse called *Ionisation.* Constructed around percussive instruments, *Ionisation* incorporates nonorchestral sound makers such as sirens, sleigh bells, and other workaday items. In addition to these unconventional instruments Varèse developed his music upon experimental thematic structures. Zappa was entranced by this new cosmos of sound. At the same time he became enamored of early rhythm and blues and amassed a huge record collection.

In 1955, at age fourteen, Zappa joined his first band, the Ramblers, as the drummer. His family moved to Antelope Valley, where Zappa's father worked at Edwards Air Force Base. Zappa attended Antelope Valley High School, where he formed a band by the name of the Black-Outs and met Don Van Vliet, later known as Captain Beefheart. To celebrate his fifteenth birthday, Zappa was allowed to place a long-distance phone call to his hero, Varèse, who lived in New York City at the time.

By the time Zappa was a senior, he had traded in his drums for a guitar, the instrument he would use for his entire rock career. He graduated from high school in 1958 and enrolled in Antelope Valley Junior College but quickly dropped out. In 1959 he enrolled in Chaffee Junior College in Alta Loma, where he studied music and met Kay Sherman, whom he married the same year. He again dropped out of college and took a succession of jobs while he played in short-lived groups and played the local bar circuit. In 1961 Zappa wrote the score for a film called *The World's Greatest Sinner,* but he never got paid for it. After earning money for writing another score for a film called *Run Home Slow* in 1964, Zappa opened a recording and film studio in Los Angeles called Studio Z. The same year, Zappa divorced Sherman. They had no children.

After creating a sexually suggestive audiotape for an undercover policeman, Zappa was arrested for conspiracy to commit pornography. Zappa later said that almost all of his professional albums were much more "obscene" than this tape, but he was convicted of a lesser charge and sentenced to ten days in jail. His arrest ended Studio Z, and made him ineligible for the draft. Soon after getting out of prison, Zappa learned that a local band called the Soul Giants were looking for a guitarist. He joined, and by the fall of 1965 he had taken over leadership of the band and renamed it the Mothers. He also convinced the other band members to perform his early songs, including "Who are the Brain Police?," "Hungry Freaks," and "Oh, No, I Don't Believe It." This new material was experimental in structure and filled with Zappa's confrontational humor. The Mothers played throughout the Los Angeles area and while playing the Whisky-A-Go-Go they were spotted by a record executive who signed the group to a record deal on Verve records.

The band lengthened its name to the Mothers of Invention and released its first album, *Freak Out!,* in 1966. A double disc packed with musical experimentation, social satire, and rhythm-and-blues–inspired pop, *Freak Out!* marked the beginning of Zappa's mix of avant-garde compositions and popular rock and roll. He announced this by quoting Varèse on the record sleeve: "The present-day composer refuses to die!" Although the album received no exposure on radio, the band went on a long tour across the United States and in June 1966 opened for Lenny Bruce, another of Zappa's heroes.

Zappa's rigorous work ethic took his band immediately back into the studio to record the Mothers' second album, *Absolutely Free* (1967). He moved the Mothers to New York City, where the band played for six months at the Garrick Theater. The beginning of 1967 also saw Zappa writing and recording an orchestral piece called *Lumpy Gravy.* Before taking the Mothers on its first European tour, Zappa moved back to Los Angeles and married Gail Sloatman in the fall of 1967; their daughter, Moon Unit, was born the same year.

In 1968 the band released its most popular album to date: *We're Only In It For the Money* was Zappa's satirical attack upon the previous year's watershed album, the Beatles' *Sgt. Pepper's Lonely Hearts Club Band.* As parody it was biting in its criticism of hippie culture; as music it was wildly experimental. The album attacked the complacency and drug use of the hippies. Although Zappa would later advocate the legalization of drugs, he never used narcotics and, unlike most musicians of the period, thought them anathema to the creative process.

Over the next two years Zappa would add to his reputation as a workaholic by expanding the Mothers' lineup to include ten musicians and putting out several albums, including one of the band's most popular works, *Uncle Meat* (1968). Zappa also organized appearances with accompanying orchestras and went on a lecture tour of American universities. In addition to his own work, he produced one of the seminal albums of the period, Captain Beefheart's *Trout Mask Replica* (1969). But by the summer of 1969 the effort of moving his large band around the globe proved too costly, and Zappa disbanded the Mothers. He immediately went to work on his first solo album, *Hot Rats* (1969). The same year the Zappa family moved into a house on Mulholland Drive in the Hollywood Hills that would remain their residence for the rest of Zappa's life.

Zappa's first son, Dweezil, was born in 1970; his second son, Ahmet, followed in 1975, and his fourth child, a daughter named Diva, was born in 1980. In addition to enlarging his family, the 1970s were an incredibly prolific period for Zappa. He released nineteen albums, ranging from a reunited Mothers work accompanied by orchestra called *200 Motels* (1971), which spawned a film of the same name, to popular work such as *Over-Nite Sensation* (1973) and *Sheik Yerbouti* (1979). Albums such as *Apostrophe (')* (1974) cemented Zappa's reputation as a musical experimenter with a caustic wit. The end of the decade also saw the release of his rock opera *Joe's Garage* (1979), which warned of censorship in the music industry, and another film, *Baby Snakes* (1979). Zappa's distinctive mustache and goatee became a pop trademark, and his comic attacks upon cultural shibboleths and his challenging stage performances made him one of the most popular rock acts of his day.

The 1980s saw Zappa concentrating on his compositions for orchestra. He released twenty-three albums over the course of the decade, ranging from the jazz-influenced instrumental *Shut Up 'N Play Yer Guitar* (1981) to the popular *Ship Arriving Too Late to Save a Drowning Witch* (1982), which included Zappa's most popular single, "Valley Girl." He also worked with many orchestras, including the London Symphony Orchestra. Several public appearances were indicative of his musical range: in 1981 he hosted "A Tribute to Edgard Varèse" in New York, and in 1983 he conducted *Ionisation* in San Francisco to commemorate the 100th anniversary of Varèse's birth. However, in 1982, Zappa's rock world hit one of its lowest points when a concert in his father's hometown in Sicily turned into a riot that resulted in the use of tear gas on the audience.

In 1985 Zappa appeared before the Senate Commerce, Technology, and Transportation Committee to speak out against the efforts of the Parents Music Resource Center (PMRC) to censor popular music. Using a Synclavier, Zappa recorded an instrumental album called *Jazz from Hell* (1986) that won a Grammy Award in 1988 for best rock instrumental performance. The same year saw the release of *You Can't Do That On Stage Anymore,* the first in a series of archival albums ranging across Zappa's entire career. In 1989 Zappa traveled to Russia to arrange for the licensing of his work; he became interested in international business and set up a consulting firm called Why Not? On a trip to Czechoslovakia, Zappa met with Czech president and Zappa fan Václav Havel, who asked Zappa to represent Czech business in the United States.

Zappa was diagnosed with inoperable prostate cancer in 1990. Although he never seemed to stop working and even wrote new compositions for the Ensemble Modern, Zappa's health quickly deteriorated. *The Yellow Shark,* a Zappa-produced recording of the Ensemble Modern performing his compositions, was released a month before his death. He died on 4 December 1993 in his home and was buried at Westwood Memorial Park in Los Angeles. At the time of his death he had released more than sixty albums.

Zappa was an iconoclast who not only challenged the form and content of pop culture but also collapsed the barriers between classical and rock music. His work combined the avant-garde dissonant counterpoint of Varèse with the harmony of American rhythm and blues to create a unique oeuvre that changed rock and influenced the popular culture of the world. The quote from Varèse on the first Mothers album—"The modern day composer refuses to die!"—continues to be felt in his recorded legacy.

★

Frank Zappa's autobiography, with Peter Occhiogrosso, *The Real Frank Zappa Book,* was published in 1989. Important biographical work includes Greg Russo, *Cosmik Debris: The Collected History and Improvisations of Frank Zappa* (1998); Neil Slaven, *Electric Don Quixote: The Story of Frank Zappa* (1997); David Walley, *No Commercial Potential: The Saga of Frank Zappa* (1996); Michael Gray, *Mother! Is the Story of Frank Zappa* (1985); and Barry Miles, *Frank Zappa—A Visual Documentary* (1993). Critical appraisals of Zappa's work and interviews with him are collected in Richard Kostelanetz, *The Frank Zappa Companion* (1997). A critical approach to Zappa's relationship to avant-garde art and thought is supplied in Ben Watson, *Frank Zappa: The Negative Dialectics of Poodle Play* (1995). An obituary is in the *New York Times* (5 Dec. 1993).

JOHN ROCCO

ZWICKER, Ralph Wise (*b.* 17 April 1903 in Stoughton, Wisconsin; *d.* 9 August 1991 in Fort Belvoir, Virginia), army general who was a prominent figure in the 1954 controversy between the U.S. Army and Senator Joseph McCarthy, chair of the Senate Subcommittee on Investigations.

Zwicker was the youngest of three children of Henry Zwicker, owner of a cigar company, and Jean Wise, a homemaker. He graduated from Madison High School in Madison, Wisconsin, in 1921 and then attended the University of Wisconsin in Madison for a year. In 1923 he was appointed to the U.S. Military Academy at West Point, New York. He graduated in 1927 and was commissioned a second lieutenant in the infantry. On 14 July 1927 he married Dorothy Harriet Stewart; they had three children.

Until World War II, Zwicker had a conventional military career while rising to the rank of major. He served with the Third Infantry Regiment at Fort Snelling, Minnesota (1927–1930 and 1933–1934); with the Thirty-fifth Infantry Regiment and later the Eleventh Tank Company in Hawaii (1930–1932); as a student at the Infantry School at Fort Benning, Georgia (1932–1933); as an instructor in drawing at West Point (1934–1939); with the Thirty-eighth Infantry Regiment at posts in Utah and Texas (1939–1940); and as an instructor at the Infantry School (1940–1942).

During World War II, Zwicker compiled a record as an outstanding combat leader and staff officer. After completing the staff officer's course at the Command and General

Ralph Zwicker testifying at the Army-McCarthy hearings, 1954. © BETTMANN/CORBIS

Staff College at Fort Leavenworth, Kansas, in June 1942, he was appointed operations officer for the Ninety-fourth Division, then organizing at Camp Phillips, Kansas. In November 1943 Zwicker was attached to the Army Ground Forces (AGF) and on 6 June 1944, while serving as an AGF observer, he led a reconnaissance mission at Omaha Beach several hours before American forces landed there as part of the D-Day invasion of Normandy. On 23 June 1944 Zwicker, holding the rank of colonel, became commander of the Thirty-eighth Infantry Regiment, part of the Second Division, and over the following weeks he led it through heavy fighting in the Normandy campaign. Later that year he was appointed the division's chief of staff, serving in this capacity during the Ardennes and Rhineland campaigns.

After the war Zwicker had a variety of assignments. He attended the Naval War College in Newport, Rhode Island, from July 1945 to December 1945 and, following a brief stint with the AGF, he was a student at the National War College in Washington, D.C. Between 1947 and 1953 he served with the operations and training division of the Army General Staff, as the deputy director of operations and training with the European Command, as the commander of the Eighteenth Infantry Regiment in Germany, as an instructor at the National War College, and as assistant commander of the Fifth Division at Indiantown Gap, Pennsylvania, which earned him promotion to brigadier general.

In July 1953 Zwicker was appointed commander at Camp Kilmer, New Jersey. The next year he was catapulted to national attention when Senator Joseph McCarthy, whose committee was looking into allegations of communist penetration of the army, decided to use the case of Captain Irving Peress to demonstrate that the army could not be trusted to weed out subversives. Peress, a dentist at Camp Kilmer and a suspected communist, had been promoted to major in the fall of 1953 and then given an honorable discharge on 2 February 1954. On 30 January, just days before, he had declined on constitutional grounds to answer questions about his alleged communist past in an appearance before McCarthy's committee. This circumstance led McCarthy to ask why this "Fifth Amendment communist" had been promoted and not court-martialed "for conduct unbecoming an officer."

General Zwicker, who shared McCarthy's concern about communist subversion and was also angry over the army's handling of the case, appeared before McCarthy's committee on 18 February to answer questions about Peress. McCarthy expected Zwicker to be a cooperative witness, but citing orders from the Department of the Army that he not testify about specific security cases, Zwicker was evasive and argumentative. As the hearing proceeded, McCarthy, believing that Zwicker had something to hide, in-

creasingly badgered him, implied that he was shielding communist conspirators, and ultimately pronounced him unfit to wear a soldier's uniform.

This treatment of a distinguished soldier triggered a rebellion against McCarthy. Since 1950, McCarthy had been a powerful and destructive force in Washington with reckless charges about communist influence in the government and the military and, until Zwicker's appearance, few had been willing to challenge him. Now army officials, furious with McCarthy's virulence toward a highly decorated combat veteran, demanded that he never again insult an officer called to testify before his committee. President Dwight D. Eisenhower publicly praised General Zwicker for his courage and patriotism. Many newspapers and even McCarthy allies judged that the senator had gone too far in his tongue-lashing of Zwicker. Support for McCarthy waned, and after the famous televised Army-McCarthy hearings he was censured by the Senate in December 1954 for his abusive tactics, effectively ending his career.

In the meantime, Zwicker was transferred to Japan, where he became the commanding general of Southwestern Command, Armed Forces Far East, Japan, and later the assistant chief of staff for personnel for Armed Forces Far East, Japan, and the Eighth Army. Zwicker again clashed with McCarthy in March 1955 when Zwicker testified in a renewed probe of the Peress case by the Senate Subcommittee on Investigations, now chaired by John McClellan. Nothing came of the investigation, but McClellan believed Zwicker had lied on the stand and asked the Department of Justice to review his testimony for possible prosecution for perjury. In the spring of 1957 it concluded there were no grounds for prosecution and shortly afterward Zwicker, whose elevation to higher rank had been delayed by the affair, was promoted to major general.

Afterward Zwicker commanded the Twenty-fourth Division, later redesignated the First Cavalry Division in Korea, and the Twentieth Corps (Reserve), headquartered at Fort Hayes, Ohio. He retired on 1 May 1960 after suffering two heart attacks and for the next ten years was employed by the Research Analysis Corporation in McLean, Virginia, a military consulting firm. Zwicker died of heart failure and is buried in Arlington National Cemetery.

A tall, trim man with a wide circle of friends, Zwicker was an able professional soldier who is remembered for his involvement in the Army-McCarthy feud.

★

A small collection of Zwicker's papers is located in the State Historical Society of Wisconsin in Madison. Extensive discussions of Zwicker's role in the Army-McCarthy controversy can be found in Thomas C. Reeves, *The Life and Times of Joe McCarthy: A Biography* (1982) and David M. Oshinsky, *A Conspiracy So Im-*

mense: The World of Joe McCarthy (1983). A number of magazine articles in 1954 touch on Zwicker's role in the controversy. Among the most important are "One Man's Army," *Time* (1 Mar. 1954); "What Hearing Revealed—McCarthy Questions a General," *U.S. News and World Report* (5 Mar. 1954); "McCarthy and Stevens—Behind Scenes," *Newsweek* (8 Mar. 1954); and "McCarthy 'Cen-

sure' Case: The Evidence is in—Verdict Yet to Come," *U.S. News and World Report* (24 Sept. 1954). Obituaries are in the *Washington Post* (11 Aug. 1991), *New York Times* (12 Aug. 1991), and the *Assembly* (July 1992).

JOHN KENNEDY OHL

DIRECTORY OF CONTRIBUTORS

AGNEW, BRAD
Northeastern State University, Tahlequah, Okla.
Walker, Edwin Anderson

ALEXANDER, EDWARD
University of Washington, Seattle
Howe, Irving

ALLEN, HOWARD
Brooklyn College of the City University of New York
(Retired)
Kemeny, John George

AMLER, JANE FRANCES
Katonah, N.Y.
Gann, Ernest Kellogg

ARETAKIS, JONATHAN G.
Editorial East, Pembroke, Maine
Meyendorff, John

BAKER, THERESE DUZINKIEWICZ
Western Kentucky University
Neumann, Vera Salaff ("Vera")

BALL, HOWARD
University of Vermont
Marshall, Thurgood

BALLARD, TERRY L.
Librarian, Quinnipiac College
Irwin, James Benson

BARBEAU, ART
West Liberty State College, West Virginia
Staggers, Harley Orrin

BELENKY, IRINA
Graduate Student in History, Rutgers University
Ford, Ernest Jennings ("Tennessee Ernie")

BELLOWS, PAMELA W.
Northwestern Connecticut Community College,
Winsted, Conn.
Barnett, Marguerite Ross

BENNETT, EVAN P.
College of William and Mary
Collins, (Thomas) LeRoy

BLICKLEY, MARK A.
Devry Institute of Technology, Long Island City, N.Y.
Gehringer, Charles Leonard ("Charlie")

BOON, LESLIE
Gettysburg, Pa.
Burr, Raymond William Stacy

BORNSTEIN, JERRY
Baruch College, City University of New York
Salant, Richard S.

BOYLES, MARY
University of North Carolina at Pembroke
Kendrick, Alexander

BRASEL, ELLEN O'CONNELL
Marshall University, Huntington, W.Va.
Humphry, (Ann) Wickett

BRILEY, RON
Sandia Preparatory School, Albuquerque, N.Mex.
Murphy, George Lloyd

BRILLER, BERT R.
Vice Chairman, Editorial Board, Television Quarterly
Daly, John Charles, Jr.

BUHLE, PAUL
Brown University
Capra, Frank

BUSTER, ALAN
Harvard-Westlake School, Los Angeles
Pasternak, Joseph Herman ("Joe")

BYRNE, JOHN J.
Adjunct Faculty, Bronx Community College
Murray, Arthur
Thomas, Danny

CAMPBELL, JIM
Bucknell University
Grange, Harold Edward ("Red")
Mosconi, William Joseph ("Willie")

CANTELON, PHILIP L.
History Associated Incorporated, Rockville, Md.
McGowan, William George

CAREY, ROBERT B.
Empire State College, State University of New York
    Dorsey, Thomas Andrew
    Snelling, Richard Arkwright
CARLIN, RICHARD
Senior Music Editor, Routledge Books
    Acuff, Roy Claxton
    Arrau, Claudio
    Miller, Roger Dean
    Twitty, Conway
CARPENTER, BRIAN B.
Sterling C. Evans Library, Texas A&M University
    Castro, Bernard
CARROLL, JOHN M.
Lamar University
    Schwartzwalder, Floyd Burdette ("Ben")
CARSTENSEN, FRED
University of Connecticut
    Ross, Steven Jay
CARSTENSEN, MILDRED G.
Doctoral Candidate, Harvard University
    Dickey, John Sloan
CASTAÑEDA, JIM
Rice University
    Herman, William Jennings ("Billy")
CASTRONOVO, DAVID
Pace University
    Barrett, William Christopher
    Yates, Richard Walden
CHABORA, ROBERT J.
Concordia College
    Serkin, Rudolf
CHAMBERS, JACK
University of Toronto
    Davis, Miles Dewey, III
CHURCH, GARY MASON
Sterling C. Evans Library, Texas A&M University
    Connors, Kevin Joseph Aloysius ("Chuck")
CICARELLI, JAMES
Walter E. Heller College of Business Administration,
    Roosevelt University
    Janeway, Eliot
CICARELLI, JULIANNE
Freelance Writer, Arlington Heights, Ill.
    Lee, Pinky
COBB, KENNETH R.
New York City Municipal Archives
    Gates, John
    Newhall, Beaumont
COCHRAN, CHARLES L.
U.S. Naval Academy
    Wildavsky, Aaron Bernard

COLBERT, THOMAS BURNELL
Marshalltown Community College
    Engle, Paul Hamilton
COLETTA, PAOLO E.
Professor Emeritus, United States Naval Academy
    (Retired)
    Hopper, Grace Brewster Murray
COMPSTON, CHRISTINE L.
Belmont, Mass.
    Freund, Paul Abraham
COPPOLA, RENEE
The Broad Art Foundation, Santa Monica, Calif.
    Arneson, Robert Carston
    Siskind, Aaron
CORPUS, MARTHA MONAGHAN
Brooklyn College of the City University of New York
    Delacorte, George Thomas, Jr.
DAMON, ALLAN L.
Horace Greeley High School, Chappaqua, N.Y.
    Bigart, Homer William
    Hersey, John Richard
    Salisbury, Harrison Evans
    Shirer, William Lawrence
    Stegner, Wallace Earle
DAVIDSON, ABRAHAM A.
Tyler School of Art, Temple University
    Diebenkorn, Richard Clifford
    Mitchell, Joan
DECKER, SHARON L.
State University of New York, Maritime College
    Gallo, Julio Robert
DEFORD, FRANK
Sports Illustrated
    Ashe, Arthur Robert
DEVINE, MICHAEL J.
University of Wyoming
    McGee, Gale William
DIAMANT, JEFFREY A.
Parsippany, N.Y.
    Valvano, James Thomas ("Jim")
DIAZ, DAVID
Freelance Writer, Woodstock, Conn.
    Koresh, David
DICK, BERNARD F.
Fairleigh Dickinson University
    Mankiewicz, Joseph Leo
DINNEEN, MARCIA B.
Bridgewater State College
University of Massachusetts at Dartmouth
    Booth, Shirley
    Kirsten, Dorothy

DOBSON, MELISSA A.
Freelance Writer, Newport, R.I.
Riding, Laura
Sabin, Albert Bruce

DOENECKE, JUSTUS D.
New College of the University of South Florida, Sarasota
Fairbank, John King

DRABELLE, DENNIS
Contributing Editor, Washington Post Book World
Arthur, Jean

DROBNICKI, JOHN A.
York College Library, City University of New York
Ruffin, Davis Eli ("David")

DYER, LEIGH
Charlotte Observer, N.C.
Ashman, Howard Elliot

EASTON, CAROL
Venice, Calif.
de Mille, Agnes George

ENDERS, ERIC E.
National Baseball Hall of Fame Library
Bell, James Thomas ("Cool Papa")

EVENSEN, BRUCE J.
DePaul University
Reasoner, Harry

FAFOUTIS, DEAN
Salisbury State University
Habib, Philip Charles

FEUERHERD, PETER
American Bible Society
Perry, Harold Robert

FISCHEL, JACK R.
Millersville University
Sachar, Abram Leon

FISCHER, WILLIAM E., JR.
U.S. Air Force
Hillcourt, William ("Green Bar Bill")

FISHER, JOHN E.
Department of Pathology, The Children's Hospital of Buffalo, N.Y.
Holley, Robert William

FITZPATRICK, JOHN
Charles Scribner's Sons
Brooks, Richard

FLEMING, THOMAS
New York City
Fenwick, Millicent Hammond

FLYNN, JOSEPH G.
State University of New York College of Technology, Alfred
Taylor, Harold Alexander

FORD, THOMAS W.
University of Houston
Guthrie, Alfred Bertram, Jr.

FRANCIS, BILL
National Baseball Hall of Fame
Durocher, Leo Ernest

FRIGUGLIETTI, JAMES
Montana State University, Billings
Gilbert, Felix

FRISCH, PAUL A.
Director of Library and Information Technology, State University of New York at Old Westbury
Drysdale, Don(ald) Scott

GAAR, GILLIAN G.
Freelance Writer, Seattle, Wash.
Wells, Mary Esther

GABOR, ANDREA
New York City
Deming, W. Edwards

GARGAN, WILLIAM M.
Brooklyn College of the City University of New York
Exley, Frederick Earl

GENTILE, RICHARD H.
Freelance Writer and Editor, South Easton, Mass.
Remick, Lee Ann

GERBER, BARBARA L.
Brooklyn College of the City University of New York
Singer, Isaac Bashevis

GERSHENOWITZ, DEBORAH
Independent Scholar, Brooklyn, N.Y.
McKissick, Floyd B.

GITELMAN, CLAUDIA
Professor Emerita, Mason Gross School of the Arts, Rutgers University
Holm, Hanya
Nikolais, Alwin Theodore

GONZALEZ, LEROY
Columbia University Graduate School of Business
Roddenberry, Eugene Wesley ("Gene")

GOOD, ELAINE McMAHON
Nassau Community College, State University of New York
Ray, Aldo
Ryan, John William ("Jack")

GOODBODY, JOAN
Sterling C. Evans Library, Texas A&M University
Brannan, Charles Franklin

GORDON, MARTIN K.
U.S. Army Corps of Engineers
University College, University of Maryland
Smith, Joseph

GOTTLIEB, JANE
The Juilliard School
Schuman, William Howard

GREENBERG, DAVID
Columbia University
Slate Magazine
 Nixon, Pat(ricia)
GREENE, KATE
University of Southern Mississippi
 Parsons, James Benton
GREENWALD, RICHARD A.
U.S. Merchant Marine Academy
 Gleason, Thomas William ("Teddy")
 Rauh, Joseph Louis, Jr.
GRISWOLD DEL CASTILLO, RICHARD
San Diego State University
 Chávez, César Estrada
GUNN, JAMES
University of Kansas
 Asimov, Isaac
HABERSKI, RAYMOND J., JR.
Marian College, Indianapolis, Ind.
 Lynes, (Joseph) Russell, Jr.
HAGER, THOMAS
University of Oregon
 Mark, Herman Francis
 Tierney, Gene Eliza
HAINES, MICHAEL F.
Dominican College, Orangeburg, N.Y.
 Luria, Salvador Edward
HANDLER, JACK
Antioch New England Graduate School, Massachusetts
 College of Liberal Arts
 Arnall, Ellis Gibbs
 Chaikin, Sol (Chick)
HANSEN, VAGN K.
High Point University
 Coleman, J(ames) P(lemon)
HARRIS, ROBERT L., JR.
Cornell University
 Haley, Alex(ander) Murray Palmer
HASKINS, JAMES
University of Florida
 Coles, Charles ("Honi")
HAWLEY, ELLIS W.
Professor Emeritus, University of Iowa
 Burdick, Quentin Northrop
HERON, DAVID W.
University Librarian Emeritus, University of California,
 Santa Cruz
 Dessauer, John Hans
 Hayakawa, S(amuel) I(chiye)
HERRMANN, LESLEY S.
Gilder Lehrman Institute of American History,
 New York City
 Berberova, Nina Nikolaevna

HODGES, GRAHAM RUSSELL
Colgate University
 Abbott, Berenice
 Sun Ra (Herman Blount)
 Yerby, Frank Garvin
HOLLI, MELVIN G.
University of Illinois at Chicago
 Rizzo, Frank Lazzaro
HOOGENBOOM, LYNN
Copy Editor, New York Times News Service
 Duke, Doris
HORN, BARBARA LEE
St. John's University, New York
 Dewhurst, Colleen
 Papp, Joseph
HOWLETT, CHARLES F.
Adelphi University
Amityville Public Schools
 Mize, John Robert ("Johnny")
IRWIN, RAYMOND D.
School of Global Studies, Just Institute, Ohio
 Ellis, John Tracy
 Taft, Robert, Jr.
JALENAK, NATALIE B.
Playhouse on the Square, Memphis, Tenn. (Retired)
 Loeb, Henry, III
JEBSEN, HARRY, JR.
Capital University, Columbus, Ohio
 Appling, Lucius Benjamin, Jr. ("Luke")
JOLLY, J. CHRISTOPHER
Corvallis, Oreg.
 Fender, Clarence Leonidas ("Leo")
KALFATOVIC, MARY
Writer and Librarian, Arlington, Va.
 Welk, Lawrence LeRoy
KASTNER, JEFFREY
Contributing Editor, Artnews
 Wojnarowicz, David Michael
KEEN, W. HUBERT
System Administration, State University of New York
 Revelle, Roger Randall Dougan
KEILER, ALLAN
Brandeis University
 Anderson, Marian
KINYATTI, NJOKI-WA-
York College, City University of New York
 Hale, Clara McBride ("Mother Hale")
 Maynard, Robert Clyve
KLOTTER, JAMES C.
Georgetown College, Kentucky
 Cooper, John Sherman

KOSTELANETZ, RICHARD
Writer, New York City
    Cage, John Milton, Jr.
KOTLOWSKI, DEAN J.
Salisbury State University, Maryland
    Connally, John Bowden, Jr.
    Dennis, Sandra Dale ("Sandy")
KREMPEL, DANIEL S.
Syracuse University
    Adler, Stella
KRINGEN, TIMOTHY
Portland, Oreg.
    Burch, (Roy) Dean
    Harken, Dwight Emary
KURTZ, MICHAEL L.
Southeastern Louisiana University
    Garrison, Jim
LAKIN, PAMELA ARMSTRONG
Research Services Librarires
    Heinz, Henry John, III
    Lorde, Audre Geraldine
LANKEVICH, GEORGE J.
Professor of History Emeritus, City University of
    New York
    Fish, Hamilton
LARSEN, CHARLES E.
Professor Emeritus, Mills College
    Lerner, Max
LAUDERDALE, KEVIN
Stanford University
    Price, Vincent Leonard, Jr.
LAUNIUS, ROGER D.
Chief Historian, National Aeronautics and Space
    Administration
    Webb, James Edwin
LEAB, DANIEL J.
Seton Hall University
    Ferrer, José
LEARY, WILLIAM M.
University of Georgia
    Quesada, Elwood Richard ("Pete")
LEVY, SHARONA A.
Borough of Manhattan Community College, City University
    of New York
    Soloveitchik, Joseph Baer
LIGGETT, LUCY A.
Professor Emeritus, Eastern Michigan University
    Lorentz, Pare
    Siegel, Don
LITTLE, JOHN E.
Princeton University
    Abravanel, Maurice

LIZZIO, JOAN
Pace University Graduate, Pleasantville, N.Y.
    Landon, Michael
LOUGHRAN, ELLEN
Hunter College, City University of New York
    Tully, Alice Bigelow
LOUGHRAN, JAMES N.
St. Peter's College, Jersey City, N.J.
    Healy, Timothy Stafford
LOUISSAINT, SABINE
Far Rockaway, N.Y.
    Parnis, Sarah Rosen ("Mollie")
LUEBBERING, KEN
Lincoln University of Missouri
    Robinson, Earl
LUFT, ERIC V. D.
State University of New York Health Science Center at
    Syracuse
    Goren, Charles Henry
    Jacoby, James Oswald ("Jim")
MACAULEY, NEILL
Professor Emeritus, University of Florida
    McCone, John Alex
McBRIDE, CARRIE C.
Writer, New York City
    Phoenix, River Jude
McDONAGH, DON
State University of New York at Purchase
New York University
    Graham, Martha
McDOWELL, MARKUS H.
Fuller Theological Seminary
Pepperdine University
    Peale, Norman Vincent
McELHENY, VICTOR K.
Massachusetts Institute of Technology
    Land, Edwin Herbert
McELWAINE, JIM
Cos Cob, Conn.
    Bauzá, Mario
McKAY, ELIZABETH
The New York and Presbyterian Hospital
    Fletcher, Joseph Francis, III
McLEAN, MICHAEL
Independent Scholar, New York City
    Speck, Richard Benjamin
MacNIVEN, IAN S.
State University of New York, Maritime College
    Boyle, Katherine ("Kay")
MADDOX, EVA M.
Texas A&M University
    Buell, Marjorie Lyman Henderson ("Marge")

MAGGIN, DONALD L.
Freelance Writer, New York City
Getz, Stan(ley)
Gillespie, John Birks ("Dizzy")

MALONEY, WENDY HALL
Brooklyn College of the City University of New York
Block, Joseph Leopold

MARC, DAVID
S. I. Newhouse School of Public Communications,
Syracuse University
Gobel, George Leslie
Goodson, Mark
Moore, Garry

MARSHALL, STEPHEN
Lincoln Park, N.J.
Graham, John
Keeler, Ruby
Ludwig, Daniel Keith

MATTISON, ROBERT SALTONSTALL
Lafayette College
Motherwell, Robert

MAYO, LOUISE A.
County College of Morris, Randolph, N.J.
Carnovsky, Morris

MEANOR, PATRICK H.
State University of New York, College at Oneonta
Milstein, Nathan

MERRON, MYRNA W.
Mount Dora, Fla.
Bloom, Allan David

MORALES, RUBIL
Brooklyn, N.Y.
Parks, Bert

MORAN, JOHN
Queens Borough Public Library, New York
Sirica, John Joseph

MORGAN, NEIL AND JUDITH
Journalists and Authors, La Jolla, Calif.
Geisel, Theodor S. ("Dr. Seuss")

MUCHNIC, SUZANNE
Art Writer, Los Angeles Times
Los Angeles Correspondent, Artnews
Simon, Norton Winfred

MURPHY, DONN B.
Georgetown University
Hayes, Helen

MYERS, R. DAVID
New Mexico State University
Beck, David

NASH, MADELEINE R.
York College, City University of New York
Dichter, Ernest
Hutchinson, G(eorge) Evelyn

NEAL, STEVE
Chicago Sun-Times
Conn, William David, Jr. ("Billy")

NELSON, ALLAN
Caldwell College, N.J.
Sulzberger, Cyrus Leo

NEWMAN, ROGER K.
School of Law, New York University
Brown, John R.
Kaufman, Irving Robert

ODERMAN, STUART
Silent Film Pianist, Museum of Modern Art, New York City
Gish, Lillian Diana

OHL, JOHN KENNEDY
Mesa Community College
Zwicker, Ralph Wise

PARASCANDOLA, JOHN
U.S. Public Health Service
Heidelberger, Michael

PARIS, BARRY
Author and Historian, Pittsburgh, Pa.
Hepburn, Audrey Kathleen

PARKER, JUDITH A.
Graduate Student, Baylor University
Tree, Mary Endicott Peabody FitzGerald ("Marietta")

PETERS, SANDRA REDMOND
Southwest Missouri State University
Page, Ruth Marian

PETERSON, ROBERT W.
Author, Ramsey, N.J.
Brown, Paul Eugene ("P. B.")

POLLOT, NAN
State University of New York College at Geneseo
Swanberg, W(illiam) A(ndrew)

PORTER, DAVID L.
William Penn College
Barber, Walter Lanier ("Red")
Chandler, Albert Benjamin ("Happy")

POTTER, BARRETT G.
Professor Emeritus, State University of New York College of
Technology, Alfred
Hawkins, Erskine Ramsay
McPartland, James Dugald ("Jimmy")

PRIMM, ALEX T.
Freelance Writer and Oral Historian, Rolla, Mo.
Kutner, Luis

PUGH, WILLIAM WHITE TISON
University of California, Irvine
Kosinski, Jerzy Nikodem

QUARATIELLO, ARLENE R.
Reference Librarian, Emerson College and Merrimack
College
Landon, Margaret Dorothea Mortenson

QUIGLEY, BRIAN
University of California, Berkeley
 Slayton, Donald Kent ("Deke")
REIDELBACH, MARIA
Author and Artist, New York City
 Gaines, William Maxwell
 Kurtzman, Harvey
REYNOLDS, CLARK G.
College of Charleston, S.C.
 Anderson, George Whelan, Jr.
RILEY, JAMES A.
Negro Leagues Baseball Museum, Canton, Ga.
 Campanella, Roy
RIPPLE, RICHARD E.
Cornell University
 Salk, Lee
ROBERTS, PRISCILLA
University of Hong Kong
 Black, Eugene Robert
ROBINSON, GREGORY K.
JazzTimes
 Eckstine, William Clarence ("Billy")
ROCCO, JOHN
State University of New York, Maritime College
 Zappa, Frank Vincent
ROCKS, BURTON E.
Author and Attorney, Stony Brook, N.Y.
 Kauffman, Ewing Marion
ROME, ROMAN
State University of New York, Maritime College
 Atwater, Harvey Leroy ("Lee")
 Foster, Vincent William, Jr.
 Haldeman, H(arry) R(obbins)
 Marcello, Carlos
 Van Fleet, James Alward
 Wagner, Robert Ferdinand
ROOT, ROBERT L., JR.
Central Michigan University
 Thomas, Lewis
ROSEN, JEFFREY S.
Spotswood High School, New Jersey
 Graham, Bill
ROSENFELD, SETH
Reporter, San Francisco Examiner
 Philbrick, Herbert Arthur
RUECKERT, WILLIAM H.
State University of New York at Geneseo
 Burke, Kenneth Duva
RUHLMANN, WILLIAM J.
Writer, New York City
 Cahn, Sammy

RUTLAND, ROBERT ALLEN
University of Tulsa
 Tower, John Goodwin
SAPIENZA, MADELINE
Independent Scholar, Washington, D.C.
 Ameche, Don
 Anderson, Judith
 Bartholomew, Frederick Llewellyn ("Freddie")
SCHANKE, ROBERT A.
Central College, Pella, Iowa
 Le Gallienne, Eva
SCHROTH, RAYMOND, S.J.
St. Peter's College, Jersey City, N.J.
Media Critic, The Nation
 Sevareid, (Arnold) Eric
SCHWARTZ, JOEL
Montclair State University
 Andrews, (Carver) Dana
SENNETT, TED
Author, Closter, N.J.
 Dietrich, Marlene
 Loy, Myrna
 Sturges, John
SEYEDIAN, MOJTABA
State University of New York, College at Fredonia
 Hazlitt, Henry Stuart
SHOR DONNER, RACHEL
Queens Borough Public Library, New York City
 Nemerov, Howard
SILVERBERG, MARK
Dalhousie University
 Schuyler, James Marcus
SMALL, CATHERINE RIFE
Nicolet High School, Glendale, Wis.
 Butts, Alfred Mosher
SMALLWOOD, JAMES M.
Oklahoma State University
 Iba, (Payne) Henry ("Hank")
SMITH, JOHN KARES
State University of New York, Oswego
 Accardo, Anthony ("Big Tuna")
 Drake, Alfred
SOFFER, JONATHAN M.
Polytechnic University, Brooklyn
 Ridgway, Matthew Bunker
SOLON, LEONARD R.
Physicist and Educator, Fort Pierce, Fla.
 Anderson, Carl David, Jr.
 Kusch, Polykarp
SPATT, HARTLEY S.
State University of New York, Maritime College
 Newell, Allen

STAHL, MARTIN JAY
Empire State College, State University of New York
   Baldwin, Hanson Weightman
STEBENNE, DAVID L.
Ohio State University
   Larson, (Lewis) Arthur
STEEN, IVAN D.
State University of New York, Albany
   Ylvisaker, Paul Norman
STEEN, SARA J.
Freelance Editor and Writer, Astoria, N.Y.
   Lazar, Irving Paul ("Swifty")
   Maleska, Eugene Thomas
STENSTROM, CHRISTINE
LaGuardia Community College, City University of
   New York
   Merriam, Eve
STERTZ, STEPHEN A.
Dowling College
Mercy College
   Hayek, Friedrich August von
STRINGER-HYE, RICHARD
Librarian, Vanderbilt University
   Dixon, Willie James
   Hearst, William Randolph, Jr.
SU, DI
York College, City University of New York
   Leinsdorf, Erich
   Vaughn, Richard Smith ("Billy")
SUCHECKI, PETER C.
Maine College of Art
   De Nagy, Tibor
TAMBORRINO, VICTORIA
St. John's University, New York
   Bardeen, John
TASSINARI, EDWARD J.
State University of New York, Maritime College
   Fine, Reuben
   Graham, William Patrick ("Billy")
   Reshevsky, Samuel Herman
THORNTON, JOYCE K.
Texas A&M University Libraries
   Robinson, Roscoe, Jr.
THORSEN, CONNIE
St. John's University, New York
   Kaye, Sylvia Fine
TINO, RICHARD L.
President, Tino Advertising and Public Relations
   Foote, Emerson
TODMAN, ANTHONY
St. John's University, New York
   Foxx, Redd
   Lewis, Reginald Francis

TOMA, YAN
Queen Library, N.Y.
   Johnson, D(aniel) Mead
TOMASINO, ADRIANA C.
Ph.D. Candidate, Graduate School and University Center,
   City University of New York
   McClintock, Barbara
TRIMBLE, PATRICK A.
Pennsylvania State University
   Shuster, Joseph E.
TSOUKAS, LIANN E.
University of Pittsburgh
   Kendricks, Eddie James
TUTOROW, NORMAN
Visiting Fellow, Hoover Institution on War, Revolution, and
   Peace, Stanford University
   Roosevelt, James
USSELMAN, STEVEN W.
School of History, Technology and Society, Georgia Institute
   of Technology
   Watson, Thomas John, Jr.
VANCE, SANDRA S.
Independent Scholar, Ridgeland, Miss.
   Walton, Sam(uel) Moore
VON WINBUSH, SAMUEL
State University of New York at Old Westbury
   McMillan, Edwin Mattison
WALD, MALVIN
School of Cinema/Television, University of Southern
   California (Retired)
   Bellamy, Ralph Rexford
WARD, RICHARD L.
University of South Alabama
   Roach, Harold Eugene ("Hal")
WATSON, GEORGE H., JR.
Air Force History Support Office
   Doolittle, James Harold
WATTEL, HAROLD L.
Professor Emeritus, Hofstra University
   Porter, Sylvia Field
WEDGE, ELEANOR F.
Freelance Writer and Editor, New York City
   Blume, Peter
WEIGOLD, MARILYN E.
Pace University, Pleasantville, N.Y.
   Grucci, Felix James, Sr. ("Pops")
WEINSTEIN, HONORA RAPHAEL
Brooklyn College of the City University of New York
   MacMurray, Fred(erick) Martin
   Picon, Molly
WEISBLAT, LEIGH BULLARD
Independent Art Historian, New York City
   Pousette-Dart, Richard Warren

WEISBLAT, TINKY "DAKOTA"
Independent Scholar, Hawley, Mass.
Fisher, M(ary) F(rances) K(ennedy)
Walker, Nancy
WEXLER, MOLLY JALENAK
Memphis Jewish Federation
Finkelstein, Louis
WHITMIRE, TIM
Charlotte Observer
France, William Henry Getty

WINECOFF, CHARLES
Author, New York City
Perkins, Anthony
YAGODA, BEN
University of Delaware
De Vries, Peter
Shawn, William
ZELIZER, JULIAN E.
State University of New York at Albany
Mills, Wilbur Daigh

OCCUPATIONS INDEX, VOLUMES 1–3

See also the Alphabetical List of Subjects beginning on p. 607.

	Volume		Volume
Author (Fiction) (*cont.*)		Ciardi, John Anthony	2
Loos, Anita	1	Coon, Carleton Stevens	1
McCarthy, Mary Therese	2	Cousins, Norman	2
MacDonald, John Dann	2	Crowther, (Francis) Bosley, Jr.	1
Macdonald, Ross	1	Daniels, Jonathan Worth	1
MacInnes, Helen Clark	1	De Man, Paul	1
Malamud, Bernard	2	Denby, Edwin Orr	1
Maltz, Albert	1	Deutsch, Helene Rosenbach	1
Mannes, Marya	2	Durant, Ariel	1
Nemerov, Howard	3	Durant, Will(iam) James	1
Percy, Walker	2	Eliade, Mircea	2
Rand, Ayn	1	Engel, A. Lehman	1
Saroyan, William	1	Fielding, Temple Hornaday	1
Schuyler, James Marcus	3	Fisher, M(ary) F(rances) K(ennedy)	3
Shaara, Michael Joseph, Jr.	2	Fixx, James Fuller	1
Shaw, Irwin Gilbert	1	Flesch, Rudolf Franz	2
Shulman, Max	2	Forbes, Malcolm Stevenson	2
Singer, Isaac Bashevis	3	Fossey, Dian	1
Stein, Aaron Marc	1	Friedrich, Carl Joachim	1
Sturgeon, Theodore	1	Gann, Ernest Kellogg	3
Wallace, Irving	2	Gardner, John Champlin, Jr.	1
Wescott, Glenway	2	Gavin, James Maurice	2
West, (Mary) Jessamyn	1	Golden, Harry	1
White, E(lwyn) B(rooks)	1	Graham, Sheilah	2
Williams, Thomas Lanier, III ("Tennessee")	1	Grosvenor, Melville Bell	1
Yates, Richard Walden	3	Guthrie, Alfred Bertram, Jr.	3
Yerby, Frank Garvin	3	Haley, Alex(ander) Murray Palmer	3
Author (Nonfiction)		Harris, Sydney Justin	2
Abbey, Edward Paul	2	Hart, Marion Rice	2
Ace, Goodman	1	Hartdegen, Stephen Joseph	2
Armour, Richard Willard	2	Hayakawa, S(amuel) I(chiye)	3
Asimov, Isaac	3	Hayek, Friedrich August von	3
Atkinson, (Justin) Brooks	1	Hazlitt, Henry Stuart	3
Baldwin, Hanson Weightman	3	Hearst, William Randolph, Jr.	3
Baldwin, James Arthur	2	Hellman, Lillian Florence	1
Barber, Walter Lanier ("Red")	3	Hemingway, Mary Welsh	2
Barnes, Djuna Chappell	1	Hersey, John Richard	3
Barr, Stringfellow	1	Hicks, Granville	1
Barrett, William Christopher	3	Hillcourt, William ("Green Bar Bill")	3
Beard, James Andrew	1	Hoffer, Eric	1
Berberova, Nina Nikolaevna	3	Holt, John Caldwell	1
Bishop, James Alonzo ("Jim")	2	Houseman, John	2
Bloom, Allan David	3	Hoving, Walter	2
Boyington, Gregory ("Pappy")	2	Hubbard, L(afayette) Ron(ald)	2
Boyle, Katherine ("Kay")	3	Hughes, Emmet John	1
Brodie, Fawn McKay	1	Huie, William Bradford	2
Burke, Kenneth Duva	3	Isherwood, Christopher William	2
Campbell, Joseph	2	Jacoby, James Oswald ("Jim")	3
Canaday, John Edwin	1	Jacoby, Oswald ("Ozzie")	1
Capote, Truman	1	Janeway, Eliot	3
Chase, Stuart	1	Jessel, George Albert ("Georgie")	1
Childs, Marquis William	2	Kahn, Herman	1

	Volume
Kardiner, Abram	1
Kendrick, Alexander	3
Kutner, Luis	3
Ladd, George Eldon	1
Langer, Susanne Katherina	1
Lash, Joseph P.	2
Levin, Meyer	1
Lichine, Alexis	2
Logan, Rayford Whittingham	1
Lynd, Helen Merrell	1
McCarthy, Mary Therese	2
Macdonald, Dwight	1
Mannes, Marya	2
Mays, Benjamin Elijah	1
Merriam, Eve	3
Milgram, Stanley	1
Mizener, Arthur Moore	2
Monroe, Marion	1
Murray, Anna Pauline ("Pauli")	1
Nearing, Scott	1
Newhall, Beaumont	3
Niel, Cornelis Bernardus van	1
Peale, Norman Vincent	3
Peter, Laurence Johnston	2
Philbrick, Herbert Arthur	3
Pool, Ithiel de Sola	1
Rand, Ayn	1
Reshevsky, Samuel Herman	3
St. Johns, Adela Rogers	2
Salisbury, Harrison Evans	3
Salk, Lee	3
Scott, Austin Wakeman	1
Sevareid, (Arnold) Eric	3
Sheed, Francis Joseph ("Frank")	1
Shirer, William Lawrence	3
Shook, Karel Francis Antony	1
Shulman, Max	2
Sloane, Eric	1
Stegner, Wallace Earle	3
Stone, Irving	2
Stuart, Jesse Hilton	1
Swanberg, W(illiam) A(ndrew)	3
Terry, Walter	1
Thomas, Lewis	3
Veeck, William Louis, Jr. ("Bill")	2
Wallace, Irving	2
Welch, Robert Henry Winborne, Jr.	1
West, (Mary) Jessamyn	1
White, E(lwyn) B(rooks)	1
Whitehead, Don(ald) Ford	1
Wojnarowicz, David Michael	3
Wright, Olgivanna Lloyd	1

Author (Poetry)	*Volume*
Armour, Richard Willard	2
Boyle, Katherine ("Kay")	3
Brautigan, Richard	1
Carver, Raymond Clevie	2
Ciardi, John Anthony	2
Cowley, (David) Malcolm	2
Duncan, Robert	2
Engle, Paul Hamilton	3
Fitzgerald, Robert Stuart	1
Guthrie, Alfred Bertram, Jr.	3
Holmes, John Clellon	2
Lorde, Audre Geraldine	3
MacLeish, Archibald	1
Merriam, Eve	3
Nemerov, Howard	3
Oppen, George	1
Rexroth, Kenneth Charles Marion	1
Rice, Helen Steiner	1
Riding, Laura	3
Schuyler, James Marcus	3
Stuart, Jesse Hilton	1
Warren, Robert Penn	2

Author (Screenplays)
Brooks, Richard	3
Chayefsky, Sidney Aaron ("Paddy")	1
Foreman, Carl	1
Goodrich, Frances	1
Lerner, Alan Jay	2
Maltz, Albert	1
Mankiewicz, Joseph Leo	3
Roach, Harold Eugene ("Hal")	3
Roddenberry, Eugene Wesley ("Gene")	3
Ryskind, Morrie	1
St. Johns, Adela Rogers	2
Salt, Waldo	2

Author (Television)
| Diamond, Selma | 1 |
| Moore, Garry | 3 |

Author (Translation)
Fitzgerald, Robert Stuart	1
Hartdegen, Stephen Joseph	2
Howe, Irving	3
Isherwood, Christopher William	2
Levin, Meyer	1

Aviator
Boyington, Gregory ("Pappy")	2
Doolittle, James Harold	3
Gann, Ernest Kellogg	3
Hart, Marion Rice	2
Quesada, Elwood Richard ("Pete")	3

	Volume		Volume
Fixx, James Fuller	1	Graham, Martha	3
Grosvenor, Melville Bell	1	Green, Edith Starrett	2
Johnson, Eleanor Murdock	2	Hanson, Howard Harold	1
Levin, Meyer	1	Harrington, (Edward) Michael	2
Lynes, (Joseph) Russell, Jr.	3	Harris, Patricia Roberts Fitzgerald	1
Macdonald, Dwight	1	Hartdegen, Stephen Joseph	2
Shawn, William	3	Hicks, Granville	1
Vreeland, Diana	2	Hoffmann, Banesh	2
Editor (Newspapers)		Hofstadter, Robert	2
Canham, Erwin Dain	1	Holland, Jerome Heartwell ("Brud")	1
Catledge, Turner	1	Holt, John Caldwell	1
Gates, John	3	Hughes, Emmet John	1
Knight, John Shively	1	Humphry, (Ann) Wickett	3
Maynard, Robert Clyve	3	Johnson, Eleanor Murdock	2
Pope, James Soule, Sr.	1	Keppel, Francis	2
Sheppard, Eugenia	1	Kline, Nathan Schellenberg	1
Sutton, Carol	1	Kohlberg, Lawrence	2
Wechsler, James Arthur	1	Koopmans, Tjalling Charles	1
Educator		Kuznets, Simon Smith	1
Albion, Robert G.	1	Langer, Susanne Katherina	1
Bainton, Roland Herbert	1	Lattimore, Owen	2
Bardeen, John	3	Lerner, Max	3
Barnett, Marguerite Ross	3	Logan, Rayford Whittingham	1
Barr, Stringfellow	1	Lynd, Helen Merrell	1
Barrett, William Christopher	3	McAuliffe, (Sharon) Christa	2
Billington, Ray Allen	1	MacLeish, Archibald	1
Bloch, Felix	1	Mays, Benjamin Elijah	1
Bloom, Allan David	3	Merriam, Eve	3
Breuer, Marcel	1	Monroe, Marion	1
Brewster, Kingman, Jr.	2	Moos, Malcolm Charles	1
Brodie, Fawn McKay	1	Murray, Arthur	3
Campbell, Joseph	2	Nagel, Ernest	1
Carnovsky, Morris	3	Nemerov, Howard	3
Cremin, Lawrence Arthur	2	Newhall, Beaumont	3
De Kooning, Elaine Marie Catherine	2	Neyman, Jerzy	1
De Man, Paul	1	Niel, Cornelis Bernardus van	1
Dickey, John Sloan	3	Padover, Saul Kussiel	1
Eisenhower, Milton Stover	1	Pendleton, Clarence Mclane, Jr.	2
Eliade, Mircea	2	Perkins, Dexter	1
Ellis, John Tracy	3	Persichetti, Vincent Ludwig	2
Ellmann, Richard David	2	Primrose, William	1
Engel, A. Lehman	1	Rafferty, Max(well) Lewis, Jr.	1
Engle, Paul Hamilton	3	Rainey, Homer Price	1
Finkelstein, Louis	3	Sachar, Abram Leon	3
Flesch, Rudolf Franz	2	Salk, Lee	3
Fletcher, Harvey	1	Schuman, William Howard	3
Fletcher, Joseph Francis, III	3	Scott, Austin Wakeman	1
Freund, Paul Abraham	3	Sessions, Roger Huntington	1
Galarza, Ernesto, Jr.	1	Stegner, Wallace Earle	3
Gardner, John Champlin, Jr.	1	Strasberg, Lee	1
Giamatti, A(ngelo) Bartlett ("Bart")	2	Taylor, Harold Alexander	3
Gilbert, Felix	3	Thompson, (Ira) Randall	1

	Volume
Bloch, Felix	1
Brattain, Walter Houser	2
Dirac, Paul Adrien Maurice	1
Feynman, Richard Phillips	2
Hagen, John Peter	2
Hoffmann, Banesh	2
Hofstadter, Robert	2
Kahn, Herman	1
Kusch, Polykarp	3
Libby, Leona Woods Marshall	2
Livingston, M(ilton) Stanley	2
McMillan, Edwin Mattison	3
Rabi, I(sidor) I(saac)	2
Rainwater, (Leo) James	2
Segrè, Emilio Gino	2
Shockley, William Bradford	2
Ulam, Stanislaw Marcin	1
Urey, Harold Clayton	1
Zacharias, Jerrold Reinach	2

Pianist. See Musician.

Playwright. See Author (Drama).

Poet. See Author (Poet).

Political Activist

Baker, Ella Josephine	2
Bowman, Thea Bertha ("Sister Thea")	2
Boyle, Katherine ("Kay")	3
Bradshaw, Thornton Frederick ("Brad")	2
Faulk, John Henry	2
Hale, Clara McBride ("Mother Hale")	3
Harrington, (Edward) Michael	2
Hoffman, Abbott ("Abbie")	2
Howe, Irving	3
Humphry, (Ann) Wickett	3
Husted, Marjorie Child	2
Jarvis, Howard Arnold	2
Kahane, Meir	2
Kent, Corita	2
King, Martin Luther, Sr. ("Daddy King")	1
Kutner, Luis	3
Lekachman, Robert	2
Lord, John Wesley	2
Lorde, Audre Geraldine	3
Mueller, Reuben Herbert	1
Nearing, Scott	1
Newton, Huey Percy	2
Perlmutter, Nathan	2
Rauh, Joseph Louis, Jr.	3
Robinson, Earl	3
Snyder, Mitch(ell) Darryl	2
Tree, Mary Endicott Peabody FitzGerald ("Marietta")	3
Welch, Robert Henry Winborne, Jr.	1
Wojnarowicz, David Michael	3

Political Adviser

	Volume
Adams, (Llewellyn) Sherman	2
Atwater, Harvey Leroy ("Lee")	3
Blaisdell, Thomas Charles, Jr.	2
Burch, (Roy) Dean	3
Burns, Arthur Frank	2
Cohn, Roy Marcus	2
Dean, Arthur Hobson	2
Gavin, James Maurice	2
Goldman, Eric Frederick	2
Green, Edith Starrett	2
Harlow, Bryce Nathaniel	2
Harriman, W(illiam) Averell	2
Hughes, Emmet John	1
Kahn, Herman	1
Keeny, Spurgeon Milton ("Sam")	2
Keyserling, Leon Hirsch	2
Martin, John Bartlow	2
Revelle, Roger Randall Dougan	3

Political Scientist

Hartz, Louis	2
Hook, Sidney	2
Lubell, Samuel	2
Padover, Saul Kussiel	1
Pool, Ithiel de Sola	1
Voorhis, Horace Jeremiah ("Jerry")	1
Wildavsky, Aaron Bernard	3

Politician (Governor)

Arnall, Ellis Gibbs	3
Baldwin, Raymond Earl	2
Barnett, Ross Robert	2
Benson, Elmer Austin	1
Bricker, John William	2
Chandler, Albert Benjamin ("Happy")	3
Clements, Earle C.	1
Coleman, J(ames) P(lemon)	3
Collins, (Thomas) LeRoy	3
Connally, John Bowden, Jr.	3
Daniel, Price Marion	2
DiSalle, Michael Vincent	1
Folsom, James	2
Grasso, Ella Rosa Giovanna Oliva Tambussi	1
Harriman, W(illiam) Averell	2
Hildreth, Horace Augustus	2
Johnson, Paul Burney	1
Jordan, Leonard Beck ("Len")	1
Landon, Alf(red) Mossman	2
Lausche, Frank John	2
Lodge, John Davis	1
McCall, Thomas William Lawson	1
Meyner, Robert Baumle	2
Ogilvie, Richard Buell	2
Russell, Charles Hinton	2

ALPHABETICAL LIST OF SUBJECTS, VOLUMES 1–3

See also the Occupations Index beginning on p. 581.

Subject	Volume	Subject	Volume
Brown, George Rufus	1	Celler, Emanuel	1
Brown, John R.	3	Chaikin, Sol (Chick)	3
Brown, Paul Eugene ("P. B.")	3	Chandler, Albert Benjamin ("Happy")	3
Broyard, Anatole Paul	2	Chapin, Harry Forster	1
Bruhn, Erik Belton Evers	2	Charney, Jule Gregory	1
Bryant, Paul William ("Bear")	1	Chase, Lucia Hosmer	2
Brynner, Yul	1	Chase, Mary Coyle	1
Bubbles, John William	2	Chase, Stuart	1
Buell, Marjorie Lyman Henderson ("Marge")	3	Chase, William Curtis	2
Buhaina, Abdullah Ibn. *See* Blakey, Arthur.		Chávez, César Estrada	3
Bundy, Theodore Robert ("Ted")	2	Chayefsky, Sidney Aaron ("Paddy")	1
Bunker, Ellsworth	1	Cheever, John	1
Bunshaft, Gordon	2	Childress, Alvin	2
Burch, (Roy) Dean	3	Childs, Marquis William	2
Burden, William	1	Church, Frank Forrester	1
Burdick, Quentin Northrop	3	Ciardi, John Anthony	2
Burke, Kenneth Duva	3	Clark, Joseph Sill, Jr.	2
Burns, Arthur Frank	2	Clark, Mamie Phipps	1
Burr, Raymond William Stacy	3	Clark, Mark Wayne	1
Burrows, Abe	1	Clarke, Kenny ("Klook")	1
Burton, Phillip	1	Claude, Albert	1
Busch, August Anheuser, Jr. ("Gussie")	2	Clements, Earle C.	1
Butterfield, Lyman Henry	1	Clifton, Nat(haniel) ("Sweetwater")	2
Butts, Alfred Mosher	3	Clubb, O(liver) Edmund, II	2
Cage, John Milton, Jr.	3	Cody, John Patrick	1
Cagney, James Francis, Jr.	2	Cohen, Benjamin Victor	1
Cahn, Sammy	3	Cohen, N(ehemiah) M(yer)	1
Caldwell, Erskine Preston	2	Cohen, Wilbur Joseph	2
Caldwell, (Janet Miriam) Taylor	1	Cohn, Roy Marcus	2
Campanella, Roy	3	Cole, William R. ("Cozy")	1
Campbell, Joseph	2	Coleman, J(ames) P(lemon)	3
Campion, Donald Richard	2	Coles, Charles ("Honi")	3
Canaday, John Edwin	1	Collbohm, Franklin Rudolph	2
Canham, Erwin Dain	1	Collingwood, Charles Cummings	1
Caniff, Milton Arthur	2	Collins, J(oseph) Lawton ("Lightning Joe")	2
Canutt, Enos Edward ("Yakima")	2	Collins, (Thomas) LeRoy	3
Capote, Truman	1	Conigliaro, Anthony Richard ("Tony")	2
Capra, Frank	3	Conlan, John Bertrand ("Jocko")	2
Carmichael, Howard Hoagland ("Hoagy")	1	Conn, William David, Jr. ("Billy")	3
Carney, Robert Bostwick	2	Connally, John Bowden, Jr.	3
Carnovsky, Morris	3	Connors, Kevin Joseph Aloysius ("Chuck")	3
Carpenter, Karen	1	Coogan, John Leslie, Jr. ("Jackie")	1
Carpenter, Robert Ruliph Morgan, Jr.	2	Cooke, Terence James	1
Carradine, John	2	Coon, Carleton Stevens	1
Carvel, Thomas Andrew	2	Cooper, Charles Henry ("Chuck")	1
Carver, Raymond Clevie	2	Cooper, Irving Spencer	1
Case, Clifford P.	1	Cooper, John Sherman	3
Casey, James E.	1	Copland, Aaron	2
Casey, William Joseph	2	Corcoran, Thomas Gardiner	1
Castro, Bernard	3	Cori, Carl Ferdinand	1
Catledge, Turner	1	Corner, George Washington	1

Subject	Volume	Subject	Volume
Goodrich, Frances	1	Harburg, Edgar Yipsel ("Yip")	1
Goodson, Mark	3	Haring, Keith Allen	2
Gordon, Dexter Keith	2	Harken, Dwight Emary	3
Gordon, Ruth	1	Harkness, Rebekah West	1
Goren, Charles Henry	3	Harlow, Bryce Nathaniel	2
Gosden, Freeman Fisher	1	Harmon, Thomas Dudley	2
Gould, Chester	1	Harriman, W(illiam) Averell	2
Goulding, Ray(mond) Walter	2	Harrington, (Edward) Michael	2
Grace, Princess, of Monaco. *See* Kelly, Grace.		Harris, Patricia Roberts Fitzgerald	1
Graham, Bill	3	Harris, Sydney Justin	2
Graham, John	3	Hart, Marion Rice	2
Graham, Martha	3	Hartdegen, Stephen Joseph	2
Graham, Sheilah	2	Hartline, Haldan Keffer	1
Graham, William Patrick ("Billy")	3	Hartz, Louis	2
Grange, Harold Edward ("Red")	3	Hassenfeld, Stephen David	2
Grant, Cary	2	Hathaway, Starke Rosencrans	1
Grasso, Ella Rosa Giovanna Oliva Tambussi	1	Haughton, Daniel Jeremiah	2
Graziano, Rocky	2	Haughton, William Robert ("Billy")	2
Green, Edith Starrett	2	Hawkins, Erskine Ramsay	3
Greenberg, Henry Benjamin ("Hank")	2	Hayakawa, S(amuel) I(chiye)	3
Greene, Lorne	2	Hayek, Friedrich August von	3
Greer, William Alexander ("Sonny")	1	Hayes, Helen	3
Grillo, Frank Raúl. *See* Machito.		Hayes, Wayne Woodrow ("Woody")	2
Grimes, Burleigh Arland	1	Haynsworth, Clement Furman, Jr.	2
Groppi, James Edward	1	Hays, (Lawrence) Brooks	1
Grosvenor, Melville Bell	1	Hays, Lee	1
Grucci, Felix James, Sr. ("Pops")	3	Hays, Wayne Levere	2
Gruenther, Alfred Maximilian	1	Hayworth, Rita	2
Gruentzig, Andreas Roland	1	Hazlitt, Henry Stuart	3
Grumman, Leroy Randle ("Roy")	1	Head, Edith	1
Guthrie, Alfred Bertram, Jr.	3	Healy, Timothy Stafford	3
Habib, Philip Charles	3	Hearst, William Randolph, Jr.	3
Hagen, John Peter	2	Hecht, Harold	1
Hagerty, James Campbell	1	Heidelberger, Michael	3
Haggar, Joseph Marion	2	Heifetz, Jascha	2
Halas, George	1	Heinlein, Robert Anson	2
Haldeman, H(arry) R(obbins)	3	Heinz, Henry John, II ("Jack")	2
Hale, Clara McBride ("Mother Hale")	3	Heinz, Henry John, III	3
Haley, Alex(ander) Murray Palmer	3	Heller, Walter Wolfgang	2
Haley, William John Clifton, Jr. ("Bill")	1	Hellman, Lillian Florence	1
Hall, Joyce Clyde	1	Hemingway, Mary Welsh	2
Halleck, Charles Abraham	2	Henderson, Leon	2
Halper, Albert	1	Henson, James Maury ("Jim")	2
Halston, (Roy Halston Frowick)	2	Hepburn, Audrey Kathleen	3
Hamilton, Margaret	1	Herman, Floyd Caves ("Babe")	2
Hammer, Armand	2	Herman, William Jennings ("Billy")	3
Hammond, E(dward) Cuyler	2	Herman, Woody	2
Hammond, John Henry, Jr.	2	Hersey, John Richard	3
Hancock, Joy Bright	2	Hickerson, John Dewey	2
Hanks, Nancy	1	Hicks, Granville	1
Hanson, Howard Harold	1	Hildreth, Horace Augustus	2

Subject	Volume	Subject	Volume
Hill, (Joseph) Lister	1	Javits, Jacob Koppel	2
Hillcourt, William ("Green Bar Bill")	3	Jaworski, Leon	1
Himes, Chester Bomar	1	Jenkins, Gordon Hill	1
Hines, Earl Kenneth ("Fatha")	1	Jenner, William Ezra	1
Hirshhorn, Joseph Herman	1	Jessel, George Albert ("Georgie")	1
Hobson, Laura Kean Zametkin	2	Jessup, Philip Caryl	2
Hoffer, Eric	1	Joffrey, Robert	2
Hoffman, Abbott ("Abbie")	2	Johnson, Clarence Leonard ("Kelly")	2
Hoffmann, Banesh	2	Johnson, D(aniel) Mead	3
Hofheinz, Roy Mark	1	Johnson, Edward Crosby, 2d	1
Hofstadter, Robert	2	Johnson, Eleanor Murdock	2
Holden, William	1	Johnson, Paul Burney	1
Holland, Jerome Heartwell ("Brud")	1	Johnson, Rachel Harris	1
Holley, Robert William	3	Johnson, Wallace Edward	2
Holm, Hanya	3	Johnson, William Julius ("Judy")	2
Holmes, John Clellon	2	Jordan, Leonard Beck ("Len")	1
Holt, John Caldwell	1	Jorgensen, Christine	2
Hook, Sidney	2	Kahane, Meir	2
Hopkins, Sam ("Lightnin'")	1	Kahn, Herman	1
Hopper, Grace Brewster Murray	3	Kardiner, Abram	1
Horowitz, Vladimir	2	Kauffman, Ewing Marion	3
Houghton, Arthur Amory, Jr.	2	Kaufman, Andrew G. ("Andy")	1
Houseman, John	2	Kaufman, Irving Robert	3
Hoving, Walter	2	Kaufman, Murray ("Murray the K")	1
Howe, Irving	3	Kaye, Danny	2
Hoyt, Homer	1	Kaye, Sammy	2
Hoyt, Waite Charles ("Schoolboy")	1	Kaye, Sylvia Fine	3
Hubbard, L(afayette) Ron(ald)	2	Keeler, Ruby	3
Hubbell, Carl Owen	2	Keeler, William Wayne	2
Hudson, Rock	1	Keeny, Spurgeon Milton ("Sam")	2
Hughes, Emmet John	1	Kelly, Charles E. ("Commando")	1
Huie, William Bradford	2	Kelly, George Lange ("Highpockets")	1
Humphry, (Ann) Wickett	3	Kelly, Grace Patricia (Princess Grace)	1
Hunter, Alberta	1	Kelman, Wolfe	2
Husted, Marjorie Child	2	Kemeny, John George	3
Huston, John	2	Kemper, James Scott	1
Hutchinson, G(eorge) Evelyn	3	Kendrick, Alexander	3
Iba, (Payne) Henry ("Hank")	3	Kendricks, Eddie James	3
Ingersoll, Ralph McAllister	1	Kennedy, William Jesse, Jr.	1
Irish, Edward Simmons, Sr. ("Ned")	1	Kent, Corita	2
Irwin, James Benson	3	Keppel, Francis	2
Isherwood, Christopher William	2	Kertész, André (Andor)	1
Jackson, Henry Martin ("Scoop")	1	Keyserling, Leon Hirsch	2
Jackson, Travis Calvin ("Stonewall")	2	Kieran, John Francis	1
Jacoby, James Oswald ("Jim")	3	Killian, James Rhyne, Jr.	2
Jacoby, Oswald ("Ozzie")	1	Kimball, Spencer Woolley	1
James, Harry Haag	1	Kinard, Frank Manning ("Bruiser")	1
Janeway, Eliot	3	King, Martin Luther, Sr. ("Daddy King")	1
Janis, Sidney	2	Kirsten, Dorothy	3
Janowitz, Morris	2	Kistiakowsky, George Bogdan	1
Jarvis, Howard Arnold	2	Kline, Nathan Schellenberg	1

Subject	Volume	Subject	Volume
Klopfer, Donald Simon	2	Levin, Meyer	1
Kluszewski, Theodore Bernard ("Ted"; "Big Klu")	2	Levine, Joseph Edward	2
Knight, John Shively	1	Lewis, Reginald Francis	3
Knight, Ted	2	Libby, Leona Woods Marshall	2
Knopf, Alfred Abraham	1	Liberace, Wladziu Valentino	2
Knott, Walter	1	Lichine, Alexis	2
Kohlberg, Lawrence	2	Licklider, J(oseph) C(arl) R(obnett)	2
Koontz, Elizabeth Duncan	2	Liebman, Max	1
Koopmans, Tjalling Charles	1	Lilienthal, David	1
Koresh, David	3	Lindsay, Goldie Ina Ruby ("Eldress Bertha")	2
Kosinski, Jerzy Nikodem	3	Lindstrom, Frederick Charles, Jr. ("Lindy")	1
Kraft, Joseph	2	Link, Edwin Albert	1
Krasner, Lee	1	Lipmann, Fritz Albert	2
Kraus, Hans Peter	2	Little, Royal	2
Kroc, Ray(mond) Albert	1	Livingston, M(ilton) Stanley	2
Kurtzman, Harvey	3	Livingstone, Mary	1
Kusch, Polykarp	3	Lodge, Henry Cabot, Jr.	1
Kutner, Luis	3	Lodge, John Davis	1
Kuznets, Simon Smith	1	Loeb, Henry, III	3
Labouisse, Henry Richardson	2	Loeb, William	1
Ladd, George Eldon	1	Loewe, Frederick	2
L'Amour, Louis	2	Loewy, Raymond Fernand	2
Lanchester, Elsa	2	Logan, Joshua Lockwood, III	2
Land, Edwin Herbert	3	Logan, Rayford Whittingham	1
Landon, Alf(red) Mossman	2	Loos, Anita	1
Landon, Margaret Dorothea Mortenson	3	Lord, John Wesley	2
Landon, Michael	3	Lorde, Audre Geraldine	3
Lane, Frank Charles	1	Lorentz, Pare	3
Langer, Susanne Katherina	1	Louis, Joe	1
Lansdale, Edward Geary	2	Lovestone, Jay	2
Lansky, Meyer	1	Lovett, Robert Abercrombie	2
Larson, (Lewis) Arthur	3	Loy, Myrna	3
Lash, Joseph P.	2	Lubell, Samuel	2
Lattimore, Owen	2	Luce, Clare Boothe	2
Lausche, Frank John	2	Ludlam, Charles	2
Lawford, Peter Sydney Vaughn	1	Ludwig, Daniel Keith	3
Lay, Herman W.	1	Luria, Salvador Edward	3
Layne, Robert Lawrence ("Bobby")	2	Lynd, Helen Merrell	1
Lazar, Irving Paul ("Swifty")	3	Lynes, (Joseph) Russell, Jr.	3
Lazarus, Ralph	2	Lyons, Theodore Amar ("Ted")	2
Lee, Pinky	3	McAuliffe, (Sharon) Christa	2
Le Gallienne, Eva	3	McBride, Lloyd	1
Leinsdorf, Erich	3	McCain, John Sydney, Jr.	1
Lekachman, Robert	2	McCall, Thomas William Lawson	1
LeMay, Curtis Emerson	2	McCarthy, Glenn Herbert	2
Lemnitzer, Lyman Louis	2	McCarthy, Mary Therese	2
Lenya, Lotte	1	McClintock, Barbara	3
Lerner, Alan Jay	2	McCloy, John Jay	2
Lerner, Max	3	McCone, John Alex	3
LeRoy, Mervyn	2	McCormick, Frank Andrew	1
		MacCorquodale, Donald William ("Mac")	2

Subject	Volume	Subject	Volume
McCracken, James Eugene	2	Matsunaga, Spark Masayuki ("Sparkie")	2
McCrea, Joel Albert	2	Matthews, Burnita Shelton	2
McCree, Wade Hampton, Jr.	2	Maynard, Robert Clyve	3
Macdonald, Dwight	1	Mays, Benjamin Elijah	1
MacDonald, John Dann	2	Means, Gardiner Coit	2
Macdonald, Ross	1	Medeiros, Humberto Sousa	1
McGee, Gale William	3	Medina, Harold Raymond	2
McGowan, William George	3	Meeker, Ralph	2
Machito (Frank Raúl Grillo)	1	Menninger, Karl Augustus	2
MacInnes, Helen Clark	1	Mercer, Mabel	1
Mack, Walter Staunton, Jr.	2	Merman, Ethel	1
Mackey, Joseph Creighton	1	Merriam, Eve	3
McKissick, Floyd B.	3	Merrill, John Putnam	1
MacLeish, Archibald	1	Meyendorff, John	3
McMillan, Edwin Mattison	3	Meyner, Robert Baumle	2
MacMurray, Fred(erick) Martin	3	Middleton, Drew	2
McNair, Ron(ald) Erwin	2	Milanov, Zinka	2
McNally, John Victor ("Johnny Blood")	1	Milgram, Stanley	1
McNamara, Margaret Craig	1	Milland, Ray	2
McPartland, James Dugald ("Jimmy")	3	Millar, Kenneth. *See* Macdonald, Ross.	
MacRae, Gordon	2	Miller, Arnold Ray	1
Madden, Ray John	2	Miller, Carl S.	2
Magnin, Cyril	2	Miller, Roger Dean	3
Magnuson, Warren Grant	2	Miller, William Mosely	2
Magowan, Robert Anderson	1	Mills, Wilbur Daigh	3
Malamud, Bernard	2	Milstein, Nathan	3
Maleska, Eugene Thomas	3	Minnelli, Vincente	2
Malone, Dumas	2	Mitchell, (John) Broadus	2
Maltz, Albert	1	Mitchell, Joan	3
Mamoulian, Rouben Zachary	2	Mitchell, John James, Jr.	1
Mankiewicz, Joseph Leo	3	Mitchell, John Newton	2
Manne, Sheldon ("Shelly")	1	Mize, John Robert ("Johnny")	3
Mannes, Marya	2	Mizener, Arthur Moore	2
Manning, Timothy	2	Mohr, Charles Henry	2
Mapplethorpe, Robert	2	Monk, Thelonious Sphere	1
Maravich, Peter Press ("Pistol Pete")	2	Monroe, Marion	1
Marble, Alice	2	Montgomery, Robert	1
Marcello, Carlos	3	Moore, Garry	3
Margulies, Lazar	1	Moore, Stanford	1
Maris, Roger Eugene	1	Moos, Malcolm Charles	1
Mark, Herman Francis	3	Morgan, Henry Sturgis ("Harry")	1
Markham, Dewey ("Pigmeat")	1	Morganfield, McKinley. *See* Waters, Muddy.	
Marks, John D. ("Johnny")	1	Moross, Jerome	1
Marriott, J(ohn) Willard	1	Morris, Richard Brandon	2
Marshall, Thurgood	3	Morton, Thruston Ballard	1
Martin, Alfred Manuel, Jr. ("Billy")	2	Mosconi, William Joseph ("Willie")	3
Martin, Freddy	1	Moses, Robert	1
Martin, John Bartlow	2	Motherwell, Robert	3
Martin, Mary Virginia	2	Mueller, Reuben Herbert	1
Marvin, Lee	2	Mulliken, Robert Sanderson	2
Massey, Raymond Hart	1	Mumford, Lawrence Quincy	1

Subject	Volume	Subject	Volume
Mumford, Lewis Charles	2	Parsons, James Benton	3
Murchison, Clint(on) Williams, Jr.	2	Parsons, Johnnie	1
Murphy, George Lloyd	3	Passman, Otto Ernest	2
Murray, Arthur	3	Pasternak, Joseph Herman ("Joe")	3
Murray, Anna Pauline ("Pauli")	1	Patriarca, Raymond	1
Myer, Dillon Seymour	1	Pauley, Edwin Wendell	1
Nagel, Ernest	1	Peale, Norman Vincent	3
Nagurski, Bronislau ("Bronko")	2	Peckinpah, David Samuel ("Sam")	1
Nearing, Scott	1	Pedersen, Charles John	2
Nef, John Ulric	2	Peerce, Jan	1
Negri, Pola	2	Pendleton, Clarence Mclane, Jr.	2
Nelson, Eric Hilliard ("Rick")	1	Pepper, Claude Denson	2
Nemerov, Howard	3	Percy, Walker	2
Neumann, Vera Salaff ("Vera")	3	Perkins, Anthony	3
Nevelson, Louise	2	Perkins, Dexter	1
Newell, Allen	3	Perkins, (Richard) Marlin	2
Newhall, Beaumont	3	Perlmutter, Nathan	2
Newton, Huey Percy	2	Perls, Laura	2
Neyman, Jerzy	1	Perry, Harold Robert	3
Niel, Cornelis Bernardus van	1	Perry, Lincoln. *See* Fetchit, Stepin.	
Nikolais, Alwin Theodore	3	Persichetti, Vincent Ludwig	2
Nixon, Pat(ricia)	3	Peter, Laurence Johnston	2
Noguchi, Isamu	2	Petrillo, James Caesar	1
Norris, Clarence	2	Philbrick, Herbert Arthur	3
Norstad, Lauris	2	Phillips, Marjorie Acker	1
North, John Ringling	1	Phoenix, River Jude	3
Northrop, John Howard	2	Picon, Molly	3
Northrop, John Knudsen ("Jack")	1	Pidgeon, Walter	1
Noyce, Robert Norton	2	Pillsbury, Philip	1
O'Brien, Lawrence Francis, Jr. ("Larry")	2	Piñero, Miguel	2
O'Brien, William Joseph, Jr. ("Pat")	1	Plough, Abe	1
Ochsner, (Edward William) Alton	1	Pollard, Frederick Douglass ("Fritz")	2
Ogilvie, Richard Buell	2	Ponselle, Rosa Melba	1
Okada, Kenzo	1	Pool, Ithiel de Sola	1
O'Keeffe, Georgia Totto	2	Pope, Generoso Paul, Jr.	2
Olin, John Merrill	1	Pope, James Soule, Sr.	1
Oppen, George	1	Porter, Sylvia Field	3
Orbison, Roy Kelton	2	Pousette-Dart, Richard Warren	3
Ormandy, Eugene	1	Powell, Eleanor Torrey ("Ellie")	1
Owings, Nathaniel Alexander	1	Powell, William Horatio	1
Padover, Saul Kussiel	1	Preminger, Otto Ludwig	2
Page, Geraldine	2	Presser, Jackie	2
Page, Ruth Marian	3	Preston, Robert	2
Paige, Leroy Robert ("Satchel")	1	Price, T(homas) Rowe, Jr.	1
Paley, William Samuel	2	Price, Vincent Leonard, Jr.	3
Palmieri, Carlos Manuel, Jr. ("Charlie")	2	Prichard, Edward Fretwell, Jr.	1
Papp, Joseph	3	Primrose, William	1
Parks, Bert	3	Prinz, Joachim	2
Parks, Henry Green, Jr.	2	Pritikin, Nathan	1
Parnis, Sarah Rosen ("Mollie")	3	Pritzker, A(bram) N(icholas)	2
Parsons, Elizabeth Pierson ("Betty")	1	Provenzano, Anthony ("Tony Pro")	2

ISBN 0-684-80620-7